# www.wadsworth.com

*www.wadsworth.com* is the World Wide Web site for Wadsworth and is your direct source to dozens of online resources.

At *www.wadsworth.com* you can find out about supplements, demonstration software, and student resources. You can also send email to many of our authors and preview new publications and exciting new technologies.

**www.wadsworth.com**
Changing the way the world learns®

KAGAN & SEGAL'S

# Psychology
# An Introduction

**NINTH EDITION**

Jerome Kagan • Julius Segal • Ernest Havemann

 As Revised by

Don Baucum • Carolyn D. Smith

**THOMSON**

**WADSWORTH**

Australia • Canada • Mexico • Singapore • Spain
United Kingdom • United States

# THOMSON

™

## WADSWORTH

Psychology Editor: Marianne Taflinger
Development Editor: Kate Barnes
Assistant Editor: Dan Moneypenny
Editorial Assistant: Nicole Root
Technology Project Manager: Darin Derstine
Marketing Manager: Lori Grebe
Marketing Assistant: Laurel Anderson
Advertising Project Manager: Brian Chaffee
Project Manager, Editorial Production: Paul Wells
Print/Media Buyer: Kristine Waller
Permissions Editor: Joohee Lee
Production Service: Lifland et al., Bookmakers
Text Designer: Detta Penna
Photo Researcher: Gail Magin/Lifland
Copy Editor: Denise Throckmorton/Lifland
Illustrator: Gail Magin/Lifland
Cover Designer: Denise Davidson
Cover Image: Rob Barker/Stock Illustration Source
Cover Printer: Quebecor World/Dubuque
Compositor: Thompson Type
Printer: Quebecor World/Dubuque

Printed in the United States of America
1 2 3 4 5 6 7 07 06 05 04 03

For more information about our products, contact us at:
**Thomson Learning Academic Resource Center**
**1-800-423-0563**
For permission to use material from this text, contact us by:
**Phone:** 1-800-730-2214
**Fax:** 1-800-730-2215
**Web:** http://www.thomsonrights.com

ExamView® and ExamView Pro® are registered trademarks of FSCreations, Inc. Windows is a registered trademark of the Microsoft Corporation used herein under license. Macintosh and Power Macintosh are registered trademarks of Apple Computer, Inc. Used herein under license.

**Wadsworth/Thomson Learning**
**10 Davis Drive**
**Belmont, CA 94002-3098**
**USA**

**Asia**
Thomson Learning
5 Shenton Way #01-01
UIC Building
Singapore 068808

**Australia/New Zealand**
Thomson Learning
102 Dodds Street
Southbank, Victoria 3006
Australia

**Canada**
Nelson
1120 Birchmount Road
Toronto, Ontario M1K 5G4
Canada

**Europe/Middle East/Africa**
Thomson Learning
High Holborn House
50/51 Bedford Row
London WC1R 4LR
United Kingdom

**Latin America**
Thomson Learning
Seneca, 53
Colonia Polanco
11560 Mexico D.F.
Mexico

**Spain/Portugal**
Paraninfo
Calle/Magallanes, 25
28015 Madrid, Spain

Library of Congress Control Number: 2003106306

Student Edition: ISBN 0-155-08114-4

Instructor's Edition: ISBN 0-534-57863-2

# Brief Contents

# Contents

CHAPTER 1

## The Science and Practice of Psychology     1

CHAPTER 2

## Brain, Body, and Behavior     52

CHAPTER 3

# Sensing and Perceiving  92

CHAPTER 4

# Conditioning and Learning  137

CHAPTER 5

# Remembering and Forgetting 181

CHAPTER 6

# Language and Thought    219

CHAPTER 7

# Intelligence and Its Assessment          256

CHAPTER 8

# Emotion and Motivation          288

CHAPTER 9

# Personality and Its Assessment    332

CHAPTER 10

# Human Development: Conception Through Childhood    370

## CHAPTER 14

# Psychotherapy and Other Treatment Approaches    544

## CHAPTER 15

# Social Psychology    584

APPENDIX

# Statistics: Description and Inference   628

# To the Instructor

The field of psychology is a constantly changing one, and the changes are reflected in this new edition of *Kagan & Segal's Psychology: An Introduction.* New and expanded sections in this edition address current trends and research in such areas as cognitive psychology, evolutionary psychology, neuroscience, and positive psychology. Chapter 2, for example, contains a new section about ethical issues in the use of neuroscience methods, and Chapter 4 has been rewritten to include more information about cognition. Chapter 8 includes a discussion of the evolutionary theory of overeating, and Chapter 12 contains a new section on well-being and positive psychology. At the same time, many familiar and "classic" topics have been retained, and the references have been extensively updated.

Throughout the text, issues of gender and diversity have been addressed where appropriate. For example, Chapter 1 includes a new section on culture, ethnicity, and diversity; Chapter 8 contains updated coverage of cross-cultural research on emotion and its expression; and Chapter 11 includes a discussion of Carol Gilligan's view on gender differences in moral development.

We have always aimed to serve instructors and students eager for a book that combines brevity, clarity, rigor, and relevance. In our effort to create a book that appeals to students, we have continued to employ a concise, straightforward writing style and have concentrated more than ever on the main thrust and meaning of psychology. To keep the book rigorous and relevant, we have constantly asked ourselves: Of all the psychological knowledge that now exists, what elements are most important to students—both those preparing for advanced courses and those who will have no further exposure to psychology? To enhance the learning process, we continue to provide a Study Guide at the end of each chapter.

If we can help students grasp the significance of key psychological principles and disabuse them of the false and often harmful beliefs about human behavior that are popular among those who have never taken a psychology course, we will feel gratified.

# MAJOR CONTENT CHANGES IN THE 9TH EDITION

The 9th edition has been extensively revised to include cutting-edge research while retaining the classic studies that constitute the building blocks of the field. Some of the substantive changes in this edition include the following.

## Chapter 1   The Science and Practice of Psychology

- Revised the definition of psychology and expanded the discussion of related disciplines.
- Revised the distinctions among kinds of psychologists and updated the related statistics.

- Included new and rewritten examples of methods throughout the chapter.
- Revised the section on Conducting Good Experiments to contrast single-subject and group designs.
- Reworked the discussion of Bandura's classic research on observational learning so that it now illustrates two-way group design.
- Reorganized the history and future of psychology primarily according to a timeline.
- Added influential theorists not formerly in the history, including Thorndike, Pavlov, McDougall, Hull, Newell and Simon, and Vygotsky, to fill in the timeline.
- Contrasted the three major historical forces in psychology.
- Added coverage of positive psychology, evolutionary psychology, and neuroscience.
- Included a new section about considerations of culture, ethnicity, diversity, and race.
- Completely revised the ethical standards with up-to-date guidelines and examples from classic research.

## Chapter 2   Brain, Body, and Behavior

- Updated the description of neuron functioning and expanded the information on glia.
- Moved the section on How Neuroscientists Study the Brain and Mind forward (it used to be at the end of the chapter) and updated it to include the latest on PET, fMRI, and QEEG.
- Streamlined and reorganized the sections on The Brain's Functions.
- Expanded the coverage of neurotransmitters.
- Added a new section on ethical issues in the use of neuroscience methods under development and on the horizon.
- Updated and expanded the feature boxes.

## Chapter 3   Sensing and Perceiving

- Expanded coverage of the role of genetics in color blindness and updated the related statistics.
- Updated information on the numbers and types of receptors and how they work.
- Credited the Gestalt psychologists for their early work on perception.
- Completely updated and rewrote the feature A Matter of Debate: A Human Scent of Sex?
- Added a Life Span Perspective feature on Taste, Smell, and Aging, which includes new research.

## Chapter 4   Conditioning and Learning

- Rewrote the chapter to include more information about cognition.
- Streamlined the history of classical conditioning, adding delayed conditioning and eliminating backward conditioning.
- Expanded coverage of biological predispositions and revised the treatment of Watson and Raynor.
- Streamlined the history of operant conditioning and revised and reorganized contingencies into positive and negative reinforcement and positive and negative punishment.

- Added cognitive qualifiers on delay of reinforcement and punishment; revised discussion of the contrast between reinforcement and punishment; and combined the coverage of superstitions and phobias, with new examples, into a single subsection preceding learned helplessness.
- Removed "old" issues in learning theory but retained the "classics."
- Included a new Matter of Debate feature about spanking children, which summarizes research on the pros and cons and cross-cultural differences.

## Chapter 5   Remembering and Forgetting

- Condensed the stages of memory to the three basics: sensory memory, short-term (now also working) memory, and long-term memory.
- Added new coverage of mood/state-dependent memory.
- Condensed coverage of mnemonics and moved it from box to text.
- Added a Psychology in the Lab and in Life feature on False Memories, which focuses on Loftus, trials, and the controversy over recovered memories of childhood abuse.

## Chapter 6   Language and Thought

- Expanded coverage of pragmatics.
- Updated treatment of language learning by other animals.
- Reorganized the material, putting "traps in problem solving" all in one section.
- Thoroughly revised the Life Span Perspective feature on Language and Thought in Babies and Toddlers.
- Added a Psychology and the Media feature about Irene Pepperberg and Alex, the African Grey parrot.

## Chapter 7   Intelligence and Its Assessment

- Split intelligence and personality into two chapters, to better reflect how psychology views these individual differences, so Chapter 7 now covers only intelligence.
- Removed coverage of Guilford and expanded and updated coverage of Gardner and Sternberg.
- Updated intelligence tests throughout and revised the aptitude/achievement discussion.
- Added range of reaction to the section on Heredity, Environment, and Intelligence.
- Completely rewrote the discussion of ethnic factors in intelligence testing.
- Added a Life Span Perspective feature that contrasts intelligence and IQ and discusses whether or not people are becoming more intelligent.

## Chapter 8   Emotion and Motivation

- Extensively rewrote and reorganized the motivation sections, reworking the definition and use of *drive*, and defining motives more generally.
- Updated coverage of Ekman and other cross-cultural research.
- Expanded discussion of homeostasis.
- Added discussion of the evolutionary theory of overeating.
- Expanded coverage of classic sleep stages and REM sleep.
- Thoroughly revised the sections on attraction and same-sex orientation.
- Eliminated power and hostility motives and motive hierarchies.

# Chapter 9   Personality and Its Assessment

- Split intelligence and personality, so Chapter 9 now covers only personality.
- Changed the definition of personality to Allport's classic one.
- Clarified contrasts between Freudian psychoanalysis and the modifed psycho-dynamic views that followed
- Moved the overview of Erikson to this chapter, with later reference in developmental chapters.
- Added coverage of Bandura and human agency.
- Added coverage of Buss and evolutionary psychology with its logic and approach to research, then examples of proposed gender differences.
- Removed situational tests and expanded coverage of Big Five theory, qualified as primarily descriptive.
- Clarified, updated, and expanded treatment of objective tests (MMPI-2, 16PF, NEO-PI-R) and projective tests.
- Included a new Matter of Debate feature on The Person and the Situation, emphasizing Mischel and closing with an example of the stability of "honesty."

# Chapter 10   Human Development: Conception Through Childhood

- Moved this chapter forward (it was formerly Chapter 12) to further emphasize the importance of development.
- Expanded general coverage of cross-cultural research and paid more attention to classics.
- Added coverage of the human genome.
- Added more material on primitive versus survival reflexes.
- Expanded coverage of object permanence.
- Expanded coverage of Harlow.
- Added a new section on Ainsworth, the strange situation test, and types of attachment.
- Updated and expanded the discussion of punishment, abuse, and neglect.
- Balanced the discussion of the effects of divorce on children aged 4–5.
- Added a section on developmental disorders that now covers mental retardation, learning disorders, and ADHD.
- Added a Matter of Debate feature asking whether or not Ritalin is overprescribed.

# Chapter 11   Human Development: Adolescence, Adulthood, and Death

- Moved this chapter forward (it was formerly Chapter 13) to further emphasize the importance of development.
- Added cultural variations in the experience of adolescence.
- Added Gilligan's views on gender differences in moral development.
- Added new coverage of teenage drug abuse, pregnancy, and STDs and a new discussion of Baumrind's parenting styles.
- Added a Matter of Debate feature about legalization of assisted suicide.

# Chapter 12   Stress, Coping, and Well-Being

- Added a discussion of student test anxiety, revised coverage of PTSD, and included a new discussion of job burnout.

- Moved biofeedback to the section on coping and stress.
- Added a new section on well-being and positive psychology that emphasizes Seligman.

## Chapter 13   Mental and Behavioral Disorders

- Thoroughly updated the entire chapter to parallel DSM-IV-TR, with updated incidence statistics, additional qualifiers, more real-life examples, and some changes in interpretation.
- Added discussion of Szasz.
- Extended discussion of paranoid schizophrenia.
- Updated statistics on mood disorders and created a more balanced discussion.
- Revised the discussion of phobias and panic attacks.
- Completely rewrote the section on substance abuse and dependence, including drugs other than alcohol.
- Added a section on sexual disorders, dissociative identity disorder, disorders of impulse control, and culture-bound syndromes.

## Chapter 14   Psychotherapy and Other Treatment Approaches

- Retained classic methods of therapy but updated the discussion to include modern therapies and research on their effectiveness.
- Thoroughly rewrote the section on behavior therapy to accommodate cognitive and newer cognitive behavior therapies.
- Included Lovaas in the coverage of aversive conditioning.
- Added exposure therapy and participant modeling and expanded the discussion of Beck and Ellis.
- Rewrote the section on psychotherapy to include clinical trials and empirically supported therapies and expand coverage of culture, ethnicity, and gender.
- Updated the material on medications used in biological therapies.
- Added a Matter of Debate feature that discusses the effects of community psychology and deinstitutionalization.

## Chapter 15   Social Psychology

- Added discussion of social schemas, enculturation versus socialization, Festinger and Carlsmith, Hovland's fourth factor, the medium, and included more on persuasive communications.
- Revised the section on attribution to include fundamental attribution error, Jones and Davis's correspondent inference theory, the actor-observer effect, the social desirability effect, and especially attribution and culture.
- Reorganized the section on conformity and obedience to include Cialdini and compliance.
- Added a section on group dynamics that includes group formation; social facilitation and impairment; diffusion of responsibility, social loafing, deindividuation, groupthink, and group polarization.
- Contrasted hostile and instrumental aggressions.
- Added Zimbardo's prison experiment and Dollard et al. on frustration-aggression.
- Added Sternberg's triangular theory of love.
- Added an epilogue designed to give better closure to the text.

## Appendix   Statistics: Description and Inference

- Rewrote and reorganized the material to emphasize the conceptual approach.
- Eliminated unnecessary statistical terms and the section on computational formulas.
- Added documentation of Galton and Pearson and correlation to the Descriptive Statistics section.
- Reorganized and reoriented the Probability, Normal Distribution, and Some Applications section, which now includes a lead-in to inferential statistics.
- Reorganized and streamlined the Inferential Statistics section, which now includes notes on ANOVA based on Bandura in Chapter 1.

# DEVELOPMENTAL THEME RETAINED

We have retained our emphasis on the changes in psychological processes from infancy through older adulthood so that the student can appreciate how experience and maturation, acting together, alter the basic mental and emotional aspects of being human. These issues are woven throughout the text and are highlighted in the Life Span Perspective features. To allow for this integration in specific contexts, we have retained the treatment of developmental psychology in two chapters. As an example of the importance and utility of the life span emphasis, consider its role in the study of memory. Although memories are subject to change and reconstruction throughout the life span, the ability to remember much beyond the very recent past is especially fragile during the first couple years of life and again during the last decade of the average life span. Memory abilities—and, more generally, cognition and the ways in which children and adults interpret their world—are by no means constants. Nor are the early temperaments and behavioral tendencies of young children comparable to the complexities of adult personalitity. We believe that the continued emphasis on this life span perspective enriches the student's understanding of psychological processes.

# PERSPECTIVES OF PSYCHOLOGY HIGHLIGHTED

The book contains four types of boxed features, designed to provide the student with a valuable perspective on especially interesting and important psychological issues within the chapter. These features are as follows:

- **A Matter of Debate.** This feature is brand-new to this edition. These boxes deal with contemporary issues in psychology and related areas that are, well, debatable. In addition to conveying that there are often two or more sides to an issue, which in its own right is important to bear in mind, these boxes also can serve as focal points for class discussion. Topics include the issues surrounding spanking children (Chapter 4) and the debate surrounding legalizing assisted suicide (Chapter 11).

- **Life Span Perspective.** These boxes, retained from the previous edition, survey how a particular phenomenon is manifested over the course of a life. The topics are designed to expand the student's appreciation of the dynamics of human development. For example, the feature in Chapter 8 explores changes in sexuality from infancy to older adulthood, and the one in Chapter 15 asks how much people can change at different ages.

- **Psychology and the Media.** Retained from the previous edition, these boxes enrich the student's insights into themes and controversies that appear in newspapers, magazines, and books. In Chapter 12, this feature highlights excerpts from an article in the *Washington Post* on Alice Isen's work and poses questions for the student about testing the hypothesis that humor can be used to fight stress.

- **Psychology in the Lab and in Life.** These new boxes explore practical applications of psychological research and show the relevance of psychology to everyday life. This feature utilizes important and relevant topics from the Psychology in Action feature in the previous edition; a number of new topics have been added as well. For example, the feature in Chapter 5 surveys the extensive research by Elizabeth Loftus, first on "false memories" and their impact on courtroom testimony and later on their impact in trials involving childhood memories of abuse.

# STUDENT AIDS ENSURE STUDENT SUCCESS

In order to help students understand the material and retain what they've learned, we have integrated a number of pedagogical features into the text.

**Focus Questions** are new to this edition. These questions, which appear at the beginning of every major section, help students understand what content will be covered in the section. They help hone critical thinking skills and then serve as an effective study tool when students are reviewing for exams. The questions are designed to help students with the Q in the SQ3R method of studying.

**Study Charts** have been added throughout the book. These tables include information about the most important aspects of certain fundamental topics.

**Test Yourself** questions have been retained and updated. Peppered throughout the margins to avoid interrupting the flow, these questions foster progressive critical thinking and application of the material. Answers appear at the end of each chapter, after the Summary.

The running **Margin Glossary,** defining key terms that are boldfaced in text, has been retained and updated. The margin glossary provides students with definitions for important terms as they are introduced in the text. The glossary also serves as a handy study tool.

The **Summary** appearing at the end of each chapter has been streamlined in this edition to highlight important topics and vocabulary without giving definitions, thus ensuring that the student will read and refer back to the text as necessary.

# TWO BOOKS FOR THE PRICE OF 1!

At the end of every chapter, students will find a **Study Guide,** an integrated tool designed to promote learning, retention, and understanding. This built-in Study Guide includes a fill-in-the-blank review of important terms (60–120 questions per chapter), a tear-out multiple-choice practice test (20 questions per chapter), and a series of exercises that expand upon important or difficult concepts within the chapter.

The Study Guide has been reordered for maximum benefit. The components are as follows:

- **Key Terms** (formerly called Review of Important Terms) are now first in the Study Guide. Accompanying this simple alphabetized list of the key terms introduced in the chapter are the numbers of the pages on which the definitions appear.

- The **Active Learning Review** (formerly called Programmed Unit) is the core of the Study Guide. This is a fill-in component that follows the structure of the text, reviewing the most important terms. The Active Learning Review consists of 60–120 questions per chapter. The fill-in answers are provided in the margin for easy review.

- The **Practice Test** follows next and consists of 20 multiple-choice questions. Answers to those questions appear at the end of the book.

- The **Exercises** are the last component of the Study Guide. Many of the exercises have been updated, and each chapter now contains at least two exercises. These exercises require students to put into action the things that they have learned. Examples are an exercise on conditioning conversation in Chapter 4, one that explores multiple intelligences in Chapter 7, and one that illustrates popular misconceptions about mental and behavioral disorders in Chapter 13.

All in all, the Study Guide offers students between 85 and 145 student review items, as well as a full list of the most important terms for each chapter.

# A PRETEST OF STUDENT UNDERSTANDING

In the next section of the Preface, To the Student, we have retained from the previous edition the set of instructions on how to study this book. The SQ3R method is detailed, and the contents of the Study Guide are reiterated. In addition, we have included an updated Test of Essential Psychological Information (TEPI), which can be used as pretest/posttest tool. It can be applied to assess the level of psychological sophistication of the students as they begin the course and the improvement that the course has helped bring about. The 30 true/false items on this test reflect key elements of content in an introductory course on psychology.

# THE ANCILLARY PACKAGE

In keeping with our desire to achieve brevity, clarity, rigor, and relevance in the 9th edition, we have gone to great lengths to ensure that the ancillaries for the 9th edition bring instructors and students the most valuable content possible. The following items are available to qualified adopters. Please consult your local sales representative for details.

## Instructor's Manual

The *Instructor's Manual* by Susan Weldon, Eastern Michigan University, and Travis Langley, Henderson State University, includes the following features:

- Detailed chapter outlines
- Learning objectives that parallel the Focus Questions in the text
- Key terms
- Language enhancement guide to help ESL students
- Lecture and activity ideas for professors
- Infotrac activities
- Internet activities
- Annotated web links
- Film and video activities
- Tie-ins to the PsychNow! 2.0 CD ROM

## Test Bank

The *Test Bank* by Susan Weldon, Eastern Michigan University, includes the following features:

- 120 multiple-choice questions per chapter
- 25 fill-in questions per chapter
- 20 true/false questions per chapter
- 5 essay questions per chapter
- All questions labeled according to type, learning objective, and difficulty level

## Multimedia Manager for Introductory Psychology, 2004

This tool, by Travis Langley, Henderson State University, makes it easy to assemble, edit, publish, and present custom lectures for introductory psychology. Through Microsoft PowerPoint, professors will have access to detailed lecture outlines, selected pieces of art straight from the book, CNN® Today video clips, and simulations. All material can be used as is, modified, or integrated with your own materials.

## Book Companion Website

The book-specific website features

- Chapter outlines
- Chapter-by-chapter quizzes linked to the text
- Flashcards for each chapter
- A crossword puzzle for each chapter
- Web links
- Instructor resources

## ExamView® Computerized Testing CD-ROM

With this easy-to-use assessment and tutorial system, you will be able to create, deliver, and customize tests and study guides (both print and online) in minutes. ExamView offers both a Quick Test Wizard and an Online Test Wizard that guide you step by step through the process of creating tests, while the unique "WYSIWYG" capability allows you to see the test you are creating on the screen exactly as it will print or display online. You can build tests of up to 250 questions using up to 12 question types. Using ExamView's complete word processing capabilities, you can enter an unlimited number of new questions or edit existing questions.

## PsychNow 2.0

For only $5 extra per copy, you can add color, depth, sound, and motion to your students' introductory psychology experience. PsychNow 2.0 offers a dynamic tool that goes beyond the boundaries of the classroom. Using this interactive CD-ROM, students can investigate many subject areas including

- Accessing Psychology
- Human Development
- The Brain and Consciousness
- Sensation and Perception
- Learning and Cognition
- Motivation and Emotion
- Personality and Abnormal Psychology
- Social Psychology

Students can also conduct 15 different interactive research experiments in areas such as

- Neurocognition
- Perception
- Memory
- Concepts
- Imagery

# ACKNOWLEDGMENTS

We would like to extend a hearty thank-you to Steven Mark Sachs of Los Angeles Valley College for contributing and revising many exercises for the Study Guide sections of the text. Most of all, we are deeply grateful to Marianne Taflinger, Senior Editor, for guiding us through the revision process, and to Kate Barnes, Development Editor, for her careful and thorough attention to every aspect of the process. We would also like to thank Paul Wells, Senior Editorial Production Project Manager, along with Sally Lifland and her staff at Lifland et al., Bookmakers, for their rendering of the text. We're also grateful to Dan Moneypenny for his careful review of all of the supplements and overseeing the entire supplements process so professionally. We would also like to thank Nicole Root, Editorial Assistant; Lori Grebe, Marketing Manager; and Laurel Anderson, Marketing Assistant.

We are especially grateful to the following reviewers, who provided much insight and inspiration for the 9th edition:

Lori Azzara, North Shore Community College
Suzanne Black, Floyd College
Michael Brady, Lansing Community College
Sheldon Brown, North Shore Community College
Patrick Butler, San Jose City College
Isabelle Cherney, Creighton University
Gail Ditkoff, California University of Pennsylvania
Robin Flaton, Hofstra University
Thomas Gerry, Columbia-Greene Community College
Jamie Goldenberg, Boise State University
John A. Greaves, Jefferson State Community College
Louise Katz, Colombia State Community College
Eileen Kaufman, Union County College
Ron Kinsman, Davenport University
John Klein, Castleton State College
Travis Langley, Henderson State University
Bettie Meachum, Cedar Valley College
Chelley Merrell, Tidewater Community College
Sandra Naumann, Delaware Tech and Community College
Robert Pellegrini, San Jose State University
William D. Phillips, The College of New Jersey
Vicki Ritts, St. Louis Community College–Meramec
William Rivero, William Carey College
Steven Sachs, Los Angeles Valley College
Kim Scheuerman, Jefferson Community College
Emily Sweitzer, California University of Pennsylvania

# To the Student

There are many possible ways to use the 9th edition of *Kagan & Segal's Psychology: An Introduction* to learn the material effectively. Your instructor may suggest methods geared to her or his classroom approach to the course. Or you may want to experiment and discover your own method, based on your individual study habits. The following suggestions are merely some general guidelines for taking full advantage of the possibilities.

## STUDYING EACH CHAPTER

The textbook and its built-in Study Guide are designed to assist you in applying the SQ3R system of studying. This system, which has proven highly effective, continues to be used by many proficient students—either after learning about the system or because they've discovered on their own the value of combining some or all of the system's five steps. SQ3R stands for the following steps: survey, question, read, recite, and review.

### 1. Survey

Before starting to read a chapter, you should get an overview of what it contains and the key points it makes. This survey need not be time-consuming. Note the title (for Chapter 1, The Science and Practice of Psychology), which is in itself a very brief description of what's to come. Then look at the outline that begins each chapter. The outline lists the main topics covered in each chapter. In Chapter 1, the first two are The Scope of Psychology and The Varieties of Psychology and Psychologists, each of which includes subsection headings to give you a clearer idea of what the section is about.

This may be enough of a survey. Or you may want to take a little more time and thumb through the chapter, noting how much space is devoted to each of the sections and subsections and looking at the illustrations (which are intended to illuminate important points or research efforts). The whole purpose of the survey is to create a framework that will help you organize the chapter's facts and ideas as you encounter them.

Make a similar survey at the start of each major section of the chapter, starting with the primary heading. Thumb through the section, examining the words printed in italics and boldface for emphasis and the points made in the illustrations. Note especially the subsections. In other words, take the time to get a general idea of what this particular section of the book is going to tell you.

### 2. Question

This step applies to the subsections in each chapter. When you come to a new subsection, before you start reading it, turn its heading into one or more questions that will pique your curiosity and orient you toward finding answers (the Focus Questions that appear at the beginning of each main section are intended to help you here). For example, when beginning the Chapter 1 subsection The Missions of Psychology, you might ask yourself: "What is this science trying to accomplish, and why?" Or you can put the question in any other way that makes you wonder why the book is going to discuss the matter and more eager to learn about it.

## 3. Read

How much to read in one chunk is largely a matter of individual preference. Some students find it best to study the entire chapter as a whole, a technique they find helpful in understanding the pattern of the materials and the way the individual topics and facts relate to one another. Some study one major section at a time (perhaps five to ten pages), others only a subsection (often a single page or so). Experiment with what works best for you—and vary the size of the chunk for various parts of the book. Some parts are more or less familiar and can be learned fairly easily. In others, ideas that are new to you may tend to crowd together and get confusing if taken in too large a dose.

Whatever you decide, read with the idea that you will make an active search for the answers to the questions you have asked about each subsection, and that you want to comprehend and remember it. As the author of the SQ3R system once pointed out, "Reading textbooks is work"—readers must know what they are looking for, find it, and then organize their thoughts about it.

## 4. Recite

You can recite what you've read by talking, either to yourself or aloud. But a much better way is to jot down notes summarizing what you have read. The notes should be brief—just a single word or a very few at most—and in your own words. They should be written *after* you have finished reading. (Many students make the mistake of taking notes as they go along, without really comprehending their meaning.)

The best method is to stop at the end of each subsection, look away from the book, and try to recite the answers to the questions you asked and any other important information you have learned. Then jot down a brief note that summarizes the subsection.

An alternative to taking notes is to go back and highlight the key words and key points in the subsection. This works for some students but is generally less helpful, in part because it does not force you to put the point into your own words. Moreover, it may lead to reading just for the sake of finding important sentences and marking them, without really attending to the meaning. You can, of course, use both techniques—first make notes and then mark the words in the book that relate to your notes, along with details that you want or figures that you need to remember.

## 5. Review

When you get to the end of a major section of the chapter, look over the notes you have jotted down on the subsections and find out how the various points are organized and related to one another. Or, if you have used highlighting instead of notes, go back through the section and examine the points you have marked. Then, because this step is closely related to the previous one, cover up your notes or look away from the book and recite the points. If you have trouble recalling any of them or what any of them mean, take another look at your notes or the book and try again. In addition, respond to the Test Yourself questions and check your answers with those provided at the end of the chapter.

Turn also to the Key Terms at the beginning of the Study Guide, making sure that you understand them, and then go to the Summary—where the most important points are presented briefly. For convenience in applying the SQ3R system, the Summary is divided into the main sections of the chapter, with each identified by the same heading used in the chapter. Read the summary for the section you have been studying and make sure that you understand everything it contains—to the extent of being able to explain the information. Wherever you can't, go back to the chapter and do some more reading of what you have missed. Your review will be of tremendous value in making sure you have grasped all the points made in the section and fixing them in your memory.

The *Active Learning Review* that forms the core of the Study Guide is a step-by-step, easily mastered summary of the most important points in the chapter. You will note that the review is divided into brief "frames," each containing blanks for you to fill in as you go along. The correct word or words to fill in the blanks are printed in the margin. When you do the review, keep the answers covered with a ruler or a strip of paper, and move it down the page each time you fill in a blank. This process serves two purposes. First, it enables you to combine the reading and reciting steps of SQ3R. Second, by letting you know right away if your answer was correct, it gives you immediate feedback on your performance and allows you to go back to the chapter to correct any mistakes.

The *Practice Test* can also be useful in your review of what you've learned, after you have finished studying the entire chapter. Taking the test offers further feedback on your performance, and checking your answers against those in the back of the book enables you to catch and correct any mistakes.

The *Exercises* at the end of each chapter are suggestions for simple demonstrations you can perform to apply or illustrate some of the scientific findings presented in the chapter.

# DIAGNOSTIC TEST: MEASURING HOW MUCH YOU WILL LEARN

As you study this book, you will be learning many facts about psychology, a sizable proportion of which may be surprising to you. Indeed, some of them may run contrary to the beliefs you now have about various aspects of human behavior. This point is discussed further at the beginning of Chapter 1.

To assess the extent to which this book enlarges your understanding of the field of psychology, we have developed the following Test of Essential Psychological Information (TEPI). The items will test your knowledge of various facets of human personality and behavior and allow you to gauge how much new information you have accumulated from this book and course.

Listed are 30 statements about various aspects of behavior and functioning that reflect the typical content of introductory courses in psychology. Facts about each of these statements are contained in this book. Read each statement carefully, and record your judgment of it by circling TRUE or FALSE.

To compare your present knowledge about the field of psychology with what you learn from this course, you may opt to take this test again at the end of the semester. A scoring guide and the correct answers are provided at the end of the test.

1. A 10-year-old has more synapses—that is, nerve connections in the brain—than does a 1-year-old.                    TRUE    FALSE

2. Acupuncture is effective in dulling subsequent pain in a patient because it may stimulate the brain's endorphins.    TRUE    FALSE

3. The tongue can detect six different pure tastes.    TRUE    FALSE

4. The sense organs that allow us equilibrium, or sense of balance, are located in the thyroid gland.    TRUE    FALSE

5. Your memory of a telephone number would remain in your mind for about only 30 seconds if you didn't repeat it to yourself.    TRUE    FALSE

6. Eyewitness testimony at a trial is generally accurate and reliable.    TRUE    FALSE

7. If you were to work with chimpanzees for a long time, they could be made to be as sophisticated with their word skills as are children.    TRUE    FALSE

8. Intelligence test scores are the best predictor of future mental health.    TRUE    FALSE

9. When a person feels frightened, the right side of the brain is likely to be more active than the left.    TRUE    FALSE

10. Our brains are sometimes more active when we are sleeping than when we are awake.    TRUE    FALSE

11. Lifetime behavior patterns are pretty much set by age 5.    TRUE    FALSE

12. Certain images in our dreams—such as fire or guns—have the same meaning for everybody.    TRUE    FALSE

13. If you're being attacked on the street, you're more likely to get help if there is one rather than six bystanders.    TRUE    FALSE

14. Firstborns are more motivated to achieve in school than are laterborns.    TRUE    FALSE

15. Sexual orientation is formed mainly as a result of experiences with one's parents in the first two years.    TRUE    FALSE

16. A person's environment can alter personality patterns that are partly genetic in origin.    TRUE    FALSE

17. Most children who are raised permissively become poor parents.    TRUE    FALSE

18. Scores on all components of intelligence tend to decrease as people grow older.    TRUE    FALSE

19. Psychological symptoms of depression are always caused by a psychological problem.    TRUE    FALSE

20. First impressions have a strong influence on interpersonal relationships.    TRUE    FALSE

21. Lie detectors generally reveal who is telling a lie.    TRUE    FALSE

22. You can overcome a phobia without understanding how it began.    TRUE    FALSE

23. The environment begins its influence the moment a person is born.    TRUE    FALSE

24. If two siblings grow up in the same home with the same parents, they usually share major personality traits.    TRUE    FALSE

25. Biofeedback is not accepted as a scientifically valid treatment.　TRUE　FALSE

26. Most creative individuals are psychologically abnormal.　TRUE　FALSE

27. Most 2-year-olds can understand the difference in meaning between right and wrong.　TRUE　FALSE

28. The suicide rate in the United States is highest among men over 85 years old.　TRUE　FALSE

29. Some young children develop better in daycare than they do at home.　TRUE　FALSE

30. Most of the time, divorce leads to longstanding psychological problems in children.　TRUE　FALSE

## Scoring

| 18 or less: | Not knowledgeable |
|---|---|
| 19–21: | Barely knowledgeable |
| 22–24: | Basically knowledgeable |
| 25–27: | Knowledgeable |
| 28–30: | Very knowledgeable |

## Answers

| 1. False | 16. True |
|---|---|
| 2. True | 17. False |
| 3. False | 18. False |
| 4. False | 19. False |
| 5. True | 20. True |
| 6. False | 21. False |
| 7. False | 22. True |
| 8. False | 23. True |
| 9. True | 24. False |
| 10. True | 25. False |
| 11. False | 26. False |
| 12. False | 27. True |
| 13. True | 28. True |
| 14. True | 29. True |
| 15. False | 30. False |

# THE AUTHORS

## Jerome Kagan

Jerome Kagan (Ph.D., Yale University) is former chair of the psychology department at Harvard University and is world renowned for his work on temperament in children. At Harvard, Dr. Kagan's research on the cognitive and emotional development of a child during the first decade of life focused on the origins of temperament. He has tracked the development of inhibited and uninhibited children from infancy to adolescence. He served on the National Institute of Mental Health and on the National Research Council. His books include *Galen's Prophecy: Temperament in Human Nature* and *Three Seductive Ideas*.

## Julius Segal

Julius Segal was a recognized authority on coping with psychological trauma and served for 30 years as director of the scientific and public information programs for the National Institute of Mental Health. Dr. Segal taught psychology at George Washington University and the University of Maryland and lectured extensively throughout the United States. Dr. Segal, the author of eight books and over 250 articles on mental health and human development, received his Ph.D. from Catholic University. Dedicated to making psychology accessible to the public, Dr. Segal served as contributing editor and monthly columnist for *Parents Magazine*.

## Don Baucum

Don Baucum is an Associate Professor and a member of the primary faculty of the Department of Psychology at the University of Alabama. His Ph.D. is in General Experimental Psychology, and he has extensive training in clinical psychology as well. He currently divides his professional time between teaching and writing. Courses include personality, social psychology, introductory statistics, research methods, developmental psychology, and psychology of learning—along with numerous offerings of introductory psychology. Writing efforts include co-authoring two other textbooks and authoring two general psychology surveys and assorted study materials.

## Carolyn D. Smith

Carolyn D. Smith, a freelance writer, is the author of *The Absentee American* and *Strangers at Home* and co-editor of *In the Field: Readings on the Field Research Experience*. She has also lent her writing expertise to other psychology texts about child development.

# 1 The Science and Practice of Psychology

© Chuck Savage/CORBIS

1

Psychology can perhaps best be characterized as a modern attempt to deal with questions that have always interested and puzzled humans: why people behave as they do, what they think and feel and how they go about thinking and feeling, how a helpless infant develops into a fully functioning adult. Thus, more than any subject you are likely to study, psychology is about a topic that should be of intense interest to you: you. It seeks answers to the kinds of questions that you have probably often asked yourself about who you are, what made you the way you are, and where you may go from here. It also seeks to answer these questions about the many people and other creatures around you.

The questions addressed by psychology are endlessly fascinating: To what extent were you born the way you are and to what extent is your personality a result of experiences you've had since birth? To what extent are you in charge of your life and to what extent are you controlled by forces in the world around you? Can you "change" if you want to? What do all people have in common? What accounts for the many variations and differences among people? What attracts people to each other? Why are some people quick to learn, others not so quick? Why do some people crumble in the face of everyday stresses while others overcome seemingly devastating crises? Why are some people generally cheerful, others generally glum; some aggressive, others passive; some withdrawn and alone, others friendly? Why do some people appear perfectly rational and in control while others behave in strange and unpredictable ways?

Such questions surface every day in popular books, magazines, radio and television talk shows, and ordinary conversations. Answers abound, often based on casual observations, old sayings, and "common sense." Sometimes folk wisdom isn't bad, although it can be contradictory. For example, for the most part, "birds of a feather *do* flock together" but "opposites *don't* attract." That is, people with similar interests and attitudes are more likely to be attracted to each other and to develop relationships than are people who are dissimilar in these respects. How do we know which adages to believe? Psychology offers *scientific* answers rather than ones that begin with "They say . . ." or ones that are based on casual observations. Psychology's insights are based on the careful, sustained efforts of researchers who continue to gather information about the nature of human behavior.

Personal experience is worth some additional comments. As you study psychology, you will find that some of your ideas and beliefs about people do indeed "fit the facts" established by research—especially if you happen to be a careful observer of people who avoids jumping to conclusions. At same time, you will almost certainly find that a lot of what has been verified (or contradicted) by scientific research clearly does not coincide with what you have come to believe. Either way, personal experience can be an important starting point in learning psychology: Information that is highly consistent with *or* sharply different from your personal beliefs is easy to remember if you sort it out accordingly. (The new information and new vocabulary you learn in a psychology course are another matter; remembering these may take considerably more work.) Here's a piece of advice that should serve you well as you take courses in psychology: Never answer an exam question based solely on personal experience!

Psychologists do not pretend to have all the answers, of course, and not all psychologists agree on the answers that have emerged. Humans and other animals are so complex that they may forever defy complete scientific analysis. But psychologists do have some important answers—plus clues to many others—and they are steadily making new discoveries. This much is certain: When you finish studying this text, you will have more objective, verifiable knowledge about the human experience than anyone in the world did back in the 19th century, when the first psychology laboratory was established and the science of psychology was born.

# THE SCOPE OF PSYCHOLOGY

Psychology has advanced by leaps and bounds over its approximately 100-year history and is now an established science, yet there remains some confusion over what the field is all about. We therefore begin with an overview of the varied domain of psychology and how it relates to the subject matter of other disciplines.

**FOCUS QUESTIONS**
- What is psychology?
- What are the missions of psychology?
- What disciplines are included in the behavioral and social sciences?

## Defining Psychology's Broad Boundaries

A good definition of **psychology** has to capture an enormous realm, and it is likely that no two psychologists will give the exact same definition. Here's one that covers the essentials: *Psychology is the scientific study of the overt and covert behavior of living organisms*—with emphasis on animals and especially humans.

   As with most definitions that you encounter as a student, each element requires some explanation. To begin with, *scientific* means that psychologists go about their studies in an orderly and systematic way, with careful attention to gathering objective evidence that others can evaluate for themselves (even though understanding and evaluating the evidence sometimes requires advanced training). In turn, "objective evidence" is in itself a broad term, and later in the chapter we have much to say about objectivity and the methods psychologists use in conducting scientific research. For now, note that psychologists—like other scientists—are inherently skeptical. They want "proof" and are disinclined to take much for granted. For example, when we noted that similarity of interests and attitudes helps in forming and maintaining relationships, we based that conclusion on research discussed in Chapter 15.

   Next, the word *behavior* can mean a host of things. In the most general sense, behavior is literally anything an organism does. Today you woke up, perhaps yawned and stretched, got up, got dressed, and started your day. Over the course of the day, you will probably attend classes, listen to and talk with other people, work, play, perhaps laugh or cry. At the end of the day, you will sleep. Then you will get up and start another cycle. Everything you do along the way—including sleeping—is behavior. These are examples of **overt behavior:** behavior that can be readily observed by someone else (or at least detected by physiological measuring instruments). But there's more. You also think about this or that while you go about your day; you experience emotions such as anger, fear, joy, and sadness; you feel hungry and thirsty at times; and ideally you learn some things in your classes. Perhaps you have stirrings of desire for accomplishment and success, friendship, even revenge; perhaps you worry about problems and seek ways to cope with them. While you sleep, you also dream. These are examples of **covert behavior:** behavior that cannot be directly observed or measured and must be inferred from overt behavior. Nearly all of modern psychology is intensely concerned with both kinds

**Psychology**
The scientific study of the overt and covert behavior of living organisms.

**Overt behavior**
Observable or otherwise measurable behavior.

**Covert behavior**
Behavior that cannot be directly observed or measured and must be inferred.

of behavior: behavior that can be observed directly and behavior that must be inferred. This was not always the case, however, as we see later in the chapter when we survey psychology's history.

Factors that influence behavior are many and varied. The most important of them is the functioning of the brain, an organ that is immensely complex in humans. The human brain is made up of many billions of intricately interconnected cells—of dozens of different kinds, performing different functions—that are constantly exchanging messages via electrical and chemical activity. But the brain would be useless without the help it gets from other parts of the body. It would not know anything about the environment without the specialized cells of the sense organs, which are sensitive to light, sound, odors, pressure, and motion. It would not even know hunger or thirst without signals provided by the bloodstream and some of the internal organs. It would not produce emotions without the aid of various chemicals in the brain and elsewhere in the body.

Psychology studies all the interrelationships between the brain and the rest of the body, along with where they come from. It investigates *heredity*—the extent to which our conduct is governed by tendencies handed down to us from the countless generations of forebears from whom we are descended—and it investigates how these tendencies evolved and were handed down. Psychology also examines the influence of *environment,* including the ways we learn from our experiences, remember them, and apply them. In particular, it looks at how the actions of other people affect our behavior and how our actions affect their behavior—effects that turn out to be much more significant and far-reaching than you might suspect.

Just as humans and members of other species are not simple creatures, devising scientific ways to study them in all their diversity is not a simple task. Psychologists cannot rely on unverifiable propositions about behavior, no matter how brilliant the reasoning. As noted earlier, psychology is skeptical and demands proof that everyone can see, based on carefully controlled experiments and on observations made with the greatest possible precision and objectivity—which requires freedom from biases or preconceived ideas of any kind. Psychology also cannot rely on metaphysical explanations based on faith and religious interpretations. This is not to say that psychologists and other scientists regard their conclusions as somehow superior to those based on philosophical or religious understanding. Science is simply a *different* way of thinking about behavior and attempting to explain it, with a distinct set of rules.

Without the scientific approach, it is difficult to reach valid conclusions about human behavior. The everyday observer is almost bound to commit mistakes of observation and interpretation and to make judgments based on faulty or insufficient evidence. Sometimes personal observations serve as a good starting point for scientific study. But all of us tend to generalize from our own feelings and experiences, and what we see in ourselves is not necessarily characteristic of people in general. Similarly, we may generalize from the actions and opinions of the people we know, which are not necessarily universal—particularly across different cultures, as we see at various points in later chapters.

## The Missions of Psychology

The field of psychology has two primary missions: (1) *to understand behavior in all its forms* and (2) *to predict its course.* Indeed, understanding and predicting are goals of all sciences. Chemists have sought from the earliest times to understand reactions among elements and molecules—for example, to predict what will happen when a substance is subjected to heat or combined with another substance in a test tube. Psychologists seek, among other things, to understand why individuals behave as they do in family or other social situations and to predict what will happen if certain changes occur—for example, to predict the effects of divorce on children.

Some scientists seek not only to understand and predict events but to control them as well. Chemists want to control the substances they work with so that they can develop useful new substances, such as the various synthetics now used in clothing, automobiles, houses, and a host of other manufactured goods. To a certain extent, some psychologists also look for ways to *control* human behavior—to direct or change it for the better—or at least to understand how it is controlled. Controlling behavior can be thought of as a third primary mission. This is especially true of those who devote their careers to treating people seeking to overcome mental and emotional problems. Mental health professionals work to "control" the behavior of their clients by trying to alleviate problems—such as an unreasonable fear of going out in public, inability to establish satisfactory sexual relationships, or alcohol abuse—or, more generally, by trying to assist them in restructuring their lives and their outlooks. Psychologists also seek to understand what factors contribute to such problems (that is, what factors control them).

But working with humans is far different from mixing chemicals in a test tube. The possibility of controlling human behavior raises thorny questions of ethics and social policy. Thus, psychologists often have mixed feelings about whether control of behavior should be considered a third primary goal of their science. Some psychologists have argued that human behavior is always under some kind of control—the control of parents and school systems over children, the control of the nation's laws over the business world—and that it would be better to have such control exercised in a scientific fashion by scientists dedicated to improving the human condition (Skinner, 1972). Most psychologists, however, shun the responsibility and the dangers of abuse inherent in general efforts to manipulate and control human behavior, believing that such efforts should be restricted to situations in which an individual freely consents to being controlled or engages in behavior that makes control essential for the public good.

## Related Disciplines

Psychology is one member of a family of sciences often called the **behavioral and social sciences.** Understanding human behavior requires that psychologists study not only individual people but also other facets of human functioning—from the activity of individual brain cells to the social and cultural settings in which people function. Thus, the subject matter of these sciences ranges from the neurochemical bases of memory and mental disorders to the dynamics of global commerce and international conflict (Gerstein, Luce, Smelser, & Sperlich, 1988). Such a broad perspective is necessary because humans are continually thinking about and affected by what is happening in the world around them. Thus, for example, the quality of a parent's sleep can be affected by a news story about an armed conflict on the other side of the world in which a son or daughter is involved—just as that son or daughter is no doubt affected by knowledge of the parents' worries.

Some scientists who work in the behavioral and social sciences come from the fields of *physiology* (the study of the biological functions and activities of living organisms) and *neuroscience* (the study of the nervous system and of relationships between brain activity and behavior). Others are involved in such seemingly different areas as the study of *cognition* (mental and intellectual processes, including memory) and *motivation* (the "why" of behavior). In turn, their endeavors often incorporate knowledge from fields such as *genetics* (the study of hereditary mechanisms and of cellular functioning at the molecular level) and *biochemistry*. The behavioral and social sciences also include *anthropology* and its subdisciplines (such as physical anthropology, the study of the evolution of humans with empha-

**Behavioral and social sciences** A family of sciences that all study behavior, from differing perspectives and with different methods.

**Test Yourself**

**(a)** A researcher has applied for a grant to carry out a project on "Patterns of Aggression and Anger in Violent Criminals and Their Relationship to Childhood Experiences." Using this book's definition of psychology, tell whether the researcher is likely to be a psychologist. Why or why not?

**(b)** A research project has been undertaken by two investigators, one of them a psychologist and the second from a related field. The title of their project is "A Study of Religious Use of Alcoholic Beverages in U.S. and Mediterranean Cultures." In which field of behavioral and social science does the second researcher most likely work?

(The answers are on page 41.)

sis on physiology, and cultural anthropology, the study of different cultures and ethnicities), *sociology* (the study of large-scale social institutions and of social problems), *linguistics, education, economics,* and *political science.* Finally, the interests of psychologists and *psychiatrists* (medical practitioners who specialize in mental and behavioral disorders) frequently overlap.

Although psychology represents a distinct field, the areas of study that psychologists focus on are so varied that they often maintain a close connection with many of their "siblings" in the behavioral and social sciences. For example, psychologists exploring the role of heredity in intelligence might work in concert with geneticists, and those studying how schooling affects children might collaborate with education specialists. In working with other professionals, psychologists seek not only to draw from other disciplines but to contribute to them as well. But what is common to all psychologists is an interest in the study of behavior and, increasingly over the past couple of decades, in the behavior of the "whole" organism—as opposed to isolated aspects. That is, psychologists now recognize that the distinct areas of the brain and other parts of the body—and the mental functions they give rise to—must be viewed as an integrated whole if complete explanations of behavior are to be developed.

# THE VARIETIES OF PSYCHOLOGY AND PSYCHOLOGISTS

**FOCUS QUESTIONS**
- How many psychologists are there and what do they do?
- What's the difference between basic and applied psychology?
- What's the difference between clinical and counseling psychology?

In the last half-century, the number of psychologists in the United States and around the world has grown dramatically, and it continues to rise. In North America, the American Psychological Association (APA) has about 84,000 members (APA, 2001), the American Psychological Society about 15,000 (Bjork, 2000), and the Canadian Psychological Association about 5,000 (Canadian Psychological Association, 2001). In Europe, the British Psychological Society is among the largest, with more than 34,000 members (Davey, 2001). Numerous other psychological associations, societies, and federations of varying size and makeup exist around the world. Many psychologists belong to more than one organization.

In the United States, the percentage of all doctoral degrees awarded to psychologists rose from 4% in 1945 to over 9% in 1987 (Coyle & Thurgood, 1989). According to data compiled by the APA's Research Office (APA, 2002), from 1975 to 1995 the number of Ph.D. psychologists in the United States increased by more than 180%, to almost 81,000. All areas of psychology posted gains, but the greatest increase by far was in "health service providers"—clinical, counseling, and school psychologists, discussed later in this section. As of 1995, about half of all Ph.D. psychologists in the United States were in this category. As of 2000, about two-thirds of APA members were health service providers (APA, 2002).

The number of books, magazine articles, and TV shows based on psychological themes has also grown. Ironically, however, the popular view of psychology can be misleading to students embarking on an introductory course and perhaps contemplating a psychology major. The field may turn out to be considerably different in both scope and content than you expected.

Who employs psychologists? As of 1997, about 40% of Ph.D. psychologists in the United States worked in colleges, universities, and other educational settings. Almost as many (about 39%) worked in the private sector, either self-employed or employed by businesses. The remainder worked either in government or for nonprofit corporations (APA, 2002).

And who are they? The majority of U.S. psychologists are still males, but the gender gap is definitely closing, as discussed in Psychology in the Lab and in Life.

## PSYCHOLOGY IN THE LAB AND IN LIFE

# Closing the Gender Gap in Psychology

Although their contributions have at times been overlooked or ignored, women have been involved in psychology since its early years. When a professional psychological organization was formed in 1892, women quickly began joining, they contributed to the new journals and presented papers at the annual meetings. Mary Calkins (1863–1930), Christine Ladd-Franklin (1847–1930), and Margaret Washburn (1871–1939) are three of the best-known female psychologists from the turn of the 20th century. In 1894, Washburn was the first woman to earn a doctorate in psychology, from Cornell University. Both Calkins and Ladd-Franklin completed the requirements for their doctorates, but they were not awarded degrees because their universities, Harvard and Johns Hopkins, at the time would not grant doctorates to women.

These female pioneers—lab researchers and theorists, published in psychological journals—all faced major obstacles in their attempts to pursue psychology. Society was opposed to the notion of a working wife or mother, so most women were forced to abandon or at least postpone their professional pursuits once they married. Even those who decided to forgo marriage faced more limited career options than did their male colleagues. Yet these early female psychologists were not relegated to "women's work," as were women in some other scientific fields. Their academic interests spanned the realm of psychology—as do those of women psychologists today.

During the 20th century, psychology proved to be a popular undergraduate major among women, attracting more women than any other science. As far back as 1950, more women earned their bachelor's degrees in psychology than in any other field. In 1997, women were awarded significantly more doctorates in psychology than in any of the other sciences (National Science Foundation, 2000). That same year, 23% of students enrolled in psychology graduate programs were women—far more than in any other science.

**Margaret Washburn (1871–1939) was the first woman to earn a doctorate in psychology.**

Over the past several decades, as more and more women have pursued higher education in all areas, the number of women earning doctoral degrees in psychology has risen markedly. In 1950, women earned 15% of the doctorates awarded in psychology. According to APA data (APA, 2002), in 1976, women earned 33% of the doctorates in psychology; by 1997, they earned a substantial majority: 69%. As of 2000, about 49% of APA members were women. Given the trends in graduate program enrollments and earned doctorates, it is safe to predict that by the time you read this book, women will be the majority.

Despite the greater opportunities for women in psychology, women today face obstacles similar to those that existed a century ago. Many people in the United States and other societies still expect women to carry most of the burden of child care, so choices between career and family are often as difficult to resolve now as they were then. Discrimination still exists, although it is more subtle than it was at the turn of the 20th century. Although institutions of higher education no longer exclude women, as of 1998 women with doctorates in psychology were still underrepresented in tenured faculty positions by more than a two-to-one ratio (APA, 2002). This situation will change, but slowly: In 1998, slightly more women than men were on tenure track.

Finally, the "salary gap" between male and female psychologists has been shrinking; among new hires, it is now gone (Williams, Wicherski, & Kahout, 2000). As of 1999, across all U.S. settings in which doctoral-level psychologists work, the median income of psychologists with 20-plus years' experience was about $4,000 to $10,000 a year more for men than for women; among psychologists with 10 to 19 years' experience, men earned $5,000 to $9,000 more; among those with 2 to 9 years' experience, men earned from no more to $2,000 more; and among those just starting out, women actually earned a bit more than men.

## "Basic" and "Applied" Psychology

**Basic science**
The pursuit of knowledge for its own sake.

**Applied science**
The pursuit of knowledge that has specific practical uses.

What the many varieties of psychologists *do* is a bit more complicated. Some psychologists are concerned with **basic science**—that is, the pursuit of knowledge for its own sake. Their chief activities are teaching and research. Their major areas of interest are shown in Figure 1.1, along with those of psychologists who focus on **applied science**—the pursuit of knowledge that has specific practical uses. Often, however, principles revealed by basic research turn out to be quite useful in applied settings.

A traditional distinction in psychology is between *experimental* and *clinical* psychologists. At one time, most experimental psychologists were interested in basic research and most clinical psychologists focused on applied work with clients. That distinction has become blurred, however. Experimental psychologists may extend their efforts into real-world applications—for example, finding ways to curb children's aggression, lessen prejudice and discrimination, or improve conditions on the job. And clinical psychologists may conduct basic research on such topics as disordered thought processes, the nature of intelligence, the structure of personality, and approaches to treatment.

It is still possible, however, to list major areas of interest of various types of psychologist. *Cognitive psychologists* are typically interested in the ways in which we perceive and understand the world around us and in such basic processes as learning and memory. *Comparative psychologists* focus their efforts on comparing the behavior of different species—and relating animal behavior patterns to those found in humans. *Physiological psychologists*, along with psychologists who specialize in *cognitive* or *behavioral neuroscience*, seek information about the structure and functioning of the brain and its connections to other bodily processes, and they examine chemical substances that influence the nervous systems and emotions. Like other psychologists, they sometimes study nonhuman animals as well as people. When studies require direct access to the

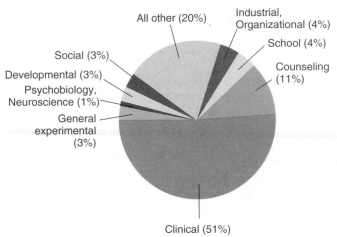

**FIGURE 1.1 The varieties of psychologists. Percentages are based on APA membership data as of 2000 (APA, 2002) and may overrepresent the number of U.S. psychologists who are health service providers; many non–health service providers belong to the APS instead.**

All other (20%)
Industrial, Organizational (4%)
School (4%)
Counseling (11%)
Social (3%)
Developmental (3%)
Psychobiology, Neuroscience (1%)
General experimental (3%)
Clinical (51%)

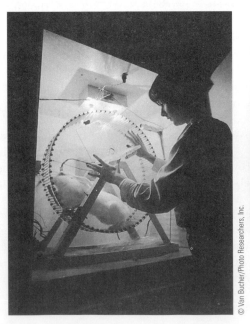

Pictured here are psychologists working in the two main areas of psychological research: basic research (left) and applied research (right).

brain through surgical techniques, laboratory animals are used as subjects in the hope that what is learned about their brains and behavior will be applicable to humans. (Of course, nonhuman animals are also studied in their own right, without regard to understanding people.) *Developmental psychologists* study all facets of how individuals grow and change throughout their lives. *Personality psychologists* study the relatively enduring characteristics of individuals and how these characteristics are formed. *Social psychologists* study how social interactions and situations influence human behavior—sometimes establishing personality characteristics and other times overriding them. Finally, *evolutionary psychologists,* who arrived relatively recently on the scene, focus on commonalities among people across cultures that might indicate psychological tendencies inherent in being human.

Along with developmental psychologists and social psychologists are many other psychologists who are likely to be found tackling life's everyday problems and trying to improve the quality of life. *School psychologists* test and evaluate students, analyze learning problems, and counsel both teachers and parents. *Educational psychologists* are concerned with the impact of educational processes and techniques, including teaching methods, curricula, and textbooks. *Industrial/organizational psychologists* deal with a wide variety of human issues in work settings. *Environmental psychologists* are interested in researching and solving ecological problems—like smog, water pollution, crowding, and noise—and with helping societies maintain and preserve the balance of nature that enables humans to thrive. *Community psychologists,* sometimes called *specialists in community mental health,* are concerned with the social environment and with how schools and other institutions might better serve individual human needs. *Forensic psychologists* work on behavioral issues that are important in the legal, judicial, and correctional systems—including evaluating "insanity" pleas. And *health psychologists* study and apply ways to improve health by altering behavior.

## The Practice of Clinical and Counseling Psychology

Most psychologists are in the fields of *clinical psychology* and *counseling psychology.* They use the findings of science to work with individuals on the diverse problems that trouble them, from deciding on a suitable line of work to dealing with marital or sexual maladjustment and overcoming debilitating depression and anxiety. As indicated in Figure 1.1, about 62% of all members of the APA are in these two fields of psychology.

The primary endeavor of clinical psychologists is the diagnosis and treatment of mental and behavioral disorders (Chapter 13), although many also conduct research on the nature and origins of such disorders and attempt to develop improved approaches to treatment. Diagnosis typically includes psychological testing, which is oriented toward assessing whether treatment is warranted and selecting the best course of treatment.

Clinical psychologists work sometimes with individuals and sometimes with small groups, including families. Their approach to treatment is known generally as *psychotherapy,* and it can take many different forms, as discussed in Chapter 14. Psychotherapy can range from systematically discussing and analyzing mental and emotional problems and trying to get at their roots, to modifying maladaptive behaviors without regard to their underlying causes. Modern psychotherapists tend to be *eclectic,* which means that they are trained in a variety of treatment approaches and employ whatever methods are known to work best with a given client's problems.

Psychotherapy in the analytical sense began with Sigmund Freud (1856–1939), an Austrian physician and neurologist who asked his troubled patients to lie on a couch and talk about themselves, their experiences, and what was troubling them.

Edmund Engleman, NY

This photograph of Sigmund Freud's office was taken in about 1895. Here Freud developed his revolutionary approach to the treatment of disturbed individuals, which he called psychoanalysis.

### Test Yourself

**(c)** Over the past 100 years, how well has psychology done, compared to other sciences, in attracting women to the field?

**(d)** Two psychologists are interested in risk-taking behavior. The first is studying the range of physiological changes people undergo when they are faced with a risky task; the second is helping the government select personnel for dangerous missions. Which psychologist's work is *basic* and which is *applied*?

**(e)** The mother of an adolescent girl is concerned about her daughter's depression and talk of suicide. If she seeks treatment for her daughter, which kind of psychologist is she likely to consult?

(The answers are on page 41.)

The premise was that if they simply let their thoughts roam in any direction, sooner or later they would get around to what was relevant—at which point Freud would begin to focus on specific issues (see Chapter 14). By analyzing this flow of thoughts and ideas, Freud tried to reveal the origins of his patients' problems and eventually lead the patients to understand and overcome these problems. Based on his clinical work, Freud also developed the first comprehensive theory of personality, with emphasis on disorders and their causes, as discussed in Chapter 9.

Psychotherapy was originally the sole province of specialists with advanced training in *psychoanalysis*, as Freud's method is called (see Chapter 14). The first psychologists who entered the field also used Freud's technique, and many of today's clinical psychologists continue to be influenced by the theories of Freud and his early adherents—although they are more likely to call their approaches *psychodynamic*. Others have developed quite different methods for treating the problems of the individuals they work with. Now, far more practitioners are eclectic than purely psychodynamic—or, for that matter, tied to any single approach. For many years now, there has been a trend toward integrating the various approaches discussed in this text (Lampropoulos, 2000).

There is some overlap between clinical psychology and *counseling psychology*, but the latter typically involves working with people who have less severe and more specific issues or problems of social and emotional adjustment. Some counseling psychologists provide guidance to people on such issues as dealing with difficulties in school or choosing a vocation. Counseling psychologists also administer psychological tests of everything from general intelligence to aptitude for specific tasks or vocations. One of psychology's most important findings is that people are usually very good at some things but only mediocre to poor at others. Thus, one secret of success, in both school and work, is to take advantage of individual strengths. Counseling psychologists attempt to reveal and encourage these strengths.

Other counseling psychologists specialize in helping married couples and other family members (such as children) overcome difficulties in their relationships—difficulties that are often caused not so much by deep-seated emotional problems as by poor communication or stressful circumstances. Yet others specialize in working with people who are recovering from substance abuse or addiction. Like clinical psychologists, these counseling psychologists work sometimes with couples, sometimes with families and other groups.

It should be noted that mental health service providers of all kinds often work together rather than alone. Practitioners such as clinical psychologists, counseling psychologists, and various kinds of *social workers*, as well as medically trained professionals such as psychiatrists and *psychiatric nurses*, may collaborate. Working as part of a team, each member contributes her or his own perspectives and expertise to developing an overall treatment approach.

# THE METHODS PSYCHOLOGISTS USE

In every science, the methods of study depend on the subject matter. Because the behavior of living organisms takes such a wide variety of forms—and in part because of ethical considerations discussed later in the chapter—psychologists use diverse approaches to research. No single method can suffice, because different methods are required to answer different kinds of research questions. Psychologists have therefore adopted an array of ways of studying their subject matter, and they are constantly seeking new ways. They have also developed or adopted increasingly sophisticated *instrumentation* suited to their research. Here we focus on the rationale and techniques of the most prominent methods of psychological research, with some notes on instrumentation. Further examples of the instrumentation that often augments psychological research appear at various points throughout the text.

**FOCUS QUESTIONS**

- What research methods do psychologists use?
- What is correlation and what does it tell us?
- What can psychological experiments tell us?

## Observation

In many cases, psychologists do what astronomers, naturalists, and certain other scientists do: They observe and record events as they occur, without intervention. For example, a psychological researcher might observe the behavior of people in various kinds of social situations. All of us casually observe the behavior of other people and draw some conclusions from their actions. If you note that a student rarely speaks up in class and has difficulty conversing in social situations in general, you might conclude that this person is shy and you might interact with him or her accordingly—if you interact with him or her at all. In a sense, psychologists are no different from everybody else, except for a preoccupation with accuracy. Psychologists make their observations and draw their conclusions in a disciplined fashion. They try to describe behavior objectively and exactly, and they don't jump to conclusions about the motives behind it. As a simple example, take a psychologist studying the reactions of students to the stress of an exam. Rather than merely recording that the students were "anxious," the psychologist might record that the "students regularly shifted position, grimaced and frowned, and tapped or chewed on their pencils."

In studying behavior through observation, psychologists try to remain apart from what is going on and thereby avoid influencing the behavior of the objects of their study in any way. In everyday settings, they practice **naturalistic observation,** trying to be as inconspicuous as possible, lest their presence affect the behavior they are studying. In laboratory settings, sometimes psychologists arrange to remain unseen behind one-way glass. Some of our most valuable knowledge

**Naturalistic observation** A method of study that involves observing behavior in normal, everyday settings.

© Cary Wolinsky/Stock Boston

Unseen behind a one-way mirror, investigators use the method of naturalistic observation to study a child at play. To the observers outside the room, the wall panel looks like a sheet of clear glass. To the child inside, it looks like a mirror.

about the behavior and development of children has come from observers who used this method. Classic and still-relevant findings regarding the sexual responses of adults who volunteered to be observed were obtained in part in this manner (Masters & Johnson, 1966). Naturalistic observation has also been used extensively in studying the behavior of species other than humans—for example, the social behavior of primates in their jungle environments (Goodall, 1986).

At times, psychologists also engage in *participant observation*. They take an active part in a social situation, perhaps deliberately "role playing" to see how other people behave, say, toward someone who seems unusually withdrawn or hostile. Participant observation has been used in a variety of settings, including schools, mental institutions, and places where homeless people congregate.

In a larger sense, accurate observation is the mainstay of psychological research and practice. All psychological research methods depend on accurate observation. Researchers systematically observe behavior as just described or when conducting experiments. Clinicians observe their clients' verbal and nonverbal behavior. When psychologists administer questionnaires or psychological tests and when they record physiological measures, they are engaging in observation.

## Interviews and Case Histories

**Interview**
An in-depth question-and-answer session in which an individual's life or problems are probed.

**Case history**
A compilation of the life history of an individual based on interviews and other sources of information.

Another way to gain insight into what people think and feel is to ask them. Psychologists—especially clinicians—often use **interviews,** in which they question clients or research participants in depth about their experiences and their ideas and feelings about those experiences. In turn, interviews are an integral part of **case histories,** in which significant experiences in a person's life are reconstructed and compiled in an attempt to show how various behavior patterns developed. Case histories may also include other information, such as family demographics and public records. Usually the first step in clinical diagnosis is to construct a case history, and thus this is the most common application of the case history. However, case histories are also useful in gaining insight into the origins of relatively rare mental and behavioral disorders or conditions that cannot, because of their rarity, be studied in other ways. Case histories are likewise useful in studying complex and long-range consequences of major life transitions, such as the effects of divorce and family breakup on parents and children (Wallerstein & Blakeslee, 1989).

## Questionnaires and Surveys

Closely related to the interview is the **questionnaire,** another way of gaining information simply by asking. A major difference between a questionnaire and an interview is that a questionnaire is a set of standardized written questions, which often are answered by filling in circles on an optical scan sheet for computer scoring and analysis. Also, unlike interviews—which can include "open-ended" questions that allow the interviewer to pursue topics of interest at length as they arise—questionnaires are usually highly structured and contain a specific list of questions that each participant answers in the same order. Although they are not as personal or flexible as interviews, questionnaires have a major advantage in that information can be gathered and processed quickly. The scoring is also more objective, in that it is obvious what a person's answers are (although determining what those answers actually *mean* can require considerable interpretation).

A popular application of questionnaires is the **survey,** in which a questionnaire is administered to a large number of people in a short period of time. Questionnaires find a special use in the study of public opinion. Scientific methods for choosing a representative sample of people to poll and then analyzing the results have made it possible to infer, with a very small margin of error, how all people across an entire nation stand on a controversial issue by questioning a mere 1,500 people. Surveys are therefore a valuable contribution to the democratic process: They shed light on what citizens think about such issues as taxation, defense expenditures, foreign policy, abortion, and laws regulating sexual conduct and drug use. Before such information was available, there was no accurate way to gauge public opinion. By waging intense publicity campaigns, small but vocal minorities were often able to convince politicians that they represented the majority view. Now political leaders can actually base their decisions on the will of the majority (which is often unorganized and silent) as expressed in polls.

Questionnaires are also routinely used in many other areas of life, as well as in smaller scale psychological research. They often take the form of *rating scales,* in which participants express opinions, beliefs, feelings, or concerns. For example, toward the end of the term, you will probably complete an evaluation of this course, using ratings—perhaps numbers between 1 and 5—to assess the quality of various aspects of the course, including the choice of textbook. Or, you may be presented with statements to which you are asked to respond "strongly disagree," "disagree," "neutral," "agree," or "strongly agree." Your response to each question will then be translated into a number for processing. Similar questionnaires are sometimes used in psychological experiments to assess emotionality, beliefs, attitudes, thought processes, and other aspects of participants' behavior that cannot be directly observed.

To produce accurate results, a questionnaire must be worded with extreme care. Creating a reliable questionnaire is a fine art, because the slightest change in the way questions are worded may completely distort the results. Questionnaire data are sometimes challenged on the ground that people do not (or cannot) respond accurately. For example, suppose you were asked questions about how many times you had sex during the previous month and what activities you engaged in. Even if you were assured that your answers would remain confidential, would you respond truthfully? If you had sex a lot during the month, would you downplay your activity? If you had very little or no sexual activity, would you ex-

**Questionnaire**
A highly structured pencil-and-paper interview.

**Survey**
The administration of a questionnaire to relatively large numbers of people.

aggerate? And if you had sex more than a few times, could you remember exactly how many times even if you tried?

Experienced investigators have ways of spotting when people are lying or exaggerating. Questionnaires cannot always reveal the complete truth, but when carefully planned and administered, they can be extremely useful.

## Standardized Psychological Tests and Physiological Measures

Among the oldest tools of psychology are tests developed to assess human abilities and achievement, as well as *traits*—supposedly stable personality characteristics. People who participate in formal schooling usually take a number of such tests over their years in school. You likely took periodic examinations that showed your teachers how your progress in basic subjects such as language and mathematics compared with that of your peers; if you scored unusually low or high, you may also have taken a test of your general intelligence. In preparing for college, you probably took an exam to assess your academic achievement. In preparing for vocational training, you would have taken tests to determine your aptitude for various kinds of work. Should you seek psychotherapy, you will be given tests to assess your personality as well as your psychological problems.

Good psychological tests measure what they are supposed to measure and do so accurately and consistently, as discussed in Chapter 7. Constructing psychological tests is much more difficult than you might suppose, and they stand in sharp contrast to the so-called psychological tests published in newspapers and magazines that claim to tell you how happy, self-fulfilled, or "disordered" you are or how good you are likely to be as a husband, wife, or parent. Except perhaps for amusement and entertainment, these tests have no value at all, because they have not been properly researched and verified. The best psychological tests also may have weaknesses, despite all the scientific knowledge and effort that go into creating them. But they do have important uses and can provide important insights when properly applied.

**Measuring Psychological Differences**   Psychology's methods have been particularly helpful in adding to our knowledge of *individual differences*. Every person is indeed unique, and physical and psychological traits, from height and muscular strength to intelligence and emotional sensitivity, vary over a wide range.

In studying individual differences, psychology relies heavily on mathematical techniques from a field known as *statistics*. (These techniques are summarized in the Appendix.) Many human traits, from height and weight to intelligence, fall into a similar pattern. Consider the heights of adult U.S. males. They range all the way from about 3 feet to about 8 feet. But most cluster around the average (about 5 feet 7 inches), and as we look up or down from the average, the number of males of each height declines steadily. Note the graph in Figure 1.2, which shows how *intelligence quotient* (IQ; see Chapter 7), as measured by certain intelligence tests, varies. The average is 100; over two-thirds of the general population score between 85 and

**FIGURE 1.2 The normal distribution applied to IQ.** As discussed in the Appendix, each 15-point interval corresponds to one standard deviation.

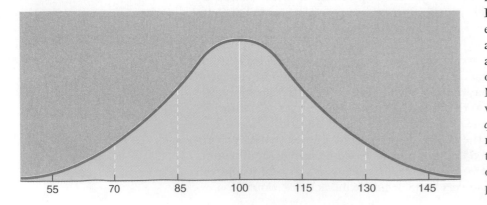

| 55 | 70 | 85 | 100 | 115 | 130 | 145 |

115, and over 95% score between 70 and 130. Only a very few people score at extreme low or high levels.

The graph in Figure 1.2 is so typical of the results generally found in physical and psychological assessments that it is known as the *normal curve* or *normal distribution*. Those who are around average have a lot of company. Those who are far removed from the average—in IQ, the geniuses and the mentally retarded; in height, the 3-footers and the 8-footers—are relatively rare.

Of course, many factors other than your score on an IQ test are involved in whether you are truly far above or far below average in intellectual ability and performance. But the normal distribution does help explain a great deal about psychological characteristics, including the general similarities displayed by most people and the distinct differences displayed by some people. The curve applies to performance in school, musical talent, athletic skill, interest or lack of interest in sex, as well as to the intensity of emotional arousal and the strength of motives for achievement, power, and friendship. These and many other individual differences underline why you can't generalize about humanity as a whole from your own traits—especially if you happen to fall at an unusually low or high point on the curve for a particular trait.

**Measuring Brain and Other Body Functioning**   Psychologists are also interested in the measurement of any physiological functioning related to behavior. They have found, for example, that certain abnormal states such as severe depression may be triggered by disturbances in the chemistry of the brain (see Chapter 13). They have shown that the feeling of hunger is caused not just by an empty stomach, as is popularly believed, but also by measurable changes in biochemicals in the bloodstream (see Chapter 8). Researchers can measure the activity of the glands that influence emotions; the way emotional arousal produces changes in heart rate, blood pressure, and breathing; and the kinds of bodily activity that occur during states of stress or relaxation.

Perhaps most intriguing are the steadily improving techniques and instruments that allow researchers to study the chemical and electrical activity of the brain directly (see Chapter 2), while an individual is engaged in a variety of activities or is experiencing unusual states of consciousness such as those produced by sleep, drugs, or hallucinations. The ability to record a person's actual thoughts is probably still a long way in the future, but even this is not beyond the realm of possibility.

## Correlation: An Important Descriptive Technique

Consider a question that has long interested psychologists: To what extent do children inherit *temperament*—basic personality tendencies—from their parents? For example, do inherited genes contribute to characteristics such as "sociability," helping to determine whether a person is shy and withdrawn or friendly and highly receptive to social interactions? The relative roles played by genetics and learning with regard to temperament, personality, and intelligence continue to be a key issue in psychology (as discussed later in the chapter and in Chapter 7). But for now, how would you go about answering the question about genes and sociability?

If you didn't read the introduction to this chapter carefully, you might be tempted to jump to a conclusion based on personal experience: "No; children obviously do not inherit their parents' temperament. My best friends are a couple who are very sociable, and their child is a loner who doesn't even have much to do with them, much less the kids at school." Or, "Sure. I know a couple who are very sociable, and their child is tight with them and has lots of friends at school." As noted earlier, personal experience is not a good basis for sound psychological answers.

A better approach, and one that has actually been used, would be to study a large group of parents and their children, use an appropriate questionnaire to assess each on sociability, and then compare their respective scores. An even better approach would be to compare the sociability scores of identical twins, nonidentical twins, and siblings who aren't twins. This approach is often used in research conducted by *behavior geneticists*—scientists who focus on the role of heredity in personality, intelligence, and other psychological characteristics. Sometimes they compare parents and children; other times they compare siblings. Their analyses can be complex, but the logic is straightforward: If identical twins are more similar to each other than nonidentical twins are on a characteristic such as sociability, and if nonidentical twins are in turn more similar to each other than other siblings are, then heredity must be a factor. This is because identical twins get virtually identical genes from their parents, nonidentical twins have fewer genes in common, and nontwin siblings have the fewest.

**Correlation**
A statistical technique for describing the extent and direction of the relationship between pairs of scores on some measure.

But how can a researcher assess "similarity"? In this type of situation and many others that appear throughout the text, psychologists apply a statistical technique called **correlation.** In essence, correlation is a mathematical way of determining the similarity or relationship between pairs of scores—such as scores on sociability for parents and their children or for siblings with differing numbers of genes in common. The computations yield a *correlation coefficient*, a number that ranges from 0 (which indicates no relationship at all) to +1.00 or −1.00 (either of which signifies a perfect relationship). Note that a *positive* correlation means that as one measure increases, the other increases too; that is, higher scores tend to be paired together and lower scores tend to be paired together. In contrast, a *negative* correlation means that higher scores tend to be paired with lower scores and vice versa—the measures behave in "opposite" fashion.

Whether a correlation is positive or negative has nothing to do with its strength or magnitude. In most research, correlations of from 0 to about +.20 (or from 0 to about −.20) are considered *weak* (or nonexistent); correlations ranging from +.20 to +.60 (or from −.20 to −.60) are considered *moderate;* and those from +.60 to +1.00 (or from −.60 to −1.00) are considered *strong.* As it happens, research on the extent to which sociability is influenced by genes has typically found moderately positive correlation coefficients for identical twins and lower correlation coefficients for children with fewer genes in common—which translates into the observation that more sociable parents *tend* to have more sociable children and less sociable parents tend to have less sociable children. But the correlations are far from perfect, so there are lots of exceptions, and genes are not all that's involved.

Consider a different possibility: Suppose researchers found that *higher* sociability among parents was associated with *lower* sociability among their children, and vice versa. This finding would be expressed as a negative correlation, although it might still be moderate. As you see correlations in this text, remember that the sign of the correlation (plus or minus) has nothing to do with its strength.

Finally, a word of caution: Correlations reveal the existence and extent of relationships, but they do not necessarily indicate what *causes* what. In the case of genetic contributions from parents to children, the cause-and-effect relationship is relatively clear. In other cases, it is not. For example, it has been consistently found that highly aggressive children tend to watch more violent TV programs than less aggressive children do. That is, there is a strong positive correlation between aggressiveness and watching violent TV programs. So does violent TV cause children to be more aggressive? A considerable body of other evidence indicates that it does (e.g., Villani, 2001) and that playing violent video games has a similar effect (Anderson & Bushman, 2001). But researchers can't know this from correlation alone. It could just as well be that children who are inherently aggressive prefer violent TV programs and games and seek them out—in which case the cause-and-effect relationship would be in the opposite direction.

Let's take another example. We would expect to find a strong positive correlation between the number of permanent teeth children have and their ability to solve difficult problems. But this certainly does not mean that having more teeth causes increased cognitive ability, nor does it mean that increases in cognitive ability cause more teeth to emerge. The correlation is strong because of a third factor: Age accounts for both additional new teeth and the cognitive development. A strong correlation *may* occur because one characteristic causes another, but on the basis of correlation alone, researchers cannot determine which characteristic causes which or whether some third factor is responsible.

The ways in which psychologists *can* verify cause-and-effect relationships are discussed next.

## The Most Conclusive Research Method: Experimentation

In an **experiment,** a researcher makes a careful and controlled study of cause and effect, first setting up differing conditions that participants (or subjects) are exposed to and then assessing whether corresponding differences in their behavior occur as a result of the different conditions they have experienced. Both the experimental conditions and the resulting behavior are called *variables.* Experiments are usually conducted in laboratories, where researchers can retain *experimental control,* eliminating or at least compensating for events that might detract from—or even void—an experiment. When the rules of good experimentation are followed carefully, laboratory experiments tend to have high **internal validity.** "Internal" refers to what goes on *within* the experiment, and internal validity refers to the extent to which the experimenter can make statements about cause and effect and be confident about them.

Laboratory experimentation is the focus of this section, but experiments can also be conducted in naturalistic settings ranging from forest habitats in which nonhuman animals live to children's classrooms and playgrounds, places where adults gather for work or play, and city streets. Experiments in nonlaboratory settings are called *field experiments.* In a field experiment, the researcher may trade some experimental control for gains in **external validity.** That is, in some areas of research, experiments conducted in the real world are more likely to yield findings that accurately apply to real-life behavior (again, provided that the basic rules of good experimentation are followed). Examples of experiments in naturalistic settings appear at various points in the text.

Although naturalistic experiments are still less common than laboratory experiments, they started becoming more popular as psychology came under fire for basing too many of its conclusions about behavior on research conducted in "artificial" laboratory settings, using a limited range of participants. As one critic stated—with implications for all of psychology—U.S. developmental psychology is "the science of the strange behavior of the child in a strange situation with a strange adult for the shortest period of time" (Bronfenbrenner, 1979). Others have made statements to the effect that psychology is the science of rats, pigeons, monkeys, and introductory psychology students (who often serve as research participants).

We do not have the space here to resolve the issue of whether laboratory experimentation has sufficient external validity; perhaps the best answer is simply "It depends." It's worth noting that the results of *basic* research on sensory-perceptual processes, learning, thought and memory processes, physiological processes of the body and the functioning of the brain, and other areas discussed in this text are not likely to be affected significantly by the fact that the research is conducted in laboratories—as it often must be because of the sophisticated instrumentation required. On the other hand, the results of certain *applied* research on real-life problems, social behaviors and interactions, and the intricacies of human devel-

**Experiment**
A careful and controlled study of cause and effect through manipulation of the conditions participants are exposed to.

**Internal validity**
The extent to which an experiment permits statements about cause and effect.

**External validity**
The extent to which an experiment applies to real-life behavior.

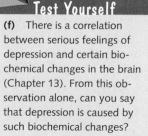

**Test Yourself**

**(f)** There is a correlation between serious feelings of depression and certain biochemical changes in the brain (Chapter 13). From this observation alone, can you say that depression is caused by such biochemical changes?

(The answer is on page 41.)

opment may be affected by laboratory settings. We'll leave this for you to decide as we go along.

# CONDUCTING GOOD EXPERIMENTS

**FOCUS QUESTIONS**
- What differences are there between experiments with individuals and experiments with groups?
- What factors must be considered in conducting meaningful, conclusive experiments?
- Why is replication of experiments important?

Effective and conclusive psychological experimentation is often a tedious endeavor, given the many potential sources of bias and other error that must be allowed for. Just as we didn't expect you to come away from the preceding section prepared to design and conduct surveys or even to compute a correlation coefficient, we don't expect you to be prepared to design and conduct experiments after you complete this section. We do want you to have the necessary background to understand the material in the chapters that follow, to be prepared for other psychology courses you may take, and to be a good consumer of psychological research when you encounter it.

## Study Chart

## Methods Used in Psychological Research

| Method | Description |
|---|---|
| Observation | A research method in which events are observed and recorded as they occur, without intervention. |
| • Naturalistic observation | Observing behavior in everyday settings or in a laboratory; the observer attempts to be as inconspicuous as possible. |
| • Participant observation | Taking an active part in a social situation and observing the behavior of others in that situation. |
| Interview | A research method in which clients or research participants are questioned about their life experiences and their ideas and feelings about them. |
| Case history | A compilation of significant experiences in a person's life. |
| Questionnaire | A set of written questions that each participant answers in the same order. |
| Survey | A research method in which a questionnaire is administered to a large number of people in a short period of time. |
| Standardized test | A test that has been developed to assess human abilities, achievement, and traits (such as personality characteristics). |
| Physiological measures | Methods for measuring any form of physiological functioning that is related to behavior. |
| Correlation | A mathematical way of determining the relationship between pairs of scores. |
| Experiment | A careful and controlled study of cause and effect in which participants or subjects are exposed to differing conditions and any corresponding differences in behavior are assessed; experiments may be conducted in a laboratory or in naturalistic settings. |

Psychological experiments come in two basic forms: those that manipulate and assess the behavior of one participant or subject at a time and those that manipulate and assess the averaged behavior of individuals in groups.

## Experiments That Focus on Individuals

In a *single-subject (or single-participant) experiment,* one individual at a time is exposed to varying *contingencies* that are expected to affect behavior. An emphasis on contingencies, which either are deliberately imposed or arise naturally from relationships between behavior and its consequences, has been typical of the work of B. F. Skinner (1904–1990) and his many adherents over the years. Much of the single-subject research follows this basic pattern: Observe and record the rate of a behavior at the beginning of an experimental session, then impose a contingency, then take it away, then impose it again. For example, to affect the behavior of a teenager (or perhaps a spouse) whose rate of doing chores was low, you would first record the rate (*baseline*) and then add rewards such as extra privileges or praise for a job well done (*contingency*); the rate of doing chores should improve. In real life, you would be finished as long as the chore performance was acceptable. As an experimenter, however, you would go further: You would discontinue the rewards and watch the chore behavior decline (*return to baseline*). Finally, you would reinstate the rewards and watch the chore behavior improve again (*return to contingency*). This way, you could verify that the rewards did indeed control the behavior—it wasn't just coincidence that the improved behavior followed the rewards.

Like other researchers, experimenters must follow rules. They must be precise in defining the behavior and then consistent with the rewards. But the rationale is as straightforward as that behind flipping a switch. Suppose you go into a darkened room (*baseline*) and flip a switch up and the lights come on (*contingency*). Then you flip the switch down and the lights go off (*return to baseline*). Finally, you flip the switch up and the lights come on again (*return to contingency*). You have conclusive scientific evidence that the switch controls the lights. That is, given that electric power is necessary too, the switch *causes* the lights to come on or go off.

Within the general approach called *operant conditioning,* Skinner set out to demonstrate that *all* behavior is governed by what happens when it occurs; he also wished to show that the same principles that govern the behavior of laboratory animals such as rats and pigeons apply equally well to humans. You probably already have some inklings about what's wrong with this view (as well as the chores example) in real life, and in the years since Skinner's pioneering work, psychologists have shown that his principles are often overstated. Where Skinner's approach came from and where it stands today, as an approach with broad utility in spite of its limitations, are discussed further in Chapter 4.

## Experiments That Focus on Groups

*Group experiments* in psychology typically use *averaging* of scores or other measures of individual behavior. A simple group experiment with humans might begin with *random assignment* of the participants to two or more different experimental groups, or treatment conditions, through a procedure that could be as simple as tossing a coin. The intent is to make the groups as equivalent overall as possible, which is important to the outcome. Each group of participants is treated the same in all respects except for the experimental manipulation—which is based on a *hypothesis* formulated by the experimenter about what specific treatment conditions will produce specific differences in behavior between the groups. That is, in accord with the hypothesis, the groups are treated differently in just this one respect. If their behavior—as assessed by their performance on a test or some other measure—differs accordingly, the hypothesis is supported. And if the experiment is conducted properly (if the groups are equivalent, if they are treated the same except for the experimental manipulation, and if their behavior is assessed precisely and objectively), the experimenter can conclude that the single difference in how they were treated *caused* the differences in behavior.

### A Group Experiment on the Learning of Aggression

Here's a concrete example based on classic and highly influential research by Albert Bandura and colleagues in the 1960s (Bandura, 1965, 1969). It's a bit more complicated than the ones discussed above, and therefore more in keeping with the kinds of experiments psychologists actually conduct. The experiment began with the hypothesis that young children's aggressive behavior could be markedly influenced by what they saw happen *afterward* to an adult "model" who behaved in aggressive ways. Three groups, composed of randomly assigned young girls and boys, saw a film in which the model "beat up" an adult-sized Bobo doll (a soft plastic doll that is inflated like a beach toy and has a weight in the bottom so that it bounces upright after being knocked over). Each of the three groups saw the same film, in which the model hit, kicked, and otherwise attacked Bobo in four very specific ways—except that the film had three different endings.

In one version, the model was praised and rewarded for doing such a good job of beating up Bobo; in another, the model was scolded and punished for beating up Bobo; and in the third, there were no consequences at all for the model. Thus, the differing consequences experienced by the model constituted the experimental manipulation, or **independent variable,** that Bandura predicted would "cause" children's behavior to differ. In general, it is through use of an independent variable that an experimenter systematically exposes participants to different conditions.

The next phase of the experiment was the *performance test,* in which each child was left alone with a smaller Bobo while hidden observers recorded the child's behavior. The test, or **dependent variable,** was how many of the aggressive model's behaviors the children in each group would spontaneously perform, on average—that is, the "effect" produced by the independent variable. More generally, a dependent variable assesses any effects of an independent variable on participants' behavior.

As illustrated in Figure 1.3, both boys and girls in the Model Rewarded group and the No Consequences group imitated significantly more of the model's behaviors than did those in the Model Punished group. (You can see this by comparing the Performance Test bars just for boys in each group, then comparing them just for girls in each group.) Whether the children were girls or boys was a *second* independent variable. In all three groups, girls imitated significantly fewer of the model's behaviors than boys did during the performance test. (Now look at each group separately and compare girls and boys.) This is not surprising, given that in the United States in the 1960s, boys were more often encouraged to be aggressive and girls not to be—a gender bias that hasn't entirely disappeared even today.

Finally, the children were given a *learning test,* in which they again spent time with Bobo but now were offered rewards based on how much of the model's behavior they could reproduce. A glance at the Learning Test bars in Figure 1.3 reveals that all the children—regardless of their experimental group and regardless of whether they were boys or girls—imitated the model's behaviors at very high rates. In Bandura's words, "The initially large sex differential . . . was virtually eliminated" (1969).

What does this experiment tell us? Among other things, it reveals that children learn more from watching aggressive behavior (or, by analogy, violent TV)

**Independent variable**
A potential "cause" in an experiment; the way in which participants are treated differently by an experimenter.

**Dependent variable**
A potential "effect" in an experiment; a measure of the behavior of participants as a result of the independent variable.

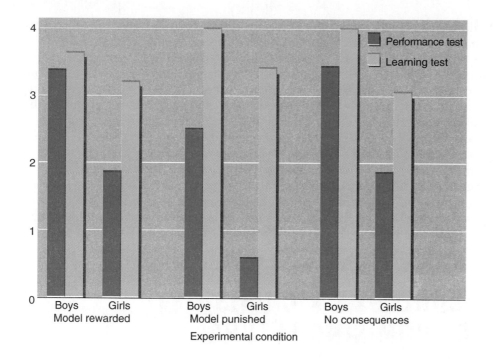
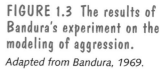

FIGURE 1.3 The results of Bandura's experiment on the modeling of aggression.
*Adapted from Bandura, 1969.*

than we might realize. The children in the Model Punished group were much less aggressive on the performance test, presumably out of fear of being punished themselves. Once fear of punishment was removed during the learning test by the offering of rewards, they became every bit as aggressive as the other children. Thus, they learned *how* to commit aggression. To the extent that Bandura's research has good external validity and generalizes to the real world, it demonstrates that children who witness aggressive acts may not display them right away but may do so later if they get the idea that "the time is right." Stated differently, this research strongly suggests that it doesn't make much difference whether the "bad guys" in TV programs and other popular media ultimately get punished. Children still remember what the bad guys do and how they do it.

### Additional Considerations in Group Experiments

Among the first things to examine when you're reading about group experiments and other psychological research are the **operational definitions.** In an experiment, an operational definition "translates" the general idea behind an independent variable into what the experimenter actually does and translates a dependent variable into what is actually measured. For example, Bandura's operational definition of "exposure to aggressive models with varying consequences" was having the children watch a particular film with different endings. As a student and consumer, you should ask yourself whether this was a reasonable operational definition of the more general concept that the researchers were interested in. Most people will say that it was, although it certainly might not apply in all cases in which children observe aggressive acts. You should also ask whether the operational definition of the dependent variable was appropriate. The extent to which the children themselves beat up Bobo appears to be a quite reasonable operational definition, but aggression can also be expressed in other ways that were not assessed by this experiment. Clearly, operational definitions are directly related to external validity and the question of how the particulars of a laboratory experiment reflect what happens in the real world.

A related issue is the need for **systematic replication** in experiments and most other kinds of psychological research. Before psychologists would be willing

**Operational definition**
The "translation" of an independent or dependent variable into what is actually done or measured.

**Systematic replication**
Reproducing experiments with variations designed to make conclusions about behavior more general.

**Test Yourself**

**(g)** If you were to do an experiment on how mathematics performance is affected by praise from teachers, which would be the independent variable and which would be the dependent variable?

**(h)** If you were a psychobiologist and were intent on studying jealousy, would you be more likely to analyze the friendship patterns of jealous individuals or the patterns of physiological change associated with feelings of jealousy?

(The answers are on page 41.)

to make broad generalizations about the relationship between exposure to aggressive models and children's aggressive behavior, they would want to see experiments similar to this one, conducted with somewhat different procedures (such as different definitions of the independent and dependent variables or different background or age requirements for the participants). Only if similar results were obtained across a variety of such replications would psychologists become confident of the general conclusions suggested here. As it happens, general conclusions are warranted in this case: The 1965 experiment discussed here was one of a series of many such experiments conducted by Bandura and others.

Advice to take with you: Always be wary of the "new," often sensational psychological research findings that appear in the popular media. These tend to draw headlines when they appear, but if it later turns out that other researchers can't replicate the findings, you probably won't see that reported—when nothing happened, it isn't "news."

# PSYCHOLOGY'S RICH HISTORY AND PROMISING FUTURE

**FOCUS QUESTIONS**

- How did scientific psychology begin?
- What were the major approaches taken by psychologists in the past?
- What are the major approaches in psychology today?

Psychological research—and psychology itself—has come a long way since the science began. Initially, the idea of taking a scientific approach to the study of the behavior of humans and other creatures required a radical shift in human thinking and the invention of new techniques of study.

Psychology is generally agreed to have been founded in 1879, when Wilhelm Wundt (1832–1920) established the first "psychological" laboratory at Germany's University of Leipzig. Wundt had studied to be a physician, but instead of practicing medicine he taught physiology. He soon lost interest in this field because, like other early European psychologists, he was much more concerned with the workings of the mind than with the workings of the body. He and his colleagues asked specially trained individuals to sit in the laboratory for hours, listening to sounds and looking at colors while also trying to report what they perceived by "looking inside themselves." In this way,

The first psychological laboratory was opened by Wilhelm Wundt in Leipzig, Germany, in 1879. Wundt's primary investigative technique was introspection, by which he meant attempting to analyze the processes occurring within the human mind.

Psychology Archives—The University of Akron

which came to be known as *introspection,* Wundt hoped to be able to discover relationships between external stimulation and various mental phenomena.

Wundt was the most popular professor at his university, and no classroom was big enough to hold all the students who wanted to hear his lectures. A few years later, similar acclaim came to Sir Francis Galton (1822–1911), one of the first British psychologists. Galton, who was interested in individual differences in mental abilities and personality and how these differences might be passed along from parents to children, invented numerous devices to test hearing, smell, color vision, and the ability to judge weights—all of which he believed comprised an index of intelligence. When he set up his equipment at an International Health Exhibition in London, people flocked in to be his participants, gladly paying an entrance fee for the privilege. Even in those early years, when psychology was just taking a few tentative steps into the vast realm of human behavior, it captured the public's imagination.

## The Era of Introspection

Like Wundt, most of psychology's pioneers concentrated on discovering the nature, origins, and significance of conscious experiences. Introspection remained their chief method of investigation. Going beyond Wundt's emphasis on sensation and perception, they tried to analyze the multitude of processes that went on inside their own minds, asked their participants to do the same, and recorded their findings as objectively as possible.

The most prominent of the early U.S. psychologists was William James (1842–1910), who came to the young science from an unusual background. Like Wundt, he studied medicine but never practiced. Indeed, he had a difficult time finding his true vocation. At one time he wanted to be an artist, then he thought of becoming a chemist, and once he joined a zoological expedition to Brazil. In his late twenties, he suffered a "mental breakdown" and went through a prolonged depression in which he seriously thought of committing suicide. But he recovered—largely, he believed, through what he called "an achievement of the will"—and went on to become a prolific writer on psychology and philosophy.

James had no doubt about the mission of the new science. He began his landmark work *Principles of Psychology* (1890) with the statement "Psychology is the study of mental life" and then proceeded to apply the results of introspection into his own mind to a long list of human behaviors. In illustrating emotion and conflict, for example, he examined many of his own emotions and reactions—at one point contrasting the warm feeling of staying in bed on a wintry morning with the dread of his feet touching a cold floor.

The distinguishing feature of mental life, James believed, was that human beings constantly seek certain results and must constantly choose among various methods of achieving them. Consistent with this approach, James embraced the works of Charles Darwin (1809–1882) and attempted to apply Darwin's principles of the evolution of species to the evolution of human mental processes. This gave rise to the first major U.S. branch of psychology, called *functionalism,* which stressed how modern human thought might result from progressive adaptations our ancestors had experienced—an idea that has been reborn in similar form in modern evolutionary psychology.

Was William James's introspective approach really scientific? The answer is "yes and no." Serious students still read his *Principles of Psychology,* which doesn't always seem as subjective as it actually is. Perhaps because of the many different realms of mental processes James explored and the groundwork he laid for more objective inquiry, many have come to regard him as the best candidate for the title of founder of modern psychology.

In the 1890s, a student of Wundt's named Edward Titchener (1867–1927) brought Wundt's approach to the United States. He dubbed it *structuralism* because of its emphasis on breaking down consciousness and mental activity into structural components and analyzing them one by one. Perhaps ironically, structuralism was displaced in the early 1900s by the functionalism of James and others, as well as by the rise of behaviorism, which will be discussed shortly.

## Psychoanalytic Theory and Its Impact

While James was pursuing introspection, Sigmund Freud was having a profound influence on many aspects of psychology. In the 1880s in Vienna, Freud turned his attention to psychological processes as a result of his experience with patients who were suffering from physical impairments—including paralysis of the arms or legs or blindness—that had no apparent physical cause. Freud described such problems as a form of *hysteria*, at the time a catch-all term for a variety of maladies that appeared to be "psychogenic" (originating in the mind). Freud believed that hysterical patients converted emotional conflicts into physical symptoms. The **psychoanalytic theory,** which he developed over a lifetime of treating many kinds of abnormal behavior and intensely analyzing his own personality, is the basis for psychoanalysis, announced to the world near the beginning of the 20th century. Psychoanalytic theory is discussed briefly below and then in more detail in Chapter 9.

> **Psychoanalytic theory** Originated by Freud, a view of personality as governed by unconscious, selfish thoughts and desires.

In his youth, Freud himself suffered from feelings of anxiety and deep depression, and he retained some neurotic symptoms all of his life. (*Neurotic* is a dated but still popular term for an assortment of anxiety disorders in people who otherwise function normally; see Chapter 13.) He smoked 20 cigars a day, was extremely nervous about traveling by train, and was given to what were probably hypochondriacal complaints about poor digestion, constipation, and heart palpitations. However, in spite of his problems, he managed to live a rich professional, family, and social life.

One of Freud's great insights in developing his psychoanalytic theory was the discovery that the human personality can be influenced by "unconscious" forces—impulses or desires of which a person is not consciously aware. At first, Freud's ideas were bitterly attacked; many people were repelled by his notion that human beings, far from being completely rational creatures, are largely at the mercy of irrational unconscious thoughts and purely selfish "animal" desires. In particular, many were shocked by his insistence on the primary role of sexuality in human behavior (which, it should be noted in fairness to Freud, was indeed a recurrent problem for people of the Victorian era in which he lived).

The initial uproar eventually died out, but among the prominent psychoanalysts and psychodynamic theorists who came after Freud, his emphasis on sexual motives always remained a point of contention. Considerable controversy also remains with regard to the effectiveness of psychoanalytic methods (see Chapter 14). And although some of Freud's theorizing about personality has survived (see especially Chapter 11), much more has been discarded. Psychoanalytic theory is discussed at various points in the text because of its historical value and because some of Freud's outmoded terms are still in popular use. (For example, have you ever referred to someone as "anal"?)

Yet Freud is generally regarded as one of the most influential figures in all of psychology. He was the first to develop a comprehensive theory of personality—flawed though it is, according to modern standards—and few would dispute that Freud was a genius. Because of the immense impact of psychoanalytic theory, it has been called **the first force in psychology.**

> **The first force in psychology** Psychoanalytic theory.

# The Rise of Behaviorism

Early in the 20th century, a new breed of psychologists began to question the usefulness of introspection and psychoanalytic theory as sources of scientific understanding. They also rejected other largely nonscientific approaches that were popular at the time, such as attempts by William McDougall (1871–1938) to catalog human behavior into a lengthy list of highly specific "instincts." This reaction—which most psychologists now regard as an overreaction—developed into what is best described as **strict behaviorism.** According to this approach, *only* overt behavior is appropriate subject matter for science and psychology. Whereas our current definition of psychology refers to both overt and covert behavior, the strict behaviorists rejected the study of covert behaviors such as thinking, reasoning, feeling, being motivated, and even learning, because none of these can be observed directly and must instead be inferred. Foremost among the early strict behaviorists were E. L. Thorndike (1874–1949) in the United States and Ivan Pavlov in Russia (1849–1936), whose work in psychology began in the late 19th and early 20th centuries, respectively.

Based on his animal research, which he initially conducted in the homes of mentors for lack of a laboratory of his own, Thorndike came up with a simple yet elegant "law of effect" that helped set the stage for strict behaviorism. In essence, he proposed that any behavior that is followed by a satisfying state of affairs tends to be repeated, and any behavior that is followed by an unsatisfying or annoying state of affairs tends not to be repeated. "Satisfying" and "unsatisfying" may sound mentalistic, or covert, but Thorndike had a way of getting around that: He simply defined "satisfying" as something an organism normally approaches and "unsatisfying" as something an organism normally avoids. We return to Thorndike's theory and research in Chapter 4.

Pavlov was another researcher who did not start out as a psychologist. During the first half of his career, he was a highly successful physiologist, winning a Nobel Prize for his work on animal digestive processes using dogs as subjects. Salivation is an initial step in digestion, and as the story goes, Pavlov became intrigued with (or perhaps irritated by) the observation that the dogs used in his research quickly developed a tendency to salivate *before* food was placed in their mouths. He initially referred to this phenomenon as "psychic secretion," but he and his followers soon abandoned such mentalistic notions in favor of describing variations of this behavior in terms of *stimulus*—any event in the environment that an organism can detect—and *response*—any observable behavior an organism engages in as a result of the stimulus. Pavlov's realization of the importance of what has come to be known as *classical conditioning* is a prime example of *serendipity* (accidental discovery) in science, and it was a sidetrack that occupied the rest of his career and influenced countless researchers who followed him. We return to the particulars of classical conditioning in Chapter 4.

In the United States, strict behaviorism soon found its spokesperson in J. B. Watson (1878–1958). Watson decreed that "mental life" is something that cannot be observed or measured and therefore cannot be studied scientifically. Instead of trying to examine such vague concepts as consciousness or mental processes, he argued, psychologists should concentrate on events and actions that are plainly visible. Extending Pavlov's approach, Watson considered all human behavior to be reducible to events in which a stimulus produces a response. Hence, Watson's approach came to be known as *S-R behaviorism*, a term that is interchangeable with *strict behaviorism.*

Watson's primary impact was to solidify, through his lectures and writings, the strict behaviorists' emphasis on overt behavior; he did little in the way of research. He believed in the overriding importance of conditioning in human development

**Strict behaviorism**
The view that only overt behavior can be studied scientifically.

and behavior and attributed little to heredity. In perhaps his best-known statement, Watson proposed,

> Give me a dozen healthy infants, well formed, and my own specified world to bring them up in and I'll guarantee to take any one at random and train him to become any type of specialist I might select—doctor, lawyer, artist, merchant, chief, and yes, even beggar-man and thief, regardless of his talents, penchants, tendencies, abilities, and race of his ancestors. (1925)

For almost six decades, strict behaviorism was the dominant force in psychology, although it gradually slipped back into the study of "unobservables," as researchers such as Clark Hull (1884–1952)—prominent among those psychologists known as *learning theorists*—formulated complex "internal" S-R sequences in an attempt to get inside the organism in a scientific way. In a sense, the efforts of Hull and his adherents heralded strict behaviorism's fall from dominance: If it was acceptable to address covert S-R "bonds" that can only be inferred, it should be acceptable to study other forms of covert behavior as well. This view never sat well with Skinner, however, who remained an ardent strict behaviorist until his death in 1990.

In all, the strict behaviorists, with their search for simple and observable knowledge, pushed psychology toward greater discipline and the realization that a science must be based on carefully thought-out, controlled experiments and other objective forms of research. This was their legacy, and it is a major part of why strict behaviorism is known as **the second force in psychology.** In the view of by far the majority of modern psychologists, overt, objective, and replicable (reproduceable) evidence is the bottom line in research and theory. However, instead of shunning the often difficult-to-study intricacies of covert behavior, modern psychologists enthusiastically embrace the challenge.

**The second force in psychology**
Strict behaviorism.

## Gestalt Psychology

**Gestalt psychology**
An approach to the study of mental processes based on the idea that the whole is more than the sum of the parts.

A movement of considerable historic importance because of its opposition to strict behaviorism—and structuralism, as well—was **Gestalt psychology,** which originated in Germany at about the same time that strict behaviorism was taking hold in the United States. Founded by Max Wertheimer (1880–1943) and his associates, the movement took its name from a German word that has no exact English equivalent. "Gestalt" can be roughly translated as "pattern" or "configuration," but it means more than that; it implies that the whole is more than the sum of the parts. This idea stood in direct opposition to the structuralists' attempts to break down mental functioning into discrete components; in so doing, according to the Gestaltists, you lose the essence.

Gestalt psychologists also stressed the importance of the entire situation, or context, in which the "whole" is found. Figure 1.4 illustrates this idea. Note how your interpretation of the bold characters is dictated by the rest of what you see in each row of characters. Although the Gestalt movement in its original form is no longer active, many of its findings survive—particularly those regarding rules of perceptual organization, discussed in Chapter 3. In a larger sense, the issues raised by the Gestaltists are still very much alive in today's emphasis on the study (or treatment) of the whole person.

**FIGURE 1.4** How the context, or "surround," influences perception, in accord with principles of Gestalt psychology. The same item is bold in each row, but what you perceive in each case is quite different.

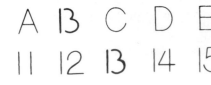

## Humanistic Psychology and Positive Psychology

Psychology has of course taken other directions, as would be expected in a science embracing such a wide field of inquiry. A movement that is still prominent today is **humanistic psychology,** which stems in part from the Gestalt school.

Humanistic psychologists take the view that human beings are different from rats, dogs, and monkeys in many respects. This view places humanists in opposition to the strict behaviorists, who focused on principles that apply to all living organisms. Humanistic psychologists likewise object to the emphasis on "animal" needs and desires that is inherent both in strict behaviorism and in psychoanalytic theory. According to humanistic psychologists, human beings have physiological needs in common with other creatures and they have selfish interests, but they also have values and goals, as well as desires to grow, express and fulfill themselves, and find peace and happiness. To humanistic psychologists, the thoughts and aspirations that the strict behaviorists considered inappropriate for study are among the most important aspects of behavior. Hence, humanistic psychology has been designated **the third force in psychology.**

Best known of humanistic psychologists are Carl Rogers (1902–1987) and Abraham Maslow (1908–1970), although the essential ideas of humanistic psychology originated earlier in work by other personality theorists (e.g., Adler, 1924; Allport, 1950). Rogers's and Maslow's theores are discussed in Chapter 9, and Rogers's humanistic approach to psychotherapy is discussed in Chapter 14.

The 1980s and especially the 1990s saw another shift in emphasis, to an approach similar to that of humanistic psychology. What is now known as **positive psychology** (e.g., Seligman & Csikszentmihalyi, 2000) arose from the observation

**Humanistic psychology**
The view that human beings are unique among animals, especially in having goals and aspirations and other positive motives.

**The third force in psychology**
Humanistic psychology.

**Positive psychology**
The view that psychological theory and research should focus in part on desirable behaviors such as happiness, satisfaction, and well-being.

# Study Chart

# Approaches and Schools of Thought in Psychology

| Approach/School | Description |
|---|---|
| Functionalism | An approach that stressed how modern human thought might result from progressive adaptations our ancestors experienced. |
| Structuralism | An approach that emphasized breaking down consciousness and mental activity into structural components and analyzing them individually. |
| Psychoanalysis | Analysis of the unconscious motives and conflicts of patients in an attempt to develop insight into their present mental or behavioral problems. |
| Strict behaviorism | An approach that considers only overt behavior to be appropriate subject matter for psychology. |
| Gestalt psychology | An approach that examines patterns of thought and behavior, emphasizing the situation or context in which they occur. |
| Humanistic psychology | An approach that emphasizes human values, goals, and desires for growth, fulfillment, and peace and happiness. |
| Positive psychology | An approach that calls attention to positive aspects of human behavior, such as happiness, satisfaction, and personal well-being. |
| Cognitive approach | A contemporary trend, based largely on the information-processing model, that emphasizes mental and intellectual processes such as learning, memory, and thought. |
| Psychobiological approaches | The study of how various facets of behavior are associated with processes in the body and especially the brain. |

© Roger Ressmeyer/CORBIS

Carl Rogers was one of the founders of humanistic psychology, which focuses on humans' desire for growth and self-fulfillment.

**Cognitive psychology**
**An approach that emphasizes the many roles of cognition in behavior.**

**Information-processing model**
**A way of studying human cognition based on computer analogies.**

by various theorists and researchers that psychologists in general, and clinical psychologists in particular, historically have paid far too much attention to the "down side" of human behavior: mental and behavioral disorders, prejudice and discrimination, rape and other sexual abuse, criminality, and the sometimes "dog eat dog" nature of human existence. In this view, far too little attention has been paid to the "up side," such as happiness, satisfaction, and personal well-being. The point made by theorists such as Martin Seligman and his colleagues is certainly not that the down side is unimportant—psychology must always be concerned with the problems of individuals and of society at large. But the up side is important too, and it has been grossly underexplored. In Chapter 12, we return to this issue and what it may portend for the future of psychology.

## The Cognitive Approach and Its Pervasive Influence

In a sense, the opposite directions taken by the strict behaviorists and the introspectionists were like the efforts of a gunner who first aims too far to the left, next too far to the right, and then, with the target bracketed, scores a direct hit. Both schools of thought were wide of the mark, yet both were essential to the growth of psychology into its present form. Many aspects of "mental life" have been drawn back into the field of study, and in recent years psychologists have been exploring language, thinking, and memory, as well as emotions, motives, and processes related to social interaction. Yet at the same time, thanks to the influence of the strict behaviorists, the study has become more disciplined and systematic, relying on observation of actual behavior rather than mere introspection.

Incorporation of **cognitive psychology** is a major trend that has now permeated most other areas of psychology. As noted earlier, *cognition* refers to mental and intellectual processes, such as the ways in which people and other animals learn about their environments, organize and store the knowledge in memory, think about it, and use it in both familiar and new situations. Much of cognitive psychology is based on the **information-processing model**, a concept that originated in the work of computer science pioneers Allen Newell (1927–1992) and Herbert Simon (1916–2001) (Newell & Simon, 1961). The process begins with input—raw data about the environment that we gather through our senses as they respond to light and sound waves, pressure and heat, and the chemicals that cause sensations of taste and smell. The brain tries to make sense out of this jumble of stimuli, comparing it to previous information and interpreting its significance (see Chapter 3). Now transformed into patterns and associated with meaning, the information is stored in memory, where it is linked with other information to which it bears some relationship. We call on the information whenever we need it—as a computer would tap its memory bank—to help us think, understand, and solve problems. This is not to say that humans "think" like computers; there are some key differences, which we consider at several points in the text. One is that most computers process information one unit at a time, in serial fashion, whereas humans are capable of simultaneous, or parallel, processing; we can attend to and think about more than one thing at a time. Another difference is that computer information storage is infallible and perfectly accurate (barring a hard-disk crash or the introduction of a computer virus). Human information storage is quite fallible, and memories are often changed or distorted with the passage of time—that is, human memories tend to "evolve." But for the most part, the information-processing model has served psychology extremely well.

Cognitive psychologists also reject another strict behaviorist idea: the idea that people are mere pawns of the environment, responding to incoming stimuli almost like automatons, as a result of prior and ongoing conditioning. Instead, cognitive psychologists view the human organism as "an active seeker of knowledge and processor of information," from which each individual actively builds "mental representations of the world" (Klatzky, 1980). These mental models of subjective reality are a core idea in cognitive psychology. They take the form of *schemas*, as discussed in Chapter 6 and elsewhere.

Basically, cognitive psychologists think of the human mind as a mental executive that organizes stimuli into perceptual patterns (for example, perceiving a girl or a boy rather than a collection of arms and legs and a body); this view is analogous to the perspective of the Gestaltists. The mind then makes comparisons and processes the information it receives into new forms and categories. It discovers meanings and uses its stored knowledge to find new principles that aid in constructive thinking, making judgments and decisions, and determining appropriate behavior. These ideas have influenced most of today's psychologists in one way or another, in all branches of the science, from the study of the senses to neuroscience and psychotherapy.

It is worth remembering that although the cognitive "revolution" in psychology first became apparent in the 1960s, early versions of cognitive psychology have been around for much longer, working quietly—and sometimes not so quietly—in the shadow of strict behaviorism. As noted earlier, the Gestaltists were cognitive psychologists, though with different perspectives and methods. Standardized intelligence testing, which is clearly about cognition and knowledge, began early in the 20th century with the work of Alfred Binet (1857–1911) in France. The first "modern" social psychology text (Allport, 1924) contained numerous references to cognitive processes, and social cognition (see Chapter 15) has been an active area of research since the 1930s. Industrial/organizational psychology, with its focus on workers' thinking and how it pertains to job performance, has always been concerned with cognitive processes. Other early cognitive psychologists were Jean Piaget (1896–1980) of Switzerland and Lev Vygotsky (1896–1934) of Russia, whose research on cognitive development in children became influential in the 1930s and remains so today (see Chapter 10). Finally, in the heyday of strict behaviorism, there were staunch opponents who were determined to tear down the prohibition against the study of cognitive processes. Notable among these was Edward Tolman (1886–1959), who devised clever experiments demonstrating that even the behavior of laboratory rats cannot be understood or predicted solely in terms of S-R conditioning; allowance must be made for the rats' thinking (see Chapter 4).

Swiss psychologist Jean Piaget gained insight into children's cognitive development by holding conversations with children of various ages.

# Psychobiology and Neuroscience

Among psychologists today are a growing number who work in an area called **psychobiology** (or, as some prefer, *biological psychology*), a general term for the study of how various facets of behavior are associated with processes in the body. Highly active among them are psychologists who focus directly on brain functioning and physical or psychological behavior and work in the areas of **cognitive and behavioral neuroscience.** References to their findings appear throughout the text—for example, in descriptions of studies of the psychological functions of various areas of the brain (Chapter 2), the influence of brain chemistry on emotions and motives (Chapter 8), the role of genetics in human development (Chapter 10), how hormonal changes affect the adjustment of adolescents (Chapter 11), the bodily

**Psychobiology**
A general term for the study of how behavior is associated with bodily processes.

**Cognitive and behavioral neuroscience**
In psychology, the study of relationships between brain functioning and physical or psychological behavior.

changes associated with stress (Chapter 12), and the use of drugs to alleviate anxiety and depression (Chapter 14).

The science of psychology is based on the assumption that all behavior is rooted in some way in the activity of the brain and nervous system; even Skinner acknowledged this. Chapter 2 describes the new and continually improving technology, which allows researchers to see what electrical and biochemical activity occurs in different areas of the brain when someone perceives an object, thinks, remembers, or experiences a hallucination. Indeed, advances in brain research have led some scientists to conclude that everything we experience and do will one day be explained by the operations of the brain. More than 20 years ago, psychologists began wondering whether "psychology is in danger of losing its status as an independent body of knowledge" (Peele, 1981). What has happened instead is that neuroscience—much like cognitive psychology—has permeated other psychological disciplines and spawned some new subdisciplines, such as *social cognitive neuroscience* and *developmental neuroscience*.

It is unlikely that neuroscience alone will ever supplant psychology. For one thing, the workings of the brain are so complex as to defy complete understanding, and thus the brain will always retain some—perhaps many—of its mysteries. This means that inferring cognitive processes from behavior rather than measuring them directly will always play a part in furthering psychologists' understanding. Moreover, no matter how completely scientists understand the brain, the workings of its structures and circuits will still depend on the external world, as the brain is an instrument through which behavior is altered by experience. Roger Sperry (1913–1994) emphasized this point when he received the Nobel Prize for his research on the brain (see Chapter 2). We cannot depend on the brain to tell us everything about the operation of the conscious mind, he noted (Sperry, 1988). Thus, psychologists will always need to know something about the prior histories and current psychological states of the people and other animals being studied.

# KEY ISSUES IN PSYCHOLOGY: YESTERDAY AND TODAY

> ## FOCUS QUESTIONS
> - What roles do heredity and environment play in behavior and development?
> - Is developmental change gradual or abrupt?
> - Why is it important to consider the context in which behavior occurs?
> - Why is it important to consider culture and ethnicity in understanding behavior?

Later chapters of this text are concerned primarily with specific knowledge that psychologists have discovered about behavior—from the role of brain cells to patterns of social interactions. Before we begin this detailed discussion, however, it is useful to examine some of the major questions addressed by psychology. By and large, these questions go to the core of human experience. Because they cut so deep, they are difficult to study—much less resolve—and there remains widespread disagreement on a number of points.

We begin with one of the oldest issues in psychology (and philosophy as well).

## Heredity and Environment: Their Relative Influence

A major issue of continuing concern to psychology is the relationship between inborn genetic factors and life experiences as they affect human development and behavior. In *science*, genetics and experience are the only two possible causes of what and who you are—metaphysical causes are ruled out—so it follows that the relative importance of each would be an important area of debate.

William James, for example, believed that many human behaviors, including pugnacity, rivalry, sociability, shyness, curiosity, acquisitiveness, and love, are regulated to a great extent by powerful instincts present at birth. Watson, on the other hand, believed that the newborn child can be turned into almost any kind of adult through environmental conditioning.

Today psychologists know that it is not possible to treat genetic makeup and life experiences as separate, independent forces (e.g., Plomin & McClearn, 1993). To become a great basketball star, for example, a child would typically have to inherit a combination of height, speed, and endurance. But without exposure to the sport and opportunity to practice—plus good nutrition—even the best-endowed child will never become a skilled player. Thus, it isn't possible when looking at a basketball hero to say exactly how much of his ability is due to what he inherited and how much to opportunities available in his environment.

This issue, formerly cast as the *nature-nurture controversy* (which implies nature *versus* nurture), has been resolved to some extent. It is now commonly accepted that *heredity* and *environment*—the modern terms—operate in *interaction* rather than in opposition. However, this acknowledgment by no means ended the debate; if anything, it intensified it. Once psychologists stopped arguing in an either-or manner, they turned to arguing about how much each contributes. Volumes of research have been published on the relative contributions of heredity and environment to just about every aspect of human development and behavior, and volumes will continue to be published.

Why is this an important issue? Except for possibilities raised by the new technologies for altering genes (which are still in their infancy as far as psychological characteristics are concerned), one's genetic makeup is essentially fixed at the point of conception and is not subject to manipulation and change. On the other hand, the myriad learning experiences people begin having even prior to birth are not fixed and are highly subject to manipulation. For example, not much can be done to improve the intelligence of a child who was born with severe neurological impairments and consequent mental retardation, but a lot can be done to prevent neurologically normal children from becoming mentally retarded as a result of growing up in impoverished environments. Here, the question of how much is directly relevant. Suppose intelligence is determined 80% by genetics and only 20% by environment, as some argue. Then whatever we do to the environment to foster the best possible outcomes for children will have to be really good and to the point in order to have much effect, but we don't risk much. On the other hand, if the genetic component is only 20% and the environmental component is 80%, we have a lot more space to work in, but what we do becomes crucial. If the environmental factors children are exposed to exert a broad influence, we have to be really careful, lest we exert a strong influence in the wrong direction.

We return to the issue of heredity and environment at various points in the text.

## Continuity and Change

Everyone would agree that you are quite different today from the human being you were at birth and from the person you will be in the closing years of your life. But how different? Is human development marked by continuity—that is, a series of gradual and cumulative changes, with the traces of each stage of life embedded in the later ones? Or is development a series of significant discontinuities—that is, changes so dramatic that some characteristics vanish and new ones emerge?

It is possible to find examples of both stability and change in behavior, and human development appears to be a mix of both. For example, psychologists who study memory claim that once a memory is formed it can never be entirely lost (barring brain damage). Similarly, studies of psychologically disordered individuals often suggest that early trauma, such as abuse in childhood, can leave emotional scars that last for life. On the other hand, the brain undergoes marked changes over time, as some circuits are phased out and new ones are added, dramatically altering a person's repertoire of behaviors. And new experiences—a different job, marriage, a sudden trauma—can dramatically shift the course of development for good or ill. Psychology must study both continuity and change. It must strive to understand to what extent we become just a different version of our earlier self and to what degree we can become "a different person," one who would be difficult to recognize as evolved from our earlier identity.

This is an especially important issue in psychotherapy (see Chapter 14). If you have bad habits, can you alter them for the better? If so, how much and how permanently? If you have a maladaptive outlook on life that prevents you from being happy and fulfilling yourself, can you change quickly or will years of "undoing" and relearning be required? Here's an even more basic question: If certain psychotherapeutic techniques don't accomplish much, is it because the techniques themselves are ineffective or because the person simply can't change? We look at these issues again as well.

## Context: The Person and the Situation

For decades, psychology was chiefly interested in the individual. Psychologists were content to separate an individual person from others—much as a zoologist might cut one elephant out of the herd for measurement and labeling—and study that person's behavior. Any characteristic was assumed to represent a consistent pattern of behavior, as stable as height or weight. A person who was found to be helpful and generous would, it was assumed, be helpful and generous under most circumstances. An aggressive person would always tend to be aggressive, an anxious person always anxiety-prone, an achievement-oriented person always focused on achievement and mastery.

It is now clear, however, that our behavior is not necessarily as consistent as was once believed. Our actions often depend on the *context*—that is, on the particular situation in which they occur. Someone may be generous at home but selfish at work, aggressive with a spouse but submissive with friends, anxious in an unfamiliar place but calm and relaxed in familiar surroundings. Another major issue in psychology, therefore, is the question of how our behavior depends on where we are—and particularly on the people around us.

The manner in which the situation and the people in it can influence behavior is a primary concern of social psychologists. But all branches of psychology have been greatly influenced by the rise of this important issue, which can be traced in large part to the research of Walter Mischel, which began in the 1960s and continued for many years (e.g., Mischel, 1965, 1990). Through his early research, Mischel became convinced that supposedly stable personality traits aren't so stable at all and that behavior across situations is much more variable than would be expected on the basis of traits. He later modified his position to acknowledge the existence of both "situation" and "person" determinants of behavior, but he maintained that it is still impossible in most cases to predict what a given person will do in a given situation based on traits alone.

Was Mischel correct? We return to this and related issues in Chapter 15, but here's an idea to ponder in the meantime. People strongly prefer predictability in the behavior of others with whom they interact; indeed, marked unpredictability is considered a sign of possible psychological problems. We like to be confident about what people will or will not do—especially the people we know. We like people to perceive us as predictable as well, particularly with regard to desirable "traits" that tend to make them like and trust us. So it may be that we and others regularly *act* as if we have stable traits because such behavior is received well. For example, you probably prefer to have others perceive you as an honest person, and you probably like to think of yourself as honest. Thus, even when you encounter a situation in which you are strongly tempted to be dishonest, you're likely to behave in an honest manner. The question of whether personality traits are stable across situations then becomes moot: If you consistently *act* honest in different situations, then you *are* an honest person—even if acting that way sometimes takes a concerted effort on your part.

## Culture, Ethnicity, Diversity, and "Race"

A final key issue in psychology today—an issue that may well be the most important of the four discussed in this section—is coming to grips with culture and other sources of diversity in human behavior.

During much of the 20th century, by far the bulk of psychological research was conducted in the United States and other Western nations. Although most research on humans used only participants from these nations, the findings often were generalized to humans everywhere. Little attention was paid to the possibility of important variations in human development and behavior attributable to **culture,** which can be defined as the composite of norms, practices, beliefs, attitudes, arts, and whatever else people regard as their heritage. (Whereas a *society* is an organized group of interacting people, culture may be thought of as a society's "personality.")

Culture greatly influences children's development, first via caregivers and later via peers, teachers, popular media, social institutions, and so on (e.g., Bronfenbrenner & Morris, 1998). Culture continues to exert its influence throughout the life span. But only in the last couple of decades have psychologists in the United States and other nations come to see the broad implications of cultural differences with regard to important aspects of human behavior such as social interactions, personality characteristics, mental and behavioral disorders, and perhaps even things as basic as cognitive functioning. That is, only in recent years have many psychologists come to appreciate fully the importance of avoiding **ethnocentrism**—an outlook bound by one's own culture and perhaps ignorant of or even disrespectful toward the cultures of others.

Consider an example of differences attributable to culture. As anthropologists and sociologists have long observed, most Western societies have a largely **individualist culture,** whereas many other societies have a largely **collectivist culture** (e.g., see Gardiner, Mutter, & Kosmitzki, 1998; Matsumoto, 2000). In individualist cultures, competition is the norm, and the good of the individual is valued more highly than that of the group. There are exceptions—in some situations, individualistic people do subordinate themselves to the greater good—but there is a consistently strong emphasis on freedom of choice and *independence.* By contrast, in collectivist cultures, cooperation and the good of the group are valued more highly than the good of the individual. There are exceptions here too—a person may feel a sense of personal pride when his or her contributions to the group help it succeed and prosper—but the emphasis is consistently on choices and goals of the group rather than those of the individual; that is, these cultures value *interdependence.* In addition to the obvious implications for many social behaviors, these orientations tend to have important implications for the way people define "self"—as an individual or as a part of something larger. Thus, Western social and personality theories based on individualistic norms have often fallen short in explaining people in general.

**Diversity and Ethnicity**    An appreciation of culture goes hand in hand with an appreciation of **diversity,** a term that refers not only to cultural and ethnic differences but also to differences in gender, age, sexual orientation, and other characteristics of social groups. Your cultural heritage is part of your ethnicity; so is your membership in a *subculture*—a smaller cultural group within a larger one. The

**Culture**
The composite of norms, practices, beliefs, attitudes, arts, and heritage.

**Ethnocentrism**
An outlook bound by one's own culture and perhaps ignorant of or even disrespectful toward the cultures of others.

**Individualist culture**
A culture that is characterized by independence and typically values the good of the individual over the good of the group.

**Collectivist culture**
A culture that is characterized by interdependence and typically values the good of the group over the good of the individual.

**Diversity**
Group differences in culture, ethnicity, gender, age, sexual orientation, and other characteristics.

United States, for example, has a history of being a "melting pot" of peoples and cultures, but many distinct subcultures remain. Each, to varying degree, is a blend of U.S. mainstream culture and the heritage that the nation's residents or their ancestors brought with them, whether a decade ago, several hundred years ago, or many thousands of years ago. Allowing for and incorporating these kinds of differences in psychology is a gargantuan task, one that researchers and theorists are just beginning to devise methods for accomplishing. For now, psychologists and other social scientists are mostly limited to highlighting examples of cross-cultural or within-culture research in areas where it seems most important. In this text, such research is discussed primarily when it sheds light on what is universally human and what can vary considerably with diversity.

**Ethnicity Versus Race**    Note that in the preceding discussion we did not use the term "race." It is now widely acknowledged that there is no scientific basis for (1) the notion that there are psychological differences associated with race or (2) the idea that different races of humans exist in the first place (see Craig & Baucum, 2002, which includes a summary of arguments on this issue). Yet the idea persists and may have considerable meaning for you. If you identify yourself as "white," for example, you belong to an extremely diverse group of peoples around the world who have light skin and other features commonly associated with being white—not to mention many who are light skinned but have features quite different from those typically associated with being white. So in calling yourself "white," you actually haven't said much, and the same applies to people who identify themselves as "black," "Asian," "Hispanic," and so on. Ethnicity is a more justifiable and accurate concept for you to use in describing yourself and for psychologists to use in categorizing the people they study. The distinguishing characteristics that groups of people display derive from ethnicity and other aspects of diversity—not from race.

Although past psychological research aimed at acknowledging and understanding ethnicity has been important historically, much of it is couched in categorizations of people that are overly inclusive and therefore meaningless. An example is the extensive research comparing "black" people and "white" people on intelligence, as measured by IQ. Research of this kind is noted in this text (and in the case of "racial" IQ differences, also refuted), but every effort is made to be as specific as possible as to whom we're talking about. Wherever the term "race" appears in the text, it is in quotes, as a reminder that the concept has no scientific basis. Terms such as "Native American," "African American," "Asian American," "Hispanic American," "European American," and the like are also kept to a minimum. Aside from the issues just discussed, there's another reason: Physical anthropologists differ on the timing and some of the particulars, but they almost unanimously agree that *all* modern humans (*Homo sapiens sapiens*) are descended from people who originated in Africa between about 40,000 and 150,000 years ago.

**Test Yourself**

**(i)**  Of the key issues in psychology, which is most relevant to avoiding ethnocentricism?

(The answer is on page 41.)

# PSYCHOLOGY'S ETHICAL STANDARDS

**FOCUS QUESTIONS**

• How do psychological researchers protect the rights and safety of human participants?

• How do psychological researchers protect the rights and safety of laboratory animals?

Consider the following examples:

• A psychologist and his assistant use loud, startling sounds to condition an 11-month-old infant to fear laboratory rats and other white, furry objects.

• A psychological research team demands that their adult participants "obey orders" and deliver increasingly painful electric shocks to another participant (who is actually a member of the team—a "confederate"—and in reality receives no shocks); about two-thirds of the participants deliver the highest—and, as far as they know, quite dangerous—level of shock.

- A psychologist subjects dogs to inescapable electric shocks, demonstrating afterward that, unless they receive additional training, they become "helpless" and do not learn to escape or avoid shocks even when given the opportunity.

Most psychological research, past and present, with humans and other species has no potential for harm. The worst that participants risk is being uncomfortable or bored for a while; experiments are more often interesting and even amusing—not distressing or painful. We began this section with extreme examples of psychological research because they highlight important considerations. The first example is J. B. Watson's notorious "Little Albert" experiment, conducted in the 1920s, which would not and could not be conducted today. The second is representative of a series of experiments carried out by Stanley Milgram in the 1960s. The third comes from research done by Martin Seligman, also in the 1960s. These examples raise different issues, to which we will return in discussing contemporary ethical standards regarding psychological research.

## Safeguarding Human Research Participants

If psychologists are to understand human behavior—both positive and adaptive behavior and negative and maladaptive behavior—experiments and other forms of research with humans are essential. But psychologists can't perform just any kind of research with humans (or with laboratory animals). They must adhere to a strict and explicit code of ethics that has evolved primarily through the efforts of the APA. The APA's *Ethics in Research with Human Participants* (Sales & Folkman, 2000) covers a broad range of ethical considerations and procedures that apply before, during, and after research with humans. It also includes consideration of the moral foundations of research with humans, along with an appendix on U.S. laws regarding ethical research.

The basic idea is that researchers should never willfully or knowingly conduct research that has the potential to cause significant or lasting harm to anyone. They shouldn't even want to, regardless of how important the research might be for understanding human behavior and furthering the public good. Psychologists can *study* the very worst human behaviors and outcomes and often do, but they cannot *cause* such behaviors or outcomes as a way of studying them. For example, psychologists are welcome to study the often-devastating effects of parental abuse and neglect on children, but no psychologist can conduct research in which parents are instructed to abuse their children in certain ways so that researchers can see what happens. Although no psychologist is likely even to want to do so, the ethical standards and laws are in place to make sure that he or she does not do so. A researcher who violates them can lose the right to call herself or himself a psychologist and may also face a lawsuit or even criminal charges.

There is a subtler reason for strict adherence to the ethical guidelines: It isn't always obvious what might cause lasting harm or otherwise violate human rights. This is where carefully defined guidelines and procedures really come into play in protecting human participants and psychologists alike.

**Informed Consent**   A basic principle of ethical research is **informed consent**. Participants in all research should be told what is going to happen to them, should agree to participate, and should continue to participate voluntarily. That is, they have to know what to expect and must be free to cease participating at any time without coercion. In the case of very young children, the parent or other caregiver

**Informed consent**
The ethical requirement that research participants be told in advance what will happen and participate voluntarily throughout.

makes the decision for the child; with older children, both the child and the parent must consent, and the parent can make the decision to remove the child from the research at any time. With regard to Watson's experiment (discussed in Chapter 4), frightening a young infant is obviously unethical, no matter what the purpose. In addition, indications are that the mother didn't even know what was going on (Harris, 1979). When she found out, she stopped the experiment. In the Milgram experiments (Chapter 15), the ethics of which have been debated extensively, the participants were commanded to continue well past the point where most of them wanted to stop—and thus they were coerced.

The Milgram experiments also illustrate the use of *deception*, less extreme versions of which are common in research with humans. Deception is ethical where it is justifiable. People cannot be deceived as to what will happen to them, but they can be deceived as to the true purpose and certain particulars of the experiment. For example, would Milgram's experiments have meant anything if the participants had known that they weren't really shocking the confederate? When deception is used, participants must be thoroughly *debriefed* afterward—they must be told the true nature of the research and allowed to ask questions. Milgram's participants, for example, were greeted afterward by the unharmed confederate and told that they hadn't actually delivered any shocks; the question was simply how far they would go. Whether this debriefing was adequate is another issue, which we return to shortly.

**Protection from Harm**   Given that considerations of informed consent are satisfied, it can be ethically acceptable to conduct research in which human participants are temporarily exposed to procedures that annoy, irritate, or otherwise disturb them or even cause them minor physical pain. How far a researcher can go is the question, along with how well a researcher can anticipate any lasting harm that might result. In Watson's experiment, the experimenters didn't actually know whether the infant would acquire a lasting fear (although this is not a justification for frightening the child). Based on extensive research in the years since, psychologists now know that *phobias* (relatively permanent irrational and unwarranted fears) can indeed be established through procedures such as Watson's. Milgram's experiments are also troubling with regard to lasting harm. Even though the participants were told that they hadn't hurt anyone, they learned something potentially very disturbing about themselves: that they would hurt someone badly if an authority figure demanded that they do so in the name of science. That is, they suffered extensive loss of dignity and self-esteem (Baumrind, 1964), which debriefing did not necessarily counteract.

**Other Protections**   Just as what experimenters do with their research participants is important, what they do with the information they obtain is important as well. Researchers can publish group results and "the numbers," but they can't disclose any personal information about the participants without express written consent. All personal information is strictly confidential, but there's more: As noted by Susan Folkman (2000), a researcher cannot force information on the participants themselves if they don't want it. This includes information that might be a source of distress for a participant, such as test results or information on behavior during an experiment. (These considerations also apply to individuals in psychotherapy.)

Finally, research-oriented organizations such as universities are now required to have **institutional review boards (IRBs)**, committees of professionals who screen all research in advance to spot potential ethical problems and decide whether the research may be conducted. If participants are determined to be "at risk" of discomfort or temporary harm within reasonable limits, the IRB may conduct a cost-benefit analysis as part of the approval process. If the benefits to science and perhaps to society at large outweigh the risks to the participants and if

**Institutional review board (IRB)**
A committee of professionals who evaluate research projects with regard to ethical considerations and decide whether the research may be conducted.

the research has the potential to add to existing knowledge, the research may be allowed to proceed. For example, Milgram's series of experiments clearly established many factors that determine participants' willingness to obey, contributing extremely important knowledge to psychologists' understanding of this aspect of human behavior (again see Chapter 15). However, similar experiments nowadays would add little and thus would probably be ruled out on these grounds alone.

## Safeguarding Research Animals

Just as the APA standards and public law protect human research participants, they protect research subjects of other species as well. (Legislation began with the U.S. Animal Welfare Act of 1966; numerous state laws have been added since.) The following is a summary of the APA's "Ethical Principles of Psychologists and Code of Conduct" as it applies to the use *and* care of animals in research (APA, 1992):

- Psychologists treat research animals humanely.

- Psychologists acquire, care for, and use research animals in compliance with legal and professional standards.

- Psychologists experienced in the care of research animals supervise all procedures and are responsible for their comfort, health, and humane treatment; they are likewise responsible for the actions of individuals under their supervision.

- Psychologists make reasonable efforts to minimize any physical or psychological suffering of research animals.

- Procedures involving "pain, stress, or privation" are used only when no alternative is available and the goals are justifiable.

- Any surgical procedures are performed under anesthesia, and they must include attention to avoiding infection and minimizing pain.

- When a research animal's life is terminated, it is done rapidly and in accord with accepted procedures, again with an effort to minimize pain.

© Mark Richards/PhotoEdit Inc.

Psychological research often requires animal subjects—but they must be treated humanely.

Issues in animal research are also monitored by a group called Psychologists for the Ethical Treatment of Animals (PSYETA). Founded in 1981, PSYETA is an animal rights organization whose overall mission is "to reduce the suffering and exploitation of both human and nonhuman animals" and, more specifically, to work toward "the replacement, refinement, and reduction of the use of nonhuman animals as models of human disorders" (PSYETA, 2002). Basically, PSYETA is opposed to animal research, particularly research that subjects animals to pain or death (e.g., see Shapiro, 1997).

One survey found that about four out of five U.S. APA members generally support animal research unless the research inflicts pain or death, in which case the acceptance rates dropped to about 34% for research with rats as subjects, 30% for research with pigeons, 19% for research with dogs, and 18% for research with primates (Plous, 1996). These findings are consistent with other survey data reported by Plous: In both the United States and Great Britain as of the early 1990s, a significant percentage of psychology programs (15–25%) had closed animal research facilities, and comparable percentages of other programs had held serious discussions about doing so—a trend paralleled by major reductions in the number of faculty and graduate students engaging in animal research.

The extent of animal research in psychology was reported to be about 7% in 1985 (Miller, 1985). The trends just mentioned suggest that the percentage was probably closer to 5% by the early 1990s and will be even lower by the time you read this, particularly with regard to primates. Animal research continues, however, and such research, past and present, is referred to throughout the text. Although space doesn't allow a debate on the issues involved, a couple of comments on the pros and cons are in order. Critics of animal research argue that members of other species should have rights comparable to those of humans and deserve to be treated accordingly—especially because it is clear that members of other species do think and feel pain. These arguments have merit. On the other hand, proponents point out from a practical perspective that considerable understanding—both medical and psychological—has resulted from research that in most cases could not have been conducted with humans (Carroll & Overmier, 2001). Pharmacological research on animals has yielded beneficial drugs too numerous to mention. Physiological research on animals has yielded an enormous store of basic understanding of the human brain. Psychological research (such as that on learned helplessness, noted at the beginning of this section) has yielded findings with direct applications to the understanding of mental and behavioral disorders, among many other areas of functioning. For example, the behavior displayed by Seligman's dogs launched an important line of research on human depression, which is typified in part by a comparable sense of profound helplessness (see Chapters 4 and 13). Notably, Seligman followed up his initial research with the development of procedures that eliminated the dogs' helplessness (Seligman, Maier, & Geer, 1968), a line of research that also had extensions to understanding human depression.

Because of the many restrictions on the care and use of research animals, as well as the strong personal orientation toward ethical behavior on the part of psychologists themselves, research proceeds with a sure sense of the humane treatment of all forms of life.

## Test Yourself

**(j)**   One psychologist is studying the effects of long-term sleep deprivation; another is studying the relative effectiveness of two approaches to treating insomnia. Which is more likely to use humans as participants?

(The answer is on page 41.)

# Chapter 1 Summary

## The Scope of Psychology

1. *Psychology* is the scientific study of the *overt* and *covert behavior* of living organisms, along with the factors that influence each form of behavior.
2. The missions of psychology are to understand behavior, to predict behavior, and perhaps to control behavior.
3. Psychology is one member of a family of sciences known as *the behavioral and social sciences.*

## The Varieties of Psychology and Psychologists

4. The number of psychologists—especially health service providers—continues to increase.
5. Many psychologists are concerned only with *basic science,* or knowledge for the sake of knowledge. Others are chiefly interested in *applied science,* or the pursuit of knowledge that has practical uses.
6. A traditional distinction is between experimental psychologists and clinical psychologists, but this distinction has become somewhat blurred.
7. Focusing primarily on basic science are the following:
    a) Cognitive psychologists, who are interested in the ways humans perceive and understand the world around them and in processes such as learning and memory.
    b) Comparative psychologists, who concentrate on relating animal behavior patterns to those found in humans.
    c) Physiological psychologists (psychobiologists and neuroscientists), who study the role of the body and especially brain functions in behavior.
    d) Developmental psychologists, who study how individuals grow and change throughout their lives.
    e) Personality psychologists, who study how people differ in their enduring inner characteristics and traits.
    f) Social psychologists, who study how people influence and are influenced by others.
    g) Evolutionary psychologists, who focus on psychological tendencies inherent in being human.
8. Focusing primarily on applied science are the following:
    a) School psychologists, who test and evaluate students, analyze learning problems, and counsel both teachers and parents.
    b) Educational psychologists, who are concerned with all aspects of the educational process.
    c) Industrial/organizational psychologists, who work on a wide variety of issues in work settings.
    d) Environmental psychologists, who deal with ecological problems such as pollution and overcrowding.
    e) Community psychologists, who deal with aspects of the social environment and how social institutions could better serve human needs.
    f) Forensic psychologists, who work on behavioral issues important in the legal, judicial, and correctional systems.
    g) Health psychologists, who focus on ways to improve health by altering behavior.
9. Clinical psychologists help diagnose and treat psychological problems through a general approach known as psychotherapy.
10. Counseling psychologists work with people who have less severe and more specific problems of social and emotional adjustment.

## The Methods Psychologists Use

11. In studying behavior, psychologists employ *naturalistic observation, interviews, case histories, questionnaires, surveys,* standardized tests, physiological measures, *correlation,* and *experiments.*
12. The normal distribution describes many physical and psychological characteristics; most people cluster around the middle, or the average, and only a few score at the extremes.
13. Correlation is a statistical tool for determining what relationship, if any, exists between different pairs of measurements or scores.
14. Experimentation, which is psychology's most powerful tool, assesses cause and effect through strictly controlled procedures and manipulations.
15. In experiments, issues of *internal validity* and *external validity* are of foremost importance.

## Conducting Good Experiments

16. Experiments may focus on individuals or on the averaging and comparison of behavior of groups.
17. Experiments begin with a prediction about conditions that will cause the participants' behavior to differ.
18. In an experiment, what a researcher manipulates is the *independent variable,* and what the researcher measures is the *dependent variable.*
19. *Operational definitions* are crucial to the value of an experiment.
20. *Systematic replication* is needed for results of an experiment to be generalized beyond the specific experimental procedures employed.

## Psychology's Rich History and Promising Future

21. Psychology was founded in 1879, when the first laboratory was established by Wilhelm Wundt; some early psychologists who followed, including William James (the founder of modern psychology), were chiefly interested in studying human functioning via introspection.

22. Sigmund Freud had a profound impact on psychology as we know it today; although many of his ideas about human nature and behavior have not survived the test of time and research, *psychoanalytic theory* has become known as *the first force in psychology.*

23. *Strict behaviorism,* a rebellion against introspection and other approaches, limited its study to overt behavior; it began with the work of Thorndike and Pavlov and has become known as *the second force in psychology.*

24. Watson was a spokesperson for strict behaviorism; he proposed that all of human and other animal behavior is a series of actions that can be explained in terms of specific stimuli and responses.

25. B. F. Skinner agreed that human beings are creatures of their environment, whose behavior depends on the contingencies they are subjected to.

26. *Gestalt psychology* took the position that that the whole is more than the sum of the parts; thus in studying any psychological phenomena—from perceptual to more general cognitive processes—psychologists must consider the phenomena themselves and the context in which they occur as a whole.

27. *Humanistic psychology* started as a rebellion against psychoanalysis and strict behaviorism; because it stresses the unique qualities of being human, it has become known as *the third force in psychology.*

28. *Positive psychology* is a more recent development; it stresses that theory and research should focus on adaptive and healthy behavior, not just maladaptive behavior.

29. *Cognitive psychology* focuses on mental and intellectual processes, such as the ways in which people and other animals learn about their environments, organize and store the knowledge in memory, think about it, and use it to act.

30. Much of cognitive psychology is based on the *information-processing model* adapted from computer science, although the study of cognition has diverse roots in the history of psychology.

31. A growing number of psychologists today focus on *psychobiology,* the study of how various facets of behavior are associated with processes in the body; psychobiology includes *cognitive and behavioral neuroscience.*

## Key Issues in Psychology: Yesterday and Today

32. There is a continuing debate (historically called the nature-nurture controversy) over the relative importance of heredity and environment in development and behavior.

33. Human development is a mix of both continuities (gradual and cumulative changes) and discontinuities (dramatic, often sudden changes).

34. Human behavior may not be as consistent as was once believed; often a person's actions depend on the context in which the behavior occurs.

35. Of foremost importance in modern psychology is coming to grips with differences in human behavior attributable to *culture,* ethnicity, and other sources of *diversity* and thereby avoiding *ethnocentrism;* of particular interest is the impact of *individualist* versus *collectivist culture* on behavior.

## Psychology's Ethical Standards

36. The code of ethics developed by the APA and enforced by law requires that researchers who use human participants pay particular attention to such issues as *informed consent* and protection of participants from physical or psychological harm.

37. *Institutional review boards (IRBs)* decide whether psychological research may be conducted.

38. The APA and public law also require that researchers take special care in the use of animals in psychological research, avoiding needless harm and exploitation; the use of animals in scientific research remains controversial.

# Chapter 1 Test Yourself Answers

(a) The researcher is likely a psychologist, since the project involves the study of overt behavior (aggression) and covert behavior (anger), along with factors (childhood experiences) that may influence them.

(b) The second researcher likely works in the field of cultural anthropology.

(c) Psychology has attracted more women than has any other science; it is perhaps the most egalitarian of the sciences in this respect.

(d) The work of the first psychologist is basic, because it primarily involves the search for scientific knowledge for its own sake. The work of the second is applied, because it involves the use of knowledge to accomplish a specific task.

(e) The psychologist is likely to be in clinical psychology, which is devoted to the diagnosis and treatment of severe psychological disorders.

(f) As with any correlation, you can't say. In this case, the depression may have caused the brain changes, the brain changes may have caused the depression, or some third factor might have caused both.

(g) The praise would be the independent variable; you would manipulate it in some manner (such as praising one group of students and not another). Mathematics performance on some test would be the dependent variable and would be expected to vary in accord with praise.

(h) You would almost certainly focus on the latter. Psychobiology is devoted to the study of how various facets of behavior are associated with the body and especially brain processes.

(i) The issues of culture and ethnicity are most relevant; understanding people requires that these be taken into account in many cases.

(j) Either researcher could ethically use humans, but the latter is more likely to. It's hard to imagine a psychological treatment for insomnia in rats or pigeons.

# Chapter 1  The Science and Practice of Psychology

## Key Terms

applied science (p. 8)
basic science (p. 8)
behavioral and social sciences (p. 5)
case history (p. 12)
cognitive and behavioral neuroscience (p. 29)
cognitive psychology (p. 28)
collectivist culture (p. 33)
correlation (p. 16)
covert behavior (p. 3)
culture (p. 33)
dependent variable (p. 20)
diversity (p. 33)
ethnocentrism (p. 33)
experiment (p. 17)
external validity (p. 17)
Gestalt psychology (p. 26)
humanistic psychology (p. 27)
independent variable (p. 20)
individualist culture (p. 33)
information-processing model (p. 28)
informed consent (p. 35)

institutional review board (IRB) (p. 36)
internal validity (p. 17)
interview (p. 12)
naturalistic observation (p. 11)
operational definition (p. 21)
overt behavior (p. 3)
positive psychology (p. 27)
psychoanalytic theory (p. 24)
psychobiology (p. 29)
psychology (p. 3)
questionnaire (p. 13)
strict behaviorism (p. 25)
survey (p. 13)
systematic replication (p. 21)
the first force in psychology (p. 24)
the second force in psychology (p. 26)
the third force in psychology (p. 27)

 *The key terms above can be used as search terms in InfoTrac, a database of readings, which can be found at http://infotrac-thomsonlearning.com.*

## Active Learning Review

### The Scope of Psychology

1. *Psychology* is the scientific study of the *overt* and *covert behavior* of living organisms—with emphasis on animals and especially humans. "Scientific study" refers to using rigorous and highly disciplined research methods rather than relying on judgments based on insufficient evidence or unwarranted generalizations; this distinguishes _____ from casual observation and "common sense."

2. Psychologists study our overt activities—everything we do from the time we wake up in the morning until we go to sleep and wake up again. Observable or otherwise measurable activities are _____ that psychologists study.

3. Psychologists also study the covert activities that take place inside of us—the ways we learn, remember, forget, feel hungry, become angry, and experience joy. These are also _____ that are studied by psychologists.

4. Factors that influence behavior are many and varied. Chief among them is the functioning of the brain, along with that of the senses and other parts of the body. Psychologists study all the _____ between the brain and the rest of the body.

5. Psychology, then, is the _____ _____ of _____ and _____ _____, including all the _____ that influence it.

6. The primary missions of psychology are (1) to understand behavior and (2) to predict its course. For example, psychologists try to _____ why individuals behave as they do in classrooms or other situations, in order to _____ future behavior in classrooms or other situations.

psychology

behaviors

behaviors

interrelationships

scientific study, overt, covert
behavior, factors

understand
predict

7. An additional mission of psychology is to control behavior or at least to understand how it can be controlled. For example, treating people who have mental or emotional problems is partly an attempt to _____ their behavior for the better, and conducting research on factors that contribute to problematic behavior is an attempt to understand how it can be _____.

**control**

**controlled**

8. Subject matter ranging from the neurochemical bases of memory and mental disorders to the dynamics of global commerce and international conflict constitutes the domain of the _____ and _____ _____.

**behavioral, social sciences**

9. Scientists who study genetics, physiology, anthropology, economics, linguistics, education, sociology, and political science are all in the _____ and _____ _____. Scientists who focus on both overt and covert behavior are most likely to be _____.

**behavioral**
**social sciences**
**psychologists**

## The Varieties of Psychology and Psychologists

10. Psychologists who are primarily interested in the way forms of energy affect the sense organs, how chemical substances influence the nervous system and emotions, how individuals grow and change throughout their lives, and how characteristics of individuals are influenced by the behavior of others are all _____ _____.

**basic scientists**

11. Other psychologists use knowledge to help people carry on everyday tasks, tackle social problems, and improve their own and others' quality of life. School psychologists, industrial/organizational psychologists, educational psychologists, environmental psychologists, community psychologists, forensic psychologists, health psychologists, and clinical and counseling psychologists are apt to be _____ _____, although they may conduct _____ research as well.

**applied scientists, basic**

12. Research motivated by the simple desire to learn about behavior often produces principles that are then used in subsequent work to improve learning in school, performance on the job, or happiness in life. In such cases, principles discovered by _____ _____ are incorporated into _____ _____.

**basic science, applied science**

13. Most applied psychologists are in the fields of _____ and _____ psychology. These psychologists use the findings of science to help people solve various problems in their lives.

**clinical, counseling**

14. Clinical psychology emphasizes the diagnosis and treatment of psychological disorders—traits and behaviors that are thought of as abnormal. Individuals with severe mental or behavioral problems should consult a _____ psychologist.

**clinical**

15. Discussing problems, trying to get at the root of them, and modifying attitudes, emotional responses, and behavior are part of _____.

**psychotherapy**

16. The analysis of a client's flow of ideas in an attempt to discover the origin of problems and lead the client to understand and overcome them is fundamental to _____ and remains one way in which modern _____ practitioners may approach treatment.

**psychoanalysis, eclectic**

17. Psychologists who specialize in resolving marital problems or the difficulties people have adjusting to the social and academic demands of school are _____ psychologists.

**counseling**

18. Psychologists who work with individuals to overcome problem behaviors are of two general kinds. Those who deal with severe problems and abnormal behavior are _____ psychologists; those who deal with less severe problems of social and emotional adjustment are _____ psychologists.

**clinical**
**counseling**

19. Clinical psychologists may treat their patients by using one of the many forms of _____, one of which originated with Sigmund Freud and is called _____.

**psychotherapy**
**psychoanalysis**

naturalistic observation

participant observation

naturalistic observation
participant observation

interview method

interview

case history

questionnaires

interviews, questionnaires

tests

individual differences

individual differences,
measurements
statistic

normal curve (or distribution)

normal
curve (or distribution)

physiological measurements
measurements
measurements

positive correlation

positive

## The Methods Psychologists Use

20. Scientists study behavior objectively, and one way to do so is to *observe* it as it occurs in *natural* settings—without being conspicuous or intruding. Valuable information about behavior can be obtained using this method, which is called _____ _____.

21. Sometimes researchers participate in groups as a way of observing the members' reactions to the researcher's behavior. This is called _____ _____.

22. Watching nursery school children play from behind a one-way mirror would constitute _____ _____. Engaging in play with the children to observe their behavior would be _____ _____.

23. Another approach is to question individual participants, perhaps with the goal of establishing a *case history* of the individual. Case histories are a good example of the use of the _____ _____.

24. Questioning participants in depth about their life experience or attitudes about a given topic constitutes an _____. Reconstructing a description of a person's life over many years to show how various behavior patterns have developed constitutes a _____ _____.

25. Instead of asking questions in person, as in the interview method, researchers may administer pencil-and-paper _____ to large numbers of people, which is a much more efficient method.

26. Public opinion *surveys* gather information about people's attitudes and opinions. They may employ either telephone _____ or written _____.

27. Many human characteristics and abilities are systematically assessed by a variety of psychological _____.

28. An important finding made through the use of tests and other measurements is that there is a wide range of individual differences in all kinds of physical and psychological traits. Each person is indeed unique, and a set of observations and measurements of behavior always yields _____ _____ that distinguish one person from another.

29. These unique _____ _____ and other _____ made by psychologists are often described and analyzed with statistics. The average grade in your class is one example of a simple _____.

30. For most characteristics measured in a large group of individuals, the graph of the frequency of particular scores forms a normal curve. In a normal distribution, scores near the average occur often, and scores both higher and lower than the average occur progressively less often. A graph of individual differences for most physical and psychological characteristics takes the form of a _____ _____.

31. The IQs of most people center around 100. Scores that indicate genius or mental retardation are relatively infrequent, in accord with the _____ _____.

32. Psychologists measure physiological phenomena that may have a bearing on behavior. Disturbances in the chemistry of the brain, for example, may produce severe depression, and electrical changes on the skin are associated with various states of anxiety. So, in addition to assessments of mental and personal behavior, psychologists also employ _____ _____.

33. Sometimes scores on one set of _____ are related to scores on another set of _____ for a group of people. When this happens, a *correlation* exists. If the relationship is in the same direction for both sets of scores, it is a _____ _____.

34. On the other hand, if the relationship is in the opposite directions for the two sets of scores, it is a negative correlation. Thus, if highly aggressive children watch lots of violent TV and nonaggressive children watch little or none, the correlation between violent TV and aggressive behavior is _____. If, instead, minimally aggressive children were to watch lots of violent TV and

highly aggressive children were to watch little or none, the correlation would be _____.

**negative**

35. A correlation coefficient between 0 and +20 or −20 reflects a weak or nonexistent correlation; one between +20 and +60 or −20 and −60 reflects a moderate correlation; and one between +60 and +1.00 or −60 and −1.00 shows a strong correlation. Thus, a correlation of +.37 is _____, and a correlation of −.72 is _____.

**moderate**
**strong**

36. Correlation alone says nothing about what causes what. For example, there is a strong positive correlation between the number of permanent teeth children have and their ability to solve difficult problems, but this does not mean that one causes the other; the correlation arises instead because of a _____ factor, which is age.

**third**

37. In sum, psychologists often study individual differences by using _____ and other _____, describing such observations by using _____ and the normal _____, and assessing whether there is a relationship, or _____, between different scores or measurements for a group of individuals.

**tests**
**measurements, statistics**
**curve (or distribution),**
**correlation**

38. When a psychologist sets up one set of conditions, determines what kind of behavior takes place under those conditions, and then changes the conditions and measures any change in behavior, the psychologist is performing an _____.

**experiment**

39. Both the change in experimental conditions and the behavior that is expected to change are called _____. Systematic manipulation of one variable and observation of whether this leads to change in another _____ constitutes an _____.

**variables**
**variable**
**experiment**

40. Laboratory experiments tend to have high *internal validity* and allow for better conclusions about cause and effect because of the high degree of experimental control that is possible in lab settings. However, they tend to be lower in *external validity*—the extent to which the results apply to the real world. Field experiments may have lower internal validity but higher external validity. Thus, for example, a well-conducted laboratory experiment on human social interactions should be higher in _____ _____, and a well-conducted field experiment on the same topic should be higher in _____ _____.

**internal validity**
**external validity**

## Conducting Good Experiments

41. A basic single-subject design typically involves changing the contingency between a behavior and its consequences—first recording the behavior (baseline), then imposing a contingency, then removing the contingency (return to baseline), and then reinstating the contingency. Thus, in an experiment on using rewards to encourage a child to clean up his or her room, you would first record the _____ for cleaning-up behavior, then impose the _____ of a reward for cleaning up, then remove the reward and expect a return to _____, and finally reinstate the _____ of a reward.

**baseline, contingency**

**baseline, contingency**

42. In a group experiment, participants are assigned to different groups at random, and the groups are treated differently in just one respect to test the experimenter's _____ or prediction about what will happen as a result. In an experiment comparing two teaching methods, for example, the experimenter's hypothesis about which is better would be tested by _____ _____ students to each method and then assessing whether the group that was predicted to learn better actually did.

**hypothesis**

**randomly assigning**

43. Bandura's experiment on aggression varied the consequences the children saw the model receive for beating up Bobo. The consequence the model received was the _____ _____, and the degree to which the children imitated the model's behavior was the _____ _____.

**independent variable**
**dependent variable**

44. Bandura also looked at differences between boys and girls in learning and performing aggressive behaviors; the children's gender was thus another _____ _____.

**independent**
**variable**

operational definition

operational definition
experiment
independent, dependent

systematic replication

systematic replication

introspection

introspection

founder

structural

psychoanalytic
theory

first force
unconscious

observable, measurable,
second force

overt (or observable)

strict behaviorism

45. *Operational definitions* translate what experimenters are interested in into what experimenters actually do and measure. For children's exposure to aggressive behaviors, Bandura used an _____ _____ of exposure to films of a model beating up Bobo. For their tendency to adopt such behaviors, he used an _____ _____ of aggressive behaviors they imitated.

46. In general, the purpose of an _____ is to observe the influence of an _____ variable on a _____ variable.

47. Researchers are reluctant to make sweeping generalizations based on a single experiment. Instead, they conduct series of experiments in which they alter procedures slightly, use different kinds of participants, and define the independent and dependent variables somewhat differently. If Bandura exposed somewhat older children to a different form of aggressive behavior and assessed their imitation of it, he would be using _____ _____.

48. If another experimenter at another time and in another place repeated Bandura's original experiment and obtained the same result, then the possibility that the original results were accidental or influenced by other factors would have been minimized by the process of _____ _____.

## Psychology's Rich History and Promising Future

49. In the early days of psychology, researchers and their participants attempted to understand sensation, perception, and, more generally, conscious experience by looking inward and trying to analyze the processes that went on inside their minds. They made a start toward the systematic study of behavior by recording as objectively as possible what they found through _____.

50. Wilhelm Wundt, a German who founded the first psychological laboratory in 1879, and William James, the most prominent U.S. psychologist around the beginning of the 20th century, were among the pioneers who relied on _____ in trying to understand conscious experiences.

51. In 1890, William James published *Principles of Psychology,* which many regard as marking the beginning of modern psychology. His approach, which incorporated Darwin's principles of evolution, was known as functionalism. Many regard James as the _____ of modern psychology.

52. Also in the 1890s, Edward Titchener brought Wundt's introspective approach to the United States, calling it structuralism. His idea was to break down consciousness and mental activity into _____ components and analyze them individually.

53. Meanwhile, Sigmund Freud's *psychoanalytic theory,* with its emphasis on the role of unconscious processes and their influence on behavior, was having a profound effect on psychology. Because of its immense impact, Freud's _____ _____ came to be known as *the first force in psychology.*

54. Freud is credited with having developed the first comprehensive theory of personality, which was the _____ _____ in psychology, but much of it has not survived—especially his extreme emphasis on _____ processes and motives such as sex.

55. *Strict behaviorism, the second force in psychology,* was in part a reaction against introspection and the psychoanalytic approach. It stressed that only overt behavior could be studied scientifically. The strict behaviorists focused exclusively on behavior that was directly _____ or otherwise _____. Their approach became known as the _____ _____ in psychology.

56. The first prominent strict behaviorists were E. L. Thorndike in the United States, with his law of effect, and Ivan Pavlov in Russia, with what came to be known as classical conditioning. Both Thorndike and Pavlov based their research on _____ behavior.

57. J. B. Watson decreed that mental life is something that cannot be studied scientifically. He became a spokesperson for _____ _____.

58. In general, the strict behaviorists focused on relationships between a stimulus presented by the experimenter and an observable response displayed by the subject or participant. Strict behaviorism is therefore also known as _____-_____ behaviorism, or simply _____ behaviorism.

**stimulus-response, S-R**

59. Like psychoanalytic theory, strict behaviorism has not survived in its original form. But because of its immense impact and especially its emphasis on the scientific method, it is known as the _____ force in psychology.

**second**

60. In their studies of conscious processes and their view that the whole is more than the sum of the parts, the *Gestalt psychologists* were opposed to both the strict behaviorists and the structuralists. In particular, they stressed that conscious experience cannot simply be broken into its _____. Instead, the _____ must be studied—along with the overall context in which behavior occurs.

**parts**
**whole**

61. Humanistic theorists such as Carl Rogers and Abraham Maslow rejected both strict behaviorism and psychoanalytic theory because of their emphasis on animal needs. They took the view that we have important needs and motives that are uniquely human. Humanistic psychology thus became known as the _____ _____ in psychology.

**third force**

62. Today's _____ _____ shares the humanistic psychologists' view that values, goals, happiness, and well-being are important to study and understand.

**positive psychology**

63. An emphasis on cognition in all its forms has been a prominent trend in most areas of psychology for several decades. The use of computer analogies and the *information-processing model* is still an important aspect of _____ psychology.

**cognitive**

64. *Cognitive psychology* rejected strict behaviorism because of its ban on studying mental processes, but also because of its view that humans are passive pawns to be understood solely in terms of reactions to stimuli. Instead, the _____ view is that humans think about what they experience and are _____ processors and users of information.

**cognitive**
**active**

65. The cognitive revolution began in the 1960s, but even in the earlier heyday of strict behaviorism the Gestalt psychologists, social psychologists, and developmental psychologists—among others—were studying _____ processes.

**mental (or cognitive)**

66. Today, a growing number of researchers within the area known as _____ are focusing on how various aspects of bodily functioning affect behavior. Prominent among them are *cognitive and behavioral neuroscientists,* who focus specifically on the brain and behavior.

**psychobiology**

67. Research on psychological functions of various areas of the brain and the influence of brain chemistry on emotions and motives is typical of the efforts of cognitive and behavioral _____.

**neuroscientists**

## Key Issues in Psychology: Yesterday and Today

68. Several issues have dominated the study of human behavior over the years. The debate over whether human behavior is controlled by heredity or environment is called the _____-_____ controversy.

**nature-nurture**

69. Nowadays, the debate has shifted to acknowledging that in most cases nature and nurture combine to determine development and behavior. That is, in modern terms, development and behavior are a result of _____ and _____ in interaction—although there is still disagreement about the relative contributions of each.

**heredity, environment**

70. Among psychology's historic figures, James believed that our behavior is regulated to a considerable extent by powerful human instincts present at birth. Thus, James took the _____ side of the controversy.

**nature (or heredity)**

71. Watson, on the other hand, believed that our behavior depends on conditioned reflexes established by various kinds of stimuli provided by the environment. Thus, he took the _____ side of the controversy.

**nurture (or environment)**

continuity, change

72. Continuity refers to how stable our traits and behaviors are as we develop throughout the life span, and change refers to how we become somewhat different at the same time. The relative contributions of _____ and _____ are important considerations in understanding human development.

aggressive
anxious

73. Another key issue concerns whether behavior is more influenced by individual traits or the context in which the behavior occurs. Some view personality traits as primary: An aggressive person would always tend to be _____ and an anxious person would always tend to be _____, regardless of context.

context

74. On the other hand, it is clear that a person's actions depend on the particular situation and that a person may be generous at home but selfish at work or aggressive with a spouse but submissive with friends. Obviously, as emphasized by Walter Mischel, a person's behavior is at least partly dependent on the _____.

75. Psychological research in recent decades has shifted away from seeing things only from the point of view of your own *culture* and toward a full appreciation of the roles of culture and diversity in understanding human development and behavior. Thus, modern psychologists avoid _____ at every turn.

ethnocentrism
individualist
collectivist

76. _____ cultures stress competition, the good of the individual, and independence, whereas _____ cultures stress cooperation, the good of the group, and interdependence.

77. Gender, age, sexual orientation, and ethnicity are important sources of *diversity*. To avoid ethnocentrism, modern psychologists attempt to take all sources of _____ into account in understanding behavior.

diversity

ethnicity

78. There is little scientific support for the idea of "race" as a way of categorizing or distinguishing people, but _____—essentially cultural heritage—can be very important in understanding people. Many psychologists therefore avoid the term "race" wherever possible, preferring the term "ethnicity" instead.

## Psychology's Ethical Standards

code, ethics

79. The American Psychological Association, backed up by public law, has developed an explicit _____ of _____ to help its members resolve ethical dilemmas they might encounter in the course of their work.

physical, psychological

80. The code of ethics states that psychologists cannot conduct any research on humans that has the potential for significant or lasting _____ or _____ harm.

81. The principle of *informed consent* includes not coercing participants in any way to continue participating in research past the point where they wish to stop. Participation must be entirely voluntary, in accord with the principle of

informed consent

_____ _____.

institutional review boards

82. Because it isn't always possible to know whether a potential for harm exists, _____ _____ _____ carefully assess the procedures that will be used in research if it is approved. Thus, these review boards are an important safeguard for human participants.

83. Psychologists must also adhere to strict guidelines in conducting research with nonhuman animals and avoid unnecessary harm; that is, laboratory animals may be subjected to considerable pain or other discomfort, but any such _____ must be justified and kept to the minimum necessary to the research.

harm

84. Animal research continues, but on a smaller scale than once was the case and with careful attention to animal rights. Psychologists continue to debate the merits of animal research, but there is no debate about whether animals have _____ in the first place.

rights

# Practice Test

____ 1. Psychology is best defined as
   a. the analysis of human behavior.
   b. the systematic study of personality and inter-personal problems.
   c. the scientific study of overt and covert behavior.
   d. the application of scientific experimentation to the study of human behavior.

____ 2. The two agreed-upon missions of psychology are to
   a. understand and control behavior.
   b. conduct controlled experiments and use the scientific method.
   c. control and manipulate behavior.
   d. understand and predict behavior.

____ 3. Psychologists who are basic scientists are mostly interested in
   a. knowledge for the sake of knowledge.
   b. understanding and controlling behavior.
   c. applying the scientific method.
   d. learning about human behavior.

____ 4. The largest group of applied psychologists are engaged in
   a. clinical and counseling psychology.
   b. school and educational psychology.
   c. industrial/organizational psychology.
   d. social and developmental psychology.

____ 5. The main difference between counseling and clinical psychologists is that counseling psychologists
   a. work with less severe disorders.
   b. work with individuals, not groups.
   c. do not conduct psychotherapy.
   d. use psychoanalysis as their main approach to treatment.

____ 6. In contrast to a laboratory experiment, naturalistic observation requires psychologists to
   a. control the situation.
   b. make interpretations about why the observed behavior occurred.
   c. be intimately acquainted with the causes of the behavior.
   d. minimize their influence on the situation.

____ 7. Questionnaires
   a. are not always answered truthfully.
   b. are not always answered accurately.
   c. take less time to administer than interviews.
   d. all of the above

____ 8. The degree of relationship between two variables for the same or related individuals is expressed by
   a. the normal curve of distribution.
   b. individual differences.
   c. the relationship index.
   d. the coefficient of correlation.

____ 9. An experiment seeks to determine the influence of
   a. the dependent variable on the independent variable.
   b. the independent variable on the dependent variable.
   c. the experimental group on the control group.
   d. not necessarily any of the above

____ 10. A major difference between an experiment and naturalistic observation is that one
   a. is objective and the other is not.
   b. studies variables and the other does not.
   c. manipulates conditions in the situation and the other does not.
   d. all of the above

____ 11. The extent to which an experiment allows for statements about cause-and-effect relationships determines its
   a. internal validity.
   b. replicability.
   c. external validity.
   d. all of the above

____ 12. Which statement is *not* likely to be associated with Freud?
   a. Behavior is governed by unconscious forces.
   b. Sex is a primary determinant of behavior.
   c. Human beings are anything but rational creatures.
   d. Psychologists should study observable stimuli and responses.

____ 13. Which of the following is most closely associated with strict behaviorism?
   a. mental life
   b. first psychology laboratory
   c. stimulus and response
   d. human goals

____ 14. The approach to psychology most likely to be associated with the statement that "the whole is greater than the sum of its parts" is
   a. humanistic psychology.
   b. Gestalt psychology.
   c. positive psychology.
   d. psychoanalytic theory.

____ **15.** The third force in psychology was
   a. humanistic psychology.
   b. Gestalt psychology.
   c. positive psychology.
   d. psychoanalytic theory.

____ **16.** A central idea in cognitive psychology is
   a. unconscious processes.
   b. information processing.
   c. self-fulfillment.
   d. the nature-nurture issue.

____ **17.** Psychologists who study how brain functioning
   and behavior are related are
   a. behavior geneticists.
   b. humanistic psychologists.
   c. strict behaviorists.
   d. psychobiologists.

____ **18.** Which of the following is *not* an approach that
   survives today?
   a. psychodynamic theory
   b. strict behaviorism
   c. structuralism
   d. humanistic psychology

____ **19.** Some people are aggressive with their spouse
   or partner but very compliant with their boss;
   this illustrates
   a. the continuity-change issue.
   b. the diversity issue.
   c. the nature-nurture issue.
   d. none of the above

____ **20.** Which of the following is accurate with regard
   to research with humans?
   a. Participants cannot be coerced to continue
      in an experiment if they wish to stop.
   b. Participants cannot be deceived as to what
      will happen to them in an experiment.
   c. Participants can experience minor discom-
      fort or pain in an experiment.
   d. all of the above

## Exercises

1. Interview two people you know well, and attempt to construct a case history for each person. Begin by asking what they think are their major personality characteristics—intelligent, outgoing, athletic, and so on. For each characteristic, such as athletic, ask about their first recollections. Why do they think they developed that characteristic, and what factors or events in their past were influential in contributing to it? Concentrate on asking why they did the things they did, what they felt might have happened to them if they had or had not done certain things, and how they felt about themselves and other people. Then try to piece together a cohesive explanation for how the particular characteristic developed in each person. Provide different interpretations of this development from the strict-behaviorist, Gestalt, cognitive, and humanistic perspectives, as well as from the standpoint of the nature-nurture, change-continuity, and individual-context issues.

2. The experimental method is the primary approach psychologists use to determine the causes of behavior. In a simple experiment, participants are randomly assigned to two groups that are treated differently in only one respect—the independent variable. If their behavior then differs by groups, the difference can be attributed to the independent variable. But research is not always this straightforward. Sometimes the difference in behavior can be explained by something other than the independent variable.

   Below are descriptions of a few hypothetical experiments and conclusions. Write a short discussion of each, pointing out the inadequacies of the experiment for drawing the stated conclusions. Try to suggest factors other than the one mentioned that might have produced the results. Also note any ethical problems that might have arisen.

   a. Back in the days of "traditional" childbirth, U.S. mothers were allowed only minimal contact with their newborns during the first several hours after birth. To assess whether mothers might be missing something important, researchers arranged for one group to have the traditional minimal contact and another to have several extra hours of contact with their babies. A year later, the "extended contact" mothers were noticeably more emotionally attached to their infants than were mothers in the "traditional" group. The researchers concluded that the first several hours after birth are a highly important period for fostering mother-to-child emotional attachment.

   b. To test the effects of marijuana on memory, some participants were asked to smoke one marijuana cigarette before memorizing a list of words; other participants instead were asked to smoke one tobacco cigarette. The marijuana group did poorly on the task compared to the tobacco group, and the researcher concluded that marijuana impairs memory.

   c. It has been found that children who play violent video and computer games are more aggressive in their play with other children than are children who do not play these games. Therefore, playing violent games makes children more aggressive toward others.

   d. An editor of a popular U.S. men's magazine published the results of a readers' survey indicating that by far the majority of men "cheat" on their spouses or partners on more than one occasion, and the longer the two are together, the more likely cheating becomes. The editor concluded that men in general are biologically incapable of being faithful and that the few exceptions in the survey "prove the rule."

❋ *For quizzing, activities, exercises, and web links, check out the book-specific website at http://www.psychology.wadsworth.com/kagan9e.*

# 2 Brain, Body, and Behavior

© Barry Mittan

- It perches on top of your spine, within your skull—3 pounds of pink, soft, strangely wrinkled tissue the size of a grapefruit.

- In weight, it makes up less than 2% of your body, yet it works so hard that it consumes about 20% of the oxygen that the body uses when at rest.

- Nature has devised ways to protect it. In addition to being encased in the thick bone of your skull, it is surrounded by a fluid that helps cushion it. And when your body is deprived of food, it is the first to get its share of whatever nutrients are coursing through the blood.

"It" is the human brain, which has been described as "the most marvelous structure in the universe" (Miller, 1990). (See Figure 2.1.) All the human capabilities discussed in this textbook—gathering information, learning and remembering, acting intelligently, moving about, developing skills, feeling emotions, coping with stress, relating to others—as well as surviving from moment to moment are managed within the brain. Think of all the things you did in the last 24 hours. Whatever you did—sleep, dream, wake up, dress, eat, study, get angry, make love—your brain was responsible.

We function through a network of brain and body systems that is surely one of the great wonders of nature. Knowledge of how these systems work and exactly what they accomplish is essential to an understanding of the entire field of psychology.

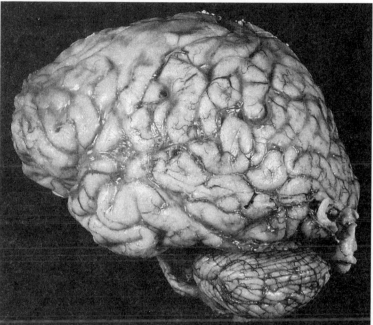

© Arthur Glauberman/Photo Researchers, Inc.

**FIGURE 2.1 A side view of the human brain.** The brain perches on top of your spine, beneath your skull—3 pounds of pinkish, soft, strangely wrinkled tissue the size of a grapefruit.

# HOW THE BRAIN GOVERNS BEHAVIOR

To appreciate the remarkable powers of the brain, it helps to understand how lower organisms manage to function. A one-celled animal such as a paramecium doesn't need a nervous system. Its entire single-celled "body" is sensitive to heat and light and capable of initiating the movements necessary for life. Larger and more complicated animals, however, must have some kind of nervous system to coordinate their internal functions and movements. This system takes the form of specialized neural fibers that extend throughout the body and are capable of transmitting information back and forth.

**FOCUS QUESTIONS**
- How do neurons work and what do they do?
- What constitutes the central nervous system?
- Why do psychologists and other scientists place so much emphasis on understanding the functions of the brain's outer surface?

**Neuron**
The neural cell; the basic unit of the nervous system.

**Hormone**
A biochemical that typically is released into the bloodstream to perform its function at locations distant from the brain, but that can also affect brain functioning itself.

**Glia**
Cells that perform a wide array of functions such as regulating the biochemical environment of the brain, helping sustain neurons, modulating neural transmission, and aiding in the repair of neurons in case of injury. They are also important in early brain development and maturation.

**Dendrites**
The primary "receiving" parts of a neuron.

**Cell body**
The part of a neuron that converts oxygen, sugars, and other nutrients into energy.

**Nucleus**
The core of the cell body of a neuron or other cell, containing the genes.

**Receptor sites**
Spots on the cell body of a neuron that, like the dendrites, can be stimulated by other neurons.

**Axon**
The fibrous body of a neuron that carries the neural impulse to the terminal branches.

**Terminal branches**
The parts of a neuron that send messages to other neurons or to muscles or glands.

**Myelin sheath**
A whitish coating of fatty protective tissue that "insulates" the axons of neurons.

The key to the human brain's mastery is a web of connected pathways running within the brain and to other parts of the body. The brain carries out its many functions through a constant exchange of information, speeding along these trillions of pathways. Indeed, without them, the brain would be helpless to direct and manage our behavior or even to keep us alive.

## The Brain's Communication System

The brain contains a staggeringly large number of **neurons,** or neural cells—certainly many billions, and perhaps as many as a few trillion (Nicholls, Martin, Wallace, & Fuchs, 2001). Each neuron can receive messages from thousands of other neurons, process these messages in various ways, and then pass its own messages along to thousands more. The total number of possible connections is so great that it defies the imagination. One estimate is 50 trillion (Rosenzweig & Lieman, 1982). Thus, the brain is an intricate tapestry of connections, interconnections, and structures. Little wonder that the brain has been described as "the most complex structure in the known universe" (Fischbach, 1992).

Although the diverse neurons of the brain primarily transmit messages, some operate like miniature glands, producing complex biochemicals called **hormones** (from the Greek word meaning "activators" or "exciters") (Nicholls et al., 2001). The various hormones, which are discussed at relevant points in the chapter, are typically released into the bloodstream to perform their functions at locations distant from the brain, but some also affect the functioning of the brain itself.

The rest of the brain is made up of cells called **glia,** from the Greek word for "glue," so named because of the 19th-century idea that they primarily bind neurons together and otherwise provide physical support. Although there is little evidence that this is one of their many roles, the idea has persisted (Purves et al., 1997). Glia—which are every bit as diverse in form as neurons and even more numerous—are known to perform a wide array of functions such as regulating the biochemical environment of the brain, helping sustain neurons, modulating neural transmission, and aiding in the repair of neurons in case of injury; they are likewise important in early brain development and maturation (Laming et al., 2000).

It is hard to imagine the amount of activity taking place in your nervous system. Right now, for example, messages rich in information are being "flashed" back and forth to every part of your body. The messages take the form of neural impulses, which resemble tiny electrical charges, each strong enough to register only on the most sensitive recording devices. The neurons start sending their messages long before birth and continue to hum with activity throughout the life span. These tiny impulses somehow account for all the accomplishments of the brain, and thus understanding neural transmission in all its complexity is the key to understanding relationships between the brain and behavior—both physical and cognitive.

Neurons come in a great many varieties and often bear little resemblance to one another, except that they generally share the characteristics illustrated in Figure 2.2. First are the **dendrites,** the primary receivers of stimulation from preceding neurons. Next is the **cell body,** which has a **nucleus,** or core, containing the genes that caused the cell to grow into a neuron in the first place. The cell body performs the process of *metabolism,* converting oxygen, sugars, and other nutrients supplied by the bloodstream into energy to both sustain the neuron and allow it to function. The surface of the cell body is dotted with numerous **receptor sites,** which—like the tips of the dendrites—are capable of responding to stimulation. When dendrites and receptor sites are sufficiently stimulated, they cause the neuron to "fire" and send an impulse down the **axon** to the **terminal branches,** which are the neuron's "senders"; they stimulate (or inhibit) the neurons next in line.

A **myelin sheath** coats the axon of many, but by no means all, neurons. Another role of the glia is to produce this whitish coating of fatty protective tissue, which functions somewhat like insulation on electrical wiring, increasing the efficiency of the neuron's operation. Transmission is further improved by the **nodes,** constrictions of the myelin sheath that act as booster stations, helping to "nudge" the neural impulse along the axon to the terminal branches.

Some neurons terminate in glands or muscles, where they stimulate or inhibit action. However, most of the neurons in the brain connect exclusively with other neurons, forming intricate *circuits* that combine to form the *systems* and *networks* that perform the specific functions of the brain.

## How Neurons Send Their Messages

A neural impulse—the tiny charge that passes down the length of the axon at perhaps 100 mph (160 kph)—can best be compared to the glowing band of fire that travels along a lit fuse. A neuron ordinarily operates on what is called the **all-or-none principle.** That is, either it fires or it doesn't. A neural impulse can only travel the length of the neuron that produced it—from dendrites or receptor sites to the terminal branches of the axon. There it stops. But when it reaches the ends of the terminal branches, it sets off events that influence the receiving neurons and deliver the message.

The key to transmission of the message is the **synapse,** the connecting point where a terminal branch of one neuron is separated by only a microscopic distance—a millionth of an inch—from a dendrite or receptor site of another neuron. At the synapse, where the two neurons almost touch, the first influences the second through the release of chemical **neurotransmitters.** When the neuron fires, a burst of these biochemically active substances is released at the synapse. The chemicals flow across the tiny gap between the two neurons (the *synaptic cleft*) and act on the second neuron, either exciting it to fire (if a sufficient amount is present) or inhibiting its firing.

Figure 2.3 is a photograph of parts of a neuron that play an especially important role in the transmission of messages—the little swellings called *synaptic knobs* at the very tips of the terminal branches of the neuron. It is these knobs that actually form synapses with other neurons at their dendrites or cell body receptor sites.

An enlarged drawing of a synapse is shown in Figure 2.4. In the first neuron, the neurotransmitter is produced in the cell body and delivered down the length of the fiber to the *synaptic vesicles*, where it is stored until called upon. When the neuron fires, the neural impulse reaching the synaptic knob causes the vesicles to release their transmitter chemicals. These neurotransmitters flow across the synaptic cleft and act on the receptors of the second neuron. Some of the neurotransmitters stimulate the second neuron to fire. Others do the opposite, instructing the second neuron to refrain from firing—that is, inhibiting activity in the second neuron.

Whether the neuron fires or not depends on the overall pattern of messages it receives. Ordinarily, it will not fire in response to a single message arriving at one of its many dendrites or receptor sites. Instead, the firing process requires multiple

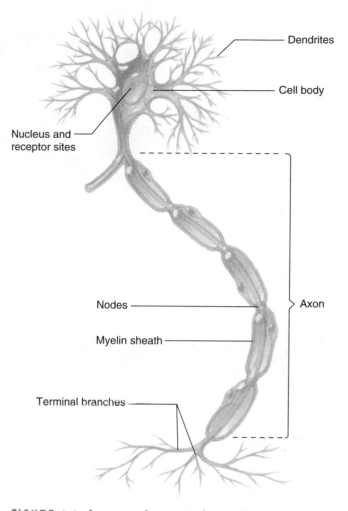

**FIGURE 2.2 A more or less typical neuron. Neurons come in many varieties. Essential features are dendrites at one end, terminal branches at the other, and a cell body and fibrous axon in between.**

**Nodes**
Constrictions of the myelin sheath of an axon that act as booster stations for neural impulses.

**All-or-none principle**
The general rule that a neuron either fires or doesn't.

**Synapse**
The connecting point where a terminal branch of one neuron is only a microscopic distance from a dendrite or receptor site of another neuron.

**Neurotransmitters**
Biochemicals released at neuron synapses that aid or inhibit neural transmission.

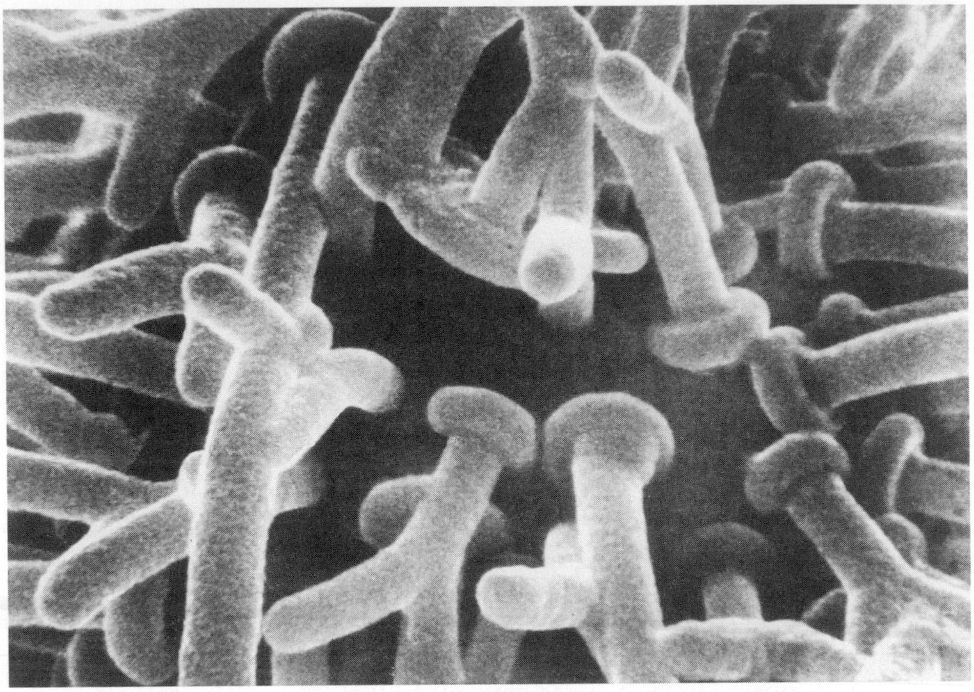

**FIGURE 2.3** Synaptic knobs. This photograph, taken at about 2,000 times life size, was the first ever made of the synaptic knobs. It shows some of the structures in a snail. *Lewis, Zeevi, & Everhart, 1969.*

American Association for the Advancement of Science

**FIGURE 2.4** Where neuron meets neuron: the synapse. The terminal branch of the first neuron ends in a synaptic knob, separated from the second neuron by only a tiny gap called the synaptic cleft.

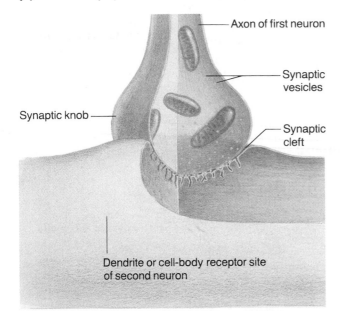

Axon of first neuron

Synaptic vesicles

Synaptic knob

Synaptic cleft

Dendrite or cell-body receptor site of second neuron

**Spinal cord**
The thick cable of neurons that mostly connects PNS neurons to the brain.

**Central nervous system (CNS)**
The brain and the spinal cord.

**Peripheral nervous system (PNS)**
The network of neurons outside of the CNS.

stimuli—a whole group of messages arriving at once or in quick succession from the other neurons with which it has synaptic contact. The overall stimulation must outweigh the overall inhibition if the neuron is to fire.

Although the electrochemical messages travel in complex ways, the process is highly organized. Neural cells are arranged in ways that permit those engaged in similar tasks to work together. The chemical receptors on the neurons are quite specific; they recognize only certain kinds of neurotransmitters. Neurons that send or receive the same neurotransmitters form special circuits, or pathways. Small wonder that the human nervous system is capable of so much.

## The Links of the Nervous System

The neurons of the brain can affect our behavior only because there are links between them and other parts of the body. These links constitute the rest of the nervous system, which is composed of neurons of various kinds. The neuron fibers of the nervous system—the axons identified in Figure 2.2—extend throughout the body. Together, the brain and the **spinal cord** are known as the **central nervous system (CNS).** The spinal cord is like a master cable that connects the brain with much of the rest of the body. The neurons that lie outside these structures constitute the **peripheral nervous system (PNS),** a network that extends throughout the body, all the way to the fingertips and toes.

Neurons differ greatly, as noted earlier, but they can be grouped into three classes based on their function, which is fixed and unchanging: (1) *Afferent neurons* originate in the sense organs and body, and they carry messages from our eyes, ears, and other sense organs toward the central nervous system. (2) *Efferent neurons* carry messages from the central nervous system in an outward direction—ordering muscles to contract and directing the activity of the body's organs and glands. (3) **Interneurons,** which are the most numerous, connect only with other neurons. Every moment of our lives, day and night, afferent neurons carry information to the brain and efferent neurons dispatch the brain's decisions and directions. At the center of this ceaseless activity of the nervous system, the interneurons of the brain and spinal cord perform all the essential functions that maintain our lives—and, in some as-yet-undetermined way, provide the basis for "mind."

## The Cerebral Cortex and How It Makes Us Human

If the top of a person's head were transparent and you looked down from above, you would see the brain as shown in Figure 2.5: a mass of tissue so rich in blood vessels that it takes on a pinkish cast. It resembles a rather large walnut, but it is soft and pulsing with life. This is the part of the brain that is chiefly responsible for thinking, remembering, and planning—the activities that make humans more intelligent than other animals. It is called the **cerebral cortex,** and nature has made it larger in proportion to body size in human beings than in other species. As can be seen in Figure 2.6, it would be too large to fit into the human skull if it didn't have *convolutions*—the intricate foldings and refoldings apparent in Figure 2.5. What you see in the photograph is in fact only about a third of the cerebral cortex. The rest is hidden in the creases.

The cortex (from the Latin word for "bark") is actually the outer surface, about one-eighth of an inch (3 mm) thick, of the brain's largest single structure, the **cerebrum.** As illustrated in Figure 2.5, the cerebrum is split down the middle into a left half, or *left hemisphere*, and a right half, or *right hemisphere*.

Although the two hemispheres look like mirror images, they differ slightly in form and are often engaged in different activities—it is almost as if we had two brains. This arrangement has provoked a number of fascinating questions, to which we return later in the chapter.

**Interneuron**
A CNS neuron that carries messages between neurons.

**Cerebral cortex**
Among its many other functions, the part of the brain responsible for thinking, remembering, and planning.

**Cerebrum**
The large brain mass that is covered by the cerebral cortex.

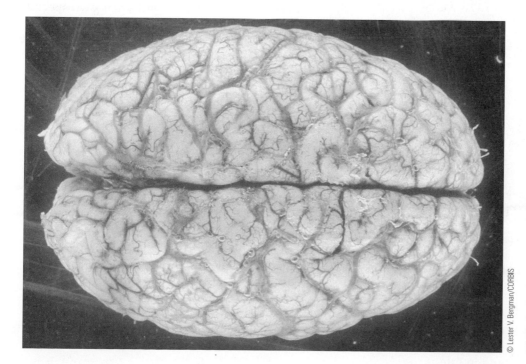

**FIGURE 2.5 A top view of the human brain.** Note especially the vertical line, resembling a narrow ditch, that runs down the middle from the right of the photo (the front of the brain) to the left. This deep fissure divides these upper areas of the brain into two separate halves, called hemispheres.

© Lester V. Bergman/CORBIS

## PSYCHOLOGY IN THE LAB AND IN LIFE

# How the Brain Restores Its Functions

We have all heard about cases in which surgeons have reattached severed fingers and toes, which then regained their function. Although similar feats have not yet been accomplished in the damaged human brain and its connecting neural fibers, there is evidence that the brain and its functions can undergo renewal—and that they can sometimes be helped to do so.

Following harm to some areas of the brain, adjoining areas may eventually appropriate a number of the lost functions. The healthy neighboring neurons may make up for the loss by forging new connections that substitute for those that were erased. As we grow older, for example, the dendrites of certain neurons increase in length, allowing them to receive messages despite the age-related destruction of neighboring neurons (Selkoe, 1992). And there is now considerable evidence—based largely on functional brain imaging research—that areas of the brain's cortex can shift their functions when neural pathways connected to them are damaged (Hallett, 2001; McEwen, 2000; Pizzamiglio, Galati, & Committeri, 2001; Stiles, 2001).

From a different perspective, numerous studies over the past couple of decades have demonstrated that, at least with rats and mice, grafting healthy normal tissue or genetically modified tissue to damaged areas of the brain can restore or at least improve cognitive functioning in the affected areas (e.g., Kim et al., 2001; Rolobos et al., 2001; Tarricone, Simon, Li, & Low, 1996; Triarhou, 1995). It has also been known for some time that the brain is generally less likely to reject newly grafted tissue than are body organs (Wyatt & Freed, 1983).

What are the prospects for restoring behavioral functions and health through such research? Techniques remain experimental, and considerable research is still necessary before new technologies can be widely applied. But the possibilities are there, including transplantation of tissue to portions of the brain affected in the neurological disorder known as Parkinson's disease (Olson et al., 1998) and restoration of tissue that produces brain chemicals to treat Alzheimer's disease (Aisen & Davis, 1997) and schizophrenia (Jaber, Robinson, Missale, & Caron, 1996). Perhaps we are truly on the threshold of an era in which research on the operations of the brain will be translated into enormous help for millions of incapacitated people.

• • • • • • • • • • • • • • • • • • • • • • • • • • • • • • • • • • • • • • • • • • • • • • • • •

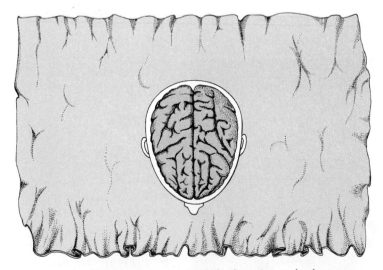

**FIGURE 2.6 The surprising size of the brain's cerebral cortex. If it were laid flat with its many folds "ironed out," the cortex would measure about 1.5 square feet (0.14 square meter) in area (Ornstein & Thompson, 1984).**

**Plasticity**
The power of the brain to reorganize and shift functions.

Beneath the cerebrum, and totally hidden when the brain is viewed from above, lie a number of other structures with their own special functions. We share many of these structures—for example, structures that maintain basic life functions—with other forms of animal life. But it is the cerebrum and its cortex, comprising 80% of the human brain, that make us special. Without them, we would be "almost a vegetable, speechless, sightless, senseless" (Hubel & Wiesel, 1979).

Because of the brain's vast and complex responsibilities, injury to it—for example, from a hard blow to the head or from a bullet—can critically affect vital psychological and physical functions. For the most part, damage to the brain is permanent. In contrast to some neurons in the PNS, such as motor neurons, the neurons of the CNS do not regenerate (e.g., Nicholls et al., 2001). Once CNS neurons suffer damage, they are gone for good and with them whatever behavioral functions they made possible. Nevertheless, neuroscientists continue to study the brain's **plasticity**—its flexibility and power to reorganize and shift functions. Their work is discussed in Psychology in the Lab and in Life.

# HOW NEUROSCIENTISTS STUDY THE BRAIN AND MIND

Neuroscience—especially cognitive neuroscience—is a fusion of various areas of psychology, including cognitive and experimental psychology, neuropsychology, psychophysiology, developmental psychology, and clinical psychology, plus other disciplines such as neurology, neurobiology, and biophysics (Müller & Mayes, 2001). As indicated in Chapter 1, the role of psychology in this family of sciences has grown considerably in recent years, focusing on mental and physical functions of the brain.

> **FOCUS QUESTIONS**
>
> • How does brain imaging work and what does it tell us?
>
> • How do neuroscientists measure electrical changes and what do they tell us?

Scientific research on the structure and functions of the brain dates back to the 19th century, when it took the form of studying changes in behavior that were attributable to known brain damage. A later and much more systematic approach was *electrical brain stimulation (EBS),* in which tiny harmless electrical charges are delivered to specific areas of the exposed cortex to see what thoughts or other behaviors they evoke. Foremost among the early neuroscientists who "mapped" the human brain in this fashion was Wilder Penfield (1891–1976), who did much of his research while performing neurosurgery to alleviate severe epilepsy. (Perhaps needless to say, invasive procedures such as EBS are not performed except as an adjunct to necessary brain surgery, greatly limiting this approach.) Nowadays, neuroscientists (and neurosurgeons) use much more sophisticated and much less invasive instrumentation and methods, which are opening up entire new realms in our understanding of how the brain works. It is safe to predict that the shift to these techniques will also reduce the need for research on laboratory animals in which various brain structures are deliberately lesioned (cut) or otherwise destroyed so that researchers can observe what happens to behavior.

The findings on brain structures and functions presented in this chapter and at other points in the text are based on both the physiological research of the past and the brain imaging research of the present. Much of the latter began during the 1990s, which has been heralded as "the decade of the brain" (see Wagemans, Verstraten, & He, 2001).

## Structural Brain Imaging

A major breakthrough in brain imaging was **computerized tomography (CT),** or CAT scanning, which developed out of the traditional X-ray procedure. In CT, brief bursts of X-rays are sent through the brain as the scanning apparatus rotates around the participant's head. The X-rays are "absorbed" differently depending on the density of the tissues, which means that different intensities of X-rays pass through to the film on the other side and the exposure varies accordingly. Computer processing then yields a series of *tomograms,* or visual "slices" of the brain along different planes, revealing many of its structures as well as tumors or other brain damage.

CT has limited resolution, however; the images are fuzzy, and small structures are hard to see. Much more detailed pictures can be obtained through **magnetic resonance imaging (MRI),** which can produce either flat or three-dimensional images of the brain from any angle—again, through computer processing. Here, however, the brain's tissues are exposed to harmless magnetic fields and pulses of radio-frequency waves, which make their atoms "resonate" and give off magnetic energy. This energy is recorded by a special detector coil placed around the head of the participant or patient (Gazzaniga, Ivry, & Mangun, 1998; Oldendorf & Oldendorf, 1988).

**Computerized tomography (CT)**
A structural brain imaging method that uses X-rays to produce two-dimensional images.

**Magnetic resonance imaging (MRI)**
A structural brain imaging method that uses the magnetic properties of brain tissue to produce two- or three-dimensional images.

# Functional Brain Imaging

Both CT and traditional MRI have the disadvantage that they produce still pictures, which provide considerable information about brain structures but do not tell us anything about their functioning. This led researchers to develop additional approaches that can assess what the brain is doing.

**Positron emission tomography (PET)** was the first of these approaches, arriving on the scene in the 1980s (Beatty, 2001). PET takes advantage of neural cell metabolism with regard to *glucose* (the form of sugar that the brain uses for energy). For example, glucose treated with minute amounts of a radioactive isotope may be injected into the participant's bloodstream. A good portion of it travels to the brain, where it is broken down primarily by clusters of neural cells that are actively engaged in processing, setting off chemical chain reactions that are picked up by special detectors placed around the head. Computer enhancement then yields ongoing displays of the areas of the brain that are active when the participant is exposed to different stimuli or asked to engage in different kinds of thought, as illustrated in Figure 2.7. The images occur almost in real time; there is a delay of just a minute or two because of the time required for the metabolism to occur (Purves et al., 1997; Savoy, 2001).

Another—and currently the most promising—approach is **functional magnetic resonance imaging (fMRI),** which has several advantages over PET (Savoy, 2001). With fMRI, precision detectors measure and localize minute magnetic changes that occur when oxygen is naturally metabolized by active clusters of neural cells. No radioactive substances are necessary, making this approach completely noninvasive. It produces ongoing images similar to those in Figure 2.7, except that it allows finer resolution than PET and also faster displays—a delay of seconds rather than minutes (Purves et al., 1997). Even so, the finest resolution possible is on the order of millimeters and reflects the activity of perhaps several hundred thousand neurons that aren't necessarily engaged in related activities (Grill-Spector & Malach, 2001). Thus, researchers are continuing to pursue methods that would produce ever finer measures.

In the future, researchers are expected to extend the uses of functional brain imaging beyond such current applications as mapping and understanding the

**Positron emission tomography (PET)** A functional brain imaging method that uses the brain's metabolism of substances containing radioactive isotopes to produce ongoing brain images.

**Functional magnetic resonance imaging (fMRI)** A functional brain imaging method that uses the brain's natural metabolism of oxygen to produce ongoing brain images.

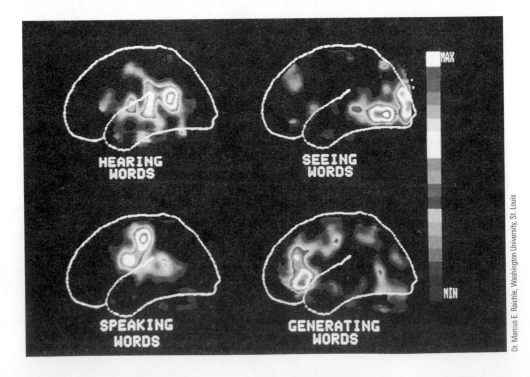

**FIGURE 2.7 The brain in action.** These **PET** scans reveal how various portions of the brain are activated while a participant is performing a series of verbal tasks. They reveal that blood flow shifts to different areas of the brain according to the type of task being performed.

Dr. Marcus E. Raichle, Washington University, St. Louis

brain. The ethical implications of brain imaging and other neuroscience techniques in the not-too-distant future are considered in Psychology and the Media.

## PSYCHOLOGY AND THE MEDIA

## Neuroscience in the Future

 The potential for improving people's lives through techniques derived from neuroscience research is undeniable. Brain imaging, for example, has long been used in identifying brain damage and shedding light on mental disorders. Drugs that improve memory in people with amnesia are on the horizon, and someday it may be possible to "cure" Alzheimer's disease. The list of possible benefits goes on and on.

But there is also the potential for misuse of neuroscience research, a subject pondered by leading neuroscientists, bioethicists, and other concerned professionals at the first-ever conference on "neuroethics," held in San Francisco in May 2002. The following are excerpts from an overview by William Safire (2002a), *New York Times* columnist and chairman of the board of directors of the conference's sponsor, The Dana Foundation (www.dana.org).

Neuroethics, in my lexicon, is a distinct portion of bioethics, which is the consideration of good and bad consequences in medical practice and biological research. But the specific ethics of brain science hits home as no other research does in any other organ. It deals with our consciousness, our sense of self, and as such is central to our being. What distinguishes us from each other beyond our looks? Answer: our personalities and behavior, and these are the characteristics that brain science will soon have the ability to change in significant ways.

Let's face it: one person's liver is pretty much like another. . . . Our brains, on the contrary, give us our intelligence and integrity, our curiosity and compassion, and—here's the most mysterious one—our conscience. . . .

Zach [W. Hall, a prominent neuroscientist] has made the point to me that when we examine and manipulate the brain—unlike the liver . . . whether for research, for treatment of disease, or for more sinister personal or political ends, we change people's lives in the most personal and powerful way. The misuse or abuse or failure to make the most of this power raises ethical challenges unique to neuroscience.

In an article published after the conference (2002b), Safire articulated some of the ethical issues facing neuroscientists and those who will apply what neuroscientists discover how to do:

For example, few will dispute the benefits of the regulated use of drugs to treat diseases of the brain. But what about drugs to enhance memory or alertness, to be taken before a test—isn't this akin to an athlete unethically taking steroids before a race? If we quiet the broadest range of inattentive, hyperactive children with compounds like Ritalin, do we weaken the development of adult concentration, character and self-control?

How about a future use of imaging to pinpoint a brain area indicating a traumatic memory—should we expunge a victim's ability to recollect, say, a rape? Do we outlaw implantation of a memory of an event that never happened? Should brain imagers give law enforcement a "lie detector" far more reliable than the mechanical polygraph, and if so, is the reading of a mind of a resistant terrorist akin to torture? . . .

[And] what of the hooking-up of software with what computerniks call "wetware" (the human nervous system) to combine human imagination with a machine's computational speed? Is this the next logical step of evolution, or an invitation to a controlling organization, as a NASA neuroethicist put it, "to hack into the wetware between our ears"?

Our generation has outlived science fiction. Just as we have anti-depressants today to elevate mood, tomorrow we can expect a kind of Botox for the brain to smooth out wrinkled temperaments, to turn shy people into extroverts, or to bestow a sense of humor on a born grouch. But what price will human nature pay for these nonhuman artifices? What does the flattening of people's physical and mental differences, accompanied by a forced fitting of mental misfits, do to the diversity of personality that makes interpersonal dynamics so fascinating?

Safire's article was aptly titled "The But-What-If Factor." Neuroscience is advancing at a geometric pace, and the potential benefits defy the imagination. At the same time, each step forward may indeed have an unsettling "But what if . . ." attached to it.

## Electroencephalography

**Electroencephalography (EEG),** in which a few electrodes are placed on the scalp to measure relatively global brain wave patterns, has been around for many years. EEG, for example, has long been the standard measure of overall brain activity during different states of consciousness and stages of sleep (see Figure 8.5 on page 305). More recently, however, researchers have refined this approach by greatly increasing the number of electrodes, standardizing their locations by fitting them into a skull cap, and subjecting the much more specific measurements to computer analysis—yielding what is now called **quantitative electroencephalography (QEEG).** QEEG allows assessment of the tiny voltage fluctuations in the brain, known as *event-related potentials (ERPs),* that result, for example, from sensory stimuli such as sights and sounds (see Friedman, Cycowicz, & Gaeta, 2001). ERPs are studied in their own right—for example, to assess brain activity when there is no corresponding overt behavior or to assess infants' perceptual capabilities (e.g., see de Haan, Pascalis, & Johnson, 2002). ERPs also can be localized in the brain and increasingly are being used in conjunction with procedures such as fMRI, because the time delay in their occurrence is on the order of milliseconds (Wilding, 2001). That is, ERPs can be used as "time markers" when cross-referenced with fMRI images.

As with functional imaging, we can predict that QEEG and variations on this method will continue to be refined.

# THE BRAIN'S FUNCTIONS, I: EXPERIENCING THE WORLD

**FOCUS QUESTIONS**

- **What brain structures process incoming sensory stimulation?**
- **What brain structures initiate and coordinate body movements?**

You're driving down the street and a child darts into the path of your car. In a twinkling, the muscles of your leg tense and your foot hits the brake, bringing your car safely to a stop. Or, you're sound asleep, when suddenly there are shouts of "Fire!" You awake with a start, jump up, and dash to safety.

Although we tend to take our behavior in such situations for granted, it is actually remarkable. Such acts require the teamwork of millions of neurons, receiving and sending messages with blinding speed. Our abilities to attend to information from the world, process it, and respond to it all depend on the intricate functioning of the brain—the cerebral cortex and the interrelated structures below it, as well as the brain's links to the peripheral nervous system.

## Sensing and Interpreting the Environment

Most of the information picked up by our senses—if we attend to it—is eventually transmitted to the cerebral cortex. The cortex has specialized areas, some of which are shown in Figure 2.8. It also contains a long strip known as the **somatosensory cortex,** which receives messages on touch from the feet (at the top) to the head (at the bottom). These specialized areas analyze and interpret incoming messages, allowing the brain to decide which messages are important and what they mean. The sounds of speech—which are of particular importance because language plays such a large role in human behavior—have an area of their own that is concerned with understanding the meanings of words and sentences.

---

**Electroencephalography (EEG)**
A method of measuring overall brain electrical activity using electrodes placed on the scalp.

**Test Yourself**

**(b)** Would a researcher engaged in neuroscience be more likely to study the role of genetics or of brain chemistry in cognitive development?

**(c)** If researchers wanted to know what portions of your brain were especially active when you tried to remember a set of facts, what brain imaging technique or techniques would they be most likely to use?

*(The answers are on page 81.)*

**Quantitative electroencephalography (QEEG)**
A method of assessing brain activity that uses a large array of electrodes in a skull cap to measure and localize minute electrical reactions of areas of the brain.

**Somatosensory cortex**
The specialized area of the cerebral cortex responsible for analyzing and interpreting messages from the sense organs.

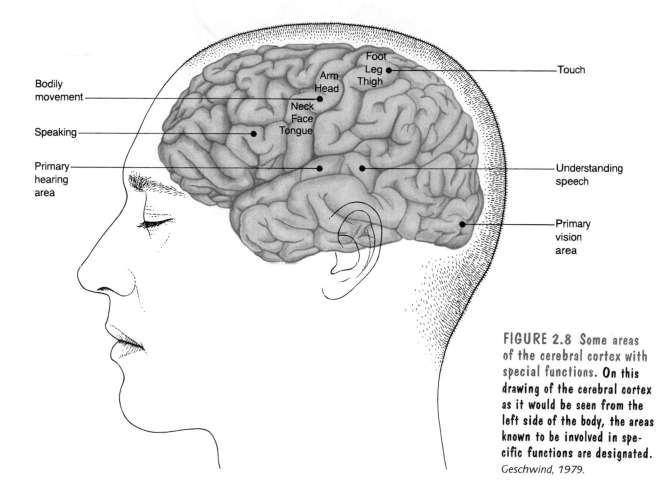

**FIGURE 2.8** Some areas of the cerebral cortex with special functions. **On this drawing of the cerebral cortex as it would be seen from the left side of the body, the areas known to be involved in specific functions are designated.** *Geschwind, 1979.*

The importance of the cerebral cortex in registering and processing sensory information becomes dramatically clear in cases of damage to any of these portions of the brain. For example, depending on the location and extent of injury to the back part of the cortex, which is responsible for vision, an individual might suffer varying degrees of blindness, even though the eyes and their muscles and nerves remain intact. With damage to a different area of the cortex, a patient may be unable to recognize a familiar person's identity from his or her face but retain the capacity to recognize the person from his or her walk. Thus, different parts of the brain and different neural circuits appear to be responsible for acquiring different types and levels of knowledge about the same entity (Damasio, 1990).

If the area for understanding speech is injured, an individual might no longer be able to interpret what is being said, even though all parts of the ear are healthy and the sounds of the words spoken are clearly heard. In such cases, the afflicted individuals seem to be incapable of getting the words "through their heads."

## Processing and Transmitting Sensory Information

Sensory information from the outside world is processed and organized in the lower parts of the brain a few milliseconds before it reaches the cortex. Serving as a relay station for sensory messages from the body to the cortex is the **thalamus,** which can be seen in Figure 2.9. (The thalamus also acts as a relay station for some of the messages traveling in the opposite direction, especially those calling for body movements, described in the next section.)

**Thalamus**
**The brain's relay station for messages to and from the body.**

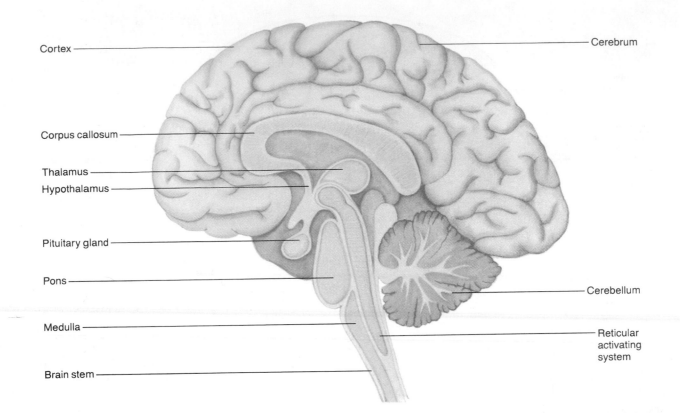

Cortex

Corpus callosum

Thalamus

Hypothalamus

Pituitary gland

Pons

Medulla

Brain stem

Cerebrum

Cerebellum

Reticular
activating
system

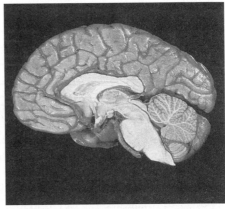

**FIGURE 2.9  A sectional view of the brain.**
**Parts of the human brain are shown here as they**
**would be seen if the brain were sliced down**
**the middle from front to back. The inset shows**
**a photograph of the brain taken from the same**
**perspective.**
*London, 1978. Inset courtesy of the Warder*
*Collection.*

Warder Collection

**Reticular activating system**
**(RAS)**
**A network of neural cells in**
**the brain stem that serves as a**
**way station for messages from**
**the sense organs.**

Sensory information is also processed in a network of neural cells near the base of the brain called the **reticular activating system (RAS).** This structure gets its name from its appearance under a microscope as a criss-crossed (reticulated) pattern of neural fibers. As shown in Figure 2.9, it extends downward to the brain stem, where the brain and spinal cord join.

Nerve pathways carrying messages from the sense organs to the cerebrum have side branches in the RAS. These stimulate the system to send its own neural impulses upward to the cerebrum, arousing it to a state of alertness and activity. Animals whose RAS has been destroyed remain permanently comatose for lack of such arousal. If the RAS is electrically stimulated, sleeping animals will awaken immediately (Rosenzweig & Lieman, 1982).

The RAS also helps us focus selectively on those sensory signals that are most important. For example, when you are reading a newspaper, the RAS blocks unimportant messages—the sounds in your room or flashes of lightning outside—and prepares the cortex to receive the ones that matter.

# Generating Body Movements

Sometimes the reactions of the nervous system are immediate—as when you quickly move your hand away from a hot stove. Such responses do not require commands from the brain. Instead, they are processed by connections in the spinal cord, as are many basic reflexes, referred to as *involuntary*. But the movements you make deliberately—from the gross muscular adjustments of the arms and legs when lifting things or running to the tiny adjustments of finger muscles when threading a needle or playing a guitar—are initiated in the cerebral cortex.

The actual sequence of events in the brain that results in *voluntary* movements is complex and not yet completely understood, but we do know that many parts of the brain are engaged in the process. A specialized strip on the cortex (Figure 2.8) controls body movements from feet to head. Known as the **motor cortex,** it initiates body movements in response to orders from other parts of the brain. In the case of the simple act of picking up a glass, for example, you must first have the intention of performing the act before actually executing the action (Libet, 1985).

The motor cortex also has an area for speaking, which moves the vocal folds and muscles associated with them in a way that produces meaningful sounds. When a stroke or other injury damages this area of the cortex, the result is often loss of the ability to formulate and utter words that convey ideas. This portion of the brain also manufactures the sounds that give voice to feelings—a shriek of delight when you see your home team score, a groan of despair when you hear about the death of a friend, or a sigh of contentment when you feel the embrace of a loved one.

## Test Yourself

**(d)** On March 30, 1981, James Brady, press secretary to President Ronald Reagan, was shot above the left eye by would-be assassin John Hinckley. The bullet went through Brady's brain and lodged in the right hemisphere. Why is it unlikely that Brady will ever fully recover his lost abilities to function—for instance, to walk, speak, and express himself as as he did before the shooting?

**(e)** Is a combat soldier who suffers a gunshot wound to the back of the brain more likely to have problems speaking or seeing?

**(f)** Why is a perfectly functioning cerebellum so important to both a guitar player and a ballet dancer?

(The answers are on page 81.)

# Managing Coordination and Balance

As shown in Figure 2.9, below the cerebrum and attached to the back of the brain stem is a bulging structure that looks like a tree in full bloom. Called the **cerebellum,** it is essential for many aspects of movement. The cerebellum, which has been called a "magnificently patterned, orderly and fantastically complex piece of machinery" (Hubel, 1979), has many connections with parts of the cerebral cortex that initiate muscular activity.

One of the special roles of the cerebellum is to coordinate all the finely regulated muscular movements we are capable of, such as playing a musical instrument or manipulating a small tool. If the cerebellum is damaged, movements become jerky, and great effort and concentration are required to perform even activities that were once automatic, such as walking. Victims of damage to the cerebellum have difficulty speaking, which requires well-coordinated movements of the muscles of the vocal cords, windpipe, and mouth.

The cerebellum also controls body balance and is the part of the brain that keeps us right side up. It plays an important role in allowing us to do things that require great equilibrium. An example is shooting a pistol at a target. Studies of champion marksmen in the Russian army showed that, although many parts of their body moved, the pistol remained virtually immobile (Evarts, 1979). With millions of neurons sending their billions of messages to and fro—from the eyes, the cerebral cortex, the arms and fingers—somehow the brain, thanks largely to the cerebellum, is able to integrate all these messages into an act of exquisite balance and precision.

Like the cerebrum, the cerebellum is divided into two lobes, or hemispheres. The left and right lobes are connected by the **pons,** which gets its name from the Latin word for "bridge." The neurons of the pons transmit messages between the two hemispheres of the cerebellum.

**Motor cortex**
The specialized strip on the cerebral cortex that controls body movements.

**Cerebellum**
A brain structure involved in controlling balance and movement.

**Pons**
The brain structure connecting the two hemispheres of the cerebellum.

# THE BRAIN'S FUNCTIONS, II: OVERSEEING EMOTIONS AND SURVIVAL

**FOCUS QUESTIONS**

• What brain structures are involved in experiencing emotions?

• How are our body functions regulated to keep us alive?

The remarkable feats of the brain described thus far, which allow us to make sense of our environment and move about in the world, are impressive in their own right. But even with them, our lives would be flat and barren were it not for the deeply moving experiences we call emotions. True, emotions such as fear and anger are often upsetting and sometimes destructive. However, they also help us cope with the world and meet its crises, motivating us to action. Other emotions, such as love and joy, greatly enrich our lives. All these feelings are produced by the brain working in concert with the body. (The components of an emotion, such as the physiological changes and the conscious or unconscious experiences that accompany them, are discussed in detail in Chapter 8.)

The brain not only regulates our emotions; it also ensures our physical survival by keeping our bodies in healthy working order. It oversees the fundamental functions of breathing, pumping blood, and maintaining adequate blood pressure. It tells us when we need food or drink, and it keeps our body chemistry in balance. The brain seems to watch out for our survival as a species, too; it is deeply involved in sexual development and behavior. Our lives end only when the brain ceases its last flicker of activity.

**Limbic system**
**The set of interconnected structures and pathways in the brain involved with emotion and memory.**

## The Wellsprings of Passions and Feelings

Of special importance in emotional life is a network of structures and pathways near the center of the brain known as the **limbic system.** It makes up about one-fifth of the brain (see Figure 2.10).

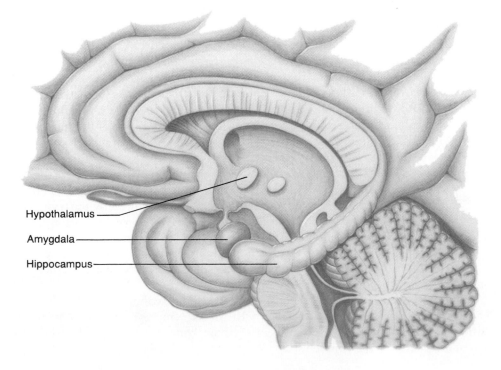

**FIGURE 2.10** The brain's limbic system. *Limbic* means "bordering," and the limbic system is so named because its parts form a border or loop around the deepest core of the cerebrum. Because it is in close contact with both the frontal lobes of the cortex and the brain stem, the limbic system is strategically located for its role in vital brain functions.

Hypothalamus

Amygdala

Hippocampus

The limbic system consists of many components, one of which—the *hippocampus*—plays a primary role in memory, as discussed later in the chapter. In effect, the hippocampus receives information and "decides" whether the information is familiar or unfamiliar. If it is unfamiliar—and therefore potentially significant or threatening—another structure, the **amygdala,** comes into play. The amygdala has neurons that are connected to other parts of the brain and body. The activity of these parts leads to the experience of intense emotions such as anger and fear (Davis, 1997). Through its connections with other portions of the brain, particularly the areas associated with taste and smell, the amygdala can also trigger actions that are appropriate to a positive emotional state—in response, say, to good food (Rolls, 2000).

In one experiment, researchers showed that the startle reaction of rats in response to a sudden, very loud noise is greater when the rats have been conditioned to fear a shock in advance of the noise. That is, the state of fear leads to a larger startle response. But when the amygdala is surgically removed, the exaggerated startle response produced by the fear vanishes, demonstrating that the amygdala mediates the fear experience (Hitchcock & Davis, 1991). As portrayed in Figure 2.11, it is the right amygdala, rather than the left, that is especially activated when fear is present. (As discussed later, the right hemisphere of the brain is especially involved in regulating negative emotions.)

The limbic system includes another key player in our emotional lives and our physical survival: the **hypothalamus,** the brain's most direct link to the glands that are active in fear, anger, and other emotions. The hypothalamus is attached to the "master gland," the **pituitary gland** (see Figure 2.9, p. 64), which it partly controls. The pituitary gland is one of the *endocrine glands*, discussed below. Working in concert with other portions of the limbic system and the cortex, the hypothalamus delivers messages that help produce the "stirred up" bodily processes that accompany emotion.

In lower mammals, the limbic system appears to contain the programming that directs the instinctive behaviors involved in feeding, mating, fighting, and escaping from danger. There is evidence that when animals learn to anticipate that a stressful experience—such as a shock—is coming, the limbic system becomes active (Herrmann, Hurwitz, & Levine, 1984). Laboratory experiments have shown that surgery on or electrical stimulation of various parts of the limbic system can cause animals to behave in unusually docile or unusually aggressive ways. Damage to one part of the limbic system will reduce the fear and avoidance that many animals display when faced with a novel stimulus; damage to another part will remove inhibitions on attack behavior and make many animals vicious.

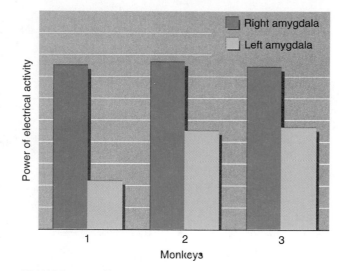

**FIGURE 2.11 The amygdala and painful emotion.** When squirrel monkeys were placed in a room where they had experienced earlier shock, the increase in delta waves—slow brain waves that typically emerge during extreme emotional arousal—was more marked in the right amygdala than in the left.

*Adapted from Lloyd & Kling, 1991.*

**Amygdala**
The part of the limbic system that plays a role in intense positive or negative emotions.

**Hypothalamus**
The portion of the limbic system that serves as a mediator between the brain and the body and helps control metabolism, sleep, hunger, thirst, body temperature, sexual behavior, and emotions.

**Pituitary gland**
The master endocrine gland, which secretes hormones controlling growth and sexual development at puberty and regulating other endocrine glands.

## Staying Alive and Physiologically in Tune

The body's well-being depends on keeping its many functions on a reasonably even keel, despite the numerous events and environmental changes it continually encounters. For example, the body must keep its internal temperature stable through all seasons and levels of exertion, and it must maintain a proper supply of oxygen, water, and various other substances that cells need to function well. The state of dy-

These photographs show the effect of electrical stimulation of the brain of a cat through electrodes planted in or around the limbic system. At left, under stimulation at one particular spot, the cat calmly ignores its traditional prey, the rat. At right, stimulation at another spot makes the cat assume a hostile posture toward a laboratory assistant with whom it is ordinarily on friendly terms.

© Arthur Leipzig

**Homeostasis**
A state of equilibrium, or balance, in the physiological systems within the human body.

**Medulla**
The structure in the brain stem that helps regulate breathing, heartbeat, blood pressure, and digestion.

**Autonomic nervous system (ANS)**
The neural network connecting the central nervous system with glands and smooth muscles, involved in maintaining homeostasis.

**Endocrine glands**
Glands that discharge hormones directly into the bloodstream, bringing about a variety of physiological and psychological changes.

namic equilibrium achieved when these processes are working right and all physiological systems are balanced is called **homeostasis.**

The air we breathe, the water we drink, and the foods we eat are the raw materials required to keep our cells properly supplied and working correctly. We need a central management system to order these supplies, make sure they arrive on time, distribute them where they are needed, and see that they are processed properly. The brain provides that management.

Besides being a center for emotional behavior, the hypothalamus helps maintain homeostasis by signaling when the body needs more food or water and by regulating states of wakefulness and sleep. It also acts like a highly accurate thermostat, keeping body temperature normal by reacting to messages from temperature sensors in the skin and from its own temperature-sensing cells.

Our continuing survival depends as well on the **medulla,** which can be seen in Figure 2.9 (p. 64). This structure in the brain stem is responsible for coordinating vital bodily processes such as breathing, heartbeat, blood pressure, and digestion.

## The Autonomic Nervous System: The Brain's Busy Deputy

In controlling bodily processes, the brain has an effective assistant in the form of the **autonomic nervous system (ANS).** The word *autonomic* means independent or self-sufficient, and in many ways the autonomic nervous system does operate on its own, without much, if any, conscious control. Unless we are hooked up to biofeedback equipment that tells us what our body is doing (see Chapter 12), we cannot command our stomach muscles to make the movements that help digest food, nor can we order the muscles of the blood vessels to redirect the flow of blood toward the muscles of the arms or legs when we have to do physical work. But the ANS can do all these things and does so constantly, even when we are asleep.

In addition, the ANS exercises considerable independent influence on important bodily structures called **endocrine glands**—glands of internal secretion—which are also resistant to conscious control. Unlike the sweat glands that deliver perspiration to the skin or the salivary glands that deliver fluids to the mouth, the endocrine glands discharge their products directly into the bloodstream. These biochemical substances, as noted earlier, are called hormones. They influence many body processes, including those associated with emotional behavior. As illustrated in Figure 2.12, the endocrine glands include the pineal, pituitary, parathyroid, thyroid, and adrenal glands, as well as the pancreas, ovaries, and testes.

The autonomic nervous system exerts its influence on important body processes through a number of centers called *ganglia,* as shown in Figure 2.13. These

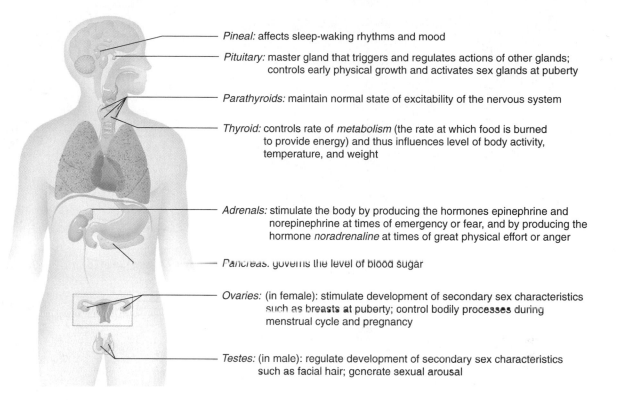

*Pineal:* affects sleep-waking rhythms and mood

*Pituitary:* master gland that triggers and regulates actions of other glands; controls early physical growth and activates sex glands at puberty

*Parathyroids:* maintain normal state of excitability of the nervous system

*Thyroid:* controls rate of *metabolism* (the rate at which food is burned to provide energy) and thus influences level of body activity, temperature, and weight

*Adrenals:* stimulate the body by producing the hormones epinephrine and norepinephrine at times of emergency or fear, and by producing the hormone *noradrenaline* at times of great physical effort or anger

*Pancreas:* governs the level of blood sugar

*Ovaries:* (in female): stimulate development of secondary sex characteristics such as breasts at puberty; control bodily processes during menstrual cycle and pregnancy

*Testes:* (in male): regulate development of secondary sex characteristics such as facial hair; generate sexual arousal

are like small brains scattered throughout the body. They consist of masses of neural cells packed together and connected with one another—as in the brain itself, but on a much smaller scale. Some of these neurons have long fibers over which they send commands to the glands, the heart muscles, and the muscles of the body's organs and blood vessels. Others are connected to the brain and the spinal cord— which means that the ANS, though independent in many ways, does take some orders from above. For example, if you are wakened by shouts of "Fire!" your ears send a message to your brain, which then sends an emergency command to the ANS, which in turn springs into action through its various connections to the glands and muscles.

As is also shown in Figure 2.13, there are two divisions of the ANS, which differ in structure and function: the parasympathetic and the sympathetic.

**The Parasympathetic Division: Running the Ordinary Business of Living**   The **parasympathetic division of the ANS** is connected to the stem of the brain and the lower part of the spinal cord. It is made up of a number of widely scattered ganglia, most of which lie near the glands or muscles of organs to which it delivers its messages. Because it is so loosely constructed, it tends to act in piecemeal fashion, delivering its orders to one or several parts of the body but not necessarily to all at once.

In general, the parasympathetic division plays its most important role during those frequent periods when no danger threatens and the body can relax and go about the ordinary business of living. It tends to slow down the work of the heart and lungs. It aids digestion by stimulating the salivary glands, producing wavelike motions of the muscles of the stomach and intestines, and encouraging the stomach to produce digestive acid and the liver to produce the digestive fluid called bile. It also brings about elimination of the body's waste products from the intestines and bladder. At times, however, the parasympathetic division abandons these usual tasks and helps mobilize the body for emergency action. When it does this— operating in ways that are not yet understood—it seems to assist and supplement the work of the other part of the autonomic system, the sympathetic division.

**FIGURE 2.12 The human endocrine glands.** The endocrine glands receive messages from the brain and ANS that tell them to speed up or slow down hormone production. They influence the excitability of the brain and the rest of the nervous system and are directly involved, for example, in emotional experiences.

**Parasympathetic division of the ANS**
A part of the nervous system made up of scattered ganglia near the glands or the muscles of organs. It helps maintain functions such as heartbeat and digestion.

**FIGURE 2.13 The autonomic nervous system. A long chain of ganglia of the sympathetic system extends down each side of the spinal cord (one side is shown here). The parasympathetic system has ganglia near the glands and smooth muscles that both divisions of the ANS help control, although in different ways.**

*Adapted from Crosby, Humphrey, & Lauer, 1962.*

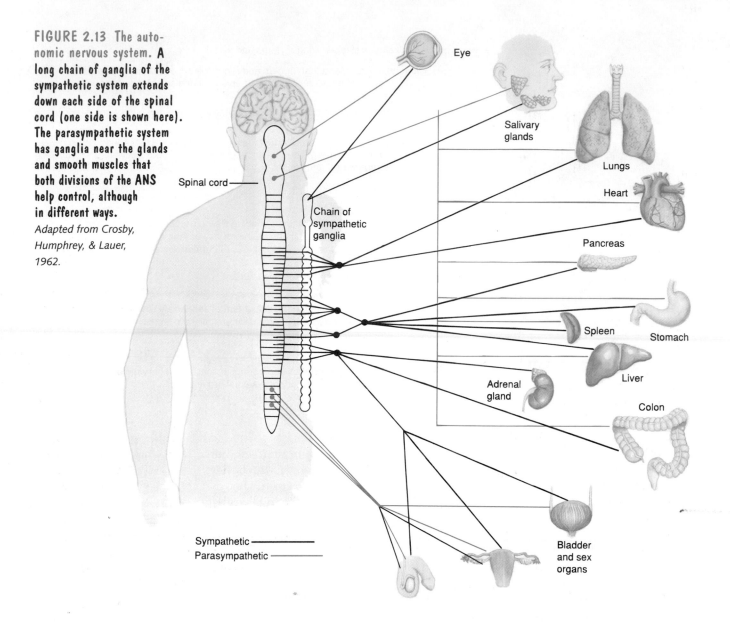

Eye

Salivary glands

Spinal cord

Chain of sympathetic ganglia

Lungs

Heart

Pancreas

Spleen

Stomach

Adrenal gland

Liver

Colon

Sympathetic ————

Parasympathetic ————

Bladder and sex organs

**Sympathetic division of the ANS**

**Long chains of ganglia that extend down the sides of the spinal cord and activate glands and smooth muscles for "fight" or "flight."**

**The Sympathetic Division: Meeting Emergencies** The **sympathetic division of the ANS** is shown in Figure 2.13 as a long chain of ganglia extending down the side of the spinal cord. There is a similar chain, not shown, on the other side of the cord. All the many ganglia of the sympathetic division are interconnected. Note that many of the neural fibers going out from the chains of ganglia meet again in additional ganglia in other parts of the body, where they again form complex interconnections with neural cells that finally carry commands to the glands and smooth muscles. For this reason, the sympathetic division, unlike the parasympathetic division, tends to function as a unit.

When the sympathetic division springs into action, as it does when we experience fear or anger, it does many things all at once. Most notably, it commands the adrenal glands to spill their powerful stimulants—such as norepinephrine, discussed later in the chapter—into the bloodstream. By acting on the adrenal glands, liver, and pancreas, it increases the level of blood sugar, thus raising the rate of metabolism and providing additional energy. It causes the spleen—a glandlike organ in which red blood cells are stored—to release more red blood cells into the bloodstream and thus enables the blood to carry more oxygen to the body's tissues. It changes the size of the blood vessels, enlarging those in the heart and the muscles that control body movement and constricting those in the muscles of the stomach and intestines. It makes the lungs breathe harder. It enlarges the pupils of the eyes, which are controlled by muscles, and slows the activity of the salivary glands. ("Wide eyes" and a dry mouth are characteristic of strong emotions such as fear.) It also activates the sweat glands and contracts the muscles at the base of the hairs on the body, producing gooseflesh in humans and causing the hair on furry animals to rise. In general, the changes triggered by the sympathetic division prepare the body for emergency action, such as fighting or running away.

Clearly, there is a very close marriage between the brain and the body, linked together as they are through numerous physical and chemical connections. The implications of this link for our state of mind, emotions, and physical and mental well-being are discussed throughout this book.

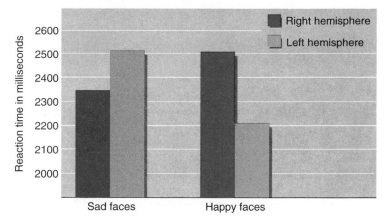

**FIGURE 2.14  Right for sad, left for happy?** When pictures of sad faces were presented to their left visual field, which connects with the right hemisphere of the brain, participants reacted significantly faster than when the same pictures were presented to their right visual field, which connects with the left hemisphere. The opposite was the case for pictures of happy faces.
*Adapted from*
*Reuter-Lorenz & Davidson, 1981.*

## The Brain's Hemispheres and the Regulation of Emotion

As described later in the chapter, many psychologists have concentrated on studying the differing roles of the two brain hemispheres in cognition. Other research points to differences between the two sides of the brain in the regulation of emotional behavior as well. In general, the frontal area of the right hemisphere appears to be more active in regulating negative emotions such as sadness and fear. The frontal area of the left hemisphere appears to be more active in regulating positive emotions such as happiness (Davidson & Tomarken, 1989). The results of a laboratory experiment demonstrating the roles of the brain hemispheres in emotion are illustrated in Figure 2.14. The figure shows that stimuli with an unhappy connotation get a faster response from the right hemisphere; the opposite is true of stimuli with a happy connotation (Reuter-Lorenz & Davidson, 1981).

The pattern appears to hold for both infants and adults. For example, it has been found that 10-month-old infants who cried when separated from their mothers were more likely in earlier testing to have displayed relatively high activity in the right frontal area (Davidson & Fox, 1989). And in studies of adults, it has been found that those who respond with intensely negative feelings to emotion-arousing films were more apt to display high activation of the right frontal area (Tomarken, Davidson, & Henriques, 1990; Tomarken, Davidson, Wheeler, & Doss, 1992).

Research suggests that differences in the activation levels of the two hemispheres are related to the function of the immune system. The *immune system* is the body's intricate defense network of organs and tissues that produces antibodies, or so-called killer cells, to help fight infection and disease, as well as protective cells such as lymphocytes (white blood cells). Researchers have found, for example, that adult women with relatively high activation of the right frontal area had lower levels of natural killer-cell activity than did women with greater left frontal activation, who showed a much more vigorous immune response (Kang et al., 1991). This finding is of special interest, given the evidence that an upbeat, optimistic mood is associated with good health (Seligman, 1991).

**Test Yourself**

**(g)** "His hormones are raging" is a description sometimes applied to an adolescent boy who is beginning to take an intense interest in sex. What gland is in charge of this development?

**(h)** A friend tells you that she spent a relaxing period last evening finishing a crossword puzzle—but that later on in the evening, while getting ready for bed, she kept hearing strange sounds in the basement and experienced a period of intense panic. In which of those two periods was the sympathetic division of your friend's autonomic nervous system more likely to have been active?

**(i)** Which of the two hemispheres of your brain is typically more active when you are feeling happy?

**(j)** Who is likely to show more activity in the right hemisphere of the brain than the left—a stand-up comic or an architect?

(The answers are on page 81.)

# THE BRAIN'S FUNCTIONS, III: MANAGING THOUGHT AND MEMORY

**Association cortex**
Diverse areas of the cortex that contribute to self-awareness and the ability to think about the past and imagine the future.

**Frontal lobes**
The front portions of the brain that play a key role in problem solving and planning.

The areas of the brain responsible for monitoring sensations and controlling movements make up only about a quarter of the cerebral cortex. The rest of the cerebral cortex, mostly the undesignated parts in Figure 2.8 (p. 63), helps us reason, relate past experiences to present ones, and plan for the future; in other words, it is responsible for all the higher cognitive processes that raise us far above the level of other organisms.

These unspecified areas, known generally as the **association cortex** or *secondary cortical areas*, contribute to our ability to be aware of ourselves and our relationship to the world, as well as our ability to contemplate what has been and what might yet be. No other species has so much of its cortex devoted to association areas—a clue to their importance in uniquely human abilities.

## Thinking and Planning

The association areas in the front portion of the brain, called the **frontal lobes**, seem to play a key role in such abilities as solving complex problems, planning, and relating the past to the present. Although we take our conscious processes for granted, they are a strange and wonderful thing, allowing us to examine our own lives, understand the lives of others, and create the ideas, arts, and technologies that are the hallmarks of human culture.

Evidence of the importance of the frontal lobes in higher mental processes comes in part from observations of individuals in whom the area has been injured or damaged. Such individuals may be able to remember facts and score well on intelligence tests, but they cannot plan ahead or initiate an activity. Such a person, for example, might easily remember her child's birthday but be incapable of taking the steps necessary to plan the child's party. Individuals with damaged frontal lobes also lose their normal social inhibitions and begin saying and doing inappropriate things, as if propelled by momentary impulses rather than thinking through a particular situation. For example, after losing the area of the frontal cortex responsible for processing information on emotional state, one man changed dramatically from a model citizen to an impulsive and irresponsible human being (Damasio, Tranel, & Damasio, 1990).

Further evidence comes from studies of early development. Very young children typically behave impulsively; they are not very good at thinking things through or purposefully planning ahead. Significantly enough, at this stage the frontal lobes are not yet fully developed, and their connections with other important centers of the brain have not yet been established (Diamond, 1991).

## How Memories Are Stored and Retrieved

In recent years, researchers have made notable progress in understanding the role of the brain in memory (as well as in emotions, as discussed earlier). For many years, it was thought that memory could be tracked to a single location in the brain. Now, however, it appears clear that multiple areas are involved. For example, the name of a person and a schematic representation of that person are stored in separate parts of the brain—which explains why, with age, we may forget the names of people but still be able to call up images of their faces (Hart & Gordon, 1992). Of course, it is also possible that we are "prewired" to remember faces better than names—of all the senses, vision is our primary system and audition is second.

A variety of studies have shown that memory is managed primarily in the association areas of the cortex, especially the frontal lobes (Goldman-Rakic, 1992). Here resides the capacity to store newly gained information and link it to relevant information stored long ago (Baddeley, 1986). Patients suffering from damage to the frontal lobes are unable to use the knowledge they gain to guide how they behave from moment to moment.

The complex task of storing and retrieving information seems to require the cooperation of other parts of the brain as well—most notably the **hippocampus** (Murray & Mishkin, 1985; Passingham, 1985; Riedel & Micheau, 2001). The hippocampus lies beneath the cortex, close to the area involved in processing speech, as shown in Figure 2.8 (p. 63), but it's difficult to illustrate clearly. It appears to be essential in transforming new information into long-lasting memories (Mishkin & Appenzeller, 1987). Research with laboratory animals suggests that certain older memories aren't affected when the hippocampus is destroyed, but newer ones either aren't formed or can't be retrieved (Squire, 1992).

Studies have shown that people suffering from amnesia display patterns of forgetting very much like those exhibited by monkeys with damage to the portion of the brain that includes the hippocampus—for example, forgetting objects they have just seen (Squire, Zola-Morgan, & Chen, 1988). From studies of both humans and laboratory animals, it appears that the hippocampus is essential for forming *semantic memories*, which include memories for people's names, words, facts, and ideas, and *episodic memories*, or memories for personal experiences (see Chapter 5), although the hippocampus is not the actual site where such memories are stored (Rolls, 2000; Squire, 1992). However, the hippocampus is not essential for *procedural memory*, which includes the ability to remember motor skills and habits such as how to tie shoelaces or play sports (Squire, 1992).

A primary role of the hippocampus is to *consolidate* new memories—that is, to relate them to other memories and permanently store them, as when we relate an event to the place where it occurred (McDonald & White, 1993). On the other hand, the frontal cortex is more essential for retrieving prior facts, names, and rules from long-range storage in the association cortex, for use in solving problems.

**Hippocampus**
**The part of the brain that transfers information from short-term memory to long-term memory.**

**Test Yourself**

**(k)** When an aging grandfather complains that his memory constantly fails him, what structure in his brain is likely undergoing change?

(The answer is on page 81.)

## The Growing Brain and the Developing Intellect

From what we have said so far, it's clear that the highly developed abilities of human beings depend in large measure on the cerebrum and its cortex. Even before birth, these structures grow so rapidly that they almost seem to explode. Growth continues at a furious pace after birth—so much so that a baby's brain triples in weight in the first 6 months of life. By age 2, the brain has reached three-quarters of its ultimate weight (which is finally achieved in the late teens to early twenties), and it is during these early years that the child makes remarkable strides in motor skills, speech, and the ability to remember and reflect. All the various stages of children's intellectual development, described later in the text, are dependent on the progressive growth and maturation of the cerebral cortex—in interaction, as always, with environmental experiences.

Although the number of neurons remains relatively constant, the number of synapses peaks early in the first two years of life. Indeed, as a child learns more information and new skills, the number of synapses actually decreases (Trentin, 2001; Webb, Monk, & Nelson, 2001). Experience appears to "prune" the cortex into a more efficient form in the same way that a sculptor chips away at an unformed

© Jose Luis Pelaez, Inc./CORBIS

A stimulating environment may speed the rate at which the young brain grows.

piece of marble to develop a final product containing less substance than the original. For a further discussion of the brain's development over time, see the Life Span Perspective on page 75.

# Left Brain, Right Brain

As you saw in Figures 2.5 (p. 57) and 2.9 (p. 64), the topmost part of the brain—the cerebrum and the cerebral cortex—is divided into two hemispheres. Each half seems to have somewhat different responsibilities for memory, reasoning, and language, although it is important to bear in mind that the brain generally functions as a whole, not a set of distinct entities. That is, in most cases, the hemispheres are in close communication with each other.

Most of the neural fibers that connect the brain with parts of the body through the spinal cord cross from one side to the other. This means that the left hemisphere ordinarily receives sensory messages from and controls movement in the right side of the body and the right hemisphere deals with the left side of the body. If you write with your right hand, it is your left hemisphere that directs the movements. The left hemisphere also has greater control over the use of language: speaking and understanding the speech of others. Thus, in most people, the left hemisphere is the dominant one—and the one that is used and relied on most heavily.

The two hemispheres cooperate very closely. They have numerous interconnections, especially through a structure known as the **corpus callosum** (shown in Figure 2.9, p. 64), which resembles a thick telephone cable between the two hemispheres. Thus, each half of the cerebrum and cerebral cortex can communicate efficiently with the other half.

What would happen if the corpus callosum were cut or missing and the two halves of the brain could not communicate? We know the answer to this question because at times surgeons have cut the connecting link as a last resort to relieve patients of debilitating epileptic seizures. This split-brain operation produces some

**Corpus callosum**
The structure of the brain that connects the right and left hemispheres of the cerebrum and enables these hemispheres to interact.

Various aspects of the brain are altered over the course of life. Those changes are often reflected in behavior and well-being. Three examples follow.

One notable change takes place in the levels of the neurotransmitter dopamine in the brain (Rosenzweig & Lieman, 1982). Concentrations of dopamine rise during childhood, with major changes taking place during adolescence with regard to dopamine production by different cortical systems (Spear, 2000). As described in Chapter 13, a significant increase in dopamine may be associated with schizophrenia, a serious mental disorder that often surfaces during late adolescence or early adulthood. Some researchers have suggested that the timing of the disorder may be more readily understood in the light of developmental changes in the brain's chemistry: A large increase in dopamine—or a change in the areas in which it is produced—in the brain of a young person who is genetically predisposed to schizophrenia might well produce the bizarre symptoms characteristic of this disorder.

At a much later period in the life span, changes in the brain, again involving dopamine, lead to the development of a neurological disorder. Parkinson's disease, appearing in late adulthood and old age, causes tremors to occur and body movements—even walking—to become uncoordinated. The disorder appears to be caused by damage to an area of the brain where neurons normally secrete dopamine (Miyawaki, Meah, & Koller, 1997; Wyatt & Freed, 1983), as well as serotonin. When patients are given replacement therapy that leads to increased levels of dopamine or serotonin, their symptoms are relieved.

A second developmental change in the brain is revealed in sleep. As discussed in Chapter 8, a major component of sleep is *REM (rapid eye movement) sleep*, which is often marked by dreaming. This is a period of intense physiological activity, which is prominent even during prenatal life and consumes about half of a newborn's sleep. The proportion of sleep time spent in REM sleep diminishes dramatically in later infancy and early childhood, and it decreases still further, to less than 20%, in adulthood. There are numerous theories about the role of REM sleep and dreaming in human development and behavior, but it appears that the REM period is essential "exercise" for the rapidly developing nervous system of the fetus and infant (Hobson, 1989; Mirmiran, 1995).

A third change takes place in the weight of the brain itself. Almost all the brain's neurons are present at birth. After birth, the number increases by only a small amount and only in certain areas (Gazzaniga et al., 1998). Yet the brain quadruples in weight from birth to adulthood, with the most rapid growth taking place in the first 5 years of life. Some of the added weight comes from the growth of glia. But perhaps more important is the growth of new offshoots from neural cells—much as a young tree develops new branches. By sprouting new branches, neurons increase their interconnections with other neurons, thus providing new pathways for messages in the brain.

As new interconnections and pathways form, presumably unused neurons and especially synapses are pruned away. At birth, the neurons of an infant's brain average about 2,500 synapses each, peaking at about 15,000 by age 2 to 3 years; the number then gradually decreases, as cognitive activity becomes more efficient (Gopnik, Meltzoff, & Kuhl, 1999).

• • • • • • • • • • • • • • • • • • • • • • • • • • • • • • • • • • • • • • • • • • • • • • • • • •

strange results. Patients may show little change in intelligence, personality, or general behavior, yet careful testing reveals that in some ways they act as if they have two independently functioning brains. One consistent finding is that they are largely unable to transfer visual information from one hemisphere to the other—what one side of the brain sees, for example, is not recognized by the other side (Corballis & Corballis, 2001).

Experiments with individuals who have undergone split-brain surgery show that the two hemispheres, when separated, perform different functions. Although the hemispheres look symmetrical overall, certain areas are slightly larger on the left side, others slightly larger on the right side. These physical differences have been seen even in unborn fetuses, an indication that they are innate rather than acquired through experience and learning (Galaburda, 1984).

A number of psychologists have concluded that the left hemisphere is more involved in dealing with symbolic information, such as words and numbers, considered one by one in a logical sequence. This is the kind of mental work that we call "reasoning," in which we arrive at logical conclusions in a step-by-step fashion. The left hemisphere is also particularly adept at language, in which sounds are put together in logical order into words and words are arranged into sentences.

© Peter Beck/CORBIS

Many psychologists believe that the left hemisphere of the brain is more involved in dealing with symbolic information, whereas the right hemisphere is more involved in considering whole patterns and therefore is better at perceiving visual information such as an architect's blueprint or model.

By contrast, the right hemisphere appears to be more involved in considering whole patterns—seeing the forest, not the trees. For example, it excels at the perception of visual information such as paintings or spatial locations, the melodies in a song or symphony, and the tone of a person's voice.

However, our knowledge about the division of labor between the two hemispheres in normal people remains incomplete. There is evidence that both hemispheres are active in most of the things we do, although for specific tasks one may be more active than the other. For example, in a study in which a normal person was trying to master the delicate feat of judging space and movement so as to get a steel ball through a maze (a spatial task), measurements of his brain's electrical activity indicated that his right hemisphere was doing most of the work. When he switched to writing a letter (a language task), there was more activity in the left hemisphere (Ornstein, 1978).

# THE BRAIN-BEHAVIOR LINK

## FOCUS QUESTIONS
- What effects do the major neurotransmitters and other biochemicals have on behavior?
- Why can't the physical processes of the nervous system tell us everything we want to know about behavior?

One of the great mysteries in psychology—perhaps the greatest mystery of all—is how the electrical and chemical activity of the brain can produce thought and emotion. Barring some sudden breakthrough, we have a ways to go to solve the mystery. This chapter closes with some observations on the subject.

## Transforming Electricity and Chemistry into Meanings and Feelings

We know from neuroscience studies that neural impulses, the tiny electrical charges discussed earlier, represent the basic activity that goes on inside the nervous system. Each neuron ordinarily produces only one kind of impulse, its own little unvarying "beep." Yet somehow these monotonous beeps—by the rate at which they are produced, the patterns they form, and the way they are routed through the brain—manage to account for human cognition and consciousness. They tell us what our eyes see and our ears hear. They enable us to learn and to think. They direct our glands and internal organs to function in harmony. They direct our muscles to perform such intricate and delicate feats as driving an automobile and playing a violin. Taken as a whole, they are the basis for what we call "mind."

Different neurons, in transmitting their neural impulses, release different kinds of neurotransmitter chemicals at the synapse. These biochemicals must be properly balanced if the whole system is to function properly. Anything that affects the amount and effectiveness of these biochemicals in the brain cells is likely to profoundly influence our thoughts, feelings, and activities.

A growing number of brain chemicals are generally recognized as neurotransmitters. Some investigators have suggested that there are as many as 300 (Kandel & Schwartz, 1985), but at present the actual number isn't known. Neurotransmitters are necessary for normal brain functioning and behavior, and when the balance is disturbed, serious biological or psychological problems may arise.

**Acetylcholine,** one of the best-known neurotransmitters, is involved in PNS functions such as motor activity, as well as a variety of CNS functions (Beatty, 2001). **Glutamate** is an abundant neurotransmitter known to play a primary role in learning and memory (see *Psychology and the Media* in Chapter 5 on page 192). The *catecholamines*—a chemically related set of neurotransmitters—have been studied extensively. They include **norepinephrine,** which plays a role in arousal as well as depression, and **dopamine,** an abundant neurotransmitter involved in goal-related motor behaviors, as well as Parkinson's disease, schizophrenia, and attention-deficit/hyperactivity disorder (Vallone, Picetti, & Borrelli, 2000). We return to the roles of the catecholamines in Chapter 13, along with that of **serotonin,** another major neurotransmitter implicated in various mental and behavioral disorders, including depression.

**Peptides** are biochemicals that are important in neural transmission and bodily regulation. Some of these—the *neuropeptides*—act like neurotransmitters; others regulate the functioning of neurotransmitters. Some peptides are more like hormones; they are released into the bloodstream and affect both parts of the nervous system, as well as distant organs. Scientists first discovered some of these substances in locations far from the brain, such as the intestines.

Peptides can be as powerful in their effects as synthetically manufactured drugs prescribed by doctors. Some seem to affect parts of the brain associated with pain and with emotion and mood (Bloom, Lazerson, & Hofstadter, 1985). Others have profound influences on behavior—including, for example, drinking and muscular movement (Iversen, 1982) and learning and memory (de Weid, 1997). One important neuropeptide, called **corticotrophin-release factor (CRF),** is secreted by the hypothalamus. By stimulating the pituitary, it leads to production by the adrenal gland of **cortisol,** a hormone that helps in alleviating emotionally stressful events and pain. More than 100 peptides have been identified, and new ones are continually being discovered; over 50 of these appear to function directly as neurotransmitters (Pinel, 2003).

One group of neuropeptides has been named **endorphins,** from the Greek word meaning "the morphine within," because they are similar in structure and effect to the powerful painkiller morphine (Thompson, 1989). The endorphins may help explain the mystery of acupuncture, an ancient technique widely used today by Chinese physicians to reduce pain and treat physical ailments. Through the insertion of fine needles into various parts of the body, acupuncture seems to increase production of the brain's own brand of morphine. It appears as if a natural pain barrier is set up when the needle is inserted (Murray, 1995), although the explanation is probably not nearly this simple (e.g., see Wall, 2000).

**Acetylcholine**
A neurotransmitter involved in motor activity and numerous CNS functions.

**Glutamate**
An abundant neurotransmitter known to play a primary role in learning and memory.

**Norepinephrine**
A neurotransmitter involved in arousal and depression.

**Dopamine**
An abundant neurotransmitter involved in goal-related motor behaviors and various mental and behavioral disorders, including schizophrenia.

**Serotonin**
A neurotransmitter involved in various mental and behavioral disorders, including depression.

**Peptides**
Essential biochemicals that may function like neurotransmitters or hormones.

**Corticotrophin-release factor (CRF)**
A neuropeptide secreted by the hypothalamus.

**Cortisol**
The hormone secreted by the adrenal gland during emotional upset or in response to pain.

**Endorphins**
Neuropeptides that serve as natural painkillers.

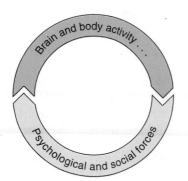

**FIGURE 2.15** Biological and behavioral forces: A reciprocal relationship. **Just as the functioning of the brain and body can affect behavior, the reverse is true as well.**

Our understanding of endorphins and the other peptides has been accelerating by leaps and bounds. But because much of this knowledge is quite new (the first endorphins were discovered in 1975), our picture of the number of brain peptides and what they do is still sketchy. It is clear, however, that they play an important part in our feelings and behavior.

## The Interplay of Biological, Psychological, and Environmental Forces

As this chapter has shown, biological factors such as hormone levels, neurotransmitter activity, and brain injury affect behavior. However, it is important to remember that behavioral factors such as environment and social interactions also affect our biological states. As indicated in Figure 2.15, the relationship between biological and psychological forces is reciprocal.

Consider this example, drawn from research with laboratory animals. It is known that the sexual activity of male monkeys reflects the levels of *testosterone*, the male sex hormone (which also exists in females to a lesser extent), in their bodies. Studies have shown, however, that levels of testosterone vary as a function of the social situation in which an animal finds himself. If a male is placed in contact with female monkeys in an environment that excludes other males, his testosterone level will increase—as will his sexual activity. On the other hand, if the male is placed in a situation in which he is dominated by other males, his testosterone level will decrease—leading, in turn, to a lower level of sexual activity. Thus, although hormones affect behavior, hormonal activity appears to be regulated by the social milieu (Moberg, 1987; see also Bernhardt, 1997).

A similar reciprocal relationship between biological and psychological factors is evident in many studies of humans. As described later in the text, it is known that biological factors such as genetic inheritance and brain malfunctions play a role in the development of serious forms of mental and behavioral disorders. But it is equally true that these vulnerabilities are triggered when individuals encounter experiences that give rise to psychological turmoil and stress (National Institute of Mental Health, 1989).

Such studies serve as an important reminder of the danger of trying to reduce all behavior to its biological correlates. Seymour Kety, a leading investigator of the biological foundations of behavior, acknowledged that remarkable progress has been made in understanding the structures of the brain, the relationships among its parts, and the effects of brain chemistry on behavior. But he maintained that biology alone cannot unravel the mysteries of human personality and experience (Kety, 1982). Nobel Prize–winning brain scientist John Eccles observed: "I go all the way with my fellow scientists in understanding the brain physically. But it doesn't explain me, or human choice, delight, courage, or compassion. I think we must go beyond. . . . There is something apart from all of the electricity and chemistry we can measure" (Facklam & Facklam, 1982). And as Roger Sperry put it, "the events of inner experience" are important to study in their own right as causal factors in human behavior (Sperry, 1988).

Psychologists work to understand human behavior at many different levels—from the minutest workings of brain cells to the broad interactions of people in groups, from observing behavior in other species to plumbing the breadth and depth of human feelings. All these approaches are needed to answer the central question: How and why do we behave as we do? Understanding how the brain works is an essential part of the picture, but it is only one part. The remaining chapters show how other aspects of psychology also help answer the same question.

# Chapter 2 Summary

## How the Brain Governs Behavior

1. The brain governs all physical and psychological functions through its connections with other parts of the body.

2. The brain contains many billions of *neurons,* or neural cells; each neuron receives messages, processes them, and transmits them to thousands of other neurons throughout the body.

3. Some neurons act as glands and transmit into the bloodstream various *hormones,* which affect bodily functioning in areas distant from the brain.

4. The brain also contains even more billions of *glia,* which perform functions such as regulating the biochemical environment of the brain, helping sustain neurons, modulating neural transmission, and helping guide early brain development and maturation.

5. Each neuron in the nervous system is a fiberlike cell with receivers called *dendrites* at one end and senders called *terminal branches* at the other. Stimulation of the neuron at its dendrites—or at *receptor sites* on its *cell body*—sets off an electrical impulse that travels the length of the *axon* to the terminal branches. There the stage is set for stimulation or inhibition of other neurons, as well as muscles or glands. Other important structures include the *nucleus, myelin sheath,* and *nodes.*

6. A neuron ordinarily fires in accord with the *all-or-none principle.*

7. The key to the transmission of nervous messages is the *synapse,* a junction where the sender of one neuron is separated by only a microscopic distance from the receiver of another neuron.

8. When a neuron fires, it releases *neurotransmitters,* which flow across the synaptic cleft and act on receiving neurons.

9. The *central nervous system (CNS)* is made up of the brain and the *spinal cord.* The neurons of the CNS affect functions and behavior throughout the rest of the body through the *peripheral nervous system (PNS).*

10. Afferent neurons carry information from the sense organs to the brain; efferent neurons carry messages from the brain to the glands and muscles; and *interneurons* are the intermediaries between other neurons in the CNS.

11. The topmost and largest area of the brain is the *cerebrum,* which is covered by the *cerebral cortex;* each is divided down the middle into a left hemisphere and a right hemisphere.

12. The cerebral cortex, which is larger in relation to body size in human beings than in any other species, is the part of the brain primarily responsible for higher processes such as thinking, remembering, and planning. When damaged, it sometimes displays remarkable *plasticity.*

## How Neuroscientists Study the Brain and Mind

13. In mapping the brain and studying its structures and functions, researchers once had to rely on changes in behavior that were attributable to brain damage. They later began studying brain lesions in laboratory animals and using electrical brain stimulation (EBS) in humans.

14. *Computerized tomography (CT)* and *magnetic resonance imaging (MRI)* are methods of studying brain structures but not brain functioning.

15. *Positron emission tomography (PET)* and *functional magnetic resonance imaging (fMRI)* are methods of studying brain structures and pathways, as well as what they do, in an ongoing manner.

16. *Electroencephalography (EEG)* is a method of measuring overall brain electrical activity. *Quantitative electroencephalography (QEEG)* allows measurement of precise event-related potentials (ERPs).

## The Brain's Functions, I: Experiencing the World

17. The specialized area of the cerebral cortex responsible for analyzing and interpreting messages from the sense organs is referred to as the *somatosensory cortex.*

18. The *thalamus* is a relay and processing center for incoming sensory messages and outgoing bodily commands.

19. The *reticular activating system (RAS)* is another sensory processing center; it helps keep the upper parts of the brain in an appropriate state of arousal, attention, and activity.

20. The specialized strip on the cerebral cortex that controls body movements and speech is the *motor cortex.* The *cerebellum* controls body balance and the coordination of complex muscular movements; its two lobes are connected by the *pons.*

## The Brain's Functions, II: Overseeing Emotions and Survival

21. The *limbic system,* a network of brain structures and pathways, helps regulate emotional behavior.

22. One of these structures, the *amygdala*, comes into play in the experience of such intense emotions as anger, fear, and joy.

23. A prominent part of the limbic system is the *hypothalamus*—the brain's most direct link to the body glands that are active in emotions. The master gland, the *pituitary*, is connected to the hypothalamus.

24. The hypothalamus plays a role in maintaining *homeostasis*, the state of dynamic equilibrium among physiological processes.

25. The *medulla* is also responsible for coordinating a number of essential bodily processes, including breathing, heart rate, and digestion.

26. The *autonomic nervous system (ANS)* exercises more or less independent control over the *endocrine glands*, the heart muscles, and the muscles of the body's organs and blood vessels. It helps regulate breathing, heart rate, blood pressure, and digestion, and in times of emergency it works in conjunction with the endocrine glands to mobilize the body's resources.

27. The endocrine glands influence behavior by secreting hormones into the bloodstream. The most important endocrine glands are the following:
    a) The pineal, which affects sleep-waking rhythms and mood.
    b) The pituitary, which produces hormones that control growth, cause sexual development at puberty, and regulate other glands.
    c) The parathyroids, which maintain a normal state of excitability of the nervous system.
    d) The thyroid, which regulates metabolism and affects levels of body activity, temperature, and weight.
    e) The adrenals, which secrete the powerful stimulants epinephrine (active in states of emergency or fear) and norepinephrine (active during physical effort or anger).
    f) The pancreas, which governs blood sugar level.
    g) The female ovaries and male testes, which regulate sexual characteristics and behavior.

28. The autonomic nervous system is composed of two parts: the *parasympathetic division*, which is most active under ordinary circumstances, and the *sympathetic division*, which is active in emergencies.

29. There may be differences between the two sides of the brain in the regulation of emotion. The right hemisphere appears to be more active in regulating negative emotions and the left hemisphere in regulating positive emotions.

## The Brain's Functions, III: Managing Thought and Memory

30. The *association cortex*, which makes up the unspecified areas of the cerebral cortex, is concerned with consciousness—awareness of self and the ability to think about the past and imagine the future.

31. The association areas called *frontal lobes* play a key role in such human capabilities as solving problems, planning, and relating the past to the present.

32. The *hippocampus* appears to be essential in transforming new information into semantic and episodic memories, but not procedural memories.

33. The right hemisphere of the brain deals with the left side of the body. The left hemisphere controls the right side of the body and the use of language; in most people, it is the dominant hemisphere.

34. The two hemispheres are in constant communication through the *corpus callosum*, a thick cable of interconnecting neurons.

35. Experiments with patients whose corpus callosum has been cut—split-brain patients—indicate that the left hemisphere specializes in individual items of information, logic, and reasoning; the right hemisphere specializes in information about form, space, music, and entire patterns and is the intuitive half of the brain.

## The Brain-Behavior Link

36. Anything that alters the amount and effectiveness of neurotransmitters in the brain is likely to profoundly influence thoughts, feelings, and behavior in general.

37. Among the best-known neurotransmitters are *acetylcholine*, involved in PNS activities such as motor functions and also many CNS activities, and *glutamate*, known to play a role in learning and memory.

38. The catecholamines include *norepinephrine* (involved in arousal as well as depression) and *dopamine* (involved in goal-directed motor behaviors and numerous mental and behavioral disorders). *Serotonin* is also involved in mental and behavioral disorders, including depression.

39. *Peptides* act like neurotransmitters or like hormones. One important peptide, *corticotrophin-release factor (CRF)*, is secreted by the hypothalamus, stimulates the pituitary, and leads to production of *cortisol* by the adrenal glands. Another important group is the *endorphins*, the body's natural painkillers.

40. Just as biological factors affect human behavior, psychological and environmental forces (behavioral factors), in reciprocal fashion, affect biology.

# Chapter 2 Test Yourself Answers

(a) The afferent neurons were likely affected. They carry messages from the sense organs—including the skin—to the brain. In contrast, the efferent neurons carry messages from the brain outward, thus directing the activities of the body.

(b) The researcher would be more likely to study the role of brain chemistry. Neuroscience focuses on the relationship between the brain—including its chemical activity—and behavior.

(c) The researchers would be most likely to use fMRI, perhaps in conjunction with QEEG. This would allow them to see which areas of your brain were involved as you engaged in specific activities, with ERP time markers.

(d) Jim Brady's brain was badly damaged, and damage to the brain is lasting because its neurons cannot regenerate—although other neurons may to some extent take over the functions of the damaged ones.

(e) The soldier is more likely to have problems seeing. The back part of the cortex is responsible for vision.

(f) The cerebellum coordinates the kind of finely regulated finger movements a guitar player uses and the kind of body balance and equilibrium a ballerina requires.

(g) The pituitary gland (see Figure 2.12, p. 69) stimulates the body's sex hormones to begin to flow more actively at puberty.

(h) The second experience undoubtedly caused the sympathetic division to spring into action; it does so whenever we feel intense emotions such as fear or anger.

(i) The left hemisphere is likely to be more active when you're feeling happy.

(j) The right hemisphere of the brain is more heavily involved than the left in dealing with visual and spatial information; it is therefore more active in the work of the architect.

(k) The grandfather's hippocampus is probably involved. It is a structure of the brain with a key role in storing and retrieving information.

(l) The neurotransmitter diminished in the brain would most likely be dopamine.

# Chapter 2  Brain, Body, and Behavior

## Key Terms

acetylcholine (p. 77)
all-or-none principle (p. 55)
amygdala (p. 67)
association cortex (p. 72)
autonomic nervous system (ANS) (p. 68)
axon (p. 54)
cell body (p. 54)
central nervous system (CNS) (p. 56)
cerebellum (p. 65)
cerebral cortex (p. 57)
cerebrum (p. 57)
computerized tomography (CT) (p. 59)
corpus callosum (p. 74)
corticotrophin-release factor (CRF) (p. 77)
cortisol (p. 77)
dendrites (p. 54)
dopamine (p. 77)
electroencephalography (EEG) (p. 62)
endocrine glands (p. 68)
endorphins (p. 77)
frontal lobes (p. 72)
functional magnetic resonance imaging
   (fMRI) (p. 60)
glia (p. 54)
glutamate (p. 77)
hippocampus (p. 73)
homeostasis (p. 68)
hormones (p. 54)
hypothalamus (p. 67)
interneuron (p. 57)
limbic system (p. 66)

magnetic resonance imaging (MRI) (p. 59)
medulla (p. 68)
motor cortex (p. 65)
myelin sheath (p. 54)
neuron (p. 54)
neurotransmitters (p. 55)
nodes (p. 55)
norepinephrine (p. 77)
nucleus (p. 54)
parasympathetic division of the ANS (p. 69)
peptides (p. 77)
peripheral nervous system (PNS) (p. 56)
pituitary gland (p. 67)
plasticity (p. 58)
pons (p. 65)
positron emission tomography (PET) (p. 60)
quantitative electroencephalography
   (QEEG) (p. 62)
receptor sites (p. 54)
reticular activating system (RAS) (p. 64)
serotonin (p. 77)
somatosensory cortex (p. 62)
spinal cord (p. 56)
sympathetic division of the ANS (p. 70)
synapse (p. 55)
terminal branches (p. 54)
thalamus (p. 63)

The key terms above can be used as search terms in
InfoTrac, a database of readings, which can be found
at http://infotrac-thomsonlearning.com.

## Active Learning Review

### How the Brain Governs Behavior

1. The human brain contains many billions of individual neural cells, or *neurons*,
   that account for all human capabilities—from processing information and
   feeling emotion to coping with stress and relating to other people. Everything
   we do is accomplished by the remarkable powers of the human _____.

**brain**

2. The brain's neural cells, or _____, are intricately connected with each
   other and with other neural cells throughout the body.

**neurons**

3. The primary job of most of the brain's neurons is transmitting messages through
   trillions of pathways. Some cells in the brain operate much like miniature
   glands, producing complex chemicals called *hormones*, from the Greek word
   meaning "activators" or "exciters." Other brain cells—called *glia*, from the Greek
   word for "glue"—perform a variety of functions including aiding transmission
   by _____.

**neurons (or neural cells)**

4. The chemicals produced and directed by the brain, which travel through the bloodstream and influence many physical and psychological activities, are known as _____. The cells in the brain that assist in neural functioning are called _____.

    hormones
    glia

5. At one end of a neuron are _____, which are branching structures that receive messages. Neural impulses can also be received along the *cell body* at numerous *receptor sites*.

    neurons (or neural cells)

6. A neuron can thus be stimulated at the _____ as well as at other _____ _____. When sufficient stimulation is present, the nervous impulse travels down the fiberlike *axon* to the *terminal branches* and the *synapse* with the next neuron—the point at which two neurons almost touch.

    dendrites, receptor
    sites

7. The sending end of a neuron consists of the _____ and the _____ _____. Above them lies the cell body, which contains the neuron's *nucleus*.

    axon, terminal
    branches

8. Receptor sites are located along the _____ _____; the cell's genetic material is contained in the _____.

    cell body
    nucleus

9. The protective tissue that covers the neuron's axon and increases the speed at which the neural impulse travels along the neuron is called the _____ _____.

    myelin
    sheath

10. Impulses are transmitted from one neuron to another across the _____.

    synapse

11. When a neuron fires, the sending structures of the neuron release _____ at the _____, which excite or inhibit the next neuron in line.

    neurotransmitters
    synapse

12. The synaptic knobs form the actual synapse with another neuron. The neurotransmitter is released by the synaptic _____, travels to the synaptic _____, and bridges the synaptic _____ to stimulate the receptors of another neuron.

    vesicles
    knobs, cleft

13. In sum: The primary cells of the nervous system, the _____, receive impulses at their _____ or at _____ _____ located along the _____ _____. The impulses travel down the neuron's cell body, past the cell's genetic material contained in the _____, and toward the sending end, or _____, which contains the _____ _____.

    neurons
    dendrites, receptor sites
    cell body
    nucleus
    axon, terminal branches

14. The speed of the impulse along the cell body is increased if the axon is wrapped with a _____ _____.

    myelin sheath

15. The neural impulse is sent to another neuron at the _____. Biochemicals called _____ are stored in the synaptic _____. They are transferred to the synaptic _____ and released into the synaptic _____ to facilitate the transmission of the impulse to the next neuron.

    synapse
    neurotransmitters, vesicles
    knobs, cleft

16. Whether a neuron fires or not depends on the overall pattern of messages it receives. A neuron may be stimulated simultaneously at different _____ or _____ _____. Some neurotransmitters excite the neuron to fire; others inhibit its firing. The result depends on the total pattern of such impulses.

    dendrites
    receptor sites

17. Generally, if a neuron fires at all, it fires as hard as it can, according to the _____-_____-_____ _____.

    all-or-none principle

18. The brain, with its many billions of intricately interconnected _____, is one part of the *central nervous system (CNS)*.

    neurons

19. The brain and the _____ _____ make up the _____ _____ system, which has many elaborate interconnections with the outlying neural cells of the body, from the head to the fingertips and toes.

    spinal cord, central nervous

20. The central nervous system, consisting of the _____ and the _____ _____, gets messages from and controls movements in all parts of the body, because it connects with the wide-reaching network of the _____ nervous system.

    brain, spinal
    cord
    peripheral

21. All the neurons in the brain, the spinal cord, and the _____ _____ _____ fall into three classes. One class is afferent neurons, which carry messages from the eyes, ears, and other sense organs to the brain.

    peripheral nervous
    system

afferent

efferent

afferent

efferent

interneurons

brain

cerebral

cortex

cerebrum

cerebral cortex

cerebrum, hemispheres

cerebral

cortex

plasticity

22. In addition to the neurons that carry messages toward the brain, known as _____ neurons, there are efferent neurons, which carry messages away from the brain and spinal cord to the body's muscles, organs, and glands.

23. The brain's messages are directed outward toward the rest of the body through _____ neurons.

24. The third class of neurons—besides the _____ neurons, which carry messages toward the brain, and the _____ neurons, which carry messages away from the brain—is the *interneurons*, which carry messages between other neurons.

25. Neural cells that carry messages between other neural cells are _____.

26. If you could look down through the top of the skull, you would see the important part of the _____ called the *cerebral cortex*. It is larger in proportion to body size in human beings than in most other species, and it is chiefly responsible for the ability to remember, think, and plan—all skills that make human beings more intelligent than other animals.

27. Human skill at all kinds of information processing is governed by the _____ _____, which—like the thick wrinkled skin of a prune—is the surface of the brain's largest single structure.

28. The largest single structure of the brain, overlaid by the cerebral cortex, is the _____.

29. The cerebrum and its covering, the _____ _____, are split down the middle into a left hemisphere and a right hemisphere.

30. The two halves of the _____ are the left and right _____.

31. Damage to the higher brain areas—especially the outer part or _____ _____—is permanent.

32. The ability of the brain to recapture functions after being damaged is referred to as its _____.

## How Neuroscientists Study the Brain and Mind

electrical brain stimulation

computerized tomography

magnetic resonance imaging

structural

positron emission

tomography

functional magnetic

resonance imaging

functional

electroencephalography,

quantitative

electroencephalography

33. An early systematic approach to studying the brain and how it works was _____ _____ _____, in which tiny harmless electrical charges are delivered to specific areas of the exposed cortex during necessary surgery.

34. Images of the brain can be obtained through _____ _____, which uses X-rays to record visual "slices" of the brain's structures, or through higher-resolution _____ _____ _____, which uses magnetic fields to produce either slices or three-dimensional views. The older and fuzzier approach of computerized tomography and the newer and sharper three-dimensional approach of magnetic resonance imaging are forms of _____ brain imaging.

35. Images of the brain's actual functioning in response to environmental events or stimuli can be obtained through _____ _____ _____, which is based on recording the brain's metabolism of glucose that has been treated with a radioactive isotope, or through _____ _____ _____ _____, which is based on recording tiny magnetic changes that occur when oxygen is metabolized by the brain. Both techniques record what the brain is doing in an ongoing manner, although fMRI is faster and completely noninvasive. Both are examples of _____ brain imaging.

36. *Electroencephalography (EEG)* has been used for many years as a method of recording overall or global brain activity (such as during sleep cycles). A newer and much more refined technique is *quantitative electroencephalography (QEEG)*, which can measure tiny voltage fluctuations in specific areas of the brain. Using electrodes placed on the scalp, both _____ and _____ _____ record brain activity; the latter records specific event-related potentials (ERPs) in response to stimuli.

37. In sum: With the aid of computers, structural brain imaging can be accomplished by _____ _____ and _____ _____ _____, functional brain imaging can be accomplished by _____ _____ _____ and _____ _____ _____ _____, overall brain electrical activity can be assessed by _____, and more specific brain electrical activity can be assessed by _____ _____.

computerized tomography, magnetic resonance imaging, positron emission tomography, functional magnetic resonance imaging, electroencephalography, quantitative electroencephalography

## The Brain's Functions, I: Experiencing the World

38. Most of the information picked up by our senses is eventually transmitted to the cerebral cortex, especially to a long strip known as the _____ _____.

somatosensory cortex

39. Information from the outside world is processed and organized in the lower parts of the brain before it reaches the cortex. A relay station for messages from the body to the cortex is the _____.

thalamus

40. Sensory information is also processed in the network of neural cells near the base of the brain called the *reticular activating system (RAS)*. Neural pathways from the senses to the cerebrum have side branches to an area near the base of the brain, which under a microscope appears to be a criss-crossed pattern of neural fibers known as the _____ _____ _____.

reticular activating system

41. Once the brain receives information from the _____ _____ _____, the *motor cortex* may instruct the muscles of the body to act.

reticular activating system

42. Initiating and controlling bodily movements is accomplished by the _____ _____, but the *cerebellum* plays an important part in coordinating the finely regulated muscular movements needed to use a computer keyboard or play a musical instrument.

motor cortex

43. People have great difficulty performing such coordinated muscle movements as walking or talking if they suffer damage to the brain structure called the _____.

cerebellum

44. Like the cerebrum, the cerebellum is divided into two lobes, or _____; these are connected by the _____.

hemispheres
pons

## The Brain's Functions, II: Overseeing Emotions and Survival

45. Of special importance in emotional life is the _____ _____, which makes up about one-fifth of the brain and controls anger and fear as well as sexual behavior.

limbic system

46. One part of the limbic system is the hippocampus, which is involved in memory. If the _____ indicates that a stimulus or situation is threatening, then the *amygdala* may come into play.

hippocampus

47. The part of the _____ _____ that is involved in intense emotions such as anger and fear is the _____.

limbic system
amygdala

48. The brain's most direct link to the body's glands—especially the *pituitary gland,* or "master gland"—is the _____.

hypothalamus

49. The organs secreting substances that help produce the "stirred up" bodily processes that accompany fear, anger, and other emotions are the _____ _____.

endocrine glands

50. The hypothalamus—in addition to playing a role in emotion in cooperation with other parts of the _____ system and the _____ _____— contributes to physical well-being by keeping the body in a state of *homeostasis,* or stability, with regard to bodily processes that sustain life.

limbic, endocrine glands

51. For example, the hypothalamus signals when the body needs oxygen, food, or water, thus contributing to the state of bodily stability or balance called _____.

homeostasis

52. In addition to signaling when the body has needs, the _____ acts like a thermostat, controlling bodily temperature.

hypothalamus

homeostasis

medulla

autonomic nervous system

autonomic nervous

hormones

ganglia

sympathetic
division, parasympathetic
division, endocrine

parasympathetic

sympathetic

parasympathetic division

hemisphere
hemisphere

hemisphere
system

cortex

association

53. Our physical well-being requires not only a state of _____ in nutrients and temperature, but also the steady performance of vital bodily processes such as breathing, heartbeat, and digestion.

54. Coordinating vital processes such as breathing and heartbeat is the responsibility of the _____.

55. In controlling bodily processes, the brain has a valuable assistant in the _____ _____ _____, which operates largely on its own, without much conscious control.

56. The autonomic nervous system can command the heart to beat faster or slower and the blood vessels to redirect the flow of blood toward the arms and legs when physical work is being done. The largely self-sufficient system called the _____ _____ system exercises considerable power over the body's *endocrine glands*, which also operate without much direct conscious control. These glands secrete into the bloodstream _____ that affect many bodily activities—including those associated with emotional behavior.

57. The autonomic nervous system exerts its impact on important bodily processes through a number of neural centers called _____, which are "small brains" composed of masses of connected neural cells packed together and distributed throughout the body.

58. There are two *divisions* of the autonomic nervous system: the _____ _____ and the _____ _____. Both are connected to the _____ glands and other organs.

59. The sympathetic division acts in various ways to prepare the body for emergency action, such as fighting or running away. The other part of the autonomic nervous system, the _____ division, seems to play its most important role when no danger threatens and the body can relax and go about the ordinary business of living.

60. Meeting emergency situations—by taking such steps as ordering the glands to pour powerful stimulants into the bloodstream and enlarging the blood vessels that carry oxygen to the heart and the muscles involved in body movement—is the function of the _____ division.

61. When no danger threatens and the body can relax, the autonomic nervous system's _____ _____ slows down the heart and encourages digestion by ordering the stomach to make wavelike motions and produce digestive acid.

62. The hemispheres of the brain perform different functions in cognition and language, but they have more basic functions in regulating emotion and the *immune system*. The frontal area of the right _____ is more active during negative emotional states; the frontal area of the left _____ more active during positive emotional states.

63. Greater activation of the left _____ has been found to be associated with a stronger response of the immune _____.

## The Brain's Functions, III: Managing Thought and Memory

64. The brain's function of sensing the world and taking action is performed largely by the specialized areas of the cerebral _____. These specialized areas make up about a quarter of the cortex; the remaining three-quarters, called the *association cortex*, is primarily responsible for our intellectual processes.

65. The ability to remember, think, plan for the future, and process information in ways that raise human beings far beyond the level of other organisms is controlled by unspecified areas that make up the _____ cortex.

66. The front portion of the _____ _____ includes the _____ _____, the areas apparently involved in solving problems, planning, and relating the past to the present.

**association cortex, frontal lobes**

67. A brain-damaged person who can remember his child's birthday but cannot plan the child's birthday party may have a disability in the _____ _____ of the _____ _____.

**frontal lobes**
**association cortex**

68. A brain structure that may be damaged in some people with amnesia who cannot form long-term memories is the _____.

**hippocampus**

69. The hippocampus appears to be essential for semantic memory and episodic memory, but not for procedural memory. A person with damage to the _____ might have difficulty with names, words, facts, ideas, and other kinds of _____ memories, plus personal experiences and other kinds of _____ memories, but not tying shoes, playing golf, or other kinds of _____ memories.

**hippocampus**
**semantic**
**episodic**
**procedural**

70. The _____ half of the cerebrum is dominant in most people; it controls language and the right side of the body. The _____ half of the cerebrum controls the left side of the body; it seems to specialize in interpreting form and space.

**left**
**right**

71. That is, the left hemisphere controls the right side of the body and _____, while the right hemisphere controls the left side of the body and the _____ of form and space.

**language**
**processing**

72. Although the two hemispheres have different responsibilities, most functions we perform use both sides of the brain. The two sides are very closely coordinated through numerous interconnections—especially through a cable called the *corpus callosum*, which connects the left and right hemispheres of the _____.

**cerebrum**

73. The master cable between the two halves of the cerebrum and its cortex is the _____ _____.

**corpus callosum**

## The Brain-Behavior Link

74. In addition to studying areas and specific functions of the brain, cognitive and behavior _____ also study the roles of various chemicals in brain functioning.

**neuroscientists**

75. Impulses are transmitted from one neuron to another with the help of chemical neurotransmitters. Four of these are *acetylcholine, glutamate, norepinephrine,* and *dopamine.* In addition to these _____, there are other essential chemicals known as *peptides.* Some act like neurotransmitters, but most are like hormones: They are released into the bloodstream and affect both parts of the nervous system and organs outside of it.

**neurotransmitters**

76. One of these _____ is *corticotropin-release factor (CRF).* Secreted by the hypothalamus, _____-_____ _____ leads to the production of *cortisol,* which helps in alleviating emotionally stressful events and pain.

**peptides**
**corticotropin-release factor**

77. Another group of _____ operating within the brain are similar in structure and effect to the powerful painkiller morphine. These biochemicals are called _____.

**neuropeptides**
**endorphins**

78. Just as biological factors affect behavior, psychological and environmental factors, in reciprocal fashion, affect biological functioning. An understanding of the reciprocal relationship among _____, _____, and _____ factors is necessary to a complete understanding of behavior.

**biological, psychological, environmental**

# Practice Test

_____ **1.** Within a neuron, an impulse travels from
   **a.** axon to dendrites.
   **b.** cell body to dendrites.
   **c.** dendrites to terminal branches.
   **d.** nucleus to cell body.

_____ **2.** The principal function of the myelin sheath is to
   **a.** make the neuron more sensitive.
   **b.** increase the strength of the neural impulse.
   **c.** protect the dendrites.
   **d.** increase the speed of the neural impulse.

_____ **3.** The all-or-none principle is that
   **a.** a neuron stimulates all the other neurons in the ganglion if it stimulates any one of them.
   **b.** a neuron will not fire unless all its receptor sites are stimulated.
   **c.** all neurotransmitters are secreted at the synapse.
   **d.** if a neuron fires at all, it fires as hard as it can.

_____ **4.** The part of the brain that does most of our remembering, thinking, and planning is the
   **a.** cerebral cortex.
   **b.** medulla.
   **c.** cerebellum.
   **d.** limbic system.

_____ **5.** The spinal cord is part of the
   **a.** peripheral nervous system.
   **b.** central nervous system.
   **c.** reticular activating system.
   **d.** parasympathetic system.

_____ **6.** The brain imaging method that provides ongoing images of brain activity and is the least invasive is
   **a.** computerized tomography (CT).
   **b.** magnetic resonance imaging (MRI).
   **c.** functional magnetic resonance imaging (fMRI).
   **d.** positron emission tomography (PET).

_____ **7.** The major relay station for sensory messages passed from the body to the cortex is the
   **a.** thalamus.
   **b.** hypothalamus.
   **c.** reticular activating system.
   **d.** corpus callosum.

_____ **8.** A sleeping animal can be awakened immediately by electrical stimulation applied to the
   **a.** hypothalamus.
   **b.** reticular activating system.
   **c.** limbic system.
   **d.** cerebellum.

_____ **9.** The brain structure that coordinates the finely regulated muscular movements of a musician is the
   **a.** sympathetic nervous system.
   **b.** limbic system.
   **c.** cerebellum.
   **d.** medulla.

_____ **10.** An adult whose hippocampus has been damaged might have trouble
   **a.** remembering childhood events.
   **b.** remembering a new telephone number.
   **c.** speaking clearly.
   **d.** walking in a straight line.

_____ **11.** As a child develops into an adult,
   **a.** the number of neurons increases dramatically.
   **b.** the number of neurotransmitters and peptides increases.
   **c.** experiences have less effect on the brain.
   **d.** the number of synapses decreases.

_____ **12.** The two hemispheres of the cerebrum communicate through the
   **a.** corpus callosum.
   **b.** hippocampus.
   **c.** pons.
   **d.** cerebellum.

_____ **13.** The left hemisphere is more skilled at
   **a.** seeing the forest, not the trees.
   **b.** interpreting speech and language.
   **c.** analyzing the melodies in a song.
   **d.** judging the symmetry in a photograph.

_____ **14.** The part of the brain chiefly responsible for emotion is the
   **a.** limbic system.
   **b.** reticular activating system.
   **c.** thalamus.
   **d.** hippocampus.

____15. The master gland is the
   a. thyroid.
   b. adrenal.
   c. endocrine.
   d. pituitary.

____16. Homeostasis refers to
   a. biochemical balance within the body.
   b. a stable relationship between the brain and the endocrine system.
   c. an equal dominance of right and left hemispheres.
   d. the ability to keep physical balance and to know up from down.

____17. Coordination of vital bodily processes, such as breathing, heartbeat, and digestion, takes place in the
   a. synapse.
   b. medulla.
   c. somatosensory cortex.
   d. frontal lobes.

____18. The part of the nervous system that plays its most important role during periods of quiet when there is no threat or need for unusual action is the
   a. sympathetic division.
   b. ganglia.
   c. parasympathetic division.
   d. autonomic nervous system.

____19. The parasympathetic and sympathetic divisions are part of the
   a. limbic system.
   b. central nervous system.
   c. peripheral nervous system.
   d. autonomic nervous system.

____20. Acetylcholine, glutamate, norepinephrine, and dopamine are all
   a. peptides.
   b. hormones.
   c. endorphins.
   d. neurotransmitters.

## Exercises

1. Trace the path of a neural impulse from its initiation in a single neuron through its transmission to another neuron. Specify the parts of the neuron and their functions, consider the role of chemicals in the process, and indicate what factors influence the speed or course of the impulse.

2. Consider a person who is driving to work in the morning. The driver is relaxed and perhaps daydreaming while on an open and fairly clear stretch of freeway. Then the driver reaches the city, exits the freeway, and has to deal with traffic. At one point, the driver is startled by the horn and screeching tires of another car in a near miss, but then the driver gradually settles down again. At another point, the driver just makes it through an intersection as the light changes from amber to red. Then, suddenly noticing flashing lights in the rearview mirror, the driver becomes aroused again, pulls over, and stops. Now the driver also becomes nauseated as a police officer approaches with ticket book and pencil in hand. Eventually the driver makes it to work, but remains rattled and unable to concentrate for the first couple of hours.

Discuss the actions of this person in terms of what you know about the nervous system. Be specific about which structures may have played a part in each action and in what way.

✳ For quizzing, activities, exercises, and web links, check out the book-specific website at http://www.psychology.wadsworth. com/kagan9e.

# 3 Sensing and Perceiving

All around us in our daily lives is a wealth of information that is vital to our well-being. Effortlessly, we experience constant interaction between the information coming to us from the environment and our reactions to it. It is a process that we take completely for granted. The information-gathering structures of the nervous system are, in their own way, as remarkable as the brain itself.

Our senses are our windows on the world. In studying **sensation,** we are exploring the process by which the sense organs *transduce,* or translate, stimulation from the environment (or from within the body). The way in which the sense organs send their information to the brain for further processing is another of the marvels of the nervous system.

Somehow, we automatically make sense of the ever-shifting stimulation the world provides to our sense organs. As illustrated in Figure 3.1, much of the time our central nervous system (CNS) allows us to extract the precise information that is important to us without any conscious effort on our part. We know almost instantaneously what it all means. The key to this remarkable accomplishment is

**Sensation**
The process by which sense organs transduce stimulation from the environment.

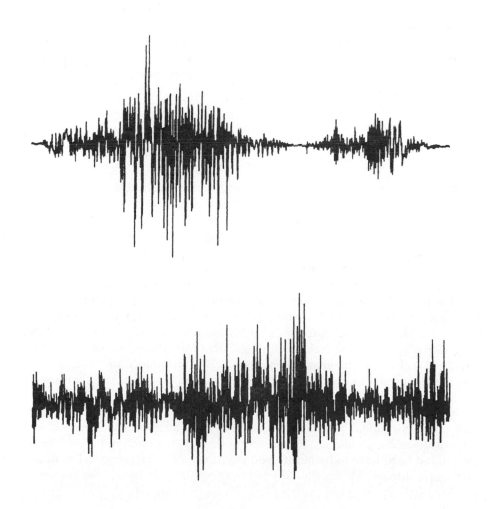

FIGURE 3.1 Making out a word in a din of conversation. Both sound waves shown here depict the actual sound pressure generated by a person saying the word "science." The top figure resulted when the person spoke the word in the stillness of a soundproof chamber. The bottom figure resulted when the person's voice was masked by noise that simulated a roomful of people talking. Neither the human eye nor any computer can detect the top wave form embedded in the bottom one; neither can extract the sound waves made by saying "science" from the jumble of additional waves made by the noise. But, amazingly, a normal listener has no trouble at all hearing and understanding the word in spite of the accompanying noise.

**Perception**
The process by which we select, organize, and interpret information from our senses.

**perception,** the process through which we become aware of our environment by selecting, organizing, and interpreting information from our senses.

First we consider some general principles of sensation. Then we look at both sensory and perceptual processes for each of the senses. The remainder of the chapter focuses on general principles of perception, including the extent to which it is innate or learned, what factors are involved in what we attend to, and how perceptions are organized and interpreted.

# HOW OUR SENSES FUNCTION: SOME GENERAL PRINCIPLES

**FOCUS QUESTIONS**

- What do all our senses have in common?
- How are thresholds in sensation measured?
- How does sensory adaptation work?

**Receptor**
A sensory neuron that responds to specific stimuli such as light waves, sound waves, or chemicals.

Our sense organs obviously vary in the sensations they produce, but they all work according to a few basic principles. They have to be activated by a stimulus—the particular form of energy that the sense organ is designed to detect. Take vision, for example. The visual stimuli you are experiencing at this moment are the light waves reflected off this book. Sense organs have **receptors,** neural structures that are capable of responding to specific kinds of stimuli. When you read, the process begins with the light-sensitive receptors in your eyes. When you hear, the receptors are sound wave–sensitive cells in your ears, and when you taste and smell, they are chemical-sensitive cells on your tongue and in your nasal tract.

When receptor cells for vision are activated by light stimuli, they set off bursts of neural impulses that are routed to the visual areas of the cerebral cortex of the occipital lobes. There, they are deciphered into our conscious sensation of vision. The same basic process—with different stimuli, receptors, and translation—applies to all the other senses.

## Thresholds for Sensory Experience

**Absolute threshold**
The minimum amount of stimulus energy to which a receptor can respond. It is traditionally defined as the energy level at which a participant can detect a stimulus 50% of the time.

All of the senses are activated only by an appropriate stimulus that is at or above their **absolute threshold,** defined as the minimum amount of energy to which a receptor can respond. Stimuli that are too weak have no effect and therefore go unnoticed. If someone were to test your hearing by noting how far away you could be from a watch and still follow its ticking, he or she would be making a rough assessment of your absolute threshold of hearing.

Much more precise measurements are used in scientific studies of the relationship between physical stimuli and sensations. These show that stimuli of borderline intensity are sometimes detected and sometimes missed. As illustrated in Figure 3.2, the absolute threshold is traditionally defined as the energy level at which a participant can detect a stimulus 50% of the time. However, the absolute threshold will vary somewhat depending on the conditions under which the stimulus is presented. For example, background noise may affect whether a sound is detected.

**Difference threshold**
The smallest change in the intensity of a stimulus that can be detected; the JND.

The senses also have a threshold for the ability to discriminate between two stimuli that are similar but not identical in strength. Suppose you see a flash of light that is followed immediately by a different flash. How much more intense would the second light have to be before you could notice a difference? The answer is 1.6% more intense. This is the **difference threshold** for light, also known as the

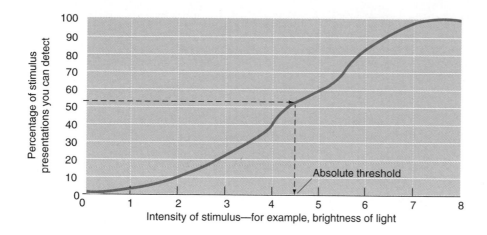

**FIGURE 3.2 Estimating the absolute threshold. As this figure indicates, the absolute threshold is actually not absolutely fixed. At times, you may be able to detect a stimulus of a given intensity; at other times, you may not. Your absolute threshold is the intensity required for you to make out the stimulus—in this case, a light—50% of the time.**

*just noticeable difference (JND)*. For sound, the difference threshold is about 10%, with slight variations for high- versus low-pitched sounds.

The rule that the difference threshold is a fixed percentage of the original stimulus is called *Weber's law*, in honor of the physiologist who discovered it more than a century ago. The law holds over a large part of the range of stimulation. In practical terms, it means this: The more intense the sensory stimulation to which the human organism is subjected, the greater the increase in intensity required to produce a recognizable difference. In a room where there is no sound except perhaps the soft buzz of a mosquito, you can hear a pin drop. On a noisy city street, you can hear the loud honk of an automobile horn but may be completely unaware of a friend's shouts to you from down the block.

## Sensory Adaptation

When you undress at the end of the day, you may notice marks on your skin caused by a wristwatch, belt, or elastic band in your clothing. These areas of skin have been subjected to a considerable amount of pressure all day. Why didn't you feel it?

The answer is **sensory adaptation**, which means that after a time your senses adjust to a stimulus—they become accustomed to it, so to speak—and the sensation produced by the stimulus tends to disappear. If you hold saltwater or a bitter fluid in your mouth for a while, the taste goes away. The strong smell that greets you when you enter a fish market goes away, although it may take a while. Your eyes may strike you as an exception, because your vision never goes blank no matter how long you stare at an object, but this is only because the eyes are never actually still. The muscles controlling the eyeballs produce tiny, spontaneous movements at the rate of up to 100 per minute, which means that light waves never stimulate the same receptor cells for long. When researchers attach a miniature slide projector to the eyeball, casting a continuous image on the same receptor cells despite the eye's movements, the image quickly fades from sight (Pritchard, 1961).

All the senses demonstrate adaptation in one way or another, unless the stimuli are too intense (such as blinding light, a deafening roar, or something that causes severe pain). In practical terms, the principle of adaptation means that our sensory equipment is built to inform us of changes in the environment—exactly the kind of information that is most valuable. Sensory adaptation is essential in allowing us to focus our attention. You would find it quite difficult to concentrate on what you were reading if you were aware of the many pressures your body was experiencing from your clothing, jewelry, chair, and so on.

### Test Yourself

**(b)** You are walking across a parking lot toward a restaurant where you plan to have dinner. At some point, you suddenly experience the smell of food. In psychological terms, what is that point called?

**(c)** A friend in an adjoining room says, "Please turn the music up a little louder." You boost the volume and announce that you did so. But a few minutes later, your friend enters your room to complain, saying "If you turned it up, it wasn't even a JND." What is your friend trying to tell you?

**(d)** You have been driving on the highway for a long time and are so lulled by the constant hum of traffic that you no longer hear it. Suddenly you hear the loud rumble of a truck behind you, and you are immediately alert. In terms of sensation, what state have you just left?

(The answers are on page 125.)

**Sensory adaptation**
**The tendency of sensory receptors to stop responding to a continuing stimulus.**

# THE POWER OF VISION

**FOCUS QUESTIONS**

- What attributes of light define color?

- How do our eyes work?

- How do we perceive color?

Perhaps the most remarkable thing about our eyes is the vast number of sensations and perceptions they can produce. You can concentrate your vision on a single black word on a white page of this book—or look out the window and see an entire landscape full of objects in what seems to be an infinite variety of shadings and colors. You can see a whole range of brightness, from pure white through various grays to jet black, plus all the colors of the rainbow, in hues from vivid blue to muddy red. It is estimated that our eyes are capable of distinguishing among 350,000 JNDs in color and brightness.

## Light: The Visual Stimulus

The stimuli for vision are light waves, which are pulsations of electromagnetic energy. Light has three qualities that determine the sensations and perceptions it produces:

**Hue**
The color we perceive.

**Brightness**
A characteristic of light determined by the intensity of the stimuli.

**Saturation**
The purity of a color.

1. *Wavelength,* the distance between the peaks of the waves, determines **hue**—the scientific term for the color we see. White light is a mixture of all the hues.

2. *Intensity* or *amplitude,* the amount of energy in the light wave, mostly determines **brightness.** The same intensity of light ordinarily produces greater brightness at the yellow and green wavelengths.

3. *Complexity,* the extent to which the predominant wavelength is mixed with other wavelengths, determines **saturation.** The purer the wavelength, the greater the saturation and the more vivid the hue. When other wavelengths are mixed in, we see a hue that might be described as duller or less vivid. A pure or saturated red is strikingly colorful. If other wavelengths are added and the saturation is reduced, what we see is "less red."

Light-wave energy can travel over long distances—as when light from a star reaches us across the vast expanse of space. Light waves travel at 186,000 miles per second (300,000 kps), the fastest speed known. This is such a great velocity that a light wave, if you could somehow manage to reflect it around the world, would make the journey and get back to you in less than one-seventh of a second.

In the broad range of wavelengths of electromagnetic energy in all its forms, light occupies only a very small niche. The range of waves that we can see is a *continuous* one, from about 380 nanometers (billionths of a meter; nm) to about 780 nm. That is, we can perceive color when we sense any wavelength in this range. The shortest waves, which are seen as violet, are just a little longer than the invisible ultraviolet rays that cause sunburn. The longest, which are seen as red, are just a little shorter than the invisible infrared waves produced by a heating lamp.

## The Structures of the Eye and How They Work

**Iris**
The circular arrangement of smooth muscles that contract and expand to make the pupil smaller in bright light and larger in dim light.

If you are familiar with cameras—especially those that must be manually set and focused before the shutter is snapped—you should feel right at home with the diagram of the eyeball in Figure 3.3. The cornea acts as a sort of preliminary lens, gathering light waves from a much wider field of vision than would be possible if the eyeball merely had a perfectly flat window at the front. Then the **iris** serves the same purpose as the diaphragm in a camera. (It is also what we are referring to

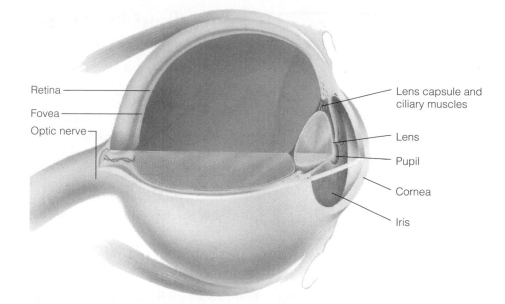

Retina

Fovea

Optic nerve

Lens capsule and ciliary muscles

Lens

Pupil

Cornea

Iris

**FIGURE 3.3 The structure of the eye.** Light waves first strike the cornea, a transparent bulge in the outer layer of the eyeball. The light waves then pass through the pupil, which is an opening in the iris. Behind the pupil lies the transparent lens, the shape of which is controlled by the ciliary muscles. The lens focuses the light rays on the retina, which contains the light-sensitive receptors of the eye. The receptors are most tightly packed in the fovea, where visual acuity is the greatest. Messages from the receptors are transmitted to the brain by way of the optic nerve, which exits from the back of the eyeball, a little off center.
*Bloom & Fawcett, 1968.*

when we talk about someone's eye color.) When the smooth muscles of the iris are fully expanded, as they are under dim conditions, the **pupil**—the small opening in the center of the iris—admits about 17 times as much light as when the iris muscles are fully contracted. (When you look at your eyes in a mirror, the pupil is the dark, almost-black circle at the center.) The **lens** of the eye serves the same purpose as the lens of a camera, but in a way that would not be possible with even the most carefully designed piece of glass. The lens of a camera has to be moved forward and backward to focus on nearby or faraway objects. The lens of the eye remains stationary but changes shape. The action of the *ciliary muscles* makes the lens thinner to bring faraway objects into focus and makes it thicker to focus on nearby objects. If you get eye strain and symptoms such as headaches and blurred vision from working at a computer all day, fatigue of the ciliary muscles is partly responsible—especially if you continually change viewing distances from the screen to papers or books and back again (Tapley, Weiss, & Morris, 1985). Finally, sharp images created by the lens are cast on the **retina,** the eye's equivalent of film or the electronic "photosites" of a digital camera.

The receptor cells in the retina trigger neural impulses that leave the eyeball by way of the **optic nerve.** At the point where this thick cable of neurons exits, there is a "blind spot" that contains no receptors. We ordinarily don't notice this gap because it is not in our visual field, but you can experience it by examining Figure 3.4. Also attached to the eyeball are muscles that enable us to look up, down, and sideways. The space inside the eyeball is filled with a transparent substance, as is the space between the cornea and the iris.

The optic nerve terminates in the thalamus, which serves as a relay station for visual stimuli. Neurons in the thalamus send the information on to the visual cortex. This visual pathway is portrayed in Figure 3.5.

**Pupil**
The opening in the iris that admits light waves into the eye.

**Lens**
The transparent structure of the eye that changes shape to focus images on the retina.

**Retina**
Tissue at the back of the eyeball containing the rods and cones that are the receptors for vision.

**Optic nerve**
The bundle of neurons that constitutes the visual pathway from the eye to the brain.

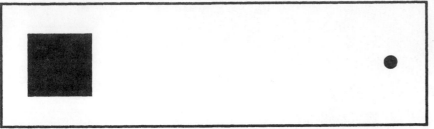

FIGURE 3.4   A demonstration of the blind spot. Hold this book at arm's length, close your right eye, and look at the circle on the right. Now move the book slowly closer. When the image of the square at the left falls on the blind spot of your left eye, it will disappear. To demonstrate the blind spot of the right eye, repeat with the book held upside down and your left eye closed; concentrate your gaze on the circle at the left.

## The Visual Receptors— in Good Light and Bad

Each retina, if flattened out, would be an irregular ellipse with a total area of just about three-fourths of a square inch (slightly under 5 cm$^2$). Packed into this small area are well over 100 million receptors of the kind shown in Figure 3.6. The great majority of the receptors are long and narrow **rods**; the rest, numbering about 5 million, are somewhat thicker and tapered **cones** (Torre, Ashmore, Lamb, & Menini, 1995).

Both rods and cones respond to different intensities of light. The rods function chiefly under conditions of low illumination, sending information to the brain about movement and about whites, grays, and blacks, but not about color. Our eyes are so sensitive that on a clear, black night they can spot a candle flame many miles away. The cones function in strong illumination, providing sensations not only of movement and brightness from white to black but also of hue, or color.

The cones are most numerous toward the middle of the retina. The area near the center of the retina, called the **fovea**, contains only cones (about 100,000). The cones are packed together more tightly in the fovea than anywhere else, so this is where our vision is sharpest. When we read or do anything else that requires a very sharp image, we keep the object in the center of our field of vision so that its light waves strike the fovea.

How light waves stimulate the receptors of the retina was discovered many years ago when physiologists managed to extract a substance called **rhodopsin**

**Rods**
The receptors that function primarily under low illumination.

**Cones**
The receptors for colors.

**Fovea**
The part of the retina that contains only cones and produces the greatest visual acuity.

**Rhodopsin**
A light-sensitive substance associated with the visual receptors and dark adaptation.

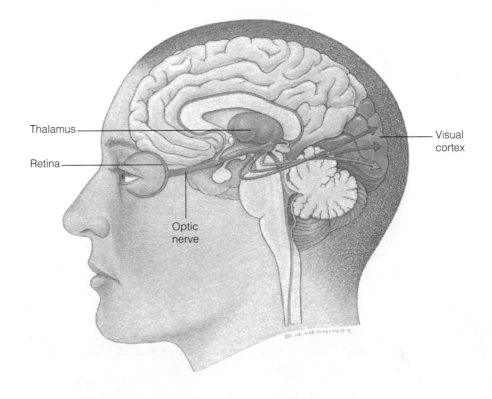

FIGURE 3.5 The neural pathway for vision. Light travels from the retina of the eye to the optic nerve and via the optic nerve to the thalamus, from which it is relayed to the visual cortex.

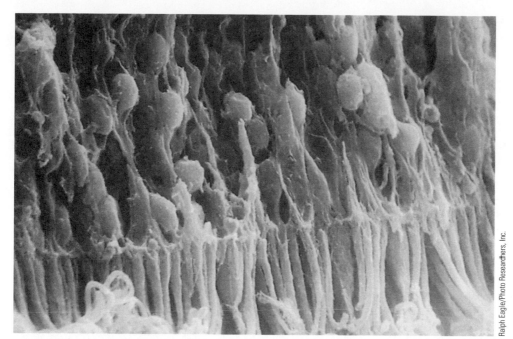

FIGURE 3.6 The retina's receptor cells. The shapes that give the names to the eye's light-sensitive rods and cones can be seen clearly in this photograph of the retina, magnified about 45,000 times.

Ralph Eagle/Photo Researchers, Inc.

from the rods. Rhodopsin is a pigment that absorbs light. The intensity and wavelength of the light determine the rate at which it bleaches the rhodopsin. Thus, light waves striking the retina produce chemical changes in the rhodopsin, and these changes act to stimulate the neurons that are next in the pathway carrying messages from the receptors to the brain (Wald, 1951).

The cones contain certain pigments that operate in much the same way, except that there are three different types. The first is most sensitive to blue wavelengths, the second to green, and the third to waves in the red portion of the spectrum. However, all three types are broadly tuned, and their pigments respond to some degree to many wavelengths.

One of the most valuable aspects of our visual equipment is its ability to function under an extremely wide range of illumination. Note what happens when you walk through bright afternoon sunlight into a movie theater where there is only dim background lighting. At first, the theater seems pitch-black, and you can hardly find your way down the aisle to an empty seat. But after a while, your eyes undergo what is called *dark adaptation*, and you can clearly see the aisle, the seats, and the people around you.

Dark adaptation depends mostly on the rods, although the cones adapt as well. Rhodopsin builds up to high levels when it goes unbleached by strong light for a time. Full adaptation to dark takes about 30 minutes, by which time the eyes are about 100,000 times more sensitive to light than they were in the bright sunlight. Note that you do not see colors in the objects around you in a dimly lit place such as a movie theater—you see only shades of gray. This is because the color-sensitive cones cannot function at low intensities of light. However, you do see full color on the screen by virtue of the cones—attesting to the dual functioning of the retina's receptors.

## Seeing in Full Color

Color does not actually exist in objects themselves. Instead, it is a psychological phenomenon—an aspect of sensory/perceptual experience that is created when the brain processes the wavelengths contained in light.

The three types of cones, each responding in its own way to different wavelengths, permit us to distinguish the hues of the rainbow. But this ability also depends on the coding that takes place in the complex pathway of neurons leading from the eye to the visual cortex by way of several switching points, including a major relay station in the thalamus.

The pathway begins with neurons in the retina that make contact with one or more receptor cells and are stimulated to a greater or lesser degree by the chemical activity of the receptors. In turn, these neurons stimulate the neurons of the optic nerve, which send their impulses to the thalamus. There appear to be four kinds of cells responsible for color vision in the thalamus, each of which behaves in a different way in response to the messages it receives.

One type of nerve cell fires a rapid burst of impulses in response to messages indicating a blue stimulus but is turned off by a yellow stimulus. Another does just the opposite—it shows a high rate of activity in response to yellow and is turned off by blue. The third type is activated by red and slowed by green; the fourth type is activated by green and slowed by red. There are also two other types of neurons that appear to be responsible for black-and-white sensations and brightness. One is turned on by white or bright stimuli and turned off by black or dark stimuli. The other works in the opposite fashion: on for dark and off for bright (De Valois & Jacobs, 1968).

This explanation is known as the *opponent-process theory of color vision*. Its basic elements have been understood since the 19th century (see Lennie, 2000). A visual stimulus sets up a pattern of chemical response in the rods and the three kinds of cones in the retina. This pattern, in turn, stimulates the neurons of the visual system to engage in their pattern of neural activity, with the six opponent-process cells for blue-yellow, red-green, and bright-dark all behaving in different ways. It is this pattern of neural impulses arriving at the visual centers of the brain that determines what we see.

## Color Blindness

**Color blindness**
**Inability to discriminate all or certain specific colors.**

Some people are deficient in the ability to discriminate colors. A small proportion of people never experience the sensation of hue at all; they are totally **color blind** and see the world only in shades of gray, like a black-and-white photograph. The rest are partially color blind. The most common difficulty is distinguishing reds and greens. Less common is reduced sensitivity to blues and yellows.

Most color-blind people are male, because the disorder is caused by a gene on the 23rd chromosome pair (Hubel, 1988; Pasternack, 1999). As discussed in Chapter 10, genes exist in matched pairs except on the 23rd, or "sex," chromosomes, where in males one of the chromosomes is much smaller and doesn't contain nearly as many genes. Males have no gene on that chromosome to offset color blindness if the gene for it occurs on the other chromosome. In the U.S. population, over 8% of males are at least partly color blind, whereas less than 1% of females are (Adams, Hendershot, & Marano, 1999). The same data also indicate ethnic differences, which are probably attributable to differences in overall gene pools for those who identify themselves as black or white: Just over 1% of blacks are at least partly color blind, compared to almost 5% of whites.

People who are color blind do not necessarily realize it. One reason is that light waves reaching the eye are seldom a fully saturated single wavelength. Both blue and yellow paints, for example, reflect some green. Most red objects reflect some yellow, and most green objects some blue. (Traffic lights are deliberately designed with some yellow in the red and some blue in the green, to help people who have difficulty distinguishing red and green.) Color-blind people learn to use subtle dif-

### Test Yourself

**(e)** If the ciliary muscles of a person's eye were suddenly to become totally rigid, what would be the result for the person's vision?

**(f)** In a discussion of vision, someone tells you that if forced to choose, she would rather do without rods than without cones. What might that indicate to you concerning the individual's feelings about color?

(The answers are on page 125.)

ferences in saturation—as well as brightness and other cues—to recognize and name hues that they never see the way a person with normal vision does. Their deficiencies can be readily detected, however, with tests that are useful in steering people away from jobs in which color blindness would be a disability (or, as in the case of flying an airplane, a hazard).

# THE POWER OF HEARING

Our hearing is just as versatile as our vision. We can distinguish tones ranging from the lowest notes of a subwoofer to the highest notes of a shrill whistle, changing in loudness from the merest hint of a whisper to the most deafening clap of thunder, and taking such diverse and varied forms as the tick of a watch, a human voice, and the blended richness of a hundred instruments in a symphony orchestra. Our world contains many kinds of sound stimuli—and our ears, like our eyes, have a remarkable ability to sense all these stimuli in ways that allow us to tell them apart.

> **FOCUS QUESTIONS**
>
> • What attributes of sound waves define sound?
>
> • How do our ears work?
>
> • How do we perceive sound?

## How Is Sound Made?

The stimulus for hearing is sound waves, traveling unseen through the atmosphere. The waves are little ripples of contraction and expansion of the air. They have three qualities that determine the sensations they produce:

1. *Frequency,* or the number of sound waves per second, determines **pitch.** The lowest note on a piano measures about 27 Hertz (Hz). (Hertz is the scientific term for the number of cycles of contraction and expansion per second.) The highest is around 4,200 Hz. Our full range of hearing extends from about 20 to 20,000 Hz, which is the frequency range covered by a good sound system.

2. *Amplitude,* or the strength of the wave, largely determines the degree of **loudness** we hear. However, our hearing is most sensitive to frequencies between about 400 and 3,000 Hz, a range that corresponds to the range of the human voice and is therefore likely a result of evolution. Higher or lower frequencies don't sound as loud, even when they have exactly the same amplitude. A wave of 1,000 Hz sounds louder than one of 10,000 Hz, which in turn sounds louder than one of 100 Hz, because we are least sensitive to sounds at the extremes—especially the low end of our range. The ways in which waves vary in amplitude and frequency are illustrated in Figure 3.7.

3. *Complexity* determines **timbre,** which is the quality that distinguishes a middle C on the piano from the same note on a clarinet or guitar. Complexity occurs because virtually all sources of sound produce not just a single frequency but others as well. For example, while the middle C piano string is vibrating at 256 Hz, sections of the string are vibrating at higher frequencies, though with lower amplitude. Each half vibrates at 512 Hz, twice the basic frequency; each third at 768 Hz; and so on. All the various frequencies combine into a complex sound wave such as the one illustrated in Figure 3.8, which produces the sensation of a middle C with the timbre characteristic of its source. One of the hallmarks of a fine piano, violin, or other stringed instrument is the blend it produces.

**Pitch**
A characteristic of sound determined by the frequency of incoming waves.

**Loudness**
A characteristic of sound determined by the amplitude of incoming waves.

**Timbre**
A characteristic of sound determined by the complexity of incoming waves.

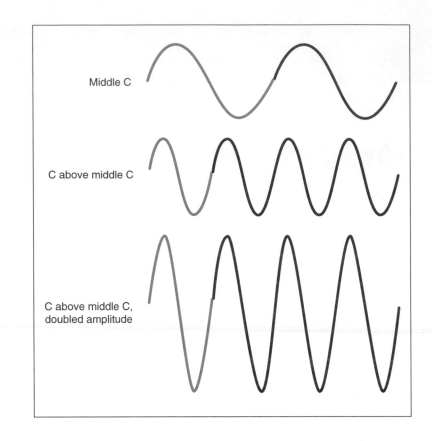

**FIGURE 3.7 Sound waves: frequency and amplitude.** The wave at the top, for the pure tone of middle C, has a frequency of 256 Hz. The wave in the middle, for the C above middle C, has twice as many cycles of contraction and expansion per second, or 512 Hz. Sounding this same note with twice the force produces the wave at the bottom, which has a frequency of 512 Hz but double the amplitude, as indicated by the height of the wave. The colored portions of the wave (to the left) show a single cycle of contraction and expansion.

Middle C

C above middle C

C above middle C, doubled amplitude

**FIGURE 3.8 A pattern of complexity and timbre.** The waves that usually reach our ears are much more complex than the "pure" waves shown in Figure 3.7. The note shown here comes from a violin. It maintains a basic frequency that produces our sensation of pitch, but each cycle of contraction and expansion is modified by overtones that change the pattern of the wave and result in our sensation of the violin's own special timbre.

**Outer ear**
The visible portion of the ear that collects sound waves and directs them to the hearing mechanisms.

**Eardrum**
The membrane between the outer ear and the middle ear.

**Middle ear**
An air-filled cavity containing three small bones that conduct vibrations.

# The Ear and Its Hearing Receptors

What we call the ear—the flap of tissue on each side of the head—is in fact the least important part of our hearing equipment. The working parts, including the receptors, lie hidden inside the skull.

The structure of the ear is shown in Figure 3.9. The **outer ear**—the visible part—merely collects the sound waves. The waves create vibrations of the **eardrum** that are passed along through the **middle ear,** an air-filled cavity containing three small bones that conduct vibrations. The last of these bones, called the *stapes,* is mounted like a piston on the *cochlea*—a bony structure about the size of a pea and shaped like a snail's shell. It is the cochlea, receiving the vibrations transmitted by the stapes, that contains the **inner ear's** receptors for hearing.

The cochlea is filled with fluid. Stretched across it and dividing it more or less in half is a piece of tissue called the *basilar membrane.* When the vibrations of sound reach the cochlea, they set up motions of the fluid inside, thus bending the basilar membrane. Lying on the membrane is the *organ of Corti,* a collection of hair cells that are the receptors for hearing.

## How the Hearing Receptors Work

With over a million working parts, our auditory receptor organ, the cochlea, has been described as "the most complex mechanical apparatus in the human body"

## PSYCHOLOGY IN THE LAB AND IN LIFE

# Loud Noises

Arlene Bronzaft, a psychologist, found that exposing children to chronic noise "amplifies aggression and tends to dampen healthful behavior." In a study of the reading levels of pupils in grades 2–6 at an elementary school in Manhattan, she showed that, by their sixth year, children assigned to classrooms on the side of the building facing the elevated train tracks were 11 months behind children in classrooms on the quieter side of the building. After the New York City Transit Authority installed noise abatement equipment on the tracks, a follow-up study showed no difference in the two groups. Yet 11-month retardation in the course of only four years of school can be disastrous. A child would have to struggle hard to catch up.

In addition to disrupting learning, it is worth emphasizing that regular exposure to extreme loudness can cause permanent damage to the hearing apparatus—as when young people attend ear-shattering concerts or "crank up" the volume in high-powered car sound systems. The damage caused by such levels of sound may not be immediately apparent but will almost certainly show up in the form of hearing difficulties in later adulthood.

*Primary source: Ackerman, 1990.*

(Hudspeth, 1985). Sound waves cause the entire basilar membrane to respond to wavelike, up-and-down motions that travel along its length and breadth, in turn activating the hearing receptors resting on the membrane. The unique feature of these receptor cells is a bundle of protruding hairs. When the floor beneath the receptors moves, the hairs move and bend like tiny dancers. This stimulates the neurons of the **auditory nerve,** to which the receptors are connected, producing the neural impulses that are routed to the thalamus and eventually to the auditory areas of the cerebral cortex of the temporal lobes. The potential impact of loud, irritating sounds in the environment is the subject of Psychology in the Lab and in Life (above).

Figure 3.10 illustrates how the basilar membrane operates. The code of neural impulses in which hearing messages eventually reach the cerebral cortex depends

**Inner ear**
The part of the ear that contains the cochlea, vestibule, and semicircular canals.

**Auditory nerve**
The auditory pathway from the ear to the brain.

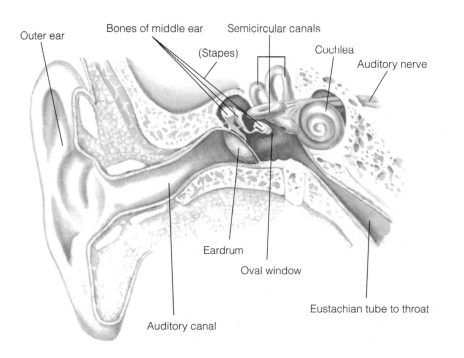

**FIGURE 3.9 A diagram of the hearing apparatus.** Sound waves enter the outer ear, pass through the auditory canal, and set up vibrations of the eardrum. The three bones of the middle ear transmit the vibrations to the cochlea through its oval window. The auditory nerve carries messages from the hearing receptors inside the cochlea to the brain. The eustachian tube, traveling from middle ear to throat, keeps the air pressure inside the middle ear at the same level as outside. The semicircular canals play no part in hearing but are responsible for our sense of equilibrium.

FIGURE 3.10 Waves of sound along the basilar membrane. The basilar membrane, shown in the top part of the figure, is narrowest and stiffest along its base, where vibrations caused by the sound waves first enter the cochlea, at its oval window. The membrane then becomes progressively wider and more flexible toward its other end, or apex. As the lower part of the figure shows, the narrower portions of the membrane—and the receptor cells at those points—move most vigorously in response to high-frequency sound waves, and the wider portions in response to low frequencies. Loudness is represented on the basilar membrane by the size and expansiveness of the waves.

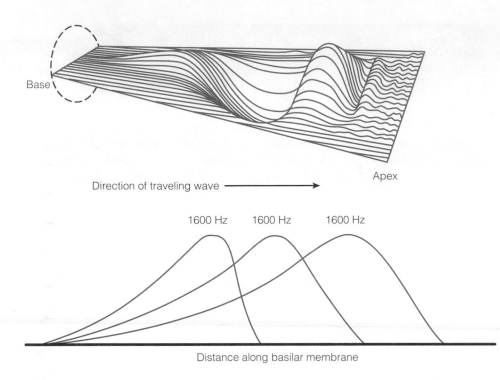

Base

Direction of traveling wave ⟶

Apex

1600 Hz    1600 Hz    1600 Hz

Distance along basilar membrane

in part on which receptors at which locations along the membrane are stimulated. The code in which hearing messages reach the cerebral cortex—and are translated into sensations of pitch, loudness, and timbre—also depends on the number of receptors stimulated, the rate at which each sets off neural impulses, and especially the entire pattern of the impulses. In fact, for very low frequencies (those below about 400 Hz) the code doesn't seem to depend at all on the exact location of the receptor, because these frequencies make the basilar membrane move as a unit.

## Determining Where Sounds Come From

If you hear an automobile pass by, you can tell at once which way it's going. The sound waves and the manner in which they stimulate your hearing receptors tell you where they come from and in what direction they are moving. The ability to determine location depends on slightly different sound waves reaching the two ears. A sound wave from the left arrives at the left ear a tiny fraction of a second before it strikes the right ear, and in a slightly earlier phase of its cycle of contraction and expansion. By the time the sound wave reaches the right ear, it has slightly less amplitude because it has traveled farther. And, because high frequencies are more likely than low ones to be absorbed by any object that gets in the path of sound waves, the pattern of overtones is altered by contact with the head, thus slightly changing the timbre.

The structure of the outer ear also plays a role. Its intricate shape bounces sound waves around, much as the walls and furniture in a room affect music being played. The two outer ears, receiving waves from different directions, reflect them toward the eardrum differently. Thus, for a number of reasons the receptors in the two ears produce slightly different patterns of neural impulses, which the brain can usually decode in order to make an instant judgment about the location of the sound. We are probably less skillful at locating sounds than are species that have movable outer ears—like dogs and horses, which prick up their ears when they are curious about a noise—but we manage well enough.

**Test Yourself**

(g) In older people, the bones in the middle ear harden and become less flexible. Why would this impair hearing?

(The answer is on page 125.)

# TASTE, SMELL, TOUCH, AND THE TWO UNNOTICED SENSES

It is commonly assumed that we are endowed with five senses: vision, hearing, taste, smell, and touch. These traditional five senses are our sole sources of inputs from the outside world, but we have two other senses—bodily movement and equilibrium—that provide us with essential information about our own bodies. Without these two senses, we would find it difficult to walk or even keep from falling down, and impossible to play sports or manipulate a computer keyboard. All seven senses are important to our ongoing existence, and life can be a great deal more difficult for people with disabilities involving any of them

> **FOCUS QUESTIONS**
> - What stimuli are involved in taste, smell, and touch?
> - How do our taste, smell, and touch senses work?
> - What senses help regulate our body movement and maintain balance and how do they work?

## Taste and Its Many Inputs

Although we can recognize a great variety of foods and be either delighted or disgusted by them, taste is probably the least efficient of our senses. The flavor of food actually depends to only a small extent on our taste receptors. Much of the sensation is produced by other factors—warmth, cold, the consistency of the food, the mild pain caused by certain spices, and, above all, smell.

The taste receptors are more or less out in the open. If you examine your tongue in a mirror, you will see that it's covered with little bumps, some tiny, others a bit larger. Similar bumps are also found at the back of the mouth and in the throat. Inside each of the bumps are **taste buds,** the receptors for the sense of taste. Your tongue contains about 10,000 taste buds, and each taste bud contains about 20 receptors that are sensitive to chemical stimulation by food molecules. Food dissolved in saliva spreads over the tongue, enters small pores in the surface of the bumps, and sets off reactions in the receptors. These reactions trigger activity in adjacent neurons, which fire off neural impulses to the brain.

The taste receptors respond to many kinds of chemical stimulation, but they respond most vigorously to four basic taste qualities: sweet, salty, sour, and bitter. The receptors are present and functional at birth—even newborn infants can discriminate the four basic tastes.

**Taste buds**
The receptors for the sense of taste.

## Smell and Its Powers

Just as newborns are prepared to detect differences in taste, they are also prepared to detect subtle differences in smell—apparently as a result of evolution (Porter & Winberg, 1999). Mother's milk historically was the sole source of nutrition for newborns, so being able to locate the mother's breast would have had high survival value. Newborns can do just that: Within minutes after birth, they respond to breast odors, and they soon learn to discriminate their own mother's breast odors from those of other lactating women.

As shown in Figure 3.11, the receptors for the sense of smell lie at the very top of the nasal passages leading from the nostrils to the throat. As we breathe normally, the flow of air from nostrils to throat takes a direct path, but a certain amount rises gently to the top of the nasal passage. There, it encounters the **olfactory epithelium,** which contains the receptor cells for smell. Sensitivity to odors depends largely on the total number of receptors. Animals that have more receptors have keener senses of smell. Humans, who are at the lower end of the scale of smell

**Olfactory epithelium**
The part of the nasal passage that contains receptor cells for smell.

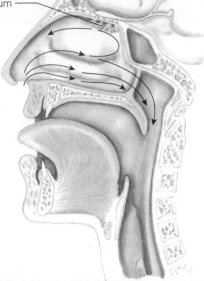

Receptors in the olfactory epithelium

**FIGURE 3.11 The nose and its smell receptors.** This cross section of the human head shows the position of the sensory receptors for smell. An odor, an assortment of molecules floating in air, goes in the nose and makes its way (see arrow) to the very top of the nasal passages, where it meets a collection of nerve cells making up the olfactory epithelium, which has direct connections to the brain. The odor is converted into neural signals matching the molecules being smelled, and these signals are transmitted to the brain.

**Odorants**
Chemical molecules that stimulate the receptor cells for smell.

**Pheromones**
Odorants secreted by animals that affect the behavior of other animals, especially other members of the same species.

sensitivity, have about 10 million olfactory receptors. In contrast, dogs, which are extremely sensitive to smell, have about 200 million such receptors.

The roughly 1,000 different kinds of olfactory receptors are stimulated by small chemical molecules called **odorants** (Araneda, Abhay, & Firestein, 2000). Odorants may travel directly to the receptors via inhaled air. Or, they may be carried from the tip of the nose to the receptors, via the mucus of the nasal tract, by other molecules called *olfactory binding proteins*. It was once believed that each receptor was sensitive to a specific odorant, but it is now clear that most, if not all, receptors can be stimulated by multiple odors and that most odors can stimulate more than one kind of receptor (Araneda, Abhay, & Firestein, 2000). This helps explain why we potentially can discriminate many thousands of different odors.

Many species rely on smell to track their prey, to detect the approach of an enemy, and even to communicate with each other. They "speak" through **pheromones,** volatile chemical secretions whose odors have powerful effects, primarily on others of the same species. Frightened animals, for example, produce a pheromone that serves as a warning signal to others of their species. Cats secrete a pheromone in their urine that tells other cats to stay away from their territory. And the females of many species release pheromones that signal when they are ready to mate.

Comparable studies in humans have been less compelling, but there is evidence that pheromones can influence human behavior. One study of dormitory residents at a women's college produced provocative results. When the college term began, the participants reported wide differences in the dates on which their menstrual periods began. Six months later, however, those who were spending a lot of time together as roommates or close friends reported that the dates were considerably closer together, as if there was a growing tendency for their menstrual cycles and ovulation to coincide (McClintock, 1971; also see Stern & McClintock, 1998). Perhaps pheromones secreted during the cycle had a mutual effect on the timing—a possibility that has been supported by experiments on the role of pheromones in synchronizing the estrous cycles of groups of rats (McClintock, 1984). The power of smell in influencing sexual activity is discussed in A Matter of Debate on page 107.

## The Taste-Smell Connection

A major factor in the experience of flavors of food and drink is the odor involved (Murphy & Cain, 1980). Smell's operation as a partner with taste becomes obvious when we have a head cold or sinus infection. The food we eat has little flavor—although our tongue and its taste receptors are undisturbed, our clogged nasal passages interfere with the work of the smell receptors. As shown in Figure 3.12, some of the most easily identified tastes become difficult to recognize when our sense of smell is hampered.

One way to demonstrate the smell-taste connection is to pinch your nostrils before approaching a food or drink that you are about to taste. (This will work even better if you have someone blindfold you, to eliminate visual taste associations.) Then place some of the substance in your mouth, move it around, and try to determine its flavor. The difficulty you experience in doing so disappears once you let go of your nostrils and begin allowing air to enter normally.

## → A MATTER OF DEBATE ←

# A Human Scent of Sex?

Many female animals, including dogs, cats, and most primates, secrete pheromones that signal when they are sexually receptive. In female rhesus monkeys, for example, chemical substances called *copulins* affect vaginal odor—and indicate to the male that mating is potentially welcome. A female moth emits a pheromone that is sufficiently strong and compelling to attract males from miles away. Males also exude pheromones that signal sex: a family of steroids called the *androstenes*. The boar produces androstenes in its testes, and when it secretes them in its saliva, the odor causes the sow to become immobile—and thus more amenable to the boar's sexual advances.

Because androstenes are also secreted by humans, particularly from underarm glands, and because humans can discriminate among various underarm odors, pheromones have been thought to be a factor in human sexual attraction as well. Several studies have yielded intriguing results. In one, women in photographs were rated as more appealing sexually by both men and women wearing surgical masks saturated with an androstene than by those wearing masks without it (Kirk-Smith, Booth, Carroll, & Davies, 1978). And when a seat in the waiting room of a dentist's office had been sprayed with the substance, more women than men chose to sit in it (Kirk-Smith & Booth, 1980). Evidently women can detect musk-like odors—which are characteristic of the sex pheromones secreted by male animals—more readily than men can. Moreover, their sensitivity to these odors is greatest during the time in their menstrual cycle when the amount of the hormone estrogen in their bodies is at its peak (Vierling & Rock, 1967).

More recent research also supports the idea that human behavior is affected by pheromones—or "chemosignals," as some researchers prefer to call such substances. In one series of experiments, researchers found that *androstadienone*, the most prominent of the underarm androstenes in men, could alter autonomic ner-

Many perfume ads present romantic images, suggesting that use of their product will enhance sexual attraction and behavior. However, there is no scientific evidence that this is the case.

© Jean-Pierre Lescourret/CORBIS

vous system activity in women and reduce their tension and nervousness (see Grosser, Monti-Bloch, Jennings-White, & Berliner, 2000). Another experiment, however, found that both androstadienone and *estratetraenol*, a prominent female chemosignal, had a positive effect on the mood of women and a negative effect on that of men, contrary to what would be expected if the biochemicals were "sex specific" (Jacob & McClintock, 1999). That is, although it was clear that the substances affected the participants, they did not affect them in a way apparently linked to sexual interest or activity. But other studies support the idea that sex-specific pheromones increase sexual interest in both men and women (see Thornhill & Gangestad, 1999).

Overall, although it is possible that scents can affect human sexual responses, there is no reason to conclude that our sex life is regulated by them to nearly the same degree as that of lower animals and insects (Jacob & McClintock, 1999; Rogel, 1978). Human responses to odors are quite variable, and human sexual behavior is determined by many factors, not the least of which is cognition. For humans, visual stimulation can be equally exciting, as can prior memories and associations. In effect, "human sexual choice, contrary to the claims of some perfume manufacturers, is apt to be more a matter of higher mental processes than of primitive responses to sexual odors" (Coren, Ward, & Porac, 1989).

What do you think? Can people be sexually aroused by "natural" body scents? Have you ever been aroused by someone's underarm odors? Could this have something to do with why so many people use underarm deodorants?

To research this topic further, go online with InfoTrac and use your own term or the following suggestions:
- pheromones
- smell

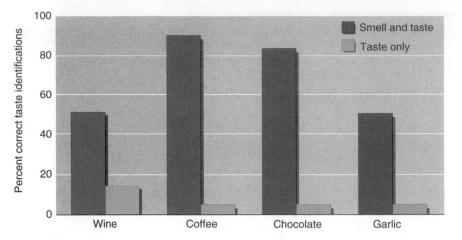

**FIGURE 3.12 The role of smell in taste.** Note the sharp decline in the capability to identify some common foods when the sense of smell is absent.

*Adapted from Mozel et al., 1969.*

**Test Yourself**

**(h)**  If someone told you that your male dog was extremely sensitive to pheromones, what might this tell you about the dog's sexual behavior?

(The answer is on page 125.)

Taste and especially smell become less sensitive with age. In one survey, about three-fourths of the respondents reported at least occasional problems with smell, and many of them—often older people—reported difficulties quite often (Gilbert & Wysocki, 1987). It is likely that such difficulties in older individuals help account for their frequent complaint that foods have lost their flavor, as discussed in the Life Span Perspective on page 109.

# The Subtle Nature of Touch: Skin Senses

The receptors for the skin senses are nerve endings scattered throughout the body, just under the surface of the skin. They are sensitive to four basic types of stimulation: *pressure, pain, cold,* and *warmth.* As with the other senses, the sensation they produce depends on the pattern of neural impulses set off by a number of broadly tuned nerve endings. Indeed, manipulation of the pattern can fool us into experiencing a sensation that is totally at odds with the actual stimulation. This has been demonstrated with the device illustrated in Figure 3.13. When cool water is passed through both coils, the device feels cool to the touch. When warm water is passed through both coils, it feels warm. But when one coil is warm and the other is cool, the device produces a sensation of heat so great that anyone who grasps it immediately pulls away. Somehow, the pattern of neural impulses set up by this kind of stimulation completely fools the sense of touch.

There are variations across the body in sensitivity of the skin to pain. The nerve endings in the back of the knee and the neck region, for example, are more

These wine tasters are well aware of how the sense of smell contributes to the sense of taste.

Human infants are born well equipped to taste and smell things, although perceptions based on these senses become more refined with development and experience. And unlike the receptors for the other senses, smell receptors regenerate—that is, new ones form to replace those that become damaged or die (Doty, 2001). So why is it that older people often say that foods don't taste as good as they once did and find themselves using more salt and spices?

Research implicates an assortment of factors, including normal biological aging, medications older people are more likely to take, and diseases older people are more likely to contract. With regard to biological change, reductions in taste and smell are modest in healthy people who are aging normally. As Susan Schiffman explained (1997), detection thresholds and recognition thresholds for taste do increase somewhat with age—that is, sensitivity decreases—for reasons that aren't well

understood. Researchers sometimes find reduced numbers of taste buds in older people, but not always. Decreased receptor functioning is another possible culprit. Sensitivity to smell also declines progressively with normal aging because of declines in functioning of the olfactory epithelium and a variety of brain structures associated with the perception of smells.

In each case, however, it is difficult to disentangle the effects of normal aging from the effects of the prescription medications older people take and the diseases they contract. Medications are a major factor. Apart from side effects that interfere with taste (such as decreased salivation and a "dry mouth"), many medications simply taste so bad that they block normal taste sensations (Schiffman, Zervakis, Suggs, Shaio, & Sattely-Miller, 1999). In turn, the bad tastes may become associated with foods eaten before taking the medications, creating conditioned taste

aversions (see Chapter 4) that interfere with normal enjoyment of those foods (Bernstein, 1999).

With regard to diseases, loss of sensitivity to taste and smell often accompanies Alzheimer's disease and other forms of dementia—as the disease progresses, areas of the cortex and other parts of the brain associated with processing taste and smell degenerate (Murphy, 1999). But declines in taste and smell can also occur because of more specific conditions, such as diseases of the teeth, gums, and throat (Ship, 1999).

In sum, some decline in taste and smell is normal with increasing age; more is not. Efforts to improve the palatability of the medications older people take are much needed, as are efforts to remedy preventable oral health problems among older people. Loss of enjoyment of eating is not inevitable, and neither is the corresponding loss of appetite many older people experience.

---

sensitive than those in the ball of the thumb and the tip of the nose (Coren, Porac, & Ward, 1984).

Nerve endings for pain are also found in muscles and internal organs. Indeed, some of the most excruciating pains come from muscle cramps or from distention of the intestines by gas. Yet the receptors in most of the internal organs do not respond to stimuli that would cause pain if applied to the skin. The intestines, for example, can be cut or even burned without arousing any sensation of pain.

Pain sensations pose many questions. Athletes in the heat of competition may suffer blows severe enough to produce deep bruises, yet feel no pain until later. People with intense and long-term pain can sometimes find relief through hypnosis (Barber, 1996). Techniques vary, but in essence the pain sufferer is induced to enter a hypnotic trance and then is given a *posthypnotic suggestion* that she or he will no longer feel the pain. That is, the patient is instructed under hypnosis not to feel the pain either during the session or after it is over. However, pain reduction through hypnosis does not work for everyone.

Some Chinese surgeons use no anesthetic, just the technique of acupuncture, in which small needles are stuck in the patient's skin at various spots, as shown in Figure 3.14. These points are often far removed from the part of the body undergoing the operation. Finally, electrical stimulation applied to the spinal cord or brain—or, for that matter, even a placebo, which is a mere sugar pill with no medical effect—may make severe pain disappear. Why?

The answer is not known. One theory is that these phenomena in one way or another induce the brain to increase its output of endorphins, discussed in Chapter 2 (Murray, 1995; Wall, 2000). Another theory is based on indications that there

**FIGURE 3.13** When you touch this harmless coil, watch out! This device can fool the skin senses. The coils are separate and can be connected to different sources of water. The surprising result described in the text is obtained by running cool water through one coil and warm water through the other.

may be two different pathways carrying pain messages through the spinal cord and into the brain—and one is made up of *"large"* *fibers* that inhibit the transmission of pain messages to the brain and *"small"* *fibers* that facilitate it (Melzack & Wall, 1995). These two kinds of fibers interact at a *gate-control mechanism* in the spinal cord, either opening it to let pain messages through or shutting it to cut off the sensations (Melzack, 1973; Wall, 2000). Such a gate might be activated by neural impulses set up through acupuncture or electrical stimulation. In the case of hypnosis or placebos, the brain might send signals to the control mechanism.

Although we can only theorize about the way pain operates, we do know that it serves a crucial purpose. Without the warning provided by pain, we might hold a hand in a flame until the tissues were destroyed or cut off a finger while peeling an apple. Even the pain of headache, though we cannot attribute it to any specific cause, may be a warning that we have been under too much physical or psychological strain. By forcing us to slow down or even take some time off, the headache may temporarily remove us from a situation that might otherwise cause serious damage to the tissues of our bodies or to our mental stability.

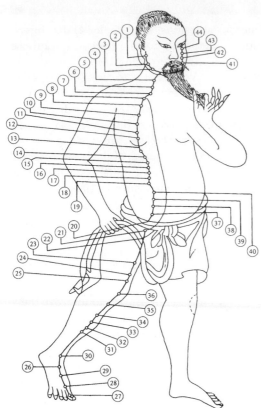

**FIGURE 3.14 An acupuncture chart. The numbers shown here indicate the spots at which needles can be inserted into a person's skin to relieve pain.**

## Bodily Movement and Equilibrium

Even in a pitch-black room, you know exactly how to move your hand to point up, down, or to either side, and to touch the top of your head or your left knee. This may not seem like much of an accomplishment, but it would be completely impossible without the generally ignored and unappreciated sense of bodily movement, which keeps us constantly informed of the position and motion of our muscles and bones.

The receptors for the sense of bodily movement—the unnoticed sense known as *kinesthesis*—are nerve endings found in three parts of the body: the muscles, the tendons, and the joints. The nerve endings in the muscles are stimulated when the muscles stretch. The nerve endings in the tendons that connect the muscles to the bones are stimulated when the muscles contract and put pressure on the tendons. Apparently most important are the nerve endings in the linings of the joints between the bones; they are stimulated by movements of the joints. Without the information provided by these three kinds of receptors, we would have difficulty performing any of the bodily movements we take for granted. Even to walk, we would have to concentrate on using our eyes to guide our legs and feet into the right position for each step.

The other unnoticed sense is equilibrium, which keeps our bodies in balance and oriented to the force of gravity. Thanks to this sense, our bodies stay erect—and if we start to fall, we can catch our balance through reflex action without even thinking about it.

**Vestibular sacs**
**The areas of the inner ear that contain receptors for the sense of equilibrium.**

The receptors for the sense of equilibrium are hairlike cells found in fluid-filled passages that are part of the inner ear, as illustrated in Figure 3.15. The three semicircular canals lie at such angles to one another that any movement of the head moves the thick fluid in at least two of them, stimulating the receptors they contain. In the **vestibular sacs,** the receptors are matted together, and tiny pieces of stonelike crystal are embedded in the mattings. The crystals are heavy enough to be pulled downward by the force of gravity, putting pressure on the receptors. Thus, the receptors in the vestibular sacs keep us aware of being upright even when we are not moving. The vestibular system in cats is what allows them to land on their feet most of the time after a fall.

The receptors for the sense of equilibrium constantly monitor the position and movements of the head. Besides keeping us right side up and in balance, they provide information that is essential to our sense of vision. By stepping toward a mirror, you can observe that your head bobs around when you walk—as it also does in many other circumstances. If the muscles controlling movement of the eyeballs did not make constant adjustments to hold your gaze steady, your field of vision would jiggle and blur. These adjustments are made by reflex action in response to messages from the sense of equilibrium. No matter how much you bob or shake your head, the world you see remains firmly in place.

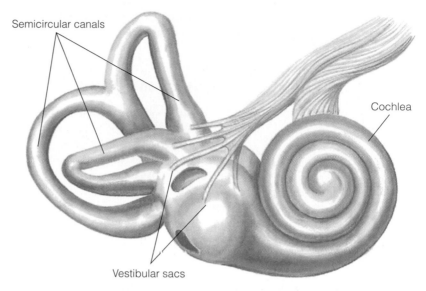

Semicircular canals

Cochlea

Vestibular sacs

**FIGURE 3.15 The sense organs for equilibrium. The receptors for the sense of equilibrium lie in these passages of the inner ear.**

# PERCEPTION AND SURVIVAL

**FOCUS QUESTIONS**

- What are perceptual feature detectors?

- To what extent are our perceptual abilities prewired versus learned?

- How do we perceive changes and motion around us?

Despite our ability to sense changes in light or loudness, it is our perceptual processes that permit us to make sense of the constantly shifting stimuli in the outside world. Consider, for example, the familiar act of crossing the street. To do so, we must perceive the shapes of objects accurately and detect their movement and speed. How long would you last in big-city traffic if you had to keep asking yourself: "That patch of blue light waves out there—is it a car or something else? Is it moving? How fast and in what direction? Is it dangerous or can I ignore it?" Or, consider the act of calling out for help. If you were in trouble and pleading for a friend to come to your side, it would be absolutely essential that the listener be able to make out that the voice was yours—no matter how loud or soft, whether high-pitched or low, whether on the phone or in the next room.

How long do you suppose it would take you to read this page if you had to work at deciphering every visual stimulus that reached your eyes—that is to say, if you had to figure out each time that a vertical line with a little horizontal dash across it was a *t*, a vertical line with a curve was an *h*, a partial circle with a horizontal line across it was an *e*, and a combination of *t*, *h*, and *e* meant *the*? But you do not have to stop and think. You perceive a *the*—or a moving car or a familiar voice—without even trying. In fact, in many cases you cannot help perceiving what you do, even if you make

Acrobats have a highly developed sense of equilibrium, without which they would be unable to perform their amazing balancing acts.

© Bettmann/CORBIS

a deliberate effort. Perception is a process over which we sometimes have little conscious control.

## The Built-in "Wiring" of Feature Detectors

Part of our skill in perceiving the world depends on the structure of the nervous system—the way it is "wired" to extract information from the environment. The nerve pathways from the sense organs to the brain, and the sensory areas of the brain, contain a great number of specialized cells that automatically detect important features of the environment. In the visual system, these cells, called **feature detectors,** are especially sensitive to patterns and movement. In hearing, the feature detectors are especially sensitive to pitch and changes in pitch. Thus, the cells are ideally suited to respond immediately to stimuli that represent such important information as the direction of a line, the shapes and motion of objects, and the flow of conversation.

Much of our knowledge of feature detectors originated with the research of David Hubel and Torsten Wiesel, who shared a 1981 Nobel Prize for their work. Hubel and Wiesel measured the neural impulses in individual cells of the visual cortex of cats and monkeys while the animals looked at a screen on which various kinds of stimuli were flashed. They found that some of the brain cells responded vigorously to a vertical bar on the screen but did not respond at all to a horizontal bar, as shown in Figure 3.16. Other cells acted in the opposite fashion, responding to a horizontal bar but not to a vertical one. Others responded most vigorously to angles, and still others to movement (Hubel & Wiesel, 1965).

Similarly, it has been found that the sensory areas of the brains of laboratory animals—and presumably those of humans as well—contain feature detectors that are specialized to respond to various characteristics of sound waves. Some are activated most strongly by low-pitched sounds, others by high-pitched sounds, and still others only by a change in pitch (Whitfield & Evans, 1965).

## The Skills of Perception: Inborn or Learned?

A long-standing controversy continues over the relative contributions of the CNS we are born with versus experience in explaining our perceptions. One view is that inborn structures in the brain allow us to perceive size and color. A contrasting view is that our perceptions are the result of accumulated psychological interpretations of the sensations we experience over time. Neither of these extreme views is likely to be correct.

On the one hand, there is evidence for inborn wiring. In the case of feature detectors, Hubel and Wiesel studied both newborn and very young monkeys kept from any visual stimulation since birth—and found feature detector cells in full operation. These cells were activated by the very first stimulation of the eye's receptors, and they responded in much the same way as the cells of older animals with visual experience (Wiesel & Hubel, 1974). The human nervous system may be wired the same way. It appears that the pathways of the sensory system not only receive the inputs provided by the sense organs but begin the information processing by making an initial selection and interpretation of these inputs. It has been said that they "condense the information present in the world down to certain features that are essential to the organism" (Levine & Shefner, 1981). Even young infants, although they have had very little experience, can perceive a variety of visual stimuli.

On the other hand, we know that in complex perceptual situations, especially when the stimuli are ambiguous, we must rely on past experience. When you are driving at dusk, for example, and try to make out an object on the road,

**Feature detectors**
Cortical cells that are sensitive to certain patterns of stimuli.

**FIGURE 3.16** How a feature-detector cell works. The spikes in the graph lines are recordings of the neural impulses in one of the feature-detector cells of a cat's brain. In response to a horizontal bar, the cell displays only its normal amount of spontaneous activity. There is a small response to an oblique bar. In response to a vertical bar—the kind of feature to which this cell is specifically sensitive—there is a sharp burst of activity.
*Hubel, 1963.*

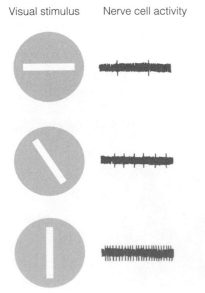

Visual stimulus    Nerve cell activity

you will be influenced by what you have learned previously. The most appropriate way to view perception, therefore, is as a skill that is derived from basic, inborn physiological mechanisms but is also shaped and modified by learning experiences.

## Perceiving Change, Movement, and Contrast

Our prewired skills are particularly suited to spotting any *change* in stimulation, which is often the most useful information of all. In general, change in stimulation is the most potent way to attract the attention of a baby. This makes sense from an evolutionary standpoint because the elements of change—for example, of temperature or brightness—usually contain the most useful information about the environment and any dangers it may contain. Throughout our daily lives, our nervous system finds it impossible to ignore change. If a TV is playing softly in the background while you are reading, you may pay no attention to it, but you cannot help noticing if the sound stops—or if a commercial comes on and the volume increases. You are instantly aware of a change if the light in the room becomes brighter or dimmer. And you recognize even extremely subtle variations in the appearance of a face, such as a narrowing of the mouth or eyes (Haig, 1984).

*Movement*, which is a form of change, is such a compelling stimulus that even very young babies try hard to follow any moving object with their eyes. Newborn infants arrive with a built-in tendency to select and pay attention to movement. When you look at a pasture full of horses, you are most aware of those that are running. An advertising sign that has items in motion commands your attention far more than a sign that remains stationary.

The reason movement leaps immediately to awareness probably also relates to inborn characteristics of the nervous system. It appears that the wiring of the visual system contains separate cells for motion (Sekuler & Levinson, 1977). This characteristic has great potential value for survival, as there are many situations in which it is more important to detect and respond quickly to the movement of an object than to know what the object may be. To our ancestors, for example, the sudden approach of a wild animal meant danger, regardless of whether the animal happened to be a lion or a bear.

Another compelling stimulus is *contrast*—any sharp difference in the intensity of light reflected by one or more objects in the field of vision. Even babies are attracted by contrast (Salapatek & Kessen, 1966). Newborns recognize and react to dark-light contrast, as well as to changes in loudness and pitch. It has long been known that infants are especially attracted to characteristics of the human face (e.g., Fantz, 1958), particularly its edges, contours, and dark-light contrasts (Roskinski, 1977). These and other apparently prewired perceptual preferences would be highly adaptive in an evolutionary sense, in that they assist in the infant's early recognition of the mother or other caregiver (e.g., Carpenter, 1974) and therefore set the stage for infant-caregiver emotional attachment, as discussed in Chapter 10.

Our perception of the relative brightness of an object often depends on differences in the amount of light reflected from adjacent objects (Shapley, 1986). This perceptual effect, called *simultaneous brightness contrast*, is demonstrated in Figure 3.17.

Besides change and contrast, two other stimulus characteristics influence perception. One is *size*, with large objects being more compelling than small ones. When you look at the front page of a newspaper, you notice the biggest headlines first. The second is *intensity*. When you drive at night along a business street where all the signs are of equal size, the brightest one is the most

**FIGURE 3.17** The same but different: a study in contrasts. The central squares of the four larger squares are exactly the same gray. The amount and wavelength of the light reaching your eye from each one are the same. (You can easily see this if you take a piece of paper, cut out a square the same size as the centers, and place it over them.) But the perceived levels of brightness of the squares are not equal. The grays printed on dark backgrounds appear lighter than those printed on light backgrounds.
*Adapted from Coren, Porac, & Ward, 1984.*

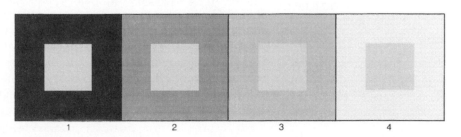

Advertisers assume that we will pay more attention to large signs than to small ones, and we usually do.

### Test Yourself

**(i)** If you hung a white mobile decorated with dark Xs and Os over an infant's crib, you would be likely to draw the baby's focused attention. What two inborn perceptual skills would the infant be displaying?

*(The answer is on page 125.)*

compelling. When you stand in a crowded subway car, you may ignore the pressure of the people pressed against you, but you quickly notice if someone accidentally pokes an elbow in your ribs.

# SELECTION AND ATTENTION

### FOCUS QUESTIONS

• What kinds of things determine what we attend to?

• Can we attend to more than one thing at a time?

Of the various functions of perception, such as selection, organization, and interpretation, **selection** heads the list. This is because we cannot possibly cope with all the varied and changing stimuli that bombard our senses. To avoid confusion, we have to select and attend to specific stimuli. What we select depends on many factors, ranging from the automatic and involuntary to the conscious and deliberate.

**Selection**
**The perceptual process by which we attend to certain stimulation and ignore other stimulation.**

## What's Behind the Selection Process?

What we select from the environment depends not only on choices dictated by the inborn tendencies of our nervous system but also on choices influenced by experience. As an example of the latter, consider the kinds of choices that might be made by a woman working as a forest ranger as she stands on an observation tower, looking out over a wide expanse of hills, valleys, open spaces, trees, and streams. Scanning the scene, she thinks she spots a plume of smoke. She raises her binoculars and focuses her eyes on this single aspect of the landscape. Only then, after selecting this small spot on which to concentrate, can she try to find some organization in the stimuli reaching her eyes (do they represent a plume of smoke or something else?) and make an interpretation (if it is smoke, is it coming from a cabin or is it the start of a forest fire?). Between the two extremes are many gradations that are difficult to classify. The in-between choices seem to depend partly on inborn tendencies and partly on learning and experience; often it is hard to say whether we make them consciously or unconsciously.

Because so many factors can influence selection, people looking at the same event in the environment may perceive it in different ways. We are likely to pay attention to events that interest us or are relevant to us for one reason or another. For example, classic research indicates that when people look at words flashed only briefly for their inspection, they are better at recognizing terms related to their own special interests than unrelated terms. Participants who are interested in religion are quick to perceive words like *sacred*. Participants who are interested in economics are quick to perceive *income* (Postman, Bruner, & McGinnies, 1948).

You can observe for yourself how mood affects selection. When you are feeling out of sorts, you are likely to pay attention to anything in the environment that is potentially irritating—a noise in the next room, a watchband that feels too tight, another person's frown. When you are feeling on top of the world, you may be especially aware that the sun is shining, everyone seems to be friendly to you, and there are a great many attractive people walking around. As the old saying goes, where a pessimist sees a glass that is half empty, an optimist sees a glass that is half full.

## Trying to Attend to Simultaneous Inputs

As we all have noticed at one time or another, it is difficult to pay attention to more than one event in the environment at a time, and selecting one stimulus usually means losing perception of the other possible inputs. In spite of this, modern civilization readily lends itself to attempts at *multitasking*—doing more than one thing at a time—because people are often bombarded with simultaneous inputs. A common example occurs in driving a car. As you drive along a highway where the traffic is light, you are listening to the radio—to a ball game or to a news broadcaster who is about to give a weather report. But now you come to a busy intersection. The traffic lights are changing. You have to slow down, veer into another lane, and watch out for a car that has moved into your path. When all this activity ends, you find to your surprise that the score in the ball game has changed or that the news is over and you've missed the weather report. Your attention was directed elsewhere, and although the radio was just as loud as before, your perceptual processes missed it entirely.

Laboratory experiments have shown that it is very difficult to process two different inputs, especially if they arrive in the same sensory channel. In studying the perception of two sounds heard at the same time, experimenters have used earphones that deliver one spoken message to the right ear and a completely different one to the left ear. Participants can pay attention to and understand either one of the two messages, but not both at once. The same applies to visual stimuli—for example, trying to take in what is happening in two films simultaneously, one showing a boxing match and the other a football game (Neisser & Becklen, 1975).

It is somewhat easier to pay attention to two things at once when two different senses are being stimulated. You can drive a car and talk on your cell phone at the same time reasonably well—where "reasonably well" means that it is still dangerous to do so, which is why it's illegal in many places. Apparently the cognitive processes required for perception can operate more efficiently with two different kinds of sensory information than with two messages in the same sensory channel. It's as if the brain has more than one area for paying attention (Wickens, 1984).

## Selection and Exploration

What selection does is help us perceive what is likely to be important to us, ignore all the many other inputs provided by our senses, and concentrate on using the

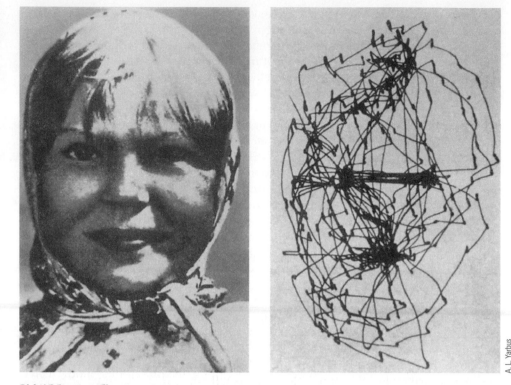

**FIGURE 3.18  The scanning process.** The pattern of lines was made by bouncing a light beam off the white of one man's eye, thus recording his eye movements as he looked for a few minutes at the photograph of a girl. Note how many movements took place and how they provided information about all the important elements of the photo.
*Yarbus, 1967.*

A. L. Yarbus

rest of our information-processing talents to the best possible advantage. When we notice something unusual out of the corner of an eye—usually because of movement or contrast—we move our eyes to bring the image to the center of the retina, where our vision is sharpest. Then we make a series of scanning movements, as illustrated in Figure 3.18. These scanning movements occur even when we think we are staring fixedly at a stimulus like the photograph in the figure; in fact, the eyes send the brain information about first one part of the photo, then another, and then still others. Somehow the brain manages to piece together this rapid succession of bits of information into a perception of the photograph as a whole. The process resembles the creation of a mosaic from tiny bits of tile—but exactly how it is done is only poorly understood.

# ORGANIZING OUR PERCEPTIONS

When we select a stimulus in the environment for further exploration, often the first thing we want to know is "What is it?" To answer this question, we have to see or hear the stimulus as something that hangs together as a unit of some kind, separate and distinguishable from all the other stimuli the environment provides. We must see visual inputs as *organized* into some *whole* object—an animal, a car, a face. We must hear auditory inputs as organized into the meaningful pattern of human speech, or a rap at the door, or an approaching car. Perhaps not surprisingly, much of what we know about organization in perception derives from the work of the Gestalt psychologists (see Chapter 1). With their emphasis on the "whole," perceptual principles and phenomena were their primary area of study.

In vision, we organize stimuli into an object largely by the perceptual principle of **figure and ground.** As you read this page, for example, your eyes are stimulated by the white space and many little black lines, curves, squiggles, and dots. Your perceptual process organizes these stimuli into dark figures—letters, words, and punctuation marks—seen against a white background. This is also the way you perceive a chair, a face, or the moon. The figure hangs together, forming an organized shape. The ground is a neutral and formless setting for the figure. What separates the two, setting the figure off from the ground, is a clearly perceived dividing line called a *contour*. The separation depends in part on our inborn skill at perceiving contrast, probably because of the way feature detectors operate. An interesting example of how we organize visual stimuli into figure and ground is shown in Figure 3.19. In the drawing, you initially may perceive some strange shapes against a white ground. Study the figure, however, and you will perceive white shapes forming the word TIE against a black ground.

## Some Principles of Organization

Although the same stimuli can sometimes be grouped into different patterns, there are several principles of organization that usually predominate. Among these are closure, continuity, similarity, and proximity.

**Closure** means that we do not need a complete and uninterrupted contour to perceive a figure. If part of the contour is missing, our perceptual processes fill in the gaps. This principle of perception is illustrated in Figure 3.20. The principle of closure also operates for sounds. A tape recording of a spoken message can be doctored so that many of the sounds are missing—consonants, vowels, syllables, or entire words. Yet if you hear the tape, you will still be able to perceive much of or even the entire message.

**Continuity,** the tendency to perceive continuous lines and patterns, is closely related to closure. An example is shown in Figure 3.21. The two lines at the left, seen separated in space, have their own continuity, but when they are put together at the right, a different kind of continuity makes us perceive them quite differently. In looking at any kind of complex visual stimulus, we are likely to perceive the organization dictated by the most compelling kind of continuity.

Similarity and proximity are illustrated in Figure 3.22. The checkerboard to the left, with blocks all the same color and equal distances apart, has no real pattern inside it. If you keep looking at it and shift your eyes from one point to another, your tendency to find organization is likely to make you perceive some patterns—vertical rows, horizontal rows, or groups of squares arranged in pairs, squares, or rectangles—but these patterns are not compelling and are likely

**FIGURE 3.19 The principle of figure and ground.** When you first look at the drawing, you probably perceive some shapes that look like pieces of a jigsaw puzzle. But you can also perceive something quite different, as explained in the text.

**Figure and ground**
In perception, the tendency to see an object as a figure set off from a background.

**Closure**
The tendency to fill in the gaps when perceiving figures.

**Continuity**
The tendency to perceive continuous lines and patterns.

**FIGURE 3.20 Some examples of closure.** Though the figures are incomplete in one way or another, we perceive them as "wholes."

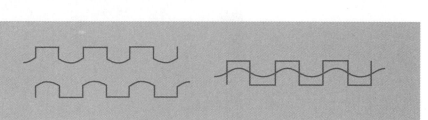

**FIGURE 3.21 An example of continuity.** At the left, we clearly perceive two continuous lines with straight and curved segments. When the two lines are put together at the right, however, we find it difficult to perceive the original pattern. Instead, we perceive a continuous wavy line running through another continuous line of straight horizontal and vertical segments.

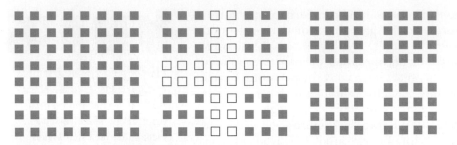

**FIGURE 3.22  The effects of similarity and proximity.** The drawing to the left has a simple pattern. But note what happens to your perception when some of the colored blocks are changed to white, as in the drawing in the middle, or moved closer together, as in the drawing to the right.

**Similarity**
In perception, the tendency to group objects that resemble each other.

**Proximity**
In perception, the tendency to group objects that are close to each other.

to keep shifting. In the drawing in the middle, however, removing the color from some of the blocks makes a white cross fairly leap off the page. This demonstrates the principle of **similarity**, which states that we tend to group together stimuli that are alike.

In the variation of the checkerboard to the right, some of the colored blocks have been moved closer together, and now a pattern of four squares can be clearly perceived. This demonstrates the principle of **proximity**, which states that we tend to group together stimuli that are close together in space. The principle also applies to sounds. When we hear a series of sounds that are all alike, the pattern we hear depends on the timing. When we hear click-click . . . click-click . . . click-click (with the dots indicating a pause), the principle of proximity dictates that we organize the sounds into pairs. When we hear click-click-click . . . click-click-click, we perceive groups of three. Even different sounds presented this way—click-buzz-ring . . . click-buzz-ring—are perceived in groups of three.

## Finding Stability and Consistency

In trying to answer the question of what something is, we often have to overcome some potentially serious difficulties. Although the objects visible in the world may have definite and unchanging shapes, the light rays they reflect to our eyes form many different patterns, depending on the angle from which we view them. A dinner plate on a table, for example, casts its true circular image only when we look straight down at it. From other angles it casts different images—ovals or el-

**FIGURE 3.23  What the world would look like without size constancy.** This is how two people on a beach look to a camera held at close range. Your eyes would detect the same images—hands of different sizes, exaggerated torsos, undersized heads—but you would not perceive the distortions.

David Moscowitz

lipses. A door is a rectangle only when seen at right angles to the eyes. From other angles, such as when it swings open or shut, it forms various trapezoids.

However, this variation seldom bothers us. Regardless of the shape of the image cast on our eyes, we know immediately that we are looking at a round plate or a rectangular door. Thanks to what is called **perceptual constancy,** we perceive a stable and consistent world. The form of perceptual constancy demonstrated by the plate and the door is called **shape constancy.** Another form is **size constancy,** which is the tendency to recognize the actual size of an object regardless of whether the image it casts on the eye is large, as when the object is seen close up, or small, as when the object is seen from a distance. Figure 3.23 demonstrates how the actual size of the image creates a distorted view of the world in a photo. If we were to view the same scene from the same place as the camera lens, we would perceive everything in proper perspective. You can experience an even more convincing demonstration of size constancy by trying the experiment illustrated in Figure 3.24. If you follow the instructions, the images cast on your eyes by the small salad plate and the large dinner plate will be exactly the same size. Yet you will find that what you perceive—and, in fact, cannot help perceiving—is a small plate fairly close to you and a larger plate farther away.

## Perceiving Distance and Depth

Another important question we ask as we explore the world is "Where is it?" To avoid bumping into walls and other people, we must perceive not only *what* objects are but also *where* they are in relation to us. Before we step off a bus, we must know how far it is to the pavement. Fortunately, we also perceive distance and depth without thinking.

This ability appears to depend partly on inborn wiring, as has been demonstrated with the apparatus shown in Figure 3.25. This device, known as a visual cliff, consists of a piece of heavy glass suspended above the floor. Across the middle of the glass is a board covered with checkered cloth. On one side of the board, the same kind of cloth is attached to the bottom of the glass, making this side look like the solid, or shallow, side of the cliff. On the other side, the cloth is laid on the floor so that to all appearances there is a drop on that side.

As the figure shows, a 6-month-old crawls without hesitation over the shallow-looking side but hesitates to crawl on the deep side (Gibson & Walk, 1960). Also, although they do not show distress, infants who are too young to crawl show interest when placed on the deep side, again indicating that they perceive depth (Campos, Langer, & Krowitz, 1970). Newborns of other species show depth perception before any kind of learning presumably has had time to take place. Baby lambs and goats that are tested as soon as they can walk avoid the deep side. This ability seems to be the secret of how even very young animals—such as mountain goats born into an environment full of sharp and dangerous drops—manage to avoid falls. Other factors that aid the perception of depth and distance are difficult to classify as either inborn or learned. They seem to be a combination of the two (Hochberg, 1978).

One influential factor is **binocular** vision: The two eyes receive different images because of the distance between them, which is about $2\frac{1}{2}$ inches (64 mm). Somewhat like the two lenses of a three-dimensional camera, the eyes view objects in the visual field from slightly different angles. The images they receive are put together by the brain into a three-dimensional pattern that greatly assists the perception of depth and distance.

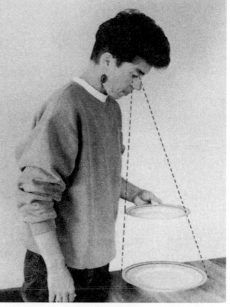

© David Hewitt/Anne Garrison

**FIGURE 3.24 Salad plate or dinner plate?** For a clear demonstration of size constancy, put a dinner plate on the table. Then move a salad plate up and down until its image exactly blots out the dinner plate. Without changing the height at which you hold the salad plate, move it to one side. The images cast on your eyes by the two plates are exactly the same size—but what do you perceive?

**Perceptual constancy**
The tendency to see objects as the same, regardless of the vantage point.

**Shape constancy**
The tendency to perceive objects as retaining their shape, regardless of the vantage point.

**Size constancy**
The tendency to perceive objects in their correct size, regardless of the vantage point.

**Binocular**
Using both eyes.

**FIGURE 3.25  A baby avoids a fall on the visual cliff.** At left, a baby fearlessly crawls toward the mother on the glass covering the shallow-looking side of the visual cliff. But at right, the baby stops—reluctant to cross the glass that covers the apparently deep side. *Gibson & Walk, 1960.*

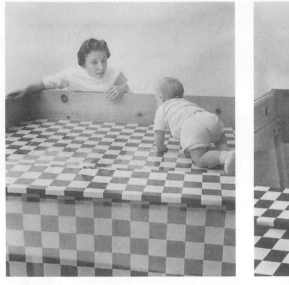

William Vandivert

**Monocular**
Using one eye.

**Interposition**
A monocular cue for distance, based on the phenomenon that objects that block off part of the view of other objects appear closer.

**Linear perspective**
A monocular cue for distance, based on the phenomenon that parallel lines appear to draw closer together as they recede into the distance.

**Relative size**
A monocular cue for distance, based on the perception that larger objects are closer and smaller objects more distant.

**FIGURE 3.26  Fooling the eye with interposition.** Two ordinary playing cards, arranged as shown in A, are the only objects visible in an otherwise dark room. You perceive clearly that the 2 of clubs is farther away. Now a corner is clipped from the 2 of diamonds, as shown in B, and the stand holding this card is moved to the right. If you now look at the cards through one eye, you perceive them as shown in C: a small 2 of clubs close by and a larger 2 of diamonds farther away. *Krech, Crutchfield, & Livson, 1969.*

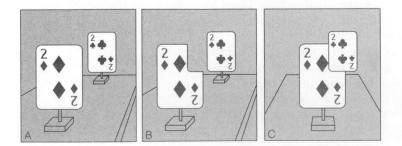

However, even people with only one working eye can perceive depth and distance through **monocular** cues. These are the same cues that allow us to perceive depth and distance in photos and cartoons. One of them is **interposition,** in which nearby objects block off part of our view of more distant objects; Figure 3.26 illustrates interposition and shows how it can lead our perceptions astray. Others include **linear perspective**—a distance cue based on the phenomenon that parallel lines, like highway lanes, seem to draw closer together as they recede into the distance—and **relative size,** which refers to the perception that larger objects are closer and smaller ones are farther away.

## When Illusions Lead Us Astray

The process of perception, aided by the inborn characteristics of the nervous system, is the source of our first quick impressions of what is going on around us. It is usually quite accurate, but it isn't perfect; our first impressions are not always in accord with the facts. For example, while walking along a path you may have had the experience of being sure you saw a small dog in the bushes ahead—only to discover, as you got closer, that it was just a piece of rumpled newspaper. Your perceptual process, in its effort to make sense out of the visual stimulation reaching your eyes, signaled "dog" when in fact there was no dog. Students of perception have shown that we can be fooled in many ways. Several optical illusions are illustrated in Figure 3.27.

Perceptual illusions also occur in senses other than vision. The Greek philosopher-scientist Aristotle (384–322 B.C.) called attention to an illusion of touch, illustrated in Figure 3.28. Perceptual illusions also take place during *altered states of consciousness*—for example, during dreams, under hypnosis, or under the influence of alcohol or other drugs. These states are described at various points later in the text.

# Interpreting What We Perceive

Selection answers the question "Which one of all the many objects and events in the environment is worthy of attention and exploration?" Organization helps answer "What is it?" and "Where is it?" But an important question remains: "What does it mean?" Finding the answer requires *interpretation*.

Of all the elements just mentioned, interpretation is the one that is most clearly dependent on learning rather than on inborn characteristics of the nervous system. We compare new information provided by the senses with old information acquired in the past. Note the symbols in Figure 3.29. You may never have seen anything exactly like them before, but as an English user, you perceive at once that all of them are the letter *E*. You have stored in memory what students of perception call a *prototype* or *schema*—a sort of generalized picture of what the letter *E* looks like. You can identify the new symbols because they resemble this prototype. Similarly, you have prototypes that help you recognize human faces, trees, animals called dogs, and all the other objects and events you have become familiar with.

Experience leads us to expect certain events to happen in familiar ways. We have a mental set toward the environment. What we perceive and how we interpret it depends to a considerable extent on our mental set—in other words, on our *perceptual expectations*. Laboratory experiments have shown that manipulating people's expectations can greatly affect their perceptions. Would you believe, for example, that two people could look at exactly the same drawing, and yet one would see a man and the other a rat? To see for yourself, try the demonstration illustrated in Figure 3.30. The psychologists who devised this experiment found that 85–95% of their participants perceived the final drawing as a man if they saw the other human heads first and as a rat if they saw the animals first—even though the final drawings are exactly alike.

The drawing in Figure 3.30 is, of course, specially designed to look like either a man's face or a rat—you can just as easily perceive either. But many of the sights we encounter in real life are also ambiguous, and the way we perceive them is likely to depend on what we

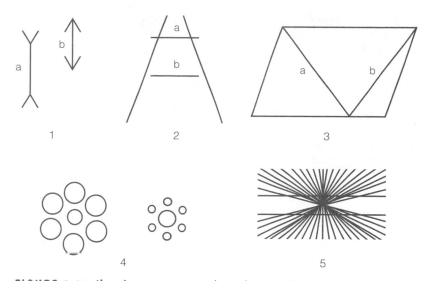

**FIGURE 3.27** How do you perceive these drawings? Is line a or line b longer in drawing 1? In drawing 2? In drawing 3? Which of the two inner circles in drawing 4 is larger? In drawing 5, are the horizontal lines straight or curved? After you make your judgments, determine with a ruler that the pairs of lines a and b are the same size, as are the two circles in drawing 4. The lines in drawing 5 are straight and parallel.

**FIGURE 3.28** One pencil or two? If you hold your fingers as pictured in the drawing to the left and touch the point between them with a pencil, you will perceive one pencil. But if you cross your fingers as shown in the drawing to the right and touch the pencil, you will perceive two distinct pencils. (If you keep your eyes closed, the effect may be even stronger.) The best explanation of the illusion is that when the pencil is stimulating the inside of the two fingers, as on the left, the touch information is being sent to adjacent or overlapping areas of the cortex responsible for touch sensations. But when the pencil is stimulating the outside of the two fingers as on the right, the information is being sent to two separate areas of that part of the cortex.
*Adapted from Coren, Porac, & Ward, 1984.*

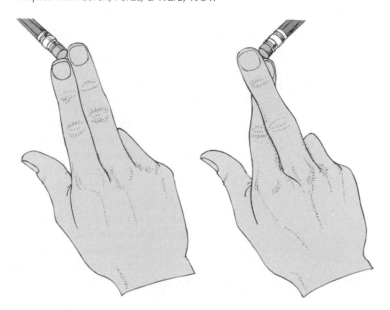

**FIGURE 3.29 You know what these are—but how do you know?** These symbols may be unlike any *Es* you have seen before, yet you recognize them at a glance.

**FIGURE 3.30 Some perceptual magic: Now it's a man, now it's a rat.** Cover both rows of drawings, and then ask a friend to watch while you uncover the faces in the top row one at a time, beginning at the left. The friend will almost surely perceive the final drawing as the face of a man. Then try the bottom row in similar fashion on another friend. The friend will almost surely perceive the final drawing as a rat.
*Bugelski & Alampay, 1961.*

**FIGURE 3.31 Same symbol, different context, different interpretation.**

THE CAT

**FIGURE 3.32**

expect to see. In a similar way, interpretation depends on the situation in which we encounter a stimulus—that is, the *context* in which it is found. For a demonstration, look at Figure 3.31. There you see exactly the same unusual symbol in the middle of each of the two words. If you saw it set apart by itself, you would hardly know what it was supposed to be. You might even guess that it was a set of goal posts. In the context of the words, however, you immediately perceive the first of the identical symbols as an *H* and the second as an *A*.

To see how mental set can affect interpretation, experimenters once asked participants to describe pictures that they were told they would see dimly on a screen. There were no real pictures, only blurs and smudges. But hungry participants, who had gone 16 hours without eating before the experiment, thought that they saw all kinds of foods and food-related objects (McClelland & Atkinson, 1948). It appears that we begin our information processing by perceiving not only what we expect to see and what the situation indicates we are likely to see but also what we want to see.

Thus, it is clear that our inborn sensory and perceptual skills, so important to our survival, are enriched and given meaning by the experiences we encounter throughout our lives (Rock, 1984).

# Chapter 3 Summary

## How Our Senses Function: Some General Principles

1. *Sensation* is the transduction of environmental stimulation for processing by the nervous system.
2. *Perception* is the process through which we become aware of our environment by selecting, organizing, and interpreting information from our senses.
3. The two basic requirements for all sensation are a stimulus and a *receptor*.
4. The information that a sense organ receives travels to the brain as millions of tiny impulses, which are deciphered at specialized locations within the brain.
5. To activate a sensory receptor, a stimulus must be at or above the receptor's *absolute threshold*.
6. To be distinguished as different, two stimuli must vary by at least the amount of the *difference threshold*—also called the just noticeable difference (JND)—based on Weber's law.
7. All the senses display *sensory adaptation*, up to a point.

## The Power of Vision

8. The stimuli for vision are light waves, a pulsating form of electromagnetic energy. Light waves occupy a small portion of the range of electromagnetic radiation.
9. Light waves vary in wavelength, intensity, and complexity, which determine *hue, brightness*, and *saturation*, respectively.
10. Light waves enter the eye through the cornea and then the *pupil*, the opening in the *iris*. Then they pass through the *lens* and are focused on the *retina* at the rear of the eyeball. Neural impulses leave the retina via the *optic nerve*.
11. The retina contains the receptors for vision—neural structures called *rods* and *cones*—as well as neurons for further processing. Rods are present throughout the retina, except in the *fovea*, which contains only cones.
12. The rods function chiefly under low illumination, sending information to the brain about whites, grays, and blacks but not color. They and the cones contain *rhodopsin*, which is the basis for dark adaptation.
13. The cones function primarily in strong illumination, sending information to the brain about movement and brightness plus color. The three kinds of cones are broadly tuned but are most sensitive to either blue, green, or red.
14. One explanation of color vision is the opponent-process theory, which holds that neural impulses set off by the rods and cones enter a pathway to the brain containing neurons that respond differently to different-colored stimuli.
15. The ability to distinguish colors varies among individuals; about 2% of people are *color blind* to varying degrees.

## The Power of Hearing

16. The stimulus for hearing is sound waves, which are ripples of contraction and expansion of the air that vary in frequency, amplitude, and complexity, giving rise to perceptions of *pitch, loudness*, and *timbre*, respectively.
17. Sound waves are collected by the *outer ear*. The waves create vibrations of the *eardrum*, which are then passed along by the three bones (including the stapes) of the *middle ear* to the cochlea of the *inner ear*. In the cochlea, the vibrations set up complex motions of the basilar membrane, which activate the hairlike receptors for hearing in the organ of Corti.
18. The bending of the hairlike receptors stimulates the neurons of the *auditory nerve* to produce impulses that are routed to the cerebral cortex.
19. Receptors at the narrow end of the basilar membrane, where sound enters the cochlea, respond most vigorously to high-frequency waves. The other end is wider and more flexible, with receptors that are more responsive to low frequencies.
20. Our ability to determine which direction a sound comes from depends on the hearing receptors in our two ears receiving slightly different patterns of stimulation.

## Taste, Smell, Touch, and the Two Unnoticed Senses

21. The receptors for taste lie mostly in the *taste buds* of the tongue. They are broadly tuned to respond to chemical stimulation, especially sweet, salty, sour, or bitter qualities.
22. The *olfactory epithelium* contains the receptors for smell, which are sensitive to thousands of *odorants*.
23. Many animals—including humans—respond to *pheromones*. Whether pheromones influence human sexual interest and activity remains a subject of debate.
24. The senses of taste and smell are closely intertwined in the perception of flavors.
25. The receptors for the skin senses are nerve endings that account for our sensations of pressure, pain, cold, and warmth.

26. The sense of bodily movement (kinesthesis) depends on receptors in the muscles, tendons, and joints.
27. The sense of equilibrium depends on hairlike receptors in the inner ear's three semicircular canals and *vestibular sacs.*

## Perception and Survival

28. Our perceptual skills depend on the inborn structure of the nervous system and specialized nerve cells called *feature detectors,* as well as on learning and experience.
29. Our inborn perceptual skills are particularly adept at spotting change, movement, and contrast.

## Selection and Attention

30. *Selection* is a key element in perception, enabling us to focus on only a few of the many stimuli that constantly bombard our senses. It depends on inborn structures, as well as on learning and current motivational states.
31. Attending to two different inputs is especially difficult if they arrive in the same sensory channel.
32. Selection helps us explore the environment, perceive what is likely to be most important, and ignore the rest.

## Organizing Our Perceptions

33. Organization is a key element of perception; through it we perceive meaningful shapes and patterns. One of the questions it answers is "What is it?"

34. An important factor in organization is *figure and ground,* which involves the perception of contours.
35. Organization typically is based on the following principles:
    a) *Closure,* not needing a complete and uninterrupted contour to perceive a figure.
    b) *Continuity,* the tendency to perceive continuous lines and patterns.
    c) *Similarity,* grouping together stimuli that are alike.
    d) *Proximity,* grouping together stimuli that are close together.
36. *Perceptual constancy* enables us to perceive a stable and consistent world. It includes *shape constancy* and *size constancy.*
37. In perceiving distance and depth, we rely on both *binocular* and *monocular* cues; the latter include *interposition, linear perspective,* and *relative size.*
38. Our perceptions of the world are usually accurate. Among the exceptions are perceptual illusions and distortions during altered states of consciousness.
39. Interpretation is a key aspect of perception. It answers the question "What does it mean?"
40. We interpret and identify stimuli in part by matching them to prototypes or schemas.
41. Our interpretations can be influenced by perceptual expectations and mental sets, as well as by context and mood.

# Chapter 3 Test Yourself Answers

(a) Your acquaintance is describing the ability called perception—that is, the ability to select, organize, and interpret evidence from the senses.

(b) It is called the absolute threshold—the point at which there is enough stimulus energy (in this case, the odor of food) for sensory receptors (in this case, receptors for smell) to respond.

(c) Your friend is trying to tell you that it was impossible to discriminate between the loudness of the sound before and after you raised the volume. To your friend's ears, the change was not enough to pass the difference threshold, or JND.

(d) You have just left the state of sensory adaptation. After a while, your ears adjusted to the constant hum of traffic sufficiently for the sensation of the sound to disappear.

(e) The resulting defect would be an inability to focus clearly by altering the shape of the lens.

(f) The statement indicates that the person puts a higher priority on the sensation of color than on the sensation of whites, grays, and blacks. Cones are responsible for the former, rods for the latter.

(g) The hardening of the bones would make them less capable of conducting the vibrations of sound on their way from the eardrum to the inner ear's receptors for hearing.

(h) The dog is likely to be adept at locating any sexually receptive female dogs in the vicinity.

(i) The infant would be demonstrating the inborn skills of spotting movement (the rotation of the mobile) and contrast (the contrast between the dark decorations and the white background).

(j) It reflects selection—the ability to perceive only a limited number of the stimuli that bombard our senses and compete for attention.

(k) She is describing the principle that the selection process depends in part on a person's emotional state.

(l) The second would be easier by far. We can pay attention to dual sources involving different senses better than to dual sources involving the same sense.

(m) It demonstrates size constancy—the ability to recognize the actual size of an object regardless of the size of the image it creates on the retina.

(n) You did so by using a prototype—a generalized model of what a human profile looks like—and then fitting the drawing to the prototype.

# Chapter 3  Sensing and Perceiving

## Key Terms

absolute threshold (p. 94)
auditory nerve (p. 103)
binocular (p. 119)
brightness (p. 96)
closure (p. 117)
color blindness (p. 100)
cones (p. 98)
continuity (p. 117)
difference threshold (p. 94)
eardrum (p. 102)
feature detectors (p. 112)
figure and ground (p. 117)
fovea (p. 98)
hue (p. 96)
inner ear (p. 102)
interposition (p. 120)
iris (p. 96)
lens (p. 97)
linear perspective (p. 120)
loudness (p. 101)
middle ear (p. 102)
monocular (p. 120)
odorants (p. 106)
olfactory epithelium (p. 105)
optic nerve (p. 97)

outer ear (p. 102)
perception (p. 94)
perceptual constancy (p. 119)
pheromones (p. 106)
pitch (p. 101)
proximity (p. 118)
pupil (p. 97)
receptor (p. 94)
relative size (p. 120)
retina (p. 97)
rhodopsin (p. 98)
rods (p. 98)
saturation (p. 96)
selection (p. 114)
sensation (p. 93)
sensory adaptation (p. 95)
shape constancy (p. 119)
similarity (p. 118)
size constancy (p. 119)
taste buds (p. 105)
timbre (p. 101)
vestibular sacs (p. 110)

*The key terms above can be used as search terms in InfoTrac, a database of readings, which can be found at http://infotrac-thomsonlearning.com.*

## Active Learning Review

**Sensation**
1. _____ is the process by which the sense organs gather and transduce information about the external or internal environment. The eyes, ears, nose, tongue, and other sense organs provide us with information and are the crucial detection instruments for this process.

**Perception**
2. _____ is the process through which we select, organize, and interpret the evidence from our senses, finding meaning in sensory information.

**sensation**
**perception**
3. Transducing information is the province of _____; interpreting that information is the role of _____.

### How Our Senses Function: Some General Principles

**stimulus**
**receptors**
4. A sense organ contains *receptors*, special structures that are sensitive to a particular form of energy called a stimulus. Light is the _____ that energizes special _____ in the eyes.

**stimulus**
**receptors**
5. For each of the senses, there is an *absolute threshold*, the minimum amount of stimulus energy to which the receptors can respond. If a clock ticks close to your ear, you hear it. If the clock is moved farther and farther away, eventually you will no longer hear it because the _____ has become so weak that the ear's _____ do not respond.

**absolute threshold**
6. The minimum amount of stimulus energy to which a receptor can respond is called its _____ _____.

7. The senses also have a threshold, which determines the minimum amount of change needed to discriminate between two stimuli that are similar but not exactly alike. If first one light is flashed and then a second light, the second must be 1.6% brighter (or dimmer) for the eyes to notice a difference. A second sound must be 10% "louder" (or "softer") than the first. So 1.6% is the _____ _____ for light.

   **difference threshold**

8. It was Weber who discovered that 10% is the _____ _____ for sound.

   **difference threshold**

9. The difference threshold is also called the just noticeable difference, or JND for short. The rule that the JND, or difference threshold, is a fixed percentage of the original stimulus is _____ _____.

   **Weber's law**

10. In practical terms, Weber's law means that the more intense the stimulation that a sense organ receives, the greater the increase in intensity required to produce a detectable difference. On a noisy city street, you may notice the loud honk of an automobile horn but be unaware that a friend is shouting to you from down the block. This is because the horn, but not the voice, has enough energy above and beyond the stimulation you already hear to produce a _____ _____ _____, or to reach your _____ _____.

    **just noticeable difference, difference threshold**

11. When you enter a fish market, you experience a strong smell of fish at first, but eventually the fishy smell seems to go away. This is because of *sensory adaptation*, which means that our senses adjust, or _____, to a stimulus after a time.

    **adapt**

12. The tendency of our conscious sensations to fade away after steady and continued stimulation is called _____ _____.

    **sensory adaptation**

## The Power of Vision

13. The energy or _____ for vision are light waves, which consist of pulsations of electromagnetic energy that have three important qualities: wavelength, intensity or amplitude, and complexity.

    **stimuli**

14. The first quality of light waves is the distance between the pulsations or waves, which is called _____. It determines our sensation of *hue*, or color.

    **wavelength**

15. Wavelength produces our sensation of _____, which is the scientific name for color.

    **hue**

16. The second quality of light waves, the amount of energy, is called _____ or _____; it determines *brightness*. A 100-watt light bulb looks _____ than a 50-watt bulb because the light waves have greater intensity, or amplitude.

    **intensity**
    **amplitude, brighter**

17. In addition to color, which is determined by _____, and brightness, which is determined by _____, light waves also have complexity, which is determined by the number of other wavelengths that are mixed together.

    **wavelength**
    **intensity**

18. The relative purity of the light wave, called its _____, determines the sensation of *saturation*. A source of light that is very pure is seen as a vivid hue. If other wavelengths are mixed in, we see the color as duller or muddier and as having less _____.

    **complexity**

    **saturation**

19. Figure 3.3 (page 97) is a diagram of the human eye. Light passes through the _____, the opening you see in your mirror as a small black circle surrounded by the colored _____, which is muscle tissue. Like the diaphragm of a camera, the muscles of the _____ contract in response to strong illumination, minimizing the size of the _____ to admit less light.

    **pupil**
    **iris**
    **iris**
    **pupil**

20. After light passes through the _____ formed by the colored _____, it then goes through the transparent *lens*. The lens, like that of a camera, focuses the light waves sharply on the back of the eyeball.

    **pupil, iris**

21. Light waves are focused by the _____, the shape of which is controlled by the ciliary muscles.

    **lens**

pupil

ciliary muscles

lens
retina
retina

rods
cones
retina
cones

rods
retina, fovea

fovea

optic nerve

blind spot

retina

rhodopsin

dark adaptation
rhodopsin

dark adaptation

cones

opponent-process

sex

color-blind

sound waves

22. The iris controls the size of the _____ and thus the amount of light that enters the eye. The shape of the lens, which focuses the waves, is controlled by the _____ _____.

23. The receptors for vision are light-sensitive neural cells packed tightly together in the *retina* at the back of the eyeball. The ciliary muscles adjust the _____ to focus the image on the light-sensitive _____.

24. The visual receptors, located at the back of the eyeball in the _____, are of two kinds. *Rods* are sensitive to movement, blacks, grays, and whites but not to color; *cones* are sensitive to color as well as to brightness and movement.

25. The visual receptors that are sensitive only to movement and brightness from black to white are the _____. The visual receptors that are sensitive to hue, and are therefore responsible for color vision, are the _____.

26. The cones are most numerous toward the middle of the _____, especially in an area at the very center called the *fovea*, which contains only _____ packed together more tightly than anywhere else. In contrast, the periphery of the retina contains mostly _____.

27. It is in the center part of the _____, called the _____, that we see color and our vision is sharpest.

28. When we read or do anything else that requires a very sharp image, we keep the object in the center of the field of vision so that its light waves fall on the _____.

29. The impulses from the rods and cones leave the eyeball by way of the _____ _____, the connector between the nerves from the eyes' receptors and the brain.

30. The place on the retina where the optic nerve is connected has no receptors and constitutes a _____ _____. It is difficult to see an image that falls there.

31. The rods and cones, located in the light-sensitive _____, contain pigments that absorb light. The light bleaches the pigments at a rate that depends on the intensity and wavelength of the light; these chemical changes cause the neurons to fire. When light strikes the rods, it bleaches a pigment called _____, causing the neurons to fire.

32. The visual system operates under a wide range of illumination. The fact that you see better in a darkened movie theater after several minutes illustrates the process of _____ _____.

33. When you spend time in the dark, the rods' light-sensitive pigment _____ builds up, producing extra sensitivity—almost 100,000 times more sensitivity after 30 minutes of _____ _____.

34. Opponent-process theory helps explain the way vision operates. This pattern theory is based in part on the differences in sensitivity among the rods and the three types of _____.

35. We see the great variety of images and colors that we do because of patterns of firing from the receptors, according to the _____-_____ theory of color vision.

36. In the United States, over 8% of males but less than 1% of females are *color blind*—that is, they have at least some difficulty discriminating colors. Thus, color blindness is a _____-linked disorder.

37. Inability to detect the difference between reds and greens is more common than reduced sensitivity to blues and yellows among individuals who are _____-_____.

### The Power of Hearing

38. Compressions and expansions of the air, called _____ _____, vary in a number of ways that affect sensation and perception. One is frequency, or the number of waves per second, which determines *pitch*.

39. The number of sound waves per second, called frequency, is responsible for the _____ of the sound we hear, from the lowest boom of a foghorn to the highest tweet of a piccolo.

**pitch**

40. *Loudness* is determined by the sound wave's amplitude, or strength. If you touch the piano key for middle C gently and then strike it hard, the second sound wave has greater _____ than the first, even though both have the same physical _____.

**amplitude**
**frequency**

41. Virtually all sources of sounds produce not just a single frequency but other frequencies as well. When a piano string vibrates at middle C, parts of the string also vibrate with reduced amplitude at other frequencies; these additional vibrations cause _____, which reflects the physical _____ of the sound wave.

**timbre, complexity**

42. Because human vocal cords vibrate in different ways and produce different patterns of complexity, their sound waves also vary in the _____ they create.

**timbre**

43. You may have noted a resemblance between the ways in which the physical qualities of light and sound waves affect vision and hearing. Just as the frequency of sound waves determines _____, the wavelength of light determines _____.

**pitch**
**hue**

44. Just as the amplitude of sound waves determines _____, the intensity of light determines _____.

**loudness**
**brightness**

45. And just as the complexity of sound determines _____, the complexity of light waves determines _____.

**timbre**
**saturation**

46. Figure 3.9 (page 103) is a diagram of the parts of the human ear. Sound waves gathered by the _____ _____, or visible portion, cause vibrations to travel to the _____, which moves three small bones in the *middle ear*.

**outer ear**
**eardrum**

47. The three bones of the _____ _____ amplify the sound. The last bone, called the stapes, is mounted like a piston on the cochlea.

**middle ear**

48. After amplification, the sound vibration is conducted via the last bone of the middle ear, the _____, to the _____ of the *inner ear*.

**stapes, cochlea**

49. A bony structure that is the size of a pea and shaped like a snail's shell is the _____, which contains the receptors for hearing in the _____ _____.

**cochlea, inner ear**

50. The cochlea is divided roughly in half by the basilar membrane, stretched across it from one end to the other. The hearing receptors lie atop the _____ membrane, which makes wavelike motions as the fluid inside the cochlea responds to vibrations.

**basilar**

51. It is the wavelike motions of the _____ _____ inside the _____ that jiggle the hearing receptors, called the organ of Corti.

**basilar membrane, cochlea**

52. The hair cells, or _____ of _____, which are located atop the _____ _____, dance in sympathetic vibration with the sound wave and send neural impulses along the *auditory nerve* to the brain to produce hearing.

**organ, Corti**
**basilar membrane**

## Taste, Smell, Touch, and the Two Unnoticed Senses

53. Taste is typically associated with the *taste bud* receptors that line the tongue and back of our mouth. But the flavor of food is influenced by its temperature, smell, and other factors, in addition to sweet, sour, salty, and bitter characteristics detected by the _____ _____.

**taste buds**

54. The receptors for smell are in the _____ _____, located at the top of the nasal passage. The receptors' sensitivity to biochemical *odorants* appears to depend in part on the number of receptors contained in the olfactory epithelium.

**olfactory epithelium**

55. Nonhuman animals often give off biochemical _____ called *pheromones* that signal danger, territory, or sexual receptivity. Humans may also produce sexual _____, but the effects of these are debatable.

**odorants**

**pheromones**

bodily movement
equilibrium

vestibular sacs, semicircular
canals, equilibrium

perception
sensation (or sensations)

feature detectors

change, feature detectors

change

movement
change, movement

feature detectors
contrast, size
intensity

selection

selection

mood

sensory
channel, select
simultaneous
sensory

select

56. Often unnoticed are the senses of bodily movement (kinesthesis) and equilibrium. Receptors in the muscles, tendons, and joints provide information about our _____ _____; receptors in the *vestibular sacs* of the semicircular canals of the inner ear help us to keep our _____.

57. Tiny pieces of stone-like crystal whose movement can be detected by receptors in the _____ _____ of the _____ _____ help us stay balanced, or in a state of _____ with respect to the force of gravity.

## Perception and Survival

58. The process by which we become aware of our environment by selecting, organizing, and interpreting sensory information is called _____, and our ability to add meaning to physical _____ is greatly assisted by the presence of specialized cells called *feature detectors*.

59. Cells that respond immediately to stimuli representing important information—such as the shapes of objects, motion, and the changes in sound that make up the flow of conversation—are called _____ _____.

60. Our inborn skills are particularly suited to spotting any change in stimulation, which is often the most useful information in survival. Our ability to perceive _____ sometimes depends on special cells called _____ _____ and other prewired characteristics of the nervous system.

61. One important form of _____ in stimulation is movement. To our ancestors, the sudden approach of a wild animal meant danger, regardless of whether the animal was a lion or a bear. Thus, there was survival value in rapid detection of _____.

62. Besides _____ and _____, other compelling stimulus attributes are contrast, size, and intensity. Apparently inborn characteristics of the nervous system, including _____ _____, make us sit up and take notice of a _____ in brightness, the _____ of objects in our field of vision, and the _____ of stimuli that are bright or loud.

## Selection and Attention

63. Of the three functions of perception—selection, organization, and interpretation—*selection* heads the list. This is because perception must start with the _____ of stimuli to attend to.

64. Although much selection of stimulation depends on the inborn structure of the nervous system, learned dispositions, such as interests, motives, and moods, also influence our _____ process.

65. You have probably noticed that when you are feeling on top of the world, you are aware that the sun is shining and everybody seems to be smiling. But when you are out of sorts, you are quick to notice anything that is potentially irritating, like noise outside the window or a watchband that feels too tight. This is an example of how perception is influenced by your _____ of the moment.

66. Selection is difficult if two simultaneous inputs arrive in the same sensory channel. Using earphones that deliver one spoken message to the right ear and a different message to the left ear, experimenters have found that subjects cannot pay attention to and understand two messages from one _____ _____ at the same time. They must _____ one message only.

67. Attending to _____ inputs is somewhat easier if the stimuli arrive in different _____ channels, such as vision and hearing.

## Organizing Our Perceptions

68. After we _____ one of the many sensory inputs from the environment for further exploration, we strive to find organization that forms the stimulus into some kind of meaningful unit.

69. Arranging visual inputs into a "whole," such as a face or a car, and forming auditory inputs into a pattern, such as meaningful speech or a rap at the door, are examples of how we _____ sensations into meaningful units.

organize
organization

70. In vision, determining what an object is through _____ depends in part on the perceptual principle of *figure and ground*. As you read this page, your eyes are stimulated by the white space and many little black lines, curves, squiggles, and dots. You perceive all this as black _____—letters and words—seen against a white _____. What separates the figure from the background is clearly perceived dividing lines called contours.

figures
ground

71. With the aid of figure and ground, a number of other principles help to _____ our perceptions into _____.

organize, wholes

72. We will perceive an object as a circle even if portions of the curved figure are missing because of the principle of _____.

closure

73. We are more likely to see a line as wavy than as a series of scallops because of our tendency toward _____.

continuity

74. In addition to using the principles of _____ and _____, we organize stimuli according to their *similarity* and *proximity*.

closure, continuity

75. Instead of seeing three shaded and five white blocks as a set of eight, we are more likely to see two sets of different blocks because of the _____ of coloring.

similarity

76. Pausing after commas and periods when we read a sentence out loud helps the listener to group the words between these punctuation marks by the principle of _____.

proximity

77. In sum, the principles of perceptual _____ include _____, _____, _____, and _____. But alone they are not sufficient; we also perceive a stable and consistent world because of our tendency toward *perceptual constancy*.

organization, closure,
continuity, similarity,
proximity

78. For example, no matter what angle we look at a dish from, we perceive it as round. The dish does not seem to change its shape, regardless of the image it casts on our retinas, because of the tendency toward _____ constancy.

shape

79. We perceive a dish as having not only a *constant shape*, but also a *constant size*, regardless of whether it is near or far. Two examples of _____ constancies are that of _____ and _____.

perceptual
shape, size

80. Not only must we organize perceptions to determine what stimuli are; we also need to know where objects are located. Just to walk around without bumping into chairs and other people, we must be able to perceive _____ and _____, for example.

distance
depth
perception

81. Two factors that aid distance and depth _____ are *binocular* vision (in which the two eyes receive slightly different images) and *monocular* vision, which uses visual cues for which only one eye is necessary. These cues include *interposition* (nearby objects block our view of what seem to be more distant ones), *linear perspective* (two parallel lines seem to draw closer together as they recede into the distance), and *relative size* (larger objects seem closer than smaller ones).

82. The two eyes receive slightly different images, a cue to distance and depth perception known as _____ vision.

binocular

83. If we see a boy blocking off part of our view of a tree, we know that the boy is closer than the tree. If the tree obscures part of the boy, we know that the tree is closer. This _____ cue is called _____.

monocular, interposition

84. In a photograph, two railroad tracks seem to draw closer together as they recede into the distance, illustrating how _____ _____ contributes to the perception of distance and depth. Similarly, larger objects are usually perceived as closer than smaller ones because of the principle of _____ _____.

linear perspective

relative
size

selection
organization

interpretation

prototype, schema

perceptual
expectation

85. In attaching meaning to our sensations, we pick particular stimuli to attend to by the process of _____, we determine what and where an object is by the process of _____, and we attach further meaning through the process of interpretation.

86. The perceptual process of finding meaning, called _____, is clearly more dependent on learning than on inborn characteristics of the nervous system. For example, you know that the object you have selected for attention and organized into a pattern of head, furry body, and wagging tail is a dog and not a tree because you have stored in memory what is called a prototype or schema—a sort of generalized picture of what a dog looks like.

87. Because the stimulus resembles the _____ or _____ you have acquired, you can quickly interpret what the stimulus means.

88. In quickly deciding what a stimulus means, we are often influenced by perceptual expectations. The mental set we have, which is the result of learning to expect certain things to happen in our environment, constitutes a _____ _____.

# Practice Test

____ 1. Weber's law states that
   a. the absolute threshold is the same for all stimuli.
   b. repeated exposure to a stimulus makes the sensation for that stimulus progressively weaker.
   c. the just noticeable difference is always the same fraction of the absolute threshold.
   d. the difference threshold is a fixed percentage of the original stimulus over a wide range of stimuli within a given sense.

____ 2. Which of the following is *not* correct?
   a. Intensity is to brightness as amplitude is to loudness.
   b. Complexity is to saturation as timbre is to pitch.
   c. Wavelength is to hue as frequency is to pitch.
   d. All of the above are correct.

____ 3. When you first enter the perfume section of a department store, the smell is strong and perhaps overwhelming. If you stay for a long time, the odor seems to go away. This demonstrates
   a. the difference threshold.
   b. just noticeable difference.
   c. sensory adaptation.
   d. broad-tuned receptors.

____ 4. When many other different wavelengths are added to a green, the light appears
   a. to have more timbre.
   b. more complex.
   c. less intensely green.
   d. more saturated.

____ 5. The eye's ciliary muscles control
   a. the way the eyeball is oriented.
   b. the size of the pupil.
   c. the sense of bodily movement.
   d. the shape of the lens of the eye.

____ 6. Relative to rods, cones are
   a. more numerous.
   b. more sensitive to dim light.
   c. more concentrated toward the center of the retina.
   d. filled with more rhodopsin, which, when stimulated by light, produces impulses corresponding to the three basic color types.

____ 7. The pitch of a sound is most closely associated with what aspect of light?
   a. wavelength
   b. hue
   c. intensity
   d. complexity

____ 8. The correct sequence in which sound is transmitted to the brain is
   a. cochlea, bones of the middle ear, basilar membrane.
   b. stapes, organ of Corti, eardrum.
   c. eardrum, stapes, cochlea, basilar membrane, organ of Corti.
   d. outer ear, eardrum, middle ear, cochlea, stapes.

____ 9. Neural cells that respond to a vertical line but not a horizontal line exemplify
   a. feature detectors.
   b. a linear perspective system.
   c. pattern analyzers.
   d. a selection and organization process.

____ 10. Cells in the neural pathways from eye to brain are especially sensitive to
   a. pattern and movement.
   b. color.
   c. brightness and saturation.
   d. distant objects.

____ 11. Which of the following aspects of a stimulus is likely to get your attention very quickly?
   a. movement
   b. size
   c. contrast
   d. all of the above

____ 12. Perception begins with
   a. organization.
   b. interpretation.
   c. selection.
   d. adaptation.

____ 13. If you are trying to follow two ball games on different TV sets, you will do best if you
   a. watch one game with the sound turned off, and listen to the other game.
   b. use single earphones that send the sound from one set to the right ear and from the other set to the left ear.
   c. close your eyes and listen to the two games.
   d. turn off the sound on both sets and watch both games.

____**14.** When you listen to a person speaking in another language with which you are familiar but not entirely fluent, you may miss some words but understand the meaning because of
  **a.** similarity.
  **b.** closure.
  **c.** perceptual constancy.
  **d.** continuity.

____**15.** As you walk toward the breakfast table, the dishes cast oval images on your eyes, yet you always perceive the dishes as circular. This is an example of perceptual
  **a.** closure.
  **b.** constancy.
  **c.** illusion.
  **d.** interpretation.

____**16.** Three-dimensional movies, but not other films, utilize
  **a.** binocular vision.
  **b.** perspective.
  **c.** movements of the eye muscles.
  **d.** interposition.

____**17.** Railroad tracks that seem to draw closer together as they recede into the distance are an example of
  **a.** linear perspective.
  **b.** relative size.
  **c.** binocular vision.
  **d.** feature detection.

____**18.** The element of perception most clearly dependent on learning rather than on inborn traits is
  **a.** organization.
  **b.** selection.
  **c.** interpretation.
  **d.** feature detection.

____**19.** A generalized picture or model of an object or event—learned in the past and stored in memory—is
  **a.** a perceptual expectation.
  **b.** a prototype or schema.
  **c.** a shape constancy.
  **d.** an opponent process.

____**20.** Our interpretation of a stimulus may be affected by
  **a.** our body chemistry.
  **b.** our mood or physical condition at the moment.
  **c.** our personality.
  **d.** all of the above

# Exercises

1. Weber's law states that the stimulus change needed for a *just noticeable difference,* or JND, is tiny when the initial stimulus magnitude is small and much bigger when the initial stimulus magnitude is large. For example, when a stereo is playing softly, only a slight increase in volume is required for you to hear it get louder. However, when the music starts out loud enough to rattle your neighbors' windows, the volume must be cranked up much more for you to notice an increase in loudness.

   This imprecise but interesting exercise will give you experience in determining a JND—in this case, a difference of pressure on the forearm.

   Here's what you'll need:

   - 70 quarters or 150 nickels
   - Seven (if you use quarters) or 15 (if you use nickels) pieces of aluminum foil, each about 3 inches square
   - A regular saucer, such as a porcelain or glass one
   - A paper saucer about the same size
   - A piece of string about 6 inches long
   - A blindfold
   - Four willing experimental participants

   First, prepare the weights by placing a stack of ten quarters (or, if you're low on funds, ten nickels) in the center of each piece of aluminum foil and then drawing up and twisting the foil so that the package looks something like a chocolate candy "kiss." Then wrap the twisted top of the kiss partway around a pencil so that it becomes a hook whose tip points down. You'll end up making either 7 stacks of quarters or 15 stacks of nickels.

   Have your first participant lay his or her forearm on a table, with the inside of the forearm facing upward. Then place the blindfold on your participant.

   Instruct the participant as follows: "I'm going to place a saucer on your forearm. Notice how heavy it feels. I'll be adding and removing weights from the saucer. Please tell me as soon as you notice the saucer get heavier."

   Put the empty *paper* saucer on the participant's upturned forearm, halfway between the wrist and the elbow.

   Holding the string at each end, gently lift a coin stack by its hook and place it on the saucer. Ask, "How about now? Did you notice a weight increase?"

   If the participant doesn't notice that the saucer got heavier, remove the stack using your string and then, after a short delay, place two stacks on the saucer at the same time. Ask the same question again.

   If the participant doesn't notice the increase in weight, remove the weights and then place three stacks on the saucer, and so on. Eventually, your participant will notice that the saucer got heavier. Using the data table, write down the number of coin stacks that had to be added for the difference—the JND—to be noticed.

   Now, repeat the same steps, except this time use the heavier regular saucer (which has greater initial stimulus magnitude) instead of the paper one. Again, write down the number of coin stacks that were necessary for the participant to notice that the saucer got heavier.

   Follow the same procedures (paper saucer first, then heavier saucer, each time writing down the number of weights necessary) for your next three participants.

   **Results Table**

   | Participant Number | Number of Weights with Paper Saucer | Number of Weights with Regular Saucer |
   |---|---|---|
   | 1 | | |
   | 2 | | |
   | 3 | | |
   | 4 | | |

   When the table has been filled in, separately total the Weights with Paper Saucer and Weights with Regular Saucer columns. Then divide each total by 4 (the number of participants) to get the average for each.

   Compare the averages, and answer the following questions, indicating whether you used quarters or nickels.

   a. What explains the difference between the averages?
   b. Is the difference between the averages in the expected direction, given your knowledge of Weber's law? Why or why not?
   c. Using Weber's law, explain how a person's accuracy in perceiving the threat posed by an oncoming vehicle with headlights on would depend on whether the vehicle was traveling down a road in the daytime or down a dark road at night.

2. Figures 3.33 and 3.34 are diagrams of the eye and ear, with several parts located but not labeled. Write in the correct name for each part indicated.

Then, without looking at the diagrams, write two paragraphs—one for vision and one for hearing—that describe the path a stimulus takes from receptor to brain. Mention as many parts of the sensory system as you can and tell the role each part plays.

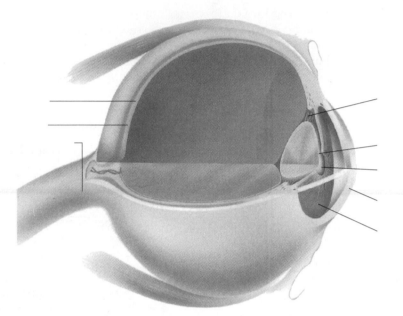

**FIGURE 3.33**

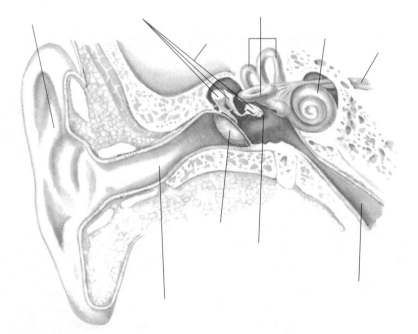

**FIGURE 3.34**

# 4

# Conditioning and Learning

© Jeff Greenberg/Index Stock Imagery

**Conditioning**
The establishment of a relationship between stimuli and responses, or vice versa.

Our behavior depends to a large extent on the process of *learning*—a subject that has been a central concern of psychology from the very beginning. Indeed, every chapter in this text includes some discussion of the role of learning. In this chapter, we look at basic principles and phenomena in learning that have been studied for over a century and continue to be studied, though nowadays from a different perspective.

During the first half or so of the 20th century, learning processes were considered primarily from the viewpoint of **conditioning,** which emphasizes the establishment of overt associations between stimuli and responses or between responses and stimuli. The early learning theorists thought that *all* behavior—human or otherwise—could be understood in terms of conditioning. They were wrong, as discussed at various points in the chapter, but their error was mainly one of degree. Just as there are some important differences between humans and other animals where learning is concerned, we do have some things in common, and a fair amount of learning can indeed be understood in terms of conditioning. This is especially true when we allow for the often-intricate cognitive processes that occur in between stimuli and responses—processes that are mentioned throughout the chapter where they shed light on learning and conditioning phenomena.

As noted in Chapter 1 and discussed further at the end of this chapter, even during the heyday of strict behaviorism, some psychologists believed that learning could not be fully understood without considering the subtle workings of the brain. The rise of cognitive psychology has popularized this view of learning as the acquisition of knowledge—one of the steps in "the human being's active interaction with information about the world" (Klatzky, 1980). It is this process that allows us

Although much learning takes place in school classrooms, learning also occurs in a variety of other situations, including the home, the workplace, and social and recreational settings.

to accomplish the learning necessary, for example, to play a musical instrument, devise a computer program, or write a textbook.

Thus, both approaches to studying learning have been fruitful. Together, they represent what is today a generally accepted definition of **learning:** a relatively permanent change in behavior potential resulting from experience. "Relatively permanent" means that once something is learned, it typically is not "unlearned" or forgotten. Forgetting is more likely caused by an inability to retrieve something from memory, as discussed in Chapter 5. "Behavior potential" emphasizes that learning does not necessarily yield a change in what a person thinks or does at the time the learning occurs. For example, specific things that you learn in this text may or may not have an effect on your behavior as you learn them, but they have potential for affecting your behavior at some future time. Finally, *experience* is included in the definition to rule out changes such as those attributable to biological development.

In this chapter, we first consider *classical conditioning*, then turn to *operant conditioning*, and wind up with a survey of the theories of early researchers who studied learning processes from a cognitive perspective. Along the way, we explore what conditioning does and does not explain well, along with the role of *predispositions*—built-in tendencies in learning and behavior that humans as well as members of other species display.

> **Learning**
> A relatively permanent change in behavior potential as a result of experience.

# CLASSICAL CONDITIONING

Many of us have seemingly inexplicable preferences for certain things, especially certain people. You may be instantly attracted to men who have beards or men who don't, to small women or women who are tall and broad shouldered. You may feel unexplained warmth toward a certain tone of voice or the way a person walks, gestures, or dresses. You know that these matters have nothing to do with what the person is really like, yet you find yourself attracted—or perhaps repelled.

> **FOCUS QUESTIONS**
> - What is classical conditioning and how did Pavlov study it?
> - What basic procedures are involved in classical conditioning?

Similarly, many of us are troubled by intense, unreasonable fears. You may be utterly terrified of snakes, dogs, rats, spiders, bees, cockroaches, or other animals or situations that *might* be dangerous but much more often aren't. Collectively, such extremely disproportionate fears are known as *phobias* (see Chapter 13).

Likes, dislikes, fears, and more may be learned in various ways (e.g., see De Houwer, Thomas, & Baeyens, 2001), but one basic way is through pairings of an initially neutral stimulus—one that does not produce a certain response—with another stimulus that does. To see how this works, we begin with the research of Ivan Pavlov.

## Pavlov and the Salivating Dogs

Pavlov conducted his experiments in the early years of the 20th century in Saint Petersburg, Russia. After spending half of his career as a physiologist, he serendipitously turned to the study of how "automatic" responses such as **reflexes** can become associated with stimuli other than those that normally produce them (see Chapter 1). Reflexes do not require thought. In humans, one reflex is the knee jerk: When you have your legs crossed, with one foot dangling in the air, a sharp tap just below the kneecap makes the lower part of your leg jump. Another reflex makes your pupils smaller whenever a bright light strikes your eyes. It is important

> **Reflex**
> A built-in or otherwise automatic response to a specific stimulus.

Ivan Pavlov (at center) is shown in his laboratory with his assistants, his experimental apparatus, and one of the dogs that served as subjects in his research on conditioning.

### Classical conditioning
**The establishment of a relationship between two stimuli, typically one that evokes a reflex response and one that is initially neutral with regard to this response.**

to note that emotional responses can also be reflexive. In response to a sudden loud noise nearby, even a baby will be startled and fearful, producing the bodily changes and cognitive reactions characteristic of fear.

Pavlov's subjects were dogs, and his experimental apparatus was the simple but effective device illustrated in Figure 4.1. When he began to realize the significance of what is now called **classical conditioning,** which in essence consists of establishing a learned association between two stimuli, Pavlov began studying the conditioning of salivation—a reflex action of the mouth's salivary glands. He strapped a dog into the harness shown in Figure 4.1 and then used sounds as a stimulus. (Initially he used the beat of a metronome, but later he changed to more manageable bells and tones.) The dog made a few movements called *orienting responses*, but, as expected, no salivation occurred. The primary stimulus for salivation is the presence of food in the mouth—not the sound of a bell. When food was delivered and the dog took it into its mouth, drops of saliva flowed freely down the tube shown in the figure.

Now Pavlov set about associating the neutral stimulus of the sound with the reflex action of the salivary glands. When the bell was sounded, he gave the dog a small amount of food and the dog salivated. After a number of instances in which the sound was paired with the food, he sounded the bell without presenting food—and saliva flowed anyway (Pavlov, 1927/1960). Thus, the dog had learned an association between the two stimuli—specifically, that the sound would usually be followed by food.

Over the years, psychologists have studied classical conditioning with a wide variety of techniques and with various species of animals—mostly rats, pigeons, and rabbits. Such learning has been shown to be possible even in the primitive sea snail (Carew, Hawkins, & Kandel, 1983). One technique—for conditioning a rabbit to blink—is illustrated in Figure 4.2. Similar procedures have been used to study the reflexive eyeblink response in humans.

**FIGURE 4.1** Pavlov's apparatus. A tube attached to the dog's salivary glands collects saliva, and the number of drops from the tube is recorded on a revolving drum outside the chamber. The experimenter can watch the dog through a one-way mirror and deliver food to the dog's feed pan by remote control. Thus, there is nothing in the chamber to get the dog's attention except the food and whatever other stimulus the experimenter wishes to present, such as the sound of a bell. *Yerkes & Morgulis, 1909.*

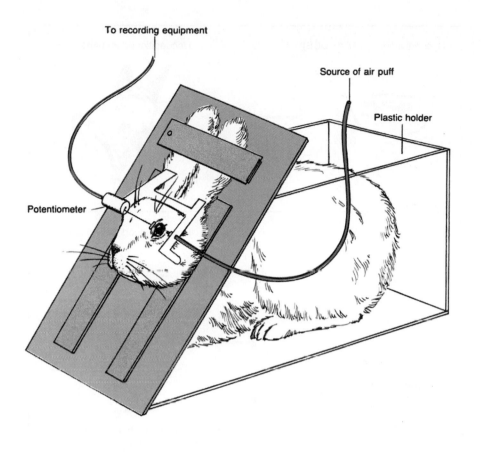

To recording equipment

Source of air puff

Plastic holder

Potentiometer

**FIGURE 4.2 Conditioning the eyeblink.** The rabbit's head is held stationary, and one end of a fine string is attached to the upper lid of one eye. The other end is attached to a small potentiometer—an electrical device through which eyelid movements can be translated into impulses and recorded. The stimulus for the eyeblink reflex is a light puff of air to the surface of the eye. In various conditioning experiments, rabbits have learned through classical conditioning to blink in response to totally new stimuli—including lights, tones, and even vibration of the animal's abdomen with a hand massager.
*Adapted from Domjan & Burkhard, 1986.*

## Classical Conditioning: The Basics

To understand how classical conditioning occurs, we first consider its five basic elements. These elements, illustrated in Figure 4.3, are common to all instances of classical conditioning.

1. The food was the **unconditioned stimulus (UCS)** that produced salivation. Any stimulus that automatically and reliably produces a particular response can serve as a UCS.

2. The sound of the bell was initially a neutral stimulus ($S_N$) with respect to salivation. But after repeated pairings with the UCS, it became a **conditioned stimulus (CS)** that also elicited salivation. In principle, any stimulus a subject or participant can detect may be the CS—although, as discussed later in the chapter, certain CSs work better than others with certain UCSs.

3. The response of the salivary glands to the food was the **unconditioned response (UCR)** because it occurred without prior learning.

4. The response of the salivary glands to the sound of the bell was the **conditioned response (CR),** which was learned. Although both the CR and the UCR are salivation, they differ in two important ways. First, the CR is slower to occur; for example, the dog doesn't salivate quite as quickly in response to the sound as it does to the food. Second, the CR is "weaker"; the dog doesn't salivate as much in response to the sound as it does to the food.

5. The UCS and the CS-to-be are repeatedly presented together; each such pairing is called a *conditioning trial.* What is learned in classical conditioning is an association between the CS and the UCS. To assess whether classical conditioning has occurred, the CS is presented by itself. This is called a *test trial.*

**Unconditioned stimulus (UCS)**
Any stimulus that automatically and reliably produces a particular response, such as a reflex.

**Conditioned stimulus (CS)**
An initially neutral stimulus that comes to elicit a response similar to that elicited by a UCS.

**Unconditioned response (UCR)**
The automatic response to an unconditioned stimulus.

**Conditioned response (CR)**
The learned response to a conditioned stimulus.

FIGURE 4.3 The basic
elements of classical conditioning. **Although there may
be many variations in such
specifics as the timing of the
stimuli, the same basic steps
are followed in all instances
of classical conditioning.**

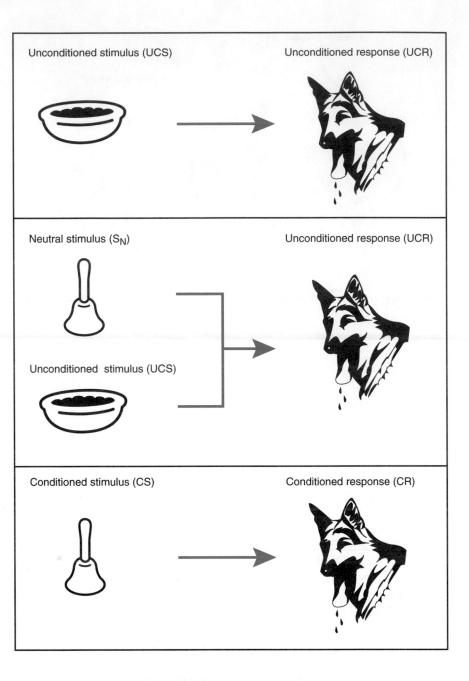

**Test Yourself**

**(a)** Juan, a 4-year-old, became nauseated and vomited
when he sat in the dentist's
chair for the first time. Since
that episode, he feels queasy
whenever he sees anyone
in a white coat. What conditioning might explain Juan's
reaction?

**(b)** In the previous question, what would you call the
dentist's garb?

(The answers are on page 170.)

# CLASSICAL CONDITIONING PHENOMENA AND APPLICATIONS

**FOCUS QUESTIONS**
- Why is the timing of the CS and UCS important in classical conditioning?
- Why is it important for the CS to "predict" the UCS?
- How do generalization and discrimination work?
- How do biological predispositions affect classical conditioning?

The rate at which classical conditioning occurs and the strength and persistence of the conditioned response are affected by a variety of factors, including the timing of the CS and UCS, the number of conditioning trials, the consistency of the CS-UCS pairings, and biological predispositions of the learner. These factors and some interesting phenomena in classical conditioning—both in laboratory animals and in humans—are discussed in this section.

## Timing and the Number of Conditioning Trials

In general, the conditioning process is most effective when the CS (the bell, in Pavlov's experiment) is presented just before the UCS (the food)—an arrangement called **delayed conditioning.** For many stimuli, a very brief delay of about 0.5 sec works best. Less effective are **simultaneous conditioning,** in which the CS and the UCS are presented at exactly the same time, and **trace conditioning,** in which the CS is presented and discontinued before the UCS. Each type of conditioning is illustrated in Figure 4.4.

The number of trials necessary to establish a CR varies according to the behavior being conditioned. For example, fear reactions are readily conditioned in the laboratory and in everyday life. After only a few trials in which a neutral stimulus is paired with a painful UCS such as electric shock, the now CS will produce bodily reactions symptomatic of fear—crouching, trembling, urination, defecation—indicating that the animal has learned that the CS signals that a shock is coming. Human phobias can be acquired in much the same way. If you're phobic of dogs, it could be that as a small child you were repeatedly menaced by a large dog and thereby conditioned to be terrified at the very sight of one—perhaps for life. The question of why phobias can be so enduring, however, requires an understanding of operant conditioning, discussed later in the chapter.

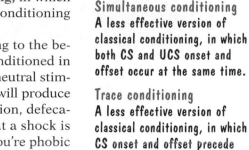

**Delayed conditioning**
The most effective version of classical conditioning, in which CS onset precedes UCS onset and the offset of both stimuli is typically at the same time.

**Simultaneous conditioning**
A less effective version of classical conditioning, in which both CS and UCS onset and offset occur at the same time.

**Trace conditioning**
A less effective version of classical conditioning, in which CS onset and offset precede UCS onset.

## Extinction and Recovery of Conditioned Responses

Once Pavlov had established the conditioned salivary response, he wanted to find out how long and under what circumstances it would persist. When he merely kept sounding the bell without presenting food, he found that within a very short time the flow of saliva in response to the sound began to decrease. Soon it stopped altogether, as shown in Figure 4.5. In the same way, your dog or cat would eventually stop getting agitated and salivating at the sound of a can opener if you stopped feeding it canned food. In Pavlov's terminology, this disappearance of the conditioned response is called **extinction.** When Pavlov occasionally followed the sound with food—thus providing the UCS some of the time but not every time—he found that he could make the conditioned response continue indefinitely.

Pavlov also demonstrated another phenomenon related to extinction. He withheld the UCS and let the CR disappear as usual, then gave the dog a rest away from the experimental apparatus. After a period of time, he put the dog in the apparatus again to see if a response to the bell would occur. Under these circumstances, the CR that had seemed to be completely gone reappeared. Pavlov called this **spontaneous recovery;** it is a clear illustration that behaviors that cease to occur are not simply unlearned or forgotten.

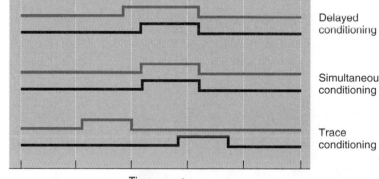

Time ⟶

**FIGURE 4.4 The importance of timing in classical conditioning.** Each pair of lines represents one conditioning trial. The top line in each pair represents the stimulus being conditioned, and the bottom line represents the unconditioned stimulus. Stimulus "onset" occurs when the line goes up; stimulus "offset" occurs when the line goes back down. Thus, in delayed conditioning, CS onset occurs before UCS onset; offset for both stimuli is typically at the same time. In simultaneous conditioning, CS and UCS onset occur at the same time, as do CS and UCS offset. In trace conditioning, CS onset and offset both occur before UCS onset.

**Extinction**
Disappearance of the CR upon discontinuation of the UCS.

**Spontaneous recovery**
Reappearance of an extinguished CR after the passage of time.

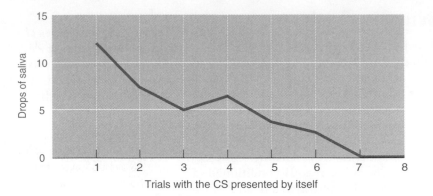

FIGURE 4.5 The conditioned response: going, going, gone. The graph shows what happened to Pavlov's dogs when the conditioned stimulus of sound was no longer accompanied by the unconditioned stimulus of food. The conditioned salivary response, very strong at first, gradually grew weaker. By the seventh time the bell was sounded, the conditioned response was extinguished—at least for this session.

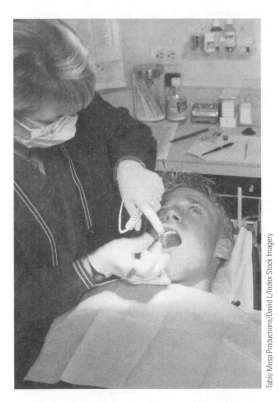

A person who has experienced painful dental procedures may develop a conditioned fear of dentists.

**Stimulus generalization** The tendency of a CR to occur to CSs that are similar to the original CS.

# Predictability of the Unconditioned Stimulus

For most conditioned responses, the crucial factor is not the number of times a CS is paired with a UCS but rather the reliability with which the CS *predicts* the occurrence of the UCS (Rescorla, 1988; Rescorla & Holland, 1982). In one experiment, dogs were first trained to jump back and forth in a "shuttle box" to escape an electric shock. (A shuttle box is simply a dog-sized enclosure divided in the middle by a short barrier to distinguish its two compartments.) After the dogs had learned to jump, they were divided into two groups. For one group, a tone CS and the electric shock UCS were presented randomly, so that a tone might occur before a shock just as often as it occurred after it. For the second group, the tone was usually followed by a shock. All the dogs were then presented only with the tone CS—that is, with no shock UCS. If learning an association between hearing a tone and feeling a shock required only that tones and shocks occur together, the first group should have learned to jump as quickly as the second group—both groups had experienced the same *number* of tones and shocks. But if learning to jump was easier when the tone usually *predicted* when the shock would occur, then the second group should have learned more quickly. The results showed that the dogs in the second group did indeed learn more quickly because of the relatively consistent relationship between the CS and the UCS.

This study suggests that we are more likely to develop a conditioned response—for example, a dislike for a particular type of person or physical appearance—if our encounters with that stimulus are consistently followed by unpleasant experiences. If exposure to the person and unpleasant experiences occur together but in a random rather than a predictable fashion, it is less likely that the conditioned dislike will develop.

# Stimulus Generalization and Discrimination

In Pavlov's experiments, there was nothing special about the sound produced by the bell. He later used many other kinds of stimuli and found that he could just as easily condition the salivary response to the sound of a tone or the flash of a light. He also discovered that a dog that had been conditioned to the sound of a bell would also salivate to the sound of a bell with a different tone. This phenomenon is called **stimulus generalization.** Once an organism has learned to respond to a particular stimulus, it tends to display that behavior toward similar stimuli as well—although to a progressively lesser extent as the stimuli become less similar. Thus, a dog or a cat displays a generalized response to the sound of any can being opened or bag being rustled—not just one that contains food or treats.

Stimulus generalization is essential to life because we never encounter the very same stimulus twice. Two portions of a food you like are never exactly the same; two chairs you sit on are never exactly the same. But as a result of generalization, you know what to do when you encounter the food or a chair.

After Pavlov had established the principle of stimulus generalization, he went on to demonstrate **stimulus discrimination.** By continuing to present food when he rang the original bell and omitting food when he sounded a different bell, Pavlov soon trained the dog to salivate much less to the sound of other bells than to the sound of the first bell. The dog had learned to discriminate between the training bell and the other ones. You may have noticed that pets have a generalized response to any sound that might be associated with food, but they also discriminate and respond less to the rustle of a grocery sack or the opening of a plastic container than to the rustle of a food bag or the opening of a can—assuming, of course, that the former have not been associated with food.

Pavlov also discovered that by taking advantage of the stimulus discrimination effect he could condition dogs to behave in abnormal ways. First, he projected a circle and an ellipse on a screen and conditioned dogs to discriminate between the two. Then he gradually changed the shape of the ellipse so that it looked more and more like a circle. Even when the difference in appearance was very slight, the dogs still discriminated successfully. When the difference became too small for the dogs to see and discrimination was impossible, the dogs acted strangely disturbed. Some became restless and aggressive; others became apathetic and developed muscle tremors and tics. Experiments like this suggest that some forms of abnormal human behavior may result from problems and difficulties that occur through classical conditioning—being unable to discriminate an object or a situation leaves you not knowing what to do, which can be highly frustrating and stressful.

**Stimulus discrimination** The tendency of a CR to be weaker or not to occur to CSs that are dissimilar to the original CS or that have undergone extinction.

## Nature versus Classical Conditioning

Up to this point, our discussion of classical conditioning has focused on general principles that might apply to all species and all behaviors. However, the power of classical conditioning depends on the degree to which the organism is prepared by its biological makeup to learn to associate a particular pair of stimuli—an issue that wasn't investigated until the latter part of the 20th century.

Researchers have now shown that it can be extremely difficult or even impossible to establish certain conditioned responses. For example, it is easy to condition a rat to avoid water with a distinctive taste when the drinking of that water is followed by sickness induced by the experimenter. Rats are prewired to associate taste (and smell) with foods. On the other hand, for rats and other animals that rely on taste, sounds are not a cue associated with eating. So when researchers paired a sound with the act of drinking unflavored water and then made the rats sick, the rats did not learn to avoid the water when they heard the noise (Holder, Bermudez-Rattoni, & Garcia, 1988). Rats are, however, prewired to associate sounds with danger and pain. In the same series of studies, John Garcia and colleagues verified this by easily conditioning the rats to avoid plain water by again pairing it with the sound but this time following the pairing with electric shock.

Thus, psychologists now know that each species is predisposed by heredity to learn to react to some stimuli but not others. For example, the ease with which *taste aversions* are learned is highly adaptive for all animals that use taste as a cue for what to eat. Such aversions are a special case of classical conditioning that "violates" the principles of timing and repeated trials discussed earlier, in that they can be learned in a single trial that spans several hours (e.g., see Welzl, D'Adamo, & Lipp, 2001).

## Test Yourself

**(c)** After 5 years, Kate—having been conditioned to feel weak and dizzy at the prospect of visiting her pediatrician—no longer gets such a reaction on entering the doctor's office. In classical conditioning, what term is used to describe this turn of events?

**(d)** Duane ate "Zesto" potato chips once and happened to become severely nauseous a couple of hours later. Now he won't eat any kind of potato chips. What classical conditioning phenomena is Duane displaying?

(The answers are on page 170.)

In evolutionary terms, those species that did not readily learn to avoid foods that made them sick were much less likely to survive long enough to reproduce. Birds use visual cues for eating, and experiments have shown that they can easily relate sickness to shapes, patterns, and perhaps colors, but not to taste. In humans, too, conditioning is easier and CRs are stronger with certain stimuli. Like rats, humans usually learn taste and food aversions as a result of sickness—not when eating the food is associated with accidents such as breaking a limb or getting cut. Also, sickness is much more likely to result in conditioned aversion to the actual foods involved than to aversion to related stimuli such as where the food was eaten (Garb & Stunkard, 1974; Logue, Ophir, & Strauss, 1981).

## Other Classical Conditioning Phenomena

We saw earlier that phobias and other fears can be acquired through classical conditioning. Here we look at an example of how this happens, in the context of a classic (and nowadays unethical) experiment conducted in the early 1920s. Other phenomena discussed in this section relate to the relationship between conditioning and illness, immune responses, and drug reactions.

**Conditioned Terror: The Baby Who Feared Santa Claus**    What salivating dogs and blinking rabbits tell us about more complicated forms of human behavior was demonstrated in a famous (most would say infamous) experiment performed by J. B. Watson and Rosalie Rayner and initially reported in 1920. Watson and Rayner's subject was an 11-month-old boy known as "Little Albert." The experiment was designed to demonstrate that unwarranted and persistent human fears (such as phobias) could be established through classical conditioning. This wasn't known at the time—psychoanalysts, for example, were offering quite different explanations for such fears, based on unresolved Oedipal complexes or the like (see Chapter 9).

Albert initially had no fear of white laboratory rats, one of which served as the CS. Each conditioning trial consisted of one experimenter presenting the rat to Albert as the other stood behind him and made a loud, frightening noise (the UCS) by hitting a steel bar with a hammer. Before long, the rat alone caused Albert to become afraid and cry, and thus the CR was established. To an extent, the fear also generalized to other things such as a dog and a fur coat—as well as a white Santa Claus beard worn by Watson. The experiment was actually relatively haphazard, and Albert's fear wasn't always consistent and predictable, but Watson and Rayner did for the most part succeed in what they had set out to accomplish: Albert's behavior closely resembled a phobia for just about anything white and furry (for the details of the experiment, see Harris, 1979).

Watson and Rayner intended to remove Albert's fearful behavior through "counterconditioning"—that is, by presenting a treat along with the rat. But at that point Albert's mother, who apparently had been unaware of what was going on, removed him from the study. Nothing is known about Albert or his fears after that. If the fear persisted, Albert may even have come to be afraid of sidewalk or department store Santa Clauses—without ever knowing why.

Although the Little Albert experiment was categorically unethical according to today's APA guidelines (see Chapter 1) and indeed anyone's standards, it did cast light on the unexplained fears we often display as adults. At least some of them are conditioned responses, learned in childhood through some long-forgotten pairing of stimuli—perhaps an experience that did not even impress us much at the time. Similarly, the experiment helps explain many of our unreasonable preferences. A liking for certain kinds of people may go back to a childhood experience in which a person with that kind of face or body build or mannerisms elicited responses of warmth and pleasure.

**Conditioned Illness**     Classical conditioning can cause illnesses that have no physical basis. In one experiment, rats were put into a coma with a heavy dose of insulin, producing the severe reaction known as insulin shock (due to depletion of glucose, the blood sugar used by the brain). The drug was administered with a hypodermic syringe while a bright light was on. The association of the syringe and light CSs with the insulin UCS and the resulting coma resulted in a spectacular kind of conditioning. When the same light was turned on and the same syringe was used to inject a harmless salt solution, the animals went into a coma characteristic of insulin shock (Sawrey, Conger, & Turrell, 1956). More recent research has demonstrated that by pairing the injection of insulin with normally irrelevant stimuli such as a strange odor, noise, and light, it is possible to condition a decrease in blood sugar level in humans (Fehm-Wolfsdorf, Gnadler, Kern, Klosterhalfen, & Kerner, 1993).

Such experiments indicate the ways in which classical conditioning can produce some of the strange physical symptoms that may bother us as adults. An asthma sufferer may have been conditioned—not in the laboratory but by some real life experience—to have an attack upon walking into a particular room, seeing a particular person, or even looking at a certain kind of picture on TV. Events that occur in our lives, unimportant in themselves but associated with past experiences, may make us develop headaches or become sick to our stomachs. We may suddenly and inexplicably show all the symptoms of having a cold, or we may experience heart palpitations, high blood pressure, dizziness, or cramps.

**Conditioning and Other Physiological Effects**     Other studies have shown that the immune system, which produces antibodies to help fight infection and disease, can be influenced by conditioning. Rats were conditioned to associate a novel taste with unpleasant physical reactions to a drug that suppresses the immune system. Later, when the animals were exposed to the novel taste but not to the drug, the production of antibodies was suppressed (Ader, Cohen, & Bovbjerg, 1982). This research demonstrates that each of us is potentially vulnerable to changes in our resistance to disease as a result of classically conditioned responses occurring without our being aware of them.

Conditioning plays a role in the development of some of life's more pleasant physical responses as well. Think, for example, of your reaction to the mention of a restaurant in which you have enjoyed a series of memorable dinners. Do you salivate? Or think of the pleasure that you might feel in response to a fragrance that you associate with an attractive friend or romantic partner. Do you become aroused?

The power of such conditioning was demonstrated in a study of male rat pups that suckled females whose nipples and vaginal odors had been altered with a distinct lemon scent CS. The rats were then weaned and never again exposed either to females or to the lemon scent until they were sexually mature. At that point, they were paired with sexually receptive females. The vaginal areas of some females were treated with lemon scent; those of others were not. The contrast in sexual response was dramatic (see Figure 4.6). A male rat placed with a lemon-scented female approached her readily and ejaculated quickly; male rats placed with females that had no lemon scent were considerably slower to respond (Fillion & Blass, 1986).

In another study, 5-day-old rats were exposed to an orange scent followed by an injection of morphine. When they were 10 days old, they showed a marked preference for the scent of orange, a preference that could be reversed by injecting a drug that blocks morphine's effects. Thus, it appeared that previous association of the orange scent CS with the morphine UCS caused a release of morphine-like chemicals in the brain (see Chapter 2). This conclusion is strengthened by the data shown in Figure 4.7. The conditioned rats, when later exposed to the orange scent alone, had a higher threshold for pain. These and many studies like them confirm that early conditioning can have powerful effects on later behavior.

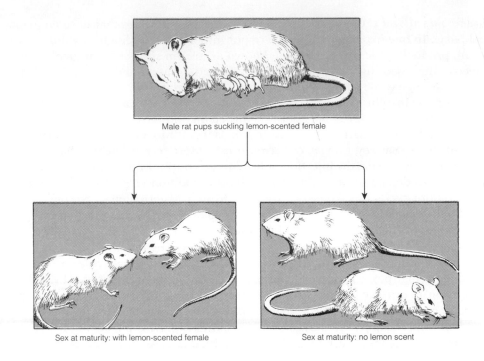

Male rat pups suckling lemon-scented female

Sex at maturity: with lemon-scented female

Sex at maturity: no lemon scent

**FIGURE 4.6 Early conditioning of later sexual behavior.** Male rat pups that suckled females treated with a lemon scent became much more sexually aroused by the lemon smell when they reached puberty.

**Expectancy**
The subject's expectation that the UCS will follow the CS—the basis for the cognitive explanation of classical conditioning.

**The Power of Expectation: Drug Reactions without Drugs** In the view of many psychologists, conditioning can be best explained by the learning of **expectancies.** In other words, what animals and humans learn in classical conditioning is the expectation that a particular conditioned stimulus will be followed by an unconditioned stimulus (Bolles, 1972). In humans, for example, it is possible to condition the "sweaty palms" measured by the galvanic skin response (GSR) simply by telling research participants that they will receive a shock every time they hear a tone. It is not necessary for the experimenter to deliver the shock; the expectation of the outcome is sufficient to produce the response.

It is now believed that Pavlov's dogs learned to salivate to the sound of the bell because they learned to expect the sound to be followed by the food. Indeed, Pavlov himself concluded that all organisms respond not only to stimuli but also in *anticipation* of the stimuli. In one series of experiments, Pavlov paired the sound of a bell CS with injection of a drug UCS; the drug was apomorphine, a stimulant that in high doses produces symptoms such as agitation and vomiting. It turned out that anticipation of the drug on hearing the bell produced the symptoms. After a period of time, even the bell sound wasn't essential. Simply opening the container of hypodermic syringes was sufficient to produce the symptoms (Siegel, 1983).

A dramatic example of this phenomenon has been observed among former drug addicts, who begin to show withdrawal symptoms and a desire to return to drug use when they are exposed to drug paraphernalia, other individuals who use drugs, or even the neighborhood where they secured their drugs. This is why people involved in rehabilitation of drug addicts suggest that they move to a new setting where encounters

**FIGURE 4.7 When the smell of orange can act as a painkiller.** Three groups of 10-day-old rat pups were placed on a heated surface while being exposed to the scent of orange, and the delay in their lifting of their paws to escape the heat was measured. Note that the rats that had been conditioned 5 days earlier to associate orange scent with morphine took almost twice as long to lift their paws as did those rats that had been conditioned with a simple salt solution and those that had not been conditioned.

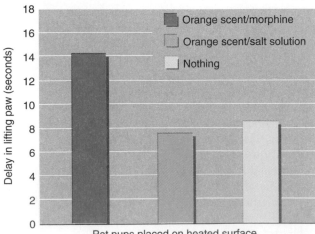

Rat pups placed on heated surface

with the cues for drug use are less likely to occur—that is, where the environment does not elicit anticipation of a "high."

# OPERANT CONDITIONING

Classical conditioning primarily concerns reflexive behavior, but reflexes certainly aren't the only form of behavior that is involved in learning. If a rat is placed in a cage, for example, it exhibits many behaviors that seem to be spontaneous and self-generated, not predetermined responses to specific stimuli. It may sniff at the cage, stand up to get a better look at things, scratch itself, wash itself, and touch various parts of the cage. Similarly, babies in a crib display many spontaneous actions. They move their arms and legs, try to turn over or grasp a blanket or the bars of the crib, turn their heads and eyes to look at various objects, and make sounds with the mouth and vocal cords.

**FOCUS QUESTIONS**

• What is operant conditioning and how did Skinner study it?

• What basic terms and procedures are involved in operant conditioning?

The actions exhibited by the rat or the babies are prewired in part. Rats, babies, and most other animals have a natural tendency to explore their environment—especially if it's a novel one. But exploratory behavior and the like are initiated *voluntarily* instead of reflexively. The organism "operates" on its environment and often brings about some kind of change in it. Hence, this type of activity is called *operant behavior,* a term coined by B. F. Skinner (1938) (also see Chapter 1). Like inborn reflexes, operant behavior can be modified through learning. Here, however, it is the relationship between behavior and its consequences—that is, the **contingency**—that is of primary interest. Why do you go to school or work (or both) each day and perform the appropriate behaviors? In Skinner's terms, you do so because you expect a payoff.

This **operant conditioning** occurs both in the lab and in everyday life. That is, in addition to contingencies imposed by experimenters, there are natural contingencies imposed by the environment. Animals—including humans—learn to perform behaviors necessary to survival, such as those that produce nourishment or avoid danger. Even animals that have prewired behaviors associated with survival must still learn *where* to look for food. And humans, of course, are subject to countless contingencies imposed by other humans at home, at school, at work—indeed, throughout everyday life. We don't always behave as predictably as other animals, though. As discussed later in the chapter, in addition to thinking about consequences, we often think about the contingencies themselves, which can wreak havoc with predictions based on operant conditioning principles alone.

**Contingency**
The relationship between behavior and its consequences.

**Operant conditioning**
The imposition of contingencies, either deliberate or natural.

## B. F. Skinner's Magic Box

Skinner revolutionized the study of learning and conditioning with the special apparatus shown in Figure 4.8, designed for rats. (Similar apparatuses have been devised for many other research animals.) When Skinner first placed a hungry rat in the apparatus, it engaged in many kinds of spontaneous operant behavior as it "checked out" its new surroundings. Eventually, besides doing other things, it happened onto the bar and caused it to move, at which point the apparatus dropped a pellet of food into the feeding cup beneath. However, little or no learning took place at this point. In cognitive terms, we could say that the animal did not "notice" a relationship between the bar and the food, so it simply ate the food and continued its explorations as before. Eventually, it accidentally pressed the bar again, causing another pellet to drop. After a number of these instances, the rat finally formed

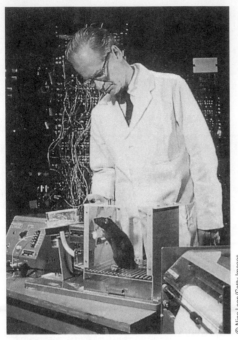

© Nina Leen/Getty Images

**FIGURE 4.8 Learning in the Skinner box. With this simple but ingenious invention—a box in which a barpress response automatically releases a pellet of food or other reward—Skinner (shown in the photo) demonstrated many of the principles of operant behavior that survive today. In the past, electric relay equipment controlled the apparatus and a "cumulative recorder," such as the one in the bottom right corner of the photo, tallied responses. Nowadays, computers are used instead. Note the steel grid bars the rat is standing on: These can be used to deliver electric shocks.**

Shaping and successive approximations
A procedure for quickly establishing a contingency, such as barpressing by rats or keypecking by pigeons, by rewarding successive approximations to the target behavior.

an association between the act of pressing the bar and the appearance of food. It now began pressing the bar as fast as it could (Skinner, 1938, 1953).

The Skinner box prompted a host of new studies of learning. These studies showed that operant conditioning had many parallels with Pavlov's classical conditioning. Like conditioned reflexes, conditioned operant behavior is subject to *extinction*. That is, if the rat no longer receives food for pressing the bar, it eventually stops. *Spontaneous recovery* also occurs: After barpressing is extinguished and the rat is removed from the Skinner box for a while, if the rat is then returned, it starts pressing the bar again.

Experiments with pigeons clearly demonstrated that *stimulus generalization* occurs in operant conditioning. A pigeon that had learned to obtain food by pecking at a white key would also peck at an off-white or perhaps even a red or green key. But if only the white key produced food, the pigeon learned *stimulus discrimination* and ignored the keys of other colors.

## Shaping and Successive Approximations

On its own, as described earlier, a rat might take quite some time to "figure out" the relationship between barpressing and its consequences—that is, getting food. Therefore, when conducting operant conditioning experiments, psychologists usually begin with **shaping and successive approximations,** a procedure that significantly reduces the time required for a rat to learn to press a bar or a pigeon to peck a key. This procedure is also used in training animals to perform much more complex behaviors, including the spectacular ones you see in stage or aquarium acts. It can likewise be effective therapeutically, as discussed in Chapter 14.

As noted earlier, a rat will move around and explore a Skinner box when first placed in it. However, instead of waiting for the rat to "blunder" into the bar, the researcher can shape the rat's behavior by using successive approximations to the target behavior of barpressing. The conditioner uses a manual switch to release a food pellet: at first when the rat heads in the direction of the bar, then when it touches the bar, then when it touches the bar and causes it to move, and finally only when it presses the bar sufficiently to trigger the food release mechanism. When shaping is complete, the automated equipment takes over. With careful attention to consistency and timing, a rat's barpressing can be shaped in less than an hour. In real life, many of our behaviors are shaped by natural contingencies or simply by feedback. An infant's behavior of eating with utensils is gradually shaped into perfection by success in getting food from bowl or plate to mouth. Similarly, based on feedback from others and from the sounds produced, a person who plays a musical instrument gradually makes better and better music.

Note, however, that *how* the rat presses the bar usually isn't the important thing. Although a rat can be shaped to press the bar in a highly specific manner, such as with the tip of its left front paw, it is the *fact* of the barpress than constitutes the operant. That is, an operant is a *class* of behaviors that "get the job done," and it doesn't matter whether the rat presses the bar with its right paw, its left paw, both paws, its nose, or even by sitting on it. As Skinner pointed out, this is an important concept in the generalization of operant conditioning principles across many different situations, behaviors, and organisms. Just as we never encounter the exact same stimulus twice, we never perform a behavior the exact same way twice. What is most important is what satisfies the contingency—along with what variations in the contingency increase or decrease the likelihood of the behavior. This is why a rat pressing a bar might be comparable to a human performing a host of behaviors that produce tangible or social reinforcement.

The technique of shaping is used to train animals like these dolphins to perform tricks.

© Philip Gould/CORBIS

The same procedure applied to shaping pigeons is illustrated in Figure 4.9. A hungry pigeon is led step by step, again using food, to perform a behavior that it might never have performed by accident.

**FIGURE 4.9 Shaping a pigeon's behavior.** How can a pigeon be taught to peck at that little black dot in the middle of the white circle on the wall of its cage? When first placed in the box, the bird merely looks about at random (A). When it faces the white circle (B), it receives food in the tray below (C). The pigeon is rewarded first for looking at the circle (D), then not until it approaches the circle (E), and then not until it pecks at the circle (F). The final step (not shown) is to deliver the food only when the pigeon pecks at the dot.

Courtesy of M. S. Terrace; Columbia University

# Reinforcement and Punishment: The Basics

Skinner and his many followers popularized the concepts of reinforcement and punishment and studied them extensively with regard to variations in quality, timing, and consistency. However, the concepts derive from Thorndike's law of effect, introduced in Chapter 1: (1) Any behavior that is followed by a satisfying state of affairs tends to be repeated (to be strengthened), and (2) any behavior that is followed by an unsatisfying or annoying state of affairs tends not to be repeated (to be weakened or suppressed) (Thorndike, 1911). The first half of the law of effect corresponds to reinforcement, the second half to punishment.

But there's more. Skinner's early research culminated in a clear distinction between "positive" and "negative" reinforcement (Skinner, 1953). Others later added a distinction between positive and negative punishment. All operant conditioning is based on these four basic contingencies, as defined in this section and illustrated in Figure 4.10. It is important to understand these contingencies because each has quite different effects on behavior. (In learning them, bear two things in mind. First, forget about other areas of psychology that use *positive* and *negative* to apply to emotions, moods, or the like. Here, *positive* simply means that something is *added* or presented, and *negative* means that something is *subtracted* or removed. Second, consider only what happens when the behavior actually occurs; if you think in terms of what happens when the behavior doesn't occur, you're likely to get these terms backward.)

**FIGURE 4.10** The four basic operant conditioning contingencies. The contingency depends on whether the stimulus or event is appetitive or aversive and whether it is presented or removed.

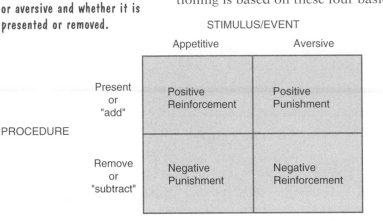

STIMULUS/EVENT

|  | | Appetitive | Aversive |
|---|---|---|---|
| **PROCEDURE** | Present or "add" | Positive Reinforcement | Positive Punishment |
|  | Remove or "subtract" | Negative Punishment | Negative Reinforcement |

**Positive reinforcement** An operant conditioning contingency in which behavior is strengthened because it results in presentation of an appetitive stimulus; also known as *reward training.*

In **positive reinforcement,** a "goody"—technically, an *appetitive stimulus*—is presented whenever the desired behavior occurs. ("Appetitive" is not restricted to food; it refers to *any* stimulus or event the organism likes, seeks, will approach, etc.) The behavior then tends to be repeated, become more likely, or increase in frequency. That is, the behavior is *strengthened.* Positive reinforcement is also known as *reward training,* and it is taking place whenever an organism engages in a behavior that produces something it likes and wants. In a Skinner box, a rat presses a bar to get food. More generally, positive reinforcement occurs with as simple and immediate an activity as opening the refrigerator door to get something to drink or flipping a switch to turn on a light and as complex and prolonged an activity as working for a week or even a month to get a paycheck or completing years of coursework to earn a diploma.

**Negative reinforcement** An operant conditioning contingency in which behavior is strengthened because it results in removal of an aversive stimulus; also known as *escape* or *active avoidance training.*

**Negative reinforcement** means that something aversive (unpleasant or fearful) is removed, goes away, or doesn't happen whenever the desired behavior is performed. Again, the behavior is strengthened. In the version called *escape training,* the aversive object or event is actually experienced, and the desired behavior makes it go away. In contrast, in *active avoidance training,* the aversive thing is not actually experienced—the desired behavior prevents it from occurring at all. A rat might press the bar to turn off an electric shock (escape), or if it has some way of predicting when the shock will occur—such as a light that precedes the shock—it may soon learn to press the bar in advance and not have to endure the shock (active avoidance). However, this particular training can be very difficult to accomplish with rats because of their built-in responses to pain. It works much better in an experimental setup such as that illustrated in Figure 4.11. When a dog is placed in the wired compartment and electric shock is administered, the dog quickly learns to jump across the hurdle to the other side to escape the shock. If some kind of warning is given, such as a light or tone that occurs before the shock is admin-

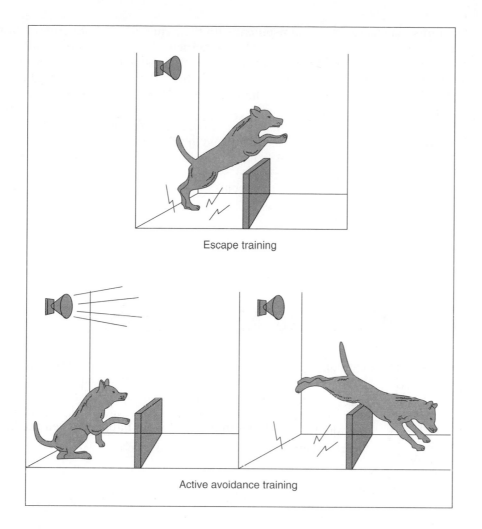

Escape training

Active avoidance training

**FIGURE 4.11** Negative reinforcement. The dog, placed in a shuttle box, first learns to escape and then learns to avoid the shock entirely.

istered, the dog will quickly learn to jump the hurdle when the stimulus occurs and avoid the shock entirely. In humans, a simple example of negative reinforcement is nagging a child to clean up his or her room; when the room is cleaned up, the nagging stops. Somewhat more complex examples are superstitions and phobias, discussed later in the chapter.

**Positive punishment** is what we normally think of as punishment and is applied to behaviors that we want to eliminate. Something aversive or unpleasant follows when the behavior occurs, and the behavior tends not to be repeated, to become less likely, or to decrease in frequency—that is, it is either *weakened* or *suppressed*. Another term for this type of punishment is *passive avoidance training* because the aversive object or event isn't experienced if the subject or participant simply does nothing (but remember, focus on what happens when the behavior does occur). If a rat that had been previously trained to barpress for food was instead shocked whenever it pressed the bar, barpressing should decrease. A human example is scolding or spanking a child for misbehaving—or having an accident while driving and talking on your cell phone. The use of positive punishment as a way of controlling children's behavior and directing their development has long been criticized by some psychologists, but certainly not by all, as we see later in the chapter.

Finally, in **negative punishment,** a "goody" (or appetitive stimulus) is removed or taken away, and the target behavior is weakened or suppressed. Traditionally this type of punishment is called *omission training*. A rat that was previously trained to press a bar for food now gets food automatically *unless* it presses the

**Positive punishment**
An operant conditioning contingency in which behavior is weakened or suppressed because it results in presentation of an aversive stimulus; also known as *passive avoidance training.*

**Negative punishment**
An operant conditioning contingency in which behavior is weakened or suppressed because it results in removal of an appetitive stimulus; also known as *omission training.*

bar. Parents may use negative punishment with their children without even realizing that they are using punishment. They give their children privileges, allowances, and other goodies freely, regarding themselves as being very "rewarding" toward their children. There is no actual contingency in effect until the child misbehaves—then negative punishment kicks in along lines of "No TV for a week," "There goes your allowance," or "You're grounded." Another example of negative reinforcement is the long-standing *time-out* procedure that teachers sometimes use in working with children who "act out" and are disruptive in class. Because it is believed that disruptive behavior is maintained by giggles from classmates and attention from the teacher—even scolding can be reinforcing for children who get little other attention from adults—the child is temporarily isolated from the classroom. Thus, attention from the teacher and classmates is removed, and the disruptive behavior declines.

# OPERANT CONDITIONING PHENOMENA AND APPLICATIONS

**FOCUS QUESTIONS**
- How are the timing and consistency of operant conditioning contingencies important?
- Why is reinforcement preferable to punishment?
- What maintains superstitions and phobias?
- How do biological predispositions affect operant conditioning?

As with classical conditioning, many variables determine the effectiveness of operant conditioning, the rate at which the behavior occurs, and the persistence of the behavior if the contingency is no longer in effect (that is, if the reinforcer or punisher is discontinued). These and other important considerations in operant conditioning are discussed in this section.

## Delay of Reinforcement and Punishment

It has been found in most laboratory animal experiments that immediate reinforcement produces the most rapid learning. Any delay reduces the amount of learning, and too long a delay produces no learning at all, as is shown in Figure 4.12. The same holds true for very young children and for extremely mentally retarded persons. For example, it is difficult to teach an 18-month-old to stay away from electrical plugs and outlets unless the child is immediately punished for the behavior or distracted and reinforced for some alternative acceptable behavior. "Wait until your father (or mother) gets home" has little, if any, effect on a very young child.

With older children and normal adults, however, delays can be quite long and the contingency is still effective. As noted earlier, you may work for a month or even longer to get a paycheck, and you may work for years to get a college degree. And with older children, the threat of punishment at the end of the day when one or the other parent gets home from

**FIGURE 4.12 Oops . . . the reinforcement came too late.** The steep drop in the curve shows how rapidly learning fell in an experiment in which a food reinforcer was presented when rats pressed the bar in a Skinner box. Different rats received reinforcement delays ranging from a few seconds to about 2 minutes. Note that there was no learning at all by the rats that received delays of about 100 seconds.

*Perin, 1943.*

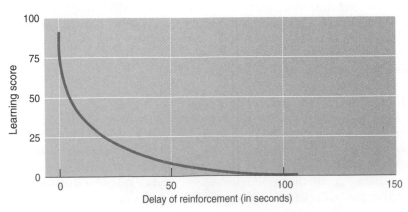

work can be very effective—perhaps even more effective than immediate punishment if the child truly fears what might happen and ponders it all day.

In each case, a good explanation is *verbal mediation*—"bridging the gap" between behavior and its consequences by thinking about and reminding oneself through "self-talk" that the consequences will eventually occur. Laboratory animals and very young children lack the necessary language and memory skills, so they consistently behave in accord with the curve in Figure 4.12. Older children and adults who have the necessary cognitive skills easily mediate very long time delays.

## The Power of Partial Reinforcement

Experimenters have compared the effects of **continuous reinforcement** (reinforcement for each instance of a behavior) with those of **partial reinforcement** (reinforcement on some occasions but not on others). They have found that although learning generally takes place more rapidly with constant reinforcement, the behavior is more persistent (that is, more resistant to extinction) with partial reinforcement (e.g., see Robbins, 1971). That is, when reinforcement is discontinued, partially reinforced behavior takes a lot longer to extinguish than continuously reinforced behavior does.

To understand why, consider the following. You have two TV sets, one that turns on every time you press the button on the remote (continuous reinforcement) and one that—unpredictably—turns on sometimes the first time you press the button, sometimes after several presses, and sometimes after half a dozen or more (partial reinforcement). Now, suppose that something unknown goes wrong with both sets and prevents them from coming on at all (extinction). Which remote will you continue to press longer before giving up and calling a service technician? Clearly, the partially reinforced one. With that remote, it will take you much longer to "discriminate" that the set truly is broken—that it isn't just the button on the remote (e.g., see Capaldi, 1966).

This finding has many applications to real-life situations. For example, in the wild, animals don't get rewarded for every instance of hunting for food. But if an animal learns that food is occasionally available in a particular place, it will continue to return there "just to make sure," perhaps long after food is unavailable.

In humans, a powerful example is what parents sometimes do when their child throws a temper tantrum. Suppose a little boy starts having temper tantrums whenever he asks for something and his request is denied. His parents try to ignore his behavior—but every once in a while, just to quiet him down, they give in and let him have what he wants. What they have done is set up a situation in which the operant behavior of temper tantrums (the very thing they would like to eliminate) produces the candy, toy, or whatever else the child wants, on a schedule of partial reinforcement. When they eventually get around to realizing that they must ignore or otherwise not reinforce the tantrums every single time they occur, they find that the tantrums are extremely hard to eliminate. The child has come to expect to be reinforced only on some occasions, and it may take him quite a long time to figure out that the tantrums don't work anymore. This is even more likely if the parents—with the best of intentions—hold out longer and longer before occasionally giving up and giving in to the child. Here, the parents are *shaping* progressively more intense tantrums at the same time that they are inadvertently teaching the child, "Keep trying long enough and hard enough and it might work."

Psychologists differentiate between two basic types of partial reinforcement schedules, as indicated in Table 4.1. In the first type, called **ratio schedules,** the reinforcement is delivered only after the subject responds a certain number of times: A rat would receive a food pellet only after pressing the bar several times or more.

**Continuous reinforcement**
Reinforcing every instance of a behavior.

**Partial reinforcement**
Reinforcing only some instances of a behavior.

**Ratio schedule**
A partial reinforcement schedule in which reinforcement occurs only after a number of responses.

Partial reinforcement may be administered in four basic ways.

**TABLE 4.1**
**Schedules of Partial Reinforcement**

| Type of Schedule | When Reinforcement Occurs | Everyday Example |
|---|---|---|
| **Ratio** | | |
| Fixed | For a specific number of responses | You're paid "piece rate" for, say, every 10 chopping boards you make in a woodworking shop. |
| Variable | For a varying number of responses around some average | You get a payoff after differing numbers of plays on a slot machine (the average number is based on probability). |
| **Interval** | | |
| Fixed | For the first response after a specific amount of time has passed since the last one | Your mail comes at the same time each day, so that's when you check your box for a magazine or a friend's letter. |
| Variable | For the first response after a varying amount of time, on average, has passed since the last one | E-mail from a friend may come at any time, so you only occasionally retrieve one when you check (the average is determined by your friend). |

**Interval schedule**
A partial reinforcement schedule in which reinforcement occurs only for the first response after an amount of time has elapsed.

**Fixed schedule**
A partial reinforcement schedule in which reinforcement occurs after a specific number of responses or for the first response after a specific amount of time.

In the second, **interval schedules,** the reinforcement is delivered for the first response after a certain amount of time has elapsed since the last response: A rat would receive a food pellet for, say, making a response every few seconds or more.

Both types of schedules are subject to another kind of differentiation. If either the ratio or the interval is the same each time, the schedule is termed a **fixed schedule.** Thus, the rat might be reinforced for exactly 5 barpresses or after ex-

Slot machines provide a good example of variable reinforcement. Because players cannot tell when a jackpot will occur, they often continue to play until they run out of money.

actly 30 seconds. On the other hand, if the ratio or interval changes unpredictably around some "average" value, the schedule is termed a **variable schedule.** Here, the rat might be reinforced for anywhere from 1 to 9 barpresses, in the long run averaging 5, or might have to wait anywhere from 5 to 55 seconds for a barpress to be reinforced, in the long run averaging 30.

Either kind of variable schedule produces greater resistance to extinction than either kind of fixed schedule. Predictability is the key, as in the example of parents who occasionally reinforce temper tantrums. On a variable ratio schedule in particular, the child cannot tell which instance of a tantrum might be rewarded, and again may take a long time to learn that none will be—when the parents "change" the contingency to extinction.

**Variable schedule**
A partial reinforcement schedule in which reinforcement occurs after a varying number of responses or for the first response after a varying amount of time, in each case around some average value.

## When There's a Choice: Reinforcement versus Punishment

Skinner (1953) strongly favored using positive reinforcement as a way of controlling children and teaching them appropriate behavior. For misbehavior—which he viewed as always maintained by consequences of some kind—he recommended extinction (ignoring the behavior) followed by positive reinforcement for appropriate alternative behavior that achieves the same end. Thus, for example, rather than scold, spank, or isolate a child who behaves aggressively to get a toy away from another child or acts disruptively to get attention from a parent or teacher, Skinner suggested that we ignore such behavior while at the same time reinforcing the child for using appropriate ways to get what she or he wants. Praise and otherwise reinforce the child for politely asking for a toy and for taking turns and sharing; likewise, reinforce a child for properly asking questions and doing work that results in attention from adults.

Beyond the much more pleasant atmosphere and "good feelings" that positive reinforcement tends to foster, Skinner and others emphasized its advantage of being more *informative*—that is, it tells the child or adult or pet specifically *what to do*, whereas punishment conveys only *what not to do*. Thus, punishment alone may eliminate or suppress one misbehavior, only to allow another misbehavior to crop up in its place. A child who is punished for aggressively going after a toy may become sneakier and try to steal the toy. An adult who is imprisoned for mugging people to get money may turn to burglary upon release. A dog who is hit with a rolled-up newspaper for urinating on the rug in one part of the home may simply urinate in another room. It is much better, Skinner and others have said, to reinforce appropriate behaviors by teaching children appropriate ways to get what they want, by teaching people who engage in criminal behavior how to earn money legitimately, and by shaping a dog to go to the door and "ask" to go outside—and initially following the desired behavior with treats and praise.

Beyond teaching only what not to do, punishment has a number of other well-documented problems. For one, it may simply teach the child to suppress the behavior when the parent or other adult is around, the same way you might lower your speed when a police car is on the highway but exceed the speed limit when one is not. Other potential effects of punishment—especially corporal or physical punishment—on children are discussed further in A Matter of Debate on page 158.

So positive reinforcement is preferable to punishment. However, as you may have noticed, the picture painted earlier is somewhat rosy. Some behaviors can't simply be ignored, because they are too dangerous and harmful—such as a young child playing with knives or matches or running out into the street. A slap on the hand when a child reaches toward a forbidden object may be the only way to prevent damage or even serious injury. Likewise, societies worldwide can't ignore criminal behavior while they try to teach muggers and other criminals alternative ways to obtain money. Use of punishment appears to be unavoidable at times,

## → A MATTER OF DEBATE ←

# Spanking Children

In July 2002, psychologist Elizabeth Gershoff of Columbia University's National Center for Children in Poverty published a journal article on the effects of corporal punishment on children. It was a major effort that reviewed and analyzed some 6 decades of research, and it was picked up and described by various news media under headlines like "Spanking Is a No-No" and "Spanking May Make Kids Violent." Here, we briefly describe Gershoff's findings and leave the matter for you to decide.

The article began by noting others' findings that although eleven nations now ban the use of corporal punishment such as spanking children, support for corporal punishment remains strong in the United States—with 94% of U.S. parents spanking their children by the time the children are 3 or 4 years old. Moreover, in spite of hundreds of studies pro and con, psychologists remain sharply divided on the issue. Articles and debates have yet to resolve the ongoing controversy or even to draw a clear line between what might constitute reasonable and appropriate corporal punishment and what constitutes physical child abuse. With that as a backdrop, Gershoff went on to review prior research on the effects of corporal punishment, including spanking. The following is a summary of what she found.

- It can be highly effective in stopping misbehavior in the immediate sense (which Skinner also acknowledged regarding punishment in general).
- Used alone, it does not tend to foster children's "internalization" of moral standards of right and wrong; among other things, it may instead teach them to focus on not getting caught.
- It models aggression (as noted in Chapter 1 of this text) and has consistently been shown to be associated with a wide variety of factors related to aggression—including legitimizing violence as a way of dealing with problems, which can surface later in adult relationships with spouse and children.
- It has been strongly implicated in the development of subsequent delinquent, antisocial, and criminal behavior—and, to a lesser extent, adult mental health problems.

- It evokes in children anxiety and anger that can seriously disrupt family relationships, and it can create a vicious cycle within a family in which the child misbehaves, the parent punishes, and the punishment leads to further misbehavior and harsher punishment; such escalation can lead to physical child abuse by the parents.

This is not a pretty picture. The subsequent analysis by Gershoff largely verified each of these points, after which she went on to describe problems with this kind of research—such as the need for further study of the frequency and severity of corporal punishment, the effects of different kinds of corporal punishment (spanking versus slapping, paddling, or whipping), whether the parents administer the punishment systematically or impulsively, what other forms of discipline are used in conjunction with corporal punishment, and how the child perceives the punishment and reacts to it.

Yet another important factor noted was culture and ethnicity. In some ethnic groups (as in the United States as a whole), corporal punishment of children is viewed as quite acceptable and the child may therefore view it as acceptable as well and not react in the negative ways noted.

Gershoff was also careful to point out that much of the research was correlational in nature, which means that clear-cut conclusions about cause and effect cannot be drawn. As has often been pointed out, for example, "naturally" aggressive children may elicit physical punishment by parents.

Still, the sheer volume of the research pointing the other way seems overwhelming. Based on your knowledge and personal experience, what do you think?

To research this topic further, go online with InfoTrac and use your own term or the following suggestions:
- Gershoff, Elizabeth
- spanking children
- internalization

although it should always be kept to the minimum necessary and, in the case of children, accompanied by explanations appropriate to the child's level of comprehension. Finally, like ignoring undesirable behavior, punishment is most effective when combined with reward—when the "wrong" behavior is punished and the "right" behavior is reinforced.

# The Power of Superstitions and Phobias

Do you have a "lucky" sweater that you always wear to exams because it helps you get good grades? Do you win more ball games when you wear a certain pair of socks and carefully pull on the right one before the left one? Do you always perform some sort of ritual if you spill salt or break a mirror? Do you avoid walking under ladders? That is, do you have superstitions?

Or, as noted earlier in the chapter, are you deathly afraid of certain insects or other animals or of certain situations, such as being in a confined space or being out in an open one? That is, do you have phobias?

Superstitions and phobias have some things in common. For one, although superstitions may be handed down from one generation to the next as "dos" and "don'ts" and phobias may be learned by observing others behaving in a fearful manner, each also can be acquired and maintained through conditioning. For another, they are wholly irrational and yet they persist, often for life—and conditioning principles help explain why.

Skinner (1953) described the establishment of **superstitious behavior**—behavior that occurs and persists in the absence of any actual contingency—in pigeons as follows. Give a pigeon food every 15 seconds regardless of what it is doing; that is, reinforce whatever behavior the pigeon happens to be engaged in. Eventually, and at random, some particular behavior will be reinforced more often and the pigeon will in turn perform it more often, in a cycle that leads to the pigeon's performing the behavior much of the time. This might be "hopping from one foot to the other and back, bowing and scraping, turning around, strutting, [or] raising the head" (Skinner, 1953).

Thus, the pigeon's behavior has been partially reinforced, and we might say that the pigeon "thinks" that the behavior is related to getting food. Sometimes this appears to be the case, as when the food just happens to follow the behavior. The extension of this principle to some human superstitions should be obvious: If you wear your lucky sweater every time you take an exam or perform the sock ritual every time you play ball, *sometimes* it will work—you'll get a good grade or you'll win. Borrowing from cognitive psychology, we know that we have a tendency to remember occasions when something we do works much better than occasions when it doesn't; this tendency is known as the *fallacy of the positive case.* Thus, through partial positive reinforcement, we become convinced that the superstitious behavior we engage in is meaningful and helpful.

Phobias and superstitious behaviors that involve negative reinforcement work differently. The common elements are *fear,* which may have been acquired through instances of aversive classical conditioning or in other ways, and negative reinforcement of behaviors that reduce the fear (Mowrer, 1951). In the case of superstitions, if you've been taught to be fearful of the imagined consequences of spilling salt or breaking mirrors, you perform the appropriate ritual and the fear goes away. The ritual behavior thus is negatively reinforced and tends to be repeated. In the case of phobias, when you encounter the feared object or situation, you "escape" from it by running away, calling for help, or—in the case of dangerous snakes and insects—perhaps attacking the object and killing it. What these behaviors have in common is that the fear again goes away, along with the object that caused it, providing negative reinforcement and making it likely that you'll engage in the behavior in the future. You may take things a step further and never venture into places (such as fields and forests) where snakes and other dangerous things tend to live—thus avoiding the object entirely.

In each case, the fear may be with you for life because you never "test" the outcome by skipping the superstitious ritual or staying around long enough to discover that the feared object usually isn't harmful. Fear reduction through negative

**Superstitious behavior**
Behavior that occurs and persists in the absence of any actual contingency.

reinforcement makes a powerful and lasting impression indeed, although phobias can be treated very effectively, as discussed in Chapter 14.

# When There Is No Escape

Most of the time, when we expect or encounter unpleasant experiences, we do whatever we can to avoid them. In addition to extreme cases such as people who avoid normal activities because of phobias, students manage to avoid taking difficult courses and people who are allergic to ragweed stay away from it in the fall. But there are some conditions in which such coping responses can't occur, and in such situations we may become apathetic and feel helpless.

This was demonstrated in a series of experiments in which dogs were strapped into the kind of harness used by Pavlov. In one experiment, one group of dogs received a series of 64 electrical shocks, lasting 5 seconds and delivered at random intervals. There was no way the dogs could avoid the shocks or escape from them before the 5 seconds were up. The next day, each of the dogs was placed in a shuttle box. From time to time the light inside the box was dimmed, and a few seconds later a shock was administered through the floor of the compartment in which the dog had been placed. The animal could avoid the shock altogether by jumping over the hurdle into the other compartment when the warning light was dimmed, or it could escape the shock by jumping after the electricity was turned on. If the dog did not jump into the other compartment, the shock continued—this time for a full 50 seconds.

**FIGURE 4.13 Results of an experiment in learned helplessness.** The rapid rise in the solid line shows how quickly "normal" dogs learned how to cope with an electric shock delivered in a shuttle box. The dashed line shows the very different behavior of animals that had acquired learned helplessness—and therefore seemed incapable of learning how to do anything about the shock.

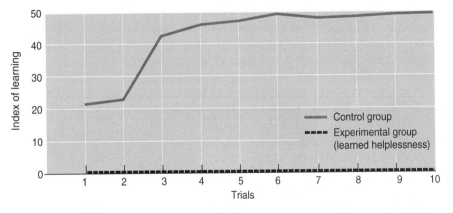

The results of the experiment, shown in Figure 4.13, were dramatic. A number of dogs were used in the experiment, and all had 10 trials in the shuttle box, during which they could learn to avoid or escape the shock. The comparison group—dogs with no prior experience with shock—learned the behavior quickly. But the previously shocked dogs mostly failed to learn at all. Most of them simply accepted the shock for the full 50 seconds, making no attempt to leap over the hurdle and instead crouching and cringing in ways that served only to minimize the shock a bit.

How can we account for the failure of the experimental dogs to learn to escape or avoid a severe and long-lasting shock? The experimenters attributed it to what they called **learned helplessness.** That is, while the dogs were in the harness, they learned that nothing they could do would have any effect on whether or how long they received a shock. In cognitive terms, they had no hope that they could do anything about the shock, even when they were moved to the shuttle box, so they didn't try (Maier, Seligman, & Solomon, 1969; Seligman & Maier, 1967).

Humans can also be led to acquire learned helplessness through simple laboratory procedures. In one experiment, college volunteers were subjected to a very loud (but safe) noise. They were told that they could stop the noise by learning how to manipulate some control devices, but actually these devices had no effect. Later, when they were placed in another situation where it would have been easy to move a control lever and turn off the noise, the participants made no effort and simply put up with the noise until the researcher stopped the experiment (Hiroto, 1974).

**Learned helplessness**
The belief that no behavior will be effective in escaping or avoiding unpleasant or painful consequences.

Children who are continually yelled at or spanked no matter what they have done may very well acquire learned helplessness. They may decide that they have no control over when, how, or why they are punished and may give up trying to learn what their parents are trying to teach them. In such a case, attempts to punish them into learning the difference between good behavior and bad become self-defeating. Some theorists believe that children who grow up in deprived, deteriorating neighborhoods and see no way to escape are also vulnerable to learned helplessness.

There are antidotes. As noted in Chapter 1, the original experiments on learned helplessness were questionable with regard to ethics, but they did open up a new line of psychological investigation. Punishment, it has been found, is not the only possible cause of learned helplessness. An even more common cause is repeated failure at any of the tasks we face throughout life—in the classroom, on the job, in social contexts, or in the world at large. Although everyone experiences failure, not everyone suffers drastic consequences. Studies of learned helplessness offer some clues as to when, how, and why this often-tragic result is likely to occur—and what might be done about it.

The inevitable failures experienced in life can produce learned helplessness under certain conditions.

Suppose you're in love, but the object of your affections rejects you (unrequited love). It makes a great deal of difference whether you blame yourself, blame her or him, or blame women or men in general. Blaming yourself usually results in loss of self-esteem and is associated with lack of confidence in the future (Garber & Hollon, 1977). Sometimes it produces significant depression (Rizley, 1978). The particular way in which you blame yourself is also important. If you merely blame your behavior in that one particular relationship, your feelings of helplessness will probably be less severe. But if you blame yourself in general—perhaps your own worth and character—you are much more likely to be in trouble (Peterson & Seligman, 1984). Thus, it is better to think "Well, I just did the wrong thing that time" than to decide "That's the way I am, and it seems I'm just plain undesirable."

## Behavior Modification and Token Economies

Parents who want their children to stop throwing temper tantrums and animal trainers who want their dolphins to jump through hoops have something in common: Both are trying to condition behavior. All of us constantly try to influence behavior—our own actions as well as those of the people around us (Stolz, Wienckowski, & Brown, 1975). We try to lose weight, quit smoking, get higher grades, or perform better on the job (Boice, 1982). This may be a matter of self-discipline, but operant conditioning reminds us that we're also subject to the contingencies we encounter. We try to influence other people to give us a good grade or a raise, to show us more appreciation and respect, or to stop doing things that annoy us. In so doing, we often informally practice what psychologists call **behavior modification,** a technique that is based primarily on operant conditioning principles.

As psychologists use the term, behavior modification refers to any deliberate program designed to influence and change behavior by manipulating its consequences. If a certain type of behavior works—that is, if it results in reinforcement through rewards or praise or even just a boost to self-esteem—it is likely to be repeated. If it does not produce satisfactory results, it will tend to be abandoned. In this fashion, it has been possible, for example, to raise the level of children's social

**Behavior modification**
**A technique for changing behavior, based on operant conditioning principles; also called behavior therapy in clinical settings.**

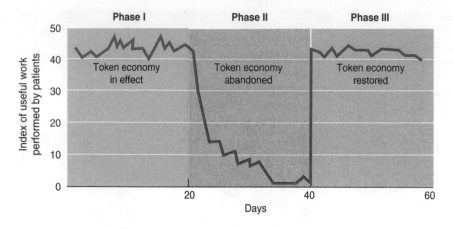

FIGURE 4.14 Behavior modification revolutionizes a mental institution. With the token economy, patients worked actively at useful jobs and helped run the institution (phase I). When the token economy was temporarily discontinued from day 20 to day 40 (phase II), to attest to its effectiveness, the patients quickly went back to their passive and apathetic ways. When the token economy was reinstated (phase III), their work returned to its previously high level.

*Adapted from Ayllon & Azrin, 1968.*

**Token economy**
A behavior modification procedure in which adaptive behavior is reinforced with tokens that can later be exchanged for privileges and other rewards.

**Instinctive behavior**
As defined by ethologists, a behavior that occurs in all normal members of a species, in response to specific releasing stimuli, and in essentially the same way every time.

**Ethology**
The study of instinctive behaviors in the lab and in natural environments.

skills (Yule, 1985) and to teach brain-damaged patients to reduce their socially inappropriate behaviors (McGlynn, 1990). In general, behavior modification—or *behavior therapy*, as it is called in clinical settings (see Chapter 14)—has thrived over the years (Sloan & Mizes, 1999).

Experiments in behavior modification have produced some dramatic results. One experiment assessed its effectiveness with a 3-year-old girl in nursery school who was too shy and withdrawn to take part in any of the group activities. Instead, she tried to hide by staying on the floor, either motionless or crawling. How could she be led to get up, start moving around, and join the other children? The procedure turned out to be simple. As long as she was on the floor, her teachers ignored her. As soon as she got up on her feet, they showered her with attention. Given this reinforcement, she quickly became an active member of the group—eventually, "natural" social reinforcers took over and the extra praise could be discontinued (Harris, Johnston, Kelley, & Wolf, 1965).

The same kind of behavior modification—ignoring undesirable actions and rewarding desirable ones—has been successful in many other situations. One special kind of behavior modification, in which the reinforcement is a form of payment for desirable behavior, is called a **token economy.** It has been used in mental institutions (as well as many other settings), where it originated as an attempt to improve the general well-being and daily lives of patients. For dressing properly, eating in an acceptable manner, and working at useful jobs, patients in mental health institutions are rewarded with "tokens" that they can exchange for privileges such as treats, movies, rental of radios or TV sets, and greater opportunities for privacy. The tokens are usually checkmarks on clipboards kept by attendants so that the patients won't lose them or possibly have them stolen. These token economies have produced some remarkable changes in behavior, such as those illustrated in Figure 4.14.

Institutional token economies have some critics, however (e.g., see Glynn, 1990). In addition to the enormous investment of time and resources required, there is a human rights issue. Granting extras to patients who "go along with the program" means denying them to patients who don't or simply can't. There is also the question of whether token economies are truly therapeutic and beneficial for the patients in the long run, after they leave the institution and no longer receive explicit rewards for appropriate behavior.

## Nature versus Operant Conditioning

Some of the creatures that inhabit our earth manage to go about their lives without learning a lot about consequences. Much of what they need to know to subsist and reproduce is already present in the prewiring of their nervous system—they require only limited experience to deal with life. Guided primarily by **instinctive behaviors,** they can find food, build shelters, mate, and survive as species. **Ethology** is the study of instinctive behaviors in animals. These behaviors have been studied extensively, both in the laboratory and in natural environments, by ethologists such as Konrad Lorenz (1903–1989) (1952). In their scientific definition, to be instinctive a behavior must meet the following criteria at a minimum:

- It must occur in all normal members of a species.

- It must occur in response to demonstrable "releasing" stimuli.
- It must occur in essentially the same way every time.

Thus, there is some room for learning and modification of instinctive behavior, but not much. For example, not all birds of a species sing *exactly* the same song, but what they sing occurs in the same kinds of situations and they all recognize what it means—food, safety, sexual interest, danger.

Human beings are quite different. To be sure, there are certain basic behaviors—sucking is one example—that appear at the very start of life without any apparent learning. Such reflexes, however, are much simpler than instincts. In turn, evolutionary psychologists continue to expand the list of human predispositions that might have evolved because they were adaptive, such as certain preferences exhibited by women and men with regard to physical characteristics and behaviors of potential mates (e.g., see Buss, 1999a). These, though, are viewed as "whisperings" in our biological makeup that can easily be overcome by culture and learning (Barash, 1979). We certainly have no inborn wiring in our nervous system that can steer us through life on "automatic pilot." We have to learn almost from scratch how to find food, keep warm, and build shelters; without this learning over an extended portion of our early lives, we don't survive. We also must learn to form social relationships and institutions that enrich our lives by providing through joint effort what no individual could manage alone. We may well be predisposed to form relationships with others—we are social creatures—but the form this behavior takes is largely learned.

However, in operant conditioning with nonhuman animals—especially nonprimates—it is now recognized that instinctive and often powerful biological predispositions must always be taken into account. As noted earlier in the chapter, rats have extreme difficulty learning to press a bar to escape or avoid shock. This has nothing to do with rats' level of intelligence; instead, it's because their built-in responses to pain include jumping and fleeing as fast as they can, behaviors that are incompatible with staying in one place and pressing a bar.

Particularly compelling demonstrations of how biological predispositions can be at odds with principles of conditioning were described by Keller and Marian Breland (1961, 1966), whose primary careers involved training animals to perform entertaining and often complex stage acts. What they found was that some of the trick behaviors could be learned easily by their animals, but then deteriorated because of *instinctual drift* back to predisposed behavior. For example, their raccoons could be conditioned to insert tokens into a slot for a food reward, but as the tokens became more strongly associated with the food—through classical conditioning pairings in which the tokens became CSs—the raccoons became unable to insert the tokens and instead reverted to holding on to them and "washing" them, as raccoons normally do with food. Similar results were obtained with pigs and tokens—pigs instinctively "root" their food and soon began doing this with tokens as well.

> ## Test Yourself
>
> **(h)** Your car's ignition switch is unreliable and unpredictable. Your car starts sometimes the first time you turn the switch, sometimes after you turn it two or three times, and sometimes after as many as nine or ten turns. One day your engine's starter goes bad, and you sit there turning the switch again and again for an hour before you finally give up. What operant conditioning phenomenon accounts for your persistence?
>
> **(i)** Having been badly stung by bees, your dog now freaks and runs whenever it sees or hears a bee. What operant conditioning contingency is maintaining this behavior?
>
> (The answers are on page 170.)

# COGNITIVE LEARNING: A CONTEMPORARY VIEW ROOTED IN THE PAST

> ### FOCUS QUESTIONS
> - Why is it important to consider cognition in studies of conditioning?
> - Can learning occur when there is no reinforcement or punishment?
> - What is the modern view of processes in learning and conditioning?

For several decades, the supposed laws of classical and operant conditioning dominated psychology's view of learning. The strict behaviorists thought of all human behavior as conditioned by events in the environment. The prevailing belief was that there is little difference between humans going

FIGURE 4.15 You can't keep a good chimp down. Faced with the problem of reaching a banana suspended high overhead, the chimpanzee on the left balanced a long stick beneath it and quickly climbed up. In a different situation, the chimpanzee on the right hit upon the "insight" of piling three boxes on top of one another to reach a banana. *Köhler, 1925.*

about their daily lives and a rat negotiating its way through a "T maze," in which it proceeds down a runway to an intersection where it must turn left or right to obtain a reward. The rat's behavior could be predicted if we knew which turn it had previously been rewarded for making and which turn it had previously been punished for or received no reward for making. The view was that we could also predict people's behavior fairly well if we simply knew which of their actions had been rewarded in the past and which had been punished, and in what way and to what extent (Miller & Dollard, 1941; Skinner, 1953). It was even thought that human personality could be explained entirely in terms of "reinforcement (and punishment) history." Nor is this approach dead—studies of human operant conditioning have continued to be published at a high rate over the years since (Dymond & Critchfield, 2002).

Even during the heyday of this view, however, there were dissenters. Some experimental results, even with rats, did not mesh with the principles of conditioning. Even in apparently simple stimulus-response learning, some researchers realized that it was essential to account for the perceptions and thoughts that take place between the stimulus and the response, as discussed in Chapter 1.

Thus, even in the early days of learning research, there was a concept that is now widely accepted: Higher organisms are far from passive products of experience and simple associations between stimuli and responses; they are always actively interacting with their environment and thinking about and interpreting what they observe. Rather than associations, they acquire knowledge (Gallistel & Gibbon, 2002).

## The Case of the Ingenious Chimps

One of the first influential experiments along cognitive lines was reported by the German psychologist Wolfgang Köhler as far back as the 1920s. Köhler worked with chimpanzees, creating situations in which they had to demonstrate considerable ingenuity to get at a banana placed tantalizingly just out of reach. Sometimes the food was just a little farther than arm's length away from a chimp behind a barrier. Sometimes it was suspended overhead, too high to reach by jumping. So near and yet so far.

Could the chimpanzees learn to get the food? As it turned out, they managed to do so in a number of clever ways. The animals behind the barrier figured out that they could use sticks to rake in the bananas. The animals who saw the food overhead hit upon several strategies, two of which are illustrated in Figure 4.15. To Köhler, this kind of learning went far beyond any stimulus-response connections established by conditioning—the chimps had no such prior training. He held that the animals had learned through relatively sudden **insight** (Köhler, 1925), or what today would be called cognition in the form of problem solving (see Chap-

**Insight**
Cognitive learning as a result of problem solving.

ter 6). That is, they evaluated the situation, called on whatever past knowledge they could muster, and processed all this information in terms of cause and effect. It is important to note that they did not solve the banana problems through the trial-and-error approach proposed by Thorndike, and they had no prior operant conditioning for this kind of task; they solved them by thinking about them until they hit upon a solution.

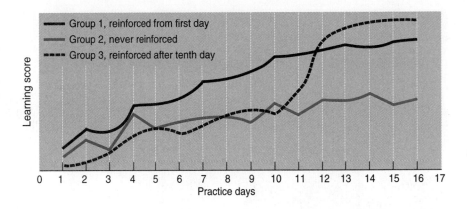

**FIGURE 4.16 A funny thing happened on the way through the maze.** The graph shows the behavior of three groups of rats placed in a maze, two under different conditions of reinforcement and one under no reinforcement. Note in particular the dotted line. *Adapted from Tolman & Honzik, 1930.*

## Learning in the Absence of Reinforcement

Another influential series of experiments, performed with rats in mazes (laid out like the ones you may have worked with a pencil as a child), produced results that contradicted the learning theorists' principle that reinforcement is essential to learning and cognition can be ignored. In one classic version (Tolman & Honzik, 1930), the rats were divided into three groups. Group 1 always found a food reward at the end of the maze, and their performance gradually improved until they were running through the maze as fast as they could and making almost no "wrong turns." Group 2 rats were simply placed in the maze and allowed to move around and explore, with no reward throughout the experiment. They did so, of course, because rats naturally explore any new environment they find themselves in (and besides, they had nothing else to do). Group 3 was treated the same way as Group 2 for the first 10 days, but for the remaining days they were switched to the food reward that Group 1 had been receiving all along.

How the three groups performed, as measured by how direct a route they took to the end of the maze, is illustrated in Figure 4.16. Note that the rats in Group 1 learned gradually and progressively, improving each day right from the beginning. As was also predicted, the never-rewarded rats in Group 2 displayed little learning. But note the behavior of Group 3. For the first 10 days this group also *displayed* little learning, but on the eleventh day the rats immediately began running the course like veterans now that they were being rewarded. In just wandering around the maze without any reinforcement, they apparently had learned a great deal about it. As soon as a reward was provided, they began to demonstrate this knowledge.

The experiment showed that even rats can learn without the immediate reinforcement that the strict behaviorists believed to be essential to conditioning—in fact, without any reinforcement at all. In cognitive terms, the rats moved around the maze and acquired knowledge about it, which they could call on when it was useful in helping them get to food as rapidly as possible.

Such experiments, along with many others, suggest that reinforcement is better viewed as an event that attracts and focuses attention (Rescorla & Holland, 1982). Think, for example, of the sudden taste of food when an animal is hungry or an unexpected frown from a teacher when a student has given a wrong answer. Both are events that alert the organism, leading it to concentrate on the behavior just performed. The effectiveness of a reinforcing event thus is related to its attracting attention to the behavior just displayed—and providing feedback about it.

Yet another basic form of learning that requires no reinforcement and occurs in humans and many other species is **observational learning**—or, as some psychologists prefer, *learning through modeling* or *learning by imitation*. Each term refers to the process through which we learn by observing the behavior of others.

**Observational learning** Cognitive learning as a result of watching others perform a behavior. It extends to learning by listening or reading.

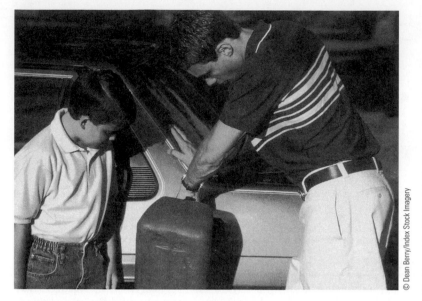

Children learn from observation of the adults around them.

It has been known for some time that many animals learn by observation and imitation. In one early experiment, a cat was placed in a Skinner box and conditioned to obtain food by pressing the bar when a light went on. Another cat had been watching and was then placed in the box. This second cat began very quickly to press the bar when the light went on. Through observation, it had learned much faster than the first cat (John, Chesler, & Bartlett, 1968). Subsequent experiments have demonstrated many kinds of observational learning by many animals, from mice to dolphins.

With humans, some of the most dramatic examples of observational learning, such as the classic "Bobo dolls" experiment described in Chapter 1, were demonstrated by Albert Bandura. Cognitive theorists do not think of observational learning as an automatic and unthinking imitation of what we have seen. Instead, they believe that we begin in early childhood and continue throughout our lives to observe what goes on around us and to store the information that the observation provides. We observe what other people seem to value, how they go about getting what they value, their behavior in general, and the results of their behavior. At the same time, we make judgments. We may or may not decide to value what they value. We may imitate their behavior, adopt some but not all of it, or reject it entirely. As Bandura stated, learning by observation is "actively judgmental and constructive rather than a mechanical copying" (Bandura, 1974).

Much of the time, we also learn how to do things by observing others, both directly and indirectly. If you can ride a bicycle, swim, propel a ball precisely with a bat or your foot, fish, or dance—you name it—you probably learned the skill with the help of someone's showing you, as well as telling you, how. That is, in a general sense, observational learning includes listening and reading and mentally *visualizing* in addition to watching. It includes the kind of learning you are doing at this moment. In our information processing, we benefit not just from the knowledge stored in our own memories but also, through language, from all the knowledge possessed by our fellow human beings—in fact, from all the wisdom accumulated throughout history as recorded in our libraries and computers. Indeed, this handed-down knowledge, in all its forms and all its complexity, is the very basis of modern civilization and technology as we know it—for better or for worse.

## Test Yourself

**(j)** Josh uses "bad" words whenever he gets angry at school—just as his father does at home. What kind of learning is Josh demonstrating?

(The answer is on page 170.)

## Cognitive Maps, Expectancies, and Knowledge

Experiments such as the ones described in this chapter—Köhler's chimpanzees and their insight, the rats that learned without reinforcement, the children who learned how to beat up a Bobo doll—led many psychologists to seek a new approach to understanding learning. Granted, humans as well as lower animals often establish simple stimulus-response and behavior-consequences associations through classical and operant conditioning, with reinforcement a part of the process. Much of life is governed by the consequences of what we do, and there is no denying it (try not paying taxes and see what happens). But in cases in which other kinds of learning occur, in ways not accounted for by the principles of conditioning, just what is it that the organism learns—and how does the learning take place?

Although we are born with all the neurons we will ever have, the overall mass of the infant's brain totals only about one-fourth that of the adult brain. Initially, the brain grows bigger because its neurons grow in size and—until about age 2—new glia cells are formed and grow. The story is a bit different with neuron synapses. These average about 2,500 per neuron at birth, peak at about 15,000 each by age 2 to 3, and are "pruned" back throughout the remainder of childhood to just those that are actively being used—with the effect that a child's brain has many more synapses than an adult's brain does (Gopnik, Meltzoff, & Kuhl, 1999). Thus, the brain specializes and becomes more efficient at processing information during childhood—and beyond. Because of such changes, we should expect that the ease of learning new ideas and skills and achieving insights should also change dramatically over the life span.

During the first year of life, before a child has acquired much in the way of language, learning consists primarily of acquiring new perceptual skills and new behaviors. If the new skill is one for which the infant is biologically prepared, learning takes place quickly. An example is visually guided reaching for objects. Infants learn rapidly to reach for a rattle when its sounds are close by, and to ignore it when the sounds are from a distance. However, if the task is not one for which the infant is innately prepared—for example, successfully grasping and holding the reached-for object—progress is slower. Thus, ease of learning is clearly a function of the nature of the task and, in this case, muscular maturation as well.

After age 2 or 3, the child can use language and mental symbols and can relate new experiences to a very large and complex set of ideas. From age 3 to 7, there is an obvious improvement in the speed of learning new skills and rules. If the task is to reach for the one object of three that is different from the other two (for example, a cup but not the two adjacent glasses), an older child will learn the new rule much more quickly than a 2-year-old.

Many researchers believe that from adolescence to about age 30 the brain is in optimal shape for learning new ideas and manipulating complex concepts. It is noteworthy, for example, that many mathematicians and physicists make their most important discoveries in their 20s. Many of the Nobel laureates in physics made their important discoveries before they were 30 years old.

New skills and knowledge can be acquired throughout the life span, but the learning of middle and older adulthood is more likely to involve the integration of past experiences, or what many would call wisdom. A 60-year-old cannot learn as quickly as a younger person. For example, if the task is to learn a series of 100 digits by learning 10 new digits each day, a 30-year-old can master the assignment much more quickly than an older person. But the older person has accumulated a richer set of experiences, permitting greater insights into complex events (see Chapter 11). Freud's most important ideas came after he had reached midlife, and George Bernard Shaw wrote some of his best plays in his "later years."

An idea proposed by Tolman (1948), based on his studies of rats in mazes, is that the rats learn **cognitive maps,** both in the lab and in their natural environments. In other words, he concluded that although animals do learn responses that result in reward, they also acquire knowledge of the spatial features of their environment—of where things are and what leads to what. Reinforcement does not produce the learning as much as it causes organisms to use what they have learned (this is the same learning-performance distinction that was demonstrated with children in Bandura's experiments). If a reward is provided in one part of the cognitive map, they will go there. If there is punishment, they will avoid the spot. We do the same.

Subsequent experimenters, working with types of learning that did not pose the spatial problems found in mazes, enlarged Tolman's interpretation into the idea of acquiring expectancies, as pointed out earlier in the chapter. What is important is the subject's anticipation, or belief, about what will take place—both in classical and operant conditioning and in other forms of learning.

Today's cognitive psychologists have expanded these suggestions into the all-embracing term *knowledge.* What is learned, according to the cognitive school, is all sorts of knowledge—the "maps" of pathways acquired by Tolman's rats, the expectancies about food acquired by Pavlov's dogs, and a human's knowledge that Main Street is one block north of Broadway, an aspirin can relieve a headache,

**Cognitive map**
**A mental representation of the spatial features of an environment.**

$2 \times 4 = 8$, "Thanks" in English is "Gracias" in Spanish and "Merci" in French, and the earth is round.

Cognitive psychologists regard "the human organism as an active seeker of knowledge and processor of information," with learning being the step in which we acquire information that we then modify, manipulate, store, and use in various ways (Klatzky, 1980). We are not passive pawns of our environment. Learning is one element in a closely related series of processes—such as perception, memory, and language and cognition—that are discussed in other chapters of the text, especially the next two.

Psychologists are also aware that learning abilities differ at various points in our lives, as discussed in the Life Span Perspective on page 167.

# Chapter 4 Summary

1. *Conditioning* emphasizes the establishment of associations between observable stimuli and responses, although underlying cognitive processes are now allowed for as well.

2. *Learning* is a relatively permanent change in behavior potential resulting from experience.

## Classical Conditioning

3. Ivan Pavlov is the originator of what is now called *classical conditioning*, a form of learning based primarily on stimuli that cause *reflexes*, such as salivation in response to food.

4. In classical conditioning, the stimulus that naturally produces the reflex response is the *unconditioned stimulus (UCS)*, which is repeatedly paired with an initially neutral stimulus until the latter becomes a *conditioned stimulus (CS)*. What is learned in classical conditioning is a CS-UCS association; the original reflex response is the *unconditioned response (UCR)*, and the response produced by the CS is the *conditioned response (CR)*.

## Classical Conditioning Phenomena and Applications

5. *Delayed conditioning* is the most effective form of classical conditioning. Less effective are *simultaneous conditioning* and *trace conditioning*.

6. After conditioning, *extinction* of the CR occurs when the UCS is discontinued. Allowing time to pass and returning the subject to the apparatus is typically accompanied by *spontaneous recovery*.

7. The crucial factor in classical conditioning is the consistency with which the CS predicts the occurrence of the UCS.

8. *Stimulus generalization* occurs when a stimulus similar to the original CS also produces a CR. *Stimulus discrimination*, its complement, occurs when dissimilar stimuli produce a lesser CR or none at all.

9. Biological predispositions are often apparent in classical conditioning. Because of prewiring, some CS-UCS associations can be established much more easily than others and some not at all.

10. Taste aversion experiments provide an example of how biological predispositions affect conditioning. The learning of taste aversions is easy for animals that naturally associate taste with food but difficult to impossible for animals that use other cues, such as visual ones, for food.

11. In Watson and Rayner's "Little Albert" experiment, the loud sound was the UCS, the rat was the CS, and a fear response was the UCR and CR.

12. In the experiment on conditioned illness in rats, the insulin was the UCS, the light and syringe were CSs, and the coma was the UCR and CR.

13. In the experiment on conditioning the immune system in rats, the drug was the UCS, the novel taste was the CS, and production of antibodies was the UCR and CR.

14. In the experiment on conditioning sexual behavior in rats, normal female odors were the UCS, the lemon scent was the CS, and sexual arousal was the UCR and CR.

15. In the modern view, conditioning can be best explained by the development of *expectancies*—that is, what animals and humans learn is the expectation that a particular CS will be followed by a UCS.

16. Classical conditioning by past events may account for many of the fears and preferences displayed by human adults—and also for physical symptoms such as unexplained headaches or nausea and the intense desire to return to drug use that is sometimes displayed by former addicts.

## Operant Conditioning

17. Operant behavior "operates" on the environment in accord with *contingencies*. *Operant conditioning* is based on contingencies that are arranged in the lab or occur in real life.

18. The controlled environment of the Skinner box revolutionized the study of learning and conditioning.

19. Parallels between classical and operant conditioning occur in the areas of extinction and spontaneous recovery, as well as stimulus generalization and discrimination.

20. *Shaping and successive approximations* is an efficient procedure for training subjects to perform specific behaviors.

21. An operant is a class of behaviors—not a specific behavior.

22. The first half of Thorndike's law of effect corresponds to *positive reinforcement* and *negative reinforcement;* the second half corresponds to *positive punishment* and *negative punishment*.

23. In operant conditioning contingencies, *positive* means that a stimulus is presented or "added" and *negative* means that a stimulus is removed or "subtracted." The effect on behavior is then determined by whether the stimulus is appetitive or aversive.

## Operant Conditioning Phenomena and Applications

24. Laboratory animals, young children, and others who lack cognitive and language skills cannot mediate delays in reinforcement or punishment, so delayed

contingencies tend to be ineffective. Older children and adults can mediate, and so delays do not void effectiveness.

25. Learning is faster with *continuous reinforcement,* but *partial reinforcement* produces behavior that is more resistant to extinction. Parents who partially reinforce tantrum behavior eventually find it very difficult to eliminate.

26. *Ratio schedules* require a number of responses before reinforcement occurs; *interval schedules* require that an amount of time pass before reinforcement occurs.

27. *Fixed schedules* require a specific number of responses or amount of time; *variable schedules* require a number of responses or amount of time that varies around an average value.

28. Skinner strongly favored positive reinforcement over punishment, because of the atmosphere it creates and especially because it tells the organism what to do.

29. Punishment, in contrast to reinforcement, only tells the organism what not to do and also has a long list of undesirable side effects—especially if the punishment is corporal.

30. Punishment may be necessary in the case of dangerous or harmful behavior, but it is best used in conjunction with positive reinforcement for acceptable behavior.

31. *Superstitious behavior* persists in the absence of any actual contingencies.

32. Phobias, as well as some superstitions, are maintained by escape and avoidance—that is, the reduction of fear through negative reinforcement.

33. *Learned helplessness* has been demonstrated in dogs by subjecting them to inescapable electric shocks; their reaction has direct parallels to human feelings of helplessness and depression.

34. Learned helplessness can be counteracted by providing success experiences.

35. *Behavior modification* refers to any program designed to alter behavior for the better by manipulating its consequences.

36. *Token economies,* which reward helpful and adaptive behavior, can be highly effective, although they sometimes raise ethical issues.

37. *Ethology* defines *instinctive behavior* in a highly specific and scientific way. Humans have reflexes and perhaps evolutionary "whisperings," but nothing in the way of instinctive behaviors as defined by ethologists.

38. In laboratory and stage animals, biological predispositions have been found to interfere with operant conditioning procedures.

## Cognitive Learning: A Contemporary View Rooted in the Past

39. In the heyday of the view that human behavior and personality could be explained in terms of reinforcement history, there were dissenters who insisted that an understanding of cognition was also essential.

40. Learning by *insight* was one early demonstration that trial-and-error learning and stimulus-response associations were inadequate in explaining behavior.

41. Rats' learning of mazes in the absence of reinforcement was another difficult phenomenon for the strict behaviorists to explain.

42. Demonstrations of *observational learning* by humans and other species also contradicted the idea that learning could be explained solely in terms of reinforcement or punishment; thus, the learning-performance distinction emerged.

43. Modern civilization and its technology exist because of direct and indirect observational learning.

44. In addition to being conditioned, we learn *cognitive maps* and expectancies—in general, knowledge. We are active seekers of learning and not passive pawns of our environment.

# Chapter 4 Test Yourself Answers

(a) Classical conditioning with prior doctors who meant well but inflicted pain

(b) A conditioned stimulus that Juan has learned to associate with pain

(c) Extinction, the eventual disappearance of a conditioned response

(d) A biological predisposition to learn taste aversions after a single instance of sickness, plus stimulus generalization to potato chips other than the ones that made him sick

(e) Operant learning—probably accompanied by observational learning, as discussed later in the chapter

(f) Shaping and successive approximations, accompanied by positive reinforcement

(g) Negative punishment; being late results in the removal of a goody, or appetitive stimulus.

(h) Partial reinforcement, which produces the greatest resistance to extinction

(i) Negative reinforcement; running makes the bees "go away," thus maintaining your dog's phobia.

(j) Observational learning, which can crop up at the most inappropriate times

# Chapter 4  Conditioning and Learning

## Key Terms

behavior modification (p. 161)
classical conditioning (p. 140)
cognitive map (p. 167)
conditioned response (CR) (p. 141)
conditioned stimulus (CS) (p. 141)
conditioning (p. 138)
contingency (p. 149)
continuous reinforcement (p. 155)
delayed conditioning (p. 143)
ethology (p. 162)
expectancy (p. 148)
extinction (p. 143)
fixed schedule (p. 156)
insight (p. 164)
instinctive behavior (p. 162)
interval schedule (p. 156)
learned helplessness (p. 160)
learning (p. 139)
negative punishment (p. 153)
negative reinforcement (p. 152)
observational learning (p. 165)

operant conditioning (p. 149)
partial reinforcement (p. 155)
positive punishment (p. 153)
positive reinforcement (p. 152)
ratio schedule (p. 155)
reflex (p. 139)
shaping and successive approximations (p. 150)
simultaneous conditioning (p. 143)
spontaneous recovery (p. 143)
stimulus discrimination (p. 145)
stimulus generalization (p. 144)
superstitious behavior (p. 159)
token economy (p. 162)
trace conditioning (p. 143)
unconditioned response (UCR) (p. 141)
unconditioned stimulus (UCS) (p. 141)
variable schedule (p. 157)

 *The key terms above can be used as search terms in InfoTrac, a database of readings, which can be found at http://infotrac-thomsonlearning.com.*

## Active Learning Review

1. The early learning theorists thought that all human behavior could be understood in terms of _____.

   **conditioning**

2. When we take too large a sip of a hot beverage, the experience teaches us to sip slowly in the future—a lasting change in our behavior potential called _____.

   **learning**

3. *Learning* is a relatively permanent change in behavior potential resulting from _____. But learning can also be applied to behaviors that originally are not learned but are inborn.

   **experience**

### Classical Conditioning

4. A *reflex* is an inborn response to a specific _____. Whenever a bright light strikes your eyes, it makes your pupils smaller. This type of inborn and automatic response is called a _____.

   **stimulus**

   **reflex**

5. Although reflexes and instincts are inborn and not _____, Ivan Pavlov, a Russian scientist, studied a form of learning through which a reflex could be made to occur in response to a stimulus that originally did not evoke it.

   **learned**

6. The process of learning to associate a reflex with a new stimulus—the kind of learning studied by the Russian scientist _____—is called *classical conditioning*.

   **Pavlov**

7. Pavlov _____ dogs to respond to a sound with a salivary reflex, which originally occurred only in response to food in the dog's mouth. This procedure is called _____ conditioning.

   **conditioned**

   **classical**

reflex

8. In the procedure for associating a _____ with a new stimulus, the stimulus that naturally sets off the reflex is called the *unconditioned stimulus,* or *UCS.*

unconditioned stimulus
UCS

9. In Pavlov's experiments, food was the natural stimulus for the reflex of salivation. In classical conditioning terms, food was the _____ _____, or _____.

reflex

10. The unconditioned stimulus naturally produces a _____. In classical conditioning terms, this unlearned reflex to a stimulus is called the *unconditioned response,* or *UCR.*

unconditioned response, UCR

11. In Pavlov's experiment, salivation was the _____ _____, or _____.

12. Classical conditioning involves establishing an association between a new, initially neutral stimulus and an _____ _____, or _____. When the new stimulus elicits a response such as salivation, it is called a *conditioned stimulus,* or *CS.* The sound of a bell was often used as the _____ _____, or _____, in Pavlov's experiments.

unconditioned stimulus,
UCS
conditioned stimulus
CS

13. Each pairing of stimuli such as a bell and food is called a conditioning trial. Eventually, after several _____, the bell presented alone produced salivation—a behavior that is called the *conditioned response* because it is learned.

trials

14. When salivation occurs as an unlearned reflex to the food stimulus, it is called the _____ response, or UCR. When it occurs as a learned response to the bell stimulus, it is called the _____ response, or CR.

unconditioned
conditioned

15. In sum, in the form of learning called _____ _____, a previously neutral stimulus is associated with another stimulus, the _____ _____, or _____, which reflexively produces the _____ _____, or _____. When the previously neutral stimulus produces this response, it is now the _____ _____, or _____, and the response is called the _____ _____, or _____.

classical conditioning
unconditioned stimulus
UCS, unconditioned
response, UCR
conditioned stimulus, CS
conditioned response, CR

## Classical Conditioning Phenomena and Applications

classical conditioning

16. Simple associative learning such as _____ _____ is influenced by several factors. One is the sequence in which the CS and UCS are presented. The most effective sequence is to present the _____ stimulus followed quickly by the _____ stimulus, a sequence called *delayed conditioning.*

conditioned
unconditioned
delayed conditioning

17. Learning occurs most rapidly under conditions of _____ _____. Less effective are *simultaneous conditioning,* in which the stimuli are presented at exactly the same time, and *trace conditioning,* in which there is a time period between the two stimuli.

delayed conditioning
simultaneous conditioning

18. If the CS precedes the UCS, the process is called _____ _____; if the stimuli are presented at the same time, it is called _____ _____; and if the CS is presented and then removed before the UCS is presented, it is called _____ _____.

trace conditioning

19. If the UCS is discontinued—that is, if the CS is no longer followed by the _____ stimulus—the learned _____ weakens and eventually no longer occurs.

unconditioned, CR

20. In Pavlov's experiments, if the sound is no longer followed by food, the dog will eventually cease to salivate to the sound. When this happens, the conditioned response has undergone _____.

extinction
UCS, CS

21. In short, when Pavlov discontinued the _____, the _____ underwent *extinction.* After a rest period away from the experimental apparatus, however, a conditioned response may reappear.

22. After a period of rest, if an extinguished CR reappears following the next presentation of the CS, the phenomenon is called _____ _____.

spontaneous recovery
conditioning
classical

23. The finding that delayed, simultaneous, and trace _____ differ in effectiveness underscores that the crucial factor in _____ conditioning is the reliability with which the CS predicts the occurrence of the UCS.

24. The subject or participant learns that the CS _____ the UCS; thus, the most effective procedure is briefly _____ _____.

predicts
delayed conditioning

25. Once a CR has been established to a specific stimulus, it may also occur in response to other stimuli similar to the original one, in a process called *stimulus generalization.* If a dog learns to salivate to the sound of one bell, the dog may also salivate to the sound of a different bell through the process of _____ _____.

stimulus
generalization

26. But if an experimenter continues to present the UCS after the original bell and never after the different one, the CR will eventually occur mostly only in response to the original bell. This phenomenon is called stimulus _____.

discrimination

27. _____ _____ are "prewired" tendencies that can either enhance or interfere with conditioning. For example, rats readily associate taste and smell with food, so it is easy to condition a rat to avoid foods or liquids with a distinctive taste by making the rat sick afterward.

Biological predispositions

28. In general, conditioned taste aversions are learned easily and quickly by many animals because of _____ _____, which enable conditioning to occur in a single trial that can span several hours. Thus, a rat or a human can learn a _____ _____ to a certain food in a way that "violates" the principles of classical conditioning.

biological predispositions

taste aversion

29. In Watson and Rayner's experiment, Albert initially learned to fear a white rat, but he also became apprehensive about a Santa Claus beard—evidence of _____ _____. If Albert had then been given experience with Santa's beard when it was not paired with the UCS, eventually his apprehension about the beard, but not the rat, would have undergone _____ and Albert would have learned _____ _____.

stimulus generalization

extinction
stimulus discrimination

30. In real-life situations, it may be that we learn accidental associations through _____ conditioning and then become ill when we encounter the CS. For example, we may develop a headache or become sick for no medical reason when a situation includes a previously established _____ stimulus that we don't even remember.

classical

conditioned

31. Based on the principle that classical conditioning works best when the CS reliably _____ the occurrence of the UCS, a cognitive explanation of classical conditioning is that we acquire an expectancy about what will happen next when a given stimulus occurs. Thus, a former drug addict may begin experiencing craving and withdrawal effects when simply exposed to drug paraphernalia, because of conditioned _____.

predicts

expectancies

## Operant Conditioning

32. In addition to reflex behavior, which is the subject of _____ conditioning, another form of behavior important in the study of learning is _____ _____—an activity that is voluntarily initiated by the organism and that somehow "operates" on the environment.

classical
operant
behavior

33. When a rat is placed in a new environment, it may explore, sniff, and climb about. Exploring the environment is a form of _____ behavior.

operant

34. A _____ is a relationship between operant behavior and its consequences, and _____ conditioning is the process through which organisms learn about contingencies—whether in the lab or in real-life settings. A rat learns what to do to obtain food and a human learns what to do to obtain a paycheck, through contingencies and operant conditioning.

contingency
operant

35. The process by which an animal learns to increase or decrease frequency of an operant behavior because that behavior is followed by a certain _____ is called _____ _____.

consequence
operant conditioning

36. When a rat in a Skinner box learns to press a bar to produce food, _____ conditioning has occurred. Through such conditioning, animals can be taught

operant

to perform novel or complex tasks by the process of *shaping and successive approximations,* which consists of rewarding them for the successful completion of each step leading to the target behavior.

37. A rat in a Skinner box might be given a food pellet at first when it heads in the direction of the bar, then when it touches the bar, then when it touches the bar and causes the bar to move, and finally only when it presses the bar sufficiently to trigger the food release mechanism. Such a process would be an example of _____ and _____ _____.

**shaping, successive approximations**
**reinforcement**
**punishment**

38. Translating Thorndike's law of effect into Skinner's terms, we might say that _____ occurs when a behavior leads to a satisfying state of affairs, and the behavior tends to be strengthened; _____ occurs when a behavior leads to an unsatisfying or annoying state of affairs, and the behavior tends to be weakened or suppressed.

**reinforcement**
**punishment**

39. When a rat presses a bar to obtain food, barpressing is strengthened and the contingency is _____. When a rat instead receives an electric shock, barpressing is weakened or suppressed and the contingency is _____.

**strengthened**

40. In operant conditioning terminology, *positive* means that something is presented or "added" when the behavior occurs. Thus, when a rat presses a bar and receives food, barpressing is _____ and the contingency is *positive reinforcement;* when the rat instead receives an electric shock, barpressing is _____ or _____ and the contingency is *positive punishment.*

**weakened, suppressed**
**positive**
**reinforcement**
**positive punishment**

41. If a child is praised for doing something good, the contingency is _____ _____. If a child is scolded for doing something bad, the contingency is _____ _____.

42. In operant conditioning terminology, *negative* means that something is removed or "subtracted" when the behavior occurs. Thus, when a rat presses a bar and escapes or avoids shock, barpressing is _____ and the contingency is *negative reinforcement;* when the rat instead has food postponed or taken away, barpressing is _____ or _____ and the contingency is *negative punishment.*

**strengthened**

**weakened, suppressed**

43. If a child is nagged until the child cleans up his or her room, the behavior is _____ and the contingency is _____ reinforcement. If a child loses privileges as a result of misbehavior, the behavior is _____ or _____ and the contingency is _____ punishment.

**strengthened, negative**
**weakened, suppressed**
**negative**

44. In sum, with regard to the consequences of behavior, presenting an appetitive stimulus, or goody, is _____ _____; removing an aversive, or unpleasant, stimulus is _____ _____; presenting an aversive, or unpleasant, stimulus is _____ _____; and removing an appetitive stimulus, or goody, is _____ _____.

**positive reinforcement**
**negative reinforcement**
**positive punishment**
**negative punishment**

## Operant Conditioning Phenomena and Applications

45. Delay of reinforcement or punishment greatly interferes with _____ _____ of laboratory animals or very young children, but older children and normal adults can span very long delays through verbal mediation, or self-talk. Young children are not capable of _____ mediation, whereas older children and normal adults regularly use it.

**operant**
**conditioning**

**verbal**

46. Learning generally takes place more rapidly with *continuous reinforcement,* in which each instance of the behavior is reinforced. When reinforcement follows each instance of the desired behavior, reinforcement is _____. But learning is more resistant to extinction if it is acquired with *partial reinforcement,* which is the delivery of reinforcement on some occasions but not on others.

**continuous**

47. In the wild, animals don't get rewarded for every instance of hunting for food; they only occasionally get rewarded, which is an example of _____ reinforcement.

**partial**

48. If parents occasionally give in and, in effect, reward their children's tantrums, they are engaging in _____ _____.

    **partial reinforcement**

49. Behaviors are learned more rapidly when reinforcement is _____, but behaviors are more resistant to _____ when reinforcement is _____. There are two types of partial reinforcement schedules. With a *ratio schedule*, reinforcement is delivered only after the subject responds a certain number of times. With an *interval schedule*, reinforcement is delivered only for the first response after a certain period of time.

    **continuous**
    **extinction, partial**

50. If a rat receives food only after pressing a bar three times, reinforcement is on a _____ schedule; if the rat receives food every two minutes, reinforcement is on an _____ schedule. For both types of schedules, if the ratio or interval is always the same, the *schedule* is *fixed;* if it changes over time, the *schedule* is *variable*.

    **ratio**
    **interval**

51. Partial reinforcement given for a specific number of responses is on a _____ schedule; partial reinforcement given for the first response after so much time is on an _____ schedule. When the ratio or interval is constant, the schedule is called _____; when it is changing, the schedule is called _____.

    **ratio**
    **interval**
    **fixed, variable**

52. Skinner strongly favored using rewards for appropriate behavior combined with ignoring inappropriate behavior; thus, he favored _____ _____ combined with _____.

    **positive reinforcement**
    **extinction**

53. Skinner emphasized that reinforcement is preferable in part because it is more informative; that is, reinforcement teaches what _____ _____, whereas punishment only teaches what _____ _____ _____.

    **to do**
    **not to do**

54. In the operant conditioning explanation, *superstitious behavior* occurs in the absence of any actual consequences, and phobic behavior occurs because of prior bad experiences. Wearing a certain sweater to an exam or throwing salt over your shoulder after you spill it is _____ behavior because it has no actual consequences; desperately avoiding certain objects or situations is _____ behavior learned through bad experiences.

    **superstitious**

    **phobic**

55. In the case of phobias, the behavior in response to the feared object or situation has the effect of making it go away and reducing the fear, and a person will be likely to continue to engage in behavior that has these effects. Phobic behavior is therefore maintained by _____ _____.

    **negative reinforcement**

56. Unavoidable _____, especially if it is painful, can lead in both laboratory animals and humans to *learned helplessness*, or a tendency to believe that events cannot be controlled and to give up trying to learn or act.

    **punishment**

57. Frequent experiences with failure or unavoidable consequences can lead to a belief that events cannot be controlled and to giving up, a condition called

_____ _____.

    **learned helplessness**

58. Principles of operant conditioning—especially positive reinforcement—have been applied in many situations to change behavior for the better. *Behavior modification* is a general term for applying _____ _____ to behavioral change.

    **operant conditioning**

59. Deliberately "teaching" people to change their behavior is known as _____ _____, a special form of which is *token economy*. This method, used in mental institutions and many other settings, provides _____ _____ for desirable and adaptive behavior in the form of tokens that patients can exchange for privileges and other rewards.

    **behavior**
    **modification**
    **positive reinforcement**

60. When the awarding of tokens—typically checkmarks on a clipboard—for good behavior is applied on a large scale within an institution, the approach is called a _____ _____.

    **token economy**

61. _____ is the study of *instinctive behavior,* which is defined as behavior that occurs in all normal members of a species, occurs in response to demonstrable "releasing" stimuli, and occurs in essentially the same way every time.

    **Ethology**

species
stimuli, every
time

62. To qualify as an instinctive behavior according to ethologists, the behavior must occur in all normal members of a _____, must occur in response to specific _____, and must occur in essentially the same way _____ _____. Humans have no behaviors that meet these criteria, although we may have subtle biological predispositions that can be overcome by culture and learning.

predispositions
instincts
biological

63. Biological _____ may exist in humans, but these do not qualify as _____.

64. In training animals to perform tricks such as circus acts, _____ predispositions can get in the way. For example, raccoons can be trained to insert tokens in a slot to obtain a food reward, but the behavior soon deteriorates because of classical conditioning; the raccoons try to wash the tokens instead—as raccoons normally do. That is, the tokens become so closely associated with food through _____ _____ that instinctual drift occurs and the raccoons can no longer perform the trick.

classical conditioning

drift
classical conditioning,
biological predispositions

65. Instinctual _____, which can interfere with operant conditioning, is a result of the interplay between _____ _____ and _____ _____.

### Cognitive Learning: A Contemporary View Rooted in the Past

operant, classical

66. Historically, the strict behaviorists thought that essentially all human learning was acquired through _____ and _____ conditioning. But not all learned behavior can be explained by these principles, as is illustrated by the example of *insight,* or what today would be called cognition in the form of problem solving.

67. In one early experiment, chimpanzees—faced with food placed beyond their reach and given some sticks—"figured out" how to use the sticks to reach the food. This form of cognition is called _____.

insight

operant, reinforced

68. The chimps had never before used sticks to reach food, so this behavior did not constitute _____ behavior that was _____ by food.

reinforcement

69. In another classic experiment, cognition and learning in the absence of _____ were demonstrated. First, a group of rats were simply allowed to explore a maze, with no reward provided. Later, when the rats were reinforced, they displayed knowledge of the maze comparable to that of rats that had been reinforced all along for finding their way through the maze. The interpretation was that the first group of rats, while exploring, had acquired *cognitive maps* of the maze.

cognition
insight, cognitive maps
classical, operant

70. In the absence of any reinforcement, both the chimpanzees and the rats displayed thinking, or _____. For the chimpanzees, the cognition was _____; for the rats, the cognition was the learning of _____ _____.

71. Another form of learning that cannot be explained by _____ or _____ conditioning is *observational learning.* Humans and many other animals learn simply by watching and perhaps imitating the _____ they see.

behavior
observational

72. In a general sense, _____ learning includes reading and mentally visualizing in addition to watching, and the knowledge handed down in this manner over the generations is the basis for modern civilization.

# Practice Test

____ **1.** Which statement is *not* true with regard to learning?
 a. A reflex response can become associated with a stimulus that did not originally produce the response.
 b. Learning can occur without observable behavioral activity.
 c. Learning differs from instinctive behavior because of the role of experience.
 d. Reflexes and instincts are inborn and are not modifiable by learning.

____ **2.** In general, fears can be learned and maintained through
 a. classical conditioning.
 b. stimulus generalization.
 c. operant conditioning.
 d. all the above

____ **3.** In Pavlov's experiments, the CR was
 a. the food.
 b. salivation to the bell.
 c. the bell.
 d. salivation to the food.

____ **4.** In the "Little Albert" experiment, the UCS was
 a. fear of the sight of the rat.
 b. the rat.
 c. the loud noise.
 d. Santa's beard.

____ **5.** A type of learning that is not initially dependent on a specific stimulus to produce a specific response is
 a. operant conditioning.
 b. reflex learning.
 c. discrimination learning.
 d. classical conditioning.

____ **6.** Human beings prone to asthma attacks because of an allergy to dust or pollen could suffer an attack when exposed to a harmless substance because of
 a. operant conditioning.
 b. stimulus discrimination.
 c. classical conditioning.
 d. spontaneous recovery.

____ **7.** Which of the following illustrates the role of biological predispositions?
 a. the learning of taste aversions
 b. the learning of superstitious behavior
 c. stimulus generalization
 d. all of the above

____ **8.** Insight and cognitive maps are concepts most closely associated with
 a. strict behaviorism.
 b. Pavlov.
 c. cognitive psychology.
 d. Thorndike.

____ **9.** A concept that is closely related to classical but not operant conditioning is
 a. stimulus discrimination.
 b. spontaneous recovery.
 c. stimulus generalization.
 d. none of the above

____ **10.** Pavlov discovered that he could make dogs restless, destructive, or apathetic by
 a. reinforcing these behaviors.
 b. giving the dogs an impossible discrimination problem.
 c. giving the dogs an impossible stimulus generalization problem.
 d. all the above

____ **11.** Phobias are maintained by
 a. positive reinforcement.
 b. negative reinforcement.
 c. positive punishment.
 d. negative punishment.

____ **12.** Omission training and the time-out procedure are examples of
 a. positive reinforcement.
 b. negative reinforcement.
 c. positive punishment.
 d. negative punishment.

____ **13.** Learning is likely to occur most rapidly and be most persistent if
 a. partial reinforcement is used.
 b. constant reinforcement is used.
 c. partial reinforcement is used first, followed by constant reinforcement.
 d. constant reinforcement is used first, followed by partial reinforcement.

____ **14.** The schedule of reinforcement that operates in gambling games such as playing slot machines is a
 a. variable ratio schedule.
 b. variable interval schedule.
 c. fixed ratio schedule.
 d. fixed interval schedule.

____15. Older children and normal adults "bridge the gap" and overcome delay of reinforcement through
   a. cognitive maps.
   b. insight learning.
   c. verbal mediation.
   d. trial-and-error learning.

____16. A parent who deliberately ignores a child's temper tantrums is attempting to discourage tantrums through
   a. negative reinforcement.
   b. extinction.
   c. active avoidance.
   d. learned helplessness.

____17. The assumption that behavior is controlled to a considerable degree by its consequences underlies
   a. behavior modification.
   b. reinforcement contingencies.
   c. token economies.
   d. all the above

____18. If a light is illuminated in a shuttle box just before an electric shock is delivered, a dog learns
   a. escape and then active avoidance.
   b. escape and then passive avoidance.
   c. active avoidance and then escape.
   d. passive avoidance and then escape.

____19. Punishment is most effective when combined with
   a. positive reinforcement for appropriate behavior.
   b. negative reinforcement for appropriate behavior.
   c. extinction of inappropriate behavior.
   d. not necessarily any of the above

____20. Learned helplessness in children may be caused by
   a. frequent and inconsistent punishment.
   b. frequent failure.
   c. continually being pressured to do better than they are able to do.
   d. all the above

From *Psychology: An Introduction* © 2004 Thomson Learning

# Exercises

1. This exercise will require you to be a bit of an actor. It is designed to demonstrate the effects of positive reinforcement in a conversational environment. Read through the entire exercise before starting the procedure.

   You will need a tape or digital recorder with at least a 5-minute capacity. You will need a person who is willing to talk about a subject of interest to her or him on two consecutive days while you record what the person says. You will also need a stopwatch or other device to time the 5-minute span.

   Through casual conversation, determine an area in which your participant has an interest. It can be almost anything: cars, music, food, politics, books, television, classes (!), fitness, etc. Explain that you will be asking your participant to talk about two areas of interest, one on each day. For example, if your participant is interested in cars, then the first day's topic might be U.S. cars and the second day's topic Japanese cars. If the area of interest is music, on each of the two days your participant might discuss a different band or a different kind of music.

   Confirm that your participant is willing to be recorded and is willing to talk for at least 5 full minutes each day while you listen attentively. Ensure that the participant knows that you will not be speaking during her or his monologues.

   *Naturally, do not tell your participant what this exercise is actually about until the second session has been completed.*

   ## First Session

   After having established what your participant will be talking about, start the tape recorder, record the start time, and begin. As you listen, do what you ordinarily would do while listening attentively, but try to minimize smiling and head nodding. If the participant seems to want you to talk, you may want to gesture to your closed lips as a reminder of how this exercise works.

   ## Second Session

   Having reminded the participant about today's topic, record a second 5-minute session, without erasing the first session. This time, however, behave differently: Every time your participant uses the personal pronoun *I* or *you*, emit a brief smile that your participant can see. This will require some finesse, and you may benefit from a little practice with someone else beforehand. Your smile must look natural. You must not leer, stretch your lips tightly over your teeth, blind your participant with too broad a smile, or otherwise allow your smile to appear contrived. *Natural* is the key word here. Your participant *must not realize* that you are producing the smiles deliberately.

   ## Analysis

   People are social animals, and smiles tend to act as appetitive stimuli. You will determine how effective your social approval smiles were in reinforcing the use of the personal pronouns by analyzing the two taped segments.

   For each taped segment separately, tally the number of times the person said either "I" or "you." Now, compare the total for the first segment (without smile reinforcement) with that for the second segment (with smile reinforcement). Answer these questions:

   a. What were the numbers for the two sessions?

   b. What was the difference in frequency (number) of those personal pronouns between the first and the second session?

   c. What does this difference suggest? Were the smiles actually appetitive stimuli or something else?

   d. How might knowledge of such tactics affect the conduct of a salesperson? A teacher? A politician? A sibling? A business client?

   e. Some people have involuntary facial expressions (tics, smiles, grimaces, and the like). What are the implications of your findings for them?

2. Suppose you're a psychologist who helps people with their problems through the use of behavior modification. Think about the following situations:

   a. You're a school psychologist, and a teacher reports to you that Sally is a very shy first-grade girl who rarely plays with other children. Most of the time she plays alone in the corner or tries to do special favors for the teacher. What would you suggest the teacher do to help this child become more social and less of a pest for the teacher?

   b. You're in charge of a ward in a hospital for mentally retarded children. Many of these youngsters have not learned to dress themselves, eat properly, wash themselves, brush

Exercises

th, or refrain from hitting other chil-
...ow would you design a token econ-
...elp these children? Describe not only
...u would do, using proper learning terminology, but why it should work.

c.  You're a child psychologist, and some parents come to you because their 3-year-old son
throws a temper tantrum whenever he does
not get his way. He yells and screams, throws
himself on the floor, kicks, and pounds. How
would you explain to the parents how such
behavior might have developed in the first
place, and what would you suggest be done
about it?

Bear in mind, of course, that there may be some
circumstances you aren't aware of. And it is understood that you probably have had no actual
experience with such cases. Moreover, although
actual psychologists would apply some of the
principles you have studied in this chapter, they
might treat some cases differently from others,
depending on their individual characteristics.
Thus, you cannot offer universally "correct" answers to these questions.

3.  There is considerable debate about the ethics of
using behavior modification in schools, in hospitals, and at home. Some people claim that this
constitutes manipulating individuals against their
will and that no one has the right to exert such
control over others in a free society. In contrast,
those who favor the use of behavioral principles
argue that children who disrupt classrooms and
patients in mental institutions are already coerced and manipulated in one way or another,
whether behavioral principles are used or not.
They claim that behavior modification is singled
out—and receives more blame than does sending
a child to the principal's office—simply because
behavior modification is more likely to be effective. Write a discussion presenting details and examples of both these opposing arguments, and
then state your personal position and justify it.

✱  *For quizzing, activities, exercises, and web links, check out the
book-specific website at http://www.psychology.wadsworth.
com/kagan9e.*

180

# 5 Remembering and Forgetting

© Jose Luis Pelaez, Inc./CORBIS

"I'm sorry. What's your name again?"

"I knew the answer, but I couldn't remember it."

"I meant to send you a birthday card, but I just forgot."

"You're right—it *is* our anniversary. How could it have slipped my mind?"

Each of us has had occasion to make statements like these. We sometimes have trouble remembering a familiar phone number, the name of a song, or what time we said we would meet a friend. It's little wonder that human memory is often blamed, apologized for, and agonized over.

Yet, no matter how imperfect our memories and no matter how frustrated we feel when we forget, we each have an enormous amount of knowledge stored somewhere—and somehow—within our nervous system. It is common for adults to know the meanings of many thousands of words in their own language and at least a few in other languages, plus rules of mathematics and basic facts about geography, history, and the universe—not to mention such practical matters as how to ride a bicycle, drive a car, read a map, operate a calculator, make a phone call, and shop for food and clothing. The marvel is not how much we forget but how much we remember.

Psychologists and other scientists have devoted considerable effort to studying just how human memory works—indeed, the scientific study of memory is as old as psychology itself. How is it that people can keep "in their heads" items as fleeting as a childhood conversation, the smell of a spring rain, or a ball player's scoring average even for a short time, let alone for many years? One thing seems clear: Human memory, rather than being a single ability, as psychologists once

A spelling bee tests participants' memory for the spellings of certain words.

thought, is made up of different kinds of memory (e.g., see Mitchell, 1989; Solso, 2001). For example, the memory you use in learning the content of this chapter is quite different from memory for events you have experienced, memory that allows you to find your way to a store, and memory for faces, sounds, and smells. This idea of multiple memories is underscored by considerable evidence that the various memory systems and functions are represented in specific areas distributed throughout the brain (Markowitsch, 2000).

Some of these forms of memory are amenable to some degree of improvement through techniques described later in the chapter. But first we consider the nature of the remarkable ability to remember.

# THE RANGE AND CONTENT OF HUMAN MEMORY

To cognitive psychologists, with their emphasis on knowledge as a key part of the human experience, learning and memory are of course closely related. *Learning* refers to the ways in which we acquire the many forms of knowledge that we possess and utilize. *Memory* has two distinct meanings. First, it is the set of "storehouses" in which we keep our knowledge—carefully organized (for the most part) so that we can find information quickly when we need it. Second, memory is the *process* by which we retrieve the information we have accumulated.

**FOCUS QUESTIONS**

- How do psychologists define memory?
- What are the stages in the information-processing view of memory and what role does each play?
- How do the stages of memory interact?

As you know, you do not always succeed in your efforts to remember. Sometimes a piece of information eludes you, and you say you've forgotten—perhaps permanently, perhaps only for the time being. How well you remember information depends in large part on how well you learned it and stored it away in the first place. Consider these three examples, each of which deals with memory for verbal material:

- You're driving to the beach and hear on the radio that the temperature is 87 degrees. But just as you hear this, you have to swerve to avoid an oncoming car. When the crisis is over, you try to remember what the temperature is, but you find that you have completely forgotten. It seems as if the information never registered in your memory.

- You're in a phone booth and look up a friend's phone number. You repeat the number to yourself as you turn from the phone book, drop coins into the phone, and make the call. You have successfully remembered the number—so far. But you get a busy signal, and by the time you fish the coins out of the return slot, drop them back into the phone, and wait for the tone, the number is gone from your memory.

- Like most people, you aren't very good at remembering names, but at a party you meet a guy named Demetrius Carson. You remark on the coincidence: His first name is the same as your brother's, and his last name is the same as your best friend's. Two years later, you meet the guy again. You have absolutely no trouble saying "Hi; you're Demetrius Carson, aren't you?"

As these examples suggest, the time span over which memories persist varies over an extremely wide range, from a fraction of a second (for the weather report heard while driving) to less than a minute (for the telephone number you forgot

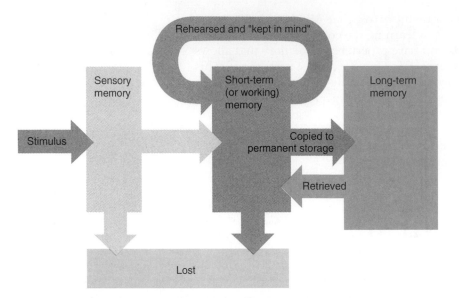

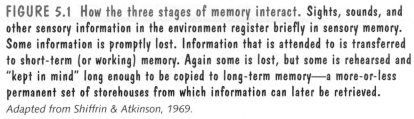

**FIGURE 5.1 How the three stages of memory interact.** Sights, sounds, and other sensory information in the environment register briefly in sensory memory. Some information is promptly lost. Information that is attended to is transferred to short-term (or working) memory. Again some is lost, but some is rehearsed and "kept in mind" long enough to be copied to long-term memory—a more-or-less permanent set of storehouses from which information can later be retrieved.

*Adapted from Shiffrin & Atkinson, 1969.*

**Sensory memory**
The memory system that briefly holds sensory information for transfer to short-term memory.

**FIGURE 5.2 The fleeting nature of sensory memory.** Arrangements of twelve letters and numbers were shown briefly to participants. The amount of information they held in sensory memory was then analyzed. As the bars show, the amount was quite high at the start but declined very quickly.

*Adapted from Sperling, 1960.*

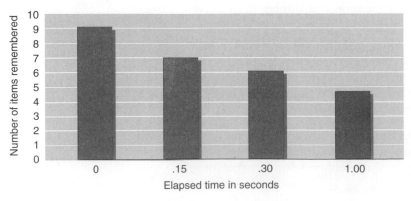

right after looking it up) to a lifetime (for a name that has a special meaning for you). This section emphasizes the interaction between time and memory—that is, the range of times over which we remember information like words, numbers, and sentences. For convenience, psychologists divide this range into three stages of memory, illustrated in Figure 5.1. You may find it helpful to refer back to this figure during the discussions that follow.

## Sensory Memory: Gone in an Instant

Every event that impinges on our sense organs remains available for at least a brief instant, but sometimes no longer. These extremely brief memories, of which we are typically unaware, are called **sensory memory.** They contain just the lingering traces of a great deal of information transduced by the senses (see Chapter 3), and there is a different memory system for each of the senses.

The existence of visual sensory memory was demonstrated many years ago by George Sperling (1960); it was later dubbed *iconic memory* by Ulric Neisser (1967). In Sperling's experiments—which are still cited by theorists trying to unscramble how iconic memory works (see Dosher & Sperling, 1998)—participants were briefly shown twelve letters and numbers in three rows and then asked how many of the letters and numbers they could remember. Without any help, participants remembered an average of four symbols. But if participants were given a signal indicating that they were to try to remember the letters and numbers on one particular row, they could usually recall at least three, and often all four, of the symbols in that row. This was true no matter which of the three rows was signaled, suggesting that the participants retained a brief impression of almost the entire pattern of stimuli.

While the experiments showed that people can briefly retain a fair amount of visual information, they also showed that information in sensory memory deteriorates very rapidly (see Figure 5.2). There is probably a sensory memory process for each of the senses, so, for example, we can remember for an instant the sight of lightning after it has flashed across the sky, the scent of flowers in a garden we have just walked by, or the sound of a car's horn after the car has passed us. But these stimuli begin to vanish very quickly—within a fraction of a second for something we have seen (Loftus, Duncan, & Gehrig, 1992) and within a fraction of a second to several seconds (in what Neisser called *echoic memory*) for something we have heard (Cowan, 1984). To retain the information longer, we must transfer it to the second of the three stages of memory.

## Short-Term (Working) Memory: How Information Is Retained Temporarily

The second of the three temporal stages is **short-term memory,** which some cognitive psychologists prefer to define somewhat differently as **working memory.** Those who use the latter term envision working memory as including a *central executive* that controls all cognitive processing and also directs attention—they view this stage of memory as actively involved in processing information rather than simply storing it temporarily (Baddeley, 1998). Either way, short-term, or working, memory is whatever you are consciously thinking about at any given time. It can be fresh information from sensory memory or information retrieved from permanent storage. Typically, it is a combination of the two. For example, when you encounter something new in your environment, such as an oddly colored bird, you immediately start comparing it to birds you know from past experience.

Classic research has demonstrated that if you do not engage in some form of thinking about new sensory information, it deteriorates and is lost completely within 15 to 30 seconds (Peterson & Peterson, 1959). So much information is lost in this way that some psychologists have described short-term memory as a "leaky bucket" (e.g., Miller, 1964). However, this tendency to lose information is far from a disadvantage. For example, a bank teller remembers only briefly that she or he is cashing a customer's paycheck for $352.89. By the time the next customer steps up to the window, the figure $352.89 has vanished from memory and the teller's working memory is "clear" to deal with the next transaction.

In addition to a limited time span, short-term memory has quite a limited capacity, as illustrated in Figure 5.3. The traditional view is that an adult's short-term memory can hold seven plus or minus two *unrelated* items (Miller, 1956). When short-term memory is near capacity with five to nine items, new items can be added only by dropping some of the old ones (or by grouping items into "chunks," as described later in the chapter). The central executive often discards the old items deliberately, by manipulating short-term memory processes (Sperling, 1967). Although we are unaware of it, the brain apparently engages in a kind of internal scanning of the information that is being held briefly in sensory memory. From the constant flow of sights, sounds, and other messages from the senses, some particular items are selected as worthy of attention—a process that is still poorly understood in spite of years of research and attempts to describe how it works.

**Short-term (working) memory**
The conscious memory system that holds information only for about 15 to 30 seconds unless it is rehearsed or otherwise processed.

**FIGURE 5.3 The brief life span of short-term memory.** Even individuals with a relatively good memory span have a limited ability to recall digits or other stimuli immediately after they are presented. And however good or poor the memory span, the ability gets weaker when the digits are presented more rapidly.

*Adapted from Lyon, 1977.*

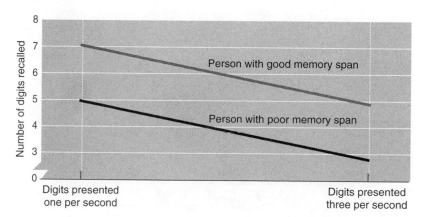

**Encoding**
The process by which information is entered into memory in either acoustic, visual, or semantic form.

Information is entered into short-term memory in ways designed to make it as easy to handle as possible. This process is called **encoding,** and it can take various forms (Solso, 2001). *Acoustic,* or *auditory, encoding*—as when you talk to yourself—appears to be the primary form. Information may also be encoded *visually,* by retaining a mental image of something, or *semantically,* by retaining "meanings." For example, suppose you're walking down the street and notice a large stranger coming toward you. You could encode the stimulus acoustically by saying to yourself "Here comes a stranger," you could encode the stimulus visually by thinking in terms of a series of pictures of the person, or you could encode the stimulus semantically by thinking in terms of what he or she might represent, such as danger. Much of the time we use all three forms of encoding, but the prevailing view is that acoustic encoding—especially when it uses words and language—is the predominant form of short-term retention (Leahey & Harris, 2001; Solso, 2001).

**Rehearsal**
A process in which information is deliberately repeated so that it can be retained temporarily or copied to long-term memory.

**Long-term memory**
The memory system in which information is stored more or less permanently.

The preceding discussion also implies that we use deliberate **rehearsal** to retain information in working memory. This is clearest in the case of acoustic encoding, as when you look up a phone number and repeat it to yourself just long enough to make a call. However, if you rehearse the phone number enough times, you may remember it indefinitely. Rehearsal is also a common way of "copying" information into **long-term memory** for more or less permanent storage, discussed next.

## Long-Term Memory: An Overview

The initial stages of memory are fascinating, but long-term memory is truly amazing, and its intricacies have received by far the most research attention over the years. Thus, long-term memory is the primary topic of the remainder of the chapter (also see Chapter 2 for more of what is known about the biological basis of long-term memory).

How long is long-term? Sometimes months or years, as illustrated in Figure 5.4, and sometimes even for life. Upon hearing a tune, an older person may remember lyrics learned decades earlier or vividly recall an incident from childhood. Although it is unclear exactly how much information we can store, long-term memory is, for all practical purposes, unlimited. That is, your brain never gets "full"—contrary to how you may feel at the end of a term or an academic year. For example, most people have the meanings of tens of thousands of words stored in memory, and many continue to acquire new words throughout life. Some people have vocabularies that run into the hundreds of thousands of words and span several languages. The same applies to the millions of facts and other kinds of knowledge people accumulate in a seemingly never-ending manner.

**FIGURE 5.4 The surprising staying power of long-term memory. From groups of four titles, three of which were made up, participants were asked to identify the actual title of a TV program that had been shown nationally for a single season within the past 15 years. As indicated in the graph, the percentage of correct identifications dropped steadily the older the program was. But even after 15 years, the chance of remembering the title of a long-discontinued TV program was still better than 50-50.**

*Adapted from Squire, 1989.*

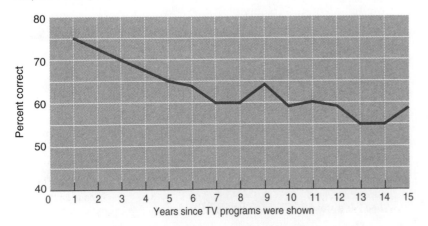

### How Long-Term Memories Are Encoded
Just as short-term memories are encoded in specific ways, information that is copied into long-term memory is "re-encoded" in ways suitable for relatively

permanent storage, as well as for use in the future. What forms does this encoding take?

Cognitive psychologists are not entirely in agreement on how many and what kinds of long-term memory systems there are, but they do agree that human memory systems store several distinct kinds of information. One distinction is between **procedural memory** and **declarative memory.** Procedural knowledge is "how to" knowledge, which can be anything from how to climb a ladder to how to ride a horse to how to drive a car. The interesting thing about procedural knowledge is that we often have difficulty verbalizing just how we do something—and yet, with practice, we can perform the behavior well without even consciously thinking about it while we're doing it.

When you look up a phone number and repeat it just long enough to make the call, you are engaging in rehearsal.

Declarative memory, on the other hand, is knowledge that can be put into words. This includes the gamut of facts, ideas, beliefs, attitudes, principles, laws, concepts, problem-solving skills, and general knowledge we have of self and the physical and social world around us.

In turn, cognitive psychologists make a distinction between two types of declarative memory: **semantic memory,** which is made up of meanings and understandings that were acquired independent of any particular context, and **episodic memory,** which includes the context in which the memory was acquired (Tulving, 1989, 1993). For example, although you may remember that Vancouver is in British Columbia and hence in Canada, you probably have no idea where you learned these facts. Nonetheless, your memory of them—a semantic association—may persist for life. In contrast, if you visited Vancouver, you would surely learn some facts about the city and about Canada that include the episode of your being there—such as streets you walked along and historical buildings and other sights you saw.

The difference between the two is dramatically illustrated by the now-classic case of K.C. Extensive brain injuries as a result of a motorcycle accident left K.C. in a state of amnesia, or severe breakdown of memory abilities. As described by memory researcher Endel Tulving (1989), K.C.'s case was unique in that, although he was unable to remember *any* events or experiences from his own life—he had no episodic memory—he did know many things about the world. He had knowledge of history, geography, politics, music, and various other fields. But he knew about his own life only from the point of view of an observer. For example, he retained his knowledge of how to play chess, but he couldn't remember ever having played chess with anyone. A similar pattern has been found in other people with amnesia suffered as a result of brain disorders or injuries. Among these in-

**Procedural memory**
Memory for how to do things.

**Declarative memory**
Memory for knowledge that can be put into words.

**Semantic memory**
Memory for knowledge that is independent of the context in which it was acquired.

**Episodic memory**
Memory that includes the context in which the knowledge was acquired.

Despite massive brain injuries, K.C. remembers how to play chess, but he has totally forgotten all his past experiences as a chess player. *(Tulving, 1989)*

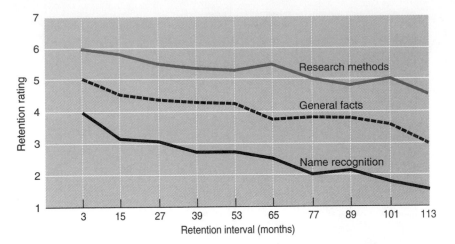

**FIGURE 5.5** Remembering a psychology course 10 years later. What students in a cognitive psychology course retained best over a 10-year period was material dealing with research methods. They retained general facts less well. Retention was poorest when they were tested on recognition of names of cognitive psychologists.
*Adapted from Conway, Cohen, & Stanhope, 1991.*

dividuals, there is often little correlation between remembering facts, or semantic memory, and remembering the sources of the facts, or episodic memory (Squire & Knowlton, 2000).

Long-term retention also depends to some extent on the nature of the material learned earlier. In a study that is especially relevant to students of psychology, nearly 400 former students in a psychology course were given memory tests to assess their retention of the material. As expected, the longer the elapsed time, the poorer their retention was—although overall, even after 10 years, the students did fairly well (Conway, Cohen, & Stanhope, 1991). As shown in Figure 5.5, there were some differences in retention depending on the topic.

**The Retrieval Process**   We cannot possibly be conscious at any given moment of the many millions of items of information we hold in long-term memory. Most of the information just lies there, unused. Then there comes a time when a situation requires the use of a particular piece of information. Suppose that one evening you're reading by the light of a single lamp. Suddenly the light goes out and you are in the dark. The situation calls for action based on the knowledge you have stored in long-term memory about lamps, electricity, and alternative sources of light—including where to look for a new light bulb.

An order has arrived at your memory's storehouse, calling for the immediate delivery of some of the items held there. You need information, and to get it you must engage in the process called **retrieval**. That is, you must find the right items and pull them into working memory, where you can actively think about them. Back in Figure 5.1 (p. 184), this retrieval process is depicted by the arrow pointing from long-term memory back to short-term memory, or consciousness.

The human memory retrieval process operates in wondrous ways. We do not have to rummage through all the items stored in memory to find what we need. Instead, we are capable of what has been called *direct-access retrieval* (Wickelgren, 1981). Our storehouses are organized in such a way that ordinarily we can go directly to the right "place," find the items we need, and deliver them promptly to working memory. The ways in which we accomplish this highly efficient organization are discussed later in the chapter.

**Retrieval**
The process of extracting knowledge from long-term memory.

# WHY WE FORGET

We cannot discuss remembering without also discussing forgetting. They are opposite sides of the same coin. When we learn something, we store a piece of information in our memory. Sometimes this information persists, and we can call on it whenever we need it. When we're able to do so, we say that we remember. But sometimes the information seems to disappear or to elude us—and then we say we've forgotten. Why do we remember some things and forget others?

## How Remembering and Forgetting Are Measured

Attempts to investigate the intertwined processes of remembering and forgetting face many obstacles. Psychologists and other scientists have not yet found any clear-cut way of examining the brain to see what kinds of changes have been made in it by specific instances of learning and how well these changes persist in memory. Although researchers can devise tests to determine how much is remembered and how much is forgotten, unfortunately these tests cannot measure memory directly. All they can measure is how well people *perform* on the tests—and their performance may not be an entirely accurate indication of what or how much they remember. Memory may be adversely affected by poor motivation, anxiety, distractions, and many other factors. Therefore, tests of remembering and forgetting must always be viewed with reservations. But in their effort to do the best they can, psychologists have devised three basic methods for measuring what is remembered: recall, recognition, and relearning.

**Recall**   If you want to show that you have learned Hamlet's famous soliloquy that begins "To be or not to be," you can recite it—thus demonstrating **recall,** or the ability to bring it out intact from wherever it is stored in your memory. In school, a common way of testing recall is the essay question. A professor who asks, "What is classical conditioning?" is calling on you to recall the essential details of what you have learned, with only the question as a cue.

**Recognition**   Often we cannot recall what we have learned, at least not completely, but we can prove that we remember something about it by demonstrating our **recognition** of it. For example, you may not be able to recall Hamlet's soliloquy, but if someone asked you what speech begins with the words "To be or not to be," you might immediately recognize these words as somehow related to Hamlet or to Shakespeare—thus demonstrating that you do remember something about the soliloquy. As shown in Figure 5.6, even patients suffering from amnesia can recognize words that they have learned but cannot recall (Graf, Squire, & Mandler, 1984).

Easy multiple-choice exams give extensive cues, requiring only that the test-taker choose the right answer from among several possible ones. Thus, the test-taker simply needs to recognize the answer. More difficult multiple-choice exams, such as those that employ the vocabulary of a particular field to ask about a concept, involve both recall and recognition. Because recognition generally is easier than recall, many students would rather take a multiple-choice exam than answer essay questions.

**Relearning**   The most sensitive method for measuring memory is to measure **relearning,** or **savings.** This method is seldom used except in research because it is cumbersome, but the existence of memory savings is very important for real-world learn-

**Recall**
Retrieval of detail given minimal cues, as in essay exams.

**Recognition**
Retrieval of limited amounts of information given extensive cues, as in some multiple-choice exams.

**Relearning, or Savings**
A measure of memory obtained by having a participant relearn something that she or he learned previously and assessing how long it takes to learn the material the second time.

**FIGURE 5.6 The difference the test makes.** Individuals suffering from chronic amnesia did only about a third as well as normal participants when the memory task was to recall words learned earlier. But they did just as well when the task was to complete the words after recognizing a few of the letters. *Adapted from Graf, Squire, & Mandler, 1984.*

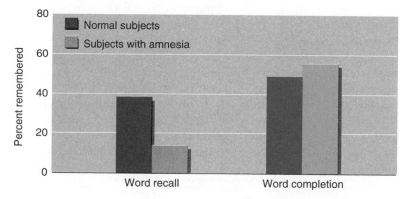

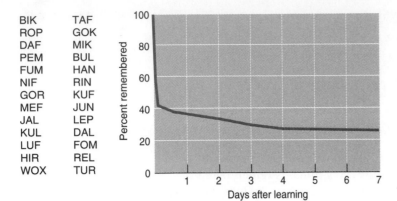

| | |
|---|---|
| BIK | TAF |
| ROP | GOK |
| DAF | MIK |
| PEM | BUL |
| FUM | HAN |
| NIF | RIN |
| GOR | KUF |
| MEF | JUN |
| JAL | LEP |
| KUL | DAL |
| LUF | FOM |
| HIR | REL |
| WOX | TUR |

**FIGURE 5.7** Ebbinghaus's famous curve of forgetting. Ebbinghaus memorized lists of 13 nonsense syllables similar to the ones shown, then measured how many he could recall after various time intervals. After 20 minutes, he recalled only 58% of the syllables, and after about an hour, only 44%. After the initial sharp decline, however, forgetting became much more gradual. After a day, he remembered about 34% of the syllables, after 2 days, about 28%, and after a week, about 25%. He still recalled 21% of the syllables after a month.

*Adapted from Ebbinghaus, 1913.*

**Memory trace**
The basic unit of memory, according to those who emphasize the changes in the nervous system brought about by learning.

**Decay**
The fading of a memory trace with the passage of time.

ing. Even when we think we remember virtually nothing of some information or skill learned, say, in childhood, we find that we can relearn it faster than we originally did. It may seem that what we learned in grade school is lost, but in fact, when we need to reacquire something previously learned, we make good use of the residue of knowledge that remains. Suppose that some years ago you were required to memorize Hamlet's soliloquy and recite it in class. You very well might not be able to recite it now, at least not in its entirety, so you would not pass a test of perfect recall. You probably would recognize it if you heard it again, but this would not be much of a test of how well you remember it. The most sensitive test would to measure the length of time or the number of attempts it would take you to learn the soliloquy to perfection again.

## Theories of Forgetting

Relearning was the measure used in psychology's earliest and most famous studies of forgetting, conducted by the German researcher Hermann Ebbinghaus (1850–1909). In addition to inventing the relearning, or savings, method, Ebbinghaus pioneered the use of "nonsense syllables," consonant-vowel-consonant (CVC) combinations that look like words but have no meaning in a given language. Examples are *XOG, JEK, QUN,* and *RIS.* Ebbinghaus learned lists of such syllables and then measured how long it took him to relearn the lists to perfection after various time intervals. His experiments yielded the *curve of forgetting,* shown in Figure 5.7. The curve does not always apply, because we learn some things so thoroughly that we never forget them. However, it tells a great deal about the forgetting of such varied kinds of learning as motor skills, poems that have been memorized, and college subject material. Its message is this: When we learn something new, we often forget much of it quickly, but we remember at least some of it for a long time.

As to why we forget, a number of factors are involved. Each may be important in at least some situations, for forgetting may be such a complex process that it takes place in different ways under different circumstances. Four general theories of forgetting are discussed here.

**Theory 1: Fading of the Memory Trace**  Every time we store a new piece of information in long-term memory, physiological changes of some kind occur in our brain and, as a result, we can do something new—recall a new fact or engage in a new kind of behavior. Obviously, something has happened inside. But what?

One way of looking at this question relies on the idea of **memory traces** as the basic units of memory. Perhaps when we learn something, neural impulses are routed over a particular pathway, passing through a number of synapses in a particular pattern. The various kinds of neural activity that take place along this pathway presumably have a lasting effect, making it possible to reactivate the pattern on future occasions—and thus remember what we have learned.

One of the oldest ideas about forgetting assumes that memory traces, whatever their neurological nature, are subject to **decay.** They fade with the passage of time and sometimes disappear entirely. In this view, the memory trace resembles a path through a forest. The trace can be kept alive through use, just as a pathway can be kept clear by continuing to walk on it. Without use, the memory trace may vanish, as a pathway disappears when it is abandoned. Some memory theorists continue to believe that the memory trace has some physical quality that changes with the passage of time, reducing the likelihood that the memory can be retraced or reactivated.

Counteracting the process of decay is **consolidation** of the trace, which might be compared with the hardening, or "setting," of a newly laid concrete sidewalk. The consolidation process takes place most rapidly in the first minutes after learning, but it continues, at a gradually slowing rate, over time—especially if the person rehearses or otherwise uses the information. Consolidation was once thought to "strengthen" the trace, but more recent evidence suggests that consolidation somehow changes *how* the trace is stored in memory (Reber, Alvarez, & Squire, 1997). The possibility of enhancing the process through biochemical means is discussed in Psychology and the Media on page 192.

**Consolidation**
**The process of establishing memory traces in long-term memory.**

**Theory 2: Failure of Retrieval**    Once established as part of long-term memory, some memories may persist for a lifetime but be unavailable for recall. If a person cannot retrieve a memory, we say that he or she has forgotten it—although the memory presumably still exists. Thus, forgetting may be due not to the loss of a memory but instead to a failure of retrieval, perhaps because of inadequate "cues" for specific memories.

Temporary forgetting caused by failure of retrieval is an everyday experience. There undoubtedly have been many occasions when you have found yourself unable to remember some item of information that seemed to be "on the tip of your tongue," then later recalled it perfectly—with or without something happening to jog your memory. Evidence suggests that what we need in recovering from temporary forgetting may depend on the kind of material involved. In one study, researchers compared what adult participants could remember after having viewed first words and then pictures on a screen. When the participants were asked simply to recall what they had seen, they did better with the pictures; however, when they were tested by means of a word-completion test (for example, having to remember "lemon" when shown only the letters "l-e-m"), recall was much better for the words than for the pictures (Rajram & Roediger, 1993).

Riding a bicycle is an example of a behavior that may depend on memory traces established many decades earlier.

Similarity between conditions at the time of retrieval and those at the time of learning and encoding may serve as a cue that stimulates the memory. The now well-established concept of **context-dependent memory** has been stated thus: "When the conditions of encoding and recall are most similar, then recall will be best" (Klatzky, 1980). Some kinds of information are retrieved more easily in the physical setting in which the learning took place (for example, the same classroom)—or even through visualizing the setting (Smith, 1979). Thus, when trying to remember a person's name, you might find it helpful to try to recall the physical circumstances in which you met or last saw that person.

**Context-dependent memory**
**Memory that is facilitated by similarity of conditions during storage and retrieval.**

Memory associated with context has been offered as an explanation for the phenomenon of *déjà vu*—a feeling that you've been in a particular situation before when you couldn't possibly have been. For example, suppose you're in a park in a new city you're visiting when déjà vu kicks in. It may be that some element of the park, such as a particular tree or bench, is very similar to one in another park that you have visited and serves as a cue. You don't consciously notice the element, but you feel a sense of familiarity just the same because the element reminds you of the other park.

## PSYCHOLOGY AND THE MEDIA

## Memory-Enhancing Drugs

 It has long been known that many drugs can impair memory. Scientists now know that some drugs can enhance memory.

Since the 1970s and especially during the 1990s, advances in unraveling the neurochemistry and molecular genetics of brain functioning have led to the discovery of drugs that enhance memory not only in laboratory animals but in humans as well. Among these is a class of drugs called the Ampakines (licensed by Cortex Pharmaceuticals), which stimulate production of the neurotransmitter glutamate. The glutamate, in turn, produces changes in the postsynaptic receptors of neurons involved in the formation of long-term memories (Baudry & Lynch, 2001; Davis et al., 1997; Lynch, 1998). A large body of research indicates that these drugs do indeed work—for some people, some of the time.

But don't call your doctor or go to your pharmacist just yet. Use of drugs that improve memory is still limited to people with mental disorders such as Alzheimer's disease (Tsai, Falk, Gunther, & Coyle, 1999) and schizophrenia (Goff et al., 2001; Heresco-Levy, 2000). There's no question that future generations of these drugs will be of tremendous value if they are shown to be safe and effective in treating mental disorders. It also has been proposed that they will be of benefit to children with cognitive impairments (Capone, 1998).

The problem is that "normal" people will probably take them too. In 1998, Stephen Hall thoroughly explored the subject in a *New York Times* article that included interviews with several leading researchers in the field. Among his observations were the following:

Drugs based on the molecular genetics of memory are probably 10 to 15 years away—just about the time when aging baby boomers will be grumbling in unison, "Now where did I put those damn keys?" Nearly every major pharmaceutical company has a fast-track program for developing memory drugs, and some 200 cognitive enhancers are being actively pursued. . . .

A future with memory enhancers, according to experts who have begun to wrestle with the issue, means Pandora's got a brand-new box. Will companies someday require employees to use these drugs to improve on-the-job performance? Will society demand that professionals to whom we entrust our safety, like airline pilots and surgeons, use memory enhancers during training? Will students have to submit a urine sample when they turn in their S.A.T.'s? Will parents feel compelled to slip smart drugs into their children's lunch boxes? (Several of the biologists I interviewed for this article have already been asked by friends to recommend or provide drugs that would enhance their children's school performance.) . . .

Alzheimer's disease and other age-related dementias tend to be the fig leaf that researchers, biotech entrepreneurs and drug companies hide behind when they talk about "cognitive enhancers." Alzheimer's afflicts nearly four million Americans, and that number may double in 20 years. But there's a much larger market out there, and it's made up of people like me: baby boomers who are still pretty sharp but beginning to wonder about those little memory lapses. . . .

The possibilities are limited only by one's imagination. I began to picture a new generation of recreational esthetes . . . popping a pill and replaying in excruciatingly self-absorbed detail every aspect of an otherwise unremarkable day. . . . Or consider the 21st-century day-tripper who wants to use a memory enhancer the way hippies used to drop LSD, to gild the lily of special events—first or last days at college, the birth of a child, seeing the Rolling Stones on their Wheelchair Tour. Who needs a camera for a Kodak moment when you have pharmaceutically moved the developing room inside your head? . . .

I even began to think about odd mnemonic side effects: some poor pre-med student is cramming for the M.C.A.T.'s late into the night, his brain revved on a memory enhancer, when a horde of mosquitoes begins to torment him; the image and sound burn into his memory, the hideous whine replayed again and again. Or you're in a car accident. Or you get hooked on "Psycho" while channel-surfing. Or happen to be prepping for a work presentation when the phone rings with bad news. . . .

What do you think? Would you really want to remember *everything* in this textbook?

**Theory 3: Interference**   Another well-researched explanation for forgetting is that the ability to remember any given piece of information is interfered with by other information stored in memory. Our memory for what we learn today can be adversely affected by what we learned in the past and what we will learn in the future. That is, there are two major types of interference: proactive and retroactive.

*Proactive Interference*   When old information causes us to forget new information, the process is called **proactive interference.** The phenomenon of proactive interference can be demonstrated through simple laboratory procedures, such as asking participants to try to learn and remember a series of lists of words. The results of one experiment in "paired-associate" learning are illustrated in Figure 5.8. Participants learned successive lists of adjective pairs, and the memory test was to present the first word of each pair and see if the participant could remember the second. Note the steady decline in the participants' ability to remember new material, caused by more and more proactive interference from prior learning.

The reason for proactive interference is debatable, but it is known to be most likely to occur when we try to learn new information that is similar to old information already stored in memory—as was the case with the word lists used in the experiment shown in Figure 5.8. For example, suppose your native language is English and you study Spanish and then French. Chances are that your Spanish vocabulary will interfere with your ability to learn the many similar words in French; you would experience considerably less proactive interference if you studied Spanish and then Japanese.

Proactive interference is less troublesome when the new information is substantially different from the old, as shown by the experiment illustrated in Figure 5.9. One group of participants watched four videotaped broadcasts of news stories that all fell into the same general category—for example, national political developments. Another group watched three videotaped broadcasts of

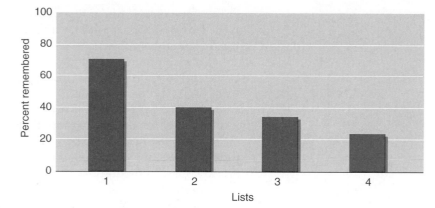

**FIGURE 5.8** How the old interferes with the new. Two days after learning list 1, participants were tested on their recall of list 1 and then asked to learn list 2. Two days later they were tested on list 2 and then asked to learn list 3. Two days after that, they were tested on list 3 and then asked to learn list 4. After a final 2-day interval, they were tested on list 4. The steady decline in the height of the bars shows that learning list 1 interfered with memory for list 2, learning lists 1 and 2 interfered with memory for list 3, and so on.
*Adapted from Underwood, 1957.*

**Proactive interference**
Interference that occurs when old information causes a person to forget new information.

**FIGURE 5.9** Changing the subject as an antidote to proactive interference. The bars show the results of an experiment in which participants watched a series of four videotapes of old news broadcasts. After each tape, participants were tested on how much they remembered. For both groups, the recall scores began a steady decline, as watching tape 1 interfered with their ability to remember tape 2 and watching tapes 1 and 2 interfered with their memory for tape 3. But note the discrepancy between the two groups on tape 4. Group 1 participants continued to show a decline, but group 2 suddenly displayed a sharp improvement.
*Adapted from Gunter, Berry, & Clifford, 1981.*

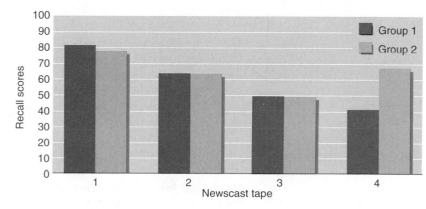

similar news stories and a fourth broadcast on a totally different subject—for example, foreign affairs rather than national politics. As the figure shows, both groups remembered less and less over the first three trials. On the final trial, the first group continued to display a decline caused by proactive interference, but the second group, with proactive interference reduced because of the change to a different topic, did much better. The same phenomenon is apparent when we try to remember the lyrics to a number of songs we have heard in the past. We have the least difficulty remembering those that are least similar to others (Halpern, 1984).

In everyday life, you experience proactive interference when you have been studying the same course material—for example, this chapter on memory—for several hours. In the third hour, your ability to remember what you have read becomes poorer. The reason is not just fatigue. If you were to turn to entirely new material—for example, world history—it is likely that you would remember more from your third hour of study.

**Retroactive interference**
**Interference that occurs when new information causes a person to forget old information.**

*Retroactive Interference*   With proactive interference, old information gets in the way of remembering new information. The opposite situation, in which new information causes us to forget old information, is called **retroactive interference.** Again, the similarity between old and new materials plays an important role in recall. When the words in a new list to be learned have the same meanings as the words in a previously learned list (they are synonyms), research participants experience more retroactive interference than when the new list contains very different materials, such as Ebbinghaus's CVC nonsense syllables. Similarly, for the English speaker studying Spanish and then French, the French words may retroactively interfere with the Spanish ones—again, much more so than if the person were to study Spanish and then Japanese.

Perhaps the most interesting—and consoling—fact about retroactive interference is that it has a greater effect on unimportant materials that are not worth remembering anyway (such as lists of words learned in a psychology experiment) than on important and meaningful materials. Retroactive interference often makes us forget the specific details of what we have learned, especially if the details are not essential, but it is not nearly so likely to make us forget the basic theme and meaning of what we have learned (Christiaansen, 1980). Thus, you will probably forget some of the things that you learn in this course because of retroactive interference from information you will learn in future courses and from your life experiences. You may not remember the exact meaning of such terms as *working memory*, but you may remember the general principles of memory indefinitely—and you'll most likely be able to relearn the vocabulary quickly. Moreover, there is evidence that while you may have difficulty recalling old information because new information interferes, your ability to *recognize* the old material will be less affected (Graf & Schacter, 1987).

### Test Yourself

**(d)** You're preparing for exams in German, Spanish, and history. To minimize retroactive interference so that you can do your best on each exam, in what order should you study the three subjects?

**(e)** You meet someone who has the same distinctive name as someone who treated you very badly several years ago. Within a few minutes, you have trouble remembering the name of your new acquaintance. What kind of forgetting has taken place?

(The answers are on page 209.)

**Motivated forgetting**
**Deliberate forgetting; in psychodynamic theory, repression.**

**Theory 4: Motivated Forgetting**   As mentioned earlier, we seem to forget some things in short-term, or working, memory deliberately. Many theorists believe that at times we also forget information stored in long-term memory because, whether consciously or not, we want to forget it. It may be emotionally uncomfortable to remember a person whom you somehow hurt or painful experiences you had at the hands of someone else.

**Motivated forgetting** is often referred to as *repression* by psychodynamic theorists (see Chapter 12), who believe that it frequently plays a part in dealing with anxiety stemming from emotional trauma or guilt. They find that people can be motivated not only to forget upsetting events but to distort their recollections in numerous ways. Indeed, most of us are troubled by persistent memories of embarrassing and painful events that we would gladly forget if only we could.

# FACTORS IN ENCODING AND STORAGE

The factors that help explain why we forget offer some valuable hints on how we can avoid the problems and embarrassments of forgetting. We will be most efficient at remembering if we can manage to store information in such a way that memories are consolidated and can be retrieved when we want them—that is, so that they remain more or less intact despite interference from previous and future learning. Everything depends on how we encode information and copy it to long-term memory. Knowing in principle how encoding and storage work, how can we do the processing more effectively, and thus learn and remember better?

**FOCUS QUESTIONS**

• How can short-term memory be enhanced?

• Why is long-term memory often inaccurate?

• How do emotional states affect memory?

**Chunking**
Combining information into units in order to increase the amount that can be held in short-term memory.

## Chunking—Putting Many Little Items into One Neat Package

One of the important elements in encoding can best be explained by taking another look at short-term memory, with its ability to store about seven unrelated items. Note what happens if you look briefly at this string of letters:

tvciamabasatnasacnn

You will probably find it impossible to remember all 19 letters—or anywhere near that number—after just one look. But note what happens with a slight change:

tvCIAmaBAsatNASAcnn

The 19 letters have been turned into a mere seven units, each containing a familiar combination of initials, and seven items fall well within the limits of short-term memory. You would have no trouble remembering the units after a few seconds of study (adapted from Bower, 1970).

This process, in which individual units of information are combined into larger units, is called **chunking** (Miller, 1956). Chunking greatly increases the amount of information that can be retained in short-term memory, which can hold about seven big packages of information just about as well as it can handle seven small individual items. We encode many forms of information into chunks—letters into words (as illustrated in Figure 5.10), words into phrases (*frying pan, kung pao chicken*), phrases into sentences (*Mary had a little lamb*), individual digits into memorable dates (1776, 1879), and so on.

Chunking obviously requires some interaction between short-term and long-term memory. For example, you would not readily form the chunks

**FIGURE 5.10 A classroom demonstration of chunking.** The instructor first shows the blackboard you see in the upper photo. How many of the 49 letters can the class possibly remember after studying the board for a minute or two? Not many, because each line contains 7 letters—and 7 is the approximate capacity of short-term memory. But then the instructor rearranges the letters, as shown in the lower photo. The task of remembering becomes much easier, because each line of letters has been rearranged into a familiar word that constitutes a single chunk, so there are now just 7 chunks to deal with instead of 49.

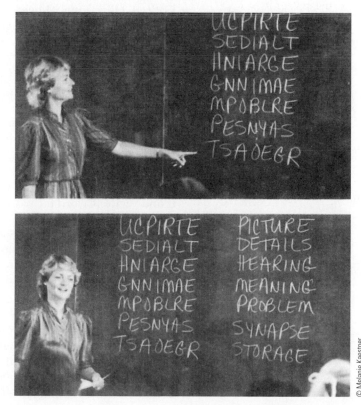

© Melanie Kaestner

The increased emotion and motivation that occur when students study together sometimes results in better retention of the information.

TV and CIA from the string of letters given earlier unless you were already familiar with these combinations of letters. And, obviously, much of the information in long-term memory has been encoded and stored there in chunks. For example, a student of paleontology or physical anthropology who was trying to understand a body of knowledge such as the evolutions that occurred during the current Cenozoic era and led to modern humans might divide the era into epochs: Paleocene, Eocene, Oligocene, Miocene, Pliocene, Pleistocene, and Holocene. This makes it easier to remember the many specific facts and events associated with each time period.

## What We Encode, Remember, and Retrieve

In encoding and storing memories, we add new knowledge. But just what is it that we add? Is it an exact copy of something we have done, seen, or heard—like a movie or a tape recording? Or is it something else?

In some cases, what we encode is virtually an exact copy of the original, such as Hamlet's soliloquy. If we memorize the soliloquy well enough, we can retrieve it and recite it word for word. But this kind of verbatim encoding and retrieval is the exception rather than the rule. In most cases, we engage in what is called *constructive* processing. We encode and retrieve not an exact copy of the information we receive from, say, a printed page or a lecture or a conversation, but whatever meanings and associations we attach to the information. We remember not what was "out there," but what we ourselves "did during encoding"—that is, the way we processed the information and related it to the knowledge already held in long-term memory (Craik & Tulving, 1975).

In most cases, we remember what we consider important in what we read or hear—the theme or underlying meaning—and forget or distort many of the details, such as the exact wording. One study suggested this analogy: When we read or hear something, we make mental notes, like those you might jot down in your notebook while listening to a lecture. It is these notes, not the actual words we read or hear, that we store in some appropriate "pigeonhole" in memory. While the notes are stored in the pigeonhole, the various factors involved in forgetting may cause some of them to become smudged or distorted. Some of them may even get lost. Thus, when we try to retrieve the information, we find that it is incomplete—only a sketchy reminder of what we actually read or heard. All we can do is "fetch the notes from their pigeonhole and from this fragmentary information reconstruct what . . . was in the original message"—or, rather, what we now have come to believe was in it (Clark & Clark, 1977). The same process applies to our memories of other items, such as melodies heard, scenes observed, and interactions with people.

We do the best we can with these brief and sometimes smudged or incomplete mental notes. We try to make sense out of them by filling in the missing details—sometimes accurately and sometimes not. Sometimes, new and contradictory information gets in the way, leading us to believe in the accuracy of erroneous memories (Loftus, 1993). Thus, a great deal of what we think we remember never really happened—or, if it did, it happened differently in many respects from the way we remember it. Memory, as one scholar said, is often "unreliable, given to invention, and even dangerous" (Bower, 1978). Such omissions and distortions pose serious problems at times—especially in legal trials in which precise details may be crucial to the outcome. Such distortions are discussed in more detail in Psychology in the Lab and in Life on page 198.

For large numbers of people in the United States and around the world, images of the attack on the World Trade Center on September 11, 2001, will stay with them as flashbulb memories throughout their lives.

## Emotional States and Retrieval

Many experiments have been performed in an effort to identify factors that might affect memory for better or worse. One such factor is the emotionality associated with memories.

Like most people, you undoubtedly have graphic recollections of events in your life that carried great emotional impact. For example, many married people possess a series of mental photographs of their wedding day. Others can tell you precisely what they were doing and where they were when they heard that a loved one had died. If you have a strong emotional reaction to an event—as many did, for example, to the sight of airplanes crashing into the World Trade Center buildings in New York on September 11, 2001, and the buildings' subsequent collapse—it is likely that you will remember many details about the event (Pillemer, 1984). Indeed, so many people can remember their experience of emotional events in photographic detail that the phenomenon has been called **flashbulb memory** (Brown & Kulik, 1977, 1982), a term that has survived even though photographic flashbulbs have not.

Such vivid recollections may exist because memory is closely tied to the limbic system and especially to the amygdala (see Chapter 2), the area of the brain that is primarily responsible for the processing of emotions (Dolan, 2000; Mishkin, 1986). Indeed, there is evidence that emotional elements of memory may be stored in their own distinct regions of the brain, separate from informational ones (Mishkin & Appenzeller, 1987). There is also evidence that neurotransmitters released during emotional arousal enhance learning and memory (McGaugh, 1983).

However, the preceding discussion does not mean that flashbulb memories are necessarily accurate over time. In the years since the discovery of the phenomenon, researchers have determined that, although such memories may be quite accurate for up to a year or so after the event, they—just like other memories—may become distorted over longer intervals. This was demonstrated in a study of flashbulb memories associated with the announcement of the verdict in the 1995

**Flashbulb memory**
**A highly detailed memory of an emotionally charged event or experience.**

## PSYCHOLOGY IN THE LAB AND IN LIFE

# False Memories

For over a quarter of a century, psychologist Elizabeth Loftus and colleagues have been demonstrating how false memories can occur—that is, how a memory of a past event can be distorted by subsequent events, information, or even the wording of the questions a person is asked about the memory. This phenomenon is similar to retroactive interference, except that the memory for things past is apparently *altered* in important ways—or created entirely from scratch. Either way, the memory becomes a false one that the person nevertheless believes to be true.

For example, in a now-classic experiment on "eyewitness" testimony (Loftus & Palmer, 1974), participants were shown a film of a car accident and then asked questions about it, including one question whose wording was altered slightly for different participants: "About how fast were the cars going when they (*smashed into, collided with, bumped into, hit,* or *contacted*) each other?" Not only did the participants who were asked questions with the stronger wording give significantly higher estimates of speed; they were also much more likely to answer "Yes" to another question about whether there was any broken glass (when in fact there was none). The implications of this research were clear. In a jury trial, how a defense attorney or prosecutor words questions can alter what an eyewitness remembers, potentially to the extent of altering the outcome of the trial—if, for example, witnesses describe the actions of a defendant inaccurately.

Loftus's research on the creation of false memories has been replicated many times (e.g., see Loftus, 1997), and the implications of the research extend beyond matters such as proper courtroom examination to police interrogations and "line-ups" (Fruzzetti, Toland, Teller, &

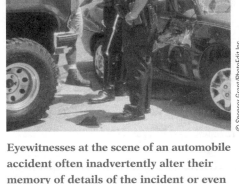

**Eyewitnesses at the scene of an automobile accident often inadvertently alter their memory of details of the incident or even create new memories from scratch.**

© Spencer Grant/PhotoEdit Inc.

Loftus, 1992; Wells, 1993). In the world of eyewitness memory, the possibility of error abounds.

Another focus of research by Loftus and her colleagues has been the accuracy of adults' "repressed" memories of childhood sexual or other abuse (Hyman & Loftus, 1998; Ornstein, Ceci, & Loftus, 1998a). The researchers have focused on the techniques psychotherapists use to unearth these and other memories (see Chapter 14), including dream interpretation (Mazzoni, Lombardo, Malvagia, & Loftus, 1999). They question whether real memories of such abuse can be pushed out of retrievable memory and later reinstated. And even if this could happen, how many of the reinstated memories would be accurate and how many would be false—having inadvertently been "implanted" by the techniques used to try to reinstate the real ones (Loftus & Polage, 1999; Ornstein, Ceci, & Loftus, 1998b)?

Although Loftus and colleagues have clearly demonstrated that all manner of false memories *can* be implanted in adults through relatively simple procedures (e.g., Thomas & Loftus, 2002), this by no means leads to a conclusion that all or even most adult survivors' memories of being abused as children *are* implanted. As yet, there is simply no way to know which memories of childhood abuse are real and which are not, and it is important to bear in mind the suffering both of those who were abused and of those who are wrongly accused of abuse. The controversy continues (see Conway, 2002; Crook & Dean, 1999a, 1999b; Loftus, 1999).

Similar effects on memory when children themselves are questioned are discussed in Psychology and the Media in Chapter 10 (page 384).

O. J. Simpson murder trial (Schmolck, Buffalo, & Squire, 2000), an event that aroused strong emotions in many people. College students completed questionnaires 3 days after the verdict and again 15 months and 32 months later. Although their memories at 15 months were reasonably accurate—consistent with findings by other researchers studying memories of other events—major memory distortions had occurred by 32 months. Indeed, only 17.5% of the participants even remembered filling out the first questionnaire.

Emotions affect memory in other ways as well. Our ability to remember is in part a function of our mood when we are trying to remember (Eich & Metcalfe, 1989). As shown in Figure 5.11, when people are depressed, their recall is less sharp than when they are not depressed (Ellis, Thomas, McFarland, & Lane, 1985). Barring extreme emotional states, however, memory may be facilitated if a person is in the same mood or emotional state—whether happy or sad—during storage and later retrieval (Bower, 1981). Numerous studies have demonstrated this **mood dependent memory,** although researchers are still trying to figure out how it works (Eich, 1995; Ucros, 1989).

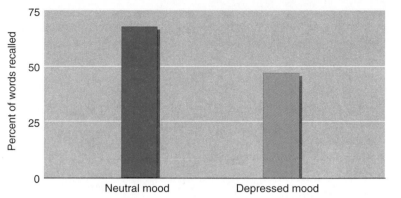

**FIGURE 5.11 How mood affects memory.** In one study, college students were asked to study a list of sentences. A depressed mood was induced in some of the students by having them read a series of depressing statements; the other participants remained in a neutral mood. The results showed that the depressed participants were significantly poorer at recalling selected words in the sentences that they had studied.
*Ellis et al., 1985.*

# LINKAGES IN LEARNING AND MEMORY

**Mood-dependent memory** The phenomenon that remembering is easier when a person is in the same mood he or she was in during learning.

Long-term memory is like a large and complex network, with linkages so intricately interconnected that tugging at one strand can produce far-reaching and sometimes unpredictable results. Suppose, for example, that you are asked to remember everything you can about the word *computer.* You might begin by remembering information about your PC or MAC, such as its speed, the amount of memory it has, and the quality of its monitor. Maybe you also remember ads you've seen for upgrades and the great new sound card and speakers you'd like to have. Then you're back to your computer's operating system and the programs you have installed, including games. Remembering the games could lead you in a number of directions, but you move on to movies you've seen in which computers took over or otherwise ran amok. Back to computers per se: Now you recall what you know about the Internet and service providers, including their servers. . . .

Suddenly you realize that this could go on indefinitely. The progression of associations could lead almost anywhere, and if you were asked to do the same thing tomorrow, the process might take an entirely different route. Associations also vary from one person to another. To someone else, the word *computer* might immediately suggest a computer course she or he took and intensely hated, then other courses in which it was necessary to use a computer, then the computer system in the library, and so on.

As these examples of retrieval indicate, items of information in long-term memory are often associated with many other items, which in turn have innumerable other associations. How likely you are to remember and retrieve any new information depends on how well you manage to add it to this network—that is, how many strong associations you form between the new information and linkages that already exist. Effective encoding sometimes takes place without much effort. You do not have to make any deliberate attempt, for example, to remember important events in your life or the names and faces of people who have played signifi-

**FOCUS QUESTIONS**

• How do meaning and organization enhance long-term memory?

• Why is learning rules superior to learning by rote?

• How does overlearning affect memory?

**Test Yourself**

**(f)** "I'm going to try to chunk this list of words so that I can remember them better," says a classmate in your French course. What is your classmate going to do?

**(g)** "I can still recall every detail of my scary first-grade classroom 60 years ago," says your grandfather. What does this indicate about the relationship between emotional states and memory?

(The answers are on page 209.)

cant parts in it. But other times—especially when trying to master a new subject or learn a new skill—you have to work hard to form associations.

## The Role of Meaning and Organization

In studying a page of text, it would be futile just to read and reread the words without making any attempt to understand them. The words might eventually begin to seem familiar, like old friends or enemies—but mere familiarity, without careful attention and analysis, is no guarantee of successful encoding. We sometimes remember surprisingly little about familiar objects and events. What counts in memory is something quite different:

> The crucial thing for most of the material you learn in school is to understand it, which means encoding it in a way that makes it distinctive from unrelated material and related to all the things it ought to be related to for you to use it. . . . [T]hinking about material you are reading and relating it to previously stored material is about the most useful thing you can do in learning any new subject matter. (Wickelgren, 1977)

To put this another way, the key to successful encoding is to figure out the meaning of new information and organize it into some unified and logical pattern so that it can be readily associated with other information. Because meaning is so important, some things are naturally easier to encode into memory than others. If the new information makes sense—that is, if it is intrinsically meaningful—your memory has a good head start on processing. Thus, it is much easier to remember lists of actual three-letter words than lists of three-letter nonsense syllables. In turn, it is easier to remember lists of nonsense syllables that resemble real words than lists of syllables that are truly nonsensical. An experiment performed many years ago showed that participants are about 50% better at remembering syllables like DOZ, SOF, LIF, and RUF, all of which remind most English speakers of actual words, than totally unfamiliar syllables like ZOJ, JYQ, GIW, and VAF (McGeoch, 1930). Similarly, people are better at encoding and remembering passages of poetry than prose, because poetry has not only meaning but also an internal logic and organization provided by the cadence and rhymes.

Successful encoding may take a variety of forms, depending on the material. If you were a teacher of physics, for example, you could help your students understand scientific concepts by presenting relevant analogies along with the facts. For example, if the concept were a pulsar, students would be better able to make accurate inferences about the nature of a pulsar if they understood that it was analogous to a beam of light emitted by a rotating beacon in a lighthouse (Donnelly & McDaniel, 1993).

## Using Rules to Learn and Remember

**Rule learning**
Learning by trying to understand the principles or logic underlying information.

**Rote learning**
Learning through memorization, by mentally repeating information over and over.

Both meaning and organization help account for why our memory is better if we employ **rule learning** (that is, try to understand the principles or logic underlying what we wish to remember) than if we engage in **rote learning** (try to memorize materials simply by repeating them mechanically without regard to what they mean).

Some things, of course, have to be memorized by rote. There is no other way to store the sequence of letters in an alphabet or new vocabulary in your own language or a second one. And, as these examples suggest, some information acquired by rote is never forgotten. But the material in most college courses would be almost impossible to encode into lasting memory by rote. Fortunately, the material in most courses readily lends itself to learning by rules. Patterns of meaning and organization can be built around underlying principles, and lectures and textbooks are designed to help you find, understand, and analyze those patterns. Thus, the material can be studied and encoded effectively through logical approaches like the SQ3R system described in the Preface to this book.

It has long been known that memory often depends more on the kind of cognitive processing and encoding we do than on the amount of time we spend (Craik & Tulving, 1975). Thus, spending even a small amount of time finding meaning, organization, and relationships is generally more effective than devoting a great deal of time to merely rehearsing what is on a page.

However, time is an important factor. Effective encoding typically requires deliberate effort *and* a certain amount of time. You can safely assume that the more time you spend, the more you are likely to remember—provided, of course, that you use the time effectively. There are no good shortcuts in most forms of memorizing. For example, little is gained through "speed reading," the popular name for techniques that are supposed to enable you to read a printed page much faster while still comprehending everything the words mean. Another long-standing research finding is that the faster you read, the less you are likely to understand and remember (Graf, 1973).

There are certain advantages, of course, to saving time by rapidly scanning materials that you do not need to remember, such as a long and complicated article in which you want to concentrate on only a few specific pieces of information. But in general, any increase in reading speed beyond your normal rate will be at the expense of remembering. Like the weaving of a strong net, the kind of encoding that results in long-lasting memory simply cannot be rushed. Of course, you can also read too slowly, which can lead to getting bogged down in details, daydreaming, or dozing off—especially if you're studying material that you aren't really interested in. "Lazy" reading hampers learning and memory at least as much as speed reading does.

Even after new information has been encoded into memory, it usually pays to spend some additional time studying it—possibly because practice and repetition somehow increase the strength and retrievability of the memories in the network. This fact is expressed in the principle of **overlearning,** which states that after you have learned something, further study tends to increase the length of time you will remember it. Overlearning explains why we never forget things like the alphabet and nursery rhymes. Long after we knew these things by heart, we continued to recite or hear them over and over again. In other words, we overlearned them.

For learning course material, overlearning is much better than cramming before an exam. By cramming, you may acquire enough information to get a passing grade, but you are likely to forget almost everything soon afterward. A little overlearning, on the other hand, is like time spent trying to understand new materials and relate them to previous information. It is a good investment in the ability to remember for a long time and truly learn.

**Overlearning**
Increasing the amount of time a memory will last by engaging in extra learning.

## Building Storehouses for Memory

Another practical implication of psychological studies of encoding is this: The more you already know, the easier it is to learn and remember something new. As you go through school and college, you acquire a bigger vocabulary, more mathematical symbols and rules, and more knowledge of science, human behavior, and the workings of society. All this previously stored information helps you understand new information, relate it to past knowledge, and encode it solidly in memory.

The principle that memory builds on memory has never been expressed more eloquently than by William James (see Chapter 1), even though James wrote his

## Life Span Perspective    Remembering and Forgetting in Older Adulthood

Does the ability to retain routine information decline with age? In one experiment, both young adults and older adults kept diaries of occasions when they could not readily come up with a familiar word that was "on the tip of their tongue." The older adults reported many more such episodes (Burke & Harrold, 1988). Older adults also have more trouble than younger adults in recalling the names of people to whom they have been introduced (Crook & West, 1990), as illustrated in Figure 5.12.

Such findings, however, do not provide a full picture of the memory abilities of older people. To begin with, not all aspects of memory ap-

pear to be equally affected by the passing years. Aging seems to affect the ability to retrieve previously stored information rather than the storage ability itself. In other words, although older people often have problems *recalling* items that they have learned, they do no worse than younger people in *recognizing* those items.

Equally significant is the ability of older people to apply the information they have learned over the years in solving problems. Researchers asked young, middle-aged, and older adults to think aloud about how they would solve several difficult life problems faced by fictitious individuals of various ages. The researchers

were trying to measure wisdom, which they defined as uncommon insight into human development and exceptional judgment about difficult life problems, based on remembering past experiences. There was little difference between the age groups, with older adults contributing an equal share of wise responses (Smith & Baltes, 1990).

Such data demonstrate that human memory is far more than simply a matter of remembering isolated facts—and, equally important, that some common stereotypes about the limited intellectual abilities of older people are untrue and unfair.

*Principles of Psychology* (1890) long before the discovery of most of what is now known about encoding and memory:

> *The more other facts a fact is associated with in the mind, the better possession of it our memory retains.* Each of its associates becomes a hook to which it hangs, a means to fish it up by when sunk beneath the surface. Together, they form a network of attachments by which it is woven into the entire tissue of our thought. The "secret of a good memory" is thus the secret of forming diverse and multiple associations with every fact we care to retain.

Of course, the possession of a great deal of information increases the possibility of proactive and retroactive interference. But any tendency to forget that is

**FIGURE 5.12 "I'm sorry, what's your name again?"** More than 1,000 people were tested on their ability to recall the names of people they had been "introduced to" via videotape. No matter what age the participants were, memory for the names improved after repeated introductions—but the older the participant, the fewer the names remembered. *Adapted from Crook & West, 1990.*

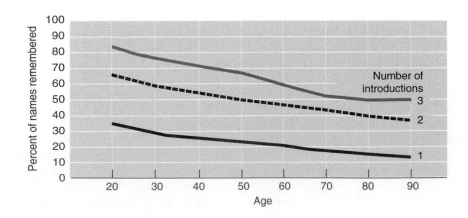

created by these kinds of interference is more than offset by the chances of finding more associations between new and old and thus weaving the new information more solidly into the memory network.

We continue to form mental associations throughout life. However, memory processes do change in certain ways as we grow older, as discussed in the Life Span Perspective on page 202.

# LEARNING HOW TO LEARN AND REMEMBER

All of us get better and better at encoding and remembering new information as time goes on. Our classroom work and life experiences provide us with something that is perhaps even more valuable than facts and general principles: We learn *how* to learn.

This fact has been demonstrated both in humans and in other animals. Even the monkey shown in the photo in Figure 5.13 learned how to learn. When the photo was taken, the food was always under a funnel and never under a cylinder, regardless of which was on the left or right. At other times, Harlow (1949) used other shapes. For example, the food was always under a circle and never under a rectangle; always under a cube and never under a sphere; always under a black object and never under a white object; and so on. At first, the monkey was slow in learning where to find the food. But after the experiment had gone on long enough—with several hundred pairs of objects—the monkey mastered the problem on the very first trial. Whether or not it found the food under the first object it examined, it went almost unerringly to the correct object the next time the pair was presented. The monkey

> **FOCUS QUESTIONS**
> * What do psychologists mean by "learning to learn"?
> * How do categorization and clustering enhance long-term memory?
> * What are mnemonic devices and how do they work?

FIGURE 5.13 What is this monkey learning? What the monkey seems to be learning is that it will find food under one of the two objects in front of it but not under the other. It is acquiring a learning set.
*Harlow, 1949.*

Harlow Primate Lab

**Learning set**
**A learned strategy for approaching a learning task.**

developed what is called a **learning set**—a successful strategy for approaching the tasks. In an experiment with humans, using a similar but more difficult series of problems, the results were much the same. Asked to perform a long series of learning tasks that were similar in form but different in detail, they showed remarkable improvement. It has also been found, as might be expected, that college students are quicker to develop effective learning sets or strategies than are fifth-graders. In turn, fifth-graders are quicker to do so than preschool children (Levinson & Reese, 1967).

## How Categories Help

**Categorization**
**Learning by arranging related items of information in a hierarchy.**

One useful learning strategy that all of us adopt in one way or another to help us deal with materials that do not at first seem to be related is to organize and encode information by arranging it into a hierarchy—a method known as **categorization.** Look at the examples shown in Figure 5.14. Note that the 18 words in part (a) at the top of the figure, arranged at random, do not seem to have much in common. They do not fall into any kind of obvious pattern, and you might think that if you wanted to encode them you would have to memorize them by rote. This is the way one group of research participants went about trying to memorize the words—a tedious process that was not completely successful.

Another group got some help. The words were presented to these participants as shown in part (b) of Figure 5.14. The participants were able to see that all the words fell into the general category of minerals, that this category could be broken down into the subcategories of metals and stones, and that these subcategories could themselves be divided into three different kinds of metals (rare, common, and alloys) and two different kinds of stones (precious stones and masonry stones).

The two groups were asked to try to memorize several such lists, containing 112 words in all, within four trials. The difference in their success was striking. As Figure 5.15 shows, the performance of participants who had been presented words organized into categories was far superior. They remembered all 112 words perfectly by the third trial—a level of success never even approached by the participants who tried to learn the words by rote (Bower, Clark, Lesgold, & Winzenz, 1969).

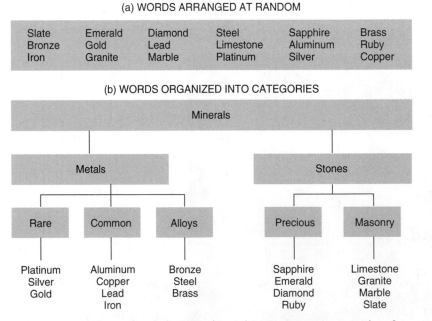

(a) WORDS ARRANGED AT RANDOM

| Slate | Emerald | Diamond | Steel | Sapphire | Brass |
| Bronze | Gold | Lead | Limestone | Aluminum | Ruby |
| Iron | Granite | Marble | Platinum | Silver | Copper |

(b) WORDS ORGANIZED INTO CATEGORIES

Minerals

Metals — Stones

Rare — Common — Alloys — Precious — Masonry

| Platinum | Aluminum | Bronze | Sapphire | Limestone |
| Silver | Copper | Steel | Emerald | Granite |
| Gold | Lead | Brass | Diamond | Marble |
| | Iron | | Ruby | Slate |

**FIGURE 5.14 A sample of the stimuli used in an experiment on the effectiveness of using categories as an aid to encoding and storage. One group of participants saw the words presented at random (part a). The other group saw the words arranged in a hierarchy of categories (part b).**

## Clustering—Packaging Information for Long-Term Memory

Organizing materials into categories bears considerable resemblance to the process that enables us to hold seven large packages of information in short-term memory as readily as seven small individual items. In both cases, a number of small units of information are lumped together into a single unit. The version of this process used for short-term memory is *chunking,* as discussed earlier. The version for long-term memory, called **clustering,** is a method of organizing information into categories by meaning, by logic, or in other ways. Information stored in some form of cluster tends to hang together in a unit that becomes a strong part of a person's network of memories.

Clustering therefore aids retrieval. Within each tightly bound and cohesive cluster are a number of individual items of information. In the search of memory that goes on during retrieval, we have a much better chance of finding one of many items than any single item. And when we manage to find this one item, we can summon up the whole cluster of information with it.

Suppose an essay question asks you to define the term *stimulus generalization.* At first, the meaning of the term eludes you. You seem to have forgotten it. But then, as you continue to search your memory, the word *stimulus* leads you to the term *conditioned stimulus*—and thus to the whole cluster of information about classical conditioning. Now you can retrieve all the facts you have clustered there, including the meaning of *stimulus generalization.*

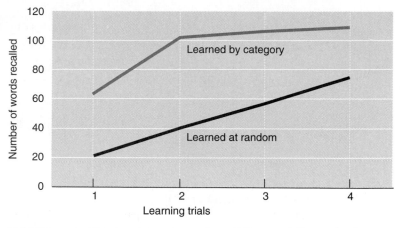

**FIGURE 5.15 Did the categories make a difference? Yes, indeed.** The top line shows how rapidly participants memorized words such as those in Figure 5.14 when the words were arranged in categories. Participants who memorized words arranged at random did not do nearly so well across the four learning trials.

*Adapted from Bower et al., 1969.*

**Clustering**
Learning by organizing related items of information into meaningful groups.

One interesting way to investigate how we encode clusters into long-term memory is to look at how much we remember of what we read. If a story moves in a straight line, with one event leading logically to the next, we can usually remember a good deal of it. If the story jumps around, switching from one point of view to another, we are less likely to remember it (Black, Turner, & Bower, 1979)

In other words, we are particularly adept at clustering together materials with a cause-and-effect relationship that binds them into a logical entity. This finding was demonstrated in an experiment in which two groups of college students studied slightly different versions of the same story. Version 1 contained pairs of sentences like these:

> He lowered the heat and walked over to the refrigerator, seeing a bowl he had left on the table. Suddenly it fell off the edge and broke.

> While he was sitting on a huge log he found an old pocket knife. He felt sad as he took a few more pictures and headed back.

In version 2, the sentence pairs were changed to read like this:

> He lowered the heat and walked over to the refrigerator, bumping a bowl he had left on the table. Suddenly it fell off the edge and broke.

> While he was sitting on a huge log he lost an old pocket knife. He felt sad as he took a few more pictures and headed back.

Note that the changes, though small, create in version 2 cause-and-effect relationships that do not exist in version 1. Bumping a bowl (version 2) is a logical reason for the bowl to fall off the table; seeing a bowl (version 1) is not. Someone who lost an old pocket knife is likely to feel sad, while someone who found an old pocket knife is not. As illustrated in Figure 5.16, establishing cause-and-effect relationships pro-

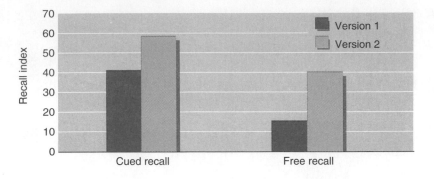

**FIGURE 5.16** If one event causes another, you are likely to remember both. The bars show the results of a memory experiment with two versions of the same story. Note how much more was remembered by participants who read version 2 (the cause-and-effect version) than by participants who read version 1, both when tested for "free recall" (how well they remembered without prompting) and when tested for "cued recall" (how well they could remember the second of each pair of sentences after the first was read to them).
*Adapted from Black & Bern, 1981.*

duced significantly better memory for the version 2 sentences (Black & Bern, 1981).

Similarly, it has been demonstrated that one good way to remember a list of unrelated items is to make up a story about them that ties them all together. Say, for example, that you are going to the supermarket to buy the following 10 items, listed in the order in which you would find them along the route you take through the aisles:

| | |
|---|---|
| 1. coffee | 6. light bulbs |
| 2. hamburger | 7. matches |
| 3. charcoal | 8. facial tissues |
| 4. milk | 9. broom |
| 5. plastic cups | 10. dog food |

One way you can be almost sure of remembering everything in proper order is to make up a story like the following, forming mental images like those in Figure 5.17.

> I was sitting in my kitchen drinking a cup of *coffee* when my neighbor came in with her child to invite me to a Saturday cookout. She said we would grill *hamburgers* over *charcoal*. I asked her to join me for coffee, and I poured the child some *milk* in a *plastic cup*. While we were talking, the *light bulb* burned out, and my neighbor lit some *matches* to help me replace the bulb. In the darkness, the child spilled some milk, and we wiped it up with *facial tissues*. I heard my dog at the door and went to let it in. It tracked in some trash, which I swept up with a *broom*. Then I fed him his *dog food* while my neighbor and I finished our coffee. (Adapted from Bower, 1978.)

Such stories have been found to be remarkably helpful. The experiment illustrated in Figure 5.18, for example, found an extremely large difference in recall of word lists between participants who wove the words into stories and participants who did not.

## Preserving Visual Information

Made-up stories are particularly helpful if you form a mental picture, or image, of what you are trying to remember. Research has shown that there are many situations in which the use of **imagery** helps in encoding and retrieving information (Bower, 1972). One reason is that we have an extraordinary ability to remember visual information. This was demonstrated in a classic experiment in which participants looked at a set of more than 600 color pictures and then were tested on how many they could recognize when the pictures were shown again, each now paired with another picture that participants had not seen before. In all, the participants spotted 97% of the original pictures—a far better performance than could ever be attained with the same large number of words (Shephard, 1967).

The ability to encode visual information and imagery easily is the basis for techniques known as **mnemonic devices.** In ancient Greece, orators developed devices to help them remember the points they wanted to make in their long speeches. We now call such devices *mnemonic* after the Greek word for "memory." One method

**Imagery**
A mental picture of an event.

**Mnemonic device**
A technique for encoding unrelated items of information so as to make them easier to remember, typically through adding imagery and humor.

**FIGURE 5.17** Remembering a shopping list. You can easily recall the 10 supermarket items listed in the text, in the correct order, by making up a story and accompanying it by mental images.

**FIGURE 5.18** How well do made-up stories work? Extremely well. The graph shows the results of an experiment in which one group of students made up stories to help them remember a dozen lists of words; another group was merely asked to try to memorize the lists. When tested for recall, the participants who made up stories remembered their lists almost perfectly. The other participants forgot most of the words on their lists.

*Adapted from Bower & Clark, 1969.*

the Greeks used, called the *method of loci*, was based on the spatial arrangement of a temple with which they were thoroughly familiar—that is, the order in which they walked past the doorways, rooms, statues, and other objects within the temple. An orator would create a mental image, associating each location with a topic in his speech. For example, if he wanted to start by discussing medicine, he might visualize a famous physician of the day walking through the temple entrance.

To try this method yourself, you might associate a list of unrelated grocery items with pieces of furniture and other objects in your room. If you make the associations between the items and the objects *humorous,* you can also take advantage of your ability to remember things associated with emotions, as discussed earlier. For example, if the first item on your grocery list is bread and the first object you see in scanning the room is a chair, picture a loaf of bread sitting in the chair with its "legs" crossed. If the next item is milk and the next object is a lamp, picture a carton of milk with a lampshade on it. If the third item

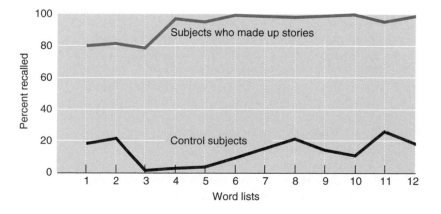

## Test Yourself

**(h)** Suppose a student in a biology course has to memorize the parts of the body. Would she do better if she simply listed all the parts alphabetically and then began to memorize them or if she instead tried to learn them according to where in the body they are found?

**(i)** How does clustering help memory?

**(j)** If a law student formed a mental picture of a law case so as to remember the details of the case better, what technique would the student be using?

(The answers are on page 209.)

is a six-pack of soda (or whatever) and the next object is the table the lamp is on, turn the table into the six-pack. And so on. If you try this, you'll find that you can memorize lists of dozens of items and recall them in the original order.

Similar systems are the secret behind the seemingly incredible stage feats performed by "memory experts" who quickly learn long lists of objects or people's names. For remembering things that do not hang together through any organization or logic, mnemonic devices are unquestionably useful. When it comes to logically organized material (such as for a college course), however, they are no match for strategies such as categorization and clustering. As noted earlier, there are no good shortcuts in learning what things mean and how they are interrelated. Mnemonic aids are useful only for remembering materials that would otherwise have to be encoded and stored by rote.

# Chapter 5 Summary

## The Range and Content of Human Memory

1. Memory is both the set of "storehouses" for information we learn and the process by which we learn it.
2. Memories may last from a fraction of a second to a lifetime. The range is divided into three stages: *sensory memory, short-term (or working) memory,* and *long-term memory.*
3. Sensory memory is made up of the lingering traces of information sent to the brain by the senses. Depending on the sense, the information will be forgotten within about a fraction of a second to several seconds unless it is transferred to short-term memory.
4. Short-term (working) memory can hold about seven unrelated items of information, which will be forgotten within about 15 to 30 seconds unless additional processing occurs.
5. Information processing in short-term memory includes several steps:
   a) scanning the information in sensory memory and selecting some of it as worthy of attention,
   b) *encoding,*
   c) *rehearsal,* and
   d) further encoding that allows the information to be copied to long-term memory.

6. Encoding can be acoustic, visual, or semantic.
7. Through rehearsal, information can be kept in short-term memory as long as desired, although the amount of information that can be kept there is quite small.
8. Long-term memory is the more-or-less permanent set of storehouses of information.
9. Long-term memory is divided into *procedural memory* and *declarative memory;* the latter includes *semantic memory* and *episodic memory.*
10. *Retrieval* is the process of extracting information from long-term memory.

## Why We Forget

11. Because *recall* is more difficult than *recognition,* recall is a more thorough measure of memory. *Relearning* is the most sensitive measure of memory.
12. Ebbinghaus established the basic curve of forgetting in the 19th century.
13. Exactly what happens inside the nervous system when we store information in long-term memory is not known. A traditional way of viewing memory is in terms of *memory traces,* which sometimes persist and sometimes disappear.
14. *Consolidation* refers to how memory traces are established in long-term memory.

15. Theories of forgetting include *decay* of memory traces, simple failure of retrieval, *proactive* and *retroactive interference*, and *motivated forgetting*.
16. Generally, memories are more easily retrieved in the physical setting in which they were learned.

## Factors in Encoding and Storage

17. The manner in which we encode information and copy it to long-term memory determines how well we can remember and retrieve it.
18. *Chunking* increases the amount of information that can be retained in short-term memory, because short-term memory can hold about seven items, whether small or large.
19. Sometimes we encode and can retrieve virtually an exact copy of the information stored in long-term memory. More often, memory is constructive and not particularly accurate.
20. When extreme emotionality is associated with an event, a *flashbulb memory* may result. Flashbulb memories tend to become less accurate with the passage of time.
21. Depressed people often have memory problems, but less extreme variations in mood can help with memory because of the phenomenon of *mood-dependent memory*.

## Linkages in Learning and Memory

22. How well we remember information generally depends on how well we learned it in the first place.
23. Finding meaning and organization and using *rules* are more effective ways of learning than learning by *rote*.
24. *Overlearning* tends to increase how long a memory will last.
25. According to William James, *"The more other facts a fact is associated with in the mind, the better possession of it our memory retains."*

## Learning How to Learn and Remember

26. The term *learning set* refers to a strategy for learning.
27. *Categorization* and *clustering* increase the efficiency of encoding and retrieval.
28. We are particularly adept at clustering material that involves cause-and-effect relationships.
29. Making up stories improves memory for unrelated items, as do *mnemonic devices* based on *imagery* and humor.

# Chapter 5 Test Yourself Answers

(a) Sensory memories are very brief, containing only fast-disappearing traces of information received by the brain from the senses.
(b) Procedural, or "how to," memory, which often can't be verbalized
(c) Declarative semantic memory
(d) You should study one of the two languages, then history, then the second language. Old information gets in the way of new information—especially if what is to be learned is similar—so breaking up the language studies with history makes the most sense.
(e) Motivated forgetting (or repression)
(f) Your classmate is going to combine a number of related words into discrete packages.
(g) Highly emotional experiences tend to stay in memory for very long periods, often for life.
(h) She would do better if she took the second approach. It helps to organize information into some uniform pattern that makes sense so that the information can be readily associated with other information.
(i) Clustering organizes information into smaller and more meaningful units for long-term memory.
(j) The student would be using a technique known as imagery.

# Chapter 5  Remembering and Forgetting

## Key Terms

categorization (p. 204)
chunking (p. 195)
clustering (p. 205)
consolidation (p. 191)
context-dependent memory (p. 191)
decay (p. 190)
declarative memory (p. 187)
encoding (p. 186)
episodic memory (p. 187)
flashbulb memory (p. 197)
imagery (p. 206)
learning set (p. 204)
long-term memory (p. 186)
memory trace (p. 190)
mnemonic device (p. 206)
mood-dependent memory (p. 199)
motivated forgetting (p. 194)

overlearning (p. 201)
proactive interference (p. 193)
procedural memory (p. 187)
recall (p. 189)
recognition (p. 189)
rehearsal (p. 186)
relearning, or savings (p. 189)
retrieval (p. 188)
retroactive interference (p. 194)
rote learning (p. 200)
rule learning (p. 200)
semantic memory (p. 187)
sensory memory (p. 184)
short-term (working) memory (p. 185)

*The key terms above can be used as search terms in InfoTrac, a database of readings, which can be found at http://infotrac-thomsonlearning.com.*

## Active Learning Review

### The Range and Content of Human Memory

1. The range of memory is divided into three stages. The first, *sensory memory*, is made up of the lingering traces of information transduced by the senses. The way the image of an irrelevant license plate number remains in your mind for less than a second illustrates the operation of _____ _____.

*sensory memory*

*sensory*

*memory*

2. Some, but by no means all, of the information that arrives in _____ _____ is transferred to the second system, *short-term* (or *working*) *memory*.

3. Information that you retain for perhaps 15 to 30 seconds—such as a telephone number that you remember just long enough to make a call—is held in _____-_____, or _____, memory, which stores information somewhat longer than sensory memory does.

*short-term, working*

4. When you walk through a crowd, many images come into your mind and are immediately forgotten. They have entered and left your _____ memory. However, if you observe a street sign and remember the name long enough to check a map, the name probably was held in _____-_____ memory.

*sensory*

*short-term*

5. Short-term memory has been described as a "leaky bucket," because much information is quickly lost unless you make an effort to process and retain it. Processing activities begin with scanning the information briefly held in _____ memory.

*sensory*

6. A person unconsciously subjects the information in sensory memory to _____, which determines items selected for further attention, and perhaps *encoding*, which involves transforming information in ways designed to make it easier to handle.

*scanning*

7. Information from sensory memory is transformed acoustically as sounds and words (the primary way), visually as mental images, or semantically in terms of meaning. Each of these is an example of _____.

*encoding*

*acoustic, visual*

8. Much of the time, we use all three forms of encoding—_____, _____, and _____—but the primary form is _____.

*semantic, acoustic*

9. If you notice a large stranger approaching you on the street, you might encode the stimulus _____ by forming a mental image of the person, _____ by thinking about what the person might mean, or _____ by saying to yourself "A stranger is coming."

visually

semantically, acoustically

10. In addition to the processes of encoding, people may use _____ to keep information active in short-term memory for a longer period of time and perhaps to help transfer it to *long-term memory*, where it is stored more or less permanently.

rehearsal

11. When you silently repeat a phone number until you have finished entering it, you are using _____ to keep information active in short-term memory.

rehearsal

12. Only a small amount of information can be maintained in _____-_____, or _____, memory, even when it is maintained there through _____. Some information will simply be lost, and some information will be copied to _____-_____ memory.

short-

term, working

rehearsal

long-term

13. The third kind of memory—along with _____ and _____-_____, or _____, memory—is _____-_____ memory, where information can be stored for months, years, or a lifetime.

sensory, short-term

working, long-term

14. Normally, your name and birth date are stored unforgettably in _____-_____ _____.

long-

term memory

15. Information is _____ from short-term memory to _____-_____ memory by processes that include additional encoding and relating the new information to information that already exists in long-term memory.

copied, long-term

16. Cognitive psychologists disagree on the number and nature of long-term memory systems, but they agree that long-term memories take distinct forms. Among these are *procedural memory*, which is "how to" knowledge, and *declarative memory*, which is knowledge that can be put into words. That is, psychologists _____ on the kinds of information that are stored, but they _____ on the characteristics of memory systems.

agree

disagree

17. Remembering how to ride a bicycle is an example of _____ memory; remembering facts and other information that can be put into words is an example of _____ memory. There are two types of declarative memory: *semantic memory*, which involves general information and understanding, and *episodic memory*, which includes the situation or context you were in when you acquired the information or knowledge.

procedural

declarative

18. If you acquired information about a city or nation from books and lectures, it is part of your _____ memory; if you actually visited the city or nation, acquired information about it, and remember being there as well, the information is part of your _____ memory.

semantic

episodic

19. K.C., who had extensive brain injuries, retained knowledge of facts and how to play chess, so his _____ memory remained intact; but he remembered no personal experiences in his life, so his _____ memory was severely damaged.

semantic

episodic

20. Information is also transferred from long-term to short-term memory by _____ processes.

retrieval

21. One aspect of the recall process is direct-access *retrieval*, which allows a person to go into long-term memory, directly locate information that was _____ there, and recall the material immediately.

copied (or stored)

## Why We Forget

22. Tests of memory can only measure how well people perform on the tests, which may or may not be an accurate indication of how much they actually know or remember. How well you score on a history quiz may be influenced by anxiety, distractions, and other factors. So a test score should be regarded primarily as a measure of how well you _____ on the test.

perform

recall

recall, recognition

recognition

recognition, recall

semantic memory

relearning, savings
relearning
savings

curve, forgetting

memory trace

decay, trace

consolidation

memory trace
differently

memory trace

failure, retrieval

retrieve

retrieval, context-
dependent

déjà vu

23. There are three principal ways to measure learning and memory. The first is through tests of *recall*, which ask people to remember information when given only a minimal cue such as a question. Performance on an essay test is measured by the _____ method.

24. Another approach is to measure *recognition*, as is done with relatively easy multiple-choice questions. Harder, more complex multiple-choice questions measure both _____ and _____.

25. If you did not study much for a history test, you might be able to pick out the correct answer to a multiple-choice question, but you would be likely to have a harder time writing an essay in which you had to produce the facts yourself, because recall tends to be more difficult than _____.

26. Thus, a poorly prepared student might prefer to be tested by the method of _____ than by the method of _____.

27. Multiple-choice exams like the Practice Test in this Study Guide tend to involve the clear-cut intentional retrieval of information, independent of the context in which it was learned. Thus, they measure _____ _____.

28. A third method of measuring memory performance is the *relearning*, or *savings*, method. If it takes you less time to memorize something the second time you study it than the first time, the difference reflects how much you remembered from the first time and is a measure of _____, or _____.

29. Ebbinghaus used this very sensitive method of measuring _____, or _____, to plot a curve of forgetting. He discovered that when we learn something new, we quickly forget much of what we have learned, but we remember at least some of it for a long time.

30. A graph of Ebbinghaus's results showed a rapid drop in memory performance followed by a leveling off, which is the typical shape of a _____ of _____.

31. Why do we forget? One possibility is that forgetting is caused by fading of the *memory trace*. According to this idea, just as a path through a field will disappear with time unless it is continually used, a _____ _____ will be subject to fading, or *decay*.

32. Counteracting fading, or _____, of a memory _____ requires what memory theorists call *consolidation*. This is a process through which the memory "sets." The hardening of newly poured concrete is analogous to the _____ of a memory trace, although researchers now believe that the trace is not exactly "strengthened." Instead, something about how the trace is stored may change.

33. Consolidation of a _____ _____, then, may mean that the trace is stored _____.

34. A second explanation of forgetting is that it is essentially a failure in retrieval rather than a failure to maintain the _____ _____.

35. Once established, a memory trace may be permanent, but it may not always be available because of a _____ in _____ of the information stored in memory. Evidence for this phenomenon includes the experience of being unable to recall information "on the tip of your tongue," but then retrieving it easily later.

36. Being unable to retrieve information that is on the tip of your tongue but being able to _____ it easily at some other time supports the idea that forgetting may result from a temporary failure to retrieve. Memory may also be *context-dependent* in that similarity of conditions during encoding and retrieval facilitates memory.

37. Sometimes being in the place where the original learning occurred or even visualizing that place helps to facilitate _____, because of the _____-_____ nature of memory. Similarity in context may also explain the phenomenon of déjà vu, in that some element of a situation you've never been in before triggers a feeling of familiarity.

38. Context-dependent memory may explain why you sometimes feel that you've been somewhere before when you haven't, a feeling called _____ _____.

39. A third possible explanation of _____ is that the ability to remember any given piece of information may suffer from interference from other information stored in memory.

**forgetting**

40. There are two general kinds of _____. _____ interference occurs when old information causes us to forget new information. For example, the fact that learning a list of fruits is made more difficult by having previously learned a list of vegetables.

**interference, Proactive**

41. The second kind of interference, _____ interference, occurs when new information causes us to forget old information. When the words in a new list they are learning are synonyms of words in a list previously learned, individuals find it more difficult to remember the original words.

**retroactive**

42. Suppose a student learns first Spanish and then French. If having previously learned Spanish makes remembering French more difficult, _____ _____ has occurred. If the memory for Spanish is disturbed by the subsequent learning of French, then _____ _____ has occurred.

**proactive interference retroactive interference**

43. A fourth possible cause of _____ is *motivated forgetting*, in which a person deliberately forgets information that he or she does not want to remember.

**forgetting**

44. Inability to remember emotionally uncomfortable or painful experiences is seen by psychodynamic theorists as evidence of _____.

**repression**

45. Gamblers are notoriously prone to remember the times they won and to forget the times they lost. Their distorted recollection of how well they have done over the years illustrates _____ _____.

**motivated forgetting**

46. In sum, the four theories that help explain forgetting suggest that forgetting may consist in part of fading, or _____, of the _____ _____; a failure to recall, or _____, information; a disturbance caused by the _____ of other material; and selective, or _____, _____.

**decay, memory trace retrieve, interference motivated, forgetting**

## Factors in Encoding and Storage

47. Information from short-term memory is _____ to long-term memory with the help of some _____ process. One such process is _____, in which a number of individual units of information are combined into one package for storage in long-term memory.

**copied encoding, chunking**

48. Sometimes we _____ an exact copy of information in memory, but more often encoding is constructive; that is, we encode meanings and associations rather than exact representations of events, through _____ processing.

**encode**

**constructive**

49. During recall, filling in details that are missing from one's sometimes sketchily encoded mental notes is an example of _____ _____.

**constructive processing**

50. A _____ _____ occurs when a special linkage causes you to remember emotional events in graphic detail. Remembering a horrific event in special detail, along with where you were and what you were doing when it occurred, is an example of this phenomenon.

**flashbulb memory**

51. Even vivid _____ memories are subject to becoming less accurate with the passage of time. A phenomenon that is related to flashbulb memory is *mood-dependent memory:* You remember things better if you are in the same mood when you try to recall them as you were when you _____ and stored them.

**flashbulb**

**encoded**

52. If you are in a good mood when you encode a piece of information, you will recall it better if you are also in a good mood when you try to recall it—a phenomenon that is known as _____-_____ _____.

**mood-dependent memory**

## Linkages in Learning and Memory

53. How well we remember often depends on how well we have stored, or _____, information in our vast network of long-term memories. Encoding is easier if we can find meaning and organization in the material.

**encoded**

54. Syllables that are real words are much easier to learn than nonsense syllables, and material that can be put into a coherent sequence is easier to remember

meaning,
organization, encoding
meaning, organization

rote
rule

rote, rule

principle
overlearning

than material that cannot be. These examples illustrate the importance for later recall of _____ and _____ during initial _____.

55. Finding _____ and _____ in information helps a person learn material by *rule* rather than by *rote*.

56. Memorizing nonsense syllables through simple repetition is learning by _____; trying to attribute some meaning or logic to the nonsense syllables is learning by _____.

57. The principle of *overlearning* states that after you have learned something, either by simple _____ or by applying a meaningful _____, continuing to work at learning the material will tend to increase the length of time you will remember it.

58. The alphabet, nursery rhymes, and other information that is frequently repeated during childhood may be remembered for life because of the _____ of _____.

### Learning How to Learn and Remember

learning set

learning set

categories

categorize
short-term

clustering
long-term

clustering

logical

organized

story

imagery

imagery

humorous
mnemonic, method
of loci

mnemonic devices

59. As individuals continue to learn the same general kind of material, they develop a _____ _____, which helps in encoding.

60. First-year college students are often overwhelmed by the amount of material they are expected to learn, but with practice they become able to handle the same amount or even more material quite efficiently, because they have developed a _____ _____ for it.

61. Sometimes information cannot be organized into a single unit, but the elements of the information can be broken down into distinct _____, another aid to encoding.

62. If you are required to learn a list of terms, for example, it may be helpful to _____ the terms first.

63. Chunking consists of organizing material in _____-_____ memory. In long-term memory, the same process is called *clustering*.

64. If a _____ process can be used to organize information by categories, by meaning, by logic, and in other ways, the result is better _____-_____ memory and retrieval.

65. People seem particularly adept at _____ materials together if the materials have a logical relationship. Cause-and-effect sequences and narrative stories are often easy to encode and remember because they involve _____ relationships among elements of the material.

66. Not all material is readily _____, so sometimes meaning must be imposed on it. Creating a made-up story about the material is one way to do this. If you wanted to remember the words *coffee, idea,* and *light,* you might say to yourself, "After a cup of coffee, I had an idea that struck me like a light bulb turning on in my head." That is, to cluster the items, you have created a _____ about them.

67. *Imagery* is also helpful during encoding. If you can create a mental picture of events, memory can be improved through the use of _____.

68. Another way to impart meaning to material is to use *mnemonic devices*. In the method of loci, for example, you use visual _____ to associate unrelated items with familiar ones in your environment, such as furniture and other objects in your room. It helps to make these associations humorous.

69. Creating _____ mental images in which items are associated with familiar objects in your environment is a _____ device known as the _____ _____ _____.

70. In their stage acts, memory experts quickly memorize long lists of objects or people's names through the use of _____ _____, but in learning college material, these are no match for strategies based on meaning and organization.

## Practice Test

____ 1. The human memory system that has been described as a "leaky bucket" because it typically retains material for less than 30 seconds is
   a. sensory memory.
   b. short-term memory.
   c. long-term memory.
   d. none of the above

____ 2. Working memory is capable of holding approximately _____ items of unrelated information.
   a. one
   b. two to four
   c. five to nine
   d. ten to twelve

____ 3. The process through which we associate information in short-term memory with information in long-term memory is called
   a. scanning.
   b. copying.
   c. rehearsal.
   d. chunking.

____ 4. A very brief mental image of the color of a fast-moving car constitutes a
   a. short-term memory.
   b. sensory memory.
   c. semantic memory.
   d. procedural memory.

____ 5. Someone who compares memory to a path worn into a plot of grass likely thinks of forgetting as
   a. the fading of the memory trace.
   b. a failure of retrieval.
   c. a lack of consolidation.
   d. failure to achieve overlearning.

____ 6. The most sensitive test of memory is
   a. relearning.
   b. recall.
   c. a multiple-choice test.
   d. an essay examination.

____ 7. If you have "crammed" for an examination, you will probably prefer a test requiring
   a. recall.
   b. recognition.
   c. relearning.
   d. procedural memory.

____ 8. The typical curve of forgetting indicates that we
   a. continue to forget substantial amounts of information long after we originally learn it.
   b. forget nearly everything we learn within a very short time.
   c. do not forget very much immediately after learning but forget rapidly thereafter.
   d. forget very rapidly immediately after learning but retain some information for very long periods of time.

____ 9. A process that occurs following learning, during which a memory becomes more firmly established, is called
   a. consolidation.
   b. overlearning.
   c. transfer.
   d. constructive processing.

____ 10. Compared to younger people, older people
   a. have generally poorer memories for most things.
   b. have better recall of explicit rather than implicit material.
   c. have more problems recalling material but recognize items equally well.
   d. have more wisdom, meaning better insight and judgment.

____ 11. You can't recall the name of a city you once visited in Mexico or anything about it. Then the name strikes you—and suddenly you also remember the name of your hotel, the street it was on, and your favorite shop. This illustrates
   a. procedural memory.
   b. the "tip of the tongue" phenomenon.
   c. motivated recall.
   d. clustering.

____ 12. Learning French after having learned Spanish may make French harder to remember because of
   a. retroactive interference.
   b. proactive interference.
   c. motivated forgetting.
   d. overlearning.

____ **13.** Flashbulb memory and episodic memory are similar in that they both are likely to involve
   a. a memory for an event in a person's experience.
   b. associations with extreme emotions or significant life events.
   c. both semantic and procedural memories.
   d. all of the above

____ **14.** Failure to remember an unpleasant experience may be a result of
   a. retroactive interference.
   b. motivated forgetting.
   c. a failure of retrieval.
   d. constructive processing.

____ **15.** Memory for information independent of where or when you learned it is called
   a. semantic memory.
   b. sensory memory.
   c. procedural memory.
   d. episodic memory.

____ **16.** Memory for particular events is called
   a. semantic memory.
   b. sensory memory.
   c. procedural memory.
   d. episodic memory.

____ **17.** Chunking occurs in short-term memory; a similar process that occurs in long-term memory is
   a. clustering.
   b. categorization.
   c. rote learning.
   d. rule learning.

____ **18.** People who learn and remember well and efficiently often have
   a. a rich associative network.
   b. more knowledge and information in general.
   c. well-developed learning sets.
   d. all of the above

____ **19.** Studies of speed reading indicate that
   a. increases in reading speed beyond normal rates result in declines in memory.
   b. speed and comprehension can both be increased markedly over normal rates with sufficient practice.
   c. very rapid readers are more efficient information processors.
   d. slow readers spend too much time on the important points.

____ **20.** People who must frequently learn different examples of the same general type of material may become very efficient at such learning because of
   a. learning sets.
   b. the law of overlearning.
   c. procedural memory.
   d. improved relearning potential.

From *Psychology: An Introduction* © 2004 Thomson Learning

# Exercises

1. Figure 5.19 contains a list of 10 nonsense syllables and a list of 10 words. Ask a friend to study
the list of nonsense syllables for 30 seconds; then
have the friend write down as many of the nonsense syllables as he or she can remember within
1 minute. After a rest of 15 seconds, have the
friend study the list again for 30 seconds and then
again write down what he or she can remember.
Repeat this procedure until the friend has recalled
all the words correctly on two consecutive trials—or until 10 trials have been attempted. Keep
track of how many syllables were recalled on
each trial, plot the scores on the graph provided
in Figure 5.20, and connect the points with a
solid line.

   Now spend 5 minutes talking to your friend
about the weather, sports, an international event,
or some other matter unrelated to nonsense syllables. Then ask the friend to write down the
syllables again. Plot on the graph the number of
syllables he or she recalls on this retest. Also ask

whether the friend used any special kind of strategy in trying to remember the list.

   Follow the same procedure with another friend,
but use the list of words rather than the list of
nonsense syllables. Plot the results as before, but
use a dashed line.

   Now consider the following questions:

   a. Are the graphs for the nonsense syllables and
   the words the same? If there are any differences, what might account for them? What do
   the graphs tell you about memory processes?

   b. Which task—memorizing the nonsense syllables or memorizing the words—seemed easier? Explain why. Which list was remembered
   better on the retest following the 5-minute
   break? Why? Did your two friends apply any
   techniques that gave the list more meaning,
   such as making up a story, using a mnemonic
   device, clustering, or the like? Did such techniques seem to help?

2. In this exercise, you will test the efficacy of chunking and adding meaning. You will need two participants, neither of whom has taken a psychology
class (so that they have not studied these memory strategies). For this imprecise study, we will
assume that your participants are equally capable at memory tasks.

   You will also need a watch or other timer, a
piece of scratch paper and a pencil for yourself,
and two specially prepared pieces of paper for
your participants. Prepare each piece of paper by
neatly printing one of the following on it:

   Paper #1:   T   A   C   T   A   E   I   P   M
               E   A   L   W   O   N

   Paper #2:   TAC   TAE   EIP   M
               EAL   WON

## Method

Please note: *The second participant must not be
present when you perform the following procedure
with the first participant.*

   Tell your participant that you will be giving
him or her a piece of paper and that he or she is
to memorize—in the correct order—what is on
the paper within 15 seconds. Hand the participant paper #1, and when the time is up, take the
paper back. Now ask Participant 1 to recite all
the letters. Write down the letters exactly as they
are recited to you.

**FIGURE 5.19**

| Memory Lists | |
|---|---|
| TAF | FAN |
| MIH | JOB |
| BOK | HIP |
| WIS | SKY |
| RUP | CAT |
| FEQ | TOP |
| DUS | BAR |
| HOL | MOP |
| CUK | WIN |
| JAD | DAY |

**FIGURE 5.20**

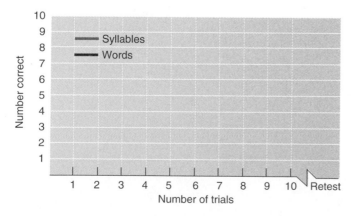

Follow the same procedure with paper #2, except this time tell the participant that *most of the entries are words spelled backward*. After 15 seconds, again write down the letters as they are recited to you.

Finally, follow the same two procedures with Participant 2.

## Scoring

For each of your four results (*before* and *after* chunking and adding meaning for both Participant 1 and Participant 2), count the number of letters that were recalled in the right order. Ignore any extra letters.

## Results and Analysis

Compute the average score for both *before* conditions by adding the two scores and dividing the sum by 2. Do the same for both *after* conditions.

Then answer the following questions:

a. What was the *before* average?

b. What was the *after* average?

c. What was the difference between the averages?

d. What can you conclude about this difference?

e. What are the implications for chunking and adding meaning?

f. How might these findings be applied to studying?

✽ For quizzing, activities, exercises, and web links, check out the book-specific website at http://www.psychology.wadsworth. com/kagan9e.

# 6 Language and Thought

## Chapter Outline

Guilland Jean Michel/CORBIS SYGMA

How do we acquire and use language? This question has puzzled philosophers, scientists, and educators for ages. Their intense interest in the subject is understandable. Somehow, we can produce and understand a virtually limitless number of statements that we may never have spoken or heard before. Indeed, we can identify every familiar spoken word we hear in a fraction of a second, drawing on the many thousands of word forms stored in our "mental dictionary." For those who know more than one language, the feat is even more awesome. Moreover, as we process the sounds we hear or the characters we read, we can almost instantaneously assemble them into meanings that correspond to the message intended by the speaker or writer.

The everyday wonders of language are possible in part because the human brain is prewired to acquire it and the human vocal apparatus is constructed to speak it. Granted, as discussed later in the chapter, some animals other than humans can understand certain symbols and even combine them to an extent. But no other species can communicate information back and forth with others of its kind in a way that approaches human use of language. And all human societies use language, no matter how isolated they may be from the larger world.

The two topics covered in this chapter—language and thought—are intricately interrelated. To be sure, thinking does not necessarily require language. Other animals obviously think, as do human babies before they have learned to speak. An artist working on a painting thinks in terms of mental images—a mind's-eye picture of what the details and final results should look like. Musicians compose and orchestrate by manipulating "sounds" that they hear inside their heads. But most of the time, we think in words and use acoustic and semantic encoding (see Chapter 5). Thus, the use of language greatly enlarges the scope of our thinking. Indeed, much of the thinking we do would be impossible without the use of words and the ideas they represent. Together, the abilities to generate complex thoughts and communicate them in language represent one of the supreme attainments of our species.

Most linguists agree that there are between 5,000 and 7,000 distinctly different languages spoken around the world, although some put the number at more than 7,000 (Gibbs, 2002). Many of these—perhaps as many as half—face extinction within this century as younger people opt for "majority" languages and either aren't taught or don't bother to learn the traditional language of their parents and ancestors. The reasons for this are often social: People believe that speaking the mainstream language of their nation will be an aid in improving their social or economic status, and at the same time their nation's majority-language speakers often pressure them to conform (Gibbs, 2002).

# THE FUNCTION AND STRUCTURE OF LANGUAGE

The origins of human language are probably lost in the mists of prehistory—before written or painted language, words didn't leave fossils. Various competing theories have been offered to explain how human language may have evolved (e.g., see Leahey & Harris, 1997). There is little scientific agreement except on two points: (1) Language evolved in conjunction with thought and other forms of cognition. (2) At some point, it gave our ancestors a distinct survival advantage—perhaps in communicating detailed information about food and danger, perhaps simply in allowing them to communicate without hand gestures while walking upright and carrying their possessions across the savannahs and through the forests. It may even have been a fortunate by-product of other aspects of cognitive evolution, one that meant little at first but later became supremely adaptive.

**FOCUS QUESTIONS**
- What is grammar?
- What are the building blocks of language?
- How are our utterances affected by the social context in which they occur?

Whatever the mysterious origins of language, a given language has the power to communicate messages that all its speakers understand, enabling people to work, play, and live together. We use language to tell each other how we feel, what we need, what we think, what we desire. We use it to amuse ourselves in conversation, to form friendships, and to help one another grow and transport food, build houses and office buildings, and manufacture and distribute clothing. Language makes possible the expression of everything, from a child's simple request for a glass of milk to a lover's declaration of passion to the most complex scientific theories.

Moreover, through reading we not only gather knowledge and information but also gain a greater sense of identification with our society and culture. Language helps us acquire information by providing labels for objects and events in the environment. It allows us to reason—to make inferences and deductions. And it helps establish and maintain social relationships. It helps us encode information into memory by providing many of the linkages in the network of memories. It helps us think and solve problems.

**Grammar** refers to the structure of a language in its entirety—everything from the specific sounds and written characters of the language to the different levels at which they are combined to produce meaning. Each language, including sign languages used by people with hearing impairment, has its own implicit grammar. Languages differ in many ways, including the sounds or signs they use, what constitutes a word, and how words are combined, but they all have a set of rules that their users must follow fairly closely if communication is to be possible. In this chapter, we focus on examples from the grammar of what is called American Standard English (after all, this textbook is written in that language), but we could just as well have used any other language for which the grammar has been described. This is because there appears to be a "universal grammar"—again, based on evolution—from which all the many variations of today's languages are thought to derive (Nowak, Komarova, & Niyogi, 2001). Thus, a child is born equipped to learn whichever of the world's thousands of languages she or he is exposed to.

**Grammar**
The structure of a language in its entirety.

## Phonemes: The Basic Sounds of Language

In effect, a language is an agreement among those who speak it that certain sounds, put together according to rules that they all know and use, convey meaningful

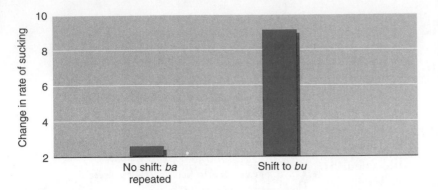

**FIGURE 6.1 The early ability to discriminate speech sounds. Researchers measured the rate at which infants engaged in sucking while they heard the speech sound *ba* repeated. As the infants became bored with hearing the sound, their rate of sucking decreased. At this point, a slightly different sound was introduced. The hypothesis was that if the infants could discriminate the new sound, they would become more aroused and, as a consequence, increase their sucking rate. That is precisely what happened. A significant increase in sucking rate occurred when there was a shift from *ba* to *bu,* indicating that the infants did indeed differentiate one sound from another.**

*Adapted from Bertoncini, Bijeljac-Babic, Jusczyk, Kennedy, & Mehler, 1988.*

messages intended by the speaker and understood by the listener. The sounds that constitute a language depend on the ability of the brain and vocal apparatus to produce them—and the number is limited. This may seem hard to believe, in view of the apparent complexity and variety of sentences that can be heard in various countries and cultures of the world, but it's true. No known language contains more than about 85 basic sounds, and some contain as few as 15. American English has about 45.

The basic sounds of a language are **phonemes.** The phonemes include the letters of the alphabet plus the variations in vowels and some special combinations of letters that are pronounced as one sound—for example, the *ch* in *chip*, the *th* in *the*, and the *sh* in *shop*. Thus, *mat* contains three phonemes. By changing any of the three (and allowing for accompanying spelling changes), you can produce many different words.

**Phonemes**
**The basic sounds of a language.**

For example, changing the first phoneme will give you *bat, cat, that,* and many other words.

As shown in Figure 6.1, infants only 1 week old already have the ability to discriminate between very similar simple speech sounds, which sets the stage for making them later in infancy. Numerous other studies over the years have demonstrated the remarkable abilities of very young infants in this respect (e.g., Shi, Werker, & Morgan, 1999).

## Morphemes: The Units of Meaning

By themselves, phonemes have no meaning (exceptions in English are the first-person pronoun *I* and the article *a*). But they can be put together in combinations of two or more to form meaningful units. For example, if we start with the phoneme *t*, add the phoneme *ea* (pronounced as a long *e*), and then add the phoneme *ch*, we arrive at *teach*. The result is called a **morpheme**—a combination of phonemes that has meaning in and of itself. Many morphemes are actual words. Others are prefixes or suffixes, which cannot stand alone but can be combined with other morphemes to form words. For example, we can combine the two morphemes *teach* and *ing* (a suffix) to form *teaching*. The plural *s* is one of the most commonly used morphemes; another is *ed* to indicate the past tense of a verb (talk*ed*, walk*ed*). Other morphemes are used to form irregular past tenses, such as *taught*. The second morpheme in *taught* is the spelling change for the past tense.

**Morpheme**
**A combination of phonemes that possesses meaning in and of itself.**

The rules for combining phonemes and morphemes into meaningful units are specified by the **semantics** of a language. The building blocks of language, though simple, make possible a tremendous variety of expressions. The 45 or so American English phonemes are combined in various ways to produce more than 100,000 morphemes. These, in turn, are combined with one another to produce the hundreds of thousands of words found in a good dictionary, all of which constitute the language's **vocabulary.**

**Semantics**
**The rules for combining phonemes and morphemes into meaningful units such as words.**

**Vocabulary**
**The words of a language.**

## Syntax: Building Phrases and Sentences from Words

True language is not possible with words alone. There must also be rules for stringing the words together into meaningful utterances such as phrases, statements, and questions. Thus—in one form or another—every language also has **syntax**. The rules of English syntax regulate the ways in which elements may be placed in order to form phrases, plus the ways in which phrases may be combined to form sentences that convey meanings people can understand. Without these rules, language would be a jumble.

For example, even very young children may know the meanings of individual names and words such as

> Nathan, quickly, who, the, down, was, sidewalk, noticed, walking, Shalini, sweater, wearing, yellow, friend, his, her.

But when presented in this order, the words do not create a coherent statement. Rearranged according to the rules of syntax (including proper punctuation), they become the meaningful sentence

> Shalini, who was walking quickly down the sidewalk, noticed her friend Nathan wearing his yellow sweater.

If that is the message you want to convey about Shalini and Nathan, you have to arrange the words in that order. Changing the arrangement might convey an entirely different meaning. English syntax allows you to use these words to create several different sentences, including:

> Nathan noticed his friend Shalini, who was walking quickly down the sidewalk wearing her yellow sweater.

The rules of syntax vary considerably from one language to another. Thus, English speakers place adjectives before nouns (*white house*), whereas French and Spanish speakers place them after nouns (*maison blanc, casa blanca*). We may be unaware of many of the rules, either as children or as adults, but we follow them nonetheless. Grammar—in all its complexity—is the key to human communication. Using it, we can construct an apparently limitless number of utterances that can express a limitless variety of meanings. In this textbook alone, there are thousands of sentences that you have never encountered, yet you understand them immediately.

**Syntax**
A language's rules for stringing words together into meaningful utterances such as phrases, statements, and questions.

We tend to use different language in public settings than in less formal ones. The language used in a courtroom, for example, is much more formal than that used in everyday settings.

## Pragmatics: The Effects of Social Context

There is another important aspect of language that affects the nature of our communications. The actual meaning of what we say may depend largely on the social situation in which we say it, and the social situation may also determine *how* we say it. Together, these variations constitute **pragmatics**.

Consider the following question: "How much money do you need?" Without knowing the context in which it was asked, you might think that the question was addressed by a kindly person to an individual in need of cash. In fact, however, it was asked by tennis star John McEnroe of fellow professional Ivan Lendl during a stormy meeting in which Lendl expressed concern over a possible decrease in tournament fees (Vecsey, 1989). Far from a kindly inquiry, the communication

**Pragmatics**
How language changes according to the social situation or context.

### Test Yourself

**(a)** In the word *pet*, is the *e* sound an example of a phoneme or a morpheme?

**(b)** How do rules of syntax help humans communicate with one another?

**(c)** When a Spanish-speaking child addresses a friend as "tú" (the familiar form of "you") and a parent as "usted" (the formal form), what aspect of language is the child displaying?

(The answers are on page 248.)

was actually belligerent in the social setting in which it was uttered. This aspect of pragmatics also extends to variations between spoken and written language. When speaking with someone, we often use incomplete sentences and "incorrect" syntax; when writing, we are much more careful about how we word things.

With regard to the second aspect of pragmatics, we often alter our utterances depending on the person we're talking to (or, more formally, the person to whom we are talking). If a friend asked you, an English speaker, to do something you might say "Sure" or "Okay." By contrast, if someone in authority asked you, you might say, "Yes, sir" or "Yes, ma'am." Many languages make a distinction between familiar and formal second-person pronouns—the former are used with friends, the latter with higher-status individuals. English once made this distinction as well; *thee* and *thou* were familiar, *you* was formal. Finally, you are certainly likely to express yourself differently when in public than you do when alone with your lover or spouse. In the latter situation, you may even find yourself using "baby talk," the way parents do with their infants—yet another example of pragmatics.

The study chart below summarizes linguistic terminology.

# THE CHALLENGE OF GENERATING AND COMPREHENDING LANGUAGE

### FOCUS QUESTIONS

- What's involved in making statements and other utterances?
- What's involved in comprehending them?

Many signs are commonly used in public places and on highways in various parts of the world to convey simple messages: "No smoking here," "Curvy road ahead," "Pedestrians may be crossing." Suppose that language worked the same way. For each idea that you wanted to express—everything from "Let's eat" to "Psychology is the scientific study of behavior"—you would need a separate sign of some kind, in the form of a spoken or written word. How many signs, each conveying only one simple message, would you need to convey everything that you now say in the course of an ordinary day? How long would it take just to tell a classmate that you would

## Study Chart

### The Language of Language

| Term | Definition | Example |
|------|-----------|---------|
| Phoneme | A basic sound of a language | *a, m, th* |
| Morpheme | A combination of phonemes that possesses meaning in and of itself | *math (m-a-th)* |
| Semantics | The rules for combining phonemes and morphemes into meaningful units such as words | To make the past tense of many verbs, add *-ed*. |
| Syntax | A language's rules for stringing words together into meaningful utterances such as phrases, statements, and questions | Adjectives come before nouns. |
| Grammar | All of the above | |

like to go along to a movie but you have a psychology exam tomorrow and must study, and besides, you have to do laundry and return books to the library—so, all in all, though you appreciate the invitation and would like a rain check, you feel you must say no?

The number of signs you would need, each conveying its own message, is almost beyond imagination. Most of the thoughts you express in the course of an ordinary day take the form of sentences you have never used or heard before—sentences you make up on the spot. In many cases, your listeners have never before heard the same combinations of words. Language enables us to exchange an unlimited number and variety of messages just by combining simple building blocks— a small number of phonemes—according to the established rules of grammar. It is difficult to imagine a more elegant system than the implicit structure of the world's many languages.

However, producing language—speaking or writing new sentences   requires thinking and planning. Understanding language also demands the most complex kind of mental activity. In the case of the spoken word, communication also requires close cooperation between speaker and listener. The speaker, having a purpose in mind, must choose words and produce sentences that will get the message across. The listener then must interpret the meaning and intention of the combination of sounds reaching the ear. A similar situation exists regarding the interaction of writer and reader, although the reader can go back over a sentence or paragraph if he or she misses something. Once spoken in a conversation, words are soon gone.

For both speaker and listener, the use of language often requires the full application of our varied cognitive abilities. When either the speaker or the listener becomes cognitively "sloppy" with regard to language, the correct message often fails to get through.

Feedback provided by students helps instructors determine which ideas and concepts need to be clarified or explained more fully.

## The Speaker

One way to get some idea of the difficulty of producing language is to make a recording of some of your own utterances, especially when you are trying to explain something fairly complicated. Hearing the tape afterward, you will probably be shocked at how tongue-tied you sound, because the spoken word is not nearly so smooth and fluent as you might think. As we talk, we often have to stop and think. Our speech is frequently full of interjections that reflect this—such as "uh . . ." and "um . . ." (Clark & Fox Tree, 2002). We make mistakes or fail to express ourselves clearly and, in response to feedback from a listener, have to amend our utterances with phrases like "What I meant was . . . ." Sometimes we stop in the middle of a sentence, leave it unfinished, and start over. We make "slips of the tongue" and end up saying something quite different from what we intended, often when we are preoccupied or distracted (Reason, 1984). (This is not the same as making slips in the context of psychoanalysis, discussed in Chapter 14; slips of the tongue normally don't imply anything.)

To produce sentences, we must first think of the meaning we want to convey— perhaps a message that will be several sentences long. Then we have to plan each sentence and each part of each sentence. We have to find the right words to flesh out the sentence and then put the words in their proper places. Finally, we have to command all the muscles we use in speech to carry out the program we have planned—even as we are mentally racing ahead to decide what we want to say next (Clark & Fox Tree, 2002). And we typically do all this so easily and so fast that we aren't even aware of it.

## → A MATTER OF DEBATE ←

# Bilingualism and Schoolchildren

Many children growing up in homes characterized by *bilingualism*—the speaking of two languages—rapidly learn to use both. In the second year of life, children already can understand that a certain word in, say, English has the same meaning as another word in a different language. One U.S. mother kept a diary describing her child, who was learning both English and Estonian. By age 2, the child knew enough to use English when speaking to people outside the home and Estonian when speaking to relatives inside (Vihman, 1985).

Theorists and researchers have debated the merits of bilingualism over the years. Most have come to agree that it is advantageous to grow up speaking two languages (e.g., see Diaz, 1985; Goncz, 1988), as many children around the world do. For one thing, the ability to pronounce unused language sounds decreases with age (Werker, 1989). For another, most people who acquire a new language after childhood never manage to speak it without an accent (Oyama, 1973). You can learn a new language at any point in your life span, but the older you are, the harder it is.

This has obvious implications for education, where today the challenge in the United States centers mostly on the growing Spanish-speaking population—which includes many children who live in homes where only Spanish is spoken. These children, like their predecessors from homes where only Italian or German or Yiddish or Chinese or one of many other languages was spoken, often face serious difficulties in acquiring knowledge in schools where the language of instruction is American Standard English.

How can these children receive equal educational opportunity? One possible way—urged by many Spanish-speaking parents—is to have them taught in Spanish by Spanish-speaking teachers. It has been suggested that this be done throughout the early grades of elementary school and English be introduced and taught later as a second language (as Spanish or French is now taught to many English-speaking children). Even after the children began to learn English, they would continue to devote as much time to Spanish and their ethnic history and culture as to U.S. history and English literature.

The suggestion has considerable appeal. It would preserve a cultural heritage—that is, fluency in the language of origin and familiarity with the traditions and customs of the Spanish-speaking world. Especially for children in the early grades, it would avoid the dislocations and difficulties of attending schools that use an unfamiliar language—and possibly the loss of self-esteem caused by failures.

But to function fully and efficiently as members of a society in which the only official language is English, all children must eventually become adept at English. Research raises some serious questions about delaying the process. For example, studies of children who spoke a dialect of Spanish and only a little English, but were expected to use English in their classrooms, have shown that they often had difficulty making the switch—and that many became discouraged and left school (Hall, 1986).

Thus, it would seem that Spanish-speaking schools represent a trade-off, with certain advantages but also some dangers. The same applies to the education of black children whose parents and friends speak what is sometimes called Black English, a rich subdialect of Standard English. Children who initially learn two languages may get off to a slow start, but they become attuned to the flexibility of language and do well over time (Hall, 1986).

To research this topic further, go online with InfoTrac and use your own term or the following suggestions:
- bilingualism and the brain
- Black English
- learning and bilingualism

# The Listener

When you listen to statements and try to interpret their meaning and intent, you engage in what is probably an even more complex form of information processing. The only raw data you have are the sound waves produced by the speaker's voice and transmitted through the air to your ears. Ordinarily, these waves meet with considerable competition from other sounds in the vicinity. Other people may be carrying on conversations in the same room. There may be coughs and sneezes, a shuffle of feet on the floor, or the sound of traffic outside. A cell phone rings. A door slams. You may think you hear every word and every syllable uttered

© Elizabeth Crews

Exposure to two languages during childhood need not interfere with school success, especially in the long run.

by the speaker—but, in fact, you typically do not. Many of the individual phonemes and morphemes often don't get through.

Even if you hear all the words, your ears may not identify them immediately. Many American English words, for example, sound very similar—such as *beach* and *peach*, *writer* and *rider*. Some sound exactly the same: *wave* and *waive*, *right* and *write*. Moreover, most of us use variations in speech that we typically don't use in writing. We say, "I'm gonna" instead of "I'm going to," "gimme" instead of "give me," "woncha" instead of "won't you." Indeed, we use condensations such as these so frequently in speech that the grammatically correct form often sounds odd. In addressing people, instead of saying "you," some American English speakers say "younse," "youse guys," or "y'all."

In listening, we carry out many mental processes at the same time. We simultaneously try to recognize sounds, identify words, look for syntactic patterns, and search for semantic meaning. When sounds and words are in themselves vague or unintelligible—as so often happens in everyday speech—the processing for syntax and semantics creates order and meaning. All this takes place so smoothly that we are not even conscious of the mental work we do when listening or the difficulties we overcome.

How do children fare when they are exposed to one language at home and another at school? See A Matter of Debate on page 226.

## Test Yourself

**(d)** With your skills of sensation intact, you can see the person who is talking to you and can hear clearly every word spoken. Is that enough for you to understand what that person is telling you?

(The answer is on page 248.)

# HOW WE LEARN LANGUAGE

Given the cognitive processing necessary to speak and understand language, it seems remarkable that children learn to use it at all. Yet they do—and quickly.

Most infants begin to understand words late in the first year—many more words than they can produce. This gap be-

## FOCUS QUESTIONS
- What role does an infant's babbling play in language development?
- How do parent-child interactions influence the child's language development and use?
- How do young children acquire their vocabularies and the elements of grammar?
- To what extent can animals other than humans learn and use language?

**Receptive vocabulary**
Words you understand when other people use them.

**Expressive vocabulary**
Words you use in speech or writing.

tween **receptive vocabulary** and **expressive vocabulary** continues for life. You will always understand more words than you find occasion to use in speaking or in writing.

Assessing this difference is harder with infants than it is with older children or adults. Parental reports have been found to be accurate to some extent (Ring & Fenson, 2000), but more objective techniques are available. For instance, one investigator showed 8-, 14-, and 20-month-old infants pairs of slides—for example, one of a kitten and the other of a tree—and then asked, "Show me the kitty. Where is the kitty?" The investigator reasoned that if the infant responded by fixing his or her gaze on the slide containing the "kitty," this would mean that the infant understood the word. The results showed that infants do indeed comprehend words very early—well before they begin to use them (Reznick, 1990).

During the second year of life, children begin acquiring words at an accelerating rate, and the order in which they acquire certain kinds of words—such as nouns before verbs and adjectives—is apparently universal (e.g., Caselli et al., 1995). By the end of their second year, many children are already speaking such sentences as "Baby drink milk." Classic research indicates that by age 5, they understand the meanings of about 2,000 words (Smith, 1926). By about age 6, they have learned virtually all the basic rules of grammar. They can string words together according to the rules of their language to create meaningful sentences of their own. And they understand the meaning of sentences they have never heard before. By the time they are 10, children speak a veritable torrent of language—about 20,000 to 30,000 words each day (Wagner, 1985).

Along the way, children also learn to make remarkably subtle interpretations of the language they hear. Until about the third year, children use language literally—that is, they use it to describe concrete, real-world events. Moreover, they assume that other people who speak intend their words to have a literal meaning. For example, when the grandfather of one young child died, the youngster heard his mother say, "They're flying the body home tomorrow." His response was immediate: "What happened to Grandpa's head?" he asked. By their fourth birthday, children begin to understand the nonliteral meanings of words and phrases, and by age 6, some are even good at appreciating irony. For example, when a child hears her father say, "Well, this sure is a *nice* morning!" as rain clouds gather, she has no problem understanding the intended meaning. Beyond the contradiction between the statement and the conditions outside, such irony usually involves cues such as a change in intonation—as implied by the emphasis on *nice*. Reaching comprehension as sophisticated as this requires a phenomenal amount of learning in a short time.

## Infants and Babbling

The specifics of the use of language must be learned, but how to create the sounds is an inborn ability. Early in life, babies begin to produce many sounds that resemble the phonemes of language. This **babbling** occurs spontaneously. It is not an attempt to imitate sounds that they have heard, because infants who are born deaf babble just like babies who can hear (Lenneberg, 1967)—up to the point at which infants who can hear start narrowing down their babbling to only the phonemes of the language being spoken around them.

**Babbling**
The early sounds babies produce spontaneously, which can include all possible human phonemes.

Further evidence of the prewired nature of babbling is that children of all nationalities make the same sounds in their earliest babbling—potentially all the sounds the human vocal apparatus can make. For example, there are no differences in the babbling of infants born to families that speak English, Russian, or Chinese (Atkinson, MacWhinney, & Stoel, 1970). Soon, however, babies begin to concentrate on the sounds appropriate to their own language, which they hear from their parents and others around them. The other sounds disappear through disuse. As shown in Figure 6.2, infants have a remarkable ability to discriminate between syllables in a strange language. Adults, on the other hand, have great difficulty with sounds far removed from the ones they are used to hearing and using (Werker, 1989). Thus, over the course of development, the ability to produce certain phonemes or to discriminate between them effectively declines.

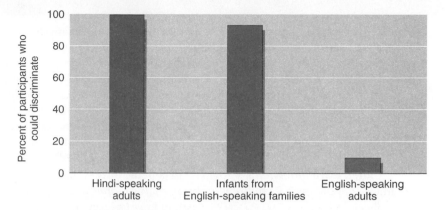

**FIGURE 6.2 Infants can, adults can't.** Infants from 6 to 8 months old were tested on their ability to discriminate two Hindi syllables not used in English and rare in the world's languages—one made with the tip of the tongue touching the front teeth, the other made with the tongue curled under the palate. These infants from English-speaking families did nearly as well as Hindi-speaking adults. But English-speaking adults were extremely poor at the task.

*Adapted from Werker, Gilbert, Humphrey, & Tees, 1981.*

## How Human Interaction Affects Language Skills

Psychologists and other language researchers have some strong clues and theories about how children learn the many other skills required for using language, but no single theory will suffice. For example, mere exposure to language without interaction—such as watching television—isn't sufficient for a child's acquisition of language (Hall, 1986). More important are the everyday social interactions between adult and child. The more time a mother spends pointing out objects to her child and gesturing and talking about them while they're playing together, the greater the child's vocabulary is likely to be at 18 months (Smith, Adamson, & Bakeman, 1988). Mothers and other caregivers who verbally interact with their children, read them stories, and teach from the stories have a strong impact on the children's vocabularies (Rebello Britto, 2001). Children who become relatively good at narrating events in their lives grow up in homes where their mothers interact with them frequently and provide a great deal of information to them in everyday conversation (Snow & Dickinson, 1990).

From the very beginning, when the child and the mother or other intimate caregiver interact, the two communicate. In speaking to their babies, mothers and other caregivers use a special tone of voice, rhythm, and style called *motherese*—a misnomer, of course, because adults of both genders use it with babies. This seems to help stimulate linguistic development because it is especially well suited to the young infant's perceptual and attentional abilities (Fernald, 1983). When mothers of infants a few days old are asked to speak in this fashion without their children present, they actually speak quite differently (Fernald & Simon, 1984).

The reciprocal interaction between caregiver and infant—that is, the give and take interaction in which the caregiver stimulates the child and vice versa—continues well beyond the first months of life. One thing parents of toddlers do is follow their children's lead in using words that connote internal feeling states. For example, as toddlers begin to show a growing understanding of what it means to feel empathy and compassion toward others, their mothers begin to use words like *good* and *bad* more frequently (Lamb, 1991).

Partly as a result of such early interactions, and also as a result of their developing cognitive abilities, children quickly acquire a grasp of the structure of language and a mastery of the processes for pro-

Talking directly to an infant and responding to the infant's babbling makes an important contribution to the child's language development.

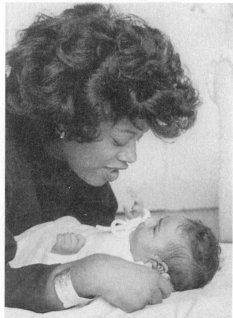

© Elizabeth Crews

Typically, the first accomplishment of babies is to speak a few meaningful single words that name objects: *baby, mama, milk, papa.* Within a few months, they begin to string two words together by adding a verb: "Baby walk," "See mama." The average length of their utterances increases at a steady rate from there. Some children learn more quickly than others, but all normal children show consistent progress.

After their second birthday, the tendency of toddlers to use speech rather than gestures to communicate becomes increasingly strong (Shore, O'Connell, & Bates, 1984). Children's acquisition of words proceeds in interaction with their efforts to solve the puzzles posed by the world around them. Thus, for example, the word *gone* appears only when a child be-

gins to grapple with the mystery of objects that disappear and later reappear (Gopnik, 1984). Similarly, children begin to speak words connoting success at a task ("There!") or failure ("No—oh!") only when they become aware of right and wrong solutions to problems and think about them (Gopnik & Meltzoff, 1984).

In general, during the first 2 years, brain maturation is a major determinant of language development. There has been no report of an infant under 8 months old who could speak and understand words. Once the brain's growth permits language use, environmental experiences begin to assume a greater role. It has been shown, for example, that the tendency of children in the second year of life to point to and name objects such as a dog, cat, or bird is an outgrowth of

interactions in the previous year with mothers who labeled these objects in the environment as they interacted with their children (Goldfield, 1990).

The interplay between language and cognition is also evident in young children's increasingly refined use of categories for objects. A child's first nouns are often *overextensions*—the child applies words for specific things beyond their actual meaning. For example, if the family cat's name is Tigger, the child may at first call *all* cats Tigger. As the child's ability to categorize improves and the child learns additional words such as *kitty-cat, doggie,* and *moo-cow,* the tendency to overextend gradually diminishes. Tigger becomes the family cat and no other (except perhaps the *Winnie-the-Pooh* character).

ducing and understanding it (Gleitman, Newport, & Gleitman, 1984). Some of the steps are described in the Life Span Perspective above.

## Discovering Grammar

At an early age, children acquire some of the rules of grammar used by the adults around them. At about age 2, for example, children are likely to say such things as "Gooses swimmed." Even though the statement is not put correctly, it shows that they have learned something about the rules. They have discovered that ordinarily a noun can be made plural by adding an *s* and a verb can be turned into the past tense by adding an *ed.* We can hardly blame them for not knowing that the English language, which is not always consistent, decrees that the plural of *goose* is *geese* and the past tense of *swim* is *swam.*

Children learn the rules of grammar in a remarkably consistent way. Whether they are fast or slow learners and regardless of the size or nature of their vocabularies, they acquire their knowledge in a predictable order. In English, one of the first morphemes learned is usually *ing,* added to a verb to denote an action going on at the moment. Somewhat later comes the addition of an *s* to words to make them plural. Still later comes the use of an *'s* to indicate possession. Most children learn to use some of the articles—*the, a, an*—before they learn to add an *ed* to a verb to convey past tense (Brown, 1973).

In general, the order in which morphemes are learned is determined by the distinctiveness of their sounds and the regularity with which they are used. The English sounds *ing* and *s,* for example, satisfy both criteria and therefore tend to be learned early (Slobin, 1985).

With minor variations, children's first two-word utterances are similar regardless of whether they are learning to speak English, Russian, or Samoan (Slobin,

1971). In languages where nouns usually occur before verbs, children tend to put nouns before verbs ("Mommy eat," not "Eat mommy") and verbs before objects ("Throw ball," not "Ball throw"). They seem to go about learning the rules in much the same way (Slobin, 1973)—with the ultimate aim of using them to make sense.

## Theories of Language Learning

At one time, some psychologists believed that the manner in which language is learned could be explained fully in terms of operant conditioning (Skinner, 1957). They thought that some of the sounds babies make in their early babbling are reinforced by their parents' smiles or other forms of approval. These sounds tend to be repeated. The same process of reinforcement was believed to account for the manner in which toddlers start to string sounds together into meaningful sentences.

Later, psychologists who approached the question from the viewpoint of observational learning proposed a different theory. They suggested that grammar is learned more through imitation of the way parents combine phonemes into meaningful morphemes and then string morphemes together into meaningful words and sentences.

Both of these theories account for some language learning, but neither offers a complete explanation. It is difficult to see how operant conditioning could lead children to acquire *rules* that would enable them to create new sentences of their own—especially because researchers have found that children may receive positive reinforcement in the form of approval for grammatically incorrect utterances that are factually right, such as "Mama isn't boy" or "She a girl," and disapproval when their grammar is okay but the facts are wrong, as in "Sesame Street comes on afternoons." It is also difficult to see how imitation could result in completely new and original sentences. In fact, there is evidence that children who do very little imitating learn language just as well as children who do a lot of it (de Villiers & de Villiers, 1978; 1999).

Former linguist Noam Chomsky looked at language learning more in terms of inborn skills. Chomsky (1965) suggested that the human brain is wired in such a way that we are born with some kind of **language acquisition device (LAD)** for learning and using language. This innate mechanism—which is theoretical, not an actual neural structure or network—enables us to acquire rules of language quickly and efficiently, based on what we hear. Our ideas of the rules are imperfect at first, but we modify and expand these notions as we become more experienced at communicating with others. Eventually, we are using the rules of grammar in such a sophisticated fashion that we can understand or express almost anything. Chomsky's theory holds that, in a sense, we cannot help learning language and using it the way we do. This is simply the way our brains operate—a behavior for which we are prewired. Just as fish are born to swim and moles to burrow, we are born to speak and understand language; we are innately motivated to do so.

In sum, some aspects of language development clearly involve conditioning and imitation. For example, we aren't born knowing which phonemes and morphemes our native language uses, and we aren't born knowing the vocabulary of our language or how to write it. Although parents typically don't reinforce the use of correct grammar with very young children, they do reinforce the use of correct words for objects and events. Later, language teachers use reinforcement a great deal with regard to both vocabulary and grammar. And children do imitate words they hear—often without knowing what they mean and at times displaying some of what they have heard on the worst possible occasions, to the embarrassment of parents who use expletives around the home. But the concept of some kind of LAD

**Language acquisition device (LAD)**
A proposed mechanism in the brain, prewired to help humans learn language.

does a much better job of explaining the acquisition of language by "extracting" rules from what is being heard. The universal nature of language development—first babbling, then single words, then two-word utterances, and so on—also supports the idea that a built-in device of some kind is responsible, although theorists are still arguing about its nature.

## Can Other Animals Learn Language?

Many attempts have been made over the years to determine whether other animals, especially chimpanzees, can acquire and use language. One problem is that even chimpanzees are unable to use their vocal apparatus to make the sounds of human speech. Researchers have therefore tried substitutes such as sign language. This was the basis for studies by Beatrix Gardner (1933-1995) and Allen Gardner, initially with a chimpanzee named Washoe.

After about 4 years of training, Washoe had learned a vocabulary of more than 130 signs, including *you, please, cat, enough,* and *time.* Moreover, she could string the signs together into statements like "hurry gimme toothbrush" (Gardner & Gardner, 1972). She even made up a word of her own using the signs available to her—*water-bird* to describe a duck—almost as if she had learned sign language in much the same way a human child learns the spoken word. Years of subsequent research by the Gardners and their colleagues with Washoe and other chimps have indicated that the chimps are capable of quite sophisticated and conversational communication—not only with the researchers but also between themselves (e.g., see Jensvold & Gardner, 2000).

David Premack took another approach with a chimpanzee named Sarah, teaching her to communicate by using symbols made of plastic cut into various shapes. Each piece represented a word, and the words could be arranged in order on a mag-

A chimpanzee talks: Washoe, age $2\frac{1}{2}$, makes the sign language signal for hat.

B. T. Gardner

netized board. Sarah learned the meanings of numerous words and "sentences," such as "Mary give apple Sarah." Once she understood the meanings of the words *take, dish,* and *red,* she obeyed a command expressed in a sentence she had never seen before: "Sarah take red dish" (Premack, 1976).

Many psychologists believe, however, that there is a qualitative difference between humans' ability for communication and that of apes (Premack, 1985). This was the conclusion of Herbert Terrace, who conducted a long-term study of a chimpanzee named Nim Chimpsky(!). Terrace began with high hopes of showing that Nim could acquire human facility with language. After 5 years, though, he reluctantly concluded that most of Nim's communication was little more than a "subtle imitation" of his teachers', learned for the sake of obtaining rewards. There seemed to be no indication of any knowledge about syntax or of any growing ability to produce longer and more complex messages (Terrace, 1985; Terrace, Petitto, Sanders, & Bever, 1979). (Remember that it is primarily syntax that allows for the tremendous flexibility and range of human language.)

However, a chimp named Kanzi has demonstrated even more sophisticated linguistic abilities. For example, in a limited way, Kanzi readily learned to use symbols to identify ideas and to request items such as food and drink that were out of his sight. Over the years, Kanzi has also acquired limited ability to learn and use syntax, at least in the interpretation of the researchers (Savage-Rumbaugh, Rumbaugh, & McDonald, 1985; Savage-Rumbaugh, Shanker, & Taylor, 1998).

Thus, the issue of true language learning by chimpanzees and other animals remains unresolved (see Kako, 1999; Pepperberg, 1999; Savage-Rumbaugh, Shanker, & Taylor, 1998). It is clear that these and many other animals *communicate,* and that they do so without special training. Whether they truly can acquire the subtleties of human language is another matter.

As for the particular animal, chimpanzees do at least seem to be plausible candidates for language learning—they are our closest relatives. But would you believe, a parrot? See A Matter of Debate on page 234.

**Test Yourself**

**(e)** Johann says that communication between chimps is just as effective as communication between humans. Izza says it isn't. Who is right?

(The answer is on page 248.)

# WORDS AND CONCEPTS

One aspect of languages deserves special attention because it makes possible great flexibility in the use of words for both communication and information processing. For example, in English, relatively few words are names of specific one-of-a-kind objects, such as the planets Earth and Mars; most words represent whole groups of objects, events, actions, or ideas. Even a simple word like *water* means not only the colorless fluid in a glass but also any somewhat similar substance anywhere, including the salty contents of the oceans and the raindrops that fall from the sky. The word *justice* represents many different abstract ideas held by people around the world at various times in history and embodied in various legal codes and practices.

Such words are called **symbolic concepts,** defined roughly as mental representations of similarities between objects or events that we know are also different from one another. For example, to know the concept *water* is to know that the substances in drinking glasses, oceans, and raindrops, though they take different forms, are in fact similar in a basic way.

Many kinds of similarities can contribute to the formation of concepts. Some concepts grow out of the physical attributes of objects as they appear to our senses—

**FOCUS QUESTIONS**
- What are concepts?
- How are concepts involved in thinking, learning, and memory?
- How does language interact with knowledge?
- How does new knowledge affect language?

**Symbolic concept**
A mental representation of the similarities between different objects and events, based on language.

## → A MATTER OF DEBATE ←

# Talking with Parrots

A 1998 special issue of *Scientific American,* on the topic of exploring intelligence, included an article by Irene Pepperberg on her 20-plus years of research with the renowned Alex, an African Grey parrot. Pepperberg became convinced that Grey parrots—especially Alex—could acquire language skills rivaling those of chimpanzees and other animals that have been the primary subjects of research on nonhuman language learning. The following are excerpts that focus on the somewhat unusual teaching method she devised and some of the remarkable skills Alex apparently acquired in *referential speech*—using word "keys" to identify objects and understand and respond to questions about them.

**Irene Pepperberg with her African Grey parrot, Alex.**

The technique we use most frequently involves two humans who teach each other about the objects at hand while the bird watches [based on research on observational learning by Bandura in the 1970s].

In a typical training session, Alex watches the trainer pick up an object and ask the human student a question about it: for example, "What color?" If the student answers correctly, he or she receives praise and is allowed to play with the object as a reward. If the student answers incorrectly, however,

the trainer scolds him or her and temporarily removes the object from sight. The second human thus acts as a model for Alex and a rival for the trainer's attention. The humans' interactions also demonstrate the consequences of an error: The model is told to try again or to talk more clearly.

We then repeat the training session with the roles of trainer and model reversed. As a result, Alex sees that communication is a two-way street and that each vocalization is not specific to an individual. . . . Alex will respond to, interact with, and learn from just about anyone. The fact that Alex works well with different trainers suggests that his responses are not being cued by any individual—one of the criticisms often raised about our studies. How could a naive trainer possibly cue Alex to call an almond a "cork nut"—his idiosyncratic label for that treat? . . .

Of course, not every item is equally appealing to a parrot. To keep Alex from refusing to answer any question that doesn't involve a nut, we allow him to trade rewards once he has correctly answered a question. If Alex correctly identifies a key, he can receive a nut—a more desirable item—by asking for it directly, with a simple "I wanna nut." Such a

for example, similarities in the appearance of roses and tulips (*flowers*), the sound of a singing voice and a brass band (*music*), and the feel of a piece of paper and a windowpane (*smooth*). Some are based on similarities in relationships between physical attributes; *bigger* applies to such diverse pairs of objects as fly-to-gnat, adult-to-child, and Texas-to-Delaware, and *louder* applies to shout versus whisper and thunderclap versus shout. Other concepts take note of similarities in function. *Home,* for example, embraces a one-family house, a high-rise apartment, a tepee, and an igloo. An abstract concept like *justice* lumps together events that share the idea that a person is treated fairly by an authority—whether the person is a criminal and the authority is a judge, the person is a minority member and the authority is a state, or the person is a ball player and the authority is an official.

Whether two words or ideas are viewed as belonging to the same concept depends on the individual's knowledge and on her or his ability to detect an aspect of similarity (Murphy & Medin, 1985). Thus, for a child *robin* and *Paris* do not belong to a concept, but for many adults they are linked to the concept of spring.

protocol provides some flexibility but maintains referentiality of the reward.

I began working with Alex when he was 13 months old—a baby in a species in which individuals live up to 60 years in captivity. Through his years of training Alex has mastered tasks once thought to be beyond the capacity of all but humans and certain nonhuman primates. Not only can he produce and understand labels describing 50 different objects and foods but he also can categorize objects by color (rose, blue, green, yellow, orange, gray, or purple), material (wood, wool, paper, cork, chalk, hide, or rock), and shape (objects having from two to six corners, where a two-cornered object is shaped like a football). Combining labels for attributes such as color, material, and shape, Alex can identify, request, and describe more than 100 different objects with about 80 percent accuracy. . . .

In addition to understanding that colors and shapes represent different types of categories and that items can be categorized accordingly, Alex also seems to realize that a single object can possess properties of more than one category—a green triangle, for example, is both green and three-cornered. When presented with such an object Alex can correctly characterize either attribute in response to the vocal queries "What color?" or "What shape?" Because the same object is the subject of both questions, Alex must change each query appropriately. . . .

Alex has also learned the abstract concepts of "same" and "different." When shown two identical objects or two items that vary in color, material, or shape, Alex can name which attributes are the same and which are different. If nothing about the objects is the same or different, he replies, "None." He responds accurately even if he has not previously encountered the objects, colors, materials, or shapes. . . .

Alex also comprehends at least one relative concept: size. He responds accurately to questions asking which of two objects is the bigger or smaller by stating the color or material of the correct item. If the objects are of equal size, he responds, "None." . . .

One last bit of evidence reinforces our belief that Alex knows what he is talking about. If a trainer responds incorrectly to the parrot's requests—by substituting an unrequested item, for example—Alex generally responds like any dissatisfied child: He says, "Nuh" (his word for "no"), and repeats his initial request. Taken together, these results strongly suggest that Alex is not merely mimicking his trainers but has acquired an impressive understanding of some aspects of human speech.

Do you agree? Based on the discussion in the text, do you think Alex actually uses language?

• • • • • • • • • • • • • • • • • • • • • • • •
To research this topic further, go online with InfoTrac and use your own term or the following suggestions:
- Irene Pepperberg
- language learning by animals

These 3-year-olds in a Head Start program are learning abstract concepts—letters of the alphabet—by associating them with specific shapes.

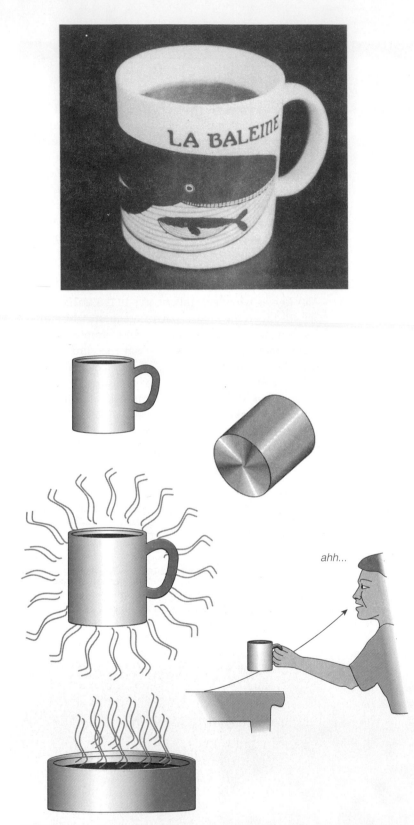

## Concepts Without Words: Perceptual Concepts

Although words that express concepts make up a large part of our vocabulary, concepts can be formed without language. Such concepts are called **perceptual concepts** or **schemas;** the elements of a relatively common human perceptual concept are illustrated in Figure 6.3. Many experiments have shown that nonhuman animals can acquire perceptual concepts of shape and other qualities of objects in the absence of language. Dogs obviously have some concept of tree and will behave toward a tree they have never seen before just as they behave toward more familiar trees. Pigeons display a similar skill. For example, they can detect a tree in pictures of scenes containing a wide variety of trees (Herrnstein & de Villiers, 1980).

Many of our concepts are, of course, both symbolic and perceptual in nature. Thus, for example, our schema for a bird involves language—words such as *feathers, beak,* and *song*—along with perceptual representations of birds, including their shape and texture.

## How Language Enriches Our Concepts—and Vice Versa

If language is not essential for acquiring concepts, it is certainly a great help. Much of our communication and thinking depends on words that represent complex concepts embedded within other concepts, in a way that would be impossible without language. Note, for example, the term *human being.* What the term means to us goes far beyond any physical attributes (having two legs, an upright stance, and so on) or functions (being students, working at jobs). We have a far richer overall concept of human being in terms of several interwoven concepts, including, for example, (1) *the most intelligent* (2) *mammal,* which is (3) *an organism* that (4) *produces* (5) *its babies* (6) *inside* (7) *the body* of (8) *the mother,* who (9) *nurses* the baby after (10) *birth.*

Language helps us find meanings, relationships, and similarities and thus build concepts on top of concepts or schemas

**FIGURE 6.3** It all adds up to a coffee mug. The perceptual concept of a coffee mug may entail representations of its shape and texture, as well as the smell and taste of coffee and even the movements of your hand in bringing the mug to your lips. All such representations, stored in various parts of the brain, are reconstructed instantaneously and "add up" to a coffee mug.
*Adapted from Damasio & Damasio, 1992.*

within schemas. Without language, it would be difficult to find much resemblance between a human being walking on the land and a whale swimming in the ocean. *Mammal*, however, includes both of them.

Just as language enriches our symbolic concepts, so do perceptual concepts enrich language. Concept words make it possible to use the 26 letters and 45 or so phonemes of the English language to express an unlimited number of messages. Suppose an English speaker lacked the concept *people* and had to talk about each individual by a different and distinct name, had no concept *home* and had to use a different word for each place where someone lived—and so on for every piece of furniture, every appliance, every utensil, and every other object.

## Concepts and Inferences

The use of both symbolic and perceptual concepts lends a tremendous variety and versatility to the kind of information processing we call "thinking." When we encounter a new object or experience, we do not ordinarily have to deal with it as a unique event that we have no prior knowledge of and must learn about from scratch. Instead, we can fit it into some already existing concept. A snake of a species we have never seen before is instantly recognizable as a snake. Concepts "give our world stability. They capture the notion that many objects or events are alike in some important respect, and hence can be thought about and responded to in ways we have already mastered" (Smith & Medin, 1981). This process is also reflected in Piaget's idea of *assimilation*, discussed in Chapter 10, which refers to how we "fit" new objects or situations we encounter to those for which we have previously acquired concepts or schemas.

One important way in which concepts help us think is demonstrated by the following example. Someone says to you, "There's a bird in Brazil called a cariama. Does it have wings?" Almost immediately, you answer in the affirmative. Assuming that you don't know this from your own experience, you reach your answer through the useful form of thinking called **inference**—or drawing logical conclusions from facts already known. You have been told that a cariama fits the concept *bird*. Your concept of bird includes the knowledge that birds have wings. It is therefore reasonable to infer that a cariama has wings.

Inference enables you to think about many matters without having any direct knowledge of the situation. At the end of a long day's drive, you feel confident that you will find a motel room if you push on another 50 miles toward Tucson. You can make this inference because, even though you have never been there before, you know Tucson is a city and your concept of cities includes the presence of motels on their outskirts.

Inferences are sometimes wrong, of course. Suppose, for example, that the question about the Brazilian bird was "Does a cariama fly?" Again, you would probably answer "yes," because your concept of birds includes flight. But there are a few birds that do not fly. As it happens, cariamas can fly if they absolutely must, but normally they don't.

Most inferences, however, are correct and valuable. Just as the rules of grammar enable us to generate sentences we have never spoken before and understand sentences we have never heard before, inference enables us to think about all kinds of matters that we have never actually encountered—including abstract concepts such as truth, beauty, and love. We can generalize about the new and unfamiliar from what we have observed about similar objects, events,

**Perceptual concept**
A concept based on physical similarities instead of language.

**Schema**
An alternative term for perceptual concept.

**Test Yourself**

**(f)** Is having language skills a prerequisite to forming concepts?

(The answer is on page 248.)

**Inference**
Drawing logical conclusions from facts you already know.

A Brazilian cariama.

© D. Roberson

or abstractions. Most of what we know—or think we know—is based on inference rather than on direct observation.

## Concepts, Learning, and Memory

While reading this discussion of concepts, you may have been reminded of a topic discussed in the chapter on memory—that is, the way categories help us organize information and encode it into long-term memory. Concepts are one of the means by which language helps us learn and remember. They make possible all kinds of chunking and clustering that help us process information in short-term memory and encode it efficiently into networks of long-term memories.

As we acquire more information, we change our symbolic and perceptual concepts in many ways, refining or enlarging them and forming new ones. Out of our simplest concepts, such as faces, food, and furniture, we build increasingly complex ones that serve as high-level clusters of related information and ideas. Thanks to these new and increasingly complex combinations of simpler ideas, we can think about complex subject matter almost as easily and efficiently as we could previously think about simpler subject matter (Wickelgren, 1981).

Language accounts to a great extent for how learning builds on learning—or, in William James's words, for how new items of information "cluster and cling like grapes to a stem" (1890). It does so both by helping us acquire concepts and by giving us specific words that help us remember and think about specific details. It is difficult to imagine, for example, how a surgeon could be trained without all the words that medical science has developed to describe the human body—some representing the general principles of how the body is put together and functions, others identifying specific anatomical structures. Effective surgery might well be impossible without an "effective language."

## A Lingering Puzzle: What Exactly Is a Concept?

Although concepts play a large part in our learning and thinking and have been studied extensively by psychologists and linguists, they continue to be something of a puzzle. The exact nature of concepts is not clear, and there are a number of conflicting points of view.

One view, suggested by Eleanor Rosch, is that from our observations of events in the world we form a notion of a typical bird (or vegetable or fruit or anything else). Based on both symbolic and perceptual concepts, many people in the United States think of the prototypical bird as being something like a robin—between a crow and a finch in size, with two shortish legs and two wings and a tendency to hop along the ground in search of worms and insects and then fly up into a tree and sing. Then we lump other creatures into our prototype of bird or reject them, depending on how much they resemble a robin. We know immediately that thrushes and song sparrows, which are similar to robins, fit into our concept of bird. We need a little more time to decide that a chicken is a bird, because it is a good deal larger than a robin and normally does not fly or sit in trees (Rosch & Mervis, 1998).

Sometimes, Rosch has pointed out, the boundary lines for family resemblances are extremely "fuzzy." Therefore, we may have trouble deciding whether a bat fits the concept of bird or that of mammal and whether a tomato is a vegetable or a fruit (Rosch, 1988). The same fuzziness in the way we form concepts makes it difficult to classify an 18-year-old female as a girl or a woman and rheumatism as a disease or something else. Our concepts and categories—indeed, our thoughts in general—are not always as neat as we would like them to be. But perhaps this simply reflects the reality that our world does not perfectly match the concepts we invent and therefore is not easy to describe in cut-and-dried terms.

To establish what is typical, sometimes we rely on factors other than family resemblances—including the degree to which the item represents an ideal or how often we encounter it (Barsalou, 1985). The typical food you might eat while on a diet, for example, is determined not by its physical features but by ideas about nutrients in a category of foods.

It appears that we are more likely to notice similar features in things that are in many ways dissimilar when our information is symbolic—that is, verbal rather than visual. In one experiment, when participants were asked to read pairs of sentences about people of two distinct ethnicities, they judged the two groups to be more similar than they did when asked to look at pictures of the two (Gati & Tversky, 1984). Because a concept or schema contains a "bundle" of features, the specific ones we pick out and use change with the context—as illustrated in Figure 6.4.

FIGURE 6.4  What does the concept "hot" mean? "Hot" contains features that vary considerably from one context to another. For example, it can mean overheated, cool(!), or on a winning streak.

## Does Language Shape Our View of the World— or Vice Versa?

Is it possible that language restricts our information-processing abilities? Is language analogous to a pair of faulty eyeglasses through which we get only a limited and sometimes distorted view of the world?

A prominent early-20th-century anthropologist and linguist, Benjamin Whorf (1897–1941), discovered that people who use different languages have very different ways of looking at the world and different concepts about the similarities and relationships that it displays. In studying many languages, Whorf found one group of Native Americans who lump together with a single word things that fly—insects, airplanes, and even airplane pilots. He found other languages that do not have any devices for distinguishing the past, present, and future tenses of verbs (Whorf, 1956; published posthumously). In Whorf's view, such differences markedly affect the way people who speak these languages conceive of the world, organize it, and think about it. For example, they may affect the personalities of people of a given culture, as proposed by anthropologist and linguist Edward Sapir (1884–1939). What has come to be known as the *Sapir-Whorf hypothesis of linguistic relativity* has continued to be studied in detail across ethnic groups with different languages (e.g., Davies, Sowden, Jerrett, Jerrett, & Corbett, 1998; Jessel, 1978; Kay & Kempton, 1984).

This is an intriguing theory—and it receives a certain amount of support from some of the findings discussed earlier in the chapter. A physiology professor, with an effective language of anatomy, looks at and thinks about the human body differently than the rest of us do. Children who start school with impoverished vocabularies may conceive of the world in a more limited fashion than their more fortunate classmates do. It would appear that information processing can be influenced not only by the use of different languages but also by differences in the vocabularies of people who speak the same language.

However, among all the many languages of the world there are more basic similarities than differences (Nowak, Komarova, & Niyogi, 2001). Certainly people everywhere seem to perceive physical objects and everyday events, find names for them, organize them into concepts and categories, and think about them in ways that are often very similar. Some colors, for example, seem particularly striking—doubtless because of the way the eyes and the process of perception operate. Although languages differ in the number of colors for which they have names, the names usually refer to the colors that "stand out," like red and yellow, not to the many other hues and shades we see in nature (Kay, 1975; Kay, Berlin, Maffi, & Merrifield, 1997). Similarly, most languages have terms for shapes that human perception seems to find compelling, such as squares and circles. Most languages also have terms for basic emotions like fear and anger, for dimensions like height and length, and for distance and direction.

Rosch has suggested that our concepts about the physical world are based on what is actually "out there" in nature. That is, they are molded by and reflect the physical realities of the environment. Objects just naturally fall into groups like birds and mammals or vegetables and fruits—and human language acknowledges this (Rosch & Mervis, 1998). Our brains are wired to notice certain attributes of the objects and events we encounter, and family resemblances in these attributes form the basis of our concepts.

## How New Knowledge Yields New Language

Another indication that language is tailored to human thinking is the way language changes when people's knowledge changes. Note, for example, all the new words modern technology has engendered. In the mid–19th century, there were no terms such as *helicopter, jet engine, gigabyte,* or *space shuttle.* Nor were there everyday items such as *televisions, stereos, telephones,* or even *light bulbs.* All grew out of the need to refer to new terms for new concepts developed by inventors.

The rapid development of new technologies in recent years has resulted in the coining of numerous new words. Examples include *laser, modem,* and *byte.*

When we need a new word, we coin it or sometimes borrow it from another language. (Many everyday "English" words are borrowed—*goulash* from Hungarian, *whiskey* from Gaelic, *filet mignon* from French.) And as additions to the language become more and more widely used, we often shorten them to make them more convenient (Zipf, 1949). Thus, the original term *moving pictures* has been condensed to *movies, gasoline* to *gas, telephone* to *phone.* Specialists in certain areas of knowledge, such as economics or political science, coin or borrow their own vocabulary and often use their own methods to shorten terms for simplicity and convenience. Creating acronyms is a commonplace way of condensing language, and acronyms sometimes replace the words they originally stood for. Do you even know exactly what *NASA* is short for? How about *PDQ* and *QED*? Or *SNAFU*?

In sum, although thinking may in some ways be molded and limited by language, as Whorf pointed out, the human brain seems remarkably capable of adapting this useful tool to its own advantage. "Apparently when people lack a word for a useful concept, they soon find one. . . . What this suggests is that language differences

reflect the culture and not the reverse" (Clark & Clark, 1977). The lesson for all of us is that we have in language a tool of virtually infinite possibilities—limited, for all practical purposes, only by how well we learn to handle it.

# THINKING AND PROBLEM SOLVING

Sometime when you are engaged in thinking—about anything at all, from your plans for your next meal to your ideas about religion or politics—stop yourself and examine what kind of process has been going on. Most likely you will find that you have been talking to yourself—using language, especially words that represent concepts.

**FOCUS QUESTIONS**
- How do rules and premises sometimes help us and sometimes lead our thinking astray?
- What sorts of mental shortcuts do we use in solving problems?
- What kinds of things get in our way in attempting to solve problems?

*Thinking* is one of those terms that everybody understands; it has already been used numerous times in this text. But there is no single definition of thinking that everyone agrees on. It is probably best described as mentally manipulating information. In the learning and memory stages of information processing, we build a store of knowledge about the objects and events we have encountered—mental representations of the world and the way it operates, including concepts and schemas. In the thinking stage, we process these inner representations in various ways to add to our understanding of the world and solve the problems it presents. Our thinking is often entirely independent of physical objects and actual events. We can think about objects that are not present at the moment (a house that doesn't yet exist), about events that occurred in the past (a childhood birthday party), or about extremely abstract concepts (the universe).

We think about many things in different ways. As we observe the world around us, we seek to find some kind of order in its objects and events. We look for meanings and relationships that enable us to form more concepts and categories. As we accumulate more knowledge, these concepts change and become more and more refined and elaborate.

## Some Tools of Thinking: Rules and Premises

Among the important pieces of information we process during our thinking are the rules that govern the relationships and interactions among objects and events in the environment—in other words, the facts that we have learned about the way the world operates. We have learned from experience that water, if heated enough, will boil and turn into steam. We have also discovered that when an egg is placed in boiling water, the insides will start to thicken and, if left long enough, will become hard-boiled. In thinking about cooking, we employ a great many rules. In a sense, this is the "syntax of daily living."

Some of the rules we use come from our own observations—that is, from the kinds of pragmatic schemas, based on everyday experience, that help us reason and solve problems (Cheng & Holyoak, 1985; 1989). Others represent the pooled observations of many people—the kinds of information found in libraries. When we think about the solar system, we utilize observations from astronomy. When we think about the distance around a circular lake that we know to be 200 yards (about 183 m) wide, we use the mathematician's rule that the circumference equals the diameter times the constant pi (3.1416).

We also base much of our thinking on **premises,** or basic beliefs that we accept as a starting point—even though they aren't guaranteed to be accurate. The

**Premises**
The basic beliefs we accept and use in thinking even though they cannot be proved.

line between a premise and a rule can be difficult to draw, because many generally accepted beliefs may not be true. It is universally believed, for example, that no object can be in two places at the same time—even though modern physics teaches that the tiniest particles of matter, called photons, can indeed accomplish this. In other areas of science, such ideas as the theory of natural selection and many advanced mathematical theories are still only premises, although they are in accord with the best observations currently possible and have considerable evidence to support them.

Many premises are the result of individual experience. They are not necessarily based on objective observation, and they vary greatly from one person to another. Some of us, from what we have observed, believe that most people are honest—and our thinking about other people and interactions with them are based on this firmly held premise. Others hold just as firmly to the premise that most people are dishonest. Some believe that there are important differences in people that are attributable to their "race," as discussed in Chapter 1; others do not, preferring instead to think in terms of ethnicity or to dismiss the notion of such differences altogether.

## Logical and Illogical Ways of Thinking

When you express an opinion and explain why you have reached it, a friend may say, "That makes sense; I agree" or, on the contrary, "No, you're wrong; I disagree." Logical thinking means drawing conclusions that follow inescapably from the rules we have learned and the premises we have adopted. Suppose, for example, you were a contestant on a quiz show and were asked, "Does a whale nurse its young?" If you had learned the rule that all mammals nurse their young and if you knew that a whale is a mammal, it would follow logically that, yes, a whale must nurse its young.

Illogical thinking, in contrast, means drawing conclusions that are not justified by such evidence as rules, facts, and premises. For example, a young person may decide to become a schoolteacher as a result of this line of thought: "My mother says she was extremely happy when she was teaching. Therefore, I will be happy teaching." The person's thinking is illogical because she or he may have very different interests and talents and the teaching profession may have changed over the years. A person with a stomachache takes a pill that was once prescribed for a friend, thinking, "The pill helped my friend, and therefore it will help me." But his or her stomachache may have an entirely different cause and may be made worse by the pill.

When we accuse people of being illogical, we are often incorrect. Their logic is perfectly sound, given their premises; it is the premises that we disagree with. Was it illogical for medieval Europeans to believe that sailing far enough west would result in falling off the world? No, because they based their reasoning on the premise that the earth was flat—and if that were so, ships would indeed fall off like plates pushed to the edge of a table. Their logic was right, but their premise that the earth is flat was wrong. Moreover, many people don't apply the same logical rules of reasoning in every situation; instead, much depends on the subject matter at hand—as well as any emotionality it may invoke. Thus, for example, a person might reason correctly about the economy but not about social inequality. An individual's prior knowledge and beliefs vary from one issue to another—and thus the content at hand typically affects the line of reasoning (Gigerenzer & Hug, 1992).

Many arguments and misunderstandings among diplomats and nations, as well as among friends and family, are caused not so much by fallacies in thinking as by starting from different premises. One economist, using flawless logic, may conclude that taxes should be raised. An equally brilliant economist, using equally

# Taking Steps to Solve a Problem

As a student, you must solve not only the theoretical problems in your math courses but also many everyday problems. You have a certain amount of money available for tuition, books, clothes, housing, food, and entertainment. How can you best allot the money among these expenses?

A person starting a long automobile trip must ask: What highways will provide the best route? Into how many days on the road can the trip best be broken up?

A mechanic looking at a stalled automobile must ask: What's wrong? What's the best and quickest way to fix it?

There have been many studies of problem solving—the traps to avoid and the most effective ways to go about it. One finding is that the process requires four distinct steps. Knowing about them is one way to improve your skills (Wessels, 1982). (These apply quite well to writing term papers, too.)

1. *Define the problem.* Clarify both the nature of the problem and the solution or goal that will suffice.
2. *Devise a strategy.* Come up with a plan that shows reasonable promise of reaching the goal.
3. *Carry out the strategy.* This is best done by calling on any rules and other knowledge you have that may be useful, while avoiding distractions and focusing attention on the task.
4. *Evaluate progress toward the goal.* Stop from time to time to see if you are getting closer to the solution. (It's often a good idea to ask someone who can be objective to help you with this.)

If you detect slow progress or failure at any point, start over. Never hesitate to rethink a problem.

---

flawless logic, may conclude that taxes should be lowered. After much thought, one person decides that the stock market will go up. Another person, after equal consideration, decides that it will go down. Which of the opinions on the economy and on the stock market is right and which is wrong? We can't really say, because we have no way of establishing the validity of the premises on which they are based.

We cannot be sure that a premise is wrong unless it clearly violates "truth," and this is seldom the case. We now know for a fact that the earth is spherical rather than flat. If a man claims to be *the* Napoleon of the French Revolution, we know that he is unquestionably wrong and we doubt his grip on reality. But mostly we hold our premises more or less on faith. We can agree or disagree with another person's premises but cannot usually prove them right or wrong. Thus, people whose thought processes are totally logical can reach entirely different conclusions.

## Using Algorithms and Heuristics

Much human thinking is directed at solving problems or making decisions—that is, attempting to cope with the innumerable problems, large and small, that are faced by all human beings. Some practical suggestions on this subject are provided in Psychology in the Lab and in Life (above).

The most effective overall strategy, when it is available, is to use what is called an **algorithm.** The word originally was used to describe mathematical formulas and procedures—which, of course, guarantee a correct solution to any problem that deals with numbers, provided that we understand the problem and know the proper algorithm to apply. The term has been broadened to include any specific technique that can be followed step by step and will produce a correct solution without fail. Consider the problem of calling a friend who is not listed in the phone book. You know that his number begins 445-57, but you have forgotten the last two digits. You could use an algorithm by trying every possible number from 445-5700

**Algorithm**
A problem-solving technique that produces a correct solution every time if we follow the specified steps.

through 445-5799. This method might keep you busy for a while—especially if the correct number turned out to be 445-5799—but it can't fail.

However, in daily living and thinking, algorithms are the exception rather than the rule. For most of the problems we face, we rely instead on **heuristics.** These are mental shortcuts that have worked for us in the past, in somewhat similar situations, and may work again—although there is no guarantee that they will. If you were driving down an unfamiliar country road, trying to get to a town known to be somewhere toward the west, and you came to a fork, you would probably choose the path that seemed, based on the position of the sun, to head more westerly—though it might later curve and turn south. A chess player, who cannot possibly predict all the potential moves in the game, follows the heuristic of trying to control the center of the board—which does not guarantee winning but usually helps.

**Heuristics**
Mental shortcuts that may produce accurate solutions but don't guarantee them.

## Traps and Obstacles in Problem Solving

Sometimes we fail to solve problems because of a sort of cognitive laziness that may include making unwarranted assumptions, taking unwarranted assumptions at face value, and attacking problems only in familiar and inflexible ways. Examples of such "traps"—and notes on how to avoid them—are the subject of this section.

**Failure to Analyze the Problem**   One of the most common dangers we face in our efforts to solve problems is failing to analyze the situation thoroughly and jumping to an incorrect view of the nature of the problem and the possible solution. This trap is beautifully illustrated by the problem shown in Figure 6.5. Try it yourself before going on to the next paragraph.

The problem presented in the figure appears simple—yet very few people manage to solve it, as most people erroneously select cards I and III (Oaksford & Chater, 1994; Wason, 1971). The first thing to note is the word *violating* in the question: You are being asked only to *disprove* the statement, not to prove it. Card I can do this if there is no 6 on the other side. Card II is irrelevant because it has an M instead of a C. Card III can't help—it could only prove the rule, which is what leads people who misread the question astray. Card IV is the other necessary card: If it has a C on the other side, the statement is disproved. So you just need to see the other sides of cards I and IV.

Researchers have found that the tendency to jump to unwarranted assumptions about the nature of the problem is most pronounced when the problem at hand is an unfamiliar and abstract one—as in Figure 6.5. Consider a more familiar-sounding problem (similar to one used by Cox & Griggs, 1982, which has the same form as the previous one). For card I, substitute "drinking beer"; for card II, substitute "drinking soda"; for card III, substitute "23 years old"; and for card IV, substitute "19 years old." Now pretend that you're a police officer and test the following statement about whether the four people represented by the cards are violating the law: "If a person is drinking beer, then the person is over 21." Now it becomes much easier to see that cards I and IV are the only ones relevant to disproving the statement.

**FIGURE 6.5 Can you solve this problem?** Four cards, which have symbols on both sides, lie on a table so that you can see only one side, as shown here. You know that each card has a letter on one side and a number on the other. You're told, "If a card has a C on one side, it has a 6 on the other." Which of the cards would you have to turn over to determine conclusively whether the cards violate the rule? (For the answer, see the text.)
*Adapted from Cox & Griggs, 1982; Wason, 1971.*

**Thinking What You Want to Think**   Closely related to the error of failing to analyze the problem and making unwarranted assumptions is the tendency to let personal biases get in the way. We try hard—and sometimes against all the weight of evidence and logic—to find the answer we would like to find (Metcalfe, 1986). The ways in which this tendency can affect problem solving have been demonstrated by the experiment in Figure 6.6. Try it yourself before going on.

A    B    C

**FIGURE 6.6** The problem of the dishonest coin salesman. This problem was posed, as an experiment, to students taking an introductory psychology course: "A stranger approached a museum curator and offered him an ancient bronze coin. The coin had an authentic appearance and was marked with the date 544 B.C. The curator had happily made acquisitions from suspicious sources before, but this time he promptly called the police and had the stranger arrested. Why?" Students were then asked, "On a scale of 1 to 10, how sure are you that you know the correct answer?" (See Figure 6.7 for the correct answer—plus the results of the experiment.)

Not every participant solved the problem, of course. But there was an interesting difference between those who succeeded and those who failed: Those who succeeded showed much less confidence that they were onto the correct solution. On the average, those who felt more certain about the answer were less likely to be right, as Figure 6.7 shows. We all have a tendency to reach conclusions based on our intuitions and on what we would prefer to be the case. Seeing a problem the way we would like to does not always lead to the best solution.

**Functional Fixedness**    Another tendency we all share is the tendency to get into a rut in our view of the world and the way it operates. In particular, we tend to think of an object as functioning only in a single way and ignore its other possible uses. This pitfall, called **functional fixedness,** is best demonstrated in the classic experiment illustrated in Figure 6.8. Before going on to the next paragraph, examine the figure and see if you can solve the problem. The problem is especially difficult when you have only a photograph and cannot actually manipulate the objects— but, with some effort, you may figure it out.

**Functional fixedness**
The tendency to think of objects in terms of their usual functions rather than other possible functions.

**FIGURE 6.8** Problem: how to mount the candle on a door so that it won't drip on the floor. Participants in an experiment were asked to figure out a way to turn these objects into an improvised candle stand. Try the problem yourself before looking at Figure 6.9 for an illustration of how it can be done.

**FIGURE 6.7** Dead certain? Dead wrong. The correct answer to the problem is that the coin could not have been authentic because it would have been impossible for someone who lived in 544 B.C. to know that the Western calendar would change on a date that was still 544 years in the future. Note that those students who got the answer wrong were more likely to say that they were certain they had the right answer.

*Adapted from Metcalfe, 1986.*

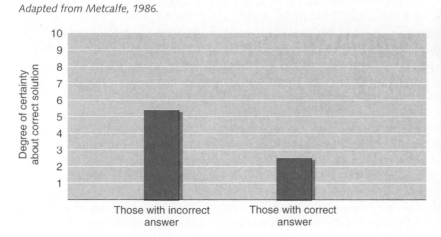

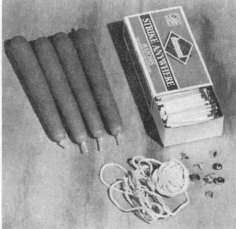

© David Hewitt/Anne Garrison

**FIGURE 6.9 The candle stand solution.** The problem posed in Figure 6.8 can be solved only by finding an unusual way of using the box holding the matches. Just use the thumbtacks to fasten it to the door—and, lo, you have a candle stand to catch the drippings.

**Persistence of set**
The tendency in problem solving to develop a mental set that leads to solving problems in a habitual way.

The problem can be solved, as shown in Figure 6.9, only by forgetting about the way a box is ordinarily used. You have to empty the box of all the matches, tack it to the door, and turn it into a candle stand. Although this seems simple enough once you know it, fewer than half the participants thought of it when the experiment was first performed (Duncker, 1945).

Functional fixedness reduces our efficiency at solving many everyday problems. A nail file is for filing nails; we may completely overlook the possibility of using it to tighten a screw and thus repair a loose hinge. A goldfish bowl is for holding fish; the first person who converted one into a terrarium for growing house plants had to break some powerful old associations.

Functional fixedness is one form of a more general phenomenon called **persistence of set.** Over the years, we develop a mental set toward problems—that is, our own habitual way of approaching them. We tend to follow the same approach even in situations in which other methods would be more appropriate. One almost sure way to improve your ability to solve new problems is to try from the very beginning to think of several possible ways to define the problem and the goal, as well as a number of different strategies that might work.

**Relying Solely on Information That Readily Comes to Mind**   The fourth common pitfall is best explained by indulging in a bit of fantasy. Suppose your life depended on a modern-day version of one of those old mythical tests devised by a king seeking a worthy heir to his throne. Your test is this: The king pulls a book from his library shelves. He turns at random to a page and circles the first word he finds that either begins with an *r* (like *road*) or has an *r* as its third letter (like *carpenter*). You have to guess which he finds. If you are right, the kingdom is yours. If you are wrong, off with your head.

How would you go about deciding? Most people start by trying to figure the odds. They see how many words they can recall that begin with *r*, then how many they can recall with *r* as the third letter. They find it much easier to think of words starting with *r*, decide that the chances are heavily weighted in that direction, and make the wrong guess. As it happens, more words have *r* as the third letter than as the first letter. But we pay much more attention to the first letter than to any other when encoding words into memory, and therefore words like *road* and *rock* are more readily available than words like *cork* and *farm* (Tversky & Kahneman, 1973).

Much of our real-life thinking and problem solving depends on the availability of information we have stored in memory. Recent events are likely to have an especially strong and sometimes undue influence on our thinking. A good example comes from the world of sports, where we are often influenced by what we know about the recent performance of athletes. Both basketball players and fans believe that a player's chances of making a shot are greater if he has just made one than if he has just missed. But the actual records of players on two professional teams show that this belief in a player's "hot hand" or "streak shooting" is not supported by the facts (Gilovich, Vallone, & Tversky, 1985).

We are also more influenced by an event that has a personal impact than by something we read in a newspaper. For example, a homeowner is more likely to buy additional fire insurance after watching a neighbor's house burn down than after reading about fires in other parts of the city.

Our reliance on the most readily available information often serves a useful purpose, because by and large our memory operates to make the most important information easiest to recall. But there are times when relying on what is readily available prevents us from solving a problem or causes an error (Tversky & Kahneman, 1973). Note this common occurrence: If we associate with people who lean strongly toward a certain lifestyle and certain opinions, we may accept their judgment as representative of the wisdom of all humanity—and be influenced accordingly in important decisions about career, purchases, marriage, and values. In actual fact, their behavior and beliefs may not be typical of most people—and not at all suitable for us.

Like functional fixedness, the availability pitfall can be avoided by being flexible in approaching a problem. Somewhere in your memory storehouse you have many kinds of information that might help. The first information that comes to mind as you start searching your memory may or may not help. You may do better if you think: What else do I know that bears on the problem? How can I think about the problem in a way that will help me find this other information? Thinking, as has been said, is the manipulation of information—and in problem solving, the more we manipulate the information, the better.

---

**Test Yourself**

**(g)** If you were lost in the forest in the late afternoon and you looked at the position of the sun in the sky to head east toward home, what kind of problem-solving approach would you be using?

**(h)** Your friend is trying to open a bottle of soda but can't locate an opener. So she gives up on the idea of having a drink—even though she is standing at the sink and could use the edge of the sink to open the bottle. Your friend's behavior is an example of what pitfall in problem solving?

(The answers are on page 248.)

---

# Chapter 6 Summary

## The Function and Structure of Language

1. The origins of human language are unknown, but language must somehow have been highly adaptive.
2. *Grammar* refers to the structure of a language in its entirety.
3. *Phonemes* are the basic sounds of language. English has about 45; some languages have fewer, and some have more. The phonemes of a written language don't necessarily correspond to the letters of its alphabet.
4. Phonemes are combined into *morphemes* to produce words that have meaning.
5. *Semantics* refers to the meaning of a language's morphemes and words; words constitute a language's *vocabulary*.
6. The *syntax* of a language refers to the way words are combined to produce phrases and statements or questions.
7. *Pragmatics* refers to how language often changes in accord with the social context in which it is used.

## The Challenge of Generating and Comprehending Language

8. Language goes a long way in making modern human interactions efficient, and even possible.
9. When we produce sentences, we must quickly think of the meaning we wish to convey, plan each sentence and part of a sentence, find the right words to flesh out our thoughts, and put the words in their proper order.
10. In listening, we carry out many mental processes all at the same time. We simultaneously try to recognize sounds, identify words, look for syntactic patterns, and search for semantic meaning.
11. When we listen to speech, the individual sounds and words are often vague or unintelligible, but our information processing creates order and meaning—so smoothly that we are not even aware of the mental work we do.
12. Bilingual children often have difficulty in U.S. schools, but there may be some remedies.

## How We Learn Language

13. The gap between *receptive vocabulary* and *expressive vocabulary* continues for life.
14. At age 2, most children speak three-word sentences. At age 5, they understand the meanings of about 2,000 words. At age 6, they have acquired virtually all the basic rules of grammar. At age 10, they produce about 20,000 to 30,000 words each day.
15. *Babbling* is the first sign of language use that infants display, and it is universal across cultures.
16. Communication and interaction between child and parent (or other intimate caregiver) is essential to language development.
17. Learning the grammar of a language appears to proceed in much the same fashion for babies the

world over, regardless of what language they are learning to speak.

18. Some theorists have suggested that language is learned through conditioning, others that it is acquired through observational learning and imitation, and still others that there is an innate learning acquisition device (*LAD*). No single explanation accounts for all language learning.

19. Animals other than humans may learn some of the basic elements of language, but their abilities are very limited.

## Words and Concepts

20. Some words name one-of-a-kind objects, but most are *symbolic concepts*—mental representations of similarities between objects or events.

21. Concepts that do not involve words are called *perceptual concepts* or *schemas.*

22. Young babies and nonhuman animals can acquire concepts without language, but language enables us to build concepts on top of concepts and adds tremendous variety and versatility to our thinking and communication.

23. Our concepts enable us to make *inferences*, drawing logical conclusions about new and unfamiliar objects and events from what we already know.

24. Many concepts represent categories or groupings that help us organize information and encode it into long-term memory.

25. Various theories have been proposed to explain the nature and formation of concepts. It may be that we form ideas of prototypical objects or events and then lump others into our concepts based on their degree of resemblance.

26. The Sapir-Whorf hypothesis proposes that people who use different languages have different ways of looking at the world, organizing it, and thinking about it.

## Thinking and Problem Solving

27. Thinking is a difficult process to define scientifically; it is probably best described as mentally manipulating information.

28. Among the important pieces of information we use in our thinking are the rules we have learned that govern the relationships and interactions among objects and events.

29. We also base our thinking on *premises*, which are basic beliefs that we accept even though they usually cannot be proved.

30. The most effective strategy in problem solving is to use an *algorithm*—a mathematical formula or other procedure that will guarantee a correct solution if followed step by step.

31. When an algorithm is not available, we use *heuristics* that have worked in similar situations and may work again, but they do not guarantee a correct solution.

32. Traps in problem solving include failure to analyze the problem; thinking what you want to think; *functional fixedness*, which is part of a more general phenomenon called *persistence of set;* and relying solely on information that comes readily to mind.

33. Traps and obstacles can often be avoided by greater flexibility in analyzing a problem, thinking of various ways to define the problem and the goal, seeking different strategies that might work, and searching memory for additional information that may help—as well as being willing to start over.

# Chapter 6 Test Yourself Answers

(a) It is a phoneme—one of the many basic sounds that are the building blocks of language.

(b) They regulate the way words are placed in proper order to form phrases—and the way these phrases are combined to form sentences. Without established rules of syntax, language would be incomprehensible.

(c) Pragmatics—variations in language use according to status

(d) It is not enough. To understand speech, you must carry out the varied perceptual and cognitive tasks—for example, recognition, understanding, and interpretation—involved in information processing.

(e) Izza is likely to be right. Although there are some points of similarity between chimp communication and human language, there is only limited evidence that chimps can learn syntax.

(f) It is not. Language is the basis for our symbolic concepts—words that connote our mental representations of distinct classes of objects or events. But we are also capable of developing concepts without words—called perceptual concepts—through a sensory awareness of the attributes of a class of objects.

(g) You would be using a heuristic—a rule of thumb or approach that has worked for you in the past in similar situations.

(h) It is an example of functional fixedness—the tendency we have to get into a rut in our view of the world and of how things operate.

# Chapter 6  Language and Thought

## Key Terms

algorithm (p. 243)
babbling (p. 228)
expressive vocabulary (p. 228)
functional fixedness (p. 245)
grammar (p. 221)
heuristics (p. 244)
inference (p. 237)
language acquisition device (LAD) (p. 231)
morpheme (p. 222)
perceptual concept (p. 237)
persistence of set (p. 246)
phonemes (p. 222)

pragmatics (p. 223)
premises (p. 241)
receptive vocabulary (p. 228)
schema (p. 237)
semantics (p. 222)
symbolic concept (p. 233)
syntax (p. 223)
vocabulary (p. 222)

*The key terms above can be used as search terms in InfoTrac, a database of readings, which can be found at http://infotrac-thomsonlearning.com.*

## Active Learning Review

1. Language is a communication system that enables human beings to exchange an almost infinite variety of messages. Although other animals can _____ with one another, human beings alone can convey an almost endless number of messages through _____.  **communicate**  **language**
2. Communication is the basic function of human _____.  **language**

### The Function and Structure of Language

3. Scientists agree on two points about the origins of language: It evolved in conjunction with thought and other forms of cognition, and it had survival value. Thus, language is intricately involved with _____ and has helped us to _____.  **cognition**  **survive**
4. We influence people with language—for example, we inform, warn, order, and question them. These purposes all serve the _____ function of language.  **communication**
5. _____ refers to the structure of a language in its entirety, including its basic sounds, called _____, and the rules by which they are combined to convey meaning.  **Grammar**  **phonemes**
6. In English, *b, ing,* and *th* are basic sounds among the language's 45 or so _____.  **phonemes**
7. _____ are combined into basic units of meaning—whole words, plus prefixes and suffixes—called *morphemes.*  **Phonemes**
8. *Hat, pre,* and *ed* are _____.  **morphemes**
9. English has about _____ meaningless _____ and more than 100,000 meaningful _____.  **45, phonemes**  **morphemes**
10. The way meaning is communicated and understood is specified by the rules of _____, within the larger framework and structure of language called _____.  **semantics**  **grammar**
11. Every language must have these essential elements for _____ to take place. *Vocabulary*—the words of a language—is created according to the rules of _____.  **communication**  **semantics**
12. Among the most important rules governing the framework and structure of a language, called its _____, are those that specify how phrases and sentences are put together, called its *syntax.*  **grammar**
13. The rules governing how nouns, verbs, adjectives, and adverbs are placed in proper order to form phrases and how phrases are combined into sentences that convey meaning readily understood by anyone who speaks the language is the _____ of a language.  **syntax**

**syntax**

**semantics**
**syntax**

**pragmatics**
**grammar**
**phonemes, morphemes**
**semantics**
**syntax**
**pragmatics**

**cognition**
**think**

**cognitive**

**semantics**
**syntax**

**receptive**
**expressive**

**babbling**

**inborn (or prewired)**
**phonemes**
**babbling**

**babbling**

**language**

**verbal interaction**

**rules, grammar**
**language**

**operant conditioning**

**observational**

14. In English, an adjective is placed before a noun (for example, *white house*); in French and in Spanish, the adjective is placed after the noun (*maison blanc, casa blanca*). This illustrates a difference in _____ between the languages.

15. In addition to meaning, or _____, and sentence structure, or _____, a third aspect of language is *pragmatics,* or how language varies according to the situation.

16. The question "How much money do you need?" means one thing when a parent is talking to a child who is about to go to the store and another thing when the parent is complaining about the child's demands for an increase in allowance. This difference reflects the workings of _____.

17. In sum, the structure of a language in its entirety is its _____. The basic sounds are its _____ and the basic units of meaning are its _____, which are combined according to its rules of _____ and put together into statements according to its _____. Meaning also can be affected by the context in which language occurs, which is referred to as _____.

### The Challenge of Generating and Comprehending Language

18. Communication requires the cooperation of both speaker and listener, each of whom often must engage in considerable cognitive activity. Thus, we say that language and _____ are intricately interrelated.

19. As we talk, we often have to stop and _____ about the meaning we want to convey, yet we do this so easily that we typically aren't aware of it.

20. A listener often must engage in considerable _____ activity to interpret what is being said, using the language's rules for establishing meaning, called _____, and the language's rules for creating statements, called _____.

### How We Learn Language

21. Among both young children and adults, _____ vocabulary is much larger than _____ vocabulary. That is, we understand more words than we actually use.

22. Before they can talk, infants from completely different language environments all engage in _____. The observation that they spontaneously make more or less the same meaningless sounds indicates that this is not a learned behavior but instead is _____.

23. Technically, *babbling* consists of a great many elementary sounds, or _____. Infants of all nationalities make the same sounds in their earliest _____, but eventually sounds that do not belong to the language the infant hears no longer occur in the infant's _____.

24. Although psychologists and linguists sometimes disagree on how children learn their _____, a crucial factor appears to be verbal interaction between the child and caregivers.

25. Instead of simply listening to language—for example, by watching television—the child must participate in active _____ _____ with someone who speaks the language.

26. The developmental sequences in which children use articles (in English, *the, a, an*), make different verb tenses (*go, going, went*), and form plurals (*dog, dogs*) are very similar in different languages, illustrating the universality of how children learn the _____ of _____.

27. Various theories have been offered to explain how children learn _____.

28. The idea that parents, for example, reward their children's language with praise and understanding is at the heart of the _____ _____ theory.

29. Other theorists have emphasized that children acquire language by imitation and _____ learning because presumably they hear language spoken and then repeat it.

30. Neither _____ conditioning nor _____ _____ provides a complete account of language learning, as was pointed out by Noam Chomsky, among others. He proposed that children have an innate mechanism for language learning, called the *language acquisition device* or *LAD*.

**operant, observational learning**

31. Chomsky's idea of a _____ _____ _____, or _____, was based on observations that children appear to actively extract the rules of their language's _____—along with observations that the sequence of language development is the same, or _____, across cultures.

**language acquisition device, LAD**
**grammar**
**universal**

32. The issue of true language learning by species other than humans, such as chimpanzees, remains unresolved. It is obvious than many animals communicate, but the extent to which they can acquire human _____ remains unclear.

**language**

## Words and Concepts

33. Only a few words in any language are names of specific one-of-a-kind objects. Most words represent whole groups of objects, events, actions, or ideas and are called _____ _____.

**symbolic concepts**

34. Whether in physical attributes, functions, or some more abstract way, individual examples of a single _____ _____ all possess certain _____.

**symbolic concept, similarities**

35. Among humans, concepts are represented primarily by words and phrases; such concepts are called _____ concepts. But concepts can be formed without language, even among lower animals.

**symbolic**

36. Although dogs have no language, they have a concept of a tree; this illustrates a _____ _____ or _____.

**perceptual concept, schema**

37. Symbolic concepts are often complex, with concepts imbedded within concepts. The term *human being* is an extremely _____ concept.

**complex**

38. Concepts help us think, and one kind of thinking is making *inferences*, that is, drawing logical conclusions from what you already know. When you encounter a species of snake that you have never seen before, you easily make the simple _____ that it is a snake.

**inference**

39. If someone tells you that there is a bird in Brazil called a cariama, you immediately decide that it has wings even though you have never seen such a bird. You conclude this by making an _____ on the basis of your _____ of bird.

**inference, concept**

40. Many concepts represent categories or groupings that help us organize information by chunking and clustering material. Many categories are _____, and many concept words describe _____.

**concepts, categories**

41. Because learning builds on _____, it is helpful to have a broad "effective language." Surgeons probably could not perform effective surgery without the _____ language of medicine and anatomy.

**language**

**effective**

42. The Sapir-Whorf hypothesis of linguistic relativity proposes that the distinctions a language makes in words markedly affect the thinking of its speakers. However, in contrast to the idea of linguistic _____, others have proposed that there are more _____ than differences among the vocabularies of the world's languages, which implies that there are more similarities than _____ in thinking as well.

**relativity**
**similarities**

**differences**

43. Another indication that thinking can govern language is the observation that new knowledge and concepts often cause the creation of new words. Words such as *space suit* and *light bulb* provide examples of how language is influenced by _____.

**thinking (or knowledge)**

## Thinking and Problem Solving

44. Thinking is the mental manipulation of information. Among the important pieces of information we manipulate during our _____ are the rules that govern relationships and interactions among the objects and events in the environment.

**thinking**

rules

rules, premises

logical thinking

rule, premise

premise
logical

problem solving
problem solving

algorithm

algorithms, heuristics

failure, analyze, problem
failure, analyze, problem

personal
biases

functional fixedness
fixedness

persistence, set
problem solving

solving

rely, readily available

45. What we have learned about the way the world operates determines some of the _____ we use during thinking. We also base much of our thinking on beliefs that we accept whether or not they can be proved.

46. Logical thinking involves drawing conclusions that follow inescapably from the _____ that we have learned and the _____ that we use as a point of departure.

47. If you know the rules that all mammals nurse their young and that a whale is a mammal, then concluding that whales nurse their young is an example of _____ _____.

48. A false conclusion may be reached because of illogical thinking or because an incorrect _____ or _____ was used. Critics who argued that Columbus would fall off the earth if he sailed west from Europe were wrong because they thought the world was flat, a faulty _____, but their thinking was _____.

49. Much of human thinking—for example, determining how best to arrange your room or how to balance your budget—is an attempt at _____ _____.

50. The most effective strategy for _____ _____ is to use a mathematical formula or other procedure that will guarantee the solution if followed step by step.

51. Most of the time, no certain, step-by-step _____ is available, and we must rely on shortcuts that have worked previously in similar situations and may work again.

52. Determining how to get to a distant town by using a map is an approach based on _____. Doing it with no map would involve _____ and a lot of trial and error.

53. One common trap in problem solving is failure to analyze the problem thoroughly. It is crucial to know exactly what the task is, what facts are available, and what constraints there are; otherwise, the problem will be difficult to solve because of a _____ to _____ the _____.

54. In addition to _____ to _____ the _____ thoroughly, another reason we have difficulty solving problems is that we may let our personal biases get in the way.

55. People often seem to find flaws in even the most logical reasoning if they disagree with the conclusion; this is an example of letting our _____ _____ interfere with our logical thinking. Another problem-solving trap, called *functional fixedness,* is the tendency to think of objects as functioning only in a certain way and to ignore their other possible uses.

56. People who cannot think of a variety of creative uses for a cup or paper clip are displaying _____ _____.

57. Functional _____ is one form of a more general phenomenon called *persistence of set,* which refers to the tendency to rely on habitual ways of approaching problems or situations.

58. The "this is the way we have always done it" approach to problem solving works well in many situations but can prove to be an obstacle to solving problems that appear similar to our previous experience but actually are not. When that happens, we attribute the error to _____ of _____.

59. Another trap in _____ _____ consists of relying solely on the most readily available information. Often we adopt a solution based on information that we have recently acquired or believe strongly, even though that information may be no more relevant to _____ the problem than other information available to us.

60. The tendency to drive more carefully after seeing an accident or to buy more insurance after a neighbor's house burns down illustrates our inclination to _____ solely on the most _____ _____ information.

## Practice Test

_____ **1.** The main difference between the communication systems of humans and those of lower animals is that human beings
   a. use sounds.
   b. use gestures.
   c. communicate meaning.
   d. communicate a greater variety of thoughts.

_____ **2.** A phoneme is
   a. a basic sound.
   b. the smallest meaningful unit of language.
   c. a syllable.
   d. all of the above.

_____ **3.** American English has about how many phonemes?
   a. 85
   b. 45
   c. 35
   d. 20

_____ **4.** A morpheme is
   a. a word.
   b. a combination of phonemes.
   c. a prefix.
   d. all of the above

_____ **5.** Semantics is most closely associated with
   a. grammar.
   b. meaning.
   c. syntax.
   d. word order.

_____ **6.** Syntax
   a. does not contribute to the meaning of a sentence.
   b. is not usually learned by children before age 6.
   c. is more concerned with word order than with word meaning.
   d. reflects meaning rather than grammar.

_____ **7.** Which is *not* accurate with regard to children's language learning?
   a. They typically speak in two- or three-word sentences by about age 2.
   b. They learn all the basic rules of grammar by about age 12.
   c. They understand the meaning of about 2,000 words by about age 5.
   d. They can string words together to create meaningful new sentences by about age 6.

_____ **8.** The early babbling of infants
   a. begins at birth.
   b. is a learned ability.
   c. does not occur in babies who are born deaf.
   d. contains potentially all possible language sounds.

_____ **9.** Which of the following is *not* accurate with regard to bilingualism?
   a. Children exposed mostly to Spanish in their home had difficulty switching from Spanish to English in school.
   b. Children exposed to two languages have no particular language problems.
   c. It is generally advantageous to grow up speaking two languages.
   d. People who learn a second language after childhood can usually speak it without an accent.

_____ **10.** Perhaps the most crucial experience in acquiring a first language is
   a. active language interaction with another speaker.
   b. sheer exposure to a language.
   c. listening to a parent who speaks slowly, in simple sentences, and repeats key words.
   d. none of the above; the "innate mechanism" is sufficient.

_____ **11.** Language is acquired through
   a. operant conditioning.
   b. observational learning.
   c. an innate mechanism specific to language.
   d. all of the above

_____ **12.** Attempts to teach apes language have demonstrated that
   a. it is impossible to teach an ape the language skills of even a 3-year-old child.
   b. apes are as capable of understanding symbols, communicating with them, and engaging in various kinds of information processing as many primary schoolchildren.
   c. apes can use language to produce long and complex messages.
   d. apes are able to create sentences they have never experienced before by combining words or symbols they already know into a new sequence.

____13. Concepts
    a. require language.
    b. cannot be learned by nonhuman animals.
    c. are first learned when babies begin to talk.
    d. none of the above

____14. Drawing logical conclusions from existing knowledge is a thought process called
    a. semantics.
    b. imitation.
    c. inference.
    d. none of the above

____15. The notion of "effective language" is most closely associated with
    a. the principle that learning builds on learning.
    b. skills in public speaking.
    c. proper syntax.
    d. schematic concepts.

____16. The idea that the nature of language influences how people conceive the world, organize it, and think about it is primarily associated with
    a. Whorf.
    b. Aristotle.
    c. Rosch.
    d. Chomsky.

____17. A false conclusion may derive from
    a. incorrect facts.
    b. faulty premises.
    c. illogical thinking.
    d. all of the above

____18. One noted economist argues that taxes must be lowered; another says taxes must be raised. They probably disagree on
    a. rules.
    b. premises.
    c. logic.
    d. semantics.

____19. A rule is to a premise as
    a. an algorithm is to a heuristic.
    b. illogical thinking is to logical thinking.
    c. an assumption is to a conclusion.
    d. a schematic concept is to a symbolic concept.

____20. Functional fixedness is a
    a. motor impairment.
    b. special form of persistence of set.
    c. type of personal bias.
    d. lack of mechanical ability.

## Exercises

1. Developers of the longest-running science fiction television and movie series, *Star Trek*, hired professional linguists to create a language named after one of the show's alien races. The language was constructed from the bottom up, from vocalizations to grammar; actors playing the aliens had to learn small segments of it.

   Assume for the moment that you have been hired by your government to serve as ambassador to an alien race named the Zingerons. Of course, you need to know their language intimately. Assume further that there is no textbook for Zingeron, but some members of that race have been hired to tutor you in the language. Unfortunately, none of the tutors is a professional language instructor, and none has any command of English.

   Based specifically on what you have learned in this chapter, what kinds of experiences or arrangements would you create to help ensure that you learn Zingeron as rapidly and effectively as possible? Describe in a minimum of one sentence each at least three different things you would do in your quest for proficiency in Zingeron. Also indicate why you chose each activity.

2. Figures 6.10 and 6.11 present two problems to solve. Have several friends attempt to solve these problems. After they give their first answer, ask them to explain their reasoning. If they are wrong, tell them that they are wrong and have them try

```
  DONALD
+ GERALD
---------
  ROBERT
```

**FIGURE 6.11** *An addition problem in which the digits are represented by letters. Given that each instance of a letter corresponds to the same digit from 0 to 9 (and only to that digit) and that* **D** = 5, *substitute for the other letters digits that will make the addition problem correct. (One of many possible routes to solving the problem is given in the text of Exercise 2.)* Adapted from Bartlett, 1958.

again and explain their next answer. From their wrong answers, try to determine what error or common trap they fell into attempting to solve the problem. The solution for Figure 6.11 follows. The answer for Figure 6.10 is in the caption for Figure 6.7 on page 245.

To get started solving Figure 6.11, make a column with the letters that are used, then fill in possible digits next to the letters as you deduce them. Given that **D** = 5, you know that **T** = 0 with a carryover of 1 to the fifth column. Now, avoid the trap of trying to continue working from right to left as you normally would in addition. What can you deduce elsewhere in the problem? For one thing, there can be no carryover from the first column, so with **D** = 5 and **T** = 0, **G** can be only 4, 3, 2, or 1, and **R** can be only 6, 7, 8, or 9. For another, note in the fifth column that the carryover plus **L** + **L** equals **R,** and the only way this can happen is if **R** is odd— so now **R** can be only 7 or 9. Then, in the second column, the only way that **O** + **E** can equal **O** is if 0 or 10 is added to **O.** **E** can't be 0 because **T** is, and 10 isn't permissible, so **E** must be 9 with a carryover from the third column. Then all that's left for **R** is 7. Does **E** = 9 also tell you something about **A** in the fourth column and **G** in the first? Does **R** = 7 tell you something about **L** in the fifth?

You're about halfway there. The complete solution is printed below.

❋ *For quizzing, activities, exercises, and web links, check out the book-specific website at http://www.psychology.wadsworth.com/kagan9e.*

**FIGURE 6.10** *The problem of the dishonest coin salesman. A stranger approached a museum curator and offered him an ancient bronze coin. The coin had an authentic appearance and was marked with the date 544 B.C. The curator had happily made acquisitions from suspicious sources before, but this time he promptly called the police and had the stranger arrested. Why? On a scale of 1 to 10, how sure are you that you know the correct answer?*

A            B            C

A = 4, B = 3, D = 5, E = 9, G = 1, L = 8, N = 6, O = 2, R = 7, T = 0

# 7 Intelligence and Its Assessment

© Annie Griffiths Belt/CORBIS

Up to this point, we have dealt primarily with universal qualities of humans—that is, what they have in common. Among such characteristics are the neurochemistry of the brain; sensation and perception; and the processes of conditioning, memory, language, and thought. Although these characteristics may vary from one person to another, all human beings possess them.

Another interest of psychology, however, is the study of *individual differences*. No two members of any species—not even identical twins—are exactly alike, and psychologists continue to study how this variation works. In humans, what is it that causes one person to be verbose and another hesitant to speak, one to be friendly and another withdrawn, one to be timid and another bold? This chapter considers differences in *intelligence*, which generally refers to variation in cognitive processes and abilities. Intelligence is one of the two major domains of human functioning widely considered to be most important in understanding and interacting with others. The second is *personality*, which generally refers to people's distinct motives, moods, and ways of behaving toward others; we turn to personality in Chapter 9. Both domains are influenced by the interaction of heredity and environment, factors that cannot readily be teased apart.

Ron Chapple/gettyimages/Taxi

Psychologists are interested in both the similarities and the differences among individuals. Two important areas in which individuals differ are intelligence and personality.

# WHAT IS INTELLIGENCE?

Try asking some of your friends and acquaintances what they mean when they use the word *intelligence*. You're almost certain to get a somewhat different definition from each, just as you would if you asked several psychologists. Perhaps the most practical definition of intelligence was proposed by David Wechsler, the developer of several of today's most widely used intelligence tests. He defined **intelligence** as the ability to understand the world and the resourcefulness to cope with its challenges. In other words, you're intelligent if you know what's going on around you, can learn from experience, and act in ways that are adaptive and successful in your particular environment. Your behavior is intelligent if it has meaning and direction and is rational and worthwhile (Wechsler, 1975).

Clearly, what is rational and worthwhile will vary with where and when a person lives. What Wechsler's definition points out is that a person who was consid-

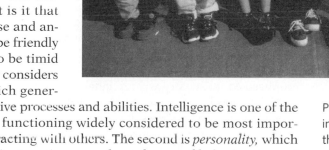

FOCUS QUESTIONS

• Is intelligence a single general ability?

• Are there multiple forms of intelligence, and if so, what are they?

**Intelligence**
The ability to understand the world and the resourcefulness to cope with its challenges.

**257**

Some psychologists believe that there are several different kinds of intelligence. The skills required to navigate a canoe are quite different from those required to pass a verbal or mathematical aptitude test.

ered highly intelligent in ancient Egypt, for example, would not be considered so in the modern industrialized areas of the world, which highly value technological and language skills. Nor would a person alive today likely be considered as intelligent if she or he were somehow transplanted to the world that may exist 3,000 years from now. A problem plaguing all investigators is that intelligence means different things to different people—and has done so from one time to another and from one place to another throughout human history. The ancient Greeks considered a talent for oratory to be a hallmark of intelligence. Until the 20th century, the Chinese emphasized mastery of written language. Some people who live in remote regions of Africa, South America, and other parts of the world are likely to attribute intelligence to a person with good hunting, gathering, and other day-to-day survival skills. Some Pacific islanders emphasize that a person who can navigate an outrigger canoe is highly intelligent.

Coming up with a broad definition of intelligence raises five basic questions:

1. Is intelligence better viewed as a single ability or as a combination of different abilities?

2. Can a person be highly skilled in some areas of mental ability but well below average in others?

3. What is actually measured by intelligence tests? If, for example, a person scores well above or well below average on one of today's intelligence tests, how much does that tell us about the person's chances of doing well in school—or of being successful and happy in life?

4. Is intelligence related to creativity, and if so, how?

5. Assuming that intelligence is a meaningful concept and some people are more intelligent than others, what roles do heredity and environment play in explaining differences in intelligence?

A great deal of psychological research has been devoted to these questions, and many are still topics of considerable debate.

## Intelligence as a General Ability

One influential theory of intelligence was suggested many years ago by Charles Spearman (1863–1945). After applying sophisticated statistical analysis to scores on tests of many kinds of abilities—from reading comprehension to visualization of spatial relationships—Spearman concluded that one's test score on any task depends in part on an *s* **factor,** meaning a specific kind of skill for the task. But people with a high level of *s* factor on one task also tend to make high scores on other tasks—a phenomenon that Spearman believed could be explained only by the presence of a pervasive general mental ability that he called the *g* **factor,** or general intelligence (Spearman, 1927).

Psychologist L. L. Thurstone (1887–1955) rejected the idea of general intelligence and set out to discredit it. He too gave dozens of tests that measured individuals' abilities on a wide range of tasks. But despite his original aim, he wound up convinced that a *g* factor does affect many diverse skills. Thurstone (1944, 1948) proposed that intelligence consists of a general factor plus seven specific skills that he called **primary mental abilities.** Those skills are as follows:

1. *Verbal comprehension*—indicated by size of vocabulary, ability to read, and skill at understanding analogies and the meanings of proverbs. (Example: *How are cotton and wool alike?*)

2. *Word fluency*—the ability to think of words quickly, as in making rhymes or solving word puzzles. (Example: *In the next ten seconds, think of as many words as you can that have to do with a car.*)

3. *Number*—the ability to solve arithmetic problems and manipulate numbers. (Example: *If seven shirts cost $126.00, how much does one shirt cost?*)

4. *Space*—the ability to visualize spatial relationships, as in recognizing a design after it has been placed in a new context. (Example: *Using the four blocks illustrated here, make the design shown below.*)

5. *Associative memory*—the ability to memorize quickly, as in learning a list of paired words. (Example: *Memorize these pairs of words—dog-pencil, leaf-ocean, cup-pipe—so that if you hear one word of a given pair, you can remember the other.*)

6. *Perceptual speed*—the ability to grasp visual details quickly and observe similarities and differences between patterns and pictures. (Example: *What is missing from this picture?*)

7. *General reasoning*—skill at the kind of logical thinking that was described in Chapter 6. (For example, see Figure 6.11 on page 255.)

Studies of intelligence carried out in recent decades have tended to support Thurstone's view. Contemporary theories, discussed next, specify different types of intelligence but are consistent with earlier researchers' idea that intelligence is not best understood as a single characteristic.

## Intelligence as Multiple Abilities

Most of today's intelligence tests measure performance on the primary abilities proposed by Thurstone, at least indirectly. But people who are skillful at any one of

**Test Yourself**

**(a)** How did Spearman explain why a person who gets a high score on a test of reading comprehension also usually gets a high score on other tasks such as spatial visualization and memory?

(The answer is on page 278.)

*s* factor
A specific kind of skill for a particular task.

*g* factor
A pervasive general mental ability.

Primary mental abilities
The seven basic abilities that, in addition to g, make up intelligence, according to Thurstone.

those abilities do not always do well on others. The correlations between them are so low that some psychologists continue to question the existence of the *g* factor.

Prominent among these psychologists is Howard Gardner (Gardner, 1983; Gardner, 1999; Gardner & Walters, 1993). Gardner's **theory of multiple intelligences** has generated considerable interest over the past 2 decades, especially among educators (e.g., Beachner & Pickett, 2001)—although not all agree on its utility for education (Klein, 1997). Gardner's theory is not based on statistical analyses such as those conducted by Spearman and Thurstone. Instead, Gardner developed his theory by first setting criteria from biology, logic, developmental psychology, and traditional psychological research on intelligence, and then "combing" the literature for evidence of distinct and separate intelligences—both within and across cultures. Gardner's theory is therefore primarily conceptual.

Gardner originally specified seven intelligences; in his most recent extension of the theory, he suggested that there might be at least three more (1999). These are presented in Table 7.1.

**Theory of multiple intelligences**
Gardner's view that there are as many as ten distinct forms of intelligence.

The first seven are the ones first proposed in 1983; the last three are provisional. Note that for some endeavors facility in more than one intelligence is necessary.

---

### TABLE 7.1
### Gardner's Multiple Intelligences

| Form of Intelligence | Abilities | Examples |
|---|---|---|
| 1. Linguistic | Learning language and using it effectively | Highest in people such as lawyers, writers, and speakers |
| 2. Logical-mathematical | Analyzing problems logically and scientifically | Highest in mathematicians, logicians, and scientists |
| 3. Musical | Composing or performing music | Highest in musicians, of course, but also those who simply appreciate music |
| 4. Bodily-kinesthetic | Using gross- or fine-motor movements to do and make things | Highest in dancers and other performers, but also craftspersons, mechanics, and the like |
| 5. Spatial | Recognizing and manipulating spatial patterns, from wide to narrow | Highest in pilots and navigators, architects, sculptors, and surgeons—plus chess players |
| 6. Interpersonal | Understanding others and working effectively with them | Highest in salespersons, teachers, clinicians, and leaders of all kinds |
| 7. Intrapersonal | Understanding oneself, including one's desires, fears, and abilities | Highest in people who effectively make decisions and regulate their own life |
| 8. Naturalist | Recognizing and classifying flora, fauna, and other elements of the environment | Highest in people who care for or interact with other species, including naturalists, but also people who hunt, fish, farm—or cook |
| 9. Spiritual | Seeking to know and understand the metaphysical or achieving some understanding of truths that go beyond material concerns | Highest in people who are genuinely religious |
| 10. Existential | Placing oneself in the world and understanding where one is going in life and why | Perhaps highest in people who have attained Erikson's sense of identity and continue to elaborate it (page 342) |

*Source: Adapted from Gardner, 1999.*

| TABLE 7.2 |  |
|---|---|
| **Essentials of Sternberg's Successful Intelligence** |  |
| Definition of successful intelligence | The ability to achieve success in life<br>According to one's personal standards<br>Within one's sociocultural context |
| Types of processing skills contributing to successful intelligence | Analytical<br>Creative<br>Practical |
| Uses of processing skills for successful intelligence | Adaptation to environments<br>Shaping of environments<br>Selection of environments |
| Mechanisms for utilization of processing skills in successful intelligence | Capitalization on strengths<br>Correction of weaknesses<br>Compensation for weaknesses |

*From "The Theory of Successful Intelligence" by R. J. Sternberg. Review of General Psychology, 3, 292–316.*
*Copyright © 1999 American Psychological Association. Reprinted with permission.*

Note the parallels with the definition of intelligence by Wechsler on page 257.

Another view, advanced by Robert Sternberg, proposes a **triarchic** (three-part) **theory of intelligence.** The three parts are (1) *practical intelligence,* or the ability to adapt to and function in the particular physical and social environments in which we find ourselves; (2) *creative intelligence,* or the ability to deal with new tasks or situations; and (3) *analytical intelligence,* which is part of what is measured by the traditional intelligence tests discussed next (Sternberg, 1985; Sternberg, Castejon, Prieto, Hautamaeki, & Grigorenko, 2001). Sternberg has long contended that traditional intelligence tests measure samples of the third type of intelligence and perhaps to some extent the second type but little if any of the practical intelligence that is so important to everyday life in the real world. His theory is well grounded in both statistical analysis and cross-cultural research (e.g., Sternberg et al., 2001).

A prolific researcher and theorist, Sternberg has applied this view to an array of issues, such as understanding the relationship between intelligence and creativity (Sternberg & Lubart, 1993; Sternberg & O'Hara, 2000), what constitutes "common sense" (Sternberg, Wagner, Williams, & Horvath, 1995), how intelligence varies according to culture (Sternberg, 1999c), and how intelligence may have evolved—with emphasis on environmental adaptation (Sternberg & Kaufman, 2002). The essentials of Sternberg's recent formulation of what constitutes "successful" intelligence are presented in Table 7.2.

Both Gardner's and Sternberg's approaches remain "works in progress." Thus, it is not possible at present to say which—if either—will become the prevailing view.

**Triarchic theory of intelligence**
Sternberg's view that there are three basic intelligences: practical, creative, and analytical.

# INTELLIGENCE TESTS

Despite the work of Thurstone, Gardner, and Sternberg, for the most part the measurement of intellectual ability has been restricted primarily to assessing analytical skills and the sorts of knowledge a person might be expected to have accumulated at a given point in the life span—that is, domains that are important in formal education. Thus, when psychologists and educators talk about intelligence, they are most often referring to people's *scores* on tests of this kind of knowledge.

**FOCUS QUESTIONS**
- How did intelligence testing get started?
- How do intelligence tests work, and what exactly is IQ?
- What's the difference between aptitude and achievement?

Alfred Binet (1857–1911) pioneered the development of intelligence tests as part of an effort to identify less capable students and place them in separate classes or schools.

Bettmann Archive

**Intelligence test**
A way of measuring the various factors that make up intelligence, typically with emphasis on *g*.

**Stanford-Binet Intelligence Scales (SBIS)**
A well-known intelligence test that began with the work of Binet and Simon and was imported to the United States by Stanford researcher Terman.

**Individual test**
A test given to one person at a time by a trained examiner.

**Wechsler Preschool and Primary Scale of Intelligence (WPPSI)**
A test for children from about age $2\frac{1}{2}$ to just over age 7.

**Wechsler Intelligence Scale for Children (WISC)**
A test for the age range from 6 to just over 16.

**Wechsler Adult Intelligence Scale (WAIS)**
A test for ages 16 through 89.

# A Brief History of Intelligence Testing

**Intelligence tests** began as an attempt to solve a problem faced by Paris educators about a century ago, a problem that arose as a result of the adoption of compulsory education. Many classrooms were crowded, and less capable students were holding up the progress of more capable ones. One solution, it seemed, was to identify the children who lacked the abilities required by the standard curriculum and put them in separate classes or schools. But how could those students be identified?

The French government assigned this task to Alfred Binet and Theodore Simon (1873–1961). The researchers immediately realized that identifying the ill-equipped students could not safely be left to teachers. There was a danger that teachers would show favoritism toward children who were well behaved and would be biased against those who were troublemakers. There was also the question of whether teachers could correctly classify children who were quiet and shy and seemed incapable, but who in fact could do the work if they received extra encouragement to try (Cronbach, 1949).

Thus, Binet and Simon spent several years developing a test designed to measure each child's potential ability at school tasks objectively and to produce accurate scores regardless of the biases of those who gave the test or the personalities of those who took it. The first Binet-Simon Scale was released in France in 1905 and revised in 1908. In 1916, Lewis Terman (1877–1956) of Stanford University completed the first U.S. version, which he called the Stanford Revision of the Binet-Simon Scale. Over the years, the test has undergone several major revisions; it is now called the **Stanford-Binet Intelligence Scales (SBIS).** The latest edition was scheduled to be released by the time this textbook went to press.

The SBIS is an **individual test,** which means that an examiner administers it to one person at a time. It continues to be widely used for children (from about age 2) and adults (to over age 90), and most modern intelligence tests bear a noticeable resemblance to it.

The other most widely used, individually administered intelligence tests were developed by Wechsler, beginning in the 1930s. Unlike the SBIS, the Wechsler tests are designed to cover three age ranges. Each has undergone revisions and refinements over the years and is currently in its third edition. The **Wechsler Preschool and Primary Scale of Intelligence (WPPSI)** is designed for children from about age $2\frac{1}{2}$ to just over age 7, the **Wechsler Intelligence Scale for Children (WISC)** for the age range from 6 to just over 16, and the **Wechsler Adult Intelligence Scale (WAIS)** for ages 16 through 89.

# Intelligence Tests: Some Specifics

The SBIS use simple physical equipment such as a paper doll and various toys with younger children, and questions and more abstract problems for older children and adults. In addition to a Full Scale, or overall, intelligence score, the test also yields a Verbal intelligence score, based on language-related items such as vocabulary and verbal comprehension, and a Nonverbal intelligence score, based on functions such as visual perception and manipulation of objects. The five domains of intellectual functioning assessed by the SBIS are Reasoning, Knowledge, Working Memory, Visual, and Quantitative. Taken together, the three intelligence scores and the five domain scores cover Thurstone's primary mental abilities (page 259) thoroughly—although the arrangement and the labels are different. A sample of the kinds of test items used at various age levels is presented in Table 7.3.

In Terman's original Stanford Revision, an individual's score on the test was his or her **mental age (MA)**, divided by actual **chronological age (CA)** and multiplied by 100 to move the decimal place. The result was that person's **intelligence quotient (IQ).** That is,

$$IQ = \frac{MA}{CA} \times 100$$

Thus, a child of 10 who scored an MA of 10 would have an IQ of 100, or average intelligence. If the child scored an MA of 8, the IQ would be below average at 80. If the child scored an MA of 13, the IQ would be well above average at 130.

This approach made the most sense with children, whose intellectual development proceeds with a fairly orderly series of intellectual accomplishments at school, and it continued to be used with children for many years. But it was problematic with adults, whose intellectual development may proceed in many different directions. Thus, later editions of the SBIS switched to the **deviation IQ,** which was developed by Wechsler for his tests. (The term is derived from a statistic called the *standard deviation,* described in the Appendix.) In essence, a person's overall IQ or other score is determined by comparing the actual, or "raw," score on the test to the average for those of other people in the same age range. The percentages of people who score at different levels on the SBIS are presented in Table 7.4. (Bear in mind that the classifications used are arbitrary and should not be thought of as rigid labels.)

The Wechsler tests are also widely used, perhaps more so than the SBIS for older children and adults. As with the current SBIS, a person receives a Full Scale IQ, a Verbal IQ, and a Performance (nonverbal) IQ—an arrangement that originated in Wechsler's work. The materials and items differ across the three Wechsler tests, although the structure is much the same. On the current WAIS, for example, Verbal IQ is assessed by subtests on general knowledge and information, memory span, vocabulary, arithmetic, social comprehension, ability to detect similarities between concepts, and ability to concentrate—related to Thurstone's factors 1, 2,

**Mental age (MA)**
In the original formula for IQ, a person's score on the IQ test.

**Chronological age (CA)**
A person's actual age.

**Intelligence quotient (IQ)**
A numerical value assigned to an individual as a result of an intelligence test. Originally, IQ was defined as MA/CA × 100; later, it was defined as the deviation IQ.

**Deviation IQ**
A numerical value for IQ, determined by comparing an individual's raw score to those of others in the same age range.

---

TABLE 7.3

### Items Similar to Those on the Stanford-Binet Intelligence Scales

| | |
|---|---|
| Two years old | On a large paper doll, points out the hair, mouth, feet, ear, nose, hands, and eyes. |
| | When shown a tower built of four blocks, builds one like it. |
| Four years old | Fills in the missing word when asked, "Brother is a boy; sister is a _____" and "In daytime it is light; at night it is _____." |
| Nine years old | Answers correctly when examiner says, "In an old graveyard in Spain they have discovered a small skull which they believe to be that of Christopher Columbus when he was about ten years old. What is foolish about that?" |
| | Answers correctly when asked, "Tell me the name of a color that rhymes with head." "Tell me a number that rhymes with tree." |
| Adult | Can describe the difference between laziness and idleness, poverty and misery, character and reputation. |
| | Answers correctly when asked, "Which direction would you have to face so your right would be toward the north?" |

As these examples show, the items asked of very young children do not demand fluency in language. The items increase in difficulty, particularly in matters of language and reasoning, at higher age levels.

Administering the Stanford-Binet Intelligence Scale to thousands of people has shown that one person in a hundred scores over 139 and is classified as *very superior* or a "genius." Three in a hundred score below 70 and are classified as *mentally retarded* (if they also meet the other criteria discussed in Chapter 10). Almost half of all people have IQs in the *average* range of 90 to 109.

**TABLE 7.4**
**Ranges of IQ and Numbers of People Found at Each Level**

| IQ | Classification | Percentage of People |
|---|---|---|
| Over 139 | Very superior | 1 |
| 120–139 | Superior | 11 |
| 110–119 | High average | 18 |
| 90–109 | Average | 46 |
| 80–89 | Low average | 15 |
| 70–79 | Borderline | 6 |
| Below 70 | Mentally retarded | 3 |

**Group test**
A test—typically a pencil-and-paper test—given to more than one person at the same time.

**Aptitude test**
A test intended to measure a person's ability to learn new skills or perform unfamiliar tasks.

**Achievement test**
A test that measures how much learning or skill a person has acquired.

3, 5, and 7. Performance IQ is assessed by subtests on recognizing what's missing in pictures, arranging pictures in a logical order, copying designs with blocks, working puzzles, substituting unfamiliar symbols for digits, matching geometric shapes, and searching for certain symbols in groups. These are closely related to Thurstone's factors 4, 6, and 7.

As noted earlier, the SBIS and the Wechsler tests are individual tests. The advantage of individual tests is that the examiner can readily determine whether the results are being influenced by such factors as poor vision, ill health, or lack of motivation. Their disadvantage, of course, is that they cannot conveniently be used to test large numbers of people. **Group tests** of intelligence date to the Army Alpha, which was used as a quick screen for recruits in World Wars I and II. Contemporary group intelligence tests are used primarily in elementary, middle, and high schools as a quick but reasonably accurate way of assessing entire classes or schools.

In one performance item on the WISC, the child is asked to copy a design, using blocks of different colors and shapes. The examiner notes whether the child completes the task as well as how long the child takes to do so.

© Lew Merrim

## Aptitude versus Achievement

Intelligence tests have also been called **aptitude tests** because, in addition to certain other aspects of intellectual functioning, they measure a person's ability to learn new skills or perform unfamiliar tasks. Aptitude tests—in theory—are different from **achievement tests,** which measure how much learning or skill a person has acquired at a given point in time. In practice, however, there is always considerable overlap between general aptitude tests, such as those for intelligence, and achievement tests, such as those that assess progress in school. Each, for example, assesses language skills and various types of knowledge. The main difference is that intelligence tests attempt to be more general, whereas academic achievement tests are more focused on specific skills and knowledge acquired at school.

Currently, academic achievement tests are used extensively in evaluating the quality of school programs—local news media regularly feature articles on whether schools are

© Jose Luis Pelaez, Inc./CORBIS

The Scholastic Assessment Test is widely used as a criterion for college admission. However, it has been shown that SAT scores are not good predictors of academic performance beyond the first year of college.

improving or declining based on the average scores of their students. Among the most widely used achievement tests is the Stanford Achievement Test Series, currently in its ninth edition. Language and math skills are emphasized, as they are on most academic achievement tests.

The college entrance exam you may have taken is also an achievement test. Foremost among such tests is the Scholastic Assessment Test (SAT)—formerly known as the Scholastic Aptitude Test, which was something of a misnomer. The SAT yields a Verbal score and a Mathematics score, which are added to produce an overall score that students hope exceeds the minimum set by some colleges for admission. If you go on to graduate school, you will probably take yet another achievement test, such as the relatively general Graduate Record Examination (GRE), or a more specific one, such as one designed for advanced study in business, law, or medicine.

> **Test Yourself**
>
> **(b)** What is the essential difference in intent between tests of intelligence and tests of achievement?
>
> (The answer is on page 278.)

# WHAT INTELLIGENCE TESTS DO AND DO NOT TELL US

The first thing to note about what IQ test scores tell us is that they measure only *current* intellectual functioning in certain areas. Contrary to what many people believe, they do not measure general intellectual *potential*, although, as noted earlier, they do predict to some extent a person's ability to learn new things. Another point is that heredity and environment can conspire to set limits on intelligence, but most people's intelligence as measured by IQ can vary across a wide range—as discussed later in the chapter. It can also change

> **FOCUS QUESTIONS**
> - Is there a relationship between IQ and success in school?
> - Does IQ predict occupational status and success?
> - Does IQ predict success in life?
> - Is there a relationship among intelligence, IQ, and creativity?

over time, for better or for worse, depending on whether or not you continue to learn and grow by exercising your intellectual skills (Ceci, 1999). Many parents react with joy if they learn that their child has an above-average IQ, or with disappointment and sadness if their child is below average. Both are overreactions; nothing in life is as simple as a score on a test.

Western societies and certain other societies value intelligence and are highly competitive. Given these two characteristics, the significance that such societies attach to IQ test scores is not surprising. And IQ tests have many legitimate uses, but intelligence test scores are by no means infallible predictors of achievement or success in life.

## IQ and Accomplishment in School

Wechsler (1975) pointed out that the word *intelligence* represents a value judgment. We call people intelligent when they have qualities that we ourselves—or our society as a whole or the part of it in which we live—consider resourceful and worthwhile. Of necessity, many industrialized societies admire fluency in language and talent for mathematics and science. The most intelligent people, according to the consensus, are those who can analyze facts, reason about them logically, and express their conclusions in convincing terms. These are the very qualities that are associated with doing well in formal schooling—and as it turns out, intelligence tests measure academic abilities better than they do anything else.

Intelligence tests cannot hope to measure an individual's "capacity to understand the world," as Wechsler (1975) put it. Nevertheless, IQ is a good indication of how well a person will do in school. Many studies of the relationship between IQ and grades in school—from elementary school to the university level—have found correlations ranging from .40 to .80 (e.g., Ceci, 1991).

IQ is a good predictor of school grades, and the reverse is also true: The extent and quality of an individual's school experience affects IQ (Ceci, 1999). This is because schooling has a direct impact on accumulation of knowledge and development of the cognitive skills that underlie performance on most IQ tests. In taking an IQ test, a person has the opportunity to apply information gained in the classroom and to use test-taking skills honed through academic experience—for example, the ability to categorize and manipulate information, to focus on questions posed, and to monitor and time one's own responses to questions, all of which can affect the test outcome (Ceci, 1991).

Scores on intelligence tests also depend on many personality characteristics—for example, cooperativeness, attention, persistence, and ability to sit still (Scarr, 1981). Motivation is especially important. Therefore, it is not surprising that children in middle-income homes, who are strongly encouraged to take pride in their mastery of reading, writing, spelling, and arithmetic, make higher scores on the average than those in lower-income homes, who tend to be less motivated toward academic success.

The relationship between IQ and school achievement stems from Binet's basic aim in designing the original test items—to assess how well an individual student was progressing. It would perhaps be more fitting to say that his test and its modern counterparts measure an individual's "AQ," or academic quotient, rather than IQ, or intelligence quotient. Because the SBIS and the Wechsler tests are called measures of intelligence, rather than something more modest, the quest for more comprehensive tests continues.

## IQ, Occupational Status, and Success on the Job

Although IQ is a good predictor of success in school, there is some question as to how well it predicts anything else. What about jobs, for example? Does a high IQ mean that you are destined for a high-level occupation and a low IQ that you are better suited for a low-level job?

A massive body of evidence bearing on these questions comes from a study of the thousands of men who took the Army's group intelligence test during World War II (Harrell & Harrell, 1945). The results indicate that there is a relationship between IQ and occupation—but often less than might be expected. The average IQ of such professionals as accountants and engineers was around 120, and the average for truck drivers and miners was below 100. But there was a wide range of IQs in every occupation.

One explanation for these findings undoubtedly is the amount of education the men in the study had received. Of two people with equal IQs, the one who can go to college may become an accountant or engineer. The other, unable for some reason to go to college or even complete high school, may have to settle for a job with lower prestige. Many studies have shown that education is a much better predictor of occupational status than is IQ (e.g., see Scullin, Peters, Williams, & Ceci, 2000).

In general, college graduates have better paying and more challenging jobs than high school graduates, who in turn have better jobs than those who have not completed high school. The relationship between IQ and job status, such as it is, seems to occur chiefly because people with higher IQs generally manage to acquire more education, barring such circumstances as illness or financial problems. Performance and advancement in one's job and career, however, frequently depend not so much on IQ level as on the kind of practical intelligence proposed by Sternberg—which involves using an appropriate style in thinking about issues, getting along with people, and grappling with problems effectively. Individuals with high practical intelligence can manage to reconcile and integrate a number of goals simultaneously—an ability that often comes from down-to-earth, on-the-job experience rather than academic knowledge.

## Does IQ Foretell Achievement in Life?

One of the most important questions about IQ is the extent to which it relates not just to classroom grades or choice of occupation but to successful living. This is a difficult question to answer: Success in life is an elusive concept. It can hardly be defined in terms of income, for many people do not have the motivation or opportunity to make a great deal of money. Other types of success—efficiency and pleasure in one's job, good human relations, happiness and well-being—are hard to measure.

One longitudinal study has led many psychologists to consider a high IQ to be a great asset in achieving success of any kind. The study involved a group of 1,500 California schoolchildren who qualified as mentally gifted, with IQs of 140 or more, putting them in the top 1% of the population. The study was begun in 1921 by Terman and continued by him, and later by others, as the children grew into adulthood.

As children, Terman's participants were superior in many respects other than IQ. They were above average in height (by about an inch), weight, and appearance. They were well adjusted and showed superiority in social activity and leadership. In later life, despite some exceptions, the group was generally successful. A large proportion went to college, achieved above-average and often brilliant records, and went on to make important contributions in fields ranging from medicine and law to literature and from business administration to government service. They also seemed to display a high level of physical and mental health, a lower than average death rate, and a lower than average divorce rate (Terman, 1954). Most of these findings continued in middle adulthood, although a small but significant percentage were not as happy or successful as they had been earlier in life (Shurkin, 1992). In their 80s, many felt that they had not lived up to the potential implied by being a member of a "gifted" study, but those who had remained active and retained good health were still faring well (Holahan & Holahan, 1999; Holahan, Holahan, & Wonacott, 2001). The study continues.

## PSYCHOLOGY IN THE LAB AND IN LIFE

# Why Some Smart People Fail

We all know seemingly intelligent people who consistently fail at what they do. As Sternberg has pointed out, many people come into the world with remarkable intellectual gifts, but because of other factors that get in their way, they find that their native abilities are of little consequence. Here's a list of 20 such factors (Sternberg, 1986):

1. Lack of motivation
2. Lack of impulse control—for example, "shooting from the hip" with the first solution to a problem instead of thinking about other possibilities
3. Lack of perseverance
4. Using the wrong abilities—that is, not capitalizing on strengths
5. Inability to translate thought into action
6. Unwillingness to apply oneself to produce a tangible product
7. Inability to complete tasks and to follow through
8. Failure to take the initiative—usually out of unwillingness to make a commitment
9. Fear of failure
10. Procrastination
11. Blaming others—or oneself—for no reason
12. Excessive self-pity
13. Excessive dependency
14. Wallowing in personal problems
15. Distractibility and lack of concentration
16. Spreading oneself too thin or too thick
17. Inability to delay gratification
18. Inability or unwillingness to see the forest for the trees
19. Not applying the right abilities in the right situation
20. Too little self-confidence—or too much

Undoubtedly, you can think of other factors to add to this list. In any case, few would argue with Sternberg's view that what really matters is not so much intelligence but how intelligence is managed. Our goal, he maintains, should be to realize fully whatever abilities each of us has.

---

**Creativity**
**The ability to solve new problems or fashion new products in one or more domains of activity; the products must be adaptive.**

Some researchers have concluded that IQ bears on success only to the extent that an IQ in the lower ranges may make it impossible for a person to complete high school, perform successfully in college, or qualify for certain demanding jobs. The issue of real-life success in relation to IQ is discussed further in Psychology in the Lab and in Life (above).

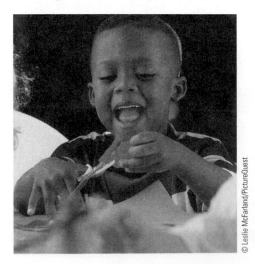

Although creativity is difficult to define, it is clear that a stimulating environment encourages creative activity.

© Leslie McFarland/PictureQuest

## Intelligence and Creativity

Although we can all point to individuals who would be universally regarded as creative, the exact nature of creativity is elusive. As in the case of intelligence, people tend to use the term casually—in contexts as diverse as schools, industry, advertising, and the arts—as if there were a common understanding of its meaning. Nevertheless, most people would agree on a definition of **creativity** as the ability to solve new problems or fashion new products in one or more domains of activity (Gardner, 1988; 1999). We might add that "a broad definition of creativity recognizes that creative ideas need to be not only novel but adaptive in some sense" (Sternberg & O'Hara, 2000).

There would appear to be considerable overlap between intelligence and creativity in general (Gardner, 1999; Sternberg & O'Hara, 2000), but the amount of overlap depends on the form the creativity takes. Among painters and sculptors, for example, there seems to be little if any correlation between intelligence as assessed by IQ scores and creative ability (Barron, 1968). Among creative writers, the relationship between creativity levels and intelligence test scores is modest. Most fields seem to require what has been called a "threshold" IQ, which is higher in the sciences than in literature or music. But above that minimum requirement, creativity depends less on intelligence than on other factors such as the motivation to sacrifice other pursuits in favor of the creative endeavor (Sternberg & O'Hara, 2000).

A frequent characteristic of those whose lives are marked by creative pursuits is the quality of their motivation. Creative individuals tend to display **intrinsic motivation**—that is, the incentive to pursue an activity because it is inherently compelling, enjoyable, and satisfying. They are less influenced by **extrinsic motivation**—the desire for tangible rewards offered by others (Amabile, 1989). Later in life, creative individuals tend to stand out from others not only in the quality of their output but in the style with which they approach their work. They emerge as more independent, self-confident, and unconventional. They also display a greater sense of alertness, ambition, and commitment to work (Gardner, 1988)—characteristics that are not necessarily tied to traditional measures of IQ.

> **Intrinsic motivation**
> The incentive to pursue an activity because that activity is inherently compelling, enjoyable, and satisfying.
>
> **Extrinsic motivation**
> The desire for tangible rewards for pursuing an activity.

# HEREDITY, ENVIRONMENT, AND INTELLIGENCE

Like many other human characteristics, intelligence is influenced by heredity as well as environment. Most psychologists agree that the two forces work in concert—a child's inherited predispositions *interact* with environmental factors to shape the development of intelligence. Although there is still some disagreement on the relative contribution of each, theorist Robert Plomin has pointed out that where intelligence is concerned psychology has taken a new direction, away from the battle over heredity and environment: The emphasis has shifted to identifying genes that contribute to the various cognitive abilities (Plomin & Petrill, 1997). This, along with more sophisticated research on how environment operates to influence intelligence, may eventually resolve the nature-nurture question entirely.

> **FOCUS QUESTIONS**
> * What evidence is there for the relative roles of heredity and environment in determining intelligence?
> * How do heredity and environment interact to determine intelligence?
> * What relationship is there between intelligence and ethnicity, and why does it occur?

Psychologists are now generally content to go with an estimate of 50-50 for the relative contributions of heredity and environment—awaiting firm evidence that might change this balance. That is, for the time being, the controversy seems to have abated, and the lines are no longer clearly drawn (Plomin & DeFries, 1999; Sternberg & Grigorenko, 1997). An important problem is that such estimates are based on the traditional "additive" view of the relative roles of heredity and environment, instead of the "interactive" view discussed in Chapter 1 and elsewhere in the text. That is, genes set the stage, but from there intellectual development is a function of a complex give-and-take between what you might be capable of neurologically and the multitude of environmental influences to which you are exposed from conception on—including nutrition, diseases, favorable or unfavorable learning experiences, and what you as a thinking being make of it all.

However, this view is relatively recent, and ways of describing the full complexities of heredity-environment interactions are still evolving. Here, we review the issues raised in the last several decades and some conclusions that may contribute to a more comprehensive understanding.

> **Test Yourself**
>
> **(c)** Which do traditional IQ tests predict better—the grades a child will get in school or the success a child will attain in life?
>
> **(d)** Mark insists that you have to be extremely intelligent to be creative. Leon disagrees. Who is right?
>
> **(e)** If, in her work, Connie is driven mainly by a yearning for praise and higher pay, is she likely to be creative?
>
> (The answers are on page 278.)

## Family Resemblances in IQ

Many studies have indicated that the more closely related two people are—that is, the greater their similarity in genetic makeup—the more similar their IQs are likely to be (DeFries, Plomin, & LaBuda, 1987). Several such studies are summarized in Figure 7.1. Note the bar showing the relationships found between parents and children: The correlations range up and down from a midpoint of about .40. The average of correlations between brothers and sisters reared together (with their parents) is a bit higher, at about .50. Children of the same parents, even when separated and brought up in different homes, still display a moderate correlation, with the figures clustering around .35. Identical twins, who have inherited the same genes, show very high correlations when brought up together, and impressively high correlations even when reared apart from each other (having been separated because of adoption).

Much of the case for the nature side of the debate rests on these data—especially on correlations between identical twins reared in different homes. If people with virtually the same genes show a correlation of somewhere between .62 and .77 even when they grow up in different environments, the influence of heredity on IQ would appear to be strong indeed.

The correlations, however, do not convince those on the nurture side of the debate. The figures on identical twins who grew up in different homes, for example, have been challenged on a number of grounds—including the small number of participants (twins separated at birth are difficult to find), the kinds of intelligence tests that were used, and possible bias in the way the tests were administered and scored. Leon Kamin, who has examined the studies carefully, also concluded that the environments in which the twins grew up were probably more similar than the term "reared apart" would imply. For instance, when adoption agencies separate twins, they tend to place them in homes that are similar with regard to parents' education and income level. This tendency toward similarity in environment might be just as responsible as the identical genes for the high correlations in IQ (Kamin, 1981). Moreover, as various theorists have also pointed out, even when identical twins are separated at birth, they still share the same environment during the prenatal period—during which nutrition, health, and other factors can directly affect brain development.

The nurture side has also pointed to correlations averaging about .25 and ranging up to .50 between adoptive parents and their adopted children, to whom they were genetically unrelated. Note in Figure 7.1 the bar for unrelated children who were brought up together, usually through adoption into the same home. One study found a zero correlation for such children—the figure that would be expected for unrelated people chosen at random—but other findings have ranged as high

**FIGURE 7.1 Family resemblances in IQ. The bars show the range of correlations— from lowest to highest—found in various comparisons of IQ between genetic relatives and also between unrelated people who lived in the same home. The correlation between unrelated people who grew up in different homes should, of course, be zero.**
*Erlenmeyer-Kimling & Jarvik, 1963; Jencks, 1972; Walker & Emory, 1985.*

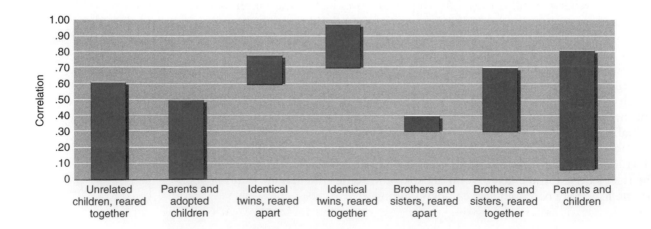

© Mary Kate Denny/Pho oEdit

Studies have found strong correlations in intelligence between identical twins, even when the twins were raised in different homes.

as about .60. The latter values clearly favor the influence of environment on IQ (Walker & Emory, 1985).

One widely accepted suggestion emerging from the various studies is that inherited genes set upper and lower limits on an individual's possible intelligence and environment then determines where within this range the score will actually fall. That is, genetic endowment sets a *range of reaction* for intellectual functioning (Gottesman, 1963b; Hunt, 1988), a principle that remains especially useful in understanding how heredity and environment may interact at different levels. If a child is born with a severe neurological impairment related to cognitive functioning, the range of reaction is narrow and environment plays only a small role—special training and environmental enrichment may benefit the child somewhat, but the child will always be severely to profoundly mentally retarded (see Chapter 10). In contrast, if a child is born genetically "normal," or average, environmental influences play a much larger role—perhaps to the extent of 20 to 25 IQ points (Scarr-Salapatek, 1971b). That is, the child might develop an IQ in the mid to high 80s if reared in a deprived environment or an IQ of over 110 if reared under optimal conditions—a dramatic difference. Finally, if a child is genetically superior, the range of reaction is broadest; environment can make the difference between being below-average to average and being a genius. In other words, environmental factors such as malnutrition and early intellectual deprivation can still "cancel out" the child's genetic potential; at the other extreme, such a child can benefit most when the environment is at its best.

## Further Interactions Between Heredity and Environment

There is some evidence that not all the components of intelligence as measured by IQ tests are equally influenced by heredity. Among identical twins, for example, a greater similarity in verbal than in nonverbal skills has been found (N. L. Segal, 1985), suggesting that the former are more heavily influenced by genetic factors. One idea is that many genetic traits influence the environmental experiences that a child will encounter. Sandra Scarr has suggested that these influences take three different forms. First, parents who are themselves intelligent, and therefore likely to pass along to their offspring the genes associated with a high IQ, are also likely to provide a favorable environment. Second, children who have inherited favorable genes, for intelligence as well as for appearance and temperament, are more likely to evoke favorable responses from their environment. And third, as children grow older, they take an active part in creating their own environments—and in choosing what aspects of the environment they will respond to and learn from. Thus, their inherited tendencies are related to their environmental encounters, which in turn enhance the original tendencies in reciprocal fashion (Scarr, 1981; 1988).

Some psychologists have challenged Scarr's view of the importance of genetic factors. For example, Diana Baumrind has contended that the role of genes is not fixed and that the IQ level any individual can reach depends on how facilitating the environment is. Citing research suggesting that genetic inheritance has a much greater degree of "plasticity" than was once believed, Baumrind has argued that the functional intelligence of some children who have very low IQ scores can be greatly improved by a suitably enriching environment (Baumrind, 1993).

Thus, the psychological environment is important. For example, middle-income mothers tend to spend more time than lower-income mothers talking to their young children, playing with them, and encouraging them to learn and to solve problems on their own. A high correlation of .76 has been found between children's IQs and parents' scores on a scale that measures how much encouragement and help they offer in using language and increasing vocabulary, how much motivation and reward they provide for intellectual accomplishment, and what opportunities for learning they provide in the home, including personal help, books, and other forms of stimulation (Wolf, 1963).

In turn, IQs change. This was demonstrated in a study done over four decades ago in which the progress of 140 girls and boys was carefully followed over a 10-year period, from the time they were 2 years old until they were 12 (Sontag, Baker, & Nelson, 1958). Intelligence tests given every year revealed that half of the children experienced changes in IQ either upward or downward, changes that in some cases reached striking proportions. Individual records from this study note that one child's IQ rose from about 110 to 160, and another's dropped from 140 to 110. The study found some other differences between the children who showed increases and those who showed declines. The children whose IQs went up were more independent, competitive, and likely to take the lead in conversation. They showed stronger motivation to master intellectual problems, worked harder in school, and persisted at even the most difficult tasks.

Thus, intelligence as measured by IQ is by no means a constant, unchanging trait like a person's fingerprints, and a score achieved on any given day is by no means an unerring guide to the future. This should be a warning to parents and teachers not to give up on a child who has a low score on an intelligence test or to expect too much from a child who has a high score. "Although genetic endowment will always influence the acquisition of intellectual skills, the environments and opportunities we create for children do make an important difference" (Weinberg, 1989).

For more on intelligence, IQ, and change, see the Life Span Perspective on page 273.

## Intelligence and Ethnicity

In 1969, educator Arthur Jensen launched an extended and heated controversy with his claim—based on statistical analysis—that intelligence as measured by IQ is 80% inherited and only 20% a result of environment. Fanning the flames were

# Are People Becoming More Intelligent?

Intelligence is among the more fluid characteristics of individuals; unlike certain other qualities, such as temperament, it tends to increase throughout most of the life span. If we define intelligence as the ability to understand the world and the resourcefulness to cope with its challenges, it is clear that over time, as a person accumulates more education and experience, she or he will gain in intelligence. In older adulthood, as you will see in Chapter 11, there is a gradual decline in what is known as *fluid intelligence,* the ability to deal with new problems that require such skills as perception and memory span. However, older people can function well using their *crystallized intelligence,* employing an accumulated body of information to make judgments and solve problems. This is sometimes referred to as wisdom.

Sometime during their school years, most children are given an intelligence test of some kind (see the descriptions in the chapter). The resulting score is converted into an intelligence quotient, or IQ. Notwithstanding research discussed in the text, for most individuals IQ remains relatively stable through adolescence and adulthood, and IQ is a factor in selecting students for special programs ranging from remedial classes to gifted-and-talented programs.

But if intelligence increases through the life span, why do IQ scores remain relatively stable? A fourth-grader who achieves an IQ between 120 and 125 will probably have a similar score when retested in junior high school. The reason is that IQ scores are age-adjusted: An individual's IQ at a given age is determined by comparing his or her score on the test to those of other people in the same age range.

Despite the relative stability of IQ scores, a person's IQ can increase in adolescence and young adulthood as a result of high-quality education (including the special programs just mentioned), as well as continued reading, mentally challenging work, and the like. Like the body, the mind responds positively to exercise.

Interestingly, average raw scores on IQ tests have risen in recent decades. It's not clear, however, whether this means that the overall level of intelligence in the population is actually increasing. Robert Howard (2001) has attempted to answer this question by examining several real-world indicators for evidence of a general rise in intelligence. He has discovered several significant trends:

- The prevalence of mild mental retardation in the United States and elsewhere has been declining steadily.

- Players of various intellectual games, such as chess, bridge, and go, are reaching high performance levels at earlier ages.

- Scientific productivity (measured by numbers of journal articles published and patents awarded) has risen greatly.

On the other hand, Howard found that high school teachers with 20 years of experience perceive that their students' average intelligence and ability to do school work have not risen. They note, however, that this may be due to a decline in student motivation.

There are other possible explanations for the rise in IQ scores besides an overall increase in intelligence. It is argued, for example, that IQ gains may be due in part to faster cognitive development, coinciding with accelerated physical development resulting from better diet and health (Flieller, 1999). Another explanation is improved test-taking ability; children who get a lot of practice in taking tests can add several points to their scores (Kulik, Kulik, & Bangert, 1984). Moreover, as we have seen, intelligence involves more than the abilities tested by IQ tests. Some individuals who do not score well on tests are able to function quite well at the normal tasks of everyday life, such as learning language and social skills, even if they do less well at school learning.

In sum, IQ is a useful measure for some purposes, but it is an imperfect instrument for evaluating general intelligence. As for whether the overall intelligence of the population is increasing, the indicators identified by Howard suggest that this may indeed be the case, although further study is warranted.

his contentions that the genetic pool of U.S. blacks was intellectually inferior to that of U.S. whites and that early intervention programs for disadvantaged black children were therefore a waste of time and money (e.g., see Jensen, 1969). This claim produced a torrent of rebuttals and outright rebukes by other researchers, along with something of a backlash against considering any genetic contributions to intelligence (Kamin, 1974). But Jensen persisted in his views (e.g., see Nyborg & Jensen, 2000).

At the time, it was widely recognized—based on research in the 1950s and 1960s—that U.S. blacks scored on average 10 to 15 points lower than U.S whites

The intelligence of any given individual is strongly affected by the environment in which he or she is raised. A deprived environment can severely limit intellectual development; a more positive environment can facilitate it.

on intelligence tests (e.g., see Reynolds & Gutkin, 1981), so it took some years for Jensen's ideas to be discredited. Among those who had the final word were Jeanne Brooks-Gunn and colleagues (1996), who convincingly made the case that "adjustments for economics and social differences in the lives of black and white children all but eliminate differences in the IQ scores between these two groups." To be fair, we must note that prominent developmental researcher Sandra Scarr (1998) said that Jensen's research has always been characterized by honesty and integrity. This is striking, in view of the professional rejection he has experienced for many years—but it does not make his conclusions any more credible.

The "test-score gap" between blacks and whites cited by Jensen later narrowed considerably, although it still remains and is a matter of concern (Williams & Ceci, 1997). It appears that the progress of a significant number of black children—along with children of other ethnicities—is hampered by unstimulating home environments, failure and criticism in the early years of school, or both. For example, compared to whites, a larger percentage of black children live in low-income homes, and they may become so discouraged that they never reach their full potential. Their environments can lead them to make low scores on intelligence tests, in turn convincing both them and their teachers to have lower expectations. The low expectations produce apathy toward displaying the skills measured by the tests.

It is important to bear in mind that although environments in lower-income homes are often unstimulating, this is by no means a rule. Lack of money and other resources does not necessarily result in a poor intellectual environment, and it is quite possible for parents or other caregivers to compensate by spending quality time with their children, providing toys and educational tools from meager materials, and so on. Poverty sets the stage for a deprived home environment—including malnutrition, which can have pronounced effects on brain and intellectual development—but by no means guarantees it.

It is also important to keep in mind that both blacks and whites show wide and overlapping distributions of individual differences in IQ. Even if statistical information indicates some average difference between any ethnicities, it is never possible to make an accurate statement about the intelligence of an individual standing before you based on this information. To do so is to display prejudice.

**Test Yourself**

**(f)** Is it possible to say that either heredity or environment is primarily responsible for a person's level of intelligence?

(The answer is on page 278.)

# PSYCHOLOGICAL TESTING— THE SCIENTIFIC WAY

There remain many unanswered questions about the origins and elements of intelligence—as well as about personality, as discussed in Chapter 9. But practicing psychologists must deal with these topics even in the absence of definitive answers. Thus, it is all the more important that psychological tests of intelligence and personality meet certain scientific criteria. These include reliability, validity, and standardization.

**FOCUS QUESTIONS**

- What criteria must a psychological test satisfy to be a good one?

- How are these criteria assessed?

## Requirement 1: Reliability

To see why **reliability** of psychological tests is important, consider an analogy between a test and the thermometer that senses the level of heat in an oven. If the thermometer is reliable—that is, if it gives the same reading every time for the same amount of heat and passes the information along to the control system that turns the heat on and off—the cook can count on casseroles and pies to come out of the oven in good shape. If the thermometer is unreliable, reading 300 degrees on one occasion and 400 degrees on the next, it will cause the heat to go on and off inappropriately and allow the temperature to vary widely. In this case, the food is likely to be disappointing or perhaps even inedible.

Just as a good thermometer produces consistent temperature readings, a good test produces consistent scores from one testing occasion to another. One way of assessing this is to evaluate *test-retest reliability:* Give the test to a large group of people twice, then correlate their scores on the two occasions. A high positive correlation indicates good reliability; a low or negative correlation means that the test is useless. A better method is to assess *split-half reliability,* which—if the format of the test allows it—can be accomplished on a single testing occasion. Here, for example, each person's scores on all the odd-numbered items might be correlated with her or his scores on all the even-numbered ones. Again, the correlation should be positive and relatively high.

Split-half reliability is better than test-retest reliability for several reasons. When two testing occasions are required, some examinees may improve from one testing occasion to the next, but others may not. The examinees may also differ in alertness, motivation, and the like across the two testing occasions. In each case, the numbers for reliability may be lowered in ways that have nothing to do with the test itself.

**Reliability**
A criterion for good tests, requiring that they provide results that are consistent from one testing occasion to the next.

## Requirement 2: Validity

Another important requirement is **validity.** That is, a test should actually measure what it is intended to measure. There are a number of ways to determine this. Common sense is one; the items in the test should bear a meaningful relationship to what is being measured. Such a relationship is called *face validity.* Giving a prospective word-processing employee a test on a manual typewriter has some face validity because of the keystrokes required for each task, but there the resemblance ends. Giving the test on a computer has much better face validity.

But common sense is not enough. A better way is to assess what is called *concurrent validity,* which involves looking at correlations between scores on a new

**Validity**
A criterion for good tests, requiring that they measure what they are intended to measure.

test and scores on some other measure of the same characteristic. The other measure might be a prior, well-established test. Or, in the case of intelligence, the new test might be administered to a group of students and the scores correlated with their current grade point averages. In the latter case, remember that intelligence tests were originally designed to assess academic ability and progress. This is still what they do best, as discussed earlier. Test designers therefore expect to find at least a moderate positive correlation between intelligence test scores and school performance.

Another way to assess validity is to observe the behavior of people who have taken the test and determine whether they perform as their test scores indicate. This relationship is called *predictive validity*. Predictive validity is used to assess the validity of a college entrance exam. Scores on the test are later correlated with examinees' grade point averages in college, with test designers hoping for a moderate positive correlation. The standard is a bit lower in the case of entrance exams because no "paper and pencil" test of what a high school student *can* do is capable of predicting what the student *will* do after the often-dramatic transition to college and the life changes that ensue. That is, such tests cannot assess the extent to which a student will remain motivated to attend classes and study or instead cut classes and party.

**Test Yourself**

**(g)** Is it possible for a test to be high in reliability but low in validity?

(The answer is on page 278.)

## Requirement 3: Standardization

**Standardization**
Criteria for good tests, requiring that they be objective, have carefully defined procedures for administration, and have a comparison population.

**Standardization** refers to two key issues in psychological testing. The first is *objectivity*—tests should provide results that aren't affected by the opinions or biases of the examiner who administers and scores it or by the manner in which the examiner gives the test. Binet and Simon's intelligence test was created in an attempt to obtain a more objective measure of a child's ability to benefit from schooling than could be provided by the opinion of the teacher. To achieve objectivity—as well as to improve reliability and validity—good psychological tests include detailed instructions on how to administer the test and how to score the results. Deviations or errors by the examiner can cause significant inaccuracy in an examinee's score, and giving some tests requires extensive supervised training.

As for the other key issue in standardization, first imagine this situation. A psychologist has created a 100-question test that can be given and scored objectively. The test has proved to be reliable, and it seems to be a reasonable and valid measure of people's ability to read and comprehend. A trained examiner gives the test to a student, who answers 60 of the items correctly. What does this score of 60 tell the examiner? By itself, not very much. The examiner cannot know, after giving the test to a single person, whether a score of 60 indicates exceptional aptitude, very low aptitude, or something in between.

Thus, the results of a test are generally not very useful unless they can be compared with the scores of other people through the establishment of *norms*. Before most tests are considered ready for use, they are administered to a large and representative sample of the population of people who will take them. An analysis is then carried out to determine norms, or the numbers of people scoring at all the possible levels from highest to lowest—with adjustments, as necessary, so that for most tests the resulting distribution of scores closely resembles the normal distribution (shown in Figure 1.2 on page 14).

Using tables provided by the test designers, an examiner can translate a person's raw score on, say, an IQ test into a score that corresponds to the units of measurement given in Figure 1.2. This makes it possible to determine whether the individual's score is average, low, or high. Then, by using statistical tables and a simple formula, the examiner can pinpoint the score precisely. An IQ score of 120, for example, corresponds to about the 91st percentile—a high score indeed, because it means that about 91% of the population has scored at or below this level.

All the widely accepted intelligence and achievement tests, and some personality tests, have been standardized on large samples of the population. As you will see in Chapter 9, some personality tests are not standardized in this manner, but they remain useful because of important insights that they can reveal to trained clinicians.

# Chapter 7 Summary

## What Is Intelligence?

1. *Intelligence* is the ability to understand the world and the resourcefulness to cope with its challenges.
2. Spearman believed that intelligence is composed of a *g* factor and a number of *s* factors.
3. Thurstone believed that intelligence is composed of a *g* factor and seven *primary mental abilities.*
4. Gardner's *theory of multiple intelligences* specifies seven distinct intelligences; Gardner later suggested three additional ones.
5. Sternberg's *triarchic theory of intelligence* specifies three forms of intelligence, with emphasis on practical intelligence.

## Intelligence Tests

6. *Intelligence tests* provide a measure of the various factors that make up intelligence, typically *g*.
7. An *individual test* is given by a trained examiner to one person at a time. Widely used individual intelligence tests are the *Stanford-Binet Intelligence Scales (SBIS)* and the three Wechsler intelligence scales: the *Wechsler Preschool and Primary Scale of Intelligence (WPPSI)*, the *Wechsler Intelligence Scale for Children (WISC)*, and the *Wechsler Adult Intelligence Scale (WAIS)*.
8. The original way of determining a person's *intelligence quotient (IQ)* was to use the formula IQ = MA/CA × 100; the current way is to use *deviation IQ*.
9. The average IQ is 100, and almost half of all people score between 90 and 109.
10. A *group test* of intelligence can be given to many people at the same time; a classic example is the Army Alpha.
11. Intelligence tests are also called *aptitude tests*.
12. In theory, aptitude tests are different from *achievement tests* such as the SAT and GRE.

## What Intelligence Tests Do and Do Not Tell Us

13. IQ tests measure current intellectual functioning but not intellectual potential.

14. IQ tests are relatively good predictors of academic success.
15. Psychologists disagree about the extent to which IQ is related to occupation and general success in life.
16. In some cases, there is considerable overlap between *creativity* and intelligence as measured by IQ.
17. Creative individuals tend to display *intrinsic motivation* rather than *extrinsic motivation*.

## Heredity, Environment, and Intelligence

18. Psychologists agree that intelligence is clearly influenced by heredity and environment in interaction, but disagree about the relative contribution of each.
19. Theorists disagree about what to make of family resemblances in IQ as assessed by correlation—studies have found the highest correlations for identical twins reared together.
20. The idea of range of reaction is that genes set an upper and lower limit on intelligence; environment then determines what level a person reaches within the range established by genetic potential.
21. Scarr has suggested that genetics and environment may interact in three ways:
    a) Parents likely to pass along favorable genes are also likely to provide a favorable environment.
    b) Children with favorable genes are likely to evoke favorable responses from the people around them.
    c) As children get older, they play an active part in creating their own environments.
22. IQ is not fixed and can change considerably as development proceeds.
23. The controversy that once raged over "racial" differences in IQ is now dormant. The idea of genetic differences has been discredited, and any differences instead appear attributable to environment.
24. Three criteria for a good psychological test are *reliability*, *validity*, and *standardization*.

# Chapter 7 Test Yourself Answers

(a) Spearman believed that our specific skills are related to an overall mental ability, which he termed general intelligence or the *g* factor.

(b) Achievement tests place much more emphasis on specific forms of learning.

(c) IQ tests predict grades better because they are typically designed to get at the very qualities that figure heavily in school success—for example, reasoning, verbal ability, and number skills. Success in the world outside the classroom, however, depends on a variety of factors not measured in IQ tests.

(d) Leon is right. Although creativity in most pursuits requires some "threshold" level of intelligence, the overall correlation between creativity and IQ is not very high.

(e) Not likely. Creative people are not typically influenced by such extrinsic motivation—that is, the desire for tangible awards offered by others. Instead, they are "turned on" by intrinsic motivation.

(f) It is not possible, because both factors constantly interact. Heredity may set the range within which an individual's IQ is likely to fall, but environmental factors help determine where within that range the individual's IQ level will actually fall.

(g) Yes. For example, a test intended to measure mechanical aptitude may produce consistent scores, meaning that it is highly reliable. But it may be measuring little in the way of mechanical aptitude, meaning that it is low in validity.

# Chapter 7  Intelligence and Its Assessment

## Key Terms

achievement test (p. 264)
aptitude test (p. 264)
chronological age (CA) (p. 263)
creativity (p. 268)
deviation IQ (p. 263)
extrinsic motivation (p. 269)
g factor (p. 259)
group test (p. 264)
individual test (p. 262)
intelligence (p. 257)
intelligence quotient (IQ) (p. 263)
intelligence test (p. 262)
intrinsic motivation (p. 269)
mental age (MA) (p. 263)
primary mental abilities (p. 259)

reliability (p. 275)
s factor (p. 259)
standardization (p. 276)
Stanford-Binet Intelligence Scales (SBIS) (p. 262)
theory of multiple intelligences (p. 260)
triarchic theory of intelligence (p. 261)
validity (p. 275)
Wechsler Adult Intelligence Scale (WAIS) (p. 262)
Wechsler Intelligence Scale for Children (WISC) (p. 262)
Wechsler Preschool and Primary Scale of Intelligence (WPPSI) (p. 262)

*The key terms above can be used as search terms in InfoTrac, a database of readings, which can be found at http://infotrac-thomsonlearning.com.*

## Active Learning Review

1. Much of psychology is oriented toward understanding the universal characteristics that people have in _____. However, psychology is also interested in how people differ, or the study of individual _____.

**common**
**differences**

2. Intelligence generally refers to a person's cognitive processes and abilities, and personality to a person's distinct motives, moods, and ways of behaving toward others. These are the two major domains in the study of _____ _____.

**individual differences**

3. In the study of individual differences, the two major domains are _____ and _____.

**intelligence**
**personality**

### What Is Intelligence?

4. _____ is a complex quality that has been defined as the ability to understand the world and the resourcefulness to cope with its challenges. Knowing what's going on around you, learning from experience, and behaving rationally and in worthwhile ways are some of the elements of a general definition of *intelligence*.

**Intelligence**

5. What constitutes behaving _____ and in _____ ways varies according to time and place. At different times in history and even today in different cultures, definitions of _____ vary considerably.

**rationally, worthwhile**

**intelligence**

6. Industrialized nations value technological and language skills. A person who is good at math and fluent in his or her language is viewed as _____ in these nations.

**intelligent**

7. Spearman believed that _____ is made up of a *g factor*, for general intelligence, and a number of specific skills, or *s factors*. His theory was based on tests of many kinds of abilities, from reading comprehension to the visualization of spatial relationships.

**intelligence**

8. His finding that people who scored well on one test also tended to do well on others convinced Spearman of the existence of general intelligence, which he called the _____ _____.

**g factor**

9. Spearman also found that people's scores varied somewhat for different kinds of abilities, suggesting the existence of specific skills, or _____ _____.

**s factors**

general

primary mental abilities

Thurstone

intelligences

ten

three

practical

practical intelligence

Intelligence

Stanford-Binet Intelligence Scales

WPPSI

WISC

WAIS

overall (or general)

MA

CA

IQ

below average

above average

deviation

IQ

numbers

intelligence

aptitude

10. Thurstone expanded on Spearman's work by defining seven specific skills. Like Spearman, Thurstone also emphasized an overall mental ability, or _____ intelligence.

11. Thurstone identified seven distinct skills—verbal comprehension, word fluency, number, space, associative memory, perceptual speed, and general reasoning—that he called the _____ _____ _____.

12. The classic theory that intelligence is made up of a *g* factor plus seven primary mental abilities was proposed by _____.

13. In recent years, Gardner's *theory of multiple intelligences* has generated considerable interest. His theory proposes seven distinct _____—linguistic, logical-mathematical, musical, bodily-kinesthetic, spatial, interpersonal, and intrapersonal—plus perhaps naturalist, spiritual, and existential, bringing the total number of intelligences to _____.

14. In the *triarchic theory of intelligence* proposed by Sternberg, intelligence has _____ components: practical, creative, and analytical. The first component is a person's ability to adapt to and function in his or her particular environment; hence the term _____ intelligence.

15. Sternberg has contended that popular intelligence tests measure little in the way of everyday _____ _____.

## Intelligence Tests

16. The first *intelligence test* was created in France by Binet and Simon, who devised a wide range of items that increased in difficulty step by step. The Binet-Simon Scale was imported to the United States by researchers at Stanford University; the current version is called the *Stanford-Binet* _____ *Scales*, or *SBIS*.

17. The current version of the _____ _____ _____ _____, or SBIS, is widely used to assess intelligence across most of the life span. Also popular are the *Wechsler Preschool and Primary Scale of Intelligence*, or _____, for children from about age $2\frac{1}{2}$ to just over age 7; the *Wechsler Intelligence Scale for Children*, or _____, for the age range from 6 to just over 16; and the *Wechsler Adult Intelligence Scale*, or _____, for ages 16 through 89.

18. The SBIS and the Wechsler tests are *individual tests*. Each yields a Full Scale, or _____, score for intelligence, as well as scores that assess specific areas of intellectual functioning.

19. In Terman's original Stanford Revision, an individual's score on the test was her or his *mental age*, or _____, divided by actual *chronological age*, or _____, and multiplied by 100 to move the decimal place. The result was that person's *intelligence quotient*, or _____. That is,

$$IQ = \frac{MA}{CA} \times 100$$

20. Thus, a child of 12 who scored an MA of 12 would be average in IQ, a child of 12 who scored an MA of 10 would be _____ _____ in IQ, and a child of 12 who scored an MA of 15 would be _____ _____ in IQ.

21. Wechsler switched to assessing *deviation IQ*, which tells how much a person's score "deviates" from the average for the person's age range. The _____ _____ approach made it possible to assess adults in a more meaningful way.

22. There are also *group tests* of IQ, usually pencil-and-paper tests that can be administered to large _____ of people at the same time.

23. All _____ tests discussed fall into the general class of *aptitude tests*, meaning that they are intended to measure how well the individual can learn new skills or unfamiliar tasks.

24. By definition, tests that estimate your ability to learn or perform in the future are called _____ tests. In contrast, tests—such as college entrance exams—

that assess what you have already learned are called *achievement tests*. There is, however, much overlap between the two.

25. Tests that measure primarily what knowledge and abilities you have acquired in the past are called _____ tests. — achievement

26. A college entrance exam is an _____ test. In contrast, the SBIS is an _____ test. — achievement / aptitude

## What Intelligence Tests Do and Do Not Tell Us

27. Although IQ tests do predict to some extent a person's future learning abilities, they actually measure here-and-now, or _____, intellectual functioning. No IQ test can measure what you might ultimately be capable of—that is, your intellectual _____. — current / potential

28. Because intelligence tests tap abilities and knowledge associated with doing well in school, they tend to measure _____ abilities better than they do anything else. — academic

29. Just as IQ scores are good predictors of school _____, school grades are good predictors of _____ scores. — grades / IQ

30. It can be argued that tests such as the Stanford-Binet _____ Scales do not measure an intelligence quotient as much as they measure an _____ quotient, or AQ. — Intelligence / academic

31. Performance in an occupation frequently depends less on a person's IQ score than on, in Sternberg's terms, his or her _____ intelligence. — practical

32. The longitudinal study of gifted California children initiated by Terman indicated that having a high _____ can be associated with achievement and success in life in middle adulthood. However, the study by _____ found that this relationship did not persist for all of the participants into older adulthood. — IQ / Terman

33. *Creativity* has been defined as the ability to solve novel or _____ problems or fashion novel or _____ products in one or more domains of activity, given that the problems and products are adaptive and useful. Having a "threshold" level of IQ seems important, but motivation may be even more important. — new / new

34. The ability to solve new problems or fashion new products is an indication of _____, which seems to be related more to _____ than to IQ. — creativity, motivation

35. Creative individuals tend to pursue an activity because they find it to be inherently compelling, enjoyable, and satisfying; that is, they are driven by _____ *motivation*. They are less influenced by *extrinsic motivation*, or the desire for tangible rewards offered by others. — intrinsic

36. Creative people are more influenced by _____ than _____ motivation, meaning that they pursue activities because they really like them rather than out of a desire for tangible _____. — intrinsic, extrinsic / rewards

## Heredity, Environment, and Intelligence

37. Like most human traits, intelligence is influenced by the pattern of genes we have inherited, which influences the way our nervous system and brain operate. In general, almost all psychologists agree that intelligence depends in part on _____. — heredity

38. But intelligence is also influenced by our experiences in the world around us—or, more generally, our _____. — environment

39. Psychologists disagree on the relative contributions of _____ and _____ to intelligence, but they agree that the two work in concert; that is, heredity and environment _____ to determine intelligence. — heredity / environment / interact

40. One argument for the influence of heredity is that IQ tends to "run in families." It has been established that the more closely related two people are—that is, the more similarity there is in the patterns of _____ they have inherited—the more similar their IQs are likely to be. — genes

genes

.40
.50
.90

heredity

environment

range
heredity
environment

80s

110

environment

IQ

environment
intelligence
low-income

inferior

environment

predict

tests

reliable

valid

valid
reliable

41. Correlations in IQ between parents and children cluster around .40; between brothers and sisters in the same home, they average around .50. For identical twins, who have almost exactly the same pattern of _____, studies have shown correlations of .70 to more than .90.

42. The correlations in IQ between parents and children average around _____; between brothers and sisters in the same home, they cluster around _____. For identical twins, studies have found correlations of .70 to more than _____.

43. For identical twins separated and brought up in different homes, correlations have been found to run between .62 and .77. Such high correlations even when people are brought up in different environments are a strong argument for the influence of _____.

44. However, children not related by heredity who are brought up in the same home also have IQs that are significantly correlated, a strong argument for the influence of _____.

45. Many psychologists have concluded that heredity probably sets upper and lower limits on the IQ of an individual and the environment then determines where within this range the IQ will actually fall; this is known as the _____ of reaction principle. Thus, the possible range of IQ is set by _____, and the actual IQ within this range by _____.

46. Some psychologists believe that for a genetically average child, heredity sets a possible range of around 20 to 25 points. This would mean that an average child might wind up with an IQ in the mid to high _____ if brought up in a very unfavorable environment—but in an ideal environment, the child might reach the high end of her or his range, somewhat above _____.

47. IQ sometimes goes up or down by as much as 50 points over time, even when the child remains in the same home _____. There are indications that the changes in IQ are related to motivation and other personality factors, physical health, and emotional adjustment. Thus, in predicting a child's chances of succeeding in school, one should consider the child's overall personality as well as his or her present score on an _____ test.

48. Children from low-income homes may become so discouraged by an unstimulating _____ or by failure and criticism in their early schooling that they fail to take advantage of their abilities and display less _____ than they could have. However, growing up in a _____-_____ home is no guarantee that the environment will be unstimulating.

49. Historically, U.S. blacks and whites showed significant differences in average IQ, a finding that Jensen took to mean that blacks were genetically _____. However, this idea was eventually discredited by researchers who demonstrated that economic and social differences—that is, differences in _____—more than accounted for the average differences in IQ.

50. Even given average differences in IQ between ethnicities, it would not be possible to _____ the IQ of a particular individual.

Psychological Testing—The Scientific Way

51. Constructing useful psychological _____ is a science in itself. A first requirement is that a test produce scores that are consistent from one testing occasion to the next.

52. A test that produces consistent scores is said to be _____. Another important requirement is that a test actually measure what it is intended to measure.

53. A test that purports to assess creativity but instead assesses verbal fluency cannot be said to be _____.

54. An IQ test predicts grades in school fairly well, but it does not predict adult income accurately; therefore, the test is _____ as a measure of school performance but not as a measure of income, even though it may be highly _____.

55. A final requirement of psychological _____ is *standardization,* which refers to two issues. The first is objectivity—the administration and scoring of the test should not be influenced by any biases on the part of the _____ or by the manner in which the examiner gives the test.

56. In addition to evidence of _____, the examiner needs something to compare the examinee's performance to. This something is norms, which are derived by giving the test to large groups of participants. How well the individual does on the test is determined by comparing the individual's score to the _____ for the test.

57. Standardization also enables an examiner to evaluate an individual's performance on a test in terms of percentiles. Scoring at the 78th _____ means that the individual has done as well as or better than 78% of the people who originally participated in the _____ of the test and the establishment of its _____.

58. In sum, the three requirements for a good psychological test—such as a test of intelligence or personality—are _____, _____, and _____.

testing

examiner

objectivity

norms

percentile

standardization
norms

reliability, validity, standardization

# Practice Test

____ **1.** Wechsler's definition of intelligence emphasized the ability to
a. do well in school.
b. communicate.
c. understand and cope with the world.
d. think logically.

____ **2.** Mary gets good grades in all her classes but does better at mathematics than at reading comprehension. Her performance is in line with
a. Spearman's theory of intelligence.
b. Thurstone's theory of intelligence.
c. both of the above
d. none of the above

____ **3.** The number of primary mental abilities proposed by Thurstone was
a. 6.
b. 7.
c. 8.
d. 9.

____ **4.** Gardner's theory of multiple intelligences proposes that the number of intelligences may be as high as
a. 7.
b. 8.
c. 9.
d. 10.

____ **5.** With regard to his triarchic theory of intelligence, Sternberg has contended that popular intelligence tests measure very little
a. practical intelligence.
b. creative intelligence.
c. analytical intelligence.
d. all of the above

____ **6.** The first intelligence test was created by
a. Binet.
b. Spearman.
c. Thurstone.
d. Wechsler.

____ **7.** In Terman's original approach, IQ = MA/CA × 100; thus, a child of 9 with an MA of 11 would be
a. below average.
b. average.
c. above average.
d. not necessarily any of the above

____ **8.** Deviation IQ is used in assessing
a. mentally retarded persons.
b. emotionally disordered persons.
c. gifted persons.
d. all of the above

____ **9.** The SBIS is
a. a group test.
b. an achievement test.
c. an individual test.
d. none of the above

____ **10.** The Army Alpha is
a. a group test.
b. an achievement test.
c. an individual test.
d. none of the above

____ **11.** Intelligence tests primarily measure
a. potential intellectual functioning.
b. accumulated knowledge.
c. current intellectual functioning.
d. capacity to understand the world.

____ **12.** IQ is a consistently good predictor of
a. occupational success.
b. grades in school.
c. achievement in life.
d. all of the above

____ **13.** Creative individuals tend to display
a. extrinsic motivation.
b. intrinsic motivation.
c. inherited motivation.
d. learned motivation.

____ **14.** The correlation between the IQs of parents and their children is around
a. .30.
b. .40.
c. .50.
d. .60.

____ **15.** Of the following choices, the highest correlations in IQ are found between
a. parents and children in the same home.
b. brothers and sisters, reared together.
c. adopted children, reared together.
d. identical twins, reared in different homes.

____**16.** Most psychologists agree that heredity accounts for about
  a. 50% of a person's intelligence.
  b. 60% of a person's intelligence.
  c. 70% of a person's intelligence.
  d. 80% of a person's intelligence.

____**17.** Intelligent or gifted people may fail because of
  a. lack of motivation.
  b. fear of failure.
  c. excessive dependency.
  d. all of the above

____**18.** Heredity combines with environment in contributing to intelligence in which way?
  a. Intelligent parents provide better environments for their children.
  b. Genetically bright children provoke encouragement from other people.
  c. Genes dispose a child to seek environments that promote intellectual growth.
  d. all of the above

____**19.** Which of the following is important in scientific psychological testing?
  a. reliability
  b. validity
  c. standardization
  d. all of the above

____**20.** In scientific psychological testing, norms are derived through
  a. objectivity.
  b. standardization.
  c. validity.
  d. none of the above

# Exercises

1. On page 257 there was a suggestion that you ask several of your friends what they mean when they describe someone as "intelligent." Extend the number to 20 or 30 friends and acquaintances, and keep a record of the various definitions given. When you have collected a fair number, try to group the criteria cited into a smaller number of categories (5–10). How do these categories compare with Thurstone's seven primary mental abilities on page 259? Do you believe that most of the people you interviewed see intelligence as a single general ability (like Spearman) or as several distinct abilities (like Sternberg and Gardner)? What is your own view of the most appropriate and meaningful definition of intelligence?

2. Intelligence test items vary in type. They include questions with multiple-choice answers ("Which of the following is the largest . . . ?"), questions with free-form or open-ended answers ("Describe as many things as you can to do with a brick"), and performance tasks (assembling various kinds of puzzles). In this exercise, you are asked to develop 15 items that you think might reasonably assess certain forms of intelligence. (Don't worry—we won't ask you to standardize them!)

Table 7.1 on page 260 describes Gardner's multiple intelligences. The last three intelligences, *Naturalist*, *Spiritual*, and *Existential*, were added recently and are currently considered "provisional." Review all of Table 7.1 to get a feel for Gardner's theory. Then write five test items for each of the three provisional intelligences. The types of items you develop and the approach you take are up to you.

After developing your items, review the three provisional intelligences. What are your thoughts about the suitability and appropriateness of each as a *different* intelligence? Do you see any possibility of overlap among the three?

✱ *For quizzing, activities, exercises, and web links, check out the book-specific website at http://www.psychology.wadsworth. com/kagan9e.*

# Emotion and Motivation

© Reuters NewMedia Inc./CORBIS

After the tragic death of England's Princess Diana in 1997, thousands of mourners came to her home, Kensington Palace, to leave bouquets and express their grief.

During the 1998 Winter Olympic games, figure skater Tara Lipinski broke into joyful tears after finishing her performance and realizing that she had probably won a gold medal.

In 2001, when terrorists attacked the World Trade Center and the Pentagon, people throughout the United States reacted with shock, anger, and a surge of patriotism.

These examples illustrate the striking ways in which emotions can influence behavior. Occasionally we hear about more extreme episodes, such as people fleeing from an erupting volcano in a state of panic or people in the grip of rage "going ballistic" and committing senseless murders.

In more ordinary situations as well, emotions affect our behavior. For example, moderate excitement or eagerness often helps us learn faster or perform a task more efficiently. At the same time, emotions involving fear and anxiety can make us forget everything we studied when we sit down to take an important exam or make us go blank when we get up and try to make a speech.

Often interrelated with emotions are motives. **Motives** may be defined in a general sense as the "why" of behavior. Some arise from basic physiological needs such as for oxygen, nourishment, and sleep, creating psychological **drives** to satisfy these needs. Other motives are primarily psychological. Examples of each of these kinds of motives are discussed in this chapter.

Hunger, for example, is a partly physiological, partly psychological motive that can make us jumpy, jittery, and unable to concentrate. Indeed, when we are hungry or thirsty, the urge to find food or water can be just as strong as the tendency to run away in fear or strike back in anger. In the famous case of a party of pioneers stranded by an 1846 blizzard in the Donner Pass of the Sierra Nevadas, the urge to eat overrode their normal constraints and turned some of them into cannibals. And the need for sleep can cause a sleep-deprived prisoner of war to turn from defiance to submission.

Unlike motives based on physiological needs, motives that are primarily psychological direct behavior toward goals such as power, friendship, and achievement. Although these motives are not essential to life on a daily basis, desires such as the desire to achieve or to "belong" can be so intense that people will devote a great deal of planning and effort to satisfying them. It is not clear to what extent such motives are universal and to what extent they are learned. It is clear, however, that culture helps determine how they are expressed. For example, as we saw in Chapter 1, achievement takes different forms in individualist versus collectivist cultures.

**Motives**
The psychologically potent ideas that direct behavior toward goals such as power over others, friendship, and achievement.

**Drives**
Physiological states (such as hunger, thirst, and fatigue) that have a pronounced effect on behavior.

# BIOLOGICAL UNDERPINNINGS OF EMOTION

**FOCUS QUESTIONS**

• What are the components of an emotion?

• What bodily changes take place when we experience an emotion?

**Emotion**
Changes in physiology that are evaluated cognitively and may lead to a change in conscious feeling.

Although there is some disagreement on the best definition of an **emotion,** most psychologists would agree that an emotion consists of (1) a precipitating event that is (2) accompanied by changes in physiology that are (3) evaluated cognitively and (4) may lead to a change in feeling. The qualifier "may lead to a change in feeling" is important. Although some physiological changes produced by an event are consciously felt—and are interpreted as fear, sadness, or joy—similar changes can occur without being consciously felt. In the second case, although behavior may change, the person is not aware of being in an emotional state. For example, a person who has been rejected by a friend may become preoccupied and forgetful without consciously feeling angry or sad. These two types of emotional states are quite different.

It should also be noted that the event that leads to an emotion is not always clearly identifiable. You may, for example, find yourself feeling angry at someone close to you, not because that person has just hurt or insulted you but because over time he or she has treated you in ways you dislike and now as you get to thinking about the person you decide that you "can't stand it anymore"—perhaps without the person even being present.

Because the most salient feature of an emotion is a change in the body's physiology, this section addresses the biological underpinnings of emotional states; cognitive aspects are discussed in the next section. At the outset, it is worth noting that there is much disagreement on how many basic emotions there are. One prominent psychologist has suggested that there are ten basic emotions (listed in Table 8.1), which combine to form more complex ones (Izard, 1977).

As the definition makes clear, the most important characteristic differentiating emotions from other psychological states—for example, perception or thought—is that they are accompanied by widespread and pronounced bodily changes that can alter blood circulation, heart rate, stomach activity, muscle tension, and concentrations of neurotransmitters and hormones. You can assume, for example, that you are in an emotional state when you blush or become pale, when your muscles grow taut, or when your mouth turns so dry that you can hardly speak. You also know that you are in an emotional state, even if you can conceal all outward signs, when you feel that you are shaking inwardly, when you are "hot under the collar," or when your pulse is racing.

The fundamental human emotions, according to one investigator, are those listed in the two left-hand columns. Other emotions that we frequently experience, notably those in the right-hand column, are combinations of fundamental feelings.

**TABLE 8.1**
**One Psychological View of the Range of Emotions**

| The Ten Basic Emotions | | Four Important Complex Emotions |
|---|---|---|
| anger | guilt | anxiety (fear plus anger, distress, guilt, interest, or shame) |
| contempt | interest-excitement | |
| disgust | joy | depression (distress plus anger, contempt, fear, guilt, or shame) |
| distress | shame | |
| fear | surprise | hostility (a combination of anger, contempt, and disgust) |
| | | love (interest plus joy) |

*After Izard, 1977.*

There are also quieter emotions that occur when the body seems to be especially relaxed. These are the calm and contented feelings you experience when you enjoy a beautiful piece of music or a satisfying meal. In these cases, too, the body is changed in a specific manner.

## Pinpointing Bodily Changes in Emotion

"I could hardly breathe."

"I had butterflies in my stomach."

"I was shaking like a leaf."

People who have been emotionally aroused often make statements like these, which raise the question of whether particular emotions are linked to changes in particular areas of the body. One team of investigators attempted to answer this question by asking research participants to reminisce about specific emotions they had felt and to indicate on detailed diagrams of the body where, especially, they had sensed each one (Nieuwenhuise, Offenberg, & Frijda, 1987). In general, the participants could indeed identify the "location" of specific emotions. For example, most people said that they felt disgust especially in the stomach and throat; fear in the abdomen, legs, genitals, and stomach; contempt and shame in the face; surprise in the lower back; joy in the arms and legs; and anger virtually everywhere, but mainly in the arms and legs.

The tendency to associate specific emotions with parts of the body may be the result of actual physiological responses related to particular feeling states. For example, disgust is likely to be ascribed to the stomach and throat because of sensations of nausea and gastric upset. Shame may be located in the face as a result of the tendency to blush. Such associations originate in the different physiological changes that accompany specific emotional experiences.

## Hidden Physiological Changes

Evidence that emotion is accompanied by changes in different parts of the body is most apparent in the behavior of nonhuman animals. It is often less obvious among humans, for most of us have learned to hide many outward signs of emotion. But the changes can be measured reliably with laboratory equipment. When we experience a strong emotion, such as fear, our heartbeat may increase from the normal rate of around 72 beats per minute to as high as 180. Blood pressure may rise sharply, and blood is often diverted from the stomach to the muscles of movement and to the surface of the body, resulting in flushed cheeks and a sensation of warmth. The composition of the blood changes: The number of red corpuscles, which carry oxygen, increases markedly. Secretion of hormones by the endocrine glands produces changes in the level of blood sugar, the acidity of the blood, and the amount of epinephrine and norepinephrine (powerful stimulants secreted by the adrenal glands into the bloodstream under the control of the autonomic nervous system, or ANS).

The normal movements of the stomach and intestines, associated with the digestion and absorption of food, usually stop under conditions of intense emotional arousal. Some emotional states may lead to nausea or diarrhea, a higher metabolic rate to create additional energy, and gasping or panting. The salivary glands may stop working, causing a feeling of dryness in the mouth that is often associated with fear and anger. The sweat glands, on the other hand, may become overactive, as shown by the dripping forehead that may accompany em-

An angry cat shows many outward bodily signs of emotion. It crouches and growls. Its hair stands on end, its ears are laid back, and its eyes are wide and staring (Young, 1961).

© Walter Chandoa

barrassment or the "cold sweat" that sometimes accompanies fear. The tiny muscles at the base of the hairs may contract and raise goose bumps. Finally, the pupils of the eyes may enlarge, causing the wide-eyed look that is characteristic of fear, rage, excitement, and pain. Of course, all of these reactions do not necessarily take place in every episode of strong fear or anger (Stenberg, Campos, & Emde, 1983), but they do tend to form a pattern.

## The Role of the Autonomic Nervous System and Glands

Some bodily changes that accompany emotion are regulated by the ANS and the endocrine glands, over which we ordinarily have no conscious control. When the sympathetic division of the ANS is activated, we experience physiological changes such as a rise in heart rate and blood pressure, muscle tension, dilation of the pupils, and inhibition of stomach and intestine activity.

It is not surprising, therefore, that we don't seem to have much control over our emotions once they have begun, although at times we may be able to head them off (see the discussion of rational-emotive therapy in Chapter 14). Typically, they seem to boil up of their own accord, and we feel them even if we manage to hide all outward signs. Even in situations in which we are determined to remain calm, we often find ourselves unaccountably angry, frightened, or overcome with joy. Note, however, that although we often can't control our emotions, we *can* control our behavior to a large extent. The experience of intense emotion is no excuse for episodes of violent irresponsible behavior such as so-called crimes of passion, road rage, and school shootings.

**Cortisol**
**A hormone secreted by the adrenal gland.**

Although a pattern of bodily changes characterizes each of the major emotions, certain changes are linked to several different emotions. For example, when we are angry, the adrenal glands produce the hormone **cortisol,** but they also produce cortisol when we are emotionally upset. Our pupils dilate when we experience fear, but they also dilate in response to milder emotions such as interest or the excitement of a tennis match (Rose, 1980). For these reasons, psychologists have found it difficult to match a particular bodily state with a particular emotional experience.

Moreover, a person who reports feelings of joy on two separate occasions may show a different pattern of bodily changes on each occasion. And two people who report feeling exactly the same emotion (joy or distress) may show different patterns. Thus, it is difficult to determine through physiological measurement alone what particular emotion a person is experiencing. Nevertheless, a variety of physiological measures are used in conducting lie detector tests, discussed in Psychology in the Lab and in Life on page 293.

## The Role of the Facial Muscles

A number of bodily changes that accompany emotion do not involve the ANS, glands, or visceral organs. These changes represent activity of the muscles of movement, over which we ordinarily do have conscious control. You're familiar with many of them—for example, muscular tension (as when the teeth are clenched in anger) or trembling (which occurs when two sets of muscles work against each other). When emotionally excited, many people have a tendency to blink or make nervous movements, such as brushing back their hair or drumming their fingers.

Emotions are often expressed vocally in laughter, snarls, moans, and screams—or revealed by changes in the speed, pitch, and loudness of speech. Speech patterns often vary sharply depending on the emotion expressed, as shown in Table 8.2. The patterns are so consistent that some emotional states can be identified with surprising accuracy just from the sound of a person's voice (Scherer, 1986). From

## PSYCHOLOGY IN THE LAB AND IN LIFE

# How Truthful Are Lie Detectors?

It has been estimated that each year at least 1 million people in the United States are asked to take a lie detector test. Some are defendants, plaintiffs, or witnesses in legal cases. Others are job applicants or workers in chain stores, banks, supermarkets, or other companies that try to spot dishonesty. Still others are executives in industrial firms or government agencies that require periodic loyalty checks.

The lie detector device is a *polygraph recorder,* which produces a continuous record of bodily processes—breathing, blood pressure, sweating—that often change at a minute level when a person experiences a particular emotional state. Many people believe that the polygraph is an infallible scientific instrument and place absolute confidence in its results, particularly since many criminal suspects confess after failing a polygraph test (Iacono & Patrick, 1999). The test is certainly based on a sound principle—namely, that people are likely to become physiologically "stirred up" when they feel so threatened by a question that they answer it untruthfully.

But psychologists have found that a perfectly innocent person may react emotionally to a "loaded" question—and thus appear to be lying when actually telling the truth. In turn, veteran liars can tell outrageous untruths without showing the slightest emotional ripple. This can and often does lead to seriously mistaken conclusions

(Kleinmuntz & Szucko, 1984). The most important thing to keep in mind is that polygraph lie detectors measure changes correlated with emotions that might be associated with lies; they do not assess lies directly.

To complicate matters, the scoring of test results may be influenced by the purely subjective impressions of the examiners. Their interpretation of the physical reactions to test questions may be colored by personal biases about an individual's age, sex, social class, or race. All in all, the great weight of psychological evidence supports the argument that lie detector tests have no real claim to being "scientific" or infallible—one expert notes that "they are about as accurate as tossing coins" (Lykken, 1998)—and we should never reach a final conclusion about whether a person is lying based solely on the results of a lie detector test (Ekman & Friesen, 1986). Based on these findings, the American Psychological Association has issued a policy statement arguing against the use of lie detection programs.

Lie detector testing is a thriving industry in the United States, and it is likely that a significant number of legal and administrative decisions are unfairly influenced by the results. This is a good example of psychology misapplied—how the science can be warped when its findings are used without sufficient safeguards and caution.

the opening "hello" of a telephone conversation, for example, we can often tell whether the person on the other end is happy or sad.

Emotions are also revealed in facial expressions, such as smiles, grimaces, and frowns. In fact, even just thinking about experiences that are happy, sad, or infuriating can produce strikingly different patterns of activity in the muscles of the face. Although the changes are often too small to be seen, they can be detected by measuring the electrical activity of the muscles (Schwartz, 1982).

Psychologists who maintain that facial expressions are a key factor in emotional experience hold that every basic emotion is accompanied by a characteristic facial pattern that occurs automatically because of the manner in which our bodies and brains are programmed by heredity (Izard, 1977). The various patterns,

**TABLE 8.2**
**Examples of Speech Patterns That Reflect Emotion**

| Emotion | Patterns of Speech | | |
| | Tempo | Pitch | Volume |
| --- | --- | --- | --- |
| Happiness | Fast | High | Loud |
| Sadness | Slow | Low | Soft |
| Contempt | Slow | Low | Loud |

**Speech patterns often vary sharply, depending on the emotion experienced.**

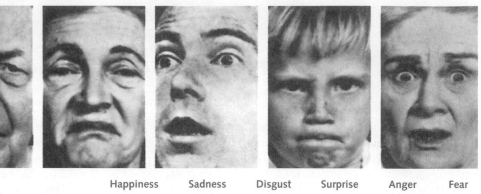

© Ekman

FIGURE 8.1 Strong agreement across cultures. These photos of faces showing different emotions were shown to participants in the countries listed. Note the high percentages of participants who linked the photos with the emotions.

*Ekman, 1973.*

|  | Happiness | Sadness | Disgust | Surprise | Anger | Fear |
|---|---|---|---|---|---|---|
| United States | 97% | 84% | 92% | 95% | 67% | 85% |
| Brazil | 95% | 59% | 97% | 87% | 90% | 67% |
| Chile | 95% | 88% | 92% | 93% | 94% | 68% |
| Argentina | 98% | 78% | 92% | 95% | 90% | 54% |
| Japan | 100% | 62% | 90% | 100% | 90% | 66% |

they believe, are the product of evolution—an idea that dates back to Charles Darwin (1872). Without language, it is an advantage to be able to avert aggression through a facial expression signaling friendliness or submission. Facial expressions of fear can alert other members of the group to the presence of danger. Thus, the process of natural selection has favored the survival of individuals who carry genes for specific facial expressions (Andrew, 1965).

This view is based in part on a study that used photographs of individuals exhibiting certain emotions. The photos were shown to people in a number of very different societies; the participants were asked to identify the emotions being displayed in the photos. As shown in Figure 8.1, there was remarkable agreement on the specific emotion on the face, not only among participants in the United States but among participants in a variety of countries and cultures around the world (e.g., Ekman, 1971; Rosenberg & Ekman, 1995). The various facial expressions are sufficiently unique that even pigeons can be trained to differentiate among them (Bhatt, Wasserman, Reynolds, & Knauss, 1988).

The study summarized in Figure 8.1 indicates that the facial expressions that accompany some emotions seem to be universal and unlearned, as if they were genetically programmed. Similar agreement across cultures has been found in judgments of the facial expression of contempt (Ekman & Friesen, 1986). However, an extensive review of cross-cultural studies pointed out that there are some problems with the methods used in those studies. For example, participants are typically asked to assign emotion labels to a specific set of stimuli—usually a set of preselected photos of people expressing various emotions. When the stimuli are not preselected, the amount of agreement on the emotions displayed may decrease. Moreover, when participants are allowed to choose their own labels, rather than selecting from a list supplied by the researcher, they don't always specify an emotion for each facial expression (Russell, 1994).

When researchers focus on evidence that is independent of language—such as infants' facial expressions—they find considerable consistency across cultures (Izard, 1994). Most adults, for example, agree on the emotions they believe are reflected by the different facial expressions of young babies (Izard, 1994), such as those shown in Figure 8.2. "Reading" the facial expressions of older individuals is more difficult for all of us, although women appear to be better at this task than men. Research has also shown that certain emotions—for example, amusement or peacefulness—are easier to read than others, such as happiness, sadness, anger, or disgust (Wagner, 1990). Despite these differences, the evidence supports the claim that certain facial expressions of emotion are innate and universal (Izard, 1994).

## Culture and the Experience of Emotion

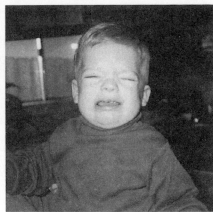

The expression of emotion may be universal, but there are cultural differences in the experience of emotion. A recent study (Mesquita, 2001) found significant differences between individualist and collectivist cultures in the way people respond emotionally to events in their lives. Collectivist cultures emphasize the person's relationship to his or her social group and to the society at large, whereas individualist cultures see the person as unique and independent. For people in collectivist cultures (Surinam & Turkey), emotions tend to be grounded in assessments of social worth and in perceptions of the outside world rather than the person's inner world. Thus, a young Turkish man who was admitted to a competitive university felt pride in his accomplishment because it enhanced the status of his family. In contrast, people in individualist cultures tend to focus on their own subjective feelings about an event rather than its social consequences. For example, a Dutch student who had just earned a master's degree in civil engineering said, "*I* had set myself this deadline, and it made me feel really good that *I* made it this time."

**FIGURE 8.2 Emotions of infants, written all over their faces. Notice the similarity of these facial expressions to those of the happy and sad adults pictured in the first two photos of Figure 8.1**

© Neil Robinson

## Can We Hide Our Emotions?

The difficulty of concealing the facial movements that accompany some emotional experiences was demonstrated by a team of investigators who attached electrodes to the facial muscles of individuals during an interview and, by measuring the electrical activity of these muscles, detected the intensity of reaction to emotionally toned material (Cacioppo, Martzke, Petty, & Tassinary, 1988). Because certain facial muscles are difficult to control voluntarily, they sometimes provide clues to an emotion that the individual is fighting to hide. When we are worried or under stress, for example, we may try to act as if nothing is wrong—but there is a fair chance that we won't be able to keep at least one clue from revealing our actual state of tension: The inner part of the eyebrows tends to rise (Ekman & Friesen, 1986).

There are times, of course, when the face does not reveal an individual's internal emotional state. In one experiment, 72 women experienced intense pain when they immersed their hands and arms in extremely cold water. Initially, they showed the facial changes that usually accompany pain: cheeks raised, eyelids tight, eyes closed in a blink, and upper lips raised, with the corners pulled back. But even though the participants experienced increasing pain as the experiment went on, their facial displays of "pain" became much less apparent as they became **habituated,** or accustomed, to their uncomfortable situation (Craig & Patrick, 1985). But by and large, the face can be more revealing than spoken words. And sometimes words aren't needed at all—as when we say to a friend, "I could tell something was wrong just by looking at you."

The judgments we make about people by "just looking" at them can often be uncannily reliable, even if time permits only a swift first impression. For example, psychologists have examined the impact that people's nonverbal, unconscious "body

**Habituated**
**Accustomed to a stimulus.**

### Test Yourself

**(a)** Suppose you encounter a shadowy figure while walking in the park at night. The thought passes through your mind that this might be either another innocent walker or a criminal bent on doing harm. But, somehow, your thought is not accompanied by any changes in your body—for example, increased heart rate, heavy breathing, sweating, or goose bumps. What emotion are you experiencing?

(The answer is on page 322.)

### FOCUS QUESTIONS

• **What theories have been developed to explain the experience of emotion?**

• **What factors give rise to individual differences in the arousal and display of emotion?**

language" has on the emotional attitudes of others toward them. When female college students were asked to form an impression of a teacher on the basis of three 10-second silent videotape segments of that teacher in a classroom, their impressions were highly correlated with end-of-semester evaluations of the teacher by his or her students (Ambady & Rosenthal, 1993). Empathy, too, plays a role in our ability to judge the emotional states of others. In one study, participants were asked to identify the emotions being expressed by a couple videotaped in conversation. The participants' ability to recognize when the conversing couple was angry was greater when the participants themselves experienced a high level of cardiovascular arousal—a physiological state shared by the couple at that point in their conversation (Levenson & Ruef, 1992).

# MECHANISMS OF EMOTION

One of the earliest and most challenging questions to confront the fledgling field of psychology in the late 19th century involved the origins of emotion. What causes changes to take place in the body, welling up without conscious control and often despite our desire to suppress them? The commonsense answer to this—that we cry because we are sad, strike out because we are angry, tremble and run because we are afraid—begs the question. Are emotions a product of brain activity or of "heart"? As we will see in this section, several theories have been proposed in an attempt to answer this question.

## Early Theories of Emotion

Well over a century ago, William James proposed that emotion occurs when specific stimuli in the environment set off physiological changes in the body. These changes, he said, stimulate sensory nerves leading to the brain, and it is the brain's reaction to these sensory messages that we perceive as emotion. In other words, we do not cry because we are sad. On the contrary, we feel sad because we are crying (James, 1890).

James's idea complemented the thinking of the Danish researcher Carl Lange. He too reasoned that physiological changes in the body come first and that the perceived conscious emotion is the result of feedback from those changes. In the absence of any plausible opposition, the **James-Lange theory** of emotion held sway for many years. Not until half a century had passed did psychologists refine the theory by linking it to the role of the facial muscles. The new thinking held that feelings of emotion are influenced by feedback from the muscles of the face, which were believed to be programmed by nature to respond in definite ways to certain events in the environment (Tomkins, 1962).

Building on this proposal, researchers have suggested that the muscle movements that accompany changes in facial expression modify the pattern of blood flow from the face to the brain, thus affecting the release of neurotransmitters by the brain—and that these in turn affect mood (Zajonc, 1989). For example, when student participants were asked to adopt either a "worried" (negative) or a "smiling" (positive) facial expression while recollecting events in their lives, students who had assumed a "worried" expression tended to rate themselves as less self-assured at the time of a given event than did those who were smiling (Stepper & Strack, 1993). And researchers have found that the activation of specific facial muscles in smiling can generate some of the changes in regional brain activity that are known

**James-Lange theory**
A physiologically based theory of emotion suggesting that stimuli in the environment set off physiological changes in an individual and these are followed by the perceived conscious emotion, which results from the perception of feedback of those changes.

to occur during spontaneous enjoyment (Ekman & Davidson, 1993). Thus, it may be that emotions do not necessarily "happen to" an individual but may be produced voluntarily.

The increasing specificity of these ideas does not solve the main problem with the James-Lange theory: the difficulty involved in matching any particular facial expression to the experience of a specific emotion. Proponents of the facial feedback theory believe that matches exist (Izard, 1984), but other psychologists have been skeptical (McCaul, Holmes, & Solomon, 1982).

As early psychologists grappled with the concept of emotions as the result of bodily feedback, two U.S. researchers emphasized the fact that brain activity changes with emotion. According to the **Cannon-Bard theory,** certain events in the environment trigger hypothalamic activity. Neurochemical events in the hypothalamus lead to arousal of the ANS, which in turn produces the various physiological changes associated with emotion and alerts the cerebral cortex. There, the message is translated into conscious feelings of emotion. Thus, the experience of emotion does not follow the body's response to a stimulus; instead, both the response and the emotion occur simultaneously. This theory considers the physiological changes accompanying emotion to be a sort of side effect—useful in preparing the body to take appropriate action but not essential to the conscious experience of emotion.

**Cannon-Bard theory**
A neurologically based theory of emotion suggesting that stimuli in the environment set off patterns in the hypothalamus and these patterns cause bodily changes in emotion and conscious awareness of the feelings of emotion simultaneously.

## The Cognitive Perspective

Among contemporary psychologists, the James-Lange and Cannon-Bard theories have been largely supplanted by the **cognitive theory** of emotion, which holds that the cortex plays the commanding role by simultaneously appraising both events that occur in the environment and feedback from the body. At any given moment, the information received by the cortex from both sources may be neutral in terms of emotional impact; in this case, we make a cognitive decision that we are not in an emotional state. On the other hand, the sensory information may lead the cognitive process to decide that we are in a state of joy, anger, or fear. We experience a change in our internal sensations, which we then try to appraise and interpret, given the context (Schachter & Singer, 1962). For example, when a student sitting alone in the library at night becomes aware of unusual bodily sensations, he or she may interpret them as feelings of loneliness. A student who has the same pattern of sensations the night before a difficult examination may interpret them as anxiety. Another student, who has put in an unusually hard day's work, may decide that he or she is tired.

**Cognitive theory**
A contemporary theory of emotion suggesting that the mind plays a commanding role in emotion and leads the individual to appraise and interpret events that occur in the environment.

A classic experiment testing this theory was conducted by Schachter and Singer in 1962. Participants received an injection of epinephrine, which causes arousal of the ANS. Some of the participants were informed that their symptoms—increased heart rate, more rapid breathing—were due to the drug, while others were given no information. The researchers predicted that the uninformed participants, who did not know why they were feeling aroused, would interpret their symptoms according to the situation in which they found themselves. Participants were left in a waiting room with another person whom they believed to be another participant but who was actually one of the experimenters. That person created either an angry situation (by complaining, tearing up a questionnaire, etc.) or a happy one (by making paper airplanes, joking around, etc.). The results were as predicted: The uninformed participants who were placed in the happy situation interpreted their feelings as happier than the informed participants did, and the uninformed participants who were placed in the angry situation interpreted their feelings as angrier than the informed participants did.

As indicated earlier, sometimes physiological states are detected consciously, sometimes not. Imagine, for instance, two mothers, both of whom are dealing daily with the troubled behavior of a preschool child and experiencing similar physiological changes. One mother, aware of her physiological state, recognizes that her emotional state is one of worry. The other mother, who fails to detect the subtle changes in her physiology, may not be able to recognize the depth of her distress.

Our cognitive appraisal of the environment is often immediate and automatic—something like the rapid first impression that occurs in perception. If you find a snake in your path, for example, everything seems to happen at once. Your heart jumps. You feel afraid. You leap back. All of this *seems* to occur without any conscious processing, although, as discussed in Chapter 14, the processing may simply occur so fast that we overlook it. At other times, our appraisal of the environment is more complex and deliberate. An example is the "slow burn" we sometimes experience when we hear an offensive remark. We may have no immediate reaction, but when we think about it and decide that it was insulting, we become angry.

In sum, the cognitive view maintains that bodily states alone are not enough to account for the different emotions we experience. When we become aware of bodily changes, what determines our emotion is our cognitive evaluation of the changes and the environmental situation in which those changes occur. (See the study chart below.)

## Individual Differences in Emotions

Some differences in emotional behavior appear to be inborn, as discussed more fully in Chapter 10. Studies of infants have shown, for example, that some are more inclined to smile than others and some have a pronounced tendency to cry at the slightest provocation.

There is considerable evidence that one inborn difference that affects emotions is the sensitivity of the ANS, which controls many of the bodily changes associated with emotion. Some people seem to react to weaker stimulation of the ANS than others—and to react more rapidly and with greater intensity. Patterns of ANS activity also vary. In the same kind of emotional situation, one person may experience a rapid heartbeat while another may experience only a small change in heart rate but a pronounced increase in skin temperature (Lacey & Lacey, 1958). Differences of this kind can be observed in children (Tennes & Mason, 1982). When they feel challenged, 2-year-olds who are chronically anxious, timid, and shy have been found to have a heart rate that is unusually high and stable. In similar circumstances, 2-year-olds who are far less fearful usually have a heart rate that is low and more variable (Kagan, 1989).

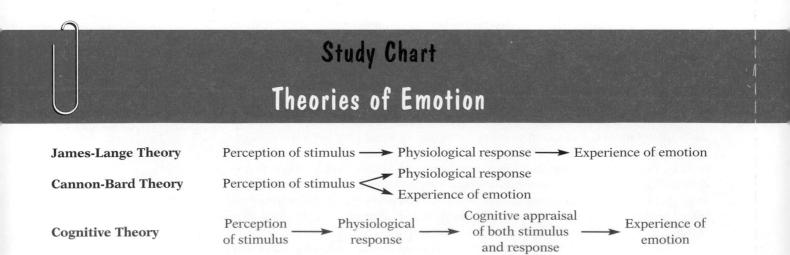

## Study Chart

## Theories of Emotion

| | |
|---|---|
| **James-Lange Theory** | Perception of stimulus ⟶ Physiological response ⟶ Experience of emotion |
| **Cannon-Bard Theory** | Perception of stimulus < Physiological response / Experience of emotion |
| **Cognitive Theory** | Perception of stimulus ⟶ Physiological response ⟶ Cognitive appraisal of both stimulus and response ⟶ Experience of emotion |

Any abnormality of the glands or nervous system can have significant effects on emotional experience. In humans, for example, malfunctioning of the pancreas as a result of an undiagnosed cancer can produce symptoms that mimic severe psychological depression (Goodwin & Jamison, 1990). And in laboratory animals, an interruption of the flow of information from the visual areas of the cortex to the brain's limbic system has been shown to disrupt emotional reactions, causing the animal to treat once-feared stimuli—for example, a threatening gesture—in a casual manner (National Institute of Mental Health, 1988).

We all know people who seem to "overreact" to even minor events in their lives, and others who don't seem to be fazed by even major upheavals. One individual, after losing his wallet, may be upset for days; another, upon learning that she needs serious surgery, may go on with her normal routine with little expression of emotion. Such differences between individuals are apparent at the very beginning of life and tend to remain as a major dimension of personality. Some people seem to crave variety and novelty in their lives. Described as "sensation-seekers," they tend to pursue a more complex existence than do most individuals (Zuckerman, 1991). Still other people respond to life events with more intense reactions regardless of whether the events evoke positive or negative emotions (Larsen, Diener, & Emmons, 1986).

Unfortunately, unpleasant emotional experiences tend to stay with us longer than pleasant ones do. In one study, students were asked to try to remember the last time something happened to them, either good or bad, that affected them emotionally. They remembered negative episodes and their emotional fallout more clearly and reported them more than twice as often as positive experiences (Scherer & Tannenbaum, 1986). Perhaps we remember negative episodes more clearly because they are exceptional rather than commonplace. Or perhaps it has proved adaptive for animals and humans to remember events that harm them more clearly than events that give pleasure. Avoiding the mountaintop where you almost fell and experienced extreme fear is more important than remembering the mountaintop where you saw a lovely sunset and felt serenity.

## Test Yourself

**(b)** You have just spilled soup on your clothes at a fancy dinner. Your face becomes flushed with embarrassment. What theory would hold that you felt embarrassed because you became flushed, not the other way around?

**(c)** If someone were to argue that the hypothalamus plays a critical role in emotions, whose theory would that person be supporting?

**(d)** If you are convinced that it is your thoughts about an event that are critical in the experience of emotion, what theory of emotion are you supporting?

**(e)** People clearly differ in the way they experience and express emotions. Are people born with such differences, or are they learned in the course of life?

(The answers are on page 322.)

# MOTIVES THAT ORIGINATE IN PHYSIOLOGICAL NEEDS

As pointed out at the beginning of the chapter, emotions are not the only states that involve changes in the body and behavior. We turn now to motives, which do so as well. Keep in mind that *needs* such as those for oxygen, food, and liquids give rise to the *drives* that underlie the motives discussed in this section.

There is no clear dividing line between emotions and motivational states like hunger and thirst. Like an emotion, a drive typically has three components: an environmental situation (e.g., food deprivation), internal changes (changes in the body's stores of fat), and a cognitive component (thoughts about food and the search for it). Both emotions and drives produce strong bodily sensations, and both trigger behavior. For example, just as an insult produces the bodily reactions and brooding behavior that we call anger, lack of food produces the physiological responses and cranky behavior of hunger.

Yet there is a difference, and even in ordinary conversation we don't refer to hunger as an emotion. Unlike an emotion, physiological motives involve the process

## FOCUS QUESTIONS

- What is meant by motives?
- How does homeostasis work to regulate body temperature and other needs?
- What factors are involved in hunger and thirst?
- What are the stages of sleep?
- What theories have been developed to explain the functions of sleep and dreams?

**Homeostasis**
A state of equilibrium or balance in any physiological system.

of **homeostasis,** the maintenance of bodily stability. An example of the physiological processes that attempt to maintain homeostasis is the mechanism by which the body's inner temperature is regulated. When we get too hot, the hypothalamus sends messages that cause us to sweat (cooling the body through evaporation) and also cause more blood to move toward the surface of the body, where it loses heat more quickly. When we get too cold, the hypothalamus sends messages that cause us to shiver (helping to generate heat) and cause blood to be routed toward the vital organs so that the body will not lose heat. Similarly, a home air-conditioning system automatically turns on when the temperature in the house rises above a certain point and automatically shuts off when the temperature falls below that point. In the case of humans and other animals, however, the process doesn't necessarily stop there. When basic homeostatic processes aren't sufficient to reduce body temperature, a person becomes motivated to shed clothing or find a cool place; when body temperature remains too low, a person becomes motivated instead to don extra clothing or find a warm place.

As explained in Chapter 2, one of the brain's functions is to preserve homeostasis by making sure the body has a constant supply of the substances that all cells need if they are to perform efficiently. When the body lacks any of these substances, homeostatic mechanisms motivate overt behavior intended to correct the imbalance. Two major sources of such motivation are **hunger** (caused by lack of nutrients) and **thirst** (caused by lack of water, which makes up two-thirds of our bodies). A third major source is sleep deprivation, which motivates us to get some rest.

**Hunger**
A major drive caused by lack of food.

**Thirst**
A major drive caused by lack of water.

## Hunger

All infants respond to an important fact of life: Taking in nutrients is vital to survival and well-being. Because food is crucial for all living creatures, our bodies must have the means to signal to us that it is time to eat. But how do we actually know that we are hungry?

Common sense suggests that we become aware of hunger through hunger pangs in the stomach, which feels empty and overactive and sometimes actually growls for food. This explanation is partially true. There are nerve fibers that carry messages to the brain from the stomach, mouth, throat, and intestines. Moreover, sustained distension of the stomach will indeed make us feel satiated and affect our eating behavior (Stellar, McHugh, & Moran, 1985).

But the role of the stomach is not so simple. Animals stop eating when they have eaten a substance that is especially nutritious, even if their stomachs are far from full. If the stomach is filled with an equal amount of nonnutritious bulk, the animal will continue eating. This indicates that the stomach's walls contain receptors that are sensitive to nutrients dissolved in the stomach acids. Evidently, these receptors relay the message that nutritious material is on its way into the system. The message is probably facilitated through the action of an intestinal hormone (Stellar et al., 1985). Whatever the mechanism of communication, more is involved in hunger than the state of the stomach and its messages to the brain.

**Set point**
An innate physiological mechanism that keeps an individual's body weight at a genetically "programmed" level.

**The Body's Set Point**    The drive to eat involves a number of interrelated physiological mechanisms that are governed by the body's **set point**—an innate physiological mechanism that keeps an individual's body weight at or above a genetically "programmed" level. In effect, the set point is part of a homeostatic mechanism that attempts to return us at least to our "natural" body weight, especially after we have gone below it (by dieting or being deprived of food). This is why fad diets or diet drugs rarely have lasting effects.

Until recently, it was widely believed that maintenance of the set point is facilitated by hunger messages originating in the liver, which manages the body's food metabolism. The evidence seemed clear enough: After we eat, there is an overly generous supply of glucose in the blood; the extra glucose is converted to **glycogen,** or "animal starch," in the liver. When the liver is actively manufacturing glycogen, we aren't hungry. But when we haven't eaten for a while, the liver begins to pour glucose into the blood from its store of glycogen, and this change in glucose level in the blood leads to hunger and to eating (Le Magnen, 1984).

However, a new view suggests that blood sugar is less important than the amount of fat stored in the body as a primary regulator of eating behavior. The body contains a large number of cells, at various locations, that are designed for the storage of fatty compounds. In evolutionary terms, survival of the species presumably depended on the ability of these **fat cells** to store energy that would tide the body over the prolonged periods of starvation that humans experienced frequently in the past (and still do in many places), as discussed in more detail later in this section. Under ordinary circumstances, hunger motivates us to eat and keep these cells filled to an appropriate level with fatty molecules. But when the body lacks other sources of food and energy, the fat cells are emptied and their contents used to produce energy. This raises the level of fatty compounds in the bloodstream, and this change, like the change in glucose in blood, serves as one of the triggers for hunger.

The current view is that the amount of fat in the body is represented in some way in the brain—and that the brain directs eating behavior to maintain the individual's optimal fat level. In effect, each person's brain tries to maintain a certain level of fat within her or his body. One piece of evidence for this view is that when an animal is starved and loses weight, if it is then allowed to eat as much as it wants, it will overeat until it has gained back the fat that was lost and, therefore, approach—or go beyond—its usual fat level.

**The Psychology of Hunger**   Hunger is also affected by external stimuli called **incentives.** These include such stimuli as the smell of food from a restaurant kitchen and the sight of pastries in a bakery window, as well as our eating habits and the social relationships we have built around eating. We tend to feel hungry around our usual dinner time regardless of our physiological condition, and we usually eat more when we are with family or friends than when we are alone. Moreover, like many other animals, humans learn from experience. We learn what kinds of food are nutritious, how much food will be available at a particular meal, what foods make us feel more energetic, and so forth. This knowledge enables us to seek out the food we need before we actually feel hungry; in other words, we don't always wait for homeostatic mechanisms to tell us we should eat (Ramsay, Seeley, Bolles, & Woods, 1996).

Although the physiological mechanisms involved in hunger are the same in everyone, there are wide variations in the ways in which we seek to satisfy hunger. Some people snack continuously; others generally eat only one meal each day. Individuals whose eating is initiated more readily by the presence of food in their environment than by internal physiological needs are referred to as "externals." Such individuals, when exposed to the smell and sight of inviting food, undergo an increase in the hormone **insulin** in their blood (Rodin, 1985). Since insulin acts to reduce blood glucose and may be the primary medium for signaling "I'm hungry" to the brain (F. E. Bloom & Lazerson, 1988), this finding provides another example of how external factors can affect internal physiology.

Clearly, hunger appears to be the result of an intricate system of bodily and psychological states—among them, the action of intestinal hormones, the level of glucose in the blood, the activity of the brain, the amount of fat in the body, the presence of cues for eating in the envi-

**Glycogen**
The "animal starch" in the liver that is converted from glucose in the blood after eating.

**Fat cells**
Cells designed for the storage of fatty compounds.

**Incentives**
The stimuli that arouse a drive or motive.

**Insulin**
A hormone secreted by the pancreas that metabolizes blood sugar to provide the body with energy.

Displays of food can act as incentives, stimulating feelings of hunger and leading us to eat more than we normally would.

© Bill Gallery/Stock Boston

ronment, and our reactions to these cues. Here, once again, we encounter one of the major issues in psychology described in Chapter 1: the interaction of biological and psychological forces in shaping behavior.

**Obesity** It is estimated that more than one-third of all adults in the United States are obese, meaning that they are at least 20% over their ideal weight—some by as much as 50 or even 100 pounds. Even more startling is the fact that in the last two decades the prevalence of obesity in the U.S. population increased by 57% (Jeffery, 2001). The reason is a mystery that many psychologists have spent years trying to unravel—in part because obesity can lead to severe psychological problems as well as to physical disorders such as high blood pressure, diabetes, and heart disease (Grinker, 1982). One study has shown that the adverse social and economic consequences of obesity, especially for women, often are greater than those of other chronic physical conditions (Gortmaker, Must, Perrin, Sobol, & Dietz, 1993). In this longitudinal study, women who were overweight (above the 95th percentile in weight for age and sex) were found to complete fewer years of school, earn significantly less per year, and have higher rates of household poverty. Overweight men were 11% less likely to be married than their slimmer counterparts.

As mentioned earlier, the set point is a homeostatic mechanism that stimulates us to eat when we need to restore an appropriate balance in the levels of nutrients in our bodies. Why, then, do some of us eat when we don't need to? One answer is evolutionary in nature: It is argued that because of the scarcity and unpredictability of food under natural conditions, many animals, including humans, have evolved to eat as much as they can whenever food is available, storing excess energy in the body to be drawn upon when food supplies are low. Hunting-and-gathering bands, for example, would feast on windfalls of game or berries whenever possible and endure long periods of hunger when no food was available. Today, however, for people who have continuous access to a variety of good-tasting foods, the urge to eat whenever food is available leads to overconsumption and in some cases obesity— because we have not yet had time to evolve mechanisms to counteract overeating (Pinel, Assanand, & Lehman, 2000). Of course, we can choose not to eat everything that is available, but such choices are easier for some people than for others.

In some cases, obesity seems to stem from metabolic disturbances. Instead of turning food into energy at the normal rate, the body stores an excessive amount in fat. In most cases, however, obesity is simply the result of eating too much and exercising too little (Stunkard, 1985). Sometimes the reason seems to be **emotional stress.** Clinical psychologists have found that many overweight patients overeat to relieve anxieties over competition, failure, rejection, or sexual performance. A study of both lower-income urban residents and Native Americans showed that individuals who undergo a great deal of stress and have an opportunity to eat will do so—and that this process, maintained over time, will lead to obesity (Pine, 1985).

The eating patterns of many overweight people are unusual in several respects. For one thing, overweight adults tend to eat whenever they have the opportunity, even if they have already had a meal and shouldn't be hungry. They are particularly likely to eat a lot when the food tastes unusually good—and more likely than people of normal weight to be turned off by food that tastes bad. This was demonstrated in a classic study by Stanley Schachter (1971), illustrated in Figure 8.3. The experimenter worked with two groups, one of normal weight and the other anywhere from 14% to 75% overweight. When the participants arrived at the laboratory, having skipped the previous meal, half from each group were fed sandwiches, the other half nothing. They then took part in what they thought was an evaluation of the taste of five different kinds of crackers presented to them in separate bowls. They were told that they could eat as few or as many of the crackers as they wished in making their judgments. As the graph shows, the amount eaten by the normal-weight participants was considerably lower if they had just eaten sandwiches. The overweight participants, however, actually ate somewhat

**Emotional stress**
The wear and tear on the body created by the physical changes that result from emotional states.

more on a full stomach than on an empty stomach.

It is possible that overweight people have a brain abnormality that affects the hypothalamus. Or it may be that the bloodstream of overweight people carries some kind of chemical that overstimulates the hypothalamus and thus creates more frequent and more intense feelings of hunger. Many experts believe that obesity stems from a complex combination of genetic and behavioral factors (Drewnowski, 1998). Whatever the source of obesity, the condition is best dealt with through programs that manage eating behavior (Stunkard, 1985).

For some obese people, even rigorous adherence to good nutrition practices will not yield great dividends. For these individuals, the problem may lie in the cells that store fatty compounds. It has been found that at least some overweight people have an unusually large number of these cells in their bodies (Björntorp, 1972). These cells may be voracious consumers of fatty compounds carried by the bloodstream. Thus, because of their excessive number of fat cells, overweight people may be constantly hungry for reasons they can't control. Their hunger may become particularly intense if they try to diet. It has been suggested that because of the social pressure against obesity, many "fat" people are actually underweight rather than overweight in terms of their bodies' requirements (Nisbett, 1972).

Why do some people have more fat cells than others? The answer seems to lie partly in heredity. Identical twins, who have inherited the same genes, are twice as likely to be in the same weight range as are fraternal twins (Stunkard, Foch, & Hrubec, 1986). Additional evidence for a strong hereditary factor comes from studies of adopted children, as illustrated in Figure 8.4.

One approach to solving the obesity problem may be to urge mothers not to push babies to overeat during the early months, when the number of fat cells is being established. But this approach comes too late for overweight adolescents and adults. Although weight loss programs appear to have more long-term efficacy in preadolescent children than in adults, extending treatment length and putting more emphasis on energy expenditure have modestly improved long-term weight loss in adults (Jeffery et al., 2000). Another approach is to stress fitness over fatness. There is considerable evidence that overweight people who follow a prudent eating and exercise plan can be healthy despite excess weight. Health care professionals therefore might be well advised to focus on helping people of all sizes develop healthful eating and exercise habits rather than focusing on weight loss alone (W. C. Miller, 1999; Rothblum, 1999).

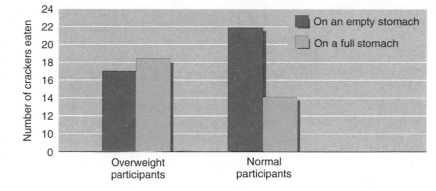

**FIGURE 8.3 One clue to overeating.** Overweight people tend to eat more on a full stomach than on an empty stomach.
*Schachter, 1971.*

**FIGURE 8.4 Overweight parents, overweight children.** Adults who had been adopted as children turned out to be thin, plump, or fat according to the size of their biological mothers rather than the size of the mothers who reared them. The pattern applies in the case of fathers as well.
*Stunkard, Foch, & Hrubec, 1986.*

## Thirst

Thirst resembles hunger in many respects. The commonsense explanation that we get thirsty when our mouths are dry again turns out to be partially true (Brunstrom, Tribbeck, & MacRae, 2000). Thirst does depend in part on messages carried to the brain from the mouth—as well as from the throat, which seems to signal how much liquid has passed through, and from the stomach, which signals whether it is empty or full. But this is not the full explanation.

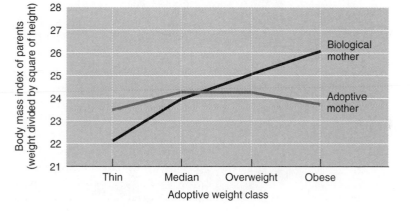

As with hunger, the hypothalamus plays an important role. Lack of water causes the body's cells to become dehydrated, and certain neurons in the hypothalamus appear to be sensitive to this change (Rolls & Rolls, 1982). Moreover, when water is lost, the body immediately activates mechanisms designed to conserve it. Lack of water reduces the volume of blood flowing through the body, causing sensory receptors in the heart and blood vessels to send signals to the brain. The reduced volume of blood also causes the kidneys to produce a chemical that stimulates the hypothalamus. Water loss results in the release of a hormone that helps prevent further loss through urination (Rolls & Rolls, 1982). Thus, thirst is triggered by various signs of imbalance in the body's water supply.

## Sleep

All humans sleep. Between the darkness out of which we are born and the darkness in which we end, there is a tide of darkness that ebbs and flows each day of our lives. A third of life is spent in sleep—that most usual yet profoundly mysterious realm of our existence.

It is almost impossible to find a living creature whose activity does not subside for at least one period each day. Lobsters become immobile. Butterflies fold their wings at night, attach themselves firmly to a blade of grass, and refuse to budge until morning. At night, some fish lie on their sides at the bottom of their aquarium; others float on the surface of the sea. Frogs, lizards, and turtles grow still for long periods. Birds and mammals sleep. In its alternation between activity and rest, every creature seems to reflect the biological necessity for sleep.

Why do we and other animals plunge into these periods of stillness? Why does the need for sleep play such an important part in the rhythm of our daily lives? And what causes us to experience dreams? Scientists have not yet answered these questions fully, but they have made considerable headway in tracking some of the unseen forces that govern the sleep-wake rhythm.

**Stages of Sleep**    Sleep may feel like a blanket of darkness punctuated by a remembered dream, a time when the mind is totally "out of it." Nothing could be less true. Studies have shown clearly that sleep is by no means a state of suspended animation in which the body and brain are shut down for a time. Instead, it is an activity in its own right. The brain continues to be highly active, though in a different way than while awake. All night a person drifts through different levels, or stages, of consciousness and brain activity. Using the electroencephalogram (EEG), which traces the pattern of the brain's electrical changes, along with measures of body temperature, pulse, and respiration, researchers have charted the stages of the average person's journey into sleep.

Imagine that you're watching your own descent into sleep, looking over the sleep researcher's shoulder. You are about to observe a journey that you make each night, yet one that you're scarcely aware of. As graph paper slowly moves under the pens of the EEG,

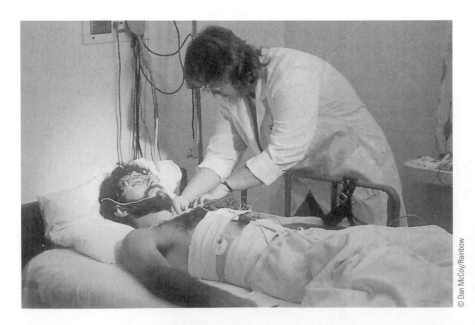

Hundreds of thousands of volunteers and patients have slept in sleep laboratories while researchers recorded the changes taking place in the brain and body. Here, a participant is prepared for observation during a night of sleep.

© Dan McCoy/Rainbow

a small pinched scrawl emerges. From the shapes of these waves the researcher can see when you closed your eyes. There, on one line, the rise and fall of your breathing has become even. On another line is the metronome flick of your pulse, also steady and even. Body temperature is gradually going down. The brain waves are showing a very definite, even frequency of about 9 to 13 waves per second, known as the **alpha rhythm.** Seeing this, the researcher knows that you are in a state of relaxation. You're awake but serene, and soon you will pass into sleep.

A sudden spasm of your body may now awaken you for a fraction of a second. This is a sign of neural changes. Known as the **myoclonic jerk,** it results from a tiny burst of activity in the brain. Children often describe it as a feeling of "falling off the bed." This phenomenon is normal in human sleep. It is finished in a fraction of a second, and the descent continues. Even if your eyes were partly open, you would be blind now. If an object were held before your eyes for a moment and you were awakened, you would not remember having seen it.

Your journey includes four **sleep stages (I, II, III, IV).** From the threshold of sleep, you sink into *Stage I.* The pens of the EEG trace waves that are small and pinched, showing that the voltage from the sleeping brain is small and rapidly changing. Your muscles relax and your pulse slows, but you might not feel asleep. If awakened, you might insist that you were wide awake. (See Figure 8.5.)

If you are not disturbed, in a few minutes you will sink into *Stage II,* during which the EEG pens trace out quick bursts of brain activity, with brain waves that are rapidly growing larger. The lines recording eye movements show shallow waves as your eyes slowly roll from side to side. If you were awakened now, you might still say that you had been awake all along—but you might be much less certain of that. At this point, you've been asleep for about 10 minutes. You might recall vague thoughts that could be as mundane as shopping lists, intermixed with strange images.

You are now descending into deeper sleep and are growing progressively harder to awaken. Within about 30 minutes, you will probably be immersed in *Stage III.* Now the pens trace brain waves that resemble a profile of buttes and mountains. As these brain waves show, the voltages are now much higher, and the changes are occurring more slowly. You may move or mutter, but your muscles are relaxed. Your breathing is even. Your temperature and blood pressure are still falling slightly, and it would take a loud noise to awaken you.

**Alpha rhythm**
A pattern of brain waves with a dominant frequency of about 9 to 13 waves per second, usually occurring when the person is relaxed, with eyes closed.

**Myoclonic jerk**
A sudden spasm in the body caused by a tiny burst of brain activity.

**Sleep stages (I, II, III, and IV)**
The levels of sleep from light to very deep, characterized by changes in the brain waves.

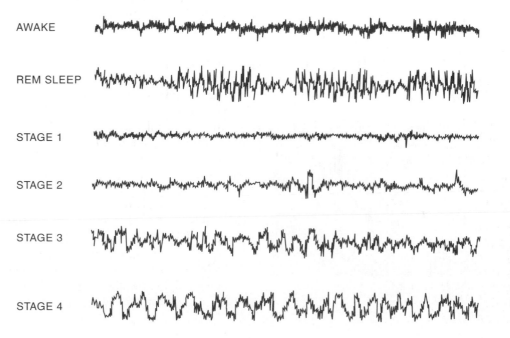

AWAKE

REM SLEEP

STAGE 1

STAGE 2

STAGE 3

STAGE 4

**FIGURE 8.5** Electrophysiological activity during sleep. EEG recordings show that brain waves display very different patterns during the various stages of sleep and wakefulness.

**Delta sleep**
The deep sleep of Stage IV, indicated by large but slow delta brain waves.

Stage III soon merges into *Stage IV.* It is the bottom of the lagoon, also called **delta sleep** for the large but slow brain waves known as delta waves. These have the profile of mountain ranges, and they signify the silent darkness of the ultimate depths of sleep. Stage IV seems to be a relatively dreamless oblivion. Sounds that might have awakened you 10 minutes ago may not penetrate your consciousness now. If someone shook you, rang a bell, or called your name, you would reluctantly rise to the surface. Most likely you would remember nothing and would say that your mind was blank. This is the sleep of the weary, and probably the state that most people like to consider sleep. Yet it represents only a fraction of the total night of sleep. You don't remain in the lower depths. After about 20 minutes, you start drifting upward into lighter sleep.

About 70 to 90 minutes after falling asleep, you approach the surface. You may turn over in bed or even thrash around for a moment. However, you do not break through into wakefulness or simply float on the threshold of consciousness; instead, something odd happens. You are so removed from the world that it would take a loud sound to awaken you. The EEG script, irregular and small, is a low-voltage, rapidly changing brain wave that resembles the pattern associated with waking. You are entering **REM (rapid-eye-movement) sleep**—so named because, among other changes in the body, the eyes begin darting rapidly under closed eyelids. During REM sleep, your physiology reflects a state of great excitement. Your heart beats irregularly. Your blood pressure fluctuates as it might during a period of intense waking emotion. Your genitals may indicate arousal—an erection if you are a male or vaginal lubrication and congestion if you are a female—even though the content of your dreams may be bland. Despite the storm of internal activity, your body is as relaxed as a piece of cloth. Because the brain's activity is similar to that of the waking state but the muscles are almost totally relaxed, this period is also referred to as **paradoxical sleep.**

**REM (rapid-eye-movement) sleep**
The period of the sleep cycle during which the brain waves resemble those associated with the waking state and the eyes dart rapidly under closed eyelids.

**Paradoxical sleep**
Another term for REM sleep, referring to the fact that the brain waves resemble those associated with the waking state but the muscles of the body are in an almost totally relaxed state.

As shown in Figure 8.6, during the night you repeat the entire sleep cycle four or five times, as if slowly sinking and rising on a recurrent tide; and if you have a bed partner who falls asleep when you do, chances are that you both enter and leave each stage of sleep at about the same time (Hobson, 1989). Toward morning, you no longer sink to the bottom in delta sleep, and your REM periods become longer. Sleep is lighter. Your body temperature begins to rise, and your blood chemistry changes. Soon you will awaken. You may remember a dream fragment, a moment of awakening, or nothing at all. Yet your mind was active throughout that time, and you were dreaming for a total of several hours. Altogether, about a quarter of the night is spent in this period, marked by dreaming, which is such a unique aspect of sleep that its possible functions will be described in more detail shortly.

**The Need for Sleep** The amount of sleep an individual needs varies considerably from one period of life to another. At birth, an infant sleeps as much as 18 hours a day. By age 4, the amount has decreased, on the average, to 9 to 10 hours, and by adolescence, to $7\frac{1}{2}$ hours—after which it declines gradually to about $6\frac{1}{2}$ hours in older adulthood (Hauri, 1982).

**FIGURE 8.6** The cycles of a night of sleep. During a normal night, the sleeper moves through the various stages of sleep in a series of cycles, each lasting about 90 minutes.

At any age, however, sleep seems to be one of the most essential needs of higher mammals. Merely lying in bed and resting is no substitute for real sleep (Mendelson, Garnett, Gillin, & Weingartner, 1984). In fact, any lack of sleep, whether from insomnia or other causes, is likely to make you feel tired, irritable, and generally below par. Despite the profound importance of sleep, millions of

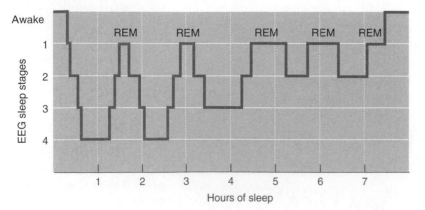

people don't get enough of it, a deficit that often has severe repercussions, including heart disease and fatigue-related accidents. In fact, sleep has been proven to be the single most important factor in predicting longevity—it is more influential than diet, exercise, or heredity (Dement & Vaughan, 1999). (See Psychology and the Media on pages 308 and 309.)

Although some people have been known to go without sleep entirely for a number of days without suffering any apparent damage (Webb & Cartwright, 1978), the older we grow, the more our performance and well-being suffer if we don't get enough sleep. A person can survive starvation for over three weeks, but three weeks' loss of sleep can produce symptoms that resemble mental illness. Prolonged sleep deprivation can lead not only to loss of mental efficiency but also to disturbances of perception and hallucinations—effects that are quickly overcome once the individual is allowed to sleep (Horne, 1988).

Even when only the normal cycles of sleep and waking are disrupted, we pay a price. This can be seen whenever our schedule changes significantly—for example, when we travel across time zones and experience jet lag. Investigators have found that shift work has the same effect, creating inefficiency, irritability, fatigue, physical symptoms, depression, and reduced mental acuity (Akerstedt, Torsvall, & Gillberg, 1982).

The need for sleep appears to be triggered by imbalances in brain chemistry, and possibly in body chemistry as well, that build up when we are awake and active. When we sleep, we correct the chemical imbalances, and we wake up ready to function again at full efficiency. Moreover, a sleep-producing chemical substance, acetylcholine, has been found in the brains of animals and in human urine. Injecting even very tiny amounts of this chemical into the brains of other animals causes about a 50% increase in very deep, dream-free sleep (Maugh, 1982). If the chemical factor could be produced synthetically, it might solve the problems of people who experience sleep disorders. At present, however, investigators have to process more than 4 tons of urine to obtain about a millionth of an ounce of the chemical.

**What Are the Functions of REM Sleep?**   As described earlier, the period known as REM sleep is different from the rest of the night. It can easily be observed in the sleep laboratory. When it occurs—roughly every 90 minutes—your eyes make large, jerky movements, and there's an 85% chance that you're experiencing a vivid or at least describable dream.

The content of dreams that occur during REM sleep has been used by psychologists and psychiatrists since Freud to delve into some of the hidden emotional aspects of a person's life. But the REM period is also a unique physiological state that is common to all mammals. Because the duration of REM sleep is longer in the young, psychologists reason that its functions must be "strictly and deeply biological" (Hobson, 1989) and that it may spur neural growth in young organisms. The rate of protein synthesis in the brain is at its highest during REM sleep, supporting this hypothesis (Hobson, 1989). By restoring brain proteins that are essential for learning and memory, REM sleep may work to keep brain tissues in good working order.

Both humans and other animals have more than their normal amount of REM sleep when, in their waking lives, they are involved in novel situations that require learning or new challenges. Moreover, a higher proportion of REM sleep occurs among individuals who are experiencing significant psychological problems (Hartmann, 1984).

Yet another function of REM sleep may be, to borrow a term from computer technology, "file maintenance" for the brain's memory banks. REM sleep may afford an opportunity for the brain to arrange memories in a hierarchy of psychological and emotional importance—and to discard items that are no longer needed (Crick & Mitchison, 1995).

---

**Test Yourself**

**(f)**   A friend whose pattern of eating varies periodically says that it's all a function of the body's set point. What is your friend saying?

**(g)**   Your roommate pleads with you not to expose him or her to any incentives in the refrigerator. What is being asked of you?

**(h)**   "All day my brain has been getting signals of imbalances in my body's water supply." How would you make that statement in simpler terms?

**(i)**   If someone is extremely difficult to awaken, what stage of sleep is that person likely to be in?

**(j)**   What physiological features of REM sleep account for its also being called paradoxical sleep?

(The answers are on page 322.)

## The Great American Sleep Debt

Americans are sleepy people. That is the conclusion of the National Commission on Sleep Disorders Research. . . . The commission, which was established by Congress to research sleep and its impact on society, estimated that 40 million Americans have sleep disorders and millions more suffer from a simple lack of sleep that can have grave repercussions.

The resulting sleepiness, according to commission chairman William Dement, chairman of the Stanford University Sleep Disorders Center, "makes them extremely vulnerable to inappropriate and often catastrophic sleep episodes and undermines their intellectual and emotional capacity."

Those episodes include serious traffic accidents caused by drowsy drivers, industrial accidents and lost productivity from employees who fall asleep on the job. The commission estimated that in 1990 sleep problems cost at least $16 billion in lost productivity, medical costs and sick leave. This does not include costs of catastrophic disasters in which sleep deprivation played a role.

The commission report said that the study of sleep has been neglected and what is available is fragmented and uncoordinated. It called for leadership in sleep research, including the establishment of a center for sleep disorders and research at the National Institutes of Health.

Commission officials said sleep disorders are commonly overlooked by physicians and their patients. They identified 17 specific disorders such as sleep apnea (re-peated cessation of breathing during sleep causing numerous wakenings each night and leading to cardiovascular complications), narcolepsy (uncontrollable sleep episodes) and chronic insomnia. They estimated 95% of cases go undiagnosed.

"A river of seriously ill sleep-disordered patients [is] flowing past the unseeing eyes of physicians, [and therefore] the lives and health of literally millions of Americans are in jeopardy," said Dement.

But just as important, Dement and other commission members said, is "the American sleep debt," the chronic scrimping on sleep that affects uncounted millions. The resulting fatigue can erode performance, interpersonal relations, child rearing, learning, psychological well-being, and behavior, they argued.

"The sleep debt, we believe, is every bit as important as the national debt," said commission member James K. Walsh, a special commission adviser and sleep specialist at Deaconess Hospital in St. Louis. Walsh is president of the American Sleep Disorders Association. "Whether it is caused by sleep disorders or sleep deprivation or daily rhythm factors, sleepiness is extremely prevalent . . . , and the consequences in the workplace and on the roads . . . are very costly."

"Using any yardstick," he said, "whether it be pain and suffering, profit and loss or life and death, our country is paying a steep price."

# THE SPECIAL CASE OF SEX AND SEXUALITY

**FOCUS QUESTIONS**

- What roles do biological, psychological, and social influences play in human sexual behavior?

- How does sexuality differ in males and females?

- What is meant by sexual orientation?

Unlike hunger, thirst, and other motives that arise from essential physiological needs, sex is something that, as individuals, we don't actually need—contrary to what some people might think. Sex is nonetheless a powerful motivator; sexuality pervades many aspects of our lives.

## The Role of Hormones and the Brain

If this were a book about animals other than humans, sex could be discussed in much simpler terms. Among nearly all nonhuman mammals, for example, sex is almost as direct a drive as hunger, though much less frequently triggered. The female sex drive is quiescent most of the time, and the female is not sexually attracted to males of her species. At regularly recurring intervals, however, the ovaries re-

The commission said that 56% of night workers report falling asleep on the job at least once a week, and more than 50% of these report errors by themselves or coworkers that are caused by lack of sleep.

Sleep researcher Mary Carskadon, from Brown University and a member of the commission, said that the brain has an inherent daily rhythm of sleepiness, for most people during two periods, the main one between 2 a.m. and 6 a.m. and another during the midafternoon. Studies have shown that night-shift workers, even those who have slept well during the day, often notice these drowsy periods.

Walsh said his studies have found that someone working at night is roughly as sleepy as a day worker who had 4 hours of sleep the night before.

The researchers said the sleep deficits have gradually developed in this century, in large part as a response to the flexibility in lifestyle that followed the introduction of electric lights. Carskadon, who specializes in sleep problems of children and adolescents, noted that in 1910, children ages 10 to 12 averaged $10\frac{1}{2}$ hours of sleep a night. In 1990, the average was closer to 9 hours. In 1910, teens between 13 and 17 slept about $9\frac{1}{2}$ hours a night. In 1990, it was a bit over 8 hours in 13-year-olds and $7\frac{1}{2}$ hours in 17-year-olds.

"We do not fully know all the consequences of this chronic sleep insufficiency, but we do know about 25% of teens report falling asleep in school at least once a week and more than 10% say they're late for school at least once a week because they've overslept," she said.

"Sleepiness," she said, "is not caused by a warm room, a dull lecture, a big meal, a long drive. These situations simply unmask or uncover the brain's sleepiness that is already present."

Carskadon said surveys show that fewer than half of American adults get 8 hours of sleep each day and a quarter get less than 7 hours. The exact amount needed varies, of course, from individual to individual, and there is a debate about the exact needs of the population as a whole. Carskadon believes that nearly all adults require at least 7 hours of sleep "to avoid accumulating a sleep debt," and most adults require at least 8 hours.

Among the most dramatic examples of problems caused by lack of sleep cited by the commission members were

- The 1989 *Exxon Valdez* oil spill in Alaska, in which transportation officials found that the third mate who was piloting the ship had fallen asleep.
- The 1979 Three Mile Island nuclear plant accident, in which fatigued workers at 4 a.m. did not respond to a mechanical failure.

Source: *From Sandy Rovner, "The Great American Sleep Debt,"* Washington Post, January 12, 1993. © 1993, The Washington Post. *Reprinted with permission.*

lease hormones that activate a sex control mechanism centered in the hypothalamus. During these periods, which vary in frequency and length from one species of mammal to another, the female seeks sexual contacts and engages in the courtship and copulation behavior that is characteristic of the species. The female's readiness is apparent from such cues as odors, vocal signals, body movements, or changes in the color and size of the genitals. These cues, in turn, prompt the male to initiate sexual behavior—although males may attempt copulation at any time in the female's cycle and be rebuffed if she is not receptive.

The hormones that determine animal sexual behavior are present in humans as well. Estrogen and testosterone—the primary female and male sex hormones—circulate in us as they do, for example, in mice. And, as in mice, they influence the activity of certain neurons in the hypothalamus and other parts of the limbic system. These, in turn, influence the production of additional hormones. But this is where the basic similarity between humans and animals ends. The specifics of human sexual behavior are quite different from those of other animals (F. E. Bloom & Lazerson, 1988; Crooks & Baur, 1999).

Sexual responsiveness, especially in human females, does not seem to be strongly tied to hormones. To begin with, the desire for sex among women is not significantly keyed to monthly fluctuations in hormone levels (Harvey, 1987). Among

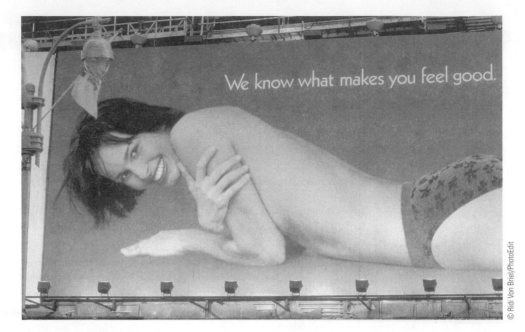

Many ads attempt to take advantage of sexual attraction to sell products or services.

**Menopause**
**The time in a woman's life when the ovaries cease to function and menstruation ends.**

most mammals, a female without ovaries is totally unreceptive to sex and typically fights off the male's overtures. But a woman without ovaries—and, therefore, without a supply of estrogen—is still potentially motivated for sexual activity. After **menopause,** when the ovaries no longer function and menstruation ends, sexual interest and activity not only do not wane but may actually increase, perhaps in part because the woman need no longer be concerned about becoming pregnant.

Although it is true that human males who lack male sex hormones are less active sexually, such effects are hardly universal. Again, there is a marked contrast between humans and other mammals. In rats, for example, castration leads to a progressive reduction in—and, eventually, an end to—sexual activity. In human males with cancer of the testicles who undergo chemical treatment that prevents the formation of male sex hormones, the effect is far less clear. Although some of these men no longer pursue sex, others maintain their usual sex life (P. A. Walker, 1978).

Clearly, the extent to which hormones determine sexual behavior is less pronounced for humans than it is for other animals. Nor does human sexual behavior depend on some "sex center" in the brain that operates like an on-off switch. Thus, biology alone cannot explain all of human sexual behavior. For example, in many cases the emotional fallout of marital conflict—not hormonal changes—is the cause of reduced sexual desire among couples.

## The Power of Psychological Influences

Sexual expression is influenced not just by basic biological urges but by a whole array of desires and preferences that we begin to learn in childhood and may continue to revise throughout our lives. For a discussion of how sexual behavior varies over the years, see the Life Span Perspective on page 312.

Sexual excitement can arise without physical contact. Some people find that even fantasizing about a sexual encounter can bring about not only sexual arousal but orgasm (F. E. Bloom & Lazerson, 1988), and lack of interest in sex can be reversed simply by thoughts of novel sexual experiences. In one study, a group of women and men saw a sexually explicit film on four consecutive days. At the end of the fourth day, they became bored, and some even reported a negative effect. Half the participants then saw a film with the same actors performing different sex acts, and the other half saw a film with different actors performing the same acts. All of the participants reported being aroused again by the novelty (Kelley & Musialowski, 1986).

Conversely, the excitement phase of the sexual cycle is often aborted by purely psychological factors—especially anxiety—or by distracting stimuli such as a knock on the door or a ringing telephone. From the study of college-age men portrayed in Figure 8.7, it would seem that the more distracting the outside stimulus, the greater the impact on arousal.

Even in nonhuman mammals—especially primates—sexual functioning can be strongly influenced by the environment. For example, research on monkeys has shown that levels of testosterone vary as a function of the social situation in which the monkey finds itself. If a male is placed in contact with female monkeys in an environment that includes other subordinate males, his testosterone level will increase—and this increased level is accompanied by increased sexual activity. On the other hand, if the male is placed in a setting in which he is dominated by the other males, his testosterone level will decrease—leading, in turn, to lower levels of sexual activity (Moberg, 1987). Thus, although hormones affect behavior, hormonal activity in turn is regulated by the social milieu.

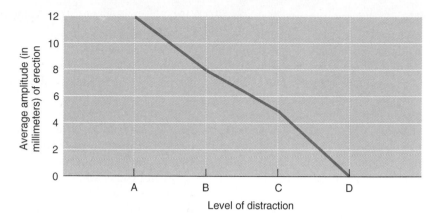

FIGURE 8.7 The effect of distractions on sexual arousal. A group of men listened through earphones to an erotic audiotape—first without any distractions (A) and then simultaneously with each of three tapes containing increasingly distracting material. The distracting tapes required the participants to write down a series of numbers (B); add successive pairs of digits and write down the results (C); and classify pairs of digits according to a complex scheme (D). Note that as the level of distraction rose, penile erection faltered.
*Adapted from Geer & Furh, 1976.*

## Social and Cultural Influences

In the United States, thin women are regarded as sexually attractive, at least among most ethnic groups. But in parts of Africa, lanky fashion models would be viewed as revolting. There, women spend a period before their marriage in a "fattening hut," where they are placed on a diet intended to increase their bulk—and thus enhance their sexual seductiveness (Gregersen, 1983).

Petting, or foreplay, as a prelude to intercourse is virtually universal in the Western world, but among some Polynesians petting follows rather than precedes sexual union. In turn, to most people in the United States, sexual intercourse with a close relative—parent, sister, brother—is repugnant. Not so to the Kubeo tribe of South America, who *require* that a boy have intercourse with his mother to officially highlight the start of his sex life (Gregersen, 1983).

Those are just a few examples of how human sexual behavior is shaped by the values and standards of the society in which people live—a potent reminder of the role of cultural context in human behavior. To social and cultural historians, this would hardly be surprising. Over the centuries, every shade of sexual attitude has been enthusiastically adopted in some settings but condemned in others. Homosexual acts were punishable by death among the ancient Hebrews but taken for granted by the Greeks. The early Christians held that abstinence was the only way to deal with the sex urge—at about the same time that the Romans were indulging in orgies. In the early 20th century, mention of sex, either in print or in conversation, was virtually taboo. Today, there is almost complete freedom to discuss and write about sex, and movies and television programs often present sex as a major theme.

Evidence of the revolution in attitudes toward sexual behavior in the United States is not hard to find. Fifty years ago, most people viewed marriage as the main avenue to sexual activity; today, premarital and extramarital sex are more widely accepted (Crooks & Baur, 1999). Most people are no longer mortified when someone in public life acknowledges that he or she is same-sex-oriented or bisexual—and the gay liberation movement is prominent in many cities and colleges.

Like many other human behaviors, sexual behavior evolves across the life span. Changes reflect not only biological capacities for sex at various stages of life but also the different psychological and social meanings attached to the sexuality during distinct periods.

Ultrasound photographs of male fetuses revealing erections in the womb (Calderone, 1983) suggest that the basic physiological activities symptomatic of sexual arousal are in place at the very start of life. Although it is not clear how prevalent or purposeful masturbation is among young children, it does seem that the motive for sex exists in rudimentary form well before puberty. Still, although many infants and children exhibit sexual behavior, they don't do so in a goal-directed way (Offir, 1982). Observations and interviews with children suggest that a motivated interest in sex—playing "doctor" and asking questions about body parts and the "facts of life"—must await cognitive maturation.

Adolescence brings the first serious attempts to build relationships with the opposite sex. Sexuality emerges as a prominent concern, not only because of the physical changes of puberty but also because adolescents must establish their sexual identities as they cope with all the other difficulties of becoming adults. The challenges of these years intensified beginning in the 1960s, when much of society adopted more permissive attitudes toward sex. By the 1990s, about one-third of self-identified white females and half of self-identified black females were having intercourse before age 18 (U.S. Census Bureau, 2001). The figures for teenage boys—which traditionally have been higher—have not changed as much, but today fewer male adolescents have sexual experiences exclusively with prostitutes or "bad" girls, and more with friends or classmates.

During young adulthood, there is less peer pressure to engage in sex and fewer demands from parents to set limits—new freedoms that present opportunities for sexual experiences dictated from within rather than without. Yet external factors still influence sexual behavior. Despite more liberal attitudes, young adults in the United States in the mid-1980s appeared to be exercising growing care in the selection of partners (Ehrenreich, Hess, & Jacobs, 1986)—a trend that continues today. Indiscriminate, casually initiated sexual encounters—among heterosexual as well as homosexual couples—have decreased, mainly in response to the threat of AIDS. At the same time, however, sex outside of marriage has become more common. This trend is especially apparent among women, whom some studies indicate are as likely as their mates to engage in extramarital relationships (Wyatt, Peters, & Guthrie, 1988).

Through the adult years, many people remain happily active sexually with their mates of many years. A complex interplay of physical and psychological factors can enrich a sexual relationship in adulthood. For others, motivation for sex with one's mate may diminish at this time, and sexual dysfunctions may appear that often are regarded as symptomatic of marital tensions and the accompanying feelings of anger (Clifford & Kolodny, 1983). Seeking to understand the factors at work makes the topic endlessly puzzling to individuals and societies—and challenging to scientists.

Sexuality in older adulthood continues to reflect an interplay of physiological changes and social attitudes. Biologically, the sexual response changes. Older men take longer to become sexually excited, and erections tend to be less frequent and less firm. Some women experience a decrease in vaginal lubrication, making sexual intercourse painful (Sarrel, 1990). Other earlier signs of sexual excitement—nipple erection and clitoris enlargement—may abate. And for both sexes, the orgasm is marked by fewer contractions. Social attitudes, too, exert an effect. In a youth-oriented culture, older people are not expected to be sexually active and may be looked upon as strange if their sexual motives are still strong (Crooks & Baur, 1999). Despite the problems, the zest for sex—and the pleasure of the experience—are not universally extinguished with age. Studies following individuals over long periods reveal that earlier patterns of sexual interest and ability often are maintained. For individuals in reasonably good health, sexual activity can play a vibrant role throughout the "declining" years (Adams & Turner, 1985).

• • • • • • • • • • • • • • • • • • • • • • • • • • • • • • • • • • • • • • • • • • • • • • • • • • • • • • •

Whether in a remote African village or a teeming Western city, social and cultural forces clearly shape sexuality.

An evolutionary perspective is useful in linking the various influences, as well as in clarifying certain gender-based differences in sexual attitudes and emotions. In a study addressing this point, male and female college students were asked to visualize their partner engaging in sexual relations with another person and, separately, forming a strong emotional relationship with another person. The students' responses to each scenario were recorded, using several physiological measures—skin conductance, pulse rate, and muscle activity. Participants of both sexes were distressed over both types of infidelity, but men were more upset by the notion of sexual infidelity of a mate than by the notion of emotional infidelity, as depicted in Figure 8.8. Women responded in the opposite way (Buss, Larsen, Westen, & Semmelroth, 1992). The researchers ascribed the differences to evolution-based sex roles: Women are more threatened by the loss of a mate's investment in the task of rearing offspring; men are more

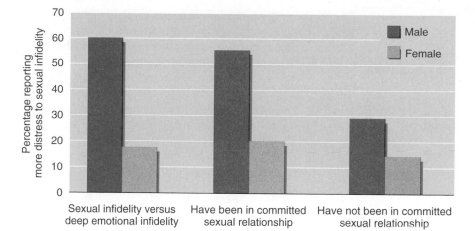

threatened by the risk of investing their resources in genetically unrelated offspring.

## Sexual Orientation

The direction taken by the motive for sex defines our **sexual orientation**—the attraction we feel toward individuals of a given sex. The large majority of men and women are **heterosexual,** feeling strong sexual attraction to members of the opposite sex. Those who are **homosexual,** or **same-sex-oriented** (gay if male, lesbian if female), are drawn to members of their own sex. Those who are open to both same-sex and opposite-sex experiences are **bisexual.**

Most people develop a sense of themselves as male or female very early in life. This *gender identity* usually remains stable throughout life. During adolescence, most people also form a stable *sexual identity;* they can say clearly, "I am a woman and I am attracted to men" or "I am a man and I am attracted to women." Such an identity is generally accepted and supported by family and peers. A small but significant minority, however, discover that they are sexually oriented wholly or in part to members of the same sex. The realization that one is potentially lesbian, gay, or bisexual tends to be accompanied by feelings of being different from others, an intense process of self-examination, and a struggle to reconcile this aspect of the self with one's overall identity (Carrion & Lock, 1997; Diamond, 1998; Patterson, 1995). Moreover, those who "come out" and openly acknowledge their sexual orientation are subjected to a variety of negative reactions from the heterosexual majority in the form of *homophobia*—aversion and prejudice that set the stage for verbal and at times physical aggression against same-sex-oriented or bisexual people. As a result, gay, lesbian, and bisexual adolescents show higher rates of depression, substance abuse, and risk of suicide than do heterosexual adolescents (Faulkner & Cranston, 1998; Remafedi, 1999; Remafedi, French, Story, Resnick, & Blum, 1998; Safren & Heimberg, 1999). In addition, those who internalize the society's prejudicial views of them live with a sense of shame and lowered self-esteem (Allen & Oleson, 1999).

What causes an individual to become gay or lesbian? This question, which has long attracted the interest of researchers in psychology and other behavioral sciences, is now being addressed by neuroscientists as well. No definitive answers have yet been found, but it is worthwhile to explore some of the extensive research that has been conducted in this area.

Some research suggests the possibility of a biological basis for homosexuality. Exposure to an abnormal level of sex hormones during a critical period of prenatal development may predispose a person to same-sex sexual activity. For example,

**FIGURE 8.8** Sex differences in jealousy. Men said they would be more distressed by sexual infidelity in a mate than by emotional infidelity, and men who actually had experienced a committed sexual relationship were most likely to be distressed over the thought of a mate's sexual infidelity. In contrast, women were more distressed by a partner's emotional infidelity than by his sexual infidelity, a response that held true whether or not the women had experienced a committed sexual relationship.

**Sexual orientation**
The attraction felt toward persons of a given sex.

**Heterosexual**
Sexually attracted to members of the opposite sex.

**Homosexual or same-sex-oriented**
Sexually attracted to members of the same sex.

**Bisexual**
Sexually attracted to members of both sexes.

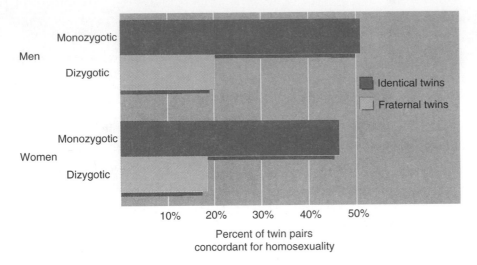

**FIGURE 8.9 Is sexual orientation an inherited trait?** Over the years, reports of the rate of *concordance*, or agreement, in sexual orientation among identical twins has ranged from 100% to 10%. *The data for women are from Bailey et al., 1993; those for men are from Bailey & Pillard, 1991.*

As the stigma attached to same-sex orientation has diminished, increasing numbers of gay couples are formalizing their union in marriage or equivalent ceremonies.

animal studies have revealed that stress during pregnancy can affect the concentration of male hormones in the brain of the fetus, leading to the "feminization of offspring" (Jacobowitz, 1989). And when gay men are injected with estrogen, many show a biochemical response of the pituitary gland that is typical of women—a response that is not found among heterosexual men (Gladue, Green, & Hellman, 1984). Despite such findings, however, the actual levels of sex hormones within any given individual do not correlate with that individual's sexual orientation.

The possibility of a biological basis for some aspects of homosexuality appears to be buttressed by reports of specific anatomical differences in the brains of gay and heterosexual men. For example, a part of the anterior hypothalamus in gays is anatomically more similar to the brain structure typically found in women than to that found in heterosexual men (LeVay, 1991). Because the hypothalamus is known to govern sexual behavior, this finding may be more than simply a correlation—but, as noted in Chapter 2, more research is needed to enable us to determine whether the difference is a cause or an effect of being gay.

A different approach to assessing biological underpinnings of homosexuality is to study identical and fraternal twins, nontwin biological siblings, and adoptive siblings, in samples of men (Bailey & Pillard, 1991) and women (Bailey, Pillard, Neale, & Agyei, 1993). As shown in Figure 8.9, these well-publicized studies suggest a substantial—but not exclusive—genetic contribution to sexual orientation. The finding of significantly higher *concordance*, or agreement, for same-sex orientation among identical (monozygotic) twins than among nonidentical (dizygotic) twins is consistent with what would be expected for a heritable trait. But among both men and women, more than half of identical twins—who share genes, as well as prenatal and, presumably, family environments—are *discordant* for the "trait" in question. Thus, even if the existence of a specific "homosexual gene" were proven, more sophisticated models for the interaction of biological, psychological, and social-environmental factors would be required to answer the question.

Subsequent to these reports, investigators at the National Cancer Institute described a preliminary genetic linkage analysis in which the DNA of 33 out of 40 pairs of gay brothers pointed to the possible role of a maternally transmitted gene in influencing same-sex orientation (Hamer, Hu, Magnuson, Hu, & Pattatucci, 1993). Although the researchers issued a number of caveats about the finding and called for replication studies, the study generated considerable media attention.

Neuroscientists, like other researchers, emphasize that lesbians and gays are far from uniform, not only in their biological makeup but also in their early development, family histories, and personality characteristics. As is the case for so many human traits, sexual orientation undoubtedly arises from a complex interaction among biological, psychological, and social factors (Money, 1987). Some researchers emphasize that it is impossible to disentangle the biological and psychological contributions to the behavioral differences that constitute sexual orientation (Baumrind, 1995) and that understanding what it means to be a member of the homosexual minority is much more important than understanding what causes homosexuality (e.g., Cohler & Galatzer-Levy, 2000; Schueklenk & Ristow, 1996).

The recognition of diversity among gays and lesbians has been partly responsible for reducing the stigma associated with a same-sex or bisexual orientation. Although far from erased, negative attitudes have waned as a more accepting attitude toward sexual orientation has emerged. Today, it is generally acknowledged that we do not choose our sexual preferences, nor can we readily alter them. In addition, homosexuality is *not* considered a sexual or mental disorder. It was removed from the American Psychiatric Association's *Diagnostic and Statistical Manual* as of the 1973 printing.

> **Test Yourself**
>
> **(k)** If a friend were to argue that sex is no different in humans than in other animals, what are two facts you might use to argue otherwise?
>
> **(l)** One friend argues that homosexuality arises from purely biological factors; another says that it arises from purely psychological and social factors. Who is right?
>
> (The answers are on page 322.)

# MOTIVES THAT ARE PRIMARILY PSYCHOLOGICAL

"I want so much to win at tennis, I can taste it."

"If I work hard enough, I'm sure I can graduate with honors."

"If only she would lose that client—then *I* would make partner!"

> **FOCUS QUESTIONS**
>
> • What kinds of motives are primarily psychological in their origins?
>
> • How do psychological motives influence behavior?

Feelings like these are familiar to most people. A hallmark of being human is an ability and propensity to strive for symbolic goals. For some, the self-imposed pressure to achieve a psychologically valued goal can be as relentless as a biologically based motive, although biology certainly does not press a person to make the dean's list, amass a fortune, or see a competitor suffer an embarrassing loss. Rather than a physiological need, the impetus is the cognitive appraisal of the desirability of a given goal. As we will see in this section, the motives that compel our behavior have diverse roots and can lead in unexpected directions, with both positive and negative outcomes.

## Achievement Motivation

Most of us are motivated to use our talents to master certain skills and goals. Beginning in childhood, we want to improve our ability and performance at tasks that are valued by significant others and by society at large—whether the task be farming, hunting, or learning to read. This urge to attain optimal levels of performance on valued tasks is called **achievement motivation.**

Very few people, of course, have a uniformly high standard of achievement in all their undertakings. For some people, the achievement motive is directed mostly at athletic prowess; for others, at intellectual mastery, musical skills, or making money. People with a strong achievement motive tend to work hard at the things they tackle and to make the most of their talents. They engage in "competition with a standard of excellence" (McClelland, 1985; McClelland & Koestner, 1992). They seek to master specific skills and to display a high level of performance when applying those skills—for example, in sports contests or musical performances (Barron & Harackiewicz, 2001; Rawsthorne & Elliott, 1999).

**Achievement motivation** The urge to attain optimal levels of performance on valued tasks.

© Mauduit Chantal/CORBIS SYGMA

Most people are motivated to use their talents to master certain skills or goals, although few go so far as to attempt to climb Mount Everest without oxygen.

The impetus to realize certain talents can be so strong that individuals manage to overcome serious obstacles. Some people devote themselves single-mindedly to achieving their "personal best" despite poverty, lack of education, or even threats of bodily harm and psychological pain. An example of the latter can be found in a study of six of the world's highest-ranking stunt performers—five men and one woman—who regularly performed dangerous feats for television and the movies. Contrary to popular expectation, they were motivated not by the thrill of courting danger, but rather by the desire to achieve mastery over the specific challenge they faced (Piet, 1987).

Achievement is especially significant, of course, in academic settings, and numerous studies have focused on achievement motivation in college students. One recent study (Covington, 1999) explored the tension between the desire to learn particular subjects (the alleged purpose of education) and the desire to achieve high grades (necessary to find good jobs after graduation). Five separate yearly cohorts of 500 undergraduate students were observed and interviewed. The results showed that students are more likely to value what they are learning when they are attaining their grade goals, when what they are studying is of personal interest, and when the dominant reasons for learning do not involve competition with others or fear of failure. In other words, when the academic setting emphasizes self-improvement, discovery, and creativity, rather than the need to increase one's own status at the expense of others and to avoid failure, students are more likely to care about what they are learning.

Regardless of the setting, achievement motivation depends to a great extent on the individual's perceptions of his or her abilities (often based on what others, especially teachers, appear to believe about those abilities), along with the person's expectations of success in a particular context (which may be affected by culture or gender roles) and how much he or she values a particular task (is the task useful or enjoyable enough to make it worthwhile to overcome the difficulties involved?). Researchers have found that children's ability beliefs, expectancies for success, and subjective values change across the school years: Younger children have more positive achievement-related beliefs than do older children. This pattern is a source of concern for educators and psychologists, who are conducting ongoing research to determine why it occurs (Wigfield & Eccles, 2000).

**Origins of Achievement Motivation**   Why do some of us develop a stronger desire for achievement than others? There are many reasons, including our experiences in the home and at school, what we read and what we see on television, and the people we come to admire (and therefore imitate) or dislike. Our estimate of our own abilities, which may be accurate or distorted, also plays a part. We tend to be motivated to persist with tasks in which we are talented, and to withdraw when we feel that we can't attain a goal because we lack sufficient skill (Reeve, Cole, & Olson, 1986). In some instances, even if a required skill or aptitude is present, the way we define ourselves—or allow society to define us—helps determine our level of achievement motivation. One study found that intelligent women whose quantitative SAT scores in mathematics would make pursuit of a career in science a reasonable goal nonetheless tended to shy away from that choice simply because they had a low expectation of success or a high level of anxiety about their mathematical ability (Chipman, Krantz, & Silver, 1992).

The way our parents treated us as children may be a crucial factor. In one early study, a group of children was divided into those who scored high and those who scored low on achievement motivation. Their mothers were then asked at what ages they had demanded that the children start to show signs of independence—that is, go to bed by themselves, entertain themselves, stay in the house alone, make their own friends, do well in school without help, and later earn their own spending money and choose their own clothes. Questions were asked about 20 forms of independent behavior. The children who turned out to be high in achievement motivation had been urged to be independent at much earlier ages than the other children (Winterbottom, 1953). Subsequent studies have reinforced the conclusion that encouraging independence in early childhood seems to strengthen achievement motivation—and that parents who make few demands for mature behavior seem to discourage it (Mussen, Conger, Kagan, & Huston, 1990).

Parents who cultivate high achievement motivation in their children leave little doubt in the child's mind about the value of achievement, rewarding their children when they perform well and admonishing them when they do not. They talk about achieving individuals as the kinds of people they admire, holding them up as models. Moreover, they make their own aspirations obvious. And in their young they stimulate not only self-reliance but curiosity and exploration (Segal & Segal, 1985). There is evidence, too, that parents who endure financial hardships and are dissatisfied with their own accomplishments increase the achievement motivation of their children (Flanagan, 1989).

The nature of achievement motivation, like that of many other characteristics, is often a function of social context—another reminder of one of the basic psychological issues introduced in Chapter 1. For example, the relatively poor performance in mathematics of U.S. high school students compared with certain Asian students has been explained in part by cultural contrasts in achievement motivation. Compared with children in China and Japan, more U.S. children grow up in families that value "happiness" to a greater degree than they value achievement in academic skills (Stevenson & Lee, 1990). (This cross-cultural research is discussed more fully in Chapter 10.)

But research across diverse racial and ethnic groups shows that the influence of parents and family values on academic achievement is strongly modified by the influence that a student's peers exert on the motive to achieve. In a study examining academic achievement among self-identified white, black, Asian, and Hispanic students, the value that peers attached to academic success could either augment or undermine a student's achievement motivation. For the Hispanic and white students, parents were the most potent sources of influence, but the low value attached to school success by Hispanic students' ethnically similar peers diluted the parental influence. The high value attached to achievement by Asian students and peers augmented a motive to achieve instilled by family values (Steinberg, Dornbusch, & Brown, 1992).

## Motivation for Affiliation and Dependency

Most young children seek close attachments with caregivers and, later, friendly relationships with others, but the strength of this tendency varies widely. Some people maintain close ties with their parents throughout their lives and are extremely sociable in general. They are "joiners," who like to be part of a group and prefer to work at jobs where they cooperate with and have the help of others. Other people prefer to spend their time alone and to work apart from others. Still others appear to be "loners," who care very little for human companionship.

The desire to be around other people and have close relationships with them is called **affiliation motivation**. It is particularly noticeable in people who are experiencing unpleasant emotions, for there seems to be considerable truth in the adage that "misery loves company." This fact was demonstrated by an experiment in which university students were asked to visit a psychology laboratory. When they arrived, they found a frightening apparatus awaiting them and were told that it was designed to deliver severe electrical shocks. After having been made anxious about the nature of the experiment, they were told that they could wait their

**Affiliation motivation**
The desire to be around other people and have close relationships with them.

Affiliation motivation leads us to spend time with other people, join groups, and make friends.

**Dependency motivation**
The desire to rely on others.

**Motivation for certainty**
The desire to feel at home in one's world, to know where one stands, and to avoid the discomfort of unfamiliar and surprising events.

turn either alone or in company. Fully 63% preferred to have company while waiting, with most of the rest saying that they did not care one way or the other. In a control group of students who had not been made anxious about the experiment, the proportion who preferred to have company while waiting was only 33% (Schachter, 1959).

In jobs that call for a group effort, it has been found that people with a strong affiliation motivation would rather be with their friends even when they could work with strangers who were more competent and could offer more help. They are more pleased by signs that their group is getting along well than by its accomplishments. There is some evidence that students who are high in affiliation motivation make better grades in classes where everyone is friendly and the instructor takes a personal interest in the students. For those who are low in affiliation motivation, grades appear to deteriorate under comparable conditions (McKeachie, Lin, Milholland, & Isaacson, 1966).

Closely allied to the desire for affiliation is **dependency motivation.** Dependency motivation probably stems from our experiences as babies, when we are completely dependent on our parents. This tendency to rely on others—at least at certain times and for certain things—never leaves us. We continue to have a strong urge to depend on others to organize our lives, set up our schedules, help us with our work, comfort us, and give us support and pleasure. Like affiliation, dependency motivation is especially prominent in troubling situations. Hospital patients, for example, often have mixed feelings. Despite their illness and worry, they may seek opportunities to be dependent on their physicians and nurses.

Behavior that stems from dependency motivation has been found to be more common among women than among men in the United States. This is probably because until recently our society considered dependency to be more appropriate for women. Men are less likely to display dependency because society has frowned on such behavior in males. They are more likely to display their dependency in subtle ways—perhaps by taking their problems to a professor or a boss (though usually under the guise of being logical rather than emotional).

## Motivation for Certainty

Even very young children display a strong **motivation for certainty**—that is, a desire to feel at home in their world, to know where they stand, to avoid the discomfort of unfamiliar and surprising events. They clearly enjoy the certainty represented by their own bed, their own toys, and the presence of familiar people and objects in their environment. As they grow a little older, most like to have rules set for their conduct; they like the certainty of knowing what they are permitted and not permitted to do. The prospect of uncertainty—being taken care of by a strange baby-sitter, going to school for the first time—is likely to upset them.

Adults, too, tend to be motivated toward the known and away from the unknown—to avoid inconsistency and novelty that they can't handle well. Although some individuals, such as explorers and astronauts, seem to thrive on novelty, most people operate with a strong desire for certainty most of the time. We like to feel that we know how our relatives and friends will act toward us, what is likely to happen tomorrow in the classroom or on the job, and where and how we will be living next year.

In some people, motivation for certainty is so strong that they seem to avoid any kind of change, even when the price of inaction is very high—for example, some people persist in marriages that they have long since decided are hopeless. Apparently, they would rather stay with the known, no matter how unpleasant, than face the unknown. For most of us, however, the desire for certainty is not overpowering and simply operates to keep our lives on an even keel.

## Motivation to Meet Standards

All of us, as we grow up, begin to set rules for our own behavior. Through learning what society values and through identification with our parents and other adults, we acquire inner standards of many kinds. We also acquire a strong **motivation to meet standards.** Most people want to be attractive, responsible, friendly, skillful, generous, honest, and fair. Some, because of a difficult early environment, have standards that motivate them to be domineering, tough, rebellious, or even asocial.

Our standards form our **ego ideal**—our notion of how we would always think and act if we were perfect. Some of us acquire such high standards that we can't possibly live up to all of them at all times. In fact, the motive to live up to inner standards often requires us to suppress other powerful motives. Our standards may tell us that we should not take food from another person even if we are hungry, that we should be kind even to people toward whom we feel hostile, that we should play fair no matter how much we want to win. As a result, we may feel shame and guilt over our thoughts, if not our actual conduct. Our self-esteem—that is, our evaluation of ourselves—suffers when we fail to meet our standards, and the result may be anxiety or depression. On the other hand, when we do at least approach our standards, we get to feel good about ourselves.

## Motives versus Behavior

We often are not very good at detecting the motives of other people because motives may not necessarily result in any actual behavior. For one thing, action may be thwarted by circumstances over which we have no control. Achievement motivation, for example, is often the victim of lack of opportunity. A young woman may want very badly to have a professional career, but for lack of money or other resources she cannot get the necessary education. A young man, even with the necessary education, may want very badly to work in advertising but be unable to find an advertising firm that will hire him.

Lack of opportunity may also thwart affiliation. For example, young people who seek the companionship of the opposite sex may live in a community where young men greatly outnumber young women, or vice versa. For older people, lack of opportunity stems from the fact that women on average live longer than men, thus creating a shortage of men among the elderly.

Whether we act on our own motives depends on our estimate of our chances of gaining what we want. We are not likely to try very hard unless we feel that we have a reasonable expectation of success. A college student who is invited to try out for the campus play will probably turn down the suggestion if she believes that she has absolutely no chance—even though she wants to get a part. Another student may be highly motivated to call up a woman he has met in one of his classes. But if he feels shy and awkward around women and considers himself unattractive and uninteresting, he will probably take no action.

In gauging our chances of success, we try to make a realistic appraisal of the situation. We may decide not to try out for a campus play because we have no acting experience. We may abandon any thought of a career in accounting because we always have trouble in math courses. But often we are influenced not so much by the facts as by our self-image—our perceptions of ourselves and our abilities. Some people have an exaggerated opinion of their talents and are inclined to try anything (a tendency that may bring them one disappointment after another).

**Motivation to meet standards**
The desire to live up to inner standards acquired from parents, other adults, and society in general.

**Ego ideal**
Our notion of how we would always think and act if we were perfect.

> ### Test Yourself
>
> **(m)** If a person has a high achievement motivation in undertaking one task, can you be sure this motive will be high with respect to other tasks as well?
>
> **(n)** What motive is lacking in a "loner"?
>
> **(o)** "When my 5-year-old sleeps over at a friend's house," says one father, "I suddenly realize how strong his motive for certainty is." What might this father be referring to?
>
> (The answers are on page 322.)

Others tend to be pessimistic about their chances, regardless of the situation. In some instances, even if a required skill or aptitude is present, low expectations may be a decisive factor. Some individuals may be capable of far more success—at fulfilling their motives for achievement, affiliation, and other goals—than they themselves believe.

# Chapter 8 Summary

## Biological Underpinnings of Emotion

1. An *emotion* usually consists of (a) a precipitating event, (b) changes in physiology, (c) a cognitive evaluation of those changes, and (d) a change in feeling.
2. *Motives* are often interrelated with emotions and may be defined as the "why" of behavior. Some motives arise from basic physiological needs, creating psychological drives to satisfy these needs.
3. Many of the bodily changes in emotion are controlled by the autonomic nervous system (ANS) and the endocrine glands. These produce changes in heart rate, blood pressure, blood circulation, the composition of the blood, activity of the digestive organs, metabolic rate, breathing, salivation, sweating, goose bumps, and pupil size.
4. Other bodily changes related to emotion are controlled by the muscles of movement. These changes include muscular tension, trembling, eye blinking and other nervous movements, vocal expressions of emotion, and facial expressions.
5. One theory holds that every basic emotion represents in part a characteristic pattern of facial expression programmed by heredity and it therefore is often difficult to hide our emotions from others.

## Mechanisms of Emotion

6. According to the *James-Lange theory*, emotions occur when a stimulus in the environment sets off physiological changes. Feedback from these changes, sent to the brain from the body's sensory nerves, is then perceived as emotion. We do not tremble because we are afraid, but rather we feel afraid because we are trembling.
7. According to the *Cannon-Bard theory*, emotions occur when a stimulus in the environment sets off patterns of nervous activity in the hypothalamus. These patterns have two simultaneous effects: In the ANS, they trigger the bodily changes characteristic of emotion; in the cerebral cortex, they cause the perception of emotion.
8. Cognitive psychologists regard emotions as composed of many complex factors. These include information about events in the environment that is delivered to the cerebral cortex by the sense organs; the brain's ability to store information that helps in the appraisal and interpretation of new events; patterns of nervous activity in the hypothalamus and the rest of the brain's limbic system, which trigger the ANS to produce bodily changes; and feedback from the bodily changes.
9. The *cognitive theory* agrees with the James-Lange theory that feedback on physiological changes is important—and with the Cannon-Bard theory that activity of the hypothalamus plays a part. But it holds that neither theory provides the full explanation. What really determines emotions is the cognitive activity resulting from the stimulus that has produced the bodily changes, along with the environmental situation in which those changes occur.
10. Some individual differences in the experience of emotion are the result of learning. Others are the result of inborn factors, including the sensitivity of the ANS and the size and activity of the endocrine glands.

## Motives That Originate in Physiological Needs

11. A drive is a pattern of brain and bodily activity that results from physiological imbalances that threaten *homeostasis*—the maintenance of bodily stability. Some motives arise from drives.
12. *Hunger* depends on the activity of the hypothalamus, as well as on incentive objects in the environment (the sight or smell of food) and eating habits and social relationships built around eating.
13. The urge to eat involves a number of interrelated physiological mechanisms that are governed by the body's *set point*—an innate physiological mechanism that keeps an individual's body weight at a genetically "programmed" minimum level.

14. A primary regulator of eating behavior is the condition of *fat cells* in the body. When the fat cells are emptied and their contents are used to produce energy, the level of fatty compounds in the bloodstream rises, triggering hunger.

15. Hunger is also affected by external stimuli called *incentives*. Some individuals undergo an increase in the hormone *insulin* in their blood when exposed to incentives such as the sight of inviting food; the increased insulin acts to reduce blood glucose, thus signaling hunger.

16. Although hunger mechanisms operate to keep most people at a normal weight, it is estimated that more than one-third of U.S. adults are at least 20% overweight. Possible explanations of obesity include metabolic disturbances, *emotional stress*, overeating simply as a matter of habit, an unknown chemical in the bloodstream, an excess of the bodily cells that store fatty compounds, and an evolved tendency to overeat when food is available.

17. *Thirst* depends on neurons in the hypothalamus that are sensitive to dehydration, signals sent to the brain from the heart and blood vessels when the volume of blood is lowered by lack of water, and stimulation of the hypothalamus by a chemical produced by the kidneys.

18. Sleep plays an important role in the rhythm of daily life. Rather than being a state of suspended animation, sleep is a brain and body activity in its own right, marked by different stages. The stages in a normal night's sleep include the initial state, characterized by the *alpha rhythm; sleep stages (I, II, III, and IV),* marked by increasingly deep levels of sleep; and *rapid-eye-movement (REM) sleep,* marked by vivid dreaming.

19. Functions of sleep are thought to include allowing the brain and body to recuperate from the wear and tear of daily activity, conserving limited supplies of energy, and correcting imbalances in brain chemistry incurred during waking life.

20. REM sleep may spur neural growth in young organisms. Adults engage in more than their normal amount of REM sleep when they are involved in novel situations or are experiencing psychological problems. REM sleep may also allow the brain to process memories.

## The Special Case of Sex and Sexuality

21. Sex is among the major human motives (goal-directed tendencies that have either a physiological or a psychological basis).

22. The primary hormones that determine sexual behavior are estrogen in the female and testosterone in the male.

23. Sexual expression in humans is influenced not only by basic biological urges but also by desires and preferences first learned in childhood and by the social and cultural environment.

24. The direction taken by the motive for sex defines *sexual orientation*—that is, the attraction felt toward persons of a given sex. The majority of men and women, described as *heterosexual,* feel strong sexual attraction to members of the opposite sex. Those described as *same-sex-oriented,* or *homosexual* (gay or lesbian), are drawn to those of their own sex. Those who seek both same-sex and heterosexual experiences are *bisexual.*

## Motives That Are Primarily Psychological

25. *Achievement motivation* involves attempting to attain optimal levels of performance on valued tasks. Among the factors that determine the strength of achievement motivation are experiences at home and school, whom we choose as role models, and the estimates we make of our own abilities.

26. *Affiliation motivation, dependency motivation, motivation for certainty,* and *motivation to meet standards* can also shape our behavior.

27. Often a motive cannot be fulfilled because of lack of opportunity. In particular, we may never have the opportunity to gratify all our desires for achievement.

28. A key factor in determining whether we will try to fulfill a motive is the way we perceive our chances of success.

# Chapter 8 Test Yourself Answers

(a)  You are experiencing no emotion. In order for an emotion to occur, bodily changes must be present—linked to an event (in this case, perception of the shadowy figure) and to thoughts triggered by the event (in this case, the question of the figure's identity). Because no physical changes occur, there is no emotion.

(b)  The James-Lange theory of emotion holds that it is the feedback of physiological changes sent to the brain that is perceived as emotion.

(c)  The Cannon-Bard theory emphasizes the role of the hypothalamus in arousing the ANS, which triggers the various physiological changes associated with emotion.

(d)  You support the cognitive theory of emotion.

(e)  Such individual differences—like others discussed throughout the book—are the result of both innate patterns and learning.

(f)  Your friend is saying that the drive to eat is regulated by an inborn physiological mechanism—the so-called set point—that keeps our body weight at a predetermined level. It leads us to return to our natural body weight after we have gone above or below it.

(g)  You are being asked not to stock the refrigerator with too many tempting food items, which—like other incentives, such as the smell of food or even talk of food—are among the outside stimuli that can affect the hunger drive.

(h)  You might say, "I've felt thirsty all day." Thirst is triggered by such imbalances.

(i)  The person is likely to be in Stage IV sleep—the deepest stage of the sleep cycle.

(j)  It is termed "paradoxical" because the brain's activity is similar to that associated with the waking state, but the muscles are almost totally relaxed.

(k)  You might use any two of the following facts: (1) Unlike sex in lower animals, human sex is not altogether tied to glandular cycles. (2) In humans, just thinking about sex can lead to arousal. (3) For both men and women, psychological factors can act as a powerful "turn-off." (4) Sexual practices differ widely from one human society to another.

(l)  Neither is right. Homosexuality appears to develop from a complex interaction of all three factors.

(m)  You can't be sure. For a variety of psychological reasons—for example, ability, interest, self-concept—some individuals tend to be motivated to persist with some tasks but not with others.

(n)  Affiliation motivation is lacking.

(o)  He is undoubtedly referring to evidence that, in sleeping away from home, his son shows discomfort at being in an unfamiliar environment, preferring the certainty of being in the presence of familiar things and people.

# Chapter 8  Emotion and Motivation

## Key Terms

*The key terms above can be used as search terms in InfoTrac, a database of readings, which can be found at http://infotrac-thomsonlearning.com.*

## Active Learning Review

### Biological Underpinnings of Emotion

1. An *emotion* occurs when an event is accompanied by thoughts associated with the event and by bodily changes. When John thinks about the unfairness of his boss, his heart beats faster and his mouth turns dry—suggesting that John is experiencing an _____.

   **emotion**

2. Many of the bodily changes accompanying _____ are regulated by the autonomic nervous system and are not ordinarily under conscious control.

   **emotion**

3. Louisa tries as hard as she can not to blush when she is embarrassed. But she always does anyway because, like the rest of us, she cannot consciously _____ the bodily changes associated with emotion.

   **control**

4. Without any command from the brain, our emotions are accompanied by changes in such functions as heart rate, blood pressure, breathing, and stomach activity—all controlled by the _____ nervous system.

   **autonomic**

5. The _____ changes accompanying emotion are also controlled by the endocrine glands, which secrete powerful hormones into the bloodstream.

   **bodily**

6. Many of the physical changes we feel in emotion are controlled by both the autonomic _____ _____ and the _____ glands. Eye blinking and finger drumming are examples of bodily changes in emotion that are consciously controlled by the muscles of movement.

   **nervous system, endocrine**

7. The emotions of anger or fear lead to production of the hormone _____ by the adrenal glands.

   **cortisol**

8. The facial expressions that accompany emotions are examples of bodily changes that are ordinarily under _____ control. Some psychologists maintain that every basic emotion represents in part a characteristic facial pattern "programmed" by heredity.

   **conscious**

heredity

habituated

emotion

James-Lange

emotion
feedback

bodily

brain

Cannon-Bard
hypothalamus

mental

cognitive

differences

inborn

emotional

sensitivity

differences

emotions

homeostasis

stability
set point

9. The facial expressions typical of certain emotions seem to be universal and unlearned, lending support to the theory that such characteristic expressions are programmed by _____.

10. Facial displays of pain may become less apparent as one becomes accustomed, or _____, to an uncomfortable situation.

## Mechanisms of Emotion

11. The *James-Lange theory* held that the bodily changes accompanying _____ send feedback messages to the brain and that these messages produce emotional feelings.

12. If feedback from bodily changes is the key to emotion—which is what the _____-_____ theory held—it follows that we do not tremble because we feel afraid, but instead feel afraid because we are trembling.

13. The James-Lange theory of _____ emphasized the importance of bodily changes, especially the _____ of such changes to the brain.

14. Unlike the James-Lange theory, which held that emotion is caused by the feedback of _____ changes to the brain, the *Cannon-Bard theory* held that emotion originates in patterns of brain activity.

15. The Cannon-Bard theory stressed the role of _____ activity in emotion—specifically the activity of the hypothalamus, which arouses the autonomic nervous system to produce the bodily changes associated with emotion and also sends messages to the cerebral cortex that result in our feelings of emotion.

16. According to the _____-_____ theory, emotions result from patterns of nervous activity in the _____. *Cognitive theory* emphasizes the role of mental processes in such feelings as joy, anger, and fear rather than the role of bodily changes and the brain.

17. Cognitive theory emphasizes the role of _____ processes in emotion.

18. Feedback of bodily changes and the role of the hypothalamus, although important, cannot fully explain emotion, according to the _____ theory.

19. Both the stimuli that arouse emotions and the behavior that results from emotion are subject to wide individual _____ that are partly the result of learning.

20. Some individual differences in emotion may reflect _____ differences rather than different learning experiences.

21. Any abnormality of the glands or nervous system can have significant effects on _____ experience.

22. The fact that some people seem to "overreact" to minor events while others are unmoved even by major upheavals appears to suggest differences from person to person in the _____ of the autonomic nervous system.

23. The fact that such contrasting reactions are apparent at the very start of life suggests the importance of inborn _____.

## Motives That Originate in Physiological Needs

24. Just as _____ depend on bodily activities, so too do psychological conditions called drives. Psychologists define a drive as a pattern of brain activity resulting from physiological imbalances that threaten *homeostasis*—or the maintenance of the body's stability.

25. *Hunger* and *thirst* are aroused when lack of food or water threatens the body's _____.

26. Drives center on the process of homeostasis, or the maintenance of the body's _____.

27. The drive to eat is governed in part by the body's _____ _____, an innate physiological mechanism that keeps an individual's body weight at a genetically "programmed" level.

28. As the liver manages the body's metabolism of food, it helps maintain the set point by converting extra glucose into _____ for long-term storage of energy.   **glycogen**

29. Another view holds that the primary trigger for the hunger drive is not blood sugar (glucose) or glycogen but the level of fatty compounds in the bloodstream, which is regulated when _____ _____ recognize that the body needs fat for fuel and empty their contents into the bloodstream.   **fat cells**

30. Hunger, in addition to being aroused by physiological mechanisms, is affected by outside stimuli—called _____—such as the sight or smell of food.   **incentives**

31. Pastries seen in a restaurant window that arouse the hunger drive can be classified as _____.   **incentives**

32. When exposed to incentives, some people experience an increase in the hormone _____ in the blood; the resulting reduction in blood sugar may be the primary mechanism for alerting the brain to hunger.   **insulin**

33. Some obesity may result from _____ _____, as people overeat to relieve anxieties over competition, failure, rejection, or sexual performance.   **emotional stress**

34. _____ is triggered by various signs of imbalance in the body's water supply.   **Thirst**

35. Like hunger, thirst centers on the process of _____, or the maintenance of bodily stability.   **homeostasis**

36. Like hunger, thirst depends in part on the activity of nerve cells in the hypothalamus—in this case, nerve cells that are sensitive to _____.   **dehydration**

37. Both hunger and thirst depend on activity of the hypothalamus. Thirst depends as well on signals sent to the brain from the heart and blood vessels when the volume of blood is _____ by lack of water.   **lowered**

38. Although sleep may feel like a blanket of darkness, the brain continues to be active during sleep, which proceeds through different _____, or *sleep stages*.   **levels**

39. During the brief phase of serene relaxation that immediately precedes sleep, the pulse is steady, body temperature is dropping gradually, and brain waves show an even frequency called the _____ rhythm.   **alpha**

40. Just before one enters the first stage of sleep, neural changes may generate a fleeting sensation of "falling"; this normal phenomenon is called the _____ _____.   **myoclonic jerk**

41. During sleep, the _____ continues to be very active, as the sleeper proceeds through a series of levels, or _____ _____. The deepest of these is stage IV, or *delta sleep*.   **brain** **sleep stages**

42. A sleeper who is extremely difficult to awaken is probably engaged in the deep sleep of stage IV, also known as _____ sleep.   **delta**

43. The period of sleep marked by dreaming is known as *REM (rapid-eye-movement) sleep*. Because the brain's activity during this period is similar to that associated with the waking state but the muscles are almost totally relaxed, this period is also known as _____ sleep.   **paradoxical**

44. A person who is in the midst of REM sleep is probably having a _____. This period is regarded as essential in restoring the brain's ability to function.   **dream**

44. The brain's ability to function appears to be restored as a result of REM _____, also known as _____ sleep because the brain appears active yet the muscles are relaxed.   **sleep, paradoxical**

46. The need for sleep appears to be triggered by _____ in brain and body chemistry.   **imbalances**

## The Special Case of Sex and Sexuality

47. Among nonhuman mammals, sex is almost as direct a drive as hunger and is triggered by the release of the sex _____, testosterone in males and estrogen in females.   **hormones**

48. In humans, especially females, sexual responsiveness does not seem to be tied to hormones. Instead, sexual activity is influenced by an array of _____, social, and cultural factors.   **psychological**

| | |
|---|---|
| estrogen, testosterone | 49. The female and male sex hormones—_____ and _____—are present in humans and influence activity of the brain's hypothalamus. But hormonal activity is not required for sexual behavior, nor is it a sole or sufficient impetus for such behavior. |
| menopause | 50. When monthly fluctuations in a woman's hormone levels end with cessation of menstruation, or _____, sexual activity may actually increase. |
| psychological | 51. In humans, sexual activity is colored by _____ factors as well as by social and cultural factors. |
| sexual orientation | 52. The direction taken by the motive for sex defines our _____ _____—that is, the attraction we feel toward persons of a given sex. |
| orientation | 53. Sally feels strongly attracted to members of her own sex—which defines her sexual _____. The majority of men and women, described as *heterosexual*, feel strong attraction to members of the opposite sex. |
| heterosexual<br>homosexual,<br>same-sex-oriented<br>bisexual | 54. Those people who feel strong attraction to members of the opposite sex are described as _____. In contrast, people drawn to those of their own sex are described as _____ or _____-_____-_____.<br>55. Those who seek both same-sex and heterosexual experiences are termed _____. |
| bisexual | 56. Mark, who seeks sexual contact with both men and women, can be described as _____. |
| interaction | 57. Sexual orientation, like sexual activity in general, is determined by an _____ among biological, psychological, and social factors. |
| biological | 58. Like later patterns of sexual behavior, sexual behavior in childhood is an outgrowth of both _____ and psychological factors. Sexuality is a prominent concern during the adolescent years. |
| adolescent | 59. Sexuality plays a significant role during the _____ years, partly because of the physical changes of puberty. |
| puberty | 60. The physical changes of _____ help usher in a heightened awareness of sexuality. |
| response | 61. Although the zest for sex is not universally extinguished with age, biologically the sexual _____ changes in some respects. |

## Motives That Are Primarily Psychological

| | |
|---|---|
| achievement | 62. Among the most important motives influencing our behavior is _____ motivation, or the desire to perform well and succeed. |
| achievement motivation | 63. If you tend to try harder than others and to attain more success in many kinds of situations, you are likely to have a strong _____ _____—the result of many factors, including experiences in home and at school and your estimate of your own abilities. |
| school | 64. The strength of a person's *achievement motivation* depends on many factors, among them experiences in home and at _____. |
| abilities | 65. The strength of our achievement motivation depends also on our estimate of our own _____. |
| Affiliation | 66. _____ motivation is the desire to be around other people and have close relationships with them. |
| affiliation<br>motivation | 67. Judy, who constantly yearns for the company of others, has a strong _____ _____. |
| dependency | 68. Closely allied to affiliation motivation is _____ motivation, the desire to rely on others to fill our needs, as our parents did when we were young. |
| dependency motivation | 69. Our urges to have other people organize our lives, help us with our work, and comfort us in our troubles are examples of _____ _____. |
| motives | 70. In addition to the desires for achievement, affiliation, and dependency—all of them strong human _____—there are other desires that influence all of us. One is the desire to feel at home in the world, to know where we stand, and to |

avoid the discomfort of unfamiliar and surprising events, called *motivation for certainty.*

71. The desire to know how our friends will behave toward us and what will happen at school tomorrow is an example of motivation for _____.  **certainty**

72. Yet another powerful motive is *motivation to meet* _____, which is the desire to behave in accordance with our own ideas of what is right and wrong.  **standards**

73. Yolanda, who is motivated by the belief that she should play fair no matter how hard she wants to win, is displaying motivation to meet_____.  **standards**

74. Our notion of how we would always think or act if we were perfect is called our ego _____.  **ideal**

75. One key factor that influences whether or not a _____ will affect behavior is expectation of success.  **motive**

76. A man who wants to be a doctor but thinks he could never get through medical school will probably never try to satisfy the motive because he has a low _____ of success.  **expectation**

77. People who believe they have no chance of satisfying their motives may refrain from acting on them because they have a low expectation of _____.  **success**

## Practice Test

_____ 1. All the emotions we experience include
   a. a particular event or memory.
   b. changes in the body or brain.
   c. thoughts generated by the event.
   d. all of the above

_____ 2. Some of the changes in the body that take place during times of high emotion are controlled by the
   a. thyroid gland.
   b. right hemisphere of the brain.
   c. autonomic nervous system.
   d. cerebral cortex.

_____ 3. Research has shown that facial expressions characteristic of some emotions
   a. are very similar in different cultures.
   b. are easier to interpret in women.
   c. need to be learned.
   d. are uncommon among animals other than humans.

_____ 4. While walking in the forest, you are suddenly confronted by a bear. You begin to tremble and say to yourself, "I've never been so scared in my whole life." According to the James-Lange theory, you are afraid because you
   a. have a conditioned fear of bears.
   b. are uncertain what the bear will do next.
   c. are trembling.
   d. have generalized your fear of other animals to bears.

_____ 5. The Cannon-Bard theory of emotion stresses the importance of
   a. physiological changes.
   b. the hypothalamus.
   c. the individual's perception of the situation.
   d. all of the above

_____ 6. Two students drink several cups of coffee at lunch, and the caffeine in the coffee arouses them. One student, who has just failed a test, interprets the effect as unusual anger. The other student, who has done well on the test, feels unusually happy. What theory of emotion best explains the difference?
   a. stimulus variability theory
   b. Cannon-Bard theory
   c. cognitive theory
   d. James-Lange theory

_____ 7. Lie detector test results can be influenced unduly by
   a. the time of day when the test is given.
   b. subjective impressions of the examiner.
   c. the age of the person being tested.
   d. the sex of the person being tested.

_____ 8. Homeostasis is most closely associated with
   a. drives.
   b. emotions.
   c. perception.
   d. arousal.

_____ 9. The center for the thirst drive is the
   a. hypothalamus.
   b. stomach.
   c. mouth.
   d. right hemisphere of the brain.

_____ 10. A sudden spasm experienced while drifting off to sleep is known as the
   a. alpha rhythm.
   b. myoclonic jerk.
   c. sleep reflex.
   d. waking reflex.

_____ 11. REM sleep is associated with the experience of
   a. insomnia.
   b. dreaming.
   c. Stage IV sleep.
   d. ordinary sleep.

_____ 12. The primary female sex hormone is
   a. testosterone.
   b. cortisol.
   c. estrogen.
   d. glycogen.

_____ 13. The direction taken by the motive for sex defines our
   a. sexual orientation.
   b. sexual attitudes.
   c. degree of inhibition.
   d. sexual energy.

_____ 14. Changes in sexuality in older adults are partly the result of
   a. biological changes.
   b. bereavement.
   c. retirement.
   d. inhibitions.

____**15.** The desire to attain a psychologically valued goal is
   a. dependency motivation.
   b. affiliation motivation.
   c. achievement motivation.
   d. motivation for certainty.

____**16.** The desire to be close to other people is
   a. affiliation motivation.
   b. dependency motivation
   c. motivation for certainty.
   d. motivation to meet standards.

____**17.** Dependency motivation is
   a. the desire to attain a psychologically valued goal.
   b. the tendency to rely on others.
   c. the desire for close relationships.
   d. none of the above

____**18.** A child's preference for familiar things in the environment is related most directly to motivation for
   a. certainty.
   b. achievement.
   c. affiliation.
   d. dependency.

____**19.** The ego ideal is a key factor in motivation for
   a. dependency.
   b. meeting standards.
   c. affiliation.
   d. achievement.

____**20.** Achievement motivation may be hampered by
   a. lack of opportunity.
   b. low expectations.
   c. an unrealistic appraisal of the situation.
   d. all of the above

# Exercises

1. Figure 8.1 (p. 294) shows photographs of six faces expressing various emotions. After covering the rest of the page, show these photographs to at least a dozen individuals who are as different in age and background as possible. Ask them to try to identify the emotions being displayed. Give each individual a list of emotions from which to choose, and ask them to record their judgments. You may want to create a table to expedite recording and tallying. Make the list twice as long as the actual emotions—for example,

   a. anger
   b. disgust
   c. fear
   d. joy
   e. sadness
   f. anxiety
   g. love
   h. contempt
   i. shame
   j. guilt
   k. interest-excitement
   l. surprise

   When you have finished collecting the responses, tally the number of individuals who identified each emotion correctly. Then consider these questions:

   a. Did most of your participants agree about the emotions expressed?
   b. Which facial expressions, if any, were especially difficult for them to identify correctly?
   c. Which ones were the easiest?
   d. Are you convinced, as one theory maintains, that facial expressions of emotions are universal?

2. Rapid-eye movement (REM) sleep is intriguing in part because most dreaming *apparently* occurs during this period. But do the eye movements track the action in a dream, or are they just random motions?

   For this "sleep clinic" exercise, you will need a willing participant (probably a very good friend or a romantic partner) who is willing to let you observe the initial stages of sleep and interrupt the sleep cycle. You will also need a watch or other timer and a pad and pencil.

   Once set up, you will need to watch your participant's face for up to 2 hours, preferably in the person's normal sleep room. You should design and *pretest* an arrangement that provides sufficient illumination for you to see your participant's eyelids. This may involve a low-light lamp on the far side of the room, nightlights, a very dim flashlight, or some other device that will not interfere with the participant's sleep.

   Set up the study so that you can move around the room. Ask your participant to tell you when he or she begins drifting off to sleep. Write down the time when the participant says that he or she is drifting off. Try to determine when the participant actually falls asleep and write down this time as well.

   Watch for the first REM episode. It will probably occur about an hour after sleep commences, but individual differences are such that you will need to check frequently after about 20 minutes. From this time on, perform a visual check of the participant about once per minute to see if REM is occurring. REM is indicated by obvious and quick movement of the eyes beneath the eyelids, which may or may not be accompanied by noticeable relaxation or a change in breathing. Once you notice REM, *write down the time when it began.*

   Allow the participant to remain in REM sleep for 5 minutes. Just before awakening your participant, observe and note on your pad the motion of the eyes. Left-to-right? Regular? Irregular? Any up-down motion? Some slow sweeps? Vibrations? Regular or irregular pauses?

   Now awaken your participant quickly but gently, remind him or her who you are, and ask, "Please tell me about your dream."

   Dreaming does not occur in all REM sleep, so there may be nothing to report. Or the participant may be unable to report. If you do not get a dream report, allow your participant to return to sleep and try again after another 5 minutes of REM sleep, following the same procedures.

   If you do not receive a dream report, answer items a, b, c, and f below the way you expect they would be answered, based on the discussions of sleeping and dreaming in the text and in class. If you do receive a dream report, answer all the items.

   a. How long did it take for the person to fall asleep?
   b. How long did it take for the person to enter REM sleep?
   c. How does this time span compare to the normal amount of time required to achieve REM sleep?
   d. What was the person's dream report?
   e. What was the relationship—if any—between the eye movements you observed and the dream report?
   f. How might your presence have affected the results you obtained?
   g. How accurate might a new "dream science" be if it relied entirely on eye movements to understand and interpret dreams?

❋ For quizzing, activities, exercises, and web links, check out the book-specific website at http://www.psychology.wadsworth.com/kagan9e.

# 9 Personality and Its Assessment

© John Neubauer/PhotoEdit

# WHAT IS PERSONALITY?

As noted in Chapter 7, the second major domain of individual differences among people is *personality*, which generally refers to their distinct motives, moods, and ways of behaving toward others. How would you describe your own personality? What factors in your life do you think helped shape your personality? Is it essentially the same as it was, say, 10 years ago?

FOCUS QUESTIONS

* How do psychologists and personality theorists define personality?

* What elements do personality theories have in common?

If you have trouble answering such questions, don't be discouraged. The human personality is one of the most baffling of psychological phenomena, one that has been discussed and argued about at least since the time of the ancient Greeks. What we casually refer to as personality is such a complex phenomenon that the English language has about 18,000 adjectives to describe the myriad characteristics that comprise it (Allport & Odbert, 1936). These characteristics are based on the intricate processes covered thus far in this textbook: the patterns of emotions and motives, the characteristics of temperament with which you were born, the surges of anxiety and stress that you experience and the diverse efforts you make to cope with them, and your beliefs about and attitudes toward the people and the world around you. Small wonder that the concept of personality is so difficult to understand and describe.

Psychologists and others have attempted to create comprehensive theories of personality—in other words, sets of general principles that explain why people are alike in some ways and very different in others. Some theorists stipulate which personality traits are the most important, the patterns of relationships among these traits, the manner in which these patterns become established in individuals, and (at least by implication) how they can be changed. Some of the theories developed over the years have been accompanied by techniques for treating people suffering from mental and behavioral disorders, as described in Chapter 14.

Just as the theories discussed in this chapter had different aims, they were devised during different eras, characterized by markedly different cultural and social contexts. Bearing this in mind as you read will help you to understand the differences in emphasis of the theories and especially the contradictions that inevitably arose in describing and understanding personality.

We begin with an attempt to define personality and explain in detail what personality theories try to accomplish.

## Defining Personality

A classic definition of personality, devised by the prominent theorist Gordon Allport (1897–1967), is stated as follows: **Personality** is the dynamic organization within the individual of those psychophysical systems that determine his [or her] characteristic behavior and thought (1961). Here, "dynamic" refers to the idea that personality is ongoing and always changing, although some changes may be gradual and slow. Personality is about *individuals*, each of whom is unique. "Psychophysical systems" refers to the interaction between mind and body. And

**Personality**
The dynamic organization within the individual of those psychophysical systems that determine his or her characteristic behavior and thought.

**333**

"characteristic behavior and thought" states more specifically what constitutes the individuality that each of us displays.

Although these elements are essential, they are not the whole story. For example, suppose a woman always wears a ring that is a family heirloom and the only one of its kind in the world. Wearing the ring is therefore both individual and characteristic of her behavior. But it would hardly be considered part of her personality (unless perhaps she attached some deep significance to the ring, regarding it as a symbol of self-esteem and social acceptance). To be a part of personality, a characteristic or trait must play a role in how a person goes about relating to the world, and especially to other people. It is because of this element of "relating" that personality traits are often thought of as positive or negative, desirable or undesirable—within a given culture. In most cultures, a positive trait, such as friendliness, helps an individual relate to people and events in constructive ways. A negative trait, such as fear of social interactions, may produce isolation and loneliness.

Finally, we possess a multitude of traits to varying degrees. It is the organization of the characteristics that we possess and display that is the essence of personality.

## Test Yourself

**(a)** After seeing Ivan hand a homeless man a bag of fruit, Pedro concluded that Ivan has a generous personality. Why might this conclusion be premature?

(The answer is on page 360.)

## Traits That Stand Out: The Personality Hierarchy

The various traits that make up a person's personality—the characteristic behavior and thought—exist in a hierarchy from salient and strong to less salient and weak. Salient qualities are easily and frequently aroused; less salient ones are less likely to be evoked. In a social situation, for example, an individual can be talkative or quiet, friendly or reserved, boastful or modest, domineering or acquiescent, more at ease with men or more at ease with women. One person may characteristically withdraw into the background, and we say that such a person is shy. Another may characteristically display warmth and try to put others at ease, and we say that such a person is outgoing. Another may be talkative, boastful, and "pushy," and we say that such a person is aggressive. In each individual, certain behaviors are higher in the personality hierarchy and more easily aroused.

Personality does evolve and change, but each person's hierarchy of qualities is *relatively* stable over time and consistent—at least in similar situations. A shy person is usually quiet with many different strangers; a domineering person is consistently aggressive with friends. But these qualities are often limited to particular situations and may not be seen when the circumstances change in a major way. For example, a young person who is typically shy and anxious with some people may be sociable and relaxed with others, such as family or close friends.

## Four Components of Personality Theory

Many theories of personality—some general, some more specific—have been proposed over the years. The more influential ones are presented in this chapter. They differ in many respects, but they all have four elements in common (Maddi, 1972; also see Maddi, 1996):

**Core of personality**
**The tendencies and traits common to all human beings.**

1. Almost every theory is based on some fundamental view of the basic quality of human nature. It assumes that there is a **core of personality** composed of tendencies and traits that are common to all of us. Different theories take different views of this common core, but almost all acknowledge that it exists and is a force in shaping personality.

2. Each theory that acknowledges a common core of personality maintains that the tendencies and traits are channeled in various directions for different individuals by the process of development—all the experiences we encounter throughout our lives. Thus, various theories agree that personality is the prod-

uct of both nature (the common core that is part of our genetic heritage) and nurture (the effect of individual experiences).

3. Every theory that acknowledges a common core of personality is concerned with what are called **peripheral traits**—that is, all the distinctive ways in which people relate to the environment. The peripheral traits are viewed as the inevitable result of the way individual development has acted on the common core of personality.

4. Finally, almost every theory is concerned with the task of identifying and defining the inner processes by which the peripheral traits are laid down and maintained.

**Peripheral traits**
The distinctive ways in which people relate to their social environment.

# PSYCHODYNAMIC VIEWS: FREUD AND THOSE WHO FOLLOWED

The best known of all views of personality is Sigmund Freud's psychoanalytic theory. Freud was the first to develop a comprehensive theory of personality. Although there are few "classical" psychoanalysts today, his views have had a profound influence on many later personality theorists, referred to as **psychodynamic theorists**—a general term for those are concerned with understanding and analyzing the inner functioning and processes that yield personality and behavior. In this section, we consider the basics of Freud's theory; we then discuss other theories that followed and departed from it—often drastically.

**FOCUS QUESTIONS**
- What was Freud's basic view of personality and how it develops?
- What major contributions did Freud make to the study of personality?
- What aspects of Freud's psychoanalytic theory were changed by psychodynamic theorists who came after him?

## Freud's Psychoanalytic Theory

A key idea in Freud's theory of personality is that all humans—children as well as adults—possess a basic energy called **libido** that is directed at satisfying needs, maximizing pleasure, and minimizing pain. Many of the acts that bring pleasure, however, cause *conflict* as well, which Freud saw as the core of personality. Examples are promiscuous sexual behavior, revenge to relieve anger, and retaining dependent ties with parents beyond childhood. As a result, some of the motives that arise from the libido are *repressed*—removed from conscious awareness. In Freud's view, this is what causes the kinds of adjustment problems and abnormal symptoms discussed in Chapters 12 and 13.

**The Unconscious**   Freud believed that anxiety is so painful an emotion that we will go to almost any length to eliminate from conscious awareness an impulse, thought, or memory that threatens to cause anxiety.

The **unconscious mind,** composed in part of repressed motives and thoughts, was one of Freud's most influential concepts. He was the first to suggest the now widely held theory that the human mind and personality are like an iceberg, with only a small part visible and the rest submerged and concealed (1923/1961).

One idea that has influenced many psychologists is that human activities are often a result of the unconscious—that is, impulses, motives, wishes, or memories that we are not aware of but that influence our behavior nonetheless. The idea of unconscious motivation raises some thorny psychological issues, including the question of how a wish that is unconscious can operate to produce actual behav-

**Psychodynamic theorists**
Those theorists, including psychoanalytic theorists, who are concerned with understanding and analyzing the inner functioning and processes that yield personality and behavior.

**Libido**
A basic energy source in all humans that is directed at maximizing pleasure and surviving.

**Unconscious mind**
The part of the mind composed mainly of repressed motives and thoughts.

ior. But this idea explains some aspects of human behavior that would otherwise be baffling.

One example of an unconscious motive comes from the phenomenon known as *posthypnotic suggestion.* Suppose that a patient, while under hypnosis, is told that after he awakens from the trance he will raise a window the first time the hypnotist coughs. Even though he will not remember having received this instruction (if told not to), when the hypnotist later coughs, sure enough, the person will go and open a window. If asked why, he may say that the room was getting stuffy. He has no idea that the reason for his action is the hypnotist's suggestion.

Other examples are all around us. A mother may seem to believe sincerely that she has generous, affectionate, and even self-sacrificing motives toward her daughter. Yet an objective observer might say that the mother's real motives are to dominate the daughter, keep her from marrying, and hold on to her. A man may earnestly deny that he has any hostile motives. Yet we may observe that he performs subtle acts of aggression against his spouse, his children, and his friends. Of course, the idea that the roots of our everyday behavior lie submerged in the unconscious unfortunately gives rise to a good deal of naive psychology. Even in "classical" psychoanalytic theory, it is not always the case that a behavior has some hidden and undesirable cause.

The details of Freud's theory are difficult to summarize, because he revised and enlarged on them throughout a career that spanned 4 decades. Moreover, Freud's followers have continued to refine his ideas, especially his later ones. The following discussion is confined to the basic principles (especially those that have had the greatest influence), some of which continue to be endorsed, others of which have been rejected outright but continue to show up from time to time in everyday conversation.

**Id, Ego, and Superego**   Freud conceived of the human personality and mind as having three major components, which he called the id, the ego, and the superego (1920/1950; 1923/1961).

**Id**
A basic and primitive part of the mind that is the origin of survival motives and sexual desires, as well as motives for self-destruction and aggression.

1.  The **id,** the most basic and primitive of the three components, springs from two sets of inborn biological impulses that Freud believed all humans possess. One of these sets is *eros,* driven by libido and consisting of sexual impulses but also of those that lead to being well-fed and comfortable. Eros is oriented toward self-preservation. The other set of impulses, called *thanatos,* is directed toward self-destruction—a later addition to Freud's theorizing, intended to explain why we eventually "self-destruct" and die. In developing this idea, Freud cited philosopher Arthur Schopenhauer (1788–1860), who observed that "the aim of all life is death" (Freud, 1920/1950). In turn, this self-destruction is often turned outward and is the force behind *aggression,* which Freud also saw as basic to human nature.

**Pleasure principle**
The demand of the unconscious id for gratification of desires.

Thus, impulses originate in biological needs, and they arouse the id to a state of excitement and tension. In seeking to relieve the tension, the id operates on what Freud called the **pleasure principle.** Our id impels us to seek satisfactions. Indeed, in Freudian theory, healthy psychological adjustment involves keeping these "animal" impulses in check or finding socially acceptable outlets for them. But the id has no contact with the external world, which contains things that will satisfy its needs. Gratification of needs is the job of the next component, the ego.

**Ego**
The conscious part of the mind that includes our knowledge, skills, beliefs, and conscious motives.

**Reality principle**
The principle by which the conscious ego operates as it tries to mediate and balance the demands of the unconscious id and the realities of the environment.

2.  The conscious part of the mind that develops as we grow is called the **ego.** This is the "real" us as we think of ourselves, including our knowledge, skills, beliefs, and conscious motives. The ego operates on the **reality principle.** The ego is the source of our thinking as we try to get along in the world, and its primary function is to obtain objects that will gratify the id. Freud believed

that our intellectual and social skills develop because we must learn, beginning in childhood, how to cope with the biologically based demands of the id. To the extent that these demands can be satisfied in some reasonable way, the ego permits satisfaction. But when the id's demands threaten to cause us to be rejected by society, the ego represses them or tries to provide substitutes that are socially acceptable. Freud held that artistic creativity, for example, represents a channeling of the libido away from open sexual expression and into the production of paintings and literature.

3. The ego, in its struggle to meet the animalistic demands of the id in some rational way, has a strong but at times troublesome ally in the **superego,** the third component of the mind as conceived by Freud. The superego can be said to operate according to the **morality principle.** In addition to desires and the ability to gratify them, in Freud's view we also possess an *ego ideal*—a sense of "right"—and a *conscience*—a sense of "wrong." The superego is at times conscious and at times unconscious, exerting a far greater influence over our behavior than we realize, as it imposes guilt for even thinking about transgressing and violating our sense of right and wrong.

**Superego**
The often unconscious part of the mind that includes the conscience and the ego ideal.

**Morality principle**
The principle by which the superego tries to govern the ego in accord with the conscience and the ego ideal.

**Psychosexual Development**    Of the many aspects of human development and behavior that Freud proposed, none has been more roundly criticized and rejected than his theory of **psychosexual development.** Freud believed that human development takes place in a series of stages in which the sexual energy of the libido and, therefore, impulses from the id focus on different parts of the body. These are listed in Table 9.1, along with various examples of *fixation*—his idea that the original focus of an impulse would persist to an abnormal degree into adult life if it were gratified improperly by the parents or other caregivers. For example, fixation in the oral stage might result from being either overfed or underfed; fixation in the anal stage from either excessive or lax toilet training.

Aside from Freud's insistence that sexual motives were at the bottom of nearly everything we do, perhaps his most controversial idea was that the superego is ac-

**Psychosexual development**
Freud's view that child development revolves around sexual desires in one form or another—particularly as in his oral, anal, and phallic stages.

**TABLE 9.1**
**Freud's Psychosexual Stages**

| | | |
|---|---|---|
| **Oral**<br>Birth to about 18 months | Impulses to be gratified focus on the mouth and tongue; expressed in activities such as sucking and eating. | Fixation can result in an adult's engaging excessively in oral activities, such as eating, smoking, drinking, or talking, and being overly dependent on others. |
| **Anal**<br>About 18 months to 3 years | Impulses to be gratified focus on the anal region; expressed in activities such as eliminating or refraining from it. | Fixation can result in an adult's being exceedingly stubborn, overly concerned with cleanliness, and meticulously orderly and concerned with minute details (The latter is probably closest to what people mean when they refer to someone as "anal.") |
| **Phallic**<br>About 3 to 6 years | Impulses to be gratified focus on the genitals. | This is the period for resolving the Oedipus complex; fixations may affect sexual orientation. |
| **Latency**<br>About 6 to 12 years | Sexual impulses become dormant. | |
| **Genital** | Sexual impulses begin to reawaken with entrance into puberty and express themselves in adult form. | |

**Oedipus complex**
The conflict between mingled love and hate for the same-sex parent experienced by boys and girls between the ages of about 3 and 6.

quired largely as a result of the **Oedipus complex.** His theory holds that all children between the ages of about 3 and 6 (the phallic stage) have strong feelings of mingled affection and resentment toward their parents. The young boy's libido drives him to want to possess his mother sexually and take his father's place with her. Fearing retaliation from his father in the form of "castration" and frustrated by his inability to obtain his mother or to replace his father in her affections, he becomes overwhelmed with feelings of love, rage, and fear—especially toward his father. Girls, according to Freudian theory, go through similar torments, except that their lust becomes directed toward their father. Here Freud also proposed that girls, lacking a penis—to Freud, the most cherished thing a person can have—develop "penis envy." Thus, in addition to lusting after the father, they desire to possess his penis symbolically.

The Oedipus complex is resolved through the process of *identification* with the parents. That is, we resolve our feelings of love and hate for our parents by becoming like them, by convincing ourselves that we share their strength and authority and the affection they have for each other. In this process, we adopt what we believe to be the values and standards of our *same-sex* parent. What we conceive to be their moral judgments shapes our superego, which helps us restrain the demands of the id. For boys, according to Freud, the driving force behind this identification is *castration anxiety*—"The more I'm like my father, the less likely he is to castrate me"—and normal resolution of the stage results in a well-developed superego. Girls, however, lacking this impetus, develop weaker, inferior superegos. They identify with their mother as a result of penis envy, seeking to possess their father's penis symbolically through the mother—and later, as adults, through transferring their feelings toward their father to their mate. They may, however, be afflicted with a degree of penis envy for life, which causes them to strive for "masculine" things such as a "masculine" mode of dress or occupation. We return to what's wrong with this picture later in the chapter when we discuss the views of Karen Horney.

**The Internal Battle**   The three parts of the mind are often in conflict, and Freud regarded this *intrapsychic* conflict as the essence of human personality. One result of the conflict is anxiety, which is produced in the ego whenever the demands of the id are dangerous or the disapprovals of the superego are intense. Anxiety arouses the ego to fight the impulses or thoughts that have created it. In one way or another—by using repression and the other *defense mechanisms* (see Chapter 12), by turning the mind's attention elsewhere, by gratifying some other impulse of the id—the ego defends itself against the threat posed by the id or the superego and minimizes the anxiety.

If the ego is not strong enough to check the id's drives, a person is likely to be selfish, impulsive, and antisocial. But if the ego checks the id too severely, other problems may arise. Too much repression of the libidinal force can make a person incapable of enjoying a normal sex life or of giving a normal amount of affection. Too much repression of aggression can seriously hamper a person in acceptable competitive pursuits. If the ego is not strong enough to check the superego, the result may be vague and unwarranted feelings of guilt and unworthiness, even an unconscious need for self-punishment. Thus, according to Freud, it is the conflict among the ego, id, and superego that often results in abnormal behavior.

**After Freud: Voices of Dissent**   Freud was an important innovator who made many contributions to understanding human personality. He was the first to recognize the role of the unconscious and the importance of anxiety and defenses against it. He also dispelled the myth, widely accepted before his time, that children did not have sexual urges or hostile impulses. He was a pioneer in recognizing the effects of childhood experiences on personality development and in highlighting the conflict between our private impulses and the need to adapt to society.

Freud's theory, however, has many critics, especially today, and belief in his ideas has declined in recent years. To begin with, it isn't possible to demonstrate scientifically that an id, an ego, or a superego actually exists. There is also no scientific support for the idea of psychosexual development and fixations. For example, if you or someone you know qualifies as "anal," there is no reason to believe that it has anything to do with toilet training during childhood.

Many critics believe that Freud overemphasized the role of sexual motivation and conflict by generalizing from the experiences of patients who had grown up in Europe during the sexually repressed Victorian age. Changes in Western societies provide support for this view. Although recent decades have seen considerable relaxation of social restraints on sexual behavior (and presumably much less repression of sexual wishes), there has not been an accompanying decrease in the incidence of anxiety and related symptoms.

Primarily because of what they saw as Freud's overemphasis on sexuality, several of his prominent adherents broke from him and established quite different psychodynamic theories.

## Jung versus Freud: Sexuality Isn't Everything

Originally a protégé of Freud, Carl Jung (1875–1961) came to believe that Freud didn't give nearly enough emphasis to the importance of culture and inherited tendencies. Thus, he broke from Freud and developed his own **analytical psychology.** Anticipating modern research, Jung viewed differences in temperament as related to the mind's ability to deal with new experiences and stress.

Jung believed that Freud overestimated the importance of sexuality. He felt that the libido was far richer and more complex—an all-encompassing life force that included a person's views of life, death, virtue, and religion. Jung placed more emphasis than Freud on intellectual and especially

Carl Jung was originally a protégé of Freud, but eventually he broke from Freud and developed his own view of human personality, known as analytical psychology.

metaphysical qualities of the human personality, and less on sex and aggression. Whereas Freud was relatively pessimistic about human nature, Jung perceived heroism as well as idealism and romanticism in humanity and took a much more optimistic view. He was the first to stress the idea of the ongoing process of *self-realization*—acquiring harmony among the elements of personality, understanding yourself, and, in essence, striving for positive goals and becoming the person that you have the potential to be. In doing so, he gave early voice to the humanistic views of personality described later in the chapter.

Jung proposed that we all possess a **collective unconscious**—a set of inherited mental structures that represent past events in the history of the human species. In a distant sense, modern neuroscience supports this idea. As we saw in Chapter 3, the brain enables us to perceive and experience the world in ways that are universal. The collective unconscious contains traces of humanity's fears, superstitions, beliefs in magic, and search for a god. Because of the collective unconscious, every person embodies a great deal of past human experience. Jung believed that each of us possesses elements of both woman and man, mother and father, hero, prophet, sage, and magician. These he called **archetypes.**

Freud viewed psychological symptoms such as anxiety or depression as the outcome of conflicts within the individual. Jung anticipated contemporary views by being more sensitive to the role that culture and the individual's social environment play in the development of such problems. This emphasis on the impact of

**Analytical psychology**
The term for Jung's approach to psychoanalytic theory.

**Collective unconscious**
A set of inherited mental structures that Jung thought were universal and the result of accumulated human experiences across time.

**Archetypes**
Jung's term for the inherited mental elements in the collective unconscious.

**Introverts**
Individuals who prefer to live with their own thoughts and avoid social interactions.

**Extroverts**
Individuals who are highly interested in other people and the social world around them.

social factors on personality was carried considerably further by other psychodynamic theorists.

Jung coined the terms **introvert** and **extrovert** (you may see the latter term spelled as *extravert* by other theorists). Introverts prefer to live with their thoughts and avoid socializing. Extroverts are highly interested in other people and in the social events around them. The human personality requires a combination of both introversion and extroversion, but in each person one of these traits tends to develop more fully, at the expense of the other.

## Adler, Horney, and Erikson: Social Influences

Like Jung, Alfred Adler (1870–1937) had an initially close relationship with Freud that later fell apart. Karen Horney (1885–1952) was trained in classical psychoanalysis, although not by Freud. She, too, sharply disagreed with him, especially with regard to his views about women. Erik Erikson (1904–1994) was trained by Freud's daughter Anna, a child psychoanalyst. Erikson managed to develop his own theory of personality development, one that didn't exactly disagree with Freud's but wound up quite different from it. Along with Jung, these three theorists all emphasized how social interactions and culture help determine personality—a topic largely ignored by Freud.

**Individual psychology**
The term for Adler's approach to psychodynamic theory.

**Adler's Individual Psychology**   Rejecting Freud's focus on sexuality, Adler's **individual psychology** emphasized instead the innate tendency to be cooperative and psychologically tuned in to other people (1927, 1931). Adler believed that individuals encounter problems in life because they develop inappropriate goals and patterns of living that block the realization of their social interest. Although this theory remains largely unsupported, psychologists have attempted to differentiate among various groups of individuals—for example, felons as contrasted to church volunteers—in terms of their degree of concern for the social welfare of others (Crandall, 1980).

Adler also proposed that we are born with a tendency to overcome innate feelings of inferiority and strive for superiority—not in terms of influence or success in competition with others, but rather in terms of being useful and contributing members of society and being on the road to self-realization, in much the same sense as Jung and later the humanistic psychologists used the concept. Those who become stifled in this process and are unable to overcome or compensate for their feelings of inferiority may develop an *inferiority complex*—a term coined by Adler. You still hear the term used today to refer to persons who are severely lacking in self-confidence and generally have low self-esteem.

Adler viewed aggression as a distortion of the more basic urge for personal fulfillment. Adler observed that many people appear to be engaged in continual efforts to overcome feelings of inferiority, based not only on physical flaws but on perceived psychological and social ones as well. Such efforts often begin early, based, for example, on the young child's perceptions of the superior abilities of an older sibling. One of Adler's most influential observations was the importance of birth order in shaping personality—a subject of research described in the Life Span Perspective on page 344.

**Social psychoanalytic theory**
The term for Horney's approach to psychodynamic theory.

**Basic anxiety**
The feeling of being isolated and helpless in a potentially hostile world.

**Horney's Social Psychoanalytic Theory**   In establishing her **social psychoanalytic theory,** Horney broke with the Freudian tradition of emphasizing sexuality. Her view of the human personality, like Jung's and Adler's, was essentially optimistic. She believed humans to be capable of growth and self-realization. This trend can be blocked, however, if as a child an individual acquires a sense of **basic anxiety**—a feeling of being isolated and helpless in a potentially hostile world (Horney, 1945)—which Horney saw as stemming from neglect or abuse by parents during early childhood. Horney's views on the importance of a child's early experiences of love and security are reflected in much of the research on early attachment described in Chapter 10.

Horney was among the first psychodynamic theorists to shift the view of women in society away from the male perspective that had dominated earlier theories (Feshbach & Weiner, 1986). For example, she took exception to Freud's notion that penis envy is a state shared by women as a result of their biological nature; she contended that Freud did not appreciate how society's view of women at the time produced problems of self-confidence and self-fulfillment. That is, any inferiority women feel with respect to men has nothing whatsoever to do with wishing they had a penis; it is instead attributable to the traditionally inferior roles and status assigned to women in Western and other cultures. Horney was, in the view of one of her biographers, "the first, and perhaps the best, critic of Freud's ideas about women" (Quinn, 1987).

In departing from Freud's theories of personality, both Adler and Horney turned away from the internal struggles of the individual and focused instead on the importance of the ways in which we relate to others in society—a modern emphasis of psychology that is discussed in the final chapter of this text. Although their contributions survive, few theorists after Freud have been as influential in this respect as Erikson.

**Erikson's Psychosocial Theory**   The idea that personality growth depends on dealing with personal and social crises is the basis of Erikson's theory of **psychosocial development.** Erikson based his conclusions on observations of people he treated, some in childhood and others at various stages of adulthood. He viewed development as a twofold process in which individuals' psychological development (their personality and view of themselves) proceeds hand in hand with the social interactions they experience as they go through life. He suggested that this development can be divided into eight stages; in each stage, individuals face new social situations and encounter new problems to work through—called *psychosocial crises* or turning points. In Erikson's view, successfully resolving these crises results in greater maturity, a richer personality, and a stronger ego. Failing to resolve them successfully results in arrestment and a weaker ego. The stages described by Erikson are shown in Table 9.2. We return to Erikson's theory in Chapters 10 and 11, with regard to development across the life span.

Karen Horney believed that humans are capable of growth and self-realization, but that growth can be blocked if the individual acquires a sense of basic anxiety during childhood.

**Psychosocial development** Erikson's twofold process in which individuals' psychological development proceeds hand in hand with the social interactions they experience as they go through life.

Erik Erikson developed a theory of personality development involving eight stages, in each of which the individual must face and resolve new social situations and problems, called psychosocial crises.

## Fromm's Social Psychoanalytic Theory

In recent years, psychodynamic theorists have added to and in some ways completely revised Freud's ideas. In particular, they have tended to move away from Freud's emphasis on the id and its biologically determined impulses, toward greater concern with the ego and its attempts to deal with reality—as, for that matter, Erikson also did to a major extent.

Along with Adler, Horney, and Erikson, other psychodynamic theorists turned their attention to the cultural and social influences on personality, which Freud neglected. One prominent member of this group was Erich Fromm (1900–1980), who suggested that personality problems are caused by conflicts between basic human needs and the demands of society. The core of personality, according to Fromm, is the desire to fulfill oneself as a human being—that is, to achieve a kind

Erikson viewed the life cycle of development from cradle to grave as having eight stages. Each stage brings new social experiences and new crises—which, if surmounted successfully, lead to continuous, steadily enriched personality growth.

**TABLE 9.2**
**Erikson's Psychosocial Stages**

| Stage | Crisis | Favorable Outcome | Unfavorable Outcome |
|---|---|---|---|
| **Childhood** | | | |
| First year of life | Trust versus mistrust | Faith in the environment and future events | Suspicion, fear of future events |
| Second year | Autonomy versus doubt | A sense of self-control and adequacy | Feelings of shame and self-doubt |
| Third through fifth years | Initiative versus guilt | Ability to be a "self-starter," to initiate one's own activities | A sense of guilt and inadequacy to be on one's own |
| Sixth year to puberty | Industry versus inferiority | Ability to learn how things work, to understand and organize | A sense of inferiority at understanding and organizing |
| **Transition Years** | | | |
| Adolescence | Identity versus confusion | Seeing oneself as a unique and integrated person | Confusion over who and what one really is |
| **Adulthood** | | | |
| Early adulthood | Intimacy versus isolation | Ability to make commitments to others, to love | Inability to form affectionate relationships |
| Middle age | Generativity versus self-absorption | Concern for family and society in general | Concern only for self—one's own well-being and prosperity |
| Aging years | Integrity versus despair | A sense of integrity and fulfillment; willingness to face death | Dissatisfaction with life; despair over prospect of death |

Source: *Adapted from Erikson, 1963.*

## Test Yourself

(b) "For the life of me, I can't figure out why I got so angry at my friend." If Freud were to hear you say those words, what would he probably conclude about the nature of your motives for having gotten angry?

(c) Does the term *libido* refer only to sexual urges?

(d) If you refer to someone as an introvert or an extrovert, whose personality theory are you drawing from?

(e) Why do you think Karen Horney's view of personality would be widely endorsed by today's feminist leaders?

(The answers are on page 360.)

of unity with nature in the special way that is dictated by the human ability to think abstractly. People must seek unity through their own efforts; they must fulfill what Fromm regarded as the five basic and uniquely human needs (listed in Table 9.3).

It would be possible, Fromm believed, to create a society in which these needs could be fulfilled harmoniously. But no such society has ever existed. Therefore, all of us tend to experience frustrations and personality problems. It is society, Fromm said, that is "sick"—and it will remain so until people can relate to one another "lovingly" and "in bonds of brotherliness and solidarity," transcend nature "by creating rather than by destroying," and gain a sense of self through their own individual powers "rather than by conformity" (Fromm, 1955).

**TABLE 9.3**
**Fromm's Five Basic Human Needs**

| | |
|---|---|
| 1. Relatedness | This need stems from the fact that human beings have lost the union with nature that other animals possess. It must be satisfied by human relationships based on productive love (which implies mutual care, responsibility, respect, and understanding). |
| 2. Transcendence | The need to rise above one's animal nature and to become creative. |
| 3. Rootedness | The need for a feeling of belonging, best satisfied by feelings of affiliation with all humanity. |
| 4. Identity | The need to have a sense of personal identity, to be unique. It can be satisfied through creativity or through identification with another person or group. |
| 5. A frame of orientation | The need for a stable and consistent way of perceiving the world and understanding its events. |

Source: From *The Sane Society* by Erich Fromm, © 1955 by Erich Fromm. Reprinted by permission of Holt, Rinehart and Winston Publishers.

Fromm's theory holds that the core of human personality is the desire to fulfill these needs. Personality problems arise when the attempt to gratify them is frustrated.

# POSITIVE GROWTH: HUMANISTIC THEORIES OF PERSONALITY

Much closer to the theories of Adler, Horney, and Fromm than to those of Freud are the humanistic theories of personality. These theories assume a core of personality almost opposite to the one Freud assumed. Freud believed that the core was conflict, springing in large part from the ruthless and pleasure-seeking demands of the id. Humanistic theories, on the contrary, hold that human nature is basically good and that the core of personality is the desire to perfect our skills and find peace and happiness.

**FOCUS QUESTIONS**
- According to humanistic psychology, what lies at the core of personality?
- What is unconditional positive regard and how is it important?
- What is self-actualization?

## Rogers and Self-Worth

Among the prominent humanistic theorists was Carl Rogers, who stressed the crucial role of the self-image we all have. This **phenomenological self** represents the way we perceive ourselves as functioning human beings. It consists of our judgments about our abilities, accomplishments, attractiveness, and relationships with other people. In part, it is based on our own observations of our behavior and the reactions of other people. But it is also highly subjective, depending on our feelings about ourselves and the way we evaluate ourselves. Thus, the phenomenological self does not necessarily correspond to reality. Many people who are considered successful and are highly respected by others perceive themselves as unworthy failures—but succeed in hiding their feelings (Rogers, 1961).

To be happy and to develop normally, we must grow up in a family and social environment that treat us with what Rogers called **unconditional positive regard.** That is, we must be valued and trusted for ourselves and accepted uncondi-

**Phenomenological self**
The self-image that represents the way we perceive ourselves as functioning human beings.

**Unconditional positive regard**
Total acceptance of individuals for who and what they are, even if one disagrees with their actions.

Were you the firstborn in your family, or did you come along later? This may seem like an odd question to ask in a discussion of personality, but it is more relevant than it may appear.

Firstborn children—on average—are more likely than others to have high achievement motivation. For example, students who are firstborns get higher grades than those who are laterborns. They are also more competitive and have higher educational aspirations (Falbo, 1981). Their high achievement motivation has led many firstborns to become outstandingly successful. They are more likely to become national merit scholars, get Ph.D.s, and be listed in *Who's Who* (Sutton-Smith, 1982). Any list of prominent people—eminent scholars, even presidents of the United States—contains a high proportion of firstborns.

One possible explanation is that parents treat firstborn children differently than they do later children. They devote more time to the firstborn, are more protective, play a greater part in the child's activities, interfere more, and expect more (Scarr & Grajek, 1982). The firstborn child is criticized more often and expected to conform to adult standards (Baskett, 1984). Laterborn children receive less attention and guidance from their parents and are influenced more by their relations with other children, including their siblings.

Among other possible explanations is that firstborns may be driven to do better than laterborns because they feel anxious about being cast aside—in Adler's words, "dethroned"—upon their siblings' arrival. The motive to excel is thus driven by the wish to retain parental approval (Adler, 1928). The tendency toward achievement by firstborns may also occur because they are likely to do better in school at earlier ages and go on to college (Sutton-Smith, 1982). Again, strictly on average, firstborn children score higher on intelligence tests—probably because they enjoy special benefits in their family relationships. They are the ones who benefit most from enriching, one-to-one contacts with their parents. From studies of large populations of children, one investigator found that the more children there are in a family—especially without wide gaps between them—the lower their average intelligence level is likely to be (Zajonc, 1986).

Psychologists have sought to identify other characteristics, in addition to achievement and intelligence patterns, common among firstborns. Firstborn children, again perhaps because of their early close interactions with their parents, have been found to be more trusting of authority than laterborn children (Suedfeld, 1969). Because of this characteristic and the related tendency to conform, firstborns are more reluctant than laterborns to generate or accept beliefs that depart from those of the majority. Among scientists, for example, firstborns are more likely to support the status quo, whereas laterborns are more likely to come up with ideas that threaten "the establishment." Copernicus, who insisted that the earth revolved around the sun rather than the other way around, was a laterborn, as was Charles Darwin, who argued against religious beliefs in creation and suggested that humans evolved from animals. The overall chance that a firstborn will support a scientific revolution is only half the chance that a laterborn will do so. A similar preponderance of laterborns is found among social reformers—whether the issue is civil rights or egalitarianism (Sulloway, 1990).

Another pattern: Just as the youngest child in the family seems to fear and shun power, firstborns often rate high in the desire to attain power. There seems to be some truth in Adler's description of the firstborn child as a "power-hungry conservative" (Adler, 1928).

There are, of course, many exceptions to these generalities. Each

---

**Conditions of worth**
Conditions that make being considered a worthwhile human being contingent on behaving in certain ways.

tionally as worthwhile human beings. Our opinions and behavior must be respected. We must be accepted and loved for who we are, even when we do things of which others disapprove. Unfortunately, Rogers (1992) observed, few people grow up in such a favorable atmosphere. Most are treated with what Rogers called **conditions of worth** that tend to be perfectionistic and unattainable standards for behavior. Their families and society at large respond warmly to only some of their thoughts and actions, respond disapprovingly to others, and tell them that their worth as a human being depends on "doing right."

All of us, said Rogers, try to perceive our experiences and behave in a way that is consistent with our phenomenological self. When we are confronted with new experiences or new feelings that seem inconsistent with the image, we can take one of two courses: We can recognize the new experiences or feelings, interpret them clearly, and somehow integrate them into our image of self—which is a healthy reaction—or we can deny the experiences or feelings or interpret them in distorted fashion.

human being is unique—and the product of many more factors than simply the order in which his or her birth happened to occur. As with other characteristics, it is never appropriate to draw conclusions about an individual based simply on knowledge of that person's birth order.

Each of these high-achieving individuals was a firstborn child. Clockwise from top left, they are Wayne Gretzky, Hillary Rodham Clinton, Martin Luther King, Jr., Candice Bergen, Spike Lee, and Eleanor Roosevelt.

Rogers believed that the second course of action is likely to cause trouble. He concluded that maladjusted people tend to regard as a threat any experience that is not consistent with their self-image. Their phenomenological self, as they conceive of it, does not match their true feelings and the actual nature of their experiences. They must set up more and more defenses against the truth, and more and more tension results. Well-adjusted people, on the other hand, are those whose self-image is consistent with what they really think, feel, do, and experience—and who are willing to accept themselves as they are. Instead of being rigid, their phenomenological self is flexible and changes as new experiences occur.

## Maslow and Self-Actualization

Humanistic psychologists believe that the most powerful motivating force in human beings is the aspiration toward benevolent and spiritual goals. The humanists' view of human personality is expressed in the idea of **self-actualization,**

**Self-actualization**
A humanistic view that people will pursue the highest and most idealistic aims unless their development is thwarted by a malevolent social environment.

Self-actualizers like Oprah Winfrey are characterized by intelligence, drive, boldness, and energy.

Abraham Maslow believed that humans are innately inclined to seek the fullest possible development of their own unique potentialities.

which holds that people will pursue the highest and most idealistic aims unless their development is thwarted by a malevolent social environment.

As noted earlier, this view actually originated with Jung and other theorists, but it was articulated the most thoroughly by Abraham Maslow. He believed that humans are innately inclined to seek beauty, goodness, truth, and the fullest possible development of their own unique potentialities for perfection and creativity. For Maslow, self-actualization meant striving for an all-encompassing self-fulfillment, in an ongoing process that never quite achieves its goal. Self-actualizing people—a tiny minority of adults— achieve satisfactions through their ongoing search for such aesthetic pleasures as order, symmetry, and beauty. They accept themselves and others and the realities of existence, and they rejoice in the experience of living. Self-actualizers are spontaneous and creative and have a keen sense of humor. They are making the most of their abilities and becoming all they are capable of becoming (Maslow, 1970). All this represents the goal toward which all humans by their very nature are motivated—although deprivation and social pressures prevent most people from making the progress of those Maslow identified as self-actualizers.

## Test Yourself

**(f)** If you were to say, "I seem to be having trouble with my phenomenological self," on what view of personality would you be basing your statement, and what would you believe to be the problem?

(The answer is on page 360.)

# FURTHER PERSPECTIVES ON PERSONALITY

## FOCUS QUESTIONS
- In Skinner's operant conditioning view, what does personality consist of?
- In Bandura's social cognitive view, what factors influence personality and behavior?
- In the view of evolutionary psychologists, how has natural selection influenced human personality?

The days of the "grand" theories of personality have come and gone, but a rich legacy of useful ideas about human nature and how to understand people and the things they do remains. Thus, the theories live on, and the next grand theory may be just over the horizon.

In the meantime, however, many personality and related theorists have turned to *describing* important personality characteristics and factors rather than attempting to specify a "core" or "structure" of personality such as those proposed by the classic theorists discussed thus far. Another shift of emphasis, in keeping with current trends, has been a return to examining the role of biological and genetic factors in personality. The classic theorists were all aware that biology plays an important role in who we are and what we become, but, given the limited scientific understanding of heredity during the late 19th and early 20th centuries, they largely acknowledged the assumption and went on from there. They paid little attention to the details of the interaction between heredity and environment or how biological commonalities and differences pertaining to personality might have arisen in the first place.

In this section, the first approach we consider is that of learning theory—especially B. F. Skinner's ideas of operant conditioning. This approach is purely descriptive in that Skinner did not acknowledge the existence of "entities" such as personality. The second approach is that of social learning and social cognitive theorists, with emphasis on the work of Albert Bandura, which is also largely descriptive. "Big Five" theory, which proposes that personality can be described in its entirety on the basis of five dimensions and which is currently the dominant theory of personality (Kagan, 2002), is discussed in the next section because of its emphasis on assessment.

The section closes with consideration of certain genetically based tendencies in personality that may have arisen through natural selection and evolution, noting the theory and research of David Buss. Another important biological approach, focusing on infant "temperament" and its role in personality development, is considered in detail in Chapter 10.

## Skinner and Operant Conditioning

Humanistic theories hold that the core of personality is the tendency toward positive growth. Classical psychoanalytic theory holds that the core is conflict. Another prominent group of theories takes still another view. These are the strict behavioral theories, which pay little heed to Freud's notion of the primitive drives of the id and do not take a stand on the question of whether human nature is basically good and positive or selfish and negative. Instead, these theories regard personality as composed largely of habits—that is, of habitual ways of responding to the situations that arise in each individual's life. Beginning at birth, our experiences mold us in accordance with the principles of learning and conditioning discussed in Chapter 4. Depending on what responses we have learned to make to events in the environment, we may either cope successfully or become helpless and troubled by anxiety or depression.

B. F. Skinner was among the best-known advocates of the strict behavioral approach to personality, although he did not accept personality as a meaningful concept (Skinner, 1953). Skinner maintained that we can understand behavior and what others call personality only by applying the operant conditioning principles described in Chapter 4 to understanding what a person does. Rejecting the belief that humans possess free will, Skinner (1972) argued that we learn to be a particular kind of person in the same way that we learn anything else in life—through positive or negative reinforcement and punishment or, in his terms, *reinforcement history*. External circumstances and consequences, not some inner self, ultimately define personality. In effect, we could predict a person's behavior if we knew which of this person's actions had been rewarded by society and which ones had been punished.

Although Skinner's view has been attacked for portraying humans as passive "pawns" of the environment, it does open up possibilities for change. Once we know what reinforcers maintain a certain pattern of behavior, logic dictates that we could cause extinction of that behavior by withdrawing them and could shape alternative ways of behaving by using new reinforcers, as discussed in Chapter 4.

Operant conditioning procedures are an integral part of behavior therapies, as described in Chapter 14.

With regard to understanding overall personality, however, operant conditioning falls short in another important respect: It's never possible to know a given person's entire reinforcement history, so it's not possible to understand and predict what the person might do in a particular situation based on operant conditioning principles. This leaves us with little choice but to try to discern motives, traits, and other covert characteristics that provide a richer understanding of people in general, as well as individuals.

## Bandura and Human Agency

At the time that behavioral theories of personality based on learning were formulated, most of psychology's knowledge of learning was confined to classical and operant conditioning. Thus, the theories originally stressed the way unreasonable fears can be acquired through classical conditioning and the role of reinforcement in molding operant behavior. As noted, the rewards and punishments provided first by the family and later by society in general were considered especially important.

Today, most learning theorists take a more cognitive view of how experience creates patterns of behavior. They agree that rewards and punishments influence learning, but they believe that people learn by means other than direct reinforcement. And factors inside the person—such as perceptions, beliefs, attitudes, and values—are also important.

**Reciprocal interaction**
A concept suggesting that humans are highly active processors of information who are continually interacting with the environment.

Albert Bandura, a prominent social learning and social cognitive theorist, developed the concept of **reciprocal interaction,** in which humans are regarded as highly active processors of information who are continually interacting with the social environment (Bandura, 1977). The environment affects us, but the opposite is true as well. For example, losing a game may cause your friend to behave in a hostile manner—and eventually lead you to respond the same way, causing friction in the friendship. But your friend would create a far different environment if she were a "good sport" and lost graciously. What this implies is that we are not

According to the concept of reciprocal interaction, humans are continually interacting with the social environment. In this example, the behavior of one of the card players will influence the other's reactions—and vice versa.

© Norbert Schaefer/CORBIS

just passive responders—we can choose how we want to affect the world around us. We have a "uniquely human capacity" for self-direction (Bandura, 1974).

After his early research on observational learning (see Chapter 1) and its role in behavior and personality, Bandura turned to developing his theory of **self-efficacy,** which refers essentially to what you are actually capable of doing in specific contexts or, more generally, who you may become as a person. This stands in contrast to **perceived self-efficacy**—that is, what you *think* you can do or become. To Bandura, your set of beliefs about what you can do and the extent to which you see yourself as having control over your life are by far the most central and pervasive aspects of your personality (Bandura, 1989). Perhaps through what we observe others succeed and fail at, perhaps through what we decide about ourselves on the basis of personal experiences with success and failure, we acquire a sense of perceived self-efficacy that often determines what we will or will not attempt in an immediate sense and in life. Phobias are a simple example: Barring disability, anyone is physically capable of holding and stroking a snake. Yet many people perceive themselves as incapable of doing so and will not attempt to do so. Thus, they are low in perceived self-efficacy (a treatment for phobias based on this view is discussed in Chapter 14). In turn, they are likely to be easily frustrated, to give up easily, to avoid challenges, and to be low in self-esteem as well.

Self-efficacy theory has generated considerable research over the years, and Bandura has extended the theory to many realms of human endeavor and consolidated it within the term *human agency* (Bandura, 1989, 2001). In his words, "To be an agent is to intentionally make things happen by one's actions. . . . The core features of agency enable people to play a part in their self-development, adaptation, and self-renewal with changing times" (Bandura, 2001). High on the list in achieving agency is, of course, the belief that you can do so, or perceived self-efficacy. In turn, the concept extends to *collective self-efficacy*—the beliefs of groups, from small local organizations to entire nations, about what they can accomplish and the positive sense of agency that results when these beliefs are optimistic (and realistic).

Bandura notes that the importance of efficacy beliefs appears to be universal, although such beliefs manifest themselves differently in individualist and collectivist cultures (Bandura, 2001). In the former, self-efficacy beliefs pertain more to individual personal accomplishments; in the latter, they pertain more to accomplishments of the group.

**Self-efficacy**
What a person is actually capable of doing in specific contexts or of becoming as a person.

**Perceived self-efficacy**
What a person thinks she or he can do or become.

# Buss and the Evolution of Personality

If various *physical* characteristics and differences have evolved in humans—and this is no longer disputed by scientists—why not *psychological* characteristics such as those pertaining to personality? Has natural selection favored certain tendencies in human personality that were more adaptive in our evolutionary history?

Not everyone agrees, but evolutionary psychologists such as David Buss and colleagues insist that there are such characteristics and tendencies and that studying them from an evolutionary perspective will eventually yield the first comprehensive view of "human nature" (Buss, 1999a). These researchers have invested a considerable amount of effort in assessing psychological commonalities among people who live in diverse cultures around the world, and they have turned up some likely candidates for "shared" personality characteristics—two of which we discuss here. But first, having alluded to evolutionary processes at various points in the text, we take a brief look at how these processes are thought to work, both for physical and psychological characteristics. The following analysis is adapted from Buss, 1999a:

1.  Within a species, individuals differ in various ways.

2. Some of these differences can be passed along from parents to children and succeeding generations through genetics.

3. Some are associated with survival or reproduction.

4. Those that contribute to a better chance of survival or greater reproduction are more likely to be passed along to succeeding generations.

5. Those that repeatedly enhance survival or reproduction tend to displace those that either don't enhance it or interfere with it.

Note that the above process is not limited to a single individual directly passing along his or her personal genes. For example, as discussed in Chapter 15 with regard to altruism, members of families or other genetically related groups pass along at least a portion of their genes when their relatives survive and reproduce. Thus, characteristics such as being helpful and cooperative and being willing to sacrifice yourself to save your kin could have an evolutionary basis too.

In specifying what psychological adaptations might have occurred over the perhaps 7-million-year history of *hominids—homo sapiens* and all of our human-like ancestors—evolutionary psychologists are careful to avoid unwarranted assumptions. Thus, in addition to requiring that diverse individuals display similarities on a given psychological characteristic, they also require that the particular "problem" solved by an adaptation be identifiable. The more scientific evidence they compile that points to how the adaptation could have solved the problem, the more confident evolutionary psychologists become that the psychological adaptation did indeed occur. In this sense, evolutionary psychology is still evolving, and a complete understanding of the role of evolution in human psychology and personality is a long way away. But considerable progress has been made in identifying likely candidates for evolved tendencies in personality and behavior. Each of the following theories involves possible personality differences between females and males that could pertain to reproductive success.

**Mate Attraction and Selection**   Building on his own research and that of other evolutionary theorists, Buss has proposed that women and men have evolved different strategies with regard to selecting long-term mates—based on the biological fact that women, by virtue of being the bearers of children and in ancestral times the primary caregivers, make a much greater investment in children than men do (Buss, 1999b). Women also can have only a limited number of children in their lifetime. Thus, especially in the time prior to civilization and agriculture, when survival and successful reproduction and childrearing depended much more on day-to-day subsistence, selection favored females who chose long-term mates who could and would take care of and provide for them and their children. That is, those females who chose their mates according to "resources" and the willingness to share them were more likely to pass their genes along to succeeding generations. This evolved tendency translates into a female preference for males who—compared to other males—are taller and stronger, are more emotionally stable and dependable, convey a stronger sense of commitment to the relationship, are somewhat older and more mature, and have better financial prospects (Buss, 1999b). This is not to say that every woman in the world is out there actively looking for a large, strong, older man with lots of money. Like any evolved psychological characteristic, this kind of preference takes the form of a "whispering" that we aren't necessarily aware of and that can readily be overcome by culture and learning based on personal experiences (Barash, 1979).

For men, in Buss's view, the best reproductive strategy is quite different. Lacking women's investment in childbearing and childrearing, and being able to produce an extremely large number of children in their lifetime, ancestral men were more likely to pass along their genes if they (1) chose women who were healthy, fertile, and therefore typically younger and (2) had sex with as many women as possible. The first point translates into male preferences for physical attractiveness in females, to the extent that this is a cue for health and fertility (Buss, 1999b). The second point is borne out by two observations: First, far more societies sanction multiple wives for men than multiple husbands for women (Wilson, 1978). Second, there has long been a "double standard" in many cultures regarding sexual infidelity—it is viewed much more negatively when committed by women than when committed by men. But, of course, this does not lead to a generalization that every man is out there trying to have sex with every attractive woman he sees, and it certainly does not mean that men are incapable of long-term relationships and fidelity. If true, the preference is again a whispering. It is also the case that selection would favor men who stuck around and made sure that their offspring were provided for.

**Jealousy**    Closely related to the proposed male-female differences in mate preferences is a proposed difference in what makes men and women the most jealous of their partners. As analyzed by Buss and thoroughly researched across cultures (Buss, 2000), men have a stronger tendency to be jealous over sexual infidelity, and women over emotional infidelity. In the case of men, who in our evolutionary past could never be absolutely sure that a child was theirs, jealousy over sexual infidelity and the behaviors it engendered—such as a man's keeping close tabs on what his mate was up to—would have been favored by selection. In Buss's words, "From an ancestral man's perspective, the single most damaging form of infidelity his partner could commit . . . would have been a sexual infidelity." This is because his partner's sexual infidelity meant that he risked investing years in raising another man's child and, if he remained faithful to his partner, not having his genes passed along at all.

For ancestral women, who then as now could always be sure that a child was genetically theirs, sexual infidelity would have been much less of a concern with regard to selection. Instead, they stood to lose the most if their partner was emotionally unfaithful, fell in love with another woman, and left—taking his resources with him and decreasing the chances that their children would survive and reproduce. As Buss put it, "A husband's one-night sexual stand is agonizing, of course, but most women want to know: 'Do you love her?'"

The book by Buss that we've been citing on the evolution of jealousy has as its primary title *The Dangerous Passion*, which underscores the horrors that can result when jealousy gets out of control—such as in cases of spouse abuse or even murder. But in moderation, it would appear to be an adaptive passion in evolutionary terms, regardless of the gender differences in what triggers it.

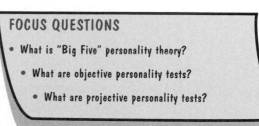

## Test Yourself

**(g)**  How much emphasis did Skinner place on conditioning as a basis of personality?

**(h)**  If you're terrified of dogs and convinced that you could never pet one, how would Bandura's theory of human agency explain this?

**(i)**  If you're male and find yourself attracted primarily to beautiful young women, how might an evolutionary psychologist explain this?

**(j)**  If you're female and find yourself attracted primarily to strong and dependable men with favorable prospects, how might an evolutionary psychologist explain this?

(The answers are on page 360.)

# PERSONALITY ASSESSMENT— AND ITS LIMITS

The idea of personality "types" has been around for quite a long time—indeed, centuries. The ancient Greeks, for example, believed that fluids inside the body determined whether people were happy or depressed, hot-tempered or lethargic.

In the 20th century, in the absence of physical descriptors of personality, the theories of Freud and those who followed him dictated the personality traits that were considered most important—traits described by terms like anxious,

## FOCUS QUESTIONS

• What is "Big Five" personality theory?

• What are objective personality tests?

• What are projective personality tests?

obsessive-compulsive, paranoid, repressed, and fixated. But as psychoanalytic theory lost its popularity and psychologists abandoned their faith in the personality characteristics that Freud emphasized, it became necessary to seek new ideas. No strong theory, however, was available to replace psychoanalytic concepts. As a result, a different strategy was chosen. Psychologists decided to be less theoretical and to let the observable and measurable evidence decide which traits were most important. They devised questionnaires in which people were asked to describe their behaviors and moods, and then they analyzed the results of these studies to ascertain which personality traits were most significant and, importantly, relatively stable. The personality questionnaires in use today derive from those developed in the mid-20th century.

## Big Five Theory

Most recent on the scene is the "Big Five" approach, which describes personality in terms of five sets of complementary factors that determine traits (McCrae & Costa, 1986, 1999). These are (1) extraversion versus introversion, (2) emotional stability, (3) openness to experience, (4) agreeableness, and (5) conscientiousness. Examples of specific characteristics that make up each factor are given in Table 9.4.

Despite the widely acknowledged conceptual value of the Big Five, this approach is not without its critics. Among the principal criticisms has been that the five factors constitute a "psychology of the stranger" (McAdams, 1992). That is, information about the five factors would enable one to make a quick appraisal of

This portrayal of five principal dimensions of personality reflects a continuing effort to define the essential ways in which individuals differ—and to do so in as meaningful and economical a way as possible.

**TABLE 9.4**
**Dimensions of Personality: The Big Five**

| Dimension | Definition of Extremes | |
|---|---|---|
| Extraversion/ introversion | Outgoing | Withdrawn |
| | Fun-loving | Serious |
| | Affectionate | Aloof |
| | Spontaneous | Inhibited |
| Emotional stability | Calm | Fearful |
| | Secure | Uncertain |
| | Strong self-concept | Weak |
| | Easygoing | High-strung |
| Openness to experience | Imaginative | Down-to-earth |
| | Likes variety | Likes *status quo* |
| | Independent | A follower |
| | Inquisitive | Disinterested |
| Agreeableness | Kind | Mean |
| | Trusting | On guard |
| | Cooperative | Unamenable |
| | Courteous | Thoughtless |
| Conscientiousness | Careful | Careless |
| | Organized | Chaotic |
| | Rigorous | Haphazard |
| | Self-disciplined | Without resolve |

Source: Adapted from McCrae & Costa, 1986, 1999.

personality features, but would not provide a comprehensive perspective on the many elements of personality. Psychologists have cautioned that it is important not to be lulled into thinking that the availability of terms, however accurate, to describe personality implies an understanding of the actual structure of personality (Briggs, 1992).

So is Big Five a scientific theory of personality, given that it is based entirely on statistical analysis of verbal self-reports (answers to questions), as discussed later in the chapter? Advocates say yes; critics say not necessarily. As with questionnaires in general (Chapter 1), there are often marked discrepancies between what people say, what they believe and feel, and what they actually do. (See Kagan, 2002, for a detailed discussion of this problem as it applies to approaches such as Big Five.) In the absence of more objective measures such as physiological ones and observations of overt behavior, Big Five theory at best falls short.

Big Five theory has also been criticized as being oriented specifically toward Western cultural and ethical values (e.g., Kagan, 2002), but its contemporary proponents, Robert McCrae and Paul Costa, have gone to great lengths in recent years to test its universality across cultures using translations of their NEO Personality Inventory–Revised (NEO-PI-R), described in the next section. They have amassed evidence that the *structure* of personality from the Big Five perspective is the same, based on comparisons of U.S. samples with samples of people who speak German, Portuguese, Hebrew, Chinese, Korean, and Japanese (McCrae & Costa, 1997), and then with Filipino and French samples (McCrae, Costa, Del Pilar, Rolland, & Parker, 1998), a People's Republic of China sample (Yang et al., 1999), and further samples from Germany, Italy, Portugal, Croatia, and South Korea (McCrae et al., 1999). Based on these and other studies, McCrae and Costa have concluded not only that personality structure is universal but also that personality *development* proceeds in much the same way across cultures (e.g., Costa et al., 2000).

These claims may or may not hold up in the long run, but the evidence is impressive, and it is clear that Big Five theory is here to stay. In the last decade alone, there have been hundreds of publications supporting it or applying it to the study of various personality types and mental and behavioral disorders.

Psychologists also wonder about the number of qualities that constitute the essential dimensions or categories of human personality. Some argue that five is much too small a number; others believe that the number might be even smaller. One classic effort to depict the human personality in even simpler terms was undertaken by Hans Eysenck (1916–1997), who proposed that many variations in personality can be

**FIGURE 9.1** Eysenck's two personality dimensions. Shown here are various traits that make up the two major personality dimensions proposed by Eysenck. Note that the combinations correspond to the four basic personality types shown in the center, which were proposed by the ancient Greek physician Galen (circa 129–199) and later considered by renowned German philosopher Immanuel Kant (1724–1804).

explained by just two key dimensions (Eysenck, 1981; also see Eysenck, 1994). These two dimensions—extraversion-introversion and emotional stability—are among the Big Five summarized in Table 9.4 on page 352. As shown in Figure 9.1, Eysenck defined these two dimensions by a variety of specific personality traits.

If psychologists had a test that measured all of personality accurately and reliably, it would be one of their most valuable tools. Clinical psychologists could quickly analyze their clients' strengths and weaknesses; pinpoint sources of stress, anxiety, and other problems; and determine the most effective approach to treatment. Guidance counselors would have a surefire guide to jobs and careers—personality is a major factor in determining whether a person will be happy and successful as a salesperson, teacher, police officer, or accountant. Research psychologists would have an invaluable aid in studying the conditions that foster or inhibit favorable personality development.

Psychologists have spent a great deal of time, effort, and ingenuity on the creation of personality tests. Their goal, unfortunately, has been elusive. They have devised hundreds of tests that are useful in many ways, but they have yet to find the perfect set of tests. Perhaps they never will. Personality is such a complex matter—the product of a tangled weaving together of genetics, prenatal experiences, and life experiences—that the difficulties in measuring it should be readily apparent.

All the personality tests now in use have both strengths and limitations. The major tests fall into two classes: objective tests and projective tests.

## Objective Tests

**Objective test**
A personality test whose results are not affected by the opinions or prejudices of the examiner.

Many people have attempted to devise measures of personality that meet the requirements for any psychological test, as discussed in Chapter 7: reliability, validity, and standardization. They have come up with **objective tests,** whose scores are not affected by the opinions or prejudices of the examiner when the test is administered properly—although the *interpretation* of the scores can be another matter. Because the procedures are standardized and the examinees respond to true-false or multiple-choice statements or questions, the results should be the same regardless of who gives the test or scores it.

### The Minnesota Multiphasic Personality Inventory
The most widely used and widely researched objective test of adult personality is the Minnesota Multiphasic Personality Inventory–2 (MMPI-2), which is used to help diagnose mental or behavior disorders. The inventory was revised in 1989 to reflect cultural and language changes in the half-century since it was first developed (Hathaway & McKinley, 1992).

The MMPI-2 is made up of nearly 600 statements somewhat like those shown in Table 9.5. For each statement, examinees are asked to check whether or not it is true of their own behavior or to mark "cannot say." The MMPI-2 is an extensively standardized and normed test in which the method of scoring is to compare an individual examinee's patterns of responses with those made in the past by large numbers of other people—including people known to have such personality traits as tendencies toward pessimism and depression, anxiety about health, emotional excitability, and tendencies toward various mental and behavioral disorders. The MMPI-2 also permits assessment of characteristics of more general interest, such as tendencies toward anger, cynicism, low self-esteem, and difficulty functioning on a job, although it is most often used for clinical diagnosis.

An examinee's responses are sorted and tallied into separate *scales*, which in turn yield an overall *profile* that is used for interpreting the results. Because some examinees might want to fake being psychologically healthy to avoid diagnosis or fake being psychologically unhealthy to avoid criminal prosecution or obtain abusable medications, the MMPI-2 includes, in addition to the ten primary diagnostic

| | | Cannot | |
|---|---|---|---|
| T | F | say | |
| ☐ | ☐ | ☐ | At times I get strong cramps in my intestines. |
| ☐ | ☐ | ☐ | I am often very tense on the job. |
| ☐ | ☐ | ☐ | Sometimes there is a feeling like something is pressing in on my head. |
| ☐ | ☐ | ☐ | I wish I could do over some of the things I have done. |
| ☐ | ☐ | ☐ | I used to like to do the dances in gym class. |
| ☐ | ☐ | ☐ | It distresses me that people have the wrong ideas about me. |
| ☐ | ☐ | ☐ | The things that run through my head sometimes are horrible. |
| ☐ | ☐ | ☐ | There are those out there who want to get me. |
| ☐ | ☐ | ☐ | Sometimes I think so fast I can't keep up. |
| ☐ | ☐ | ☐ | I give up too easily when discussing things with others. |

**TABLE 9.5**
**Some Items from a Possible Personality Test**

*Source: Schultz & Schultz, 2001. Reprinted by permission.*

The Minnesota Multiphasic Personality Inventory–2 is made up of statements somewhat like these, which examinees are asked to mark true, false, or cannot say. These are not actual items from the test.

or "clinical" scales, nine "validity" scales that assess the truthfulness of an examinee's responses. Numerous additional scales have been developed and standardized for special purposes, such as assessing a person's propensity for abuse of alcohol and other drugs.

**The Sixteen Personality Factor Questionnaire** Another long-standing and widely used objective test was developed by personality theorist Raymond Cattell (1905–1998) in the 1960s. Currently in its fifth edition, the Sixteen Personality Factor Questionnaire (16PF) has a structure similar to that of the MMPI-2, in that an examinee's responses to the 185 items are tallied into scales and produce an overall profile describing personality. As its name indicates, it primarily assesses the 16 factors that Cattell (1965) considered necessary for an adequate description of personality. Of these, 15 are personality or temperament characteristics; the remaining factor is basic intelligence.

The 16PF can be used for clinical purposes, but it is more often used in business settings for screening job applicants, and in guidance, vocational, and rehabilitation counseling. That is, whereas the MMPI-2 is oriented primarily toward assessing people with mental and behavioral disorders, the 16PF primarily assesses the personality make-up of relatively normal, well-functioning people.

**The NEO Personality Inventory–Revised** As noted earlier, the NEO-PI-R, based on Big Five theory, is the relative newcomer in objective personality testing. Like the 16PF, it is oriented toward describing normal personality, although it too can be used in clinical settings. An examinee rates 240 self-descriptive statements on a 5-point scale from "strongly agree" to "strongly disagree," and an additional 3 items assess the validity of the examinee's responses. Five "domain" scales represent the Big Five factors (on the test, "Emotional Stability" is called "Neuroticism"), and 30 "facet" scales provide a more specific description of personality characteristics. The result is a profile analogous to that of the MMPI-2 and the 16PF.

## Projective and Other Tests

The term *projection* originated as the name for a Freudian defense mechanism (see Chapter 12) in which people attribute to others some of their own anxiety-causing impulses and desires. **Projective tests** of personality assume that analogous mental processes occur when people are presented with *ambiguous* stimuli—they project their own emotional state and thought processes onto the stimuli. These responses can then be analyzed to reveal personality characteristics, along with mental and behavioral problems. Throughout its history, projective testing has had both adherents and harsh critics, but it remains widely used in clinical settings. Two popular approaches to projective testing are described here, along with several informal procedures.

**Projective test**
A personality test in which participants are expected to project aspects of their own personalities into responses to ambiguous stimuli.

### The Thematic Apperception Test

In the 1940s, personality theorist Henry Murray (1893–1988) published the Thematic Apperception Test (TAT) (Murray, 1943), which is still used in its original form today. (The TAT was also used extensively by David McClelland in assessing achievement and other psychological motives discussed in Chapter 8.) In essence, the examinee is asked to make up stories about pictures like the one in Figure 9.2, which you might want to look at and think about before reading on.

The picture in Figure 9.2, like each of the 31 pictures in the set, is deliberately ambiguous. It could depict almost any sort of interaction. Thus, in responding to it, you are likely to project some of your own personality traits. The story you make up may reveal something about your own motives, feelings, anxieties, and attitudes. Sometimes the amount of self-revelation is dramatic, as in this hypothetical story:

> The older woman represents evil, and she is trying to persuade the younger one to leave her husband and run off and lead a life of fun and adventure. The younger one is afraid to do it—afraid of what others will think, afraid she will regret the action. But the older one knows that she wants to leave, and so she insists over and over again. I am not sure how it ends. Perhaps the younger woman turns and walks away and ignores the older woman.

**FIGURE 9.2 A projective test.** What story does this picture tell? What led to the situation? What is happening? How will events turn out? These are the questions asked in the *Thematic Apperception Test* (TAT), which uses drawings similar to this one. Try making up your own story about the picture.
*Reprinted by permission of the publishers from Murray, 1971, Plate 12F. Copyright © 1943 by the President and Fellows of Harvard College, © 1971 by Henry A. Murray.*

As it typically is used today, the TAT does not rely on standardization and norms. Its chief value is that examinees, in telling stories about the pictures, will sometimes reveal problems and issues that they cannot express directly. It can also serve as a vehicle for interaction between examiner and examinee—a sort of "warming up" exercise during psychological assessment.

### The Rorschach Inkblot Test

The Rorschach, as it is familiarly called, uses symmetrical images like the one shown in Figure 9.3. If your reaction to the picture is that it's a blot made by splattering ink on a piece of paper and then folding it in half, this is not a coincidence. In the early 1900s, in the absence of radio or TV programs for entertainment, making inkblots and telling stories about them was a popular evening pastime and parlor game. The ten cards that constitute the Rorschach were carefully selected by Swiss psychiatrist Hermann Rorschach (1885–1922) because the responses they elicited from mentally disordered patients seemed distinctly different from those of normal people. He published the set in 1921, with some ideas about how to interpret responses to the cards (Rorschach, 1921/1942), and the International Rorschach Society has been faithfully reproducing them ever since.

When participants are asked what they see in the blots, they typically mention more than one thing. Their responses are then analyzed or scored for various characteristics, such as emotional state and thinking. For example, a tendency to respond to the blot as a whole may indicate that the participant thinks in terms of abstractions and generalities; a tendency to pick out minor details that most people ignore may indicate overconcern for detail. Most early interpretive systems for the Rorschach were psychoanalytic and highly subjective, but a breakthrough occurred in the 1970s when John Exner and colleagues began publishing a standardized scoring system with norms (e.g., see Exner, 1997) that some view as fairly objective. Because of the test's history, however, its reliability and validity remain controversial.

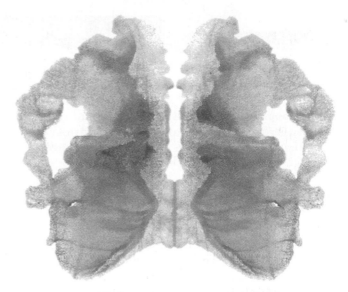

**FIGURE 9.3 Another projective test: what do you see?** This is an image like those used in the *Rorschach Inkblot Test.* Examinees are asked to look at it and report what they see. *Klopfer & Davidson, 1962.*

**Nonstandardized Tests**    A number of less formal and nonstandardized clinical techniques for personality assessment have been developed. The first *word association test* was developed by Jung, who spent a great deal of time and energy refining it for use in working with patients (Jung, 1919). The examiner says a word such as *mother* or *bad* or *money,* and the patient is asked to respond as quickly as possible with the first word that comes to mind. The examiner notes the nature of the associations that the test words suggest and also the speed with which the participant responds. Any unusual delays in responding, as well as other behaviors of interest, are taken to indicate that the test word arouses some kind of conflict. This later becomes a focus of psychotherapy.

In a *draw-a-person test,* the examinee is simply asked to draw a picture of a person on a blank sheet of paper. The sex of the person drawn, the size, the facial expression, and other characteristics may contain clues to the examinee's personality.

In a *sentence-completion test,* the examiner gives the participant a series of partially completed sentences such as the following:

I sometimes feel _____.
When by myself _____.
When I was young _____.

The examinee is asked to complete the sentences with the first thoughts that come to mind. The responses, like TAT stories, may suggest hidden motives, conflicts, and other areas of therapeutic concern.

**Test Yourself**

**(k)** If a clinical psychologist gave you a form with a series of statements and asked you to say whether each statement applied to you by marking "True," "False," or "Cannot say," what kind of personality test would he be giving you?

**(l)** If a clinical psychologist asked you to make up a story about each of a series of pictures, what kind of personality test would she be giving you?

(The answers are on page 360.)

## Limitations of Psychological Testing

Even if a personality test is high in reliability, validity, and standardization, it appears unlikely that it can capture the "whole" person. Tests measure the specific traits and characteristics that they are designed to measure, and even the most comprehensive tests that we have discussed are intended to describe a person *adequately,* according to a defined purpose, but not *entirely.*

There is also the question, raised by Bandura and others, of whether each of us is the same person in the different social contexts we encounter. That is, if an instance of behavior is strongly influenced by the environment in which it occurs,

# → A MATTER OF DEBATE ←

# The Person and the Situation

Throughout this chapter, we presented personality theories and approaches to assessment that assume that personality is relatively stable and largely consistent from one situation to the next. In most personality theories, there is the assumption that certain traits or other characteristics predict what a person will do across a variety of different situations.

But many people behave differently at home, at work, and while dining out. Theorists such as Walter Mischel have argued that personality is neither very stable across time nor consistent across situations (Mischel, 1968, 1969). Mischel later softened his position to include both "person variables" and "situation variables" as determinants of behavior (1984, 1990), but he always maintained that the situation was every bit as important as the person—consistent with Bandura's idea of reciprocal interaction, discussed in the text on page 348.

From a social cognitive perspective, stable personality can be seen as something of an illusion—perhaps one that we actively strive to maintain, rather than something that maintains us. That is, we greatly prefer consistency and predictability both in ourselves and in others, because it makes the world a much easier and safer place to be. So it may be that we regularly make a conscious effort to behave consistently—regardless of our true motives or momentary impulses. In a sense, perhaps we "manufacture" our personality characteristics to make them more consistent than they actually are.

As an example, consider the following thought experiment with regard to a personality trait that people tend to view both as highly important in themselves and others and as stable across a broad variety of situations: honesty. You're an honest person, in class with a group of other students whom you see as being honest—so much so that they wouldn't even take a pencil someone left behind. Your instructor places a coin on a table at the front of the room and turns off the lights, with a guarantee that no one will be searched should the coin disappear. The room goes completely dark. Will the coin still be there a few minutes later when the lights are turned back on? Sure. Honesty prevails; no one steals the coin. Now suppose that instead of a coin, your instructor places a stack of small-denomination bills on the table and darkens the room. Will the money still be there when the lights come back on? Well, probably. Honesty prevails again. Then your instructor places an appealingly thick stack of large-denomination bills on the table and proceeds as before. Will the money stay there? Now you're probably not so sure. In the end, your instructor places a priceless diamond on the table, one worth enough money to provide for you well for the rest of your life—with plenty left over for your children to inherit. Will the diamond be there when the lights come back on? Maybe, if you and your classmates aren't convinced that the diamond is real or that they won't be searched or otherwise caught. But if you and they *were* convinced, ask yourself honestly: Would you be in the stampede toward the table?

We return to this issue in Chapter 15 in the contexts of attitudes versus behavior, conformity, and other topics.

To research this topic further; go online with InfoTrac and use your own term or the following suggestions:
- personality
- Walter Mischel

to what extent can there be stable "traits" that yield consistency in behavior from one context to the next—such as the traits that tests attempt to measure in describing personality?

For more thoughts on this issue, see A Matter of Debate above.

# Chapter 9 Summary

## What Is Personality?

1. *Personality* is the dynamic organization within the individual of those psychophysical systems that determine his or her characteristic behavior and thought.
2. Personality theories are concerned with four aspects of human behavior. They make the following assumptions:
   a) There is some *core of personality* common to all human beings.
   b) These common tendencies and characteristics of human beings are channeled in various directions by the process of development.
   c) The core of personality, as modified by development, makes each person a unique individual, displaying a unique pattern of the *peripheral traits* that are generally known as personality.
   d) Identifying and defining inner human qualities can help to explain the peripheral traits.

## Psychodynamic Views: Freud and Those Who Followed

3. Freud's psychoanalytic theory assumes that the core of personality is conflict—springing from a basic pleasure-seeking energy called the *libido*. This theory was the first of what are now called psychodynamic theories.
4. Psychoanalytic theory holds that the human mind has three parts, or forces: the *unconscious mind*, which includes the *id*, with its *pleasure principle*; the conscious *ego*, with its *reality principle*; and the often unconscious *superego*, with its *morality principle*.
5. The primitive id contains the person's instinctive drives toward sensuality and aggression.
6. Freud believed that human *psychosexual development* takes place in five stages: *oral, anal, phallic, latency,* and *genital*.
7. The superego is acquired as a result of the *Oedipus complex*, which all children are assumed to undergo between the ages of 3 and 6.
8. The central problem in mental disorders, according to classical psychoanalytic theory, is anxiety.
9. The following are among Freud's successors who made major modifications to his theory:
   a) Jung, with his *analytical psychology*, rejected Freud's emphasis on sexuality, introduced the concept of the *collective unconscious* with its *archetypes*, and coined the terms *introvert* and *extrovert*.
   b) Adler, with his *individual psychology*, rejected Freud's emphasis on sexuality and instead emphasized striving for superiority and social interest.
   c) Horney, with her *social psychoanalytic theory*, rejected Freud's emphasis on sexuality and his views on women and introduced the concept of *basic anxiety*.
   d) Erikson put forth his theory of *psychosocial development*.
   e) Fromm emphasized social and cultural influences on personality.

## Positive Growth: Humanistic Theories of Personality

10. Humanistic theories hold that human nature is basically good and that the core of personality is the desire to perfect our skills and find peace and happiness.
11. Rogers's humanistic theory stresses the self-image, or *phenomenological self*, in conjunction with *unconditional positive regard* and avoidance of *conditions of worth*.
12. Maslow formulated the theory of *self-actualization*.

## Further Perspectives on Personality

13. The operant conditioning approach of B. F. Skinner rejects the idea of personality in favor of positive and negative reinforcement and punishment as predictors of behavior. Skinner viewed reinforcement history as a better way of looking at what others call personality.
14. Along with observational learning, social learning theories now stress *reciprocal interaction*, a concept developed by Albert Bandura.
15. Bandura's social cognitive theory of human agency stresses the role we ourselves play in our development and successful functioning in the world around us. Central to his conceptualization of human agency are *self-efficacy* and *perceived self-efficacy*.
16. Evolutionary psychology looks at commonalities in people across cultures and views personality characteristics that humans share as adaptations to problems with survival or reproduction in our distant past.
17. Two proposals by evolutionary psychologists such as Buss are as follows:
   a) Females are attracted to particular males more because of the males' resources; males are attracted to particular females more because of the females' fertility.

b) Males are more inclined to become jealous over their partner's sexual infidelity; females are more inclined to become jealous over their partner's emotional infidelity.

## Personality Assessment—and Its Limits

18. "Big Five" theory attempts to describe personality in terms of five general factors; it also proposes universals in personality structure and development. Two of the factors, extraversion-introversion and emotional stability, originated in the work of Hans Eysenck.

19. *Objective tests* minimize bias in scoring. Widely used objective tests include the MMPI-2, the 16PF, and the NEO-PI-R.

20. *Projective tests* assume that an examinee projects personality characteristics onto the ambiguous stimuli. Popular projective tests include the TAT and the Rorschach Inkblot Test.

21. Other useful but informal tests are word association tests, draw-a-person tests, and sentence-completion tests.

22. The extent to which personality characteristics remain stable over time and across situations remains debatable.

# Chapter 9 Test Yourself Answers

(a) Pedro based his conclusion on only one episode. To be considered a part of personality, a particular behavior must be characteristic of the individual.

(b) Freud would probably conclude that your motives in this case were unconscious. He believed that we are often unaware of our true wishes and desires—but that our behavior is, nonetheless, influenced by them.

(c) That is how the term is popularly used, but Freud meant it to stand for a basic energy force—embracing sexual urges, but also such related desires as the urges to be kept warm, well fed, and content.

(d) You are drawing from Carl Jung, who coined the terms and considered the balance between the two to be an important element in the human personality.

(e) Horney took issue with Freud's view of the importance of women's biological nature, contending that Freud did not sufficiently emphasize how society's view of women can produce problems with self-confidence and barriers to self-fulfillment.

(f) You would be basing your statement on the humanistic view of personality as expressed by Carl Rogers, and you would be convinced that you were having a problem with your self-image—the way you feel about and evaluate yourself.

(g) Skinner was convinced that learning through positive and negative reinforcement and punishment is the entire basis for what others call personality.

(h) You would be displaying a discrepancy between your self-efficacy and your perceived self-efficacy where dogs are concerned.

(i) The explanation would involve an evolved adaptation in which males are attracted to females who are most likely to be fertile.

(j) The explanation would involve an evolved adaptation in which females are attracted to males who can and will provide for them and their children.

(k) He would be giving you an objective personality test.

(l) She would be giving you a projective personality test.

# Chapter 9  Personality and Its Assessment

## Key Terms

analytical psychology (p. 339)
archetypes (p. 339)
basic anxiety (p. 340)
collective unconscious (p. 339)
conditions of worth (p. 344)
core of personality (p. 334)
ego (p. 336)
extroverts (p. 340)
id (p. 336)
individual psychology (p. 340)
introverts (p. 340)
libido (p. 335)
morality principle (p. 337)
objective test (p. 354)
Oedipus complex (p. 338)
perceived self-efficacy (p. 349)
peripheral traits (p. 335)
personality (p. 333)

phenomenological self (p. 343)
pleasure principle (p. 336)
projective test (p. 356)
psychodynamic theorists (p. 335)
psychosexual development (p. 337)
psychosocial development (p. 341)
reality principle (p. 336)
reciprocal interaction (p. 348)
self-actualization (p. 345)
self-efficacy (p. 349)
social psychoanalytic theory (p. 340)
superego (p. 337)
unconditional positive regard (p. 343)
unconscious mind (p. 335)

*The key terms above can be used as search terms in InfoTrac, a database of readings, which can be found at http://infotrac-thomsonlearning.com.*

## Active Learning Review

### What Is Personality?

1. *Personality* is the dynamic organization within the individual of those psycho-physical systems that determine his or her characteristic behavior and thought. Thinking logically or illogically and behaving in a friendly or unfriendly manner are two of many elements of the human _____.   **personality**

2. Personality is always developing and changing. Its organization is therefore _____, although the changes may be gradual and slow. A person's characteristic _____ and _____ correspond to the person's traits.   **dynamic** **behavior, thought**

3. To constitute a trait, a person's behavior and thought must be _____ of the person. We do not describe a man as bad-tempered if he "goes off" once in 10 years. But if he displays a bad temper often and under a variety of circumstances, it is a personality _____ because it is _____ of him and it involves how he relates to the social environment.   **characteristic** **trait, characteristic**

4. Magaly wears an unusual ring. Although her wearing of this ring may be characteristic and distinctive, it is not a personality _____ because it plays no significant part in how she _____ to her social environment.   **trait** **relates**

5. Magaly is also friendly and outgoing. This constitutes a personality trait because it does play a significant part how she relates to her _____ _____.   **social environment**

6. Although there are many theories of personality—defined as the total pattern of _____ behavior and thought, along with ways of relating to the environment—almost all of these theories assume that there is some kind of *core of personality* composed of tendencies and characteristics common to all of us.   **characteristic**

7. A theory that assumes human nature is basically good views goodness as the core of _____.   **personality**

8. Almost all personality theories assume that there is some kind of _____ of personality and also that development channels the core characteristics in different directions for different people.   **core**

development
core

development
peripheral

personality

psychoanalytic
personality

Freud
libido

conflict
anxiety

psychodynamic

unconscious mind
unconscious

posthypnotic

unconscious

id, pleasure
pain
eros, preservation
self-
destruction, aggression

pleasure

id

ego, reality

psychoanalytic

9. Personality theories have to do with the way the core tendencies are channeled by experience—in other words, with the _____ of personality.

10. Personality theories, in addition to being concerned with _____ characteristics and their development, are also concerned with the *peripheral traits* of personality, or the way we think, feel, and behave at any given moment.

11. The personality characteristics we display at any given moment, resulting from the way our core of personality has been modified by _____, are our _____ traits.

## Psychodynamic Views: Freud and Those Who Followed

12. Sigmund Freud was the first to develop a comprehensive theory of _____, which he called psychoanalytic theory. Those who followed in his tradition but differ in important ways are called *psychodynamic theorists.*

13. Freud, in his _____ theory, proposed that the tendencies or characteristics common to human nature, or the core of _____, are the result of conflict that derives from the energy of the *libido*—which is directed toward maximizing pleasure and minimizing pain.

14. Psychoanalytic theory, developed by _____, emphasizes how the energy of the _____ causes conflict and how anxiety is the central problem in mental and behavioral disorders.

15. Freud believed that the core of human personality is _____ and that the central problem in mental and behavioral disorders is _____.

16. Freud, whose psychoanalytic theory is one version of the more general approach called _____ theory, proposed the concept of the *unconscious mind*—which is where repressed motives, thoughts, and memories reside.

17. Marcus, who is not aware of his hostile motives but reveals them in ways that others can see, is displaying the influence of the _____ _____.

18. The existence of _____ motives is demonstrated when a person who has been given a posthypnotic suggestion during the course of a hypnotic trance acts upon the instruction without realizing why.

19. When a person acts on a _____ suggestion, the person is unaware of having received the instruction during the trance.

20. According to Freud, the primary component of the _____ mind is the *id.* The id consists of inborn biological impulses called eros, which are oriented toward obtaining pleasure and avoiding pain (that is, self-preservation), plus those called thanatos, which are oriented toward self-destruction and give rise to aggression.

21. Freud believed that the primary component of the unconscious and of personality, the _____, contains our instinctive impulses to obtain _____ and avoid _____ in accord with the *pleasure principle.* This set of impulses is called _____ and is oriented toward self-_____.

22. The other set of impulses, called thanatos, is oriented toward _____-_____. Turned outward, these impulses yield _____.

23. In acting to relieve the tension created by its quest for material and sexual gratification, the id acts on the _____ principle.

24. A second part of the human mind and personality proposed by Freud is the *ego.* The ego, unlike the _____, is largely conscious and is the person's contact with external reality; it acts in accord with the *reality principle* in its attempts to gratify the impulses of the id.

25. According to psychoanalytic theory, the conscious part of the mind and personality is the _____, which operates according to the _____ principle.

26. The third component of the mind and personality proposed by Freud in his _____ theory is the *superego*—a stern and powerful judge that threatens guilt even for thoughts of transgression. The superego consists of an ego ideal—

our sense of what is right—and a conscience—our sense of what is wrong—and it operates according to the *morality principle*.

27. In the case of sex, Freud said that the _____ produces an impulse to obtain a sexual object, the _____ attempts to satisfy the impulse in some way, and the _____ exerts its _____ principle in determining whether the ego's approach is acceptable.

28. Freud believed that during the first three and most important _____ of human *psychosexual development*, which he termed oral, anal, and phallic, libido focuses on different parts of the body—respectively, the mouth, then the anal region, and then the genitals.

29. The gratification that an infant gets from sucking and eating occurs during the _____ stage of development. During the _____ stage, a toddler derives gratification from activities involving elimination. During the latter part of early childhood, the _____ stage, gratification for both males and females involves the _____.

30. In Freud's phallic stage, children attempt to resolve the *Oedipus complex*, or mixed feelings of sexual attraction and resentment toward parents. Through a process called identification, which is driven by castration anxiety in boys and penis envy in girls, children adopt what they believe to be their parents' values and standards as the core of _____.

31. During the _____ stage, girls resolve their _____ _____ through identification with the mother, and boys resolve their _____ _____ through identification with the father.

32. Freud's psychoanalytic theory of _____ emphasizes conflict between our private _____ and the need to get along with others. It has had many critics—beginning with Carl Jung, who developed what he called *analytical psychology*.

33. Jung's _____ _____ included the view that Freud placed too much emphasis on sexuality and too little on the importance of culture and inherited tendencies, or the *collective unconscious*—which is composed of *archetypes*.

34. In emphasizing the cultural and metaphysical qualities of human personality, Jung proposed that humans possess an inheritance of experiences that have occurred throughout human history. This _____ _____ is composed of _____. Jung is also the originator of the terms introvert and extrovert. Introverts tend to prefer to live with their thoughts and avoid socializing; extroverts are highly interested in other people and in the social events around them.

35. Lavonia has lots of friends and spends much time with them; in Jung's terms, she is an _____. Harold is bookish and shy; in Jung's terms, he is an _____.

36. Another early disciple who rejected Freud's emphasis on _____ was Alfred Adler. Adler placed great emphasis on the tendency of people to be cooperative and psychologically tuned in to the lives of others—which he called social interest.

37. According to Adler's _____ _____, we must overcome innate feelings of inferiority and strive for superiority in the sense of having _____ interest, being contributing members of society, and being on the road to self-realization.

38. Those whose strivings for superiority are blocked or stifled may develop an _____ complex.

39. Another psychoanalyst who broke with Freudian theory was Karen Horney, who objected to Freud's emphasis on _____ and his view of women. Her *social psychoanalytic theory* focused on individuals who acquire a sense of *basic anxiety*—a feeling of being isolated and helpless in a potentially hostile world—as a result of childhood abuse or neglect.

40. According to Horney's _____ psychoanalytic theory, bad parenting practices such as _____ and _____ can create feelings of isolation and helplessness, or a sense of _____ _____, in the child and later the adult.

| |
|---|
| id |
| ego |
| superego, morality |
| stages |
| oral, anal |
| phallic |
| genitals |
| personality |
| phallic, penis envy |
| castration anxiety |
| personality |
| impulses |
| analytical psychology |
| collective unconscious |
| archetypes |
| extrovert, introvert |
| sexuality |
| individual psychology |
| social |
| inferiority |
| sexuality |
| social |
| abuse, neglect |
| basic anxiety |

Freud

penis envy
inferior

different

eight, psychosocial
development

psychodynamic

Jung, Adler, Horney
Erikson, Fromm

conflict

positive
humanistic

phenomenological

unconditional
positive
unconditional
positive regard

conditions, worth
humanistic

self-actualization

core

41. Horney also strongly rejected _____'s idea of penis envy, instead attributing any strivings on the part of women toward masculine pursuits to cultural views of women as inferior.

42. In Horney's view, if a woman intensely wants to hold a traditionally masculine, high-status job, it is not because of _____ _____; it is because women are viewed as _____ in some cultures and want to better their status.

43. Erik Erikson developed his own version of Freud's theory. In the end, it was quite _____ from Freud's theory because of Erikson's emphasis on social interactions and the person's interpretations along the way.

44. Each of the _____ stages in Erikson's theory of _____ _____ is characterized by a crisis or turning point, which—if resolved successfully—leads to increasing maturity, a richer personality, and a stronger ego.

45. Theorists who have added to and revised Freud's theorizing are called _____ theorists. With his view that conflicts between basic human needs and the demands of society are the cause of human problems, Erich Fromm continued the emphasis on cultural and social influences on personality.

46. One way or another, social and cultural influences on personality figured strongly in the views of Carl _____, Alfred _____, Karen _____, Erik _____, and Erich _____.

## Positive Growth: Humanistic Theories of Personality

47. In contrast to Freud, who believed that the core of personality is _____ over sexual and aggressive impulses, humanistic theories hold that human nature is basically good and that the core of personality is the desire to grow in positive ways—to perfect our skills and find peace and happiness.

48. Carl Rogers was among the prominent advocates of humanistic personality theory, which holds that the core of personality is the desire to grow in _____ ways.

49. As a leading proponent of _____ personality theory, Rogers stressed the importance of the self-image.

50. The _____ self, or self-image, includes the way we see ourselves, our abilities, and our relationships with other people. In particular, a healthy self-image results when we are valued and trusted for ourselves and accepted unconditionally as worthwhile human beings.

51. If those around us when we are growing up value and trust us and respect our opinions and behavior, we benefit from what Rogers termed _____ _____ regard.

52. Rogers observed that unfortunately most people do not receive _____ _____ _____. Instead, they grow up in a social environment in which they must meet certain conditions if they are to be regarded as worthwhile human beings; these are called _____ of _____.

53. According to _____ psychologists, the most powerful motivating force for human beings is making progress toward achieving and realizing benevolent and spiritual goals for the self.

54. Humanistic psychologist Abraham Maslow perceived an innate tendency of people to pursue beauty, goodness, and truth and to fulfill their own potential, which he called _____-_____.

## Further Perspectives on Personality

55. In contrast to the humanistic theories, which hold that the _____ of personality is to grow in positive ways, behavioral theories take no stand on whether human nature is basically good and positive or selfish and negative. They hold instead that personality is simply the habitual ways we have learned to respond to environmental events, through such mechanisms as operant conditioning.

56. B. F. Skinner took the view that the principles of _____ conditioning and a person's reinforcement history are more helpful than the concept of _____ in understanding and predicting what people do.

**operant**

**personality**

57. Skinner's view that _____ history provides a better way to look at things has been attacked on the grounds that it regards humans as too passive and also that it is not possible to know a person's entire _____ _____.

**reinforcement**

**reinforcement history**

58. Today, most learning theorists take a cognitive view of the manner in which experience creates habitual forms of _____. Although they acknowledge the importance of reinforcement and punishment in shaping personality, they also emphasize the roles of perceptions, beliefs, attitudes, and values in _____.

**behavior**

**personality**

59. Social _____ theorist Albert Bandura introduced the term *reciprocal interaction* as a means of emphasizing that not only does the environment affect us, but the opposite is true as well. Our style of reciprocal _____ helps to establish the nature of the social environment in which we interact.

**learning (or cognitive)**

**interaction**

60. Bandura's more recent theorizing has lead to the concept of human agency as an important and pervasive force in _____. Two key factors in agency are *self-efficacy*—what you can do—and *perceived self-efficacy*—what you think you can do.

**personality**

61. In Bandura's theory of _____ agency, discrepancies between actual _____-_____ and _____ self-efficacy are a major source of problems. If you are physically capable of picking up a snake but believe that you can't, there is a gap between your _____-_____ and your _____ _____-_____.

**human**

**self-efficacy, perceived**

**self-efficacy, perceived**

**self-efficacy**

62. The importance of beliefs about self-efficacy appears to be universal across cultures, although they manifest themselves differently in individualist _____ and collectivist ones. In the former, efficacy beliefs pertain more to _____ accomplishments; in the latter, more to the accomplishments of the _____.

**cultures**

**individual**

**group**

63. David Buss and other evolutionary psychologists propose that certain _____ characteristics have been favored by natural selection because they were more adaptive in our _____ history.

**personality**

**evolutionary**

64. For a personality characteristic to be a product of _____, it must be capable of being passed along to succeeding generations through genetics, it must be associated with the survival or reproduction of individuals or groups, and it must have solved a particular adaptive problem.

**evolution**

65. If it is true that women tend to prefer mates on the basis of their resources and men tend to prefer mates who appear to be fertile, this could be a result of _____ because in each case it solved an _____ problem for our ancestors: Women make a greater investment in their limited number of _____ and need to ensure that the children will survive long enough to _____, whereas men can conceive an extremely large number of _____ and achieve greater _____ success by winning _____ mates.

**evolution, adaptive**

**children**

**reproduce**

**children**

**reproductive, fertile**

66. Men appear to be more likely to become jealous over sexual infidelity by their partners; women appear to be more likely to become jealous over emotional infidelity. This could have evolved because a man risks not passing along his _____ if he raises a child who is not his because of his mate's _____ infidelity, whereas a woman risks not passing along her children's _____ if her mate's _____ infidelity causes him to leave and take his resources with him, endangering her children's survival.

**genes, sexual**

**genes**

**emotional**

## Personality Assessment—and Its Limits

67. Assessing _____ is oriented toward describing people in terms of how, rather than why, they differ with respect to stable traits. Most recent on the scene is Big Five theory, which specifies five factors thought to determine sta-

**personality**

traits

high
low, high
low, low


extraversion, introversion
emotional


personality
assessment
relatively stable


objective


profile
patterns, personality traits
objective

personality

profile
objective

normal
profile


personality
MMPI-2


projective


personality tests


personality
norms


stable

ble _____: (1) extraversion versus introversion, (2) emotional stability, (3) openness to experience, (4) agreeableness, and (5) conscientiousness.

68. A person who is outgoing and likes to be around people, is uncertain and unpredictable, likes new things, is often mean and thoughtless toward others, and tends to be careless and haphazard would score _____ on extroversion, _____ on emotional stability, _____ on openness to experience, _____ on agreeableness, and _____ on conscientiousness.

69. Psychologist Hans Eysenck proposed that many variations in human behavior can be explained by just the first two dimensions in Big Five theory. One is _____ versus _____; the other is _____ stability.

70. Because personality is such a complex matter, its measurement is difficult. An important assumption in assessing personality is that there are relatively stable traits that make up each individual's characteristic behavior and thought—that is, an individual's _____.

71. An important assumption in personality _____ is that personality is composed of _____ _____ traits. *Objective tests*, which constitute one category of personality tests, produce scores least likely to be affected by the views of the examiner.

72. One widely used _____ test is the Minnesota Multiphasic Personality Inventory-2, or MMPI-2, a clinically oriented test in which an individual's responses to statements are compared with the responses of large numbers of other people known to have certain patterns of personality traits.

73. On the widely used MMPI-2, an examinee's responses are sorted and tallied into separate scales, which in turn yield an overall profile that is used for interpreting the results. This _____ is then compared to the profiles of other people known to have certain _____ of _____ _____.

74. Another long-standing and widely used _____ test is Raymond Cattell's Sixteen Personality Factor Questionnaire (16PF), which is oriented toward describing the _____ of relatively normal people for guidance, vocational, and rehabilitation counseling. Like the MMPI-2, it produces an overall _____ of the examinee's personality.

75. A third, more recently developed _____ test is the NEO Personality Inventory–Revised (NEO-PI-R). Like the 16PF, it is oriented primarily toward describing relatively _____ people; like both the MMPI-2 and the 16PF, it produces an overall _____ of the examinee's personality.

76. On *projective tests*, examinees are thought to project their own emotional state and thought processes onto ambiguous stimuli. The responses are analyzed to reveal _____ characteristics along with mental and behavioral problems. Thus, projective tests are clinical tests, just as the _____ is.

77. The Thematic Apperception Test (TAT), in which a person is asked to make up stories about ambiguous pictures, invites the attribution to others of the person's own motives, emotional states, and thought processes; it is therefore in the category of _____ tests. Another well-known test in this category is the Rorschach Inkblot Test, in which people are asked to describe what they see in inkblots.

78. Nonstandardized _____ _____ include word-association tests, in which an examinee responds to a word with the first word that comes to mind; draw-a-person tests, in which an examinee does just that, and sentence-completion tests, in which an examinee completes leading sentence fragments. These tests can provide a clinician with clues about _____, but being nonstandardized, the tests lack the _____ that exist for objective personality tests.

79. An important question in considering traits and the tests designed to measure them is the extent to which personality characteristics remain relatively _____ across time and social situations.

Name _____  Section _____  Date _____

# Practice Test

____ **1.** To be considered part of a person's personality, a way of thinking or behaving must be
a. innate.
b. characteristic.
c. unchanging.
d. observable.

____ **2.** Personality theories that acknowledge a core of personality maintain that the core tendencies and traits are channeled in various directions by the process of
a. development.
b. differentiation.
c. maturation.
d. fixation.

____ **3.** Which of the following is a psychodynamic theory of personality?
a. Freud's psychoanalytic theory
b. Erikson's psychosocial theory
c. Jung's analytical psychology
d. all of the above

____ **4.** According to Freud, the main element of the unconscious is
a. the id.
b. the ego.
c. the superego.
d. none of the above

____ **5.** Which of the following best describes the dynamics of the human personality as seen by Freud?
a. The superego is caught between the id and the ego.
b. The id is caught between the superego and the ego.
c. The ego is caught between the id and the superego.
d. not necessarily any of the above

____ **6.** In Freud's theory, the superego consists of
a. the conscience.
b. the ego ideal.
c. both of the above
d. none of the above

____ **7.** In Freud's theory, the ego operates according to
a. the pleasure principle.
b. the reality principle.
c. the morality principle.
d. all of the above

____ **8.** Freud's Oedipus complex is said to occur during
a. the oral stage.
b. the anal stage.
c. the phallic stage.
d. the genital stage.

____ **9.** Striving for superiority is a key element in
a. Freud's psychoanalytic theory.
b. Adler's individual psychology.
c. Erikson's psychosocial theory.
d. Jung's analytical psychology.

____ **10.** The existence of a collective human unconscious is a key element in
a. Freud's psychoanalytic theory.
b. Adler's individual psychology.
c. Erikson's psychosocial theory.
d. Jung's analytical psychology.

____ **11.** Horney agreed with Freud that
a. women are inferior.
b. women are often afflicted by penis envy.
c. human personality is basically selfish and negative.
d. none of the above

____ **12.** Unconditional positive regard is central to
a. Fromm's social psychoanalytic theory.
b. Rogers's humanistic theory.
c. Maslow's humanistic theory.
d. Freud's psychoanalytic theory.

____ **13.** In Skinner's operant conditioning view, people are best understood in terms of
a. reinforcement history.
b. unconscious processes.
c. reactions to basic anxiety.
d. accumulated habits.

____ **14.** In Bandura's theory of human agency, the most central and pervasive aspect of personality is
a. self-efficacy.
b. resolution of crises.
c. perceived self-efficacy.
d. not necessarily any of the above

____ **15.** According to evolutionary psychologists,
a. men are attracted to women primarily on the basis of fertility, women to men primarily on the basis of resources.
b. women are attracted to men primarily on the basis of fertility, men to women primarily on the basis of resources.
c. both men and women are attracted to potential mates primarily on the basis of fertility.
d. both men and women are attracted to potential mates primarily on the basis of resources.

____16. In which of the following are adaptations thought to be determinants of personality?
a. Bandura's theory of human agency
b. Maslow's theory of self-actualization
c. Buss's evolutionary theory
d. all of the above

____17. In general, personality assessment is primarily oriented toward
a. determining what causes personality traits.
b. determining how many personality traits there are.
c. describing personality traits.
d. diagnosing mental and behavioral disorders.

____18. Which of the following is an objective personality test?
a. the MMPI-2
b. the 16PF
c. the NEO-PI-R
d. all of the above

____19. Which of the following produces a personality profile and has norms?
a. the MMPI-2
b. the 16PF
c. the NEO-PI-R
d. all of the above

____20. Which of the following uses ambiguous stimuli?
a. the TAT
b. the Rorschach
c. both of the above
d. none of the above

## Exercises

1. Reliability—consistency in results from one test occasion to the next—is essential to standardized psychological assessment, as discussed in Chapter 7. Reliability is normally assessed through correlation of item responses and scores, but in this exercise you are asked to take an informal approach and assess reliability simply by looking at the correspondence between different raters on personality items. This type of reliability is called inter-rater reliability.

   ### Method

   Identify three people (including yourself, if you like) who watch the same television series regularly and believe themselves to be very familiar with one of its characters. Have each rater study Table 9.4 on page 352 and rate this character on each of the 20 subdimensions of the Big Five. Explain that the raters are to use a scale of 1 to 5, where 1 represents the extreme at the far left and 5 represents the extreme at the far right. Each rater should use a separate sheet of paper, and none of the ratings should be seen by others or discussed until they're complete.

   ### Results

   For each subdimension, make a combined master list of all three scores.

   ### Analysis

   Review the master list for subdimensions where scores are very similar and for those where scores are very dissimilar. Also, note whether score similarity seems to be stronger within some of the five main dimensions than within others.

   On the basis of your observations, answer each of the following:

   a. What might account for the subdimensions with low inter-rater reliability?

   b. What might account for the subdimensions with high inter-rater reliability?

   c. Given the informal nature of your study, what can you conclude about Big Five theory?

2. We all have things about ourselves that we readily share with others and things that we'd rather other people not know, and we all present an image to others that may not be exactly who we are.

   Write either a detailed paragraph or a set of lists about your own personality. This self-analysis should include about three statements for *each* of the following:

   - What I'm like
   - What I like to do
   - What I don't like to do
   - What bothers me a lot
   - What experiences—good or bad—I remember most clearly
   - How I am different when alone versus with others
   - Where I'm going in life

   Now, go over your statements and circle those that describe things that your friends or relatives probably are *not* aware of. Leave uncircled those items that describe attributes you believe are clearly evident to your friends or relatives.

   How do you believe that your friends or relatives would view you if they somehow became aware of the "secret" items you circled? Might their view of you be different if you revealed these items rather than just those that are "socially acceptable"?

   On the basis of the above, explain how a psychotherapist's understanding of a client might be enhanced by using a well-constructed personality test instead of relying entirely on the therapist's observations and the self-reports of the client. Why?

*For quizzing, activities, exercises, and web links, check out the book-specific website at http://www.psychology.wadsworth.com/kagan9e.*

# 10

# Human Development: Conception Through Childhood

## Chapter Outline

Maria Taglient/Index Stock Imagery

ook into a hospital nursery filled with newborn babies. It may be difficult to distinguish one baby from another. But within a few weeks, many differences among these infants will begin to emerge: One may be cranky and hard to soothe, another calm and easy-going. One prefers lots of excitement and stimulation; another requires quiet and tranquility. With each passing month, more and more clues to each child's personality will appear. The forces shaping these young individuals are both biological and environmental in nature.

As a result of biological forces, children normally begin to speak before they are 2 years old, feel guilt by their fourth birthday, and reason logically by the time they reach adolescence. These forces also contribute to marked personality differences among children—for example, whether the child is shy or gregarious, high-strung or placid. At the same time, profound environmental influences arise from both within and outside the family. In the early years, family experiences predominate. Daily interactions with parents and siblings help determine the child's motives, values, sources of anxiety, and ways of coping with conflict. Once children venture outside the home, environmental experiences outside the family—with peers, teachers, even television and movies—begin to exert their powerful influence.

As the child grows, biological and environmental forces become so closely intertwined that it is virtually impossible to distinguish between their effects. Indeed, one of the three central themes of psychology first raised in Chapter 1—the interaction of heredity and environment—is nowhere better illustrated than in the development of the child, as we will see throughout this chapter.

# LIFE'S BEGINNINGS: FROM CONCEPTION TO BIRTH

The overture to human development, played out in the mother's womb, is brief but awesome. In only 9 months, a single microscopic cell transforms itself into a fully formed human infant. Psychologists recognize that the future of each of us is shaped to a large degree during this period. The study of children's physical, mental, and emotional development is known as *developmental psychology*.

To begin with, the impact of heredity is felt at the moment of union between the mother's egg cell and the father's sperm cell. Then, from the instant of conception, the environment begins to leave its mark. When babies give up their home in the womb, they have already undergone experiences that can influence how the characteristics they inherit will actually unfold in the outside world.

**FOCUS QUESTIONS**

- What is developmental psychology?

- What potential influences do diet, alcohol, drugs, and stress during pregnancy have on the infant and child?

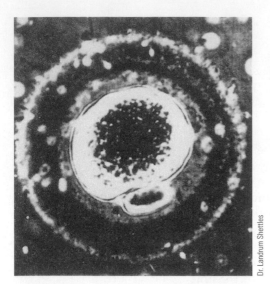

Dr. Landrum Shettles

**FIGURE 10.1 The moment of conception.**
The large round object is a human egg cell. In this photo, it is being fertilized by a male sperm cell that has worked its way deep inside and can no longer be seen. Other sperm cells, with small heads and long tails, are also attempting to pierce the egg but have arrived too late.

**Chromosomes**
The 23 pairs of tiny structures, found in all human cells, that make up the mechanisms of heredity.

**X chromosome**
One of the two chromosomes that determine the sex of an offspring; an X-X pairing produces a female.

**Y chromosome**
One of the two chromosomes that determine the sex of an offspring; an X-Y pairing produces a male.

**Genes**
The smaller structures of a chromosome, composed of molecules of DNA, that are responsible for inherited individual differences.

# The Mechanics of Heredity

The development of each individual begins when the egg cell produced by the mother is penetrated and fertilized by the sperm cell of the father, as shown in Figure 10.1. This fertilized egg contains the key to life. Something inside it directs the entire process of development, from single cell to baby to fully mature adult. Something in the cell helps determine the inherited characteristics of the individual to be born—the color of the eyes and hair, facial features, height, and other physical characteristics, as well as psychological characteristics such as potential intelligence and patterns of behavior.

That "something" is the set of **chromosomes** within the cell. Figure 10.2 shows how chromosomes appear when seen under a powerful microscope just prior to cell division. The original fertilized cell contains 46 chromosomes, arranged in 23 pairs with one member of each pair from each parent. When the cell splits, the chromosomes also divide and replicate themselves. Thus, most cells in the human body contain exactly the same 46 chromosomes that were present in the fertilized egg. The only exceptions are the cells involved in reproduction—the female egg and the male sperm. In these cells, the chromosome pairs split apart and remain divided, forming new cells with only half the normal complement of chromosomes. Fertilization of an egg by a sperm rejoins the chromosomes into the normal complement of 46.

One of the pairs in the fertilized egg cell determines whether the fertilized egg will be a girl or a boy. If you look back at Figure 9.2, you will note that two chromosomes are pointed out by arrows. The larger one is called an **X chromosome,** and the smaller one a **Y chromosome.** The chromosomes in Figure 10.2 are from a cell taken from a male. The X-Y pairing normally produces a male; an X-X pairing normally produces a female.

This is how sex is determined: When the mother's X-X cells split, the resulting cells contain an X chromosome. When the father's X-Y cells split, the result is a mix of cells with X or Y chromosomes. If a sperm cell with the X chromosome fertilizes the egg, the result is an X-X pairing and a girl. If a sperm cell with the Y chromosome fertilizes the egg, the result is an X-Y pairing and a boy. The sex of the baby depends on which sperm, an X or a Y, penetrates the egg.

Each chromosome, though tiny in itself, is composed of hundreds to perhaps thousands of much smaller structures called **genes,** each of which is a molecule of a complex chemical called DNA (deoxyribonucleic acid). Estimates of the number of genes in each normal cell range from 30,000 to 120,000, with a best guess at between 65,000 and 80,000 (Strachan & Read, 1999). Each is responsible—sometimes by itself, but more often in combination with other genes—either for some aspect of everyday functioning or for some phase of development.

Genes give the cell coded instructions that cause it to perform a specific function, such as manufacturing a particular protein. During the process of development, the cell turns on some genes and turns off others. Thus, if the cell turns on "muscle genes," it will produce substances that cause it to develop into a muscle cell rather than another type of cell such as a neuron.

The entire collection of genes in a human being is known as the human *genome,* and it is universal across all human groups. However, the specific combination of genes in any given individual is unique. Like chromosomes, genes occur in pairs, one coming from the sperm and the other from the ovum. As a result, a child receives only half of its genes from each parent. Because there are so many genes in human cells, the chance that two human beings will inherit the exact same set of genes is infinitesimal. The only exception is identical twins, who develop from the same fertilized egg and therefore have virtually the exact same set of genes.

## The World Inside the Womb

The environment, like heredity, begins to exert its influence at the very start of life's journey. Over the approximately 280 days of prenatal development, the tiny speck of matter that will one day become a child undergoes a remarkable series of changes. During the first 8 weeks—between the instant of fertilization and the moment at which a recognizable embryonic human being is formed—the infant-to-be increases nearly 2,000,000% in size. Alterations in the size, shape, and type of body cells take place with remarkable speed. The number of body cells (not counting neurons) increases from 1 to many billions as body structures increase in size and complexity.

All the while, the central nervous system (CNS) is taking root. During each minute in the womb, the brain gains tens of thousands of new cells. As early as 7 weeks after conception, some sections of the developing brain can already be discerned, and the nerves that feed electrical impulses from the brain to various parts of the body are in place and beginning to work. The budding arms of the fetus will now move in response to tapping on the sac that protects it. By the time the fetus is 20 weeks old, the nervous system is mature enough to make the developing baby sensitive to touch, pain, and changes in temperature. Surprisingly, the brain waves of a fetus look much the same at 30 weeks as they do after birth. The brain is clearly "turned on" long before normal delivery.

The findings from studies of prenatal life show that, starting at the very instant of conception, the development of a child can be affected dramatically by the quality of the environment in the womb. The implications of these findings are discussed in Psychology in the Lab and in Life on page 374.

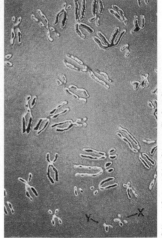

**FIGURE 10.2** Human chromosomes, enlarged 750 times. These human chromosomes are from a man's skin cell, broken down and spread out into a single layer under the microscope. The labels point out the X and Y chromosomes, which determine sex.

## The Birth Process

The vast majority of babies are born healthy and normal. Nevertheless, certain events surrounding the birth process can affect the child's later development.

The ease or difficulty with which a baby is born and how quickly it begins to breathe can affect its immediate well-being, as well as its long-range development. From the time the first contractions of labor begin and the baby's head starts to squeeze its way into the world, the tiny brain is vulnerable. If there is very strong pressure on the head, the blood vessels in the brain may rupture, leading to **anoxia,** or a loss of oxygen supply to the nerve cells. If the baby fails to begin to breathe soon after being separated from the mother, the resulting anoxia may affect the brain's metabolism and result in motor paralysis, often called *cerebral palsy* (Rosen, 1985).

Even when complications in the birth process occur, however, most babies do not suffer long-term damage. A lot can depend on what happens later. A group of Hawaiian children who underwent stresses at birth were studied over a period of 18 years. Their early impairments were linked to later problems in physical and psychological development only when combined with persistently poor environmental circumstances such as chronic poverty, family instability, or maternal

**Anoxia**
Loss of the oxygen supply to nerve cells, which may negatively affect the brain's metabolism and lead to motor paralysis.

## At Risk in the Womb

Many factors can affect the future well-being of children while they are still taking shape in their mother's womb. If the mother's diet during pregnancy lacks proper nutritional value and vitamins, the baby may have difficulty attaining the IQ level that its genes might otherwise have made possible. Mothers who eat contaminated foods may give birth to children who are less responsive and more easily upset than other children (Jacobson et al., 1984). Mothers who experience prolonged anxiety or anger during pregnancy may have babies who are smaller than average, overactive, or inclined to digestive problems—as if they, too, had been subjected to damaging stress.

Mothers who smoke may pollute the unborn baby's blood supply with carbon monoxide and thus deprive the baby of oxygen and nutrients essential for healthy development. Smoking during pregnancy has been associated with a number of adverse effects on the growth, cognitive development, and behavior of the child (Cornelius & Day, 2000). Marijuana use during pregnancy can have negative effects on attentional behavior and problem-solving ability in children age 3 and older (Fried & Smith, 2001).

Infants born to alcohol-abusing mothers are likely to suffer from fetal alcohol syndrome, which causes serious mental and physical handicaps (National Institute on Alcohol Abuse and Alcoholism, 2000). Even limited alcohol consumption by a pregnant woman may damage her baby's central nervous system. A group of 4-year-olds whose mothers drank moderately during pregnancy still revealed impaired abilities on tests of motor skills such as grasping and manipulating objects or pouring water into a glass (Barr, Streissguth, Darby, & Sampson, 1990). Recent research has shown that alcohol exposure during development may affect social as well as cognitive abilities; for example, infants exposed to alcohol before birth show deficits in attachment behavior (Kelly, Day, & Streissguth, 2000).

Use of illicit drugs, especially crack cocaine, is also harmful to the developing fetus. Children whose mothers smoked crack during pregnancy may have difficulty concentrating, interacting with others, and playing by themselves. The most common effects are an increased risk of premature birth, decreased birth weight, and smaller head circumference (Hawley & Disney, 1992).

Despite these grim facts, the great majority of babies are born healthy—even those of mothers who have smoked moderately, eaten a less-than-perfect diet, received medication, or experienced emotional upsets during pregnancy. Moreover, newborns have a surprising capacity to recover from all but the most severe prenatal stress. The effects of many, but not all, early complications can eventually be reversed if the baby's later experiences are good ones (Werner & Smith, 1982). Nevertheless, expectant parents need to take every reasonable precaution they can to make sure that their babies get off to the best possible start. If they smoke or drink, this clearly is a good time to quit.

### Test Yourself

(a) How many chromosomes are present in a fertilized cell?

(b) Infants born to mothers who have abused alcohol during pregnancy may suffer from what disorder?

(The answers are on page 404.)

health problems. Children who were raised in more affluent homes, with an intact family and a well-educated mother, showed few, if any, negative effects of the stresses endured at birth—unless, of course, there was severe damage to the CNS (Werner & Smith, 1982).

Prematurity may also affect the course of the baby's development. The more premature and underweight a newborn is, the greater the likelihood of physical and mental impairment. Premature babies weighing less than 3.3 pounds have significantly more health problems at school age than their normal-weight peers (McCormick et al., 1992). But once again, the eventual outcome is likely to be influenced by later environment. Early intervention programs have shown great promise in helping premature babies overcome potential disabilities. The simple power of touch in the first weeks after birth can dramatically help premature infants. For example, it has been found that those who are gently massaged three times a day show significantly more weight gain, more rapidly maturing nervous systems, higher rates of activity, and greater responsiveness than those who are left untouched in incubators (Field, 1989).

# NEWBORN INFANTS: SIMILARITIES AND DIFFERENCES

Newborns are miraculous creations. If born healthy, they are remarkably competent—most of their senses are working well, and their reflexes will help them adjust to the world. From the moment the first breath is drawn, all normal babies are sensitive to stimuli in their environment. Babies only a few hours old can follow a moving object with their eyes. After only a week, newborns can differentiate the smell of their own mother from that of another woman (Makin & Porter, 1989).

> **FOCUS QUESTIONS**
>
> • What are the infant's most important survival reflexes?
>
> • What is meant by temperament?

A newborn inherits a marked preference for the human voice and certain features of the human face. One of the reasons babies gaze so intently into their mother's or father's eyes is that all babies focus on dark contour lines, such as the dark pupils of a parent's eyes (Haith, 1980). When 3-day-old infants were compared to 3-day-old chimpanzees, the humans and the chimps showed the same reactions to a variety of stimuli. An exception was the face and voice, which human babies greeted with greater attention (Hallock, Worobey, & Self, 1989).

Babies respond to stimuli with a wide range of inborn reflexive behaviors that allow them to escape pain, avoid harsh stimuli, and obtain food. These reflexes can be classified as *survival reflexes* and *primitive reflexes*. Survival reflexes, as the term implies, are necessary if the infant is to survive in the first few weeks of life. Breathing is a survival reflex. So is the **rooting reflex** (turning the head toward the mother's nipple), illustrated in Figure 10.3. Primitive reflexes, in contrast, do not appear necessary for survival but may have been important at some point in the past. For example, the Moro, or startle, reflex might have had survival value: If an infant was dropped, this reflex would cause it to grasp its mother's body hair and hold on. Some of the infant's reflexes are permanent; others either come under voluntary control or simply disappear within a few months. The major reflexes of the newborn are listed in Table 10.1.

**Rooting reflex**
An inborn reflex in which a newborn turns toward the stimulus when touched near the mouth.

**FIGURE 10.3** The newborn's rooting response. When the side of an infant's mouth is touched (A), the reflex response is to turn the head toward the stimulus (B) and then try to suck the finger (C), as if it were a source of food.

## Differences in Temperament

The concept of inherited psychological factors pertaining to personality is synonymous with the idea of human *temperament* (Kagan, 2001, 2002). This idea has

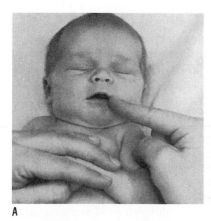

A

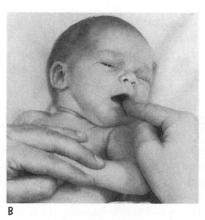

B

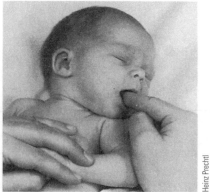

C

Heinz Prechtl

At birth, the baby exhibits a variety of reflexes, some of which are essential for survival.

**TABLE 10.1**
## The Reflexes of Healthy Newborns

| | |
|---|---|
| **Survival Reflexes** | Breathing: Infants inhale to obtain oxygen and exhale to eliminate carbon dioxide. These reflexive actions continue throughout life. |
| | Eye-blink: Infants blink if an object moves quickly toward their eyes. This is a permanent reflex. |
| | Rooting: When touched on the cheek, an infant turns its head in that direction and opens its mouth. This reflex disappears after 3 or 4 months. |
| | Sucking: When touched on the mouth, infants respond by sucking. This response begins as a reflex but gradually becomes voluntary. |
| **Primitive Reflexes** | Moro (startle): When startled by a loud sound or by being dropped, infants spread their arms and stretch out their fingers, then bring their arms back to the body and clench their fingers. This reflex disappears after about 4 months. |
| | Palmar: When its palm is touched, an infant grasps tightly. This reflex disappears after about 5 months. |
| | Plantar: When an object is placed on the sole of its foot, an infant responds by trying to flex the foot. This reflex disappears after about 9 months. |
| | Stepping: When held upright with their feet against a flat surface and moved forward, infants appear to walk. This reflex disappears after 2 or 3 months. |
| | Swimming: When placed in water in a prone position, infants attempt to swim. This reflex disappears after about 6 months. |

been around since the days of the ancient Greeks, as discussed in Chapter 9, but it fell into disfavor during the first part of the 20th century because of the strict behaviorists' pronounced emphasis on overt behavior and environmental factors (see Chapter 1). A return to serious consideration of temperament was marked by now-classic research by Alexander Thomas and Stella Chess, beginning in the late 1950s (see Thomas & Chess, 1977).

Although all normal babies are aware of their environment and can react to the stimuli it presents, they differ in degree of sensitivity and style of response. They differ also in level of activity, mood, adaptability, and other ways that parents are quick to recognize and describe as their baby's "nature." These characteristic styles of behavior, called **temperament,** are displayed so early that they almost surely represent hereditary differences in the physiology of the brain.

Studies have shown wide individual differences in sensory threshold. With some babies, even the most gentle stroking of the skin produces a muscular reflex. Other babies do not respond unless the stroking is fairly firm. There are also differences in how rapidly babies adapt to sensations. Some babies appear to become bored with a stimulus more quickly than others. If a series of pictures of the human face is projected on a screen above their crib, some infants pay close attention for a long time. Others soon stop looking, as if they had rapidly tired of the repetitive stimulus. Similarly, some babies are more attentive and alert than others.

**Temperament**
The characteristic styles of behavior displayed by young babies, which probably represent hereditary differences in the physiology of the brain.

Two fundamental temperamental qualities in which infants differ are the ease with which they become aroused by stimulation and the ways in which they regulate, or try to cope with, their arousal. The signs of arousal are motor activity, babbling, and crying. Methods of regulation include turning away from the stimulus, retreating, becoming extremely distressed, and approaching an exciting stimulus.

Another important difference among infants is their degree of irritability. Some babies begin to fret, whine, or cry at the slightest provocation. Others do not fret unless their discomfort or pain is intense or lasts a long time. Even then, they may fret only for a half minute or so and then stop, as if they possessed some mechanism that inhibits the buildup of extreme upset.

Infants between 3 and 5 months of age differ greatly in the degree of both motor arousal and irritability they display when exposed to a stimulus such as a moving mobile. Some babies remain very relaxed, showing little movement in their arms and legs. About 20% become very aroused: Their tongues protrude from their mouths, their arms and legs pump vigorously, and they often begin to cry. Infants who become highly aroused and irritable are more likely to be fearful and emotionally restrained when they are 2 years old. The approximately 40% of infants who remain calm, often smiling at the same stimulus, tend to become outgoing and sociable children with little fear of unfamiliar events (Kagan, 1994).

The tendency toward irritability seems to be a fairly stable trait. Compared to nonirritable newborns, children who were irritable as infants were rated as more upset, less attentive, and less responsive to adults when they were 2 years old (Reite, 1987).

## Easy, Slow-to-Warm-up, and Difficult Babies

One group of investigators (Chess & Thomas, 1999; Thomas, Chess, & Birch, 1970), after studying more than 100 children from birth through elementary school, came to the conclusion that most newborns in the United States fall into three distinct temperamental groups:

1. *Easy children*, who make up about 40% of healthy babies, are generally cheerful. Their reactions to stimuli are low to moderate in intensity. They establish regular habits of eating and sleeping and are quick to adapt to new schedules, foods, and people.

2. *Slow-to-warm-up children*, who make up about 15%, are less cheerful; indeed, their mood seems slightly sad and tense. Their responses are low in intensity. Their eating and sleeping habits vary, and they tend to withdraw initially from new experiences, such as unfamiliar people or unfamiliar toys. They take time to adjust to change.

3. *Difficult children*, who make up about 10% of infants, become very irritable and cry at unfamiliar events—for example, when given a bath. Because of this, they are difficult to soothe, and their parents find them hard to please. They show little regularity in eating and sleeping and are easily upset by new experiences.

The remaining 35% of children have mixed reactions and are not easily categorized in terms of temperament.

A striking example of the difference between an easy and a difficult baby is shown in Figure 10.4. The photographs, which were taken several years apart, are of an older sister and a younger brother—an indication that early differences in temperament do not necessarily reflect the parents' personalities or childrearing methods.

The three types of temperament require different treatment during infancy and in the early years of school. Easy children thrive in most family situations in

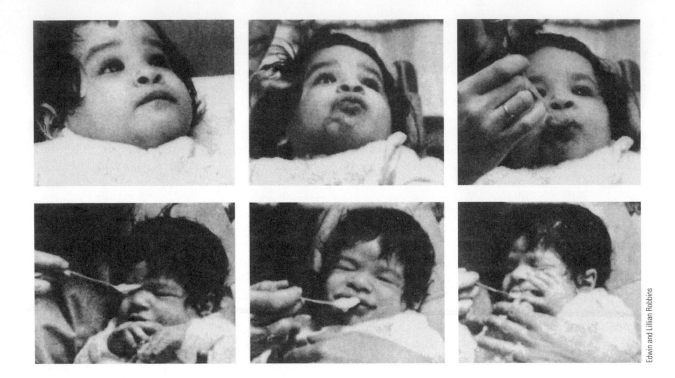

Edwin and Lillian Robbins

**FIGURE 10.4 A contrast in infant temperament. Both these babies are 3 months old and are being offered a new kind of cereal for the first time. The girl at the top, an easy baby, eagerly accepts the new experience. The boy at the bottom, a difficult baby, fights it.**

early childhood. Slow-to-warm-up children require considerable patience. They do their best when encouraged to try new experiences but allowed to adapt at their own pace. Too much pressure heightens their natural inclination to withdraw.

Difficult children present a special problem. Because of their irregular habits, resistance to adjustment, and negative attitude, they are hard to live with—a trial to their parents and later to their teachers (Guerin, Gottfried, & Thomas, 1997). There is evidence that mothers of difficult and irritable 1-year-old boys tend to back off from their natural attempts to teach and train (Maccoby, Snow, & Jacklin, 1984). Attempts to force such babies to behave like other children may only make them more difficult. Their parents must exercise exceptional understanding and tolerance to bring them around—slowly and gradually—to getting along with other individuals.

Knowledge about inborn differences in temperament, together with information about variations in sensitivity, activity, and irritability, is of potential value to parents, day-care-center staff, and teachers, especially in the early grades. The findings contradict the popular assumption that all young children are more or less alike. Infants require individual treatment if they are to develop to their maximum capability.

## The Durability of Early Traits

Two relatively enduring temperamental traits are the excessive cautiousness of a timid child and the sociable nature of an outgoing child. Timid children comprise about 20% of healthy infants. They are easily aroused as young infants and usually become irritable when stimulated at 3 or 4 months of age. Two-thirds of these "highly reactive" infants become timid, shy, and inhibited in their second, third, and fourth years. On the other hand, about 40% of 4-month-old infants are very relaxed when stimulated and rarely cry. Almost three-quarters of these children are sociable, outgoing, easy children during their preschool years (Kagan, 1997).

These traits appear to be a result of inherited physiological tendencies involving the neurochemistry and physiology of the brain. One research team that followed these two types of children through age 13 found that about one-third of the very shy, fearful, inhibited 2-year-olds were still dour, serious, and moderately tense as adolescents, while half of the formerly outgoing, sociable, uninhibited 2-year-olds were still exuberant, minimally fearful, and unusually extraverted in their relationships with others (Kagan, 1994).

The evidence of change in temperament should offer comfort to parents who are worried or pessimistic if a child is difficult, shy, irritable, overactive, or seemingly unable to pay attention. The research findings suggest not pessimism but optimism about children and their potentialities. Babies who are difficult—boisterous, stubborn, and headstrong—often quiet down as they grow older. Babies who seem restless and inattentive in the cradle often learn to concentrate and become star pupils in school. Even babies who seem anxious may turn out to be perfectly normal. If parents can bear in mind that babies show a wide range of individual differences, need individual treatment, and thrive on warmth and love—and if they can tolerate behavior that at the moment may hardly be ideal—their patience will usually be rewarded.

The environment always plays an important role in determining whether an inherited temperamental tendency develops into a permanent personality trait. If a highly reactive infant is raised with parents who do not overprotect their child and who impose reasonable demands for obedience and socialization, at age 2 and 3 the child will be less fearful than a highly reactive infant who is raised with an overprotective, anxious parent who is reluctant to impose any stress on the child.

> ### Test Yourself
>
> **(c)** What do we call characteristic styles of behavior, such as level of activity, mood, and adaptability?
>
> **(d)** In terms of temperamental type, how would you classify an infant who is slightly sad and tense and who tends to withdraw from new experiences?
>
> (The answers are on page 404.)

# THE EARLY DEVELOPMENT OF BODY AND MIND

Most new parents are quick to recognize their infant's outward physical growth. The baby's birth weight doubles in the first 3 months and triples in 1 year. By the end of the first year, the baby's height typically has increased by almost 50%. But there are internal changes as well. The fibers of the nervous system grow and form myriad additional connections to other fibers, and they become faster and more efficient messengers of information to and from the brain. The brain itself grows in size and weight. In fact, it grows more rapidly during the first 3 months than at any other time.

> ### FOCUS QUESTIONS
>
> • What role does maturation play in physical, perceptual, and intellectual development?
>
> • What are the stages of cognitive development identified by Piaget?

The results of all this are some of nature's most spectacular events: the growth of the newborn baby into an eager toddler (sometime after the first birthday); the child's early experiments with language (starting near the end of the second year); and later, the child's mastery of the mysteries of reading and writing. How many and varied are the accomplishments of those early years. How many new worlds are faced and conquered.

Part of this rapid early development is the result of **maturation**—the physical changes taking place after birth that continue the biological growth of the organism from fertilized egg to adult. Almost day by day, simply as a result of growing older, babies become capable of new feats of physical, perceptual, and mental skill—although practice is always necessary as well.

**Maturation**
The physical changes taking place after birth that continue the biological growth of the organism.

## Physical Maturation

Even before birth, babies begin to use their muscles. Their movements can usually be felt in the womb beginning in the 20th week of pregnancy. Newborn babies have all the muscle fibers they will ever possess, but the fibers still have a lot of growing to do. Eventually, at full maturity, the muscles will weigh about 40 times as much as they weighed at birth. As shown in Figure 10.5, the muscles of posture, creeping, and standing must mature before the baby can walk alone, which occurs at about 15 months. (There are, however, considerable variations both across individual children and across cultures, the latter as a result of differences in child-rearing practices and children's opportunities to practice skills leading up to walking.) Similarly, as they mature, the muscles of the hands and arms produce increased skill at reaching and grasping.

At birth, the skeleton is composed largely of cartilage, which is softer and more pliable than bone but gradually hardens. The fibers of the nervous system grow and form additional synaptic connections to other fibers, and some of them develop protective myelin sheaths that make them faster and more efficient conductors of nervous impulses. The brain, in particular, grows in size and weight—very rapidly during the first 2 years, then more slowly until growth is complete. At the same time, however, unused neural pathways are "pruned" during the early years of life as an individual child's brain becomes specialized (e.g., see Webb, Monk, & Nelson, 2001).

Much of the baby's remarkable progress in the early months of life reflects maturation of the body and the nervous system. Thus, regardless of childrearing practices, children all over the world tend to display some behaviors at about the same age. They begin to smile at the sight of a human face at about 4 months, show vocal excitement in response to a new voice at 6 to 7 months, and search for a hidden object that they saw being covered by a piece of cloth at 8 to 12 months. They begin to utter some of the basic sounds of language in the first few days of life, but they can't really use speech until around 18 months—although "first words" may appear at age 12 months or even earlier. Evidence suggests that their brains may be mature enough earlier but that their vocal systems are not yet ready (Bonvillian, Orlansky, & Novack, 1983).

**FIGURE 10.5 How the muscles of movement mature. The process of maturation accounts for the increasing ability of babies to move around. Shown here is the progress from birth to walking alone.**

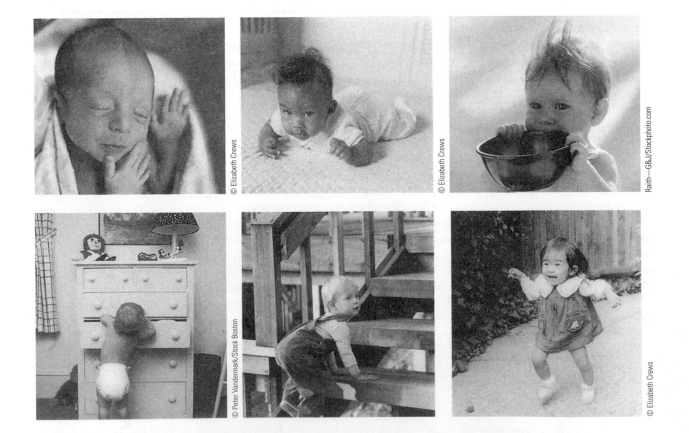

# The Unfolding of Intellectual Abilities

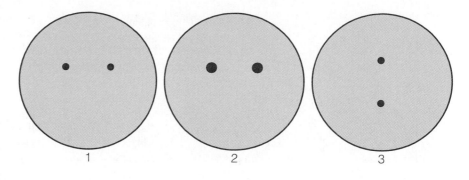

During the opening years of life, children reveal a dazzling succession of intellectual capacities, each more advanced than the one before. When they are only a few hours old, babies can distinguish between two designs as subtly different as those shown in Figure 10.6. Although we take such skills for granted in adults, they are remarkable in infants who have only just begun to function in the world. Equally remarkable is the rapid and steady pace at which a given skill develops. The ability to recognize a familiar stimulus, for example, gets better with the passage of time. One-month-old infants who have learned to recognize a frequently repeated word lose that ability if a day passes without their hearing that word spoken. Only 3 months later, however, they can recognize a familiar word after interruptions of as long as a week or two. The ability to recall past events also becomes more solidly entrenched over the space of only a few months, as shown in Figure 10.7. Such changes appear to be correlated with the maturation of the frontal lobe of the brain, as indicated in Figure 10.8.

As early as 3 to 4 months of age, young infants quickly learn to anticipate an event that will happen in the future. In one study, a baby was observed while it lay on its back looking at pictures, which were placed alternately on the infant's right and left sides. Within a short time, the infant learned to look to the alternate side before the picture appeared, in anticipation of seeing a new scene (Kagan, 1994). Researchers have also found that when infants are presented with a possible event (e.g., a small box supported by a platform) and an impossible event (a box with no support), they show a preference for the possible event, indicating that they have gained some understanding of physical relationships (Baillargeon, 1994).

Do these early cognitive skills predict later intelligence? A review of the literature on early intelligence indicates that the encoding, storage, retrieval, discrimination, and recognition skills measured by the tests just described may be related to the vocabulary, abstract reasoning, and memory skills measured by childhood intelligence tests (McCall & Carriger, 1993).

Many factors contribute to intellectual development. One is improvement in the process of perception. As children grow older, they begin to know what to search for in their environment and how to go about searching for it. They develop strategies for seeking important information and ignoring irrelevant information. Their attention becomes more selective, and they are able to maintain it over a longer time span. Their scanning of the environment becomes more systematic and orderly. Progress in perceptual efficiency has been charted by recording children's

**FIGURE 10.6 The visual skills of newborns. Infants are capable of detecting differences between the pattern shown in circle 1 and variations of that pattern, such as those shown in circles 2 and 3.**
*Adapted from Linn, Reznick, Kagan, & Hans, 1982.*

Figure 10.7 The baby's progress in short-term memory. The bars show the percentages of 10- and 12-month-old babies who could recall, after brief delays, where a toy was hidden. The babies watched a toy being placed under one of the cloths, and a screen was then lowered to block their view for 1 second or 7 seconds. The task of finding the toy gets harder, of course, as the delay gets longer. But no matter how long the delay, note how sharply the ability to find the toy improved with the passage of only 2 months.
*Kagan, Kearsley, & Zelazo, 1978.*

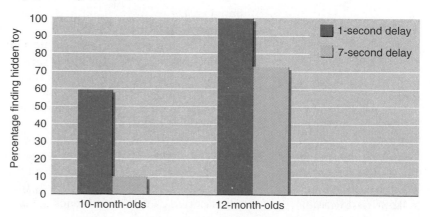

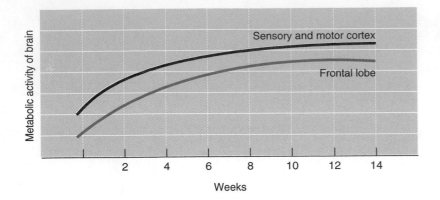

**FIGURE 10.8 Changes in brain function during the first year. In the opening months of life, the sensory and motor areas of the brain's cortex are more active than the frontal lobe, which does not become significantly active until about 8 months.** *Adapted from Chugani & Phelps, 1986.*

eye movements. When 1-month-olds are shown a design, they are likely to scan whatever feature their eyes encounter first—usually part of the external border. Only 1 month later, they scan the essential elements of the design. As children grow older, they become increasingly efficient in searching for information. They also become more adept at perceiving details and organizing them into meaningful patterns and entities.

Another important factor in intellectual development is the baby's growing skill in understanding and using language. There is some evidence that parents can help advance this skill by talking to their babies, especially one to one (Olson, Bates, & Bayles, 1984). In turn, skill with language facilitates the formation of concepts, which help organize information into categories and facilitate the mental processing that eventually creates long-lasting memories.

## Piaget's Theory of Cognitive Development

During the 20th century, psychologists' views of intellectual development in children were dominated by the thinking of the Swiss psychologist Jean Piaget. Piaget spent his entire career studying the mental development of his own and other children as they grew from infancy through adolescence. His observations have greatly influenced psychologists' ideas about how we reason, solve problems, and use our intelligence to understand and adapt to our world.

Piaget concluded that our mental growth—which he defined as increases in the ability to adapt to new situations—takes place because of two key processes: assimilation and accommodation. **Assimilation** is the process of incorporating a new event into one's existing cognitive view of the world. **Accommodation** is the process of changing one's cognitive view and behavior when new information requires such a change.

As a simple example, consider a young boy who has a number of toys. To these familiar old toys we add a new one, a magnet. The boy's initial impulse will be to assimilate the new toy into his existing knowledge of other toys; he may try to bang it like a hammer, throw it like a ball, or blow it like a horn. But once he learns that the magnet has a new and unprecedented quality—the power to attract iron—he accommodates his view of toys to include this previously unfamiliar fact. He now behaves on the basis of the revised assumption that some toys are designed not for banging, throwing, or making noise but for attracting metal objects.

Piaget concluded that there is always some tension between assimilation (which involves using old ideas to meet new situations) and accommodation (which involves changing old ideas to meet new situations). The resolution of this tension results in intellectual growth. Thus, we can develop our cognitive skills only through active interaction with objects and people in our world. We need an environment that exposes us to new situations and problems and thus challenges us to exercise and increase our mental skills.

Another key word in Piagetian theory is *operations*. This term is difficult to define. Roughly, an **operation** is a sort of dynamic mental rule for manipulating objects or ideas into new forms and then back to the original forms. An example is the rule that four pieces of candy (or the mere figure 4) can be divided into two parts of two each, then put back again into the original four.

**Assimilation**
The process of incorporating a new event into one's existing cognitive view of the world.

**Accommodation**
The process of changing one's cognitive view and behavior when new information requires such a change.

**Operations**
Dynamic mental rules for manipulating ideas or objects into new forms and then back to the original forms.

## Four Stages of Cognitive Development

Piaget proposed that mental growth takes place in a series of four stages, in each of which the child thinks and behaves in a quite different fashion than before. He maintained that the child grows intellectually not like a leaf, which simply gets larger every day, but like a caterpillar, which is eventually transformed into a butterfly (Piaget, 1952). Let's take a closer look at each of Piaget's stages, bearing in mind that the stages are not discrete; that is, a particular stage represents the child's *dominant* way of thinking at that age, not the *only* way the child is capable of thinking (Siegler & Ellis, 1996). (See the study chart below.)

**The Sensorimotor Stage**    In the first stage, the **sensorimotor stage,** which continues for the first 2 years of life, children have not yet learned to use language and symbols to represent the objects and events in their environment. Infants begin to know the world in terms of their own sensory impressions of its sights, sounds, tastes, and smells. But soon they begin to discover the relationship between their actions toward the objects they perceive and the consequences that follow from their actions. By 4 to 6 months, babies are aware that they can produce results through physical activity. They will repeatedly kick at toys hanging over their cribs, apparently to make them swing and thus produce a change of stimulus that they find interesting. By 12 months, they have acquired the concept of *object permanence;* that is, they act as if they know that objects are permanent and do not mysteriously disappear. If a toy is shown to them and then hidden behind two pillows lying side by side, they know how to find it. They look first behind one of the pillows. If the toy is not there, they look behind the other. If they cannot find the toy at all, they are surprised, indicating that they expect an object that they saw earlier to be somewhere.

**Sensorimotor stage**
According to Piaget, the stage of intellectual development in the first 2 years of life when the child knows the world only in terms of sensory and motor activities.

**The Preoperational Stage**    From age 2 through age 6, children are in the **preoperational stage.** They have acquired language and can manipulate symbols. They may behave toward a doll as if it were a child and toward a stick as if it were a gun. They often put objects together in appropriate groups—for example, all the red blocks into one pile and all the blue blocks into another. But their actions are still dictated largely by the evidence of their senses. They have not yet developed

**Preoperational stage**
According to Piaget, the stage of intellectual development, from ages 2 through 6, when the child's ability to use language and manipulate symbols dominates intellectual development.

## Study Chart
## Piaget's Four Stages of Cognitive Development

| Stage | Age | Cognitive Abilities |
|---|---|---|
| **Sensorimotor** | Birth to 2 years | Awareness of relationships between actions toward objects and the consequences of those actions |
| **Preoperational** | 2–6 years | Ability to use language and manipulate symbols Autobiographical memories |
| **Concrete operational** | 7–11 or 12 years | Ability to reason about concrete objects and relate objects and events to a larger context Understanding of operational rules and conservation |
| **Formal operational** | 11 or 12 years and over | Ability to reason logically about abstract ideas and possibilities Preoccupation with own thought processes |

## PSYCHOLOGY AND THE MEDIA

# Influencing Children's Memories

 Can a child's memory be influenced by an adult's questions? According to researchers led by Stephen Ceci of Cornell University, persistent questioning may lead young children to develop and believe a description of an event that never happened.

Parents of children between the ages of 4 and 6 helped researchers compile a list of two events that had really happened and eight that had not. Each week, a researcher went through the list with each child, asking him or her after each event, "Did this ever happen?" One of the children was asked whether he had been to the hospital because he had gotten his finger caught in a mousetrap. The first time the child was asked the question, he answered that he had never even *been* to a hospital. The second time he was asked the question, he "remembered" crying when his finger got caught. By the eleventh week, he had developed an elaborate account of how his brother had pushed

his finger into the mousetrap. By that same week, 56% of the children reported at least one false event as being true, and some reported all of the false events as being true.

The children not only believed these stories but also described them in such detail that when researchers showed the videotaped accounts to colleagues, the other professionals were convinced that the events had really happened. The researchers also found that persistent questioning led children to make up new "facts" about false events.

A question that concerns judges is whether children elaborate on their memories in this way when they are being interviewed about possible abuse. But those who defend existing procedures for questioning children have pointed out that children need to be coaxed or else they will not report upsetting events.

*Source: Clyman, Friedman, & Weiss, 1993.*

---

the kinds of concepts that would enable them to form meaningful categories and are not yet capable of thinking in terms of the dynamic rules of operations.

Preoperational children do, however, begin to display autobiographical memories. Although children as young as age 2 remember incidents from months before, true autobiographical memories that last into adulthood usually don't begin until about $3\frac{1}{2}$ to 4 years of age (Nelson, 1993). Autobiographical memories seem to form lasting impressions only after children begin to converse with others about what has happened to them. Shaping events into a story makes it easier to retrieve the memory many years later. Reenactment also seems to reinforce memories: Recent research has found that when 18-month-old children reenact certain activities (e.g., making a teddy bear talk by pressing its paw or finding Mickey Mouse in a toy chest) after 2 weeks, they can recall those activities up to 10 weeks later (Hudson & Sheffield, 1998). Apparently, the child's age is not the primary determinant of whether an event will be recalled; instead, recall is determined mainly by what the child is asked to remember, the number of exposures to the event, and the availability of cues or reminders of the event (Bauer, 1996).

Young children are also easily influenced by suggestions from adults, a fact that takes on particular importance when children are called upon to testify in court trials (Bruck & Ceci, 1999; Schachter, Kagan, & Leichtman, 1995). The implications are discussed in Psychology and the Media, above.

**Stage of concrete operations** According to Piaget, the stage of intellectual development, beginning at 6 to 8 years of age, when children can reason logically about objects they see but cannot yet deal with rules in the abstract.

**Conservation** The principle stating that qualities such as mass, weight, and volume remain constant regardless of changes in the object's appearance.

**The Stage of Concrete Operations**  Sometime between the ages of 6 and 8, children enter the **stage of concrete operations**—the period during which, as the name implies, they first begin to reason about concrete events. They can now relate a particular object or event to a larger context. Thus, in the **conservation** experiment illustrated in Figure 10.9 the child can relate what he or she sees in beaker C to what he or she saw originally in beaker B.

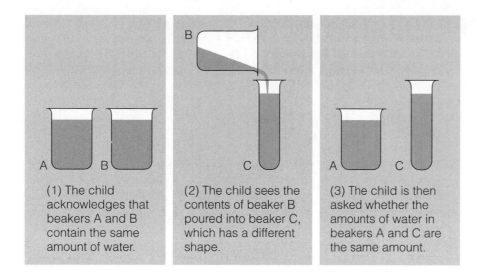

(1) The child acknowledges that beakers A and B contain the same amount of water.

(2) The child sees the contents of beaker B poured into beaker C, which has a different shape.

(3) The child is then asked whether the amounts of water in beakers A and C are the same amount.

**FIGURE 10.9 Figuring out the conservation rule. A 5-year-old child, still in the preoperational stage, will say that the taller beaker has more water. In contrast, a 7-year-old child, who has entered the concrete operations stage, will say that the beakers still have the same amount of water. The ability to reverse events mentally—for example, to see that it is possible to pour the water from beaker C back to B—is a key advance in concrete operations.**

Now children display understanding of a variety of operational rules. They know, for example, that if object 1 is heavier than object 2 and object 2 is heavier than 3, object 1 must be heavier than object 3. They have also acquired considerable sophistication in the use of concepts and categories. They realize, for example, that "all the pets that are dogs" plus "all the pets that are not dogs" make up a category called "all pets." They also realize that objects or attributes can belong to more than one concept. They know that animals can be tame or wild, furry or feathered. Thus, children in the stage of concrete operations show an ability to reason logically and apply operational rules.

But as the term *concrete* implies, children in this stage reason more effectively about objects that they can see or feel than about verbal statements. Suppose, for example, that children of this age are given the following problem: A is the same size as B, but B is smaller than C. Which is bigger, A or C? They may not be able to answer, for the question requires that they think about an abstract idea rather than about concrete objects.

**The Stage of Formal Operations**    The fourth and final period of cognitive growth—the **stage of formal operations**—begins around age 11 or 12. In a giant leap toward intellectual skill, children in their adolescent years ideally acquire the ability to reason logically, not just about concrete objects but also about abstract ideas and possibilities. Not everyone acquires formal operational abilities, but those who do can now apply operations to all kinds of situations, real or imagined. They can assume hypothetical conditions and make correct inferences, thus manipulating their own thoughts as readily as they once manipulated colored blocks. It is probably not a coincidence that the emergence of this stage is associated with maturation of the portions of the brain's frontal cortex that play an important role in thought processes (Stuss & Benson, 1986).

One prominent characteristic of the stage of formal operations is preoccupation with one's own thought processes. Adolescents think about their own thoughts and are curious about how these thoughts are organized and where they will lead. This inquiring attitude often brings them into conflict with the standards of the adult world. Adolescents become keenly aware that people do not always practice what they preach, and they begin to question such ideals as democracy, honesty, and self-sacrifice. They may decide that many of the beliefs and values they have been taught are "phony" and that they want to search instead for a different set of moral principles and a new philosophy of life.

**Stage of formal operations** According to Piaget, the stage of intellectual development, beginning at about age 11 or 12, when the child becomes capable of thinking in the abstract.

**Test Yourself**

**(e)** What word do we use to describe the physical changes that take place after birth?

**(f)** Piaget described two key processes that define children's mental growth. What are they?

**(g)** True autobiographical memories that last into adulthood don't usually begin until about what age?

(The answers are on page 404.)

# PERSONALITY DEVELOPMENT: BIRTH TO 18 MONTHS

**FOCUS QUESTIONS**

• What is meant by attachment, stranger anxiety, and separation anxiety?

• What effects does day care have on young children?

Like intellectual progress, the development of the personality seems to proceed in an orderly way, through a series of gradually merging stages. All aspects of personality—emotions, motives, and ways of coping with conflicts—first appear and then undergo change. During each stage, important qualities develop in all children. Variations in those qualities (which is what is meant by *personality*) are a function of what is happening in the child's environment—in interaction with the child's innate temperament, as discussed earlier.

During the first stage of personality development, which lasts from birth to about 12 months, one of the child's most important tasks is to develop attachment to his or her parents or other caregivers. **Attachment** is an emotional bond between parent and child characterized by mutual feelings of love and closeness. Although inner states such as "feeling close" can be difficult to measure, researchers have devised means for assessing the quality of attachment, such as the "strange situation" procedure discussed later in this section.

Attachment protects a child from too much fear or anxiety. But there is variation in the degree or security of an infant's attachment to caregivers. This variation depends on the predictability, availability, and sensitivity of the caregiver. When caregivers have these three qualities, thus providing what is generally termed *responsive caregiving,* children will develop a strong and secure attachment to them. Without these qualities, children become anxious and insecure in their attachment. Moreover, attachment is closely related to trust, which, as we noted in Chapter 9 in the discussion of Erikson's theory of psychosocial development, is essential if the child is to develop faith in the environment and future events. Children who develop secure attachment to a caregiver in childhood are more successful emotionally and socially in adulthood than those who do not.

**Attachment**
An emotional bond between a child and his or her caregiver(s) characterized by mutual feelings of love and closeness.

## The Process of Attachment

For a long time, psychologists believed that attachment occurred automatically as a result of the caregiver's fulfillment of the infant's basic needs. According to learning theorists, the child was conditioned to associate the nearness of the caregiver with food. According to Freud and other psychoanalytic theorists, gratification of the infant's needs caused the infant to form a positive image of the caregiver. But these views were challenged by the findings of a remarkable series of experiments by Harry F. Harlow.

Harlow took newborn monkeys from their actual mothers and placed them with doll-like **surrogate mothers.** As shown in Figure 10.10, Harlow gave his baby monkeys two such surrogate mothers. One was made of bare wire, with a bottle and nipple from which the monkey was always fed. The other was covered with terry cloth; it was an object that the baby monkey could cling to but from which it was never fed.

As the photographs show, the baby monkeys strongly preferred the terry cloth doll to the wire doll. They clung to the terry cloth "mother" even when feeding from the other doll. When a new object was placed in the cage, they clung to the terry cloth mother while making their first hesitant and tentative attempts to discover what this strange and at first frightening object might be (Harlow, 1961). Obviously, something about the terry cloth surrogate provided the baby monkey

**Surrogate mother**
A mother substitute.

Fred Sponholz

with what humans might call comfort, protection, and a secure base from which to explore new aspects of the environment.

It is important to note, however, that monkeys reared with surrogate mothers did not develop normally. As adults, they attacked other monkeys and did not engage in normal sexual activity. Later research found, however, that infant monkeys that were raised with surrogate mothers but had opportunities to interact with other infant monkeys developed more normally. It is clear that social interaction is essential for normal development in monkeys, and it seems safe to assume that this is true of human children as well.

During the first 2 years of a human infant's life, the quality of the child's attachment influences her or his tendency to approach particular people, to be receptive to care and consolation from them, and to be secure and unafraid in their presence. Human babies, like monkeys, seem to be born with an innate tendency to become attached to the adults who care for them. They show a strong preference for those who have served as continuous caretakers—especially when they are bored, frightened, or distressed by the unfamiliar or unexpected.

One study has shown that young children who were separated from their mothers during the birth of another child became more agitated, depressed, and withdrawn; they also cried more and experienced increased heart rate and awakenings from sleep. As illustrated in Figure 10.11, when the mother returned, the symptoms abated (Field & Reite, 1984).

**FIGURE 10.10** Baby monkey and surrogate mothers. The baby monkey has been taken from its own mother and placed with two surrogate mothers. Note how it clings to the terry cloth mother, even when feeding from the wire mother and especially when exploring a new and unfamiliar object that has been placed in the cage

**FIGURE 10.11** Baby's response to mother's absence. The average heart rate of babies during play sessions rose sharply when the mother was hospitalized and then dropped back when she was home once again.
*Field & Reite, 1984.*

### The Strange Situation Procedure

Mary Ainsworth and colleagues developed a procedure for studying children's responses to separation from their mother and the strength of their attachment. This procedure, called the *strange situation*, consists of the following steps (Ainsworth, Blehar, Walters, & Wall, 1978):

1. A mother and child enter a room. The mother places the baby on the floor, surrounded by toys, and sits in another part of the room.
2. A female stranger enters the room and sits, converses with the mother for a minute, and then attempts to play with the baby.
3. The mother leaves the room. If the baby is not upset, the stranger sits quietly. If the baby is upset, the stranger tries to soothe him or her.

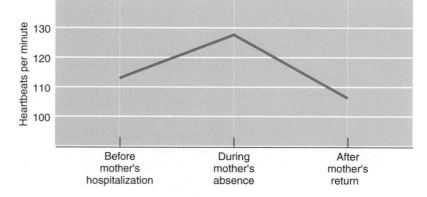

4.  The mother returns and plays with the baby; the stranger leaves the room.
5.  The mother leaves the room, leaving the baby alone.
6.  The stranger returns. If the baby is upset, the stranger tries to soothe him or her.
7.  The mother returns and the stranger leaves the room.

During the entire procedure, researchers observe the baby through a one-way mirror and record her or his behaviors.

## Patterns of Attachment

On the basis of observations of numerous babies in the strange situation, researchers have identified three distinct patterns of attachment. Babies may be categorized into one of the following groups:

*Securely attached.* These babies seek to interact with the mother when she returns to the room. Some simply acknowledge her presence while continuing to play with a toy. Others seek physical contact with her, and still others attempt to stay near her through the entire session and show intense distress when she leaves. Between 60% and 65% of babies in the United States are securely attached.

*Insecurely attached: avoidant.* These babies do not interact with the mother when she returns. Some ignore her; others display mixed behavior, both seeking and avoiding interaction. Avoidant babies often do not show distress when the mother leaves and are easily soothed by the stranger. They account for about 20% of U.S. babies.

*Insecurely attached: ambivalent.* Another group of babies simultaneously seek and resist physical contact with the mother when she returns. They may cry to be picked up and then squirm until they are put down again. About 10% of U.S. babies fall into this category.

Because not all babies fit these categories, researchers have developed a fourth category: *disorganized* (Main & Solomon, 1986). Babies in this category show contradictory behaviors, such as approaching the mother while not looking at her or suddenly crying after having settled down.

It is important to note that there may be cultural differences in patterns of attachment. For example, cross-cultural research using the strange situation procedure has found that the percentage of insecure-ambivalent babies is higher in Japan than in the United States, whereas the percentage of insecure-avoidant babies is higher in the United States than in Japan. However, these findings need to be interpreted within the context of the cultures in which they occur. In Japan, for example, insecure-ambivalent behavior is not as closely associated with incompetence as it is in the United States. Some researchers believe that theories and measures of attachment that are appropriate in one culture do not necessarily apply in other cultures (Rothbaum, Weisz, Pott, Miyake, & Morelli, 2000).

## Courage for Exploration

Although attachment and exploration seem to be conflicting tendencies, they actually work hand in hand. Note in Figure 10.10 how the baby monkey engages in both activities at once—cautiously exploring a new object while clinging to its terry cloth surrogate mother. Human babies also seem to gather courage for exploration from their attachment to their mothers. In one experiment, babies just under a year old were placed in a strange room that contained a chair piled high with and surrounded by toys. When the baby and mother were in the room together, the baby actively looked at the toys, approached them, and touched them. All this exploratory behavior dropped off, however, if a stranger was present or if the mother left the room (Ainsworth & Bell, 1970).

## The Appearance of Anxiety

Along with the development of attachment comes a related phenomenon—the first appearance of signs of anxiety. When babies are left alone in a room, many soon begin to cry, frantically search for the mother, or both. These babies are exhibiting **separation anxiety,** a characteristic that usually appears around the age of 8 months.

Separation anxiety seems to emerge as an outgrowth of the child's newly developed intellectual skills. At 8 months, most babies can not only recall past events but also compare them with the here and now. When the mother departs, they can recall her former presence—and at the same time realize that she is no longer there. Since they don't understand the inconsistency, they become anxious and cry. Later, when babies can also anticipate that the mother will return, the inconsistency is more easily resolved, and separation anxiety begins to fade.

Separation anxiety appears to be universal regardless of childrearing practices, as shown in Figure 10.12. However, the infant's temperamental qualities influence how intense the child's separation anxiety is and how long it lasts. Infants who have a temperamental disposition to become highly fearful will show more intense separation anxiety than those who are relaxed and less vulnerable to anxiety (Kagan, 1989).

Shortly before separation anxiety becomes apparent, babies display **stranger anxiety.** This first appears at about 7 months, increases until around the first birthday, then declines. Infants will usually smile if the mother shows her face above the crib. But if a stranger appears, they often show anxiety by turning away and perhaps breaking into tears. Again, the explanation is that the appearance of the strange face creates uncertainty. The baby has acquired a mental representation or perceptual expectation of familiar faces. This representation is violated by the unfamiliar face, and as a result the child becomes fearful. Behavior that seems to indicate stranger anxiety can sometimes be produced by showing the baby a distorted mask of the human face. Although all infants show fear of strangers, they differ in the intensity of their fear, how long it lasts, and the ease with which they can be soothed.

The fear that babies show in the presence of strangers reflects a more general principle in psychological development: Anxiety is less likely to be generated by an event if the event can be anticipated. For example, 1-year-old infants are less frightened by mechanical toys that produce noises on a predictable schedule than by toys that produce noises on an unpredictable schedule (Gunnar, Leighton, & Peleaux, 1984).

**Separation anxiety**
A form of anxiety, appearing at about 8 months of age, in which the infant cries when separated from a caretaker.

**Stranger anxiety**
A form of anxiety, appearing at about 7 months of age, in which the infant cries at the appearance of an unfamiliar person.

**FIGURE 10.12 The emergence of separation anxiety: a universal pattern.** In widely different cultures, babies younger than 7 months rarely cry when their mothers leave them. Between 12 and 15 months, however, the experience is almost sure to bring distress and tears—and then the impact begins to weaken. The pattern shown here applies equally everywhere children have been studied, including isolated villages in the Guatemalan highlands and remote areas of the Kalahari Desert in Africa. *Kagan, Kearsley, & Zelazo, 1978.*

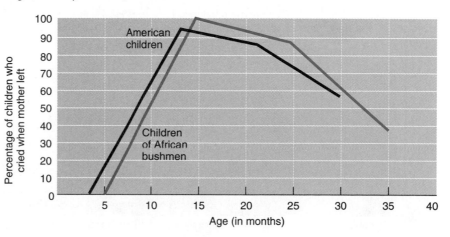

In most infants, stranger anxiety develops around the age of 7 months and diminishes toward the end of the first year.

# The Effects of Day Care

Findings like those discussed in this section have raised many questions in the minds of parents about the advisability of day-care programs. In recent years, especially with both parents frequently working outside the home, day-care programs for young children have become popular. What are the effects on the children? Some theorists have warned that the consequences are likely to be dangerous for the child's emotional development (Dreskin & Dreskin, 1983). But the evidence points to a more qualified conclusion: The consequences depend on the quality of the day-care program itself—on what goes on inside the program. Day-care programs are not universally good or bad.

In one study, illustrated in Figure 10.13, children who had experienced either high-quality or low-quality day care in their first year of life were studied during preschool or kindergarten. The results showed that children who had experienced high-quality programs were more compliant, capable of self-regulation, task-oriented, and considerate. Those who had experienced low-quality programs had greater difficulties with peers and were more distractible and hostile (Howes, 1990).

Another recent study focused on the effects of differing amounts of nonparental care (i.e., day care). The researchers studied two groups of children: one consisting of children who received 30 or more hours of nonparental care per week beginning around 4 months of age, the other of children who never experienced more than 10 hours per week of nonparental care. When the children were evaluated at ages 2 and 3, there were no significant differences in cognitive and socioemotional development between the two groups. Factors that appeared to be more important than the amount of day care the children received included higher family income, less authoritarian child-rearing attitudes, and more sensitive parenting. In short, children who are raised in comfortable, stimulating environments and receive loving attention from parents and other caretakers tend to show positive cognitive and socioemotional development, regardless of the amount of nonparental care they receive (NICHD Early Child Care Research Network, 1998, 2002).

In well-run centers, one caretaker is responsible for only three or four infants or five or six toddlers. The selection of playthings and learning materials for the children is also important. Infants, for example, should be exposed to many kinds of stimulation and have opportunities to practice new abilities as they mature. One study focused on nine day-care centers that differed in the degree of stimulation

**FIGURE 10.13 The results of day care: it all depends.** When children were divided into two groups based on the quality of the day care they had experienced as infants, differences in outcome were observed. *After Howes, 1990.*

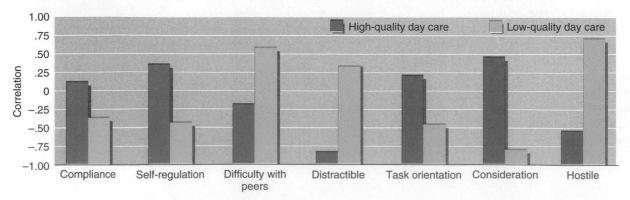

they offered for language development. Children in centers where the caregivers talked a lot performed best on tests of language development (McCartney, 1984).

If day care is good, it may even help children in their later adjustment to school (Howes, 1988). Children from disadvantaged homes—particularly those with a single caregiver, several children, and very limited resources—seem to especially benefit from high-quality day care. A study of disadvantaged 4-year-olds found that those who attended high-quality day-care programs had IQs more than 15 points higher than those of children who had minimal exposure to day care (Burchinal, Lee, & Ramey, 1989). However, if day-care conditions are poor—if the program is understaffed, provides little variety and few pleasures, and restricts the child's explorations—the child's development can indeed be affected adversely.

# LEARNING SOCIETY'S RULES: 18 MONTHS THROUGH 3 YEARS

The second important period in personality development, roughly from 18 months through the third year, involves the child's first appreciation of right and wrong: the notion that some behaviors will be met with punishment and disapproval and others with praise and approval. All children are expected to acquire an initial moral sense by their second birthday. The role of the environment is to determine what actions or behaviors the child regards as good and proper and what actions he or she regards as bad. Also important during this period is the development of autonomy—that is, a sense of self-control and adequacy (see Chapter 9); children who fail to develop autonomy may become mired in feelings of shame and self-doubt.

**FOCUS QUESTIONS**

- What important events occur during the child's early social development?

- How do parental practices influence the development of morality?

The "good" and "proper" behaviors that children are expected to learn differ from one culture to another. In villages in developing countries, for example, where there are no toilets or bathrooms, it is not considered wrong for a child to urinate outside. In contrast, in most developed countries such behavior is likely to be corrected. Thus, the environment determines what the child will regard as right or approved. Variations among children will be due primarily to the particular standards their families promote. In the United States, parents typically are concerned with teaching their children to control elimination and defecation, to inhibit aggression and destruction, to be clean, and not to cry at every minor frustration.

## Initial Moral Sense

The process of teaching children to adhere to society's rules is given a boost by a dramatic change within the child that occurs around age 2. This is when children first develop a sense of right and wrong; that is, they develop inner standards and the desire to live up to them. In one study, 2-year-olds watched someone play in a complicated manner—for example, pretending to use toy kitchenware to cook a meal for a family—and then were told that it was their turn to play with the toys. Just a few months earlier, the process had passed without incident. Now, however, many of them broke into tears or ran to their mother. Apparently they felt obligated to play with the toys in an equally sophisticated manner, yet were unsure of their ability.

This newly developed uncertainty over living up to a self-imposed standard creates anxiety and distress (Kagan, 1981). Even subtle violations of standards appear to be disturbing. Children will now point to a cracked toy, dirty hands, torn clothing, or a missing button and show concern. They can discern—even from small changes in the sound of their father's voice or the shape of their mother's eyes—that their own behavior elicits judgmental responses from others.

## Parental Practices and the Development of Morality

Rewards and punishments also play a part in the process of learning to meet social demands. Children are usually rewarded with praise and hugs when they use the toilet successfully or refrain from playing with an object after being told "no." And they may be punished, with disapproval if not physically, when they soil themselves, break something, or get into forbidden places. But the desire to live up to standards of proper conduct appears at about the same time that children learn to be anxious about possible punishment.

During their first year, babies act without any strong focus on the consequences of their actions and show little emotional reaction when they achieve a specific outcome. But at about 20 months, they become more interested in the results of their actions, reflecting the desire to meet inner standards. By age 3, the outcome of their efforts has become important to them. They are proud of success and frustrated by failure (Bullock & Lutkenhaus, 1988).

In addition to parental approval and disapproval, the child's own temperament plays an important role in the development of a moral sense. One researcher has proposed that temperament contributes to two aspects of conscience: (1) guilt and feelings of discomfort about doing something wrong and (2) the ability to restrain one's behavior to accord with the rules of society (Kochanska, 1993).

## Punishment, Abuse, and Neglect

Punishment can upset the delicate balance between a child's natural urge to explore the environment and the requirement of social discipline. (See Chapter 4 for a discussion of the role of punishment in learning.) This early period of life holds exciting possibilities for children as they form a self-image as active, competent, and increasingly self-sufficient human beings. By moving about in the world for the first time, they acquire all kinds of fascinating information about the environment. By handling objects—and sometimes, unfortunately, destroying them—they learn that they have some power over their environment. They discover that they can roam about the world and perhaps rearrange it to their liking. They learn that they can satisfy many of their own desires. By reaching into the cookie jar, they can relieve hunger. By crawling under a blanket, they can find warmth. One of the responsibilities of parents is to aid children in their explorations and discoveries while at the same time setting appropriate limits on their behavior.

When and how children are punished varies by culture. For example, Japanese parents rarely punish their young children because they are afraid of making them angry or anxious. (However, they also adhere to a strict tradition of family secrecy, making it difficult to gauge how much physical punishment actually occurs; Kozu, 1999.) In the United States, on the other hand, the majority of parents believe that punishment is necessary. Although U.S. attitudes regarding obedience have relaxed over time, many people still favor the use of corporal punishment such as spanking as a disciplinary technique.

Parents who use corporal punishment are usually convinced that their methods make sense. But the notion that physical pain is an effective teaching device is not supported by evidence from psychological research. Indeed, one study after another has shown that the opposite is true. Unsparing use of corporal punishment makes children less prone to obey in the long run and angrier and more aggressive than other kids. Research shows that corporal punishment can create pent-up feelings of resentment—along with the dangerous conviction that, once you're big enough, power and physical force are the best means for getting your way (Leach, 1989). In fact, the psychological effects of physical punishment can range from apathy to obsessiveness, paranoia, and extreme dissociation (Greven, 1991). Parents who are tempted to hit their children should keep in mind that, as they grow, children tend to follow the guidance of those who arouse affection and admiration, not loathing and fear.

When does corporal punishment become child abuse? All physical punishment of a child by an adult has the potential to become abusive and carries with it the possibility of lasting harm. Children growing up on a diet of beatings are vulnerable to a variety of mental health problems later in life, including depression and alcohol abuse (Holmes & Robins, 1987) and possibly more severe problems such as schizophrenia (Read, 1997). Investigators have also found that "the more children are hit by their parents, the more likely they are to hit others" (Straus, Gelles, & Steinmetz, 1981). Small wonder that, as shown in Figure 10.14, physically abused children find it relatively difficult to maintain good social relationships (Salzinger, Feldman, Hammer, & Rosario, 1993).

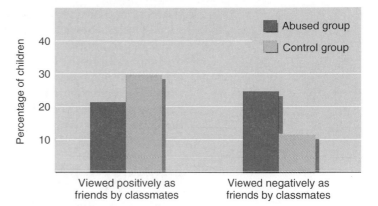

**FIGURE 10.14 The effects of physical abuse on peer relationships.** Researchers compared the social popularity of a large group of abused children between the ages of 8 and 12 with that of an otherwise comparable group of nonabused children. Note that the abused youngsters were considerably less likely to be accepted—and more likely to be spurned—by their peers. They were seen as more aggressive and less cooperative.

*Salzinger, Feldman, Hammer, & Rosario, 1993.*

Abuse can be psychological as well as physical. Parents who continually tell their child that she or he is "no good" or "a klutz" can inflict lasting psychological harm. Neglect, too, is a form of abuse. Lack of adequate nutrition or medical care can cause severe damage to a child's physical, mental, and emotional development—as can lack of love and responsive caregiving.

What causes parents to be abusive? A number of explanations have been proposed, including mental illness, a culture that condones violence, and problematic family interactions. None of these factors has been shown to directly cause child abuse, but researchers have identified several factors that seem to increase the chances that abuse will occur. Chief among these is whether the parent experienced abuse as a child: Many child abusers were abused themselves, and in this way they seem to have learned that abusive behavior is an appropriate way of disciplining children (Ney, 1988). In addition, children whose parents engage in physical violence toward each other are at risk of being abused (Appel & Holden, 1998). Other risk factors for child abuse are family poverty, parental unemployment, and characteristics of the child such as a difficult temperament. Programs for preventing child abuse therefore focus on providing social support for parents and teaching them more appropriate disciplinary techniques.

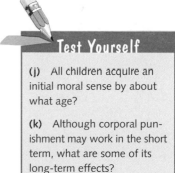

**Test Yourself**

**(j)** All children acquire an initial moral sense by about what age?

**(k)** Although corporal punishment may work in the short term, what are some of its long-term effects?

(The answers are on page 404.)

# VENTURING INTO THE WORLD: AGES 4 AND 5

**FOCUS QUESTIONS**

- What is meant by identification?
- How does sex typing occur?
- What effects can divorce or loss of a parent have on children?

By age 4, children venture outside the home to play with other children, and they may go to nursery school or kindergarten. This increasing social experience appears to be essential to normal development; according to Erikson (see Chapter 9), this is when children develop initiative—the ability to be "self-starters," and initiate their own activities. Moreover, as children move into broader social circles, they learn, among other things, that the world is made up of males and females, for whom society decrees different kinds of behavior. Although sex role expectations are less distinct today than they were in the past, they still influence children's behavior. Boys begin to take on the characteristics that society considers appropriate for males, and girls take on the characteristics considered appropriate for females. This is also the time when children begin to identify with their parents.

## Emulating a Parent

At age 4 or 5, children have entered a stage of development in which they are mature enough to detect similarities between their parents and themselves, and they begin to feel vicarious emotions—that is, emotions that are inherent in their parents' behavior and interactions with others. For example, when a 5-year-old perceives that her mother is competent, popular, and loved by the child's father, she feels pride because she identifies with her mother.

Children detect many kinds of similarity between themselves and their parents. They have the same last name, they are told that they look like one or both of their parents, and they begin to imitate their parents, which leads to an increase in perceived similarity. As this perception increases, the child begins to experience the emotions that come from recognizing the parent's strengths, virtues, and skills or, on the other hand, the parent's failures and undesirable traits.

Children with intelligent parents often come to think of themselves as intelligent. A boy whose father holds a job that requires physical strength usually begins to think of himself as strong. One study has shown that the mother's clearly stated attitudes about the importance of learning during the child's preschool years are reflected in a higher level of school achievement 6 years later (Hess, Holloway, Dickson, & Price, 1984).

Unfortunately, children identify with their parents' faults as well as their virtues, and it is not unusual for children to become aware of their parents' defects. They may see that their father is unable to hold a job or that their mother drinks too much. They may hear relatives criticize their parents. Or they may hear warring parents criticize each other. Under such circumstances, many children begin to believe that they, too, are unworthy, unlovable, hateful, stupid, lazy, or mean.

This identification with undesirable qualities can be a burden, especially for children from disadvantaged or minority backgrounds. Children may identify with what they perceive as undesirable qualities of their social class or ethnic group, and as a result they will experience anxiety. Not all children react this way, of course—ethnicity can just as easily be a source of pride in its own right. Finally, for tens of thousands of homeless children, any sense of healthy identification is at a premium—as reflected in the drawings shown in Figure 10.15.

## Same-Sex Identification

Young children typically identify with the parent of their sex. Even 3-year-olds reveal their understanding of the differences between mom and dad—a boy may lather his face with shaving cream and pretend he is shaving; a girl may stuff a pillow beneath her shirt and announce that she has a baby inside.

Social experiences are very influential. Children learn to act in what their culture defines as masculine or feminine ways through a process called **sex typing**. Even parents who say that they believe in treating the two sexes the same way make distinctions between them.

**Sex typing**
The process through which society molds its members into its traditional patterns of femininity and masculinity.

Knowledge of gender differences is present among children as young as 2 years old. In one study, a group of 2-year-old boys and girls were shown sequences that portrayed stereotyped males and females, and the boys remembered more of the male stereotypes than the female ones. The girls remembered the male and female sequences equally well (Bauer, 1993).

Pressures for sex typing can emerge from television, books, and school. The message sinks in very early. When offered a choice, girls as young as 3 or 4 years old display their femininity in the kinds of toys they select. In Western nations, these are likely to be dolls, toy stoves, and dish sets; boys shun such toys and prefer games and trucks. When opportunities arise, boys are more likely than girls to take risks (Ginsburg & Miller, 1982). But even if books, television, and schools were to abandon sex stereotyping, children would probably still show sex-typed differences. Boys and girls differ in major traits around the world, even in cultures where there are no schools, no television, no books, and no toys.

Recent research has found that sex typing is more systematic in children's activities and interests than in their attitudes and personalities. Moreover, families differ in the extent to which they promote sex typing in their children. Some parents have more traditional views of appropriate activities for boys and girls than do others, with the result that their children are more likely to be steered toward "gender-appropriate" activities. As the researchers point out, "To the extent that children's activity patterns and preferences mean that they practice different kinds of skills (e.g., sewing versus soccer) and that they become exposed to different opportunities, sex-typing around everyday activities may have long-term and pervasive developmental consequences" (McHale, Crouter, & Tucker, 1999, p. 1002).

Sex differences become prominent when children are among peers. If a fight breaks out, odds are good that it will be the boys rather than the girls who are in the thick of things. Aggression remains more stable in boys than in girls. U.S. society has traditionally characterized males as aggressive, independent, and dominant and females as unaggressive, dependent, and submissive. Hence, girls are more likely than boys to be punished for showing aggression; as they approach kindergarten, aggressive behavior among girls diminishes (Cummings, Iannotti, & Zahn-Waxler, 1989). But girls are certainly not incapable of aggression; they are simply more likely to display it through verbal means or by ostracizing other children (Cairns, Cairns, Neckerman, Ferguson, & Gariépy, 1989).

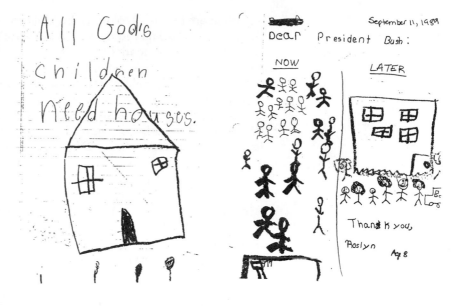

**FIGURE 10.15 The yearning for identification. These drawings were made by children in the Homeless Children's Tutorial Project in Washington, D.C.**

*Courtesy Broderick Johnson, Homeless Children's Tutorial Project, Washington, D.C.*

## The Influence of Television

Long before children begin socializing with classmates and peers, another major outside influence enters their lives: television. By the time they are a year old, children are watching and paying attention to the TV. Many parents prop their infants in front of the television to quiet or entertain them, and babies as young as 6 months of age become upset when the TV picture becomes fuzzy or the sound is distorted. Children in the United States spend more time watching television than they do in any other activity except sleeping.

What are the effects of this powerful medium on children? The answer is mixed. On the one hand, its influence can be deadening, even destructive. On the other hand, TV has the potential to be a valuable educational tool (Huston, Wright, Rice, Kerkman, & St. Peters, 1990).

Much of what children watch on television does not have positive effects. According to one estimate, a child who watches an average of 2 to 4 hours of television daily will have witnessed 8,000 murders and 100,000 other acts of TV violence by the time he or she graduates from elementary school (Huston, Donnerstein, Fairchild, Fesbach et al., 1992). There is considerable evidence that portrayals of violence on TV tend to stimulate aggressive behavior (e.g., Bok, 1998; Liebert & Sprafkin, 1988). Indeed, one study showed a positive correlation between the amount of time children spend viewing television and the seriousness of later criminal behavior (Eron, 1987). These findings are not unique to the United States; cross-cultural research has found that "the extent and omnipresence of media violence contribute to the development of a global aggressive culture" (Groebel, 2001, p. 267). Watching television can also reinforce sex stereotypes, although sex stereotyping has decreased in recent years.

When parents watch television along with their children, they can harness its power in their children's behalf. With very young children, programs like *Sesame Street* can be treated as talking picture books that parents and children discuss (Lemish & Rice, 1986). In addition to its avowed goal of teaching children numbers, the alphabet, and concepts such as *near* and *far*, *Sesame Street* may improve children's vocabulary (Rice, Huston, Truglio, & Wright, 1990). For parents of older children, television offers an opportunity to discuss values as well as news and noteworthy facts.

The effects of television are not likely to be the same for every child. They depend on the child's temperament—for example, his or her level of anxiety or aggressive tendencies—and on what else may be going on in the child's environment. Clearly, however, all children can use help in learning to relate wisely to what they see on television. Children can be taught "critical viewing skills" such as how to distinguish between fictional portrayals and factual presentations and how to recognize ways in which violence is portrayed unrealistically (S. L. Smith & Donnerstein, 1998), as well as to understand the real consequences of behavior portrayed on TV.

This need for critical viewing applies as well to the increasingly sophisticated new media to which children are exposed today. The Internet in particular has opened up vast new possibilities for both positive and negative influences on children. Unsupervised children have no difficulty gaining access to content that is pornographic, extremely violent, or both. Parental oversight and participation in their children's use of new media technologies is essential to avoid the most negative aspects of those technologies (Subrahmanyam, Kraut, Greenfield, & Gross, 2001; Tarpley, 2001).

## Divorce and Loss of a Parent

Because most children identify strongly with their parents during the early years, the death of a parent is a keen loss. Although it is not clear what the most vulnerable age is (Garmezy, 1983), it would appear that the loss of a parent is often especially painful when it occurs during the preschool years. Of the many ways in which the removal of a parent can hamper a child's development, one is interference with the identification process. But what happens subsequently matters. One study showed that the effects of early loss of the mother may be mitigated if the father remarries and the new marriage brings stability to the child's life, along with a good relationship with the stepmother (Birtchnell, 1980).

The fate of children of divorce isn't uniform either. Some children of divorced parents experience high levels of anger, fear, and depression. Many children treated for psychological problems have experienced the distress of parental discord and divorce (Hetherington & Camara, 1984), and the impact on school achievement and emotional well-being may reverberate even in late adolescence and early adulthood (Wallerstein & Blakeslee, 1989). One study, however, reported that although many children showed some loss of well-being after their parents split up, the differences were too small to be considered very significant (Allison & Furstenberg, 1989).

A study of a group of 7- to 11-year-old boys whose parents had divorced found that, although the boys showed more behavioral problems than boys from intact homes, most of the problems existed before the divorce occurred (Cherlin et al., 1991). In other words, a significant portion of what are usually considered the ill effects of divorce on children may be due to living in a family in which the parents' marriage was troubled for a long time. Thus, couples who attempt to stay together "for the kids" may be making a mistake (Hetherington & Stanley-Hagan, 1999).

As in the case of bereavement, the results depend on what happens afterward. One study found that among girls who were in preschool when their parents separated, school achievement depended on a continuing strong identification with a competent mother and a solid relationship between mother and child. For boys, the key factor was the father's continuing interest or the presence of an involved and committed stepfather (Wallerstein & Kelley, 1980).

**Test Yourself**

**(l)**  Little Joey tries to copy his father in every possible way—wearing similar clothes, walking the same way, imitating his speech. How would you describe Joey's behavior?

(The answer is on page 404.)

# EXPANDING SOCIAL INFLUENCES: AGES 6 TO 10

As children approach their sixth and seventh birthdays and enter the stage of concrete operations, they can compare an event with its broader context. At a personal level, this means that the child will compare him- or herself with others on traits that the child values, such as intelligence, bravery, physical attractiveness, and ability to deal with stress. The child arrives at a conception of self: smart or dumb, pretty or plain, brave or timid. In U.S. culture, two important environmental determinants of the child's self-concept are achievement in school and acceptance by peers. Children who do well in school and are popular with their peers will develop a self-concept that does not arouse anxiety. On the other hand, those who fail in school and have few friends may develop a self-concept that arouses anxiety and will influence personality development in a major way. According to Erikson (see Chapter 9), in the school years it is essential for children to resolve the crisis of industry versus inferiority. They must acquire the ability to learn how things work, to understand and organize; if they do not, they may develop a sense of inferiority that can have lasting negative effects.

**FOCUS QUESTIONS**

- What influences are exerted by a child's teachers and peers?

- What factors cause some children to become dominant and others submissive?

It is worth noting, however, that not all children base their self-concept primarily on achievement in school. Many low-achievers still manage to develop a positive view of themselves in other areas and activities, as well as through positive interactions with family and peers. This is also true for minority children, who must develop a positive self-concept in spite of the prejudice and discrimination they often experience (Spencer, 1988).

## The New World of School

Teachers usually play a dual role in their pupils' development. First, they teach the intellectual skills required in our society. Second, and perhaps more important, they encourage intellectual mastery. It is in the early years of school that children

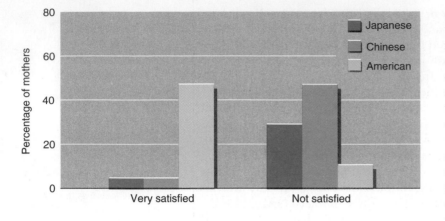

**FIGURE 10.16 Differing cultural expectations for achievement. Despite their children's lower scores in mathematics, U.S. parents said they were very satisfied with their performance. In contrast, Japanese and Chinese parents, whose children had scored higher, reported lower satisfaction.**

*Stevenson, Chen, & Lee, 1993.*

crystallize their inner standards of intellectual mastery and begin to feel anxiety if they don't live up to those standards. By age 10, some children have developed expectations of success that are likely to bolster their self-confidence throughout life. Others have developed expectations and fears of failure.

Many children who are actually very competent academically develop disparaging self-perceptions and illusions of incompetence (Phillips, 1984). Such outcomes depend largely on the school experience, including the expectations of teachers. Much has been made, for example, of sex differences in intellectual abilities, especially in reading and math. These differences may have more to do with expectations than with innate ability. One team of researchers studied the intellectual performance of kindergartners and first- and fifth-graders in the United States, Taiwan, and Japan. They found little evidence that boys and girls differed in their abilities in either reading or math (Lummis & Stevenson, 1990).

As a group, however, children in the United States lag behind their counterparts in Japan and China in achievement in mathematics, and the decline becomes more apparent as children progress in school (Stevenson, 1998; Stevenson, Chen, & Lee, 1993). Part of the reason for this disparity may be the contrasting expectations of parents in different cultures. Japanese and Chinese parents had much higher expectations than U.S. parents for what their children should achieve, as shown in Figure 10.16. Japanese and Chinese parents were also more likely to attribute their children's academic success to hard work, whereas U.S. parents attributed it to innate ability.

An extensive study of schools in London attempted to isolate the school factors that make a difference in the child's development. The results showed that physical factors—the size of the school, the age of the buildings, or the amount of space available—do not seem to matter very much. What does matter is the way pupils are dealt with in the school. Children accomplish more and display fewer behavior problems when they are given positions of responsibility and opportunities to help run the school and are rewarded and praised for their work, and when staff members are available for consultation and help. They also do better when teachers emphasize their successes and potential rather than focus on their shortcomings (Rutter, 1983a).

## The Importance of Peers

Besides adjusting to teachers and schoolwork, children must learn to live with their schoolmates. During the years from 6 to 10, peers have a particularly strong influence. For one thing, children in school can now evaluate themselves in relation to their classmates (Marsh & Parker, 1984). They can determine their rank on such attributes as intelligence, strength, and various kinds of skills. For another thing, among their peers they can freely express the rebelliousness and hostility they often feel toward the adult world.

Unfortunately for some children, 1 child out of 10 is abused by aggressive peers, and girls are as much at risk as boys are. Two kinds of youngsters tend to be targets of aggression: those who are bullies themselves and those who are generally passive and frightened (Perry, Kusel, & Perry, 1988).

Happily, most children benefit from their relations with other children. Peers can provide models for learning such traits as generosity, empathy, and helpful-

Children often serve as models for their peers, helping them learn new skills and traits such as generosity and helpfulness.

ness. They can teach other academic skills with surprising effectiveness, and sometimes they do a better job than parents of relieving the anxieties and agitation encountered in growing up (Furman, Rahe, & Hartup, 1981).

Early friendships can leave lasting impressions. When presented with pictures of their nursery school playmates, 9- and 10-year-old children said that they did not recognize them. But measurement of subtle changes in skin conductance showed that on some unconscious level they did recognize them (Newcombe & Fox, 1994). Although early memories fade, some events and people are not completely forgotten.

## Becoming Dominant or Submissive

One personality trait that is partially set by the end of the early school years is the tendency to be dominant or submissive in relations with other people. Ten-year-olds who actively make suggestions to the group, try to influence and persuade others, and resist pressure from others often tend to remain dominant in their social relations later in life. Children who are quiet and like to follow the lead of others often remain passive and submissive.

The tendency to be dominant or submissive is, in part, a function of group acceptance. Children who believe that they are admired by the group are likely to develop enhanced self-confidence and to be dominant. Children who do not consider themselves admired by the group are likely to develop feelings of inferiority and to be submissive. Physical attributes play an important part. The attractive girl and the large, strong boy are more likely to be dominant; the small, frail boy and the unattractive girl are likely to be submissive. Other factors are identification with a dominant or submissive parent and the kind of control exercised by the parents. Permissive parents tend to produce children who are more dominant; parents who restrict their children's activities tend to produce more submissive youngsters.

## The Doorway to Adolescence

By age 10, children have made remarkable progress from their helpless days in the crib. Their bodies and nervous systems have grown to near maturity. They are

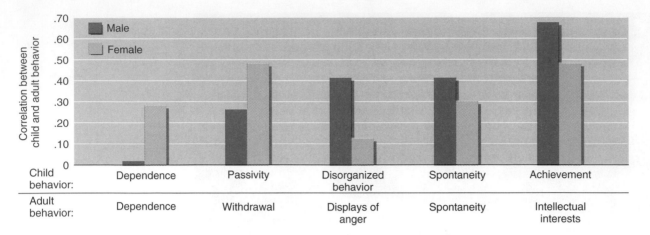

FIGURE 10.17 Some relationships between childhood traits and adult personality. The correlations were obtained by rating the behavior of children aged 6 to 14, then rating the same participants after they had become young adults. For males, note that dependence in childhood shows almost no correlation with dependence as an adult—but striving for achievement shows a high correlation. For females, disorganized behavior in childhood shows little correlation with displays of anger in adulthood—but both passivity and striving for achievement show a fairly high correlation.
*Kagan & Moss, 1962.*

capable of many physical skills. Intellectually, they are well along in the stage of concrete operations and perhaps about to enter the stage of formal operations. Their personalities have blossomed.

As children approach adolescence, the emotional road becomes rockier. A study of children ranging in age from 9 to 15 found that as children grow older they report fewer occasions of feeling on top of the world and more instances of feeling mildly negative (Larsen & Lampman-Petraitis, 1989). Cultural beliefs, values and traditions, and associated childrearing and socialization practices shape the kinds of problems youngsters experience. One comparison of 11- to 15-year-olds from Kenya, Thailand, and the United States (both white and black) found strong differences in the youngsters' behavioral and emotional problems from one cultural context to another (Weisz, Sigman, Weiss, & Mosk, 1993). U.S. adolescents were more likely to display problems like disobedience and cruelty, which are often due to insufficient parental control. Kenyan adolescents, in comparison, displayed more fear and guilt, problems often due to too much control by parents.

In some ways, the 10-year-old child offers a reasonably accurate preview of the future adult. The trend of physical development and the pattern of mental processes have been established. Personality traits have emerged and may persist through adolescence and into adulthood, as indicated by the correlations shown in Figure 10.17. But note that the correlations are by no means perfect; indeed, some are very low. The child's personality is still subject to change—for development, though it proceeds rapidly and dramatically through the first 10 years, does not end at that point. The experiences of adolescence and adulthood may move development into entirely new channels.

**Test Yourself**

**(m)** How would you describe a child who actively makes suggestions to a group, tries to influence and persuade others, and resists pressures from peers?

(The answer is on page 404.)

**FOCUS QUESTIONS**

• What are the most common developmental disorders?

• Why are children with ADHD at a disadvantage relative to other children?

# DEVELOPMENTAL DISORDERS

Although the majority of children experience little psychological distress in their early years, there are some who suffer from certain disorders that are usually first diagnosed in infancy, childhood, or adolescence. Prominent among these are mental retardation, learning disorders (which some refer to as learning disabilities), and attention-deficit/hyperactivity disorder.

## Mental Retardation

Children suffering from mental retardation have significantly subaverage intellectual functioning, with IQs of approximately 70 or below, accompanied by significant limitations in adaptive functioning in such areas as communication, self-care, home living, social and interpersonal skills, work, health, and safety. *Adaptive functioning* refers to how effectively individuals cope with common life demands and how well they meet the standards of personal independence expected of people in their age group. Usually, it is deficits in adaptive functioning, rather than low IQ per se, that give rise to a diagnosis of mental retardation. Finally, mental retardation must arise during the developmental period—that is, before age 18. It is estimated that approximately 1% of the U.S. population suffers from this disorder (American Psychiatric Association [APA], 2000).

The American Psychiatric Association distinguishes among four levels of mental retardation: mild, moderate, severe, and profound. Mildly retarded individuals account for 85% of all people with this disorder (APA, 2000). They have IQs ranging from 50–55 to approximately 70 and are considered "educable." They typically develop social and communication skills during the preschool years and are not distinguishable from normal children until a later age, when it becomes clear that they are limited in their ability to acquire academic skills. As adults, they can develop additional social and vocational skills, but they may need supervision, guidance, and assistance.

Moderately retarded individuals, about 10% of the total (APA, 2000), have IQs ranging from 35 to 55. They, too, acquire communication skills in early childhood, but academically they are unlikely to progress beyond the second-grade level. They can benefit from vocational training and, with moderate supervision, attend to their personal care. As adults, they can perform unskilled or semiskilled work under supervision in sheltered workshops or in the general workforce.

Severely and profoundly retarded individuals have minimal intelligence and are seriously limited in their adaptive functioning. Most are cared for by their families or in group homes.

## Learning Disorders

Approximately 5% of students in public schools in the United States are identified as having a learning disorder (APA, 2000). These disorders, which include reading disorder, mathematics disorder, and disorder of written expression, are diagnosed when the individual's achievement on standardized tests is substantially below that expected for his or her age, schooling, and level of intelligence. Perhaps more serious than the low academic performance of these children is the demoralization, low self-esteem, and lack of social skills that may accompany the learning disorder. Children with learning disorders drop out of school at far higher rates than other children, and as adults they may have significant difficulties in employment or social adjustment.

## Attention-Deficit/Hyperactivity Disorder

The central feature of attention-deficit/hyperactivity disorder (ADHD) is a persistent pattern of inattention and/or hyperactivity and impulsivity that is more severe than is typical of individuals at a comparable level of development. It is possible

## → A MATTER OF DEBATE ←

# Is Ritalin Overprescribed?

Children with attention-deficit/hyperactivity disorder (ADHD) are certainly hard to handle. Frequently described as "bouncing off the walls," they are in constant motion. Impulsive and inattentive, they present a challenge to their parents and teachers. For adults who must deal with such children, stimulant drugs like Ritalin can make a significant difference. Although one might expect a stimulant to make the symptoms of ADHD even worse, it actually has the opposite effect: It helps the child calm down and pay attention. For some, the medication makes it possible to sit still long enough to learn. "It's made differences that are monumental in the lives of these kids and their parents," notes Howard Abikoff, director of research at the Child Study Center of New York University (quoted in Zernicke & Petersen, 2001).

In recent years, however, there has been widespread concern that Ritalin and similar stimulants are overprescribed. Prescriptions for these drugs increased from about 13 million in 1995 to almost 20 million in 2000. Some observers feel that excessive reliance on medication is driving parents away from traditional forms of discipline and from alternative forms of treatment such as behavioral therapy and family counseling. Others point out that the diagnosis of ADHD is based on a set of subjective judgments of a child's inattention, distractibility, and impulsivity, making it likely that some evaluators diagnose the disorder in children who don't actually have it. In fact, some critics believe that what used to be viewed as normal childhood activity has increasingly come to be considered abnormal. They accuse psychiatric organizations and drug companies of "manufacturing a disease" by promoting the diagnosis of ADHD and the use of Ritalin to treat it.

To make matters worse, some public schools now inform the parents of hard-to-handle children that they will not allow the children to attend conventional classes unless they are medicated, based on "diagnoses" by teachers. This is especially likely when children first enter school and do not behave appropriately in the classroom.

Some researchers point out that there are significant differences among communities in the extent to which stimulants are prescribed for the treatment of ADHD, and while there may be places where the drugs are overprescribed, there are undoubtedly others where they are underprescribed. Reports of overdiagnosis and overprescribing thus do not describe a general phenomenon but are specific to particular communities. Taken out of context, such reports may mask the problem of unrecognized and untreated children with ADHD in some parts of the country and may discourage some parents from seeking treatment (Jensen, 2000).

It thus appears that the most important step that could be taken to alleviate concerns about overuse of Ritalin is to ensure that great care is taken in diagnosing the disorder in the first place. In addition, some experts believe that more consideration should be given to alternative forms of treatment before resorting to medication.

To research this topic further, go online with InfoTrac and use your own term or the following suggestions:
- attention-deficit/hyperactivity disorder
- Ritalin
- stimulants and children

to have attention deficit without hyperactivity, and vice versa, but most often the two occur together. Children with this disorder may fail to pay attention to details or may make careless mistakes in schoolwork or other tasks. They often have difficulty sustaining attention in tasks or play activities and find it hard to persist with tasks until completion. They may begin a task, move on to another, and then turn to yet another before completing any one task, and they often fail to complete schoolwork, chores, or other duties. They find tasks that require sustained mental effort unpleasant and seek to avoid such tasks. They are easily distracted, forgetful, and inattentive. As adults, they will have difficulties in relationships as well as on the job.

Children with ADHD often fidget and squirm or engage in excessive running or climbing. They have difficulty engaging in quiet activities and may talk incessantly. They may also be impatient—making comments out of turn, failing to listen to directions, interrupting others excessively, grabbing objects from others, and clowning around, behaviors that may cause difficulties in social, academic, or occupational settings. It is estimated that about 3% to 7% of school-age children suffer from ADHD (APA, 2000).

Clearly, children with ADHD are at a significant disadvantage. They may do poorly in school, at least until the disorder is diagnosed and treated. They may have trouble getting along with other children, and as adults they may experience difficulties on the job. It therefore is not surprising that the need for proper diagnosis and treatment of the disorder has taken on greater urgency in an increasingly competitive society. However, the primary means of treatment, a stimulant known as Ritalin, is a subject of considerable controversy, as can be seen in A Matter of Debate on page 402.

# Chapter 10 Summary

## Life's Beginnings: From Conception to Birth

1. Developmental psychology studies children's physical, mental, and emotional development.
2. The mechanisms of human heredity are the 23 pairs of *chromosomes* that are found in the fertilized egg cell and repeated, through the process of division, in every cell of the body that grows from the egg—except for sperm and ova, which contain half of each pair.
3. An individual's sex is determined by the *X* and *Y* *chromosomes*. An X-X pairing in the fertilized egg cell creates a female. An X-Y pairing creates a male.
4. Each chromosome is made up of a large number of *genes*, which direct the growth of cells into parts of the body, account for the individual differences we inherit, and maintain daily functioning.
5. The development of a child can be affected dramatically by the quality of the environment in the womb.
6. Over approximately 280 days of prenatal development, the developing baby undergoes a remarkable series of changes. During the first 8 weeks, an infant increases nearly 2,000,000% in size. As early as 7 weeks, the nervous system, brain, and parts of the body can be discerned. By 20 weeks, the child is sensitive to touch, pain, and changes in temperature.
7. The ease or difficulty with which a baby is born, how quickly the baby begins to breathe, and the length of the pregnancy can affect the baby's well-being. *Anoxia*, or loss of oxygen supply to the nerve cells, may result in motor paralysis.

## Newborn Infants: Similarities and Differences

8. All babies respond to stimuli with a wide range of inborn reflex behaviors that allow them to escape pain, avoid harsh stimuli, and seek food. For example, if the side of the mouth is touched, they display the *rooting reflex*.

9. Studies have shown wide individual differences among infants in how rapidly they display sensory adaptation and quit responding, as well as in degree of irritability and vulnerability to stress.
10. Most newborns fall into three categories of *temperament*: easy, slow-to-warm-up, and difficult.
11. Traits displayed in infancy endure for varying periods of time. Most early traits are altered by childhood environment, although one trait that appears to be relatively persistent is timidity.
12. Human infants are extremely impressionable. An unfavorable environment may produce drastic and sometimes long-lasting abnormalities. But infants are also resilient and malleable—capable of changing when circumstances change.

## The Early Development of Body and Mind

13. Physical development, including the acquisition of such skills as walking and talking, depends on the process of *maturation*, in interaction with practice.
14. Factors contributing to intellectual development include improvement in the process of perception and growing skill in understanding and using language.
15. Piaget concluded that intellectual growth is basically an increased ability to adapt to new situations. The key processes in development, he found, are *assimilation* (incorporating a new event into one's existing cognitive view of the world) and *accommodation* (changing one's cognitive view and behavior when new information dictates such a change).
16. A key word in Piaget's theory is *operation*, which refers to a dynamic mental rule for manipulating objects or ideas into new forms.
17. Piaget charted children's intellectual development through four stages: (a) the *sensorimotor stage* (birth to 2 years), in which children know the world only through their sensory impressions and the results of their motor (or muscular) movements; (b) the *preoperational stage* (age 2 through about age 6), in which they have acquired language and can manip-

ulate symbols but do not yet grasp the dynamic rules of operation; (c) the *stage of concrete operations* (age 6 to about age 12), when they can manipulate ideas mentally, translate them into concrete terms, and understand *conservation;* and (d) the *stage of formal operations* (beginning at about age 12), when they begin to apply operational rules and logical reasoning to abstract ideas and possibilities.

## Personality Development: Birth to 18 Months

18. Personality development from birth to 18 months is characterized by *attachment* to the mother or other caretakers. This period is marked by the appearance of *separation anxiety* and *stranger anxiety* at about 8 months of age.
19. The effects of day-care programs on children depend on the quality of the program. If the program is understaffed, provides little stimulation, and restricts the child's explorations, development can be affected adversely.

## Learning Society's Rules: 18 Months Through 3 Years

20. The second important period in personality development, roughly from 18 months through the third year, is dominated by a child's first important experiences with the demands of society.
21. Children in the second year develop inner standards and desire to live up to them. In learning to meet social demands, rewards and punishment play a part in influencing behavior. However, physical punishment has the potential to become abusive and cause lasting harm.

## Venturing into the World: Ages 4 and 5

22. The preschool years, ages 4 and 5, are characterized by identification with the parents, the first notions of *sex typing* and conduct appropriate to males and females, and the first feelings of guilt and conscience.
23. The effects of television can be positive or negative. TV can be a valuable educational tool, but there is considerable evidence that portrayals of violence on TV tend to stimulate aggressive behavior.
24. Divorce or the death of a parent is especially stressful during the preschool years. Some children of divorced parents experience high levels of anger, fear, and depression.

## Expanding Social Influences: Ages 6 to 10

25. From age 6 to age 10, children come under the strong influence of their peers. Peers provide evaluation, a social role, and an opportunity for rebellion against the adult world. During this period children acquire a tendency to be dominant or submissive. They also develop strong inner standards that call for being valued by parents, teachers, and peers; mastering physical and mental skills; and achieving harmony between thoughts and behavior.
26. By age 10, a child offers a reasonably accurate preview of the future adult.

## Developmental Disorders

27. A small percentage of children suffer various kinds of developmental disorders, of which the most common are mental retardation, learning disorders, and attention-deficit/hyperactivity disorder.

## Chapter 10 Test Yourself Answers

(a) There are 46 chromosomes in a fertilized cell.
(b) They may suffer from fetal alcohol syndrome.
(c) The term is *temperament.*
(d) The description is of a slow-to-warm-up infant.
(e) The term is *maturation.*
(f) The two key processes described by Piaget are assimilation and accommodation.
(g) Autobiographical memories usually don't begin until about age $3\frac{1}{2}$ to 4.
(h) This process is called attachment.
(i) Separation anxiety usually appears at about 7 months.
(j) A moral sense develops by about the age of 2 years.
(k) Corporal punishment can lead to disobedience, aggression, resentment, apathy, depression, obsessiveness, and paranoia.
(l) Joey has identified with his father.
(m) This child is dominant in social relations.

# Chapter 10  Human Development: Conception Through Childhood

## Key Terms

accommodation (p. 382)
anoxia (p. 373)
assimilation (p. 382)
attachment (p. 386)
chromosomes (p. 372)
conservation (p. 384)
genes (p. 372)
maturation (p. 379)
operations (p. 382)
preoperational stage (p. 383)
rooting reflex (p. 375)
sensorimotor stage (p. 383)

separation anxiety (p. 389)
sex typing (p. 394)
stage of concrete operations (p. 384)
stage of formal operations (p. 385)
stranger anxiety (p. 389)
surrogate mother (p. 386)
temperament (p. 376)
X chromosome (p. 372)
Y chromosome (p. 372)

*The key terms above can be used as search terms in InfoTrac, a database of readings, which can be found at http://infotrac-thomsonlearning.com.*

## Active Learning Review

### Life's Beginnings: From Conception to Birth

1. *Conception* is the instant at which a sperm and egg unite to form a new individual. The child's heredity is determined at the moment of _____.
   **conception**

2. The characteristics of the parents passed on to the child through _____ are carried in 46 *chromosomes* arranged in 23 pairs. Each chromosome is composed of hundreds of smaller *genes*.
   **heredity**

3. Each body cell contains 46 _____, 23 from each parent.
   **chromosomes**

4. Each cell's chromosomes, in turn, contain from 30,000 to 120,000 _____, which—alone or, more likely, in combination—influence a particular phase of development and specific physical and behavioral characteristics.
   **genes**

5. The sex of the new individual is determined by one particular pair of _____. One member of the pair is an X chromosome; the other is either an *X chromosome* or a *Y chromosome*.
   **chromosomes**

6. If the pair of sex chromosomes is X-X, the child will be a _____. If the pair is X-Y, the child will be a _____.
   **female**
   **male**

7. The mother, being a female, has only X _____ to give to her child. The father, being a male, has either an _____ or a _____ chromosome to give to his child.
   **chromosomes**
   **X, Y**

8. Therefore, the sex of the child will depend on whether the child receives an X or a Y chromosome from the _____.
   **father**

9. A child's heredity is determined at _____, and the influence of environmental factors also starts at this time.
   **conception**

10. Whether the mother eats properly, smokes, drinks coffee or alcohol, uses drugs, or is stressed during pregnancy contributes to the prenatal _____ of the fetus, which can influence the child's physical and behavioral characteristics. At birth, a condition called *anoxia,* a shortage of oxygen to the brain, may lead to later problems.
    **environment**

11. Some types of physical paralysis, such as that associated with cerebral palsy, may be caused by _____, insufficient oxygen to certain parts of the brain, at birth.
    **anoxia**

12. Whether prenatal factors such as substance use or anoxia produce long-term effects in the child may depend on whether the child grows up in a stimulating, supportive _____ after birth.
    **environment**

inborn

inborn

rooting

rooting

temperament

temperament

arousal

coping

copes, arousal

irritability

temperament

easy

easy

slow to warm up

slow to

warm up

difficult

easy, slow to

warm up, difficult

temperament

irritable, change

406

## Newborn Infants: Similarities and Differences

13. Newborn infants display many inborn abilities and behaviors. The ability to follow a moving object with the eyes and the tendency to pay more attention than chimpanzees do to the human face and voice are _____ tendencies.

14. Newborns also have reflexes that are _____. For example, the tendency of a newborn to turn toward and suck on a finger that strokes the corner of the mouth is called the _____ reflex.

15. While babies learn to improve the efficiency of their sucking with practice, the _____ reflex helps get them started.

16. Newborn infants differ a great deal in behavior. For example, they differ with respect to *temperament,* or their general pattern of responding to people and events. A baby's general activity, mood, adaptability, and irritability define its _____.

17. Two fundamental qualities of _____ are how easily the infant becomes aroused by stimulation and, once aroused, how the infant copes with the arousal.

18. Motor activity, babbling, and crying are signs of _____. Turning away from the arousing stimulus, becoming extremely distressed, and approaching an exciting stimulus are methods of regulating or _____ with arousal.

19. How an infant _____ with _____ contributes to the temperamental characteristic of irritability. That some infants whine or cry at the slightest provocation while others rarely do so illustrates differences in _____.

20. Investigators have found that infants can be grouped into three general types based on _____. One type consists of easy infants, who are cheerful, react to stimuli with low to moderate intensity, have regular eating and sleeping habits, and are quick to adapt to new schedules, foods, and people. Approximately 40% of babies are like this, and parents find these children _____ to deal with.

21. Less cheerful than _____ infants are slow-to-warm-up babies, a category that applies to approximately 15% of infants. Their responses are low in intensity, they seem slightly sad and tense, they may withdraw from their first exposure to a new stimulus, and their eating and sleeping habits vary. They seem cautious or _____ _____ _____ _____.

22. In addition to the easy infants and those who are _____ _____ _____ _____ are the approximately 10% of infants who are termed difficult. They seem hard to please, they become very irritable and cry at unfamiliar events, they are difficult to soothe, and they have little regularity in eating and sleeping. For their parents, they are _____.

23. Although 35% of babies have mixed characteristics and are difficult to classify, the rest fall into three groups based on: _____, _____ _____ _____ _____, and _____.

24. For some infants, these temperamental characteristics persist into adolescence, while for others they change. For example, about one-third of very shy, fearful, inhibited 2-year-olds become dour, serious, and moderately intense adolescents, and approximately half of the outgoing, sociable, uninhibited 2-year-olds become extraverted adolescents; the remainder do not show such consistency in _____.

25. It should come as some comfort to parents who must cope with difficult or _____ infants that most will grow out of it, or _____ in temperament, during childhood.

## The Early Development of Body and Mind

26. *Maturation* refers to the physical changes that continue the biological growth of the organism from fertilized cell to adult. As infants and children get older,

they become capable of new feats of physical, perceptual, and mental skill that are associated with _____.    **maturation**

27. These biological processes cannot be speeded up to any great extent. Children from all over the world, regardless of childrearing practices, tend to display various skills at about the same ages because of biological _____.    **maturation**

28. Intellectual, as well as physical, development is influenced by _____. Many factors contribute to intellectual development, including improvements in the process of perception and skill in understanding and using language.    **maturation**

29. As children grow older, their attention becomes more selective, they can maintain it longer, they scan the environment more systematically, and they become increasingly efficient in searching the environment for information—all because of improvements in the process of _____.    **perception**

30. The increasing use of words and concepts helps children organize information into categories and facilitates the type of information processing that creates long-lasting memories. These processes reflect the emerging use of _____.    **language**

31. Study of the intellectual development of infants and young children has been dominated by the theories of the Swiss psychologist Jean Piaget. According to _____, mental growth is the result of an increased ability to adapt to new situations.    **Piaget**

32. The theories of _____ emphasized the processes of *assimilation* and *accommodation*.    **Piaget**

33. The process of incorporating a new event into one's existing cognitive view of the world is called _____.    **assimilation**

34. The process of changing one's cognitive view and behavior when new information dictates such a change is called _____.    **accommodation**

35. If a young boy is given a new toy—for example, a magnet—he may try to throw it like a ball or bang it like a hammer. These are behaviors he has practiced with other toys, and he is trying to _____ the new toy into existing behavior patterns.    **assimilate**

36. On the other hand, he may discover the power of the magnet to attract iron and use the magnet to pull other toys toward him, thus _____ his own behavior to fit the unique characteristics of the new object.    **accommodating**

37. _____ believed that there is always a tension between _____ and _____, and the resolution of this tension produces intellectual growth. As growth proceeds, the child learns *operations*.    **Piaget, assimilation accommodation**

38. A mental rule for manipulating objects or ideas into new forms and then back to the original is an _____.    **operation**

39. As children grow older, the sophistication of the _____ of which they are capable increases. According to Piaget, this mental growth occurs in four stages. The first, covering approximately the first 2 years of life, is called the *sensorimotor* _____.    **operations**    **stage**

40. The period during which infants come to know the environment primarily through their own sensory impressions and the discovery of the relationship between their actions toward physical objects in their environment and the consequences of those actions is called the _____ _____.    **sensorimotor stage**

41. Following the _____ stage, from approximately age 2 through age 6, children are in what Piaget calls the *preoperational stage*.    **sensorimotor**

42. During the _____ _____, children have acquired language and can manipulate symbols, but their actions are still dictated largely by the evidence of their senses. They are not capable of forming meaningful categories or thinking according to rules.    **preoperational stage**

43. After the _____ stage, beginning at approximately 6 to 8 years of age, children enter the *stage of concrete operations*.    **preoperational**

44. Children become capable of mentally manipulating ideas about actual events in the world during the stage of _____ _____.    **concrete operations**

concrete operations

45. During the stage of _____ _____, children acquire an understanding of *conservation* of volume, mass, number, and weight. That is, they understand that these attributes of objects do not change when other attributes are altered.

46. A child who recognizes that the volume of liquid is the same when the liquid is poured from a short, wide beaker into a tall, narrow beaker has achieved an awareness of _____ of volume.

conservation

operational rules

47. During the stage of concrete operations, children also learn a variety of _____ _____. For example, if they know that object 1 is heavier than object 2 and object 2 is heavier than object 3, they can conclude that object 1 is heavier than object 3.

concrete operations

48. Following the stage of _____ _____, beginning around the age of 11 or 12, children enter the *stage of formal operations*. The ability to reason logically, not just about actual objects but also about abstract ideas and possibilities, is the hallmark of the stage of _____ _____.

formal operations

49. Children who can assume hypothetical conditions and make correct inferences, thus manipulating their own thoughts as readily as they once manipulated colored blocks, are in the stage of _____ _____.

formal operations
Piaget
sensorimotor
preoperational, concrete
formal operations

50. According to the Swiss psychologist _____, the child's mental development goes through four stages, beginning with the _____ stage. This is followed by the _____ stage and then by the _____ and _____ _____ stages.

## Personality Development: Birth to 18 Months

attachment

51. Personality development, like mental development, seems to occur in stages. A major feature of the first period of personality development is the growing _____ between the infant and the person who constitutes the main source of interaction, comfort, and care.

attachment

52. In the first 2 years of life, the infant's strong tendency to approach particular people, to be receptive to care and consolation from them, and to be least afraid when in their presence are signs of _____.

predictable
available
sensitive

53. Attachment in the infant is promoted by a caregiver who is predictable, available, and sensitive to the infant's signals and needs. A caregiver who behaves in a similar manner from day to day is _____; one who spends a good deal of time with the infant and responds when needed is _____; and one who adjusts responses to fit the infant's changing needs and abilities is _____.

54. The characteristics of the caregiver are more important for attachment than the satisfaction of other basic needs, such as the need for food. This was demonstrated in an experiment in which baby monkeys were given two doll-like *surrogate mothers*, one of which was made of wire with a bottle and nipple to feed the infant monkey and one of which was made of sponge rubber and terry cloth to which the infant could cling. The infants preferred the _____ surrogate over the _____ surrogate, especially when frightened.

cloth
feeding
attachment

55. The desire of most infants to be near their parents is a sign of _____. If a parent leaves the infant, *separation anxiety* may occur.

separation anxiety

56. At around 8 months of age, infants may become upset and cry as soon as a parent leaves them. They are displaying _____ _____.

separation

57. In addition to _____ anxiety, infants of approximately the same age show *stranger anxiety*.

stranger
anxiety

58. If an unfamiliar person suddenly appears, especially one who approaches the infant rapidly, the baby may become upset and cry because of _____ _____.

attachment

59. One of the first events in personality and social development is the formation of _____ between infant and principal caretaker. Later, at approximately

8 months of age, the infant may become upset and cry if the caregiver leaves (thereby exhibiting _____ _____) or if a new person approaches (thereby exhibiting _____ _____).

separation anxiety
stranger anxiety

60. In view of the factors that contribute to attachment, many have wondered whether day care is damaging to infants and toddlers. The answer seems to depend on the quality of care—the extent to which the circumstances are similar to those in good homes with attentive parents. Thus, research seems to indicate that _____-_____ day care is not damaging and may be good for some infants and toddlers.

high-quality

## Learning Society's Rules: 18 Months Through 3 Years

61. In the second phase of personality development, from 18 months through 3 years, children learn to be disciplined members of society by encountering _____ _____ such as toilet training and rules against destroying property.

social demands

62. One aid to parents in imposing discipline is the fact that by 2 years of age most children have learned what they are allowed and not allowed to do in particular situations; in other words, they have acquired their own _____ of behavior.

standards

63. In part, standards of behavior are created by _____ and _____.

rewards, punishments

64. Parents praise, hug, and kiss children for desirable behaviors and scold them for undesirable behaviors. These _____ and _____ contribute to the establishment of the children's own behavioral _____.

rewards, punishments
standards

65. The task for the parent during this period is to construct a balance between encouraging exploration, independence, and learning about the child's own effects on the environment on the one hand and learning and obeying the rules of family and society on the other. Creating this delicate balance between _____ and _____ is the parent's task in the period when children meet their first _____ _____.

rewards, punishments
social demands

## Venturing into the World: Ages 4 and 5

66. Children during this period begin the process of identification with their parents. That is, they see themselves as similar to their parents in many different respects. Behaving like and believing themselves to be similar to their parents constitutes part of the _____ process.

identification

67. One aspect of the process of _____ is that children come to understand that society considers somewhat different behavior appropriate for males and females, and children of each sex learn the appropriate kind of behavior. This training is called _____ _____.

identification

sex typing

68. U.S. children spend more time _____ _____ than in any other single activity except sleeping.

watching television

69. The average child, who watches 2 to 4 hours of television per day, will witness 8,000 murders and 100,000 other acts of violence before leaving elementary school. On the other hand, if children watch educational programs, they will be exposed to educational information and positive social behavior. Depending on what children watch, how much they watch, their temperament and personality, and whether their parents watch with them and encourage positive behaviors, the effects of television on children can be _____ and _____ or _____ and _____.

negative, destructive
positive, beneficial

70. Another factor influencing a child's _____ with parents is divorce. The effects of parental separation are not uniform for all ages, sexes, and individual children, and negative effects seem to be associated with the amount of _____ _____ before and after divorce.

identification

parental conflict

### Expanding Social Influences: Ages 6 to 10

teachers

71. A great deal of children's development from ages 6 to 10 is influenced by the fact that they must conform to the discipline and seek the acceptance of new adults in their lives, especially their _____.

intellectual skills
intellectual mastery

72. Partly as a result of the practices of teachers, children may develop an expectancy for success or for failure, a situation that may have substantial consequences. A child's intellectual future may be influenced by a teacher's emphasis on, expectancy for, and encouragement of _____ _____ and _____ _____.

evaluate
peers
evaluation

73. Children must also learn to live with their peers. For one thing, peers provide a standard of evaluation. Children decide whether they are competent or incompetent, good or bad, excellent or poor on the basis of how they _____ themselves relative to their _____.

peers

74. By providing a standard of _____, peers advance each other's development. Children who remain isolated from peers often have problems in social relations, because _____ provide models and encouragement that may be necessary for development.

dominant
submissive

75. Some children have self-confidence and become accustomed to influencing other children, while others do not. These patterns of being _____ or _____ develop during the school years.

skills
mastery
evaluation
dominant, submissive

76. During the early school years, an important influence on child development is the teacher, who serves to promote intellectual _____ and encourage or discourage motivation for intellectual _____. At the same time, peers provide children with a standard of _____. As a result of interacting with peers, children acquire the trait of being socially _____ or _____.

## Practice Test

____ **1.** The sex of a baby is determined by
  a. the mother.
  b. the father.
  c. both the mother and the father.
  d. a single gene, X.

____ **2.** Which of the following feats can 1- or 2-week-old infants *not* accomplish?
  a. Follow a moving object with their eyes.
  b. Differentiate between the smell of their own mother's milk and that of milk from another mother.
  c. Display a marked preference for the human face and voice.
  d. Remember for a few seconds where an attractive object is hidden.

____ **3.** The rooting reflex occurs when
  a. the corner of a newborn human's mouth is lightly touched.
  b. baby pigs dig for roots and mushrooms.
  c. the heel of a baby is pricked with a pin.
  d. a bright light is suddenly directed in a baby's eyes.

____ **4.** Differences in temperament between babies in their first months of life
  a. reflect the personalities of their parents.
  b. are permanent dispositions that last in one form or another for most of the child's life.
  c. reflect differences in childrearing and infant care practices.
  d. tend to change as the infant gets older.

____ **5.** Infants showing a slightly sad and tense mood and low-intensity responses, especially to new experiences, are said to be temperamentally
  a. easy.
  b. slow to warm up.
  c. difficult.
  d. none of the above

____ **6.** Psychology's "optimistic message to parents" is that
  a. everything will turn out fine.
  b. it is difficult to predict from the way infants behave how they will behave as children and adolescents.
  c. almost all harmful experiences will be overcome in time.
  d. most characteristics are established early, so mistakes parents make later do not matter much.

____ **7.** The most persistent early personality trait seems to be
  a. timidity.
  b. irritability.
  c. activity level.
  d. readiness to smile.

____ **8.** For parents, the most important implication of differences in the temperaments of babies is that
  a. a single style of childrearing may not be the most appropriate for all babies.
  b. genetics plays a large part in personality development.
  c. babies come with different personalities and little can be done to change them.
  d. babies who are extremely irritable are likely to be a problem for many years.

____ **9.** Extremely poor early experiences can
  a. lead to maladjustment later in life.
  b. be counteracted by positive environments later.
  c. both a and b
  d. neither a nor b; the result depends on other factors.

____ **10.** The physical changes that continue the biological growth of the organism throughout life are called
  a. growth trajectories.
  b. maturation.
  c. socialization.
  d. identification.

____ **11.** Which of the following is *not* true of early physical growth?
  a. Newborn babies have all the muscle fibers they will ever possess.
  b. At birth, the skeleton is composed largely of cartilage, which is softer and more pliable than bone.
  c. Some of the fibers of the nervous system develop protective sheaths that make them faster and more efficient conductors of nervous impulses.
  d. The process of maturation can be speeded up to a great extent by exercise and stimulation.

____ **12.** Jason is a quiet and somewhat unresponsive child who tries to avoid new experiences. His parents can probably help him most if they
  a. gently encourage him to try new experiences at his own pace.
  b. treat him like any other child.
  c. create many new experiences for him.
  d. reprimand him for being so timid.

___13. Harlow's experiment with surrogate mothers showed that
   a. attachment in monkeys was not simply a matter of who fed the infant monkey.
   b. infant monkeys would cling to a soft surrogate when hungry.
   c. infant monkeys would cling to either surrogate when scared.
   d. attachment is different in monkeys than in humans.

___14. Placing young children in out-of-home day care typically produces
   a. different outcomes in different children, depending on the nature of the care.
   b. little effect on the children.
   c. better social skills.
   d. improved language performance.

___15. Separation anxiety commonly occurs
   a. in understaffed nurseries and institutions.
   b. in infants who have insecure attachment relationships with their caregivers.
   c. when a stranger rapidly approaches a baby.
   d. at approximately 8 months in most infants.

___16. A magazine warns that children will be permanently retarded unless they receive proper stimulation during their first year. Findings on early experience indicate that this advice is incorrect because
   a. babies under 1 year of age do not know language.
   b. the critical period for learning comes at about 4 or 5 years of age.
   c. mental maturation starts at 18 months of age.
   d. development requires continuing encouragement and support, and changes can occur at most ages under appropriate circumstances.

___17. The similarity in attitude and behavior between a child and his or her same-sex parent is most closely associated with the process of
   a. socialization.
   b. identification.
   c. stranger anxiety.
   d. maturation.

___18. Peers
   a. often teach a child academic skills.
   b. can relieve anxieties and agitation in children better than parents can.
   c. abuse about 1 in 10 of their classmates.
   d. all of the above

___19. A child $2\frac{1}{2}$ years old who becomes upset because a button is missing or a toy is cracked may be exhibiting
   a. excessive anxiety.
   b. inner standards.
   c. separation anxiety.
   d. a reaction to stimulus discrepancy.

___20. Loss of a parent through death or divorce
   a. is more serious for the child if it occurs during middle childhood than if it occurs at other ages.
   b. is made worse for the child if the remaining parent remarries.
   c. typically leads to poorer school performance and delinquency in children.
   d. may or may not lead to problems in children, depending on the quality of the relationship between the child and the remaining parent.

# Exercises

1. Boys and girls are reared differently, even by parents who profess to believe in sexual equality. For example, we teach boys to be physically and socially aggressive, to achieve, to get ahead, and to be independent. We teach girls to get along with other people, to value friendship, and to be a good person.

   Ask several students of both sexes to participate in this exercise. Tell them that all they need to do is to write a short story—one paragraph—using the following topic sentence:

   Miguel/Latisha has just been named first in his/her medical school class at a convocation and reception for the class.

   Use Miguel for male participants and Latisha for female participants. (If you have time, also ask some male participants to respond to Latisha and some female participants to respond to Miguel.) Examine the stories written by male and female respondents separately.

   Consider these questions:

   a. How many positive and how many negative or concerned responses did you get? Were these rates different for males and females?

   b. What kinds of reasons for positive and negative feelings were mentioned by males and females? Were there any differences?

   c. Was there any hint that one sex was more concerned about losing friendships or disturbing social relationships as a result of being first in the class whereas the other sex tended to see the advantage to career and future in this situation?

   d. If you had males and females respond to both Miguel and Latisha, did they differ in how they viewed a successful male versus a successful female?

   e. Speculate on how the male-female differences you observed might have developed. You might ask some of your participants why they answered as they did and what experiences led them to believe as they do.

2. Based on what you have learned in this chapter, write a brief paragraph describing how you suspect several of your own prominent personality characteristics developed. Start by identifying three or four traits, both good and bad. Then speculate on how they were created by considering such possible factors as heredity; parental practices and attitudes; the roles of siblings, peers, and teachers; and particular experiences. In view of this exercise and the material in this chapter, what advice would you give to new parents about rearing their children? What should they do and not do? Write a brief statement as if you were giving advice to parents in a newspaper or magazine.

❋ *For quizzing, activities, exercises, and web links, check out the book-specific website at http://www.psychology.wadsworth. com/kagan9e.*

# Human Development: Adolescence, Adulthood, and Death

© Zack Gold/CORBIS

At 30 a man should know himself like the palm of his hand, know the exact number of his defects and qualities, know how far he can go, fore-tell his failures—be what he is. And above all accept these things.

—Albert Camus, *Carnets*

Do most 30-year-olds fit this description? Adult development, unlike child development, has few clear biological markers. Once adolescents have passed through the physical changes of puberty, most of the influences on a person are the result of experience, not of biology. Bernice Neugarten, a pioneer in the field of human development, has pointed out that as we enter adulthood, chronological age is an increasingly unreliable indicator of what people will be like at various ages. Newborns or 6-year-olds show less psychological variation than 35- or 60-year-olds in a particular culture.

Although the words *adolescent* and *adult* are frequently used, they are difficult to define. In many nonindustrial cultures, there is a clear transition from childhood to full membership in the community, which is often marked by a prescribed ceremony called a puberty rite. Individuals are then treated as adults; they marry, start a family, and set about establishing their role in their community. In industrialized societies, the situation is much more complex. Most young people remain in school until they are at least 16 years old. Over half go on to college or trade school, where they remain until they are 21, 22, or even older. During this period or shortly afterward, they make decisions about a job and a career. Many postpone marriage and children until they are in their 30s, and a few forgo these milestones altogether.

Studies of adulthood have not always been of interest to developmental psychologists. But today it is understood that development does not end when we leave adolescence behind. At age 18, people in developed nations have lived less than a quarter of today's average lifetime. And regardless of our culture, we will face new crises, sometimes solving them and sometimes not, and we may still change remarkably in many respects. As adults, we take on new roles, address new tasks and challenges, enter and leave new relationships. As we do so, we react, learn, and change—sometimes in surprising ways—channeling development into entirely new patterns even in the later years of life. For psychologists interested in **life span development,** it is essential to study the various physical, psychological, and social changes that accompany not only the early years but also the adult years—the longest period of human life.

**Life span development**
The physical, psychological, and social changes that occur throughout life.

# ADOLESCENCE: A TIME OF TRANSITION

Some parents approach their child's adolescence with anxiety; they fear that adolescence is a synonym for rebellion and conflict. As shown in Table 11.1, a number of dramatic changes do mark the adolescent's passage from childhood to adulthood.

**FOCUS QUESTIONS**
- How does adolescents' physical development influence their behavior?
- What are the stages of moral development identified by Kohlberg?
- What problems do adolescents face in attempting to achieve independence?

Psychologists use various markers to distinguish adolescence from childhood on the one hand and adulthood on the other.

**TABLE 11.1**
**The Adolescent Years**

| Area of Development | When Adolescence Begins | When Adolescence Ends |
|---|---|---|
| Biological | Beginning of growth spurt | End of growth spurt |
| Emotional | Beginning of detachment from parents | Reaching separate sense of identity |
| Interpersonal | Shifting interest from parents to peers | Development of intimate relationships |
| Cognitive | Start of more advanced reasoning abilities | Full development of advanced reasoning |
| Educational | Entry into junior high school | Completion of schooling |
| Moral | Becoming tuned in to the expectations of others | Making some judgments according to dictates of personal conscience |

*Steinberg, 1985.*

© Peter Menzel/Stock Boston

Adolescence is characterized by new reasoning abilities and increased freedom, but sometimes by new conflicts as well.

**Primary sex characteristics** The developed reproductive organs, such as the ovaries in females and the testes in males.

**Secondary sex characteristics** Such characteristics as enlarged breasts and hips in females and deep voice and facial hair in males.

Keep in mind, however, that there is no single, strict definition of adolescence. Moreover, although adolescence is regarded as spanning roughly the period between ages 10 and 20, there are wide variations.

Adolescence has traditionally been viewed as a difficult period. In the 1960s, for example, many people, looking back on their lives when they had reached the age of 30, felt that their adolescent years were the time when they were most confused and their morale was at its lowest ebb. They mentioned such difficulties as striving for acceptance from peers of their own and the opposite sex, feeling anxiety due to parental pressure for academic achievement, and trying to establish their independence while remaining financially dependent on their parents (Macfarlane, 1964).

Today, psychologists are reaching different conclusions. A number of studies have shown that many families with adolescents experience less serious conflict than earlier generations did and there is less of a "generation gap." If this difference is real, it may be because today's parents give their adolescents considerably more freedom and society is more accepting of very different lifestyles. As a result, there may be less conflict over failing to meet family and community standards of behavior.

## Physical Changes in Adolescence

Puberty is marked by the start of menstruation and ovulation in the female and the production of viable sperm in the male. This typically occurs sometime between the ages of about 11 and 16—on average, a couple of years earlier in girls than in boys. The onset of puberty is preceded by a spurt in physical growth. A girl may suddenly grow 3 to 5 inches in height in a single year, a boy 4 to 6 inches. Along with growth comes a change in physical proportions and strength. As illustrated in Figure 11.1, the girl begins to look like a woman, the boy like a man. The **primary sex characteristics,** or reproductive organs, develop significantly, and the **secondary sex characteristics**—enlarged breasts and hips in girls, a deeper voice and facial hair in boys—appear soon afterward. All these changes are set in

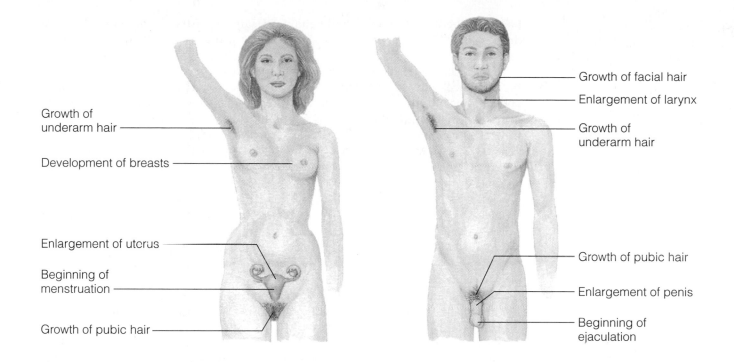

Growth of
underarm hair

Development of breasts

Enlargement of uterus

Beginning of
menstruation

Growth of pubic hair

Growth of facial hair

Enlargement of larynx

Growth of
underarm hair

Growth of pubic hair

Enlargement of penis

Beginning of
ejaculation

motion by increased activity of the pituitary gland, which stimulates the sex glands (ovaries in girls and testes in boys) to produce large quantities of the hormones estrogen (in the female) and testosterone (in the male).

The first menstrual period, known as **menarche,** is the benchmark of physical maturity in girls, although fertility often does not arrive until after the first few cycles—perhaps as much as a year or more later. The average age of menarche in the United States is 11. In the past, many girls entered adolescence with ambivalent feelings—a mixture of excitement and fear. More recently, however, studies have found that the attitudes of adolescent girls toward menarche are less negative than was the case a couple of decades ago. The change is probably due to a more open and less defensive presentation of information about menstruation in homes, schools, and the media (Grief & Ulman, 1982), a trend that continues today. It is noteworthy that girls with negative feelings about their first menstruation are more likely to be growing up in a family characterized by lack of openness in discussing physical and sexual issues (Brooks-Gunn, 1987). When asked how the presentation of information about menarche could be improved, a sample of ninth-grade girls indicated that the focus should be on the personal and subjective aspects of the experience rather than on the biology of menstruation (Koff & Rierdan, 1995).

The timing of puberty is important psychologically. For boys, reaching puberty early seems to be advantageous in both social and emotional terms. Although later maturation provides added time for both sexes to prepare emotionally for changes in social status, it also means a continued childlike appearance and short stature. This tends to be a particular problem for boys. If they are slow to show the growth spurt, they continue to be treated as "little boys" and are not accepted by peers, while their bigger, stronger, and more mature classmates are gaining new respect.

However, along with early sexual maturation comes early sexual activity. Boys who reveal secondary sex characteristics, such as facial hair, deeper voice, and enlarged genitals, earlier than their peers are more likely to become sexually active earlier. Contrary to expectations, increased levels of the male hormone testosterone are not responsible for the greater sexual activity. Instead, the boys' feelings of being sexually mature because of their physical development are the main

**FIGURE 11.1 The onset of puberty. With the beginning of puberty, primary and secondary sex characteristics begin to appear.**

**Menarche**
**The first menstrual period.**

basis for the initiation of sexual behavior (Halpern, Udry, Campbell, & Suchindran, 1993). Moreover, in many cultures, early sexual activity is a status symbol for boys.

For girls, early puberty tends either to have little effect or to be a disadvantage, for it reduces the time 12- and 13-year-olds have to prepare for their new status and responsibilities (Brooks-Gunn, 1987). Early-maturing girls have been found to have the highest rate of depressive symptoms during adolescence (Ge, Conger, & Elder, 2001) and to be more likely than later-maturing girls to engage in delinquency (Caspi, Lynam, Moffitt, & Silva, 1993). For girls, therefore, reaching puberty at the same time as peers and classmates would appear to permit the smoothest transition (Powers, Hauser, & Kilner, 1989).

A number of factors can affect the timing of menarche and its meaning. For example, athletic girls as a group tend to mature late and thus are likely to view themselves as being on schedule rather than behind their peers (Brooks-Gunn, 1987). There is evidence, too, that aspiring dancers are often more successful in that field if they mature late (Petersen, 1987). Differences in age at puberty exist as well among girls from various countries and different subcultures within a country. For example, Czechoslovakian girls mature later than U.S. girls. In the United States, black girls tend to reach menarche earlier than white girls (Powers, Hauser, & Kilner, 1989).

### Distorted Body Image: The Path to Eating Disorders

Because adolescence brings dramatic changes in physical appearance, it is a time when self-image is highly dependent on body image. Adolescents who see themselves as deviating from the "ideal" physique may lose self-esteem. In many cultures, being overweight can be particularly devastating to teenagers who are concerned about how they appear to others (Ricciardelli & McCabe, 2001; Steinberg, 1985). However, this concern appears to be more prevalent in Western than in Eastern cultures (Lake, Staiger, & Glowinski, 2000).

The concern with weight can lead to the development of a variety of eating problems, including compulsions about food. It is also regarded as one of the factors that lead some adolescents—particularly white adolescent and young adult women—to take abnormal, and ultimately life-threatening, steps to remain thin (Attie & Brooks-Gunn, 1989; Wildes & Emery, 2001). The result in some cases is a disorder known as **anorexia nervosa,** in which the already emaciated individual continues to diet and exercise excessively, to the point of potentially fatal weight loss. Even more common is **bulimia nervosa,** a disorder in which the person engages in eating binges and then purges or takes laxatives. Although a person suffering from bulimia does not usually experience significant weight loss, the damaging effects of regurgitating stomach acids and emptying the gastrointestinal tract by taking laxatives can be severe.

Both anorexia and bulimia undoubtedly have complex causes. For example, the disorders may arise out of a biological predisposition such as a hormone imbalance or from chronic anxiety and depression (Graber & Brooks-Gunn, 2001; Keel, Leon, & Fulkerson, 2001). (See the discussion of eating disorders in Chapter 13.)

An adolescent girl whose self-image is fragile can be especially sensitive to comments about her body. One study found that girls with eating disorders were much more likely than girls of normal weight to have mothers who urged them to lose weight (Pike & Rodin, 1991). These mothers were also more likely to have eating disorders themselves.

The issue of body image in boys has not received as much research attention as that of body image in girls. The relatively few studies that have been conducted have found that although boys generally display less concern overall than girls, many boys report dissatisfaction with their bodies. Whereas girls typically want to be thinner, boys frequently want to be bigger. Small size in relation to peers is often associated with reduced self-esteem (Cohane & Pope, 2001). In recent years, physicians and school authorities have expressed concern over the increasing use

**Anorexia nervosa**
An eating disorder in which an already emaciated person continues to diet and exercise excessively to the point of potentially fatal weight loss.

**Bulimia nervosa**
An eating disorder in which a person engages in eating binges and then purges or takes laxatives but does not experience significant weight loss.

of steroids by boys as young as age 10 seeking to "bulk up." These substances, many of which are illegal, can lead to side effects that interfere with normal physical development (Labre, 2002).

All adolescents can be emotionally hurt when teased or criticized about their appearance by parents, older siblings, teachers, coaches, or other significant people in their lives. Those who were teased between the ages of 8 and 16 are most likely to be dissatisfied with their bodies when they grow up, revealing low self-esteem, depression, and a distorted body image—all factors linked to the development of eating disorders (Thompson, Penner, & Altabe, 1990).

## The Adjustment to Junior High School

The physical changes that accompany the end of childhood are not the only ones that affect the self-concept of adolescents. So, too, do changes in the social environment—notably the junior high school experience, which imposes a host of challenges that can affect self-esteem. For one thing, students who attend junior high school must learn to deal with a more bureaucratic educational institution. They must adapt to a changing cadre of teachers rather than a single teacher who was often perceived as a substitute parent. Moreover, they must respond to heavier academic demands that, if not met, will change other people's views of their potential (Eccles, Midgley, Wigfield, & Reuman, 1993).

During the transition to junior high school, adolescents are especially vulnerable to troubles at home. Junior high school students whose parents lose their jobs or have their employment status threatened tend to become more disruptive at school (Flanagan, 1993).

The transition to junior high seems to take an especially high toll on the self-esteem of adolescent girls. As boys grow, their feelings of self-esteem tend to rise, while the opposite tends to be true for girls (Block & Robins, 1993). And the characteristics that lead to high self-esteem differ for boys and girls. As Table 11.2

**TABLE 11.2**
**Self-Esteem among Boys and Girls**

| Observer Judgments of Personality at Age 14 | Correlation with Increase in Self-Esteem |
|---|---|
| Females | |
| Is moral | .47 |
| Responds to and appreciates humor | .46 |
| Is protective of those close to her | .42 |
| Is turned to or sought out for advice and reassurance | .38 |
| Is cheerful, happy | .37 |
| Has a clearcut personality; is relatively easy to understand | .36 |
| Behaves in a sympathetic and considerate manner | .36 |
| Initiates humor; makes spontaneous funny remarks | .34 |
| Is giving, generous toward others | .34 |
| Males | |
| Is socially at ease; has social poise and presence | .36 |
| Feels satisfied with self; is unaware of self-concern | .34 |
| Regards self as physically attractive | .33 |
| Is calm, relaxed in manner | .30 |
| Behaves in masculine style | .27 |

*Block & Robins, 1993.*

Once they reach junior high school, boys tend to have higher self-esteem than girls do, and the qualities associated with high self-esteem differ for males and females.

shows, the girls whose self-esteem rose as they approached adulthood were, at age 14, most likely to be regarded as being moral, appreciating humor, and being nurturant and cheerful. For boys, on the other hand, the important predictors of later high self-esteem were social poise, self-satisfaction, belief in one's attractiveness, and behaving in a masculine way.

Problems of self-esteem may affect girls' performance in school. Girls show the same aptitudes for math as boys until about the seventh grade, when many girls begin to do less well in math than boys. At about the same time, boys begin to catch up with girls in verbal skills.

## Developing a Set of Morals

An individual's moral standards usually undergo important and often lasting change during adolescence. Specifically, these standards become a more permanent part of an adolescent's philosophy. This is especially likely if the adolescent is entering the stage of formal operations, which motivates the development of a set of consistent philosophical premises.

The development of moral judgments was studied extensively by Lawrence Kohlberg, who presented boys and young men with a number of hypothetical situations involving moral questions such as the following: If a man's wife is dying for lack of an expensive drug that he cannot afford, should he steal the drug? If a patient who is fatally ill and in great pain begs for a mercy killing, should the physician agree? By analyzing the children's answers and, particularly, the reasoning they used to reach their answers, Kohlberg determined that moral judgments develop through a series of six stages, as shown in Table 11.3. People in the two stages of the *preconventional level* base their ideas of right and wrong largely on self-interest. They are concerned chiefly with avoiding punishment and gaining rewards. Next, in the two stages of the *conventional level*, they become concerned with the approval of other people. Finally, in the two stages of the *postconventional level*, they become concerned with abstract moral values and the dictates of their own consciences. Thus, the considerations the participants cited for determining what is good or bad ranged from concrete external consequences at the lower levels to abstract internalized principles at the higher levels.

Among 7-year-olds, almost all moral judgments are made at the preconventional level. By age 16, only a few are made at this level, and judgments made at the postconventional level become important (Kohlberg, 1963, 1967). However, it is important to note that—as with Piaget's stage of formal operations—not all adults operate at Kohlberg's higher levels of moral reasoning. Although Kohlberg initially presented his theory as universal, he later acknowledged that Stage 6 in particular may not apply to all people in all cultures (Kohlberg, 1978).

Kohlberg's studies have been criticized for focusing too heavily on the behavior of males and not devoting enough attention to possible differences in moral reasoning among females (Gilligan, Ward, Taylor, & Bardige, 1988; Wren, 1997). Carol Gilligan has demonstrated that females are likely to base their moral judgments on considerations of caring as well as the factors identified by Kohlberg. More than males, females confronting moral dilemmas tend to look for solutions that also serve to maintain relationships. They therefore are more likely to seek caring solutions that consider the needs of both sides (Gilligan & Attanucci, 1994).

This difference is illustrated in research by Kay Johnston (1988), in which adolescent boys and girls were presented with dilemmas taken from Aesop's fables. The young people were read a fable that presents a moral dilemma and then asked what they understood the problem to be and how they would solve it. In the fable of the dog in the manger, for example, a dog has taken over an ox's manger (food trough). Some adolescents judged the situation purely in terms of which an-

TABLE 11.3
## Kohlberg's Stage Theory of Moral Development

**Preconventional Level**

Seven-year-old children are oriented to the consequences of their behavior.

**Stage 1.** Defer to the power of adults and obey rules to avoid trouble and punishment.

**Stage 2.** Seek to satisfy their own needs by behaving in a manner that will gain rewards and the return of favors.

**Conventional Level**

At around 10, children begin to become oriented to the expectations of others and to behave in a conventional fashion.

**Stage 3** Want to be "good" in order to please and help others and thus receive approval.

**Stage 4.** Want to "do their duty" by respecting authority (parents, teachers, God) and maintaing the social order for its own sake.

**Postconventional Level**

Adolescents become oriented to more abstract moral values and their own consciences.

**Stage 5.** Think in terms of the rights of others, the general welfare of the community, and a duty to conform to the laws and standards established by the will of the majority. Behave in ways they believe would be respected by an impartial observer.

**Stage 6.** Consider not only the actual laws and rules of society but also their own self-chosen standards of justice and respect for human dignity. Behave in a way that will avoid condemnation by their own consciences.

*Kohlberg, 1963, 1967.*

imal had the right to the space, making statements like "It's [the ox's] ownership and nobody else had the right to it." Others sought a caring solution that would take into consideration both animals' needs, making statements like "If there's enough hay, well, this is one way, split it. Like, if they could cooperate." Boys were more likely than girls to give solutions based on rights, whereas girls were more likely than boys to choose solutions that emphasized caring.

It should be pointed out, however, that all of these investigators studied the verbal reasons children and adolescents give for moral and immoral actions. They did not study actual moral behavior. As children and adolescents grow, they offer more abstract reasons why people should not be cruel or dishonest, but they may actually display more cruelty and dishonesty.

## Establishing an Identity

Adolescence takes different forms in different societies and is affected by the cultural context in which young people grow up (Portes, Dunham, & Del Castillo, 2000). In isolated villages in Latin America and Africa, for example, the main concerns of adolescents have to do with interpersonal relationships and how their

**Identity**
**A secure sense of self.**

choices may affect their rapport with family members. And, as noted earlier, in nonindustrialized societies adolescence may be a relatively brief period that offers few individual choices. In U.S. culture, however, adolescents think of themselves as possessing a distinct and unique personality, of being people in their own right—different from their parents and siblings. Adolescents in the United States crave independence and seek to establish a secure and steady sense of self, called an **identity.** The quest for a sense of self is surrounded by difficult questions: *Who am I? What am I? What do I want to do with my life?*

As an example, in their quest for identity many adolescents explore the world of work through part-time jobs. Adolescent work experience may have negative consequences, however. One study of more than 70,000 high school seniors found a positive association between number of hours worked and a set of undesirable behaviors, including poor school performance, drug use, aggression, fighting with parents, and failing to engage in healthy behaviors such as eating a good breakfast and getting enough exercise and a good night's sleep (Bachman & Schulenberg, 1993). A recent study of high school students that assessed the benefits and costs of part-time employment found that working did encourage a sense of personal responsibility—punctuality, dependability, and self-reliance. But at the same time, working reduced commitment to family and friends and led to cynical attitudes toward work, acceptance of unethical work practices, increased use of cigarettes and marijuana, and increased risk-taking behavior in general (Steinberg & Avenevoli, 1998).

In any event, many adolescents now begin to think in abstract terms about their identity. They form theories about the meaning of life and contemplate what society might be, rather than what it seems to be. Their new cognitive abilities may make them critical of the values held by society and by their parents.

As they seek an identity, adolescents tend to emphasize not only personal concerns such as those dealing with privacy, self-expression, and self-fulfillment but also moral values like friendship, love, and tolerance. Among girls, there is a shift from earlier feelings of certainty and self-confidence to feelings of confusion and self-doubt about what they believe is right and wrong.

According to Erikson (see Chapter 9), the key crisis to be overcome by adolescents is the *identity crisis.* During this important decision-making period, the individual makes a commitment to a career and a set of values. When this process is completed successfully, the individual sees himself or herself as a unique and integrated person. Failure to complete the process and resolve the identity crisis leads to confusion over who and what one really is, which may interfere with subsequent crisis resolution and haunt a person for life.

James Marcia (1980) built on Erikson's theory, noting at the outset that not all adolescents experience much in the way of turmoil in forming an identity. He identified four different ways in which the process of identity formation may be played out. The four "identity statuses" are foreclosure, diffusion, moratorium, and identity achievement. (See the study chart on page 423.) An adolescent who has attained *foreclosure* status has made commitments but has not done much decision making or experienced much distress. She or he may have chosen a career and a set of values, but those choices were made early and based mainly on the opinions of parents and teachers. Adolescents who seem to have little motivation to make major life choices are in a state of *diffusion;* they avoid making important decisions and may continually shift among different attitudes and values. Adolescents who are in the midst of an identity crisis—who are concerned with "finding themselves"—are in a state of *moratorium.* They are taking a long time to make a commitment to a particular career or set of values, and it is these adolescents who experience the difficulties emphasized by Erikson. Finally, young people who have passed through an identity crisis and made the necessary decisions are said to have reached the status of *identity achievement*. They have chosen a career and developed a set of values to guide their lives. This status is usually viewed as a sign of maturity (Marcia, 1980).

The search for identity may be complicated by ethnicity, with some young people embracing their ethnic roots while others seek to distance themselves from them, often because of the experience of prejudice at school and in their communities (Lee, 1999). The quest for identity may be even more complex for adolescents of mixed ancestry, who must constantly struggle with a sense of being "different" (Friedlander et al., 2000; Gillem, Cohn, & Throne, 2001). In addition, cross-cultural research has found some differences in how the search for identity is experienced in different societies. For example, Norwegian youth show more moderate tendencies toward exploration and commitment than U.S. teenagers, perhaps because of a greater tendency toward conformity in Norwegian society (Jensen, Kristiansen, Sandbekk, & Kroger, 1998; Stegarud, Solheim, Karlsen, & Kroger, 1999).

The search for identity may be complicated by ethnicity. Some young people embrace their ethnic roots, while others seek to distance themselves from them.

# Study Chart

# Identity Statuses

| Status | Description | Example |
| --- | --- | --- |
| **Foreclosure** | Has internalized parents' standards without considering alternatives | A young man who enters his father's accounting firm and adopts his views on politics, religion, and morality |
| **Diffusion** | Has considered various careers and explored different belief systems but has not made any major commitments | A young woman who works at several different jobs and experiments with alternative lifestyles but does not choose a career or develop a specific set of values |
| **Moratorium** | Is struggling with issues of identity without making much progress toward resolving conflicts between parents' values and his or her own | A young man who drops out of college to "find himself" |
| **Identity achievement** | Has considered alternative life courses and value systems and made a commitment to a particular path | A young woman who decides that she wants to be a doctor and applies to medical school, after having developed her own set of values while in college |

## The Troubles of Adolescence

Some adolescents feel alienated from their society. This may help explain the increase in drinking, delinquency, sexual promiscuity, drug abuse, and even suicide in the last few decades.

An especially serious problem for adolescents in the United States is drug abuse. According to the annual National Household Survey on Drug Abuse sponsored by the Substance Abuse and Mental Health Services Administration (SAMHSA, 2001), 10.9% of youths ages 12–17 use illicit drugs. Marijuana is the most frequently abused drug, with 7.7% of youths using it. (See Table 11.4.) Also increasing in frequency is abuse of the synthetic drug ecstasy, a psychoactive drug with hallucinogenic and amphetamine-like characteristics. Use of ecstasy can have serious physical and psychological effects, including nausea, blurred vision, faintness, confusion, severe anxiety, and depression. More than 750,000 people in the United States report that they are currently using ecstasy.

Even more serious is alcohol abuse: Even though consumption of alcoholic beverages is illegal for those under 21 years of age, 10.4 million current drinkers are between the ages of 12 and 20; of these, 2.1 million are heavy drinkers. On the positive side, there has been a slight decrease in drug abuse by youths ages 12–17 since 1997. Surveys of teenagers indicate that increasing numbers of young people perceive drug use as risky (SAMHSA, 2001). (Drug abuse is discussed more fully in Chapter 13.)

*Over 10% of youths between the ages of 12 and 17 use illicit drugs, primarily marijuana.*

TABLE 11.4

**Percentages of Persons Aged 12 to 17 Reporting Use of Illicit Drugs in Lifetime, Past Year, and Past Month: 1999**

| | Time Period | | |
|---|---|---|---|
| Drug | Lifetime | Past Year | Past Month |
| Marijuana and Hashish | 18.7 | 14.4 | 7.7 |
| Cocaine | 2.4 | 1.6 | 0.5 |
| Crack | 0.6 | 0.4 | 0.1 |
| Heroin | 0.4 | 0.3 | 0.2 |
| Hallucinogens | 5.7 | 3.8 | 1.1 |
| LSD | 3.8 | 2.4 | 0.6 |
| PCP | 0.9 | 0.4 | 0.1 |
| Inhalants | 9.1 | 4.6 | 1.9 |
| Nonmedical Use of Any Psychotherapeutic[1] | 10.9 | 7.0 | 2.9 |
| Pain Relievers | 8.2 | 5.3 | 2.2 |
| Tranquilizers | 2.5 | 1.5 | 0.5 |
| Stimulants | 3.9 | 2.1 | 0.7 |
| Methamphetamine | 1.4 | 0.7 | 0.3 |
| Sedatives | 0.8 | 0.5 | 0.2 |
| Any Illicit Drug[2] | 27.6 | 20.3 | 10.9 |
| Any Illicit Drug Other Than Marijuana[3] | 18.3 | 12.0 | 5.3 |

[1]*Nonmedical use of any prescription-type pain reliever, tranquilizer, stimulant, or sedative; does not include over-the-counter drugs.*

[2]*Any Illicit Drug indicates use at least once of marijuana/hashish, cocaine (including crack), inhalants, hallucinogens (including PCP and LSD), heroin, or any prescription-type psychotherapeutic used nonmedically.*

[3]*Any Illicit Drug Other Than Marijuana indicates use at least once of any of these listed drugs, regardless of marijuana/hashish use; marijuana/hashish users who also have used any of the other listed drugs are included.*

*SAMHSA, 2001.*

Another problem for many adolescents is early pregnancy. Although rates of teenage childbearing have fallen significantly in the last 40 years, they remain higher in the United States than in many other advanced industrial nations. Because teenage mothers are more likely than nonteenagers to be single mothers and to be living in poverty, a major consequence of teenage childbearing is that many babies are born into homes in which they will not receive adequate care and nourishment.

A related problem is the high rate of sexually transmitted diseases (STDs) among adolescents. One out of six sexually active teenagers contracts an STD, and if the disease is not treated, adverse consequences ranging from urinary tract infections to sterility can result. The major STDs include chlamidia, gonorrhea, herpes, and syphilis. By far the most serious STD, however, is HIV/AIDS. Over one-fifth of HIV infections in the United States originate in adolescents who engage in irresponsible sexual behavior, although symptoms may not become apparent until young adulthood. In an effort to prevent the spread of this deadly disease, most states now require AIDS education in public schools.

In addition to the problems discussed so far, growing numbers of adolescents are experiencing depression, sometimes leading to suicide. Suicide accounts for 11.4 deaths per 100,000 people among those ages 15 to 24, and it is the third leading cause of death in this age group (U.S. Census Bureau, 2001). In a recent study of 580 adolescents, 14% of the girls and 7% of the boys reported suicidal thoughts or preoccupations at age 16 (Sourander, Helstela, Haavisto, & Bergroth, 2001). Issues involving teenage suicide are discussed in Psychology in the Lab and in Life on page 426.

Research results call into question the popular belief that adolescents engage in risky behaviors because they believe they are protected from catastrophe (e.g., Quadrel, Fischhoff, & Davis, 1993). In one study, adolescents and adults were asked how probable it was that they would experience eight adverse events ranging from being in an auto accident to getting sick from radiation poisoning. The responses indicated that their perceptions of invulnerability were similar.

The frequency of serious problems among the nation's adolescents has grown, in part, because of the deteriorating environment in which many young people are raised (National Research Council, 1993). Traditional institutions for helping youth—the family, child welfare and neighborhood organizations, health care groups, schools, job-training programs—are no longer offering adolescents the support they need. Of the many factors that shape the lives of teenagers, family income is most powerful, according to these findings. Almost 16% of families headed by an adult between the ages of 25 and 34 live in poverty. And at all income levels, adolescents living in either single-parent families or stepfamilies are far more likely to engage in risky behavior, including running away from home, dropping out of school, smoking, and truancy. There is also evidence that media exposure leads to increased violent and aggressive behavior, increased high-risk behaviors (including alcohol and tobacco use), and accelerated onset of sexual activity (Villani, 2001).

## Conflicts Within the Family

Adolescents often find life going less smoothly than it was just a few years earlier, not only at school but also at home. Although many families experience little or no conflict, there is some evidence that arguments and angry confrontations are more prevalent at this time than during other periods of development. Family arguments often occur because adolescents want to apply their newly expanded freedom to many areas of life and parents want their children to act responsibly. Adolescents feel that they should be the ones deciding which friends to spend time

## PSYCHOLOGY IN THE LAB AND IN LIFE

# Teenage Suicide: A Growing Tragedy

Suicide rates among teenagers and young adults have tripled since the 1960s. Indeed, suicide is the third leading cause of death among young people after accidents and homicide (U.S. Census Bureau, 2001). Why do so many adolescents choose to kill themselves?

There is no single answer, but various studies offer different reasons for the rise in suicides.

Society may be changing in ways that have made adolescence a more difficult time, with increased demands and decreased sources of support. Adolescent stresses include the pressure to assume adult roles faster, an increasing rate of family breakup, high rates of mobility, and uncertain career opportunities (Steinberg, 1985).

Easy availability of firearms may increase suicide. A gun is used in 59% of all teen suicide cases and in three-fourths of those committed by adolescent males (Berman & Jobes, 1991).

Often there is an immediate precipitating cause, such as being the victim of abuse, experiencing a humiliation before parents and friends, or the breakup of a romantic relationship (Frazier, 1985). Significant predictors of suicide include stresses involving parents, peers, and sexuality; problems with the police; parental physical abuse; running away from home; living with neither biological parent; and knowing someone who committed suicide (A. L. Miller & Glinski, 2000; Morrison & L'Heureux, 2001; Wagner, 1997).

Evidence suggests that adolescents who are predisposed to suicide may be moved to actually commit the act as a result of watching portrayals of teenage suicides in movies or television programs (Gould & Shaffer, 1986) or in television news stories (Phillips & Carstensen, 1986).

There may be complex predisposing factors at work early in life. For example, children whose mothers were chronically ill during pregnancy and who experienced significant respiratory problems at birth appear more vulnerable to suicide years later. Such children, because they are at greater-than-usual risk for developmental problems, may be more likely to experience chronically poor relationships with their parents during childhood. Indeed, recent research has found that suicide is often the end-point of long-term difficulties extending back to childhood or early adolescence (Houston, Hawton, & Shepperd, 2001).

Most adolescents who attempt suicide have experienced bouts of serious depression. Like depressed adults, they are likely to feel helpless and hopeless and to conclude that there is never going to be a solution to their problems—and they therefore view suicide as their only way out. There are many more unsuccessful attempts at suicide by adolescents than actual suicides. Girls are two or three times more likely to attempt suicide; males are more likely to complete the act (Petti & Larson, 1987).

It is important to keep in mind that most adolescents, however unhappy they may be for a time, never consider suicide. Although the suicide rate for adolescents has risen, it is lower than the rate for individuals in their 20s and far lower than the rate for older adults.

The most effective means of preventing suicide by adolescents who are considering it is to get help for them early. Studies show that most suicidal youngsters give obvious clues to their intent (Berman & Jobes, 1991). The mental health services available in a community can be identified by calling the state or county mental health department. Many communities also have a 24-hour suicide prevention hot line, which will be listed in the telephone directory. Threats of suicide do not, of course, always result in the act—but they always deserve to be taken seriously by concerned family members and friends.

• • • • • • • • • • • • • • • • • • • • • • • • • • • • • • • • • • • • • • • • • • • • • • • • • • • • • • • • • • • • •

with, how neat to keep their room, or where to go on a free evening. Yet their parents may continue to try to exert control in these areas. Adolescents of both sexes experience more friction in relating to their mothers than in relating to their fathers, presumably because mothers spend more time managing the details of everyday life (Smetana, 1988). For both parents, however, the approach taken can make a difference in the amount and kind of conflict a family undergoes. In other words, it makes a difference whether parents are authoritarian, punitive, authoritative, or permissive (Baumrind, 1975, 1991).

*Authoritarian* parents often have serious problems with their adolescent—and younger—children. They stress obedience and fixed standards, and they do not willingly share power with their adolescent. *Punitive* parents generate anger when they use harsh discipline to curb what they view as adolescent willfulness. The behaviors of both types of parents can diminish the adolescent's feeling of self-worth.

In contrast, *authoritative* parents, who combine limit-setting with negotiation, encounter less turmoil. They do not regard either their standards or themselves as infallible; they are supportive, loving, and committed (Baumrind, 1975, 1991; Powers, Hauser, & Kilner, 1989). It has also been shown that adolescents with authoritative parents do better in high school than those with authoritarian or very *permissive* parents (Steinberg, Lamborn, Dornbusch, & Darling, 1992).

It appears that the best antidote to adolescent turmoil is having the opportunity to identify with parents who are neither too strict nor too permissive. Such parents are warm but firm, and although they are eager for their children to develop autonomy and self-direction, they leave no doubt that they are responsible for their children's behavior (Steinberg, 2001). Such parents—reasonable, fair, respectful, and eager for their children to advance to maturity—are most likely to lead the child toward adult responsibility and happiness.

In general, despite the problems, research indicates that "the great majority of teenagers share a common core of values with their parents, retain harmonious family relationships, and respect the need for discipline" (Graham & Rutter, 1985). Most are reasonably well adjusted, confident about the future, and resilient enough to work through any stresses they encounter during the transition to adulthood.

> **Test Yourself**
>
> **(a)** What is the name for the period of physical changes and sexual maturation that occurs during adolescence?
>
> **(b)** What is the distinction between primary sex characteristics and secondary sex characteristics?
>
> **(c)** What is the third leading cause of death among adolescents?
>
> **(d)** Adolescents seem to have the fewest family conflicts when their parents exhibit what type of parenting style?
>
> (The answers are on page 446.)

# ADULTHOOD: THE PRIME TIME

As described in the preceding chapter, maturation of the brain and body during the first few years of life sets the path of human development. But with the passage of time, personal life events begin to make it harder to anticipate the course of development. Marriage and parenthood, divorce and remarriage, career choices and changes are among the many critical experiences that help shape the dynamic flow of the adult years.

> **FOCUS QUESTIONS**
> * What factors influence the choice of a career and a marriage partner?
> * How does stereotyping of men's and women's sex roles create conflicts in their careers and social relationships?
> * In what ways is parenthood both a demanding and a rewarding experience?

As a result, the personality and behavior of young adults sometimes seem to bear little relation to those of the earlier years. Although the threads of childhood temperament and adolescent behavior may still be visible, some traits become transformed in many respects—raising once again the major theme of continuity and change over the life span introduced in Chapter 1.

The beginning and end of any one stage of adult life are very difficult to detect. Individuals move at a different pace—and sometimes imperceptibly—from one period to another as they choose careers, marry and build a family, and engage in the world of work. The adult years bring on gradual physical alterations as well. We may continue to look the same to ourselves, but not to our acquaintances. (Indeed, people who attend a 40th college reunion often have difficulty recognizing old classmates.)

## New Beginnings

As a child, he was placed in one foster home after another by his widowed father, who was going through difficult times. When he was 16 and his father could finally reassemble his family, he started his first year of high school. But after having been on his own for so many years, he could stand neither the mothering of his three sisters nor the school environment, so he dropped out and ran away from home to join the Marines. Following 3 years of service, including World War II combat, he enrolled as a freshman in the University of Southern California, where the admissions personnel failed to notice that he hadn't completed high school. When they discovered their mistake, they were going to expel him, but then they relented and let him remain as a special student. He stayed on for 3 years and became editor of the college humor magazine—but to this day he has earned neither a high school diploma nor a college degree.

His name? Art Buchwald.

The case of this famous humorist and writer is not as unusual as it may seem. Some of the most startling about-faces have been observed among people who were troubled, sometimes seriously, as adolescents. It has been found that even the most maladjusted adolescent—a failure in school, unsuccessful in social contacts, unpopular and despondent—may turn into a successful, happy, well-liked, and highly respected adult. In one classic study, 166 boys and girls were observed from shortly after birth until they were 18 years old and then observed again at the age of 30. About half the participants were living richer and more productive lives as adults than could have been predicted from the nature of their adolescent personalities (Macfarlane, 1963).

What causes such marked changes between adolescence and age 30? One possibility is that some people are naturally "late bloomers." It takes a long time—and often a change of environment that gets them away from their parents and to a new community—for them to "find themselves."

Taking a meaningful job may help young people find purpose and direction in their lives. So may marriage, with all its responsibilities and its opportunities for forming an abiding, supportive relationship. In one study, researchers reconstructed the lives of a group of young women who had been born into abusive and broken families, had been placed in foster care, and had encountered mostly trouble as adolescents. As young adults, a sizable number of them were found to be contented, productive, and free of the grinding problems they had faced earlier in their lives. In many cases, it turned out, they were lucky enough to find supportive and caring husbands, and as a result they were now enjoying stable family lives far removed from the misery of their younger years (Quinton & Rutter, 1983).

Sometimes a troubled adolescence proves a blessing in disguise. If adolescents go through a period of painful experiences but manage to survive them, they may gain greater insight and stability in the long run. In effect, for some individu-

Helpful role models on the job can lead to greater job success, which in turn improves job satisfaction and self-esteem.

© Larry Williams/CORBIS

als, stress-filled events can have a "steeling" effect that increases their resilience and adaptability as adults (Rutter, 1983b).

## Choosing and Succeeding at a Career

Early adulthood demands many new adjustments. Many young people believe that while they are still in their early 20s they must pick an occupation and begin a well-defined path of work. In reality, however, the process is more complicated. The course of a career is usually based on the ebb and flow of decisions made over time.

A number of factors can influence a person's choice of occupation (Kimmel, 1980). These include (1) background factors, such as socioeconomic level, intelligence, sex, and prior education, which set boundaries on the range of occupational choice; (2) role models, such as an older sibling whom the individual identifies with and wishes to emulate; (3) unique life experiences—for example, deciding to become a doctor because of the early death of a parent from cancer; (4) interests and personality traits that can be realized and expressed in a particular occupation; (5) rational assessments of the job market and areas of opportunity; and (6) personality difficulties, which can limit career choices and hamper success in the world of work. One study found that individuals who exhibited explosive temper tantrums as children were significantly less successful as adults in both their jobs and their marriages (Caspi, 1987).

Work can affect a person's sense of well-being. Success on the job can have a potent impact on self-esteem, marital satisfaction, and physical health. There is evidence that job satisfaction increases over the years and that it is dependent on such factors as willingness to accept challenges and exercise independence (Gruenberg, 1980).

Until recently, psychologists focused their studies on the role of work in the lives of men, but increased attention is now being given to the role of work in the lives of women. The changed role of women in society, combined with an increase in life expectancy and length of marriages, a lower birthrate, and a decline in the real value of family income, has brought about a remarkable increase in the number of married women—currently over 70%—who are paid employees in jobs outside the home (U.S. Census Bureau, 2001).

A majority of married women hold jobs because they need or want the money, but many others say that they work in order to have something interesting to do. An in-depth study of about 300 35- to 55-year-old women in the Boston area revealed a strong relationship between working for a salary and a sense of pride and mastery (Baruch, Barnett, & Rivers, 1983). But because of the persistence of gender-role stereotypes, the path for women in the world of work is not always smooth.

## Workplace Inequities: Struggles for Women

Women have never shared equally in society's esteem, praise, privileges, and rewards. In one way or another, they have been treated as the inferior sex in most civilizations to date. In fact, sex discrimination may have been the first form of social inequality, practiced before people ever thought of discriminating against one another on the basis of race or social class. The division of labor between the sexes has varied from society to society, but no matter how tasks were split up, the jobs assigned to men have always been considered more important (Goode, 1965).

Even today, despite affirmative action programs, fewer women than men pursue careers in scientific and technical fields. Although girls do as well as boys in mathematics in the early grades, fewer females take advanced math courses in high school and college and become physicists, engineers, or computer scientists

(Meece, Parsons, Kaczaia, & Goff, 1982). Overall, women have lower rates of employment, more intermittent employment, and lower earning power than men. The median income of male workers is $27,275; that of female workers is $15,311 (U.S. Census Bureau, 2001). Women are also at a disadvantage with regard to both private pension plans and social security benefits. Through the year 2055, women's benefits are expected to be only two-thirds of those for men (U.S. Public Health Service, 1985).

Psychological studies suggest why such differences continue to exist. **Gender-role stereotypes** have changed somewhat in the past few decades. But in the United States and many other nations, significant numbers of both sexes continue to view men as more forceful, independent, stubborn, and reckless than women, and to view women as more well-mannered, kind, emotional, and submissive than men (Werner & LaRussa, 1985). In their day-to-day behavior, many men seem to reinforce the stereotype. They display greater concern with power than women do (Gaeddert, 1985). They also continue to associate sex with power (Hendrick, Hendrick, Slapion-Foote, & Foote, 1985) and, perhaps because of their higher status, take prerogatives at work that women do not. For example, men are much more likely to behave in a dominating fashion toward their female coworkers and to use intimate gestures and sexual innuendos on the job (Radecki & Jennings, 1980). A survey of women lawyers revealed that half find opportunities at their firms better for men and that nearly two-thirds are the targets of unwanted sexual teasing, jokes, remarks, or questions (Couric, 1989). To be sure, blatant sexual harassment has declined in recent years as men have become more aware of the possible consequences, but harassment cases still appear regularly in the media.

## Gender Roles in Adulthood: Confusion and Conflicts

Perhaps the greatest problem is that women feel compelled to give full expression to their motivations for affiliation and dependency but are under some pressure to suppress their motivation for achievement in the world of work. In the past, it was common for women, even the most capable ones, to conceal their intelligence, abandon interest in such "masculine" subjects as mathematics and science, and either shun a career or settle for such traditionally feminine jobs as nursing. One study has shown that the proportions of males and females who take bachelor's degrees in mathematics are exactly the same. Yet more men than women earn Ph.D.s in mathematics (Lubinski & Benbow, 1992).

A common stereotype is that women are inherently more verbal and men are naturally better at math. In the past, studies suggested that, on the average, females outperform males on tests of verbal ability such as vocabulary, spelling, and verbal comprehension. Today, however, indications are that both sexes do equally well. On the Scholastic Assessment Test (SAT), for example, males and females achieve similar scores (U.S. Census Bureau, 2001). As for mathematics, there is evidence that males do somewhat better; however, in one area of math—computation—females do as well as males or slightly better (Hyde, Fennema, & Lamon, 1990; Wilder & Powell, 1989). Some researchers believe that the differences that exist stem from the fact that parents and teachers expect boys to be better at math and therefore treat them differently at home and in school.

Such issues are not of merely academic interest. Many people still do not consider it feminine to be too successful and competent at tasks that have been regarded as reserved for men. Nor is it considered feminine to be too competitive and aggressive on the job, especially when these behaviors conflict with a desire to help and support others (Gilligan, 1982).

Men also have problems with their assigned gender roles. The typical male conflicts are the opposite of the usual female conflicts. Boys and men are encouraged to express their motivation for achievement. They are expected to welcome every opportunity to leap into competition and assert their status and position so that they will not appear weak. But they are expected to muffle their motivations for affiliation and dependency and to suppress their emotions of sympathy, tenderness, and vulnerability. They have to keep a "stiff upper lip"—avoiding any show of fear or grief—even in the face of serious disappointment and tragedy.

The struggle to play the masculine role can be fraught with anxiety. The motivations for affiliation and dependency (discussed in Chapter 8) are universal. So are the emotions that accompany them. One study showed that men, although they are quite ready to have close social interactions with other men when the situation warrants, actually enjoy fewer close interactions with other men than women do with other women (Reis, Senchak, & Solomon, 1985). Society's demands to suppress motivations for affiliation and dependency run counter to human nature, and hence such efforts can never completely succeed (Stevens, 1974).

Successful women like Hewlett-Packard chief executive Carleton Fiorina must overcome stereotypes such as the idea that women should not be competitive or aggressive on the job.

## The Quest for Love, Intimacy, and Commitment

As noted in Chapter 9, Erikson believed that the critical event of early adulthood centers on moving into a relationship marked by love, intimacy, and commitment. This often means marriage. In the United States, about 95% of adults get married sooner or later—increasingly later in recent decades. Between 1960 and 2000, the median age at first marriage increased from 20 to 25 for women and from 23 to almost 27 for men (see Figure 11.2).

Many people have wondered what leads to the development of a loving interaction culminating in marriage. Aristotle was among the first to point out that "we like those who resemble us and are engaged in the same pursuits." Indeed, we are more likely to fall in love with and choose as a mate someone who shares our beliefs and attitudes. Moreover, most people pick a spouse who is of the same religion and ethnicity and is similar in intelligence, age, educational level, and economic status—although, as interreligious and interracial marriages increase, we see many more exceptions to the pattern.

It is not universally true, of course, that love is a prerequisite for marriage. In a number of non-Western cultures, marriage is based on a contract or on a financial arrangement outside the boundaries of romantic love. In U.S. culture, how-

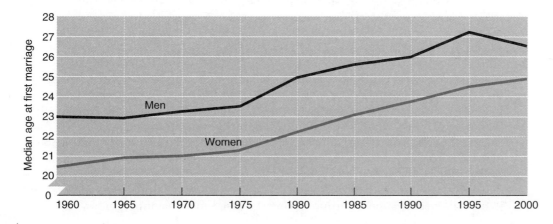

**FIGURE 11.2** Marriage and age. Many people are waiting longer to get married.

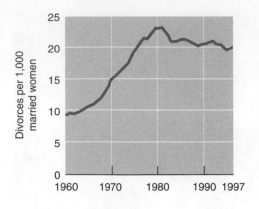

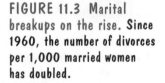

FIGURE 11.3 Marital breakups on the rise. Since 1960, the number of divorces per 1,000 married women has doubled.

Cohabitation
Living together and having a sexual relationship without being married.

ever, the connection between love and marriage is strong. One survey found that only 15% of men and women would agree to marry someone they didn't love (Simpson, Campbell, & Berscheid, 1986).

Whatever the motive, marriage seems to enhance physical and mental health. People who are either married or living together are ill less often and have fewer chronic conditions that limit their activity than single individuals (Schoenborn & Wilson, 1988). Married people feel less lonely, less depressed, and less emotionally disturbed than those who remain single (Cargan & Melko, 1982). And for women, being married and having children can serve as a buffer against job stress (Barnett, Marshall, & Singer, 1992a, 1992b).

Divorced individuals are especially vulnerable to anxiety, and unfortunately the number of unsuccessful marriages is high. In 1998, for example, there were 2,244,000 marriages and 1,135,000 divorces (U.S. Census Bureau, 2001). As shown in Figure 11.3, in 1960 there were about 10 divorces for every 1,000 married women. By 2000, that number had doubled.

For most people, "unlucky in love" means selecting the wrong partner. Yet one team of researchers has suggested that the divorce rate is high not because people make foolish choices but because they are drawn together for reasons that change as time goes on. What brings a couple together at the beginning appears to become less important as the years go by, and the qualities that matter most later on are rarely the ones that figure heavily in the early romantic stages of the relationship. Passion is quick to develop, but it fades quickly as well. Feelings of intimacy develop more slowly, and a sense of commitment grows even more gradually. No relationship is stable over time, but the basic underlying ingredient of a loving and enduring marriage appears to be the ability to communicate and to satisfy the partner's needs (Sternberg, 1986; Sternberg & Grajek, 1984).

**Cohabitation**—living together and having a sexual relationship without being married—has become more prevalent in recent decades. In the United States, there were about 4.5 million cohabiting heterosexual couples in 2000—about three times as many as in 1980 (U.S. Census Bureau, 2001).

Two researchers analyzed data on cohabition, marriage, and divorce gathered from more than 13,000 people. They found that few people in their 50s had ever cohabited, but that almost half of those in their 30s had done so. One-fourth of the couples living together married within a year, and another quarter married within 3 years (Bumpass & Sweet, 1989). There is no good evidence, however, that living together first leads to more satisfying marriages (DeMaris & Leslie, 1984). Indeed, it would seem that couples are more likely to get divorced if they have lived together before marriage—perhaps because those who cohabit are likely to be less religious and less subject to family pressure to begin with than those who do not do so. Given the same level of unhappiness, couples who cohabited before marriage may be more willing to see divorce as a solution (Bumpass & Sweet, 1989).

# Raising Children: Stressful but Rewarding

The birth of a first child often alters family life more than anticipated. For about half the couples participating in two studies, the birth of a first child was followed by more arguments and less satisfaction with the marriage (Belsky & Pensky, 1988; Cowan & Cowan, 1988). The arrival of a baby, however, did not turn a good marriage into a bad one. The relationships that were most harmonious before the birth of a baby continued to be so afterward (Belsky & Pensky, 1988). Although arguments may be inevitable after a baby arrives, the availability of emotional and social support seems to help couples weather the stress. Couples who participated in a small weekly support group during the last 3 months of pregnancy and until the baby was 3 months old reported more satisfaction with their marriage than comparable couples who did not participate in such a group, and they were far more likely to remain married as much as 3 years after the group had stopped meeting (Cowan & Cowan, 1988).

Having a child creates complex and sweeping changes in the roles wife and husband play in the marriage and in their lifestyles. Parenthood is hard work; it requires a sense of responsibility; it is often stressful; and once you have begun, you can't quit when you feel like it (LeMasters & DeFrain, 1983). Most of all, parenting requires various kinds of skills: sensitivity to children's cues and needs at various stages of development; ability to help them cope with stresses and adversity; knowledge about how to talk and play with them and how to use appropriate disciplinary techniques (Rutter, Quinton, & Liddell, 1983).

Such requirements are easier to satisfy, of course, when parents collaborate. Although we tend to think of parenting as a joint venture undertaken with a spouse, more and more families are headed by just one parent. Single-parent families rose from 12% of all families with children in 1980 to 28% in 1999. Among blacks, the figure is nearly 60%, and for portions of the black community, single parenthood is becoming the norm. Most of the single parents are mothers, and many of them have never been married (U.S. Census Bureau, 2001).

Three decades ago, most U.S. women who found themselves unmarried and pregnant headed for the altar. Today, the overwhelming majority of unmarried women who become pregnant do not marry before the baby is born, although they may do so later. This trend does not apply only to low-income, minority, or less educated women. Among white women, the percentage who became mothers without marrying increased from 26.6% in 1990 to 33.0% in 1999 (U.S. Census Bureau, 2001). Research indicates that children in single-parent families tend to have more problems than those raised by two parents, which raises questions about the future welfare of children raised by only one parent.

Even among two-parent families, the quality of the parenthood experience is affected by a number of factors. It matters how many children there are in the household (Schaffer & Liddell, 1984), whether the parents get along (Hauser, 1985), and whether there are social supports available to the family (Belsky, 1984). One study found that couples who coped best with the demands of parenthood

© Lucidio Studio Inc./CORBIS

Most couples find parenthood to be a significant and rewarding experience.

were able to communicate their feelings to each other, showed adaptability to the baby's needs, viewed parenthood as a responsibility to be shared, continued to pursue their own interests, found some time to spend away from the baby, and depended on friends and relatives for information, advice, and help in caring for the child (B. C. Miller & Sollie, 1980). All this is easier, of course, for the affluent than for the poor.

Most young adults who embark on the adventure of parenthood find it a significant and rewarding experience (Veroff, Douvan, & Kulka, 1981). Contentment in marriage does not deteriorate if the children are planned for and if the parents are psychologically prepared for their responsibilities (Feldman, Biringen, & Nash, 1981). Indeed, for many adults, raising children represents their most important achievement. For some couples, however, the opportunity to raise children is thwarted by biology. Studies indicate that as many as 1 in 6 couples will experience difficulty in conceiving a child (Griel, 1991). And research has shown that infertility can be a major life crisis for those who experience it. When those who desire children find their efforts unsuccessful, they commonly experience frustration, despair, and helplessness (Jones & Toner, 1993).

## Midlife: Radical Changes and Quiet Revelations

When the topic of "middle age" is brought up, many people think of the "midlife crisis," fraught with images of the 45-year-old husband and father of four running off to Aruba with his 20-year-old secretary. Many popular images of middle adulthood depict it as an unhappy period when people regret the loss of their youth and all the dreams that might have been. But recent research debunks these myths, showing that for many people middle adulthood is the best of times. According to sociologist Ronald Kessler of the University of Michigan's Institute for Social Research:

> When looking at the total U.S. population, the best year is 50. You don't have to deal with the aches and pains of old age or the anxieties of youth. . . . Rates of general distress are low—the incidences of depression and anxiety fall at about 35 and don't climb again until the late sixties. You're healthy. You're productive. You have enough money to do some of the things you like to do. You've come to terms with your relationships, and the chance of divorce is very low. Midlife is the "it" you've been working toward. You can turn your attention toward being rather than becoming. (Gallagher, 1993)

It is true that people sometimes make radical changes in their lifestyles during middle adulthood. Men may switch careers, moving from a job they have held because of accident or habit—or for financial reasons—to something they have always wanted to do. Or they may change careers as a result of corporate "downsizing," if they can't find work in their preferred area. Women who have spent their early years working as homemakers may take an outside job for the first time, thus encountering new problems but also finding new satisfactions. In all, surveys have shown that only 10% to 12% of respondents report that they have experienced a midlife crisis (Gallagher, 1993).

Ideally, according to Erikson, the crisis of middle adulthood produces a wider outlook on the meaning of life—a sense of kinship with one's fellow human beings, with the ebb and flow of history, with nature itself. (See Chapter 9.) Old goals, especially selfish ones, may be abandoned. New satisfactions of the spirit may be found. Research results tend to bear out Erikson's views. One researcher, for example, analyzed the responses of passersby in a shopping mall to a request by a pregnant woman for donations to help fight birth defects. Generosity increased with age—especially in the middle and later years (Midlarsky & Hannah, 1989).

One frequent shift in midlife is an inclination to begin expressing elements of personality that were suppressed earlier. With most career goals met and mastered, marital adjustments made, and children raised, many women and men begin to move out of the stereotyped gender roles they maintained during earlier decades. Men tend to become less aggressive and competitive in midlife and to take on some of the characteristics of the traditional feminine role. Women become less dependent and submissive and more independent, assertive, and competitive (Zube, 1982).

The changes are gradual. In one study, students at a women's college were asked to answer a personality questionnaire when they were seniors and then twice in later life—at about age 27 and age 43. At age 27, the women had become more self-controlled and tolerant and stronger in characteristics that have traditionally been considered feminine: sympathy and altruism, combined with feelings of vulnerability and inadequacy. By age 43, the women had become more dominant and independent and less flexible and feminine. These changes were common in women who were involved either in raising a family or in succeeding in a high-level career. Those who were engaged in neither of these pursuits showed few of the changes just described. It may be that the tasks of adulthood—which demand control of impulses, interpersonal skills, independence, perseverance, and goal orientation—propel women to change in adaptive ways (Helson & Moane, 1987).

## Women and Menopause

Another aspect of midlife that is often portrayed negatively is **menopause**—the time when women stop menstruating and lose the ability to reproduce. Stereotypical images of unhappy women going through the change of life, with hormones run amok, are not universally true. Although some women do have a difficult time physically or psychologically, most women pass through menopause without much incident or regret (Budoff, 1994). According to the Massachusetts Women's Health Study, which included more than 2,500 menopausal women, 42% of the women reported relief about ending their menstrual periods, 36% reported neutral feelings, 20% said they had mixed feelings, and only 3% conveyed regret.

The most uncomfortable symptom experienced by many women during menopause is hot flashes. These result from a decline in estrogen, which causes the part of the brain that regulates body temperature to behave as if the body were overheated. Studies show that from 50% to 85% of menopausal women experience hot flashes to some degree (Budoff, 1994).

**Menopause**
**The time when women stop menstruating and lose the ability to reproduce.**

**Test Yourself**

**(e)** If we describe a typical man as forceful, independent, stubborn, and reckless, we are describing what type of belief?

**(f)** "Opposites attract," as the old saying goes. But do they usually marry each other?

**(g)** If a couple's marriage is in trouble, would you recommend having a baby to solidify the relationship?

**(h)** "Men and women often move away from stereotyped gender roles in midlife." Is this statement true or false?

(The answers are on page 446.)

# GROWING OLD: MAINTAINING AN ACTIVE, PRODUCTIVE LIFE

U.S. society is getting older, but the old are getting younger. The activities and attitudes of a 70-year-old today are equivalent to those of a 50-year-old a few decades ago. During the past few decades, several changes have affected the lives of people over 65. First of all, the financial, physical, and mental health of older people has improved. Because of better medical care, improved diet, and increasing interest in physical fitness, more people are reaching the ages of 65, 75, and older in excellent health. A better understanding of aging has

**FOCUS QUESTIONS**
● What physical changes are associated with the aging process?
● What kinds of memory and personality problems are experienced by some older people?
● What is the difference between fluid and crystallized intelligence?
● What factors are associated with successful aging and adaptation to the closing years of life?

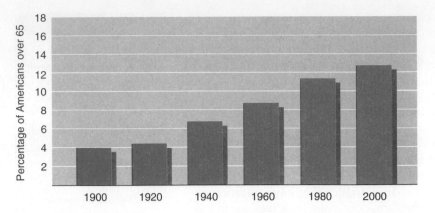

**FIGURE 11.4** The increasing U.S. population over 65. In 1900, people over 65 made up only 4% of the U.S. population. Over the course of the 20th century, their numbers increased to almost 13% of the population.

*U.S. Census Bureau, 2001*

**Ageism**
Negative stereotypes and discrimination based solely on age.

allowed researchers to sort out the inevitable results of biological aging from the effects of illness or social and environmental problems.

The potential for productive and satisfying later years takes on added importance because more and more people are living increasingly long lives. In 1900, only 1 in 25 people in the United States was 65 years old or over; by 2000, 1 in 8 was at least 65 (U.S. Census Bureau, 2001). Put another way, as shown in Figure 11.4, the percentage of people who have passed what is generally considered to be the retirement age of 65 more than tripled during the 20th century (U.S. Census Bureau, 2001).

Thanks to modern knowledge and technology, the average life expectancy for people born in the United States today is almost 77 years, and strides in curing disease are expected to increase it further. Moreover, the population age 85 and older is growing especially rapidly. It is expected to rise from 2.2 million in 1980 to more than 19 million by 2050, a ninefold increase (U.S. Census Bureau, 2001). Small wonder that the nature of the retirement years has become a major focus of psychological investigation.

The retirement years have long been viewed in an unfavorable light—so much so that the term **ageism** has come to be used to describe the negative stereotypes and discrimination that take hold solely on the basis of age. Older adults have been viewed not only as physically deteriorated but as intellectually and emotionally spent, and there has actually been a decline in the willingness of managers to employ older workers. Psychological research reveals such pessimistic perceptions to be surprisingly far from reality. Older adulthood is a time of problems for many people, to be sure, but it can be a time of great pleasure as well.

## The Aging Process

**Senescence**
The gradual weakening and decline of the body that begins in late young adulthood.

Like earlier periods of life, the aging years bring physical alterations. **Senescence,** the weakening and decline of the body, actually begins almost as soon as we stop growing during young adulthood. Although the changes are not visible, the body reaches its greatest strength in late adolescence and grows weaker throughout our adult years. But the declines—in the output of the heart, in reaction time, in frequency of sexual intercourse—are so gradual that they are of little significance in our day-to-day life.

Although there is no specific age at which these changes become obvious, many of them become apparent as we approach our seventh decade. Changes in the spinal column may result in a stooped posture. Acuity in vision and hearing deteriorates. Sensitivity to odor and taste diminishes. Blood vessels harden. The body's capacity to fight disease weakens, and changes in the CNS lead to a slowdown in behavior.

There are a number of theories that attempt to explain the aging process. Some suggest that aging is caused by the damage that occurs in various body systems throughout life—damage caused by normal "wear and tear" or by harmful substances that we breathe or eat. Another theory says that aging results from a slow buildup of damage to the DNA that directs the machinery of every body cell. Others ascribe aging to hormonal changes, and still others to the breakdown of the immune system, the body's weapon for fighting disease. There are no simple answers to the mystery of aging, and most scientists believe that it is a complex process involving many body systems, with the crucial factor being a growing inability of all the body's cells to function properly.

The facts of aging have led to a stereotype of the older person as "over the hill"—a portrait that is essentially inaccurate. True enough, in some cases, especially in extreme old age, damage to the brain's cells causes **senile dementia,** or *senility,* with symptoms such as disorientation, poor attention, loss of memory, and inability to store new information. But contrary to popular assumptions, senility is not an inevitable result of aging. Rather, it is a disease that afflicts a small proportion—from 5% to 8%—of older people.

**Alzheimer's disease,** a progressive form of dementia, is the most common cause of severe intellectual and emotional impairment in older people. It is estimated that in the United States there are 4 million older people who suffer from Alzheimer's disease; as Figure 11.5 shows, the rate increases dramatically beyond age 65 (Evans, Funkenstein, Albert, Scherr, & Cook, 1989). A million and a half older adults are incapacitated by Alzheimer's to the point of needing others to care for them continually (Light & Lebowitz, 1989), and the disease usually leads to death in 7 to 10 years (Heston & White, 1983). The causes and treatments for Alzheimer's disease are still unknown, but studies of aged primates suggest the possibility that a drug—clonidine—may one day help improve the memory capacities of older adults afflicted with this disorder (Arnsten & Goldman-Rakic, 1985). There is some evidence that memory training exercises (for example, learning facts through questions that are embedded in a narrative and then repeated as a review) can facilitate memory formation and consolidation in Alzheimer's patients (Arkin, 2000). And neuroscientists are getting closer to unraveling the genetic factors underlying Alzheimer's disease (Cowan, Harter, & Kandel, 2000; Kudo et al., 2000; Tolnay & Probst, 2001).

**FIGURE 11.5 Alzheimer's disease and age. The prevalence of Alzheimer's disease increases by 15 times during the decades from age 65 to age 85.** *Evans et al., 1989.*

**Senile dementia**
A condition of serious mental impairment that is common in older adulthood, caused by damage to brain cells, with symptoms like disorientation, poor attention, loss of memory, and inability to store new information; sometimes referred to as senility.

**Alzheimer's disease**
A progressive form of dementia that causes severe intellectual and emotional impairment in some older adults.

Contrary to widespread beliefs, intellectual capabilities do not decline significantly as people grow older.

Despite the realities of the aging body, growing old does not necessarily mean becoming weak and sick. Contrary to common stereotypes, the vast majority of older people view their health positively. Although most older people have at least one chronic condition, 7 out of 10 older adults who are not living in institutions describe their health as good or excellent compared with that of others their age (U.S. Senate Special Committee on Aging, 1988). This fact is reflected in the often surprisingly high level of intellectual and emotional functioning of older people.

## Intellectual Capabilities: Slower but Wiser

It is commonly believed that intellectual capabilities decline as people grow older—and indeed many earlier studies pointed in this direction (Willis & Baltes, 1980). One of the problems with such studies, however, is that they were based on average scores on tests by many individuals of a given age (Schaie & Hertzog, 1983). In any cross section of older people, researchers are bound to include a number who are suffering from undiagnosed physical ailments, and the atypically low test scores of these people are likely to pull down the overall average.

More revealing, therefore, are studies that follow a sample of the same people over many years. Such studies tend to present a more optimistic view of the intellectual capacities of older people. In one study, researchers tracked the mental abilities of individuals from age 22 to 67. They found only slight declines in intellectual functioning before age 60. Although more significant changes showed up later, even then there was a wide range of individual differences (Schaie & Hertzog, 1983).

Another problem with past studies of the intellectual capacities of older people is that they gave too much weight to speed of response. True enough, after age 50 we experience a decrease in the efficiency and speed with which we manipulate information (Cerella, 1985; Salthouse, 1988). But speed itself may indicate very little about the nature and quality of thought in late adulthood. Grandfathers are no match for their grandsons at playing video games, but this hardly means that they are deteriorating intellectually. (On the other hand, response speed is important for driving. Many older people either do not want to give up the independence they gain from driving or have no alternative means of going places. They therefore continue to drive when it is no longer safe for them to do so.)

**Fluid intelligence**
The capacity to deal with new problems that require such skills as perception and memory span.

**Crystallized intelligence**
The capacity to use an accumulated body of information to make judgments and solve problems.

More than three decades ago, psychologist Raymond Cattell proposed that intelligence can be divided into two major kinds of abilities. The first is **fluid intelligence,** the ability to deal with new problems that require such skills as perception (solving a picture puzzle) and memory span (remembering shopping lists and telephone numbers), as well as generally to learn new skills. The second is **crystallized intelligence,** which uses an accumulated body of information to make judgments and solve problems (Cattell, 1971; Horn, 1982). Today, it is generally agreed that as we grow older we experience a gradual decline in the first kind of intelligence but not in the second.

Research findings confirm, for example, that the ability to retain routine information does decline with age. As Figure 11.6 shows, people are more likely to lose things, have trouble recalling names, and become forgetful about recent events as they age. In one experiment, both young and older adults kept a diary of occasions on which they could not readily come up with a familiar word that was "on the tip of the tongue." The older adults reported many more such episodes (Burke & Harrold, 1988).

Despite these setbacks, the old keep up with the young in other ways. In one study, researchers asked young, middle-aged, and older adults to think aloud about how they would solve several difficult life problems faced by fictitious individuals of varying ages. The researchers were trying to measure "wisdom," which they defined as uncommon insight into human development and exceptional judgment about difficult life problems. There was little difference among the age groups; older adults contributed an equal share of wise responses (J. Smith & Baltes, 1990).

Even certain deficits in fluid intelligence—for example, in such skills as inductive reasoning and spatial perception—can be partially reversed with the use of simple mental exercises (Baltes, Sowarka, & Kliegl, 1989; Paggi & Hayslip, 1999; Schaie & Willis, 1986). It may be that despite a decline in these skills, many older people have a substantial reserve capacity that they can call into play (Baltes et al., 1989). There is also some evidence that aerobic exercise (walking, swimming, biking) can help reverse declines in cognitive functioning (C. D. Hall, Smith, & Keele, 2001; Rebok & Plude, 2001). Moreover, not all aspects of memory appear to be equally affected with the passing years. One psychologist tested younger and older adults on tasks involving two types of memory discussed in Chapter 5: **semantic memory** (retrieval of facts) and **episodic memory** (retrieval of actual experiences). He found that the older adults, aged 63 to 80, performed as well as those aged 19 to 32 on tasks of the first type (for example, remembering the names of objects shown in pictures), even exhibiting a richer vocabulary while doing so. But they did not do as well on tasks of the second type—specifically, tasks requiring them to recall the details of recent experiences (Mitchell, 1989).

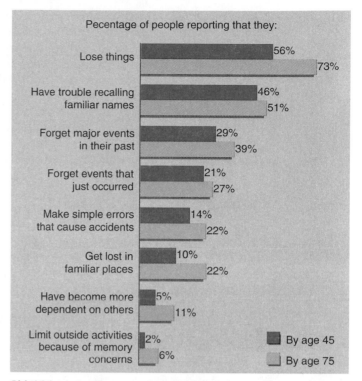

FIGURE 11.6 **Memory and aging.** Telephone interviews with more than 600 people showed that certain memory lapses increase with age. World Book Health and Medical Annual, *1994.*

**Semantic memory**
The memory or retrieval of facts or bits of information.

**Episodic memory**
The memory or retrieval of personal experiences or events.

## Aging and Mental Health

Do most people feel contentment and well-being in their aging years—or do they usually encounter a time of agitation and despair? Psychology's findings are, by and large, contrary to what is generally assumed.

In U.S. culture, "old age" is often thought of as a period of decrepitude and dissatisfaction. Younger people—with their emphasis on growth, progress, and strength—assume that life will become considerably less zestful with the passage of time. Therefore, they give the aging years the lowest rating of all for happiness and quality of life, and they view any signs of "going downhill" with fear and prejudice (Butler & Lewis, 1977). In fact, however, the vast majority of older adults are free of emotional

For many people, the ideal way to spend their last years is to live at home with caring family members.

problems and have the psychological resources necessary to manage an effective and independent life (Romaniuk, McAuley, & Arling, 1983).

To be sure, there are problems. After retiring, some people are plagued by financial difficulties. Some suffer from chronic illness. Among people 65 and over there are about 2.5 million widowers and 10.9 million widows (U.S. Census Bureau, 2001), and the stresses they encounter in adjusting to their loneliness are reflected in their mortality rates (i.e., number of deaths per 100,000 population). Men especially seem to have a difficult time. One study showed that the mortality rate was 61% higher for widowers between the ages of 55 and 64 than for those in the same age range who were married. Among both men and women who lost their mates, the death rate was higher for those who lived alone than for those who shared a household with someone else (Helsing, Szklo, & Comstock, 1981).

Like people of any age, some older adults suffer from mental health problems. Sometimes these may be associated with physical illness or with the stress of caring for a loved one. Depression, for example, is commonly associated with stroke and Parkinson's disease (Lebowitz & Cohen, 1991, citing Robinson, Lipsey, Rao, & Price, 1986). And at least 30% of people caring for spouses with Alzheimer's dis-

Some great achievers in the sunset years.

Pablo Picasso (artist)

Jessica Tandy (actor)

Nelson Mandela (statesman)

Vladimir Horowitz (pianist)

Margaret Chase Smith
(member of Congress)

Frank Lloyd Wright (architect)

ease have been diagnosed as suffering from major depression (Light & Lebowitz, 1989). Suicide rates increase with age among white males, with those over age 85 having the highest recorded suicide rate (Lebowitz & Cohen, 1992). At the same time, however, many psychiatric problems are less common among older people (U.S. Senate Special Committee on Aging, 1988).

The overall picture suggests that patterns of psychological and social adjustment are as varied in late adulthood as in earlier periods of life (Bornstein & Smircina, 1982). Indeed, some psychologists who study aging believe that diversity increases with age and that individual patterns of personality and behavior are more pronounced in the later years than at any earlier age (Schaie, 1981).

## Retirement: Freedom or Boredom?

Retirement has become an expected and significant period of a person's life. For many people, however, retirement is threatening because it is seen as formally ushering in the period of older adulthood (Glick, 1980). But most studies show that when retirees maintain their health and have an adequate income, they find this a rewarding stage of life (Barfield & Morgan, 1978). The concept of retirement often no longer means the end of employment, but rather the initiation of self-chosen and self-directed activity (Atchley, 1982). Most people seem to find that the retirement years are not nearly so bad as they were led to expect—surprisingly full of pleasures that may differ in kind and intensity but are nonetheless fulfilling. A key factor appears to be the presence of a network of friends, at least some of whom are viewed as intimates (Heller & Mansbach, 1984).

Even among people 85 and older, researchers find diversity not only in physical well-being but in emotional, behavioral, and social characteristics as well. Many people at this stage in life are infirm and dependent, but many others are still active and some still work (Suzman & Riley, 1985).

As noted in Chapter 9, to Erikson the aging years represent a fork in the road that can lead either to a heartwarming sense of integrity or to feelings of despair. Putting together a successful life picture with reminiscences from the past can be part of this process. One study has shown that in reviewing their lives, those who age successfully retrieve memories that enhance their feelings of competence and continuity—rather than experiencing guilt over the past or, at the other extreme, glorifying the past and deprecating the present (Wong & Watt, 1991).

People who succeed in negotiating Erikson's final crisis live out the last years of their lives with a sense of self-fulfillment and wisdom. They face the inevitability of death without fear or regret. Those who fail—often because they have not surmounted life's earlier crises—wind up embittered. They are dissatisfied with the way they have lived their lives. They think with regret about what might have been, and the prospect of dying fills them with despair.

**Test Yourself**

**(i)** What is the term used to describe negative stereotypes of older adulthood and the discrimination they provoke?

**(j)** What disease is the most common cause of severe intellectual and emotional impairment in older adulthood?

**(k)** What do we call the capacity to use an accumulated body of information to solve problems?

(The answers are on page 446.)

# COMING TO TERMS WITH LIFE'S END

The chief reason for today's increased life expectancy is that science has conquered diseases, such as pneumonia, that formerly killed people in the prime of life. Most deaths now result from chronic, long-lasting conditions—for example, cancer and ailments of the heart and circulatory system. Thus, people are more likely to be aware that they are approaching the end of life—and must somehow reconcile themselves to this inevitable event.

**FOCUS QUESTIONS**

• What kinds of attitudes toward death are found among older individuals?

• What factors can influence attitudes toward death?

## Attitudes Toward Death

Death is a reality throughout most of our lives. When children are between 5 and 7 years old, they already understand the concept that death is universal and irreversible (Speece & Sandor, 1984). But the challenge of facing death emerges more insistently with the passing years.

Contrary to popular assumptions, fear of death is not pervasive among older adults. Indeed, a number of studies show that with increasing age, earlier anxieties about death become muted. The nature of beliefs about dying appears to be less important in reducing anxiety than the certainty with which these beliefs are held (D. K. Smith, Nehemkis, & Charter, 1983–1984), and earlier experience with death—of a close friend or family member—tends to reduce anxiety about death (Cole, 1978–1979).

Death becomes more acceptable if, in reviewing their lives, older people experience a sense of what Erikson described as integrity and fulfillment—a feeling that they have lived a whole and satisfying life. The capacity to face death with equanimity is diminished among those who have a distinct and pervasive sense of having lived a life that was not fully realized, with tasks or goals that remain to be completed, as well as among those who feel that their control over what remains of life has slipped away (Silverberg, 1985). Older people tend to fear a slow and lonely death more than they do death itself (Rogers, 1980). Those who accept death with equanimity view it as part of the continuity of life—"as a point in a journey down an endless road full of travelers who have gone before and will follow. During the journey all leave their own unique mark along the way, enriching those they have encountered and accompanied" (Wyatt, 1985).

## Bereavement

Among people age 65 and over in the U.S. population, over 50% are married and living with their spouses (U.S. Census Bureau, 2001). In general, these are the most fortunate of older adults. Studies have shown that older people typically consider their marriage to be just as happy as (or even happier than) it was when they were younger (Foster, 1982).

Unfortunately, the marriage that prospers into older adulthood, surmounting the problems of retirement and achieving greater happiness than ever before, must inevitably end in sadness when one of the partners dies. Since women live on average about 7 years longer than men, usually it is the wife who survives and faces the new crisis of widowhood. There are about 11 million widows in the United States, most of them older adults. Indeed, almost half of all women over 65 are widows (U.S. Census Bureau, 2001). There are, of course, widowers as well, but not nearly so many—2.5 million. And because there are four times as many widows as widowers age 65 and over, the widowers have a far better chance of remarrying, and many of them do.

Many people believe that normal or "healthy" mourning follows a set pattern: an initial period of great grief or even depression followed by an eventual recovery within some specified period. Psychologists have found that responses to bereavement are considerably more varied. Grieving, even soon after a loss, can be a relatively mild experience for some; for others, its debilitating emotional and physical effects can persist for years. Moreover, some deaths, such as the sudden loss of a child, are particularly hard to recover from (Wortman & Silver, 1989).

Evidence from a number of studies suggests that men suffer more than women when their spouse dies. The death rate for widows is only slightly higher than the rate for other women, but the rate for widowers is over 60% higher than that for married men (Helsing et al., 1981). The reason probably lies in a combination of factors, including the fact that widowers are likely to find fewer sources of social support and that men, by and large, are biologically more vulnerable to stress than women (Stroebe & Stroebe, 1983). Often, however, the impact of the death of a spouse is less traumatic for older people than for younger people because the event is felt to be "on time" (Rodin, 1987).

## The Final Stage: Facing Death

A classic example of research on how people cope with death is a famous study by Elisabeth Kübler-Ross (1969). Based on intensive work with several hundred patients facing death, Kübler-Ross concluded that most people go through a series of predictable stages (Kübler-Ross, 1969). First comes denial—"I don't believe this is happening to me"; next comes anger—"Why does this have to happen to me?"; then bargaining—"If you let me survive just a few more years, dear God, I'll never get angry again"; then depression—"I'll never see my grandchildren grow up"; and finally acceptance—"I guess my number is up, and that's the way it has to be."

Kubler-Ross's theory has been the subject of much criticism. At least some of the stages she described are probably experienced by most people facing death—though not always in the same order—but they are hardly predictable for everyone. Moreover, many people for whom death is near manage to find new meaning in what remains of their lives. One investigator who worked with terminally ill cancer patients was struck by "how many of them use their crisis and their danger as an opportunity for change." Many of the patients rearranged their priorities and began to live fully in the present. They were able to communicate more deeply with loved ones than before, and they enjoyed a vivid appreciation of nature and of their relationships with family and friends (Yalom, 1980).

Some people prefer to face death in a hospital setting so that everything possible can be done to postpone the final moment. But the advent of modern medicine has brought with it the ability to sustain life in ways that many people view as a curse rather than a blessing. Contrary to popular myths, however, most older adults do not die in hospitals hooked up to machines after weeks or months in an intensive care unit; instead, they spend their last days in their own homes, surrounded by family and friends. (See A Matter of Debate on page 444.)

© ImageState-Pictor/PictureQuest

Hospice programs are designed to help dying patients maintain a decent quality of life. Family members (including pets) are encouraged to participate as much as they can.

# → A MATTER OF DEBATE ←

## Should Assisted Suicide Be Legalized?

Should terminally ill patients be allowed to end their pain and suffering through suicide? This question is a subject of heated debate and legal controversy. On one side are those who believe that people have a "right to die"—in particular, a right to die with dignity. On the other are those who believe that each human life is sacred and must not be ended by artificial means.

Those who believe in the right to die support the practice of assisted suicide, in which a physician helps a terminally ill patient self-administer a lethal drug. Opponents claim that assisted suicide does not differ significantly from euthanasia, or "mercy killing," which is legally equivalent to murder. Although polls indicate that a majority of people in the United States support the right of a patient to receive a lethal drug from a physician (Horgan, 1997), most health-related professional organizations, including the American Medical Association, oppose the practice.

Those who support assisted suicide argue that many people die in agony after a long struggle with a terminal disease such as cancer. Although they are given painkilling medications, these often are not sufficient to eliminate the pain—and in most states physicians are prohibited from prescribing excessive dosages of painkillers. Instead of forcing patients to endure long periods of hopeless suffering, why not allow them to die at a time of their own choosing and in as painless a way as possible? Witnesses at assisted suicides note, "There are no adverse effects, no seizures, no loss of bodily functions of any type. The death is very, very peaceful" (Murphy & Marshall, 2001).

Opponents of assisted suicide claim that it is just another name for euthanasia. They also point out that legalizing assisted suicide would be a step along a "slippery slope" that could lead to abuses. Who, for example, would decide whether a mentally disordered patient really wished to die? What about patients with nonterminal but incurable illnesses? "You worry that people will be manipulated into committing suicide, either through withdrawal of medical care, or being told that tomorrow will be worse because of this or that, or having medications withheld that could make a person feel better, or [the family] finally giving up or pulling away and not being supportive," notes Dr. William M. Petty of Physicians for Compassionate Care (quoted in Murphy & Marshall, 2001).

At present, Oregon is the only state with a law permitting assisted suicide. Oregon's Death with Dignity Act was approved by voters in 1994 and re-approved by a wide margin in 1997. Under the law, doctors may provide—but not administer—a lethal prescription to terminally ill adult state residents, provided that two doctors agree that the patient has less than 6 months to live, has voluntarily chosen to die, and is capable of making health care decisions. At least 70 people have made use of the law since it took effect. However, the suicides have been carried out using a federally controlled drug, and on November 6, 2001, U.S. Attorney General John Ashcroft ordered that because federal drug laws must be enforced uniformly throughout the nation, Oregon may not allow the use of those drugs in assisted suicides. Oregon sued to block Ashcroft's order, arguing that the attorney general was interpreting the Controlled Substances Act in a way that was not intended by Congress. A federal judge issued a restraining order against the directive, and at this writing it is not clear whether the Oregon law will be overturned.

Thus, the debate over assisted suicide continues, with no resolution likely in the near future. Meanwhile patients who wish to die must wait and hope. As one Oregon man suffering from liver cancer noted, "I just want the option to have assisted dying, in case I get to the point where I can't take care of any bodily functions, or do anything for myself, and I have to be drugged so heavily that I'm out of it most of the time" (quoted in Murphy & Marshall, 2001).

To research this topic further, go online with InfoTrac and use your own term or the following suggestions:
- assisted suicide
- euthanasia

---

**Hospice**
**A program through which terminally ill patients are helped to die with a minimum of pain and a maximum of dignity.**

One alternative to death in a hospital is hospice. Originally a European term meaning a sheltered place for weary travelers, **hospice** is now used to refer to programs that help terminally ill patients die with a minimum of pain and a maximum of dignity. Hospice is more a concept than a place—it may occur in a special facility or through visits to the home. Emphasizing pain management rather than "heroic measures" to prolong life, hospice addresses the needs of people who fear protracted pain and suffering more than death itself. It provides physician-directed medical services but also offers psychological, social, and religious assistance, as well as sufficient painkilling drugs to diminish suffering (Wyatt, 1985). Family members are invited to participate as much as they can and at any time. Hospice includes programs of out-patient as well as in-patient care, so that if the patient wishes to die in the familiar surroundings of home, in the midst of family, the required medical and psychological support is available.

Psychologists have only recently begun to study the cognitive and emotional processes that occur with the knowledge that death is imminent. The findings are sparse and inconclusive. But the search goes on for information that may help ease this final episode of life and surround dying with a grace and dignity befitting the human spirit and the remarkable flow of events that unfold from the cradle to the grave.

> **Test Yourself**
>
> **(l)** What two processes, described by Erikson, help people accept death?
>
> **(m)** If a terminally ill patient doesn't want to die in a hospital hooked up to machines, what setting might he or she choose in order to die with a minimum of pain and medical intervention?
>
> (The answers are on page 446.)

# Chapter 11 Summary

## Adolescence: A Time of Transition

1. A number of criteria are used to determine the boundaries of adolescence. Although the period is generally seen as extending from age 10 to age 20, adolescence has a variety of beginnings and endings across cultures and in different individuals.

2. Psychologically, adolescence may be a period of "storm and stress"—with much confusion over establishing independence, striving for recognition, and dealing with academic and social pressure. However, some studies have shown that most adolescents are well adjusted.

3. In physical terms, adolescence is usually defined as beginning with the onset of puberty—marked by menstruation in females and production of sperm in males. The onset of puberty is almost invariably preceded by rapid physical growth and accompanied by significant development of *primary* and *secondary sex characteristics*.

4. Concern about body image and being overweight can lead to eating disorders such as *anorexia nervosa* and *bulimia nervosa*.

5. The self-concept of adolescents may be affected by the social environment—notably the junior high school experience, which is the occasion for the emergence of many academic and psychological problems.

6. Moral standards usually undergo rapid change during adolescence. From his studies of boys, Kohlberg has suggested that moral development occurs in six stages, in which children's reasons for good behavior progress from sheer self-interest to desire for the approval of others and finally to concern for their own values and the approval of their own conscience. Studies of girls show that they exhibit greater concern with kind, considerate relationships than do boys, who tend to be more concerned with abstract principles of justice and fairness.

7. Adolescents seek to establish a sense of *identity*—that is, to think of themselves as possessing a distinct and unique character, of being people in their own right.

8. Some adolescents feel alienated from society and are more likely than their peers to engage in drinking, delinquency, sexual promiscuity, drug abuse, and even suicide.

9. Parental attitudes and approaches to discipline can affect the feelings of self-worth and the degree of turmoil experienced by adolescents.

## Adulthood: The Prime Time

10. Continuing development in the years after adolescence often produces striking changes. Some of the most troubled and despondent adolescents turn out to lead happy and fulfilling lives as adults, while some untroubled and self-confident adolescents do not live up to their early promise.

11. Work often deeply affects an individual's well-being. Success on the job can have a potent impact on self-esteem, marital satisfaction, and physical health.

12. *Gender-role stereotypes* are common in the workplace, where women are encouraged and often expected to act in traditional feminine roles. In different ways, the stereotyping of sex roles can affect men as well.

13. According to Erikson, the critical event in early adulthood is moving into a relationship (usually marriage) marked by intimacy, commitment, and love. The experience of love differs widely from one individual to another.

14. The quality of a marriage greatly affects the individual's psychological and physical well-being. *Cohabitation*—living together and having a sexual relationship without being married—has become much more common and socially accepted. However, there is no evidence that living together first draws a couple closer together.

15. Having a child creates complex and sweeping changes in the roles husband and wife play in their marriage. If the children are planned for and the parents are psychologically prepared for their responsibilities, contentment in marriage does not deteriorate.

16. Middle adulthood is marked by a transitional period in which people attempt to make the shift to the later stages in life. Although this shift can create conflicts and stress, it is often facilitated by the increased mellowing and self-assurance that middle adulthood may bring.

## Growing Old: Maintaining an Active, Productive Life

17. With the dramatic increase in the number of people age 65 and over, the problems and pleasures of the retirement years have become an important subject of psychological investigation.

18. Negative stereotypes of the later years have given rise to *ageism*, but psychological research reveals that negative perceptions of older adults are far from reality.

19. The later years, like earlier periods of life, bring physical changes. *Senescence*, the weakening and decline of the body, often becomes obvious during the seventh decade of life.

20. *Senile dementia*, or senility, with symptoms such as disorientation, poor attention, loss of memory, and inability to store new information, is a disease that significantly afflicts a small proportion of older people. *Alzheimer's disease*, a form of dementia, is the most common cause of intellectual impairment in older people.

21. Intelligence can be divided into two major kinds of abilities: *fluid intelligence* and *crystallized intelligence*. Fluid abilities rely on such skills as perception and memory span and are relatively independent of the impact of education and cultural influences. Crystallized intelligence, in contrast, requires the capacity to use an accumulated body of general information in making judgments and solving problems. Today it is generally agreed that as we grow older we experience a decline in fluid intelligence but not in crystallized intelligence.

22. Older adults perform well on tasks that require *semantic memory* (retrieval of facts) but less well on tasks that require *episodic memory* (retrieval of actual experiences).

23. Most people seem to cope with the problems of the retirement years and find them fulfilling. A key factor appears to be the presence of a network of friends, at least some of whom are viewed as intimates.

## Coming to Terms with Life's End

24. Fear of death is not pervasive among older adults. Death becomes more acceptable if older people experience a sense of what Erikson described as integrity and fulfillment—a feeling that they have lived a whole and satisfying life.

25. The stages many people experience in the process of facing death are denial, anger, bargaining, depression, and acceptance. However, the experiences of grief and mourning vary from one individual to another.

26. *Hospice* is a program designed to help dying patients maintain a decent quality of life and deal with the emotional trauma of dying.

# Chapter 11 Test Yourself Answers

(a) This period of physical maturation is called puberty.

(b) Primary sex characteristics represent changes involving the sexual organs. Secondary sex characteristics represent changes in appearance—that is, enlarged hips and breasts in girls and facial hair and deepening voices in boys.

(c) Suicide is the third leading cause of death among adolescents.

(d) Authoritative parents, who combine limit-setting with negotiation, usually have the least conflict with their teenagers.

(e) We are describing a gender-role stereotype.

(f) No; people tend to marry individuals with similar religious beliefs, ethnic backgrounds, education, intelligence, age, and economic status.

(g) No; the arrival of a baby, a stressful event in the best of marriages, usually will not turn a bad marriage into a good one.

(h) True; men and women often move away from stereotyped gender roles in adulthood.

(i) Ageism

(j) Alzheimer's disease

(k) We call it crystallized intelligence.

(l) The two processes are integrity and fulfillment.

(m) A hospice program

# Chapter 11  Human Development: Adolescence, Adulthood, and Death

## Key Terms

ageism (p. 436)
Alzheimer's disease (p. 437)
anorexia nervosa (p. 418)
bulimia nervosa (p. 418)
cohabitation (p. 432)
crystallized intelligence (p. 438)
episodic memory (p. 439)
fluid intelligence (p. 438)
gender-role stereotyping (p. 430)
hospice (p. 444)
identity (p. 422)

life span development (p. 415)
menarche (p. 417)
menopause (p. 435)
primary sex characteristics (p. 416)
secondary sex characteristics (p. 416)
semantic memory (p. 439)
senescence (p. 436)
senile dementia (p. 437)

*The key terms above can be used as search terms in InfoTrac, a database of readings, which can be found at http://infotrac-thomsonlearning.com.*

## Active Learning Review

### Adolescence: A Time of Transition

1. The period of adolescence, usually defined as beginning with the onset of puberty, is typically one of dynamic and often dramatic change. The teenage years usually constitute the period called _____.  **adolescence**

2. Adolescence is usually defined as beginning with the onset of _____. The period is typically preceded by rapid physical growth.  **puberty**

3. A girl may grow 3 to 5 inches and a boy 4 to 6 inches in height in a single year as they approach the period known as _____.  **adolescence**

4. The onset of _____ is marked by the beginning of menstruation in the female and the production of sperm in the male.  **puberty**

5. With puberty comes rapid development of the reproductive organs, or _____ sex characteristics.  **primary**

6. Also occurring is the development of enlarged breasts and hips in girls, and a deeper voice and facial hair in boys. These are known as _____ sex characteristics.  **secondary**

7. The first menstrual period is known as _____.  **menarche**

8. During adolescence, self-image is very much dependent on body image. Concern with weight can lead some adolescents, especially girls, to develop a disorder known as _____ _____, which is marked by the pursuit of a starvation diet by an already emaciated individual.  **anorexia nervosa**

9. Even more common is _____ _____, a disorder in which a person engages in eating binges and then induces vomiting or takes laxatives in order to avoid gaining weight.  **bulimia nervosa**

10. Nancy regularly gorges herself on food and then sticks her finger down her throat to induce vomiting. She is suffering from a disorder known as _____ _____.  **bulimia nervosa**

11. Adolescence brings a dramatic change in moral standards. The stages of moral development were extensively studied by Lawrence _____.  **Kohlberg**

12. In adolescence, there is often a shift from concern with the approval of others to concern with the approval of one's own conscience. This typifies the change taking place in _____ _____.  **moral standards**

13. Teenagers begin to think of themselves as possessing a distinct and unique character and being people in their own right. In other words, they establish a sense of _____. Often this comes down to the matter of choosing a career.  **identity**

behavior

identity

drug

pregnancy
sexually transmitted
depression
suicide

authoritarian, punitive,
authoritative, permissive
Authoritative

career

gender-role

achievement

affiliation

stereotyping
adulthood

cohabitation
roles,
lifestyles
single-parent

crisis

menopause

ageism

expectancy
senescence

cells

14. New principles of _____ emerge during adolescence, marking a change in moral standards.

15. In choosing a line of work, adolescents are demonstrating their need to establish themselves as people in their own right—that is, with a sense of _____.

16. An especially serious problem for adolescents in the United States is _____ abuse.

17. Another problem for many adolescents is early _____. A related problem is the high rate of _____ _____ diseases among adolescents.

18. Growing numbers of adolescents are experiencing _____, sometimes leading to _____.

19. The amount of conflict a family undergoes during the children's adolescence is affected by whether the parents are _____, _____, _____, or _____.

20. _____ parents, who combine limit-setting with negotiation, encounter less turmoil than parents using other approaches.

## Adulthood: The Prime Time

21. Entry into adulthood entails the choice of a _____. In today's society, this task applies equally to women and men, but because of the persistence of *gender-role stereotyping*, the path of women in the world of work is not always a smooth one.

22. Women often find it difficult to succeed in their chosen careers because of the persistence of _____-_____ stereotypes. As a result, they are under pressure to suppress their achievement motivation.

23. Women often find themselves impelled to give full expression to their motivations for affiliation and dependency but to suppress their _____ motivation. Men, in contrast, are often in conflict because society pressures them to suppress their motivations for affiliation and dependency.

24. For men, achievement—rather than the motivations for _____ and dependency—is the expected norm.

25. For both men and women, adulthood means facing gender-role _____.

26. For most people, one milestone in the period of _____ is marriage—the establishment of a relationship marked by love, intimacy, and commitment.

27. Living together in a sexual relationship without marriage is known as _____.

28. Having a child creates complex and sweeping changes in the _____ wife and husband play in the marriage and in their _____.

29. Research indicates that children in _____-_____ families tend to have more problems than those raised by two parents.

30. Surveys have shown that only 10% to 12% of respondents report having experienced a midlife _____.

31. A negatively depicted aspect of midlife is _____, or the time when women stop menstruating and lose the ability to reproduce.

## Growing Old: Maintaining an Active, Productive Life

32. The retirement years have often been viewed in a negative light, so much so that _____—the negative stereotypes and discrimination associated with aging—is a factor affecting the lives of many older adults.

33. The later years, like earlier periods of life, bring physical changes, including *senescence*, or the weakening and decline of the body. Still, the average life _____ in the United States continues to increase.

34. In older adults, the weakening or decline of the body—referred to as _____—becomes more apparent.

35. The aging process usually involves the growing inability of the body's _____ to function adequately. The facts of aging—including the onset of *senile demen-*

*tia*, or senility, among some older people—have led to an inaccurate stereotype of older people.

36. The symptoms of _____ _____ include disorientation, poor attention, loss of memory, and inability to store new information. — **senile dementia**

37. _____ _____ affects only a small proportion of older adults. — **Senile dementia**

38. Among the symptoms of senility are disorientation, poor attention, loss of _____, and inability to store new _____. — **memory, information**

39. An especially cruel form of senile dementia known as _____ disease causes severe emotional and intellectual impairment. — **Alzheimer's**

40. The most common cause of severe emotional and intellectual impairment in older people is _____ _____. — **Alzheimer's disease**

41. Growing old does not necessarily mean getting weak and sick. Most older people do not suffer the severe _____ and emotional impairment caused by senile dementia. — **intellectual**

42. Psychologist Raymond Cattell proposed that intelligence can be divided into two types of abilities—_____ intelligence and _____ intelligence—and that older people experience a decline in the first but not in the second. — **fluid, crystallized**

43. _____ intelligence relies on such skills as perception and memory span and is relatively independent of the impact of education and cultural influences. — **Fluid**

44. _____ intelligence, in contrast, requires the capacity to use an accumulated body of general information in order to make judgments and solve problems. — **Crystallized**

45. Older people experience a decline in _____ intelligence, but not in _____ intelligence. — **fluid** / **crystallized**

46. Grouping letters or numbers is an example of a task requiring _____ intelligence. — **fluid**

47. Explaining the motives of political candidates is an example of a task requiring _____ intelligence. — **crystallized**

48. *Semantic memory* involves retrieval of facts, while *episodic memory* deals with retrieval of actual experiences. Tests show that older adults perform as well as young people on _____ memory tasks, but not as well on _____ memory tasks. — **semantic, episodic**

49. To Erikson, the aging years represent a fork in the road that can lead either to a heartwarming sense of _____ or to feelings of _____. — **integrity, despair**

## Coming to Terms with Life's End

50. Death becomes more acceptable for older people if they experience what Erikson described as a sense of _____ and _____—a feeling that they had lived a whole and satisfying life. — **integrity, fulfillment**

51. An aging grandmother who feels that she has fully achieved her life's goals is more likely to accept the prospect of _____ than one who has not. — **death**

52. A common crisis among older people is the death of a _____—an experience more likely to happen to women than to men. — **spouse**

53. Statistics comparing men and women indicate that it is more likely that your spouse will die before you if you are a _____. — **woman**

54. There are many more _____ than widowers over 65 in the United States. — **widows**

55. Studies comparing men and women suggest that the experience of bereavement may be more difficult for _____. — **men**

56. Elisabeth Kübler-Ross developed a description of the _____ most people go through in facing death. — **stages**

57. *Hospice* programs can help meet the needs of the _____ _____. — **terminally ill**

58. Many people are helped to die with a minimum of pain and a maximum of dignity through a _____ program. — **hospice**

## Practice Test

_____ 1. Adolescence is marked by the onset of
  a. puberty.
  b. conflict.
  c. withdrawal.
  d. frustration.

_____ 2. The name most frequently associated with the study of moral development is
  a. Erikson.
  b. Kohlberg.
  c. Spock.
  d. Skinner.

_____ 3. According to Erikson, the key crisis to be overcome by adolescents is the
  a. integrity crisis.
  b. maturation crisis.
  c. identity crisis.
  d. attachment crisis.

_____ 4. Teenage suicide can be explained by
  a. adolescent stresses.
  b. availability of firearms.
  c. depression.
  d. all of the above

_____ 5. Kohlberg traced the stages of
  a. puberty.
  b. moral development.
  c. sexuality.
  d. hostility.

_____ 6. Lack of advancement in work by women is often due to the persistence of
  a. prejudice.
  b. gender-role stereotyping.
  c. insufficient physical strength.
  d. emotional instability.

_____ 7. Women are often urged to give up their motivation for
  a. affiliation.
  b. dependency.
  c. achievement.
  d. sex.

_____ 8. Men are often pressured to give up their motivation for
  a. dependency.
  b. aggression.
  c. achievement.
  d. power.

_____ 9. People who are married
  a. live longer than single people.
  b. die at a younger age than single people.
  c. are poorer than single people.
  d. take greater risks than single people.

_____ 10. The middle years often bring out long-hidden aspects of
  a. intelligence.
  b. personality.
  c. identity.
  d. conflict.

_____ 11. In Erikson's theory, middle age brings a decrease in concern with
  a. selfish goals.
  b. generativity.
  c. spiritual satisfaction.
  d. kinship.

_____ 12. The average life expectancy for Americans is now
  a. 68 years.
  b. 72 years.
  c. 77 years.
  d. 65 years.

_____ 13. One of the symptoms of senile dementia is
  a. poor attention.
  b. shortness of breath.
  c. stooped appearance.
  d. Alzheimer's disease.

_____ 14. An ability that does not decrease during the later years is
  a. fluid intelligence.
  b. crystallized intelligence.
  c. memory for digits.
  d. visual acuity.

_____ 15. Aging usually involves inadequate functioning of the body's
  a. synapses.
  b. cells.
  c. liver.
  d. hormones.

_____ 16. The most common cause of severe intellectual and emotional impairment in older individuals is
  a. poor attention.
  b. Alzheimer's disease.
  c. loss of memory.
  d. senescence.

____ **17.** Erikson believed that a sense of integrity in old age was most dependent on
   a. financial security.
   b. early childhood experiences.
   c. successfully coping with previous life stages.
   d. physical health.

____ **18.** The gradual weakening and decline of the body is referred to as
   a. wear and tear.
   b. aging.
   c. cell deterioration.
   d. senescence.

____ **19.** Told he is dying, a man responds, "You must be wrong!" In the view of Elisabeth Kübler-Ross, he is expressing
   a. bargaining.
   b. acceptance.
   c. denial.
   d. anger.

____ **20.** A program or facility in which terminally ill patients are helped to die with a minimum of pain and a maximum of dignity is a
   a. hospice.
   b. halfway house.
   c. Heaven's Gate program.
   d. nursing home.

# Exercises

1. Kohlberg has suggested that moral behavior is based in part on how we evaluate a situation intellectually, and that such evaluations vary in intellectual level. Table 11.3 (page 421) presents the six stages, or levels, of moral reasoning proposed by Kohlberg.

   Read the paragraph below, entitled "Moral Dilemma," to different students and have them respond, especially to explain their reasoning. Have them write their answers.

   ### Moral Dilemma

   In Europe, a woman was near death from cancer. One drug that might save her was exclusively in the hands of a druggist in the same town. The druggist was charging $2,000, ten times what the drug cost him. The sick woman's husband, Heinz, went to everyone he knew to borrow the money, but he could only get together about half of what it cost. He told the druggist that his wife was dying and asked him to sell it cheaper or let him pay later. But the druggist said, "No." The husband got desperate and broke into the man's store to steal the drug for his wife. Should the husband have done that? Why? (Kohlberg, 1969, p. 379)

   After you have accumulated responses from several students, analyze them by taking each statement or reason and attempting to determine its level according to Table 11.3. You may want to do this together with other students in your class. Count up the number of statements at each level for each participant you assess and also across all the participants you interview. Then consider these questions:

   a. What is the average level of moral reasoning in the group of participants you tested?

   b. Are there statements corresponding to more than one level within the answer from a single person?

   c. Do you think that the level of answer might depend on the specific moral dilemma posed to a participant?

   d. What are the issues raised by the people in your sample?

   e. Speculate on whether your participants would actually act the way they reasoned in this exercise.

2. The factors that are important early in a love relationship tend to differ from those that characterize a long-lasting mature relationship. In this exercise, you will conduct your own mini-study to identify some possible differences between early and mature relationships.

   Your task is to interview one member of each of four couples: two *early* couples, which we will define as couples who have been together for 6 months or so, and two *mature* couples, which we will define as couples who have been together for at least 5 years. The couples may be heterosexual or same-sex oriented.

   To simplify things, you need not analyze differences between male and female respondents. The gender of your interviewees doesn't matter—you may use all men, all women, or a mix. And you need not consider how many relationships each person has had prior to the current one.

   First, read your participants this introduction:

   We are doing a mini-study of the factors that are important in relationships—the factors that create the basis of the relationship itself. I have asked you to be one of my study participants because you are in a committed relationship at this time. I'd like you to tell me what things you believe are important at different stages of a relationship.

   Now ask and record the answers to each of the following questions, urging the respondents to list at least five factors for each question:

   a. [For all respondents] What factors were important to both of you in the first few weeks of your relationship?

   b. [For those in an early relationship] Let's assume for the moment that you two have been married for at least 5 years. What factors do you believe would be important to both of you then?

   c. [For those in a mature relationship] What factors are important to both of you now?

   Write a separate brief paragraph addressing each of the following questions.

   • What important points about early relationships were identified consistently across all participants?

- What important points about mature relationships were identified consistently across all participants?

- How do respondents in early relationships differ from those in mature relationships in their identification of early important factors?

- How do respondents in early relationships differ from those in mature relationships in their identification of mature important factors?

- What do the differences identified in the two preceding questions imply about relationships, relationship maturity, and differences among individual participants?

❋ *For quizzing, activities, exercises, and web links, check out the book-specific website at http://www.psychology.wadsworth. com/kagan9e.*

# 12 Stress, Coping, and Well-Being

© Bob Thomas/The Image Bank

**455**

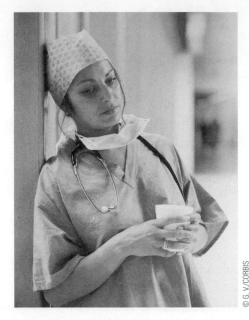

Intense stress, if prolonged, can have serious effects on both physical and mental health.

**Stress**
A physical and psychological response to a harmful or potentially harmful circumstance.

**Stressors**
The events or conditions that put a strain on the organism and pose a challenge to its efforts to adjust.

Sooner or later, all of us encounter times when either minor irritations or major problems of living pile up and seem almost unbearable. The result may be distressing physical symptoms: a racing heart, shortness of breath, trembling hands, a queasy stomach, headaches, and even lingering physical ailments. Or we may suffer troublesome psychological reactions—inability to concentrate, anxiety, or a case of "the blues." Whether our symptoms are physical or psychological, we are experiencing typical reactions to the strains and pressures of life—what we often refer to as stress.

The word *stress* has become part of our everyday consciousness and even our slang. In the United States, people talk casually about being "stressed out." As a solution, they may attend "stress management workshops." Although most people have no trouble knowing when they feel stress, little agreement exists about the precise definition of this term (Elliot & Eisdorfer, 1982; Rutter, 1983b; Selye, 1980). In everyday language, for example, many people use the word *stress* to refer to circumstances that cause stress, such as tornadoes, violent crimes, or serious illness. It is more correct, however, to refer to these conditions as *stressors* and use the term *stress* to refer to what we experience when we encounter stressors—in other words, our biological reactions to those circumstances and our conscious concern or worry about them.

Generally, psychologists define **stress** as a physical and psychological response to a harmful or potentially harmful circumstance—that is, to anything that threatened to damage the organism (Taylor, 1988). A stress reaction can be caused by a disease-carrying virus, air or noise pollution, the physical danger of an earthquake, or the psychological danger posed by the loss of a job or the death of a loved one. **Stressors** are defined as the events or conditions that put a strain on the organism and pose a challenge to its efforts to adjust. It's important to distinguish between temporary or *acute* sources of stress, such as a house fire or the loss of a spouse, and *chronic* stressors, such as life-long poverty, unemployment, or physical disabilities. Although both types of stressors can cause severe stress, their effects may differ significantly. As we will see in later sections of the chapter, acute stressors are more likely to give rise to conditions such as adjustment disorders and post-traumatic stress disorder (American Psychiatric Association, 2000), whereas chronic stressors tend to have serious and lasting effects on physical health.

Some people are convinced that there are more—and more serious—stressors in the contemporary world than ever before, while others question whether life is more difficult today than in the past, when the concept of stress was less well known to the general public (Averill, 1989). In either case, stress clearly plays a significant role in both physical and mental health. Psychologists have carefully studied the responses we make to stressors, and in doing so, they have identified ways to handle stress that can help us maintain our physical and psychological well-being.

**FOCUS QUESTIONS**
- What are some sources of stress in humans?
- Can pleasant events be sources of stress?
- How can frustration and conflict give rise to stress?
- What factors cause the stress response to vary from one individual to another?

# SOURCES OF STRESS

After 6 years of happy marriage, your spouse dies a slow death from a ravaging cancer. A few years later, you get married again—to a kind, devoted person. But after 3 contented years, your new spouse is killed while crossing the street.

You are an engineering student facing three exams, but instead of studying, you have to spend precious time hunting for a summer job or else you won't be able to pay your debts. Meanwhile, you are struggling with a conflict: Your significant other wants to get married now, but you think you should wait until you have finished school.

You are driving along the freeway, on your way to an important job interview. Suddenly, you get a flat tire. Your cell-phone battery is dead, so you try desperately to flag down a passing motorist. But by the time someone stops to pick you up, you are already late and still miles from a phone.

These three vignettes are taken from real life. They aren't unusual. Stress can be caused by a sudden overwhelming event, by the daily grind of work, or by the accumulation of a series of relatively small incidents on a day when everything seems to go wrong. What we so often refer to as "the stresses of life" range from everyday irritations to devastating catastrophes—from a lost wallet to bereavement, from being stuck in an elevator to being taken hostage, from failing to meet a deadline to losing a job.

Certainly most of us would agree that some experiences are far more devastating than others. Missing an appointment, for example, is hardly as devastating as finding out that you have incurable cancer. Yet we experience stress from both the major crises and the seemingly minor problems of life. Moreover, although most of us think of stress as the result of outside events, stress can also arise from *within* the individual—for example, as a result of conflicts between contradictory motives. The sources of stress are not restricted to any particular period of life. Instead, they are our constant companions, as detailed in the Life Span Perspective on page 458.

## Life Crises

A disabling accident, divorce, job loss, bankruptcy—at one time or another, each of us is likely to be faced with a seemingly overwhelming personal crisis. Indeed, it is probably fair to say that no life is without its episodes of trauma and loss. Eventually, we all must confront stressors that test our limits.

One investigator reviewed a number of studies and identified three kinds of events that have been found to be especially stressful for most people (Rutter, 1983b): (1) events that signal the loss of an important relationship—for example, divorce; (2) events that cannot be controlled and therefore produce a feeling of helplessness—for example, a tragic accident; and (3) events that pose a long-term threat because they have lasting consequences—for example, a lingering illness, loss of a job, or caring for a desperately ill and dying spouse (Kiecolt-Glaser, Glaser, Shuttleworth, & Dyer, 1987). Such circumstances often produce the kind of physical and psychological stress responses that can significantly affect a person's health.

When personal crises pile up, stress reactions are likely to be compounded. In a study of alcohol abusers who had completed a treatment program, chronic (constant and long-lasting) stress led to a return to heavy drinking—although less severe stress did not (S. A. Brown et al., 1990). The same pattern holds for children. Among youngsters, a single hospital experience is not likely to be associated with psychological problems, but two such experiences are more likely to be so. The same is true among children who experience parental divorce two or three times (Garmezy & Rutter, 1985).

## Transitions as Stressors

The kinds of crises just described are major life transitions, and because they are unhappy events, we can understand that they are especially likely to produce stress.

From the moment of birth, humans confront the reality of a world replete with stressors—experiences that are, for the newborn, unsettling, disturbing, and noxious (Lipsitt, 1990). During the first 3 months, pain, hunger, and cold are the primary sources of stress, manifested by irritability and difficulties in feeding and sleeping. From 4 to 12 months, unpredictable events that are hard for the infant to assimilate, such as the presence of an unfamiliar adult or a mother's departure, are the most typical stressors, leading to such behaviors as withdrawal and crying. During the second year, parental restrictions, punishment, prolonged separation, and even the presence of an unfamiliar child can evoke stress—as evidenced, for example, by clinging behavior or apathy. Later, as toddlers and schoolchildren, most youngsters eventually encounter a variety of stressors—the loss of a loved one, illnesses, separations, family conflicts, failures, or just the everyday griefs and disappointments that life inevitably brings (Garmezy & Rutter, 1985).

As noted in Chapter 11, the adolescent years are especially filled with stressful experiences. Over an average of just 4 years, the child is transformed into an adult (Petersen, 1987). These changes usher in the turbu-

lence of heightened sexuality, a striving for autonomy, and a search for personal identity. For teenagers, a host of conflicts are to be found in the disparity between the values of adolescent peers and those of the family. At the same time, society demands evidence of the transition to adulthood—for example, the achievement of independence from parents, responsible sexual behavior, the completion of required academic goals, and preparation for an occupation.

For college students, too, stress is often a major factor. Today's students feel pressured by the high cost of education, an uncertain job outlook, and stiff competition from their peers for everything from seats at a ball game to slots in a graduate program. As a result, serious stress-related illnesses such as depression, migraine headache, and eating and sleeping disorders appear—a pattern that one investigator has called "student shock" (Gottschalk, 1983).

The popular generalization that life gets easier with age hardly holds for most people. The challenges of young adulthood—establishing a career, finding a mate, becoming a parent—produce significant stress. Later on, in midlife, crises brought on by career changes, marital discord, and financial worries induce

stress reactions. And the closing years, bringing the specter of physical and psychological decline, usher in an entirely new set of stressors that challenge the coping capacities of many older adults.

Certain stressors found in contemporary society appear to affect all of us, irrespective of age. An example is the ever-present threat of violence. Each day, newspaper headlines and TV newscasts assault us with reports of violent acts threatening the well-being and lives of people at all stages of life. Countless children, for example, are frightened by stories of abductions and molestations. Many teenagers are affected by the aura of violence on the streets and even in the schools. In many communities, retirees live in fear of muggings, break-ins, and carjackings. And since the horrific terrorist attacks on the World Trade Center and the Pentagon on September 11, 2001, large numbers of people of all ages have felt constant stress as they have worried about their safety and the future of their society.

In sum, stress clearly appears to be our companion throughout the life span. At every point, however, we humans show a remarkable range of responses to the problems and crises that beset us.

But transitional milestones that are generally viewed as positive can be the occasion for stress as well. For example, stress can result from such basically joyous occasions as going off to college, getting married, or gaining a new family member. The following account by a young man who had just graduated from law school is not unusual: "I'm drowning in stress," he said. "I'm about to start a new job in a law firm, my girlfriend and I have decided to get married, and we've got our eye on the house we want to buy." Exposure to a number of such seemingly positive events within a short period can be stressful and, at least in some individuals, can lead to illness (Maddi, Barone, & Puccetti, 1987).

The characteristic shared by all such experiences is change. Today, most people in industrialized nations expect change to occur in their lives. We change schools, jobs, and places of residence, experiencing abrupt alterations of environment when we do so. The result can be considerable stress—as has been demonstrated in studies of nonhuman animals as well. In one experiment, for example, individual monkeys were moved from one social group to another so that they constantly had to fight for social position within the group. Unlike other monkeys, who were allowed to have a stable social life, these animals developed severe arterial damage (Bloom & Lazerson, 1988).

## Catastrophes

Earthquakes, hurricanes, and other natural disasters obviously produce a great deal of stress. After the Mount Saint Helens volcanic eruption and ashfall in 1980, researchers studied people living in the nearby town of Othello, Washington. As shown in Figure 12.1, emergency room visits rose by about a third compared with the same period a year earlier. Mortality rates rose by about a fifth, and rates of mental and behavioral disorders doubled (Adams & Adams, 1984).

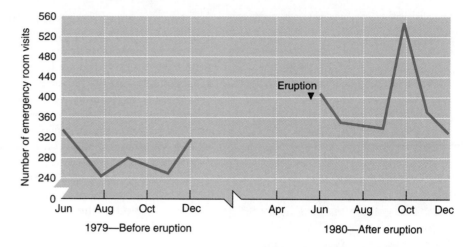

**FIGURE 12.1 Health implications of a major catastrophe.** Shown here is the rise in emergency room visits after the eruption of the Mount Saint Helens volcano near Othello, Washington. *After Adams & Adams, 1984.*

The effects of exposure to catastrophic events can be revealed in more subtle ways as well. In a study spanning a 3-week period following the 1989 earthquake in San Francisco, 40% of people living in the area reported experiencing nightmares about an earthquake. In a comparison group in Tucson, Arizona, the percentage of residents experiencing such nightmares following the earthquake was only about a tenth as large (Wood, Bootzin, Rosenhan, Nolen-Hoeksema, & Jourden, 1992).

Stress often occurs when people are exposed to a harmful substance that may cause their health to suffer at some time in the future. This happened to a group of firefighters who fought a large warehouse fire in New Jersey in 1985. Inside the warehouse was illegally stored polyvinyl chloride, which produces toxic fumes that can have long-term harmful effects. Unaware of the presence of the polyvinyl chloride, the firefighters did not at first put on masks to protect themselves; only later did they discover the risk they had endured. Researchers compared these firefighters with others a month or two after the event and again 22 months later. In contrast to the control group, those who had fought the dangerous fire were sadder and more anxious, and had more physical complaints. They were also significantly more angry and subject to confused thinking even as long as 2 years after the fire (Markowitz, 1989). As we will see shortly, uncertainty and doubt can be potent sources of stress, and these elements undoubtedly contributed to the symptoms suffered by the exposed firefighters.

Comparable reactions may follow catastrophes caused by technological failures. When an accident damaged the nuclear power plant at Three Mile Island, people living nearby were exposed to potentially devastating radiation. Although some residents of the area moved away, others stayed on. People who continued to live there after the accident experienced chronic emotional tension. As long as 17 months after the incident, they showed more physiological signs of stress and reported more depression and anxiety than did members of a control group (Kiecolt-Glaser & Glaser, 1991; Schaeffer & Baum, 1984).

## Everyday Hassles

"It's not the large things that send a man to the madhouse. . . . No, it's the continuing series of small tragedies that send a man to the madhouse . . . not the death of his love but a shoelace that snaps with no time left. . . ." This view, expressed in a poem by Charles Bukowski, is reflected in the work of a number of psychologists who have concluded that **daily hassles**, or seemingly minor irritations, can accu-

**Daily hassles**
The seemingly minor irritations that can create as much stress as major life events.

© Robert Landau/CORBIS

Daily hassles such as traffic jams and other seemingly minor irritations can accumulate to create as much stress as major life events.

mulate to create as much stress as major life events. These are the "little things" that go wrong in life—the burned toast, the washing machine that breaks down, the traffic tie-up that makes us late for work, the friend who forgets a lunch engagement. In many societies—not just modern ones—the sources of such stressors seem endless.

Taken individually, such episodes usually do no more than turn a sweet day sour (L. A. Clark & Watson, 1988). But hassles that pile up have been shown to constitute a potent stressor (Lazarus & Folkman, 1984; Weinberger, Hiner, & Tierney, 1987). The greater the number of daily hassles we encounter, the greater the number of psychological symptoms we are likely to experience (Zika & Chamberlain, 1987). Moreover, physical problems such as flu, backaches, and headaches have been tied to the stress posed by daily hassles (DeLongis, Folkman, & Lazarus, 1988).

## Conflict

Should I stay in my room and study for tomorrow's test, or go to a movie with friends?

Should I get married to that special person, or continue living a life free of obligations?

Should I let my boss know what I really think of her, or keep quiet and not risk losing my job?

**Conflict**
The simultaneous arousal of two or more incompatible motives, resulting in unpleasant emotions such as anxiety or anger.

Such choices create **conflict,** which psychologists define as the simultaneous arousal of two or more incompatible motives, resulting in unpleasant emotions such as anxiety or anger. The phrase "unpleasant emotions" is an essential part of the definition. A person whose motives are in genuine conflict experiences anxiety, uncertainty, and the feeling of being torn and distressed. This is why conflict is a significant source of stress—and, in extreme cases, a threat to mental health.

Life is full of conflicts over pairs of goals that cannot be attained. These generally fall into one of four classes:

1. *Approach-approach conflict* takes place between two motives, each of which impels us to approach a desirable goal. However, we cannot reach both goals, for attaining one means giving up the other.

2. *Avoidance-avoidance conflict* occurs between two motives, each of which impels us to avoid an unpleasant alternative.

3. *Approach-avoidance conflict* occurs when fulfilling a motive will have both pleasant and unpleasant consequences.

4. *Double approach-avoidance conflict* takes place when we are torn between two goals, each of which will have both pleasant and unpleasant consequences. For example, consider a young woman from a small community who wants to become a certified public accountant. She knows that the best opportunities in this field exist in large cities, but she is worried about the crowded and impersonal aspects of big-city life. She falls in love with a classmate who plans to go into business with his parents, who run a small-town automobile agency. She wants very much to marry this man, and she likes the idea of living with him in a small community. But she knows that this community will give her very little opportunity for her chosen career as an accountant. Which way should she turn?

Often there is no fully satisfactory solution to the conflicts we face in everyday life. But understanding their stressful nature can help us cope—and arrive at sensible resolutions.

## Uncertainty and Doubt

Whenever the future is shrouded in uncertainty and doubt, stress is likely to arise. For example, because hostages do not know whether they will ever be released, the experience of captivity is especially stressful. On a more mundane level, you may experience stress when you come to class to take an exam, sit in a doctor's office waiting to learn what your X-rays show, or drive along a highway and suddenly see the flashing light of a police car looming behind you. Even highly trained astronauts show evidence of physiological stress as they sit at their controls, knowing that in a few seconds they will blast off into the void of space.

One classic experiment showed that uncertainty affects rats as well as humans. Pairs of rats were placed in a device (shown in Figure 12.2) in which they could not move. They were then given a series of electric shocks to their tails. The shocks came at the same time and were of equal strength. However, one rat in each pair received a warning tone before each shock and the other heard meaningless random beeps. The rats that couldn't know when the shocks would come engaged in erratic eating and drinking behavior and developed severe stomach ulcers as a consequence of their stress. Those that could predict when the shocks would arrive displayed far fewer signs of stress (Weiss, 1970).

In general, the more knowledge people have as they prepare to face a stress-provoking experience, the better they feel. But the result depends in part on how apprehensive they are to begin with. For individuals who worry a lot, information about what lies in store may actually increase the impact of the stressor. In one study, a group of women who were about to have their hands immersed in painfully cold water received detailed information about what to expect. The information helped reduce the stress of those who were not overly concerned about the experience—but it compounded the stress of those who approached the experiment with extreme foreboding (McCaul, 1980).

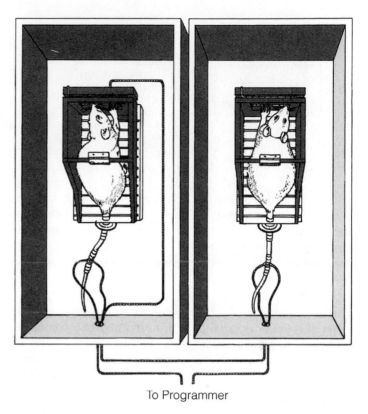

To Programmer

**FIGURE 12.2 The effects of not knowing what lies ahead. The stressor—shocks to the tail—was the same for both rats, but the experience produced different results, depending on whether the rat received a warning before each shock.**

## Stress as an Individual Experience

"Grief is a matter of relativity; the sorrow should be estimated by its proportion to the sorrower; a gash is as painful to one as an amputation is to another." These are the words of poet Percy Bysshe Shelley, writing early in the 19th century. The accuracy of his view has been documented by psychologists who have demonstrated the uniqueness of individual reactions to stressful events.

Some early investigators, who conducted studies using laboratory animals, assumed that the effects of stressors could be studied without reference to their meaning to the individual. But this view is no longer held by most psychologists. A person's **cognitive appraisal**, or subjective interpretation, of a potentially stress-

**Cognitive appraisal**
A person's subjective interpretation of a potentially stressful episode.

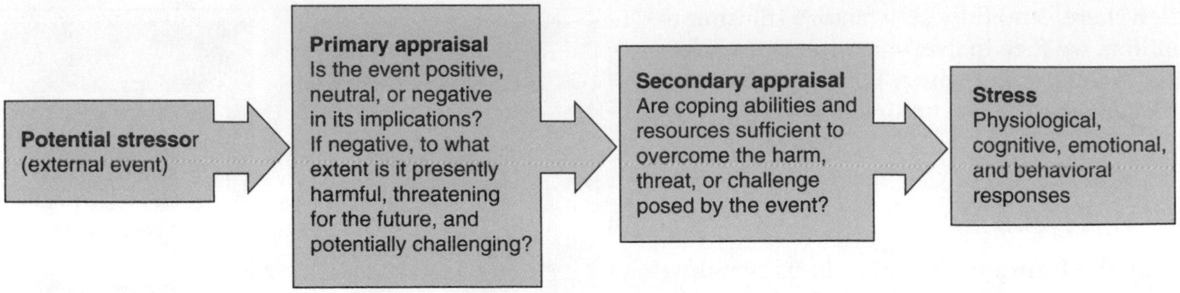

| Potential stressor (external event) | → | **Primary appraisal** Is the event positive, neutral, or negative in its implications? If negative, to what extent is it presently harmful, threatening for the future, and potentially challenging? | → | **Secondary appraisal** Are coping abilities and resources sufficient to overcome the harm, threat, or challenge posed by the event? | → | **Stress** Physiological, cognitive, emotional, and behavioral responses |

**FIGURE 12.3 The stress experience. A given event may or may not produce stress, depending on the individual's interpretation of it.**
*After Taylor, 1986.*

Primary appraisal
A type of cognitive appraisal in which the individual assesses the personal meaning of the stressor.

Secondary appraisal
A type of cognitive appraisal in which the individual assesses alternative ways of coping.

ful episode strongly influences his or her response (Lazarus & Folkman, 1984). As a result, the same event may be perceived by different individuals in widely different ways—as irrelevant, benign, and positive or as threatening and harmful.

As shown in Figure 12.3, our cognitive appraisal of a stressful stimulus takes two forms: primary and secondary. In **primary appraisal**, the individual assesses the personal meaning of a stressor. How significant is the event—the loss of a neighbor, a new job, a surprise quiz—to me? In **secondary appraisal**, the individual assesses alternative ways of coping. What can I realistically do about this situation? What are my options? Can I handle this?

Because of the range of appraisals that humans make in response to stressful events, one person may experience severe stress over an occurrence that leaves another person relatively calm. For one person, a given stressor produces chronic feelings of anxiety; for another, it leads to little tension. You doubtless know men and women who carry on in normal fashion and even appear relatively calm and cheerful despite serious physical handicaps or tragic disappointments. You probably know others who are reduced to panic or temper tantrums if their bacon is too crisp.

Even such apparently traumatic stressors as being the victim of a crime do not provoke the same responses from everyone. "The degree of violation experienced by an individual victim . . . depends on the meaning of the crime in that person's life. What seems a minor incident to one target may be a personal catastrophe for another." It is the victim's subjective interpretation of the crime that determines how traumatic that event actually turns out to be (Bard & Sangrey, 1986).

# STRESS AND PHYSICAL HEALTH

FOCUS QUESTIONS
- What is the general adaptation syndrome?
- How does stress affect the body's immune system?
- How can stress cause bodily illness?

Although we do not all respond to life's stressors in the same way (Manuck, Cohen, Rabin, & Muldoon, 1991), in general our bodies react in a fairly universal way. A number of physiological changes take place, involving the brain and various organ systems, as portrayed in Figure 12.4. These changes mobilize our physical resources for "fight or flight." That is, they enable us to fight for our survival harder and longer than would otherwise be possible or else to run away from danger faster and farther.

The fact that our physiology is altered under stress constitutes a rather mixed blessing; some of the changes produce wear and tear on the body and symptoms of illness. In the case of purely physical stress, such as sudden injury, the body will take steps to limit the damage—for example, by rushing antibodies to the site of the injury. This could mean the difference between life and death. The fight-or-flight response may be equally valuable in situations in which we must make split-second decisions and take quick action. We may, for example, need to deal with a sudden fire in the kitchen, avoid an oncoming car, or rescue a drowning friend.

Yet many of the stresses of modern life are complex, ongoing, and seemingly inescapable. How can the fight-or-flight response help us deal with an overbearing boss, a seriously ill relative, or a difficult chemistry course that we cannot drop? Such situations cannot be fought in the same way that our distant ancestors fought off a saber-toothed tiger. There are many enduring problems that we simply can't fight or run away from. It is this dilemma that so frequently gets us into difficulties. To appreciate why this is so, it is necessary to understand in more detail how the body responds to stress.

## The General Adaptation Syndrome

Much of what we know about the physiological effects of stress goes back to experiments performed on animals by Hans Selye in the 1950s and 1960s (Selye, 1956). The reactions he analyzed were much the same as those produced in humans by any type of external or internal stressor, including prolonged emotional tension. Selye exposed animals to a variety of physical stressors, such as extreme cold, fatigue, or doses of poison strong enough to make them sick but not strong enough to kill. He expected to find a different physiological response to each form of stress. Surprisingly, however, the animals responded in basically the same way no matter what he did to produce stress. Selye coined the phrase **general adaptation syndrome** to describe what he observed.

**Test Yourself**

**(a)** "I have felt totally worn out ever since that night when our house was robbed." Is the house-robbing experience referred to in that statement better described as a stress or as a stressor?

**(b)** At what age can it be said that stress is not a factor to be reckoned with in our lives?

**(c)** Students, worried about the outcome of a test, may say, "No matter what grade I got, I'd rather know it sooner rather than later." What source of stress are they trying to avoid?

**(d)** As you anxiously prepare to visit your dentist, a friend tells you, "I can't figure out why you feel so bad. Look at me. *I* never feel stress when I have to go." What important aspect of the stress experience is your friend overlooking?

(The answers are on page 489.)

Pituitary gland secretes hormones

Lungs expand

Blood vessels near skin contract

Adrenal glands secrete adrenalin

Large blood vessels dilate to speed blood flow

Hair stands on end

Pupils of eyes dilate

Salivary glands' activity slows (dry mouth)

Heart rate and blood pressure rise

Liver releases glucose for energy to muscles

Sweat glands activated (moist palms)

Muscle tension increases

*General adaptation syndrome* **According to Selye, the sequence of events involved in prolonged stress, including the alarm phase, the resistance phase, and the exhaustion phase.**

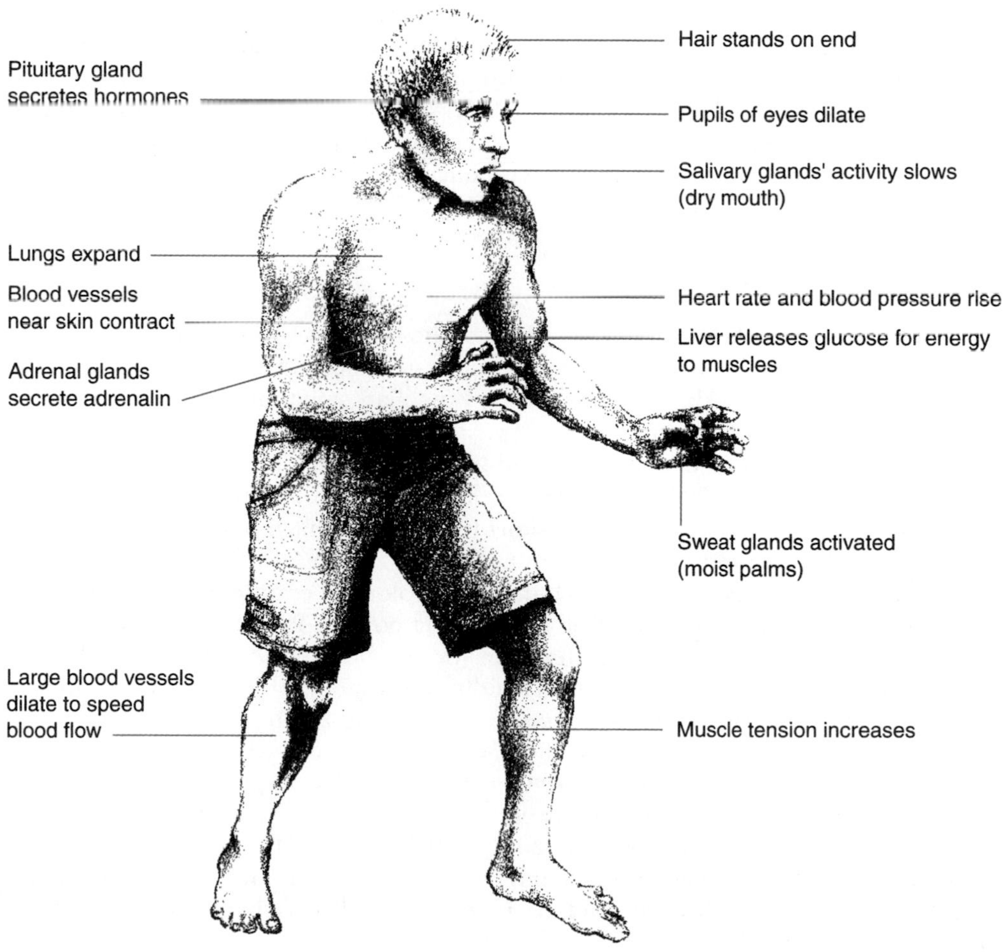

**FIGURE 12.4 Fight or flight: the body's response to a stressful event. Faced with an emergency, the body undergoes a variety of physical reactions.**

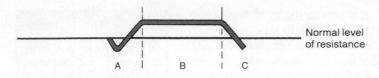

**FIGURE 12.5** The three phases of Selye's general adaptation syndrome. In the alarm phase (A), when the body first reacts to stress, resistance is lowered. As the stress continues, the body enters the resistance phase (B), in which resistance is above normal and the body appears to be doing well. In the exhaustion phase (C), resistance plummets.

*After Taylor, 1986.*

Selye distinguished among three phases in the general adaptation syndrome: the alarm stage, the resistance stage, and the exhaustion stage. (See Figure 12.5.) During the *alarm stage*, the body mobilizes its resources to meet the threat. Selye found that when an animal was injected with poison, its body automatically tried to defend itself. Most notably, its endocrine glands immediately sprang into action. The adrenal glands in particular showed striking changes. They became enlarged and produced more epinephrine and norepinephrine. They also discharged their stored-up supply of the hormones known as steroids, which help sustain the body in various ways. Because of this high level of activity of the adrenal glands, numerous physical changes occurred. For example, tissue was broken down into sugar to provide energy, and the amount of salt in the bloodstream was sharply reduced.

Selye named the second phase of the general adaptation syndrome the *resistance stage*. At this point, as Figure 12.5 shows, the body is coping. After a few days of continued exposure to stress-producing conditions, Selye's animals adapted to their situation. The adrenal glands returned to their normal size and began to renew their supply of steroids, the salt level in the blood rose to normal or even higher, and the animals appeared normal.

Yet Selye discovered that during this period the animals were not as normal as they seemed. If a second source of stress was introduced during this stage, the animals soon died. In attempting to adapt to the original stress, they had used their defenses to the maximum and were helpless against additional stressors.

Even if only the original stressors continued, the animals' recovery was temporary. After several weeks of continued resistance to stress, they entered the third stage, the *exhaustion stage*. Their adrenal glands again became enlarged and lost their store of steroids. The level of salt in the blood fell drastically. As a result of receiving an excess of hormones, the kidneys underwent some damaging changes. Eventually the animals died, as if from exhaustion. They had been killed, so to speak, by an excess of the hormones they had produced in their own defense (Selye, 1956).

## Somatoform Disorders

**Somatoform disorder**
A bodily ailment that stems, at least in part, from psychological causes.

Like Selye's animals, humans can mobilize the body's resources in order to react quickly and effectively to an immediate stressor. Yet if stress is long-lasting, the body can be severely damaged by the very mechanisms that would save it in the short run. Stress—especially psychologically induced stress—is often prolonged and not easily remedied, and it can lead to physiological damage and disease. For example, cortisol—a hormone that is released in the body when we experience stress—works to our benefit in the short run, but it is harmful if secreted at high levels over long periods.

Stress caused by frustration, conflict, or prolonged emotional upset can be as drastic as the kind Selye produced by injecting poison. The physical results often take the form of a **somatoform disorder** (or psychosomatic illness), a bodily ailment that suggests a general medical condition but stems at least in part from psychological causes (American Psychiatric Association, 2000). Research has shown, for example, that over the course of 4 decades individuals who live under tension are twice as likely to develop hypertension, or high blood pressure, as are those whose lives are relatively free of stress (Markovitz, Matthews, Kannel, Cobb, & D'Agostino, 1993; Wickrama et al., 2001). Other diseases that frequently seem to be worsened by stress include ulcers, bronchial asthma, and headache (Taylor, 1986). (Somatoform disorders are discussed more fully in Chapter 13.)

As many people have discovered, the stresses that produce illness can be related to the work environment. It has been found, for instance, that air traffic controllers, especially in high-traffic airports, are more likely than other workers to suffer from stomach ulcers and hypertension (Rose, Jenkins, & Hurst, 1978). And a study of subway train drivers showed that a major work-related crisis can erode health and well-being, as described in Figure 12.6.

The onset of health problems following stress need not be immediate. For example, during the first 3 months there was no difference between the two groups of train drivers identified in Figure 12.6. The same pattern was shown in a study of men enrolled in a Navy submarine school. The participants completed a survey of life experiences covering the past year, dating each experience and rating its desirability and impact. An analysis of this information in relation to the participants' medical records revealed a strong positive correlation between stressful life events and illnesses occurring as long as 6 months to 1 year later (Antonini, 1985).

Some researchers believe that, at least in humans, different types of stressors may affect the body differently and produce varying physiological responses (Taylor, 1990). For example, there are some indications that stressful events that evoke feelings of loss and depression are linked to higher vulnerability to cancer (Jensen, 1987). In any case, it would seem that under ordinary conditions our bodies can resist such external causes of illness as viruses and bacteria. When our usual defenses are weakened by stress, we are more likely to get sick.

## Stress and Survival

Can stress actually kill, as it killed Selye's animals? Some evidence comes from a study of the backgrounds of middle-aged men who died suddenly of heart attacks. The results showed that 4 out of 5 had been feeling overwhelmed and depressed for periods ranging from a week to several months. Moreover, just before the fatal attack, at least half of them had been in a situation that was likely to produce sud-

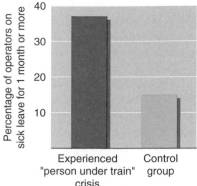

**FIGURE 12.6 Out sick after a traumatic crisis.** "Person under train!" is a shocking message sometimes heard by subway train operators. Operators who had experienced such an unfortunate event—that is, having a person hurt or killed after falling under the moving train—were far more likely to lose time because of illness during the following year.
*Theorell, Leymann, Jodko, & Konarski, 1992.*

The physical results of stress caused by prolonged emotional upset often take the form of a somatoform disorder, a bodily ailment that suggests a general medical condition but stems at least in part from psychological causes.

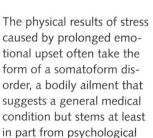

den and intense emotional arousal—in some cases, an unusually heavy workload or other bustle of activity; in others, a high level of anxiety or anger (Greene, Goldstein, & Moss, 1972).

Additional evidence comes from a study of children who experienced life-threatening asthma attacks. The researchers found significant differences between the children who died from the attacks and those who survived. The children who died were more likely to be unusually sensitive to separation or loss. Often they had experienced a recent loss through death, divorce, or abandonment. In addition, the children who succumbed were more likely to have a history of family turmoil and to have expressed hopelessness or despair within a month before the fatal attack (B. D. Miller & Strunk, 1989). For both the asthmatic children and the men who suffered heart attacks, it seems likely that stress was at least a contributing factor in the deaths.

## Are Some Stressors Worse Than Others?

Everyone undergoes stressful experiences—yet not everyone comes down with somatoform disorders. Why? Just as no two people have exactly the same physiology, no two people have exactly the same experiences. And even when they do, as discussed earlier, they may not view it in the same way. After studying the life experiences and medical records of large numbers of people, one group of investigators developed the Life Stress Scale shown in Table 12.1, which assigns numerical values to the amounts of stress created by various kinds of events (Holmes & Rahe, 1967). Note that these events include not only misfortunes but also pleasurable happenings such as getting married, achieving something outstanding, and even going on vacation or celebrating Christmas. Indeed, getting married, which was assigned a numerical value of 50, was found to be fully half as stressful as the death of a husband or wife, which tops the list at 100.

The likelihood of a somatoform disorder, the investigators concluded, was determined by the total number of stress units that occurred within a single 12-month

*These are some of the figures in the Life Stress Scale.*

### TABLE 12.1
### A Scale of Stresses Produced by Various Events

| Experience | Stress Units | Experience | Stress Units |
|---|---|---|---|
| Death of spouse | 100 | Change to new kind of work | 36 |
| Divorce | 73 | Change in work responsibilities | 29 |
| Separation | 65 | Trouble with in-laws | 29 |
| Jail term | 63 | An outstanding achievement | 28 |
| Death of close family member | 63 | Wife starts job or stops | 26 |
| Getting married | 50 | Begin or end school | 26 |
| Being fired | 47 | Trouble with boss | 23 |
| Reconciliation in marriage | 45 | Change in work conditions | 20 |
| Retirement | 45 | Move to new residence | 20 |
| Getting pregnant | 40 | Changing schools | 20 |
| Sex problems | 39 | Changing social activities | 18 |
| New member in family | 39 | Vacation | 13 |
| Change in finances | 38 | Christmas holidays | 12 |
| Death of close friend | 37 | Minor law violation | 11 |

*Holmes & Rahe, 1967*

period. When the number exceeded 200, more than half the people in the study developed health problems. And when the total exceeded 300, nearly 80% of the participants became ill.

Some critics regard the Life Stress Scale and others like it as arbitrary. For one thing, many psychologists believe that, when all other things are equal, happy events seldom lead to physical symptoms (Taylor, 1986). In addition, stress scales ignore individual differences both in the way we appraise the stressors we encounter and in the coping skills and outside emotional support available to us (Holahan & Moos, 1986). The physical effects of stress may also depend on our level of physical fitness. One investigation showed that an abundance of stress is clearly associated with poor health among people who are not very fit to begin with, but the association is less clear for those who are in good shape (Roth & Holmes, 1985). As an example, both physical and emotional stress appear to produce abnormal—and potentially dangerous—heart activity in workers with coronary artery disease but not in healthy individuals (Ganster, Fox, & Dwyer, 2001). Despite such criticisms, scales like the one in Table 12.1 remain useful tools for stress researchers and mental health practitioners (Scully, Tosi, & Banning, 2000).

## Stress and Immunity to Disease

One factor that keeps us healthy from day to day is a well-functioning **immune system**, the network of cellular organs and tissues that protect cells against disease. The immune response springs into action against any intruder that threatens the organism, from bacteria, viruses, and new growths (such as tumors) to ragweed pollen and bee venom.

The immune response is extremely complex, and researchers have only begun to penetrate its secrets. One important area of study is **psychoneuroimmunology**, a new field of research activity that focuses on the interaction of psychological and physiological processes that influence the body's capacity to fend off disease (Cohen & Herbert, 1996). Work in this field has reinforced the view that the net effect of stress is suppression of immunity—and, hence, increased vulnerability to illness.

Studies of animals that have been subjected to stress consistently demonstrate a weakening of the immune system (Coe, 1993). As noted earlier, one of the main consequences of the fight-or-flight response is the release of certain hormones: epinephrine, norepinephrine, and cortisol. These hormones, it turns out, act to suppress the body's lymphocytes, or white blood cells, reducing its ability to fight infection and disease (Marx, 1985).

There is growing evidence that the same pattern takes place in humans. Many of the stressors identified earlier in the chapter appear to be correlated with weakened immunity. For example, following the death of a spouse from cancer, bereaved survivors showed a lowered immunity level—lower even than when their spouses were critically ill and dying. Separation and divorce appear to have the same effect, as does the stress of a poor marriage. Moreover, a similar pattern has emerged in studies of individuals who have been exposed to chronic environmental stress. After the accident at the nuclear plant at Three Mile Island, residents of the area developed lower immunity than people who lived 80 miles away (Kiecolt-Glaser & Glaser, 1991).

Milder forms of stress may also reduce immune response. A study of medical students, illustrated in Figure 12.7, showed that the activity of white blood cells that help fend off viral infections such as flu was significantly lower at final examination time than it had been 1 month earlier. Even greater suppression of these protective cells was found among students who were experiencing especially stress-

**Immune system**
The network of cellular organs and tissues that protect cells against diseases.

**Psychoneuroimmunology**
A new field of research that focuses on the interaction of psychological and physiological processes influencing the body's capacity to fend off disease.

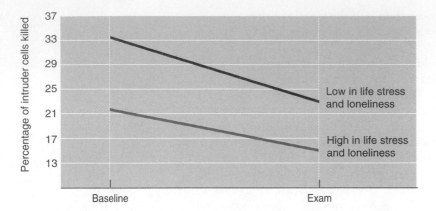

**FIGURE 12.7 The body's immune response to stress. Immune system protection (measured by the percentage of intruder cells killed) declined as students approached examination time. Protection was especially weak among students who scored high on a scale of stressful life changes, as well as on a scale of loneliness.**

*Adapted from Kiecolt-Glaser et al., 1984.*

## Test Yourself

**(e)** A doctor hears the following account from a patient who, though unhurt, has been involved in a terrifying auto accident: "For a while I seemed to be doing O.K. But then, after a few days, I began to feel so exhausted, I had trouble getting through the day." What term did Selye apply to this pattern?

**(f)** If someone were to describe your stomachache as a somatoform disorder, would that mean that the problem was purely a product of your imagination?

**(g)** A scientist is trying to find out why people who experience stress tend to be more vulnerable to colds and other illnesses. In what new field of investigation is that scientist working?

**(h)** What useful purpose can anger serve?

*(The answers are on page 489.)*

ful life events and were also especially lonely. The results suggest that there may be some truth to the popular belief that we are more likely to suffer a bout of flu or a cold in the wake of a stressful period (Kiecolt-Glaser et al., 1984).

Moreover, the drugs prescribed by doctors to protect against illness may be less helpful when we are under heavy stress. In one study, a group of medical students were given inoculations against hepatitis during examination time. Among students who had difficulty coping and were overwhelmed by anxiety, the inoculations were less effective in raising immunity against the disease (Glaser et al., 1992).

Not all bereaved spouses experience reduced immunity, of course, nor do all students taking examinations. There is evidence that individuals differ substantially in how their immune systems respond to stress. Such differences appear to depend, at least in part, on the nature of the individual's sympathetic nervous system (see Chapter 2). In one study, healthy volunteers were subjected to a 20-minute period of acute stress by being required to perform demanding cognitive tasks—for example, math problems—under time pressure and in a distracting environment. There was a suppression of immune function only in individuals whose sympathetic nervous system was highly activated—as evidenced, for example, by heightened cardiovascular activity—when under stress (Manuck et al., 1991).

## Power, Anger, and Hypertension

In a remarkable study spanning 2 decades, a group of men in their early 30s were assessed for their motivation and their tendency either to gratify or to inhibit certain motives. Twenty years later, their patterns of blood pressure were measured. The early tests of motivation were surprisingly accurate in predicting which of the men would have high blood pressure in later life. By far the greatest number of cases occurred among men who, while in their 30s, had a strong power motive that they tried to inhibit (McClelland, 1979). Presumably, "bottling up" the motivation for power produced frequent anger and chronic stress (McClelland, 1989).

This study is one of a number showing that many people with high blood pressure tend to conceal strong feelings of anger and resentment (Weiner, 1982). It has been suggested that this may be one reason why high blood pressure is twice as prevalent among blacks—many of whom resent their status in U.S. society but keep their anger in check—as among whites. In one study, black students were shown several scenes from a film. Racist scenes raised the students' blood pressure more than scenes that were anger-provoking but not racist in content, and emotionally neutral scenes did not raise their blood pressure at all. Students who tended to hold their anger in check had higher blood pressure after viewing the anger-provoking scenes than did students who were more open about their anger (Armstead, Lawler, Gorden, & Cross, 1989). Some suggestions for handling anger are presented in Psychology in the Lab and in Life on page 469.

## PSYCHOLOGY IN THE LAB AND IN LIFE

# Using Anger Constructively

Although anger is a universal emotion, some of us get angry more easily and more often than others. We now know that excessive anger may harm our bodies as well as our relationships. How can we learn to deal with anger? Here are some points to consider (Institute for Mental Health Initiatives, 1988).

*Don't be afraid that anger will drive others away.* Friendships and romantic relationships cannot endure if either party is afraid to honestly express at least some angry feelings. By a wide margin, people report that honest expression of anger is helpful rather than harmful. Even those who are targets of another person's anger frequently say that they come to realize their own shortcomings because of the angry reactions of others. Anger is not pleasant, but it need hardly spell the end of an otherwise healthy relationship.

*Avoid expressing unnecessary and corrosive anger.* The anger we waste on trivial matters is most likely to act upon the victims we least intend—ourselves. On the other hand, it is not always wise to suppress legitimate anger. Some people overcompensate for the anger they feel by becoming overly ingratiating—at great personal cost. Suppressed anger can fester and end up misdirected at a friend or coworker.

*Keep in mind that there is a vast difference between thought and action.* Everyone has a "dark side." In the privacy of our own minds, we can be infantile, petty, vicious, murderous, perversely spiteful, cruelly sadistic, and worse. Although they seem alien, these dark impulses are hardly abnormal; instead, they are an inescapable part of being human. We are allowed to think anything without feeling guilty. Fantasies never hurt anyone.

*The main purpose of expressing anger should be to improve an upsetting situation, not to gain revenge.* Anger can be used constructively to improve the quality of a relationship. It should not be manipulated to prove that one is right or used as a weapon to cause another person to feel bad or guilty.

*Accept the angry feelings of others.* Friends and intimates are quick to pick up signals that we are unprepared to accept their angry feelings. The result is often confusion and misunderstanding on both sides. If we can recognize that the anger of others often stems from a deep sense of caring and if we can accept anger without self-pity or resentment, our relationships will be significantly enriched.

*Try to convert anger into constructive action.* Too often, anger becomes a habitual springboard for feeling soured on life and resentful toward others. The usual result is unhappiness and scarred relationships. Yet we can use anger as an opportunity for growth. That is what the prophets of old did when they transformed their wrath and indignation into campaigns for social change. And that is what the great civil rights leaders did when they redirected their outrage into the service of a noble cause. We too can convert anger into constructive action—by effecting change in ourselves, in others, or in social institutions.

# STRESS AND MENTAL HEALTH

"The thought of hunting for a job makes me anxious all the time."

"I'm so upset about my parents' divorce that I can't keep my mind on my work."

"When I lost my dog, I just felt like staying in bed forever."

**FOCUS QUESTIONS**

- What kinds of psychological experiences accompany stress?

- How can anxiety affect human behavior and performance?

These statements begin to suggest the range of psychological experiences that accompany the body's responses to stress. When stressful events can be overcome, they may lead to positive feelings of mastery and self-esteem. But when they are perceived as overwhelming, they introduce painful feelings of anxiety and a draining of intellectual resources. Often, too, they lead to feelings of depression, hopelessness, and despair. Because stress influences the way we feel, think, and behave, it can powerfully affect the quality of our day-to-day lives—the way we function at work or school, how we relate to other people, and the degree to which life itself seems worth living.

## Stress and Anxiety

**Anxiety**
An unpleasant feeling accompanied by a premonition that something undesirable is about to happen.

**Adjustment disorder**
A psychological response to a stressor or stressors that results in the development of clinically significant emotional or behavioral symptoms.

One prominent response to stress, particularly prolonged or repeated stress, is anxiety. As with many other commonly used terms, there is no single, agreed-upon scientific definition of **anxiety**. For our purposes here, we can define it as an unpleasant feeling accompanied by a premonition that something undesirable is about to happen. Anxiety is closely related to the emotion of fear, but fear is the result of a specific stimulus such as a menacing intruder in the home or a large attacking dog.

Anxiety takes many forms and may be experienced differently by different individuals (Kagan, 2002). Typical symptoms include excessive worry, restlessness, difficulty concentrating, muscle tension, and disturbed sleep (American Psychiatric Association, 2000). Persistent anxiety may indicate the presence of **adjustment disorder**, a psychological response to an identifiable stressor or stressors that results in the development of clinically significant emotional or behavioral symptoms (American Psychiatric Association, 2000). When symptoms of anxiety become so severe that the individual has difficulty functioning effectively in day-to-day life, he or she may be diagnosed as suffering from an *anxiety disorder;* some of these disorders are discussed in detail in Chapter 13.

Although it is impossible to list all the potential causes of anxiety, we can identify five types of stressful situations that are likely to lead to anxiety:

1. Having conflicting motives. (We want to make sacrifices and dedicate our lives to helping others, yet at the same time we want to live comfortably.)
2. Experiencing a conflict between our behavior and an inner standard. (We believe that something is wrong, but because of situational pressures we do it anyway.)
3. Encountering some unusual event that we cannot immediately understand and adjust to. (We arrive in a new town, not knowing what life will be like there.)
4. Facing an event whose outcome is unpredictable. (We don't know how we will fare at a new job.)
5. Confronting the loss of a beloved person. (A close friend or parent becomes desperately ill.)

In each case, the feeling of anxiety is clearly related to a motive. In situations 1 and 2, it is produced by a conflict between motives or between a motive and an inner standard. In situations 3 and 4, it is produced by frustration of the desire for certainty. And in situation 5, it is produced by frustration of the affiliation motive.

### Anxiety and Cognitive Performance

Anxiety evoked by stress can put a considerable strain on our cognitive resources. One reason is that when we are under stress we devote energy to understanding what the stressful event is, as well as trying to determine whether it is likely to continue. As a result, we have less time and energy to devote to careful thought—and this leads to poor performance on tasks. Another reason is that a stressful situation requires us to stay alert for signs of danger. Like the cowboy hero in an Old West movie or a hunter in a jungle full of dangerous animals, we must always be vigilant—which reduces our ability to concentrate (Taylor, 1986).

Of particular interest to college students is the influence of anxiety on ability to learn. Although it appears that people who are high in anxiety do not do more poorly when the learning tasks are simple, their performance does suffer when the learning tasks are difficult. Presumably, their high anxiety impairs the intense focusing required to learn complex topics and remember them come exam time. They seem distracted, as if their anxiety is forcing them to concentrate on the way they feel rather than on the tasks at hand. People who are high in anxiety seem to do particularly badly at complex reasoning when they are put under pressure—such as by being required to answer test questions in what they perceive as too little time (Leon & Revelle, 1985).

*Test anxiety* is a form of general anxiety caused in part by fear of failure. It takes the form of worry and emotionality and may be triggered by a variety of factors such as time pressure, the classroom environment, and the perceived difficulty of exams (Sapp, 1999). Although some psychologists believe that inadequate performance on tests is often simply a result of ineffective test-taking habits, others emphasize that test anxiety is a genuine problem for some students and that there are a number of effective approaches for treating it (Flippo, Becker, & Wark, 2000). These include teaching students better ways to study for and take tests and helping them gain greater control over their feelings when preparing for tests. For example, here are some suggestions for effective use of time when taking tests (Flippo et al., 2000, p. 249):

1. Read all directions thoroughly.
2. Review the entire test before starting.
3. Answer the easy questions first.
4. Skip difficult items and go back to them.
5. Plan time for review at the end.
6. Change any answer if it seems appropriate to do so.

Suggestions for reducing test anxiety include the following (Flippo et al., 2000, p. 249):

1. While in a relaxed state, visualize the exam room. Remain calm while imagining yourself in the room. Imagine taking the test, going through the steps just listed.
2. Be aware of negative internal self-talk and counter it with positive, supportive self-talk.
3. Select a specific place for study, and set goals for time spent studying or number of pages read or problems solved.
4. When studying for tests, follow the SQ3R system (see the description at the beginning of this book).

Other stress-reduction techniques include increasing study time, obtaining coaching from fellow students, and dropping a particularly difficult course. In general, though, the best way to deal with test anxiety is to combine relevant problem-solving skills such as good study habits with emotion-focused skills such as relaxation. Active studying is especially important to success because it directly confronts the problem (Zeidner, 1995).

**Post-Traumatic Stress Disorder**   In the studies described earlier, the anxiety felt by participants typically arose from the kinds of stressful experiences that all of us can recognize. Some people, however, have to endure traumatic stressors that lie far outside the range of usual human experience. They include victims not only of disasters such as floods and earthquakes and fires but also of shocking experiences caused by human actions—war, captivity, torture, assault, rape, life-threatening accidents, and other severely stressful events.

Survivors of such overwhelming events—particularly people who narrowly escape death—may experience **post-traumatic stress disorder,** or **PTSD** (American Psychiatric Association, 2000; Greyson, 2001). Some seem numbed by the shock of their ordeal. Their interest in life is diminished, and they feel alienated from the people around them (Walker, 1981). Others develop a tendency to remain constantly on the alert—as if disaster might strike again at any moment. They tend also to startle easily. People who have lived through automobile accidents may panic at the sound of cars during the night. Those who have endured a mug-

**Post-traumatic stress disorder (PTSD)**
A type of anxiety disorder experienced by people reacting to a traumatic situation or experience that is far outside the usual range of human experience.

**FIGURE 12.8** When words bring back painful memories. Fifteen Vietnam combat veterans suffering from post-traumatic stress disorder (PTSD) were asked to name the color in which each of a series of randomly presented words was printed. The speed with which they responded was compared with that of 15 Vietnam veterans without PTSD. The PTSD group took significantly longer to name the colors of words associated with their Vietnam experience (PTSD words). Note that the three other categories of words used in the experiment produced no significant difference in response time between the two groups of veterans.

*McNally et al., 1990.*

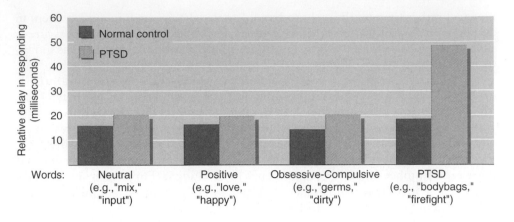

ging or rape may jump whenever they hear strange sounds; some former prisoners of war and hostages report similar reactions whenever they hear approaching footsteps. As shown in Figure 12.8, even words that evoke memories of an earlier trauma can be emotionally disturbing (McNally, Kaspi, Riemann, & Zeitlin, 1990). The participants in this experiment were Vietnam combat veterans suffering from PTSD. Words associated with their Vietnam experience, such as *bodybags* and *firefight,* appeared to activate memories that interfered with the cognitive task at hand.

Survivors of psychological trauma are also likely to keep reliving their experience. They suffer from nightmares in which the shattering episode is reenacted in all its terrifying detail. By day, whenever they are exposed to situations that even remotely resemble the original event, they find themselves suddenly overwhelmed by "flashbacks" in which they relive the experience.

PTSD occurs more often in women than in men and varies in severity and duration from one individual to another (Breslau, 2001a, 2001b). Some people recover from a traumatic experience fairly quickly, but others are troubled by symptoms for many years. One team of investigators studied 27 women who had been raped, some as much as 16 years earlier. The victims continued to suffer from episodes of depression, tension, and fatigue. They experienced not only sexual problems but also difficulties in developing close relationships. Two of the women eventually became so disordered that they had to be hospitalized, and four reported that they subsequently returned to long-abandoned patterns of alcohol and drug abuse (Ellis, Atkeson, & Calhoun, 1981). A number of concentration camp survivors broke down completely when, decades after their ordeal, they had to be hospitalized for medical reasons. The experience was sufficiently similar to imprisonment to reopen their psychological wounds (Edelstein, 1982). Research findings suggest that this lingering pattern may have a biological basis. The experience of terrorizing, traumatic events may alter the chemistry of the brain, rendering victims more vulnerable over time (Mason, Kosten, Southwick, & Giller, 1990).

Although PTSD is not a universal consequence of trauma (Helzer, Robins, & McEvoy, 1987), there is some evidence that traumatic episodes inflicted by others leave worse scars than those that occur by accident or as a result of a natural catastrophe (American Psychiatric Association, 1980). Crime victims, hostages, and combat veterans are especially likely to suffer from their ordeals. Among Vietnam War veterans, 15% have shown signs of the disorder, and their suicide rate has been considerably higher than that for the population as a whole (Roberts, 1988). Similar findings have been reported for Persian Gulf War returnees (Erickson, Wolfe, King, King, & Sharkansky, 2001; Sutker, Davis, Uddo, & Ditta, 1995) and Bosnian refugees (Mollica et al., 2001). PTSD is also widespread among people who survived the September 11, 2001, attacks on the World Trade Center and the Pentagon—especially police and firefighters who saw the towers collapse with their friends and coworkers inside. Many of the survivors report that they cannot get that day out of their thoughts, that they have nightmares about it and feel unrea-

© AFP/CORBIS

Many people who experienced the World Trade Center disaster, especially firefighters, police officers, and rescue workers, have shown symptoms of post-traumatic stress disorder.

soning fear at the sound of a plane overhead or a passing siren. Some are so traumatized that they have been unable to resume their everyday lives.

## Stress and Depression

It is sometimes difficult to separate the physical effects of stress from the psychological effects. This is especially true in the case of **depression,** a common emotional disturbance that can vary widely in severity and affects 1 in 12 people in the United States (National Institute of Mental Health, 1991b). A depressed mood, accompanied by tearfulness or feelings of hopelessness, may be a sign of an adjustment disorder (American Psychiatric Association, 2000). The diagnosis of clinical depression is usually reserved for more severe cases, as described in Chapter 13, and more often involves cases in which specific causes cannot be identified.

A tendency toward depression, especially in its more extreme forms, may be at least partly attributable to heredity. Apparently, some people have naturally low levels of norepinephrine, which could predispose them to depression (Goodwin & Jamison, 1990). At any rate, depression is an emotional disturbance in which the physical and psychological aspects of stress appear to be closely intermingled (Meyer, Chrousos, & Gold, 2001).

Even though a biological vulnerability may be present, depression is frequently precipitated by a stressful experience—especially one that is associated with a sense of loss, such as bereavement, unemployment, or family breakup. The risk of depression appears to increase with the seriousness of the stressful event (Kessler, 1997). There is some evidence that life events that produce disturbed interpersonal relationships lead to depression (Rutter, 1983b). Often, such events destroy an individual's sense of identity and feelings of worthiness (Dohrenwend, Levav, Shrout, & Link, 1987). Depression can also be one of the consequences of chronic pressure to work without adequate emotional rewards. This is one of the reasons given for the fact that 1 in 8 medical school students suffers bouts of depression (Zeldow, Daugherty, & Leksas, 1987).

Even among individuals suffering from depression that is clearly related to **endogenous causes**—that is, causes that are biological rather than exclusively environmental—stressful events apparently play a role. A study of 68 depressed

**Depression**
A common emotional disturbance that can vary widely in severity.

**Endogenous causes**
Causes of depression that are biological rather than exclusively environmental.

patients showed that the degree to which earlier life events were perceived as stressful—including events revolving around marital difficulties, childrearing, and health—was related to the severity of the depression. Moreover, individuals who were not subject to major stressors were more likely to recover from their symptoms (Reno & Halaris, 1990). Chronic stresses—such as those associated with marital and social problems, poor family relationships, continuing employment and financial crises—seem especially likely to lead to severe and recurrent depressive symptoms (Hammen, Davila, Brown, Ellicott, & Gitlin, 1992).

For some people, echoes of stressful events appear to produce depression years later, when feelings about the original events are reawakened by similar experiences. Thus, for example, the death or divorce of parents may sensitize a child and increase her or his vulnerability to depression over losses later in life (Rutter, 1983b). And long-term studies have traced the existence of depression in some individuals as long as a half-century after the economic depression and job disruptions of the 1930s (Gerstein, Luce, Smelser, & Sperlich, 1988).

## Burnout

A frequent symptom of excessive stress on the job is the condition known as *burnout,* a state of emotional exhaustion coupled with cynicism and inefficiency. Burnout is most often seen among people in the helping professions, such as teachers, social workers, and health professionals (Maslach, Schaufeli, & Leiter, 2001; Schaufeli, Maslach, & Marek, 1993), although it also occurs in a wide range of other professions and trades (Matheny, Gfroerer, & Harris, 2000). Individuals in the helping professions may be more prone to burnout because they are often highly motivated and idealistic. They seek to make a difference through their skills and efforts, and when they realize that they are having little effect on the people they are trying to help or that they have little chance of solving problems like poverty or drug abuse, they become angry and frustrated. Work becomes an unbearable burden, and they begin to show signs of physical exhaustion, low morale, and somatoform disorders, accompanied by emotional withdrawal and cynicism.

It's important to note that burnout is primarily the fault of the organization, not the individual (Maslach & Goldberg, 1998). It is generally caused by a lack of rewards in a work situation that requires great effort from workers—who start out with high hopes but finally realize that they cannot make as much of a difference as they expected to. Often it is made worse by the need to spend large amounts of time on paperwork required by government regulations, time that cannot be devoted to helping people. Little can be done to change the conditions that cause burnout, but individuals can minimize its effects by trying to be realistic about what they can achieve and making sure that they keep their work life separate from their home life and other interests. Positive social and emotional support from employers and coworkers can also be helpful (Zellars & Perrewé, 2001).

### Test Yourself

**(i)** "Luckily, my post-traumatic stress disorder just lasted for a couple hours after the earthquake." What is wrong with this statement?

**(j)** What psychological impact do stressful events involving loss—for example, bereavement or divorce—seem to have?

(The answers are on page 489.)

# COPING WITH STRESS

### FOCUS QUESTIONS

- What are the major forms of assertive coping?
- How do a sense of inner control, the availability of social supports, and an optimistic outlook contribute to coping?

The stressors we encounter can produce a wide range of responses—from depression and self-pity to optimism and heroism. Some people throw up their hands in despair; others try to fight off the stressor. Those who fail to overcome their difficulties may find a way of reconciling themselves to the situation—or they may develop physical ailments or crippling psychological symptoms. Indeed, to a considerable extent, all abnormal behavior is the result of unsuccessful coping, whatever its cause—physiological, psychological, or both. Some sort of maladjustment occurs between the individual and the environment, especially the social environment: family, friends, coworkers, bosses, teachers. The individual experiences stress and wants to relieve it but does not know how (Lazarus, 1978).

Many psychologists have focused on the factors that allow individuals to remain resilient rather than on those that cause a person to break down (Segal, 1986). Even in the face of major stressors—bereavement, severe illness, being held hostage—people show a surprising ability to cope. Some people who have been held captive as prisoners of war or hostages, for example, have used their time in captivity to teach themselves new languages, learn new skills, write poetry or books, or plan for the years ahead. Under severe stress, many people in everyday life also rise to the occasion—thus helping to protect their physical and mental health (Lazarus & Folkman, 1984).

## Coping Assertively

Some psychologists refer to constructive attempts to deal with stress as **assertive coping.** Often such responses take the form of direct attempts to change the stressful situation. Whether the stressor is as mundane as a flat tire that will make you late for an appointment, as challenging as difficulties in school, or as harrowing as being held captive, you can often do something to prevail over your predicament. A motorist who is frustrated by a flat tire can get busy changing it or phone for help. A student who wants to be an engineer but is weak in certain areas of mathematics can find a tutor. Even prisoners of war and civilians seized as hostages—brutally stripped of every physical and psychological means of defending themselves—have found ways to change their situation. U.S. servicemen who were taken prisoner during the Vietnam War coped assertively for years with the stress of isolation, loneliness, and confinement. Some adopted programs of physical exercise. Others passed the time by inventing new games or memorizing stories. A few kept a careful census of the insects in their cells. Lacking toothbrushes, they made picks of bamboo sticks and wire, and dental floss out of threads of their clothing or blankets. Similarly bold coping techniques were used by the 52 U.S. hostages who were held for 14 months in Iran. As one of them, Ambassador Bruce Laingen, said after his release, "We're like tea bags. We don't know our own strength until we get into hot water."

**Assertive coping**
Constructive direct attempts to change stressful situations.

## Three Varieties of Coping

We do not need to suffer extreme deprivation to cope assertively. We can find constructive ways to deal with the stresses of everyday life. For example, let's say that we are experiencing frustration because we cannot carry out a particular plan. We feel bad about the situation and may even suffer intense anger. Yet, if we can keep our wits about us, perhaps we can somehow manage to overcome the obstacle. We can face up to the difficulty and try to find some way through or around it. We can regard the situation as an exercise in problem solving and get busy seeking a solution, which may take one of the following three forms:

1. *Changing the environment.* A hungry animal that is prevented from getting food may try to outwit its environment by gnawing through the barrier. Adolescents growing up in an impoverished and harsh environment may work hard to build a life of greater security and comfort. Parents who are anxious

about the presence of a child molester in their community may arrange to post monitors at public playgrounds.

Coping assertively with the environment consists of making a meaningful attempt to change the situation in a constructive way that has a reasonable chance of success. Even though the attempt may fail, the effort itself helps combat the damaging effects of stress.

2. *Changing behavior.* In many cases, the stress we suffer comes not so much from the environment as from our own behavior. Failure in college can result from inattention in class or insufficient study. Social unpopularity may reflect a grumpy, timid, or overly aggressive approach to other people. (The way our own actions strongly influence other people's behavior toward us is one of the concerns of Chapter 15.) Thus, at times the only effective way to reduce stress is to change our own behavior. For example, people with financial problems often can escape only by setting up a strict budget and resisting the urge to spend. A couple who enter marriage counseling will probably find that both partners have to make adjustments in the ways they act toward each other. Indeed, people who seek counseling or therapy of any kind are in effect asking for help in changing their behavior and attitudes.

3. *Managing the internal wear and tear.* Sometimes a stressful situation persists no matter how hard we try to change the environment or our own behavior. During severe economic recessions, many people continue to suffer the strains of unemployment and lack of money no matter how far they travel in search of a job. Efforts to cope with the situation by changing their own behavior—such as training themselves for a new line of work—may fail. Similarly, a person may be helpless to do anything about such sources of stress as the illness of a family member, the breakup of a love affair, or racial discrimination.

In situations like these there is no escape from the source of stress. The only form assertive coping can take is an effort to control the effects of the stress. We must somehow keep the physical and emotional wear and tear within bounds. There is no magic formula for this kind of coping, but many people have succeeded at it—even people suffering from major personal tragedies. One element in their resilience appears to be the conviction that they have not altogether lost control of their lives.

## The Importance of Control

The capacity to exert control is important in reducing the amount of stress we experience in a potentially damaging situation. Researchers studied executives of a midwestern utility company who had experienced various stressful situations, including transfer to a new job in a new city. When a comparison was made of the personality traits of those who became ill and those who did not, the executives who avoided illness turned out to have much more of what the researchers termed *hardiness.* They tended to feel that they were responsible for their own destiny and made vigorous attempts to face and solve their problems, in contrast to the more passive approach of those who became ill (Maddi & Kobasa, 1984).

To be sure, some situations allow more latitude for control than others. One study analyzed how the stressors of routine military flight affected pilots and crews. Preflight measurements of cortisol were found to be the same for both groups. However, postflight levels were higher in crew members whose activities only indirectly affected the safety of the flight (radio operators, navigators) than they were in pilots—those with their hands literally on the controls of the aircraft (Leedy & Wilson, 1985).

Similarly, among individuals who suffer from a chronic disease or disability, those who believe that they can manage either the course of their illness or its day-to-day symptoms appear to adapt better psychologically to their condition. There is some evidence, too, that the progress of the disease itself is influenced by this attitude. For example, a number of studies suggest that cancer, once it has developed, is more likely to spread rapidly in people who "give in" and resign themselves to their fate than in those who maintain a fighting attitude (Taylor, 1990).

What happens to people who find themselves chronically in situations in which they cannot control what happens to them? Heart disease appears to be more common among people in low-level jobs—particularly jobs that are demanding but provide the worker with little opportunity for mastery, such as jobs on an assembly line (Karasek et al., 1988). A similar finding comes from a study in which researchers examined the effect of job stress on men across a range of occupations, both white- and blue-collar. Those who had both a highly demanding job and little opportunity for making decisions were more likely to suffer from high blood pressure, as well as undesirable structural changes in the heart (Schnall, Pieper, Schwartz, & Karasek, 1990). In sum, a major source of occupational stress is responsibility without accompanying authority.

## The Importance of Social Support

Another influential element in coping is the quality of our relationships with others. A number of studies have underscored the common belief that a **social support network**—including devoted family members, friends, colleagues, or fellow members of organizations—offers one of the most effective avenues through which people can escape the damaging consequences of stress (Greenblatt, Becerra, & Serafetinides, 1982; Haines, Hurlbert, & Beggs, 1996; Taylor, 1990).

The importance of social support has been demonstrated in laboratory studies of animals subjected to stress. They show, for example, that the mere presence of a familiar member of the same species lessens the impact of stress (House, Landis, & Umberson, 1988). When the social group is unstable—that is, when its composition is changed regularly—the result is a reduction in the capacity of the stressed animal's immune system to function effectively. This is especially true if the animal is by nature a "loner" that finds it difficult to affiliate with others (Coe, 1993).

The availability of social support appears to "inoculate" against depression among people facing difficult life events (Holahan & Moos, 1991)—even such major stressors as family breakup, illness, and job loss. Moreover, people who have social supports available to them recover more quickly from physical illness (House, Landis, & Umberson, 1988).

Post-traumatic stress symptoms are much less likely to take hold in the presence of strong social support. This was true, for example, even for some who survived the incredibly hideous conditions of Nazi concentration camps during World War II (Schmolling, 1984). And combat veterans of the

**Social support network**
The network of family, friends, colleagues, or fellow members of organizations who aid a person in escaping the damaging consequences of stress.

Talking with others who understand your problems can have a therapeutic effect.

Vietnam War who returned home to supportive family and friends were relatively free from the PTSD problems that so heavily afflicted their comrades (Martin, 1982).

Children also manage to weather stress better if they have social support. In a study of elementary school students, researchers found that youngsters had fewer behavior problems after stressful events such as the death of a parent, parental divorce, or a move to a new home if they received high levels of social support from their family and other children (Dubow & Tisak, 1989).

Members of a social support network can provide support in a variety of ways—for example, companionship and assistance with daily tasks and hassles (Rook, 1987); reassurance and emotional strength (Schaefer, Coyne, & Lazarus, 1981); practical advice and guidance; and, perhaps most crucial, the sense that one is important, valued, and cared about (Sarason & Sarason, 1985).

Just the simple act of confiding your thoughts and feelings to another person can have a potent stress-reducing effect. That conclusion has emerged from a variety of studies, among them one involving more than 2,000 people who had suffered various kinds of trauma, including physical abuse, rape, and the death of a loved one. Survivors were healthier if they managed to talk to someone about the event. Those who hadn't discussed their experiences more often developed illnesses, ranging from headaches to respiratory disease (Pennebaker, 1989). In another study, students who were asked to reveal, in writing, details of the most traumatic events they had suffered—physical and sexual abuse, abandonment, humiliation—showed more effective immune activity than students who were not asked to do so (Pennebaker, Kiecolt-Glaser, & Glaser, 1988).

## The Benefits of Optimism

"Each patient carries his own doctor inside him," said the famed physician and humanitarian Albert Schweitzer. There is reason to believe that a person's attitudes when under stress may indeed affect the ways in which the body responds. For example, people with a negative, pessimistic approach to life, particularly those who tend to become depressed or anxious, appear more likely than others to develop coronary artery disease, asthma, headache, ulcers, and arthritis.

We don't yet know why this happens. It may be, of course, that people with a negative outlook act in ways that harm their health, such as smoking or overeating (Taylor, 1990). But it is likely, too, that a pessimistic view of the future and the accompanying feelings of depression act to impair the immune system through biochemical changes in the nervous system (Rodin, 1980). One source of evidence is a study of a group of Harvard graduates who were evaluated over a period of 40 years. Initially, there were no significant health differences between those identified as optimists and those identified as pessimists; all were in good health at age 25. But the health of the pessimists started to deteriorate at age 45 and continued to do so through age 60 (Seligman, 1988), reflecting a weakened immunity to disease.

Optimists and pessimists make sharply contrasting interpretations of the events in their lives. As Table 12.2 shows, some people are quick to conclude that the crises they face are entirely of their own making, that their reaction will last, and that it will undermine everything they do. They are essentially pessimists. Others, who are optimists, view the crises they face as arising from external circumstances, as transient, and as unrelated to the rest of their lives. This style of reacting makes a difference in their resistance to stress when crises occur.

The sources of such contrasting attitudes are undoubtedly varied, including temperamental and environmental influences as well as cultural differences (Chang, 1996). It has been found, for example, that members of fundamentalist religious groups have more optimistic attitudes than members of moderate or liberal groups. The differences may well be accounted for by the relatively hopeful attitude toward

**TABLE 12.2**
**Contrasting Attributions for Stressful Events**

| Pessimist | Optimist |
|---|---|
| *Internal:* "I can't do these math problems. I'm just naturally stupid." | *External:* "These problems were rigged." |
| *Stable:* "Math has always been a difficult subject and always will be." | *Unstable:* "With a different teacher, things would be a lot better." |
| *Global:* "Doing poorly in math is going to undermine everything I do." | *Specific:* "One test score doesn't make a career." |

*Peterson & Seligman, 1984*

In interpreting stressful events, some individuals show a pessimistic perspective while others are decidedly more upbeat.

life that fundamentalism engenders, along with the greater optimism reflected in the actual content of religious services (Sethi & Seligman, 1993).

Whatever its sources, there is evidence that an upbeat, positive view of life can significantly enhance well-being and perhaps even longevity. The evidence comes from a study of the causal explanations of events on the field given by members of the Baseball Hall of Fame. Explanations of the outcomes of games were gathered from the sports pages of *The New York Times* and the *Philadelphia Inquirer*. Interviewed by reporters after the game, some players displayed an optimistic explanatory style—for example, "We lost because our top hitter had a sore finger, but he'll be OK in a day or two" or "We picked off the runner because my catcher and I have perfected our signals." Other players gave neutral or pessimistic explanations of events on the field—for example, "My aim is still good, but I don't have the stuff I used to." It turns out that those who interpreted game results optimistically lived considerably longer than those who didn't (Seligman, 1986).

There is growing evidence that thoughts, expectations, and hopes affect the body's stress reactions more than the stressful experience itself. Even laughter may be beneficial (Lefcourt, Davidson, Prkachin, & Mills, 1997). One researcher discovered that showing college students funny movies temporarily raised their immunity levels (McClelland, 1989). The role of humor in fighting stress is discussed further in Psychology and the Media on page 480.

There is much still to be learned about the extent to which our outlook serves as a healing force. No doctor can prescribe hopeful optimism. Yet, as illustrated in Figure 12.9, an optimistic outlook seems to aid the recovery of people with serious illnesses, occasionally to the point of enabling them to defy all medical predictions (Cousins, 1989).

Finally, if you are a pessimist, are you stuck with this attitude? Definitely not, says Martin E. P. Seligman, who has written extensively on the subject (e.g., Seligman, 1998). In his view, a pessimistic outlook (or an optimistic one) is learned in childhood and has a lot to do with how parents and others explain why undesirable events occur. At any point in the life span, pessimism can be "unlearned" and replaced by a healthy, optimistic outlook, as discussed later in the chapter.

Baseball players who interpreted their team's losses optimistically lived considerably longer than those who did not.

## PSYCHOLOGY AND THE MEDIA

## Stress? Laugh It Off

 Humor is one of the best on-the-spot stress busters around. It's virtually impossible to belly laugh and feel bad at the same time. If you're caught in a situation you can't escape or change (a traffic jam, for example), then humor may be the healthiest form of temporary stress release possible.

Even when you can change the situation, humor helps. Research by Alice M. Isen, a psychologist at Cornell University, in Ithaca, New York, shows that people who had just watched a short comedy film were better able to find creative solutions to puzzling problems than people who either had just watched a film about math or had just exercised. In other studies, Isen found that shortly after watching or experiencing comedy, people were able to think more clearly and were better able to "see" the consequences of a given decision.

The physiological effects of a good laugh work against stress. After a slight rise in heart rate and blood pressure during the laugh itself, there's an immediate recoil: muscles relax and blood pressure sinks below pre-laugh levels and the brain may release endorphins, the same stress reducers that are triggered by exercise. A hearty ha-ha-ha also provides a muscle massage for facial muscles, the diaphragm, and the abdomen. Studies show that it even temporarily boosts levels of immunoglobulin A, a virus-fighter found in saliva.

While our cave-dwelling ancestors were stressed by actual life-threatening situations like bumping into a woolly mammoth, times have changed. "Nowadays, stress is usually not caused by the situation itself, but by how we perceive that situation," says Allen Elkin, program director of Manhattan's Stress Management and Counseling Centers. Getting a new perspective is what comedy is all about. Several philosophers and writers have pointed out that comedy and tragedy are different ways of looking at the same stressful event.

Comedy works by stepping back from a situation and playing up its absurdities. The same kind of disinterested observation makes the tale of your disastrous vacation seem funny—after you get safely home. For stress busting, the trick is to find ways to laugh at the situation while it is happening. Even if you don't consider yourself much of a comedian, here are a few simple techniques you can use:

*The Bart Simpson maneuver.* How would your favorite cartoon character or comedian react to the situation? "Imagining what would happen can give you a chuckle, making the situation less annoying. You can pretend you're the star of a TV comedy, and this frustrating episode is tonight's plot," says Steve Allen Jr., an assistant professor of family medicine at SUNY Health Science Center, Syracuse (yes, he is the son of comedian Steve Allen).

*Ballooning.* In your mind, consciously exaggerate the situation: Blow it completely out of proportion and into absurdity—into a comedy routine. In that long, long checkout line, don't say, "This waiting is killing me; I hate this." Say: "I'll never get to the front of this checkout line. The woman ahead of me is covered in cobwebs. The guy in front of her grew a beard standing in line. The cashier must be part snail. The continental drift moves faster." This maneuver helps take the edge off the situation, redirects your tension, and helps you see things as not so impossible after all. Your running commentary, however, is probably best kept to yourself. If people stare at you because you seem to be laughing for no reason, pretend you're reading the scandal sheets. You don't have to be a master of one-liners to be funny. There are gentler forms of humor that can defuse anxiety in a group without making anyone feel like the butt of the joke.

*Pick a target.* Making fun of your own foibles can save face in an embarrassing situation—you'll have people laughing with you, rather than at you. Inanimate sources of frustration, like computers and copying machines, are also safe objects of humor.

*Laying it on the line.* Sometimes just telling the truth or pointing out the obvious can get a laugh. People are accustomed to exaggeration and truth-bending (too many TV commercials, perhaps), so plain speaking can come as a refreshing shock. For example, after delivering a series of lengthy explanations during a question-and-answer period, some people have been known to put everyone in stitches by simply replying to the next question with "Gee, I don't know." "This kind of humor is a way of fighting stress by accepting our shortcomings," says Joel Goodman, director of the Humor Project in Saratoga Springs, N.Y.

*Clip a cartoon.* Keep a file of jokes and cartoons that make *you* laugh. Paste a few up where you're likely to need them—at work, on the refrigerator, wherever.

*Source: From "Stress? Laugh It Off," by Stephen Lally, Washington Post, August 28, 1991.*

# Exercise as a Means of Coping

It is generally assumed that exercise makes us feel better. Millions of us engage in regular exercise routines such as walking, jogging, running, and biking or participate in exercise classes—and most of us do so, at least in part, because we feel a greater sense of well-being as a result.

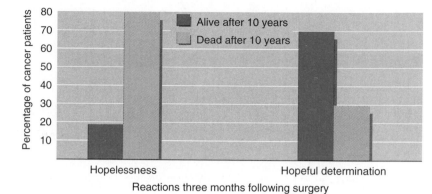

**FIGURE 12.9 Attitude and longevity after cancer surgery. After breast cancer surgery, women who felt that their cause was hopeless had a much lower survival rate than those who harbored a sense of optimistic determination.** *Pettingale et al., 1985.*

Are such subjective experiences supported by research evidence? In general, the answer is yes. People of all ages who stay fit through exercise show less evidence of stress when faced with difficult stressors than those who do not (J. D. Brown, 1991; Stephens, 1988). There is some evidence, too, that engaging in sustained exercise can be an effective way to improve mood—as illustrated in Figure 12.10. It is not clear, however, what mechanisms are involved in producing such results. Among the possibilities are that exercise produces deeper, more relaxing sleep; that it enhances the individual's self-concept and sense of worth (Hogan, 1989); and that it raises the level of mood-altering endorphins produced by the brain. Perhaps all of these mechanisms—and others as well—are involved. Even though we don't know why exercise reduces stress reactions, the pursuit of regular physical activity would appear to be a wise approach for helping us handle the variety of stressors that inevitably come our way (Baum & Posluszny, 1999).

# Biofeedback

Some people are able to deal with the effects of stress by means of *biofeedback*, a method in which control is achieved over bodily and brain functions. Attempts have been made to apply biofeedback to all the various bodily activities over which we ordinarily have no conscious control, including heart rate, blood pressure, and the movements of the stomach muscles. Perhaps one reason we cannot control

© ROB & SAS/CORBIS

Exercise won't make problems disappear, but it can help in managing the effects of stress.

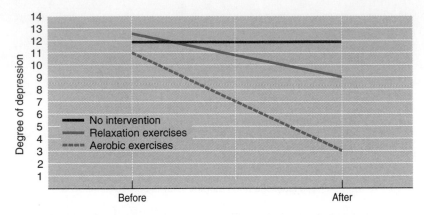

FIGURE 12.10 **Exercise and depression.** Two groups of mildly depressed women engaged in one of two self-help programs; a third group engaged in neither. As shown here, those who practiced aerobic exercise clearly enjoyed the greatest improvement.

*After McCann & Holmes, 1984.*

**FOCUS QUESTIONS**

• What are defense mechanisms?

• What are the most common defense mechanisms?

**Defense mechanisms**
The unconscious psychological processes that people develop to relieve anxiety.

these activities is that we are not usually aware of them. We do not know how fast our heart is beating, whether our blood pressure is high or low, or whether our alimentary canal is busy digesting food. Nor are we aware of many other bodily events—for example, tenseness in the forehead and neck muscles (which appears to be the cause of tension headaches), spasms of the blood vessels in the head (which are associated with migraine headaches), or the patterns of our brain waves (which may be related to epilepsy and also, in another form, to feelings of relaxation, peace of mind, and happiness).

Biofeedback procedures attempt to give the individual control over these activities by providing a moment-to-moment reading of what is going on in the body. With headache patients, for example, electrodes are attached to the muscles of the forehead and neck and connected to a device that clicks rapidly when the muscles are tense and more slowly when they begin to relax. Given this knowledge of what is going on, patients may learn to control the activity of their muscles. Similarly, through devices that monitor and report the volume of blood in the forehead, migraine sufferers may learn to direct the flow of blood away from the vessels in the head that are causing the problem.

Even in the treatment of headaches, where biofeedback has had its greatest successes, the results have varied from one patient to another and have not always been satisfactory. One reason may be that people show wide individual differences in the ability to learn to control their bodily activities, just as they differ in other skills.

# DEFENSE MECHANISMS

Not everyone handles stress in a positive fashion, using techniques of assertive coping. Many individuals use less successful ways to deal with the painful psychological consequences of stressful events. Prominent among these devices are **defense mechanisms,** which were first described by Sigmund Freud (see Chapter 9) and later expanded on and studied intensively by his daughter Anna (Freud, 1966). Freud regarded these mechanisms as unconscious psychological processes that people develop to relieve anxiety. Unlike assertive coping, defense mechanisms are not deliberate efforts to change the environment or one's own behavior or to deal realistically with stress and anxiety. All defense mechanisms are based to some degree on self-deception and distortion of reality. Yet all of us use some of them at one time or another.

By and large, defense mechanisms are not as effective as assertive coping in dealing with stress. They may serve as stopgaps in an emergency. They may even be practiced over long periods, as a sort of life strategy, with some success and without serious damage. But when carried to extremes, they pose a serious risk. They lie in a sort of gray area between successful coping and downright failure to cope—

or, in other words, between normal and abnormal behavior. In this section, we describe several kinds of defense mechanisms. (See the study chart below.) As you read these descriptions, you may think that you recognize them in yourself or people you know. But do not be tempted to play "amateur psychologist" and impute these mechanisms to others. It is essential to treat fellow human beings as entities with dignity and worth, and this includes not trying to "psychoanalyze" them.

## Repression

As discussed earlier, people sometimes feel stress because of internal conflict over their motives, especially their moment-to-moment or day-to-day impulses or desires. To deal with the anxiety this causes them, they may try to banish the offending desires from their conscious thoughts—to the point where they seem to be totally unaware of the original desires or even of having banished them. This defense mechanism—the most basic one according to Freud—is called **repression.** For example, people who at one time suffered severe stress and anxiety over unacceptable sexual desires may repress these desires so thoroughly that they no longer seem to be aware of any sexual feelings or desires at all—or at least those involving an unacceptable object. Other people may seem oblivious to the fact that they have desires for dependency or hostility. Some cases of amnesia, or loss of memory, appear to be exaggerated forms of repression.

**Repression**
A defense mechanism in which a person tries to banish offending desires from conscious thought to the point of being totally unaware of the original desires.

## Rationalization

A common defense mechanism, rationalization has been recognized ever since Aesop coined the phrase "sour grapes" with his fable about the fox. (The fox, un-

## Study Chart

# Defense Mechanisms

| | |
|---|---|
| **Repression** | The person tries to banish offending desires from conscious thought to the point of being totally unaware of the original desires. |
| **Rationalization** | The person attempts to deal with a stressful situation by claiming that the stressor was of minimal importance and may even have had beneficial effects. |
| **Sublimation** | The person unconsciously transforms conflict and anxiety into a different but related desire that is more acceptable to society and to himself or herself. |
| **Identification** | The person attempts to take on the virtues of an admired person. |
| **Reaction formation** | The person pretends to possess desires that are the opposite of the desires that are causing conflict and anxiety. |
| **Projection** | The person attributes to others the desires or thoughts that have caused personal conflict. |
| **Denial** | The person attempts to dispel anxiety by refusing altogether to accept reality. |
| **Displacement** | The person tries to escape the discomfort of unwanted ideas or feelings by transferring them onto another person. |
| **Regression** | The person retreats toward behaviors that usually characterize a lower level of maturity. |

**Rationalization**
**A defense mechanism in which a person attempts to deal with a stressful situation by claiming that the stressor was of minimal importance and may even have had beneficial effects.**

able to reach an inviting cluster of grapes, consoled itself by deciding that they probably would have been sour anyway.) **Rationalization** is an attempt to deal with a stressful situation by claiming that the stressor was of minimal importance and may even have had beneficial effects. (This is essentially a negative view, in contrast to the positive outlook of the optimist, discussed earlier.)

People often resort to rationalization to explain away their frustrations. A man who has been rejected by a woman convinces himself that she was not nearly so attractive or interesting as he had supposed. A woman who has been turned down for employment convinces herself that the job wasn't really worth having. People also use rationalization to reduce the stress and anxiety caused by conflicts between desires and inner standards. For example, a student who cheats on an exam may rationalize the action with the claim that everybody cheats, which makes cheating easier to accept.

## Sublimation

**Sublimation**
**A defense mechanism in which a person unconsciously transforms conflict and anxiety into a different but related desire that is more acceptable to society and to himself or herself.**

A desire that causes conflict and anxiety can be transformed unconsciously into a different but related desire that is more acceptable to society and to oneself. **Sublimation,** which is the closest thing to a "healthy" defense mechanism, enables a shameful or otherwise unacceptable desire to find expression in a nobler form. Freud believed that works of art are often the result of sublimation—that the Shakespeares and Michelangelos of the world may very well have channeled forbidden sexual urges into artistic creativity. Similarly, he believed that people may sublimate their urges toward cruelty into a socially approved desire to become surgeons, prosecuting attorneys, or even teachers with the authority to discipline the young.

## Identification

**Identification**
**A defense mechanism in which a person attempts to take on the virtues of an admired person.**

Another mechanism for relieving stress and anxiety is to attempt to take on the virtues of some admired person or group that seems free of such anxiety. This process is called **identification.** A man, anxious about his own lack of courage, may identify with a brave movie hero or a group of mountain climbers so that he can believe he too possesses their daring. Similarly, a woman who is anxious about her lack of social acceptance may identify with a popular roommate.

In a more complex form, identification may be established with an authority figure who is resented and feared. Thus, a young man may defend himself against the anxiety aroused by hostile feelings toward his boss by identifying with the boss, just as children resolve the Oedipus complex by identifying with the same-sex parent (see Chapter 9). He may imitate the boss's mannerisms and express the same opinions, thus persuading himself that he possesses the same power. This type of identification may also be made with a group. Young people who are anxious about their feelings of envy and hostility toward an exclusive clique may identify with the group and adopt its standards.

## Reaction Formation

**Reaction formation**
**A defense mechanism in which a person pretends to possess desires that are the opposite of the desires that are causing conflict and anxiety.**

People who display a trait to excess—that is, in an exaggerated form that hardly seems called for by the circumstances—may be using the defense mechanism called **reaction formation.** They are pretending to possess desires that are the exact opposite of the desires that are actually causing them to feel conflict and anxiety. For example, consider a woman who appears to be the soul of politeness.

She is always smiling, agreeable, and apologetic for her mistakes. This exaggerated politeness and concern for others may be a defense mechanism that she has adopted to conceal hostile desires that she finds unacceptable and that make her anxious. A man who dresses in a flamboyant manner and is constantly flirting and telling risque stories may be concealing anxiety and sexual inhibitions.

## Projection

A woman who claims that everybody is dishonest and a man who is convinced of the immorality of the younger generation may have reached their conclusions through honest examination of the evidence. On the other hand, they may be exhibiting the defense mechanism known as **projection,** in which people attribute to others—that is, project onto others—their own unacceptable desires or thoughts. The woman who complains too much about dishonesty may be concealing her own tendencies toward dishonesty. The man who talks too much about the immorality of young people may be concealing his own desire to be promiscuous.

**Projection**
A defense mechanism in which a person attributes to others the desires or thoughts that have caused personal conflict.

Projection often plays a part in disagreements between the sexes. A woman may complain that her mate is distant and remote, although a disinterested observer may clearly see that she is the one who is actually withdrawn and inaccessible. A man who is torn by sexual conflicts and urges toward infidelity may falsely accuse his partner of being unfaithful. Another example of the dangers of projection is that a person who has hostile impulses toward another may project those impulses, creating an excuse to "strike first" in self-defense.

Projection is one of the most powerful and dangerous of the defense mechanisms. It works very effectively to reduce anxiety, but it does so at the risk of a completely distorted view of the truth about oneself and others.

## Denial

**Denial** is an attempt to dispel anxiety by refusing to accept reality. (How many heavy smokers or drinkers, for example, successfully deny that their habit can cause serious problems?) Denial is particularly common among children, although they may display any of the other defense mechanisms as well. For a child, it is quite easy to "look the other way" and simply refuse to see unpleasant things as they really are.

**Denial**
A defense mechanism in which a person attempts to dispel anxiety by refusing altogether to accept reality.

## Displacement

**Displacement** is an attempt to escape the discomfort of unpleasant feelings or frustrations by "unloading" on another person, situation, or object. Thus, a woman who is angry at her boss but can't express her anger for fear of being fired may instead pick a quarrel with a friend; in that way, the friend rather than the boss becomes the object of the anger. A boy who perceives himself as having been inappropriately punished by his parents may vent his anger by kicking the family dog.

**Displacement**
A defense mechanism in which a person tries to escape the discomfort of unwanted ideas or feelings by transferring them onto another person.

## Regression

**Regression** is a retreat toward behaviors that usually characterize a lower level of maturity. Displays of regression as a reaction to frustration and stress are common. Frustrated adults may regress to childish behavior such as throwing temper tantrums. Many parents have described how, when faced with frustration, their

**Regression**
A defense mechanism in which a person retreats toward behaviors that usually characterize a lower level of maturity.

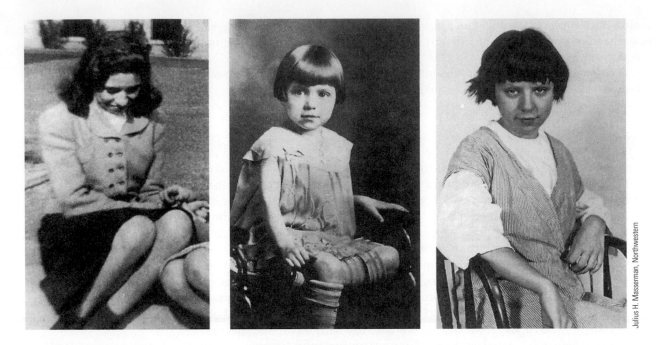

Julius H. Masserman, Northwestern

**FIGURE 12.11 A case of regression.** The girl at left, a 17-year-old psychiatric patient, found the old photograph of herself in the center, taken when she was 5. She then cut her hair, as shown at right, and made every attempt to look as she had at 5.

*Masserman, 1961.*

children begin to behave in a manner more appropriate to younger levels of development. The arrival of a new sibling can be the occasion for an older child to regress to such behavior as bed-wetting or thumb-sucking. People who have suffered extreme emotional disturbance sometimes display striking degrees of regression, as illustrated in Figure 12.11.

## When Defenses Falter

Because conflict and stress are so common, all of us use defense mechanisms from time to time—either those described in this section or others of our own invention. Although these defense mechanisms are usually irrational, they often serve a useful purpose. They may help us through crises that would otherwise overwhelm and disable us. If nothing else, they may gain us time to gather the strength, maturity, and knowledge we need to cope more realistically and constructively with our anxiety and stress. This is often true, for example, of cancer patients who practice denial until they are emotionally ready to face up to their often bleak prognosis (Breznitz, 1983).

In extreme cases, of course, the use of defense mechanisms slips over into the realm of the abnormal. When efforts to cope by employing defense mechanisms no longer work, and when such problematic devices as projection or regression get out of hand, the human personality falls apart. The result can be one or another of the psychological disorders described in detail in the next chapter.

**Test Yourself**

**(m)** If a friend who is hostile accuses you of being angry, what defense mechanism is the friend displaying?

(The answer is on page 489.)

**FOCUS QUESTIONS**

- What characteristics predispose an individual to happiness?

- What techniques can be used to overcome pessimism?

# WELL-BEING AND POSITIVE PSYCHOLOGY

In recent decades, some psychologists have called for a shift in emphasis from the negative to the positive. Instead of focusing on stress, mental or behaviorial disorders, and other psychological problems, they seek to study *subjective well-being* or satisfaction with life, otherwise known as happiness.

Several factors have been found to contribute to subjective well-being. Research has shown that married, religious, extraverted, and optimistic people are most likely to be satisfied with their lives. Economic circumstances also play a role. As one research team put it, "the happy person is blessed with a positive temperament, tends to look on the bright side of things, and does not ruminate excessively about bad events" but also "possesses adequate resources for making progress toward desired goals" (Diener, Suh, Lucas, & Smith, 1999, p. 306). Positive psychology is related to health in that it emphasizes wellness; that is, it calls for formulations of human health that go beyond disease and dysfunction to include studies of how the mind works interactively with the body to produce good health (Ryff & Singer, 1998).

Positive psychologists believe that if people are taught to be resilient and optimistic they will be less likely to suffer from depression and will lead happier lives. Instead of seeking only to find treatments for mental and behavioral disorders, they wish to identify human strengths and learn how to assess and measure them. As noted earlier, Seligman believes that "by studying the building blocks of things like courage, love, forgiveness, and hope," psychologists can not only "understand how [these strengths] grow and how best to nurture them" but also devise a set of psychological tools to facilitate their growth (*Elle Magazine*, 1998).

One area to which Seligman has given particular attention is optimism. His research has produced data showing that helping children at risk for depression learn to think more optimistically can actually prevent mental illness (DeAngelis, 1996). Seligman's learned optimism can contribute immensely to subjective well-being.

Other characteristics that predispose an individual to happiness are self-esteem, a sense of personal control, and extraversion. Happy people have healthy self-esteem and engage in purposeful or meaningful activities that they plan and schedule. They also have strong social support—numerous friends and an active social life. Positive human relations, especially mutual love, also contribute to happiness (Ryff & Singer, 1998).

There are some cultural variations in the sources of life satisfaction. One group of researchers found that financial satisfaction is more strongly associated with life satisfaction in poorer nations, whereas satisfaction with home life is more strongly associated with life satisfaction in wealthy nations. The same research team found that self-esteem plays a greater role in life satisfaction in individualist (Western) cultures than in collectivist (Eastern) cultures (Oishi, Diener, Lucas, & Suh, 1999).

What can you do to increase your feelings of well-being? According to David G. Myers (1992), a leader in the field of happiness research, a good way to start is to smile more. Smiling really does make you feel happy. Myers also suggests devoting more time to social activities ranging from phone calls to visits with friends. Still another way to increase feelings of happiness is to become involved in an activity that engages your skills— be it work, a hobby, sports, or anything else that interests you.

One way to increase feelings of happiness is to become involved in a hobby or other activity that engages your skills.

© Jose Fuste Raga/CORBIS

If you are a confirmed pessimist, it may take more than a smile or a rewarding activity to change your thought patterns. Seligman (1998) suggests three techniques for overcoming pessimism:

1. *Distraction.* When you have a pessimistic thought, try to distract yourself by thinking about something else.

2. *Disputation.* If you experience a negative event, argue with yourself about your interpretation of it. For example, if you're upset because you got a B on an exam when you had hoped to get an A, tell yourself that B is not a bad grade and you'll do better next time.

3. *Distancing.* If you have pessimistic beliefs, try to distance yourself from them long enough to judge them objectively.

Using these techniques, you can learn to be more optimistic. A more optimistic outlook, combined with social support and meaningful activities, can go a long way toward increasing your feelings of well-being and satisfaction with life.

# Chapter 12 Summary

1. Most psychologists view *stress* as a physical and psychological response to a harmful or potentially harmful circumstance.

2. The circumstances that produce stress are best referred to as *stressors*—the events or conditions that put a strain on the organism and pose a challenge to adjust.

## Sources of Stress

3. Throughout the life span, humans confront the reality of a world filled with stressors—from the hunger of the newborn to the physical and psychological decline of older adults.

4. Among the circumstances that constitute stressors are life crises such as bereavement and divorce, transitions such as getting married or starting a new job, catastrophes such as earthquakes and fires, and *daily hassles*—that is, an accumulation of seemingly minor irritations.

5. Three kinds of life crises are especially damaging psychologically: the loss of an important relationship, uncontrollable events, and events that pose long-term threats.

6. Stress can also arise from within the individual as a result of *conflict*—the simultaneous arousal of two or more incompatible motives, resulting in unpleasant emotions such as anxiety or anger.

7. Any situation that is clouded with uncertainty has a built-in potential for creating stress.

8. A person's *cognitive appraisal*, or subjective interpretation, of a potentially stressful episode strongly influences that individual's response.

9. In *primary appraisal*, the individual assesses the personal meaning of the stressor at hand. In *secondary appraisal*, the individual assesses the options available for coping.

## Stress and Physical Health

10. The damaging potential of stress was demonstrated by Hans Selye in experiments with animals subjected to small doses of poison. Selye found that the body's automatic efforts to defend itself produce striking changes in the activity of the endocrine glands, especially the adrenals. After a time, the body seems to adapt and the glands return to normal. If the stressful conditions continue, however, the recovery proves to be only temporary and the animal dies, killed by an excess of hormones the body produced in its own defense. This sequence of events—the alarm stage, the resistance stage, and the exhaustion stage—is called the *general adaptation syndrome*.

11. The bodily changes described by Selye also seem to occur in human beings, often as part of the stress caused by frustration, conflict, or any prolonged emotional upset. They often take the form of *somatoform disorders*, bodily ailments that stem at least in part from mental and emotional causes.

12. The fact that some people get sick and some do not can be attributed to differences in interpretations of a stressful event, coping skills, outside emotional support, and level of physical fitness.

13. The *immune system* is the network of cellular organs and tissues that protect cells against diseases. Studies of the impact of stress on the human immune system suggest that the net effect is a depression of immunity and, therefore, greater vulnerability to becoming ill.

14. *Psychoneuroimmunology,* a new field of research activity, focuses on the interaction of psychological and physical processes that influence the body's capacity to fend off disease.

15. How an individual fares under stress often reflects his or her overall psychological makeup, or personality.

## Stress and Mental Health

16. One prominent response to stress is *anxiety*—a vague unpleasant feeling accompanied by a premonition that something undesirable is about to happen.

17. People who are high in anxiety do as well as others at simple learning tasks but more poorly at difficult learning tasks.

18. Survivors of extremely traumatic events sometimes experience *post-traumatic stress disorder (PTSD),* which is marked by symptoms of stress that can linger for years.

19. The psychological effects of stress include *depression,* a common emotional disturbance that is often triggered by experiences that leave an individual with a sense of loss.

20. People in the helping professions often experience a state of emotional exhaustion known as burnout.

## Coping with Stress

21. *Assertive coping* is an effective defense against stress. It may take three forms: changing the environment to relieve the stressful situation, changing one's own behavior, and keeping the emotional and physical wear and tear within bounds.

22. Successful coping often depends on the ability to maintain a sense of control over the environment, the availability of a *social support network,* and an attitude of hopeful optimism.

## Defense Mechanisms

23. Among questionable forms of coping are the *defense mechanisms* described by Freud. These are unconscious psychological processes, mental or symbolic, developed to relieve anxiety. They include *repression, rationalization, identification, reaction formation, sublimation, projection, denial, displacement,* and *regression.*

## Well-Being and Positive Psychology

24. In recent decades, some psychologists have called for greater attention to the factors that produce subjective well-being or life satisfaction.

25. Among the factors that contribute to subjective well-being are optimism, self-esteem, a sense of personal control, social support, and meaningful activities.

# Chapter 12 Test Yourself Answers

(a) The experience is better described as a stressor—that is, an event that puts a strain on an individual and poses a challenge to adjustment. The speaker's physical or psychological reaction to the house-robbing would be referred to as stress.

(b) There is no such age, for stress is a factor that must be dealt with throughout the life span.

(c) They are trying to avoid uncertainty and doubt.

(d) Your friend is overlooking the importance of cognitive appraisal—in other words, the subjective interpretation of a potentially stressful episode.

(e) The term Selye applied to this pattern is *general adaptation syndrome.*

(f) Somatoform complaints are not imaginary; they concern actual bodily ailments that stem in part from mental and emotional causes.

(g) The scientist is working in the field of psychoneuroimmunology, which is devoted to the study of the interaction of psychological and physiological processes that influence the body's capacity to fend off disease.

(h) Anger can be a springboard for constructive action.

(i) Post-traumatic stress disorder is made up of a set of symptoms that tend to last for a long time—often many years.

(j) Such events typically produce depression.

(k) It might be helpful because it would give the child some sense of control over the stressful experience.

(l) All three are appropriately termed *social support networks.*

(m) The friend is displaying projection.

# Chapter 12  Stress, Coping, and Well-Being

## Key Terms

adjustment disorder (p. 470)
anxiety (p. 470)
assertive coping (p. 475)
cognitive appraisal (p. 461)
conflict (p. 460)
daily hassles (p. 459)
defense mechanisms (p. 482)
denial (p. 485)
depression (p. 473)
displacement (p. 485)
endogenous causes (p. 473)
general adaptation syndrome (p. 463)
identification (p. 484)
immune system (p. 467)
post-traumatic stress disorder (PTSD) (p. 471)
primary appraisal (p. 462)

projection (p. 485)
psychoneuroimmunology (p. 467)
rationalization (p. 484)
reaction formation (p. 484)
regression (p. 485)
repression (p. 483)
secondary appraisal (p. 462)
social support network (p. 477)
somatoform disorder (p. 464)
stress (p. 456)
stressors (p. 456)
sublimation (p. 484)

*The key terms above can be used as search terms in InfoTrac, a database of readings, which can be found at http://infotrac-thomsonlearning.com.*

## Active Learning Review

1. Most psychologists view *stress* as a physical and psychological response to a harmful or potentially harmful circumstance—in other words, to anything that threatens to damage the organism. Thus, events such as an earthquake or the loss of a loved one can produce the physical and psychological response we call _____.

**stress**
**response**

2. Stress is the _____ we make to anything that threatens to damage the organism.

3. John faces both a critical final exam and a broken romance. Such events, which put a strain on him and pose a challenge to adjustment, are known as _____.

**stressors**

### Sources of Stress

4. Whether it is an everyday irritation or a devastating catastrophe, an event or condition that produces stress is known as a _____.

**stressor**

5. *Stressors* involving personal upheavals, such as a crippling illness or the breakup of a marriage, are referred to as _____ _____. Even major life transitions, or changes, that are basically joyous—for example, getting married or beginning college—can produce stress.

**life crises**

6. Marriage as well as divorce can be a source of stress, since each is a major _____, or change.

**transition**

7. Both a job change and a damaging flood put a strain on the individual's capacity to adjust and therefore are _____. A flood, like a fire or a tornado, represents a type of _____ that can be described as a _____.

**stressors**
**stressor, catastrophe**

8. Compared to a life crisis or major catastrophe, a flat tire seems like a minor irritation. Yet such irritations, or _____ _____, can be a source of stress.

**daily hassles**

9. When two or more incompatible motives are aroused at the same time, the result is called _____.

**conflict**

10. When we are torn between studying and going to a movie, we are in *conflict* because of the simultaneous arousal of incompatible _____.

**motives**

11. The simultaneous arousal of incompatible motives results in unpleasant _____.

12. One type of _____ occurs between a motive and an inner standard.

13. When a student is tempted to cheat on an exam to get a good grade but feels inwardly that cheating is wrong, the student experiences a conflict between a motive and an inner _____.

14. When we are torn between studying and going to the movies, we are in conflict because our motives are aimed at two different and _____ goals.

15. When the aroused motives are directed toward two desirable goals but attaining one means giving up the other, the conflict is called an approach-approach conflict. As in all cases of conflict, the result is likely to be unpleasant _____.

16. A conflict between motives directed toward two desirable goals is an _____-_____ conflict.

17. A student who wants to stay up to watch a late-night movie—and at the same time wants to get a good night's sleep—faces an _____-_____ conflict.

18. Fred is a college sophomore who must now declare a major area of study. He always dreamed of being a lawyer, but he also wants to enter the field of electronics. Fred faces an approach-approach conflict, or a conflict between motives directed toward two _____ goals.

19. Jane, too keyed up to sleep, wants to avoid the unpleasantness of tossing and turning in bed—but she also wants to avoid the grogginess she will feel tomorrow if she takes a sleeping pill. Jane faces an _____-_____ conflict.

20. Mary hates going to the dentist and would like nothing better than to cancel her appointment. But she has lost a filling and knows that her tooth will soon start to hurt. She faces an avoidance-avoidance conflict, or a conflict between motives to avoid two _____ alternatives.

21. Because having a baby creates both pleasant and stressful circumstances, it can pose an _____-_____ conflict. A _____ _____-_____ conflict takes place when we are torn between two goals, each of which has both pleasant and unpleasant consequences.

22. The experience of stress depends on our subjective interpretation, or _____ *appraisal,* of a stressful event, or _____.

23. One person faces an illness with little stress; another faces the same illness with a great deal of stress. The difference lies in their cognitive _____ of the condition.

24. Our physical and psychological response to a harmful or potentially harmful circumstance is known as _____. The response depends on our _____ _____ of the event or circumstance.

25. The assessment of the personal meaning of the stressor at hand is known as _____ appraisal.

26. Martin, who is facing surgery, wonders what he can do to handle the situation. By surveying his coping alternatives, he is engaging in _____ appraisal.

## Stress and Physical Health

27. In experiments with animals subjected to small doses of poison, Selye found that the body automatically tries to defend itself from stress through activity of the endocrine glands, especially the adrenals. In these experiments, the introduction of poison was the threatening event, or what psychologists call the _____.

28. Selye described what he called the *general adaptation syndrome:* After the body is subjected for a time to stressful conditions, it seems to adapt and return to normal. But if the stressful conditions continue, the recovery process proves to be only temporary and the animal dies—killed by an excess of hormones produced in its own defense by the body's endocrine glands, primarily the _____.

emotions
conflict

standard

incompatible

emotions
approach-
approach

approach-approach

desirable

avoidance-avoidance

unpleasant

approach-avoidance, double
approach-avoidance

cognitive
stressor

appraisal

stress, cognitive
appraisal

primary

secondary

stressor

adrenals

general adaptation syndrome

Selye

poison

somatoform disorders

somatoform disorder

stress

individual differences
immune

psychoneuroimmunology

psychological

anxiety

anxiety
fear

cognitive

post-traumatic stress disorder
PTSD
depression
physical

stress

depression

norepinephrine

low

endogenous causes

stressors

29. To describe the sequence of events that takes place during prolonged stress, Selye coined the term _____ _____ _____.

30. The pattern of bodily changes by which the body attempts to adapt to stress was described by _____.

31. The stress caused in human beings by frustration and conflict can be just as drastic as the kind Selye produced by injecting _____ into animals.

32. In human beings, the workings of the general adaptation syndrome often produce bodily ailments called _____ _____.

33. Jim, who gets an attack of severe indigestion every time he is forced to work under intense pressure, is a victim of a _____ _____.

34. The likelihood of *somatoform disorders* is determined in part by the amount of _____ a person experiences—but also by individual differences in physical as well as psychological reactions to outside pressures.

35. Martina developed asthma attacks when her parents got divorced, but her twin brother apparently suffered no ill effects. This can be explained in part by _____ _____ in responses to stressful experiences.

36. Stress can affect the _____ system, which produces the body's protective cells.

37. A psychologist who studies the interaction of psychological and physical processes that influence the body's capacity to fend off disease is working in a field of research called _____.

### Stress and Mental Health

38. Along with the body's stress responses go a number of painful _____ effects.

39. Among the painful psychological effects of stress is _____, an unpleasant feeling accompanied by a premonition that something undesirable is about to happen.

40. "I go around with the sense that something bad is going to happen any minute now," says a person who is experiencing _____.

41. The feeling of _____ is closely related to *anxiety*.

42. That high levels of anxiety can keep a student from achieving his or her usual grades shows that anxiety can affect _____ performance.

43. Survivors of deadly fires or of concentration camps may be left with special anxiety problems called _____-_____ _____ _____.

44. Post-traumatic stress disorder is also known as _____.

45. Along with anxiety, stress can produce feelings of _____, a common emotional disturbance arising from both psychological and _____ causes.

46. *Depression* seems to be associated with low levels of the neurotransmitter norepinephrine in the brain, demonstrating how the physical and psychological effects of _____ are sometimes intermingled.

47. A common emotional disturbance in which the physical and psychological effects of stress are difficult to separate is _____.

48. Depression appears to be related to the brain's supply of the neurotransmitter _____.

49. Among people suffering from depression, the brain's supply of norepinephrine is _____.

50. When the causes of depression are internal, or biological, rather than only environmental, they are referred to as _____ _____.

### Coping with Stress

51. One way people try to cope is by attempting to deal with the causes of their stress, or the _____ they face.

52. Psychologists apply the term _____ _____ to constructive attempts to deal with anxiety and stress. Failure to cope may result in physical ailments or psychological problems.

53. A student who tries to overcome his anxiety over a failing grade by studying harder is engaging in _____ _____.

54. One form of *assertive coping* is to change the _____ and thus relieve the stressful situation.

55. A motorist who is feeling anxious about a flat tire that has delayed a trip can cope assertively either by changing the tire or by seeking help, both of which are attempts to _____ the environment.

56. In many cases, the stress we suffer comes not so much from the environment as from our own behavior, and changing that behavior is another form of _____ _____.

57. At times, the only effective way to reduce _____ is to change our own behavior.

58. People who seek counseling or therapy are asking for help in changing their _____.

59. Assertive coping, in addition to changing the _____ or our own _____, can take the form of managing the internal wear and tear produced by stress.

60. A person may be helpless to do anything about some sources of stress, such as the illness of a family member. In such cases, the only form assertive coping can take is to keep the internal _____ and _____ within bounds.

61. Individuals facing difficult stressors are likely to suffer less stress if they feel that they have the capacity to exert _____ over the situation.

62. The harmful effects of stress can be reduced by the availability of good relationships with family, friends, colleagues, or fellow organization members— that is, by a _____ _____ _____.

## Defense Mechanisms

63. Some ways of coping with stress lie in the gray area between successful coping and downright failure to cope. These include _____ _____, which are unconscious psychological processes based to some degree on self-deception and distortion of reality.

64. *Defense mechanisms*, first described by Freud, are _____ processes.

65. People who are feeling anxious about their motives may use the defense mechanism known as *repression*, which involves simply banishing the motives from their thoughts. Repression is an _____ psychological process.

66. John frequently behaves in ways that other people consider hostile, yet he seems totally unaware of any hostile motives. He is probably using the defense mechanism known as _____.

67. _____ is an attempt to deal with a stressful situation by claiming that it is of minimal importance or may even have a beneficial effect.

68. When the fox in Aesop's fable, unable to reach the grapes, consoles itself by deciding that they would have been sour anyway, it provides a good example of _____.

69. Unlike _____, by which people banish anxiety-provoking motives from their awareness, *sublimation* allows people to transform such motives into different but related ones that are more acceptable to themselves and to society.

70. A composer who channels forbidden sexual impulses into musical creativity is employing the defense mechanism known as _____.

71. Repression, *rationalization*, and sublimation are all defense mechanisms based to some degree on self-_____ and _____ of reality.

72. An individual who takes on the virtues of some admired person or group is displaying the defense mechanism known as _____.

assertive coping

assertive coping

environment

change

assertive coping

stress

behavior

environment, behavior

wear, tear

control

social support network

defense mechanisms

unconscious

unconscious

repression

Rationalization

rationalization

repression

sublimation

deception, distortion

identification

reaction formation

psychological process

projection

denial

displacement

regression

subjective well-being

resilient

optimistic

esteem, control, extraversion

73. When people pretend to possess motives that are the exact opposite of the motives actually causing them anxiety, they are practicing the defense mechanism called _____ _____.

74. *Projection* is a defense mechanism by which people foist off (or project) onto others their own anxiety-provoking motives or thoughts. Like other such mechanisms, it is an unconscious _____ _____.

75. A person who hides tendencies toward dishonesty by claiming that everyone else is dishonest is engaging in _____.

76. If your friend tried to dispel anxiety by refusing altogether to accept reality, you would be correct in seeing this reaction as an example of _____.

77. In the defense mechanism known as _____, the individual escapes the discomfort of unwanted ideas or feelings by transferring them onto another person, situation, or object.

78. A retreat toward behaviors that usually characterize a lower level of maturity is typical of those practicing the defense mechanism known as _____.

### Well-Being and Positive Psychology

79. Instead of focusing on stress, mental or behavioral disorders, and other psychological problems, positive psychologists seek to study _____ _____-_____, or satisfaction with life.

80. Positive psychologists believe that if people are taught to be _____ and _____, they will be less likely to suffer from depression and will lead happier lives.

81. Among the characteristics that predispose an individual to happiness are self-_____, a sense of personal _____, and _____.

# Practice Test

____ 1. Stress is defined as
   a. a response to threats to the organism.
   b. psychological discomfort.
   c. an emotional response to conflict.
   d. the frustration of a psychological goal.

____ 2. An individual's subjective interpretation of a potentially stressful episode is referred to as the individual's
   a. stressor.
   b. stress response.
   c. projection.
   d. cognitive appraisal.

____ 3. The sources of stress are referred to as
   a. primary appraisals.
   b. cognitive responses.
   c. stressors.
   d. cognitive stimuli.

____ 4. Life's seemingly minor irritations are known as
   a. minor stresses.
   b. daily hassles.
   c. stressful transitions.
   d. minor trauma.

____ 5. Stress is known to exist
   a. especially in adolescence.
   b. when we grow into adulthood.
   c. primarily in the later years.
   d. from infancy to adulthood.

____ 6. To be classified as a conflict, the simultaneous arousal of two or more incompatible motives must result in
   a. approach-avoidance.
   b. unpleasant emotions.
   c. violation of an inner standard.
   d. aggression.

____ 7. The person who first demonstrated and named the general adaptation syndrome was
   a. Selye.
   b. James.
   c. Cannon.
   d. Freud.

____ 8. In the general adaptation syndrome, the animal eventually dies from
   a. lack of oxygen.
   b. starvation.
   c. an excess of white blood cells.
   d. an excess of its own hormones.

____ 9. Somatoform disorders
   a. result in psychotic behavior.
   b. have mental and emotional causes.
   c. cause a decrease in motivation and drive.
   d. have only imaginary symptoms.

____ 10. Studies of animals that have been subjected to stress consistently demonstrate a weakening of
   a. the immune system.
   b. the fight-or-flight response.
   c. the sympathetic nervous system.
   d. all of the above

____ 11. Anxiety is most closely related to the emotion of
   a. anger.
   b. fear.
   c. grief.
   d. joy.

____ 12. Extremely stressful experiences such as military combat or captivity can result in
   a. cognitive disorders.
   b. poor appraisal.
   c. post-traumatic stress disorder.
   d. somatoform disorders.

____ 13. A common emotional illness that can be caused by stress is
   a. depression.
   b. psychosis.
   c. post-traumatic stress disorder.
   d. cognitive disorder.

____ 14. Assertive coping is a
   a. strategy to overcome depression.
   b. framework for interpersonal interaction.
   c. constructive effort to deal with stress.
   d. defense mechanism.

____ 15. Defense mechanisms are *not*
   a. mental processes.
   b. conscious.
   c. attempts to relieve anxiety.
   d. a form of self-deception.

____ 16. Defense mechanisms were first described by
   a. Selye.
   b. Maslow.
   c. Freud.
   d. Aristotle.

____ **17.** When we try to be like some admired person who seems to be free of the anxiety that troubles us, we are using the defense mechanism called
a. reaction formation.
b. sublimation.
c. rationalization.
d. identification.

____ **18.** Mark, who feels anxious about his excessive hostility, is the soul of politeness and courtesy. His behavior is an example of the defense mechanism called
a. identification.
b. sublimation.
c. repression.
d. reaction formation.

____ **19.** When we falsely accuse other people of the motives that are making us feel guilty, we are using the defense mechanism called
a. identification.
b. projection.
c. reaction formation.
d. sublimation.

____ **20.** Retreating to activities characteristic of a lower level of maturity is called
a. regression.
b. depression.
c. reaction formation.
d. withdrawal.

# Exercises

1. On pages 482 to 486 of the text you will find a description of defense mechanisms that we all use to some degree when faced with anxiety and stress. Five of them are listed here:

   a. Rationalization

   b. Reaction formation

   c. Projection

   d. Displacement

   e. Denial

   Keep a record for the next month or so of episodes in which you believe an individual has used one of these forms of coping. Among the sources you may use to gather such episodes are movies and television shows, short stories and novels, interactions with friends, conversations you overhear, experiences someone tells you about, and observations of your own behavior.

   Summarize each episode in a few paragraphs, and identify the form of coping used by assigning the appropriate letter from the above list. After you have collected 20 episodes, consider the following questions:

   a. Did certain forms of coping occur much more frequently than others?

   b. Do you think the individuals were aware of the coping techniques they were using?

   c. Was it easier to spot the coping techniques used by others or your own?

2. Every change we experience produces stress. This includes not only undesirable changes, such as illness, the death of a loved one, or divorce, but also generally desirable changes, such as getting a new job, receiving a gift, falling in love, or getting married. This exercise may give you an idea of how your level of stress compares with those of other students taking this course.

## Phase I

Each student should carry out the first phase individually. Use brainstorming to list 20 changes that have occurred in your life over the last year. Write down desirable, undesirable, and possibly neutral changes without regard to their importance to you. After you have identified 20 changes, sort them into three columns labeled *positive, negative,* and *neutral. Positive* means that you liked the change; *negative* means that you didn't like it; and *neutral* means that you were aware of the change but didn't much care one way or the other about it.

To the right of each item, place a stress score between 1 and 10, where 1 = minimum emotional impact and 10 = maximum emotional impact. Now total your stress points for each column separately. Finally, produce a grand total by adding all the column subtotals.

## Phase 2

Meet with the other classmates who did this exercise and compare your column scores and your grand total against theirs. Using the information on stress in this chapter and any lecture material you may have been given in class, respond to the following questions:

a. What differences are there in *positive* scores?

b. What differences are there in *negative* scores?

c. What differences are there in *neutral* scores?

d. What differences are there in grand total scores?

e. What are the implications of experiencing stress from *positive* events?

f. How could something seen as *neutral* affect a person?

g. Is it true that just about any kind of change is stressful?

✱ *For quizzing, activities, exercises, and web links, check out the book-specific website at http://www.psychology.wadsworth.com/kagan9e.*

# 13

# Mental and Behavioral Disorders

© Peter Turnley/CORBIS

498

When we imagine someone with a mental or behavioral disorder, we tend to picture a disheveled old man mumbling to himself while pushing a shopping cart full of tattered belongings or a withdrawn, dazed woman wandering the halls of a mental institution. Although both images do depict people suffering from such disorders, they are examples from the extreme end of the spectrum. Many people with serious depression appear to be functioning normally but are nonetheless suffering and in need of treatment. People with deep-seated personality disorders may appear charming and engaging at first glance, although time and familiarity will reveal hurtful, destructive, and even dangerous aspects of their personality.

Many of the symptoms described in this chapter will be familiar to you—who among us hasn't experienced an occasional blue mood, intense anxiety, or a nagging compulsion? Although all of us have had some of the same experiences and symptoms as people who are clearly identified as abnormal, most of us go through life without ever suffering a severe mental disorder. The task of identifying that breaking point—the point where a person's psychological functioning goes significantly awry—is among the most challenging in the field of psychology.

Shostak/Anthro-Photo File

In some hunter-gatherer societies, people spend as little as 10 hours per week earning a livelihood. In your society, would such behavior seem normal?

# ABNORMAL CHARACTERISTICS: THEIR NATURE AND SCOPE

When do people cross the line between what is normal and what is not? A psychologist wouldn't hesitate to label a belligerent person standing on a street corner screaming obscenities as abnormal. Nor would a psychologist hesitate to describe as distinctly normal people who are functioning at the peak of their powers and feeling good about themselves and others. However, in less extreme cases, it can be difficult to make a clear distinction between normal and abnormal. Moreover, it is always necessary—in keeping with one of the major themes in psychology emphasized in this textbook—to bear in mind the importance of context and culture in understanding variations in human behavior.

**FOCUS QUESTIONS**

- How is abnormal behavior defined?

- How prevalent are mental and behavioral disorders?

## Qualities That Define Disorders

Is it abnormal to believe in witches and possession by demons? It was not considered so by many peoples throughout history, including both native peoples and European colonists in the Americas, and it is not considered so by many people even today. Is it abnormal to become angry and suspicious every time you encounter disappointment and frustration? Among the Kaluli of New Guinea, such responses are the accepted norm (Schieffelin, 1985). Is suicide abnormal? To most people in the Americas and Europe, it may seem the ultimate in abnormality. Yet in East Asia, a Buddhist priest who commits suicide as a form of political protest is regarded as exhibiting strength of character rather than abnormality. Tragically for all concerned, "suicide bombings" of innocent civilians as a means of warfare have become almost commonplace in recent years—with the bombers often being revered by loved ones and others they leave behind. Clearly, even from such a limited sample of cultural variations in beliefs and behaviors we can see that abnormality is not something that can be defined universally.

From a statistical viewpoint, behavior can be called abnormal if it is uncommon and unusual—what is often referred to as "odd." But this isn't the whole story either, for even unusual forms of behavior are not generally considered abnormal unless they are regarded as undesirable by the society in which they occur. In North America, the habit of working 18 hours a day is probably rarer than heroin addiction. Yet many people consider an 18-hour workday to be admirable or at least acceptable—definitely not abnormal in the sense of disordered. In contrast, heroin addiction is considered highly undesirable and therefore thoroughly abnormal.

Because happiness is highly valued in most societies, people who are happy are generally regarded as being free of abnormality. Although this criterion is widely accepted, there are some notable exceptions here as well. People who commit vicious acts that could hardly be considered normal—such as serial killings and mass murders—may at the same time seem to be quite happy.

In general, a useful working definition of abnormal behavior embraces the three features we have mentioned. A mental or behavioral abnormality is (1) statistically unusual, (2) considered undesirable by most people, and (3) a source of unhappiness to the person who displays it. It must be admitted that this definition is not entirely satisfactory from a theoretical point of view and would not be accepted enthusiastically by some mental health professionals—chiefly on the ground that it sets up standards that might enable society to label as abnormal anyone whose behavior is disliked or considered disruptive by the "normal" majority. However, this problem is offset by the observation that most people who are regarded as abnormal satisfy all three criteria.

**Maladaptive behavior**
**A behavior that interferes with an individual's functioning.**

In addition, many psychologists view as abnormal behaviors that interfere with the individual's personal or social functioning—that is, **maladaptive behaviors.** For example, when a person becomes so anxious or depressed that going to work, attending school, or seeing friends becomes impossible, that person's behavior is not considered normal. Today, most mental disorders are characterized by the pattern, severity, and duration of clusters of symptoms and by the levels of impairment and disruption they produce in people's lives. But as we will see later in the chapter, efforts have been under way for some time to develop additional criteria—such as tests of brain structure and activity—that can aid in determining when an individual is mentally ill (Kales, Stefanis, & Talbott, 1990).

## The Prevalence and Impact of Disorders

Mental and behavioral disorders affect people of all ages, ethnicities, and walks of life. Contrary to popular belief, they are common in developing and industrialized nations alike (Léon, 1989). As the World Health Organization (2001) notes,

> Mental and behavioural disorders are found in people of all regions, all countries and all societies. They are present in women and men at all stages of the life course. They are present among the rich and poor, and among people living in urban and rural areas. The notion that mental disorders

are problems of industrialized and relatively richer parts of the world is simply wrong. The belief that rural communities, relatively unaffected by the fast pace of modern life, have no mental disorders is also incorrect. (p. 37)

Estimates vary, but it appears that at least 50 million people in the United States suffer from a diagnosable mental or behavioral disorder at any given time (e.g., see U.S. Department of Health and Human Services, 1999). Among these are people whose conditions are truly severe—individuals who experience long-term, persistent, and disabling disorders that have a profound impact on their everyday existence and on that of their families and communities. The U.S. prevalence rates of selected disorders discussed in this chapter are shown in Figure 13.1.

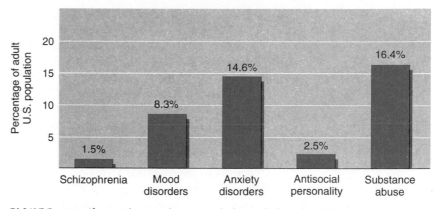

**FIGURE 13.1  How widespread are psychological disorders? From interviews with over 18,000 individuals age 18 or over, it was possible to estimate the percentage of people in the United States who have experienced major mental disorder in the course of their lifetime.**
*After Regier, Boyd, Burke, & Rae, 1988.*

No statistical data, however, can portray the full impact of these disorders in human terms. Anyone who has actually experienced periods of intense anxiety or depression knows how disabling they can be and how much pain and distress they can cause. In one study, patients in the throes of terminal cancer who also had a history of severe depression were asked to compare the two. Most reported that the physical pain was more bearable—and far preferable to the psychological pain of their mental disorder (Jamison, 1982)

# CAUSES AND CLASSIFICATION OF ABNORMAL BEHAVIORS

Although the causes of abnormal behaviors are thought to vary considerably, in general people seem to have a "breaking point" at which they lose their psychological equilibrium. That fragile point seems to depend on the kinds and amounts of environmental stressors people face and their ability to handle them. That ability, in turn, depends on their biological makeup, their personality, the kinds of support they get from other people, and their learned styles of coping.

Some people are so biologically susceptible that they seem to develop mental or behavioral disorders without any pressure from external stressors. Others, as described in the preceding chapter, seem practically invulnerable, able to endure and triumph over conditions that would break the minds and spirits of most people. Still others, for reasons not yet clear, seem to develop personalities that are enduringly abnormal. Studies of the sources of psychological disorders strongly underscore the first of the three major themes introduced at the beginning of this text: Human behavior, whether normal or abnormal, is determined by a complex interplay of biological and environmental factors, mediated by personality and cognition.

**Test Yourself**

**(a)** Unusual forms of behavior are not always considered abnormal. For instance, it is more common in this country to be a heroin addict than to be someone who works 18 hours a day. What makes the former abnormal and the latter not?

(The answer is on page 532.)

**FOCUS QUESTIONS**

• How is abnormal behavior influenced by biological, psychological, and environmental factors?

• What criteria are used to diagnose mental and behavioral disorders?

## Biological Influences

Just as people vary greatly in their outward physical makeup, they vary greatly in their inner wiring: There are wide individual differences in glandular activity and sensitivity of the autonomic nervous system, as well as in the activity of the brain centers concerned with emotion. These differences may incline one person to be more easily aroused and more intensely emotional than another. Thus, some people, because of their genetic makeup, probably experience a great deal more emotional and physical wear and tear than others.

There is considerable evidence that heredity can contribute to tendencies toward the most severe forms of abnormal behavior. For example, schizophrenia is more common among close relatives of schizophrenics than among people whose family background shows no other cases. Studies also indicate that hereditary factors may produce tendencies toward disabling forms of depression and perhaps toward other, less extreme forms of abnormal behavior as well (Neubauer & Neubauer, 1990). Nevertheless, it is unlikely that a specific gene will be identified as an isolated cause of most mental disorders (Dunn & Plomin, 1990). Where psychological characteristics are concerned, *polygenic influences* are assumed to be the rule—that is, characteristics are influenced by multiple genes in complex interactions. Moreover, genes only set the stage for development and perhaps "predispose" an individual to disorders or other psychological characteristics. The ongoing environment the person experiences then plays a major role in determining whether such characteristics will be expressed.

## Environmental Influences

Learning and experience play an important part in many mental and behavior disorders. The role of environmental stressors and other negative experiences in precipitating abnormal behavior has been recognized since the early 20th century. Research clearly indicates that unfair, harsh, and inconsistent parental discipline in childhood is related to mental and behavioral disorders in adulthood. Such experiences probably help bring on a disorder to which the child is already predisposed (Holmes & Robins, 1987). The importance of environmental factors is underscored by consistent evidence that mental disorders disproportionately affect people living in poverty (National Institute of Mental Health, 1991b). An even clearer example is the effects of PTSD, discussed in Chapter 12.

Although stressful events in a person's current social environment can increase his or her vulnerability to mental disorder, the stage may be set by the nature of earlier environments. Children who grow up in broken families, are physically or sexually abused, or live with a severely mentally ill parent may be vulnerable to mental disorder in later life (Rutter, 1986). Growing up in poverty may also contribute to later vulnerability—perhaps because of the stress-

A traumatic combat environment can leave lasting emotional scars.

UPI/Bettmann

ful experience of deprivation or because deprived conditions contribute to poor physical health and impaired capacity to cope with anxiety and stress.

## The Role of Personality and Cognition

Personality traits play a key role in determining how much anxiety and stress we are likely to experience and how much we can tolerate without succumbing to mental disorder. For example, people who have—but cannot fulfill—high needs for power, achievement, or approval may become extremely vulnerable to tense moods. From a cognitive perspective, our inner standards and our interpretations of events have a strong influence on our psychological well-being. An event such as receiving a barely passing grade on a final exam may produce little or no anxiety in a person with relatively low standards of mastery, but it may produce almost unbearable anxiety in a person with higher standards. Clinical psychologists often see people who are extremely anxious about violations of norms concerning sexual behavior, honesty, hostility, or dependency that would seem minor to others.

## DSM-IV

Some deviations from the normal are so slight that they are popularly termed *quirks;* examples include eccentricities of dress or speech that go beyond fad or fashion. People who have picked up such habits may seem a bit odd at times, but they are not seriously discomforted or prevented from functioning effectively. At the other extreme are the serious forms of mental disturbance that leave their victims out of touch with reality and incapable of conducting the ordinary affairs of life. In a sort of twilight zone between normal behavior and extreme abnormality are long-lasting emotional disturbances characterized by high levels of anxiety and depression. Their victims usually function from day to day, but well below par and without much happiness or contentment. They are the people who are most likely to seek to improve their lives through psychotherapy.

The symptoms and clusters of symptoms (or *syndromes*) that are regarded as evidence of psychological disorder have evolved over time, based on a combination of social attitudes and values, the experiences of people who treat patients, and accumulating insights into the underlying causes and patterns of abnormal behavior. The classification scheme now used by psychologists, psychiatrists, and other mental health professionals is contained in the fourth edition of the *Diagnostic and Statistical Manual of Mental Disorders,* published in 1994 and updated in 2000 by the American Psychiatric Association. Known as **DSM-IV,** the manual presents detailed descriptions of patterns of abnormal behavior, ranging from those formerly known as "neurotic" to more devastating ones often referred to as "psychotic." (See the study chart on page 504.)

The use of labels such as those in DSM-IV remains a subject of some controversy. Psychiatrist Thomas Szasz, for example, has long argued that the broadly accepted "medical model" for physical illness does not apply to mental and behavioral problems and that the very concept of "mental illness" is in most respects a myth (1960; more recently, 1993, 1998, 1999, 2000). For one thing, the diagnosis of a mental disorder suggests that the person has a malady analogous to a cancer or a virus, even though, as Szasz points out, he or she may simply be experiencing "problems of living." That is, the mental-illness approach presumes that each disorder has an underlying cause that is relevant to treatment, even though many psychologists believe that the causes of some disorders are far less important than their symptoms. Phobias, discussed later in the chapter, are a prime example:

**Test Yourself**

**(b)** Tracy and Annette, who both work for a large software company, are laid off as a result of downsizing. During the next 6 months, as the two search for new jobs, Tracy becomes severely depressed; Annette does not. What factors could account for their differing reactions to this life crisis?

(The answer is on page 532.)

**DSM-IV**
Abbreviation for the fourth edition of the American Psychiatric Association's *Diagnostic and Statistical Manual of Mental Disorders,* which presents detailed descriptions of patterns of abnormal behavior.

Never mind why a person is terrified by snakes, they say; just eliminate the terror, as discussed in Chapter 14.

Perhaps not suprisingly, the views of Szasz and his adherents have not gone uncriticized (see Dammann, 1997, for an objective review of each position). But regardless of one's point of view, DSM-IV is a thorough and extensive catalog with concise criteria and useful background information on mental and behavioral abnormality. It has greatly improved the process of identifying and treating most disorders, and it continues to serve as the standard guide for this purpose—both for those who endorse it and for those who do not.

## Study Chart

## Major Psychological Disorders

| Disorder | Description | Also Discussed in |
|---|---|---|
| Disorders first evident in infancy, childhood, or adolescence | Mental retardation, autism, attention-deficit/hyperactivity disorder, speech disorders, and other deviations from normal development | Chapter 10 |
| Schizophrenia | A disorder characterized by loss of contact with reality, disturbances of thought and perception, and bizarre behavior; frequently accompanied by delusions or hallucinations | |
| Mood disorders | Disturbances of normal mood in which the person is extremely depressed, is abnormally elated, or alternates between periods of depression and elation | |
| Anxiety disorders | Disorders in which anxiety is the main symptom or is experienced unless the person avoids feared situations or performs certain rituals or thinks persistent thoughts; includes post-traumatic stress disorder | |
| Somatoform disorders | Disorders in which the person exhibits physical symptoms for which no organic basis can be found | Chapter 12 |
| Dissociative disorders | Disorders characterized by temporary alterations in the functions of consciousness, memory, or identity due to emotional problems | |
| Sexual disorders | Problems of sexual identity, sexual performance, and sexual interest | Chapter 8 |
| Eating disorders | Disorders characterized by self-induced starvation or by binge eating followed by self-induced purging | Chapter 11 |
| Sleep disorders | Chronic insomnia, excessive sleepiness, sleep apnea, sleepwalking, narcolepsy | Chapter 8 |
| Personality disorders | Patterns of maladaptive behavior that constitute inappropriate ways of coping with stress or solving problems | |
| Substance use disorders | Excessive use of alcohol and other drugs that alter behavior, including marijuana, caffeine, and tobacco | Chapter 11 |
| Disorders of impulse control | Kleptomania, pathological gambling, and pyromania | |

The current classification scheme may change in time, of course. As our knowledge of abnormal behavior changes, disorders are added, excluded, regrouped, and relabeled. (Note, too, that people don't always fit neatly into one category or another—for example, schizophrenics may have mood problems, and depressed people sometimes hallucinate.) The sections that follow deal with today's major groupings of seriously abnormal mental, behavioral, and personality patterns.

# SCHIZOPHRENIA

The symptoms began to appear when Ralph was 19 years old. He became suspicious of his classmates, insisting that they were developing a special language so that they could carry out their secret plans to destroy him. His dress became slovenly, and sometimes, even in the heat of summer, he would wear three sweaters to protect himself from "the poisonous rays that will appear at noon." His few friends would often find him in a corner of the library, mumbling to himself. Once Ralph refused to eat for an entire week. He was convinced that the food had been poisoned in order to punish him for his grandmother's death. He imagined that she had died as a result of a magic word he had secretly thought of.

**FOCUS QUESTIONS**

• What are the major symptoms of schizophrenia?

• What are some possible causes of schizophrenia?

As time passed, Ralph's behavior became even more bizarre. He would stand at the window for hours on end, staring at passersby and mumbling nonsensical phrases like "gloop in the soup" or "brangle my strangle." He complained that neighbors were spying on him, and he would scream obscenities at them. He believed that he had enormous powers, and he wrote to the president to offer solutions for all the world's problems. He was chosen, he said, to act as peacemaker not only between nations but also between the U.S. government and the creatures that were about to arrive from outer space.

By the time he was hospitalized, nothing Ralph said or did made any sense. Once he tried to climb into the toilet and have a nurse flush him away. He ordered his doctors to leave the room because, as he explained it, "I am attending a conference with God, George Washington, and IBM."

Ralph is one of the estimated 2 million people in the United States suffering from **schizophrenia,** a devastating psychological disorder that is often chronic (Sperling, 1999). About 10% of the nation's permanently disabled population and as much as 14% of the homeless are people with schizophrenia (Rupp & Keith, 1993). The disorder is particularly common among young adults in their 20s and occurs more often among men than among women. A recent report by the Surgeon General estimates that 1.3% of adults aged 18–54 suffer from this disorder in any given year (U.S. Department of Health and Human Services, 1999).

**Schizophrenia**
A devastating psychological disorder in which the victim loses touch with reality and has hallucinations, delusions, and/or inappropriate emotion.

## Symptoms

Individuals are generally considered to be suffering from schizophrenia when they display the following types of disturbed behavior (Rosenhan & Seligman, 1984):

1. *Perceptual difficulties*—for example, inability to understand other people's speech, identify other people, gauge the passage of time, or distinguish between what is real and what is not. Often the person experiences **hallucinations,** or false sensory experiences that have a compelling sense of reality.

2. *Thought disruptions*—including incoherent speech and quick shifts from one topic to a totally unrelated one, as well as nonsensical utterances such as those

**Hallucination**
An imaginary sensation, such as seeing nonexistent things or feeling nonexistent objects under the skin.

**Delusion**
A false belief, such as the conviction that someone alive is dead.

displayed by Ralph. Schizophrenic patients may also have **delusions,** or false and inane beliefs—for example, the conviction that other people can hear their thoughts, that they no longer exist, or that their head and arms are missing. Compared to the delusions of other psychiatric patients, schizophrenic patients' delusions are much more bizarre, often involving the belief that they are being controlled by outside forces (Junginger, 1992).

3. *Emotional disturbances*—including remoteness, the absence of any feeling, and inappropriate reactions such as laughing at a sad episode.

DSM-IV defines schizophrenia as a disorder that lasts for at least 6 months and includes at least 1 month of two or more of the following: delusions, hallucinations, disorganized speech, and grossly disorganized behavior (American Psychiatric Association, 2000). *Paranoid schizophrenia*, from which Ralph is clearly suffering, is the most common form of the disorder.

In schizophrenia, many of the normal processes described in this book—from the ability to perceive the world to the capacity to relate to other people—unravel completely. People with the disorder lose touch with the real world. They hear voices that are not there, speak a language that does not exist, laugh for no reason, or sit motionless for hours on end. What could possibly cause such a condition?

## Causes

Most investigators have concluded that schizophrenia is not a single disturbance but instead is made up of several types of disturbances that have been grouped together because they exhibit certain similarities. Moreover, these different disturbances probably have different causes, manifestations, and responses to treatment.

There is mounting evidence that heredity may play a large role in who is at risk for schizophrenia. One of the possible early markers of the disease in some people is serious retardation in motor development during the first year of life; these infants are more likely to have parents with schizophrenia (Fish, 1992). Further evidence of a familial factor is the higher rate of schizophrenia in biological relatives of adoptees with the disorder, shown in Figure 13.2.

Schizophrenia is associated in some patients with increased levels of dopamine in the brain. Virtually all drugs that are effective in treating schizophrenic symptoms interfere with the action of dopamine. Techniques for observing the brain in action, such as *positron emission tomography (PET)* and new forms of *magnetic resonance imaging (MRI),* discussed in Chapter 2, offer further indications that some schizophrenics differ from normal people in brain functioning. Moreover, in some schizophrenics the brain ventricles (fluid-filled cavities) are enlarged, resulting in a shrinkage of brain tissue (Meltzer, 1987).

Researchers have found that schizophrenics show abnormal patterns of eye movements when they try to track a moving object. Many of their close relatives, though not themselves victims of schizophrenia, display the same unusual tracking pattern, as if there was a family tendency to do so (Holzman, 1992). The unusual patterns might indicate some defect in parts of the nervous system responsible for perception—possibly explaining why schizophrenics seem out of touch with reality as perceived by normal people.

Individuals with schizophrenia appear to be deficient in the capacity to focus attention—especially when beset by competing stimuli (Grillon, Courchesne, Ameli, & Geyer, 1990). Although they appear to be able to focus attention for a while, they apparently are functioning with a defect in the brain's capacity to pay sustained attention over time, especially when there are distracting inputs (Everett, Laplante, & Thomas, 1989). Research has also

**FIGURE 13.2 Heredity and schizophrenia.** Biological relatives of adoptees with schizophrenia were about 10 times as likely to be suffering from the disorder as were relatives of adoptees making up a control group.

*Kety & Ingraham, 1992.*

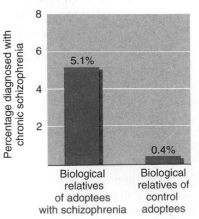

shown that the brains of some schizophrenics are smaller in volume than those of normal individuals, particularly in areas vital to perception, concentration, memory, and thinking (Suddath, Christison, Torrey, Casanova, & Weinberger, 1990).

Even if some inherited defect is the basis for the disorder, however, other factors may influence whether the inborn tendency will actually affect behavior. Environmental stressors may play a role, as might prenatal experiences or injuries during birth. Studies indicate that schizophrenia is more likely to appear in children of families with a high level of communication disorders (Mishler, 1991). The likelihood of developing schizophrenia is also greater among those who are unemployed and unmarried. A job and a spouse seem to offer some buffer against the disease, especially for men (Tien & Eaton, 1992).

People suffering from schizophrenia often go through remission phases during which they behave more or less normally, only to have the symptoms reappear unpredictably—perhaps throughout their lives. This pattern is most common among those who are inconsistent in taking their medications or combine these with alcohol or other drugs of abuse.

**Test Yourself**

(c) What physical evidence is there that the metabolic activity of the brains of schizophrenics is abnormal?

(The answer is on page 532.)

# MOOD DISORDERS

We all know from personal experience that a variety of events, both major and minor, can affect our mood. There are times when life is marred by grief—when we lose a friend or loved one to death or to a parting of the ways, when a job we've worked so hard to get is given instead to someone else. Such events can sometimes lead to **mood disorders,** of which the most common is depression. However, as is discussed later in this section, not all cases of mood disorders have an identifiable "triggering" event. Similarly, it isn't clear why some individuals react to distressing events much more profoundly than others do.

**FOCUS QUESTIONS**

- What are the major symptoms of mood disorders?

- What is the difference between unipolar and bipolar disorders?

## Depression

Everyone is "blue" or "down" from time to time; it's normal to become depressed after a significant loss or setback. Yet no matter how painful the stress or loss, we expect to bounce back after a reasonable period and feel like our "old self" again. Many people, however, experience clinical, or major, **depression**—a feeling of severe and prolonged sadness that occurs as a reaction to stress or as a result of chemical imbalances in the brain. According to DSM-IV, depression is present if five or more specific symptoms have been present during the same 2-week period and represent a change from previous functioning. The symptoms include depressed mood most of the day, nearly every day; markedly diminished interest or pleasure in all activities; significant weight loss; fatigue or loss of energy; feelings of worthlessness or excessive or inappropriate guilt; and diminished ability to think or concentrate, or indecisiveness (American Psychiatric Association, 2000).

Depression is very common. According to the U.S. Agency for Health Care Policy and Research, one in eight people in the United States will experience an episode of major depression at some time in their life. The incidence of depression has been increasing. In some countries, including the United States, the likelihood of suffering major depression is at least three times greater for people born after 1955 than it was for their grandparents' generation (Weissman, Sigman, Weiss, & Mosk, 1992).

**Mood disorders**
A form of psychological disorders characterized by abnormalities of emotion, including severe depression and swings of mood from one extreme to another.

**Depression**
A feeling of severe and prolonged sadness that occurs as a reaction to stress and chemical imbalances in the brain.

Depression is accompanied by feelings of futility, hopelessness, and apathy.

Severely depressed people appear quite different from people who are merely "unhappy." They experience not only unrelenting sadness but intense helplessness and hopelessness as well. They lose all semblance of positive self-esteem and are filled instead with grinding self-recriminations and guilt. They have no zest for either work or play. They may find that even routine acts of thinking and speaking require enormous effort. In the most severe cases, they may suffer delusions and hallucinations.

Depression causes physical problems as well. Sleep is disturbed—especially by waking up too early in the morning without feeling rested—and the desires for food and sex tend to diminish or disappear. Depressed people may also complain of poor digestion, heart palpitations, headache, visual disturbances, or dizziness. Selected indicators of severe depression are listed in Table 13.1.

People who are in the grip of a severe depressive episode feel hopeless about virtually everything. Writer William Styron's depression led him to view all the things around him as "potential devices" for his own destruction: "the attic rafter (and an outside maple or two) a means to hang myself, the garage a place to inhale carbon monoxide, the bathtub a vessel to receive the flow of my opened arteries" (Styron, 1990). With an outlook so dark, about 10 to 15% of depressed people eventually choose suicide as a way out of their misery; in fact, major depressive disorders account for about 20 to 35% of all deaths by suicide (Angst, Angst, & Stassen, 1999).

## Bipolar Disorder

**Unipolar disorder**
**A type of mood disorder that occurs without the swings in mood experienced in bipolar disorder.**

**Bipolar disorder**
**A type of mood disorder in which a person's lows alternate with exaggerated highs; formerly called manic-depression.**

When people have recurrent episodes of depression like the one just described, the disorder is called **unipolar disorder.** But there is another severe mood disorder, known today as **bipolar disorder** but referred to in the past as *manic-depression,* in which the lows typically alternate with exaggerated highs. Most of us, of course, know that our mood can shift—sometimes for no apparent reason—from bright and joyful to dark and sad. For people suffering from this disorder, however, the emotional pendulum swings wildly from intense excitement to deep melancholy, at first with long intervals in between, but later with frequent and abrupt shifts from high to low (Goodwin & Jamison, 1990). However, "excitement" can mean a variety of things, as will be discussed shortly.

It is estimated that about 1.1% of the adult population suffers from bipolar disorder (U.S. Department of Health and Human Services, 1999). Bipolar disorder affects men and women equally, and it sometimes appears during childhood. Unfortunately, if the disorder appears in childhood or adolescence, the individual is likely to experience more treatment difficulties and increased social disability. The disorder can often be managed fairly well with drug therapy (see Chapter 14), but people often delay seeking treatment when early symptoms appear, and the problem is often misdiagnosed.

Bipolar disorder magnifies common human experiences to larger-than-life proportions. Among its symptoms are exaggerations of normal sadness and fatigue, joy and exuberance, sensuality and sexuality, irritability and rage, energy and creativity. To afflicted individuals, it can be so painful that suicide seems the only means of escape.

In the manic, or "up," phase, people with bipolar disorder tend to be talkative, restless, aggressive, boastful, and destructive. At the same time, they may develop feelings of intense well-being and even ecstasy. Sexual and moral inhibitions dis-

## TABLE 13.1
### Indicators of Severe Depression

| | None or a Little of the Time | Some of the Time | Good Part of the Time | Most or All of the Time |
|---|---|---|---|---|
| 1. I feel downhearted, blue, and sad. | | | | ✓ |
| 2. Morning is when I feel the best. | ✓ | | | |
| 3. I have crying spells or feel like it. | | | | ✓ |
| 4. I have trouble sleeping through the night. | | | | ✓ |
| 5. I eat as much as I used to. | ✓ | | | |
| 6. I enjoy looking at, talking to, and being with attractive women/men. | ✓ | | | |
| 7. I notice that I am losing weight. | | | | ✓ |
| 8. I have trouble with constipation. | | | | ✓ |
| 9. My heart beats faster than normal. | | | | ✓ |
| 10. I get tired for no reason. | | | | ✓ |
| 11. My mind is as clear as it used to be. | ✓ | | | |
| 12. I find it easy to do the things I used to. | ✓ | | | |
| 13. I am restless and can't keep still. | | | | ✓ |
| 14. I feel hopeful about the future. | ✓ | | | |
| 15. I am more irritable than usual. | | | | ✓ |
| 16. I find it easy to make decisions. | ✓ | | | |
| 17. I feel that I am useful and needed. | ✓ | | | |
| 18. My life is pretty full. | ✓ | | | |
| 19. I feel that others would be better off if I were dead. | | | | ✓ |
| 20. I still enjoy the things I used to do. | ✓ | | | |

These items are from a test called the Self Rating Depression Scale. Note that a depressed person would feel that all the positive emotions and experiences mentioned in the test apply "none or a little of the time" whereas all the negative ones apply "most or all of the time." However, even if you were to mark many of the items in these ways, it wouldn't necessarily mean that you were seriously depressed—mental health professionals use interviews and other sources of information in addition to psychological tests before making a diagnosis.

appear, and life becomes one uninterrupted "high." The manic person needs little sleep and is filled with abundant energy and grandiose notions. Soon, however, most manic individuals plummet back to the depressed phase, becoming so gloomy and hopeless that they are immobilized.

As far back as the ancient Greeks, society has believed that the artistic temperament is often touched by divine madness. In recent years, evidence linking mood disorders to creativity has accumulated (Jamison, 1993). From the melancholy Lord Byron to the suicidal Sylvia Plath, biographies of celebrated poets, musicians, and artists have attested to extreme moods in creative people. Here is how writer Virginia Woolf (1978) described her divine inspiration: "As an experience, madness is terrific I can assure you, and not to be sniffed at; and in its lava I still find most of the things I write about. It shoots out of one everything shaped, final, not in mere driblets, as sanity does."

Despite the links between creativity and bipolar disorder, it is important not to glamorize or trivialize the disorder. In fact, most people with the disorder are not creative geniuses, and most talented artists are emotionally stable. Modern medicine can offer relief to those who endure the ravages of mood. In the past, artists who were in the clutches of this devastating disorder had nowhere but their art to seek solace. A further discussion of the subject appears in Psychology and the Media on page 510.

## Making Art of Madness

 On Nov. 15, 1934, Virginia Woolf began her rewrite of a novel eventually titled "The Years." "Lord! Lord!" she noted in her diary, "10 pages a day for 90 days: three months . . . . now, damnably disagreeable, as I see it will be—compacting the vast mass—I am using my faculties again & all the flies and fleas are forgotten."

Seven years later the flies and fleas and larger plagues drove Woolf, who had fought mental illness throughout her life, to suicide. An increasing number of psychiatrists, neurologists and geneticists, says an article in this week's *Science Times*, believe there's a link between the genius and madness of artists such as her. Maybe so. But as anyone who's ever read Woolf's letters and diaries can attest, it's the link between imagination and self-discipline that got her a place in literature's pantheon. Her mind may have had a grasshopper's fleetness, but her industry was the ant's.

"People who have experienced emotional extremes, who have been forced to confront a huge range of feelings and who have successfully coped with those adversities,

could end up with a richer organization in memory, a richer palette to work with," said Dr. Ruth Richards, a psychiatrist at McLean Hospital in Belmont, Mass., which often served as a haven for Robert Lowell, the fine American poet.

At least three fine English poets—Byron, Shelley and Coleridge—also suffered from manic depression or severe depression; and so did the composer Robert Schumann, who starved himself to death when he was 46. Dr. Robert M. Post, chief of the biological psychiatry branch at the National Institutes of Health, sees the link between bipolar disorder and creativity as "fortunate," because it is in so many other ways "a devastating illness." To be mad is not necessarily to be creative, or there'd be a Shelley on every street corner. And to be creative is not necessarily to be mad, or Shakespeare would not have been a monument to shrewdness and adaptability. But to be creative is almost invariably to be diligent—and, manic-depressive or no, to swing high, swing low.

*Source: Editorial published in the* New York Times, *October 15, 1993. Copyright © 1993 by The New York Times Co. Reprinted with permission.*

## Seasonal Mood Swings

Many people experience a shift in mood according to the brightness of the day. A sunny day helps raise their spirits; a cloudy day lowers them. A typical pattern is an increase in depressed mood as the day wears on, reaching its peak as darkness falls and night descends (Robbins & Tanck, 1987).

Early in the 1980s, researchers reported a form of mood disorder that exaggerates this pattern of response to light and dark. Called *seasonal affective disorder (SAD)*, it causes some people to become depressed in winter and energetic—even manic—in summer. Individuals with SAD are depressed, unproductive, and lethargic in winter; they show little interest in sex, their sleep deteriorates, and they tend to overeat. In contrast, in summer they display heightened creativity, interest in sex, and euphoric mood. A demonstration of this phenomenon emerged from a study of more than 1,600 individuals living at varying latitudes along the East Coast of the United States, including Florida, Maryland, New York, and New Hampshire. The results showed an increase in SAD in the more northern latitudes, supporting the hypothesis that light deprivation produces the decline in mood (Rosenthal, 1989).

When they are exposed to light that mimics natural sunlight, individuals suffering from seasonal affective disorder seem to emerge from their dark-induced winter depression. Within a few days, many patients experience dramatic improvements in mood. Some find that even an hour or two of bright light exposure a day is sufficient to eliminate their winter symptoms (Rosenthal, 1989).

Less disabling than SAD, but still an impediment to normal living, are the "winter blues" experienced by many people during the dark, short days of the year.

A surprising number of individuals find that their creativity, energy, and sense of well-being are depleted until the brightness of spring appears (Rosenthal, 1989).

## Untangling the Biological and Environmental Components

As with schizophrenia, there is some evidence that mood disorders have a genetic basis. The risk of developing bipolar disorder is less than 1% in the population at large. However, the risk is 6 to 8 times greater among the close relatives (parents, siblings, and children) of manic-depressives (Tsuang & Faraone, 1990). One study of depression among female twins found that genetic factors played a substantial, though not overwhelming, role (Kendler, 1992a).

There is also evidence that mood disorders are related to disturbances in the chemistry of the brain—to such an extent that the symptoms sometimes appear without any provocation. The levels of a number of neurotransmitters appear to be disturbed in depression, and various drugs used to treat the disorder (described in the next chapter) work by altering the balance of these neurotransmitters. Among depressed individuals there also appears to be a disturbance in the functioning of hormones regulated by the pituitary and adrenal glands.

It is not yet clear whether mood disorders are caused by biochemical factors or whether the disorder causes the biochemical changes. The most widely held theory is that some people are genetically vulnerable to biochemical imbalances, which are likely to occur in response to intolerably stressful experiences. One such experience, for example, would appear to be the trauma of abuse. Researchers found an atypically high rate of both physical and sexual abuse in a sample of women who had been hospitalized for depression and other abnormal symptoms (Bryer, Nelson, Miller, & Krol, 1987). The trauma and stress of illnesses ranging from strokes to cancer may also alter the brain's chemistry, leaving the person more vulnerable to depression. Even asthma has been found to be associated with depression.

Various problems within the family put people at greater risk for depression. As illustrated in Figure 13.3, unfair, harsh, and inconsistent discipline in childhood has been found to be strongly associated with adult depression (Holmes & Robins, 1987). The disruption of divorce may leave children more vulnerable to depression. One study found that children who had been separated from a parent as a result of divorce faced an increased risk of major depression, as well as anxiety; this link was not found among children who had been separated from a parent by death (Kendler, 1992b). For more details on depression among children, see the Life Span Perspective on page 512.

There also appears to be a link between familial substance abuse and the presence of depression. Children of alcohol-abusing fathers are more prone to *introjective depression*—a type of depression characterized by feelings of guilt, inferiority, self-criticism, and a sense of having failed to meet expectations (Jarmas & Kazak, 1992).

## Sex Differences in Depression

Depression is diagnosed twice as often in women as in men, and twice as many women as men take antidepressant drugs (Nolen-Hoeksema, 1990). The reason is not entirely clear. One possibility is that women are more vulnerable because of their bio-

**FIGURE 13.3 Childhood abuse and adult depression. Compared to those free of depression, depressed adults are three times as likely to have been abused as children.** *After Holmes & Robins, 1987.*

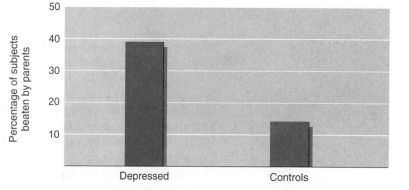

# Depression in the Early Years

Until the early 1960s, the term **childhood depression** did not appear in textbooks on child psychiatry (Cytryn, McKnew, & Bunney, 1980). In recent decades, however, it has become clear that children as well as adults can suffer from depression. A study of more than 5,500 high school students revealed that nearly 1 in 10 suffered from depression, ranging from mild to severe (Whitaker, Johnson, Shaffer, & Rapoport, 1990). Yet the ailment still goes unrecognized—and untreated—in too many cases. Childhood depression may be masked by two kinds of problems:

1. Physical complaints, such as headaches, stomachaches, and bed-wetting
2. School problems, including school phobia, truancy, and poor academic performance

Parents and pediatricians are likely to overlook the possibility that such conditions may be hiding a mood of depression. But careful observation of children by informed child psychiatrists and psychologists can often strip away the mask (Petti, 1981).

Even when the signs of depression are more obvious, the disorder is still easy to overlook in children. Because children are unaware of the meaning of depression, they do not complain of it openly in the same way that adults do. Moreover, children can still be active and show some interest in their environment even while quite depressed. But close attention shows that depression produces in children symptoms comparable to those found among severely depressed adults.

Depressed children look sad and feel even sadder, are moody, cry easily, and sleep and eat poorly. They are burdened with a sense of worthlessness, hopelessness, and guilt. Finding no pleasure in life, some entertain thoughts of suicide, and a small but increasing number actually commit the act.

Childhood depression is likely to occur as a result of both genetic vulnerability and a stressful environment. Some long-standing cases arise when children are subjected to continuous stress—repeated separations from loved ones, abuse, family strife and violence, or the daily trauma of being reared by an emotionally disturbed parent. The incidence of depression in children of seriously depressed parents is atypically high (Beardslee, Bemporad, Keller, & Klerman, 1983). Other cases are much briefer and are usually triggered by an identifiable, immediate cause, such as the sudden death of a parent, an unexpected and uprooting move to a new city, or the arrival of a new sibling. Extremely stressful events, such as divorce or a death in the family, are strong predictors of later depression (Hoeksema, 1992).

Youth is no shield against the ravages of depression, which was long regarded to be a painful consequence only of adult stress. More pediatricians, teachers, and parents need to learn to recognize the condition, bringing children and adolescents the medical treatment they need.

logical makeup. Hormonal factors may be partially responsible; for example, premenstrual and postpartum depression are common and well recognized. Another possibility is social roles. Some psychologists theorize that women are encouraged by society to devote themselves to nurturing others, in the process denying their own goals and needs (Jack, 1991). At least one study bears this out. It found that men and women are equally capable of adjusting to negative events that happen to them personally. But historically, women were more deeply affected than men by stressful events experienced by close friends and family members—particularly their spouses (Turner & Avison, 1989). As women have emerged from their traditional social roles, their rates of depression have, in fact, declined (F. Goodwin, 1993).

Increasingly unrealistic standards of beauty and thinness may be another reason for higher rates of depression among women in some cultures around the world and some subcultures in the United States. Women from cultures that promote extreme thinness have been found to be twice as likely as men to suffer from depression. In contrast, in cultures with more realistic ideals of feminine physique, rates of depression for men and women are almost equal (McCarthy, 1990). We saw in Chapter 11 that unrealistic ideals of female body type can also lead to eating disorders. The same study found that eating disorders are almost nonexistent in cultures where the feminine ideal is closer to women's actual body types. For more information on eating disorders, see Psychology in the Lab and in Life on page 513.

Another reason for higher rates of depression among women may be errors in diagnosis. In one study, clinicians were found to overdiagnose depression among

## PSYCHOLOGY IN THE LAB AND IN LIFE

# Eating Disorders: When Food Becomes the Enemy

Katherine is a 5'4" 16-year-old who weighs 80 pounds. As her body began going through the changes of puberty, Katherine put on a little bit of weight, which prompted her to begin a demanding regimen of dieting and exercise. Within a month, she had lost the excess weight. But she still saw herself as "fat" and intensified her exercise and diet program. Her daily routine now involves consuming no more than a piece of dry toast, one serving of raw vegetables, a piece of fruit, and four glasses of water and performing at least an hour of aerobic exercise.

Although Katherine doesn't believe she has a problem, clinicians would diagnose her as suffering from *anorexia nervosa,* a disorder in which an already thin person continues on a starvation diet to keep his or her weight down. People with this disorder are terrified about gaining weight even when they have already lost as much as 40% of their normal body weight. Once the individual has experienced sufficient weight loss, the physiological effects of malnutrition (such as slower emptying of the stomach) and the psychological effects (such as increasing social isolation) help perpetuate the disorder (F. E. Bloom & Lazerson, 1988).

Even more common is *bulimia nervosa,* a disorder in which the person engages in eating binges and then induces vomiting, takes laxatives, or exercises excessively in order to avoid gaining weight. Feelings of depression and shame typically run high during and after binges. As in anorexia, there is a constant preoccupation with food and a morbid fear of being viewed as overweight (Hinz & Williamson, 1987).

As we saw in Chapter 11, eating disorders are most common among young women in their teens and early twenties. A variety of causes have been proposed, rang-

The primary symptom of anorexia is self-starvation to the point of emaciation.

© William Thompson/Index Stock Imagery

ing from chemical and hormonal imbalances to societal and family pressures. Eating disorders seem to run in families (National Institute of Mental Health, 1987), although it is difficult to tease out the biological causes from the environmental causes. Often, vulnerable girls come from families that show little cohesion or mutual support (Attie & Brooks-Gunn, 1989). It has been shown that the families of individuals with anorexia are often very protective and demanding (Yates, 1990). Yet the familial link also reveals a genetic component. Among twins, if one twin has the disorder, the other is more likely to also have the disorder when the twins are identical rather than fraternal (Fichter & Noegel, 1990).

There is accumulating evidence for an underlying biological component. Researchers have found that women with bulimia tend to binge when levels of serotonin in the brain are low (Kaye, Weltzin, & Hsu, 1993). Low levels of serotonin may encourage bingeing either through a direct effect on appetite or through an effect on mood. Another study has shown that people with bulimia nervosa have unusually high levels of *vasopressin,* a brain hormone that affects learning and memory and may be released during times of stress (Demitrack, 1992). Bulimics may release higher levels of vasopressin when they are anxious, which may in turn reinforce the repetitive cycle of dieting, gorging, and vomiting.

Societal standards of thinness share some of the blame for the prevalence of eating disorders among young women. An extremely disturbed body image often underlies eating disorders (Steinberg, 1985). The feminine "ideal" as shown in fashion magazines may be setting an impossible standard against which women evaluate themselves.

women and underdiagnose it among men (Potts, Burnam, & Wells, 1991). Men may tend to deny depression and may be less likely to express their feelings openly and to seek help. In addition, health professionals may be less likely to ask men about their feelings and may tend to attribute their problems to physical causes. On top of

## Test Yourself

**(d)** What are some common symptoms of depression?

**(e)** Jeffrey, a third-grader, complains every morning of a headache or stomachache and says he doesn't want to go to school. What disorder might he be suffering from?

(The answers are on page 532.)

## FOCUS QUESTIONS

• **What are the common types of anxiety disorders?**

• **What is a phobia?**

**Anxiety disorder**
A psychological disorder in which anxiety is the dominant symptom.

that, men are much less likely to visit a doctor than women are. Instead, they may attempt to "deal" with their depression by using alcohol or other mood-altering drugs; being cranky, irritable, or falsely cheerful; or becoming workaholics or exercise addicts (Bucher et al., 1981). People are becoming more aware of the hidden symptoms of depression, however, and the gap between men and women may narrow as more men are diagnosed and treated.

# ANXIETY DISORDERS

Perfectly normal people have many anxious moments when they anticipate an undesirable event such as rejection or harm. Anxiety also gnaws at many people with disorders of all sorts—mental and physical. But in some people, anxiety is the primary symptom—either constantly or on specific occasions, it dominates their lives. These individuals suffer from one or another form of **anxiety disorder.** They outnumber virtually all other groups of mentally ill individuals; one study found that between 4.1% and 6.6% of the U.S. population had experienced a generalized anxiety disorder during their lives (Robins & Regier, 1991).

Anxiety disorders take a number of forms. In some cases, conscious worry is the most prominent symptom. In others, individuals develop maladaptive, disabling patterns of behavior—such as staying home to avoid crowds or washing their hands every half hour—as a way of coping with their anxiety (also see defense mechanisms in Chapter 12).

Many victims of anxiety disorders function well enough that even their close friends are not aware of their problem. Moreover, unlike schizophrenics and manic-depressives, they stay in touch with reality and often recognize that their feelings and behavior are illogical. However, certain anxiety disorders prevent people from functioning in their social relationships or at work. There are four common forms of anxiety disorders: (1) generalized anxiety, (2) panic, (3) phobia, and (4) obsessive-compulsive disorder. A less common anxiety disorder, post-traumatic stress disorder (PTSD), is discussed in Chapter 12.

## Generalized Anxiety Disorder

**Generalized anxiety disorder**
A type of anxiety disorder marked by unfocused feelings of tension, uneasiness, and vague fear.

As the term implies, people with **generalized anxiety disorder** feel anxious but the anxiety has no specific focus. Freud aptly described the condition as "free-floating anxiety." Each day is permeated with feelings of uneasiness, vague fears, and correspondingly unpleasant tension. People displaying this disorder often feel irritable and jumpy, and they are uncomfortable with other people. They are constantly on edge, unable to concentrate, and filled with doubts about their ability to work or study. Their level of anxiety is likely to shoot up as a result of minor events that would not affect a normal person (Hamilton, 1982). A person is diagnosed as having this disorder if he or she has experienced at least 6 months of persistent and excessive anxiety and worry (American Psychiatric Association, 2000).

Many anxious people are constantly concerned about their health—often needlessly, although they may actually develop physical symptoms. Their autonomic nervous system is overactive, producing heart palpitations, shortness of breath, hot flashes, cold sweats, nausea, diarrhea, and frequent urination. Because they find it difficult to "turn off" at night, they wake up feeling as tired as when they went to bed. They cannot seem to control the apprehension that hovers menac-

TABLE 13.2
## What Anxiety-Ridden People Typically Say

| Typical Statements | Percentage of Cases |
|---|---|
| I just can't relax. | 97 |
| I have no powers of concentration. | 86 |
| I'm tense all over. | 86 |
| I feel scared all the time. | 79 |
| I am likely to go out of control. | 76 |
| I'm afraid of being rejected. | 72 |
| I just can't control my thinking. | 72 |
| I feel confused. | 69 |
| My mind feels like a blur. | 66 |
| I feel unsteady. | 62 |
| I get weak all over. | 59 |
| I can't recall a thing. | 55 |
| I'm often terrified. | 52 |
| My hands sweat. | 52 |

*After Beck & Emery, 1985.*

Listed here are statements made by half or more of individuals suffering from generalized anxiety disorder.

ingly over them and clouds virtually every aspect of their lives. Examples of typical complaints of such individuals are presented in Table 13.2.

As with mood disorders, some people are genetically more susceptible to anxiety disorders than others. Researchers have found that when anxiety runs in families, it is more likely to be due to genetic than to environmental causes.

## Panic Disorder

Some people experience recurrent unexpected panic attacks, about which there is persistent concern. They are said to be suffering from a **panic disorder** (American Psychiatric Association, 2000). For no clear reason, they are suddenly overwhelmed with a sense of disaster and imminent death, usually accompanied by physical symptoms: pounding heart, hot flashes, nausea, dizziness, and accelerated breathing. They also may have feelings of unreality or believe that they are about to lose control and "go crazy."

The consequences of untreated panic disorder are similar to those of depression: feelings of poor physical and emotional health, alcohol or other drug abuse, increased risk of suicide, and impaired social functioning (Markowitz, 1989). Although panic disorder is usually diagnosed in adulthood, research shows that panic attacks often occur for the first time among children as young as 11 or 12 and that the onset is closely linked to the beginning of puberty in girls (Hayward, Killen, Hammer, & Litt, 1992). Some people with panic disorder become so afraid of having an attack on the street that they are reluctant to leave the safety of their home. When this happens, they are referred to as agoraphobic. (See the following discussion of phobias.) Panic disorder is uncommon in the general population, but it is diagnosed in approximately 10% of individuals referred for mental health consultation (American Psychiatric Association, 2000).

It should be noted that a panic attack is not inherently dangerous. The accelerated breathing that usually accompanies such an attack produces hyperventilation; the person "passes out" and then automatically starts breathing normally again. However, it can be extremely dangerous should the person lose consciousness and then suffer an injury due to a fall (or worse, due to an accident while

**Panic disorder**
A type of anxiety disorder characterized by a sudden and overwhelming sense of disaster or impending death, usually accompanied by physical symptoms like a pounding heart, breathing difficulties, hot flashes, nausea, and dizziness.

driving a car). Indeed, fear that such a thing will happen tends to worsen the attack once it starts or may even precipitate the attack in the first place.

## Phobias

**Phobia**
A type of anxiety disorder in which the person has an intense, irrational, and unreasonable fear of an object, situation, or activity.

**Specific phobia**
An intense fear of exposure to a specific object or situation.

**Social phobia**
An intense fear of social situations in which one might be scrutinized by others.

Sometimes anxiety becomes associated with a specific object, situation, or activity. The person is then regarded as suffering from a **phobia**—in other words, a fear that is far out of proportion to whatever danger is present. (*Phobia* is the Greek word for fear.) According to the National Institute of Mental Health, phobias are the most common mental health problem in the United States, although incidence rates are largely unknown because phobic individuals often perceive no need for treatment and therefore are not counted. Individuals with **specific phobia** experience extreme anxiety when exposed to a specific feared object or situation; this often causes avoidance behavior—or, in the case of phobic objects such as spiders, roaches, snakes, and the like, attack. Those with **social phobia** suffer anxiety when exposed to certain types of social or performance situations, which again often leads to avoidance behavior (American Psychiatric Association, 2000).

Many people describe themselves casually as having one sort of phobia or another, perhaps several. "I'm phobic about spiders," they may say, as they scrupulously survey the ground before setting up for a picnic. Others will tell you that they are terrified by thunderstorms, and they carefully check and recheck the weather forecast before starting out on a trip. Most of us manage to function quite well despite such fears. But for a person who is phobic about certain insects and lives in an area where regular encounters are unavoidable, the phobia may interfere with daily functioning and be maladaptive. The same applies to a person who is *claustrophobic* (afraid of enclosed places) and must ride elevators or a person who is *acrophobic* (afraid of high places) and must drive across bridges to get to work.

Phobias can be acquired through simple conditioning in childhood. This is how the child Albert acquired his fear of furry animals and objects (see p. 146). Similarly, a child who has terrifying experiences with dogs may become an adult who has a phobic reaction to the sound of a dog barking, even when the dog isn't within view. Phobias can also be acquired indirectly, through observational learning (Chapter 4). For example, a child who repeatedly witnesses a parent displaying intense fear of some object or situation may acquire that fear as well. This kind of learning occurs readily because there is usually an element of real danger—*some* spiders and snakes are poisonous, an enclosed space *might* turn into a trap, being in a high place *might* result in a fall, and so on.

**Agoraphobia**
An abnormal fear of being in public places.

Extreme fear of snakes is a common type of specific phobia.

© Chris Windsor/gettyimages/Stone

The most disabling of all phobias is **agoraphobia**—anxiety about or avoidance of places or situations from which escape might be difficult (or embarrassing) or in which help may not be available in the event of a panic attack (American Psychiatric Association, 2000). People with this disorder have an overwhelming fear of public places, which can include streets, stores, buses, trains—virtually anywhere outside the person's home. In fact, they often become virtual prisoners in their own homes, which they perceive as the only safe place to be. Agoraphobia typically takes hold after a number of severe panic attacks; about one-third of people diagnosed with panic disorder develop it (National Institutes of Health [NIH], 1991). The person begins avoiding situations in which the attacks happened, but this avoidance response soon spreads to other situations. Eventually, it becomes impossible to go anywhere at all—and certainly not alone. The person may display little in the way of fear when accompanied by a trusted friend who could help in case a panic attack occurred.

The main characteristic of social phobia is fear of being scrutinized by others. Sufferers are preoccupied with the notion that they will be humiliated in some type of social encounter. (Anxiety about public speaking is a mild form of social phobia.) In its most serious form, social phobia leads people to retreat from social involvement and to have extreme difficulty interacting with others at work. They often try to calm their fears through alcohol use, which can lead to excessive drinking (Kushner, Sher, & Beltman, 1990).

Phobias are more likely to be found among adolescents and young adults than among older people. Like panic attacks, they are—at least in their milder forms— also more common in females than in males (Costello, 1982). One possible explanation of this sex difference is that fearfulness has traditionally been considered more acceptable among women than among men.

## Obsessive-Compulsive Disorder

An **obsession** is an irresistible thought that keeps cropping up in a persistent and disturbing fashion. Some anxiety-ridden people are obsessed with the idea that they have heart trouble or that they are going to die by a certain age. A common obsession is the recurrent thought, while trying to sleep, that a door or window has been left unlocked or that an appliance has been left on.

A **compulsion** is an irresistible urge to perform some act over and over again. Compulsions are usually an attempt to cope with obsessions: The person who can't shake the thought that a window has been left unlocked may get up and check the windows repeatedly throughout the night. The host who cannot bear to see a knife or fork out of line at the table is exhibiting a milder form of compulsion, as is the student who cannot get any work done unless every book, paper, and pencil is "in its place."

Together, these reactions, when practiced to the extreme, make up **obsessive-compulsive disorder,** or **OCD** (American Psychiatric Association, 2000). This disorder causes an individual to experience excruciating uncertainties and perform repeated routines perhaps hundreds of times each day. Here are two typical cases, described in a government report on the disorder (Alcohol, Drug Abuse, and Mental Health Administration, 1989):

> Several times a day, a young mother is seized by the fearful thought that she is going to harm her child. However hard she tries, she cannot get rid of this painful and worrisome idea. She even refuses to touch the kitchen knives and other sharp objects because she is afraid that she may use them as weapons.

> Troubled by repeated thoughts that she may have contaminated herself by touching doorknobs and other "dirty" objects, a teenage girl spends hours every day washing her hands. Her hands are red and raw, and she has little time for social activities, but the washing continues.

OCD is not as rare as was once thought: It affects as many as 5 million people in the United States, including a large number of young people. A listing of obsessions and compulsions commonly found among people with this disorder is provided in Table 13.3.

There is considerable evidence that the disorder has a biological basis—specifically, a disruption of the pathways that link the frontal lobes of the cerebral cortex to areas of the cerebellum and brainstem that govern certain cognitive and motor functions. Moreover, about a fifth of people with the disorder have tics such as eye blinks and grimaces. Because the disorder seems to run in families, it may be transmitted genetically (Rapoport, 1989). However, this does not rule out the possibility that OCD may also be learned. For example, a person who has been terrorized by an intruder might well develop an obsession about keeping the home locked tight and a compulsion to check the locks repeatedly.

**Obsession**
A repetitive thought that occurs in a persistent and disturbing fashion.

**Compulsion**
A repetitive and irresistible urge to perform a particular act.

**Obsessive-compulsive disorder (OCD)**
A type of disorder marked by repetitive thoughts (obsessions) and repetitive urges to act (compulsions).

### Test Yourself

**(f)** A friend is suddenly overwhelmed with a sense of disaster and imminent death. He complains of a pounding heart, difficulty breathing, hot flashes, nausea, and dizziness. What disorder might this be?

**(g)** What age group suffers the most from panic disorder and phobias?

(The answers are on page 532.)

Indicated here are the symptoms found most frequently in a study of 70 children and adolescents diagnosed as having obsessive-compulsive disorder.

---

TABLE 13.3
**When Anxiety Breeds Chronic Obsessions and Compulsions**

| Symptoms of Obsessions | Percentage |
|---|---|
| Concern with dirt, germs, or environmental toxins | 40 |
| Something terrible happening (fire or death or illness of self or loved one) | 24 |
| Symmetry, order or exactness | 17 |
| Scrupulosity (religious obsessions) | 13 |
| Concern or disgust with bodily wastes or secretions (urine, stool, saliva) | 8 |
| Lucky or unlucky numbers | 8 |
| Forbidden, aggressive, or perverse sexual thoughts, images, or impulses | 4 |
| Fear might harm others or oneself | 4 |
| Concern with household items | 3 |
| Intrusive nonsense sounds, words, or music | 1 |

| Symptoms of Compulsions | Percentage |
|---|---|
| Excessive or ritualized handwashing, showering, bathing, toothbrushing, or grooming | 85 |
| Repeating rituals (going in or out of a door, up or down from a chair) | 51 |
| Checking (doors, locks, stove, appliances, emergency brake on car, paper route, homework) | 46 |
| Rituals to remove contact with contaminants | 23 |
| Touching | 20 |
| Measure to prevent harm to self or others | 16 |
| Ordering or arranging | 17 |
| Counting | 18 |
| Hoarding or collecting rituals | 11 |
| Rituals of cleaning household or inanimate objects | 6 |
| Miscellaneous rituals (such as writing, moving, speaking) | 26 |

*Rapoport, 1989.*

---

# PERSONALITY DISORDERS

**FOCUS QUESTIONS**

- What is meant by a personality disorder?
- What are the common types of personality disorders?

**Personality disorders**
A category of disorders characterized by ingrained and inflexible habits that are an integral part of the whole personality.

People suffering from schizophrenia, depression, or various forms of anxiety may have recurrent episodes of abnormal behavior and disruption of their psychological functioning, but most return to their "normal selves" the rest of the time. In contrast, some disorders involve long-standing, integral parts of the individual's personality. Known as **personality disorders,** these disturbances may arise from underlying and deep-seated conflicts, from progressive maladaptive learning experiences or mistreatment during childhood, or from as yet unidentified sources. The person may not feel any discomfort such as depression or panic—or even be aware that there is something wrong with her or his outlook and behavior. However, people with these disorders behave in ways that are often painful to others. They seem to lack the desire—or perhaps the ability—to act in ways that are socially acceptable, and they rarely try to change their behavior or seek treatment except as a means of avoiding prosecution if they commit crimes and get caught. Their patterns of behavior often surface at an early age and become so deeply ingrained that even friends and family members find it difficult to distinguish the disorder from the person.

DSM-IV defines a personality disorder as "an enduring pattern of inner experience and behavior that deviates markedly from the expectations of the individual's culture, is pervasive and inflexible, has an onset in adolescence or early adulthood, is stable over time, and leads to distress or impairment" (American Psychiatric Association, 2000, p. 685). Although personality disorders are not easy to classify, it is possible to differentiate among 10 different types (American Psychiatric Association, 2000). Discussions of three types follow, and the others are described in Table 13.4. In each case, there is no mistaking the central theme, or core, of the personality.

## Antisocial Personality Disorder

A sometimes extreme form of personality disorder is **antisocial personality disorder.** This disorder is characterized by a pervasive pattern of disregard for and violation of the rights of others, as indicated by behaviors such as deceitfulness, impulsivity, and consistent irresponsibility (American Psychiatric Association, 2000). People with this type of personality seem to lack a normal conscience or sense of social responsibility and to have little empathy for other people. *Sociopaths*—or *psychopaths,* as they are sometimes called—may seem on the surface to be quite charming, candid, and generous, but in reality they are selfish, ruthless, and addicted to lying. They have little affection for anyone but themselves and take advantage of others without a shred of guilt. The apparent absence of anxiety or guilt is one of their outstanding characteristics—and, of course, a factor that makes antisocial personality different from most other disorders. It is estimated that about 3% of males and 1% of females have this disorder (American Psychiatric Association, 2000).

People with antisocial personality disorder are likely to be in and out of trouble throughout their lives; they rarely learn from experience and appear to have no desire to help themselves. Instead of becoming independent, self-supporting adults, they are impulsive and reckless—unable to hold a job, maintain an enduring marital or sexual relationship, or act as a responsible parent. Lacking respect for the law, they often end up spending time in prison.

The causes of antisocial personality disorder remain a mystery, but antisocial behavior patterns usually begin at about age 7 or 8 and are more common in boys than in girls. It is rare for people to be diagnosed as having an antisocial personality without having displayed similar problems before they reached 18 years of age. People with the disorder have a history of school truancy, stealing, lying, irresponsibility about money, heavy involvement in sex, staying out late, or running away from home. The more antisocial symptoms children display, the more likely they are to grow up to be antisocial adults.

There is some evidence that the autonomic nervous systems of people with antisocial personality disorder are less reactive and more difficult to arouse than those of normal individuals. One study found that disruptive and antisocial children and adolescents had lower levels of serotonin and lower levels of arousal than normal children (Kruesi, 1992). This biological characteristic might lead them to seek emotional excitement and at the same time to be oblivious to danger (such as the consequences of committing a serious crime). They also seem to respond less to punishment than other people. But, as in most other forms of abnormal behavior, it is unlikely that biological factors alone account for an antisocial personality. The social environment appears to weigh heavily in the development of the disorder. The chances of developing an antisocial personality disorder are high for children raised by a parent who has the disorder. Growing up with antisocial companions and in high-crime neighborhoods are also strong factors—but these carry less weight if the parents themselves are free of antisocial behavior. The back-

**Antisocial personality disorder**
A personality disorder characterized by lack of conscience or lack of a sense of social responsibility; a person with this disorder is often referred to as a sociopath.

We all know people who have traits somewhat like the ones listed. But for people with personality disorders, the patterns are so pervasive that it becomes virtually impossible for them to adapt to the demands of the real world.

TABLE 13.4
## Characteristics of People with Personality Disorders

| Type of Personality Disorder | What the Person Is Like |
|---|---|
| Histrionic | Highly excitable, often reacting to tiny events with gigantic displays of emotion; shallow and not very genuine; quick to form friendships—but soon becomes demanding and inconsiderate; seductive and tries to dominate the opposite sex; egocentric and needs to control others, sometimes even by threatening or actually attempting suicide |
| Avoidant | Avoids work or school activities that involve significant interpersonal contact because of fears of criticism, disapproval, or rejection; avoids making new friends unless certain of being liked and accepted without criticism; will not join in group activities unless there are repeated and generous offers of support and nurturance |
| Dependent | Lacks self-confidence and initiative; manages to let other people take responsibility for everything in life—even for major decisions about job or career; cannot stand the idea of being self-reliant; needs to depend on others at all costs—even if the other person is mean and abusive; sees self as dumb and helpless |
| Obsessive-compulsive | Perfectionistic and so absorbed in trivial details as to be unable to see "the big picture"; overly serious and stingy and rarely does anything spontaneously; intent on having others conform to "my way of doing things"; indecisive, afraid of making a mistake, and unable to establish priorities; puts even routine work ahead of friends (not the same as OCD) |
| Schizoid | Unable to build close social relationships or even to feel any warmth toward others; indifferent to almost everything, including the feelings of people; reserved and withdrawn—a true "loner"; humorless, dull, and aloof; vague and indecisive; absentminded and given to daydreaming; sometimes seems removed from the real world—but without the seriously abnormal symptoms of schizophrenia |
| Schizotypal | Incorrectly interprets casual incidents and external events as having a particular and unusual meaning specifically for him or her; may be superstitious or preoccupied with paranormal phenomena; may claim to have special powers to sense events before they happen or to read others' thoughts; speech may include unusual or idiosyncratic phrasing and construction |
| Borderline | Impulsive, unpredictable, and easily upset; gets uncontrollably angry for little reason; quickly shifts mood—from depression to irritability to anxiety; feels empty and bored inside and is unable to establish a firm sense of identity; lives on the border of reality, slipping beyond it during periods of heavy pressure and stress |

grounds of those who end up as criminals reveal the same combination of biological traits and environmental circumstances (Wilson & Herrnstein, 1985).

## Paranoid Personality Disorder

All of us feel suspicious at times—and it's a good thing we do. You would be ignoring your own best interests if you were not wary upon hearing strange sounds in your basement at night or discovering that a classmate's term paper bears an uncanny resemblance to your own. But the basement prowler may turn out to be a cat and the apparent case of plagiarism a coincidence. Once normal people acquire evidence that their suspicions are not warranted, they are dispelled. Wariness decreases, and trust is established.

In contrast, people with **paranoid personality disorder** show a pattern of pervasive distrust and suspiciousness of others (American Psychiatric Association, 2000). They are unable to give up their constant suspicions and mistrust of other people—even when the facts clearly point the other way. Worse yet, they may become suspicious of anyone who tries to reason with them. They expect at any moment to be tricked, and they are always on guard and worried about the hidden motives of others. Paranoid individuals often seem to be devious and scheming. They also appear hostile and defensive—and so stubborn and rigid that they are unable to compromise. Between 0.5% and 2.5% of people in the general population have this disorder (American Psychiatric Association, 2000).

It is extremely hard to build satisfying relationships with paranoid individuals. At work, such people tend to be intensely concerned with rank, always needing to know who is in control. Moreover, they take everything personally. For example, if their company established a new regulation that required all employees to sign in and out of work, paranoid individuals would feel that the rule was specifically devised to get at them. In marriage, they may become insanely jealous for no reason (read *Othello*), yet they are incapable of intimacy because they can trust no one.

People with paranoid personality disorder are intellectually intact and often quite bright, which distinguishes them from people with paranoid schizophrenia. In their own distorted way, they display highly prized capacities such as sensitivity, quickness of thought, and great consistency. Yet underneath, paranoid individuals feel grossly inferior. Because they are always fighting off feelings of inadequacy, they tend to blame everything on others. In extreme cases, this process results in delusions of persecution.

Some paranoid individuals manage to compensate for their feelings of inferiority by developing delusions of power and grandeur. Among them are extremely disturbed paranoid people who end up actually believing that they are the pope or the president. Their delusions are as pervasive as those found in schizophrenics, with whom trying to use reasoning to deal with delusions "is like trying to bail out the ocean with a bucket" (Torrey, 1983).

**Paranoid personality disorder**
A personality disorder characterized by constant suspicions and mistrust of others.

## Narcissistic Personality Disorder

In ancient Greek legend, Narcissus was a beautiful young man who fell so deeply in love with his own reflection in a pool that he remained by the pool until he died. His name is the basis for a trait known as narcissism, or self-love, which in its extreme form may be diagnosed as **narcissistic personality disorder.**

People with this disorder display a pattern of grandiosity, need for admiration, and lack of empathy (American Psychiatric Association, 2000). They are often quite charming and attractive, but once you get to know them, they are easy to

**Narcissistic personality disorder**
A personality disorder characterized by self-love; Freud used the term *narcissistic personality* to describe total involvement with the desires of the self.

© CORBIS/Sygma

Individuals with narcissistic personality disorder crave constant attention and admiration.

dislike. They seem to have an inflated sense of their own importance, acting as if they were nature's gift to humanity. Unlike obsessive-compulsive individuals, who constantly seek perfection, narcissistic people claim it (Akhtar & Thomson, 1982). They feel entitled to everything and continually use people for their own purposes, including sex. Often they give the impression that they really like you when all they actually want is to get you to do something for them. They offer little in return and, worse still, cannot excuse others. Fortunately, the disorder occurs in less than 1% of the general population (American Psychiatric Association, 2000).

Narcissistic individuals crave constant attention and admiration because they are trying desperately to compensate for painful feelings of emptiness and worthlessness lurking beneath the surface. That is also why they tend to daydream about incredible successes in their work or in their love affairs. They are extremely superficial, totally preoccupied with appearances. They would rather be seen with the "right people" than enjoy the company of close friends. They also fake the feelings they think are appropriate in any situation to impress others. How they look is so important to them that they can easily spend hours grooming themselves. The narcissist of today stands transfixed at the mirror instead of at the reflecting pool.

Some experts believe that greater acceptance of selfish behavior in Western culture has caused this disorder to become more common (Wallach & Wallach, 1983). For example, books intended to teach us how to look out for ourselves first or how to get everything we want out of life at any cost tend to become best-sellers. But there is no evidence from research that narcissistic behavior is any more prevalent today than it was in the days of Narcissus. Moreover, it is wise to remember that, to a degree, the urge for self-enhancement can be a healthy and fulfilling goal. It's when the urge becomes overwhelming and dominates one's existence that problems begin to accumulate.

# SUBSTANCE ABUSE AND DEPENDENCE

## FOCUS QUESTIONS
- What are the major signs of substance abuse?
- What is the difference between psychological and physical dependence?
- What causes addiction?

**Substance abuse**
The voluntary, frequent, and heavy use of alcohol, heroin, or other potent addictive drugs.

So far, this chapter has dealt with alterations in thought, perception, mood, and behavior that occur as a result of disorders whose immediate precipitating causes are not always clear. In contrast, this section considers similar changes that take place as a result of an identifiable cause: voluntary, frequent, and heavy use of alcohol and other potent drugs, which is referred to as **substance abuse.**

The use of alcohol or drugs cannot itself be viewed as a disorder; otherwise countless people would be considered abnormal for sipping a drink to relax before dinner or taking a sedative to get to sleep when upset. The use of substances that affect the central nervous system is considered a disorder when it becomes so frequent and heavy that users can no longer function normally—whether in the family, at school, or at work. Moreover, such people continue to seek alcohol and drugs despite damage to their health and perhaps a threat to life itself. Although this is much more likely in the case of illegal and dangerous drugs like heroin and cocaine, as well as alcohol, it is important to recognize that people can also become excessively dependent on nicotine, caffeine, and some prescription drugs. Nicotine dependence is especially problematic because smoking can lead to serious health problems; smoking-related illnesses such as lung cancer are a leading cause of death in the United States.

An indication that alcohol or drug use is departing from normal is the development of **psychological dependence.** When this happens, users no longer view the substance as an incidental feature of life or as a way to promote temporary feelings of pleasure and well-being. Instead, they believe it to be essential in handling the day-to-day stresses of life. An executive might come to believe that he couldn't possibly endure the daily grind of corporate life without gulping a few swallows of the gin he keeps hidden in a desk drawer for "emergencies." Or a student might be convinced that without marijuana she would be unable to survive the tensions of school.

Many people who are psychologically dependent on alcohol and certain other drugs become **physically dependent**—or *addicted*—as well. Because their bodies develop a **tolerance** for the substance, they require increasingly larger doses to achieve anything like the desired effect. Moreover, they will now suffer from **withdrawal symptoms**—painful physical and psychological reactions—if they stop using the substance. Withdrawal from alcohol may result in **delirium tremens,** popularly known as the *DTs*—a state of intense panic that includes agitation, tremors, confusion, horrible nightmares, and even hallucinations. It is not unusual for alcohol abusers in the throes of the DTs to be convinced that bugs are crawling all over their bodies. Withdrawal from stimulants such as cocaine produces depression, disorientation, and irritability. Withdrawal from narcotics such as heroin has similar effects and also produces sensations of intense physical pain.

The suffering produced by withdrawal is often so great that addicts will go to any lengths to obtain the substance. Many do so despite a strong wish to "kick the habit" and return to a more normal existence.

## Consequences of Alcohol Abuse

The road from an occasional drink to dependence on alcohol is strewn with heavy physical penalties. Over the long haul, alcohol abusers run into a variety of serious health problems. Alcohol itself has little food value, and because alcohol abusers usually eat poorly, they often suffer severe malnutrition. **Cirrhosis** of the liver—in which the liver becomes scarred and hardened—may result from poor nutrition, as well as from the irritating effects of alcohol. Alcohol abusers also run a greater-than-normal risk of developing heart problems, high blood pressure, anemia, impotence, gastrointestinal disorders, and cancers of the tongue, mouth, larynx, esophagus, and liver.

Another serious problem caused by alcohol abuse is *Korsakoff's syndrome,* in which the ability to encode new memories is severely impaired. This disorder apparently is due to a deficiency in the vitamin thiamine that is associated with prolonged heavy ingestion of alcohol. It first appears as a neurological condition with such symptoms as confusion and abnormal eye movements; these gradually subside, but the memory impairment remains (American Psychiatric Association, 2000).

Heavy drinking for long periods leads to cognitive and emotional problems as well. Alcohol destroys brain cells—which is why studies of alcohol abusers show that their perceptual skills and problem-solving abilities are weakened (Silberstein & Parsons, 1981). Moreover, alcohol is a central nervous system depressant, not a stimulant: Although it gives users the idea that their feelings of depression are lighter, it actually deepens them (Aneshensel & Huba, 1983). An unusually large number of people with drinking problems commit suicide, and more than a third of all suicides involve alcohol. A significant number of industrial accidents, drownings, burns, and falls have also been attributed to drinking. So, too, have

### Test Yourself

**(h)** People with which personality disorder may have an autonomic nervous system that is insensitive and difficult to arouse?

**(l)** The incidence of narcissism in our society is increasing because of our cultural preoccupation with getting everything we want in life and being number one at all costs. True or false?

(The answers are on page 532.)

**Psychological dependence**
The feeling that the use of alcohol or other drugs is essential in handling day-to-day stress.

**Physical dependence**
A state of addiction to alcohol or drugs that exists when the body develops a tolerance for the substance and attempts to stop using it result in withdrawal symptoms.

**Tolerance**
An adaptation to a substance that causes the user to require increasingly larger doses to produce anything like the desired effect.

**Withdrawal symptoms**
Painful physical and psychological reactions experienced by individuals after they stop using the substance to which they are addicted.

**Delirium tremens**
A state of intense panic, characterized by agitation, tremors, confusion, horrible nightmares, and even hallucinations, that occurs when an alcohol abuser suddenly withdraws from drinking; also called the DTs.

**Cirrhosis**
A liver condition, caused by the excessive and prolonged use of alcohol, in which the liver becomes scarred and hardened.

Because alcohol abuse runs in families, heredity apparently plays some role in the disorder.

many cases of assault, rape, child abuse and neglect, and family violence. Alcohol consumption is implicated in 38% of all traffic fatalities, with enormous costs both to innocent victims and to society (U.S. Census Bureau, 2001).

## What Causes Alcohol Abuse?

In the United States and other nations where alcohol is legal, people from all walks of life become alcohol abusers—as any meeting of the self-help organization known as Alcoholics Anonymous demonstrates. What is the common denominator? Alcohol abuse has no single cause, but heredity apparently plays a role. As in the case of schizophrenia, the chances that twins will both become alcohol abusers are much greater for identical twins than for fraternal twins. Studies of adopted children have shown that those fathered by alcohol abusers were four times more likely to develop the disorder later in life than similar adoptees born to fathers who were not alcohol abusers. Factors in the children's upbringing—including being raised by an alcohol abuser or living in a home broken by death or divorce—did not affect the results (Goodwin, 1986).

Researchers have not identified an "alcohol-abusing personality," although there is some evidence that individuals who experience a greater-than-usual reduction in autonomic stress reactions with the help of alcohol are at higher risk for the disorder (Sher & Levenson, 1982). The popular image of the alcohol abuser as a "skid row drunk" does not hold up in real life. It is estimated that only 5% of all alcohol abusers fit this stereotype. All kinds of people can fall victim, including hard-driving politicians, high-strung performers, and anxious college students.

Cultural traditions can affect both patterns of alcohol use and the likelihood of abuse. There are significant differences in the amount and frequency of alcohol consumption in different countries. In most Asian cultures, for example, the prevalence of alcohol abuse is relatively low. In addition to cultural factors, low educational level, unemployment, and low socioeconomic status are associated with alcohol abuse, although it is often difficult to distinguish cause from effect (American Psychiatric Association, 2000).

## Gender and Alcohol Abuse

Surveys consistently indicate that men drink more heavily than women (Substance Abuse and Mental Health Services Admin. [SAMHSA], 2000). Moreover, the problems associated with the use of alcohol are much more prevalent among men. Men are twice as likely as women to show signs of dependence on alcohol and are also twice as likely to suffer adverse consequences from alcohol, such as problems with family and social relationships, encounters with police, and auto accidents (W. B. Clark & Midanik, 1982).

Women may be less prone than men to try to fight off their feelings of depression and anxiety by drinking. It may be that some women are turned off to drinking because they are more likely to suffer the adverse effects of alcohol. Recent evidence shows that the stomach lining of women manufactures smaller amounts of the enzyme **alcohol dehydrogenase,** which helps in the digestion of alcohol. As a result, more alcohol enters the bloodstream through the stomach wall and goes on to the brain, causing not only the symptoms of intoxication but also a greater threat to the liver (Frezza, di Padova, Pozzato, Terpin, & Baraona, 1990).

**Alcohol dehydrogenase**
**An enzyme that helps in the metabolism of alcohol.**

# The Highs and Lows of Substance Abuse

Humans have always been interested in finding substances that relieve anxiety, produce feelings of contentment and happiness, and result in strange experiences that make the user perceive the world in a distorted fashion. Hallucinations of imaginary sights and sounds may result, and sometimes a mystical or religious sense of oneness with the universe may be attained. Such states are referred to as **altered states of consciousness (ASC).**

Some mind-altering substances are used so routinely that they are seldom thought of as drugs. In the United States, alcohol is probably the best example. **Nicotine,** inhaled through smoking, can act in several different ways—sometimes as a stimulant, sometimes relieving feelings of anxiety. **Caffeine,** found in coffee, tea, and many cola-based beverages, is another stimulant.

Popular drugs include a number of substances whose nonmedical use is illegal, ranging from marijuana to heroin and cocaine, as well as prescription drugs like sleeping pills and stimulants taken for "kicks" rather than on a physician's orders. (In fact, addiction to prescription drugs, especially by middle-class adults, is widespread.) The use of drugs increased rapidly in the United States during the 1960s and 1970s. More recent evidence indicates that the overall use of illicit drugs has declined. Nevertheless, in 2000, an estimated 14 million people in the United States were current illicit drug users; this figure represents 6.3% of the population age 12 and older (SAMHSA, 2000). (See Figure 13.4.)

All the mind-altering drugs create their effects by temporarily changing the activity of the brain—certainly by assisting or hindering the transmission of messages at the brain's innumerable switching points, perhaps also by changing the circuits over which messages ordinarily flow. Almost invariably, the effect depends not only on the drug itself and the amount used but also on the user's frame of mind, the circumstances in which the drug is used, and the behavior of companions. The user's expectations likewise play an important part. For example, it has been found that cocaine users, who expect to get high from sniffing the powder, may not know the difference when another substance that produces the same sensation in the nose is substituted for the real thing (Van Dyke & Byck, 1982).

**Altered states of consciousness (ASC)**
States of consciousness produced by dreams, sleep, hypnosis, alcohol, or mind-altering drugs, that differ from normal waking experiences.

**Nicotine**
A drug in tobacco that acts like a stimulant and may relieve feelings of anxiety.

**Caffeine**
A central nervous system stimulant found in coffee, tea, and many cola-based beverages.

# Consequences of Drug Abuse

The most dangerous illegal substances include cocaine, heroin, hallucinogens, amphetamines, and barbiturates. Following are some of the effects these drugs may have on those who abuse them.

**Cocaine** Cocaine, which is ingested through the nasal passages, or "snorted," produces a feeling of increased strength, endurance, and intellectual power. But if used excessively, it can cause neurological disorders and seizures. This is especially true of the smokable form of cocaine known as crack. Crack produces an instant powerful "rush" that lasts about 15 minutes and causes a strong desire for another rush. As a result, this form of cocaine is highly addicting.

**Heroin** Heroin is injected intravenously with a hypodermic needle. In some users, it produces a sudden intense feeling of pleasure;

**FIGURE 13.4 Types of drugs used in the past month by illicit drug users. This chart shows what kinds of illicit drugs were used by people age 12 and older in the United States in 1999 and 2000.**
*SAMHSA, 2000.*

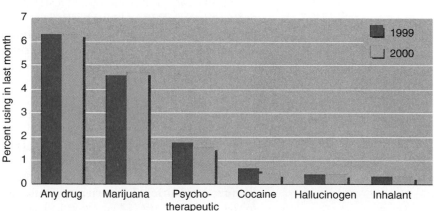

in others, self-esteem is enhanced. After the initial euphoria, however, the user becomes lethargic. Withdrawal from the drug can cause severe symptoms, which the user attempts to avoid at all costs; as a result, most users spend all their time trying to obtain additional supplies, usually through various forms of crime. Because of their propensity to share needles, heroin addicts are at high risk for AIDS.

**Hallucinogens**    LSD (lysergic acid diethylamide) is the most commonly abused hallucinogenic drug. It has the effect of distorting the user's perceptions. Studies have found that long-term adverse reactions to use of the drug occur mainly in users with preexisting mental problems; there is no evidence that LSD causes physical or psychological dependence (Ray, 1996).

**Amphetamines**    Amphetamines are legal when prescribed by a physician, and many users become addicted to them in this way. Overdose can cause coma, brain damage, and sometimes death, and withdrawal can lead to suicidal depression in heavy users.

**Barbiturates**    Barbiturates are central nervous system depressants. Long-term use in high doses can cause physical dependence; the systems are similar to those of heroin addiction and can be even more dangerous. In moderate doses, barbiturates have effects similar to those of alcohol, leading to reduced inhibition. Overdose can cause poisoning, convulsions, coma, and, in some cases, death.

## What Causes Addiction?

Over 90% of all people in the United States will at some time in their lives experiment with either legal or illegal drugs, and many of them will continue to use drugs regularly. Yet only a few will ultimately develop a substance abuse problem (Glantz & Pickens, 1992). Why do some people get "hooked"?

A crucial difference is the condition that existed before drug use started. Teenagers who become heavy drug users, for example, tend to be aggressive, have a strong tendency to seek sensation, and show a high tolerance for unconventional or deviant behavior. Other factors include poor relations between parent and child, drug use by other family members and peers, and living in an area where drugs are readily available and widely used (Glantz & Pickens, 1992).

After experimenting with drugs, some people develop the belief that they are unable to cope without them. Continued use sets up a vicious cycle. As these users rely more and more on drugs to feel in control, they repeatedly confirm their belief that they are powerless to cope on their own. Each failure to function without drugs strengthens that belief until they become addicted and are, in fact, unable to face life without chemical assistance (Gold, 1980).

In the case of heroin, one investigator identified six key characteristics of addicts (Nurco, 1979): (1) inability to cope with intense feelings of anger, usually generated by frustration; (2) need for immediate gratification; (3) inability to establish adequate sexual identity; (4) rejection of society's goals and the means typically used to achieve them; (5) proneness to take risks as a way of proving personal adequacy; and (6) constant need to deal with boredom. In another study, addicts were found to be relatively deficient in the capacity for self-regulation—that is, in the ability to plan ahead and anticipate the consequences of their actions (Wilson, Passik, Faude, Abrams, & Gordon, 1989).

One view of the road to drug abuse is based on a more general principle called the *opponent-process theory of emotion* (Solomon, 1980). According to this theory, the human nervous system seeks to balance out any deviation from normal equilibrium in emotional experience. Thus, every emotion triggers an opposing emotion that lingers after the first one is "switched off." For instance, after fearful flyers endure a frightening trip, they begin to feel ecstatic. Or, as a sequel to the pain of child-birth, many women tend to feel euphoric. In the same way, the discomfort, or "low," that a drug user feels when the effects of the drug wear off leads to the motivation for repeated use of the drug as a means of establishing the opposing "high." Ultimately, the result is the onset of tolerance—and addiction. In effect, the drug user becomes an abuser through the frequently repeated experience of contrasting unpleasant and pleasant emotional states (Solomon, 1986).

People often learn to use drugs by observing the behavior of their peers.

## Substance Abuse and Mental Disorder

Alcohol and drug abuse often coexist with mental health problems. One survey found that 37% of people with an alcohol abuse problem also had some kind of mental disorder (Regier, 1990). The causal nature of the relationship is not always clear. Many people use alcohol and drugs to find temporary relief from their depression and anxiety. A survey of people with bipolar disorder, for example, found that 49% abused alcohol or drugs during periods when their condition wasn't being treated (National Depressive and Manic-Depressive Association, 1993). On the other hand, those who abuse substances may be more prone to develop mental or behavioral disorders. Those suffering from a major mental disorder such as schizophrenia or mood disorders are also often beset by alcohol and drug abuse (Brown, Ridgley, Pepper, Levine, & Ryglewicz, 1989). The overlap has been found in nearly a third of all those suffering from depression (Goodwin, 1989).

There may be a genetic susceptibility that leaves people vulnerable to both mental disorders and substance abuse. One study found that people biologically related to depressed individuals were about twice as likely as relatives of nondepressed people to develop either a depressive or a substance abuse disorder, usually alcoholism (Ingraham, 1992).

As in the case of all mental disorders, understanding what substance abuse is and how it develops will make us less fearful of it and more compassionate toward its victims. One of the great challenges for psychology is to learn how to spare more people the pain of mental disorders, lighten the burdens of those who do succumb, and—as described in the next chapter—help society respond more appropriately to their needs.

### Test Yourself

**(j)** What type of dependence is experienced by someone who sees alcohol or drugs as essential to handling the day-to-day stresses of life?

**(k)** When individuals who are physically dependent on a drug or alcohol abruptly stop taking the substance, what will they experience?

(The answers are on page 532.)

# OTHER DISORDERS

So far we have discussed the mental disorders that are most widespread and have the greatest impact on both the individual and society. However, as indicated in the study chart (page 504), DSM-IV lists several other categories of disorders

### FOCUS QUESTIONS

- What are the basic types of sexual disorders?
- What is meant by "split personality"?
- What kinds of disorders are characterized by lack of impulse control?
- How can culture influence mental and behavioral disorders?

as well. Some of these, such as disorders first apparent in childhood and adolescence, are discussed in other chapters. Others that are worth a brief mention are described in this section.

## Sexual Disorders

*Sexual dysfunctions* involve disturbances in the processes that characterize the sexual response cycle or pain associated with sexual intercourse. They include hypoactive sexual desire disorder (lack of sexual fantasies and desire for sexual activity), sexual aversion disorder (aversion to and active avoidance of genital sexual contact with a sexual partner), female sexual arousal disorder (inability to maintain sexual excitement), and male erectile disorder (inability to maintain an adequate erection). Also included in DSM-IV are female and male orgasmic disorders, premature ejaculation, and sexual pain disorders (American Psychiatric Association, 2000). These disorders can have psychological causes, physical causes, or both. But whatever their cause, they are often accompanied by significant personal distress.

Perhaps more serious from a societal standpoint are **paraphilias,** disorders characterized by "recurrent, intense sexually arousing fantasies, sexual urges, or behaviors generally involving (1) nonhuman objects, (2) the suffering or humiliation of oneself or one's partner, or (3) children or other nonconsenting persons. The behavior must occur over a period of at least 6 months" (American Psychiatric Association, 2000, p. 566). The most serious—and dangerous—paraphilias are those that are acted out with a nonconsenting partner in ways that may be injurious to the partner.

Among the more common types of paraphilias are exhibitionism, voyeurism, and frotteurism. *Exhibitionism,* or "flashing," involves exposing one's genitals to strangers as a way of becoming sexually aroused. *Voyeurism* refers to watching strangers undress or engage in sex, without their knowledge, as a way of becoming aroused. *Frotteurism,* which typically occurs in crowded places such as elevators or subway cars, involves rubbing one's genitals against a nonconsenting person.

Other paraphilias include *fetishism* (fantasizing and masturbating while touching objects such as shoes or underwear worn by members of the opposite sex); *sadism* (inflicting humiliation, pain, and suffering as part of the sexual act), and *pedophilia* (sexual behavior by an adult with a child). Pedophilia is regarded as a disorder regardless of whether it is accompanied by personal distress, and in most parts of the world it is a serious crime, even if the child consents.

## Dissociative Identity Disorder

You may remember the movie *The Three Faces of Eve* or may have heard of other instances of so-called multiple personality. Formally known as **dissociative identity disorder,** this condition is controversial because it is not clear whether it is truly involuntary (and therefore constitutes a disorder) or whether it may be voluntary (which implies that the person is acting—albeit very convincingly).

Also called *split personality,* dissociative identity disorder is characterized by a splitting of the individual's sense of self into two or more personalities. Each personality has a different name and characteristics: One may be shy, the other gregarious; one may be timid, the other aggressive. Sometimes one personality is not aware of the other (or others), and in some cases the personalities struggle for dominance. Usually there is a primary identity that responds to the person's given name and is passive and dependent; from time to time, this identity disappears and is replaced by secondary identities with very different characteristics.

**Paraphilia**
A disorder characterized by recurrent, intense sexually arousing fantasies, sexual urges, or behaviors generally involving (1) nonhuman objects, (2) the suffering or humiliation of oneself or one's partner, or (3) children or other nonconsenting persons.

**Dissociative identity disorder**
A disorder characterized by a splitting of the person's sense of self into two or more personalities; also called split personality.

It is believed that dissociative identity disorder stems from a failure to integrate various aspects of identity, memory, and consciousness, causing the individual to appear to have several different personalities. The shift from one personality to another may be accompanied by changes in posture, tone of voice, and even physiological processes such as blood pressure (Putnam, 1991).

In recent years, there has been a significant increase in the number of cases of dissociative identity disorder reported in the United States. Some believe that the increase is due to greater awareness of the disorder and, therefore, improved diagnosis. Critics argue, however, that it is likely that the disorder is over-diagnosed in individuals who are highly suggestible (American Psychiatric Association, 2000).

Pathological gambling is among the more common disorders of impulse control.

## Disorders of Impulse Control

DSM-IV lists several disorders in the category of impulse-control disorders. These disorders are characterized by impulses to engage in behaviors that are destructive to self or others, coupled with inability to resist engaging in those behaviors. They include *kleptomania* (inability to resist stealing), *pyromania* (inability to resist starting fires), and *pathological gambling* (inability to resist gambling despite excessive losses).

Gambling itself is not necessarily destructive to self or others; the vast majority of gamblers do so recreationally, and when they lose, they keep their losses within affordable limits. However, pathological (compulsive) gambling, or gambling to excess, may be highly detrimental both to the individual and to his or her family. Pathological gamblers often abandon their work and family life and spend all their time at casinos, racetracks, and the like, incurring heavy financial losses. People with this disorder are preoccupied with gambling and with obtaining more money to gamble with—whether by borrowing, stealing, or other illegal means. They also use gambling as a way of escaping from the problems and responsibilities of everyday life. If forced to stop gambling, they become restless and irritable—symptoms similar to those of drug withdrawal.

## Culture-Bound Syndromes

In addition to the disorders discussed earlier, which are found in many different societies and affect people regardless of characteristics such as ethnicity or nationality, there are a variety of unusual disorders that for the most part appear only among members of specific cultural groups. These **culture-bound syndromes,** according to DSM-IV, are "localized, folk, diagnostic categories that frame coherent meanings for certain repetitive, patterned, and troubling sets of experiences and observations" (American Psychiatric Association, 2000, p. 898). Members of the groups in which they occur consider them to be illnesses or afflic-

**Culture-bound syndrome** A disorder that appears only among members of a specific cultural group.

TABLE 13.5
## Examples of Culture-Bound Syndromes

| Syndrome | Description | Cultural Group |
|---|---|---|
| Amok | A dissociative episode characterized by a period of brooding followed by an outburst of violent, aggressive, or homicidal behavior | Malaysia |
| Boufée delirante | A sudden outburst of agitated and aggressive behavior, marked confusion, and psychomotor excitement | West Africa, Haiti |
| Dhat | Severe anxiety and hypochondriacal concerns associated with the discharge of semen | India |
| Ghost sickness | A preoccupation with death and the deceased, sometimes associated with witchcraft | Native Americans |
| Hwa-byung | "Anger syndrome" (attributed to suppression of anger); symptoms include insomnia, fatigue, panic, indigestion, anorexia, palpitations, and generalized aches and pains | Korea |
| Mal de ojo | A condition that occurs mainly in children, symptoms include fitful sleep, crying without apparent cause, diarrhea, vomiting, and fever | Mediterranean cultures |
| Pibloktoq | An abrupt dissociative episode accompanied by extreme excitement and frequently followed by convulsive seizures and coma lasting up to 12 hours | Eskimo communities |
| Shenjing shuairuo | A condition characterized by physical and mental fatigue, dizziness, headaches and other pains, concentration difficulties, sleep disturbance, and memory loss | China |
| Susto | An illness attributed to a frightening event that causes the soul to leave the body and results in unhappiness and sickness | Latinos in North, Central, and South America |
| Taijin kyofusho | Intense fear that one's body, its parts, or its functions displease, embarrass, or are offensive to other people | Japan |

*Source: Adapted from American Psychiatric Association, 2000.*

tions, and most have local names. Although some of their symptoms overlap with those of DSM-IV categories, there is seldom a one-to-one equivalence between a culture-bound syndrome and a DSM-IV diagnostic category. Some of the more common culture-bound syndromes are listed in Table 13.5.

# Chapter 13 Summary

## Abnormal Characteristics: Their Nature and Scope

1. Abnormal behavior, though difficult to define, is generally considered to be behavior that is statistically unusual, considered undesirable by most people, and a source of unhappiness to the person who displays it. In addition, it is usually *maladaptive*, interfering with the person's social or personal functioning.

## Causes and Classification of Abnormal Behaviors

2. Abnormal behavior hinges on two factors: the amount of stress and anxiety a person experiences and the person's ability to handle that amount.

3. The ability to handle stress and anxiety appears to be determined by biological factors (such as glandular activity and sensitivity of the autonomic nervous system), psychological factors (such as motives and anxiety over failure to fulfill them), and environmental influences.

4. The *Diagnostic and Statistical Manual of Mental Disorders* (DSM) published by the American Psychiatric Association presents detailed descriptions of patterns of abnormal behavior.

## Schizophrenia

5. *Schizophrenia* is characterized by extreme disorganization of personality. Schizophrenics typically display perceptual difficulties, including *hallucinations;* thought disorders, including *delusions;* and emotional disturbances.

6. In many patients, schizophrenia is associated with increased levels of the neurotransmitter dopamine in the brain. It has also been found that schizophrenics appear to have defects in brain metabolism and in parts of the nervous system responsible for perception. There is strong evidence that genetic factors play a role in causing the disorder.

## Mood Disorders

7. Abnormal *depression* is a *mood disorder* marked by a severe and prolonged mood of sadness, helplessness, and hopelessness. Depressed individuals suffer from lowered self-esteem and motivation, guilt, sleep difficulties, physical complaints, and disturbances of perception and thought. The risk of suicide is especially high with depression.

8. Episodes of depression that recur without other abnormalities of mood are characteristic of *unipolar disorder.* Exaggerated fluctuations in mood from intense excitement to deep melancholy are characteristic of *bipolar disorder.*

9. One form of mood disorder, called seasonal affective disorder (SAD), causes people to become depressed in the winter and energetic—even manic—in the summer.

10. There is evidence that genetic and biochemical factors are involved in the development of mood disorders.

11. Mood disorders occur twice as often among women as among men. For both sexes, the chance of experiencing depressive episodes increases with age.

12. The risk of serious depression increases in the later years of life, but the disorder affects a considerable number of children as well.

## Anxiety Disorders

13. *Anxiety disorders* arise when situations that produce conflict and frustration remain unresolved. Four common types of anxiety disorders are *generalized anxiety disorder, panic disorder, phobias*—including *specific phobia, social phobia,* and *agoraphobia* and *obsessive-compulsive disorder,* characterized by extreme *obsessions* and *compulsions.*

## Personality Disorders

14. Some forms of abnormal behavior that are difficult to classify are called *personality disorders.* Unlike other forms, they are not expressed in specific symptoms or clearly related to anxiety and stress. People with these disorders seem to lack the desire or ability to act in socially acceptable ways. Three major types are *antisocial personality, paranoid personality,* and *narcissistic personality disorders.*

## Substance Abuse and Dependence

15. Voluntary, frequent, and heavy use of alcohol and other potent drugs is referred to as *substance abuse.* Indications that alcohol or drug use is departing from normal are the development of *psychological dependence* and *physical dependence,* or addiction. Because people who are physically dependent on a substance develop *tolerance* for it, they require increasingly large doses to produce the desired effect. If they stop using the drug, they suffer *withdrawal symptoms* (painful physical and psychological reactions).

16. People who abuse alcohol become strongly dependent on alcohol and lose control over the act of drinking. They continue to drink despite the serious physical and psychological problems alcohol

produces, including brain damage and *cirrhosis* of the liver, malnutrition, impaired problem-solving abilities, and disruption of family life. Withdrawal from alcohol may result in *delirium tremens*, or DTs. Alcohol abuse has no single cause, but heredity apparently plays some role.

17. *Altered states of consciousness (ASC)*, in which perception does not operate in the usual fashion, can be produced by a variety of drugs ranging from *nicotine* (in tobacco) and *caffeine* (in coffee, tea, and many cola-based beverages) to heroin and cocaine.

18. Drug abuse results from repeated use of drugs for other than medical purposes, leading to severe physical and psychological disturbances. Abusers of multiple drugs are likely to have especially serious medical, personal, and social problems.

## Other Disorders

19. Sexual dysfunctions involve disturbances in the processes that characterize the sexual response cycle or pain associated with sexual intercourse.

20. *Paraphilias* are characterized by recurrent, intense sexually arousing fantasies, sexual urges, or behaviors generally involving nonhuman objects, the suffering or humiliation of oneself or one's partner, or children or other nonconsenting persons. They include exhibitionism, voyeurism, frotteurism, fetishism, sadism, and pedophilia.

21. *Dissociative identity disorder* is characterized by a splitting of the individual's sense of self into two or more personalities.

22. Impulse-control disorders are characterized by impulses to engage in behaviors that are destructive to self or others, coupled with inability to resist engaging in those behaviors. Typical of these disorders are kleptomania (inability to resist stealing), pyromania (inability to resist starting fires), and pathological gambling (inability to resist gambling despite excessive losses).

23. *Culture-bound syndromes* are unusual disorders that appear only among members of specific cultural groups.

# Chapter 13 Test Yourself Answers

(a) Unusual forms of behavior are not considered abnormal unless they are regarded as undesirable within the culture.

(b) Tracy may have a greater biological susceptibility to depression than Annette. She may also have other environmental stressors in her life. In addition, Annette may have more avenues of support and better coping skills than Tracy.

(c) Physical evidence includes results from PET and MRI scans and the fact that all drugs that effectively treat schizophrenia affect the neurotransmitter dopamine.

(d) Unrelenting sadness, intense helplessness and hopelessness, listlessness in work or play, dis-

turbed sleep, impaired appetite, headaches, heart palpitations, and dizziness are some of the common symptoms of depression.

(e) Jeffrey might be suffering from depression.

(f) He may have panic disorder.

(g) Adolescents and young adults suffer the most from panic disorder and phobias.

(h) Those with antisocial personality disorder may have insensitive nervous systems.

(i) False; the incidence of narcissism has remained steady.

(j) Those who see alcohol or drugs as essential to handling life have a psychological dependence.

(k) They will experience withdrawal symptoms.

# Chapter 13  Mental and Behavioral Disorders

## Key Terms

agoraphobia (p. 516)
alcohol dehydrogenase (p. 524)
altered states of consciousness (ASC) (p. 525)
antisocial personality disorder (p. 519)
anxiety disorder (p. 514)
bipolar disorder (p. 508)
caffeine (p. 525)
cirrhosis (p. 523)
compulsion (p. 517)
culture-bound syndrome (p. 529)
delirium tremens (p. 523)
delusion (p. 506)
depression (p. 507)
dissociative identity disorder (p. 528)
DSM-IV (p. 503)
generalized anxiety disorder (p. 514)
hallucination (p. 505)
maladaptive behavior (p. 500)
mood disorders (p. 507)
narcissistic personality disorder (p. 521)

nicotine (p. 525)
obsession (p. 517)
obsessive-compulsive disorder (OCD) (p. 517)
panic disorder (p. 515)
paranoid personality disorder (p. 521)
paraphilia (p. 528)
personality disorders (p. 518)
phobia (p. 516)
physical dependence (p. 523)
psychological dependence (p. 523)
schizophrenia (p. 505)
social phobia (p. 516)
specific phobia (p. 516)
substance abuse (p. 522)
tolerance (p. 523)
unipolar disorder (p. 508)
withdrawal symptoms (p. 523)

 *The key terms above can be used as search terms in InfoTrac, a database of readings, which can be found at http://infotrac-thomsonlearning.com.*

## Active Learning Review

### Abnormal Characteristics: Their Nature and Scope

1. One characteristic of abnormal behavior is that it is statistically unusual. Since only a few Americans believe in witches, such a belief may be taken as an indication of _____ behavior. — **abnormal**

2. Abnormal behavior, besides being statistically _____, is regarded as undesirable by most people. — **unusual**

3. A man who walks down the street talking loudly to himself is considered abnormal partly because most people regard his behavior as _____. — **undesirable**

4. A third characteristic of abnormal behavior—in addition to being _____ unusual and considered _____ by most people—is that it is a source of unhappiness to the person who displays it. — **statistically** / **undesirable**

5. A woman who is miserable because she cannot give up drinking heavily every day is considered abnormal partly because her behavior is a source of _____. — **unhappiness**

6. Many psychologists view as abnormal those behaviors that are _____—that is, behaviors that interfere with the individual's functioning and development. — **maladaptive**

7. At least 50 million people in the United States suffer from a diagnosable psychological disorder at any given time. This indicates the widespread extent of _____ behavior. — **abnormal**

### Causes and Classification of Abnormal Behaviors

8. Abnormal behavior, though influenced to a degree by an individual's inherited _____ characteristics, also depends on acquired psychological characteristics. — **biological**

9. If we have a strong motivation for achievement that is frustrated, we become vulnerable to abnormal behavior. This shows that regardless of the biological characteristics we inherit, our acquired _____ characteristics also play a role.

psychological

10. In addition to _____ and _____ psychological characteristics, a third factor influencing the development of abnormal behavior is the environment.

biological, acquired

11. There is a high rate of mental disorder among people living in poverty. This shows that abnormal behavior is influenced in part by the _____.

environment

12. Individuals develop different kinds of abnormal behavior under stress partly as a result of differences in their _____.

environment

13. To study abnormal behavior scientifically, scientists must have a common _____ scheme. To provide this, the American Psychiatric Association developed the *Diagnostic and Statistical Manual of Mental Disorders*, now in its fourth edition and known as *DSM-IV*.

classification

## Schizophrenia

14. *Schizophrenia* is one of the major disorders in the American Psychiatric Association's classification scheme, known as _____.

DSM-IV

15. Patients with schizophrenia typically display _____ difficulties, _____ disruptions, and _____ disturbances.

perceptual, thought
emotional

16. A prominent symptom among victims of schizophrenia is a false belief, called a _____.

delusion

17. If you encountered a man who insisted that his head was missing, you would conclude that he was suffering from a _____.

delusion

18. Often, people with schizophrenia experience false sensory events, known as _____—for example, seeing things that are not actually present.

hallucinations

19. Inherited defects in the nervous system and brain chemistry seem to play an important part in the origin of schizophrenia. But the fact that not all people from the same family become schizophrenic points to the influence of psychological and environmental factors as well as inherited _____ characteristics.

biological

## Mood Disorders

20. The behavior of individuals with a *mood disorder* is marked by extreme abnormalities of _____.

mood

21. Many people react to stress with clinical, or major, _____—a plunge in mood so severe and prolonged that it overwhelms the entire personality.

depression

22. People who are constantly sad, unable to work, eat, or sleep, and feel so hopeless that they often consider suicide are likely to be suffering from major _____.

depression

23. Depressed people, unable to feel any hope for the future, are prone to view _____ as a way to end their suffering.

suicide

24. In _____ *disorder*, the individual has recurrent episodes of depression.

unipolar

25. In _____ *disorder*, the person's mood fluctuates from deep melancholy to intense excitement.

bipolar

26. A person who is depressed to the point of suicide one week and higher than a kite the next would probably be diagnosed as suffering from _____ disorder.

bipolar

27. A person suffering from bipolar disorder experiences wide swings in _____.

mood

28. A person who is depressed during the dark winter and verges on manic activity in the bright summer is probably suffering from _____ _____ _____.

seasonal affective
disorder

29. The disorder just described is also known as _____.

SAD

30. There is some evidence that mood disorders have a _____ basis.

genetic

31. Mood disorders occur among individuals showing evidence of _____ disturbances in the brain.

chemical

32. A type of depression characterized by feelings of guilt, inferiority, and self-criticism is known as _____ depression.

**introjective**

33. Unrealistic standards of beauty and thinness may be a reason for higher rates of depression in women. These standards may also lead to _____ disorders.

**eating**

34. One eating disorder, in which an already emaciated person continues on a starvation diet, is known as _____ nervosa.

**anorexia**

35. Another such disorder, in which a person engages in eating binges and then induces vomiting or takes laxatives, is called _____ nervosa.

**bulimia**

36. Evidence for a biological basis for eating disorders comes from studies showing alterations in the brain chemical _____ and the brain hormone _____.

**serotonin, vasopressin**

## Anxiety Disorders

37. Although most people suffering from a psychological disorder experience some symptoms of _____, the term *anxiety disorder* is reserved for cases in which anxiety is the outstanding symptom.

**anxiety**

38. When anxiety is the obvious and most striking symptom, the patient is suffering from an _____ _____.

**anxiety disorder**

39. One form of anxiety disorder is _____ anxiety—a sort of "free-floating" anxiety felt not toward anything in particular but to everything in general.

**generalized**

40. Marcus faces each day beset with an unfocused feeling of tension, uneasiness, and vague fear. He is constantly "on edge" and lives as if the world were about to cave in. Marcus shows signs of _____ _____ _____.

**generalized anxiety disorder**

41. In another form of anxiety disorder, patients experience episodes in which their anxiety erupts into an attack of terror. They are said to be victims of _____ _____.

**panic disorder**

42. Sara has attacks of anxiety that overwhelm her "out of the blue." She might be driving her car or walking down the street when suddenly she feels that she is about to die. Sara appears to be suffering from _____ _____.

**panic disorder**

43. In another type of anxiety disorder, the victim has a *phobia*—a crippling fear of something, such as being confined in a small space or venturing out into public places or even streets. In *specific phobia*, the anxiety is attached to a particular _____ or _____.

**object, situation**

44. A man with an intense fear of being scrutinized by others—for example, during public speaking—is suffering from a _____ phobia.

**social**

45. A crippling fear of public places is called *agoraphobia*. It is the most disabling of all the _____.

**phobias**

46. A woman who is virtually confined to her home by anxiety over venturing out in public is a victim of _____.

**agoraphobia**

47. In addition to the vague and free-floating type of anxiety disorder called _____ anxiety disorder, the attacks of terror known as _____ disorder, and the crippling fear of some object or situation called a _____, there is a fourth type of anxiety disorder called *obsessive-compulsive disorder (OCD)*. It takes the form of persistently recurring thoughts and urges.

**generalized, panic phobia**

48. An *obsession* is a thought that keeps cropping up in a persistent and disturbing fashion. A man who cannot help thinking he has heart trouble is exhibiting one of the two symptoms of _____ _____ _____.

**obsessive-compulsive disorder**

49. A woman who is constantly troubled by the thought that she will be killed in an earthquake before her 35th birthday is displaying an _____.

**obsession**

50. A persistent and irresistible urge to perform some act over and over again is a _____.

**compulsion**

51. A man who is driven to wash his hands dozens of times a day is displaying a _____.

**compulsion**

52. Obsessive-compulsive disorder, phobias, panic disorder, and generalized anxiety disorder are all forms of _____ disorder.

**anxiety**

## Personality Disorders

53. Some forms of abnormal behavior, rather than being expressed in specific symptoms, appear to exist as part of the entire personality. They are called _____ _____.

**personality disorders**

54. Among the various personality disorders, which seem to originate in childhood, is *antisocial personality disorder*—a diagnosis applied to people who seem to lack any normal conscience, sense of responsibility, or feelings for others. These traits seem to pervade their entire _____.

**personality**

55. A person who constantly behaves in an impulsive and reckless manner, has no respect for the law, and ignores the feelings of family and friends is displaying an _____ personality.

**antisocial**

56. Also listed among the personality disorders is _____ _____ _____, a diagnosis applied to people who seem consumed by a groundless distrust of others.

**paranoid personality disorder**

57. A man who is constantly suspicious that his wife is unfaithful, even though he has no real reason for his suspicion, is displaying a _____ personality.

**paranoid**

58. Just as antisocial personality and paranoid personality are forms of _____ _____, so is *narcissistic personality,* a diagnosis applied to people who crave constant attention and admiration and use others for their own purposes and gratifications.

**personality disorders**

59. A woman who never considers the needs of other people but continually manipulates and exploits them to gain attention and admiration is displaying a _____ personality.

**narcissistic**

## Substance Abuse and Dependence

60. The use of alcohol or drugs cannot itself be viewed as a psychological disorder. But _____ _____ occurs when the use of these substances becomes so frequent and heavy that users can no longer function normally.

**substance abuse**

61. One indication that users of alcohol or drugs can no longer function normally is the development of _____ dependence, or the belief that they need the alcohol or drugs to operate successfully under pressure.

**psychological**

62. George, convinced that he can handle the stresses of life only with the help of whisky, is showing signs of _____ _____.

**psychological dependence**

63. People who are physically dependent on alcohol or drugs are said to be _____. Because they develop a physical *tolerance* for whatever substance they are using, they require increasingly large doses to produce the desired effect.

**addicted**

64. Marie needs increasing quantities of whiskey to produce the effects she wants. Her body is apparently developing a physical _____ for alcohol.

**tolerance**

65. When people become physically dependent on a substance, or _____, stopping use of the substance results in painful physical and psychological reactions called *withdrawal symptoms.*

**addicted**

66. Suddenly stopping the use of alcohol often results in the _____ symptoms of *delirium tremens,* popularly known as DTs—a state of intense panic accompanied by tremors, confusion, nightmares, and even hallucinations of nonexistent sights and sounds.

**withdrawal**

67. People who are addicted to alcohol and drink large amounts because of an increased _____ for it may suffer the extreme withdrawal symptoms called _____ _____.

**tolerance**
**delirium tremens**

68. They may also suffer from _____ of the liver, a condition in which the liver is scarred and hardened.

**cirrhosis**

69. Psychological dependence, physical dependence (or addiction), and withdrawal symptoms are all indications of substance _____. Drug abuse oc-

**abuse**

curs with the repeated use of drugs for nonmedical purposes in ways that result in physical and psychological disturbances.

70. Jack uses drugs repeatedly and is now suffering chronic physical and psychological symptoms. He is likely to be a victim of _____ _____.

       **drug abuse**

71. Throughout history, people have sought mind-altering substances, or substances that produce altered states of _____.

       **consciousness**

72. Alcohol is such a substance, and so are _____, inhaled through smoking cigarettes, and _____, found in coffee, tea, and cola-based beverages.

       **nicotine**
       **caffeine**

73. One theory about the origins of drug abuse is based on a general principle called the _____-_____ theory of emotion.

       **opponent-process**

74. Alcohol and drug abuse often coexist with _____ _____ problems.

       **mental health**

## Other Disorders

75. Sexual dysfunctions involve disturbances in the processes that characterize the _____ _____ cycle or pain associated with _____ _____.

       **sexual response**
       **sexual intercourse**

76. A _____ is a disorder characterized by sexual urges or behaviors involving nonhuman objects, suffering or humiliation, or nonconsenting persons.

       **paraphilia**

77. _____ _____ _____ is characterized by a splitting of the individual's sense of self into two or more personalities.

       **Dissociative identity disorder**

78. Disorders of _____ _____ include kleptomania (inability to resist stealing), pyromania (inability to resist starting fires), and pathological gambling (inability to resist gambling despite excessive losses).

       **impulse control**

79. _____-_____ _____ are localized, folk, diagnostic categories that frame coherent meanings for certain repetitive, patterned, and troubling sets of experiences and observations.

       **Culture-bound syndromes**

## Practice Test

___ 1. Which of the following is *not* part of the definition of abnormal behavior?
   a. It is statistically unusual.
   b. It is considered undesirable by most people.
   c. It is inherited.
   d. It is a source of unhappiness.

___ 2. The number of people in the United States who are suffering from a mental disorder at any given time is estimated at
   a. 30 million.
   b. 50 million.
   c. 20 million.
   d. 10 million.

___ 3. Behaviors that interfere with functioning and development are referred to as
   a. psychotic.
   b. depressive.
   c. bipolar.
   d. maladaptive.

___ 4. The American Psychiatric Association's scheme for classifying mental disorders, now used by most psychologists and other mental health professionals, is known as
   a. DSM-II.
   b. APA-III(R).
   c. DSM-IV.
   d. APA II.

___ 5. The most devastating of all mental disorders, marked by a dramatic disorganization of personality, is known as
   a. schizophrenia.
   b. affective disorder.
   c. paranoid personality.
   d. phobic disorder.

___ 6. Which of the following is *not* a symptom displayed by people suffering from schizophrenia?
   a. delusions
   b. hallucinations
   c. phobic reactions
   d. inappropriate emotions

___ 7. Which of the following is a mood disorder?
   a. schizophrenia
   b. depression
   c. generalized anxiety
   d. alcohol abuse

___ 8. Which of the following statements about depression is true?
   a. A tendency to suffer from it may be inherited.
   b. It is not affected by experiences during childhood.
   c. Men are more susceptible than women.
   d. It is always followed by a period of manic behavior.

___ 9. An eating disorder sometimes related to depression is called
   a. narcissism.
   b. pyromania.
   c. addiction.
   d. bulimia nervosa.

___ 10. Depression that occurs mainly in the winter months is typical of a disorder known as
   a. bipolar disorder.
   b. seasonal affective disorder.
   c. schizoaffective disorder.
   d. unipolar disorder.

___ 11. Which one of the following is *not* a typical symptom of childhood depression?
   a. school phobia
   b. truancy
   c. hallucinations
   d. bed-wetting

___ 12. Individuals who are so anxious about being in a public place that they never leave home are suffering from
   a. claustrophobia.
   b. agoraphobia.
   c. generalized anxiety.
   d. acrophobia.

___ 13. A person who spends half the day checking and rechecking the doors and windows and still doubts that they are locked is suffering from
   a. a phobic disorder.
   b. generalized anxiety.
   c. depression.
   d. obsessive-compulsive disorder.

___ 14. A person with an antisocial personality is best described as
   a. suspicious and hostile.
   b. withdrawn.
   c. selfish and addicted to lying.
   d. perfectionistic and indecisive.

____15. A person with a narcissistic personality is best described as
  a. craving constant attention and admiration.
  b. suspicious and sensitive.
  c. hostile and defensive.
  d. reckless and ruthless.

____16. *Psychopath* is a term sometimes used to describe a person with
  a. paranoid personality disorder.
  b. narcissistic personality disorder.
  c. antisocial personality disorder.
  d. borderline personality disorder.

____17. Cirrhosis of the liver is associated with
  a. drug abuse.
  b. organic mental disorder.
  c. alcohol abuse.
  d. somatoform disorder.

____18. When individuals require increasingly larger doses of alcohol or a drug to produce the desired effect, they have developed
  a. withdrawal symptoms.
  b. psychological dependence.
  c. "DTs."
  d. tolerance.

____19. Delirium tremens, known as the DTs, are a symptom of
  a. tolerance.
  b. blackout.
  c. multiple drug use.
  d. withdrawal.

____20. Another term for addiction is
  a. psychological dependence.
  b. physical dependence.
  c. substance abuse.
  d. alcohol abuse.

# Exercises

1. There are often major differences between the general public's ideas about psychological disorders and the diagnostic categories used by psychologists and psychiatrists. This exercise illustrates the difference with regard to schizophrenia, which often is confused with "split personality" (dissociative identity disorder) and psychopathy (antisocial personality disorder).

   Your participants should be six people who say that they know something about schizophrenia but have never studied psychology.

   Give each participant a pencil and a piece of lined paper on which you have written the numbers 1 through 10 down the left margin, skipping a couple of lines between each number. Read your participants the following directions:

   > This is a test of what people know about mental disorders. I'll ask you for a list of symptoms. For example, a list of symptoms for a snake phobia might include (1) fear of snakes, (2) trying to avoid snakes, (3) a belief that all snakes are dangerous, (4) nervousness around worms and garden hoses.

   > Now please use the paper to list all the symptoms you believe are involved in schizophrenia. Please try to list ten items, although you may list more or fewer if you wish.

   When you have collected your lists, go through them and make a new list that includes each *different* symptom that your participants wrote down. If two or more people listed the same symptom, put it on your list once and tally the number of people who listed it.

   Using the chapter's description of schizophrenia, circle the symptoms in your list that are correct—that is, properly associated with schizophrenia. Identify the two most frequently named incorrect symptoms (not circled) and the two most frequently named correct symptoms (circled).

   Then answer the following questions:

   a. Why do you think some people believe that schizophrenics display the top two symptoms on the incorrect list?

   b. What do you think makes the top two correct symptoms easy to identify properly as schizophrenic?

   c. To what disorders do the top two incorrect symptoms belong? (*Hint:* Check the disorders mentioned at the beginning of the exercise first.)

   d. What are some of the implications of the public's misunderstandings of psychopathology? What might happen when police, schoolteachers, legislators, and other professionals harbor these misunderstandings?

2. Table 13.1 in the text (p. 509) is a brief test for depression; it shows the answers likely to be given by the most extremely depressed individual. Most of us, of course, would answer the test items in a less extreme way. Moreover, depending on our mood, our answers would undoubtedly vary if we took the test on different days.

   Two copies of the test are provided here (Figures 13.5a and 13.5b). Fill in one of them on a day when you're feeling especially "up"—when things are going just right and you're optimistic and content. Then take the test again when you're feeling "down"—at a time when you're troubled and "blue." Your answers may vary considerably. If so, you have demonstrated that all of us experience fluctuations in mood. Our spirits rise and fall in the natural course of events. (Remember that a diagnosis of true depression is impossible from the results of any single test—so don't worry if your results seem to point in that direction.)

✿ *For quizzing, activities, exercises, and web links, check out the book-specific website at http://www.psychology.wadsworth.com/kagan9e.*

FIGURE 13.5a

| | None or a Little of the Time | Some of the Time | Good Part of the Time | Most or All of the Time |
|---|---|---|---|---|
| 1. I feel downhearted, blue, and sad. | | | | |
| 2. Morning is when I feel the best. | | | | |
| 3. I have crying spells or feel like it. | | | | |
| 4. I have trouble sleeping through the night. | | | | |
| 5. I eat as much as I used to. | | | | |
| 6. I enjoy looking at, talking to, and being with attractive women/men. | | | | |
| 7. I notice that I am losing weight. | | | | |
| 8. I have trouble with constipation. | | | | |
| 9. My heart beats faster than normal. | | | | |
| 10. I get tired for no reason. | | | | |
| 11. My mind is as clear as it used to be. | | | | |
| 12. I find it easy to do the things I used to. | | | | |
| 13. I am restless and can't keep still. | | | | |
| 14. I feel hopeful about the future. | | | | |
| 15. I am more irritable than usual. | | | | |
| 16. I find it easy to make decisions. | | | | |
| 17. I feel that I am useful and needed. | | | | |
| 18. My life is pretty full. | | | | |
| 19. I feel that others would be better off if I were dead. | | | | |
| 20. I still enjoy the things I used to do. | | | | |

FIGURE 13.5b

| | None or a Little of the Time | Some of the Time | Good Part of the Time | Most or All of the Time |
|---|---|---|---|---|
| 1. I feel downhearted, blue, and sad. | | | | |
| 2. Morning is when I feel the best. | | | | |
| 3. I have crying spells or feel like it. | | | | |
| 4. I have trouble sleeping through the night. | | | | |
| 5. I eat as much as I used to. | | | | |
| 6. I enjoy looking at, talking to, and being with attractive women/men. | | | | |
| 7. I notice that I am losing weight. | | | | |
| 8. I have trouble with constipation. | | | | |
| 9. My heart beats faster than normal. | | | | |
| 10. I get tired for no reason. | | | | |
| 11. My mind is as clear as it used to be. | | | | |
| 12. I find it easy to do the things I used to. | | | | |
| 13. I am restless and can't keep still. | | | | |
| 14. I feel hopeful about the future. | | | | |
| 15. I am more irritable than usual. | | | | |
| 16. I find it easy to make decisions. | | | | |
| 17. I feel that I am useful and needed. | | | | |
| 18. My life is pretty full. | | | | |
| 19. I feel that others would be better off if I were dead. | | | | |
| 20. I still enjoy the things I used to do. | | | | |

# Psychotherapy and Other Treatment Approaches

© Ed Lallo/Index Stock Imagery

Of the many millions of people in the United States who have diagnosable mental and behavioral disorders, about two-thirds do not seek treatment (U.S. Department of Health and Human Services, 1999)—even though a bewildering array of treatments are available today, ranging from drug therapy to self-help. Unlike the case in some areas of medicine, there are no definitive formulas for curing these disorders. You can't surgically remove depression, for example, and even when a particular treatment has been successful for one person, it may not be for another. In addition, mental health care providers are often at a loss to explain the mechanisms through which treatments work.

Despite the lack of definitive answers to some treatment questions, most mental or emotional problems can be eased in some way. If you suffer from such a problem, this is a good time to live. Not more than a few centuries ago, most victims of mental and behavioral disorders were likely to be chained and beaten in rat-infested prisons and totally rejected by society. Indeed, the gap between the "treatments" of the past and those of our own time defines how far society has come in meeting the needs of people with mental or behavioral disorders in humane ways (National Institute of Mental Health, 1991b).

Punishment and incarceration as treatments of abnormal behaviors were not invented out of the blue. They were based on theories of the causes of those behaviors and how best to deal with them. For example, one notion was that the victims were possessed by demons and that brutal remedies were needed to drive the demons out (Valenstein, 1986). As recently as the opening decades of the 20th century, patients were put in padded cells and severely punished in the name of "treatment."

Current approaches to treatment are based on contemporary views of human personality such as those described in Chapter 9, along with assumptions about why personality and functioning sometimes go awry. For instance, psychologists who believe that abnormal behavior originates in negative emotional experiences of early life focus on assisting the individual in understanding and overcoming these childhood traumas. Others are convinced that abnormal behavior results

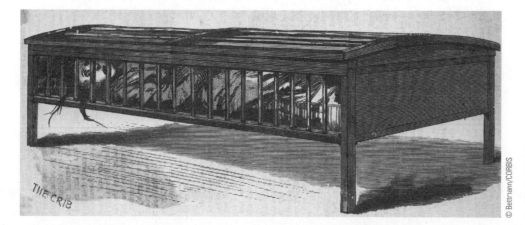

In the past, people with mental and behavioral disorders were often restrained in devices like this one, known as a crib.

## PSYCHOLOGY IN THE LAB AND IN LIFE

# How to Select a Psychotherapist

Given the number and variety of therapists, the selection of one by a prospective client is by no means an easy task. Following are some practical steps that can help in the decision:

1. *Ask for referrals.* General practitioners, as well as many medical specialists, often refer patients to psychotherapists and are likely to know who in the community is available and reputable. Others in the service professions, such as lawyers, teachers, and school counselors, may also be of help. Another good source is the local Mental Health Association.

2. *Talk to former clients.* It is better to interview people who have already completed therapy than people who are still in therapy. Psychotherapy clients can be emotionally swayed by what happened in their therapy session yesterday, and it might be difficult to correct for their momentary feelings of enthusiasm or disappointment.

3. *Ask for expert consultation.* A "diagnostic consultation" with a prominent psychologist or psychiatrist in the community—for example, the head of a university or hospital department—can be used to narrow the number of choices.

4. *Interview the prospective therapist.* With a few referrals in hand, the most direct way of learning how a particular therapist works is to spend an hour in a "feeling out" interview. In arranging an appointment, it is wise to make clear that the intent is to explore the possibilities, not to actually begin treatment. Some psychotherapists do not charge for a preliminary appointment unless therapy is actually begun.

The match between client and therapist is a distinctly personal matter. The therapist's personality and how it meshes with the client's can be even more important than the therapist's theoretical orientation and specific approach.

---

from self-defeating responses to people and situations, so they attempt to teach appropriate behavior while essentially ignoring the client's past experiences.

The therapeutic techniques used today number in the hundreds. This chapter describes the major contemporary approaches to treatment, which—with some overlap—fall into four broad categories:

1. *Psychotherapy,* referred to by Sigmund Freud as the "talking cure," is a broad term for the treatment of disorders using psychological rather than physical or biological techniques. *Psychodynamic therapy* includes detailed discussions of problems, carried out between patient (or client) and therapist to alleviate the patient's anxiety or depression—thus modifying attitudes, emotional responses, and behavior. (The term *patient* is preferred by psychiatrists and other medical practitioners; *client* is preferred by psychologists and other nonmedical mental health professionals.) Psychodynamic therapy has been characterized as "an emotionally charged, confiding interaction between a trained, socially sanctioned healer and a sufferer" (Frank, 1982). It is practiced in a group setting with several patients or clients, as well as on a one-to-one basis.

2. Another form of psychotherapy is *behavior therapy,* which focuses on problems in the here and now, with little or no concern about their origins. Behavior therapists are interested simply in what a person does and how it might be changed. *Cognitive behavior therapy* goes a step further, addressing the thinking underlying the person's behavior.

3. *Biological therapy* consists of physical interventions of various kinds, but especially the use of psychoactive medications. This approach is based on evidence, discussed in the preceding chapter, that abnormal personality and behavior arise in part from disturbances in brain functioning—particularly with regard to neurotransmitters.

4. *Community mental health approaches* include less structured techniques—self-help groups, vocational and social rehabilitation programs, telephone hotlines. Sometimes these are used in conjunction with other approaches; at other times they are the sole source of aid for people wrestling with mental health problems.

Whom does the average person turn to when he or she needs help? A survey of more than 20,000 adults found that 43% of those seeking treatment turned to a practitioner other than a psychiatrist, such as a clinical psychologist, clinical social worker, or other trained mental health professional (Regier, 1993). Finding the right person can be a daunting task, and some suggestions are contained in Psychology in the Lab and in Life on page 546.

# PSYCHODYNAMIC THERAPY: PROBING THE MIND

**Psychodynamic therapy**
Therapy based on the belief that effective treatment must focus on the underlying cognitive and emotional forces that generate a person's problems.

Practitioners who use **psychodynamic therapy** believe that effective treatment involves discovering the underlying cognitive and emotional forces that generated the individual's problems. They believe that these forces can usually be traced to early childhood, although they differ in their views on the importance of early childhood experiences and their emphasis on unconscious versus conscious sources of problems. Freud's classical psychoanalysis—the first psychodynamic approach—traced all mental and emotional problems to unconscious "residuals" of childhood experiences. Most of the psychodynamic theorists who followed shifted their emphasis to current problems—however they might have originated—and to conscious functioning (the ego).

> **FOCUS QUESTIONS**
>
> • What techniques are used in classical psychoanalysis?
>
> • How do current psychodynamic therapies differ from the classical psychoanalytic approach?

Freud believed that patients would be "cured" when they gained insight. **Insight,** in this context, is achieved by identifying the motives, emotions, and conflicts that have been repressed into the unconscious mind, with emphasis on those involving sex and aggression. Modern psychodynamic theorists downplay sex and aggression and consider a variety of issues, including how a person interacts with others in the course of daily life.

**Insight**
The uncovering of the motives, emotions, and conflicts operating in the unconscious.

**Classical psychoanalysis**
A form of psychotherapy, developed by Freud, in which free association and the study of dreams and transference are used to help the client gain insight into unconscious conflicts.

## Classical Psychoanalysis

Now known as **classical psychoanalysis,** the method of treatment developed by Freud is designed to bring to light the unconscious desires and conflicts that he believed to be sources of the abnormal anxiety and guilt that "haunt" the person. Thus, insight in itself is the "cure."

An important tool in psychoanalysis is **free association.** Patients are asked to lie on a couch, make themselves as relaxed as possible, and talk about every thought that occurs to them—no matter how foolish, obscene, or insulting it might seem. In this situation, as when you are drifting off to sleep, conscious control of mental processes is reduced to a minimum and unconscious forces become more apparent. The analyst pays particular attention to occasions when the patient's thoughts encounter **resistance**—that is, when the patient's train of thought seems to be blocked by anxiety and repressions that indicate unconscious conflicts, as evidenced by inability or outright refusal to talk about them. The analyst also pays attention to fantasies and slips of the tongue in searching for clues to unconscious desires and conflicts. Eventually, in a process that can include sessions several times a

**Free association**
A psychoanalytic tool in which patients are encouraged to let their minds wander and speak out every thought that occurs to them.

**Resistance**
The blocking of a patient's thoughts by anxiety and repression, which often indicates the presence of unconscious conflicts.

**Dream analysis**
A psychoanalytic technique in which the patient's dreams are analyzed in order to uncover unconscious motives and conflicts.

**Latent content**
The unconscious sexual and aggressive meanings of a dream.

**Manifest content**
The conscious material or actual images of a dream.

**Transference**
The tendency of a patient to transfer to the therapist the emotional attitudes felt as a child toward much loved or hated persons, such as parents or siblings.

week for months or even years, the analyst becomes more "directive" and attempts to focus the patient's thinking on what the analyst has come to believe is at the heart of the patient's problems.

Another psychoanalytic technique used to uncover unconscious motives and conflicts is **dream analysis.** Freud believed that dreams often reveal deeply hidden conflicts, though in disguised ways that require painstaking interpretation. Forbidden sexual desires in particular, he thought, are likely to crop up—often in hidden forms in which the penis is symbolized by a snake, a tower, or an airplane and the vagina by a basket or a flower. Freud identified more than two dozen symbols for the penis and more than 20 for the vagina, plus numerous others involving repressed desires to engage in sex or to harm others (see Rycroft, 1986). He used the term **latent content** to refer to the unconscious sexual and aggressive meanings of dreams and the term **manifest content** to refer to the conscious material—that is, the actual images contained in the dream. During therapy, the analyst and the patient work together to explore the manifest content of a dream and expose its latent content—thereby identifying and ultimately resolving conflicts deeply rooted in the patient's unconscious. Freud described dreams as "the royal road to knowledge of the unconscious activities of the mind" (1900/1988).

Another clue to the unconscious is what analysts call **transference.** Freud believed that, in a sense, none of us ever completely grows up. Maladjusted people in particular tend to retain their childhood emotional attitudes and combined feelings of love and hate toward their parents or other caregivers, and they often display or transfer such attitudes to the analyst. For example, a man who hated his father might transfer this attitude to the analyst and act aloof and hostile. At times, patients might try desperately to please the analyst, as they once tried to please their parents; at other times, they might resent the analyst, who has done nothing to provoke these feelings. The psychoanalyst deliberately remains passive, acting as a neutral listener during the early sessions and thus providing a blank screen onto which patients can project their feelings about key people in their lives. Transference is also an aid to establishing rapport during therapy and serves as another source of information for interpretations.

In sum, through these techniques in conjunction with reports of everyday behavior, the analyst tries to uncover the unconscious problems that give rise to the patient's real-life difficulties. The analyst then interprets the problems for the patient, who acquires insights into the unconscious causes as a way of gaining control over them. The goal of classical psychoanalysis is to inform the ego and provide what one analyst described as "freedom from the tyranny of the unconscious" (Kubie, 1950).

## Modern Psychodynamic Therapies

Practitioners of classical psychoanalytic therapy are guided by Freud's views of the origins of abnormal personality development, as described in Chapter 9. For these traditional Freudians—a dwindling number—unconscious sexual and aggressive drives and how they are handled are paramount. However, many contemporary psychodynamic therapists, taking their cues from the theories of analysts such as Adler, Horney, Fromm, and Erikson (described in Chapter 9), place greater emphasis on the importance of social and cultural forces in their patients' lives, along with their patients' conscious understanding of these forces. They still use a dynamic approach, but they believe that it is important for patients to gain insight into what is happening currently in their lives—in their work, marriage, friendships, and so forth—and to focus less on what may have happened in childhood.

A number of therapists believe, for example, that substantial changes in attitudes and behavior are possible only if the distorted perceptions and interactions of the individual are altered in the presence of the very people with whom the problems arise (Wachtel & Wachtel, 1986). They have demonstrated the importance of working with the family and spouse, as well as with the individual, in dealing with a variety of disorders, including anxiety disorders and depression (Goldfried, Greenberg, & Marmar, 1990).

Moreover, practitioners of modern psychodynamic psychotherapy recognize the impact of social and cultural forces on the therapist-patient relationship. They no longer regard the major assumptions of psychoanalytic theory as valid for all, for there are often substantial differences in their applicability depending on the cultural background of the patient. In India, for example, many people are highly attuned to their inner lives, and once they have established a trusting relationship with a therapist, they allow their associations about the most personal matters to emerge freely. In Japan, in contrast, people tend to be less intimately in touch with their private thoughts and emotions and do not reveal them as easily in therapy (Roland, 1989).

## Brief Goal-Oriented Treatment

Psychodynamic therapy today diverges from classical psychoanalysis in matters of technique as well as theory. In its classic form, psychoanalysis is a long process, requiring three to five visits a week for 2 to 5 years or more, and it is therefore very expensive. In recent years, many dynamically oriented therapists have effectively shortened the treatment period (Gingerich & Eisengart, 2000; Peake, Meyers, & Duenke, 1997; Strupp & Binder, 1984; Widen, 2000). As indicated in Table 14.1, they have adopted new and faster techniques for assisting people in achieving, if not full "freedom from the tyranny of the unconscious," at least enough insight to cope with their more serious problems. Some therapists claim that patients can be treated in just one session (B. Bloom, 1991).

Brief dynamic therapy does not aim to change a patient's basic personality—although such changes sometimes do occur. During therapy sessions, the analyst

---

**TABLE 14.1**
### The Major Features of Brief Psychotherapy

| Feature | Role of Therapist |
| --- | --- |
| Prompt intervention | Offers timely treatment to a wide range of patients |
| Limited time | Estimates the number of sessions required— usually not more than 25—after assessing the patient's problems |
| Limited goals | Helps the patient achieve rapid improvement of symptoms and provides insight into sources of problems and future coping strategies |
| Maintenance of focus | Selects the specific area to work on, such as problematic family relationships |
| High level of therapist activity | Talks as much as required to make interpretations and offer support and guidance |

*Koss, Butcher, & Strupp, 1986.*

For practical reasons, including financial ones, brief psychotherapy has become the treatment of choice for many people.

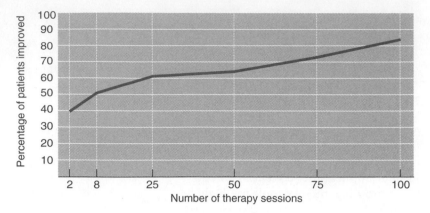

**FIGURE 14.1** The impact of brief therapy. Over a third of clients reported improvement in feelings of well-being after only a couple of sessions. Half did so after 8 sessions and two-thirds after about 25 sessions. Subsequent sessions appeared to add little benefit.

*Adapted from Howard, Pion, Gottfredson, & Flatau, 1986.*

## Test Yourself

**(a)** In analyzing dreams, Freud labeled two types of content. What are they?

**(b)** In what type of therapy would a therapist most likely take an active, directive role in getting clients to focus on maladaptive patterns of behavior and solve problems?

(The answers are on page 575.)

**Humanistic therapy**
A form of psychotherapy in which the therapist encourages the growth of self-awareness and self-acceptance.

takes an active, directive role in getting patients to focus on specific problems, such as their ways of relating to others, rather than focusing on reliving childhood memories. The traditional psychoanalytic couch is no longer used; it is replaced by face-to-face discussion between patient and therapist. And there is less emphasis on free association and more on a focused analysis of specific conflicts and anxieties.

Evidence of the sort shown in Figure 14.1 suggests that such psychotherapy can be as effective as longer-term treatment programs. Brief dynamic therapy can produce positive effects for a number of conditions, including depression in older people (Thompson, Gallagher, & Breckenridge, 1987), stress-induced disorders (Marmar & Horowitz, 1988), and certain kinds of phobias (McCullough & Andrews, 2001). There is some evidence, however, that short-term therapy is less useful when the patient is beset by family conflict or lacks a social support system (Moos, 1990). Such findings once again highlight one of the three major psychological issues raised in Chapter 1: the importance of context in understanding the nature of human personality and behavior.

Brief therapy is no longer limited to psychodynamic approaches. Its basic principles, as presented in Table 14.1, have been extended to humanistic/experiential approaches (Elliott, 2001) and cognitive behavioral approaches (Dziegielewski, 1997; Peake et al., 1997), as well as to family therapy (Schultz & Ososkie, 1999) and rehabilitation counseling (Kaslow, 2000)—approaches that are discussed later in the chapter.

# HUMANISTIC THERAPY: IMPROVING PERSONAL STRENGTHS

## FOCUS QUESTIONS

• What is humanistic therapy?

• How do the approaches of humanistic therapy differ from those used in classical psychoanalysis?

**Phenomenological perspective**
A person's unique personal understanding of the world.

Unlike classical psychoanalysis or modern psychodynamic therapy, **humanistic therapy** does not demand a rigid set of procedures. The humanistic therapist participates in the treatment in order to facilitate self-awareness and self-acceptance on the part of the client. The goals of treatment are to explore the client's inner experience from his or her own **phenomenological perspective**—the person's unique personal understanding of the world—and to encourage responsibility, freedom, and will (Rosenhan & Seligman, 1989). The traditional assumption in classical psychoanalysis is that the therapist develops an understanding of the causes and cure of the patient's symptoms and imposes that view on the patient. In contrast, the assumption in humanistic therapy is that the therapist must try to see things from the client's point of view and carefully assist, where possible, while encouraging the client to figure out solutions for herself or himself.

## Person-Centered Therapy

**Person-centered therapy,** developed by Carl Rogers and originally called *client-centered therapy,* is one of the most prominent examples of the humanistic approach. Unlike psychodynamic therapists, who see themselves as the force behind behavioral change, person-centered therapists give this responsibility to the client. As Rogers saw it, the therapist's task is to facilitate, in a "nondirective" manner, individuals' efforts to understand, control, and reshape their own lives.

Of central importance to person-centered therapy is the warmth and acceptance displayed by the therapist toward the client. Unlike psychoanalytic therapists in particular, who remain aloof, the person-centered therapist fosters a non-threatening situation in which clients explore their thoughts and feelings. In the safety of this accepting relationship, clients are expected to get in touch with their true self and gain the ability to resolve their conflicts. This process, Rogers believed (1959), requires several important steps:

1. Clients begin to experience, understand, and accept feelings and desires that they weren't previously aware of.

2. They begin to understand the reasons for their behavior.

3. They begin to see how they can undertake more positive and growth-oriented forms of behavior.

In short, they learn to be themselves. These goals are also present in psychoanalysis, but in person-centered therapy the emphasis is on the third goal—namely, that clients begin to see how it is possible to undertake more positive forms of behavior on their own.

Rogers identified three important qualities of an effective person-centered therapist: unconditional positive regard, empathy, and genuineness. As described in Chapter 9, unconditional positive regard means acceptance of individuals for who and what they are. The therapist may express frank disapproval of some of a client's *actions,* but still unconditionally accept the *person* as a worthwhile human being. Such acceptance, free from value judgments and criticism, promotes a trusting relationship between client and therapist. Indeed, some clients benefit greatly from this aspect of person-centered therapy alone—they may never have encountered another person who accepted them with no strings attached.

Empathy, according to Rogers, is the ability of the therapist to understand the feelings of the client and communicate this understanding. Finally, genuineness requires that therapists frankly describe their own feelings, including any disapproval of the client's actions, carefully distinguishing between criticism of an action and criticism of the person. Because an important aspect of humanistic treatment is for the therapist to be viewed as sincere at all times, the match between therapist and client becomes an important factor—as it is in all forms of therapy. How the client perceives and relates to the therapist can be more important than the actual form the therapy takes.

## Other Humanistic Techniques

The techniques used in humanistic therapy are based on the belief that people will grow in constructive ways if they explore and use their hidden potential. **Gestalt therapy** assists clients in exploring the past so that they can learn to understand and control the present. The goal is to become aware of the whole personality, focusing especially on how the client is feeling and behaving at the moment. Individuals treated by Gestalt therapists are sometimes urged to relive early emotional experiences as vividly as they can. They are encouraged to act out feelings, fantasies,

**Person-centered therapy**
A form of humanistic therapy developed by Carl Rogers in which the responsibility for behavioral change belongs to the client; called client-centered therapy.

**Gestalt therapy**
A type of therapy in which clients explore the past so that they can learn to understand and control the present.

**Existential psychotherapy**
A type of psychotherapy that emphasizes the importance of one's attitudes in controlling one's destiny.

## Test Yourself

**(c)**   What type of therapy gives the responsibility for behavior change to the client? Who developed this therapy?

**(d)**   What three qualities are thought to be necessary for a person-centered therapist to be effective?

(The answers are on page 575.)

or dreams in the interest of learning that they can now understand their feelings and be responsible for controlling them (Rosenhan & Seligman, 1989; Van De Riet, 2001). In confronting their emotions, clients are taking a major step toward taking charge of them.

Practitioners of **existential psychotherapy** also emphasize people's ability to take control of their lives. In direct contrast to Skinner (see Chapter 4), they believe in the importance of free will. They maintain that the events in our lives do not control our destinies—what really counts is our perceptions and interpretations of these events, which we construct for ourselves. Each of us is responsible for our own behavior. We make our own decisions and in this way control our attitudes and thoughts—and thus can rise above even the most adverse events in our environment.

This view can be seen in the Judeo-Christian ethic, as well as in that of Islam. Although Muslims believe in a form of predestination, they also believe that individuals are free to choose what path to tread and should strive to make themselves better people—consistent with humanistic psychology. Hindu beliefs are consistent as well: Hinduism stresses that each individual should strive to grow and expand his or her personal knowledge and understanding.

# BEHAVIOR THERAPY

## FOCUS QUESTIONS

• What are some techniques used in behavior therapy?

• What is meant by cognitive behavior therapy?

Whatever habits have been learned can be changed, according to **behavior therapy.** This approach employs techniques based on the principles of conditioning described in Chapter 4; the single-subject design described in Chapter 1 is often used to assess outcomes. In contrast to psychodynamic and humanistic therapy, behavior therapy makes no attempt to provide insight or restructure the individual's underlying personality. Instead, the goal of behavior therapy is to alleviate troubling symptoms—whether they involve depression, phobias, compulsions, or sexual dysfunctions.

**Behavior therapy**
A form of therapy in which the principles of learning theory and conditioning are applied to relieve the person of troubling symptoms and problems.

Some behavior therapists work directly on overt behavior rather than relying on insight or addressing underlying thoughts and attitudes; hence, their approach is useful in treating abnormal behavioral and emotional conditions that involve action. They might address, for example, a phobia that leads a client to avoid certain places, such as elevators, bodies of water, or heights, or a client's habit of responding to certain situations with anxiety or outbursts of anger. These behavior therapists attack symptoms directly by trying to break the old stimulus-response connections and substitute more effective responses.

Behavior therapy based on classical or operant conditioning procedures uses techniques such as positive reinforcement and aversive conditioning. In contrast, cognitive therapy and cognitive behavior therapy address thought patterns and emotional reactions in addition to overt behavior; techniques include systematic desensitization, exposure therapy, participant modeling, cognitive restructuring, and rational-emotive therapy.

## Reinforcement: A Positive Approach

Many of us use the technique of *reinforcement*, especially with children. A teacher might reward a child with a star whenever he completes his chores, or a parent might lavishly praise a toddler every time she successfully uses the toilet. In a clinical setting, behavior therapists do much the same thing: They offer rewards following the display of a more desirable or effective behavior.

Positive reinforcement has been used for many years to substitute desirable, adaptive behaviors for maladaptive ones—especially with young children, mentally retarded individuals, and mentally or behaviorally disordered individuals, all of whom may lack the language and cognitive abilities necessary for other forms of therapy. A classic example is the technique developed by Ivar Lovaas (1977) for getting autistic children to speak. At first, he rewarded any kind of vocal sound a child made. Then he gradually required the child to make sounds closer and closer to actual speech—in accord with shaping and successive approximations, as discussed in Chapter 4. In the end, the children were using whole words to ask for things and otherwise communicate, at which point the rewards were no longer necessary. From this technique, Lovaas went on to develop more sophisticated procedures to improve the overall emotional and intellectual functioning of autistic children (Lovaas, 1987).

Reinforcement has also been used in the form of token economies (see Chapter 4) to improve the behavior of individuals in mental institutions and schools for developmentally disabled people (e.g., Williams, Williams, & McLaughin, 1989) and in settings such as classrooms (Musser, Bray, Kehle, & Jenson, 2001), drug abuse rehabilitation programs (Silverman, Preston, Stitzer, & Schuster, 1999), and summer camps for children with ADHD (Hupp, Reitman, Northup, O'Callaghan, & LeBlanc, 2002). For aggressive or disruptive behaviors in particular, it appears that token economies and other positive behavioral approaches are an effective alternative to approaches that involve restraint or isolation (Corrigan & McCracken, 1995).

## Aversive Conditioning

**Aversive conditioning** can involve either pairing a neutral stimulus with an unpleasant one (classical conditioning) or following an undesirable behavior with an unpleasant stimulus (operant conditioning and punishment). An example of the former is a mildly aversive and well-established treatment for *enuresis* (bedwetting). An example of the latter is an effective but much more aversive and also controversial treatment for the self-injurious behaviors sometimes displayed by extremely mentally retarded or mentally disordered individuals—especially those in institutions.

The technique still known as the "bell-and-pad method" for treating enuresis dates to the 1930s (Morgan, 1938; Morgan & Witmer, 1939). Here, a child's bedwetting is viewed as resulting from the lack of an association between a full bladder and awakening (which is necessary if the child is to get up and go to the bathroom to urinate). Thus, a full bladder is initially a neutral stimulus (see Chapter 4), and the procedure involves making it a conditioned stimulus for awakening. The bell or other alarm that normally awakens the child is the unconditioned stimulus. A special pad on the bed detects the first few drops of urine and sounds the alarm, and after repeated pairings the full bladder alone causes the child to wake up—at which point the treatment is complete. Although the bell-and-pad method has been underutilized in recent years compared to medication, research indicates that it is still an effective form of treatment (Mellon & McGrath, 2000; Mikkelsen, 2001; Rajigah, 1996).

Ivar Lovaas, the researcher who devised the shaping procedure for conditioning autistic children to speak, also devised an aversive conditioning method for eliminating self-injurious behaviors such as "headbanging" (with a hand or against a wall) and "gouging" one's forehead or eyes with fingernails—both of which tend to be highly repetitive and persistent and therefore life-threatening. The causes of such behaviors are poorly understood, but the treatment devised by Lovaas and

**Aversive conditioning**
The elimination of a response through the pairing of an undesirable stimulus, such as an electric shock, with the response.

colleagues has been shown to work (Lovaas & Simmons, 1969; Simmons & Lovaas, 1969). In essence, each instance of self-injurious behavior is punished with a painful electric shock, and the behavior soon ceases—often permanently (McGlynn & Locke, 1997). Perhaps needless to say, such an approach has been criticized on grounds of ethics and humane treatment (e.g., Jacob-Timm, 1996), and the search for a better understanding of self-injurious behaviors and less drastic approaches to treating them continues.

Many other approaches to eliminating or alleviating maladaptive behavior through aversive conditioning have been attempted, such as following sips of alcohol with medication-induced nausea as a way of treating alcohol abuse. However, these approaches usually are not effective in the long run because they do not generalize beyond the immediate setting in which the conditioning takes place. For example, a problem drinker who receives aversive conditioning in a clinic knows that he or she will not be made sick for consuming alcohol elsewhere, such as at a neighborhood bar. For further discussion of how what people think can interfere with conditioning techniques, refer back to Chapter 4.

## Cognitive Behavior Therapy

**Cognitive behavior therapy** A form of behavior therapy that includes techniques designed to change the beliefs and attitudes that underlie maladaptive behavior.

Many behavior therapists have moved away from sole reliance on relatively pure behavioral techniques such as reinforcement and aversive conditioning and have added procedures designed to change the beliefs and attitudes that underlie maladaptive or disordered behavior. Like psychodynamic and humanistic therapies, **cognitive behavior therapy** is best used with intelligent clients whose thinking is basically intact. It does not work as well when a client's ability to think is disrupted, as in schizophrenia.

Cognitive behavior therapy is used to treat a diverse array of disorders and maladaptive behaviors, including anxiety disorders (Gelder, 1991), especially test anxiety (Algaze, 1995); obsessive-compulsive disorder (Marks, 1997); depression (Antonuccio, Thomas, & Danton, 1997); drug abuse (Piane, 2000; Stitzer & Walsh, 1997); and even pathological gambling (Viets & Miller, 1997). Of the major approaches to psychotherapy, cognitive behavior therapy has been the focus of the greatest increase in research interest in recent years (Killgore, 2000).

In a two-day "Achieving Flight" seminar for people who fear flying, clinical psychologists demonstrate anxiety-reduction skills. Here, a pilot explains safety features.

**Systematic Desensitization**    In the 1960s, Joseph Wolpe (1915–1997) originated **systematic desensitization** (Wolpe, 1961, 1969). Since then, this technique has evolved into a standard method for treating phobias and other unreasonable fears and anxieties that have an identifiable cause (Marx & Gross, 1998). Based primarily on conditioning principles, the method involves associating the fear-producing object or situation with relaxation. In its modern variations, a cognitive component—such as mental imagery—is often included as well.

A client first learns a relaxation technique, such as *applied relaxation*, which enables her or him to relax quickly and completely (Öst, 1987). Then the client imagines or is exposed to progressively more fearful stimuli, pausing to relax whenever fear or anxiety arises. For example, if you were to seek treatment for a phobia of spiders, the therapist might begin by asking you to imagine viewing a spider in a cage at a safe distance—a situation that should produce little or no fear. You might then be asked to imagine moving closer to the spider until you became fearful, then to relax, then to move a bit closer, and so on. At some point, a real—and harmless—spider would be introduced, and you would be asked to touch it or perhaps even allow it to crawl on your arm. Once you can do this and remain calm and relaxed, your phobia has been eliminated.

Of course, some spiders, snakes, dogs, and other animals are extremely dangerous, and being stung by a swarm of bees or wasps can hospitalize or even kill you. Learning to distinguish harmless species from dangerous ones and learning how to cope with the latter can also help in eliminating phobias.

**Exposure Therapy**    Somewhat newer on the scene as a treatment for phobias is **exposure therapy,** in which the client either simply spends time in the anxiety-producing situation (Thyer, 1983) or engages in vivid mental imagery and talks about the fearful object or distressing situation (Marks et al., 2000; Rothbaum & Schwartz, 2002) until the fear or anxiety subsides. Although clients are often extremely frightened and upset at first, in many cases exposure therapy is a highly efficient procedure. Another advantage is that it can be used with disorders as diverse as post-traumatic stress disorder and obsessive-compulsive disorder.

**Participant Modeling**    After his pioneering work on observational learning (see Chapters 1 and 4), Albert Bandura turned to developing a theory of personality and behavior based on *self-efficacy* (discussed in Chapter 9). According to many therapists, the difference between normal behavior and certain kinds of abnormal or maladaptive behavior lies in a person's beliefs about his or her ability to cope with anxiety-producing or stressful situations—including phobic ones. Beliefs about self-efficacy determine whether individuals will make efforts to cope, how hard they will try, and how long they will persist. The key to their success in therapy is enhanced regard for their own self-efficacy. The key to these feelings about themselves, in turn, is successful performance in situations that have previously caused anxiety or stress (Bandura, 1984). With this in mind, Bandura and colleagues developed a treatment approach called **participant modeling,** designed to increase beliefs about self-efficacy in the case of phobias (Bandura & Adams, 1977; Bandura, Adams, & Beyer, 1977). Suppose that you are terrified of snakes and believe that you couldn't possibly approach or handle one. Your treatment might consist first of watching (from a safe distance) while a live model handles a nonpoisonous snake and explains what to do and what not to do. At the same time, a therapist encourages you to move closer to the snake and its handler, reassuring you and reminding you to relax, until you are close enough to touch the snake. You do so, tentatively at first, then with more confidence when nothing bad happens. Your sense of self-efficacy regarding dealing with snakes increases, and in the end you find yourself capable of holding the snake. The treatment is then com-

**Systematic desensitization**
A cognitive behavioral technique used to eliminate phobias by associating the event that is feared with relaxation rather than the fearful behavior itself.

**Exposure therapy**
A form of cognitive behavior therapy in which the client either spends time in the anxiety-producing situation or engages in vivid mental imagery and talks about a fearful object or distressing situation until the fear or anxiety subsides.

**Participant modeling**
A form of cognitive behavior therapy in which the client observes the behavior of a model and then engages in progressively closer approximations of the desired behavior.

plete. You may never handle a snake again, but your phobia toward them has been eliminated—perhaps in a single session. Alongside systematic desensitization, participant modeling has become a popular treatment for phobias and other anxieties over the years (Ollendick & King, 1998).

**Cognitive Restructuring**   In treating depression, therapists may try to bring to light the unrealistically negative and self-defeating views that depressed people tend to develop about their own abilities, the world around them, and the future. This approach was pioneered by Aaron Beck, who developed a method of client questioning and probing designed to encourage clients to recognize their own unrealistic thoughts and self-fulfilling prophecies and learn to alter them—and their everyday behaviors—accordingly. This approach is termed **cognitive restructuring** (Beck, 1970, 1982), and it has become the most widely used psychotherapeutic treatment for depression (Roberts & Hartlage, 1996). The focus is on negative "self-talk" that the client may be only dimly aware of but that helps sustain depression or anxiety. In Beck's view, this self-talk takes four general forms:

1. The client sees the world as a harmful and dangerous place, ignoring rational evidence to the contrary.

2. The client overgeneralizes from normal instances of frustration and disappointment.

3. The client blows negative events all out of proportion to their actual severity.

4. The client thinks about life strictly in absolute terms, such as all good or, especially, all bad.

In therapy, the client is encouraged to identify negative self-statements and beliefs, challenge them, and change them with the therapist's guidance.

**Rational-Emotive Behavior Therapy**   **Rational-emotive behavior therapy (REBT)**, developed by Albert Ellis (Dryden & Ellis, 2001; Ellis, 1962; Ellis & Dryden, 1987), has much in common with Beck's cognitive restructuring and makes the same basic assumptions. It differs in that it places greater emphasis on how people make themselves depressed, anxious, angry, or generally unhappy by the way they interpret everyday events. Ellis describes the process in what he calls the *ABCD theory:* Something unpleasant or frustrating that happens (A) is followed by the client's irrational cognitive appraisal of the event (B), which produces an unwarranted negative emotional response (C). For example, an unkind word or gesture (A) might be appraised as awful (B), causing an emotional response of sadness and dejection (C)—especially if the appraisal includes an overgeneralization such as "Because this person apparently doesn't like me, no one does, so I'm a worthless human being." The therapeutic process (D) involves assisting the client in identifying such overreactions and overgeneralizations and looking at things more rationally at the B stage: A single instance (or even repeated instances) of people doing unkind things doesn't mean that a person *must* react with unhappiness, and it certainly doesn't mean that the person is altogether worthless.

Ellis and colleagues have identified a long list of irrational interpretations and beliefs that clients take for granted, such as the notions that every single person we encounter must like us or no one does, that we must be competent and successful in everything we do or we're a complete failure, and that it is terrible and catastrophic when something doesn't go the way we want it to. Over the years, REBT researchers and therapists have repeatedly demonstrated that clients can learn to identify irrational thoughts, counter them, and head off undesirable emotions before they occur.

---

**Cognitive restructuring**
A method of questioning and probing designed to encourage depressed clients to recognize their own unrealistic thoughts and self-fulfilling prophecies and learn to alter them—and their everyday behaviors—accordingly.

**Rational-emotive behavior therapy (REBT)**
A form of cognitive behavior therapy that exposes and challenges a client's irrational and illogical ideas.

---

**Test Yourself**

(e)   An autistic child who has never learned to sit still is rewarded with a treat or attention when he successfully sits for a few minutes. What is this technique called?

(f)   What type of therapy focuses on changing the unrealistically negative and self-defeating views depressed people have of themselves?

(The answers are on page 575.)

# THERAPY IN GROUPS

Most of the types of treatment described so far can be practiced with several clients in a group setting, as well as one-to-one. **Group therapy** was born of necessity; there are not enough trained therapists to treat every client individually. But it seems to have genuine advantages with some clients. Joining a group may relieve anxiety by showing clients that other people have some of the same problems that they do. It also creates a social give-and-take that is not possible in an individual session with a therapist. Some psychologists believe that many clients show the greatest progress when treated through a combination of group and individual psychotherapy. It is essential, however, that group therapy be conducted by competent, trained *facilitators* who steer group members away from pitfalls such as scapegoating and destructive personal attacks.

**Group therapy**
A type of psychotherapy in which several clients are treated simultaneously.

## Group Therapy: The Traditional Approach

In traditional group therapy, the therapist meets with a small number of individuals, typically six to nine. The therapist determines the composition of the group, selecting participants on the basis of what is known about their problems and how each member can be anticipated to engage in the give-and-take of the group situation. Over time, however, each group usually develops its own style and its own ways of dealing with explosive subjects like love and hate, guilt and anger, sex and suspicion. The skills of the facilitator are crucial. It takes a well-trained therapist to track the complex interactions among group members and explain what is happening as the interactions unfold.

For many people, group therapy is an effective vehicle for growth and change (Yalom, 1985). Therapy in a group gives each participant a circle of people who will share feelings and understand and deal with them. Group therapy has been described as a "living laboratory" in which therapists can zero in on clients' habitual ways of dealing with people and encourage them to try out new ones.

Group therapy has some advantages over individual therapy; joining a group may relieve anxiety by showing clients that other people have some of the same problems that they do. It is essential, however, that group therapy be conducted by competent, trained facilitators.

© Mary Kay Denny/PhotoEdit

## Group Therapy for Specific Problems

**Assertiveness training**
A technique for teaching people to stand up for their rights without violating the rights of others.

Some therapists address very specific problems with groups of clients. **Assertiveness training,** for example, is a type of cognitive behavior therapy in which people learn to stand up for their rights without violating the rights of others. A key technique in this approach is having clients role-play real-life social interactions. This allows the facilitator to provide feedback not only on what clients say and do in situations calling for assertiveness but also on their voice quality and body language.

**Family therapy**
A type of therapy based on the assumption that the family plays a key role in producing maladaptive behavior.

Analysis of relationships as played out in everyday life is at the core of **family therapy,** an approach based on the belief that the family as a dynamic system plays a key role in producing maladaptive behavior. Underlying this belief is the view that interactions among family members are often the cause of an individual's problems—the disordered behavior of one family member is a symptom of a much larger problem rooted in the dynamics of the family as a whole. Family therapy sessions typically include parents and children, although extended family members may at times be included as well. Another variation is *couple therapy* for married or cohabiting partners. In each case, the therapist's goal is to resolve each individual's problems by changing the behavior patterns of family members. In this sense, the family as a whole—its structure and organization—becomes the therapist's client (Epstein & Vlok, 1981; Reid, 2002). Thus, the therapist may play back video recordings of sessions to allow clients to see how they actually interact or even visit the home to observe the family in its natural setting. The therapist may also give homework assignments, as is done in a number of approaches to psychotherapy (Dattilio, 2002).

## Self-Help Groups

**Self-help groups**
Groups of individuals facing comparable problems who get together in the belief that they can benefit themselves as well as each other.

**Self-help groups** are based on the belief that when we come together with others who are facing the same kinds of problems that we are, we can help ourselves as well as them. Some self-help groups use professional advisers, but most do not. They are diverse in size and in the structure and frequency of their meetings (Katz, 1993; Riessman, 1984). Group meetings can take place almost anywhere—for example, in a basement, an apartment, a mental health center, or a school.

Family therapy is based on the belief that the disordered behavior of one family member is a symptom of a much larger problem rooted in the dynamics of the family as a whole. Thus, the family, rather than the individual member, becomes the therapist's client.

Probably no group more clearly reflects the beneficial effects of mutual support than Alcoholics Anonymous, or AA. Each chapter of AA is a fellowship of individuals who share their experiences, hopes, and strengths in order to help themselves and others recover from the misuse and abuse of alcohol.

It is estimated that some 2–3% of the adult U.S. population belongs to self-help groups (Borkman, 1997). Included are groups in which the jobless organize to help one another find work, burned-out professionals sustain one another, parents of young children with cancer see one another through their ordeal, and widows and widowers attempt to pick up the pieces of their lives. There are groups for couples who are infertile, parents whose children use drugs, divorced people, isolated older people, disabled people, and suicide-prone individuals. The groups are indeed diverse and also numerous. In the United States in the early 1990s, there were as many as 750,000 (Katz, 1993).

Self-help groups are effective for at least three reasons. To begin with, simply putting feelings into words can be a very positive experience. People find that expressing even their most morbid concerns helps them build a bond with others who are equally troubled. Second, communication helps people recognize that others who face similar problems manage to survive. It helps them discover models with whom they can identify. Third, people learn in self-help groups that reactions to stress are not "sick" or a sign of weakness. Being unduly anxious, sad, or upset is generally not approved of in our society, and many people struggling with problems are uncomfortable because they see themselves as more upset than they should be. The opportunity to share their concerns with others gives them the assurance that they are really not so atypical in their reactions to their problems (Segal, 1986).

> ## Test Yourself
>
> **(g)** What are some advantages of group therapy?
>
> **(h)** A group of people all suffering from cancer get together once a week to discuss their common problems and concerns. What type of program is this?
>
> **(i)** What types of problems are best addressed in these groups?
>
> (The answers are on page 575.)

# HOW EFFECTIVE IS PSYCHOTHERAPY?

Each year, many millions of people in the United States and around the world undergo some form of psychotherapy. This means that huge amounts of money are spent for various treatments, training of psychotherapists, and research into new and better methods. Are the time and money a good investment? Does therapy actually work?

> ## FOCUS QUESTIONS
> - Why is it important to evaluate the effectiveness of psychotherapy?
> - What are some of the challenges involved in evaluating treatment approaches?
> - How can people with mental or behavioral problems help themselves?

The best answer is "it depends." One issue is that studies of therapeutic outcomes are often subject to differing interpretations. Another is the "fit" between patient or client and therapist, along with the fit between the person's disorder and the approach to treatment.

## Evaluating Treatment Approaches

For the better part of a century, psychologists and other mental health professionals have struggled with the problem of demonstrating that the various approaches to psychotherapy are worthwhile. It can be hard to determine whether a client has improved, much less exactly to what extent. Often, different opinions are held by the therapist, the client, and outside observers such as the client's family and friends. Moreover, many people who experience troublesome psychological symptoms such as mild anxiety or depression eventually get over them without any treatment at all.

During the last couple of decades, however, clinical researchers began investing a tremendous amount of time and energy in defining standards for evaluating treatment approaches and conducting *efficacy studies.* This term refers to the use of rigorous scientific methodology parallel to that which is employed in clinical trials of drugs with human populations. Patients or clients with a given disorder are randomly assigned to *treatment* or *comparison* groups (whose members receive what appears to be psychotherapy but actually isn't), and both the treatment being investigated and the results are carefully operationally defined (Seligman, 1995). In other words, recent years have seen extensive use of the experimental method (see Chapter 1) in evaluating psychotherapies.

The many hundreds of efficacy studies that have been conducted on the various psychotherapies have set the stage for some scientific statements about what works for specific mental and behavioral disorders and what doesn't. Treatments that efficacy studies have demonstrated to be effective are called *empirically supported therapies,* or *ESTs* (Chambless & Hollon, 1998). Selected disorders and the ESTs that have been identified for them are presented in Table 14.2. Note that this is in no way a "final" list; EST research is truly a work in progress, and it is not free from controversies over methods and the like (Chambless & Ollendick, 2000). Of particular concern is the external validity of the tightly controlled efficacy studies and whether the findings generalize to all clinical settings and client populations (see Chapter 1).

Do some clients have a better chance of improving than others? It does not seem to matter whether the client is young or old, male or female. For most people, almost any form of attention may help, at least temporarily. But the nature of the problem does make a considerable difference. The less serious the disturbance, the greater the likelihood of improvement. Thus, people with minor disorders of recent origin usually do better than people with severe and long-standing problems. Those who are troubled only by anxiety or mild depression are much more likely to benefit than victims of schizophrenia or bipolar depression. Cases of antisocial personality are extremely resistant to treatment—perhaps because these individuals do not experience the intense anxiety that most other disordered people are eager to escape.

A desire to get rid of the psychological problem, willingness to work at eliminating it, and a firm belief that the treatment will be helpful are three factors that increase the likelihood of therapeutic success. In addition, many forms of therapy depend heavily on the client's verbal skills and willingness to communicate.

## Finding the Right Fit Between Client and Therapist

Clients improve most when they trust, respect, and like their therapist and believe that the therapist understands their problems, sympathizes with them, and is using a treatment that is likely to be effective (Strupp, 1986). The match between client and therapist thus is a distinctly personal matter. How the therapist's personality and beliefs mesh with the client's can be more important than the therapist's theoretical orientation and specific practices. The analyst, the behavior therapist, and the humanist can all be equally effective if the match between client and therapist is a good one.

A strong feeling of empathy on the part of the therapist is necessary if the client is to feel comfortable sharing troubling thoughts and anxieties. Empathy goes beyond sympathy; it involves the ability to understand the feelings the client is expressing and to see the client's problems the way the client sees them. There is evidence that many individuals who become therapists have experienced emotional pain themselves and hence can identify with a client's pain (Pope & Feldman-Sumners, 1992). Occasionally, however, a therapist's feelings toward a client can hinder treatment. In a survey of nearly 300 clinical psychologists, almost one-third

**TABLE 14.2**
**Empirically Supported Therapies (ESTs) for Selected Disorders among Adults, According to Various Task Forces in the United States and the United Kingdom**

| Disorder | Psychotherapy | Empirical Support | | |
|---|---|---|---|---|
| | | Well established | Probably to possibly efficacious | Promising |
| **Anxiety** | | | | |
| Agoraphobia/ panic disorder with agoraphobia | Cognitive behavior therapy | X | | |
| | Exposure therapy | X | | |
| Geriatric anxiety | Cognitive behavior therapy | | | X |
| Generalized anxiety disorder | Applied relaxation | | X | |
| | Cognitive behavior therapy | X | | |
| Obsessive-compulsive disorder | Cognitive therapy | | X | |
| Post-traumatic stress disorder | Exposure therapy | | X | |
| Social anxiety/ phobia | Cognitive behavior therapy | | X | |
| | Exposure therapy | | X | |
| Specific phobia | Exposure therapy | X | | |
| **Depression** | | | | |
| Geriatric depression | Behavior therapy | X | X | |
| | Brief dynamic therapy | X | X | |
| | Cognitive behavior therapy | X | X | |
| Major depression | Behavior therapy | X | | |
| | Cognitive behavior therapy | X | | |
| | Interpersonal therapy | X | X | |
| **Eating disorders** | | | | |
| Bulimia nervosa | Cognitive behavior therapy | X | X | |
| | Interpersonal therapy | | X | |
| Schizophrenia | Cognitive therapy (for delusions) | | | X |
| | Behavioral family therapy | X | | |
| **Substance abuse and dependence** | | | | |
| Cocaine abuse | Cognitive behavior therapy | | X | |
| Opiate dependence | Brief dynamic therapy | | X | |
| | Cognitive therapy | | X | |

*Adapted from Chambless & Ollendick, 2000.*

An X indicates that at least two of the task forces provided evidence that the psychotherapy belongs in the category indicated. It is important to note that the absence of a therapy does not mean that it has been found to be ineffective.

reported disliking one or more of their clients, 83% feared being attacked by at least one client, and nine out of ten reported being sexually attracted to a client (Pope & Tabachnick, 1993). Sexual relationships between a therapist and a client are, of course, strictly forbidden under the ethical standards of the American Psychological Association and other groups, so sexual attraction on the part of the therapist truly is a problem. Therapists are strongly advised to terminate the therapeutic relationship under such circumstances.

Other factors that need to be considered in the selection of a therapist include culture, ethnicity, and gender. According to Sue and Sue (1990), four factors can stand in the way of effective therapy: cultural values, social class, language, and nonverbal communication such as gestures and facial expressions. When the client and the therapist share the same ethnic and social-class background, they are likely to share many cultural values and communicate in similar ways, and this can make it easier for them to relate to each other. When they differ significantly, the therapist may misinterpret some of the client's behaviors as abnormal when they are actually normal in the client's culture (Lewis-Fernández & Kleinman, 1994). Accordingly, in each of its discussions of major psychological disorders, DSM-IV includes a section entitled "Specific Culture, Age, and Gender Features," and in cities with large immigrant populations, some therapists specialize in the treatment of patients with culture-bound syndromes.

Sexism can be a problem in some situations. Whereas women participate in psychotherapy (as clients) far more than men do, therapists are more likely to be males. Standards of mental health for men and women have been affected by traditional gender-role stereotypes, with therapists more likely to consider female clients normal if they are submissive, unaggressive, and emotional. In an effort to reduce such gender bias in therapy, the American Psychological Association and the Canadian Psychological Association have issued guidelines for providing therapy to women.

## Is One Method Better Than Another?

Granted that psychotherapy is often helpful, a vital question still remains: Is one method of therapy better than another? EST task forces approach this issue in an all-or-none fashion: Either a treatment is shown to be effective for a certain disorder or it isn't. Where two or more therapies appear to be effective—as with geriatric depression (depression among older adults) in Table 14.2 on page 561—EST compilations do not yet address which is the most beneficial. Numerous studies have been conducted to compare different treatment approaches for certain disorders, with the results sometimes favoring one therapy, sometimes another, and sometimes finding no difference.

Some of the problems encountered in this kind of research are illustrated by a large-scale longitudinal assessment of selected treatment approaches conducted by the National Institute of Mental Health Treatment of Depression Collaborative Research Program, which started in the mid-1980s and continues to date (e.g., Elkin, 1994; Elkin, Parloff, Hadley, & Autry, 1985; Gibbons et al., 2002). The project began with 250 outpatients suffering from depression. One group was treated with *interpersonal therapy*—a form of psychodynamic therapy that helps individuals understand their relationships with others and how conflicts in those relationships can result in depression. A second group received cognitive behavior therapy, described earlier. A third group was treated with imipramine (described later in the chapter), a drug designed to relieve depression. A fourth group was given only a **placebo**—a sugar pill with no remedial value at all. The two latter groups, although receiving no formal therapy, received brief (20 minutes per week) counseling with their medication. As shown in Figure 14.2, all three forms of treatment were about equally effective—and all were superior to the placebo, although the placebo, too, was effective for a noteworthy percentage of the participants (Elkin et al., 1989).

**Placebo**
A sugar pill that has no remedial or medicinal value but may relieve an illness through psychological suggestion.

However, when the data were re-analyzed according to severity of depression, the results changed (Elkin et al., 1995). As before, there were no differences among the three treatments with less severely depressed participants, but with more severely depressed patients the drug was superior, followed by interpersonal psychotherapy and then cognitive behavior therapy—with cognitive behavior therapy being no better than the placebo (Elkin, 1999).

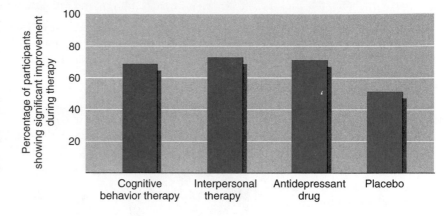

**FIGURE 14.2 Comparing treatments for depression. All three therapeutic approaches were about equally effective. Though less effective, the placebo also produced significant improvement.**
*Adapted from Elkin et al., 1989.*

To complicate matters further, the cause of the condition is important. Depression can be caused by the recent loss of a loved one, an abusive relationship that has gone on for years, lifelong tendencies toward self-blame and a poor self-concept, or a chemical imbalance. The best treatment is likely to be different in each case.

In a surprising number of instances, a physical rather than an emotional disturbance produces the abnormal condition. In such cases, the effectiveness of any form of psychotherapy may be minimal. About 10% of patients treated in psychiatric clinics suffer from medical conditions that gave rise to the psychological complaints. With appropriate medical treatment, their symptoms usually clear up rapidly. For example, people suffering from anemia (a deficiency in red blood cells) often complain of being depressed and unable to concentrate (Schwab, 1980). A diseased thyroid gland can cause rapid swings of mood, uncontrollable restlessness and agitation, disturbed sleep, anxiety to the point of panic, and even hallucinations (Hall, 1980b).

Finally, the effectiveness of various therapies must be gauged not only by the reduction of symptoms but also by other criteria, including improvement in social and vocational functioning, an increased sense of well-being, and prevention of harm to the client and people in the client's environment. For more information about how people of different ages respond to treatment, see the Life Span Perspective on page 564.

## How People Can Help Themselves

"The patient who treats himself has a fool for a doctor." Does this old saying apply to psychotherapy as well as to physical illnesses? Can we solve our own problems and correct tendencies toward abnormal or maladaptive behavior? In particular, how helpful are all the advice-giving articles and books in print and on the Internet that recommend ways to achieve better mental health and greater self-fulfillment?

There is accumulating evidence that, in the case of certain well-researched and carefully documented self-help materials in which serious therapists explain their theories and methods, reading can be as beneficial for some individuals as consulting a psychotherapist—an idea that dates to Karen Horney (1942; see Chapter 9). But there are many qualifications. For example, the person must be highly motivated and the readings must be chosen carefully, for there are many useless and even damaging self-help materials in magazines, in bookstores, and on the Internet (for a helpful review of these sources, see Norcross et al., 2000).

In one study, a group of older men and women, all mildly or moderately depressed, were given two highly regarded books on behavioral and cognitive approaches for dealing with depressed mood. Tests after 4 weeks showed that two-

Therapists do not treat clients of all ages in the same ways. Most of the treatments described in this chapter are designed for people in young or middle adulthood. Because of the special physical and developmental needs of children and adolescents—and, at the other extreme, older adults—traditional therapy techniques are often modified or refocused for them.

Until children are 4 or 5 years old, their behavioral problems are generally treated by pediatricians unless they are unusually severe. Symptoms of psychological disturbance among young children often include extreme fears and phobias. Other, less common problems include attention-deficit/hyperactivity disorders and conduct disorders such as extreme disobedience.

Most psychologists and psychiatrists assume that a young child's symptoms are caused in part by the behavior of her or his parents and the dynamics of the family. Therefore, therapists usually treat both the child and the family, as discussed in this chapter. One therapist may meet with the parents and try to provide insight into the problem and advice as to how they should behave with the child. A second therapist will see the child, often in play sessions with toys, in an effort to tempt him or her

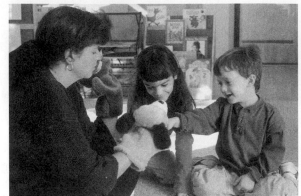

**Play sessions with dolls and other toys may encourage young children to act out the conflicts underlying their symptoms.**

to act out the conflicts that are producing the symptoms. When conflicts, fears, and concerns appear during play sessions, the therapist will encourage the child to talk about them.

When the client is an older child or young adolescent, the typical behavioral problems are more varied but may include fearfulness, shyness, difficulties in school, antisocial behavior, distractibility, and disorders such as asthma, eczema, or bulimia. The typical treatment will involve psychotherapy, psychotherapy with

drugs, or, in some cases, drugs alone. The therapy is usually closely matched to the symptom. For example, children with extreme forms of hyperactivity rarely undergo psychotherapy and are simply treated with the drug Ritalin. Children with problems in school—such as dyslexia, a reading impairment—are usually given special tutoring.

Clients between the ages of 20 and 50 are treated with the forms of therapy described in this chapter, including psychotherapy, psychotherapy with drugs, drugs alone, and group therapy.

The most common psychological problems among older adults are depression, complaints about poor memory, and distractibility. It is less common for older adults to complain of anxiety or somatoform disorders. Because many of the mental symptoms present among these individuals are partially or indirectly due to physiological changes in the brain and the body, therapy tends to rely on drugs rather than individual psychotherapy, but group therapy is often used as well, especially to counter feelings of isolation.

---

**Test Yourself**

**(j)** What types of mental problems are most amenable to treatment?

**(k)** What type of person is likely to get the most out of a reputable self-help product?

(The answers are on page 575.)

thirds of the participants had experienced substantial improvement, whereas only 20% of a nonreading control group had. After 2 years, the gains made by the book readers were almost fully maintained (Scogin, Jamison, & Davis, 1990). A similar study of people with panic disorder found that those who read a book about panic disorder and performed the exercises described in it did better after 4 weeks than participants who underwent imagery exposure therapy (Gould, Clum, & Shapiro, 1993).

Many psychotherapists recommend self-help books to their clients. In a survey of 121 psychologists in Boston and San Diego, two-thirds said that they consider self-help books helpful and encourage their clients to read them (Starker, 1988). Of course, those who get the most out of self-help products (including audio and video tapes) tend to be highly motivated and well-educated.

Readings and tapes are, of course, not the only self-help techniques available. For some people, as we saw in Chapter 12, aerobic exercise can prove beneficial in dealing with depression (McCann & Holmes, 1984; Salmon, 2001). Simple ex-

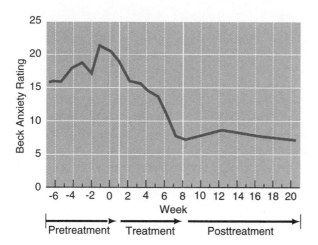

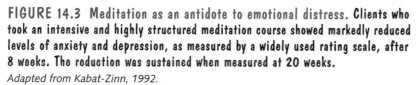

**FIGURE 14.3 Meditation as an antidote to emotional distress.** Clients who took an intensive and highly structured meditation course showed markedly reduced levels of anxiety and depression, as measured by a widely used rating scale, after 8 weeks. The reduction was sustained when measured at 20 weeks.
*Adapted from Kabat-Zinn, 1992.*

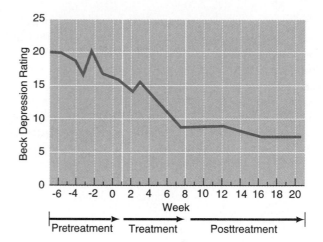

ercise such as a brisk 10-minute walk can reduce the urge to smoke or snack (Thayer, 1992). Other people deal with anxiety by practicing breathing exercises or meditation (Weil, 1990). The potential benefits of meditation are illustrated in Figure 14.3.

One difficulty with attempts at self-therapy is that they lack the support of a positive relationship, either with an understanding therapist or with members of a therapeutic group. Without such a relationship, it is often difficult to achieve real change and improvement (Strupp, 1989).

Many people find that regular meditation is a therapeutic experience that reduces stress and anxiety.

# BIOLOGICAL THERAPIES

The therapies described so far are based on interpersonal communication between patient or client and therapist—on a "specialized human relationship designed to facilitate changes in the patient's cognitions, feelings, and actions" (Strupp, 1986). As described in Chapter 13, however, biological factors can play an important role in the development of mental and behavioral disorders. Changes in glandular activity and brain chemistry are often associated with profound changes in personality and behavior. **Biological therapies** are intended to alter these underlying physiological mechanisms. Often, of course, biological approaches are used in conjunction with other therapies.

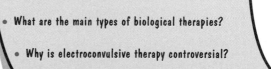

**FOCUS QUESTIONS**

● What are the main types of biological therapies?

● Why is electroconvulsive therapy controversial?

**Biological therapies**
Forms of therapy that rely on drugs or other physical treatments to alter brain chemistry.

## Drug Therapy

The most widely and successfully used form of biological treatment is **drug therapy,** also called *chemotherapy*—the use of prescribed drugs to produce specific changes in mood or behavior. The development in the early 1950s of drugs that

**Drug therapy**
A widely used form of biological treatment in which drugs are prescribed in order to produce specific changes in mood or behavior; also called chemotherapy.

control the symptoms of schizophrenia was a major breakthrough in the treatment of severely disturbed individuals. Patients who were agitated, unmanageable, and potentially dangerous to themselves or others became calm and cooperative, and the need for contraptions such as straitjackets was largely eliminated. Moreover, these drugs greatly improved the atmosphere of mental institutions, making it possible to discharge patients sooner. The introduction of drug treatment led to a drastic reduction in the number of patients in mental institutions.

In the past few decades, a variety of drugs have been shown to be helpful in combatting not only the disoriented behavior and hallucinations of schizophrenia but anxiety and depression as well. Table 14.3 identifies the three major classes of drugs used in the treatment of mental and behavioral disorders. A more detailed description follows.

## Drugs for Schizophrenia (Major Tranquilizers)

**Major tranquilizers**
A group of drugs used to reduce hallucinations, delusions, and the disordered thinking often displayed by schizophrenic individuals; also called antipsychotic drugs.

The **major tranquilizers** (also referred to as *antipsychotic drugs*) have allowed many individuals to be treated in the community rather than in mental institutions. Such drugs have proved especially effective in reducing hallucinations, delusions, and the disordered thinking typically displayed by schizophrenic individuals (National Institutes of Health, 1989). They have enabled some patients, though by no means all, to return to a more or less normal life. But they do not "cure" schizophrenia, just as drugs do not cure other mental and behavioral disorders. The beneficial effects cease when the drugs are discontinued—hence, they are called *maintenance medications.*

The therapeutic effect of some drugs is thought to be related to their impact on the neurotransmitter dopamine. As described in Chapter 13, schizophrenic patients often have unusually high levels of dopamine. By blocking dopamine receptors at the nerve synapses, these drugs reduce the activity of nerve cells that respond to dopamine. The process is illustrated in Figure 14.4.

Drugs such as the ones identified here alleviate many of the symptoms suffered by people with mental and behavioral disorders.

**TABLE 14.3**
**Some Prescribed Medications**

| Three Major Drug Groups | Trade Names (Examples) | Effects |
|---|---|---|
| Drugs for schizophrenia (major tranquilizers) | Clozaril | Fewer hallucinations and delusions; less disordered thinking; better emotional expression |
| Drugs for depression (antidepressant drugs) | Tofranil Prozac Zoloft Paxil Celexia | Improved mood, sleep, and appetite; fewer negative thoughts |
| | Eskalith* Lithobid* | Control of mood swings |
| Drugs for anxiety (minor tranquilizers) | Valium Xanax Klonopin | Sedation; muscle relaxation; less anxiety |

*Lithium

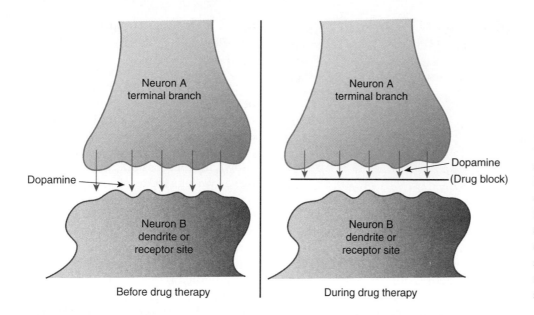

Before drug therapy    During drug therapy

**FIGURE 14.4 How drugs may act in treating schizophrenia.** Many patients with schizophrenia have an increased level of the neurotransmitter dopamine in the brain. A number of the major tranquilizer drugs—which reduce the most extreme symptoms typical of schizophrenia—prevent dopamine from crossing neuron synapses.

Although the benefits of antipsychotic drugs are well established, there is still concern about the risks involved in long-term treatment. For example, in the past, some patients who underwent treatment with major tranquilizers for many years developed **tardive dyskinesia,** a serious motor disorder characterized by involuntary movements, primarily of the face, mouth, lips, and tongue. Others developed tremors or jerking fits that required treatment with another drug. Although a reduced dosage may decrease the incidence of such side effects (Kane, 1983), it is clear that the continuous use of powerful drugs in the treatment of psychological disorders must be carefully monitored.

A newer antipsychotic drug, *clozapine (Clozaril),* has less severe side effects than earlier drugs. Introduced in 1990, it has been shown to blunt hallucinations and delusions and counteract passivity and withdrawal in about 60% of patients. An added bonus is that it does not appear to cause tardive dyskinesia (Meltzer, 1992). Clozapine continues to be the drug of choice for people with schizophrenia, although several other "atypical antipsychotics," as they are called, have been developed in recent years (National Institute of Mental Health, 2002). Each has some side effects, as does clozapine, but none that are nearly as severe as tardive dyskinesia.

**Tardive dyskinesia**
A motor disorder characterized by involuntary movements, primarily of the face, mouth, lips, and tongue (a side effect of some antipsychotic drugs).

## Drugs for Depression

People who experience major depression are often treated with **antidepressant drugs** that act as "psychic energizers." After a period of 2 to 4 weeks, individuals treated with these drugs often show significant signs of improvement, including relief from insomnia, renewed appetite, and improvement in mood. *Imipramine (Tofranil),* an antidepressant drug developed in the 1960s, has also been used successfully in treating obsessive-compulsive disorders and can relieve many of the obsessive-compulsive symptoms associated with autism (Gordon, State, Nelson, Hamburger, & Rapoport, 1993). However, because of some intensely unpleasant side effects, imipramine and other early drugs in its class are no longer the primary drugs used in treating depression (National Institute of Mental Health, 2002). Among the lengthy list of modern drugs for depression that you may have heard of are *fluoxetine (Prozac), sertraline (Zoloft),* and *paroxetine (Paxil),* each of which has minimal side effects compared to imipramine. The reason that you may have

**Antidepressant drugs**
A group of drugs, often given to depressed patients, that act as "psychic energizers."

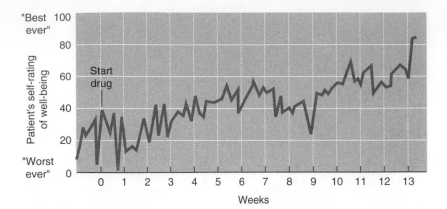

**FIGURE 14.5 The course of recovery of a patient with bipolar disorder. The efficacy of the medication is clear from this chart, but there is "an uneven, sawtooth nature to the recovery pattern."**
Adapted from Goodwin & Jamison, 1990.

heard of these is that antidepressants are among the most widely prescribed medications today.

Antidepressants are believed to work by increasing the brain's supply of two neurotransmitters—norepinephrine and serotonin—which are often found to be deficient in people suffering from depression. Some studies have shown antidepressants to be as effective as various forms of psychotherapy in overcoming depressive symptoms (Elkin et al., 1989; Elkin et al., 1995), as noted earlier in the chapter. Although they are used mainly for depression, they can also be effective in blocking repeated panic attacks (Tuma & Maser, 1985).

The salts of the metallic element *lithium (Eskalith, Lithobid)* are another treatment for depression, especially when it is accompanied by swings toward manic states—that is, bipolar disorder. This medication, taken regularly, often prevents the extreme ups and downs of mood typical of people with bipolar disorder (National Institute of Mental Health, 2002). As with all medications affecting the central nervous system, however, the dosage and possible side effects must be carefully monitored (Goodwin & Jamison, 1990). As shown in Figure 14.5, the course of improvement is likely to be uneven, with advances and regressions over time.

Although there are over-the-counter equivalents, such as St. John's wort, for some of these drugs, it is important to recognize that self-medication for mental or emotional problems is not a good idea. Dosage adjustments and monitoring by a physician are key factors in effective drug therapy.

## Drugs for Anxiety (Minor Tranquilizers)

**Minor tranquilizers**
**A group of drugs, including Valium and Klonopin, that are used as antianxiety medications.**

**Minor tranquilizers** include the *benzodiazepines* (such as *Valium* and *Xanax*). These are among the most widely used antianxiety medications and are often prescribed to alleviate symptoms associated with stress and tension. They are believed to work by inhibiting the activity of parts of the central nervous system, much as alcohol does—which is why taking these drugs while drinking can be extremely dangerous (National Institute of Mental Health, 2002). Because of concerns about chronic use and subsequent addiction, Valium and Xanax have been prescribed far less frequently in recent years than they were in the past. *Klonopin*, a much less addictive and less dangerous benzodiazepine, is more commonly prescribed today.

## Combined Therapies

We can be confident that the future will bring many new drugs that work on the biological causes of personality problems. It may even turn out that new medications will completely cure some disorders. However, it is generally believed that abnormal symptoms and behavior typically spring from both psychological and biological causes and that drug treatment should therefore be accompanied by psychotherapy. For this reason, those who treat mentally disordered people often use a combination of approaches, giving medications when they are needed but also assisting clients in understanding their problems and in coping with the feelings, individuals, and situations that they find most troublesome. In the words of one patient being treated for manic-depressive illness,

At this point in my life, I cannot imagine leading a normal life without both taking lithium and being in psychotherapy. Lithium prevents my seductive but disastrous highs, diminishes my depressions. . . . But, ineffably, psychotherapy heals . . . it is where I have believed—or have learned to believe—that I might someday be able to contend with all of this. (Goodwin & Jamison, 1990)

Dependence on a pill to dissipate painful anxiety may reduce a person's motivation to get at the underlying causes and adopt better ways of coping with stress. Many anxiety disorders therefore are best treated with a combination of drug therapy (to bring the anxiety under control) and ongoing psychotherapy (to improve the client's ability to avoid anxiety and panic).

Most clients seeking long-term relief from panic disorder benefit from a combination of drugs (usually antidepressants or minor tranquilizers) and cognitive behavior therapy. Therapists help clients re-create the feelings of an attack, then teach them to deal with those sensations. In one study, nearly 90% of participants who attended 12 sessions over a period of 8 to 12 weeks were panic-free afterward and 80% were still free of symptoms 2 years later (Craske, Brown, & Barlow, 1991).

A combination of drugs and psychotherapy has also been shown to be effective in overcoming the eating disorder bulimia nervosa. One study divided patients into groups in which they received either an antidepressant drug, cognitive behavior therapy, or a combination of the two. The group that improved the most received both the drug and the psychotherapy. The group that did most poorly received only the drug (Agras et al., 1992). Another study showed that patients with eating disorders achieve significant improvements when given an antidepressant along with either individual or group short-term therapy (Jimerson, Herzog, & Brotman, 1993).

> ### Test Yourself
>
> **(l)** What is the name for the type of treatment in which medically prescribed drugs are used to produce specific changes in behavior?
>
> **(m)** What drug can help prevent the extreme mood swings typical of bipolar disorder?
>
> **(n)** For a client who is extremely depressed and potentially suicidal, what treatment offers the quickest and possibly most effective relief?
>
> (The answers are on page 575.)

## Electroconvulsive Therapy

**Electroconvulsive therapy (ECT),** known in the past as electroshock therapy, is the quickest method available for treating severe or otherwise unresponsive cases of depression. Some patients' moods improve dramatically after only one session.

**Electroconvulsive therapy (ECT)**
A biological treatment for severe depression in which an electrical current is administered to the brain.

First used in the 1930s, ECT gained a very negative reputation, especially due to horrific depictions in later movies such as *One Flew over the Cuckoo's Nest.* Current practice is much more humane. The electrical current is administered in millisecond bursts of low voltages through electrodes attached to the skull; the patient is under general anesthesia and has been given a muscle relaxant. The result is a convulsion lasting about a minute. Although ECT's popularity has risen and the approach has lost some of its stigma, it remains controversial (e.g., McCall & Dickerson, 2001). Some believe that ECT can cause long-lasting memory impairment and possibly brain damage. However, the general consensus is that, when used with the proper med-

ECT procedures have been improved in recent years. Though still controversial, they can be beneficial for clients who are not responsive to other forms of treatment.

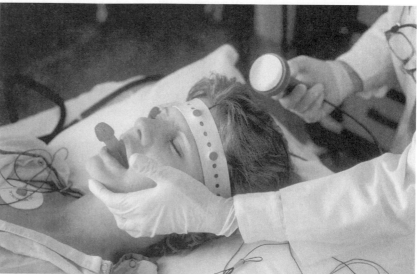

© Will McIntyre/Photo Researchers, Inc.

ical safeguards, it can work for clients who are not responsive to other approaches and can be a lifesaving technique for those on the brink of suicide.

How does ECT actually work to relieve depression? The answer is not known, but ECT probably increases the brain's supply of norepinephrine and other neurotransmitters. Because the electric current shocks the entire brain, it is difficult to identify the effective ingredient of ECT (Rosenhan & Seligman, 1989).

# MENTAL HEALTH IN THE COMMUNITY AND SOCIETY

**FOCUS QUESTIONS**
- What are the origins of the community mental health movement?
- How do community mental health programs deal with both mental health problems and related social problems?

Less than a century ago, most people believed that individuals who developed a pattern of abnormal behavior should be treated as outcasts and locked away in "asylums." Today, in contrast, we try to incorporate mentally disordered people into their communities. This movement began in the early 1960s when President John F. Kennedy called for a "bold new approach" to mental illness. A law passed by Congress in 1963 mandated the construction and staffing of hundreds of community mental health centers across the country.

The field of **community psychology** was developed not only to meet the needs of individuals who present themselves for treatment but also to provide "outreach" services to those in need of mental health services. One such service is **rehabilitation counseling,** through which individuals learn to perform the physical, intellectual, and emotional tasks necessary to function in their environment (Olfson, 1990).

Because community psychology is based in part on the premise that conditions in society can cause or worsen mental health problems, the field is also devoted to making needed changes in places where people spend much of their lives, including schools and workplaces. An important goal is to strengthen the mental health of individuals as much by preventing problems as by providing treatment after problems have begun taking their toll (Kessler & Goldston, 1986).

**Community psychology**
A branch of applied psychology that deals with the social environment and how it can better serve human needs.

**Rehabilitation counseling**
A form of mental health service through which individuals learn to perform the physical, intellectual, and emotional tasks necessary to function in their environment.

## Community Mental Health Programs

Community mental health centers were designed to permit disordered individuals to be treated in their communities rather than sent to mental institutions where they were cut off from family and society. The centers provide partial inpatient care, in which individuals receive therapy during the day but return home in the evening. Or patients can work during the day—a therapeutic force in itself—and stay overnight at the center.

Many centers operate so-called storefront clinics where staff are available day and night to respond to emergencies such as episodes of abuse in the family, suicide threats, or panic attacks. An important role of psychologists is to offer consultation and education to individuals in the community who provide psychological assistance without actually being trained to do so. Many people do not bring their personal troubles to mental health professionals, preferring instead to talk to members of the clergy, lawyers, teachers, physicians, police, or welfare workers (Cowan, 1982). These "natural caregivers" can benefit from the advice of trained psychologists.

# Crisis Intervention

Some psychologists and other mental health professionals work in **crisis intervention** programs designed to deal with situations that demand immediate attention. The crisis may be an accident, a fire, a runaway child, the loss of a job, a rape—any situation in which direct and immediate emotional support is likely to be therapeutic. Crisis intervention has been used effectively with survivors of the shootings at Columbine High School in Littleton, Colorado, in 1999 and the terrorist attack on the World Trade Center in 2001. In 2002, when nine coal miners were trapped 240 feet underground for 77 hours at the Quecreek mine in Somerset, Pennsylvania, staff from the Western Psychiatric Institute and Clinic of the University of Pittsburgh Medical Center were on the scene to provide counseling for family members while efforts were being made to rescue the men.

The goal of crisis intervention is to use any therapeutic intervention that might be effective. It can entail home visits, repeated and prolonged telephone contacts, or ensuring that an abused spouse is given shelter. The point is to focus on the immediate circumstances and reduce the impact of traumatic events. Such intervention is viewed as an important element of the **case management approach** to serving the mentally ill in the community; other elements of this approach include assisting clients in maintaining medication schedules and addressing problems of daily life.

For many people, the nearest source of assistance in a crisis is the telephone. Thus, the hotline has become an important therapeutic resource for people in crisis. Although telephones lack the intimacy and power of face-to-face contact, the delivery of advice, sympathy, and comfort via telephone can be crucial in getting a stressed person through a traumatic episode and preventing breakdown. The hotline also allows callers to be referred to appropriate individuals and agencies for help.

A rape hotline counselor responds to a distraught caller.

**Crisis intervention**
A community-based program designed to deal with stress-filled situations that demand immediate attention.

**Case management approach**
A comprehensive program to aid the mentally ill within the community.

# Supporting Clients and Their Families

It has been shown repeatedly that people who are attempting to overcome disabling psychological disorders can benefit from the support of their families and close friends. For example, people in developing nations who suffer from serious mental disorders recover more quickly and suffer fewer recurrences than do those in industrially advanced countries. With few mental health professionals available, family members are more likely to take responsibility for their care, providing the kind of support and encouragement needed to increase their chances of recovery.

Family support appears to be especially important for victims of serious disorders, such as schizophrenia and severe depression. The risk of suicide is considerably less for deeply depressed individuals who have close ties with relatives than for those who have no such ties (Slater & Depue, 1981). Other studies reveal that recovered schizophrenics are less likely to suffer a relapse if family members minimize their anxiety and exert a calming influence (Hooley, 1985).

Family members of people with mental and behavioral disorders, however, often require psychological support themselves (Backer & Richardson, 1989; Regier, 1993). Sixty-five percent of discharged psychiatric inpatients—approximately 1.5 million per year—return to live with their families. Largely owing to cost factors, many of these patients return earlier than they otherwise might and are still severely disabled. As a result, the stress and disorganization of family life become overwhelming—with a heavy overlay of financial and emotional burdens.

Psychologists can play an important role in reducing the family's burdens, not only by providing appropriate counseling and therapeutic services but also by encouraging family members to seek out support groups. One organization, the National Alliance for the Mentally Ill (NAMI), has more than 1,200 local affiliates throughout the United States and Canada and more than 210,000 members. An essential element of NAMI is its network of support groups through which burdened family members find needed emotional strength (Backer & Richardson, 1989).

## Disorders and the Homeless

The importance of a social support system for individuals suffering from psychological disorders highlights the special problems of the homeless. Although being homeless is not in itself a psychological disorder, a substantial number of street people have histories of mental and behavioral disorders. There are many more people with schizophrenia and depressive disorders in public shelters and on the streets than there are in public mental institutions. Yet they do not receive the kinds of treatment and care designed for severe psychological disorders (Levine & Haggard, 1989).

The problem is in part an outgrowth of the success of drug treatment in controlling the symptoms of severe psychological disorders and reducing the number of patients cared for in institutions. This trend is shown in Figure 14.6. But the cause-and-effect relationship may run in the opposite direction as well. That is, psychological disorders can be generated—or at least exacerbated—by homelessness (Redburn & Buss, 1985). For example, homeless individuals who appear paranoid, depressed, or agitated may be reacting realistically to the abysmal conditions of their lives. It is noteworthy that the newly homeless have atypically high rates of major depression, in part as a response to their plight (National Institute of Mental Health, 1991b).

The problem is heightened in many cities because the community mental health programs begun in the 1960s have not kept pace with the need to care for the homeless. Not since the early 19th century have so many people with serious mental health problems gone untreated (Torrey, Erdman, Wolfe, & Flynn, 1990). At the heart of the problem are public attitudes toward mental and behavioral disorders—specifically, the tendency to reject those whose behavior deviates from the norm. For more on the problems of community psychology, see A Matter of Debate on page 573.

**FIGURE 14.6 The drop in mental institution populations. In the United States in 1955, there were over a half million people in state and county mental institutions. By 1980, the total had been reduced to one-fourth that number. The sharp decline was due primarily to the development of medications that eliminate the most disabling symptoms of mental and behavioral disorders.**

*Kornblum & Julian, 2001.*

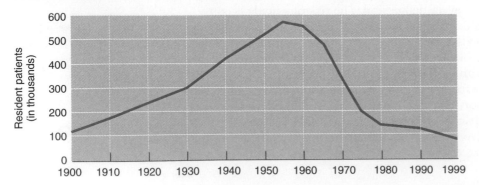

## Removing the Stigma from Mental and Behavioral Disorders

Although at any given time more than one in four people in the United States are suffering from a diagnosable disorder, seven out of ten cases are not

## → A MATTER OF DEBATE ←

# Community Psychology—A Revolving Door?

In the second half of the 20th century, our understanding of psychological disorders improved steadily as a result of research in psychology, medicine, and related disciplines. Outpatient treatment is now available for many disorders, along with increased public and private funding for such treatment. At the same time, the stigma attached to mental illness has been greatly reduced, and people are more willing than ever before to seek treatment for mental disorders.

In the case of more severe disorders, outpatient treatment has become more feasible as a result of the development of effective psychiatric drugs beginning in the 1950s and 1960s. The new drugs, along with court rulings establishing a right to treatment and humane care, led to a movement toward deinstitutionalization in which many thousands of patients were released from mental institutions. The released patients were to be returned to their communities, where they would receive outpatient treatment. Treatment in the community would be more humane and less expensive than "warehousing" patients in mental institutions.

Deinstitutionalization and community mental health programs have allowed many former patients to return to at least a semblance of a normal life. However, this has not occurred without some serious problems and repercussions. Some ex-patients don't have a "community" to return to; they have no family, or their family refuses to take them. Some find places in "halfway houses"—small, privately run residential communities where ex-patients receive therapy and are assisted in making the transition from the institution to normal life. But halfway houses suffer from lack of funds and do not have enough space to meet the demand—particularly because many people oppose the presence of such facilities in their neighborhoods, believing that their residents will disrupt community life and cause property values to decline. As a result, large numbers of people who have been released from mental institutions have ended up homeless, living on the streets and not receiving treatment for their disorders.

For many homeless ex-patients, therefore, deinstitutionalization is not a one-way process. As they experience the stress and deprivation of life on the streets, with no one to ensure that they take the medications prescribed for them, they often return to a disordered state. Eventually they reenter an institution of some kind, where they are treated and again released "into the community," and the cycle begins again.

In sum, the community psychology movement has emptied the wards of mental institutions throughout the nation, but for some ex-patients it has created a "revolving door" situation in which they are continually reentering institutions and being released to a life of loneliness and neglect.

To research this topic further, go online with InfoTrac and use your own term or the following suggestions:
* community psychology
* deinstitutionalization
* psychotropic drugs

being treated (Regier, 1993). Part of the reason may be the stigma attached to admitting that one has a disorder. In 1993, for example, Vincent Foster, a high-ranking attorney at the White House, committed suicide as a result of depression. Colleagues and friends expressed great shock at the suicide, saying that they had no idea he was depressed and might take his life. In the following days and weeks, many speculated that Foster had not sought treatment that could have saved him because of fears of how his disorder would be perceived by the public if it were revealed.

The way people receiving treatment are viewed by others can be crucial. It can help determine whether they will be overwhelmed by their symptoms and get even worse, or get well and function productively in society. Individuals who are known to have had mental problems are often caught in a vicious cycle. At work, they may be perceived as incompetent and their performance may be rated as poor for no apparent reason. Feeling alienated and unappreciated, they may become anxious and their performance may actually deteriorate (Farina, 1982). Even those who have recovered fully may face discrimination in the workplace.

A positive response can be beneficial to people who require assistance—even those with serious disturbances—as they try to resume a productive life. Therapists

### Test Yourself

**(o)** Psychiatrists who provide counseling for family members during a situation such as a school shooting are participating in what kind of program?

(The answer is on page 575.)

work hard with their clients to assist them in overcoming their symptoms, realizing their potential, and taking their rightful place in society, but full recovery requires that society be willing to accept them as fully functioning members of the community. Although it has no name, this itself is a powerful therapy.

# Chapter 14 Summary

## Psychodynamic Therapy: Probing the Mind

1. *Psychodynamic therapy* is based on the assumption that an individual's problems are generated by underlying mental and emotional forces.

2. The earliest example of psychodynamic therapy was *classical psychoanalysis*, developed by Sigmund Freud. Freud's method was designed to bring to awareness the unconscious desires and conflicts that he believed were sources of anxiety and guilt. The techniques of *free association, dream analysis,* and examination of *transference* are used to provide *insight* and thus achieve "freedom from the tyranny of the unconscious."

3. Modern psychodynamic therapies diverge from classical psychoanalysis by placing less emphasis on unconscious sexual and aggressive drives and greater emphasis on the importance of social and cultural factors.

## Humanistic Therapy: Improving Personal Strengths

4. *Humanistic therapy*—with its emphasis on self-awareness and self-acceptance—attempts to explore the client's inner experience solely from the client's own *phenomenological perspective* and encourage personal responsibility, freedom, and will.

5. Carl Rogers's humanistic approach—known as *person-centered,* or client-centered, therapy—provides an atmosphere of unconditional positive regard in which clients are free to explore all their thoughts and feelings, including those they have been unable to perceive clearly for fear of condemnation by themselves or others. Other humanistic approaches include *Gestalt therapy* and *existential psychotherapy.*

## Behavior Therapy

6. *Behavior therapy* is based on the premise that personality disturbances are learned responses that can be changed through relearning. Its techniques include reinforcement and *aversive conditioning.*

7. Many behavior therapists practice *cognitive behavior therapy,* which seeks to change unrealistically negative and self-defeating thought patterns. Approaches include *systematic desensitization, exposure therapy, participant modeling, cognitive restructuring,* and *rational-emotive behavior therapy,* whose goal is to expose and discourage irrational and illogical ideas about life.

## Therapy in Groups

8. *Group therapy* involves the treatment of several clients at the same time. Traditional group therapy allows participants to share their feelings with one another. Other group approaches include *assertiveness training* and *family therapy.*

9. *Self-help groups* are effective for three primary reasons:
   a) Simply putting feelings into words can have a healing effect.
   b) Communication allows individuals to recognize that others who face similar problems manage to survive.
   c) Individuals learn that reactions to stress are not unnatural.

## How Effective Is Psychotherapy?

10. Except in the case of clearly defined problems such as specific phobias, the results of therapy are difficult to assess. The best available evidence, however, indicates that psychotherapy benefits many people.

11. The effectiveness of therapy depends on many factors, including how motivated the client is, the nature of the problem, and the qualities of the therapist.

## Biological Therapies

12. *Biological therapies* include chemical and physical interventions that affect the brain either directly or indirectly and thus produce or inhibit certain behaviors that alter mood.

13. The most widely and successfully used form of biological treatment is *drug therapy* (chemotherapy), the prescription of drugs intended to produce specific changes in mood or behavior.

14. The three major classes of drugs are drugs for schizophrenia *(major tranquilizers),* some of which can cause *tardive dyskinesia;* drugs for depression *(anti-*

depressant drugs); and drugs for anxiety *(minor tran-quilizers)*. Treatment with drugs is most effective when combined with psychotherapy.

15. *Electroconvulsive therapy (ECT)*, a controversial treatment, has been found to be very effective in treating cases of depression that have not responded to other treatments. The patient is sedated, and a brief electrical current is administered through electrodes attached to the skull, producing a convulsion lasting about a minute.

## Mental Health in the Community and Society

16. *Community psychology* is based in part on the premise that the conditions prevailing in society can cause or worsen mental health problems. The field therefore is devoted to providing "outreach" services. One such service is *rehabilitation counseling*, through which individuals learn to perform the physical, intellectual, and emotional tasks necessary to function in their environment.

17. Community mental health centers are designed to permit mentally disturbed individuals to be treated in their communities rather than in an institutional setting and to provide outpatient care in clinics.

18. *Crisis intervention* programs are designed to deal with immediate, stress-filled situations that require quick attention. Such programs are an important element of the *case management approach*.

19. Attitudes toward people with psychological disorders can play a central role in determining whether they will recover sufficiently to function in society. Support by family members is particularly important.

20. A positive response by the community can be beneficial to people who need assistance—even those with serious disturbances.

# Chapter 14 Test Yourself Answers

(a) The two types of dream content Freud labeled are manifest content—the actual images of dreams—and latent content—the unconscious sexual and aggressive material symbolized by something else.

(b) A therapist would most likely take an active role in brief dynamic therapy.

(c) Person-centered therapy, developed by Carl Rogers, gives the responsibility for change to the client.

(d) Unconditional positive regard, empathy, and genuineness are the three qualities Rogers said a therapist must have.

(e) This technique is called reinforcement.

(f) Cognitive restructuring aims to change self-defeating and unrealistic views.

(g) Some advantages of group therapy are that it is more cost-effective; it may relieve anxiety by showing that other people have the same problem; and it provides an opportunity for social give-and-take in a therapeutic setting.

(h) People with similar problems can discuss common concerns in self-help groups.

(i) A broad spectrum of life crises can be addressed in self-help groups.

(j) Minor disorders of recent origin are the mental problems most amenable to treatment.

(k) People who are highly motivated and well-educated are most likely to get something out of a self-help product.

(l) It is referred to as drug therapy or chemotherapy.

(m) Lithium can help prevent the mood swings of bipolar disorder.

(n) Electroconvulsive therapy (ECT) offers the quickest relief in cases of suicidal depression.

(o) They are participating in a crisis intervention program.

# Chapter 14  Psychotherapy and Other Treatment Approaches

## Key Terms

antidepressant drugs (p. 567)
assertiveness training (p. 558)
aversive conditioning (p. 553)
behavior therapy (p. 552)
biological therapies (p. 565)
case management approach (p. 571)
classical psychoanalysis (p. 547)
cognitive behavior therapy (p. 554)
cognitive restructuring (p. 556)
community psychology (p. 570)
crisis intervention (p. 571)
dream analysis (p. 548)
drug therapy (p. 565)
electroconvulsive therapy (ECT) (p. 569)
existential psychotherapy (p. 552)
exposure therapy (p. 555)
family therapy (p. 558)
free association (p. 547)
Gestalt therapy (p. 551)
group therapy (p. 557)
humanistic therapy (p. 550)

insight (p. 547)
latent content (p. 548)
major tranquilizers (p. 566)
manifest content (p. 548)
minor tranquilizers (p. 568)
participant modeling (p. 555)
person-centered therapy (p. 551)
phenomenological perspective (p. 550)
placebo (p. 562)
psychodynamic therapy (p. 547)
rational-emotive behavior therapy (REBT) (p. 556)
rehabilitation counseling (p. 570)
resistance (p. 547)
self-help groups (p. 558)
systematic desensitization (p. 555)
tardive dyskinesia (p. 567)
transference (p. 548)

*The key terms above can be used as search terms in InfoTrac, a database of readings, which can be found at http://infotrac-thomsonlearning.com.*

## Active Learning Review

### Psychodynamic Therapy: Probing the Mind

**mental (or cognitive), emotional**

1. Practitioners who use *psychodynamic therapy* believe that effective treatment must focus on the underlying _____ and _____ forces that generated the individual's problems.

**psychodynamic**

2. Therapists who believe that effective treatment must focus on the underlying mental and emotional forces that generated the individual's problems employ a _____ approach.

**insight**

3. Identifying the motives, emotions, and conflicts that have been repressed into the unconscious mind leads to _____.

**classical psychoanalysis**

4. Freud's method of treatment, known as _____ _____, is designed to give individuals insight into the unconscious desires and conflicts that he considered the source of abnormal anxiety and guilt.

**unconscious**

5. In *classical psychoanalysis*, therapists attempt to bring into awareness the _____ desires and conflicts that are viewed as the source of extreme anxiety and guilt.

**insight**

6. In classical psychoanalysis, patients can overcome severe anxiety and guilt by gaining _____ into their unconscious desires and conflicts.

**conflicts**

7. In helping an individual acquire insight into unconscious desires and _____, those who practice classical psychoanalysis use the tool of *free association*, in which patients talk about every thought that occurs to them.

**free association**

8. Rosa, who is being treated by means of classical psychoanalysis, lies on a couch and reveals every thought that occurs to her, no matter how foolish or obscene. Rosa's therapist is using the tool known as _____ _____.

9. In classical psychoanalysis, the therapist pays particular attention to occasions when patients' thoughts encounter _____—that is, when their train of thought seems to be blocked by anxiety and repression.

**resistance**

10. Based on Freud's belief that dreams often reveal deeply hidden conflicts, psychoanalysts use the technique known as _____ _____.

**dream analysis**

11. Freud labeled the unconscious sexual and aggressive material found in a dream as its _____ content. In contrast, he identified the conscious material—that is, the actual images of the dream—as its _____ content.

**latent**

**manifest**

12. Freud believed that people tend to display toward the analyst those emotional attitudes they learned to display toward parents and other family members in real life—a process he called _____.

**transference**

13. Helping individuals gain insight within a short treatment period is typical of today's forms of _____ _____ therapy.

**brief dynamic**

## Humanistic Therapy: Improving Personal Strengths

14. *Humanistic therapy* is based on humanistic theories of personality—with their emphasis on self-_____ and self-_____.

**awareness, acceptance**

15. One goal of humanistic therapy is to explore the client's inner experience from his or her own _____ perspective—the person's unique personal understanding of the world.

**phenomenological**

16. An example of humanistic therapy is _____-_____. therapy, developed by Carl Rogers.

**person-centered**

17. Of central importance in *person-centered therapy* is the _____ and _____ displayed by the therapist toward the client.

**warmth**

**acceptance**

18. Person-centered therapy emphasizes three qualities of the therapist: unconditional positive regard, _____, and _____.

**empathy, genuineness**

19. Another humanistic approach is _____ therapy, in which therapists try to help individuals explore their past so that they can confront and understand their feelings and take responsibility for controlling them.

**Gestalt**

20. Practitioners of _____ psychotherapy also emphasize the ability of people to take control of their own lives, and they believe in the capacity of free will.

**existential**

## Behavior Therapy

21. Practitioners of *behavior therapy* use techniques based on principles of _____.

**conditioning**

22. _____ _____ is an attempt to change behavior rather than to achieve insight.

**Behavior therapy**

23. When a therapist provides rewards for more effective and more desirable behavior, the technique being used is _____.

**reinforcement**

24. A delinquent boy who is given praise for altruistic behavior is being treated with _____.

**reinforcement**

25. The technique of reinforcement has been used in mental institutions by offering tokens to patients who engage in desired behaviors—an approach referred to as a _____ _____.

**token economy**

26. Justin, who is suffering from alcoholism, is undergoing a treatment in which he is given a nausea-producing medication every time he sips a glass of whiskey. Justin's therapist is using the technique known as _____ _____.

**aversive conditioning**

27. Therapists who help their clients by changing the beliefs and attitudes that underlie maladaptive behavior are practicing _____ behavior therapy.

**cognitive**

28. Attempts to associate anxiety-provoking stimuli with relaxation rather than panic comprise a technique known as _____ _____.

**systematic desensitization**

29. Mary's therapist urges her to remain calm and relaxed while thinking about the exams that habitually cause her anxiety. Her therapist is using a technique known as _____ _____.

**systematic desensitization**

exposure therapy

self-efficacy
Participant

restructuring

rational-emotive

group therapy

facilitator

assertiveness

family

family

self-help
Alcoholics Anonymous

outcomes

efficacy
empathy

more
placebo

self-help materials
hyperactivity
Ritalin

biological

biological
chemotherapy

30. In _____ _____, the client engages in vivid mental imagery and talks about fearful objects.
31. Convictions about one's ability or lack of ability to cope with anxiety-producing or stressful situations add up to one's convictions about _____-_____.
32. _____ modeling involves watching a live model engaging in a feared behavior.
33. Cognitive _____ focuses on the negative "self-talk" that helps sustain depression or anxiety.
34. Some cognitive therapists practice _____-_____ behavior therapy, which aims to expose and discourage a client's irrational and illogical ideas.

## Therapy in Groups

35. Therapists of a number of different orientations have adapted their approaches for use in _____ _____, or the treatment of several patients at the same time.
36. *Group therapy* has been described as a "living laboratory" where participants can learn new ways of dealing with the world. Of extreme importance is the skill of the _____.
37. A form of group therapy intended to teach submissive people to stand up for their rights is _____ training.
38. In *family therapy,* participants typically include mother, father, and children, and the goal of the therapist is to help resolve any one individual's problems by changing the behavior patterns of the entire _____.
39. Dave, who is failing in junior high and increasingly dependent on drugs, is in a therapy group with his mother, father, and two older brothers. He is participating in _____ therapy.
40. Groups made up of individuals who share common problems are called _____-_____ groups.
41. Among the best-known *self-help groups* is _____ _____.

## How Effective Is Psychotherapy?

42. It is difficult to assess the _____ of various forms of psychotherapy, which may depend on the kind of condition being treated.
43. In recent decades clinical researchers have invested a great deal of time and energy in conducting _____ studies to evaluate psychotherapies.
44. A strong feeling of _____ on the part of the therapist is necessary if the client is to feel comfortable sharing troubling thoughts.
45. Women participate in psychotherapy (as clients) far _____ often than men.
46. A sugar pill with no remedial value at all is called a _____.
47. Self-therapy—that is, serving as your own psychotherapist by reading _____-_____ _____—can prove beneficial under some conditions.
48. Children with extreme _____ are sometimes treated with the drug _____.

## Biological Therapies

49. The preceding chapter described how mental disorders can arise not only from psychological and environmental factors but also from _____ factors such as changes in brain chemistry and glandular activity. This is why approaches to treatment include *biological therapies,* which are intended to help the patient by changing these underlying physiological mechanisms.
50. Treatments designed to alter behavior by modifying brain chemistry and glandular activity are referred to as _____ therapies. The most widely and successfully used of these is *drug therapy,* or _____—the prescription of drugs intended to produce specific changes in mood or behavior.

51. The prescription of drugs intended to produce specific changes in mood or behavior is known as _____ _____.                                    **drug therapy**

52. Drugs used to control the most disruptive symptoms of schizophrenia are called _____ tranquilizers or _____ drugs.                                **major, antipsychotic**

53. Some patients who have undergone drug therapy for a long period develop a serious motor disorder which is called _____ _____, characterized by involuntary movements.                                                         **tardive dyskinesia**

54. A newer antipsychotic drug that appears to avoid such side effects is _____.    **clozapine**

55. People suffering from depression are often treated with _____ drugs.            **antidepressant**

56. These drugs probably work by increasing the brain's supply of two _____, norepinephrine and serotonin.                                                 **neurotransmitters**

57. Janet, who is deeply depressed, is being treated with chemotherapy. She is probably taking an _____ drug.                                              **antidepressant**

58. The drug lithium, though sometimes used in depression, is used especially to smooth out the mood swings typical of _____ disorder.                     **bipolar**

59. Sean has been diagnosed as suffering from bipolar disorder. The drug he is most likely to be given is _____.                                           **lithium**

60. To treat cases of anxiety, drugs known as _____ _____ are often prescribed.                                                                     **minor tranquilizers**

61. Valium is an example of a _____ tranquilizer.                                   **minor**

62. Paula is suffering from schizophrenia. The drug she is being treated with is likely to be a _____ _____. Robert, who suffers from panic attacks, is more likely to be undergoing treatment with a _____ _____.     **major tranquilizer, minor tranquilizer**

63. With the advent of drugs for depression, patients are much less likely to be treated with *electroconvulsive therapy (ECT)*, in which an electrical _____ is administered in brief bursts of low voltages through electrodes attached to the skull.                                                                    **current**

64. In cases of serious and suicidal depression that does not respond to drugs, patients may be treated with a brief electric current applied to the skull—a treatment known as _____ _____, or _____.                      **electroconvulsive therapy, ECT**

65. In electroconvulsive therapy, or ECT, the patient experiences a _____ lasting about a minute.                                                         **convulsion**

## Mental Health in the Community and Society

66. Approaches that fall into the category of _____ _____ _____ gave rise to the field of *community psychology*.                                **community mental health**

67. Community psychology is oriented not only to meeting the needs of individuals who present themselves for treatment but also to providing _____ services to those in need of mental health services.                            **outreach**

68. One such service is _____ _____, through which individuals learn to perform the physical, intellectual, and emotional tasks necessary to function in their communities.                                                    **rehabilitation counseling**

69. Some psychologists and other mental health professionals provide an important service in *crisis intervention* programs designed to deal with stress-filled situations that require _____ attention.                              **immediate**

70. A community mental health program designed to provide help for victims under acute stress, such as rape victims, is called a _____ _____ program.  **crisis intervention**

71. The *case management approach* includes crisis intervention and also addresses everyday problems of _____.                                             **living**

72. Bill, who is recovering from schizophrenia, is being helped by a mental health team which ensures that he takes his medication and gets to work. This is an example of the _____ _____ approach.                              **case management**

# Practice Test

Name _____  Section _____  Date _____

____ 1. Psychoanalysis is an outgrowth of the theories of
    a. Freud.
    b. Adler.
    c. Rogers.
    d. none of the above

____ 2. Free association and dream analysis are elements of the form of therapy known as
    a. behavior therapy.
    b. humanistic therapy.
    c. Gestalt therapy.
    d. psychoanalysis.

____ 3. The name associated with person-centered therapy is
    a. Freud.
    b. Adler.
    c. Rogers.
    d. Frankl.

____ 4. Person-centered therapy places most emphasis on
    a. warmth and acceptance by the therapist.
    b. reinforcing desirable behavior.
    c. gaining insight into the causes of one's problems.
    d. a cognitive, problem-solving approach.

____ 5. Existential therapy fits best under the category of
    a. psychoanalysis.
    b. humanistic therapy.
    c. dream analysis.
    d. mutual support therapy.

____ 6. Which of the following is *not* a technique commonly used by behavior therapists?
    a. free association
    b. reinforcement
    c. observational learning
    d. desensitization

____ 7. Behavior therapy is an outgrowth of
    a. psychoanalytic theory.
    b. Gestalt theory.
    c. humanistic theory.
    d. none of the above

____ 8. Systematic desensitization is a technique that
    a. helps reduce feelings of inferiority.
    b. grew out of the study of aggressive animals.
    c. attempts to eliminate phobias by forming new associations.
    d. attempts to discover unconscious conflicts that cause anxiety.

____ 9. Aversive conditioning is a form of
    a. extinction.
    b. desensitization.
    c. dissonance.
    d. learning by observation.

____ 10. Henry is afraid of flying. His therapist asks him to imagine being in an airplane and having a good time. The therapist is using the technique called
    a. extinction.
    b. aversive conditioning.
    c. reinforcement.
    d. desensitization.

____ 11. Another term for drug therapy is
    a. chemotherapy.
    b. hydrotherapy.
    c. Gestalt therapy.
    d. tranquilizers.

____ 12. Antipsychotic drugs, or major tranquilizers, are used primarily in the treatment of
    a. anxiety disorders.
    b. schizophrenia.
    c. depression.
    d. bipolar disorder.

____ 13. The therapeutic effect of drugs used in treating schizophrenia is thought to be related to their impact on the neurotransmitter
    a. norepinephrine.
    b. serotonin.
    c. tardive dyskinesia.
    d. dopamine.

____ 14. Drugs used to combat depression are known as
    a. minor tranquilizers.
    b. major tranquilizers.
    c. neurotransmitters.
    d. none of the above

____ 15. A person who is suffering from bipolar disorder is likely to be treated with
    a. Valium.
    b. a major tranquilizer.
    c. lithium.
    d. norepinephrine.

____ 16. Valium is a type of
    a. antidepressant drug.
    b. minor tranquilizer.
    c. major tranquilizer.
    d. none of the above

____ **17.** Electroconvulsive therapy is most likely to be used with people who are suffering from
a. schizophrenia.
b. personality disorders.
c. depression.
d. bipolar disorder.

____ **18.** In choosing a psychotherapist, it is wise to
a. ask one's doctor for a referral.
b. talk to former clients.
c. interview the prospective therapist.
d. all of the above

____ **19.** Among the typical psychological problems for which older people seek help is
a. depression.
b. panic attacks.
c. schizophrenia.
d. obsessive-compulsive disorder.

____ **20.** A community psychologist is helping survivors of a hotel fire deal with their trauma on the scene. She is practicing a form of
a. humanistic therapy.
b. desensitization.
c. crisis intervention.
d. self-help.

# Exercises

1. If you were undergoing psychoanalysis and engaged in free association, you would be urged by the analyst to speak out every thought that occurred to you—no matter how foolish, irrelevant, hostile, or obscene it might seem. But even without the experience of psychoanalysis, it is possible to get at least some idea of what the process is like.

   Find a place where you will have privacy and are not likely to be interrupted. Bring along either a close friend or a tape recorder to record your free associations. To get started, think of something specific—a person you know, an incident that occurred to you recently, or a dream that you happen to remember. Now start the chain of free associations by saying anything and everything that comes to your mind. It may be difficult, but don't hold back any thought that occurs to you, even if it seems totally unrelated to the thought with which you started the chain. And don't be concerned if your associations seem bizarre or abnormal. The process is intended to allow "irrational" thoughts and feelings buried in the unconscious to come to the surface without any inhibition. There may be times when absolutely nothing occurs to you—when you feel "blocked." Just wait until another thought surfaces in your conscious mind, and go on with your chain of associations.

   After about 10 or 15 minutes, stop the process and review your associations, considering these questions:

   a. Did you find the process difficult? If so, why?

   b. Are you able to identify some of the links in the chain of your associations—the threads that tied one thought to another?

   c. Is there a major theme or idea that seems to "wrap up" all the thoughts that came to your mind?

   d. Do you think it's easier or harder to free associate in the presence of another person?

   e. How valuable do you think the technique of free association would be in the process of psychoanalysis?

2. You're an "intake interviewer" at an outpatient mental health center. Your job is to interview all new clients and write a case history that will serve as the starting point for diagnosis and treatment. You interview Lynda, and what you write about her includes the following:

She is a 21-year-old female. She feels like she doesn't "fit in" with her co-workers and is also very uncomfortable around her few friends and acquaintances. She can't really talk with either her friends or her co-workers because, she says, she feels that she isn't a worthwhile person. She believes that her friends wouldn't want to waste their time with her.

Whenever someone calls her, Lynda feels nauseated and gets off the phone as fast as she can. She says that every time the phone rings, it feels just like it did when she was a child and her mother tried to force her to go out and play with other children. Lynda says that her mother used to make fun of her when she refused to go out to play.

Even to this day, Lynda will only leave her apartment if there seems to be no alternative, and she does so with great trepidation. She goes to great lengths to come up with ways to avoid going out.

She never liked playing with the other girls in particular. Instead of wanting to play with the other girls, she wanted to wait for her father to come home and spend time with him. Lynda says that she loves her father dearly to this day, and she admits harboring a keen dislike for her mother.

Your clinic has three clinical psychologists. Dr. A is primarily a psychodynamic therapist and adheres closely to Freudian psychoanalysis. Dr. B leans toward Rogers's view that perfectionistic "conditions of worth" are often a major part of the problem. Dr. C tends to look for evidence of Bandura's idea of discrepancies between self-efficacy and perceived self-efficacy.

Which details of the excerpt from Lynda's case history would each of the psychotherapists be most inclined to attend to? What else might each therapist want to know about Lynda? Identify at least one specific procedure that each therapist would be likely to employ to assist Lynda. For example, you may wish to discuss how Dr. A might delve into Lynda's childhood experiences analytically, how Dr. B might explore the standards Lynda's mother imposed on her, and how Dr. C might approach Lynda's phobic behavior.

❉ *For quizzing, activities, exercises, and web links, check out the book-specific website at http://www.psychology.wadsworth.com/kagan9e.*

# 15 Social Psychology

© Jeff Greenberg/PhotoEdit

O f all the environmental influences on our behavior, none is as powerful as the people around us. Hence the importance of **social psychology**—the study of how an individual's thoughts, feelings, and actions are affected by others (Feldman, 1985). Social psychology focuses on how psychological processes, behaviors, and personalities are influenced by social processes and social settings. It thus has some similarities to sociology, which is the scientific study of human societies and human behavior in the many groups that make up a society. It differs from sociology, however, in its emphasis on people as individuals rather than as members of large groups.

Note that the definition of social psychology covers cognitive processes and emotions as well as behavior. These processes are, of course, often interrelated, but for the sake of clarity we will examine each of them in turn.

**Social psychology**
The study of how an individual's thoughts, feelings, and actions are affected by others.

# SOCIAL COGNITION: SCHEMAS AND ATTITUDES

Underlying many of the concepts discussed in this chapter are *schemas:* cognitive structures that help us perceive, organize, process, and use information. As noted in Chapter 6, we all develop a variety of schemas as we mature and learn; for example, most people have developed schemas for *mother, father, teacher, animal,* and so on. These provide systems for organizing and processing information.

Because schemas tend to be stable over time, they result in stable ways of perceiving and utilizing information. However, each individual's schemas differ from those of other people, causing each person to evaluate events and situations differently and to behave in different ways. For example, upon being introduced to a friend's father, a person who conceives of a father as a distant authority figure will react differently than will a person whose schema for *father* is that of a warm, loving "Daddy." Thus, differences between individuals' schemas account in part for differences in their personalities.

An important set of schemas, which we acquire largely through interactions with others, consists of very strong opinions and associated feelings. These are called **attitudes.** Most of us have favorable or unfavorable attitudes toward members of various ethnic groups, foreigners, rich people, poor people, males, females, children, teenagers, and older people. Political parties, unions, national defense, taxation, welfare, and crime are just a few of the issues and institutions that evoke a broad array of attitudes.

Attitudes are not off-the-cuff judgments that we make casually and change easily. Instead, they are deeply ingrained, and typically slow to change, parts of our personality. An attitude is defined as an organized and enduring set of beliefs and feelings that predispose us to behave in a certain way. Attitudes always con-

**FOCUS QUESTIONS**
- What are schemas, and how are they related to attitudes?
- How do attitudes—including prejudices and stereotypes—influence human behavior?
- What is meant by cognitive dissonance?
- What factors can lead to effective persuasive communication?

**Attitudes**
Organized and enduring sets of opinions and feelings that predispose us to behave in a certain way.

© Ed Bock Photography, Inc./CORBIS

There are many different possible schemas for *father*.

**Socialization**
The way children are deliberately integrated into the society through exposure to the actions and opinions of others.

**Enculturation**
The process by which we absorb the norms and values of the culture in which we are born and raised.

tain an *evaluative* component: You like or dislike something, you consider it good or bad. Although psychology still has much to learn about the nature and power of attitudes, some broad patterns have been established (Eagly, 1992).

## Developing New Schemas and Attitudes Throughout Life

Two major forces play a role in the formation of an individual's attitudes. The first is **socialization**—that is, the way children are deliberately integrated into the society through teaching by parents, teachers, and others. Socialization is intended to teach children how to function in society. Also playing a role in the formation of attitudes is **enculturation,** the process by which we absorb the norms and values of the culture in which we are born and raised (Segal, Dasen, Berry, & Poortinga, 1999). Much of what we think and believe is shaped by our culture. A child raised in a collectivist culture like that of mainland China, for example, will develop quite different attitudes than will a child raised in an individualist culture like that of the United States.

We tend to cling to many of our attitudes the way a child clings to a security blanket—and perhaps for some of the same reasons. Yet not all attitudes are permanent. Sometimes a lifelong miser becomes a philanthropist or a confirmed atheist becomes religious. Public opinion polls taken in recent decades have shown sharp changes in prevailing attitudes toward many institutions and issues in the United States and elsewhere in the world.

One reason attitudes change is that the process of socialization continues throughout life. In our early years, our parents are the chief agents of socialization, and we tend to adopt their attitudes as our own. But as we grow older and are exposed to friends, teachers, and others, the early influence of our parents begins to weaken. Although about 80% of elementary school children prefer the same political party as their parents, one study found that the number drops to about 55% among college students (Goldsen, Rosenberg, Robin, & Suchman, 1960). The first year in college is especially likely to produce attitude changes (Freedman, Carlsmith, & Sears, 1970).

We are particularly receptive to changes in attitude during adolescence and late adulthood (Krosnick & Alwin, 1989). This is partly because we experience more major life shifts at these times than at any other point in our lives. Changes experienced between the ages of 18 and 25 often include graduating from high school, going to college, graduating from college, starting a first job, getting married, becoming a parent, and moving—all of which can lead to changes in attitudes. Among the major changes associated with late adulthood is retirement.

When we take a job, we undergo a new kind of socialization. Each time we change jobs or get a promotion, each time we move to a new neighborhood or a new community, we come under new influences. We can also be swayed by what we read and by what we see on television. The world changes, and we change with it. Our attitudes can be compared to a house that undergoes frequent remodeling, expansion, and repainting over the years. In some ways the house never changes, yet it is never really the same.

# Illogical Attitudes: Prejudices and Stereotypes

Not all attitudes are based on objective observations. Some simply represent what we have learned in growing up and interacting with others. We often adopt attitudes from people around us without considering any evidence at all.

Nor are attitudes necessarily logical or consistent. Indeed, a remarkable thing about our attitudes is the amount of inconsistency we manage to tolerate. Moreover, we are surprisingly adept at reconciling dissimilar attributes in a given individual (Asch & Zukier, 1984). That explains why, for example, citizens sometimes vote for officials whom they like but who have been found guilty of dishonesty and wrongdoing.

Two kinds of attitudes that often contradict fact are so common that social psychologists have given them specific names: *prejudice* and *stereotype*.

1. A **prejudice** is an attitude that an individual maintains so stubbornly as to be virtually immune to any information or experience that would disprove it. (Note that prejudice is not the same as *discrimination*. Prejudice is an attitude, such as the notion that members of a particular ethnic group are inferior in some way. Discrimination is actual behavior based on prejudice, such as refusing to rent an apartment to members of a particular ethnic group.)

2. A **stereotype** is an attitude that disregards individual differences and holds that all members of a certain group behave in the same manner or share some "undesirable" characteristic. People are making judgments on the basis of stereotypes when they claim that all women are flighty or that all men are sexist pigs. Stated differently, stereotypes are stored as schemas containing "clusters" of behaviors or characteristics that a person believes always occur together. So a gender-prejudiced person might see women as being flighty as well as having an assortment of other undesirable tendencies, or men as being sexist as well as being undesirable in other ways.

We tend to cling to our prejudices and stereotypes—so much so that when we encounter a group member whose attributes run counter to our preconceptions of the group as a whole, we are likely to dismiss that person as atypical, or a "fluke" (Bargh & Ferguson, 2000; Lord, Lepper, & Mackie, 1984; Macrae & Bodenhausen, 2000). In our personal relationships, we may judge new acquaintances on the basis of stereotypes and thus become suspicious of people who might actually prove congenial if we only gave them a chance. Members of certain ethnic groups tend to be the targets of society's strongest prejudices and stereotypes. A study of Princeton students showed how irrational such stereotypes can be. The students characterized Turks as cruel, treacherous, sensual, ignorant, and dirty—despite the fact that they had never met a Turk (R. Brown, 1986).

**Prejudice**
An attitude that an individual maintains so stubbornly as to be virtually immune to any information or experience that would disprove it.

**Stereotype**
An attitude, shared by a large number of people, that disregards individual differences and holds that all members of a certain group behave in the same manner.

# Cognitive Dissonance

What kinds of new experiences and information are most likely to produce attitude changes? One answer comes from proponents of the theory of **cognitive dissonance.** This theory maintains that we strive to be consistent and rational in our thinking and to preserve agreement and harmony between our attitudes and our behavior, and that we feel uncomfortable or even anxious whenever there is a discrepancy between them. There is evidence, for example, that we are more likely to remember information that is consistent with our attitudes than information that runs counter to them (Eagly, 1992). When consistency is broken, we experience cognitive dissonance, and this makes us uncomfortable. We may manage to tolerate the inconsistency, but because of our discomfort we are strongly motivated to restore harmony by making some kind of adjustment in our attitudes.

**Cognitive dissonance**
A feeling generated by lack of consistency between our attitudes and our behavior.

Apparently it is easier to change people's attitudes by offering them just enough to get them to engage in behavior contrary to those attitudes than by offering them more; a larger reward serves to reduce dissonance and thus makes attitude change less likely. This was demonstrated in a classic experiment by Leon Festinger and James M. Carlsmith (1957) in which participants were offered a small reward ($1) or a larger one ($20) for telling another person that a dull task they had just performed was interesting. (A typical task consisted of placing a number of spools on a tray, dumping them off, and then putting them on the tray again—over and over.) After they had told the other person that the task was interesting, the participants were asked to indicate how much they themselves liked the task. Those who were given $1 for misleading the other person reported liking the task more than those who were given $20, as a result of cognitive dissonance. The $1 participants could not change the behavior that they had just engaged in, so they changed their attitudes to correspond. This sort of behavior is a lot like rationalization, discussed in Chapter 12.

In some cases, new factual information is enough to create cognitive dissonance and bring about a change in attitude. For example, some people who were once strongly opposed to birth control have been influenced by information about the rapid growth of the world population. They once believed that a growing population was a good thing, but this belief has now changed—and their attitude toward birth control has changed with it.

Events that have a strong emotional impact may also create an inconsistency that calls for change. For example, imagine what would happen if a man who had always believed that women should be subservient found himself in love with an ardent feminist. Or consider the classic laboratory experiment in which college women underwent a deeply emotional experience related to cigarette smoking. The women, all heavy smokers, were asked to act out a scene in which the experimenter pretended to be a physician and they were his patients. Each subject, visiting the "doctor," got bad news about a persistent cough from which she had been suffering: Her X ray had shown lung cancer; immediate surgery was required; before the operation, she and the doctor would have to discuss the difficulty, pain, and risk. The experimenter tried to keep the scene as realistic as possible and to involve each subject emotionally to the greatest possible degree. As a result, almost all the women quit or drastically cut down on their smoking. A follow-up 18 months later found that they continued to show significant change in their smoking habits (Mann & Janis, 1968).

## How Changes in Behavior Can Change Our Attitudes

It seems logical that a change in an attitude, caused by new beliefs or new emotional responses, should cause a change in behavior. Yet, strangely enough, the sequence of events is often exactly the opposite. In many cases, the change in behavior comes first, and the new behavior creates a change in attitude.

Many studies have shown that experimental manipulation of behavior can produce remarkable results. One such experiment concerned the highly controversial action of President Gerald Ford in extending a blanket pardon to his predecessor, Richard Nixon, for any crimes committed during the Watergate incident. College students who strongly opposed the pardon were asked to write essays taking the opposite point of view and justifying Ford's action. This simple act of writing an essay created a more favorable attitude toward the pardon (Cooper, Zanna, & Taves, 1978). A similar experiment was conducted with students who favored the legalization of marijuana. After they were asked to write an essay opposing legalization, their attitudes showed considerable change (Fazio, Zanna, & Cooper, 1977).

In our everyday lives, new social situations often push us in the direction of new patterns of behavior, and these in turn often lead to shifts in attitudes. People of different ethnicities who have attended school or worked together hold more favorable attitudes toward each other than do those who have had no such contacts. To combat ethnic animosity, researchers have been attempting to bring members of different ethnicities together at an early age, before prejudices have had a chance to harden. One successful method involves assigning diverse students to learning teams in the hope that a common purpose will lead to friendship. Such cooperative groups reduce prejudice by undercutting the categories that lead to stereotyped thinking (Gaertner, 1989).

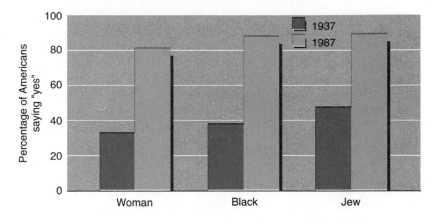

**FIGURE 15.1 Would you vote for such a person for president?** As indicated here, people in the United States have developed more accepting attitudes toward certain groups. *After Yankelovich, 1988.*

Despite highly publicized incidents of violence, people in the United States appear to be more accepting of different groups than ever before (Yankelovich, 1988). In 1937, a Gallup poll asked people if they would vote for a well-qualified person for president who was a woman, a black, or a Jew. As shown in Figure 15.1, endorsement of each was low. But by 1987, people were much more receptive—more than 80% said "yes." And today, 92% of poll respondents say that they would be willing to vote for a woman for president (White House Project, 2002).

Dealing cooperatively with members of another ethnic group—studying or working with them and treating them as companions—has undoubtedly produced attitude changes. The theory of cognitive dissonance maintains that friendly behavior produces an imbalance that can be remedied by abandoning the disapproving attitude.

## Being Persuaded to Change Our Attitudes

All of us are under constant pressure to adopt new attitudes. Politicians bombard us with speeches and press releases intended to foster favorable attitudes toward them and their party. Companies spend huge amounts every year on advertising to try to create favorable attitudes toward their products. Many organizations work hard to win support for such causes as conservation, humane treatment of animals, and pollution control. Such attempts to change attitudes by transmitting information and making emotional appeals are known as **persuasive communications.** Because persuasive communications can have significant effects on society, they have been studied in considerable depth.

**Persuasive communications** All attempts to change attitudes by transmitting information and making emotional appeals.

Attempts to influence the attitudes of large numbers of people face many obstacles. For one thing, persuasive communications do not ordinarily reach many people. A politician may make an impassioned and convincing plea for support—yet the actual speech will be heard in person by only a few thousand people at most. Even if part of the speech is shown on television, it will reach only a small proportion of the population. Newspaper accounts of a political speech reach and impress an even smaller audience, and editorials have a smaller readership still. In addition, it has been found that the audience most likely to watch or read any appeal for attitude change—and to pay attention to it—is determined largely by a factor called **selective exposure.** Because we tend to associate with people we like and to read or listen to communications we find interesting, we are exposed mostly to people and communications that we already agree with. This means that, by and large, persuasive communications reach people who are already persuaded.

**Selective exposure** The tendency to pay attention to communications with which one already agrees.

© Jeff Greenberg/PhotoEdit

Persuasive communications, such as those characteristic of political rallies, are more likely to appeal to people who are already persuaded than to people who hold opposing views.

**Belief perseverance**
**The tendency to maintain one's beliefs, even when faced with evidence to the contrary.**

### Test Yourself

**(a)** If someone were to say to you, "You won't change your mind because you're trying to avoid cognitive dissonance," what would the person be trying to convey?

**(b)** A TV ad about saving the environment is likely to be listened to with particular interest by people who are devoted to that cause. What is this characteristic of persuasive communication called?

**(c)** Does social psychology offer an optimistic or a pessimistic view of the potential for humans to change over time?

(The answers are on page 618.)

But let's assume that a persuasive communication does succeed in reaching you despite the obstacles, and that it argues for a viewpoint you're opposed to. If you are to adopt that viewpoint, your attitudes must change. Classic research has revealed several factors that help determine whether this will happen.

**The Credibility of the Source**    Some sources are likely to have considerable influence. Others are less likely to convince us and may, in fact, make us more opposed to what they are proposing. If the communication comes from someone whose knowledge or motives are suspect—in other words, from a source with low credibility—we tend to disregard it. If it comes from people who clearly know what they are talking about—in other words, from a source with high credibility—we are much more likely to accept it (Hovland & Weiss, 1951). The effectiveness of the communication is enhanced if the source seems to be fair, objective, and not particularly interested in wielding influence. Of course, it helps if the ideas being communicated match, at least to some degree, the prior beliefs of the audience (Newstead, Pollard, & Evans, 1992). Indeed, there is evidence that people often exhibit **belief perseverance**—the tendency to maintain beliefs even when faced with evidence to the contrary (Sherman & Kunda, 1989).

**The Nature of the Medium**    The channel of communication makes a difference. Face-to-face communication tends to be more effective than communication via media such as newspapers or television. We are influenced more by our friends and colleagues than by what we see on TV. This does not mean that the media have no effect, however. Even if they have little direct effect on our attitudes, they may have an indirect effect. The individuals who personally influence us must get their ideas and information somewhere, and often their sources are newspapers, television, and other media. Moreover, the more lifelike the medium, the more persuasive it tends to be; thus, face-to-face communication and television are generally more persuasive than radio and print media.

**The Nature of the Communication**    What kinds of arguments does the source present, and how and when are they presented? In general, appeals to the emotions—particularly fear—tend to be especially effective (Robberson & Rogers, 1988; Rogers, 1985), particularly if the communication includes specific recommendations for action to prevent or avoid the fear-producing event. Such appeals can change not only attitudes but behavior as well. In the experiment illustrated in Figure 15.2, college students were urged to get inoculations for tetanus. The disease was described in detail—how serious it was and that it was easy to contract—but to different degrees for each of three groups. For the first group, the descriptions were extremely vivid, and the disease was made to seem as fearsome as possible; for the second group, a moderate amount of fear was aroused; and for the third, very little. The greater the fear aroused, the more likely students were not only to say that they intended to take shots but to actually report to the university health service to be inoculated (Dabbs & Leventhal, 1966).

The arousal of excessive fear will backfire if the person cannot do anything to deal with the danger. Presumably, the listener becomes upset and tries to forget the whole matter.

The effectiveness of a communication appears to increase if it seems to present a fair argument rather than a one-sided one, especially if it is addressed to an intelligent, well-educated audience (Hovland, Lumsdaine, & Sheffield, 1949). With

# How Much Can People Change?

One of the great barriers to progress—both for individuals and for society as a whole—is that many people take a pessimistic view of the nature-nurture argument. Although there is strong evidence that most human behavior is influenced just as much by environment and learning as by heredity—and often more so—many people still cling to the belief that human nature is determined at birth and resists any attempt to alter or improve it. This belief is evident in such familiar expressions as "People don't change," "That's just human nature," or "That kid was born to be bad." About themselves, people often say, "I can't help it; I'm just built this way" or "I'm just plain unlucky."

The belief that human nature is largely inherited is a powerful deterrent to change in attitudes and behavior. In a classic experiment, university students were asked whether they thought the next 5 years might alter their attitudes about some of their personality characteristics (such as whether they regarded themselves as trusting, curious, and so on) and about various social issues (such as capital punishment and legalization of marijuana). It turned out that their answers depended largely on whether they thought their present attitudes were the result of nature or of nurture (Festinger, 1954). If they considered an attitude to be largely a matter of learning (as a majority did for being trusting and favoring legalization of marijuana), they were significantly more likely to foresee possible change than if they regarded the attitude as something innate (as a majority did for curiosity). The results of that experiment would undoubtedly hold true today.

We tend to assume that personality traits—especially any undesirable ones—are inborn and lasting (the social desirability effect). Many people become convinced that they are just naturally "dumb" or "awkward" or "bad." This makes it unlikely that they will believe change is possible, much less try to achieve it. Suppose, for example, that an adolescent boy who is constantly in trouble feels that he was "born" to be an outcast. He is likely to be totally unresponsive to any options for changing his attitudes and behavior. If he could be convinced that his problems are, at least in part, the result of environmental influences, he would be much more receptive to the possibility of change.

Perhaps the greatest potential contribution of social psychologists to human happiness and progress is the evidence they have accumulated about the influence of the social environment. No longer is it possible to assume that our innate biological makeup determines our destiny. The findings indicate that personality, attitudes, and behavior are more elastic than many people believe and that change for the better—both in human happiness and in the way society functions—is always possible.

---

a less intelligent audience, a one-sided argument may be more effective, perhaps because the listeners are confused by hearing both sides (Aronson, 1984).

**The Audience** Who is listening may be just as important as what is said and the source of the communication. Some people are more easily persuaded than others (Hovland, Janis, & Kelley, 1953). The crucial factor seems to be your opinion of yourself. People with low self-esteem tend to be much more easily persuaded than people with high self-esteem. Similarly, people who are anxious about social acceptance are more easily persuaded than those who have little anxiety. In an odd way, the possibility that listeners will change their attitudes is also affected by their beliefs

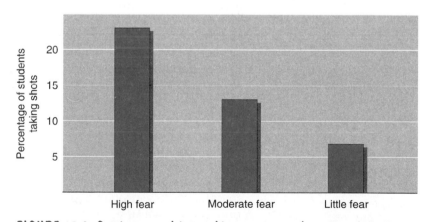

FIGURE 15.2 Getting scared into taking a tetanus shot. The graph illustrates the results of a study in which college students were urged to get inoculations for tetanus. The greater the fear aroused, the more likely students were to report to the university health service to be inoculated.
*Dabbs & Leventhal, 1966.*

about the relative influence of nature and nurture. This fact is so significant—especially as an influence that can discourage changes for the better—that its implications are discussed in the Life Span Perspective above.

# ATTRIBUTION: WHY DID YOU (OR I) DO THAT?

**FOCUS QUESTIONS**

- How do attribution theories explain our search for the reasons people act as they do?
- What is the fundamental attribution error?
- What is meant by self-fulfilling prophecies?

**Attribution theories**
Theories about how people attempt to infer the causes of behavior.

On December 3, 1979, a crowd of 8,000 people waited for hours in the bitter cold outside the Riverfront Coliseum in Cincinnati to see the rock band The Who perform. Finally, a few doors were opened and the crowd began to surge forward, pushing, shoving, knocking people to the ground, and crushing them. Eleven people were killed and many were seriously injured. In the wake of this tragedy, the citizens of Cincinnati searched for explanations for the concertgoers' behavior. Were they heartless, cruel people who would literally trample over someone else to get what they wanted? Or were they otherwise considerate people caught in a horrible accident?

To explore these kinds of questions, psychologists turn to **attribution theories**—theories about how people attempt to infer the causes of behavior. The theories vary, but they all assume that we want to know why people act the way they do because we want our social interactions to have the most favorable possible outcomes (Heider, 1944)—that is, we hope to avoid embarrassing and possibly costly mistakes and maximize satisfactions and rewards. If we can attribute behavior to some underlying motive or other cause, we have a valuable clue to where we stand, what is likely to happen next, and how we can best deal with the situation. Thus, we all perform a good deal of amateur psychology, seeking in various ways to interpret the meanings and future implications of behavior as best we can.

## Person or Situation: Attribution Errors

**Dispositional factors**
Behavior-producing factors that are deep-seated and consistent personality traits.

**Situational factors**
Behavior-producing factors that depend on the situation or circumstances of the moment.

**Fundamental attribution error**
The tendency to use dispositional factors rather than situational factors to explain other people's actions.

For almost any action, there are a number of possible explanations. Consider these simple actions: One morning, a server smiles at us and expresses the hope that we will enjoy our meal. That same morning, the person at the newsstand scowls while taking our money. One possibility is that the server is basically a warm and friendly person and that the individual at the newsstand is hostile and bad-tempered. In that case, their behavior was due to **dispositional factors:** deep-seated and consistent personality traits. It is also possible, however, that the server acted that way only to get a good tip, while hiding a basic tendency to be surly and arrogant. Perhaps the person at the newsstand, though ordinarily good-humored, had a bad headache. In this case, their behavior was caused by **situational factors,** or circumstances that forced them in that direction.

We often attribute other people's actions to dispositional factors, thus ignoring evidence that people are not nearly so consistent as is generally assumed and that their behavior often depends on the situation. The tendency to favor dispositional factors—rather than aspects of the situation that may provide a better explanation—is so powerful and widespread that it has been called the **fundamental attribution error** (Ross, 1977).

When we try to interpret our own actions, we typically take into account the shifting situations we find ourselves in. For example, we may say, "I get angry when someone tries to take advantage of me" or "I feel shy when I'm introduced to someone new." But when we try to interpret the actions of other people, we typically commit the fundamental attribution error by pinning these actions on their personality traits. For example, we may say, "She's hostile" or "He's withdrawn" (McGuire & McGuire, 1986). This tendency, known as the *actor-observer effect,* seems to occur because we are well aware of the various external factors affecting our own actions but are less aware of such factors operating on other people (Jones, 1976; Jones &

Nisbett, 1971). We are especially likely to make these kinds of attributions in situations involving failure or undesirable behavior. For example, if a fellow student fails a test, we may conclude that he or she isn't very bright, whereas if we get an F, we may complain that the test was too difficult or that there wasn't enough time to study.

The question of how we use information about other people's behavior as a basis for inferring that they possess certain traits has long been of interest to social psychologists. This question has been examined in depth by Edward Jones (1926–1993) and Keith Davis (Jones, 1990; Jones & Davis, 1965).

They developed the theory of *correspondent inference,* which states that in trying to interpret the behavior of others, we focus only on the actions that are most likely to be informative. For one thing, we consider only actions that appear to be voluntary, largely ignoring those that seem to have been forced on the person in question. (For example, if someone bumps into us, we are more likely to forgive the action if the person is on crutches or accompanied by a guide dog.) We also place more confidence in our attributions regarding actions that are low in *social desirability.* For example, if someone donates a large amount of money to a charity, it is easier to believe that the person did so to get a big tax write-off than to believe that the person is genuinely a philanthropist.

As predicted by the concept of the fundamental attribution error, we tend to believe that we drive safely and carefully but that most other people drive carelessly or aggressively.

Numerous studies have focused on the tendency to make judgments based on the degree to which an individual is perceived as being in control of his or her behavior in a particular situation (e.g., Snyder & Jones, 1974; Weiner, 1990, 1993). Researchers have found, for example, that people who do not succeed at a given task are judged more negatively if they have not tried very hard than if they lack ability (Weiner, 1993). Our notions about the degree to which other people's behavior is controllable strongly influence our conclusions about whether they are personally responsible for their own actions.

Various groups can easily be stigmatized by errors in attribution. For instance, people suffering from illnesses are often blamed for their afflictions. Certain illnesses are more likely to be seen as subject to the individual's control than others (Weiner, Perry, & Magnusson, 1988). People with physically based illnesses such as cancer and Alzheimer's disease are not considered responsible for their conditions and hence are seen as deserving help. On the other hand, those with behavioral or mental disorders, such as alcohol or drug abuse, evoke little compassion and often meet with hostility.

**Culture and Attribution**   Psychologists have long believed that basic reasoning processes such as causal attribution are the same in all cultures (Gardner, 1985). Recent research has shown, however, that people from Asian cultures are less likely to commit the fundamental attribution error than people from Western cultures (Choi, Nisbett, & Norenzayan, 1999). For example, Hindu Indians prefer to explain ordinary life events in terms of the context in which they occur, whereas people in the United States are much more likely to explain similar events in terms of the dispositions of the individuals involved (J. G. Miller, 1984). Similarly, Morris and Peng (1994) found that Chinese students in the United States tended to explain murders in terms of the situation, whereas Western students were more likely to explain them in terms of the presumed dispositions of the perpetrators.

Interestingly, these differences have been found to go beyond interpretations of human behavior. In one study (Morris & Peng, 1994), participants were shown cartoons of a fish moving in a variety of configurations in relation to a group of fish, and were asked why they thought the fish acted as it did. Chinese participants tended to attribute the individual fish's behavior to external factors—that is, to aspects of the group—whereas U.S. participants were more likely to attribute it to internal factors.

Scholars in many fields have identified significant differences between the intellectual traditions of Asia and the West, and these differences help explain the findings just described (Norenzayan & Nisbett, 2000). Western culture tends to take an analytic stance, focusing on individual objects, whereas Asian culture is more holistic, taking the overall context into account. Similarly, as we have seen in earlier chapters, Asian culture tends to be more collectivist, while Western culture is more individualistic. Thus, the effects of enculturation can be seen in the different ways in which people from Asian and Western cultures tend to interpret similar events.

## Mistaken Impressions

The fundamental attribution error may be compounded when we reach our mistaken conclusions on the basis of mistaken impressions. An example occurred in an experiment in which psychologists made a videotape, without a soundtrack, of a college woman being interviewed. They then showed the videotape to two groups of men. One group was told that the topic of the interview was sex; the other was told that the topic was politics. Afterward, the participants were asked to rate the woman on how nervous and anxious she seemed to be. Their ratings turned out to depend on what they had been told about the interview. If they thought the topic was sex, they thought the woman showed considerable anxiety. They assumed that the woman would be made anxious by a discussion of sexual behavior. If they thought the topic was politics, they felt that she showed less anxiety. Thus, exactly the same behavior—the same videotape of the same woman—created two very different impressions.

The same two groups of participants were then asked to rate the woman's general tendency to be calm or flustered—in other words, her basic disposition. The results followed the same pattern. Participants who believed that the interview was about sex and that it had flustered her decided that the woman was naturally inclined to be apprehensive, nervous, and anxious. Those who believed that the interview was about politics did not make the same judgments (Snyder & Frankel, 1976). The participants jumped to the erroneous conclusion that acting flustered during an interview about sex—a situation that might produce a certain amount of anxiety in many people—indicated a disposition to be easily flustered in general.

All of us are probably guilty of this compounded error at times. We watch person A being treated by person B in what we consider an abusive manner. Such treatment would make us angry—so we assume that A is angry. Then, on the basis of this assumption, we further assume that A tends to be hot-tempered in general. We watch person C making a fuss over person D. Such attention from C, whom we like very much, would greatly please us—so we assume that D is pleased. Then, on the basis of this assumption, we further assume that D is friendly and easily pleased in general. We could be dead wrong in thinking that A is angry or that D is pleased—and how they happen to feel in these particular situations does not necessarily reflect their basic dispositions anyway.

## Expectations and Social Relationships

It is important to recognize that we ourselves, by the way we act, may produce the very actions that we incorrectly interpret as indicating another person's deep-seated personality traits. This tendency can lead to a **self-fulfilling prophecy**—a prediction that comes true not because it was correct but simply because it was made in the first place.

Self-fulfilling prophecies based on false attributions and mistaken impressions are common, and they have important implications for the way we relate to one another. To illustrate this point, a team of psychologists conducted a now-classic experiment that was simple in design but had some surprising results. The participants were college men, each of whom was asked to become acquainted, in a 10-minute telephone conversation, with a college woman he had never met. Before the call was made, the participant was shown what he was told was a photograph of the woman. (Actually the photograph was of someone else.) Half the participants saw a picture of a woman who had been judged by an independent panel to be physically attractive. The others saw a picture of a woman who had been judged to be physically unattractive.

The phone calls were made and recorded on tape. In analyzing the tapes, the experimenters found something remarkable. There seemed to be two completely different types of women on the phone. One type—those believed by the male students to be the person in the attractive photo—sounded warm, charming, and humorous. The other type—those believed by the men to be the person in the unattractive photo—sounded cold, clumsy, and humorless. How could this be? The answer is simple: There seemed to be two very different types of men on the tapes. If the male participants thought their telephone partner was attractive, they stereotyped her as warm and charming—and they themselves were friendly, eager, and easy to respond to. If they thought she was unattractive, they expected her to be cold and humorless—and they themselves cast a pall over the phone call, inviting a chilly and stilted response. By thus setting the tone of the conversation, they pushed their partner into the very kind of behavior they expected (Snyder, Tanke, & Berscheid, 1977).

The gloomy prophecy made by half the participants was that their telephone partner would be unsociable—and because they acted accordingly, their prophecy was fulfilled. The other half of the men did exactly the opposite—and made their optimistic predictions come true.

This experiment makes a point worth remembering in social relationships: In everyday dealings with other people, it pays to be optimistic and cheerful. (See the discussion of positive psychology in Chapter 12.) When you have high hopes that the other person will be likable, your own friendly and accepting actions go a long way toward guaranteeing that the person will indeed behave in a likable manner. But if you expect to dislike someone, your own pessimistic and sour actions almost guarantee a cold and unsympathetic response. It is probably equally true that expecting other people to like us tends to be a self-fulfilling prophecy. If we expect to be liked, we behave in a likable fashion. If we fear rejection, we tend to act tense, guarded, and not likable at all—and thus bring about the very thing we dread. By and large, people treat us not only as we treat them but also as we expect to be treated.

**Self-fulfilling prophecy** A prediction that comes true not because it is right but simply because it was made in the first place.

## The Potent Effects of Self-Fulfilling Prophecies

One place where the self-fulfilling prophecy flourishes is the classroom. Sometimes the effects are positive. Teachers frequently decide very early in the school

## PSYCHOLOGY IN THE LAB AND IN LIFE

# Guidance from Attribution Theorists

Attribution theorists suggest some lessons to guide us in our day-to-day social relationships. They tell us that we should be cautious and tentative when we act as amateur analysts, looking for the reasons behind other people's actions. Yet the attempt at analysis is often useful and not necessarily doomed to failure. Despite the difficulties, we can manage to make a careful enough study to judge people more or less correctly.

- When you can, make every attempt to take situational factors into consideration. If, for example, a person seems withdrawn or confused during the weekend, try to determine whether this is his or her usual frame of mind or simply the result of anxiety about the coming Monday's demands.

- Search for any information that would indicate whether an act is typical or an uncharacteristic incident. For example, do not decide that a person is hot-tempered because of a single display of anger.
- When possible, seek and consider the opinions of other observers. These can help you determine whether your attributions are on the mark or way off.

Other people are so important to us that it is essential that we try to understand them. We have to make attributions of some kind—and we do the best we can. It is safe to assume that most of the time, a person's behavior is based on a combination of both internal disposition and the particular situation at hand.

---

### Test Yourself

**(d)** Sometimes it is difficult to know whether the behavior of an individual arises from basic personality characteristics or from the context in which that individual happens to be functioning. What do social psychologists call these two factors?

**(e)** If you were told to be careful not to make the fundamental attribution error, what would the speaker be warning you against?

**(f)** I expect my friend to be hostile, so when we meet, I manage to act in a way that elicits hostility. What is that process called?

(The answers are on page 618.)

year that some students should do well. Although their judgments are often right, as measured by test scores, a positive outcome can also be due to the influence of the teacher's expectations. It has been shown that the more favorably teachers view students at the beginning of the year, the more those students increase their grades and test scores above the levels that would have been predicted by their prior performance (Jussim & Eccles, 1992; Rosenthal & Jacobson, 1966). This occurs because teachers are more encouraging toward the favored students and spend more time working with them. Apparently, teachers communicate their expectations about individual pupils' performance through the ways in which they communicate with them—for example, teaching more, and more difficult, material to "gifted" students and giving them more opportunities to respond (Harris & Rosenthal, 1986).

Unfortunately, sometimes the effects of a self-fulfilling prophecy are negative. Teachers may decide that some students are not worth much attention. In the elementary school classroom, for example, they may make this decision on the basis of physical unattractiveness (Rist, 1970). Once teachers have made their prophecies, they tend to ignore their "dull" pupils and provide much more attention and help to the "bright" ones (Cooper, 1979). This behavior has a considerable effect on the pupils' actual progress in the classroom. The ones who have been tagged as "dull," possibly through no fault of their own, have little opportunity or encouragement to change that label (Rosenthal & Jacobson, 1996).

Compounding the problem is the fact that a prophecy about another person's behavior may *seem* to come true in the eyes of the prophecy maker, regardless of how the other person actually behaves. Once we have decided that certain individuals are likely to be "bright" or "dull" (or friendly, hostile, charming, humorless, or anything else), we are likely to interpret whatever they do as evidence of that trait. Many actions do not in themselves tell very much about the person who performs them—so an observer who starts with a bias is free to assign whatever meaning the bias dictates (Darley & Fazio, 1980). Teachers may find the very same action to be a sign of stupidity in a "dull" pupil but of intelligence in a "bright" one.

Our expectations may be created by a stereotype that certain types of behavior are characteristic of members of a particular ethnic group, social class, or gender. Or they may represent a hasty first impression or even something we have heard, true or not, about the other person's reputation. Unfortunately, such an expectation can have far-reaching and drastic results, especially when it is held by a person with the power of a teacher, employer, police officer, or mental health professional. As one study concluded, an expectation about another person can "significantly affect the life" of that person "perhaps for the better, but as many who do this research fear, often for the worse" (Darley & Fazio, 1980). Some lessons on this subject are contained in Psychology in the Lab and in Life on page 596.

# CONFORMITY, COMPLIANCE, AND OBEDIENCE

From the first interactions we have with others, usually our parents and family, we learn the ways of our own society: how to use a knife and fork, when to cross the street. Gradually, through socialization and enculturation, we learn the customs and laws that dictate a whole host of activities, from finding a mate to conducting a business deal. Social psychologists have found that most people everywhere display strong tendencies toward (1) **conformity,** or yielding to group pressures, (2) **compliance,** or agreeing to the requests of others, and (3) **obedience,** or submission to authority. These three tendencies are the subject of this section.

> **FOCUS QUESTIONS**
> * What factors lead people to conform to the wishes of others?
> * What techniques are used to induce compliance?
> * Why do people tend to obey those in authority, even if it means inflicting harm on others?

**Conformity**
Yielding by individuals to pressures from the group in which they find themselves.

**Compliance**
Agreeing to the requests of others.

**Obedience**
Submission to authority.

## The Urge to Conform

Life requires that we coordinate or subordinate our actions to fit the larger demands of society. From a very early age, children are taught to obey their parents and follow the rules of the household. As children move out into society, these rules increase in number and become more formal: Schools, organizations, and businesses all require us to follow agreed-upon rules and customs. So it is hardly surprising that most of us will go along with the requests, demands, or, in some cases, coercion of others.

There are always "mavericks" who resist the influence of society and culture and break the rules or even fail to conform to them most of the time. But most people follow the customs and rules they have learned and behave the way they believe they are expected to behave. The group that puts pressure on the individual to conform may be the society as a whole or any part of it—from family, friends, and classmates to business associates. It may even be made up of total strangers, such as the people sitting around us on a bus or in a theater. Of course, on many occasions we tend to believe that there is group pressure on us to conform when, in fact, there is none.

The tendencies toward obedience and conformity—and the difference between them—were demonstrated decades ago in a small and simple experiment built around a campus doorway that was in frequent use. On the doorway an urgent sign suddenly appeared:

ABSOLUTELY NO ADMITTANCE
USE ANOTHER ENTRANCE

The sign had been put up by a psychologist, who then sat nearby to see what happened. One person after another, even those who had been walking through the

FIGURE 15.3 Styles change over the years—but people remain look-alikes. These street scenes, photographed over a span of almost a century, show how the appearance of people in the United States has changed since 1910. Yet, no matter when the camera recorded them, they all looked more or less like their contemporaries.

doorway every day, turned back—thus conforming to society's rules. But then the experimenter arranged for confederates to appear, ignore the sign, and march right in. Given this example, others walked in too (Freed, Chandler, Mouton, & Blake, 1955). They were now conforming with the behavior of the confederates.

If you make a point of looking for similar examples, you will see them all around you. If a traffic light sticks, showing red to motorists approaching from all four directions, the drivers will all come to a halt and wait patiently for a change. But when at last one or two venture across the intersection, others will follow. When a pedestrian on a crowded sidewalk stops to stare at the upper floor of a tall building, others are likely to stop and stare too, even if they find nothing worth watching. People even manage to resemble one another in appearance. As the street scenes in Figure 15.3 show, styles change over the years—but at any given moment in history, everyone looks pretty much like everyone else.

It is amusing but not very significant that all of us tend to gawk at a building when others are doing so or that we follow the dictates of fashion in clothing and hairstyles. Often, however, conformity can affect more important aspects of our lives. A study of Princeton University undergraduates, for example, found that although most male students felt uncomfortable with the drinking habits of their peers, they believed that their fellow students did not feel the same way—and over time they shifted their attitudes toward drinking so that their behavior was more in accord with what they assumed their peers' attitudes to be. Female students didn't react in a similar fashion, but the investigators believe that if the behavior being studied had been more typical of females, they would have reacted in a similarly conforming manner (Prentice & Miller, 1993).

## Pressures to Conform

A classic experiment on conformity was performed in the 1950s by renowned social psychologist Solomon Asch (1907–1996). In this experiment, one participant, who thought the study was about perceptual discrimination, sat at a table with a group of other "participants" who were actually confederates of the experimenter. The experimenter showed pairs of white cards with black lines of varying lengths, such as those in Figure 15.4. The experimenters then asked the group which of the lines in (b) matched the test line in (a). The real participant was always seated last so that the confederates' judgments came first.

Sometimes the confederates gave the right answer, but on some trials they deliberately called out the wrong answer. On these trials, 37% of the answers given by the real participants who took part in the experiment were also incorrect. In other words, the participants conformed with the group's wrong judgment much of the time.

Only one out of four participants remained completely independent and did not conform at any time. Even those who displayed independence, however, experienced various kinds of conflict and anxiety—as is evident from Figure 15.5. Their later comments included these: "At times I had the feeling, to heck with it, I'll go along with the rest." "I felt disturbed, puzzled, separated, like an outcast from the

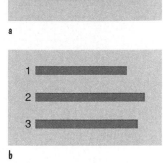

**FIGURE 15.4 Which line matches?** Which of the lines in (b) matches the line in (a)? The correct answer is line **2**. But the experimenter's six confederates at the table insisted unanimously that it was line 1—which is, in fact, the one least like the test line.

**FIGURE 15.5 An "independent" participant—shaken but unyielding.** In the first of these three scenes from the Asch experiment, student 6 is making his first independent judgment, disagreeing with the group's otherwise unanimous but incorrect verdict. His puzzlement and concern seem to increase until, preserving his independence despite the pressure from the group, he announces (at bottom), "I have to call them as I see them."

William Vandivert

rest." Thus, the urge to conform—to go along with the group—was strong, even among the most independent participants (Asch, 1956).

# Why We Conform

Why do we have a tendency to conform? Why is this tendency so powerful that it can sometimes make us behave in unexpected ways?

1. *Dependence on approval.* One reason seems to be that it is pleasant to win approval as an accepted, well-liked member of a group. It is highly unpleasant to be rejected by the group and perhaps even subjected to ridicule (Aronson, 1984). Thus, it is generally easier and more rewarding to conform—especially when we are members of a group in which there is unanimous agreement.

   It can be very difficult to stand alone as a sole dissenter in virtually any culture. In Japan, for example, the tendency to conform is even stronger than it is in the United States. Rebelling against peer values and experiencing the rejection of the group is more painful for Japanese adults than for adults in the United States (Azuma, 1982).

2. *Respect for authority and its symbols.* Another reason for conformity is the tendency we have as members of a group to accede to the requests or demands of those who appear to be in legitimate control. The tendency to respect authority develops early in life. For example, children will offer specific answers to obviously irrational questions such as "Is a cup sadder than an orange?" Instead of questioning the questioner, they respond, because the social situation is one in which it seems natural to comply (Pratt, 1990).

3. *The need for guidance.* Still another reason for conformity is that we need the help of other people in developing an accurate view of our physical and social environment. We cannot get through life successfully, and we may not even survive, if we do not understand ourselves and our world—and often other people are the only guide we have.

**Social comparison theory**
The theory that we often evaluate our own abilities, opinions, and behaviors by comparing ourselves with other people.

The need for guidance is the basis of an important psychological concept called **social comparison theory** (Festinger, 1954). Because we usually have no objective and scientific way to evaluate our abilities, our opinions, or the propriety of our actions, we judge ourselves by comparing ourselves with other people—often with friends or other people whom we consider to be similar to ourselves, but sometimes with strangers. The more uncertain we are of where we stand and how we should act, the more likely we are to make these comparisons. For example, if you go to a party where you are the only stranger, how can you fit in without seeing how the others act? On a new campus, how are you expected to dress, behave in the classroom, and get along with your fellow students?

Social comparison theory also holds that our search for guidance strongly influences our self-esteem—indeed, our entire self-image. According to the theory, we judge our abilities and our worth mostly by comparing ourselves with other people. We cannot determine whether we are good students, good teachers, or good athletes unless we compare our ability with another person's. Even children feel compelled to try to determine how they rank in comparison with their peers (Marsh & Parker, 1984). We also continually ask ourselves, "What do other people think of me?" Fear of rejection or ridicule is a strong force leading to increased conformity, which explains why peer pressure can be so powerful at times (Janes & Olson, 2000).

The opinions of other people play an important role in self-esteem. For dramatic evidence, consider the following experiment and its surprising results (Ross, Lepper, & Hubbard, 1975). The participants were women attending high school or college. They were asked to try their hand at a problem-solving task containing 25 items. After they had finished, the experimenters pretended to grade their attempts and then told them how they had scored. No grading was actually done, however. The experimenters simply told half the participants that they had done badly and the other half that they had done very well.

This false information about performance was allowed to "sink in" for a time. Then the experimenters flatly admitted their deception. The women were told that their scores had never actually been compiled and that there was no truth at all in the information that they had done badly or well. Once the truth was out, the women were asked to rate their own ability at that kind of problem solving, estimate how many problems they had in fact solved correctly, and predict how many they would solve correctly on a future trial. As shown in Figure 15.6, the results were startling. Apparently, the women who had been told that they did badly were never quite able to get over the loss of self-esteem they suffered—even though they knew that the unfavorable rating bore no relation to the facts and meant absolutely nothing. The women who had been told that they did well, on the other hand, were much more confident—even though they too knew that the information was meaningless. There could hardly be a more convincing demonstration of the way other people's opinions shape our own views—even of ourselves.

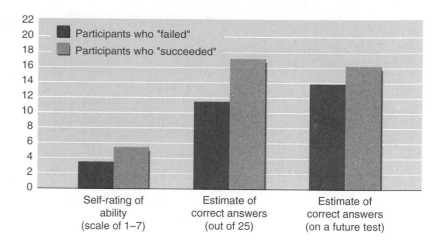

**FIGURE 15.6** It's not true—but I believe it! High school and college women who were told that they had failed at a problem-solving task had a significantly lower opinion of their ability than did those who were told that they had succeeded—even though both groups knew that the information about their performance had no relation to the facts.

*Ross, Lepper & Hubbard, 1975.*

## Compliance

In everyday life, we often comply with the requests of other people: "Would you please set the table?" "Do you mind not smoking here?" And we wonder how we can get other people to comply with our requests. Psychologist Robert Cialdini (1993) has conducted extensive studies of what he terms *compliance professionals*—people such as salespeople, lobbyists, advertisers, fundraisers, and others whose business or financial success depends on obtaining the compliance of others. He has identified a number of specific techniques that are often used to gain compliance. Among these are the foot-in-the-door, lowballing, and door-in-the-face techniques.

Perhaps the most familiar technique for inducing compliance is the *foot-in-the-door technique*. It involves getting the person to agree to a small initial request—such as accepting a free sample—and then making a larger request—such as making a purchase. The underlying principle is consistency: Once we have said yes to a small request, we are more likely to say yes to subsequent requests because refusing them would be inconsistent with our previous behavior.

Related to the foot-in-the-door technique is *lowballing*, in which a salesperson offers a customer a very good deal that is later changed to make it less advantageous. This technique is common among automobile dealers. The salesperson offers the customer a special price; the customer then test-drives the car and decides to buy it. But when the transaction is being finalized, it turns out that there was an "error" in the calculations or something was left out. The rational thing to do in such cases is to walk away from the deal; however, the tendency toward consistency leads many people to accept the less advantageous deal. As can readily be seen, both the foot-in-the-door technique and lowballing are based on commitment: Once we have made an initial commitment, it becomes more difficult to say no, even though the conditions that initially led us to say yes have been changed.

Another frequently used technique for inducing compliance is referred to as the *door-in-the-face,* or *rejection-then-retreat,* technique. It is essentially the reverse of the foot-in-the-door technique; it involves making a very large request, which is almost certain to be refused, and then following it up with a smaller request, which often produces compliance. In one experiment, Cialdini and colleagues asked college students if they would serve as unpaid counselors for juvenile delinquents 2 hours a week for the next 2 years. None of the students agreed to that request, but when the experimenters followed up by asking the same students if they would take a group of delinquents to the zoo for 2 hours, 50% of the students agreed. Less than 17% of the students in a control group agreed to this smaller request when it was not preceded by the larger one.

Knowledge of these techniques should be helpful the next time you're approached by a salesperson or find yourself in a situation that involves negotiation. In any such situation, it's helpful to keep your goals in mind and walk away from any "deal" that doesn't satisfy those goals.

## Obedience: "Just Following Orders"

Related to compliance is obedience, in which people follow the orders of individuals in positions of authority. As noted in Chapter 1, a famous series of experiments testing the limits of obedience was performed by Stanley Milgram and colleagues (e.g., see Milgram, 1963; also Milgram, 1992). Milgram's original experiments went as follows. Participants were supposedly randomly assigned to be the "teacher" in what they were led to believe was an important study of learning and memory; they were to deliver progressively stronger electric shocks whenever the "learner," in another room, made mistakes. (In reality, the learner was a confederate with a carefully scripted set of mistakes and responses, the true participant was always the teacher, and no shocks were administered.) The question was how high the teacher would go in administering shocks—via the console illustrated in Figure 15.7—when initially urged by a domineering experimenter and later commanded to continue. In the first experiment, 65% of the participants (all male) went all the way to the top level, marked XXX-Danger—even though the learner's script included complaining about the pain and, toward the end, not responding at all.

In subsequent experiments, comparable percentages were obtained with female and college student participants. But they did not do so casually. According to Milgram's description of their behavior, "profuse sweating, trembling, and stuttering were typical . . ." and some displayed "nervous laughter."

## When Independence Replaces Obedience

Is blind obedience the rule? Various observers have used Milgram's results to explain how so many "ordinary" people in Nazi Germany could have gone along with the terrible atrocities involved in the systematic murder of millions of innocent people. Although Adolf Hitler was a psychopathic monster, most of those who conducted the daily operations of the death camps were not. Social philosopher Hannah Arendt, who followed the trial of Adolf Eichmann, a Nazi war criminal ultimately executed for his crimes, claimed that Eichmann was a rather unremarkable man who simply saw himself as a cog in the bureaucratic wheel (Arendt, 1963).

The obedience displayed in the examples we have mentioned does not mean, of course, that all adults will inevitably behave in a similar fashion. Nearly two

**Test Yourself**

**(g)** You walk into a store with no plan to buy a scarf. But suddenly you notice people streaming to a counter where scarves are on sale—so you make a detour and buy one yourself. What form of social behavior are you demonstrating?

**(h)** If I am the kind of person who, without guidance, feels uncertain about what to do, what kind of behavior am I likely to display if requested to do a nasty task?

(The answers are on page 618.)

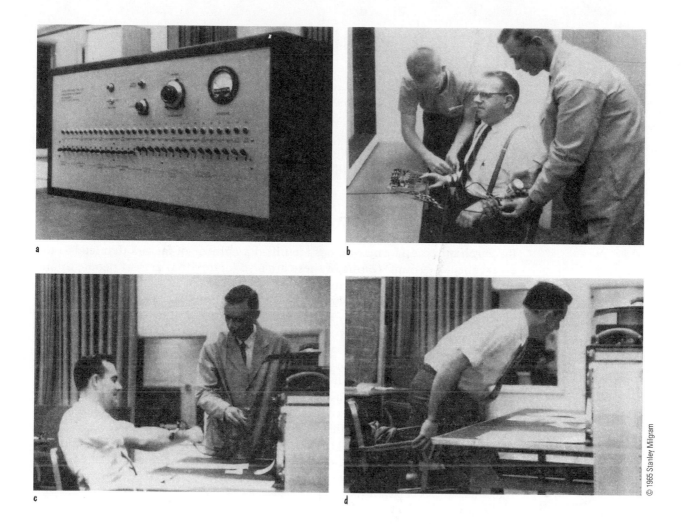

a

b

c

d

© 1965 Stanley Milgram

decades after Milgram's first experiments, a group of scientists conducted the following experiment: A group of participants, who lived in a working-class town in the Midwest, agreed to be videotaped as they discussed the merits of a legal case concerning a service station manager whose license had been revoked because of allegedly immoral behavior. After the coordinator of the experiment had asked a few members of the group to argue as if they were offended by the service station manager's behavior, he requested that all the participants sign an affidavit giving the service station the right to introduce the tapes of the group discussion as evidence in court. Several of the participants reacted with anger and rebellion (Gamson, Fireman, & Rytina, 1982). The contrast with Milgram's earlier results was probably due to at least two factors. First, changes in U.S. society have encouraged a more distrustful attitude toward authority than existed when Milgram conducted his experiments. Second, in this case there was ample opportunity for group discussion about whether the request being made was fair.

It is important to note that people do not always blindly obey authority, despite strong pressures to do so. Various factors affect the tendency to obey (Taylor, Peplau, & Sears, 2000): (1) We are less likely to obey if we are directly causing and witnessing the suffering of others. (2) If we feel personally responsible for our actions, we are less likely to obey something that we oppose. (3) If we see others disobey, we are more likely to disobey ourselves. (4) We are less likely to follow orders if we have been encouraged to question the motives, expertise, or judgment of those in authority.

**FIGURE 15.7** Following orders—a high price to pay. Photo (a) shows the panel used in the Milgram experiment, which participants believed controlled the level of shock. In photo (b), electrodes are being attached to the wrists of a "learner." In photo (c), a participant who will be at the control panel receives a sample shock of the kind he believes he will administer. In photo (d), a participant breaks off the experiment after reaching as high a shock level as he is willing to administer.

# GROUP DYNAMICS

**FOCUS QUESTIONS**

- What factors lead to the emergence of groups?

- How do groups influence the behavior of their members?

People's behavior often changes when they find themselves in groups—sometimes for the better, sometimes for the worse. To understand what factors are operating in group contexts, social psychologists devote a great deal of study to the area of research known as *group dynamics*. In this section, we look at some of the main findings of that research.

## How Do Groups Form?

Research on group formation has identified a number of factors that lead to the emergence of groups. (Some of these are also factors that attract people to one another, as discussed later in the chapter.)

Among the most prominent of these is *proximity:* People who live near one another or work together may develop into a cohesive group simply because they interact regularly and are concerned with the same issues, such as the safety of children in the neighborhood or shared tasks on the job. *Similarity* is another important factor: People who are similar in some way, such as gender or cultural background, are more likely to form groups. This is true also of people with similar religious, political, or philosophical beliefs.

*Shared interests* are another basis for group formation. These may range from recreational activities to political campaigns. Groups form around a wide variety of interests—just think of all the different kinds of groups you and people you know belong to. Of course, shared interests overlap with the factors mentioned earlier; people who are similar in other ways are also more likely to have shared interests.

## How Do Groups Influence Behavior?

We saw in the preceding section that people tend to want to conform to the opinions of others. This desire for conformity is a strong influence on the behavior of people in groups. However, the presence of other people has a number of other, more subtle effects on behavior as well.

**Social Facilitation and Social Impairment**  Have you ever noticed how your performance of various activities improves when you have an audience? You may run faster, play a musical instrument better, work more efficiently, and so on. Many researchers have found that behaviors can be facilitated by the presence of other people. Social psychologists call this effect *social facilitation.* They believe that it results from the increased arousal (tension, excitement) that occurs when we are aware that others are watching (Zajonc & Sales, 1966). The presence of an audience also appears to motivate individuals to perform well and make a good impression.

More recent research indicates that cognitive processes are also involved. One theory, known as distraction-conflict theory, holds that when an audience is present, performers must divide their attention between the audience and the task. This threatens to produce cognitive overload, causing the performer to focus more closely on the demands of the task and thus to perform better (Baron, 1986).

But there are also times when we don't perform as well before an audience as we do when alone—a phenomenon that many readers may remember from the days of the dreaded piano recital or its equivalent. This phenomenon, known as

Performance can be either improved or impaired by the presence of an audience.

*social impairment,* appears to result from overly high levels of arousal and motivation. Social impairment is more likely to occur when the behavior in question is relatively unfamiliar or complex. Thus, an accomplished musician may perform better in front of an audience, but someone who is just learning to play an instrument may do better alone.

**Diffusion of Responsibility**   Another effect of the presence of other people—discussed more fully in the next section—is *diffusion of responsibility*. This phenomenon occurs in groups of all sizes but is especially likely in relatively large groups. If you're the only person in a situation, the responsibility for any action necessary is yours alone. The more other people are present, the more the responsibility is shared. Diffusion of responsibility explains a great deal of what happens in work groups, committees, juries, and other groups that must make decisions and carry out related tasks. It also plays a role in mob violence, as we will see shortly.

Diffusion of responsibility is involved in a common behavior known as *social loafing*. Because the individual feels less responsible in a group, he or she is less inclined to act and will let others do most of the work. Moreover, the larger the group, the less likely it is that any given member—other than the group's leaders—will be involved in decision making. You can see this phenomenon at work in your college classes: The larger the class, the less likely it is that any given student will ask questions or participate in discussions. Interestingly, social loafing does not seem to occur in collectivist cultures, which value the well-being of the group over that of the individual (Earley, 1993; P. B. Smith & Bond, 1999). In such cultures, people seem to work harder in groups than alone.

Sometimes the diffusion of responsibility that occurs in large groups leads to a phenomenon known as *deindividuation*. In a crowd, individuals may lose a sense of personal identity. In the midst of a noisy, hysterical mob, they may become highly aroused and may engage in behaviors that they otherwise would never consider, such as vandalism, looting, and even violence. Afterwards, they return to normal, although they may experience feelings of guilt about their unrestrained behavior.

Also related to diffusion of responsibility is **groupthink,** in which the attitudes of individuals yield to those of the group as a whole (Janis, 1982). Groupthink is most common in cohesive, task-oriented groups and results from pressures to

**Groupthink**
A condition in which the attitudes of individuals yield to those of the group as a whole.

conform, as described earlier. In an effort to reach consensus, individual members may set aside their own opinions and go along with those of the group, even if they privately disagree quite strongly with the group's decisions. A famous example is the decision-making that led to President Kennedy's failed invasion of the Bay of Pigs in Cuba. Although several members of the President's national security team felt that the invasion was ill-advised, they were unwilling to express views that differed from those of the group as a whole. Groupthink apparently led to the conviction that the group couldn't possibly be wrong.

**Group polarization**
A condition in which a group makes more extreme decisions and takes more risks than its members would if they were acting alone.

**Group polarization** may also occur when responsibility is diffused among group members. Group polarization overlaps with groupthink, but its focus is on the actions of the group as a whole. Because no individual member is responsible for the group's actions, the group may make more extreme decisions and take more risks than its members would if they were acting alone. Committees, juries, and other decision-making groups are subject to group polarization. A committee, for example, might allocate more funds to a risky venture than individual members might if they were making the decision on their own.

# INTERPERSONAL BEHAVIOR: AGGRESSION AND PROSOCIAL BEHAVIOR

**FOCUS QUESTIONS**
- What factors contribute to aggressive behavior?
- What factors attract us to other people and make us like them?
- How is implicit personality theory related to the importance of first impressions?
- Why do some loving relationships endure for a lifetime while others do not?

In November 1990, a Brooklyn mother and member of an Orthodox Jewish community that abhors violence was arrested for the murder of her 8-year-old son. He had died on Yom Kippur day of assorted head injuries and broken bones inflicted at her hands after months, perhaps years, of suffering.

In January 1982, just after an Air Florida jet crashed into the 14th Street Bridge in Washington, D.C., Arland Williams, Jr. jumped into the icy Potomac River, where he stayed afloat until he caught a rope cast from a hovering helicopter and delivered it to at least three survivors. Williams died before he himself could be rescued.

These two episodes highlight one of the many questions about social behavior that continue to puzzle psychologists. It has to do with the basic quality of human nature (see also Chapter 9). Are humans naturally aggressive and cruel, as crime statistics, episodes of terrorism, and warfare might indicate? Or are they basically kind and helpful, as countless stories of self-sacrifice seem to say? Are people essentially selfish and mean, as newspapers and television stories so often suggest? Or are they basically nurturing and loving, as the humanistic psychologists have maintained?

In the past, such questions were answered through philosophical speculation and casual observation rather than scientific evidence. But psychologists are continually learning more about why people sometimes treat others with great kindness and generosity and sometimes treat others with apparent disregard for their well-being and even survival. They are also learning how we develop special connections of attraction and love with various individuals who cross our lives.

## The Faces of Aggression

**Aggression**
Any action that is intended to hurt others.

Psychologists usually define **aggression** as any action that is intended to hurt others. However, we can make a further distinction between hostile aggression and instrumental aggression. **Hostile aggression** is specifically intended to inflict some kind of harm on the victim. **Instrumental aggression** may also inflict harm, but its primary goal is not to harm the victim but to attain some other objective, such as money or drugs—or, for children, perhaps simply a toy in the possession of another child.

The clearest example of hostile aggression is the kind of aggressive behavior that overtly inflicts physical harm and is a major concern of society—for example, murder, rape, or child abuse. Even more common, however, are acts that are intended to hurt another person yet on the surface do not appear to do so. A husband or wife, for example, may initiate an affair that does not seem to constitute an aggressive act but actually is intended to hurt an indifferent or rejecting spouse. The hurt is psychological rather than physical, but nonetheless painful.

In contrast, some behaviors are clearly harmful to others even though the intention to inflict harm is absent. Thus, a football lineman viciously tackles the opposing team's quarterback and breaks his leg. Or, in a competitive office atmosphere, an achievement-oriented staff member works hard to impress the boss—and ends up replacing a colleague in the company hierarchy.

Many behaviors that end up hurting another person fall into a borderline area between those that clearly are intentional and those that clearly are not. Indeed, often we can know the true nature of an act only by knowing its full context. The coach who practices "tough love" with a ball team and the schoolyard bully who taunts younger children are both behaving in ways that look aggressive from the outside, but the context of one is prosocial and that of the other antisocial. Moreover, certain aggressive acts are sanctioned by some societies—for example, shooting a hostage-holding terrorist or escorting a murderer to the gas chamber. Examples of the remarkable variety of aggressive behaviors are displayed in Table 15.1.

**Hostile aggression**
Aggression that is specifically intended to inflict some kind of harm on the victim.

**Instrumental aggression**
Aggression whose primary goal is not to harm the victim but to attain some other objective, such as money.

---

**TABLE 15.1**
## Which of These Constitute Aggression?

- A soldier shoots an enemy at the front line.
- The warden of a prison executes a convicted criminal.
- A juvenile gang attacks members of another gang.
- Two men fight for a piece of bread.
- A man viciously kicks a cat.
- A man, while cleaning a window, knocks over a flower pot, which, in falling, injures a pedestrian.
- A girl kicks a wastebasket.
- Mr. X, a notorious gossip, speaks disparagingly of many people of his acquaintance.
- A man mentally rehearses a murder he is about to commit.
- An angry son purposely fails to write to his mother, who is expecting a letter and will be hurt if none arrives.
- A woman daydreams of harming her antagonist but has no hope of doing so.
- A senator does not protest the escalation of bombing to which she is morally opposed.
- A farmer beheads a chicken and prepares it for supper.
- A hunter kills an animal and mounts it as a trophy.
- A physician gives a flu shot to a screaming child.
- A boxer gives his opponent a bloody nose.
- A girl scout tries to assist an elderly woman but trips her by accident.
- A bank robber is shot in the back while trying to escape.
- A tennis player smashes her racket after missing a volley.
- A person commits suicide.

*After Benjamin, 1985.*

A creature from outer space, without knowledge of our society, would have difficulty telling which of these examples constituted aggression. An important criterion is intent.

An important experiment that revealed a great deal about aggressive tendencies was actually designed to study the power of situations in determining people's behavior. Philip Zimbardo and colleagues created a simulated prison, complete with cells and solitary confinement units, in the basement of a building at Stanford University. They then advertised for volunteers to participate in a 2-week study of prison life. Once they had selected the participants—24 students—they divided them randomly into two groups: "guards" and "prisoners." The "prisoners" were "arrested" and confined in the cells. The "guards" were given uniforms, handcuffs, and nightsticks. Neither group received any specific training.

The goal of the experiment was to determine how the participants would behave, given their conceptions of the roles assigned to them. After only 6 days, however, the experiment had to be canceled. Not only were participants in both groups performing their assigned roles, but they were no longer distinguishing between the experiment and reality. The guards began abusing the prisoners, withholding food and subjecting them to arbitrary punishments and hard labor. Their attitudes became increasingly aggressive; they were clearly enjoying their power over the "unruly and uncooperative" prisoners. The prisoners were rebellious at first, but they soon became demoralized and subservient. One became severely depressed. The researchers, shocked at what was occurring, terminated the experiment, commenting that "human values were suspended, self-concepts were challenged, and the ugliest, most base, pathological side of human nature surfaced" (Zimbardo, 1972).

This experiment was a target of harsh criticism on ethical grounds, and the researchers acknowledged that the participants had been subjected to pain and humiliation—which led to the cancelation of the experiment. However, in a recent article reflecting on their experience, they point out that such behavior could arise in many similar situations. As they note, "The negative, anti-social reactions observed were not the product of an environment created by combining a collection of deviant personalities, but rather the result of an intrinsically pathological situation which could distort and rechannel the behaviour of essentially normal individuals" (Haney & Zimbardo, 1998).

## The Origins of Aggression: Innate or Learned?

Although some theorists believe that aggressive tendencies are innate in humans as well as other animals, social psychologists tend to believe otherwise. They have concluded that, though it may have some basis in biological inheritance, human aggression is largely the result of learning and can be controlled. As Bandura's experiment, described in Chapter 1, demonstrated, children tend to imitate the aggressive behavior they observe. This is true even if the behavior occurs on television (Turner, Hesse, & Peterson-Lewis, 1986). In fact, the issue of whether exposure to media violence increases aggression among children and adults has been an important subject of social-psychological research for decades. The bulk of the evidence now strongly suggests that exposure to media violence does indeed contribute to high levels of violence in countries where large numbers of people view such violence (e.g., Anderson, 1997; Berkowitz, 1993; Paik & Comstock, 1994).

Similarly, it has been shown that people are more likely to accept and even practice aggression directed toward women after viewing pornographic materials depicting violent acts directed toward women (Donnerstein, Linz, & Penrod, 1987). Even a physically uncomfortable environment—crowded, loud, hot—apparently can elicit aggressive behavior (Anderson, 1989; Geen, 1976). An example of this phenomenon can be seen in Figure 15.8.

There is also evidence that many aggressive people come from aggressive families and were punished severely for childhood misconduct. They may be imitating the behavior of their parents, even though it was once painful to them. Others seem somehow to have learned from experience that aggression serves in some way to bring rewards, social and otherwise. Having used it successfully on one occasion, they may adopt it as a way of life.

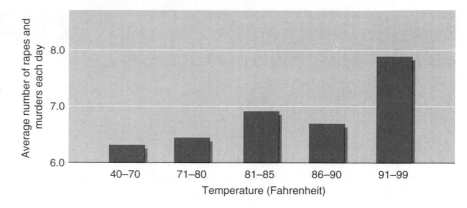

Another view of aggression is the *frustration-aggression hypothesis* (Dollard, Doob, Miller, Mowrer, & Sears, 1939). Some theorists argue that aggression results from frustration. When a person has a need that is not fulfilled, he or she becomes frustrated, and often the frustration is vented in aggressive behavior. The strength of the needs or wishes that are thwarted determines the amount of frustration the person experiences, and this in turn determines the degree of aggression expressed. This hypothesis is a popular explanation of violent behavior (Berkowitz, 1993, 2001); however, it doesn't explain why frustration leads to aggression in some cases and in some individuals, but not in others (Barker, Dembo, & Lewin, 1943). More recently, Leonard Berkowitz (1990) has proposed a more cognitive explanation, in which negative feelings tend to activate ideas, memories, and expressive reactions associated with anger and aggression. Further thought can then either intensify or suppress the initial reactions; intensification can lead to aggressive behavior.

**FIGURE 15.8 Violence and the weather.** In Houston between 1980 and 1982, more rapes and murders were committed on days when the temperature reached or exceeded 91 degrees Fahrenheit.
*Anderson & Anderson, 1984.*

## The Nature of Caring: Studies of Altruism

Social scientists use the term **altruism** to describe behavior that is kind, generous, and helpful to others. We don't hear about cases of altruism as often as we hear about cases of violence and aggression, but they take place with great frequency. People go to considerable trouble to help a sick neighbor, take in a family left homeless by a fire, or serve as volunteer firefighters and hospital attendants. And the amount of money donated to charities each year is staggering.

As in the case of aggression, some scientists see in the behavior of animals indications of a hereditary basis for altruism. Chimpanzees, for example, have been observed to share their food with another hungry chimpanzee in an adjoining cage—though they do so somewhat grudgingly (Nissen & Crawford, 1936). Many other animal studies have also produced evidence of an altruistic concern for others.

Some scientists maintain that altruism is an innate trait that has been passed along through the process of evolution. They point out that humans have always had a better chance of survival when living with other people than when trying to make it alone. So it seems likely that those who were willing to cooperate with others had a better chance of surviving and passing along their characteristics to future generations. The belief that altruism is an innate trait is somewhat strengthened by studies indicating that many children show strong tendencies to perform altruistic acts as early as the second year of life. Researchers have observed even 18-month-olds giving up food when someone around them is hungry, trying to come to the rescue of victims, consoling adults in distress, and expressing genuine anguish over another child's sorrow (Zahn-Waxler, Radke-Yarrow, & King, 1983).

Other psychologists believe that the explanation lies not in heredity but in learning. They point out that there are wide individual differences in tendencies toward altruism. Many studies have shown that the people who are most likely to be altruistic are those who have learned to experience **empathy**—the ability to feel the mental and emotional states of another person as if they were one's own.

**Altruism**
Any behavior that is kind, generous, and helpful to others.

**Empathy**
The ability to feel the mental and emotional states of another person as if they were one's own.

## PSYCHOLOGY AND THE MEDIA

## Compassionate Kids

 Contrary to past popular and professional "wisdom," children apparently begin life not as totally selfish creatures, but with a readiness to extend themselves to others in need. What can we do to encourage this potentially positive side of a child's nature? Studies by psychologists suggest five approaches.

1. It's important for parents to let children know how deeply they feel about their behavior toward others. Theoretical discussions about kindness are not as likely to encourage altruism as is evidence of its importance. The effective approach, researchers conclude, is not calmly dispensed reasoning as much as emotional and forceful displays of how much stock we put in being kind to others.

2. Fostering altruism requires also that parents convey the reasons for the importance they place on helping rather than hurting others—at a level appropriate to the child's language skills and understanding. Passion must be accompanied by persuasion. This means taking the time to explain—with intensity and clarity—the potent consequences our behavior can have on the lives of those around us.

3. Children need to be exposed to models of altruistic behavior. Where there is a contrast between the admonitions of parents and their actions ("Do as I say, not as I do"), children will model themselves on the living examples they observe rather than the words they hear. Observational learning works where altruistic behavior is concerned. Indeed, there is evidence that youngsters tend to emulate models of caring, sharing, and comforting behavior even when they observe them only on TV rather than in person.

4. It's essential to reinforce caring behavior. Parents should be on the lookout for signs of children's altruism and other prosocial behavior—and when they see them, recognize and reward them. Even a generally self-involved child will on occasion act with a surprising degree of consideration for others. An adult's task is to spot the child in the performance of an altruistic deed and then to reinforce it—with praise or, for a very young child, tangible rewards.

5. It's important to build a bridge of caring between parent and child. A child's altruistic enthusiasm may well depend on a solid and nurturing bond with caregivers. The nurturance offered by parents to their children is itself a solid model. When children are the beneficiaries of our own acts of caring—assistance when they are in need, compassion when they are in pain, forbearance in the face of their mistakes—they are likely to behave in the same way toward others.

*Source: Adapted from Segal & Segal, 1988.*

The ability to interpret the psychological states of others and to experience them emotionally appears to emerge as early as the second year of life (Zahn-Waxler & Radke-Yarrow, 1990). Having altruistic parents or other models to imitate and identify with also appears to encourage the development of altruism (Barnett, Howard, King, & Dino, 1980). Whether altruism is or is not a basic and innate human trait, there seems to be little doubt that it can be encouraged or discouraged by learning and by social influences (Radke-Yarrow, 1989). This topic is discussed in Psychology and the Media above.

## When No One Cares: Bystander Apathy

In March 1991, a man raped his 3-year-old niece about 25 feet from the highway during rush hour. According to reports, dozens of people watched the attack without intervening. In an earlier, more famous incident, a young woman named Kitty Genovese was attacked on a dark street by a stalker who stabbed and raped her. Many neighbors heard her screams for help, but none called the police until 30 minutes after the attack began—and after the attacker had temporarily retreated and then returned to attack again.

Why do people sometimes help others who are in trouble but sometimes completely ignore them, exhibiting a remarkable degree of what social psychologists term **bystander apathy?** Experiments show a close relationship between the number of people who witness an incident—such as a murder, a theft, or a fire—and the likelihood that an individual will offer assistance. Kitty Genovese and the 3-year-old girl may have been victims because, contrary to popular belief, there is not always safety in numbers. Experiments repeatedly have shown that a person who needs assistance is more likely to receive it if there is only one person around than if there are several or many (Latané & Nida, 1981). Various explanations have been suggested. First, the presence of others may relieve any single member of the group from feelings of personal responsibility. Second, apparent indifference on the part of other spectators may cause the individual bystander to downgrade the seriousness of the situation. In some cases, bystander apathy may even represent a type of conformity. If a group of people seem to be ignoring the plight of a person in need, individual members may feel strong pressure to behave the way the rest of the group is behaving. Finally, there's the possibility of *pluralistic ignorance:* If no one else is doing anything to help, maybe help isn't warranted.

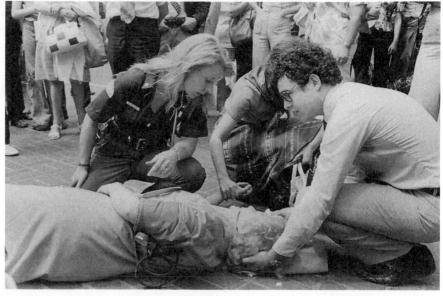

A person is much more likely to help someone in need if no one else is available to do so.

**Bystander apathy**
The tendency of people, especially under crowded conditions, to ignore others who need help or situations that call for action.

Studies also show that people who need help are more likely to receive it in a small town than in a big city (Amato, 1981). In a city, people can walk for blocks without meeting anyone they know. They are mere faces in the crowd. They do not have the intimate contact with friends and neighbors that might lead to offers of help. Figure 15.9 shows that the likelihood of getting help appears to be twice as high in a small town as in a large metropolis. The graph reflects the percentage of passersby who offered to help the investigator after he collapsed in the street, pretending to be in pain. His leg was bandaged and smeared with realistic-looking "blood." Note that the percentage of helpers drops sharply as the community size increases beyond 20,000. The same pattern emerged when the investigator asked for other kinds of help—for example, for a charitable donation or for directions when "lost" (Amato, 1983).

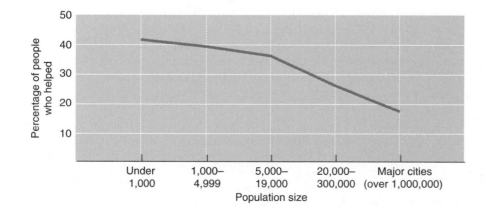

**FIGURE 15.9 Helping behavior in communities of different sizes.** This graph shows the percentages of passersby in communities of different sizes who offered to help the investigator.
*Amato, 1983.*

Any increase in the degree of intimacy serves to reduce bystander apathy. Indeed, the size of the group makes little difference when its members know each other and have a sense of group cohesiveness (Rutkowski, Gruder, & Romer, 1983). We are also more likely to empathize with strangers whom we believe to be similar to ourselves (Rushton, Russell, & Wells, 1984).

Bystander apathy is also reduced when group members merely anticipate having to interact with each other in the future (Gottlieb & Carver, 1980). This anticipation of face-to-face interaction with other bystanders may increase the possibility of being blamed for inaction. Or perhaps the expectation of future interaction induces some degree of group cohesiveness, thus enhancing members' compliance with social norms.

## Interpersonal Attraction: What Draws Us Together?

Granted that other people influence our behavior, another question arises: What determines the kinds of people who influence us most? In particular, in a diverse society, why do we become members of one group and not another? And what is the basis of the special connections we build with specific individuals?

It is, of course, the people around us—those with whom we have our closest and most frequent social relationships—who have the greatest impact on our attitudes and our behavior. Therefore, social psychologists have studied the forces that attract us to others and make us like them and associate with them. The key finding has been aptly summarized in a single sentence: "We like those who reward us, and the more they reward us the better we like them" (Berscheid & Walster, 1974). But fully understanding that sentence requires an examination of what it is that we find rewarding about other people—and why. The following are some of the factors that appear to be important.

**Proximity**
**Physical nearness (a characteristic of attraction).**

**Proximity**    Some social psychologists have concluded that **proximity**, or physical nearness, is the most powerful factor in determining who our associates will be. For example, relatively early studies conducted in college dormitories revealed that after a year of school, roommates were twice as likely as floormates to be friends. Moreover, floormates were twice as likely as residents elsewhere in the dorm to be friends (Priest & Sawyer, 1967).

**Familiarity**
**Exposure to or knowledge concerning a person or situation (a characteristic of attraction).**

**Familiarity**    The power of proximity in fostering social relationships is, of course, due partly to sheer accessibility. One experiment on the effect of such **familiarity** brought together pairs of participants who did not know each other. They did not speak but merely sat across from each other in the laboratory. Some pairs saw each other on only a few occasions, others as many as a dozen times. Afterward, they were asked how much they liked each other. The more often they had been together—even in this casual fashion—the greater the mutual attraction was (Freedman et al., 1970). The process applies to things as well as people. Researchers have shown, for example, that individuals who are repeatedly exposed to unfamiliar items—nonsense syllables, novel music or geometric patterns, human faces—experience an increased liking for them (Moreland & Zajonc, 1982; Zajonc, 1989). This phenomenon has been aptly named the **mere exposure effect.**

**Mere exposure effect**
**The phenomenon whereby repeated exposure to people or things increases one's liking for them.**

**Similarity**
**Perceived likeness (a characteristic of attraction).**

**Similarity**    Still another important factor in interpersonal attraction is **similarity**. Given the opportunity, and all other things being equal, we tend to be attracted to people who are like us—or at least whom we perceive to be similar to us. Spouses who enjoy similar interests and activities encounter less conflict and remain closer to each other than spouses who are dissimilar in such respects (Caspi & Herbener, 1989). Moreover, we tend to seek out as friends those whom we perceive to be comparable to ourselves in physical attractiveness. A study of a video dating service found that men and women alike were prone to hook up with a person who resembled them in physical attractiveness (Foulkes, 1982).

**Reciprocity**    When we believe someone is fond of us, we react with greater warmth—which, in turn, causes the person to react even more positively (Curtis & Miller, 1986). This process of **reciprocity** appears to be circular—almost in the manner of a self-fulfilling prophecy.

**Reciprocity**
A circular process whereby a positive reaction toward a person causes that person to react positively in return.

**Physical Attractiveness**    In actual fact, physical attractiveness is more influential than most people care to admit. We tend to be "turned off" by people whose appearance—especially the face—we find unattractive (Langlois et al., 2000; Mueser, Grau, Sussman, & Rosen, 1984). Even children judge one another on the basis of appearance. As early as the nursery school years, the attractive boys are the most popular, the unattractive ones the least popular (Dion & Berscheid, 1972). Later, as college students, attractive young men continue to enjoy more social interactions (Reis, Wheeler, Kernis, Nezlek, & Perri, 1982). However, it is always important to remember that, although all cultures have definitions of what constitutes physical attractiveness, the definitions themselves vary considerably.

## The Staying Power of First Impressions

Why is physical attractiveness so influential? One reason seems to be that it is immediately and obviously apparent. When we meet someone for the first time, we can only guess whether that person is similar to us in attitudes, interests, and tastes. We have no clear clues about her or his competence. We can see at a glance, however, how well the person meets our own standards of attractiveness—and thus move toward acceptance or rejection.

**First impressions** have a strong and lasting influence. If we like people from the start, even if it's just because of their physical appearance, we tend to keep on liking them—no matter if some of their subsequent behavior is objectionable. If we dislike them at the start, we are likely to continue to dislike them—even if their subsequent behavior is above reproach.

**First impressions**
Our initial reactions to a person.

In one study, the participants were 48 pairs of college roommates, all of whom were previously unacquainted. At the end of the year, some of the students decided not to live together any more and others remained roommates. Whatever the decision, however, it turned out to have been made early in the relationship (Berg, 1984). Evidently, for those who decided to part ways, the effects of bad first impressions outweighed those of familiarity.

Why are first impressions of people so strong and long lasting? Social psychologists say it is because we carry around a sort of working theory about people and their personalities. We have concluded that certain personality traits generally go together—in much the same way that characteristics associated with schemas cluster together. If something convinces us at the start that a new acquaintance is "cold," for example, we might automatically assume that this person is also irritable, humorless, unsociable, and self-centered. But if we perceive the new acquaintance as "warm," we might expect this warmth to be accompanied by a good disposition, a sense of humor, friendliness, and generosity. This belief that personality traits come in clusters is called an **implicit personality theory**. All of us seem to hold such a theory, without being aware of it (Schneider, 1973).

**Implicit personality theory**
The belief that certain personality traits are correlated with others—for example, that "warmth" of personality is associated with sociability and good humor.

Not all physically attractive people, of course, are admirable in every other respect—and the theory that desirable traits always come in clusters can lead us astray in other ways as well. For one thing, it inclines us to think of people as more consistent than they really are. But our theory has been developed through experience and is probably right more often than wrong. Either way, it is one of the heuristics (see Chapter 6) that we use in conducting the social relationships that are such an important part of our lives.

## The Elusive Nature of Love

For many years, social psychologists avoided focusing on the subject of love, believing that the phenomenon was too difficult to define and analyze scientifically. But in recent years, they have attempted to deal with this complex topic, which is usually reserved for poets, novelists, and philosophers and is subject to each person's perhaps unique interpretation.

As we know from our own lives, not everyone experiences love in the same way. Much of psychology's effort therefore has been devoted to attempts to describe various facets of a loving relationship. One meaningful distinction that has emerged is the one between passionate love and companionate love.

**Passionate love** has been portrayed as "a wildly emotional state" in which "tender and sexual feelings, elation and pain, anxiety and relief, altruism and jealousy coexist in a confusion of feelings" (Berscheid & Walster, 1974). In such a state of love, emotions run high—fueled by physiological arousal that originates, for example, in sexual longing, fear of rejection, or the anger of a quarrel (Sears, Peplau, & Taylor, 1988). In the view of some observers, the origins of passionate love lie in our biological nature, ensuring that we will unite, reproduce, and remain attached to one another (Buss, 1988). Others argue that such an orientation to love is hardly the rule in all societies—especially those characterized by communal living (Dion & Dion, 1988).

**Companionate love,** in contrast, is emotionally more tranquil and not necessarily accompanied by strong sexual feelings; it more typically produces a sense of stability (Brehm, 1985). Among its characteristics are feelings of affection rather than passion, of trust rather than turmoil (Hatfield, 1988). In contrast to passionate love, companionate love is viewed as the basis for enduring relationships. It is less likely to sizzle for a while and then fade.

Most psychologists would contend that the distinction just described hardly exhausts the varieties of love we experience. They have attempted to make finer distinctions. Basing their study on 1,300 college students, one team of investigators identified six styles of love, which are described in Table 15.2. Perhaps human expressions of love are so varied simply because they mirror the remarkable range of differences in human personality. Moreover, it seems clear that an individual's style of love may vary over the life span. Like other aspects of our social interactions, our expressions of love are marked by diversity and change.

Robert Sternberg (1999a) has devoted considerable study to the factors that cause love to last—or not to last—over time. Focusing on intimate relationships, particularly marriages, he has identified three factors that play a role in maintaining love: passion, intimacy, and commitment.

**Passionate love**
An intense emotional state in which tender and sexual feelings, elation, altruism, and jealousy coexist.

**Companionate love**
An emotionally tranquil state of affection that produces a sense of stability.

In most lasting relationships, passion tends to diminish while intimacy and commitment increase.

© Creatas/Creatas/PictureQuest

**TABLE 15.2**
**Varieties of Love**

| Love Style | Characteristic |
|---|---|
| Passionate | Early attraction and intense emotion: "I feel that my lover and I were meant for each other." |
| Game-playing | A sport to be played out with different partners: "I have sometimes had to keep two of my lovers from finding out about each other." |
| Friendship | A blurring of the borders between platonic and emotional relationships: "I did not realize that I was in love until I actually had been for some time." |
| Pragmatic | Calculation in a rational, shopping-list fashion of the desired attributes of a partner: "One consideration in choosing a partner is how he/she will reflect on my career." |
| Possessive | A feeling of uncertainty about oneself and one's lover: "When things aren't right with my lover and me, my stomach gets upset." |
| All-giving | A view of love as yielding and nondemanding: "I would rather suffer myself than let my lover suffer." |

*Hendrick & Hendrick, 1986.*

Six styles of love are differentiated here, along with typical test items (answered "yes" or "no") used by researchers to define and measure them. Women scored higher on friendship love and possessive love, while men scored higher on game-playing love.

For many couples, it's difficult to maintain the early passion as the relationship develops. Passion consists largely of physical attraction and sexuality. For the relationship to last, intimacy and commitment must be present as well. Intimacy is a sense that each partner can reveal his or her innermost feelings to the other, even as those feelings change. Commitment is a sense that each partner is permanently devoted to the other.

The most complete love—perhaps "true love"—includes all three of these components, but the level of each changes over time. Over the course of the relationship, the level of passion decreases, but intimacy develops steadily as the partners share their experiences and values. Gradually, commitment increases as well. Thus, for a relationship to last, the couple must not get so caught up in their initial passion that they fail to develop as individuals; this can cause major problems later as their passion fades. On the other hand, commitment by itself is not enough to sustain a long-term relationship. At least some degree of passion and intimacy is necessary for the relationship to be meaningful and satisfying to both partners.

# EPILOGUE

And there you have it, an introduction to psychology past and present. Human beings are social, communicating creatures, and we all have much in common. We are also individuals, with a unique genetic makeup and unique experiences that in turn are markedly influenced by our society and culture. Some things we're born with, some things not. We think of ourselves and others in terms of intelligence and personality characteristics. We define what is normal and what isn't, and we pursue ways of fixing what isn't in the hope of making life better for everyone. We worry about motives; we try to assess them in ourselves and in others. We try to cope with the life that we ourselves, as a species, define to a major extent—for ourselves and for all other species.

**Test Yourself**

**(i)** What important information do we often lack when we try to decide whether an act is aggressive simply by observing an individual's behavior?

**(j)** You are walking with a friend who says, "That person seems to be in some kind of trouble. Let's stand here and see what happens." What term do social psychologists use to describe such behavior?

**(k)** You have just met someone new who appears unkempt—so you believe that this person is also disorganized in his work, forgetful, and unreliable. What do psychologists call this view of personality?

**(l)** A friend tells you, "I'm tired of these intense relationships. I'm ready for the kind of love that's less heated—but lasts." What two types of love does your friend seem to be contrasting?

(The answers are on page 618.)

Like all living creatures, we are fundamentally biological, with physical needs and growth. We develop. The first thing we remember is that we were wide-eyed children. Then we start accumulating memories and knowledge and understanding and wisdom, which we spend a lifetime doing—if we continue to pay attention and think. We see and hear, interpret, respond, feel, remember, forget, and try to make sense of it all.

Then we pass it on to the next generation, for better or for worse. It is your authors' sincere hope that what you have learned in this textbook and what you pass on will be for the better.

We think it will be.

# Chapter 15 Summary

## Social Cognition: Schemas and Attitudes

1. Schemas are cognitive structures that help us perceive, organize, process, and use information.

2. An important set of schemas consists of strong, deeply ingrained opinions and feelings known as *attitudes*. We are very much "for" things toward which we have a positive attitude and very much "against" things toward which we have a negative attitude.

3. Two major forces play a role in the formation of attitudes: *socialization*, the way children are integrated into the society through teaching by parents, teachers, and others, and *enculturation*, the process by which we absorb the norms and values of our culture.

4. Attitudes, though powerful, are not necessarily consistent or based on evidence. Two kinds of attitudes that often contradict fact are *prejudices* (for example, against ethnic groups or religions) and *stereotypes*, which assume that all members of a certain group behave in the same manner.

5. One explanation for attitude change is the theory of *cognitive dissonance*, which maintains that we have a strong desire to preserve agreement and harmony between our attitudes and our behavior. When there is a conflict—caused by factual information, the arousal of emotions, or circumstances that push us into different behavior—we experience cognitive dissonance and may relieve it by changing our attitude.

6. Attempts by other people to change our attitudes, either by transmitting information or by making emotional appeals, are called *persuasive communications*.

7. The effectiveness of persuasive communications is affected by *selective exposure*—most such communications reach only people who are already persuaded. Effectiveness also depends on the credibility of the source, the nature of the medium, the nature of the communication, and the audience or listener. Listeners who are low in self-esteem or anxious about social acceptance are more easily persuaded.

## Attribution: Why Did You (or I) Do That?

8. All of us spend considerable time seeking the reasons other people act as they do. Why and how we make the search is the subject of various *attribution theories*.

9. Attribution theories assume that we want to know the reasons behind other people's behavior because we want our social interactions to have the most favorable possible outcomes; therefore, we seek clues to where we stand, what is likely to happen next, and how best to handle the situation.

10. We have a strong tendency to attribute other people's behavior to *dispositional factors* rather than *situational factors*, which may provide a far better explanation. Because this tendency is so common—and ignores social psychology's finding that people's behavior is not necessarily consistent and often depends on circumstances—it is called the *fundamental attribution error*.

11. One situational factor we often ignore is the influence of our own behavior on the behavior of others. Often, because we expect another person to act in a certain way (for example, to be friendly or unfriendly), we push the person into exactly the kind of behavior we expected—thus turning our expectation into a *self-fulfilling prophecy*.

12. In seeking the reasons for our own behavior, we tend to look for situational rather than dispositional factors. When we are forced to accept a dispositional cause, we may change our attitudes accordingly.

## Conformity, Compliance, and Obedience

13. Most people follow the customs they have learned and behave as they believe they are expected to be-

have. They display strong tendencies toward *conformity*, or yielding to group pressures; *compliance*, or agreeing to the requests of others; and *obedience*, or submission to authority.

14. One reason for conformity is that we depend on the people around us for many of our psychological satisfactions. It is pleasant to win approval as an accepted member of the group—and highly unpleasant to be rejected.

15. Another reason for conformity is the tendency we have as members of a group to accede to the requests or demands of those we regard as being in control.

16. Still another reason for conformity is that we need guidance from other people in developing an accurate view of our physical and social environment.

17. The need for guidance is the basis for the *social comparison theory*, which holds that to live successfully we must evaluate our own conduct, abilities, and opinions—and often can do so only by comparing ourselves with other people.

18. Compliance professionals have identified several techniques that are often used to gain compliance. These include the foot-in-the-door, lowballing, and door-in-the-face techniques.

19. Related to compliance is obedience, in which people follow the orders of individuals in positions of authority.

20. People do not always blindly obey authority, despite strong pressures to do so.

## Group Dynamics

21. Factors that lead to the emergence of groups include proximity, similarity, and shared interests.

22. Behaviors can be facilitated by the presence of other people, an effect termed social facilitation. The presence of an audience can also affect performance adversely; this phenomenon is known as social impairment.

23. Diffusion of responsibility is especially likely in large groups and can lead to social loafing, deindividuation, *groupthink*, and *group polarization*.

## Interpersonal Behavior: Aggression and Prosocial Behavior

24. The question of whether *aggression* is primarily the result of inborn tendencies or of learning is one of the unresolved issues in psychology.

25. The people most likely to display *altruism* (a tendency to be kind, generous, and helpful to others) are those who feel a personal responsibility for others and have learned *empathy* (the ability to feel the joys and pains of others as if these emotions were their own).

26. *Bystander apathy* is indicated by failure to assist another person who appears in need of help. Bystander apathy tends to be greatest when there are large numbers of other people around. It is encouraged by anonymity, lack of intimacy, and the rush of big-city life.

27. The forces that attract us to other people—and make us like them and associate with them—are important in social psychology because it is our closest associates who have the greatest effect on our attitudes and behavior. As a general principle, "we like those who reward us, and the more they reward us the better we like them."

28. The most powerful factor may be *proximity*, or physical nearness, which occurs by chance. Chance determines the family into which we are born, as well as our neighborhood, school companions, and coworkers.

29. Proximity is influential in part because of the effect of *familiarity*. In general, the better we know people, the better we like them. Just being repeatedly exposed to unfamiliar people or objects can increase our liking for them—a phenomenon known as the *mere exposure effect*.

30. We are also attracted to people because of *similarity*, especially in attitudes; *reciprocity*, an indication that they in turn like us; and physical attractiveness.

31. *First impressions* of other people have a strong and lasting effect, perhaps because we seem to hold an *implicit personality theory* that personality traits come in clusters—for example, that physically attractive people are also likely to be warm, sociable, poised, and interesting.

32. Psychologists distinguish between two types of love: *passionate love*, which is marked by strong emotions and sexual feelings, and *companionate love*, which is marked by feelings of affection, trust, and stability.

33. Three components are necessary to maintain love over a long period: passion, intimacy, and commitment.

# Test Yourself Answers

(a) The person would be trying to convey that you have a strong urge to be consistent in your attitudes—in other words, you find it hard to tolerate the dissonance, or disharmony, of inconsistent attitudes.

(b) It is called selective exposure.

(c) It offers an optimistic view of the human ability to change attitudes and behavior over the life span.

(d) They are called dispositional factors and situational factors, respectively.

(e) The speaker would be cautioning you against attributing other people's actions to dispositional rather than situational factors.

(f) It is called the self-fulfilling prophecy.

(g) You are demonstrating conformity.

(h) I am likely to display obedience.

(i) We lack information about the intent of the behavior.

(j) The term they use is bystander apathy.

(k) The belief that personality traits come in clusters is called an implicit personality theory.

(l) Your friend is contrasting passionate love and companionate love.

# Chapter 15  Social Psychology

## Key Terms

aggression (p. 606)
altruism (p. 609)
attitudes (p. 585)
attribution theories (p. 592)
belief perseverance (p. 590)
bystander apathy (p. 611)
cognitive dissonance (p. 587)
companionate love (p. 614)
compliance (p. 597)
conformity (p. 597)
dispositional factors (p. 592)
empathy (p. 609)
enculturation (p. 586)
familiarity (p. 612)
first impressions (p. 613)
fundamental attribution error (p. 592)
group polarization (p. 606)
groupthink (p. 605)
hostile aggression (p. 607)
implicit personality theory (p. 613)

instrumental aggression (p. 607)
mere exposure effect (p. 612)
obedience (p. 597)
passionate love (p. 614)
persuasive communications (p. 589)
prejudice (p. 587)
proximity (p. 612)
reciprocity (p. 613)
selective exposure (p. 589)
self-fulfilling prophecy (p. 595)
similarity (p. 612)
situational factors (p. 592)
social comparison theory (p. 600)
social psychology (p. 585)
socialization (p. 586)
stereotype (p. 587)

*The key terms above can be used as search terms in InfoTrac, a database of readings, which can be found at http://infotrac-thomsonlearning.com.*

## Active Learning Review

1. The way people influence and are influenced by others is the core of _____ psychology.                                        **social**

### Social Cognition: Schemas and Attitudes

2. Our behavior is strongly influenced by our _____, which are deeply ingrained beliefs and feelings that predispose us to behave in a certain way.          **attitudes**

3. The influence of other people begins in childhood with the process of _____,       **socialization**
   or integration into society through exposure to the actions and opinions of others, and _____, in which we absorb the norms and values of our culture.    **enculturation**

4. As children grow up, they learn from others how they are expected to behave in society. This process is known as _____.                          **socialization**

5. The deeply ingrained beliefs we acquire as part of the socialization process—about matters that we are strongly "for" or "against"—are _____ that help   **attitudes**
   shape our behavior.

6. Since we are neither "for" nor "against" pandas or polar bears, a casual, off-the-cuff belief that pandas are more interesting than polar bears is an opinion, not an _____.                                                   **attitude**

7. One kind of attitude that often contradicts fact is a _____—an attitude     **prejudice**
   that an individual maintains so stubbornly as to be immune to any information or experiences that would disprove it.

8. A _____ is an attitude, shared by large numbers of people, that disregards individual differences and holds that all members of a certain group behave in the same manner.                                                    **stereotype**

change

socialization

change

cognitive dissonance

cognitive
dissonance

harmony (or consistency)

cognitive dissonance

attitudes

persuasive communications

persuasive communication

selective
exposure

attitude

source

source

credibility

persuasive communication

9. One reason our attitudes are often inconsistent is that we have taken them over from our parents and other people around us without examining the evidence. Despite the inconsistencies, our attitudes are long-lasting and resistant to _____.

10. We may change an attitude, however, because of new experiences we have or new associates we acquire—showing that the _____ process continues throughout life.

11. One explanation of how attitudes change is the theory of *cognitive dissonance*, which maintains that we have a strong urge to preserve agreement and harmony between our attitudes and our behavior. Lack of harmony produces cognitive dissonance, which is so uncomfortable that we are strongly motivated to relieve it. To do so, we may be forced to _____ an attitude.

12. The idea that attitudes may change as a result of lack of harmony between our attitudes and our behavior is the theory of _____ _____.

13. New factual information may shake our beliefs and thus produce _____ _____.

14. Cognitive dissonance may be produced by new emotional experiences or by the discovery that we are acting in ways that are creating lack of _____ between attitudes and behavior.

15. Though it seems logical that an attitude change should cause a change in behavior, it appears that often the change in behavior, as the result of new experiences, comes first. As a result of studying or working together and treating one another as friendly companions, members of different ethnic groups have abandoned their disapproving attitude toward other groups. The reason is that the changed behavior produced _____ _____—and harmony could be restored only by changing the attitude.

16. *Persuasive communications* are attempts by other people to win our favor, usually by transmitting information or making emotional appeals. Since they want us to be "for" them, they are seeking to change our _____.

17. Attempts by other people to change our attitudes—through political speeches, advertising campaigns, or newspaper editorials—are called _____ _____.

18. The attempt to influence attitudes is handicapped by *selective exposure*, or the fact that many appeals reach only people who are already convinced. For example, a political rally for Candidate X will attract people who already favor X—and do not need to be convinced through a _____ _____ that makes a factual or emotional appeal in the candidate's behalf.

19. Since we all tend to seek out people and information with which we already agree, persuasive communications are greatly handicapped by _____ _____.

20. The effectiveness of an appeal depends in large part on the credibility of the source of the communication. The opinion of a good mechanic is more likely than the word of a salesperson to persuade us to form a favorable _____ toward a particular make of automobile.

21. The effectiveness of an attempt to influence our attitudes depends to a considerable extent on the _____ of the communication.

22. We are more likely to be influenced by a statement about medicine if a noted physician, rather than an electronics engineer, is the _____ of the communication.

23. A persuasive communication is more likely to convince us if it comes from an expert source with high _____ and if it is presented fairly and logically.

24. Some people are more easily persuaded than others to change their attitudes. Thus, the audience, as well as the credibility of the source, helps determine the effectiveness of a _____ _____.

25. The effectiveness of an attempt to change attitudes depends not only on the source of the communication but also on the _____ that receives it.  **audience**

26. The notion that persuasive communications reach people who are already persuaded is referred to as _____ _____.  **selective exposure**

27. The tendency to maintain one's beliefs even when faced with evidence to the contrary is termed _____ _____.  **belief perseverance**

## Attribution: Why Did You (Or I) Do That?

28. To ensure that our interactions with other people have the best possible outcomes, we want to know what their behavior can tell us about where we stand, what is likely to happen, and how we can best deal with the situation. Therefore, we continually try to analyze and search for the causes of people's _____.  **behavior**

29. Our search for the causes of behavior is the basis of *attribution theories,* which attempt to explain why and how we make the search. The theories assume that if we can attribute behavior to an underlying motive or some other cause, we can make our _____ with other people have the best possible outcomes.  **interactions**

30. Attempts to explain why and how we search for the causes of behavior are called _____ _____.  **attribution theories**

31. Behavior may spring from *dispositional factors* (deep-seated and consistent personality traits) or *situational factors* (circumstances that cause the actions). Thus, both dispositional and situational factors are important considerations in _____ _____.  **attribution theories**

32. If a server smiles and speaks cheerfully to us, we may decide that he has a consistently friendly personality, thus attributing his behavior to a _____ factor.  **dispositional**

33. If we happened to know, however, that the server's boss had just warned him against being his usual surly self around customers, we would attribute his warm smile to a _____ factor.  **situational**

34. We usually attribute other people's behavior to deep-seated and consistent personality traits—in other words, to _____ factors.  **dispositional**

35. The tendency to favor dispositional factors is so widespread that it is called the *fundamental attribution error.* The error lies in thinking of people as more consistent than they really are and therefore attributing their behavior to deep-seated personality traits—ignoring the particular circumstances, or _____ factors, that may offer a better explanation.  **situational**

36. The tendency to attribute behavior to dispositional factors, which often are not the real explanation, is called the _____ _____ _____.  **fundamental attribution error**

37. The tendency to attribute our own behavior to situational factors and other people's behavior to dispositional factors is known as the _____-_____ effect.  **actor-observer**

38. The theory of _____ _____ states that in trying to interpret the behavior of others we focus only on the actions that are most likely to be informative.  **correspondent inference**

39. Our actions toward other people are often determined by our expectations of how they will behave. Thus, expecting people to like us often becomes a *self-fulfilling prophecy.* Our expectations lead us to behave in a likable fashion—and the other person is likely to respond accordingly. On the other hand, we may invite rejection by being tense and guarded because of an _____ that the other person will not like us.  **expectation**

40. Fearing that someone will dislike us may make us behave in such a cold and unlikable way that our expectation becomes a _____-_____ _____.  **self-fulfilling prophecy**

41. In analyzing the behavior of others, we tend to look for dispositional factors. We usually do the opposite in analyzing ourselves—we tend to _____ our behavior to situational factors.  **attribute**

## Conformity, Compliance, and Obedience

conformity

42. We depend on the approval of the people around us, and it is generally easier and more rewarding to follow their lead. This is one explanation for _____ to the group.

approval

43. *Conformity* also develops out of respect for authority and its symbols. Thus, conformity stems from a sense of respect as well as the need for _____.

need

authority

44. A third factor leading to conformity is the need we feel for guidance from other people to help us understand the world and learn how to cope with it successfully. This factor is in addition to the _____ for approval and the respect we feel for _____ and its symbols.

guidance

45. The *social comparison theory* holds that we usually judge our abilities, opinions, and actions mostly by comparing ourselves with other people. Thus, the theory is based on the idea that conformity often stems from the need for _____.

social comparison

46. Our need for guidance, which is especially strong when we are uncertain of where we stand or how we should act, is the basis of the _____ _____ theory.

uncertain

47. We are most likely to seek guidance when we are _____ of how we should act—as on a new campus or when we are the only stranger at a party.

48. Our need for approval and guidance from the people around us helps explain our strong tendency toward _____ to the group.

conformity

compliance

49. Perhaps the most familiar technique for inducing _____ is referred to as the foot-in-the-door technique. This technique involves getting the person to agree to a small initial request—such as accepting a free sample—and then making a larger request—such as making a purchase.

lowballing

50. Related to the foot-in-the-door technique is _____, in which a salesperson offers a customer a very good deal that is later changed so that it becomes less advantageous.

51. The door-in-the-face, or rejection-then-retreat technique is essentially the reverse of the foot-in-the-door technique. It involves making a very large request, which is almost certain to be refused, and then following it up with a smaller

compliance

request, which often produces _____.

obedience

52. Related to compliance is _____, in which people follow the orders of individuals in positions of authority.

responsible

53. If we feel personally _____ for our actions, we are less likely to obey an order that we oppose.

## Group Dynamics

group

54. To understand what factors are operating in _____ contexts, social psychologists devote a great deal of study to the area of research known as group dynamics.

proximity

55. Research on group formation has identified a number of factors that lead to the emergence of groups. Among the most prominent of these is _____—people who live near one another or work together may develop into a cohesive group simply because they interact regularly and are concerned with the same issues.

similar

56. People who are _____ in some way, such as gender or cultural background, are also likely to form groups.

interests

57. Shared _____ are another basis for group formation.

58. Many researchers have found that behaviors can be facilitated by the presence of other people. Social psychologists call this effect _____ _____.

social facilitation

59. Pete had practiced the "Moonlight Sonata" until he thought he could play it in his sleep. On the day of the recital, however, he could hardly remember a note. Pete suffered from a phenomenon known as _____ _____.

social impairment

60. Another effect of the presence of other people is diffusion of _____.    **responsibility**

61. Diffusion of responsibility is involved in a common behavior known as social _____. Because the individual feels less responsible in a group, he or she is less inclined to act and will let others do most of the work.    **loafing**

62. Sometimes the diffusion of responsibility that occurs in large groups leads to a phenomenon known as deindividuation. In a crowd, individuals may lose a sense of personal _____.    **identity**

63. Also related to diffusion of responsibility is _____, in which the attitudes of individuals yield to those of the group as a whole.    **groupthink**

64. *Group polarization* may also occur when responsibility is diffused among group members. Because no individual member is responsible for the group's actions, the group may make more _____ decisions and take more _____ than its members would if they were acting alone.    **extreme, risks**

## Interpersonal Behavior: Aggression and Prosocial Behavior

65. Throughout history, people have speculated about whether human behavior is marked by *aggression* or by *altruism*. Because this issue relates to the scientific study of how people feel and behave toward one another, it is in the province of social _____. A major question is whether aggressive and altruistic behaviors are part of our biological inheritance or are learned.    **psychology**

66. Some psychologists believe that aggression is part of our _____ inheritance. Most, however, believe that the tendency toward aggression is _____. They believe that the same is true of altruistic behavior, or behavior that is kind, generous, and helpful.    **biological** **learned**

67. When a person comes to the help of a stranger in distress, we see evidence of _____.    **altruism**

68. The capacity to feel the mental and emotional states of another person as if they were one's own is called _____.    **empathy**

69. If your neighbors ignore your cries for help during a robbery, they are showing evidence of _____ _____.    **bystander apathy**

70. There is evidence that people living in _____ _____ are more helpful to others than are people living in _____ _____.    **small towns** **big cities**

71. Social psychology has devoted considerable study to the forces that _____ us to other people and make us like them.    **attract**

72. Paul is more likely to form a close friendship with students in the adjoining dorm room than with those in the next building. This is an example of the influence of _____.    **proximity**

73. The influence of proximity is related to that of _____—we are attracted to those whom we see often. This phenomenon has been aptly named the _____ _____ effect.    **familiarity**

    **mere exposure**

74. We are also influenced by _____—we tend to be attracted to people who are like us.    **similarity**

75. When we believe that someone is fond of us, we react with greater warmth—which, in turn, causes the person to react even more positively. This is called _____.    **reciprocity**

76. It has been found that _____ _____ have a strong and lasting influence on how we feel about others.    **first impressions**

77. Physical _____ plays a large part in our feelings about other people because it is immediately and obviously apparent.    **attractiveness**

78. The belief that personality traits come in clusters is called an _____ _____ _____.    **implicit personality theory**

79. In studying love, social psychologists distinguish between _____ love, a highly emotional and sexually charged state, and _____ love, which is accompanied by feelings of affection and trust.    **passionate** **companionate**

passionate, companionate

passion, intimacy

commitment

passion

intimacy

80. A person who feels aroused and emotional about another individual is experiencing _____ rather than _____ love.
81. Three factors that play a role in maintaining love are _____, _____, and _____.
82. Over the course of a relationship, the level of _____ decreases, but _____ develops steadily.

# Practice Test

____ 1. Social psychology is best described as the study of
a. the rules of society.
b. the effects of socialization.
c. how other people influence us and we influence them.
d. how social customs arise and change.

____ 2. In different parts of the world, people have different ways of expressing emotions, practicing or refraining from aggression, and behaving toward one another. A social psychologist would attribute this to differences in
a. inherited characteristics.
b. enculturation.
c. their physical environment.
d. the social structure they have established.

____ 3. Attitudes are characterized by their
a. deeply ingrained quality.
b. consistency.
c. susceptibility to change.
d. reliance on evidence.

____ 4. The theory of cognitive dissonance holds that we have a strong urge to preserve agreement between our
a. thoughts and actions.
b. beliefs and attitudes.
c. attitudes and behavior.
d. beliefs and feelings.

____ 5. Cognitive dissonance may be caused by
a. factual information.
b. emotional experiences.
c. social behavior.
d. all of the above

____ 6. A woman who has just bought a new car is likely to
a. read ads for that car.
b. read ads for other cars.
c. ask her friends what they think of that make and model.
d. wish she had taken more time to decide.

____ 7. Of the following, the best example of a persuasive communication is a
a. classroom lecture.
b. news story on the passage of a tax law.
c. coach's pep talk to the team.
d. friend's invitation to go see a movie.

____ 8. Which of the following is *not* a barrier to persuasive communication?
a. the difficulty of reaching a large audience
b. selective exposure
c. people's reluctance to change attitudes
d. the ineffectiveness of appeals to emotion

____ 9. Our attempts to explain other people's behavior are the basis of the theory of
a. cognitive dissonance.
b. attribution.
c. social comparison.
d. self-perception.

____ 10. In trying to explain other people's behavior, we are likely to pay special attention to
a. situational factors.
b. their facial expressions.
c. their apparent sincerity.
d. dispositional factors.

____ 11. Which of the following beliefs is most closely related to the fundamental attribution error?
a. People's actions are generally consistent.
b. People are often forced by circumstances to act as they do.
c. It is hard to guess a person's motives.
d. Physically attractive people are usually interesting, poised, and outgoing.

____ 12. Which of the following is *not* a result of the diffusion of responsibility that occurs in large groups?
a. social loafing
b. social facilitation
c. deindividuation
d. group polarization

____ 13. A female student is introduced to a male student. Which of the following factors is *least* likely to make him seem attractive?
a. She has seen him on the campus many times.
b. She has been assigned to work with him on a series of psychology experiments.
c. He seems similar to her in many ways.
d. He does not seem attracted to her.

____ 14. Physical attractiveness plays a big part in attracting people to one another because of the importance of
a. reciprocity.
b. first impressions.
c. proximity.
d. similarity.

____**15.** The belief that personality traits come in clusters is referred to as
  a. an implicit personality theory.
  b. a fundamental attribution theory.
  c. a social comparison theory.
  d. a cognitive dissonance theory.

____**16.** The belief that altruism is an innate trait is strengthened by evidence that
  a. aggressive behavior is rare in young children.
  b. helpful behavior declines with age.
  c. babies show compassion.
  d. none of the above

____**17.** Intimacy among individuals is likely to reduce
  a. cognitive dissonance.
  b. changes of attitude.
  c. bystander apathy.
  d. social comparison.

____**18.** The tendency to conform is
  a. closely related to the need for approval and guidance.
  b. equally strong in all people.
  c. an inherited trait.
  d. found in some cultures but not in others.

____**19.** To encourage children to behave altruistically, it is important to
  a. say little about it.
  b. avoid criticism.
  c. praise such behavior.
  d. let nature take its course.

____**20.** An important component of altruism is the capacity to feel
  a. empathy.
  b. intimate.
  c. attracted.
  d. enraged.

## Exercises

1. It's easy to conduct an informal experiment on the effect of your own behavior on the behavior of other people. For a day or at least part of a day, devote yourself to being as pleasant as you can to everyone with whom you come into contact—other students, salespeople, family members, neighbors, friends. Go out of your way to be as cheerful, warm, and friendly as you possibly can, even to the most sour and forbidding of the people you meet. Try to find something nice to say about everyone—a little compliment they might enjoy.

   Make mental notes of people's reactions—or jot down reminders—and at the end of your experiment tally the results. How many people showed no response at all? How many seemed to back off from your friendly approach? How many seemed unusually warm and friendly in return? With any luck at all, you should find that most of the reactions fell into the last of the three categories. Your own reactions may also be interesting to analyze. Did you enjoy spreading good cheer? Did the experiment tell you something important about social relationships?

   It must be emphasized that this is just an informal experiment with no real claim to being scientific. You have no objective measure of how friendly your behavior actually seemed to others or how much, if at all, it differed from your customary behavior. You're also forced to rely on your own subjective judgment of how people responded to you, and you have no way of determining whether there was any change in their customary behavior. Nevertheless, the experiment is well worth trying.

2. Along similar lines, you can try an informal attempt to show how one's expectations about another person affect the way one acts—and how these actions, in turn, influence the other person. Pick out someone you know—a Mr. or Ms. X—who is generally regarded as somewhat cranky, critical, and sharp-tongued. Then arrange to have X meet, for the first time, another of your acquaintances, whom we'll call Friend 1. Before the meeting—which preferably should occur over a meal, at a sports event, or on a long drive so that the two spend some time together—warn your friend about X's notorious cantankerousness. Note how well, if at all, the two get along. Now arrange a similar meeting between X and Friend 2. Tell this friend in advance that X, though occasionally a bit outspoken, is a warm and generous person with a delightful sense of humor. See what happens. Is there a difference in the way Friends 1 and 2 act toward X? How does X act toward each of them in turn?

❋ *For quizzing, activities, exercises, and web links, check out the book-specific website at http://www.psychology.wadsworth.com/kagan9e.*

# Statistics: Description and Inference

The field called *statistics* focuses on the application of a broad set of mathematical techniques to the interpretation of results obtained in research. As used by psychologists, it has been aptly called a "way of thinking" (Hebb, 1958)—a problem-solving approach that enables researchers to summarize observations and measurements of behavior and draw conclusions from them. Psychologists and others have developed an array of statistical techniques that range from relatively simple to thoroughly complex in terms of both computation and interpretation. Most psychological research relies on these techniques, a sampling of which are presented here as an adjunct to the research methods discussed in Chapter 1 and elsewhere in the text.

We begin with *descriptive statistics*—numbers that summarize or "describe." Then we consider probability and mathematically derived distributions, with an emphasis on the normal, or "bell-shaped," curve. This sets the stage for a conceptual understanding of *inferential statistics*—numbers that allow psychologists to "infer" what the results of their research efforts mean, particularly with regard to cause and effect.

# DESCRIPTIVE STATISTICS

The use of descriptive statistics as a tool in psychology began with Sir Francis Galton (1822–1911) in the latter part of the 19th century. A cousin of Charles Darwin, Galton was interested in the workings of evolution and heredity as they pertain to individual differences—how people vary in height, weight, and characteristics such as color vision, sense of smell, hearing, and ability to judge weights (e.g., see Galton, 1889). One of the questions that fascinated him was whether taller-than-average people tend to have taller-than-average children. Another was whether intelligence is primarily inherited—which he believed to be the case (Galton, 1891).

As Galton discovered, answering questions such as these means first making accurate measurements. Galton himself devised a number of tests for such abilities as vision and audition, and generations of psychologists in the decades since have tried to perfect ways of measuring a great many specific psychological skills and characteristics—plus, on a larger scale, ways of measuring intelligence and personality. But the results of the tests are meaningless unless they can be analyzed and compared. An important aspect of this kind of comparison is *correlation*, which largely originated with Galton. We return to correlation at the end of this section.

Descriptive statistics do two things: They provide convenient ways of summarizing the characteristics or behavior of a group under study, and they provide the starting point for inferential statistics. With regard to the former, suppose we devise a new intelligence test and administer it to 10,000 people. We wind up with 10,000 "raw" scores—that is, simple total scores on the test. To summarize what we have learned about the test, however, we need not quote every one of the 10,000 scores. Through the use of descriptive statistics, we can summarize and condense. With just a few well-chosen numbers, we can tell other people what they need to know to understand our results.

## Number

*Number* is the simplest statistic of all. It is simply the total number of scores being studied, where *score* is a general term for a measurement of an individual characteristic or instance of behavior. One reason number is important is that the chances of obtaining accurate results are greater if we study a large group than if we study only a small group. For example, if we test only three people on our new intelligence test, we may happen to select three who are above-average or below-average and do not represent the targeted group as a whole.

## Central Tendency: The Mean and the Median

Another useful piece of information is what in everyday language is called the *average*. Suppose seven students take an exam containing 100 true-false questions and receive scores of 70, 74, 74, 76, 79, 80, and 82. The average score—or the *mean*—is the sum of the scores divided by the number of scores: 535/7 = 76.4. If only whole-number scores are possible on the test, no student could actually make 76.4, but we still have a single number that summarizes the scores nicely. That is, we have what statisticians call a *measure of central tendency*, or the general "location" of a set of scores—in this case, a general location on a test where the scores could lie anywhere between 0 and 100. However, the mean alone is not enough for an adequate description of the scores. We need a second number that tells us the extent to which the scores are clustered fairly close to the mean or scattered across a wider range. We return to this shortly.

For most statistical analyses, the mean is the preferable measure of central tendency. It has several advantages over other measures, the most important being that it takes the numerical values of all the scores into account. But in some cases the *median* is preferable. This is the halfway point that separates the lower 50% of scores from the upper 50%. In the above example, the median is 76, because half the scores fall below it and the other half above it. The median is often very close to the mean, as it is here (76 versus 76.4). But the median becomes a better statistic than the mean when a set of scores includes a few that differ markedly from the rest. For example, suppose that the seven scores on the true-false exam were *20*, 74, 74, 76, 79, 80, and 82. The student who blew the exam and scored 20 brings the mean down sharply, to 485/7 = 69.3. This number is hardly a representative statistic, because six of the seven students scored noticeably higher than 69.3. The median, which is still 76, gives a better description of the scores as a whole.

The median is an especially useful statistic for describing things like the annual income of residents of a city or employees of a large corporation. In each case, there will be many people who make a relatively low to moderate amount of money and only a few people—such as business owners and corporate executives—who make a lot. As in the example with the exam scores, the mean is "pulled" in the direction of the few extreme scores—here, the high-income people. What most of the people make is more accurately represented by the median, which is mostly unaffected by the few extremely high incomes.

## Variability: The Standard Deviation

Given the general location of a set of scores as indicated by the mean, we need an additional statistic that tells us how "spread out" the scores are with respect to it. This is called a *measure of variability*. The initial true-false exam scores we considered were 70, 74, 74, 76, 79, 80, and 82, each of which is fairly close to the mean of 76.4. Thus, we say that the variability of the scores with respect to the mean is relatively small. If the scores were instead 56, 61, 74, 76, 78, 93, and 97, the variability would be considerably larger—even though the mean would still be 535/7 = 76.4.

One sensitive and highly useful statistic that we compute to describe variability with a number is called the *standard deviation (SD)*. In essence, the *SD* is computed by comparing each of the scores to the mean. If the scores cluster closely around the mean, the *SD* will be a small number. If the scores are widely spread out in each direction and many differ markedly from the mean, the *SD* will be a larger number. Computing standard deviations is a bit complicated and therefore is not covered here, but we can give you some results for perspective. For the exam scores 70, 74, 74, 76, 79, 80, and 82, *SD* = 3.8, and for the scores 56, 61, 74, 76, 78, 93, and 97, *SD* = 13.9. By themselves, these numbers may not mean much to you, except to verify that more variability results in a substantially larger *SD*. They should mean more when we consider applications of the mean and *SD* later in this appendix.

## Correlation

As discussed in Chapter 1, *correlation* is a descriptive statistical tool used to examine pairs of measurements (such as the IQs of parents and the IQs of their children) and to determine—from what would otherwise seem to be hopelessly jumbled numbers—what relationship, if any, exists between the two measurements. It is also the primary tool in assessing the reliability and validity of psychological tests, as discussed in Chapter 7.

As noted earlier, the idea of correlation can be traced back to the work of Galton. However, its formula was derived by Karl Pearson (1857–1936), a colleague of Galton who was also keenly interested in the extent to which psychological characteristics are inherited (Pearson, 1894). Pearson's *product-moment correlation coefficient*, or Pearson's *r*, remains an important tool in psychological research, and all other correlational techniques derive from it. In working out his correlation coefficient, Pearson also devised the procedure for determining the standard deviation and coined its name. The concept of the *SD*, along with that of its numerical square, the *variance*, is basic to the formula for Pearson's *r*. Here, however, we limit the discussion of correlation to some examples and details intended to augment the discussion in Chapter 1.

Some correlations are *positive*. This means that the higher a person scores on one measure (for example, IQ), the higher that person is likely to score on the other (for example, grades). Other correlations are *negative*. This means that a high score on one measure is likely to be accompanied by a low score on the other. For example, higher-income parents tend to have a lower rate of premature births; lower-income parents, a higher rate. Another example is the relationship between students' test anxiety and their scores on tests.

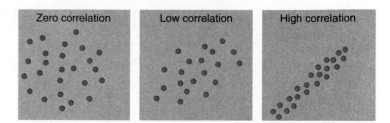

**FIGURE A.1 Scatterplots of correlation. For each participant, a dot corresponds to the point where the score on the horizontal measure and the score on the vertical measure intersect.**
*Ferguson, G. A. Statistical Analysis in Psychology and Education. New York: McGraw-Hill, 1959. Copyright © 1959 by McGraw-Hill Companies. Reprinted with permission.*

**Scatterplots**   A rough idea of the degree of correlation between two measured characteristics can be obtained by plotting each participant's score on one measure against her or his score on the other. For each participant, a dot is entered at a point that corresponds to the scores on both measures, as shown in Figure A.1. The result is what is called a *scatterplot*. If the dots are scattered completely at random, as in the left panel, the correlation is near or equal to 0.00. At the other extreme, if the dots were to be positioned exactly along a diagonal straight line, the correlation would be a perfect 1.00. Scatterplots typically fall somewhere in between. If a fairly narrow diagonal oval encloses most of the dots, as in the right panel, the correlation is relatively high. If the oval is fatter, as in the center panel, the correlation is lower—perhaps moderate, as noted in Chapter 1.

**Correlation Coefficients**   By using Pearson's $r$ or one of various other formulas that derive from it, a more precise measure of the relationship between scores on two measures can be obtained without constructing a scatterplot. As noted, a correlation coefficient can range from 0.00 (no correlation at all) to +1.00 (a perfect positive correlation) or −1.00 (a perfect negative correlation). But correlations of +1.00 or −1.00 are very rare. Even such physical traits as height and weight, which would seem to go together in almost perfect proportion, do not reach a correlation of +1.00. Some typical correlations that have been found in various studies are the following:

- Between IQ and college grades: .50
- Between parents' IQ and child's IQ: .49
- Between IQ and ability at pitch discrimination: .00
- Between height at age 2 and height at age 18: .60
- Between height at age 10 and height at age 18: .88

**Correlation and Prediction**   The correlation coefficients listed above show that there is a considerable relationship between height at age 2 and at age 18—and an even greater relationship between height at age 10 and height at age 18. Knowing that these relationships exist, we can make some predictions. We can say that a child who is taller than average at age 2—or especially at age 10—has a pretty good chance of also being taller than average at age 18. Because of the .50 correlation coefficient between IQ and college grades, we can suggest that high school seniors who make high scores on intelligence tests have a good chance of getting high grades in college, and that students with very low scores run the risk of failure.

It must always be kept in mind, however, that a correlation coefficient is less accurate as a predictor than it sounds. Only when the correlation is very close to +1.00, as in the scatterplot in the right panel in Figure A.1, does every subject tend to show a close relationship between scores on the two measures. Even for a correlation of +.75, which sounds high, there is a considerable amount of scatter, which means that some participants scored relatively low on the first measure and relatively high on the second—and vice versa. Because most correlations found in psychological studies are smaller than +.75 (or −.75), we must be quite tentative in making predictions based on this statistic.

# PROBABILITY, NORMAL DISTRIBUTION, AND SOME APPLICATIONS

The *normal distribution* or *normal curve* is defined according to a precise mathematical formula that derives from probability theory. In this section, we illustrate where the normal curve comes from and provide some examples of its uses. But first, we consider the meaning of probability.

## What Probability Is and Is Not

By way of introduction to probability, consider two possible poker hands. One is the poker player's dream—a royal flush, containing an ace, a king, a queen, a jack, and a ten, all from the same of any of the four suits (spades, hearts, diamonds, or clubs). The other is a run-of-the-mill hand containing a king, a nine, an eight, a five, and a two, of mixed suits. If you played poker tonight, which of these hands would you be *less* likely to be dealt?

Even if you don't know much about poker, your intuitive response is likely to be the royal flush. When a poker player gets such a hand—especially in five-card stud, a game where five cards are all you get—the player will probably talk about it for quite a long time afterward. This is especially likely if it turns out that the player wins a nice pile of money with the hand. And in terms of probability, a royal flush is extremely rare. As can be calculated easily, it is expected to occur only once in every 650,000 poker hands dealt—again, in any one of the four suits. You could play poker for a lifetime and never be dealt one.

But the other poker hand, whatever it is, is equally rare. The chance of getting any *specific* combination of five cards is only 1 in 650,000 hands. The reason a royal flush seems rarer than any other hand is that poker players pay attention to it, while mentally lumping together all their mediocre hands as if they were one and the same.

So what is probability? First, it is not a "law"—contrary to the commonly used expression "the law of probability." If you deal 650,000 poker hands, a royal flush may occur once or several times or it may not occur at all. There is no guarantee. If you flip an unbiased, or "fair," coin once, the chances of getting "heads" or "tails" are exactly 50-50 (ruling out the possibility that the coin might land on its edge). If you flip the coin 10 times, you might get 5 heads and 5 tails—the likeliest prediction according to probability—but you might instead get any other possible combination.

Also consider this: If you flip the fair coin 10 times and get *all* heads, what is the probability that the 11th toss will be heads? In this situation, most people realize that the chances are still 50-50 for heads or tails—the coin has no memory for what has occurred earlier, and again, there is no such thing as law where probability is concerned. If probability were a law, the chances of tails coming up would increase with each successive heads that occurred—as if probability were "trying to come true."

The same is the case with card games such as poker and casino games such as blackjack and craps—as well as with slot machines. The cards, the dice, and the machines all have no memory. Yet, where these games are concerned, many people intuitively go astray and think that after a losing streak they somehow become "overdue" for a series of wins. This belief that probability is indeed a law and that it will come true is called the *gambler's fallacy*.

Probability is a mathematical way of assigning a meaningful and often useful number to situations involving uncertainty. The number can range from 0.00, if an event absolutely can't happen, to 1.00, if the event absolutely must happen. For everything in between, the outcome is uncertain, and the number reflects its likelihood. For example, the probability of drawing a card labeled "Wizard" from a standard deck of 52 is 0.0; no such card exists. The probability of drawing a card that is a two, a three, or some other card up through an ace is 1.00; you can't miss. But for any specific card or combination of cards, the outcome is uncertain, and probability tells us what the chances are.

Computing probabilities can be anything from easy to quite complicated, but probability itself is conceptually straightforward:

$$p = \frac{\text{number of specified outcomes}}{\text{total number of outcomes possible}}$$

Thus, the probability of getting heads on a flip of a coin is 1/2 = .50. In a standard deck of 52 cards, there are 4 aces, so the probability of drawing an ace is 4/52 = .08.

In statistics, probabilities tend to be exceedingly difficult to compute, so instead we look them up in tables (or have a computer determine them for us). One way of computing probabilities involves use of a table for the normal curve. However, statisticians have tables for many other distributions as well, each of which is designed for the sole purpose of determining probabilities.

## Coin Tossing and a Normal Curve of Distribution

We noted earlier that the normal curve is based on a precise formula. Here we discuss the normal curve's origins in probability theory—without regard to the formula, whose derivation requires an understanding of integral calculus.

One of the principles of probability, as Galton was the first to note, has to do with the way many things—including psychological characteristics and behavior—are distributed in the normal course of events. Suppose you drop 10 coins into a cup, shake the cup, throw the coins on a table, and count the number of heads. If you do this 100 times, your tally is likely to resemble the one shown in Figure A.2.

What we have is a simple illustration of approximately normal distribution. When you toss 10 coins 100 times—a total of 1,000 tosses—your expectation is about 500 heads, an average of 5 heads per toss. As the tally shows, the number 5 came up most often. The numbers on either side, 4 and 6, were close seconds. The numbers farther away from 5 occurred progressively less often. The number 10 came up only once, and zero did not come up at all. (In the long run, both 10 and zero would be predicted to occur an average of once in every 1,024 tosses.) The tally shown in Figure A.2 can be converted into the bar graph shown in Figure A.3, which provides a more easily interpreted picture of what happened in the coin tossing. Note its shape—highest in the middle, then tapering off toward the left

| Number of heads | | | | | | |
|---|---|---|---|---|---|---|
| 0 | | | | | | |
| 1 | I | | | | | |
| 2 | HH | I | | | | |
| 3 | HH | HH | | | | |
| 4 | HH | HH | HH | III | | |
| 5 | HH | HH | HH | HH | HH | II |
| 6 | HH | HH | HH | HH | I | |
| 7 | HH | HH | I | | | |
| 8 | IIII | | | | | |
| 9 | I | | | | | |
| 10 | I | | | | | |

**FIGURE A.2 A tally of coin tosses.** Ten coins were shaken in a cup and tossed on a table 100 times. This is a tally of the number of heads that appeared on each toss.

**FIGURE A.3 The tally in bar form.** Here, the tally of the coin-tossing experiment has been converted into a bar graph. Note the peak at the center and the rapid falling off toward each extreme.

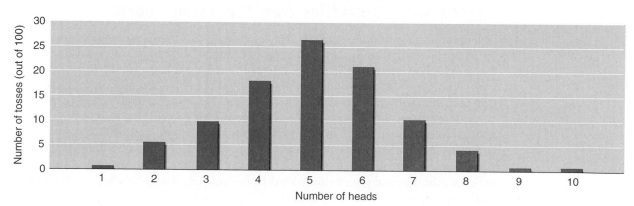

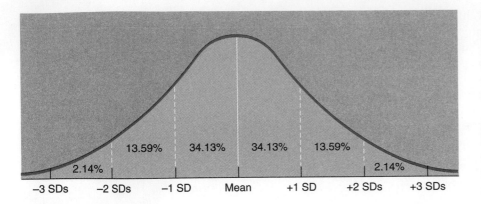

| 2.14% | 13.59% | 34.13% | 34.13% | 13.59% | 2.14% |

-3 SDs   -2 SDs   -1 SD   Mean   +1 SD   +2 SDs   +3 SDs

**FIGURE A.4 The normal distribution.** The percentages of the measurements in the various areas hold for any normal distribution, although the size of the *SD* differs from one distribution to another.

and the right. This is a rough approximation of the normal curve—which is typical of the results found in many tests and measurements of both physical and psychological characteristics.

And where does that formula for the normal curve come from? What the formula describes is the theoretical result of tossing an infinite number of coins an infinite number of times.

## Determining Percentages from the Normal Curve

The normal distribution presented in Figure A.4 is the same as Figure 1.2 on page 14, except that it is laid out with mean = 0 and *SD* = 1 instead of the mean and *SD* for IQ. Note that the curve is symmetrical, which means that if it were folded vertically down the middle (the mean), the sides would match perfectly. Also note that the "tails" don't actually touch the horizontal axis—they stretch out to infinity. This is not a problem, however: In using the normal curve, we can work outward from the mean and assess any area we wish. To get precise measurements, we use a table called the *standard normal distribution*. For illustration, however, we can simply refer to the figure.

The mean and *SD* help in determining the percentage of scores or measurements that will be found under a given part of the normal curve. For example, Figure A.4 shows that 34.13% of all the scores lie between the mean and 1 *SD* above it; 13.59% lie between 1 *SD* and 2 *SD*s above the mean; and 2.14% lie between 2 *SD*s and 3 *SD*s above the mean. The same percentages are found below the mean. If you total these percentages, you'll see that *almost* 100% of the normal distribution lies between −3 *SD*s and +3 *SD*s. As noted earlier, very extreme scores on a physical or psychological variable are rare indeed. The figure also illustrates the point made earlier about how the majority of scores tend to cluster around the mean: The area between −1 *SD* and +1 *SD* contains 34.13% + 34.13% = 68.26% of the distribution—over a two-thirds majority.

With IQ, the mean is 100 and the *SD* is 15. That is, an IQ score that is 1 *SD* above the mean is 115. Given this information and the properties illustrated in Figure A.4, we know that IQ tends to be distributed according to the percentages in Table A.1.

## Determining Percentiles from the Normal Curve

The meaning of *percentile* can best be explained by an example. A senior who wants to go on to graduate school may be asked to take the Graduate Record Examinations, which are nationally administered achievement tests used to screen applicants. Suppose the student scores 460 on the verbal test and 570 on the quantitative test, each of which in theory has a mean of 500 and an *SD* of 100—although in practice these values vary somewhat from year to year. By themselves, these scores do not mean much either to the student or to the faculty of the graduate program the student wants to attend, except that one score is below average and the other is above. Because of standardization (Chapter 7), however, and the properties of the normal curve illustrated in Figure A.4, it can easily be determined

TABLE A.1.
**Percentages of People Who Score in Different IQ Ranges**

| IQ | Percentage of People |
|---|---|
| Over 144 | 0.14 |
| 130–144 | 2.14 |
| 115–129 | 13.59 |
| 100–114 | 34.13 |
| 85–99 | 34.13 |
| 70–84 | 13.59 |
| 55–69 | 2.14 |
| Under 55 | 0.14 |

from statistical tables that a score of 460 on the verbal test corresponds to about the 35th percentile. This means that 35% of the standardization group made a lower score and 65% made a higher score. Not so good for the student. But 570 on the quantitative test corresponds to about the 76th percentile, which is much better. These figures show the student and the faculty of the graduate program how the student's abilities compare with those of other prospective graduate students: Quantitative ability is well above average, but verbal aptitude is noticeably below average.

## Determining Probabilities from the Normal Curve

An important use of the table for the normal curve—along with tables for many other distributions, according to the situation—is determining probabilities. As a simple example, refer back to Table A.1. What is the probability that someone you encounter will have an IQ of 130 or higher? Adding the percentages for 130–144 and over 144 yields 2.28%. Then shifting the decimal two places to the left (or dividing by 100) turns the percentage into a proportion—that is, a probability. The result is .0228, or just over 2 in 100. In statistics, this is a "long shot"—a relatively unlikely occurrence. Such probabilities play a crucial role in statistical inference, discussed next.

# INFERENTIAL STATISTICS: THE SCIENCE OF THE LONG SHOT

Psychologists who use statistical inference rarely look at individuals. They look instead at groups, often using the means of the groups as the starting point. For example, just as we can determine the probability of meeting an individual with a given IQ or a more extreme one, we can determine the probability of obtaining a *group* of individuals with a given *mean* IQ or a more extreme one. Sometimes we use the normal curve to obtain this probability and then make a decision based on it. Much more often, however—according to the situation and what we're analyzing—we use special statistics and distributions that are designed entirely for purposes of inference. After discussing a couple of additional considerations in conducting good research, we consider the basic logic of statistical inference and two of these special statistics.

## Populations and Samples

The method of inferential statistics is important because science is interested in what are called *populations*, that is, all people or all events in a particular category. But we cannot study or measure *all* people. For example, we cannot give an IQ test to every human being on the face of the earth, every human in a nation, or even every human in a city. Even if we were to try, we still would not reach the entire defined population, because people would die and new people would be born while we were conducting our lengthy series of tests. We must rely on *samples*—groups of convenient size taken from the population as a whole.

The rules of inferential statistics hold that we can make valid generalizations only if the sample we use is *representative* of the population we want to study. If we are seeking some general conclusions about the intelligence of North Americans, we certainly cannot use a sample made up entirely of college students or of people who live on the streets. If we want to learn about political attitudes, we cannot poll only members of one political party or voters who live in big cities or voters who have a particular socioeconomic status. Our sample must be representative of all kinds of people of the designated type.

Our best shot at obtaining a representative sample is *random sampling*. If each member of the total population has an equal chance of being chosen—and if our sample is sufficiently large—then it is *likely* that the sample will represent all segments of the population. There is of course no guarantee; even with random sampling, we could still get a nonrepresentative sample.

A survey- or other population-oriented researcher can improve the chances of getting a representative sample by using *stratified random sampling*. Here, the researcher first assesses the demographics of the population in question—for example, the age, income, and educational levels of its members, its ethnicities, its gender makeup, and other characteristics that might be relevant to the research question. (Pollsters add political affiliation as an important consideration.) Stratifying then involves seeing that the percentages for each demographic characteristic are accurately represented in the sample. For example, if a population is 60% female and 40% male—or 10% higher income, 60% middle income, and 30% lower income—these percentages should be the same in the sample. Within each designation, of course, the researcher then chooses individuals at random. Once again, there is no guarantee of getting a truly representative sample, but the chances are greatly improved.

## More on Conducting Good Experiments

The random approach is standard procedure in selecting groups that will receive different experimental or treatment conditions; here, however, it is called *random assignment*. As noted in Chapter 1, each of the two or more treatment groups should be comparable with regard to the topic being studied. This way, any meaningful differences in the dependent variable—the measure of behavior—can be attributed to the independent variable—the experimental treatment. For example, if the experiment is about memory under different conditions of noise or other distracters, the different groups should be equivalent in their memory abilities at the outset. If they are not, the researcher can't be sure whether it was the treatment conditions or the initial group differences that caused any differences in the results. When there are two or more possible causes for the outcome of an experiment, the experiment is said to be *confounded*.

Random assignment is one way that researchers attempt to eliminate such problems. Participants are simply chosen at random for the different treatment conditions, with the hope that the groups will be comparable—as they likely will be. As with random sampling, however, there is never a guarantee. Thus, in the case of a memory task, participants might be given a *pretest* in which they memorize materials somewhat similar to those to be used in the experiment. If the experiment then has two treatment groups, the researcher can assign an equivalent number of those who score high on the pretest to each of the groups, and likewise for those who score low—assigning at random except for the pretest scores.

## The Logic of Statistical Inference: Comparing Two Groups

The simplest possible group experiment involves two groups, which sometimes are designated as an *experimental group* and a *control group*. The experimental group receives special treatment of some kind; the control, or comparison, group receives a "substitute" treatment or "treatment as usual." The two groups are treated the same way in all other respects.

Imagine an experiment in which we are trying to determine whether a special intense health regimen affects students' learning. We randomly select 32 students who we hope constitute a representative sample of the population of students at a given school, and then we randomly assign them to two groups of 16 students each. One group experiences a supervised diet-and-exercise schedule, regular physical examinations, and prompt treatment of any illness. The other group experiences no health emphasis beyond what is customary for the school (an ethical consideration—see Chapter 1). At the end of the academic year, we find that the experimental group, on a scale of 0 to 4, has a mean grade point average (GPA) of 3.2 with $sd = 0.8$ (in inferential statistics, the standard deviation is computed slightly differently—the lowercase letters reflect this). The control group has a mean GPA of 2.7 with $sd = 0.7$.

The question: Does the mean difference of half a letter grade between the experimental group and the control group ($3.2 - 2.7 = 0.5$) support a conclusion that special attention to physical health actually improved learning? Although half a letter grade sounds like a lot, it could have happened entirely by chance; *any* two samples of 16 students are likely to have somewhat different mean GPAs.

More accurately, here's what we're asking in conducting a statistical analysis to make a decision about the results of the experiment: Do the two groups of students come from the *same* population, as they did at the outset? If so, any observed difference is indeed due to chance. Alternatively, do the two groups of students come from *different* populations—one that consists of students who get special health emphasis and one that consists of students who get "treatment as usual"? We started out with two groups of students from a known population—the population of the school with its usual health program. When we imposed the special health regimen for one group, we may in a sense have "created" a different population—a theoretical one consisting of students in better health who make better grades.

When students such as yourself are initially exposed to this logic, they often find it baffling. It actually isn't. The key is that the only basis we have for making a decision is to assume that the groups are the same except for chance. We then compute the chance (probability) that this assumption is correct, and if it is very small, we deem it unlikely that the groups are the same. Finally, if the groups are unlikely to be the same, the only alternative is that they're different.

By tradition in statistical inference, a probability that is less than .05 (expressed as $p < .05$) is usually considered sufficiently small. The statistical test that is appropriate for this experiment is called the *independent t-test*: The groups are "independent" in the sense that different participants are in each, and the inferential statistic we compute to assess the probability is $t$.

Finally, in case you're curious, the numbers in the experiment yield a value of $t$ that is associated with $p < .001$, much smaller than the maximum $p < .05$. We therefore easily conclude that we have obtained a *statistically significant difference*—that is, that the special health regimen was effective.

## Comparing Multiple Groups

Psychologists still use two-group experiments and other two-group comparisons with one independent variable, but they are much more likely to use experiments that simultaneously compare the effects of more than one independent variable across more than two groups of participants. They may also assess more than one dependent variable. Statistical inference has become complex indeed, and it is truly an area of expertise in its own right.

However, the logic is always the same: Assume no difference except for chance, apply the appropriate statistical test and determine the probability or probabilities, and draw conclusions accordingly. For an example of an experiment with multiple groups, we return to the classic experiment by Bandura on the learning of aggression, as described in Chapter 1 on pages 20–22 (you might want to read about the experiment again before continuing). There were two independent variables: (1) the consequences the children saw the model receive for beating up Bobo—either reward, punishment, or no consequences and (2) whether the children were boys or girls. The dependent variable was the extent to which the children later imitated the model when supposedly alone with their own Bobo. On the initial *performance test*, it was concluded that, for both boys and girls, those who saw the model punished imitated significantly fewer behaviors than those who saw the model either rewarded or receive no consequences. It was further concluded that girls in all three groups imitated significantly fewer of the behaviors than boys did. (We can skip the *learning test* here, remembering that all of the differences essentially disappeared.)

How did the researchers assess the results of the performance test? They did so through a procedure called *analysis of variance (ANOVA)*, which yields an inferential statistic $F$ as the overall test of statistical significance and also allows for closer looks at what happened in an experiment. When researchers looked only at the model-consequences variable (combining boys' and girls' behaviors), the $F$ was significant at $p < .05$. When researchers looked only at gender (combining behaviors in the model-consequences conditions), the $F$ was significant at $p < .001$. These are called "main effects" for the model-consequences variable and the gender variable, respectively. Further analysis was required to reach the conclusion that the children imitated significantly fewer behaviors in the model-punished condition than in the other conditions; this was accomplished by separately comparing each of the three possible pairs of means on the model-consequences variable.

Here's a detail that we didn't mention in Chapter 1 (think of this additional information as your reward for reading this far into the Appendix): This finding was accounted for largely by differences in the *girls'* behavior in the three model-consequences conditions. When the boys' behavior was assessed separately from that of the girls, no significant differences were obtained. This finding provided even more evidence for the note in Chapter 1 regarding gender bias in the United States in the 1960s, here with respect to girls not only being taught to be less aggressive than boys but perhaps also being taught to pay more attention to adults and consequences.

Finally, ANOVA also allows for assessing the *interaction* between two or more independent variables. An interaction occurs when, say, two variables come together to affect behavior differently than either one would have alone. Fortunately for your authors, however, the interaction between model consequences and gender in the Bandura experiment was not statistically significant, so there's no need to discuss it further.

**chapter 1**

1. c
2. d
3. a
4. a
5. a
6. d
7. d
8. d
9. b
10. c
11. b
12. d
13. c
14. b
15. a
16. b
17. d
18. c
19. d
20. d

**chapter 2**

1. c
2. d
3. d
4. a
5. b
6. c
7. a
8. b
9. c
10. b
11. d
12. a
13. b
14. a
15. d
16. a
17. b
18. c
19. d
20. d

**chapter 3**

1. d
2. b
3. c
4. c
5. d
6. c

7. b
8. c
9. a
10. a
11. d
12. c
13. a
14. b
15. b
16. a
17. a
18. c
19. b
20. d

**chapter 4**

1. d
2. d
3. b
4. c
5. a
6. c
7. a
8. c
9. d
10. b
11. b
12. d
13. d
14. a
15. c
16. b
17. d
18. a
19. a
20. d

**chapter 5**

1. b
2. c
3. b
4. b
5. a
6. a
7. b
8. d
9. a
10. c
11. d
12. b
13. d

14. b
15. a
16. d
17. a
18. d
19. a
20. a

**chapter 6**

1. d
2. a
3. b
4. d
5. b
6. c
7. b
8. d
9. d
10. a
11. d
12. d
13. d
14. c
15. a
16. a
17. d
18. b
19. a
20. b

**chapter 7**

1. c
2. a
3. b
4. d
5. a
6. a
7. c
8. d
9. c
10. a
11. c
12. b
13. b
14. b
15. d
16. a
17. d
18. d
19. d
20. b

**chapter 8**

1. d
2. c
3. a
4. c
5. b
6. c
7. b
8. a
9. a
10. b
11. b
12. c
13. a
14. a
15. c
16. a
17. b
18. a
19. b
20. d

**chapter 9**

1. b
2. a
3. d
4. a
5. c
6. c
7. b
8. c
9. b
10. d
11. d
12. b
13. a
14. a
15. a
16. c
17. c
18. d
19. d
20. c

**chapter 10**

1. b
2. d
3. a
4. d
5. b
6. b

7. a
8. a
9. c
10. b
11. d
12. a
13. a
14. a
15. d
16. d
17. b
18. d
19. b
20. d

**chapter 11**

1. a
2. b
3. c
4. d
5. b
6. b
7. c
8. a
9. a
10. b
11. a
12. c
13. a
14. b
15. b
16. b
17. c
18. d
19. c
20. a

**chapter 12**

1. a
2. d
3. c
4. b
5. d
6. b
7. a
8. d
9. b
10. a
11. b
12. c
13. a

14. c
15. b
16. c
17. d
18. d
19. b
20. a

**chapter 13**

1. c
2. b
3. d
4. c
5. a
6. c
7. b
8. a
9. d
10. b
11. c
12. b
13. d
14. c
15. a
16. c
17. c
18. d
19. d
20. b

**chapter 14**

1. a
2. d
3. c
4. a
5. b
6. a
7. d
8. c
9. a
10. d
11. a
12. b
13. d
14. d
15. c
16. b
17. c
18. d
19. a
20. c

**chapter 15**

1. c
2. b
3. a
4. c
5. d
6. a
7. c
8. d
9. b
10. d
11. a
12. b
13. d
14. b
15. a
16. c
17. c
18. a
19. c
20. a

# References

Ackerman, D. (1990). *A natural history of the senses.* New York: Random House.

Adams, C. G., & Turner, B. F. (1985). Reported change in sexuality from young adulthood to old age. *Journal of Sex Research, 21,* 126–141.

Adams, D., & Adams, G. R. (1984). Mount Saint Helen's ashfall: Evidence for a disaster stress reaction. *American Psychologist, 39,* 252–260.

Adams, P. F., Hendershot, G. E., & Marano, M. A. (1999). Current estimates from the National Health Survey, 1996. *Vital and Health Statistics Series* (National Center for Health Statistics), *10* (200).

Ader, J., Cohen, N., & Bovbjerg, P. (1982). Conditioned suppression of humoral immunity in the rat. *Journal of Comparative and Physiological Psychology, 96,* 517–521.

Adler, A. (1924). Individual psychology. *Journal of Abnormal and Social Psychology, 22,* 116–122.

Adler, A. (1927). *Understanding human nature.* Oxford, UK: Greenberg.

Adler, A. (1928). Characteristics of the first, second, and third child. *Children, 3,* 14–52.

Adler, A. (1931). *What life should mean to you.* Oxford, UK: Little, Brown.

Agras, W. S., Rossiter, E. M., Arnow, B., Schneider, J. A., Telch, C. F., Raeburn, S. D., et al. (1992). Pharmacologic and cognitive-behavioral treatment for bulimia nervosa: A controlled comparison. *American Journal of Psychiatry, 149,* 82–87.

Ainsworth, M. D. S., & Bell, S. M. (1970). Attachment, exploration, and separation. *Child Development, 41,* 49–68.

Ainsworth, M. D., Blehar, M. C., Walters, E., & Wall, S. (1978). *Patterns of attachment: A psychological study of the strange situation.* Hillsdale, NJ: Erlbaum.

Aisen, P. S., & Davis, K. L. (1997). The search for disease-modifying treatment for Alzheimer's disease. *Neurology, 48,* S35–S41.

Akerstedt, T., Torsvall, L., & Gillberg, M. (1982). Sleepiness and shift work: Field studies. *Sleep, 5,* 95–106.

Akhtar, S., & Thomson, J. A., Jr. (1982). Overview: Narcissistic personality disorder. *American Journal of Psychiatry, 139,* 12–20.

Alcohol, Drug Abuse, & Mental Health Administration. (1989). *Obsessive-compulsive disorder.* DHHS Publication No. (ADM) 89-1579.

Algaze, B. (1995). Cognitive therapy, study counseling, and systematic desensitization in the treatment of text anxiety. In C. D. Spielberger & P. R. Vagg (Eds.), *Test anxiety: Theory, assessment, and treatment.* Philadephia: Taylor & Francis.

Allen, D. J., & Oleson, T. (1999). Shame and internalized homophobia in gay men. *Journal of Homosexuality, 37,* 33–43.

Allison, P. D., & Furstenberg, F. F. (1989). How marital dissolution affects children: Variations by age and sex. *Developmental Psychology, 25,* 540–549.

Allport, F. H. (1924). *Social psychology.* New York: Houghton Mifflin.

Allport, G. W. (1950). *The nature of personality: Selected papers.* Oxford, UK: Addison-Wesley.

Allport, G. W. (1961). *Pattern and growth in personality.* New York: Holt, Rinehart and Winston.

Allport, G. W., & Odbert, H. S. (1936). Traitnames. A psycho-lexical study. *Psychological Monographs, 47,* 1–171.

Amabile, T. M. (1989). *Growing up creative.* New York: Crown.

Amato, P. R. (1981). Urban-rural differences in helping: Behavior in Australia and the United States. *Journal of Social Psychology, 114,* 289–290.

Amato, P. R. (1983). Helping behavior in urban and rural environments: Field studies based on a taxonomic organization of helping episodes. *Journal of Personality and Social Psychology, 45,* 571–586.

Ambady, N., & Rosenthal, R. (1993). Half a minute: Predicting teacher evaluations from thin slices of nonverbal behavior and physical attractiveness. *Journal of Personality and Social Psychology, 64,* 431–441.

American Psychiatric Association. (1980). *Diagnostic and statistical manual of mental disorders* (3rd ed.). Washington, DC: Author.

American Psychiatric Association. (2000). *Diagnostic and statistical manual of mental disorders* (4th ed., text revision). Washington, DC: Author.

American Psychological Association. (1992). Ethical principles of psychologists and code of conduct. *American Psychologist, 47,* 1597–1611.

American Psychological Association. (2001). *Directory of the American Psychological Association: 2001 edition.* Washington, DC: Author.

American Psychological Association. (2002). APA Research Office data on education and employment. Internet document at www.apa.org.

Anderson, C. A. (1989). Temperature and aggression: Ubiquitous effects of heat on occurrence of human violence. *Psychological Bulletin, 106,* 74–96.

Anderson, C. A. (1997). Effects of violent movies and trait hostility on hostile feelings and aggressive thoughts. *Aggressive Behavior, 23,* 161–178.

Anderson, C. A., & Anderson, D. C. (1984). Ambient temperature and violent crime: Tests of the linear and curvilinear hypotheses. *Journal of Personality and Social Psychology, 46,* 91–97.

Anderson, C. A., & Bushman, B. J. (2001). Effects of violent video games on aggressive behavior, aggressive cognition, aggressive affect, physiological arousal, and prosocial behavior: A meta-analytic review of the scientific literature. *Psychological Science, 12,* 353–359.

Andrew, R. J. (1965). The origins of facial expressions. *Scientific American, 213,* 88–94.

Aneshensel, C. S., & Huba, G. J. (1983). Depression, alcohol use, and smoking over one year: A four-wave longitudinal case model. *Journal of Abnormal Psychology, 92,* 134–150.

Angst, J., Angst, F., & Stassen, H. H. (1999). Suicide risk in patients with major depressive disorder. *Journal of Clinical Psychiatry, 60* (Suppl. 2), 57–62.

Antonini, M. H. (1985). Temporal relationship between life events and two illness measures: A cross-lagged panel analysis. *Journal of Human Stress, 11,* 21–26.

Antonuccio, D. O., Thomas, M., & Danton, W. G. (1997). A cost-effectiveness analysis of cognitive behavior therapy and fluoxetine (Prozac) in the treatment of depression. *Behavior Therapy, 28,* 187–210.

Appel, A. E., & Holden, G. W. (1998). The co-occurrence of spouse and physical child abuse: A review and appraisal. *Journal of Family Psychology, 12,* 578–599.

Araneda, R. C., Abhay, D., & Firestein, S. (2000). The molecular receptive range of an odorant receptor. *Nature Neuroscience, 3,* 1248–1255.

Arendt, H. (1963). *Eichmann in Jerusalem: A report on the banality of evil.* New York: Viking.

Arkin, S. M. (2000). Alzheimer memory training: Students replicate learning successes. *American Journal of Alzheimer's Disease, 15,* 152–162.

Armstead, C. A., Lawler, K. A., Gorden, G., & Cross, J. (1989). Relationship of racial stressors to blood pressure responses and anger expression in Black college students. *Health Psychology, 8,* 541–556.

Arnsten, A. F. T., & Goldman-Rakic, P. S. (1985). Alpha 2–adrenergic mechanisms in prefrontal cortex associated with cognitive decline in aged nonhuman primates. *Science, 230,* 1273–1276.

Aronson, E. (1984). *The social animal* (4th ed.). San Francisco: Freeman.

Asch, S. E. (1956). Studies of independence and submission to group pressure. I: A minority of one against a unanimous majority. *Psychological Monographs, 70* (416), 7.

Asch, S. E., & Zukier, H. (1984). Thinking about persons. *Journal of Personality and Social Psychology, 46,* 1230–1240.

Atchley, R. C. (1982). Retirement as a social institution. *Annual Review of Sociology, 8,* 263–287.

Atkinson, K., MacWhinney, B., & Stoel, C. (1970). An experiment on recognition of babbling. In *Papers and Reports on Child Language Development.* Stanford, CA: Stanford University Press.

Attie, I., & Brooks-Gunn, J. (1989). Development of eating problems in adolescent girls: A longitudinal study. *Developmental Psychology, 25,* 70–79.

Averill, J. B. (1989). Stress as fact and artifact: An inquiry into the social origins and functions of some stress reactions. In C. D. Spielberger, I. G. Sarason, & J. Strelau (Eds.), *Stress and anxiety.* New York: Hemisphere.

Ayllon, T., & Azrin, N. H. (1968). *The token economy: A motivational system for therapy and rehabilitation.* New York: Appleton-Century-Crofts.

Azuma, H. (1982). Current trends in the study of behavioral development in Japan. *International Journal of Human Development, 5,* 163–169.

Bachman, J. G., & Schulenberg, J. E. (1993). How part-time work intensity relates to drug use, problem behavior, time use, and satisfaction among high school seniors: Are these consequences or merely correlates? *Developmental Psychology, 29,* 220–235.

Backer, T. E., & Richardson, D. (1989). Building bridges: Psychologists and families of the mentally ill. *American Psychologist, 44,* 546–550.

Baddeley, A. (1986). *Working memory.* London: Oxford University Press.

Baddeley, A. (1998). *Human memory: Theory and practice* (revised ed.). Boston: Allyn and Bacon.

Bailey, J. M., & Pillard, R. C. (1991). A genetic study of male sexual orientation. *Archives of General Psychiatry, 48,* 1089–1096.

Bailey, J. M., Pillard, R. C., Neale, M. C., & Agyei, Y. (1993). Heritable factors influence sexual orientation in women. *Archives of General Psychiatry, 50,* 217–223.

Baillargeon, R., 1994. Physical reasoning in young infants: Seeking explanations for impossible events. *British Journal of Developmental Psychology, 17,* 9–33.

Ball, G. G. (1974). Vagotomy: Effect on electrically elicited eating and self-stimulation in the lateral hypothalamus. *Science, 184,* 484–485.

Baltes, P. B., Sowarka, D., & Kliegl, R. (1989). Cognitive training research on fluid intelligence in old age: What can older adults achieve by themselves? *Psychology and Aging, 4,* 217–221.

Bandura, A. (1965). Influence of models' reinforcement contingencies of the acquisition of imitative responses. *Journal of Personality and Social Psychology, 1,* 589–595.

Bandura, A. (1969). *Principles of behavior modification.* New York: Holt, Rinehart and Winston.

Bandura, A. (1974). Behavior theory and the models of man. *American Psychologist, 29,* 859–869.

Bandura, A. (1977). *Social learning theory.* Englewood Cliffs, NJ: Prentice Hall.

Bandura, A. (1984). Recycling misconceptions of perceived self-efficacy. *Cognitive Therapy and Research, 8,* 231–255.

Bandura, A. (1989). Human agency in social cognitive theory. *American Psychologist, 44,* 1175–1184.

Bandura, A. (2001). Social cognitive theory: An agentic perspective. *Annual Reviews of Psychology, 52,* 1–26.

Bandura, A., & Adams, N. E. (1977). Analysis of self-efficacy theory of behavioral change. *Cognitive Therapy and Research, 1,* 287–310.

Bandura, A., Adams, N. E., & Beyer, J. (1977). Cognitive processes mediating behavioral change. *Journal of Personality and Social Psychology, 35,* 125–139.

Barash, D. P. (1979). *The whisperings within: Evolution and the origin of human nature.* New York: Penguin.

Barber, J. (Ed.). (1996). *Hypnosis and suggestion in the treatment of pain: A clinical guide.* New York: Norton.

Bard, M., & Sangrey, D. (1986). *The crime victim's book* (2nd ed.). New York: Basic.

Barfield, R. E., & Morgan, J. N. (1978). Trends in satisfaction with retirement. *The Gerontologist, 18,* 19–23.

Bargh, J. A., & Ferguson, M. J. (2000). Beyond behaviorism: On the automaticity of higher mental processes. *Psychological Bulletin, 126,* 925–945.

Barker, R. G., Dembo, T., & Lewin, K. (1943). Frustration and regression. In R. G. Barker, J. S. Kounin, & H. F. Wright (Eds.), *Child behavior and development.* New York: McGraw-Hill.

Barnett, M. A., Howard, J. A., King, L. M., & Dino, G. A. (1980). Antecedents of empathy: Retrospective accounts of early socialization. *Personality and Social Psychology Bulletin, 6,* 361–365.

Barnett, R. C., Marshall, N. L., & Singer, J. D. (1992a). Job experiences over time, multiple roles, and women's mental health: A longitudinal study. *Journal of Personality and Social Psychology, 62,* 634–644.

Barnett, R. C., Marshall, N. L., & Singer, J. D. (1992b). "Job experiences over time, multiple roles, and women's mental health: A longitudinal study." Correction. *Journal of Personality and Social Psychology, 62,* 890.

Baron, R. S. (1986). Distraction/conflict theory: Progress and problems. In L. Berkowitz (Ed.), *Advances in experimental social psychology.* Orlando: Academic.

Barr, H. M., Streissguth, A. P., Darby, B. L., & Sampson, P. D. (1990). Prenatal exposure to alcohol, caffeine, tobacco, and aspirin. *Developmental Psychology, 26,* 339–348.

Barron, F. (1968). *Creativity and personal freedom.* New York: Van Nostrand Reinhold.

Barron, K. E., & Harackiewicz, J. M. (2001). Achievement goals and optimal motivation: Testing multiple goal models. *Journal of Personality and Social Psychology, 80,* 706–722.

Barsalou, L. W. (1985). Ideals, central tendency, and frequency of instantiation as determinants of graded structure in categories. *Journal of Experimental Psychology: Learning, Memory, and Cognition, 11,* 629–654.

Bartlett, F. (1958). *Thinking: An experimental and social study.* Oxford, UK: Basic.

Baruch, G., Barnett, R., & Rivers, C. (1983). *Lifeprints.* New York: McGraw-Hill.

Baskett, L. M. (1984). Ordinal position differences in children's family interactions. *Developmental Psychology, 20,* 1026–1031.

Baudry, M., & Lynch, G. (2001). Remembrance of arguments past: How well is the glutamate receptor hypothesis of LTP holding up after 20 years? *Neurobiology of Learning and Memory, 76,* 284–297.

Bauer, P. J. (1993). Memory of gender-consistent and gender-inconsistent event sequences by twenty-five-month-old children. *Child Development, 64,* 285–297.

Bauer, P. J. (1996). What do infants recall of their lives? Memory for specific events by one- to two-year-olds. *American Psychologist, 51,* 29–41.

Baum, A., & Posluszny, D. M. (1999). Health psychology: Mapping biobehavioral contributions to health and illness. *Annual Review of Psychology, 50,* 137–163.

Baumrind, D. (1964). Some thoughts on the ethics of research: After reading Milgram's "Behavioral study of obedience." *American Psychologist, 19,* 421–423.

Baumrind, D. (1975). *Early socialization and the discipline controversy.* Morristown, NJ: General Learning Press.

Baumrind, D. (1985). Research using intentional deception. *American Psychologist, 40,* 165–174.

Baumrind, D. (1991). The influence of parenting style on adolescent competence and substance use. *Journal of Early Adolescence, 11,* 56–95.

Baumrind, D. (1993). The average expectable environment is not good enough: A response to Scarr. *Child Development, 64,* 1299–1317.

Baumrind, D. (1995). Commentary on sexual orientation: Research and social policy implications. *Developmental Psychology, 31,* 130–136.

Beachner, L., & Pickett, A. (2001). *Multiple intelligences and positive life habits: 174 activities for applying them in your classroom.* Thousand Oaks, CA: Corwin.

Beardslee, W. R., Bemporad, J., Keller, M. B., & Klerman, G. L. (1983). Children of parents with major affective disorder: A review. *American Journal of Psychiatry, 140,* 825–844.

Beatty, J. (2001). *The human brain: Essentials of behavioral neuroscience.* Thousand Oaks, CA: Sage.

Beck, A. T. (1970). Cognitive therapy: Nature and relation to behavior therapy. *Behavior Therapy, 1,* 184–200.

Beck, A. T. (1982). *Depression: Clinical, experimental, and theoretical aspects.* New York: Harper.

Beck, A. T., & Emery, G. (1985). *Anxiety disorders and phobias: A cognitive perspective.* New York: Basic.

Belsky, J. (1984). The determinants of parenting: A process model. *Child Development, 55,* 83–96.

Belsky, J., & Pensky, E. (1988). Marital change across the transition to parenthood. *Marriage and Family Review, 12,* 133–156.

Benjamin, L. T., Jr. (1985). Defining aggression: An exercise for classroom discussion. *Teaching of Psychology, 12,* 40–42.

Berg, J. H. (1984). Development of friendship between roommates. *Journal of Personality and Social Psychology, 46,* 346–356.

Berkowitz, L. (1990). On the formation and regulation of anger and aggression: A cognitive-neoassociationistic analysis. *American Psychologist, 45,* 494–503.

Berkowitz, L. (1993). *Aggression: Its causes, consequences, and control.* New York: McGraw-Hill.

Berkowitz, L. (2001). On the formation and regulation of anger and aggression: A cognitive-neoassociationistic analysis. In L. Parrott & W. Gerrod (Eds.), *Emotions in social psychology: Essential readings.* Philadelphia: Psychology Press/Taylor & Francis.

Berman, A. L., & Jobes, D. A. (1991, March). *Adolescent suicide: Assessment and intervention.* Washington, DC: American Psychological Association.

Bernhardt, P. C. (1997). Influences of serotonin and testosterone in aggression and dominance: Convergence with social psychology. *Current Directions in Psychological Science, 6,* 44–48.

Bernstein, I. L. (1999). Food aversion learning: A risk factor for nutritional problems in the elderly? *Physiology and Behavior, 66,* 199–201.

Berscheid, E., & Walster, E. (1974). Physical attractiveness. In L. Berkowitz (Ed.), *Advances in experimental social psychology* (Vol. 7). New York: Academic.

Bertoncini, J., Bijeljac-Babic, R., Jusczyk, P. W., Kennedy, L. J., & Mehler, J. (1988). An investigation of young infants' perceptual representations of speech sounds. *Journal of Experimental Psychology: General, 117,* 21–33.

Bhatt, R. S., Wasserman, E. A., Reynolds, W. F., & Knauss, K. S. (1988). Conceptual behavior in pigeons: Categorization of both familiar and novel examples from four classes of natural and artificial stimuli. *Journal of Experimental Psychology: Animal Behavior Processes, 14,* 219–234.

Birtchnell, J. (1980). Women whose mothers died in childhood: An outcome study. *Psychological Medicine, 136,* 317–325.

Bjork, R. A. (2000). About APS. Internet document at www.psychologicalscience.org.

Björntorp, P. (1972). Disturbances in the regulation of food intake. *Advances in Psychosomatic Medicine, 7,* 116–147.

Black, J. B., & Bern, H. (1981). Causal coherence and memory for events in narratives. *Journal of Verbal Learning and Verbal Behavior, 20,* 267–275.

Black, J. B., Turner, T. J., & Bower, G. H. (1979). Point of view in narrative comprehension, memory, and production. *Journal of Verbal Learning and Verbal Behavior, 18,* 187–198.

Block, J., & Robins, R. W. (1993). A longitudinal study of consistency and change in self-esteem from early adolescence to early adulthood. *Child Development, 64,* 909–923.

Bloom, B. (1991). *Planned short-term psychotherapy.* Needham Heights, MA: Allyn and Bacon.

Bloom, F. E., & Lazerson, A. (1988). *Brain, mind, and behavior* (2nd ed.). New York: Freeman.

Bloom, L. M., Lazerson, A., & Hofstadter, L. (1985). *Brain, mind, and behavior.* New York: Freeman.

Bloom, W., & Fawcett, D. W. (1968). *A textbook of histology* (9th ed.). Philadelphia: Saunders.

Boice, R. (1982). Increasing the writing activity of "blocked" academicians. *Behavioral Research and Therapy, 20,* 197–207.

Bok, S. (1998). *Mayhem: Violence as public entertainment.* Reading, MA: Perseus.

Bolles, R. C. (1972). Reinforcement, expectancy, and learning. *Psychological Review, 79,* 394–409.

Bonvillian, J. D., Orlansky, M. D., & Novack, L. L. (1983). Early sign language acquisition and its relation to cognitive and motor development. In J. G. Kyle & B. Woll (Eds.), *Language in sign: An international perspective on sign language.* London: Croom Helm.

Borkman, T. J. (1997). A selected look at self-help groups in the U.S. *Health and Social Care in the Community, 5,* 357–364.

Bornstein, R., & Smircina, M. T. (1982). The status of the empirical support for the hypothesis of increased variability in aging populations. *The Gerontologist, 22,* 241–243.

Bower, G. H. (1970). Organizational factors in memory. *Cognitive Psychology, 1,* 18–46.

Bower, G. H. (1972). Mental imagery and associative learning. In L. Gregg (Ed.), *Cognition in learning and memory.* New York: Wiley.

Bower, G. H. (1978). Improving memory. *Human Nature, 1,* 64–72.

Bower, G. H. (1981). Mood and memory. *American Psychologist, 36,* 129–148.

Bower, G. H., & Clark, M. C. (1969). Narrative stories as mediators for serial learning. *Psychonomic Science, 14,* 181–182.

Bower, G. H., Clark, M. C., Lesgold, A. M., & Winzenz, D. (1969). Hierarchical retrieval schemes in recall of categorized word lists. *Journal of Verbal Learning and Verbal Behavior, 8,* 323–343.

Brehm, S. (1985). *Intimate relationships.* New York: Random House.

Breland, K., & Breland, M. (1961). The misbehavior of organisms. *American Psychologist, 16,* 681–684.

Breland, K., & Breland, M. (1966). *Animal behavior.* Oxford, UK: Macmillan.

Breslau, N. (2001a). The epidemiology of posttraumatic stress disorder: What is the extent of the problem? *Journal of Clinical Psychiatry, 62,* 16–22.

Breslau, N. (2001b). Outcomes of posttraumatic stress disorder. *Journal of Clinical Psychiatry, 62,* 55–59.

Breznitz, S. (1983). *The denial of stress.* Independence, MO: International University Press.

Briggs, S. R. (1992). Assessing the five-factor model of personality description. *Journal of Personality, 60,* 253–293.

Bronfenbrenner, U. (1979). *The ecology of human development.* Cambridge, MA: Harvard University Press.

Bronfenbrenner, U., & Morris, P. A. (1998). The ecology of developmental processes. In R. M. Lerner (Ed.), *Handbook of child psychology* (5th ed., Vol. 1). New York: Wiley.

Brooks-Gunn, J. (1987). Pubertal processes. In V. P. Van Hesselt and M. Hersen (Eds.), *Handbook of adolescent psychology.* Elmsford, NY: Pergamon.

Brooks-Gunn, J., Klebanov, P. K., & Duncan, G. J. (1996). Ethnic differences in children's intelligence test scores: Role of economic deprivation, home environment, and maternal characteristics. *Child Development, 67,* 396–408.

Brown, J. D. (1991). Staying fit and staying well. *Journal of Personality and Social Psychology, 60,* 555–561.

Brown, R. (1973). *A first language.* Cambridge, MA: Harvard University Press.

Brown, R. (1986). *Social psychology* (2nd ed.). New York: Free Press.

Brown, R., & Kulik, J. (1977). Flashbulb memories. *Cognition, 5,* 73–99.

Brown, R., & Kulik, J. (1982). Flashbulb memories. In U. Neisser (Ed.), *Memory observed.* San Francisco: Freeman.

Brown, S. A., Vik, P. W., McQuaid, J. R., Patterson, T. L., Irwin, M. R., & Grant, I. (1990). Severity of psychosocial stress and outcome of alcoholism treatment. *Journal of Abnormal Psychology, 99,* 344–348.

Brown, V. B., Ridgley, M. S., Pepper, B., Levine, I. S., & Ryglewicz, H. (1989). The dual crisis: Mental illness and substance abuse. *American Psychologist, 44,* 565–569.

Bruck, M., & Ceci, S. J. (1999). The suggestibility of children's memory. *Annual Review of Psychology, 50,* 419–439.

Brunstrom, J. M., Tribbeck, P. M., & MacRae, A. W. (2000). The role of mouth state in the termination of drinking behavior in humans. *Physiology and Behavior, 68,* 579–583.

Bryer, J. B., Nelson, B. A., Miller, J. B., & Krol, P. A. (1987). Childhood sexual and physical abuse as factors in adult psychiatric illness. *American Journal of Psychiatry, 144,* 1426–1430.

Bucher, K. D., Elston, R. C., Green, R., Whybrow, P., Helzer, J., Reich, T., Clayton, P., & Winokur, G. (1981). The transmission of manic depressive illness, II: Segregation analysis of the three sets of family data. *Journal of Psychiatric Research, 16,* 65–78.

Budoff, P. W. (1994). Straight talk about menopause. *World Book health and medical annual.* Chicago: World Book.

Bugelski, B. R., & Alampay, D. A. (1961). The role of frequency in developing perceptual sets. *Canadian Journal of Psychology, 15,* 205–211.

Bullock, M., & Lutkenhaus, P. (1988). The development of volitional behavior in the toddler years. *Child Development, 59,* 664–674.

Bumpass, L. L., & Sweet, J. A. (1989). National estimates of cohabitation. *Journal of Demography, 26,* 615–626.

Burchinal, M., Lee, M., & Ramey, C. (1989). Type of day care and preschool intellectual development in disadvantaged children. *Child Development, 60,* 128–137.

Burke, D. M., & Harrold, R. M. (1988). Aging and semantic processes. In L. L. Light & D. M. Burke (Eds.), *Language, memory and aging.* New York: Cambridge University Press.

Buss, D. M. (1988). Love acts: The evolutionary biology of love. In R. J. Sternberg & M. L. Barnes (Eds.), *The psychology of love.* New Haven, CT: Yale University Press.

Buss, D. M. (1999a). *Evolutionary psychology: The new science of the mind.* Needham Heights, MA: Allyn and Bacon.

Buss, D. M. (1999b). Human nature and individual differences: The evolution of human personality. In L. A. Pervin & O. P. John (Eds.), *Handbook of personality: Theory and research* (2nd ed.). New York: Guilford.

Buss, D. M. (2000). *The dangerous passion: Why jealousy is as necessary as love and sex.* New York: Free Press.

Buss, D. M., Larsen, R. J., Westen, D., & Semmelroth, J. (1992). Sex differences in jealousy: Evolution, physiology & psychology. *Psychological Science, 3,* 251–255.

Butler, R. N., & Lewis, M. I. (1977). *Aging and mental health.* St. Louis: Mosby.

Cacioppo, J. T., Martzke, J. S., Petty, R. E., & Tassinary, L. G. (1988). Specific forms of facial EMG response index emotions during an interview: From Darwin to the continuous flow hypothesis of affect-laden information processing. *Journal of Personality and Social Psychology, 54,* 592–604.

Cairns, R. B., Cairns, B. D., Neckerman, H. J., Ferguson, L. L., & Gariépy, J. L. (1989). Growth and aggression. *Developmental Psychology, 25,* 320–330.

Calderone, M. S. (1983, May–July). Fetal erection and its message to us. *SIECUS Report,* 9–10.

Campos, J. J., Langer, A., & Krowitz, A. (1970). Cardiac responses on the visual cliff in pre-locomotor human infants. *Science, 170,* 196–197.

Canadian Psychological Association. (2001, June). *Annual report.* Ste-Foy, Quebec: Author.

Capaldi, E. J. (1966). Partial reinforcement: A hypothesis of sequential effects. *Psychological Review, 73,* 459–477.

Capone, G. T. (1998). Drugs that increase intelligence? Application for childhood cognitive impairment. *Mental Retardation and Developmental Disabilities Reviews, 4,* 36–49.

Carew, T. J., Hawkins, R. D., & Kandel, E. R. (1983, January 28). Differential classical conditioning of a defensive withdrawal reflex in *Aplysia californica. Science, 219,* 397–400.

Cargan, L., & Melko, M. (1982). *Singles: Myths and realities.* Beverly Hills, CA: Sage.

Carpenter, G. (1974). Mother's face and the newborn. *New Scientist, 61,* 742–744.

Carrion, V. G., & Lock, J. (1997). The coming out process: Developmental stages for sexual minority youth. *Clinical Child Psychology and Psychiatry, 2,* 369–377.

Carroll, M. E., & Overmier, J. B. (Eds.). (2001). *Animal research and human health: Advancing human welfare through behavioral science.* Washington, DC: American Psychological Association.

Caselli, M. C., Bates, E., Casadio, P., Fenson, J., Fenson, L., Sanderl, L., et al. (1995). A cross-linguistic study of early lexical development. *Cognitive Development, 10,* 159–199.

Caspi, A. (1987). Personality in the life course. *Journal of Personality and Social Psychology, 53,* 1203–1213.

Caspi, A.., & Herbener, E. S. (1989). *Continuity and change: Assortive marriage and the consistency of personality in adulthood.* Unpublished manuscript, Harvard University.

Caspi, A., Lynam, D., Moffitt, T. E., & Silva, P. A. (1993). Unraveling girls' delinquency: Biological, dispositional, and contextual contributions to adolescent misbehavior. *Developmental Psychology, 29,* 19–30.

Cattell, R. B. (1965). *The scientific analysis of personality.* Oxford, UK: Penguin.

Cattell, R. B. (1971). *Abilities: Their structure, growth, and action.* Boston: Houghton Mifflin.

Ceci, S. J. (1991). How much does schooling influence general intelligence and its cognitive components? A reassessment of the evidence. *Developmental Psychology, 27,* 703–722.

Ceci, S. J. (1999). Schooling and intelligence. In S. J. Ceci & W. M. Williams (Eds.), *The nature-nurture debate: The essential readings.* Malden, MA: Blackwell.

Cerella, J. (1985). Information processing rates in the elderly. *Psychological Bulletin, 98,* 67–83.

Chambless, D. L., & Hollon, S. D. (1998). Defining empirically supported therapies. *Journal of Consulting and Clinical Psychology, 66,* 7–18.

Chambless, D. L., & Ollendick, T. H. (2000). Empirically supported psychological interventions: Controversies and evidence. *Annual Review of Psychology, 52,* 685–716.

Chang, E. C. (1996). Cultural differences in optimism, pessimism, and coping: Predictors of subsequent adjustment in Asian American and Caucasian American college students. *Journal of Counseling Psychology, 43,* 113–123.

Cheng, P. W., & Holyoak, K. J. (1985). Pragmatic reasoning schemas. *Cognitive Psychology, 17,* 391–416.

Cheng, P. W., & Holyoak, K. J. (1989). On the natural selection of reasoning theories. *Cognition, 33,* 285–313.

Cherlin, A. J., Furstenberg, F. F., Chase-Lansdale, P. L., Kiernan, K. E., Robins, P. K., Morrison, D. R., et al. (1991). Longitudinal studies of effects of divorce on children in Great Britain and the United States. *Science, 252,* 1386–1389.

Chess, S., & Thomas, A. (1999). *Goodness of fit: Clinical applications from infancy through adult life.* Philadelphia: Brunner/Mazel.

Chipman, S. F., Krantz, D. H., & Silver, R. (1992). Mathematics anxiety and science careers among able college women. *Psychological Science, 3,* 292–295.

Choi, I., Nisbett, R. E., & Norenzayan, A. (1999). Causal attribution across cultures: Variation and universality. *Psychological Bulletin, 125,* 47–63.

Chomsky, N. (1965). *Aspects of the theory of syntax.* Cambridge, MA: MIT Press.

Christiaansen, R. E. (1980). Prose memory: Forgetting rates for memory codes. *Journal of Experimental Psychology: Human Learning and Memory, 6,* 611–619.

Chugani, H. T., & Phelps, M. E. (1986, February 21). Maturational changes in cerebral function in infants determined by [18]FDG positron emission tomography. *Science, 231,* 840–842.

Cialdini, R. B. (1993). *Influence: Science and practice* (3rd ed.). New York: HarperCollins.

Clark, H. H., & Clark, E. V. (1977). *Psychology and language.* New York: Harcourt.

Clark, H. H., & Fox Tree, J. E. (2002). Using uh and um in spontaneous speaking. *Cognition, 84,* 73–111.

Clark, L. A., & Watson, D. (1988). Mood and the mundane: Relations between daily life events and self-reported mood. *Journal of Personality and Social Psychology, 54,* 296–308.

Clark, W. B., & Midanik, L. (1982). *Report of the 1979 national survey.* Port Royal, VA: National Technical Information Service, PB No. 82-156514.

Clausen, J. A. (1975). The social meaning of differential physical and sexual maturation. In S. E. Dragastin & G. H. Elder, Jr. (Eds.), *Life cycle*. New York: Wiley.

Clifford, R. E., & Kolodny, R. (1983). Sex therapy for couples. In B. B. Wolman & G. Stricker (Eds.), *Handbook of family and marital therapy*. New York: Plenum.

Clyman, R., Friedman, M., & Weiss, E. (1993, November). As they grow—0 to 13 years: Bulletin on research. *Parents, 68*, 192–193.

Coe, C. L. (1993). Psychosocial factors in immunity in nonhuman primates: A review. *Psychosomatic Medicine, 55*, 298–308.

Cohane, G. H., & Pope, H. G., Jr. (2001). Body image in boys: A review of the literature. *International Journal of Eating Disorders, 29*, 373–379.

Cohen, S., & Herbert, T. B. (1996). Health psychology: Psychological factors and physical disease from the perspective of human psychoneuroimmunology. *Annual Review of Psychology, 47*, 113–142.

Cohler, B. J., & Galatzer-Levy, R. M. (2000). *The course of gay and lesbian lives: Social and psychoanalytic perspectives*. Chicago: University of Chicago Press.

Cole, M. A. (1978–1979). Sex and marital status differences in death anxiety. *Omega, 9*, 139–147.

Conway, A. V. (2002). A forgotten topic. *Psychologist, 15*, 56.

Conway, M. A., Cohen, G., & Stanhope, N. (1991). On the very long-term retention of knowledge acquired through formal education: Twelve years of cognitive psychology. *Journal of Experimental Psychology: General, 120*, 395–409.

Cooper, H. (1979). Pygmalion grows up: A model for teacher expectation communication and performance influence. *Review of Educational Research, 49*, 389–410.

Cooper, M., Zanna, M. P., & Taves, P. A. (1978). Arousal as a necessary condition for attitude change following induced compliance. *Journal of Personality and Social Psychology, 36*, 1101–1106.

Corballis, M. C., & Corballis, P. M. (2001). Interhemispheric visual matching in the split brain. *Neuropsychologia, 39*, 1395–1400.

Coren, S., Porac, C., & Ward, L. M. (1984). *Sensation and perception* (2nd ed.). New York: Academic.

Coren, S., Ward, L. M., & Porac, C. (1989). Sensation and perception (3rd ed.). San Diego: Harcourt Brace Jovanovich.

Cornelius, M. D., & Day, N. L. (2000). The effects of tobacco use during and after pregnancy on exposed children: Relevance of findings for alcohol research. *Alcohol Research and Health, 24*, 242–249.

Corrigan, P. W., & McCracken, S. G. (1995). Contingencies for dangerous behavior. *American Journal of Psychiatry, 152*, 1696–1697.

Costa, P. T., Jr., McCrae, R. R., Martin, T. A., Oryol, V. E., Senin, I. G., Rukavishnikov, A. A., et al. (2000). Personality development from adolescence through adulthood: Further cross-cultural comparisons of age differences. In V. J. Molfese & D. L. Molfese (Eds.), *Temperament and personality development across the life span*. Mahwah, NJ: Erlbaum.

Costello, C. G. (1982). Fears and phobias in women: A community study. *Journal of Abnormal Psychology, 91*, 280–286.

Couric, E. (1989, December 11). Women in the law: Awaiting their turn. *The National Law Journal*, S-2.

Cousins, N. (1989). *Head first: The biology of hope*. New York: Dutton.

Covington, M. V. (1999). Caring about learning: The nature and nurturing of subject-matter appreciation. *Educational Psychologist, 34*, 127–136.

Cowan, C. P., & Cowan, P. (1988). Who does what when partners become parents: Implications for men, women, and marriage. *Marriage and Family Review, 12*, 105–131.

Cowan, E. (1982). Help is where you find it. *American Psychologist, 37*, 385–395.

Cowan, N. (1984). On short and long auditory stores. *Psychological Bulletin, 96*, 341–370.

Cowan, W. M., Harter, D. H., & Kandel, E. R. (2000). The emergence of modern neuroscience: Some implications for neurology and psychiatry. *Annual Review of Neuroscience, 23*, 343–391.

Cox, J. R., & Griggs, R. A. (1982). The effects of experience on performance in Wason's selection task. *Memory and Cognition, 10*, 496–502.

Coyle, S. L., & Thurgood, D. H. (1989). *Summary report 1989: Doctorate recipients from U.S. universities*. Washington, DC: National Academy Press.

Craig, G. J., & Baucum, D. (2002). *Human development* (9th ed.). Upper Saddle River, NJ: Prentice Hall.

Craig, K. D., & Patrick, C. J. (1985). Facial expression during induced pain. *Journal of Personality and Social Psychology, 48*, 1080–1091.

Craik, F. I. M., & Tulving, E. (1975). Depth of processing and the retention of words in episodic memory. *Journal of Experimental Psychology: General, 104*, 268–294.

Crandall, J. E. (1980). Adler's concept of social-interest: Theory, measurement, and implications for adjustment. *Journal of Personality and Social Psychology, 39*, 481–498.

Craske, M., Brown, T. A., & Barlow, D. H. (1991). Behavioral treatment of panic disorder: A two-year follow-up. *Behavior Therapy, 22*, 289–304.

Crick, F., & Mitchison, G. (1995). REM sleep and neural nets. *Behavioural Brain Research, 69*, 147–155.

Cronbach, L. J. (1949). *Essentials of psychological testing*. New York: Harper.

Crook, L. S., & Dean, M. C. (1999a). "Lost in a shopping mall"—A breach of professional ethics. *Ethics and Behavior, 9*, 39–50.

Crook, L. S., & Dean, M. C. (1999b). Logical fallacies and ethical breaches. *Ethics and Behavior, 9*, 61–68.

Crook, T. H., & West, R. L. (1990). Name recall performance across the adult life-span. *British Journal of Psychology, 81*, 335–340.

Crooks, R., & Baur, K. (1999). *Our sexuality* (7th ed.). Belmont, CA: Brooks/Cole.

Crosby, E., Humphrey, T., & Lauer, E. W. (1962). *Comparative anatomy of the nervous system*. New York: Macmillan.

Cummings, E. M., Iannotti, R. J., & Zahn-Waxler, C. (1989). Aggression between peers in early childhood. *Child Development, 60*, 887–895.

Curtis, R. C., & Miller, K. (1986). Believing another likes or dislikes you: Behaviors making the beliefs come true. *Journal of Personality and Social Psychology, 51*, 284–290.

Cytryn, L., McKnew, D. H., & Bunney, W. E. (1980). Diagnosis of depression in children: A reassessment. *American Journal of Psychiatry, 137*, 22–25.

Dabbs, J. M., Jr., & Leventhal, H. (1966). Effects of varying the recommendations in a fear-arousing communication. *Journal of Personality and Social Psychology, 4,* 525–531.

Damasio, A. R. (1990). Category-related recognition deficits as a clue to the neural substrates of knowledge. *Trends in Neuroscience,* 1395–1398.

Damasio, A. R., & Damasio, H. (1992, September). Brain and language. *Scientific American,* 89–95.

Damasio, A. R., Tranel, D., & Damasio, H. C. (1990). Individuals with sociopathic behavior caused by frontal damage fail to respond automatically to social stimuli. *Behavioral Brain Research, 14,* 81–94.

Dammann, E. J. (1997). "The myth of mental illness": Continuing controversies and their implications for mental health professionals. *Clinical Psychology Review, 17,* 733–756.

Darley, J. M., & Fazio, R. H. (1980). Expectancy confirmation processes arising in the social interaction sequence. *American Psychologist, 35,* 867–881.

Darwin, C. (1872). *The expression of emotion in man and animals.* London: Murray.

Dattilio, F. M. (2002). Homework assignments in couple and family therapy. *Journal of Clinical Psychology, 58,* 535–547.

Davey, G. (2001). About the British Psychological Society. Internet document at www.bps.org.uk.

Davidson, R. J., & Fox, N. A. (1989). Frontal brain asymmetry predicts infants' response to maternal separation. *Journal of Abnormal Psychology, 98,* 127–131.

Davidson, R. J., & Tomarken, A. J. (1989). Laterality and emotion: An electrophysiological approach. In F. Boller & J. Graffman (Eds.), *Handbook of neuropsychology.* New York: Elsevier Science.

Davies, I. R. L., Sowden, P. T., Jerrett, D. T., Jerrett, T., & Corbett, G. G. (1998). A cross-cultural study of English and Setswana speakers on a colour triads task: A test of the Sapir-Whorf hypothesis. *British Journal of Psychology, 89,* 1–15.

Davis, C. M., Moskovitz, B., Nguyen, M. A., Tran, B. B., Arai, A., Lynch, G., & Granger, R. (1997). A profile of the behavioral changes produced by facilitation of AMPA-type glutamate receptors. *Psychopharmacology, 133,* 161–167.

Davis, M. (1997). Neurobiology of fear responses: The role of the amygdala. *Journal of Neuropsychiatry and Clinical Neurosciences, 9,* 382–402.

DeAngelis, T. (1996). Seligman: Optimism can be a vaccination. *APA Monitor, 27* (10), 33.

DeFries, J. C., Plomin, R., & LaBuda, M. C. (1987). Genetic stability of cognitive development from childhood to adulthood. *Developmental Psychology, 23,* 4–12.

de Haan, M., Pascalis, O., & Johnson, M. H. (2002). Specialization of neural mechanisms underlying recognition in human infants. *Journal of Cognitive Neuroscience, 14,* 199–209.

De Houwer, J., Thomas, S., & Baeyens, F. (2001). Association learning of likes and dislikes: A review of 25 years of research on human evaluative conditioning. *Psychological Bulletin, 127,* 853–869.

DeLongis, A., Folkman, S., & Lazarus, R. (1988). The impact of daily stress on health and mood: Psychological and social resources as mediators. *Journal of Personality and Social Psychology, 54,* 486–495.

DeMaris, A., & Leslie, G. R. (1984). Cohabitation with the future spouse: Its influence upon marital satisfaction and communication. *Journal of Marriage and the Family, 46,* 77–84.

Dement, W. C., & Vaughan, C. (1999). *The promise of sleep.* New York: Dell.

Demitrack, M. A. (1992). Plasma and cerebrospinal fluid measures of arginine vasopressin secretion in patients with bulimia nervosa and in healthy subjects. *Journal of Clinical Endocrinology and Metabolism, 74,* 1277–1283.

De Valois, R. L., & Jacobs, G. H. (1968). Primate color vision. *Science, 162,* 533–540.

de Villiers, J. G., & de Villiers, P. A. (1978). *Language acquisition.* Cambridge, MA: Harvard University Press.

de Villiers, J. G., & de Villiers, P. A. (1999). Language development. In M. H. Bornstein & M. E. Lamb (Eds.), *Developmental psychology: An advanced textbook* (4th ed.). Mahwah, NJ: Erlbaum.

de Weid, D. (1997). Neuropeptides in learning and memory processes. *Behavioural Brain Research, 83,* 83–90.

Diamond, A. (1991). Frontal lobe involvement in cognitive changes during the first year of life. In K. Gibson & A. Petersen (Eds.), *Brain maturation and cognitive development.* Hawthorne, NY: Aldine de Greuter.

Diamond, L. M. (1998). Development of sexual orientation among adolescent and young adult women. *Developmental Psychology, 34,* 1085–1095.

Diaz, R. M. (1985). Bilingual cognitive development: Addressing three gaps in current research. *Child Development, 56,* 1376–1388.

Diener, E., Suh, E. M., Lucas, R. E., & Smith, H. L. (1999). Subjective well-being: Three decades of progress. *Psychological Bulletin, 125,* 276–302.

Dion, K. K., & Berscheid, E. (1972). *Physical attractiveness and social perception of peers in preschool children.* Unpublished research report.

Dion, K. L., & Dion, K. K. (1988). Romantic love: Individual and cultural perspectives. In R. J. Sternberg & M. L. Barnes (Eds.), *The psychology of love.* New Haven, CT: Yale University Press.

Dohrenwend, B. P., Levav, I., Shrout, P. E., & Link, B. G. (1987). Life stress and psychopathology: Progress on research begun with Barbara Snell Dohrenwend. *American Journal of Community Psychology, 15,* 677–715.

Dolan, R. J. (2000). Emotional processing in the human brain revealed through functional neuroimaging. In M. S. Gazzaniga (Ed.), *The new cognitive neurosciences* (2nd ed.). Cambridge, MA: MIT Press.

Dollard, J., Doob, L. W., Miller, N. E., Mowrer, O. H., & Sears, R. R. (1939). *Frustration and aggression.* New Haven, CT: Yale University Press.

Domjan, M., & Burkhard, B. (1986). *The principles of learning and behavior* (2nd ed.). Monterey, CA: Brooks/Cole.

Donnelly, C. M., & McDaniel, M. A. (1993). Use of analogy in learning scientific concepts. *Journal of Experimental Psychology: Learning, Memory, and Cognition, 19,* 975–987.

Donnerstein, E., Linz, D., & Penrod, S. (1987). *The question of pornography: Research findings and implications.* New York: Free Press.

Dosher, B. A., & Sperling, G. (1998). A century of human information-processing theory: Vision, attention, and memory. In J. Hochberg (Ed.), *Perception and cognition at century's end.* San Diego: Academic.

Doty, R. L. (2001). Olfaction. *Annual Reviews of Psychology, 52,* 423–452.

Dreskin, W., & Dreskin, W. (1983). *The day care decision: What's best for you and your child.* New York: M. Evans.

Drewnowski, A. (1998). The behavioral phenotype in human obesity. In E. D. Capaldi (Ed.), *Why we eat what we eat: The psychology of eating.* Washington, DC: American Psychological Association.

Dryden, W., & Ellis, A. (2001). Rational emotive behavior therapy. In K. S. Dobson (Ed.), *Handbook of cognitive-behavioral therapies* (2nd ed.). New York: Guilford.

Dubow, E. F., & Tisak, J. (1989). The relation between stressful life events and adjustment in elementary school children: The role of social support and social problem-solving skills. *Child Development, 60,* 1412–1423.

Duncker, K. (1945). On problem solving. *Psychological Monographs, 58,* 1–113.

Dunn, J., & Plomin, R. (1990). *Separate lives: Why siblings are so different.* New York: Basic.

Dymond, S., & Critchfield, T. S. (2002). A legacy of growth: Human operant research in the *Psychological Record,* 1980–1999. *Psychological Record, 52,* 99–106.

Dziegielewski, S. F. (1997). Time-limited brief therapy: The state of practice. *Crisis Intervention and Time-Limited Treatment, 3,* 217–228.

Eagly, A. H. (1992). Uneven progress: Social psychology and the study of attitudes. *Journal of Personality and Social Psychology, 63,* 693–710.

Earley, P. C. (1993). East meets West meets Mideast: Further explorations of collectivistic and individualistic work groups. *Academy of Management Journal, 36,* 319–348.

Ebbinghaus, H. (1913). *Memory.* New York: Columbia University Teachers College.

Eccles, J. S., Midgley, C., Wigfield, A., & Reuman, D. (1993). Development during adolescence. *American Psychologist, 48,* 90–101.

Edelstein, E. L. (1982). Reactivation of concentration camp experiences as a result of hospitalization. In C. D. Spielberger, I. G. Sarason, & N. A. Milgram (Eds.), *Stress and anxiety* (Vol. 8). Washington, DC: Hemisphere.

Ehrenreich, B., Hess, E., & Jacobs, G. (1986). *Re-making love.* Garden City, NY: Anchor Press/Doubleday.

Eich, E. (1995). Searching for mood dependent memory. *Psychological Science, 6,* 67–75.

Eich, E., & Metcalfe, J. (1989). Mood dependent memory for internal versus external events. *Journal of Experimental Psychology: Learning, Memory, and Cognition, 15,* 443–455.

Ekman, P. (1971). Universal and cultural differences in facial expressions of emotion. In J. K. Cole (Ed.), *Nebraska symposium on motivation* (Vol. 19). Lincoln: University of Nebraska Press.

Ekman, P. (1973). *Darwin and facial expression: A century of research in review.* Oxford, UK: Academic.

Ekman, P., & Davidson, R. J. (1993). Voluntary smiling changes regional brain activity. *Psychological Science, 4,* 342–345.

Ekman, P., & Friesen, W. V. (1986). A new pan-cultural facial expression of emotion. *Motivation and Emotion, 10,* 159–167.

Elkin, I. (1994). The Treatment of Depression Collaborative Research Program: Where we began and where we are. In A. E. Bergin & S. L. Garfield (Eds.), *Handbook of psychotherapy and behavior change* (4th ed.). New York: Wiley.

Elkin, I. (1999). A major dilemma in psychotherapy outcome research: Disentangling therapists from therapies. *Clinical Psychology: Science and Practice, 6,* 10–32.

Elkin, I., Gibbons, R. D., Shea, M. T., Sotsky, S. M., Watkins, J. T., Pilkonis, P. A., et al. (1995). Initial severity and differential treatment outcome in the National Institute of Mental Health Treatment of Depression Collaborative Research Program. *Journal of Consulting and Clinical Psychology, 63,* 841–847.

Elkin, I., Parloff, M. B., Hadley, S. W., & Autry, J. H. (1985). NIMH Treatment of Depression Collaborative Research Program: Background and research plan. *Archives of General Psychiatry, 42,* 305–316.

Elkin, I., Shea, M. T., Watkins, J. T., Imber, S. D., Sotsky, S. M., Collins, J. F., et al. (1989). National Institute of Mental Health Treatment of Depression Collaborative Research Program: General effectiveness of treatments. *Archives of General Psychiatry, 46,* 971–982.

*Elle Magazine.* (1998, December). Happy days are here again.

Elliot, G. R., & Eisdorfer, C. (1982). *Stress and human health.* New York: Springer.

Elliott, R. (2001). Contemporary brief experiential psychotherapy. *Clinical Psychology: Science and Practice, 8,* 38–50.

Ellis, A. (1962). *Reason and emotion in psychotherapy.* Oxford, UK: Lyle Stuart.

Ellis, A., & Dryden, W. (1987). *The practice of rational emotive therapy.* New York: Springer.

Ellis, E. M., Atkeson, B. M., & Calhoun, K. S. (1981). An assessment of long-term reaction to rape. *Journal of Abnormal Psychology, 90,* 263–266.

Ellis, H. C., Thomas, R. L., McFarland, A. D., & Lane, J. W. (1985). Emotional mood states and retrieval in episodic memory. *Journal of Experimental Psychology: Learning, Memory, and Cognition, 11,* 363–370.

Epstein, N. B., & Vlok, L. A. (1981). Research on the results of psychotherapy: A summary of evidence. *American Journal of Psychiatry, 138,* 1027–1035.

Erickson, D. J., Wolfe, J., King, D. W., King, L. A., & Sharkansky, F. J. (2001). Posttraumatic stress disorder and depression symptomatology in a sample of Gulf War veterans: A prospective analysis. *Journal of Consulting and Clinical Psychology, 69,* 41–49.

Erikson, E. H. (1963). *Childhood and society* (2nd ed.). New York: Norton.

Erlenmeyer-Kimling, L., & Jarvik, L. F. (1963). Genetics and intelligence. *Science, 142,* 1477–1479.

Eron, L. D. (1987). The development of aggressive behavior from the perspective of a developing behaviorism. *American Psychologist, 42,* 435–442.

Evans, D. A., Funkenstein, H. H., Albert, M. S., Scherr, P. A., & Cook, N. R. (1989). Prevalence of Alzheimer's disease in a community population of older persons. *Journal of the American Medical Association, 262,* 2551–2556.

Evarts, E. V. (1979). Brain mechanisms of movement. In Scientific American's *The brain.* San Francisco: Freeman.

Everett, J., Laplante, L., & Thomas, J. (1989). The selective attention deficit in schizophrenia: Limited resources or cognitive fatigue? *The Journal of Nervous and Mental Disease, 177,* 735–738.

Exner, J. E., Jr. (1997). The future of Rorschach in personality assessment. *Journal of Personality Assessment, 68,* 37–46.

Eysenck, H. J. (with Kamin, L.). (1981). *The intelligence controversy.* New York: Wiley.

Eysenck, H. J. (1994). Personality: Biological foundations. In P. A. Vernon (Ed.), *The neuropsychology of individual differences.* San Diego, CA: Academic.

Facklam, M., & Facklam, H. (1982). *The brain: Magnificent mind machine.* New York: Harcourt.

Falbo, T. (1981). Relationships between birth category, achievement, and interpersonal orientation. *Journal of Personality and Social Psychology, 41,* 121–131.

Fantz, R. L. (1958). Pattern vision in young infants. *Psychological Record, 8,* 43–47.

Farina, A. (1982). The stigma of mental disorders. In A. G. Miller (Ed.), *In the eye of the beholder: Contemporary issues in stereotyping.* New York: Praeger.

Faulkner, A. H., & Cranston, K. (1998). Correlates of same-sex sexual behavior in a random sample of Massachusetts high school students. *American Journal of Public Health, 88,* 262–266.

Fazio, R. H., Zanna, M. P., & Cooper, J. (1977). Dissonance and self-perception. *Journal of Experimental Social Psychology, 13,* 464–479.

Fehm-Wolfsdorf, G., Gnadler, M., Kern, W., Klosterhalfen, W., & Kerner, W. (1993). Classically conditioned changes of blood glucose level in humans. *Physiology and Behavior, 54,* 155–160.

Feldman, R. S. (1985). *Social psychology: Theories, research, and applications.* New York: McGraw-Hill.

Feldman, S. S., Biringen, Z. C., & Nash, S. C. (1981). Fluctuations of sex-related self-attributions as a function of stage of family life cycle. *Developmental Psychology, 17,* 24–35.

Fernald, A. (1983). The perceptual and affective salience of mother's speech to infants. In L. Feagans (Ed.), *The origins and growth of communication.* New Brunswick, NJ: Ablex.

Fernald, A., & Simon, T. (1984). Expanded intonation contours in mother's speech to newborns. *Developmental Psychology, 20,* 104–113.

Feshbach, S., & Weiner, B. (1986). *Personality* (2nd ed.). Lexington, MA: Heath.

Festinger, L. A. (1954). A theory of social comparison processes. *Human Relations, 7,* 117–140.

Festinger, L., & Carlsmith, J. M. (1957). Cognitive consequences of forced compliance. *Journal of Abnormal Psychology, 58,* 203–210.

Fichter, M. M., & Noegel, R. (1990). Concordance for bulimia nervosa in twins. *International Journal of Eating Disorders, 9,* 255–263.

Field, T. (1989). Stressors during pregnancy and the postnatal period. *New Directions in Child Development, 45,* 19–31.

Field, T., & Reite, M. (1984). Children's responses to separation from mother during the birth of another child. *Child Development, 55,* 1308–1316.

Fillion, T. J., & Blass, E. M. (1986, February). Infantile experiences with suckling odors determines adult sexual behavior in rats. *Science, 231,* 729–731.

Fischbach, G. D. (1992, September). Mind and brain. *Scientific American,* 48–59.

Fish, B. (1992). Infants at risk for schizophrenia: Sequelae of a genetic neurointegrative defect. *Archives of General Psychiatry, 49,* 221–235.

Flanagan, C. (1989). *Economic hardship, parents' regrets, and adolescents' achievement motivation.* Paper presented at Society for Research in Child Development, Kansas City, MO.

Flanagan, C. A. (1993). Changes in parent's work status and adolescent's adjustment at school. *Child Development, 64,* 246–257.

Flieller, A. (1999). Comparison of the development of formal thought in adolescent cohorts aged 10 to 15 (1967–1996 and 1972–1993). *Developmental Psychology, 35,* 1048–1058.

Flippo, R. F., Becker, M. J., & Wark, D. M. (2000). *Handbook of college reading and study strategy research.* Mahwah, NJ: Lawrence Erlbaum.

Folkman, S. (2000). Privacy and confidentiality. In B. D. Sales & S. Folkman (Eds.), *Ethics in research with human participants.* Washington, DC: American Psychological Association.

Foster, B. G. (1982). Self-disclosure and intimacy in long-term marriages. In N. Stinnett et al. (Eds.), *Family strengths 4: Positive support systems.* Lincoln: University of Nebraska Press.

Foulkes, V. S. (1982). Forming relationships and the matching hypothesis. *Personality and Social Psychology Bulletin, 8,* 631–636.

Frank, J. D. (1982). Therapeutic components shared by all psychotherapies. In J. H. Harvey & M. M. Parks (Eds.), *The master lecture series: Vol. 1. Psychotherapy research and behavior change.* Washington, DC: American Psychological Association.

Frazier, S. H. (1985, June 19). *Preventing youth suicide: A collaborative effort.* Paper presented at the National Conference on Youth Suicide, Washington, DC.

Freed, A. M., Chandler, P. J., Mouton, J. S., & Blake, R. R. (1955). Stimulus and background factors in sign violation. *Journal of Personality, 23,* 499.

Freedman, D. X. (1984). Psychiatric epidemiology counts. *Archives of General Psychiatry, 41,* 931–933.

Freedman, J. L., Carlsmith, J. M., & Sears, D. O. (1970). *Social psychology.* Englewood Cliffs, NJ: Prentice Hall.

Freud, A. (1966). *The ego and the mechanisms of defense* (rev. ed.). New York: International Universities Press.

Freud, S. (1900/1988). *The interpretation of dreams.* Birmingham, AL: Classics of Medicine Library.

Freud, S. (1920/1950). *Beyond the pleasure principle.* Oxford, UK: Liveright.

Freud, S. (1923/1961). *The ego and the id.* New York: Norton.

Frezza, M., di Padova, C., Pozzato, G., Terpin, M., & Baraona, G. (1990). High blood alcohol levels in women: The role of decreased gastric alcohol dehydrogenase activity and first-pass metabolism. *New England Journal of Medicine, 322,* 95–99.

Fried, P. A., & Smith, A. M. (2001). A literature review of the consequences of prenatal marihuana exposure: An emerging theme of a deficiency in aspects of executive function. *Neurotoxicology and Teratology, 23,* 1–11.

Friedlander, M. L., Larney, L. C., Skau, M., Hotaling, M., Cutting, M. L., & Schwann, M. (2000). Bicultural identification experiences of internationally adopted children and their parents. *Journal of Counseling Psychology, 47,* 187–198.

Friedman, D., Cycowicz, Y. M., & Gaeta, H. (2001). The novelty P3: An event-related brain potential (ERP) sign of the brain's evaluation of novelty. *Neuroscience and Biobehavioral Reviews, 25,* 355–373.

Fromm, E. (1955). *The sane society.* New York: Holt.

Fruzzetti, A. E., Toland, K., Teller, S. A., & Loftus, E. F. (1992). Memory and eyewitness testimony. In M. M. Gruneberg & P. E. Morris (Eds.), *Aspects of memory: Vol. 1. The practical aspects* (2nd ed.). Florence, KY: Taylor & Francis/Routledge.

Furman, W., Rahe, D. F., & Hartup, W. W. (1981). Rehabilitation of socially-withdrawn preschool children through mixed-age and same-age socialization. In E. M. Hetherington & R. D. Parke (Eds.), *Contemporary readings in child psychology* (2nd Ed.). New York: McGraw-Hill.

Gaeddert, W. P. (1985). Sex and sex-role effects on achievement strivings: Dimensions of similarity and difference. *Journal of Personality, 53,* 286–305.

Gaertner, S. (1989). Researching intergroup bias: The benefits of intercategorization. *Journal of Personality and Social Psychology, 57,* 239–249.

Galaburda, A. M. (1984). Anatomical asymmetries. In N. Geschwind & A. M. Galaburda (Eds.), *Cerebral dominance: The biological foundations.* Cambridge, MA: Harvard University Press.

Gallagher, W. (1993). Midlife myths. *The Atlantic, 271* (5), 51–68.

Gallistel, C. R., & Gibbon, J. (2002). *The symbolic foundations of conditioned behavior.* Mahwah, NJ: Erlbaum.

Galton, F. (1889). *Natural inheritance.* London: Macmillan.

Galton, F. (1891). *Hereditary genius: An inquiry into its laws and consequences.* New York: D. Appleton.

Gamson, W. A., Fireman, B., & Rytina, S. (1982). *Encounters with unjust authority.* Homewood, IL: Dorsey.

Ganster, D. C., Fox, M. L., & Dwyer, D. J. (2001). Explaining employees' health care costs: A prospective examination of stressful job demands, personal control, and physiological reactivity. *Journal of Applied Psychology, 86,* 954–964.

Garb, J. J., & Stunkard, A. J. (1974). Taste aversion in man. *American Journal of Psychiatry, 131,* 1204–1207.

Garber, J., & Hollon, S. (1977). *Depression and the expectancy of success for self and for others.* Unpublished manuscript, University of Minnesota.

Gardiner, H. W., Mutter, J. D., & Kosmitzki, C. (1998). *Lives across cultures: Cross-cultural human development.* Needham Heights, MA: Allyn and Bacon.

Gardner, H. (1983). *Frames of mind: The theory of multiple intelligence.* New York: Basic.

Gardner, H. (1985). *The mind's new science.* New York: Basic.

Gardner, H. (1988). Creativity: An interdisciplinary perspective. *Creativity Research Journal, 1,* 8–26.

Gardner, H., & Walters, J. (1993). A rounded version. In H. Gardner (Ed.), *Multiple intelligences: The theory in practice.* New York: Basic.

Gardner, R. A., & Gardner, B. T. (1972). Communication with a young chimpanzee. In R. Chauvin (Ed.), *Edition du centre national de la recherche scientifique.* Paris: Centre National de la Recherche Scientifique.

Gardner, H. E. (1999). Multiple approaches to understanding. In C. M. Reigeluth (Ed.), *Instructional-design theories and models: A new paradigm of instructional theory* (Vol. II). Mahwah, NJ: Erlbaum.

Garmezy, N. (1983). Stressors of childhood. In N. Garmezy & M. Rutter (Eds.), *Stress, coping, and child development.* New York: McGraw-Hill.

Garmezy, N., & Rutter, M. (1985). Acute reactions to stress. In M. Rutter & L. Hersov (Eds.), *Child and adolescent psychiatry: Modern approaches* (2nd ed., pp. 152–176). Oxford: Blackwell.

Gati, I., & Tversky, A. (1984). Weighing common and distinctive features in perceptual and conceptual judgments. *Cognitive Psychology, 16,* 341–370.

Gazzaniga, M. S., Ivry, R. B., & Mangun, G. R. (1998). *Cognitive neuroscience: The biology of the mind.* New York: Norton.

Ge, X., Conger, R. D., & Elder, G. H. (2001). Pubertal transition, stressful life events, and the emergence of gender differences in adolescent depressive symptoms. *Developmental Psychology, 37,* 404–417.

Geen, R. G. (1976). *Personality.* St. Louis: Mosby.

Geer, J. H., & Fuhr, R. (1976). Cognitive factors in sexual arousal: The role of distraction. *Journal of Consulting and Clinical Psychology, 44,* 238–243.

Gelder, M. (1991). Psychological treatment for anxiety disorders: Adjustment disorder with anxious mood, generalized anxiety disorders, panic disorder, agoraphobia, and avoidant personality disorder. In W. Coryell & G. Winokur (Eds.), *The clinical management of anxiety disorders.* New York: Oxford University Press.

Gershoff, E. T. (2002). Corporal punishment by parents and associated child behaviors and experiences: A meta-analytic and theoretical review. *Psychological Bulletin, 128,* 539–579.

Gerstein, D. R., Luce, R. D., Smelser, N. J., & Sperlich, S. (Eds.). (1988). *The behavioral and social sciences: Achievements and opportunities.* Washington, DC: National Academy Press.

Geschwind, N. (1979). Specializations of the human brain. *Scientific American, 241* (3), 180–199.

Gibbons, M. B. C., Crits-Christoph, P., Levinson, J., Gladis, M., Siqueland, L., Barber, J. P., et al. (2002). Therapist interventions in the interpersonal and cognitive therapy sessions of the Treatment of Depression Collaborative Research Program. *American Journal of Psychotherapy, 56,* 3–26.

Gibbs, W. W. (2002). Saving languages. *Scientific American, 287* (2), 79–85.

Gibson, E. J., & Walk, R. D. (1960). The "visual cliff." *Scientific American, 202,* 64–71.

Gigerenzer, G., & Hug, K. (1992). Domain specific reasoning: Social contracts, cheating and perspective change. *Cognition, 43,* 127–171.

Gilbert, A. N., & Wysocki, C. J. (1987). The smell survey: Results. *National Geographic, 172,* 514–525.

Gillem, A. R., Cohn, L. R., & Throne, C. (2001). Black identity in biracial black/white people: A comparison of Jacqueline who refuses to be exclusively black and Adolphus who wishes he were. *Cultural Diversity and Ethnic Minority Psychology, 7,* 182–196.

Gilligan, C. (1982). *In a different voice.* Cambridge, MA: Harvard University Press.

Gilligan, C., & Attanucci, J. (1994). Two moral orientations: Gender differences and similarities. In B. Puka (Ed.), *Caring voices and women's moral frames: Gilligan's view.* New York: Garland.

Gilligan, C., Ward, J. V., Taylor, J. M., & Bardige, B. (Eds.). (1988). *Mapping the moral domain.* Cambridge, MA: Harvard University Press.

Gilovich, T., Vallone, R., & Tversky, A. (1985). The hot hand in basketball: On the misperception of random sequences. *Cognitive Psychology, 17,* 295–314.

Gingerich, W. J., & Eisengart, S. (2000). Solution-focused brief therapy: A review of the outcome research. *Family Process, 39,* 477–498.

Ginsburg, H. J., & Miller, S. M. (1982). Sex differences in children's risk-taking behavior. *Child Development, 53,* 426–428.

Gladue, B. A., Green, R., & Hellman, R. E. (1984). Neuro-endocrine response to estrogen and sexual orientation. *Science, 225,* 1496–1499.

Glantz, M., & Pickens, R. (1992). *Vulnerability to drug abuse.* Washington, DC: American Psychological Association.

Glaser, R., Kiecolt-Glaser, J. K., Bonneau, R. H., Malarkey, W., Kennedy, S., & Hughes J. (1992). Stress-induced modulation of the immune response to recombinant hepatitis B vaccine. *Psychosomatic Medicine, 54,* 22–29.

Gleitman, L. R., Newport, E. L., & Gleitman, H. (1984). The current status of the motherese hypothesis. *Journal of Child Language, 11,* 43–79.

Glick, R. (1980). Promoting competence and coping through retirement planning. In L. A. Bond & J. C. Rosen (Eds.), *Competence and coping during adulthood.* Hanover, NH: University Press of New England.

Glynn, S. M. (1990). Token economy approaches for psychiatric patients: Progress and pitfalls over 25 years. *Behavior Modification, 14,* 383–407.

Goff, D. C., Leahy, L., Berman, I., Posever, T., Herz, L., Leon, A. C., et al. (2001). A placebo-controlled pilot study of the ampakine CX516 added to clozapine in schizophrenia. *Journal of Clinical Psychopharmacology, 21,* 484–487.

Gold, S. R. (1980). The CAP control theory of drug abuse. In D. J. Lettieri, M. Sayers, & H. W. Pearson (Eds.), *Theories on drug abuse: Selected contemporary perspectives.* National Institute on Drug Abuse, DHHS Publication No. (ADM) 80-967, pp. 8–11.

Goldfield, B. A. (1990). Pointing, naming, and talk about objects: Referential behavior in children and mothers. *First Language, 10,* 231–242.

Goldfried, M. R., Greenberg, L. S., & Marmar, C. (1990). Individual psychotherapy: Process and outcome. *Annual Review of Psychology, 41,* 659–688.

Goldman-Rakic, P. S. (1992, September). Working memory and the mind. *Scientific American,* 110–117.

Goldsen, R., Rosenberg, M. W., Robin M., Jr., & Suchman, E. A. (1960). *What college students think.* Princeton, NJ: Van Nostrand.

Goncz, L. (1988). A research study on the relation between early bilingualism and cognitive development. *Pschologische-Beitrage, 30,* 75–91.

Goodall, J. (1986). *The chimpanzees of Gombe.* Cambridge, MA: Harvard University Press.

Goode, W. J. (1965). *The family.* Englewood Cliffs, NJ: Prentice Hall.

Goodwin, D. W. (1986). Heredity and alcoholism. *Annals of Behavioral Medicine, 8,* 3–6.

Goodwin, F. (1993). Personal communication.

Goodwin, F. J., & Jamison, K. R. (1990). *Manic-depressive illness.* New York: Oxford University Press.

Goodwin, F. K. (1989, June 23/30). From the Alcohol, Drug Abuse, and Mental Health Administration. *Journal of the American Medical Association, 261,* 3517.

Gopnik, A., (1984). The acquisition of *gone* and the development of the object concept. *Journal of Child Language, 11,* 273–292.

Gopnik, A., & Meltzoff, A. N. (1984). Semantic and cognitive development in 15- to 21-month-old children. *Journal of Child Language, 11,* 495–513.

Gopnik, A., Meltzoff, A. N., & Kuhl, P. K. (1999). *The scientist in the crib: Minds, brains, and how children learn.* New York: Morrow.

Gordon, D., State, R., Nelson, J., Hamburger, S., & Rapoport, J. (1993). A double blind comparison of clomipramine, desipramine and placebo in the treatment of autistic disorder. *Archives of General Psychiatry, 50,* 441–447.

Gortmaker, S. L., Must, A., Perrin, J. M., Sobol, A. M., & Dietz, W. H. (1993). Social and economic consequences of overweight in adolescence and young adulthood. *New England Journal of Medicine, 329,* 1008–1012.

Gotlib, I. H. (1984). Depression and general psychopathology in university students. *Journal of Abnormal Psychology, 93,* 19–30.

Gottesman, I. I. (1963a). Biogenetics of race and class. In M. Deutsch, I. Katz, & A. B. Jensen (Eds.), *Social class, race, and psychological development.* New York: Holt.

Gottesman, I. I. (1963b). Genetic aspects of intelligent behavior. In N. Ellis (Ed.), *Handbook of mental deficiency.* New York: McGraw-Hill.

Gottlieb, J., & Carver, C. S. (1980). Anticipation of future interaction and the bystander effect. *Journal of Experimental Social Psychology, 16,* 253–260.

Gottschalk, E. C. (1983, June 1). Student shock. Stress is more severe for collegians today; counselors keep busy. *Wall Street Journal.*

Gould, M. S., & Shaffer, D. (1986). The impact of suicide in television movies: Evidence of imitation. *New England Journal of Medicine, 315,* 690–694.

Gould, R. A., Clum, G. A., & Shapiro, D. (1993). The use of bibliotherapy in the treatment of panic: A preliminary investigation. *Behavior Therapy, 24,* 241–252.

Graber, J. A., & Brooks-Gunn, J. (2001). Co-occurring eating and depressive problems: An 8-year study of adolescent girls. *International Journal of Eating Disorders, 30,* 37–47.

Graf, P., & Schacter, D. L. (1987). Selective effects of interference on implicit and explicit memory for new associations. *Journal of Experimental Psychology: Learning, Memory, and Cognition, 13,* 45–53.

Graf, P., Squire, L. R., & Mandler, G. (1984). The information that amnesic patients do not forget. *Journal of Experimental Psychology: Learning, Memory, and Cognition, 10,* 164–178.

Graf, R. C. (1973, December). Speed reading. *Psychology Today,* 112–113.

Graham, P., & Rutter, M. (1985). Adolescent disorders. In M. Rutter & L. Hersov (Eds.), *Child and adolescent psychiatry: Modern approaches.* London: Blackwell.

Greenblatt, M., Becerra, R. M., & Serafetinides, E. A. (1982). Social networks in mental health: An overview. *The American Journal of Psychiatry, 139,* 977–984.

Greene, W. A., Goldstein, S., & Moss, A. J. (1972). Psychosocial aspects of sudden death. *Archives of Internal Medicine, 129,* 725–731.

Gregersen, E. (1983). *Sexual practices.* New York: Franklin Watts.

Greven, P. (1991). *Spare the child.* New York: Knopf.

Greyson, B. (2001). Posttraumatic stress symptoms following near-death experiences. *American Journal of Orthopsychiatry, 71,* 368–373.

Grief, E., & Ulman, K. (1982). The psychological impact of menarche on early adolescent females: A review of the literature. *Child Development, 53,* 1413–1430.

Griel, A. (1991). *Not yet pregnant.* New Brunswick, NJ: Rutgers University Press.

Grill-Spector, K., & Malach, R. (2001). fMR-adaptation: A tool for studying the functional properties of human cortical neurons. *Acta Psychologica, 107,* 293–321.

Grillon, C., Courchesne, E., Ameli, R., & Geyer, M. A. (1990). Increased distractibility in schizophrenic patients: Electrophysiologic and behavioral evidence. *Archives of General Psychiatry, 47,* 171–179.

Grinker, J. A. (1982). Physiological and behavioral basis of human obesity. In D. W. Pfaff (Ed.), *The physiological mechanisms of motivation.* New York: Springer-Verlag.

Groebel, J. (2001). Media violence in cross-cultural perspective. In D. B. Singer & J. L. Singer (Eds.), *Handbook of children and the media.* Thousand Oaks, CA: Sage.

Grosser, B. I., Monti-Bloch, L., Jennings-White, C., & Berliner, D. L. (2000). *Psychoneuroendocrinology, 25,* 289–299.

Gruenberg, B. (1980). The happy worker. An analysis of educational and occupational differences in determinants of job satisfaction. *American Journal of Sociology, 86,* 247–271.

Guerin, D. W., Gottfried, A. W., & Thomas, C. W. (1997). Difficult temperament and behaviour problems: A longitudinal study from 1.5 to 12 years. *International Journal of Behavioral Development, 21,* 71–90.

Gunnar, M. R., Leighton, K., & Peleaux, R. (1984). Effects of temporal predictability on the reactions of 1-year-olds to potentially frightening toys. *Developmental Psychology, 20,* 449–458.

Gunter, B., Berry, C., & Clifford, B. R. (1981). Proactive interference effects with television news items: Further evidence. *Journal of Experimental Psychology: Human Learning and Memory, 7,* 480–487.

Haig, N. D. (1984). The effect of feature displacement on face recognition. *Perception, 13,* 505–512.

Haines, V. A., Hurlbert, J. S., & Beggs, J. J. (1996). Exploring the determinants of support provision: Provider characteristics, personal networks, community contexts, and support following life events. *Journal of Health and Social Behavior, 37,* 252–264.

Haith, M. (1980). *Rules babies look by.* Hillsdale, NJ: Erlbaum.

Hall, C. D., Smith, A. L., & Keele, S. W. (2001). The impact of aerobic activity on cognitive function in older adults: A new synthesis based on the concept of executive control. *European Journal of Cognitive Psychology, 13,* 279–300.

Hall, R. C. W. (1980). Medically induced psychiatric disease: An overview. In R. C. W. Hall (Ed.), *Psychiatric presentations of medical illness: Somatopsychic disorders.* New York: Spectrum.

Hall, S. S. (1998, February 15). Our memories, our selves. *New York Times Sunday Magazine.* Internet document at www.nytimes.com.

Hall, W. S. (1986). *Science and public policy seminars: Some recent developments in the study of children's language.* Washington, DC: Federation of Behavioral, Psychological and Cognitive Sciences.

Hallett, M. (2001). Brain plasticity and recovery from hemiplegia. *Journal of Medical Speech-Language Pathology, 9,* 107–115.

Hallock, M. B., Worobey, J., & Self, P. A. (1989). Behavioral development in chimpanzee and human newborns across the first month of life. *International Journal of Behavioral Development, 12,* 526–540.

Halpern, A. R. (1984). Organization and memory for familiar songs. *Journal of Experimental Psychology: Learning, Memory, and Cognition, 10,* 496–512.

Halpern, C. T., Udry, J. R., Campbell, B., & Suchindran, C. (1993). Testosterone and pubertal development as predictors of sexual activity: A panel analysis of adolescent males. *Psychosomatic Medicine, 55,* 436–447.

Hamer, D., Hu, S., Magnuson, V. L., Hu, N., & Pattatucci, A. M. L. (1993). A linkage between DNA markers on the X chromosome and male sexual orientation. *Science, 261,* 321–327.

Hamilton, M. (1982). Diagnosis of anxiety states. In R. J. Mathew (Ed.), *The biology of anxiety.* New York: Bruner/Mazel.

Hammen, C., Davila, J., Brown, G., Ellicott, A., & Gitlin, M. (1992). Psychiatric history and stress: Predictors of severity of unipolar depression. *Journal of Abnormal Psychology, 101,* 45–52.

Haney, C., & Zimbardo, P. (1998). The past and future of U.S. prison policy: Twenty-five years after the Stanford prison experiment. *American Psychologist, 53,* 709–727.

Harlow, H. F. (1949). The formation of learning sets. *Psychological Review, 56,* 51–65.

Harlow, H. F. (1961). The development of affectional patterns in infant monkeys. In B. M. Foss (Ed.), *Determinants of infant behaviour.* London: Methuen.

Harrell, T. W., & Harrell, M. S. (1945). Army general classification test scores for civilian occupations. *Educational and Psychological Measurement, 5,* 229–239.

Harris, B. (1979). Whatever happened to Little Albert? *American Psychologist, 34,* 151–160.

Harris, F. R., Johnston, M. K., Kelley, C. S., & Wolf, M. M. (1965). Effects of positive social reinforcement on regressed crawling of a nursery school child. In L. P. Ullmann & L. Krasner (Eds.), *Case studies in behavior modification.* New York: Holt.

Harris, M. J., & Rosenthal, R. (1986). Four factors in the mediation of teacher expectancy effects. In R. S. Feldman (Ed.), *The social psychology of education: Current research and theory.* New York: Cambridge University Press.

Hart, J., & Gordon, B. (1992). Neural subsystems for direct knowledge. *Nature, 359,* 60–64.

Hartmann, E. (1984). *The nightmare.* New York: Basic.

Harvey, S. M. (1987). Female sexual behavior: Fluctuations during the menstrual cycle. *Journal of Psychosomatic Research, 31,* 101–110.

Hatfield, E. (1988). Passionate and companionate love. In R. J. Sternberg & M. L. Barnes (Eds.), *The psychology of love.* New Haven, CT: Yale University Press.

Hathaway, S. R., & McKinley, J. C. (1992). *Minnesota Multiphasic Personality Inventory–2 (MMPI-2).* Minneapolis: University of Minnesota Press.

Hauri, P. J. (1982). *The sleep disorders.* Kalamazoo, MI: Upjohn.

Hauser, B. B. (1985). Custody in dispute: Legal and psychological profiles of contesting families. *Journal of the Academy of Child Psychiatry, 24,* 575–582.

Hawley, T. L., & Disney, E. R. (1992). Crack's children: The consequences of maternal cocaine abuse. *Social Policy Report, VI,* 4.

Hayward, C., Killen, J. D., Hammer, L. D., & Litt, I. F. (1992). Pubertal stage and panic attack history in sixth- and seventh-grade girls. *American Journal of Psychiatry, 149,* 1239–1243.

Hebb, D. O. (1958). *A textbook of psychology.* Philadelphia: Saunders.

Heider, F. (1944). Social perception and phenomenal causality. *Psychological Review, 51,* 358–374.

Heller, K., & Mansbach, W. E. (1984). The multifaceted nature of social support in a community sample of older women. *Journal of Social Issues, 40,* 99–112.

Helsing, K. L., Szklo, M., & Comstock, G. W. (1981). Factors associated with mortality after widowhood. *American Journal of Public Health, 71,* 802–809.

Helson, R., & Moane, G. (1987). Personality change in women from college to midlife. *Journal of Personality and Social Psychology, 53,* 176–186.

Helzer, J. E., Robins, L. N., & McEvoy, L. (1987). Post-traumatic stress disorder in the general population: Findings of the epidemiologic catchment area survey. *New England Journal of Medicine, 317,* 1630–1634.

Hendrick, C., & Hendrick, S. (1986). A theory and method of love. *Journal of Personality and Social Psychology, 50,* 392–402.

Hendrick, S., Hendrick, C., Slapion-Foote, M. J., & Foote, F. H. (1985). Gender differences in sexual attitudes. *Journal of Personality and Social Psychology, 48,* 1630–1642.

Heresco-Levy, U. (2000). N-Methyl-D-aspartate (NMDA) receptor-based treatment approaches in schizophrenia: The first decade. *International Journal of Neuropsychopharmacology, 3,* 243–258.

Herrmann, T. F., Hurwitz, H. M. B., & Levine, S. (1984). Behavioral control, aversive stimulus frequency, and pituitary-adrenal response. *Behavioral Neuroscience, 98,* 1094–1099.

Herrnstein, R. J., & de Villiers, P. A. (1980). Fish as a natural category for people and pigeons. In G. H. Bower (Ed.), *Psychology of learning and motivation* (Vol. 14). New York: Academic.

Hess, R. D., Holloway, S. D., Dickson, W. P., & Price, G. G. (1984). Maternal variables as predictors of children's school readiness and later achievement in vocabulary and mathematics in the sixth grade. *Child Development, 55,* 1902–1912.

Heston, L. H., & White, J. A. (1983). *Dementia: A practical guide to Alzheimer's disease and related illness.* San Francisco: Freeman.

Hetherington, E. M., & Camara, K. A. (1984). Families in transition: The process of dissolution and reconstitution. In R. D. Parke (Ed.), *Review of child development research: Vol. 7. The family.* Chicago: University of Chicago Press.

Hetherington, E. M., & Stanley-Hagan, M. (1999). The adjustment of children with divorced parents: A risk and resiliency perspective. *Journal of Child Psychology and Psychiatry and Allied Disciplines, 40,* 129–140.

Hinz, L. D., & Williamson, D. A. (1987). Bulimia and depression: A review of the affective variant hypothesis. *Psychological Bulletin, 102,* 150–158.

Hiroto, D. S. (1974). Locus of control and learned helplessness. *Journal of Experimental Psychology, 102,* 187–193.

Hitchcock, J. M., & Davis, M. (1991). Efferent pathway of the amygdala involved in conditioned fear as measured with the fear-potentiated startle paradigm. *Behavioral Neuroscience, 105,* 826–842.

Hobson, J. A. (1989). *Sleep.* New York: Scientific American Library.

Hochberg, J. (1978). *Perception* (2nd ed.). Englewood Cliffs, NJ: Prentice Hall.

Hoeksema, S. N. (1992). Predictors and consequences of childhood depressive symptoms: A 5-year longitudinal study. *Journal of Abnormal Psychology, 101,* 405–422.

Hogan, J. (1989). Personality correlates of physical fitness. *Journal of Personality and Social Psychology, 56,* 284–288.

Holahan, C. J., & Moos, R. H. (1986). Personality, coping, and family resources in stress resistance: A longitudinal analysis. *Journal of Personality and Social Psychology, 51,* 389–395.

Holahan, C. J., & Moos, R. H. (1991). Life stressors, personal and social resources, and depression: A 4-year structural model. *Journal of Abnormal Psychology, 100,* 31–38.

Holahan, C. K., & Holahan, C. J. (1999). Being labeled as gifted, self-appraisal, and psychological well-being: A life span developmental perspective. *International Journal of Aging and Human Development, 48,* 161–173.

Holahan, C. K., Holahan, C. J., & Wonacott, N. L. (2001). Psychological well-being at age 80: Health-related and psychosocial factors. *Journal of Mental Health and Aging, 7,* 395–411.

Holder, M. D., Bermudez-Rattoni, F., & Garcia, J. (1988). Taste-potentiated noise-illness associations. *Behavioral Neuroscience, 102,* 363–370.

Holmes, S. J., & Robins, L. N. (1987). The influence of childhood disciplinary experience on the development of alcoholism and depression. *Journal of Child Psychology and Psychiatry, 28,* 399–415.

Holmes, T. H., & Rahe, R. H. (1967). The Social Readjustment Rating Scale. *Journal of Psychosomatic Research, 11,* 213–218.

Holzman, P. H. (1992). Behavioral markers of schizophrenia useful for genetic studies. *Journal of Psychiatric Research, 26,* 427–445.

Hooley, J. M. (1985). Expressed emotion: A review of the critical literature. *Clinical Psychology Review, 5,* 119–139.

Horgan, J. (1997). Seeking a better way to die. *Scientific American, 276,* 100–105.

Horn, J. L. (1982). The aging of human abilities. In J. Woolman (Ed.), *Handbook of developmental psychology.* Englewood Cliffs, NJ: Prentice Hall.

Horne, J. (1988). *Why we sleep: The functions of sleep in humans and other mammals.* Oxford, UK: Oxford University Press.

Horney, K. (1942). *Self-analysis.* New York: Norton.

Horney, K. (1945). *Our inner conflicts.* New York: Norton.

House, J. S., Landis, K. R., & Umberson, D. (1988). Social relationships and health. *Science, 241,* 540–545.

Houston, K., Hawton, K., & Shepperd, R. (2001). Suicide in young people aged 15–24: A psychological autopsy study. *Journal of Affective Disorders, 63,* 159–170.

Hovland, C. I., Janis, I. L., & Kelley, H. H. (1953). *Communication and persuasion: Psychological studies of opinion change.* New Haven, CT: Yale University Press.

Hovland, C. I., Lumsdaine, A. A., & Sheffield, F. C. (1949). *Experiments on mass communication,* Princeton, NJ: Princeton University Press.

Hovland, C. I., & Weiss, W. (1951). The influence of source credibility on communication effectiveness. *Public Opinion Quarterly, 15,* 635–650.

Howard, A., Pion, G. M., Gottfredson, G. D., Flatau, P. E., et al. (1986). The changing face of American psychology: A report from the committee on employment and human resources. *American Psychologist, 41,* 1311–1327.

Howard, R. W. (2001). Searching the real world for signs of rising population intelligence. *Personality and Individual Differences, 30,* 1039–1058.

Howes, C. (1988). The relation between early child care and schooling. *Developmental Psychology, 24,* 53–57.

Howes, C. (1990). Can the age of entry into child care and the quality of child care predict adjustment in kindergarten? *Developmental Psychology, 26,* 292–303.

Hubel, D. H. (1963). The visual cortex of the brain. *Scientific American, 209,* 54–62.

Hubel, D. H. (1979). The brain. In Scientific American's *The brain.* San Francisco: Freeman.

Hubel, D. H. (1988). *Eye, brain, and vision.* New York: Scientific American Library.

Hubel, D. H., & Wiesel, T. N. (1965). Receptive fields and functional architecture in two non-striate visual areas (18 and 19) of the cat. *Journal of Neurophysiology, 28,* 229–289.

Hubel, D. H., & Wiesel, T. N. (1979). Brain mechanisms of vision. In Scientific American's *The brain.* San Francisco: Freeman.

Hudson, J. A., & Sheffield, E. G. (1998). Deja vu all over again: Effects of reenactment on toddlers' event memory. *Child Development, 69,* 51–67.

Hudspeth, A. J. (1985, Nov. 15). The cellular basis of hearing: The biophysics of hair cells. *Science, 230,* 745–752.

Hunt, J. McV. (1988). Relevance to educability: Heritability or range of reaction. In S. G. Cole & R. G. Demaree (Eds.), *Applications of interactionist psychology: Essays in honor of Saul B. Sells.* Hillsdale, NJ: Erlbaum.

Hupp, S. D. A., Reitman, D., Northup, J., O'Callaghan, P., & LeBlanc, M. (2002). The effects of delayed rewards, tokens, and stimulant medication on sportsmanlike behavior with ADHD-diagnosed children. *Behavior Modification, 26,* 148–162.

Huston, A. C., Donnerstein, E., Fairchild, H. H., Feshbach, N. D., Katz, P. A., Murray, J. P., et al. (1992). *Big world, small screen: The role of television in American society.* Lincoln: University of Nebraska Press.

Huston, A. C., Wright, J. C., Rice, M. L., Kerkman, D., & St. Peters, M. (1990). Development of television viewing patterns in early childhood: A longitudinal investigation. *Developmental Psychology, 26,* 409–420.

Hyde, J. S., Fennema, E., & Lamon, S. J. (1990). Gender differences in mathematics performance: A meta-analysis. *Psychological Bulletin, 107,* 139–155.

Hyman, I. E., Jr., & Loftus, E. F. (1998). Errors in autobiographical memory. *Clinical Psychology Review, 18,* 933–947.

Iacono, W. G., & Patrick, C. J. (1999). Polygraph ("lie detector") testing: The state of the art. In A. K. Hess & I. B. Weiner (Eds.), *The handbook of forensic psychology* (2nd ed.). New York: Wiley.

Ingraham, L. J. (1992). Risk for affective disorder and alcohol and other drug abuse in the relatives of affectively ill adoptees. *Journal of Affective Disorders, 26,* 45–57.

Institute for Mental Health Initiatives. (1988). *Channeling children's anger.* Washington, DC: Author.

Iversen, L. L. (1982). Neurotransmitters and CNS disease: Introduction. *Lancet, II* (8304), 914–916.

Izard, C. E. (1977). *Human emotions.* New York: Plenum.

Izard, C. E. (1994). Innate and universal facial expressions: Evidence from developmental and cross-cultural research. *Psychological Bulletin, 115,* 288–299.

Jaber, M., Robinson, S. W., Missale, C., & Caron, M. G. (1996). Dopamine receptors and brain function. *Neuropharmacology, 35,* 1503–1520.

Jack, D. C. (1991). *Silencing the self.* Cambridge, MA: Harvard University Press.

Jacob, S., & McClintock, M. K. (1999). Psychological state and mood effects of steroidal chemosignals in women and men. *Hormones and Behavior, 37,* 57–78.

Jacob-Timm, S. (1996). Ethical and legal issues associated with the use of aversives in public schools: The SIBIS controversy. *School Psychology Review, 25,* 184–199.

Jacobowitz, D. M. (1989). Personal communication.

Jacobson, J. L., et al. (1984). Prenatal exposure to an environmental toxin: A test of the multiple effects model. *Developmental Psychology, 20,* 523–532.

James, W. (1890). *Principles of psychology.* New York: Holt.

Jamison, K. R. (1982). Personal communication.

Jamison, K. R. (1993). *Touched with fire.* New York: Free Press.

Janes, L., & Olson, J. M. (2000). Peer pressure: The behavioral effects of observing ridicule of others. *Personality and Social Psychology Bulletin, 26,* 474–485.

Janis, I. L. (1982). *Victims of groupthink* (2nd ed.). Boston: Houghton Mifflin.

Jarmas, A. L., & Kazak, A. E. (1992). Young adult children of alcoholic fathers: Depressive experiences, coping styles, and family systems. *Journal of Consulting and Clinical Psychology, 60,* 244–251.

Jeffery, R. W. (2001). Public health strategies for obesity treatment and prevention. *American Journal of Health Behavior, 25,* 252–259.

Jeffery, R. W., Drewnowski, A., Epstein, L. H., Stunkard, A. J., Wilson, G. T., Wing, R. R., et al. (2000). Long-term maintenance of weight loss: Current status. *Health Psychology, 19,* 5–16.

Jencks, C. (1972). *Inequality: A reassessment of the effect of family and schooling in America.* New York: Basic.

Jensen, A. R. (1969). How much can we boost IQ and scholastic achievement? *Harvard Educational Review, 39,* 1–123.

Jensen, M., Kristiansen, I., Sandbekk, M., & Kroger, J. (1998). Ego identity status in cross-cultural context: A comparison of Norwegian and United States university students. *Psychological Reports, 83,* 455–460.

Jensen, M. R. (1987). Psychobiological factors predicting the course of breast cancer. *Journal of Personality, 55,* 317–342.

Jensen, P. S. (2000). Are stimulants overprescribed? Reply. *Journal of the American Academy of Child and Adolescent Psychiatry, 39,* 270–271.

Jensvold, M. L. A., & Gardner, R. A. (2000). Interactive use of sign language by cross-fostered chimpanzees

(Pan troglodytes). *Journal of Comparative Psychology, 114,* 335–346.

Jessel, L. (1978). Whorf: The differentiation of language. *International Journal of the Sociology of Language, 18,* 83–110.

Jimerson, D. C., Herzog, D. B., & Brotman, A. W. (1993). Pharmacologic approaches in the treatment of eating disorders. *Harvard Review of Psychiatry, 1,* 82–93.

John, E. R., Chesler, P., & Bartlett, F. (1968). Observation learning in cats. *Science, 159,* 1489–1491.

Johnston, D. K., 1988. Adolescents' solutions to dilemmas in fables: Two moral orientations—two problem solving strategies. In C. Gilligan, J. V. Ward, J. M. Taylor, & B. Bardige (Eds.), *Mapping the moral domain.* Cambridge, MA: Harvard University Press.

Jones, E. E. (1976). How do people perceive the causes of behavior? *American Scientist, 64,* 300–305.

Jones, E. E. (1990). *Interpersonal perception.* New York: Freeman.

Jones, E. E., & Davis, K. E. (1965). From acts to disposition: The attribution process in person perception. In L. Berkowitz (Ed.), *Advances in experimental social psychology* (Vol. 2). New York: Academic.

Jones, E. E., & Nisbett, R. E. (1971). *The actor and the observer: Divergent perceptions of the causes of behavior.* Morristown, NJ: General Learning Press.

Jones, H. W., & Toner, J. P. (1993). The infertile couple. *New England Journal of Medicine, 329,* 1710–1715.

Jung, C. G. (1919). *Studies in word association: Experiments in the diagnosis of psychopathological conditions carried out at the psychiatric clinic of the University of Zurich.* New York: Moffat.

Junginger, J. (1992). Mood theme and bizarreness of delusions of schizophrenia and mood psychosis. *Journal of Abnormal Psychology, 101,* 287–292.

Jussim, L., & Eccles, J. S. (1992). Teacher expectations II: Construction and reflection of student achievement. *Journal of Personality and Social Psychology, 63,* 947–961.

Kabat-Zinn, J. (1992). Effectiveness of a meditation based stress reduction program. *American Journal of Psychiatry, 149,* 936–943.

Kagan, J. (1981). *The second year: The emergence of self-awareness.* Cambridge, MA: Harvard University Press.

Kagan, J. (1989). Temperamental contributions to social behavior. *American Psychologist, 44,* 668–674.

Kagan, J. (1994). *Galen's prophecy.* New York: Basic.

Kagan, J. (1997). Temperament and the reactions to unfamiliarity. *Child Development, 68,* 139–143.

Kagan, J. (2001). The structure of temperament. In R. N. Emde & J. K. Hewitt (Eds.), *Infancy to early childhood: Genetic and environmental influences on developmental change.* New York: Oxford University Press.

Kagan, J. (2002). *Surprise, uncertainty, and mental structures.* Cambridge, MA: Harvard University Press.

Kagan, J., Kearsley, R. B., & Zelazo, P. R. (1978). *Infancy: Its place in human development.* Cambridge, MA: Harvard University Press.

Kagan, J., & Moss, H. A. (1962). *Birth to maturity.* New York: Wiley.

Kako, E. (1999). Elements of syntax in the systems of three language-trained animals. *Animal Learning and Behavior, 27,* 1–14.

Kales, A., Stefanis, C. N., & Talbott, J. (1990). *Recent advances in schizophrenia.* New York: Springer-Verlag.

Kamin, L. (1974). *The science and politics of IQ.* Hillsdale, NJ: Erlbaum.

Kamin, L. (with Eysenck, H. J.). (1981). *The intelligence controversy.* New York: Wiley.

Kandel, E. R., & Schwartz, J. H. (1985). *Principles of neural science* (2nd ed.). New York: Elsevier.

Kane, J. M. (1983). Low dose medication strategies in the maintenance treatment of schizophrenia. *Schizophrenia Bulletin, 9,* 528–532.

Kang, D.-H., Davidson, R. J., Coe, C. L., Wheeler, R. E., Tomarken, A. J., & Ershler, W. B. (1991). Frontal brain asymmetry and immune function. *Behavioral Neuroscience, 105,* 860–869.

Karasek, R. A., Theorell, T., Schwartz, J. E., Schnall, P. L., Pieper, C. F., & Michela, L. L. (1988). Job characteristics in relation to the prevalence of myocardial infarction in the U.S. Health Examination Survey (HES) and the Health and Nutrition Examination Survey (HANES). *The American Journal of Public Health, 78,* 810–818.

Kaslow, L. (2000). Continued evolution of family therapy: The last twenty years. *Contemporary Family Therapy: An International Journal, 22,* 357–386.

Katz, A. H. (1993). *Self-help in America: A social movement perspective.* New York: Twayne.

Kay, P. (1975). Synchronic variability and diachronic changes in basic color terms. *Language in Society, 4,* 257–270.

Kay, P., Berlin, B., Maffi, L., & Merrifield, W. (1997). Color naming across languages. In C. L. Hardin & L. Maffi (Eds.), *Color categories in thought and language.* New York: Cambridge University Press.

Kay, P., & Kempton, W. (1984). What is the Sapir-Whorf hypothesis? *American Anthropologist, 86,* 65–79.

Kaye, W. H., Weltzin, T. E., & Hsu, L. K. G. (1993). Serotonin and norepinephrine activity in anorexia and bulimia nervosa: Relationship to nutrition, feeding, and mood. In J. J. Mann & D. J. Kupfer (Eds.), *Biology of depressive disorders, Part B: Subtypes of depression and comorbid disorders. The depressive illness series, Vol. 4.* New York: Plenum.

Keel, P. K., Leon, G. R., & Fulkerson, J. A. (2001). Vulnerability to eating disorders in childhood and adolescence. In R. E. Ingram & J. M. Price (Eds.), *Vulnerability to psychopathology: Risk across the lifespan.* New York: Guilford.

Kelley, K., & Musialowski, D. (1986). Repeated exposure to sexually explicit stimuli. *Archives of Sexual Behavior, 15,* 487–498.

Kelly, S. J., Day, N., & Streissguth, A. P. (2000). Effects of prenatal alcohol exposure on social behavior in humans and other species. *Neurotoxicology and Teratology, 22,* 143–149.

Kendler, K. S. (1992a). Childhood parental loss and adult psychopathology in women. *Archives of General Psychiatry, 49,* 109–116.

Kendler, K. S. (1992b). A population-based twin study of major depression in women. *Archives of General Psychiatry, 49,* 257–266.

Kessler, M., & Goldston, S. E., (Eds.). (1986). *A decade of progress in primary prevention.* Hanover, NH: University Press of New England.

Kety, S. S. (1982, September). The impact of neurobiology in the concept of the mind. Paper presented at European Neuroscience Congress, Malaga, Spain.

Kety, S. S., & Ingraham, L. J. (1992). Genetic transmission and improved diagnosis of schizophrenia from pedigrees of adoptees. *Journal of Psychiatric Research, 26,* 247–255.

Kiecolt-Glaser, J. K., Garner, W., Speicher, C., Penn, G. M., Holliday, J., & Glaser, R. (1984). Psychosocial modifiers of immunocompetence in medical students. *Psychosomatic Medicine, 46,* 7–14.

Kiecolt-Glaser, J. K., & Glaser, R. (1991). Stress and immune function in humans. In R. Ader, D. Felten, & N. Cohen (Eds.), *Psychoneuroimmunology II.* San Diego: Academic.

Kiecolt-Glaser, J. K., Glaser, R., Shuttleworth, E. C., & Dyer, C. S. (1987). Chronic stress and immunity in family caregivers of Alzheimer's disease victims. *Psychosomatic Medicine, 49,* 523–535.

Killgore, W. D. (2000). Academic and research interest in several approaches to psychotherapy: A computerized search of literature in the past 16 years. *Psychological Reports, 87,* 717–720.

Kim, D., Schallert, T., Liu, Y., Browarak, T., Nayeri, N., Tessler, A., & Fischer, I. (2001). Transplantation of genetically modified fibroblasts expressing BDNF in adult rats with a subtotal hemisection improves specific motor and sensory functions. *Neurorehabilitation and Neural Repair, 15,* 141-150.

Kimmel, D. C. (1980). *Adulthood and aging: An inter-disciplinary developmental view* (2nd ed.). New York: Wiley.

Kirk-Smith, M. D., & Booth, D. A. (1980). Effects of androstenone on choice of location in each other's presence. In H. van der Starre (Ed.), *Olfaction and taste VII* (pp. 397–400). London: IRL Press.

Kirk-Smith, M., Booth, D. A., Carroll, D., & Davies, P. (1978). Human social attitudes affected by androstenol. *Research Communications in Psychology, Psychiatry and Behavior, 3,* 379–384.

Klatzky, R. L. (1980). *Human memory: Structures and processes* (2nd ed.). San Francisco: Freeman.

Klein, P. D. (1997). Multiplying the problems of intelligence by eight: A critique of Gardner's theory. *Canadian Journal of Education, 22,* 377–394.

Kleinmuntz, B., & Szucko, J. J. (1984). A field study of the fallibility of polygraph lie detection. *Nature, 308,* 449–450.

Klopfer, B., & Davidson, H. H. (1962). *The Rorschach technique.* New York: Harcourt.

Kochanska, G. (1993). Toward a synthesis of parental socialization and child temperament in early development of conscience. *Child Development, 64,* 325–347.

Koegel, R. L. (1991). Personal communication.

Koff, E., & Rierdan, J. (1995). Preparing girls for menstruation: Recommendations from adolescent girls. *Adolescence, 30,* 795–811.

Kohlberg, L. (1963). The development of children's orientations toward a moral order. I: Sequence in the development of moral thought. *Vita Humana, 6,* 11–33.

Kohlberg, L. (1967). Moral and religious education and the public schools. In T. Sizer (Ed.), *Religion and public education.* Boston: Houghton Mifflin.

Kohlberg, L. (1969). Stage and sequence: The cognitive-developmental approach to socialization. In D. A. Goslin (Ed.), *Handbook of socialization theory and research* (p. 379). Chicago: Rand McNally.

Kohlberg, L. (1978). Revisions in the theory and practice of moral development. In W. Damon (Ed.), *New direc-tions for child development, 2.* San Francisco: Jossey-Bass.

Köhler, W. (1925). *The mentality of apes.* New York: Harcourt.

Kornblum, W., & Julian, J. (2001). *Social Problems* (10th ed). Upper Saddle River, NJ: Prentice Hall.

Koss, M. P., Butcher, J. N., & Strupp, H. H. (1986). Brief psychotherapy methods in clinical research. *Journal of Consulting and Clinical Psychology, 54,* 60–67.

Kozu, J. (1999). Domestic violence in Japan. *American Psychologist, 54,* 50–54.

Krech, D., Crutchfield, R. S., & Livson, N. (1969). *Elements of psychology* (2nd ed.). Oxford, UK: Knopf.

Krosnick, J. A., & Alwin, D. F. (1989). Aging and susceptibility to attitude change. *Journal of Personality and Social Psychology, 57,* 416–425.

Kruesi, M. J. P. (1992). A 2-year prospective follow-up study of children and adolescents with disruptive behavior disorders. *Archives of General Psychiatry, 49,* 429–453.

Kubie, L. S. (1950). *Practical and theoretical aspects of psychoanalysis.* New York: International University Press.

Kübler-Ross, E. (1969). *On death and dying.* New York: Macmillan.

Kudo, T., Imaizumi, K., Tanimukai, H., Katayama, T., Sato, N., Nakamura, Y., et al. (2000). Are cerebro-vascular factors involved in Alzheimer's disease? *Neurobiology of Aging, 21,* 215-224.

Kushner, M. G., Sher, K. J., & Beltman, B. D. (1990). The relation between alcohol problems and the anxiety disorders. *American Journal of Psychiatry, 147,* 685–695.

Labre, M. P. (2002). Adolescent boys and the muscular male body ideal. *Journal of Adolescent Health, 30,* 233-242.

Lacey, J. I., & Lacey, B. C. (1958). Verification and extension of the principle of autonomic response-stereotype. *American Journal of Psychology, 71,* 50–73.

Lake, A. J., Staiger, P. K., & Glowinski, H. (2000). Effect of Western culture on women's attitudes to eating and perceptions of body shape. *International Journal of Eating Disorders, 27,* 83–89.

Lamb, S. (1991). Internal state words: Their relation to moral development and to maternal communications about moral development in the second year of life. *First Language, 11,* 391–406.

Laming, P. R., Kimelberg, H., Robinson, S., Salm, A., Hawrylak, N., Müller, C., et al. (2000). Neuronal-glial interactions and behaviour. *Neuroscience and Biobehavioral Reviews, 24,* 295–340.

Lampropoulos, G. K. (2000). Evolving psychotherapy integration: Eclectic selection and prescriptive applications of common factors in therapy. *Psychotherapy: Theory, Research, Practice, Training, 37,* 285–297.

Langlois, J. H., Kalakanis, L., Rubenstein, A. J., Larson, A., Hallam, M., & Smoot, M. (2000). Maxims or myths of beauty? A meta-analytic and theoretical review. *Psychological Bulletin, 126,* 390–423.

Larsen, R. J., Diener, E., & Emmons, R. A. (1986). Affect intensity and reactions to daily life events. *Journal of Personality and Social Psychology, 51,* 803–814.

Larsen, R. J., & Lampman-Petraitis, C. (1989). Daily emotional states as reported by children and adolescents. *Child Development, 60,* 1250–1260.

Latané, B., & Nida, S. (1981). Ten years of research on group size and helping. *Psychological Bulletin, 89,* 308–324.

Lazarus, R. S. (1978). *The stress and coping paradigm.* Paper delivered at the University of Washington conference on the critical evaluation of behavioral paradigms for psychiatric science.

Lazarus, R. S., & Folkman, S. (1984). *Stress, appraisal, and coping.* New York: Springer.

Leach, P. (1989). *Your growing child: From babyhood through adolescence.* New York: Knopf.

Leahey, T. H., & Harris, R. J. (1997). *Learning and cognition.* Upper Saddle River, NJ: Prentice Hall.

Leahey, T. H., & Harris, R. J. (2001). *Learning and cognition* (5th ed.). Upper Saddle River, NJ: Prentice Hall.

Lebowitz, B. D., & Cohen, G. D. (1991). Psychotropic drugs and geriatric patients. In C. Salzman (Ed.), *Geriatric psychopharmacology.* Baltimore: Williams and Wilkins.

Lebowitz, B. D., & Cohen, G. D. (1992). The elderly and their illness. In C. Salzman (Ed.), *Clinical geriatric psychopharmacology* (2nd ed.). Baltimore: Williams and Wilkins.

Lee, S. J. (1999). "Are you Chinese or what?" Ethnic identity among Asian Americans. In R. H. Sheets & E. R. Hollins (Eds.), *Racial and ethnic identity in school practices: Aspects of human development.* Mahway, NJ: Lawrence Erlbaum.

Leedy, M. G., & Wilson, M. S. (1985). Testosterone and cortisol levels in crewmen of U.S. Air Force fighter and cargo planes. *Psychosomatic Medicine, 47,* 333–338.

Lefcourt, H. M., Davidson, K., Prkachin, K. M., & Mills, D. E. (1997). Humor as a stress moderator in the prediction of blood pressure during five stressful tasks. *Journal of Research in Personality, 31,* 523–542.

Le Magnen, J. (1984). Is regulation of body weight elucidated? *Neuroscience and Biobehavior Reviews, 8,* 515–522.

LeMasters, E. E., & DeFrain, J. (1983). *Parents in contemporary America.* Homewood, IL: Dorsey.

Lemish, D., & Rice, M. L. (1986). Television as a talking picture book: A prop for language acquisition. *Journal of Child Language, 13,* 251–274.

Lenneberg, E. H. (1967). *Biological foundations of language.* New York: Wiley.

Lennie, P. (2000). Color vision: Putting it all together. *Current Biology, 10,* R589–R591.

Leon, C. A. (1989). Clinical course and outcome of schizophrenia in Cali, Colombia. *Journal of Nervous and Mental Disease, 177,* 593–606.

Léon, M. R., & Revelle, W. (1985). Effects of anxiety on analogical reasoning: A test of three theoretical models. *Journal of Personality and Social Psychology, 49,* 1302–1315.

LeVay, S. (1991). A difference in hypothalamic structure between heterosexual and homosexual men. *Science, 253,* 1034–1037.

Levenson, R. W., & Ruef, A. M. (1992). Empathy: A physiological substrate. *Journal of Personality and Social Psychology, 63,* 234–246.

Levine, I. S., & Haggard, L. K. (1989). Homelessness as a public mental health problem. In D. A. Rochefort (Ed.), *Handbook on mental health policy in the United States.* Boston: Greenwood Press.

Levine, M. W., & Shefner, J. M. (1981). *Fundamentals of sensation and perception.* Reading, MA: Addison-Wesley.

Levinson, B., & Reese, H. W. (1967). Patterns of discrimination learning set in preschool children, fifth-graders, college freshmen, and the aged. *Monographs of the Society for Research in Child Development, 32* (7), 1–92.

Lewis, E. R., Zeevi, Y. Y., & Everhart, T. E. (1969). Studying neural organization in *Aplysia* with scanning electron microscope. *Science, 165,* 1140–1142.

Lewis-Fernández, R., & Kleinman, A. (1994). Culture, personality, and psychopathology. *Journal of Abnormal Psychology, 103,* 67–71.

Libet, B. (1985). Unconscious cerebral initiative and the role of conscious will in voluntary action. *The Behavioral and Brain Sciences, 8,* 529–539.

Liebert, R. M., & Sprafkin, J. (1988). *The early window: Effects of television on children and youth* (3rd ed.). New York: Pergamon.

Light, E., & Lebowitz, B. (1989). *Alzheimer's disease treatment and family stress: Directions for research.* Rockville, MD: National Institute of Mental Health, DHHS Publication No. (ADM) 89-1569.

Linn, S., Reznick, J. S., Kagan, J., & Hans, S. (1982). Salience of visual patterns in the human infant. *Developmental Psychology, 18,* 651–657.

Lipsitt, L. P. (1990). Personal communication.

Lloyd, R. L., & Kling, A. S. (1991). Delta activity from squirrel monkeys *(Saimiri sciureus)*: Influence of social and environmental context. *Behavioral Neuroscience, 105,* 223–229.

Loftus, E. F. (1993). The reality of repressed memories. *American Psychologist, 48,* 518–537.

Loftus, E. F. (1997). Memories for a past that never was. *Current Directions in Psychological Science, 6,* 60–65.

Loftus, E. F. (1999). Lost in the mall: Misrepresentations and misunderstandings. *Ethics and Behavior, 9,* 51–60.

Loftus, E. F., & Palmer, J. C. (1974). Reconstruction of automobile destruction: An example of the interaction between language and memory. *Journal of Verbal Learning and Behavior, 13,* 585–589.

Loftus, E. F., & Polage, D. C. (1999). Repressed memories: When are they real? How are they false? *Psychiatric Clinics of North America, 22,* 61–70.

Loftus, G. R., Duncan, J., & Gehrig, P. (1992). On the time course of perceptual information that results from a brief visual presentation. *Journal of Experimental Psychology: Human Perception and Performance, 18,* 530–549.

Logue, A. W., Ophir, I., & Strauss, K. E. (1981). The acquisition of taste aversion in humans. *Behavior Research and Therapy, 19,* 319–333.

London, P. (1978). *Beginning psychology.* Chicago: Dorsey.

Lord, C. G., Lepper, M. R., & Mackie, D. (1984). Attitude prototypes as determinants of attitude-behavior consistency. *Journal of Personality and Social Psychology, 46,* 1254–1266.

Lorenz, K. (1952). *King Solomon's ring.* New York: Crowell.

Lovaas, O. I. (1977). *The autistic child: Language development through behavior modification.* Oxford, UK: Irvington.

Lovaas, O. I. (1987). Behavioral treatment and normal educational and intellectual functioning in young autistic children. *Journal of Consulting and Clinical Psychology, 55,* 3–9.

Lovaas, O. I., & Simmons, J. Q. (1969). Manipulation of self-destruction in three retarded children. *Journal of Applied Behavior Analysis, 2,* 143–157.

Lubinski, D., & Benbow, D. P. (1992). Gender differences in abilities and preferences among the gifted: Implications for the math-science pipeline. *Current Directions in Psychological Science, 2,* 61–66.

Lummis, M., & Stevenson, H. W. (1990). Gender differences in beliefs and achievement: A cross-cultural study. *Developmental Psychology, 26,* 254–263.

Lykken, D. T. (1998). *A tremor in the blood: Uses and abuses of the lie detector.* New York: Plenum.

Lynch, G. (1998). Memory and the brain: Unexpected chemistries and a new pharmacology. *Neurobiology of Learning and Memory, 70,* 82–100.

Lyon, D. R. (1977). Individual differences in immediate serial recall: A matter of mnemonics. *Cognitive Psychology, 9,* 403–411.

Maccoby, E. E., Snow, M. E., & Jacklin, C. N. (1984). Children's dispositions and mother-child interaction at 12 and 18 months: A short-term longitudinal study. *Developmental Psychology, 20,* 459–472.

Macfarlane, J. W. (1963). From infancy to adulthood. *Child Education, 39,* 336–342.

Macfarlane, J. W. (1964). Perspectives on personality consistency and change from the guidance study. *Vita Humana, 7,* 115–126.

Macrae, C. N., & Bodenhausen, G. V. (2000). Social cognition: Thinking categorically about others. *Annual Review of Psychology, 51,* 93–120.

Maddi, S. R. (1972). *Personality theories.* Homewood, IL: Dorsey.

Maddi, S. R. (1996). *Personality theories: A comparative analysis* (6th ed.). Belmont, CA: Brooks/Cole.

Maddi, S. R., Barone, P. T., & Puccetti, M. C. (1987). Stressful events are indeed a factor in physical illness: Reply to Schroeder and Costa (1984). *Journal of Personality and Social Psychology, 52,* 833–843.

Maddi, S. R., & Kobasa, S. C. (1984). *The hardy executive: Health under stress.* Homewood, IL: Dow Jones-Irwin.

Maier, S. F., Seligman, M. E. P., & Solomon, R. L. (1969). Pavlovian fear conditioning and learned helplessness. In B. A. Campbell & R. M. Church (Eds.), *Punishment and aversive behavior.* New York: Appleton-Century-Crofts.

Main, M., & Solomon, J. (1986). Discovery of an insecure-disorganized/disoriented attachment pattern: Procedures, findings and implications for the classification of behavior. In T. B. Brazelton & M. Yogman (Eds.), *Affective development in infancy.* Norwood, NJ: Ablex.

Makin, J. W., & Porter, R. H. (1989). Attractiveness of lactating females' breast odors to neonates. *Child Development, 60,* 803–810.

Mann, L., & Janis, I. L. (1968). A followup study on the long-term effects of emotional role playing. *Journal of Personality and Social Psychology, 8,* 338–342.

Manuck, S. B., Cohen, S., Rabin, B. S., & Muldoon, M. F. (1991). Individual differences in cellular immune response to stress. *Psychological Science, 2,* 111–115.

Marcia, J. (1980). Identity in adolescence. In J. Adelson (Ed.), *Handbook of adolescent psychology.* New York: Wiley.

Markovitz, J. H., Matthews, K. A., Kannel, W. B., Cobb, J. L., & D'Agostino, R. B. (1993). Psychological predictors of hypertension in the Framingham study: Is there tension in hypertension? *Journal of the American Medical Association, 270,* 2439–2443.

Markowitsch, H. J. (2000). The anatomical bases of memory. In M. S. Gazzaniga (Ed.), *The new cognitive neurosciences* (2nd ed.). Cambridge, MA: MIT Press.

Markowitz, J. S. (1989). Long-term psychological distress among chemically exposed firefighters. *Behavioral Medicine, 15,* 75–83.

Marks, I. (1997). Behaviour therapy for obsessive-compulsive disorder: A decade of progress. *Canadian Journal of Psychiatry, 42,* 1021–1027.

Marks, I. M., O'Dwyer, A.-M., Meehan, O., Greist, J., Baer, L., & McGuire, P. (2000). Subjective imagery in obsessive-compulsive disorder before and after exposure therapy: Pilot randomised controlled trial. *British Journal of Psychiatry, 176,* 387–391.

Marmar, C. R., & Horowitz, M. J. (1988). Diagnosis and phase-oriented treatment of post-traumatic stress disorder. In J. P. Wilson, Z. Harel, & B. Kahana (Eds.), *Human adaptation to extreme stress* (pp. 81–103). New York: Plenum.

Marsh, H. W., & Parker, J. W. (1984). Determinants of student self-concept: Is it better to be a relatively large fish in a small pond even if you don't learn to swim as well? *Journal of Personality and Social Psychology, 47,* 213–231.

Martin, J. L. (1982, August). The effects of social support on psychological distress among Vietnam veterans and their peers. Paper presented at the Annual Meeting of the American Psychological Association, Washington, DC.

Marx, B. P., & Gross, A. M. (1998). Behavioral treatment. In T. H. Ollendick & M. Hersen (Eds.), *Handbook of child psychopathology* (3rd ed.). New York: Plenum.

Marx, J. L. (1985). The immune system "belongs in the body." *Science, 227,* 1190–1192.

Maslach, C., & Goldberg, J. (1998). Prevention of burnout: New perspectives. *Applied and Preventive Psychology, 67,* 1063–1078.

Maslach, C., Schaufeli, W. B., & Leiter, M. P. (2001). Job burnout. *Annual Review of Psychology, 52,* 397–422.

Maslow, A. H. (1969). Personal communication.

Maslow, A. H. (1970). *Motivation and personality* (2nd ed.). New York: Harper.

Mason, J. W., Kosten, T. R., Southwick, S. M., & Giller, E. L. (1990). The use of psychoendocrine strategies in post-traumatic stress disorder. *Journal of Applied Social Psychology, 20,* 1822–1846.

Masserman, J. H. (1961). *Principles of dynamic psychiatry* (2nd ed.). Philadelphia: Saunders.

Masters, W. H., & Johnson, V. E. (1966). *Human sexual response.* Boston: Little, Brown.

Matheny, K. B., Gfroerer, C. A., & Harris, K. (2000). Work stress, burnout, and coping at the turn of the century: An individual psychology perspective. *Journal of Individual Psychology, 56,* 74–87.

Matsumoto, D. (2000). *Culture and psychology: People around the world* (2nd ed.). Belmont, CA: Wadsworth.

Maugh, T. M., II. (1982). Sleep-promoting factor isolated. *Science, 216,* 1400.

Mazzoni, G. A. L., Lombardo, P., Malvagia, S., & Loftus, E. F. (1999). Dream interpretation and false beliefs.

*Professional Psychology: Research and Practice, 30,* 45–50.

McAdams, D. P. (1992). The five-factor model in personality: A critical appraisal. *Journal of Personality, 60,* 329–361.

McCall, R. B., & Carriger, M. S. (1993). A meta-analysis of infant habituation and recognition memory performance as predictors of later IQ. *Child Development, 64,* 57–79.

McCall, W. V., & Dickerson, L. A. (2001). The outcome of 369 ECT consultations. *Journal of ECT, 17,* 50–52.

McCann, I. L., & Holmes, D. S. (1984). Influence of aerobic exercise on depression. *Journal of Personality and Social Psychology, 46,* 1142–1147.

McCarthy, M. (1990). The thin ideal: Depression and eating disorders in women. *Behavior Research and Therapy, 28,* 205–215.

McCartney, K. (1984). Effect of quality of day care environment on children's language development. *Developmental Psychology, 20,* 244–260.

McCaul, K. D. (1980). Sensory information, fear level, and reactions to pain. *Journal of Personality, 48,* 494–504.

McCaul, K. D., Holmes, D. S., & Solomon, S. (1982). Voluntary expressive changes in emotion. *Journal of Personality and Social Psychology, 42,* 145–152.

McClelland, D. C. (1979). Inhibited power motive and high blood pressure in men. *Journal of Abnormal Psychology, 88,* 182–190.

McClelland, D. C. (1985). How motives, skills, and values determine what people do. *American Psychologist, 40,* 812–825.

McClelland, D. C. (1989). Motivational factors in health and disease. *American Psychologist, 44,* 675–682.

McClelland, D. C., & Atkinson, J. W. (1948). The projective expression of needs, I: The effect of different intensities of the hunger drive on perception. *Journal of Psychology, 25,* 205–222.

McClelland, D. C., & Koestner, R. (1992). The achievement motive. In C. P. Smith & J. W. Atkinson (Eds.), *Motivation and personality: Handbook of thematic content analysis.* New York: Cambridge University Press.

McClintock, M. K. (1971). Menstrual synchrony and suppression. *Nature, 229,* 224–245.

McClintock, M. K. (1984). Estrous synchrony: Modulation of ovarian cycle length by female pheromones. *Physiology and Behavior, 32,* 701–705.

McCormick, M. C., et al. (1992). The health and developmental status of very low-birth-weight children at school age. *Journal of the American Medical Association, 267,* 2204–2208.

McCrae, R. R., & Costa, P. T. (1986). Clinical assessment can benefit from recent advances in personality psychology. *American Psychologist, 41,* 1001–1003.

McCrae, R. R., & Costa, P. T., Jr. (1997). Personality trait structure as a human universal. *American Psychologist, 52,* 509–516.

McCrae, R. R., & Costa, P. T., Jr. (1999). A five-factor theory of personality. In L. A. Pervin & O. P. John (Eds.), *Handbook of personality: Theory and research* (2nd ed.). New York: Guilford.

McCrae, R. R., Costa, P. T., Jr., de Lima, M. P., Simoes, A., Ostendorf, F., Angleitner, A., et al. (1999). Age differences in personality across the adult life span: Parallels in five cultures. *Developmental Psychology, 35,* 466–477.

McCrae, R. R., Costa, P. T., Jr., Del Pilar, G. H., Rolland, J.-P., & Parker, W. D. (1998). Cross-cultural assessment of the five-factor model: The Revised NEO Personality Inventory. *Journal of Cross-Cultural Psychology, 29,* 171–188.

McCullough, L., & Andrews, S. (2001). Assimilative integration: Short-term dynamic psychotherapy for treating affect phobias. *Clinical Psychology: Science and Practice, 8,* 82–97.

McDonald, R. J., & White, N. M. (1993). A triple dissociation of memory systems: Hippocampus, amygdala, and dorsal striatum. *Behavioral Neuroscience, 107,* 3–22.

McEwen, B. S. (2000). Effects of adverse experiences for brain structure and function. *Biological Psychiatry, 48,* 721–731.

McGaugh, J. L. (1983). Preserving the presence of the past: Hormonal influences on memory storage. *American Psychologist, 38,* 161–174.

McGeoch, J. A. (1930). The influence of associative value upon the difficulty of nonsense-syllable lists. *Journal of Genetic Psychology, 37,* 421–426.

McGlynn, A. P., & Locke, B. J. (1997). A 25–year follow-up of a punishment program for severe self-injury. *Behavioral Interventions, 12,* 203–207.

McGlynn, S. M. (1990). Behavioral approaches to neuropsychological rehabilitation. *Psychological Bulletin, 108,* 420–441.

McGuire, W. J., & McGuire, C. V. (1986). Differences in conceptualizing self versus conceptualizing other people as manifested by contrasting verbs used in natural speech. *Journal of Personality and Social Psychology, 51,* 1135–1143.

McHale, S. M., Crouter, A. C., & Tucker, C. J. (1999). Family context and gender role socialization in middle childhood: Comparing girls to boys and sisters to brothers. *Child Development, 70,* 990–1004.

McKeachie, W., Lin, Y., Milholland, J., & Isaacson, R. (1966). Student affiliation, motives, teacher warmth and academic achievement. *Journal of Personality and Social Psychology, 4,* 457–461.

McNally, R. J., Kaspi, S. P., Riemann, B. C., & Zeitlin, S. B. (1990). Selective processing of threat cues in posttraumatic stress disorder. *Journal of Abnormal Psychology, 99,* 398–402.

Meece, J. L., Parsons, J. E., Kaczaia, C. M., & Goff, S. B. (1982). Sex differences in math achievement: Toward models of academic choice. *Psychological Bulletin, 91,* 324–348.

Mellon, M. W., & McGrath, M. L. (2000). Empirically supported treatments in pediatric psychology: Nocturnal enuresis. *Journal of Pediatric Psychology, 25,* 193–214.

Meltzer, H. Y. (1987). Biological studies in schizophrenia. *Schizophrenia Bulletin, 13,* 77–111.

Meltzer, H. Y. (1992). Dimensions of outcome with clozapine. *British Journal of Psychiatry, 160,* 46–53.

Melzack, R. (1973). *The puzzle of pain.* New York: Basic.

Melzack, R., & Wall, P. D. (1995). Pain mechanisms: A new theory. In A. Steptoe & J. Wardle (Eds.), *Psychosocial processes and health: A reader.* New York: Cambridge University Press.

Mendelson, W. B., Garnett, D., Gillin, J. C., & Weingartner, H. (1984). The experience of insomnia and daytime and nighttime functioning. *Psychiatry Research, 12,* 235–250.

differences in children's cognitive competence. *Developmental Psychology, 20,* 166–179.

Ornstein, P. A., Ceci, S. J., & Loftus, E. F. (1998a). Adult recollections of childhood abuse: Cognitive and developmental perspectives. *Psychology, Public Policy, and Law, 4,* 1025–1051.

Ornstein, P. A., Ceci, S. J., & Loftus, E. F. (1998b). Comment on Alpert, Brown, and Courtois (1998): The science of memory and the practice of psychotherapy. *Psychology, Public Policy, and Law, 4,* 996–1010.

Ornstein, R. (1978). The split and the whole brain. *Human Nature, 1,* 76–83.

Ornstein, R., & Thompson, R. F. (1984). *The amazing brain.* Boston: Houghton Mifflin.

Öst, L.-G. (1987). Applied relaxation: Description of a coping technique and review of controlled studies. *Behaviour Research and Therapy, 25,* 397–409.

Oyama, S. (1973). *A sensitive period for the acquisition of a second language.* Unpublished doctoral dissertation, Harvard University.

Paggi, K., & Hayslip, B., Jr. (1999). Mental aerobics: Exercises for the mind in later life. *Educational Gerontology, 25,* 1–12.

Paik, H., & Comstock, G. (1994). The effects of television violence on antisocial behavior: A meta-analysis. *Communication Research, 21,* 516–546.

Parloff, M. B. (1990). Personal communication.

Passingham, R. E. (1985). Memory of monkeys *(Macaca mulatta)* with lesions in prefrontal cortex. *Behavioral Neurosciences, 99,* 3–21.

Pasternack, J. J. (1999). *Human molecular genetics: Mechanisms of inherited diseases.* Bethesda, MD: Fitzgerald Science Press.

Patterson, C. J. (1995). Sexual orientation and human development: An overview. *Developmental Psychology, 31,* 3–11.

Pavlov, I. P. (1927/1960). *Conditioned reflexes.* New York: Dover.

Peake, T. H., Meyers, T. L., & Duenke, S. D. (1997). Options for brief psychotherapy: Cognitive and psychodynamic variations. *Journal of Mental Health, 6,* 217–235.

Pearson, K. (1894). *Contributions to the mathematical theory of evolution.* London: K. Paul, Trench, Trübner, and Co.

Peele, S. (1981). Reductionism in the psychology of the eighties: Can biochemistry eliminate addiction, mental illness, and pain? *American Psychologist, 36,* 807–818.

Pennebaker, J. W. (1989). Confession, inhibition, and disease. *Advances in Experimental Social Psychology, 22,* 211–244.

Pennebaker, J. W., Kiecolt-Glaser, J. K., & Glaser, R. (1988). Disclosure of traumas and immune function: Health implications for psychotherapy. *Journal of Consulting and Clinical Psychology, 56,* 239–245.

Pepperberg, I. M. (1998). Talking with Alex: Logic and speech in parrots. *Scientific American Presents, 9* (4), 60–65.

Pepperberg, I. M. (1999). *The Alex studies: Cognitive and communicative abilities of grey parrots.* Cambridge, MA: Harvard University Press.

Perin, C. T. (1943). A quantitative investigation of the delay of reinforcement gradient. *Journal of Experimental Psychology, 32,* 37–51.

Perry, D. G., Kusel, S. J., & Perry, L. C. (1988). Victims of peer aggression. *Developmental Psychology, 24,* 807–814.

Petersen, A. C. (1987, September). Those gangly years. *Psychology Today,* 28–34.

Peterson, C., & Seligman, M. E. P. (1984). Causal explanations as a risk factor in depression. *Psychological Review, 91,* 347–374.

Peterson, L., & Peterson, M. J. (1959). Short-term retention of individual verbal items. *Journal of Experimental Psychology, 58,* 193–198.

Petti, T. A. (1981). Depression in children: A significant disorder. *Psychosomatics, 22,* 444–447.

Petti, T. A., & Larson, C. N. (1987). Depression and suicide. In V. P. Van Hesselt & M. Hersen (Eds.), *Handbook of adolescent psychology.* New York: Pergamon.

Pettingale, K. W., et al. (1985, March 30). Mental attitudes to cancer: An additional prognostic factor. *Lancet.*

Phillips, D. (1984). The illusion of incompetence among academically competent children. *Child Development, 55,* 2000–2016.

Phillips, D. P., & Carstensen, L. L. (1986). Clustering of teenage suicides after television news stories about suicide. *New England Journal of Medicine, 315,* 685–689.

Piaget, J. (1952). *The origins of intelligence in children.* New York: International University Press.

Piane, G. (2000). Contingency contracting and systematic desensitization for heroin addicts in methadone maintenance programs. *Journal of Psychoactive Drugs, 32,* 311–319.

Piet, S. (1987). What motivates stunt men? *Motivation and Emotion, 11,* 195–213.

Pike, K., & Rodin, J. (1991). Mothers, daughters, and disordered eating. *Journal of Abnormal Psychology, 100,* 198–204.

Pillemer, D. H. (1984). Flashbulb memories of the assassination attempt of President Reagan. *Cognition, 16,* 63–80.

Pine, C. J. (1985). Anxiety and eating behavior in obese and nonobese American Indians and white Americans. *Journal of Personality and Social Psychology, 49,* 774–780.

Pinel, J. P. J. (2003). *Biopsychology.* Boston: Allyn and Bacon.

Pinel, J. P. J., Assanand, S., & Lehman, D. R. (2000). Hunger, eating, and ill health. *American Psychologist, 55,* 1105–1116.

Pizzamiglio, L., Galati, G., & Committeri, G. (2001). The contribution of functional neuroimaging to recovery after brain damage: A review. *Cortex, 37,* 11–31.

Plomin, R., & DeFries, J. C. (1999). The genetics of cognitive abilities and disabilities. In S. J. Ceci & W. M. Williams (Eds.), *The nature-nurture debate: The essential readings.* Malden, MA: Blackwell.

Plomin, R., & McClearn, G. E. (Eds.). (1993). *Nature-nurture and psychology.* Washington, DC: American Psychological Association.

Plomin, R., & Petrill, S. A. (1997). Genetics and intelligence: What's new? *Intelligence, 24,* 53–77.

Plous, S. (1996). Attitudes toward the use of animals in psychological research and education. *American Psychologist, 51,* 1167–1180.

Pope, K., & Feldman-Sumners, S. (1992). National survey of psychologists' sexual and physical abuse history and their evaluation of training and competence in these areas. *Professional Psychology: Research and Practice, 23,* 353–361.

Pope, K. S., & Tabachnick, B. G. (1993). Therapists' anger, hate, fear and sexual feelings: National survey of therapist responses, client characteristics, critical events, formal complaints, and training. *Professional Psychology: Research and Practice, 24,* 142–152.

Porter, R. H., & Winberg, J. (1999). Unique salience of maternal breast odors for newborn infants. *Neuroscience and Biobehavioral Reviews, 23,* 439–449.

Portes, P. R., Dunham, R., & Del Castillo, K. (2000). Identity formation and status across cultures: Exploring the cultural validity of Eriksonian theory. In A. L. Comunian & U. P. Gielen (Eds.), *International perspectives on human development.* Lengerich, Germany: Pabst Science Publishers.

Postman, L., Bruner, B., & McGinnies, E. (1948). Personal values as selective factors in perception. *Journal of Abnormal and Social Psychology, 43,* 142–154.

Potts, M. K., Burnam, M. A., & Wells, K. B. (1991). Gender differences in depression detection: A comparison of clinical diagnosis and standardized assessment. *Psychological Assessment, 3,* 609–615.

Powers, S. I., Hauser, S. T., & Kilner, L. A. (1989). Adolescent mental health. *American Psychologist, 44,* 200–208.

Pratt, C. (1990). On asking children, and adults, bizarre questions. *First Language, 10,* 167–175.

Premack, D. (1976). *Intelligence in ape and man.* Hillsdale, NJ: Erlbaum.

Premack, D. (1985). "Gavagai!" or the future history of the animal language controversy. *Cognition, 19,* 207–296.

Prentice, D. A., & Miller, D. T. (1993). Pluralistic ignorance and alcohol use on campus: Some consequences of misperceiving the social norm. *Journal of Personality and Social Psychology, 64,* 243–256.

Priest, R. F., & Sawyer, J. (1967). Proximity and peership: Bases of balance in interpersonal attraction. *American Journal of Sociology, 72,* 633–649.

Pritchard, R. M. (1961). Stabilized images on the retina. *Scientific American, 204,* 72–78.

Purves, D., Augustine, G. J., Fitzpatrick, D., Katz, L. C., LaMantia, A-S., & McNamara, J. O. (Eds.). (1997). *Neuroscience.* Sunderland, MA: Sinauer.

Putnam, F. W. (1991). Recent research on multiple personality disorder. *Psychiatric Clinics of North America, 14,* 489–502.

PSYETA (2002). Internet home page at www.psyeta.org.

Quadrel, M. J., Fischhoff, B., & Davis, W. (1993). Adolescent (in)vulnerability. *American Psychologist, 48,* 102–116.

Quinn, S. (1987). *A mind of her own: The life of Karen Horney.* New York: Basic.

Quinton, D., & Rutter, M. (1983). Parenting behavior of mothers raised "in care." In A. R. Nicol (Ed.), *Practical lessons from longitudinal studies.* Chichester, UK: Wiley.

Radecki, C., & Jennings, J. (1980). Sex as a status variable in work settings: Female and male reports of dominance behavior. *Journal of Applied Social Psychology, 10,* 71–85.

Radke-Yarrow, M. (1989). Personal communication.

Rajigah, L. S. (1996). Treatment of choice for nocturnal enuresis: Review and recommendations. *Journal of Psychological Practice, 2,* 33–42.

Rajram, S., & Roediger, H. L. (1993). Direct comparison of four implicit memory tests. *Journal of Experimental Psychology: Learning, Memory, and Cognition, 19,* 765–776.

Ramsay, D. S., Seeley, R. J., Bolles, R. C., & Woods, S. C. (1996). Ingestive homeostasis: The primacy of learning. In E. D. Capaldi (Ed.), *Why we eat what we eat: The psychology of eating.* Washington, DC: American Psychological Association.

Rapoport, J. L. (1989, March). The biology of obsessions and compulsions. *Scientific American,* 83–89.

Rawsthorne, L. J., & Elliott, A. J., 1999. Achievement goals and intrinsic motivation: A meta-analytic review. *Personality and Social Psychology Review, 3,* 326–344.

Ray, O. S. (1996). *Drugs, society, and human behavior* (7th ed.). St. Louis: Mosby.

Read, J. (1997). Child abuse and psychosis: A literature review and implications for professional practice. *Professional Psychology: Research and Practice, 28,* 448–456.

Reason, J. (1984, September/October). The psychopathology of everyday slips. *The Sciences,* 45–49.

Rebello Britto, P. (2001). Family literacy environments and young children's emerging literacy skills. *Reading Research Quarterly, 36,* 346–347.

Reber, P. J., Alvarez, P., & Squire, L. R. (1997). Reaction time distributions across normal forgetting: Searching for markers of memory consolidation. *Learning and Memory, 4,* 284–290.

Rebok, G. W., & Plude, D. J. (2001). Relation of physical activity to memory functioning in older adults: The memory workout program. *Educational Gerontology, 27,* 241–259.

Redburn, F. S., & Buss, T. F. (1985). *Responding to America's homeless.* New York: Praeger.

Reeve, J., Cole, S. G., & Olson, B. C. (1986). Zeigarnik effect and instrinsic motivation. *Motivation and Emotion, 10,* 233–245.

Regier, D. A. (1990). Comorbidity of mental disorders with alcohol and other drug abuse. *Journal of the American Medical Association, 264,* 2511–2518.

Regier, D. A. (1993). The de facto U.S. mental and addictive disorders service system. *Archives of General Psychiatry, 50,* 85–94.

Regier, D. A., Boyd, J. H., Burke, J. D., & Rae, D. S. (1988). One-month prevalence of mental disorders in the United States. *Archives of General Psychiatry, 45,* 977–986.

Reid, W. J. (2002). Knowledge for direct social work practice: An analysis of trends. *Social Service Review, 76,* 6–33.

Reis, H. T., Senchak, M., & Solomon, B. (1985). Sex differences in the intimacy of social interaction: Further examination of potential explanations. *Journal of Personality and Social Psychology, 48,* 1204–1217.

Reis, H. T., Wheeler, L., Kernis, M. H., Nezlek, J., & Perri, M. (1982). Physical attractiveness in social interaction: II. Why does appearance affect social experience? *Journal of Personality and Social Psychology, 43,* 979–996.

Reite, M. L. (1987). Temperament stability between prenatal period and 24 months. *Developmental Psychology, 23,* 216–222.

Remafedi, G. (1999). Sexual orientation and youth suicide. *Journal of the American Medical Association, 282,* 1291–1292.

Remafedi, G., French, S., Story, M., Resnick, M. D., & Blum, R. (1998). The relationship between suicide risk and sexual orientation: Results of a population-based study. *American Journal of Public Health, 88,* 57–60.

Reno, R. M., & Halaris, A. E. (1990). The relationship between life stress and depression in an endogenous sample. *Comprehensive Psychiatry, 31,* 25–33.

Rescorla, R. A. (1988). Pavlovian conditioning: It's not what you think it is. *American Psychologist, 43,* 151–160.

Rescorla, R. A., & Holland, P. C. (1982). Behavioral studies of associative learning in animals. In M. R. Rosenzweig & L. W. Porter (Eds.), *Annual Review of Psychology, 33,* 265–308.

Reuter-Lorenz, P., & Davidson, R. J. (1981). Differential contributions of the two cerebral hemispheres to the perception of happy and sad faces. *Neuropsychologia, 19,* 609–613.

Reynolds, C. R., & Gutkin, T. B. (1981). A multivariate comparison of the intellectual performance of blacks and whites matched on four demographic variables. *Personality and Individual Differences, 2,* 175–180.

Reznick, J. S. (1990). Visual preference as a test of infant word comprehension. *Applied Psycholinguistics, 11,* 145–166.

Ricciardelli, L. A., & McCabe, M. P. (2001). Children's body image concerns and eating disturbance: A review of the literature. *Clinical Psychology Review, 21,* 325–344.

Rice, M. L., Huston, A. C., Truglio, R., & Wright, J. C. (1990). Words from "Sesame Street": Learning vocabulary while viewing. *Developmental Psychology, 26,* 421–428.

Riedel, G., & Micheau, J. (2001). Function of the hippocampus in memory formation: Desperately seeking resolution. *Progress in Neuro-Psychopharmacology and Biological Psychiatry, 25,* 835–853.

Riessman, F. (1984, June 29). *Support groups as preventive intervention.* Paper presented to Vermont Conference on Primary Prevention, Burlington, VT.

Riessman, F. (1985). Personal communication.

Ring, E. D., & Fenson, L. (2000). The correspondence between parent report and child performance for receptive and expressive vocabulary beyond infancy. *First Language, 20,* 141–159.

Rist, R. C. (1970). Student social class and teacher expectations: The self-fulfilling prophecy in ghetto education. *Harvard Educational Review, 40,* 411–451.

Rizley, R. (1978). Depression and distortion in the attribution of causality. *Journal of Abnormal Psychology, 87,* 32–48.

Robberson, M. R., & Rogers, R. W. (1988). Beyond fear appeals: Negative and positive persuasive appeals to health and self-esteem. *Journal of Applied Social Psychology, 18,* 277–287.

Robbins, D. (1971). Partial reinforcement. *Psychological Bulletin, 76,* 415–431.

Robbins, P. R., & Tanck, R. H. (1987). A study of diurnal patterns of depressed mood. *Motivation and Emotion, 11,* 37–49.

Roberts, J. E., & Hartlage, S. (1996). In P. W. Corrigan & S. C. Yudofsky (Eds.), *Cognitive rehabilitation for neuropsychiatric disorders.* Washington, DC: American Psychiatric Press.

Roberts, L. (1988). Vietnam's psychological toll. *Science, 241,* 159–161.

Robins, L. N., & Regier, D. A. (1991). *Psychiatric problems in America: The epidemiological catchment area.* New York: Free Press.

Robinson, R. G., Lipsey, J. R., Rao, K., & Price, T. R. (1986). Two-year longitudinal study of poststroke mood disorders: Comparison of acute-onset with delayed-onset depression. *American Journal of Psychiatry, 143,* 1238–1244.

Rock, I. (1984). *Perception.* Washington, DC: Scientific American Library.

Rodin, J. (1980). Managing the stress of aging: The role of control and coping. In S. Levine & H. Ursin (Eds.), *Coping and health.* New York: Plenum.

Rodin, J. (1985). Insulin levels, hunger, and food intake: An example of feedback loops in body weight regulation. *Health Psychology, 4,* 1–18.

Rodin, J. (1987). *The determinants of successful aging.* Washington, DC: Federation of Behavioral, Psychological and Cognitive Sciences.

Rogel, M. J. (1978). A critical evaluation of the possibility of higher primate reproductive and sexual pheromones. *Psychological Bulletin, 85,* 810–830.

Rogers, C. (1969). Personal communication.

Rogers, C. R. (1959). A theory of therapy, personality, and interpersonal relationships, as developed in the client-centered framework. In S. Koch (Ed.), *Psychology: A study of a science* (Vol. 3). New York: McGraw-Hill.

Rogers, C. R. (1961). *On becoming a person.* Oxford, UK: Houghton Mifflin.

Rogers, C. R. (1980). *A way of being.* Boston: Houghton Mifflin.

Rogers, C. R. (1992). The necessary and sufficient conditions of therapeutic personality change. *Journal of Consulting and Clinical Psychology, 60,* 827–832.

Rogers, R. W. (1985). Attitude change and information integration in fear appeals. *Psychological Reports, 56,* 179–182.

Roland, A. (1989). *In search of self in India and Japan.* Princeton, NJ: Princeton University Press.

Rolls, B. J., & Rolls, E. T. (1982). *Thirst.* New York: Cambridge University Press.

Rolls, E. T. (2000). Memory systems in the brain. *Annual Review of Psychology, 51,* 599–630.

Rolobos, A. S., Heredia, M., de la Feunte, J. A., Criado, J. M., Yajeya, J., Campos, J., et al. (2001). Functional recovery of skilled forelimb use in rats obliged to use the impaired limb after grafting of the frontal cortex lesion with homotopic fetal cortex. *Neurobiology of Learning and Memory, 75,* 274–292.

Romaniuk, M., McAuley, W. J., & Arling, G. (1983). An examination of the prevalance of mental disorders among the elderly in the community. *Journal of Abnormal Psychology, 92,* 458–467.

Rook, K. S. (1987). Social support versus companionship: Effects on life stress, loneliness, and evaluations by others. *Journal of Personality and Social Psychology, 52,* 1132–1147.

Rosch, E. (1988). Principles of categorization. In A. M. Collins & E. E. Smith (Eds.), *Readings in cognitive science: A perspective from psychology and artificial intelligence.* San Mateo, CA: Morgan Kaufmann.

Rosch, E., & Mervis, C. B. (1998). Family resemblances: Studies in the internal structure of categories. In

M. R. DePaul & W. M. Ramsey (Eds.), *Rethinking intuition: The psychology of intuition and its role in philosophical inquiry*. Lanham, MD: Rowman and Littlefield.

Rorschach, H. (1921/1942). *Psychodiagnostics: A diagnostic test based on perception* (3rd ed., rev.). Oxford, UK: Grune and Stratton.

Rose, R. M. (1980). Endocrine responses to stressful psychological events. *Psychiatric Clinics of North America, 3,* 251–276.

Rose, R. M., Jenkins, C. D., & Hurst, M. W. (1978). *Air traffic controller health change study.* Boston: Boston University School of Medicine.

Rosen, M. G. (1985, April). Factors during labor and delivery that influence brain disorders. In J. M. Freeman (Ed.), *Prenatal and perinatal factors associated with brain disorders.* National Institute of Child Health and Human Development, NIH Publication No. 85-1149.

Rosenberg, E. L., & Ekman, P. (1995). Conceptual and methodological issues in the judgment of facial expressions of emotions. *Motivation and Emotion, 19,* 111–138.

Rosenhan, D. L., & Seligman, M. E. P. (1984). *Abnormal psychology.* New York: Norton.

Rosenhan, D. L., & Seligman, M. E. P. (1989). *Abnormal psychology* (2nd ed.). New York: Norton.

Rosenthal, N. E. (1989). *Seasons of the mind: Why you get the winter blues and what you can do about it.* New York: Bantam.

Rosenthal, R., & Jacobson, L. (1966). Teachers' expectancies: Determinants of pupils' IQ gains. *Psychological Reports, 19,* 115–118.

Rosenthal, R., & Jacobson, L. F. (1996). Teacher expectations for the disadvantaged. In S. Fein (Ed.), *Readings in social psychology: The art and science of research.* Boston: Houghton Mifflin.

Rosenzweig, M. R., & Lieman, A. L. (1982). *Physiological psychology.* Lexington, MA: Heath.

Roskinski, R. R. (1977). *The development of visual perception.* Santa Monica, CA: Goodyear.

Ross, L. (1977). The intuitive psychologist and his shortcomings. In L. Berkowitz (Ed.), *Advances in experimental social psychology* (Vol. 10). New York: Academic.

Ross, L., Lepper, M. R., & Hubbard, M. (1975). Perseverance in self-perception and social perception. *Journal of Personality and Social Psychology, 32,* 880–892.

Roth, D. L., & Holmes, D. S. (1985). Influence of physical fitness in determining the impact of stressful life events on physical and psychological health. *Psychosomatic Medicine, 47,* 164–173.

Rothbaum, B. O., & Schwartz, A. C. (2002). Exposure therapy for posttraumatic stress disorder. *American Journal of Psychotherapy, 56,* 59–75.

Rothbaum, F., Weisz, J., Pott, M., Miyake, K., & Morelli, G. (2000). Attachment and culture security in the United States and Japan. *American Psychologist, 55,* 1093–1104.

Rothblum, E. D. (1999). Contradictions and confounds in coverage of obesity: Psychology journals, textbooks, and the media. *Journal of Social Issues, 55,* 355–369.

Rupp, A., & Keith, S. J. (1993). The costs of schizophrenia. *Psychiatric Clinics of North America, 16,* 413–423.

Rushton, J. P., Russell, R. J. H., & Wells, P. A. (1984). Genetic similarity theory: Beyond kin selection. *Behavior Genetics, 14,* 179–193.

Russell, J. A. (1994). Is there universal recognition of emotion from facial expression? A review of the cross-cultural studies. *Psychological Bulletin, 115,* 102–141.

Rutkowski, G. K., Gruder, C. L., & Romer, D. (1983). Group cohesiveness, social norms, & bystander intervention. *Journal of Personality and Social Psychology, 44,* 545–552.

Rutter, M. (1983a). School effects on pupil progress: Research findings and policy implications. *Child Development, 54,* 1–29.

Rutter, M. (1983b). Stress, coping, and development: Some issues and some questions. In N. Garmezy & M. Rutter (Eds.), *Stress, coping, and development in children.* New York: McGraw-Hill.

Rutter, M. (1986). Meyerian psychobiology, personality development and the role of life experiences. *American Journal of Psychiatry, 143,* 1077–1087.

Rutter, M., Quinton, D., & Liddell, C. (1983). Parenting in two generations: Looking backwards and looking forwards. In N. Madge (Ed.), *Families at risk* (pp. 60–68). London: Heinemann Educational.

Rycroft, C. (1986). *Psychoanalysis and beyond.* Chicago: University of Chicago Press.

Ryff, C. D., & Singer, B. (1998). The contours of positive human health. *Psychological Inquiry, 9,* 1–28.

Safire, W. (2002a, May 13–14). *Conference overview: Visions for a new field of "neuroethics."* Address presented at Neuroethics: Mapping the Field, San Francisco.

Safire, W. (2002b, May 16). The but-what-if factor. *The New York Times.* Internet document at www.nytimes.com.

Safren, S. A., & Heimberg, R. G. (1999). Depression, hopelessness, suicidality, and related factors in sexual minority and heterosexual adolescents. *Journal of Consulting and Clinical Psychology, 67,* 859–866.

Salapatek, P., & Kessen, W. (1966). Visual scanning of triangles of the human newborn. *Journal of Experimental Child Psychology, 3,* 155–167.

Sales, B. D., & Folkman, S. (Eds.). (2000). *Ethics in research with human participants.* Washington, DC: American Psychological Association.

Salmon, P. (2001). Effects of physical exercise on anxiety, depression, and sensitivity to stress: A unifying theory. *Clinical Psychology Review, 21,* 33–61.

Salthouse, T. A. (1988). Effects of aging on verbal abilities. In L. L. Light & D. M. Burke (Eds.), *Language, memory and aging.* New York: Cambridge University Press.

Salzinger, S., Feldman, R., Hammer, M., & Rosario, M. (1993). The effects of physical abuse on children's social relationships. *Child Development, 64,* 169–187.

Sands, S. F., & Wright, A. A. (1982). Monkey and human pictorial memory scanning. *Science, 216,* 1333–1334.

Sapp, M. (1999). *Test anxiety: Applied research, assessment, and treatment interventions.* Lanham, MD: University Press of America.

Sarason, I. G., & Sarason, B. R. (Eds.). (1985). *Social support: Theory, research, and applications.* Hingham, MA: Klumer.

Sarrel, P. M. (1990). Sexuality and menopause. *Obstetrics and Gynecology, 75* (Supplement 4), 26S–30S.

Savage-Rumbaugh, S., Rumbaugh, D. M., & McDonald, K. (1985). Language learning in two species of apes. *Neuroscience and Biobehavioral Reviews, 9,* 653–665.

Savage-Rumbaugh, S., Shanker, S. G., & Taylor, T. J. (1998). *Apes, language, and the human mind.* London: Oxford University Press.

Savoy, R. L. (2001). History and future directions of human brain mapping and functional neuroimaging. *Acta Psychologica, 107,* 293–321.

Sawrey, W. L., Conger, J. J., & Turrell, E. S. (1956). An experimental investigation of the role of psychological factors in the production of gastric ulcers of rats. *Journal of Comparative and Physiological Psychology, 49,* 457–461.

Scarr, S. (1981). Testing for children: Assessment and the many determinants of intellectual competence. *American Psychologist, 36,* 1159–1166.

Scarr, S. (1988). How genotypes and environments combine: Development and individual differences. In N. Bolger, A. Caspi, G. Downey, & M. Moorehouse (Eds.), *Persons in context: Developmental processes.* New York: Cambridge University Press.

Scarr, S. (1998). On Arthur Jensen's integrity. *Intelligence, 26,* 227–232.

Scarr, S., & Grajek, S. (1982). Similarities and differences among siblings. In M. E. Lamb & B. Sutton-Smith (Eds.), *Sibling relationships: Their nature and significance across the lifespan.* Hillsdale, NJ: Erlbaum.

Scarr-Salapatek, S. (1971a). Race, social class, and IQ. *Science, 174,* 1286–1295.

Scarr-Salapatek, S. (1971b). Unknowns in the IQ equation. *Science, 174,* 1223–1228.

Schachter, D. L., Kagan, J., & Leichtman, M. D. (1995). True and false memories in children and adults: A cognitive neuroscience perspective. *Psychology, Public Policy, and Law, 1,* 411–428.

Schachter, S. (1959). *Psychology of affiliation.* Stanford, CA: Stanford University Press.

Schachter, S. (1971). Some extraordinary facts about obese humans and rats. *American Psychologist, 26,* 129–144.

Schachter, S., & Singer, J. E. (1962). Cognitive, social and physiological determinants of emotional state. *Psychological Review, 69,* 379–399.

Schaefer, C., Coyne, J. C., & Lazarus, R. S. (1981). The health-related functions of social support. *Journal of Behavioral Medicine, 4,* 381–406.

Schaeffer, M. A., & Baum, A. (1984). Adrenal cortical response to stress at Three Mile Island. *Psychosomatic Medicine, 46,* 227–237.

Schaffer, H. R., & Liddell, C. (1984). Adult-child interaction under dyadic and polyadic conditions. *British Journal of Developmental Psychology, 2,* 33–42.

Schaie, K. W. (1981). Psychological changes from midlife to early old age: Implications for the maintenance of mental health. *American Journal of Orthopsychiatry, 51,* 199–218.

Schaie, K. W., & Hertzog, C. (1983). Fourteen-year cohort-sequential analyses of adult intellectual development. *Developmental Psychology, 19,* 531–543.

Schaie, K. W., & Willis, S. L. (1986). Can decline in adult intellectual functioning be reversed? *Developmental Psychology, 22,* 223–232.

Schaufeli, W. B., Maslach, C., & Marek, T. (Eds.). (1993). *Professional burnout: Recent developments in theory and research.* Washington, DC: Taylor & Francis.

Scherer, K. R. (1986). Vocal affect expression: A review and a model for future research. *Psychological Bulletin, 99,* 143–165.

Scherer, K. R., & Tannenbaum, P. H. (1986). Emotional experience in everyday life. *Motivation and Emotion, 10,* 295–314.

Schieffelin, E. L. (1985). The cultural analysis of depressive affect: An example from New Guinea. In A. Kleinman & B. Good (Eds.), *Culture and depression.* Berkeley: University of California Press.

Schiffman, S. S. (1997). Taste and smell losses in normal aging and disease. *Journal of the American Medical Association, 278,* 1357–1362.

Schiffman, S. S., Zervakis, J., Suggs, M. S., Shaio, E., & Sattely-Miller, E. A. (1999). Effect of medications on taste: Example of amitriptyline HCl. *Physiology and Behavior, 66,* 183–191.

Schmolck, H., Buffalo, E. A., & Squire, L. R. (2000). Memory distortions develop over time: Recollections of the O. J. Simpson trial verdict after 15 and 32 months. *Psychological Science, 11,* 39–45.

Schmolling, P. (1984). Human reactions to the Nazi concentration camps: A summing up. *Journal of Human Stress, 10,* 108–120.

Schnall, P. L., Pieper, C., Schwartz, J. E., & Karasek, R. A. (1990). The relationship between "job strain," workplace diastolic blood pressure, and left ventricular mass index: Results of a case-control study. *Journal of the American Medical Association, 263,* 1929–1935.

Schneider, D. J. (1973). Implicit personality theory: A review. *Psychological Bulletin, 79,* 294–309.

Schoenborn, C. A., & Wilson, B. F. (1988). *Are married people healthier? Health characteristics of married and unmarried U.S. men and women.* Paper presented to the American Public Health Association, Boston.

Schueklenk, U., & Ristow, M. (1996). The ethics of research into the cause(s) of homosexuality. *Journal of Homosexuality, 31,* 5–30.

Schultz, J. C., & Ososkie, J. N. (1999). Utilizing brief therapy principles in rehabilitation counseling. *Journal of Applied Rehabilitation Counseling, 30,* 4–8.

Schwab, J. J. (1980). Psychiatric manifestations of infectious diseases. In R. C. W. Hall (Ed.), *Psychiatric presentations of medical illness: Somatopsychic disorders.* New York: Spectrum.

Schwartz, G. E. (1982). Psychophysiological patterning and emotion revisited: A system perspective. In C. E. Izard (Ed.), *Measuring emotions in infants and children* (pp. 67–93). Cambridge, UK: Cambridge University Press.

Scogin, F., Jamison, D., & Davis, N. (1990). A two-year follow-up of the effects of bibliotherapy for depressed older adults. *Journal of Clinical and Consulting Psychology, 58,* 665–667.

Scullin, M. H., Peters, E., Williams, W. M., & Ceci, S. J. (2000). The role of IQ and education in predicting later labor market outcomes: Implications for affirmative action. *Psychology, Public Policy, and Law, 6,* 63–89.

Scully, J. A., Tosi, H., & Banning, K. (2000). Life event checklists: Revisiting the Social Readjustment Rating Scale after 30 years. *Educational and Psychological Measurement, 60,* 864–876.

Schultz, D. P., & Schultz, S. E. (2001). *Theories of personality* (7th ed.). Belmont, CA: Wadsworth.

Sears, D. O., Peplau, L. A., & Taylor, S. E. (1988). *Social psychology* (6th ed.). Englewood Cliffs, NJ: Prentice Hall.

Segal, J. (1986). *Winning life's toughest battles: Roots of human resilience.* New York: McGraw-Hill.

Segal, J., & Segal, Z. (1985). *Growing up smart and happy.* New York: McGraw-Hill.

Segal, J., & Segal, Z. (1988, September). Compassionate kids. *Parents Magazine.*

Segal, M. H., Dasen, P. R., Berry, J. W., & Poortinga, Y. H. (1999). *Human behavior in global perspective: An introduction to cross-cultural psychology* (2nd ed.). Boston: Allyn and Bacon.

Segal, N. L. (1985). Monozygotic and dizygotic twins: A comparative analysis of mental ability profiles. *Child Development, 56,* 1051–1058.

Sekuler, R., & Levinson, E. (1977). The perception of moving targets. *Scientific American, 236,* 60–73.

Seligman, M. E. P. (1986). *Explanatory style: Depression, Lyndon Baines Johnson, and the Baseball Hall of Fame.* Paper presented at meeting of the American Psychological Association, Washington, DC.

Seligman, M. E. P. (1988). *Predicting depression, poor health and presidential elections.* Washington, DC. Federation of Behavioral, Psychological and Cognitive Sciences.

Seligman, M. E. P. (1991). *Learned optimism.* New York: Knopf.

Seligman, M. E. P. (1995). The effectiveness of psychotherapy: The *Consumer Reports* study. *American Psychologist, 50,* 965–974.

Seligman, M. E. P. (1998). *Learned optimism: How to change your mind and your life.* New York: Simon and Schuster.

Seligman, M. E. P., & Csikszentmihalyi, M. (2000). Positive psychology: An introduction. *American Psychologist, 55,* 5–14.

Seligman, M. E., & Maier, S. F. (1967). Failure to escape traumatic shock. *Journal of Experimental Psychology, 74,* 1–9.

Seligman, M. E., Maier, S. F., & Geer, J. H. (1968). Alleviation of learned helplessness in the dog. *Journal of Abnormal Psychology, 73,* 256–262.

Selkoe, D. J. (1992, September). Aging brain, aging mind. *Scientific American,* 135–142.

Selye, H. (1956). *The stress of life.* New York: McGraw-Hill.

Selye, H. (Ed.) (1980). *Selye's guide to stress research* (Vol. 1). New York: Van Nostrand Reinhold.

Sethi, S., & Seligman, M. E. P. (1993). Optimism and fundamentalism. *Psychological Science, 4,* 256–259.

Shapiro, K. J. (1997). The separate world of animal research. *American Psychologist, 52,* 1250.

Shapley, R. (1986). Personal communication.

Shephard, R. N. (1967). Recognition memory for words, sentences, and pictures. *Journal of Verbal Learning and Verbal Behavior, 6,* 156–163.

Sher, K. J., & Levenson, R. W. (1982). Risk for alcoholism and individual differences in the stress-response dampening effect of alcohol. *Journal of Abnormal Psychology, 91,* 350–367.

Sherman, B. R., & Kunda, Z. (1989). *Motivated evaluation of scientific evidence.* Paper presented at meeting of the American Psychological Society, Arlington, VA.

Shi, R., Werker, J. F., & Morgan, J. L. (1999). Newborn infants' sensitivity to perceptual cues to lexical and grammatical words. *Cognition, 72,* B11–B21.

Shiffrin, R. M., & Atkinson, R. C. (1969). Storage and retrieval processes in long-term memory. *Psychological Review, 76,* 179–193.

Ship, J. A. (1999). The influence of aging on oral health and consequences for taste and smell. *Physiology and Behavior, 66,* 209–215.

Shore, C., O'Connell, B., & Bates, E. (1984). First sentences in language and symbolic play. *Developmental Psychology, 20,* 872–880.

Shurkin, J. N. (1992). *Terman's kids: The groundbreaking study of how the gifted grow up.* New York: Little, Brown.

Siegel, S. (1983). Classical conditioning, drug tolerance, and drug dependence. In R. G. Smart et al. (Eds.), *Research advances in alcohol and drug problems* (Vol. 7). New York: Plenum.

Siegler, R. S., & Ellis, S. (1996). Piaget on childhood. *Psychological Science, 7,* 211–215.

Silberstein, J. A., & Parsons, O. A. (1981). Neuropsychological impairment in female alcoholics: Replication and extension. *Journal of Abnormal Psychology, 90,* 179–182.

Silverberg, R. A. (1985). Men confronting death: Management versus self-determination. *Clinical Social Work Journal, 13,* 157–169.

Silverman, K., Preston, K. L., Stitzer, M. L., & Schuster, C. R. (1999). Efficacy and versatility of voucher-based reinforcement in drug abuse treatment. In S. T. Higgins & K. Silverman (Eds.), *Motivating behavior change among illicit-drug abusers: Research on contingency management interventions.* Washington, DC: American Psychological Association.

Simmons, J. Q., & Lovaas, O. I. (1969). Use of pain and punishment as treatment techniques with childhood schizophrenics. *American Journal of Psychotherapy, 23,* 23–36.

Simpson, J. A., Campbell, B., & Berscheid, E. (1986). The association between romantic love and marriage: Kephart 1967 twice revisited. *Personality and Social Psychology Bulletin, 12,* 363–372.

Skinner, B. F. (1938). *The behavior of organisms.* New York: Appleton-Century-Crofts.

Skinner, B. F. (1953). *Science and human behavior.* New York: Free Press

Skinner, B. F. (1957). *Verbal behavior.* Englewood Cliffs, NJ: Prentice Hall.

Skinner, B. F. (1972). *Beyond freedom and dignity.* New York: Knopf.

Slater, J., & Depue, R. A. (1981). The contribution of environmental events and social support to serious suicide attempts in primary depressive disorder. *Journal of Abnormal Psychology, 90,* 275–285.

Sloan, D. M., & Mizes, J. S. (1999). Foundations of behavior therapy in the contemporary healthcare context. *Clinical Psychology Review, 19,* 255–274.

Slobin, D. I. (1971). *Psycholinguistics.* Glenview, IL: Scott, Foresman.

Slobin, D. I. (1973). Cognitive prerequisites for the acquisition of grammar. In C. A. Ferguson & D. I. Slobin (Eds.), *Studies of child language development.* New York: Holt.

Slobin, D. I. (1985). *Cross-cultural study of language acquisition.* Hillsdale, NJ: Erlbaum.

Smetana, J. G. (1988). Concepts of self and social convention: Adolescents' and parents' reasoning about hypothetical and actual family conflicts. In M. R. Gunnar & W. A. Collins (Eds.), *The Minnesota symposia* (Vol. 21). Hillsdale, NJ: Erlbaum.

Smith, C. B., Adamson, L. B., & Bakeman, R. B. (1988). Interactional predictors of early language. *First Language, 8,* 143–156.

Smith, D. K., Nehemkis, A. M., & Charter, R. A. (1983–1984). Fear of death, death attitudes, and religious conviction in the terminally ill. *International Journal of Psychiatry and Medicine, 13,* 221–232.

Smith, E. E., & Medin, D. L. (1981). *Categories and concepts.* Cambridge, MA: Harvard University Press.

Smith, J., & Baltes, P. B. (1990). Wisdom-related knowledge: Age/cohort differences in response to life-planning problems. *Developmental Psychology, 26,* 494–505.

Smith, M. E. (1926). An investigation of the development of the sentence and the extent of vocabulary in young children. *University of Iowa Studies in Child Welfare, 3* (5).

Smith, P. B., & Bond, M. H. (1999). *Social psychology across cultures.* Boston: Allyn and Bacon.

Smith, S. L., & Donnerstein, E. (1998). Harmful effects of exposure to media violence: Learning of aggression, emotional desensitization, and fear. In R. G. Geen & E. Donnerstein (Eds.), *Human aggression: Theories, research, and implications for social policy.* San Diego: Academic.

Smith, S. M. (1979). Remembering in and out of context. *Journal of Experimental Psychology, 5,* 460–471.

Snow, C. E., & Dickinson, D. K. (1990). Social sources of narrative skills at home and at school. *First Language, 10,* 87–103.

Snyder, M., & Jones, E. E. (1974). Attitude attribution when behavior is constrained. *Journal of Experimental Social Psychology, 10,* 585–600.

Snyder, M., Tanke, E. D., & Berscheid, E. (1977). Social perception and interpersonal behavior. *Journal of Personality and Social Psychology, 35,* 656–666.

Snyder, M. L., & Frankel, A. (1976). Observer bias. *Journal of Personality and Social Psychology, 34,* 857–864.

Solomon, R. L. (1980). The opponent-process theory of acquired motivation: The costs of pleasure and the benefits of pain. *American Psychologist, 35,* 691–712.

Solomon, R. L. (1986). *The costs of pleasure and the benefits of pain.* Paper presented at meeting of the American Association for the Advancement of Science, Philadelphia.

Solso, R. L. (2001). *Cognitive psychology* (6th ed.). Boston: Allyn and Bacon.

Sontag, L. W., Baker, C. T., & Nelson, V. L. (1958). Mental growth and personality development. *Monographs of the Society for Research in Child Development, 23* (2).

Sourander, A., Helstela, L., Haavisto, A., & Bergroth, L. (2001). Suicidal thoughts and attempts among adolescents: A longitudinal 8-year follow-up study. *Journal of Affective Disorders, 63,* 59–66.

Spear, L. P. (2000). The adolescent brain and age-related behavioral manifestations. *Neuroscience and Biobehavioral Reviews, 24,* 417–463.

Spearman, C. (1927). *The abilities of man.* London: Macmillan.

Speece, M. W., & Sandor, B. B. (1984, October). Children's understanding of death: A review of three components of a death concept. *Child Development, 55,* 1671–1686.

Spencer, M. B. (1988). Self-concept development. In D. T. Slaughter (Ed.), *New Directions for Child Development, 42.* San Francisco: Jossey-Bass.

Sperling, G. (1960). The information available in brief visual presentations. *Psychological Monographs, 74.*

Sperling, G. (1967). Successive approximations to a model for short-term memory. *Acta Psychologica, 27,* 285–292.

Sperling, M. K. (1999). *Schizophrenia.* Bethesda, MD: National Institute of Mental Health.

Sperry, R. W. (1988). Psychology's mentalist paradigm and the religion/science tension. *American Psychologist, 43,* 607–613.

Squire, L. (1992). Memory and the hippocampus: A synthesis from findings with rats, monkeys, and humans. *Psychological Review, 99,* 195–231.

Squire, L. R. (1989). On the course of forgetting in very long-term memory. *Journal of Experimental Psychology: Learning, Memory, and Cognition, 15,* 241–245.

Squire, L. R., & Knowlton, B. J. (2000). The medial temporal lobe, the hippocampus, and the memory systems of the brain. In M. S. Gazzaniga (Ed.), *The new cognitive neurosciences* (2nd ed.). Cambridge, MA: MIT Press.

Squire, L. R., Zola-Morgan, S., & Chen, K. S. (1988). Human amnesia and animal models of amnesia: Performance of amnesic patients on tests designed for the monkey. *Behavioral Neuroscience, 102,* 210–221.

Starker, S. (1988). Do-it-yourself therapy: The prescription of self-help books by psychologists. *Psychotherapy, 25,* 142–146.

Stegarud, L., Solheim, B., Karlsen, M., & Kroger, J. (1999). Ego identity status in cross-cultural context: A replication study. *Psychological Reports, 85,* 457–461.

Steinberg, L. (1985). *Adolescence.* New York: Knopf.

Steinberg, L. (2001). We know some things: Parent-adolescent relationships in retrospect and prospect. *Journal of Research on Adolescence, 11,* 1–19.

Steinberg, L., & Avenevoli, S. (1998). Disengagement from school and problem behavior in adolescence: A developmental-contextual analysis of the influences of family and part-time work. In R. Jessor (Ed.), *New perspectives on adolescent risk behavior.* New York: Cambridge University Press.

Steinberg, L., Dornbusch, S. M., Brown, R. B. (1992). Ethnic differences in adolescent achievement: An ecological perspective. *American Psychologist, 47,* 723–729.

Steinberg, L., Lamborn, S. D., Dornbusch, S. M., & Darling, N. (1992). Impact of parenting practices on adolescent achievement: Authoritative parenting, school involvement, & encouragement to succeed. *Child Development, 63,* 1266–1281.

Stellar, E., McHugh, P. R., & Moran, T. H. (1985). The stomach: A conception of its dynamic role in satiety. In *Progress in psychobiology and physiological psychology* (Vol. 11, pp. 197–232). New York: Academic.

Stenberg, C. R., Campos, J. J., & Emde, R. N. (1983). The facial expression of anger in seven-month-old infants. *Child Development, 54,* 178–184.

Stephens, T. (1988). Physical activity and mental health in the United States and Canada: Evidence from four population surveys. *Preventive Medicine, 17,* 35–47.

Stepper, S., & Strack, F. (1993). Proprioceptive determinants of emotional and nonemotional feelings. *Journal of Personality and Social Psychology, 64,* 211–220.

Stern, K., & McClintock, M. K. (1998). Regulation of ovulation by human pheromones. *Nature, 392,* 177–179.

Sternberg, R. J. (1985). Implicit theories of intelligence, creativity, and wisdom. *Journal of Personality and Social Psychology, 49,* 607–627.

Sternberg, R. J. (1986). A triangular theory of love. *Psychological Review, 93,* 119–35.

Sternberg, R. J. (1999a). *Love is a story: A new theory of relationships.* New York: Oxford University Press.

Sternberg, R. J. (1999b). The theory of successful intelligence. *Review of General Psychology, 3,* 292–316.

Sternberg, R. J. (1999c). A triarchic approach to the understanding and assessment of intelligence in multicultural populations. *Journal of School Psychology, 37,* 145–149.

Sternberg, R. J., Castejon, J. L., Prieto, M. D., Hautamaeki, J., & Grigorenko, E. L. (2001). Confirmatory factor analysis of the Sternberg Triarchic Abilities Test in three international samples: An empirical test of the triarchic theory of intelligence. *European Journal of Psychological Assessment, 17,* 1–16.

Sternberg, R. J., & Grajek, S. (1984). The nature of love. *Journal of Personality and Social Psychology, 47,* 312–329.

Sternberg, R. J., & Grigorenko, E. L. (Eds.). (1997). *Intelligence, heredity, and environment.* New York: Cambridge University Press.

Sternberg, R. J., & Kaufman, J. C. (Eds.). (2002). *The evolution of intelligence.* Mahwah, NJ: Erlbaum.

Sternberg, R. J., & Lubart, T. I. (1993). Investing in creativity. *Psychological Inquiry, 4,* 229–232.

Sternberg, R. J., & O'Hara, L. A. (2000). Intelligence and creativity. In R. J. Sternberg (Ed.), *Handbook of intelligence.* New York: Cambridge University Press.

Sternberg, R. J., Wagner, R. K., Williams, W. M., & Horvath, J. A. (1995). Testing common sense. *American Psychologist, 50,* 912–927.

Stevens, B. (1974). The sexually oppressed male. *Psychotherapy, 11,* 16–21.

Stevenson, H. W. (1998, March). A study of three cultures: Germany, Japan, and the United States—An overview of the TIMSS Case Study Project. *Phi Delta Kappan,* 524–530.

Stevenson, H. W., Chen, C., & Lee, S. (1993, January). Mathematics achievement of Chinese, Japanese, and American children: Ten years later. *Science, 259,* 53–58.

Stevenson, H. W., & Lee, S. (1990). Contexts of achievement. *Monographs of the Society for Research in Child Development, 55.*

Stiles, J. (2001). Neural plasticity and cognitive development. *Developmental Neuropsychology, 18,* 237–272.

Stitzer, M. L., & Walsh, S. L. (1997). Psychostimulant abuse: The case for combined behavioral and pharmacological treatments. *Pharmacology, Biochemistry, and Behavior, 57,* 457–470.

Stolz, S. B., Wienckowski, L. A., & Brown, B. S. (1975). Behavior modification. *American Psychologist, 30,* 1027–1048.

Strachan, T., & Read, A. P. (1999). *Human molecular genetics* (2nd ed.). New York: Wiley.

Straus, M. A., Gelles, R. J., & Steinmetz, S. K. (1981). *Behind closed doors: Violence in the American family.* Garden City, NY: Doubleday/Anchor.

Stroebe, M. S., & Stroebe, W. (1983). Who suffers more? Sex differences in health risks of the widowed. *Psychological Bulletin, 93,* 279–301.

Strupp, H. H. (1986). Psychotherapy: Research, practice, and public policy (how to avoid dead ends). *American Psychologist, 41,* 120–130.

Strupp, H. H. (1989). Can the practitioner learn from the researcher? *American Psychologist, 44,* 717–724.

Strupp, H. H., & Binder, J. L. (1984). *A guide to time-limited dynamic psychotherapy.* New York: Basic.

Stunkard, A. J. (1985). Behavioral management of obesity. *Medical Journal of Australia, 142* (7 supplement), 513–520.

Stunkard, A. J., Foch, T. T., & Hrubec, H. (1986). A twin study of human obesity. *Journal of the American Medical Association, 256,* 51–54.

Stuss, D. T., & Benson, D. F. (1986). *The frontal lobes.* New York: Raven.

Styron, W. (1990). *Darkness visible: A memoir of madness.* New York: Random House.

Subrahmanyam, K., Kraut, R., Greenfield, P., & Gross, E. (2001). New forms of electronic media: The impact of interactive games and the Internet on cognition, socialization, and behavior. In D. B. Singer & J. L. Singer (Eds.), *Handbook of children and the media.* Thousand Oaks, CA: Sage.

Substance Abuse and Mental Health Services Administration. (2000). *The 2000 National Household Survey on Drug Abuse.* Washington, DC: GPO.

Substance Abuse and Mental Health Services Administration. (2001). *The 2001 National Household Survey on Drug Abuse.* Washington, DC: GPO.

Suddath, R. E., Christison, G. W., Torrey, E. F., Casanova, M. F., & Weinberger, D. R. (1990). Anatomical abnormalities in the brains of monozygotic twins discordant for schizophrenia. *New England Journal of Medicine, 322,* 789–794.

Sue, D. W., & Sue, D. (1990). *Counseling the culturally different: Theory and practice.* New York: Wiley.

Suedfeld, P. (1969). Sensory deprivation stress. *Journal of Personality and Social Psychology, 11,* 70–74.

Sulloway, F. (1990). Personal communication.

Sutker, P. B., Davis, M. J., Uddo, M., & Ditta, S. R. (1995). War zone stress, personal resources, and PTSD in Persian Gulf War returnees. *Journal of Abnormal Psychology, 104,* 444–452.

Sutton-Smith, B. (1982). Birth order and sibling status effects. In M. E. Lamb & B. Sutton-Smith (Eds.), *Sibling relationships: Their nature and significance across the lifespan.* Hillsdale, NJ: Erlbaum.

Suzman, R., & Riley, M. W. (1985). Introducing the "oldest old." *Milbank Memorial Fund Quarterly, 63,* 177–205.

Szasz, T. S. (1960). The myth of mental illness. *American Psychologist, 15,* 113–118.

Szasz, T. (1993). Crazy talk: Thought disorder or psychiatric arrogance? *British Journal of Medical Psychology, 66,* 61–67.

Szasz, T. (1998). The healing word: Its past, present, and future. *Journal of Humanistic Psychology, 38,* 8–20.

Szasz, T. (1999). Medical incapacity, legal incompetence and psychiatry. *Psychiatric Bulletin, 23,* 517–519.

Szasz, T. (2000). A plea for the cessation of the longest war of the twentieth century—the war on drugs. *Humanistic Psychologist, 28,* 67–78.

Tapley, D. F., Weiss, R. J., & Morris, T. Q. (1985). *The Columbia University College of Physicians and Surgeon's complete home medical guide.* New York: Crown.

Tarpley, T. (2001). Children, the Internet, and other new technologies. In D. B. Singer & J. L. Singer (Eds.),

*Handbook of children and the media.* Thousand Oaks, CA: Sage.

Tarricone, B. J., Simon, J. R., Li, Y. J., & Low, W. C. (1996). Neural grafting of cholinergic neurons in the hippocampal formation. *Behavioural Brain Research, 74,* 25–44.

Taylor, S. E. (1986). *Health psychology.* New York: Random House.

Taylor, S. E. (1988). *Health psychology* (4th ed.). New York: McGraw-Hill.

Taylor, S. E. (1990). Health psychology: The science and the field. *American Psychologist, 45,* 40–50.

Taylor, S. W., Peplau, L. A., & Sears, D. O. (2000). *Social psychology* (10th ed.). Upper Saddle River, NJ: Prentice Hall.

Tennes, K. H., & Mason, J. W. (1982). Developmental psychoendocrinology: An approach to the study of emotions. In C. E. Izard (Ed.), *Measuring emotions in infants and children.* Cambridge, UK: Cambridge University Press.

Terman, L. M. (1954). The discovery and encouragement of exceptional talent. *American Psychologist, 9,* 221–238.

Terrace, H. S. (1985). On the nature of animal thinking. *Neuroscience and Biobehavioral Reviews, 9,* 643–652.

Terrace, H. S., Petitto, L. A., Sanders, R. J., & Bever, T. G. (1979). Can an ape create a sentence? *Science, 206,* 891–902.

Thayer, R. (1992). *Moderate exercise and mood.* Paper presented at the American Psychological Association Convention.

Theorell, T., Leymann, H., Jodko, M., & Konarski, K. (1992). "Person under train" incidents: Medical consequences for subway drivers. *Psychosomatic Medicine, 54,* 480–488.

Thomas, A., & Chess, S. (1977). *Temperament and development.* New York: Brunner Mazel.

Thomas, A., Chess, S., & Birch, H. G. (1970). The origin of personality. *Scientific American, 223,* 106–107.

Thomas, A. K., & Loftus, E. F. (2002). Creating bizarre false memories through imagination. *Memory and Cognition, 30,* 423–431.

Thompson, C. (1989). Personal communication.

Thompson, J. K., Penner, L. A., & Altabe, M. N. (1990). Procedures, problems and progress in the assessment of body images. In T. Cash & T. Pruzinsky (Eds.), *Body images.* New York: Guilford.

Thompson, L. W., Gallagher, D., & Breckenridge, J. S. (1987). Comparative effectiveness of psychotherapies for depressed elders. *Journal of Consulting and Clinical Psychology, 55,* 385–390.

Thorndike, E. L. (1911). *Animal intelligence.* New York: Macmillan.

Thornhill, R., & Gangestad, S. W. (1999). The scent of symmetry: A human sex pheromone that signals fitness? *Evolution and Human Behavior, 20,* 175–201.

Thurstone, L. L. (1944). *A factorial study of perception.* Chicago: University of Chicago Press.

Thurstone, L. L. (1948). Primary mental abilities. *Science, 108,* 585.

Thyer, B. A. (1983). Treating anxiety disorders with exposure therapy. *Social Casework, 64* (2), 77–82.

Tien, A. Y., & Eaton, W. W. (1992). Psychopathologic precursors and sociodemographic risk factors for the schizophrenia syndrome. *Archives of General Psychiatry, 49,* 37–46.

Tolman, E. C. (1948). Cognitive maps in rats and men. *Psychological Review, 55,* 189–208.

Tolman, E. C., & Honzik, C. H. (1930). Introduction and removal of reward and maze performance in rats. *University of California Publications in Psychology, 4,* 257–275.

Tolnay, M., & Probst, A. (2001). Frontotemporal lobar degeneration: An update on clinical, pathological and genetic findings. *Gerontology, 47,* 1–8.

Tomarken, A. J., Davidson, R. J., & Henriques, J. B. (1990). Resting frontal brain asymmetry predicts affective responses to films. *Journal of Personality and Social Psychology, 59,* 791–801.

Tomarken, A. J., Davidson, R. J., Wheeler, R. E., & Doss, R. C. (1992). Individual differences in anterior brain asymmetry and fundamental dimensions of emotion. *Journal of Personality and Social Psychology, 62,* 676–687.

Tomkins, S. S. (1962). *Affect, imagery, consciousness: Vol. 1. The positive affects.* New York: Springer.

Torre, V., Ashmore, J. F., Lamb, T. D., & Menini, A. (1995). Transduction and adaptation in sensory receptor cells. *Journal of Neuroscience, 15,* 7757–7768.

Torrey, E. F. (1983). *Surviving schizophrenia.* New York: Harper.

Torrey, E. F., Erdman, K., Wolfe, S. M., & Flynn, L. M. (1990). *Care of the seriously mentally ill: A rating of state programs* (3rd ed.). Washington, DC: Public Citizen Health Research Group and National Alliance for the Mentally Ill.

Trentin, E. (2001). Networks with trainable amplitude of activation functions. *Neural Networks, 14,* 471–493.

Triarhou, L. C. (1995). The cerebellar model of neural grafting: Structural integration and functional recovery. *Brain Research Bulletin, 39,* 127–138.

Tsai, G. E., Falk, W. E., Gunther, J., & Coyle, J. T. (1999). Improved cognition in Alzheimer's disease with short-term D-cycloserine treatment. *American Journal of Psychiatry, 156,* 467–469.

Tsuang, M., & Faraone, S. V. (1990). *The genetics of mood disorders.* Baltimore: Johns Hopkins University Press.

Tulving, E. (1989). Remembering and knowing the past. *American Scientist, 77,* 361–367.

Tulving, E. (1993). What is episodic memory? *Current Directions in Psychological Science, 2,* 67–70.

Tuma, A. H., & Maser, J. D. (Eds.). (1985). *Anxiety and the anxiety disorders.* Hillsdale, NJ: Erlbaum.

Turner, C. W., Hesse, B. W., & Peterson-Lewis, S. (1986). Naturalistic studies of the long-term effects of television violence. *Journal of Social Issues, 42,* 7–28.

Turner, R. J., & Avison, W. R. (1989). Gender and depression: Assessing exposure and vulnerability to life events in a chronically strained population. *Journal of Nervous and Mental Diseases, 177,* 443–455.

Tversky, A., & Kahneman, D. (1973). Availability: A heuristic for judging frequency and probability. *Cognitive Psychology, 5,* 207–232.

Ucros, C. G. (1989). Mood state-dependent memory: A meta-analysis. *Cognition and Emotion, 3,* 139–169.

Underwood, B. J. (1957). Interference and forgetting. *Psychological Review, 64,* p. 61.

U.S. Census Bureau. (2001). *Statistical abstract of the United States.* Washington, DC: GPO.

U.S. Department of Health and Human Services. (1993). *National survey results on drug use from monitoring the future study, 1975–1992.* (NIH Publication No. 93-3497).

U.S. Department of Health and Human Services (1999). *Mental health: A report of the Surgeon General.* Rockville, MD: Author.

U.S. Public Health Service. (1985, January–February). Women's health: Report of the Public Health Service Task Force on women's health issues. *Public Health Reports, 100,* 73–106.

U.S. Senate Special Committee on Aging. (1988). *Aging in America: Trends and projections, 1987–88 edition.* Washington, DC: U.S. Department of Health and Human Services.

Valenstein, E. S. (1986). *Great and desperate cures.* New York: Basic.

Vallone, D., Picetti, R., & Borrelli, E. (2000). Structure and function of dopamine receptors. *Neuroscience and Biobehavioral Reviews, 24,* 125–132.

Van De Riet, V. (2001). Gestalt therapy and the phenomenological method. *Gestalt Review, 5,* 184–194.

Van Dyke, C., & Byck, R. (1982). Cocaine. *Scientific American, 246,* 3, 128–141.

Vecsey, G. (1989, September 11). Moral of the U.S. Open: You just never know. *The New York Times,* p. C-3.

Veroff, J., Douvan, E., & Kulka, R. (1981). *The inner American.* New York: Basic.

Vierling, J. S., & Rock, J. (1967). Variations of olfactory sensitivity to exaltolide during the menstrual cycle. *Journal of Applied Physiology, 22,* 311–315.

Viets, V. C. L., & Miller, W. R. (1997). Treatment approaches for pathological gamblers. *Clinical Psychology Review, 17,* 689–702.

Vihman, M. M. (1985). Language differentiation by a bilingual infant. *Journal of Child Language, 12,* 297–324.

Villani, S. (2001). Impact of media on children and adolescents: A 10–year review of the research. *Journal of the American Academy of Child and Adolescent Psychiatry, 40,* 392–401.

Wachtel, E. F., & Wachtel, P. L. (1986). *Family dynamics in individual psychotherapy.* New York: Guilford.

Wagemans, J., Verstraten, F. A. J., & He, S. (2001). Editorial. *Acta Psychologica, 107,* 1–7.

Wagner, B. M. (1997). Family risk factors for child and adolescent suicidal behavior. *Psychological Bulletin, 121,* 246–298.

Wagner, H. L. (1990). The spontaneous facial expression of differential positive and negative emotions. *Motivation and Emotion, 14,* 27–43.

Wagner, K. R. (1985). How much do children say in a day? *Journal of Child Language, 12,* 475–487.

Wald, G. (1951). The photochemical basis of rod vision. *Journal of the Optical Society of America, 41,* 949–956.

Walker, E., & Emory, E. (1985). Commentary: Interpretive bias and behavioral genetic research. *Child Development, 56,* 775–778.

Walker, J. I. (1981). The psychological problems of Vietnam veterans. *Journal of the American Medical Association, 246,* 781–782.

Walker, P. A. (1978). The role of antiandrogens in the treatment of sex offenders. In C. B. Qualls, J. P. Wincze, & D. H. Barlow (Eds.), *The prevention of sexual disorders* (pp. 117–136). New York: Plenum.

Wall, P. (2000). *Pain: The science of suffering.* New York: Columbia University Press.

Wallach, M. A., & Wallach, L. (1983). *Psychology's sanction of selfishness.* New York: Freeman.

Wallerstein, J., & Blakeslee, S. (1989). *Second chances: Men, women and children a decade after divorce.* New York: Ticknor and Fields.

Wallerstein, J., & Kelley, J. (1980). *Surviving the breakup: How children and parents cope with divorce.* New York: Basic.

Wason, P. C. (1971). Problem solving and reasoning. *Cognitive Psychology* (British Medical Bulletin), 27.

Watson, J. B. (1925). *Behaviorism.* New York: Norton.

Webb, W. B., & Cartwright, R. D. (1978). Sleep and dreams. *Annual Review of Psychology, 29,* 223–252.

Webb, S. J., Monk, C. S., & Nelson, C. A. (2001). Mechanisms of postnatal neurobiological development: Implications for human development. *Developmental Neuropsychology, 19,* 147–171.

Wechsler, D. (1975). Intelligence defined and undefined. *American Psychologist, 30,* 135–159.

Weil, A. (1990). *Natural health, natural medicine.* Boston: Houghton Mifflin.

Weinberg, R. A. (1989). Intelligence and IQ: Landmark issues and great debates. *American Psychologist, 44,* 98–104.

Weinberger, M., Hiner, S. L., & Tierney, W. M. (1987). In support of hassles as a measure of stress in predicting health outcomes. *Journal of Behavioral Medicine, 10,* 19–31.

Weiner, B. (1990). On perceiving the other as responsible. In R. A. Dienstbier (Ed.), *Nebraska Symposium on Motivation, 1990: Perspectives on motivation.* Lincoln: University of Nebraska Press.

Weiner, B. (1993). On sin versus sickness: A theory of perceived responsibility and social motivation. *American Psychologist, 48,* 957–965.

Weiner, B., Perry, P. P., & Magnusson, J. (1988). An attributional analysis of reactions to stigmas. *Journal of Personality and Social Psychology, 55,* 738–748.

Weiner, H. (1982). Psychobiology of essential hypertension. In R. J. Mathew (Ed.), *The biology of anxiety.* New York: Brunner/Mazel.

Weiss, J. M. (1970). Somatic effects of predictable and unpredictable shock. *Psychosomatic Medicine, 32,* 397–409.

Weissman, M. M., Sigman, M., Weiss, B., & Mosk, J. (1992). Affective disorders. In L. Robins & D. A. Regier (Eds.), *Psychiatric disorders in America.* New York: Free Press.

Weisz, J. R., Sigman, M., Weiss, B., & Mosk, J. (1993). Parent reports of behavioral and emotional problems among children in Kenya, Thailand, and the United States. *Child Development, 64,* 98–109.

Wells, G. L. (1993). What do we know about eyewitness identification? *American Psychologist, 48,* 553–571.

Welzl, H., D'Adamo, P., & Lipp, H.-P. (2001). Conditioned taste aversion as a learning and memory paradigm. *Behavioural Brain Research, 125,* 205–213.

Werker, J. F. (1989). Becoming a native listener. *American Scientist, 77,* 54–59.

Werker, J. F., Gilbert, J. H., Humphrey, K., & Tees, R. C. (1981). Developmental aspects of cross-language speech perception. *Child Development, 52,* 349–355.

Werner, E. E., & Smith, R. S. (1982). *Vulnerable but invincible.* New York: McGraw-Hill.

Werner, P. D., & LaRussa, G. W. (1985). Persistence and change in sex-role stereotypes. *Sex Roles, 12,* 1089–1100.

Wessels, M. G. (1982). *Cognitive psychology.* New York: Harper.

Whitaker, A., Johnson, J., Shaffer, D., & Rapoport, J. L. (1990). Uncommon troubles in young people: Prevalence estimates of selected psychiatric disorders in a nonreferred adolescent population. *Archives of General Psychiatry, 47,* 487–496.

White House Project (2002). Internet document at www.thewhitehouseproject.org.

Whitfield, I. C., & Evans, E. F. (1965). Responses of auditory cortical neurons to stimuli of changing frequency. *Journal of Neurophysiology, 28,* 655–672.

Whorf, B. L. (1956). Science and linguistics. In J. B. Carroll (Ed.), *Language, thought, and reality.* Cambridge, MA: MIT Press.

Wickelgren, W. A. (1977). *Learning and memory.* Englewood Cliffs, NJ: Prentice Hall.

Wickelgren, W. A. (1981). Human learning and memory. *Annual Review of Psychology, 32,* 21–52.

Wickens, C. D. (1984). *Engineering psychology and human performance.* Columbus, OH: Charles Merrill.

Wickrama, K. A. S., Lorenz, F. O., Wallace, L. E., Peiris, L., Conger, R. D., & Elder, G. H., Jr. (2001). Family influence on physical health during the middle years: The case of onset of hypertension. *Journal of Marriage and Family, 63,* 527–539.

Widen, H. (2000). Using dreams in brief therapy. *Psychoanalytic Social Work, 7,* 1–24.

Wiesel, T. N., & Hubel, D. H. (1974). Ordered arrangement of orientation columns in monkeys lacking visual experience. *Journal of Comparative Neurology, 158,* 307–318.

Wigfield, A., & Eccles, J. S. (2000). Expectancy-value theory of achievement motivation. *Contemporary Educational Psychology, 25,* 68–81.

Wilder, G. Z., & Powell, K. (1989). *Sex differences in test performance: A survey of the literature.* New York: College Entrance Examination Board.

Wildes, J. E., & Emery, R. E. (2001). The roles of ethnicity and culture in the development of eating disturbances and body dissatisfaction: A meta-analytic review. *Clinical Psychology Review, 21,* 521–551.

Wilding, E. L. (2001). Event-related functional imaging and episodic memory. *Neuroscience and Biobehavioral Reviews, 25,* 545–554.

Williams, S., Wicherski, M., & Kahout, J. L. (2000). *Salaries in psychology: 1999.* Washington, DC: American Psychological Association.

Williams, W. M., & Ceci, S. J. (1997). Are Americans becoming more or less alike? Trends in race, class, and ability differences in intelligence. *American Psychologist, 52,* 1226–1235.

Willis, S. L., & Baltes, P. B. (1980). Intelligence in adulthood and aging: Contemporary issues. In L. W. Poon (Ed.), *Aging in the 80's: Psychological issues.* Washington, DC: American Psychological Association.

Wilson, A., Passik, S. D., Faude, J., Abrams, J., & Gordon, G. (1989). A hierarchical model of opiate addiction: Failures of self-regulation as a central aspect of substance abuse. *Journal of Nervous and Mental Disease, 177,* 390–399.

Wilson, E. O. (1978). *On human nature.* Cambridge, MA: Harvard University Press.

Wilson, J. Q., & Herrnstein, R. J. (1985). *Crime and human nature.* New York: Simon and Schuster.

Winterbottom, M. R. (1953). *The relation of childhood training in independence to achievement motivation.* Unpublished doctoral dissertation, University of Michigan. Summarized in D. C. McClelland, J. W. Atkinson, R. A. Clark, & E. L. Lowell, *The achievement motive.* New York: Irvington.

Wolf, R. M. (1963). *The identification and measurement of environmental process variables related to intelligence.* Unpublished doctoral dissertation, University of Chicago.

Woolf, V. (1978). In N. Nicholson & J. Trautman (Eds.), *The Letters of Virginia Woolf: 1975–1980.* New York: Harcourt.

Wolpe, J. (1961). The systematic desensitization treatment of neuroses. *Journal of Nervous and Mental Disease, 132,* 189–203.

Wolpe, J. (1969). *The practice of behavior therapy.* Oxford, UK: Pergamon.

Wong, P. T. P., & Watt, L. M. (1991). What types of reminiscence are associated with successful aging? *Psychology and Aging, 6,* 272–279.

Wood, J. M., Bootzin, R. R., Rosenhan, D., Nolen-Hoeksema, S., & Jourden, F. (1992). Effects of the 1989 San Francisco earthquake on frequency and content of nightmares. *Journal of Abnormal Psychology, 101,* 219–224.

World Book, Inc. (1994). *World Book health and medical annual, 1994.* Chicago: Author.

World Health Organization. (2001). World health report 2001: Mental health: New understanding, new hope. Internet document at www.who.int.

Wortman, C., & Silver, R. C. (1989). The myths of coping with loss. *Journal of Consulting and Clinical Psychology, 57,* 349–357.

Wren, D. J. (1997). Adolescent females' "voice" changes can signal difficulties for teachers and administrators. *Adolescence, 32,* 463–470.

Wyatt, G., Peters, S., & Guthrie, D. (1988). Kinsey revisited, part I: Comparisons of the sexual socialization and sexual behavior of white women over 33 years. *Archives of Sexual Behavior, 17,* 201–239.

Wyatt, R. J. (1985). *After middle age.* New York: McGraw-Hill.

Wyatt, R. J., & Freed, W. J. (1983). Progress in neurografting as a treatment for degenerative brain disease: The Parkinson's model. In W. Regelson (Ed.), *Intervention in the aging process.* New York: Alan R. Liff.

Yalom, I. (1980). *Existential psychotherapy.* New York: Basic.

Yalom, I. D. (1985). *The theory and practice of group psychotherapy,* (3rd ed.). New York: Basic.

Yang, J., McCrae, R. R., Costa, P. T., Jr., Dai, X., Yao, S., Cai, T., et al. (1999). Cross-cultural personality assessment in psychiatric populations: The NEO-PI–R in the People's Republic of China. *Psychological Assessment, 11,* 359–368.

Yankelovich, D. (1988, May). The work ethic is underemployed. *Psychology Today, 16,* 5–8.

Yarbus, A. L. (1967). *Eye movements and vision* (L. A. Riggs, Trans.). New York: Plenum.

Yates, A. (1990). Current press perspectives on the eating disorders: II. Treatment, outcome, and research directions. *Journal of the American Academy of Child and Adolescent Psychiatry, 29,* 1–9.

Yerkes, R. M., & Morgulis, S. (1909). The methods of Pavlov in animal psychology. *Psychological Bulletin, 6,* 257–273.

Young, P. T. (1961). *Motivation and emotion.* New York: Wiley.

Yule, W. (1985). *Behavioral approaches.* In M. Rutter & L. Hersov (Eds.), *Child and adolescent psychiatry: Modern approaches* (2nd ed.). London: Blackwell.

Zahn-Waxler, C., & Radke-Yarrow, M. (1990). The origins of empathic concern. *Motivation and Emotion, 14,* 107–130.

Zahn-Waxler, C., Radke-Yarrow, M., & King, R. (1983). Early altruism and guilt. *Academic Psychology Bulletin, 5,* 247–259.

Zajonc, R. B. (1968). Attitudinal effects of mere exposure. *Journal of Personality and Social Psychology, 9,* 1–27.

Zajonc, R. B. (1986, August). The decline and rise of scholastic aptitude scores: A prediction derived from the confluence model. *American Psychologist, 41,* 862–867.

Zajonc, R. B. (1989). The face as a primary instrument of social process. In R. B. Zajonc & S. Moscovici (Eds.), *Social psychology and the emotions.* Cambridge, UK: Cambridge University Press.

Zajonc, R. B., & Sales, S. M. (1966). Social facilitation of dominant and subordinate responses. *Journal of Experimental Social Psychology, 2,* 160–168.

Zeidner, M. (1995). Adaptive coping with test situations: A review of the literature. *Educational Psychologist, 30,* 123–133.

Zeldow, P. B., Daugherty, S. R., & Leksas, L. (1987). A four-year longitudinal study of personality changes in medical students. *Journal of Medical Education, 62,* 992–995.

Zellars, K. L., & Perrewé, P. L. (2001). Affective personality and the content of emotional social support: Coping in organizations. *Journal of Applied Psychology, 86,* 459–467.

Zernicke, K., & Petersen, M. (2001, August 19). Schools' backing of behavior drugs comes under fire. *The New York Times,* pp. 1, 30.

Zika, S., & Chamberlain, K. (1987). Relation of hassles and personality to subjective well-being. *Journal of Personality and Social Psychology, 53,* 155–162.

Zimbardo, P. G. (1972). Pathology of imprisonment. *Society, 9,* 4–8.

Zipf, G. K. (1949). *Human behavior and the principle of least effort.* Reading, MA: Addison-Wesley.

Zube, M. (1982). Changing behavior and outlook of aging men and women. *Family Relations, 31,* 147–156.

Zuckerman, M. (1991). Sensation seeking: The balance between risk and reward. In L. P. Lipsitt & L. L. Mitmick (Eds.), *Self-regulatory behavior and risk taking: Causes and consequences.* Norwood, NJ: Ablex.

Zung, W. W. K. (1965). A self-rating depression scale. *Archives of General Psychiatry, 12,* 63–70.

# Photo Credits

# Subject Index

Terms in boldface type are defined in the marginal glossary.

## A

AA. *See* Alcoholics Anonymous
ABCD theory, 556
Abnormal behavior. *See also* Mental disorders; Psychological disorders; *entries for individual disorders*
    causes and classifications of, 501–505
    characteristics of, 499–501
    historical treatment of, 545
**Absolute threshold,** 94, 95
Abuse
    alcohol. *See* Alcohol abuse
    child, 393
    drug. *See* Drug abuse
    mood disorders and, 511
    psychological, 393
    substance, 504, 522–527
**Accommodation,** 382
**Acetylcholine,** 77
    sleep and, 307
Achievement
    academic, 316, 397, 398
    birth order and, 344
    IQ and, 266, 267–268
**Achievement motivation,** 315–317, 398
**Achievement test,** 264–265
Acoustic encoding, 186
Acronyms, 240
Acrophobic, 516
Active avoidance training, 152
Actor-observer effect, 592
Acupuncture, 77, 109, 110
Adaptation, dark, 99
Adaptive functioning, 401
Addiction, 523, 526–527
ADHD. *See* Attention-deficit/hyperactivity disorder
**Adjustment disorder,** 470, 473
Adler's individual psychology, 340
Adolescence, 415–427
    alcohol abuse in, 424
    attitude changes in, 586
    depression and suicide in, 425, 426
    drug abuse in, 424
    early, 399–400
    family conflicts in, 425–427
    identity establishment in, 421–423
    jobs in, 422
    moral development in, 420–421
    physical changes in, 416–419
    pregnancy in, 425
    sexuality in, 312
    sexually transmitted diseases in, 425
    stage of formal operations in, 383, 385, 400
    stress in, 426, 458
    thought processes in, 385
    troubles in, 424–425
Adoptive parents, IQ of children and, 270
Adrenal gland, 69, 70, 292, 464, 511
Adulthood, 427–441
    aging in, 435–441

changes between adolescence and, 428–429
    choosing a career in, 429
    gender roles in, 430–431
    intellectual capacities in, 438–439
    learning in, 167
    love, intimacy and commitment in, 431–432
    midlife phase of, 434–435
    retirement in, 436, 441, 586
    sexuality in, 312
    stress in, 458
    therapeutic strategies in, 564
Afferent neurons, 56
**Affiliation motivation,** 317–318
**Ageism,** 436
**Aggression,** 606
    Adler's view of, 340
    gender differences in, 395
    group experiment on, 20–21
    hostile, 607
    instrumental, 607
    origins of, 608–609
    psychoanalytic theory of, 336
    spanking and, 158
    television and, 396, 608
Aging
    intellectual capacities and, 438–439
    learning and, 167
    mental health and, 439–441
    process of, 436–438
    sexuality and, 311
    taste and smell and, 109
**Agoraphobia,** 515, 516
AIDS, 311, 425
Alarm stage, 464
Alcohol, 525. *See also* Alcohol abuse
    during pregnancy, 374
Alcohol abuse. *See also* Substance abuse
    in adolescence, 424
    aversive conditioning and, 554
    causes of, 524
    childhood abuse and, 393
    consequences of, 523–524
    gender and, 524
    post-traumatic stress disorder and, 472
    stress and, 457
**Alcohol dehydrogenase,** 524
Alcoholics Anonymous, 524, 559
Alex (the parrot), 234–235
**Algorithm,** 243
**All-or-none principle,** 55
**Alpha rhythm,** 305
**Altered states of consciousness (ASC),** 120, 525
**Altruism,** 609–610
**Alzheimer's disease,** 58, 437
    memory drugs and, 192
    taste and smell and, 109
American Medical Association, 444
American Psychological Association (APA), 6, 7, 8, 9, 35, 37, 38, 293, 562
    ethical guidelines of, 146
American Psychological Society, 6
American Sleep Disorders Association, 308
American Standard English, 221, 222, 226